Marketing

TENTH CANADIAN EDITION

FREDERICK G. CRANE
CEILIDH INSIGHTS LLC

ROGER A. KERIN
SOUTHERN METHODIST UNIVERSITY

STEVEN W. HARTLEY
UNIVERSITY OF DENVER

WILLIAM RUDELIUS
UNIVERSITY OF MINNESOTA

Mc
Graw
Hill
Education

Marketing

Tenth Canadian Edition

ISBN-13: 978-1-25-926880-9

ISBN-10: 1-25-926880-2

2 3 4 5 6 7 8 9 TCP 20 19 18

Printed and bound in Canada.

Care has been taken to trace ownership of copyright material contained in this text; however, the publisher will welcome any information that enables them to rectify any reference or credit for subsequent editions.

Portfolio and Program Manager: *Karen Fozard*

Product Manager: *Sara Braithwaite*

Executive Marketing Manager: *Joy Armitage Taylor*

Product Developer: *Amy Rydzanicz*

Senior Product Team Associate: *Marina Seguin*

Supervising Editor: *Janie Deneau*

Photo/Permissions Research: *Derek Capitaine*

Copy Editor: *Mike Kelly*

Plant Production Coordinator: *Sarah Strynatka*

Manufacturing Production Coordinator: *Emily Hickey*

Cover Design: *Lightbox Visuals Communications Inc.*

Cover Image: *Lightbox Visuals Communications Inc.; Chalkboard: Image Source / Getty Images*

Interior Design: *Lightbox Visuals Communications Inc.*

Page Layout: *MPS*

Printer: *Transcontinental Printing Group*

DEDICATION

This text is dedicated to my wild mustangs. My royalties from this book are being donated to support the rescue and care of wild mustangs. If you wish to help, check out non-profit organizations in your area that are involved in equine rescue.

ABOUT THE AUTHOR

Frederick G. Crane is an executive professor at the College of Business at Northeastern University, editor of the *Journal of the Academy of Business Education*, and co-founder of Ceilidh Insights LLC, an innovation training, intellectual property management, and customer insight firm. He is a former professor of marketing and entrepreneurship at the University of New Hampshire and a former full professor at Dalhousie University. He was also the founding editor of the *Journal of Promotion Management*.

Dr. Crane grew up in a family business and has also founded several of his own businesses, including successful management consulting and research firms. As a corporate consultant for more than 20 years, Dr. Crane has completed over 300 consulting assignments for companies/organizations in over two dozen countries. He has worked for both small businesses and Fortune 500 companies, assisting them with the development and execution of strategic plans, consumer research, innovation/new product development, and branding projects. He has also developed and participated in numerous corporate training and executive education programs for major corporate clients in the educational, financial services, health care, high-tech, packaged goods, pharmaceutical, and telecommunications fields.

His academic research activities have resulted in more than 100 publications, including more than a dozen books. He currently sits on the editorial boards of *Health Marketing Quarterly*, *Services Marketing Quarterly*, and *Journal of Hospital Marketing*. His current research stream intersects the domains of marketing, entrepreneurship, corporate venturing, and innovation. Dr. Crane has also received numerous awards for teaching excellence over the past 20 years.

BRIEF CONTENTS

Preface   xxii

Part 1 **Initiating the Marketing Process   1**

    1 Creating Customer Value, Relationships, and Experiences Through Marketing   1

    2 Developing Successful Marketing Strategies   26

    Appendix A: Creating an Effective Marketing Plan   54

    3 Scanning the Marketing Environment   72

    4 Ethics and Social Responsibility for Sustainable Marketing   95

Part 2 **Understanding Buyers and Markets   116**

    5 Consumer Behaviour   116

    6 Understanding Organizations as Customers   141

    7 Reaching Global Markets   162

Part 3 **Targeting Marketing Opportunities   193**

    8 Marketing Research: From Information to Action   193

    9 Market Segmentation, Targeting, and Positioning   220

Part 4 **Satisfying Marketing Opportunities   243**

    10 Developing New Products and Services   243

    11 Managing Products and Brands   267

    12 Managing Services   295

    13 Pricing Products and Services   318

    Appendix B: Financial Aspects of Marketing   350

    14 Managing Marketing Channels and Supply Chains   358

    15 Retailing   390

    16 Integrated Marketing Communications and Direct Marketing   416

    17 Advertising, Sales Promotion, and Public Relations   442

    18 Personal Selling and Sales Management   473

Part 5 **Managing the Marketing Process   500**

    19 Pulling It All Together: The Strategic Marketing Process   500

    20 Using Social Media and Mobile Marketing to Connect with Consumers   532

Glossary   GL-1

Chapter Notes   CN-1

Name Index   NI-1

Company/Product Index   CI-1

Subject Index   SI-1

CONTENTS

Preface xxii

Part 1   **Initiating the Marketing Process**   **1**

1   **Creating Customer Value, Relationships, and Experiences Through Marketing**   **1**

The Marketing of the City of Hamilton, Ontario   1

What Marketing Is and What It Is Not   3

Marketing: Defined   3

Going Online: Understanding Marketing: Terms and Concepts   *4*

Requirements for Marketing to Occur   4

The Breadth and Depth of Marketing   5

The Diverse Factors Influencing Marketing Activities   6

How Marketing Discovers and Satisfies Consumer Needs   7

Discovering Consumer Needs   7

Satisfying Consumer Needs   9

Making Responsible Decisions: Marketing and Female Body Dissatisfaction   *9*

The Marketing Program   10

A Marketing Program for the City of Hamilton   11

How Marketing Became So Important   12

Evolution of North American Businesses   12

Marketing Matters: Lessons from the Leading Edge of Customer Experience Management   *15*

Ethics and Social Responsibility: Balancing the Interests of Different Groups   17

Learning Objectives Review   18

Applying Marketing Knowledge   19

Building Your Marketing Plan   *20*

Video Case 1   Chobani: Making Greek Yogurt a Household Name   *21*

2   **Developing Successful Marketing Strategies**   **26**

Making the World a Better Place, One Scoop at a Time!   26

Today's Organizations   27

Kinds of Organizations   27

What Is Strategy?   28

Structure of Today's Organizations   28

Strategy in Visionary Organizations   30

Organizational Foundation: Why Does It Exist?   30

Organizational Direction: What Will It Do?   31

Making Responsible Decisions: The Global Dilemma: How to Achieve Sustainable Development   *32*

Organizational Strategies: How Will It Do It?   33

Setting Strategic Directions   33

A Look Around: Where Are We Now?   33

Growth Strategies: Where Do We Want to Go?   34

Marketing Matters: Filling the Shoes of Apple CEO Tim Cook: Where Will Apple's Projected Future Growth for Its Major SBUs Come From?   35

Marketing Matters: Growing by Using Multiple Market–Product Strategies   38

Tracking Strategic Performance with Marketing Analytics, Marketing Dashboards, and Marketing Metrics   39

Using Marketing Dashboards: Which Provinces Are Underperforming?   40

The Strategic Marketing Process   41

Strategic Marketing Process: The Planning Phase   42

Going Online: Ben & Jerry's Flavours: From Chocolate Fudge Brownie Ice Cream and One Sweet Whirled Novelty Bars to . . . the Flavor Graveyard   44

Strategic Marketing Process: The Implementation Phase   45

Strategic Marketing Process: The Evaluation Phase   47

Learning Objectives Review   48

Applying Marketing Knowledge   49

Building Your Marketing Plan   50

Video Case 2   IBM: Using Strategy to Build a "Smarter Planet"   50

Appendix A   Creating an Effective Marketing Plan   54

3   Scanning the Marketing Environment   72

Is "Connecting the World" an Ambitious Vision? Not If You Are Facebook!   72

The Importance of Environmental Scanning   73

Tracking Environmental Trends   73

An Environmental Scan of Canada   74

Social Forces   75

Demographics   76

Marketing Matters: How Ethnic Canadian Buyers Shop!   79

Culture   79

Economic Forces   81

Macroeconomic Conditions   81

Consumer Income   81

Going Online: Family Income in Canada by Province and Territory   82

Technological Forces   82

Technology Enables Data Analytics   83

Competitive Forces   83

Alternative Forms of Competition   83

Components of Competition   84

Using Marketing Dashboards: Assessing Competition Is a Key to Success   84

Small Business as Competitors   85

Pure-Play Online Competitors   85

Regulatory Forces   86

Protecting Competition and Consumers   86

Self-Regulation   88

Consumerism   88

Making Responsible Decisions: Cross-Device Tracking and Consumer Privacy   89

Learning Objectives Review   90

Applying Marketing Knowledge   91

Building Your Marketing Plan   91

Video Case 3   Geek Squad: A New Business for a New Environment   91

4   Ethics and Social Responsibility for Sustainable Marketing   95

Introducing Some of Canada's Most Ethical and Socially Responsible Companies   95

Nature and Significance of Marketing Ethics   96

Ethical/Legal Framework in Marketing   97

Current Perceptions of Ethical Behaviour   98

Marketing Matters: Ethical Perceptions of Canadian and American Entrepreneurs: A Cross-Cultural Study   98

Understanding Ethical Marketing Behaviour   99

Societal Culture and Norms   99

Business Culture and Industry Practices   100

Going Online: The Corruption Perceptions Index   101

Corporate Culture and Expectations   101

Personal Moral Philosophy and Ethical Behaviour   103

Understanding Social Responsibility for Sustainable Marketing   104

Concepts of Social Responsibility   104

The Social Audit and Sustainable Development: Doing Well by Doing Good   106

Making Responsible Decisions: Desjardins Group Is One of Canada's Top Corporate Citizens   107

Turning the Table: Consumer Ethics and Social Responsibility   109

Learning Objectives Review   110

Applying Marketing Knowledge   111

Building Your Marketing Plan   111

Video Case 4   Toyota: Building Cleaner, Greener Cars   111

Part 2   Understanding Buyers and Markets   116

5   Consumer Behaviour   116

Enlightened Carmakers Know What Custom(h)ers Value   116

TRIPLE-BOTTOM-LINE: PEOPLE, PLANET, PROFIT

Consumer Purchase Decision Process   117

   Problem Recognition   117

   Information Search   118

   Alternative Evaluation   118

   Purchase Decision   119

   Post-purchase Behaviour   119

   Involvement and Problem-Solving Variations   120

   Situational Influences   121

Psychological Influences on Consumer Behaviour   122

   Motivation and Personality   123

   Perception   124

   Making Responsible Decisions: The Ethics of Subliminal Messages   125

   Learning   125

   Values, Beliefs, and Attitudes   126

   Lifestyle   127

   Going Online: Identify the PRIZM5 Segment You Belong To   127

   Marketing Matters: Understanding a Canadian Lifestyle Segment from PRIZM5—Lunch at Tim's   128

Socio-cultural Influences on Consumer Behaviour   129

   Personal Influence   129

   Reference Groups   130

   Family Influence   130

   Social Class   132

   Culture and Subculture   132

Learning Objectives Review   135

Applying Marketing Knowledge   136

   Building Your Marketing Plan   136

Video Case 5   Groupon: Helping Consumers with Purchase Decisions   137

6 Understanding Organizations as Customers   141

   A New Solution to Student Housing   141

   The Nature and Size of Organizational Markets   142

   Industrial Markets   143

   Marketing Matters: Some Facts about Canada's Manufacturing Industry   143

   Reseller Markets   143

   Government Markets   144

   Global Organizational Markets   144

Measuring Domestic and Global Industrial, Reseller, and Government Markets   144

Characteristics of Organizational Buying   145

   Demand Characteristics   145

   Size of the Order or Purchase   145

Number of Potential Buyers 146

Organizational Buying Objectives 146

Organizational Buying Criteria 147

Buyer–Seller Relationships and Supply Partnerships 147

Making Responsible Decisions: Sustainable Procurement for Sustainable Growth 148

The Buying Centre: A Cross-Functional Group 148

Charting the Organizational Buying Process 150

Stages in the Organizational Buying Process 150

Buying a Machine Vision System 151

Online Buying in Organizational Markets 153

Prominence of Online Buying in Organizational Markets 153

E-marketplaces: Virtual Organizational Markets 153

Going Online: eBay Means Business, Too 154

Online Auctions in Organizational Markets 154

Learning Objectives Review 156

Applying Marketing Knowledge 157

Building Your Marketing Plan 157

Video Case 6 Trek: Building Better Bikes through Organizational Buying 158

7 Reaching Global Markets 162

Building a $2.5 Billion Business in India the Dell Inc. Way 162

Dynamics of World Trade 163

World Trade 163

Marketing Matters: Five Trade Trends and How Canada Can Take Advantage of Them 165

Competitive Advantage of Nations 166

Marketing in a Borderless Economic World 168

Decline of Economic Protectionism 168

Making Responsible Decisions: Global Ethics and Global Economics—The Case of Protectionism 168

Rise of Economic Integration 169

A New Reality: Global Competition among Global Companies for Global Consumers 171

Emergence of a Networked Global Marketspace 173

Growing Prevalence of Economic Espionage 174

A Global Environmental Scan 174

Cultural Diversity 174

Economic Considerations 177

Political-Regulatory Climate 179

Going Online: Checking a Country's Political Risk Rating 179

Comparing Global Market Entry Strategies 180

Exporting 180

Licensing 181

Joint Venture 181

Direct Investment 182

Crafting a Worldwide Marketing Program 182

Product and Promotion Strategies 182

Marketing Matters: Global Marketing and Social Media 184

Distribution Strategy 185

Pricing Strategy 185

Learning Objectives Review 187

Applying Marketing Knowledge 188

Building Your Marketing Plan 188

Video Case 7   Mary Kay, Inc.: Building a Brand in India 189

Part 3   **Targeting Marketing Opportunities 193**

8 **Marketing Research: From Information to Action 193**

Using Social Media for Marketing Research 193

What Is Marketing Research? 194

Types of Marketing Research 195

Exploratory Research 195

Descriptive Research 195

Causal Research 196

The Marketing Research Process 196

Problem Definition 197

Exploratory Research 197

Formal Research Design 200

Survey 201

Experiment 203

Observation 205

Using Marketing Dashboards: Making Sense of Online Panel Results 205

Marketing Matters: Neuromarketing: The Holy Grail of Marketing Research? 207

Is There an Optimal Research Design? 208

Sampling 208

Data Collection and Analysis 209

Conclusions and Report 209

Ethical Issues in the Marketing Research Process 210

Making Responsible Decisions: A Charter of Respondent Rights 210

Using an Intelligent Marketing Enterprise Platform to Trigger Marketing Actions 211

Going Online: The Latest News in Marketing Research 213

Learning Objectives Review 214

Applying Marketing Knowledge 215

Building Your Marketing Plan 216

Video Case 8   Carmex®: Leveraging Facebook for Marketing Research 216

9 Market Segmentation, Targeting, and Positioning 220

Segmenting the Tourism Market 220

Why Segment Markets? 221

What Market Segmentation Means 221

When to Segment Markets 223

Steps in Segmenting and Targeting Markets 224

Step 1: Group Potential Buyers into Segments 225

Marketing Matters: Segmenting the Social Media User 227

Step 2: Group Products to Be Sold into Categories 229

Going Online: Apple Inc. Product Groupings 229

Step 3: Develop a Market–Product Grid and Estimate Size of Markets 230

Step 4: Select Target Markets 230

Making Responsible Decisions: De-selection of Customers or Customer Segments 231

Step 5: Take Marketing Actions to Reach Target Markets 232

Positioning the Product 233

Two Approaches to Product Positioning 233

Writing a Positioning Statement 234

Product Positioning Using Perceptual Maps 234

Sales Forecasting Techniques 236

Judgments of the Decision Maker 236

Surveys of Knowledgeable Groups 236

Statistical Methods 237

Learning Objectives Review 238

Applying Marketing Knowledge 239

Building Your Marketing Plan 239

Video Case 9   Prince Sports, Inc.: Tennis Racquets for Every Segment 239

Part 4   Satisfying Marketing Opportunities 243

10 Developing New Products and Services 243

The Space Elevator Is No Longer Science Fiction 243

The Variations of Products 244

Product Line and Product Mix 244

Classifying Products 245

Classifying Consumer and Business Goods 245

Classification of Consumer Goods 245

Classification of Business Goods 246

What Is a New Product? 247

What Are New Services? 249

Why New Products or Services Succeed or Fail 250

Marketing Reasons for New-Product Failures 250

Marketing Matters: Some Canadian Innovation Success Stories 251

Using Marketing Dashboards: Monitoring Your New-Product Launch 252

The New-Product Process 254

Stage 1: New-Product Strategy Development 254

Stage 2: Idea Generation 255

Stage 3: Screening and Evaluation 256

Stage 4: Business Analysis 257

Stage 5: Development 258

Stage 6: Market Testing 258

Stage 7: Commercialization 259

Learning Objectives Review 261

Applying Marketing Knowledge 262

Building Your Marketing Plan 263

Video Case 10   X-1: Breaking the Barriers of Sound with New-Product Development 263

11 Managing Products and Brands 267

Canada's Most Trusted Brands 267

Product Life Cycle 268

Introduction Stage 268

Growth Stage 270

Maturity Stage 270

Decline Stage 270

Four Dimensions of the Product Life Cycle 271

Managing the Product Life Cycle 273

Role of a Product Manager 273

Modifying the Product 273

Modifying the Market 274

Repositioning the Product 275

Using Marketing Dashboards: Knowing Your CDI and BDI 275

Making Responsible Decisions: Consumer Economics of Downsizing: Get Less, Pay More 277

Branding and Brand Management 277

Brand Personality and Brand Equity 278

Marketing Matters: Top Global and Top Canadian Brands 280

Picking a Good Brand Name 281

Going Online: Have an Idea for a Brand or Trade Name? Check It Out! 282

Branding Strategies 282

Packaging and Labelling 285

Marketing Matters: Creating Customer Value through Packaging: Pez Heads Dispense More Than Candy 285

Creating Customer Value through Packaging and Labelling 286

Contemporary Packaging and Labelling Challenges 287

Product Warranty 288

Learning Objectives Review 289

Applying Marketing Knowledge 290

Building Your Marketing Plan 290

Video Case 11 P&G's Secret Deodorant: Finding Inspiration in Perspiration 291

12 Managing Services 295

Airbnb Redefines Services—and the Economy! 295

The Service Economy 297

The Uniqueness of Services 298

The Service Continuum 300

How Consumers Purchase Services 301

Purchasing a Service 301

Customer Contact Audit 302

Post-purchase Evaluation 303

*Making Responsible Decisions: Customer Behaviour Can Affect
    the Perception of Service Quality 304*

Managing the Marketing of Services: The Seven Ps 305

Product (Service) 305

Price 306

Place (Distribution) 306

Promotion 307

Going Online: Canada's North Tourism Initiative 307

People 308

Physical Evidence 308

Process 308

Using Marketing Dashboards: Are Airline Flights Profitably Loaded? 309

Services in the Future 310

Marketing Matters: Seven Steps to Creating Great Service Experiences! 311

Learning Objectives Review 312

Applying Marketing Knowledge 313

Building Your Marketing Plan 313

Video Case 12 LA Galaxy: Where Sports Marketing Is a Kick! 314

13 Pricing Products and Services 318

Vizio, Inc.—Delivering Beautifully Smart Products at a Great Value 318

Nature and Importance of Price 319

What Is a Price? 320

Price as an Indicator of Value 320

Price in the Marketing Mix 321

Step 1: Identifying Pricing Constraints and Objectives 321

Identifying Pricing Constraints 322

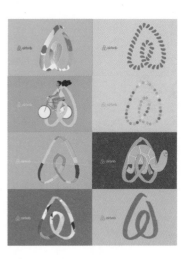

Making Responsible Decisions: Getting an Unfair Premium Price? 322

Identifying Pricing Objectives 323

Step 2: Estimating Demand and Revenue 326

Fundamentals of Estimating Demand 326

Fundamentals of Estimating Revenue 328

Step 3: Estimating Cost, Volume, and Profit Relationships 328

The Importance of Controlling Costs 328

Break-Even Analysis 328

Step 4: Selecting an Approximate Price Level 330

Demand-Oriented Approaches 330

Marketing Matters: Panera Cares Cafes: Where the Customers Decide What They Want to Pay!! 333

Cost-Oriented Approaches 333

Profit-Oriented Approaches 334

Competition-Oriented Approaches 335

Using Marketing Dashboards: Are Cracker Jack Prices above, at, or below the Market? 336

Step 5: Setting the List or Quoted Price 337

One-Price Policy versus Flexible-Price Policy 337

Company, Customer, and Competitive Effects 338

Social Media Impact on Pricing 339

Step 6: Making Special Adjustments to the List or Quoted Price 339

Discounts 339

Allowances 340

Geographical Adjustments 341

Legal and Regulatory Aspects of Pricing 341

Going Online: Checking Out Price Violations 342

Learning Objectives Review 344

Applying Marketing Knowledge 345

Building Your Marketing Plan 346

Video Case 13   Carmex: Setting the Price of the Number-One Lip Balm 346

Appendix B: Financial Aspects of Marketing 350

14 Managing Marketing Channels and Supply Chains 358

Callaway Golf: Designing and Delivering the Goods for Great Golf 358

Nature and Importance of Marketing Channels 360

Defining Marketing Channels of Distribution 360

Value Created by Intermediaries 361

Consumer Benefits from Intermediaries 361

Channel Structure and Organization 362

Marketing Channels for Consumer Goods and Services 362

Marketing Channels for Business Goods and Services 363

Internet Marketing Channels   364

Direct Marketing Channels   365

Multiple Channels and Strategic Alliances   365

A Closer Look at Channel Intermediaries   366

Vertical Marketing Systems and Channel Partnerships   367

Channel Choice and Management   368

Factors Affecting Channel Choice and Management   368

Channel Design Considerations   369

Going Online: Need Cash Fast? Check the Visa ATM Locator   369

Using Marketing Dashboards: Channel Sales and Profit at ABC Furniture   370

Global Dimensions of Marketing Channels   371

Channel Relationships: Conflict, Cooperation, and Law   372

Making Responsible Decisions: The Ethics of Slotting Allowances   373

Logistics and Supply Chain Management   374

Sourcing, Assembling, and Delivering a New Car: The Automotive Supply Chain   375

Supply Chain Management and Marketing Strategy   375

Information and Logistics Management Objective in a Supply Chain   377

Information's Role in Supply Chain Responsiveness and Efficiency   377

Total Logistics Cost Concept   377

Customer Service Concept   378

Key Logistics Functions in a Supply Chain   379

Transportation   379

Marketing Matters: Canada's Ice Road   381

Warehousing and Materials Handling   381

Order Processing   382

Inventory Management   382

Closing the Loop: Reverse Logistics   383

Learning Objectives Review   384

Applying Marketing Knowledge   386

Building Your Marketing Plan   386

Video Case 14   Amazon: Delivering the Earth's Biggest Selection!   386

15 Retailing   390

What Is Trending in Canadian Retailing?   390

The Value and Scope of Retailing   391

Classifying Retail Outlets   392

Form of Ownership   392

Level of Service   393

Merchandise Line   394

Non-store Retailing   395

Automatic Vending   395

Direct Mail and Catalogues   396

Television Home Shopping 397

Online Retailing 397

Telemarketing 398

Direct Selling 398

Retailing Strategy 399

Positioning a Retail Store 399

Retailing Mix 400

Using Marketing Dashboards: Why Apple Stores May Be the Best Retailer 403

The Changing Nature of Retailing 404

The Wheel of Retailing 405

The Retail Life Cycle 405

Five Important Trends That Are Shaping the Retail Landscape 406

Travel Retailing 406

Going Online: Welcome to the Retail Council of Canada 407

Mobile Retailing 407

Faster Retailing 408

Experience Retailing 408

Innovative Retailing 408

Marketing Matters: The Shopping Bag of the Future Is Here! 409

Making Responsible Decisions: Innovative Retailing Includes Sustainability Practices 410

Learning Objectives Review 411

Applying Marketing Knowledge 411

Building Your Marketing Plan 412

Video Case 15   The Mall of America: America's Biggest Mall Knows the Secret to Successful Retailing! 412

16 Integrated Marketing Communications and Direct Marketing 416

Taco Bell Loves Twitter! 416

The Communication Process 418

Encoding and Decoding 419

Feedback 419

Noise 419

The Promotional Elements 420

Advertising 420

Personal Selling 421

Public Relations 421

Sales Promotion 422

Direct Marketing 422

Integrated Marketing Communications—Developing the Promotional Mix 423

Marketing Matters: Sears Canada Goes Integrated! 423

The Target Audience 424

The Product Life Cycle 424

Product Characteristics   425

Stages of the Buying Decision   426

Channel Strategies   427

Developing the IMC Program   429

Identifying the Target Audience   429

Specifying Promotion Objectives   429

Setting the Promotion Budget   430

Using Marketing Dashboards: How Much Should You Spend on IMC?   430

Selecting the Right Promotional Tools   431

Designing the Promotion   432

Scheduling the Promotion   432

Executing and Evaluating the IMC Program   432

Going Online: Canadian Agencies Adopt IMC Approaches   433

Direct Marketing   433

The Growth of Direct Marketing   434

The Value of Direct Marketing   434

Technological, Global, and Ethical Issues in Direct Marketing   435

Making Responsible Decisions: Consumer Privacy and Direct Marketing in the Future   436

Learning Objectives Review   437

Applying Marketing Knowledge   438

Building Your Marketing Plan   438

Video Case 16   Taco Bell: Using IMC to Help Customers Live Más!   438

17 Advertising, Sales Promotion, and Public Relations   442

Virtual Reality Is the New Reality for Advertising   442

Types of Advertisements   443

Product Advertisements   444

Institutional Advertisements   444

Developing the Advertising Program   445

Identifying the Target Audience   445

Specifying Advertising Objectives   446

Setting the Advertising Budget   446

Designing the Advertisement   446

Selecting the Right Media   448

Using Marketing Dashboards: What Is the Best Way to Reach 1,000 Customers?   450

Different Media Alternatives   450

Going Online: Mobile Advertising Is Growing in Canada   456

Scheduling the Advertising   456

Executing the Advertising Program   457

Pre-testing the Advertising   457

Carrying Out the Advertising Program   457

Evaluating the Advertising Program   458

Post-testing the Advertising   458

Making Needed Changes   459

Marketing Matters: Consumers' Perspectives on Advertising in Canada   459

Sales Promotion   460

The Importance of Sales Promotion   460

Consumer-Oriented Sales Promotions   460

Trade-Oriented Sales Promotions   463

Public Relations   464

Public Relations Tools   464

Making Responsible Decisions: Ethics and PR Activities   465

Learning Objectives Review   467

Applying Marketing Knowledge   468

Building Your Marketing Plan   469

Video Case 17   Google, Inc.: The Right Ads at the Right Time   469

18 Personal Selling and Sales Management   473

Meet Today's Sales Professional   473

Scope and Significance of Personal Selling and
Sales Management   474

Nature of Personal Selling and Sales Management   475

Pervasiveness of Selling   475

Personal Selling in Marketing and Entrepreneurship   475

Creating Customer Value through Salespeople: Relationship and
Partnership Selling   476

The Many Forms of Personal Selling   477

Order Taking   477

Order Getting   477

Customer Sales Support Personnel   478

The Personal Selling Process: Building Relationships   479

Prospecting   479

Preapproach   479

Approach   481

Presentation   481

Close   483

Follow-Up   483

The Sales Management Process   483

Sales Plan Formulation: Setting Direction   483

Making Responsible Decisions: The Ethics of Asking Customers about Competitors   484

Sales Plan Implementation: Putting the Plan into Action   488

Going Online: What Is Your Emotional Intelligence?   489

Salesforce Evaluation: Measuring Results   490

*Using Marketing Dashboards: Tracking Salesperson Performance at Moore Chemical &
Sanitation Supply, Inc.   491*

Salesforce Automation and Customer Relationship Management 492

Marketing Matters: How to Use Twitter as a Sales Tool 493

Learning Objectives Review 495

Applying Marketing Knowledge 496

Building Your Marketing Plan 496

Video Case 18   Xerox: Building Customer Relationships Through Personal Selling 497

Part 5   **Managing the Marketing Process 500**

19 **Pulling It All Together: The Strategic Marketing Process 500**

Strategic Marketing Helps General Mills Adapt to New Tastes! 500

Marketing Basics: Doing What Works and Allocating Resources 502

Finding and Using What Really Works 502

Allocating Marketing Resources Using Sales Response Functions 503

The Planning Phase of the Strategic Marketing Process 506

The Vital Importance of Metrics in Marketing Planning 506

The Variety of Marketing Plans 507

Marketing Planning Frameworks: The Search for Growth 508

Marketing Matters: Canada Goose's Differentiation Strategy Is Working 509

Marketing Matters: A Key Strategy Issue: Finding Synergies 511

Some Planning and Strategy Lessons 513

Making Responsible Decisions: Strategy Includes Good Citizenship and Sustainable Development 515

Going Online: Want to Be a BCG Consultant? Solve the Trevor's Toys Online Case 516

The Implementation Phase of the Strategic Marketing Process 516

Is Planning or Implementation the Problem? 516

Increasing Emphasis on Marketing Implementation 517

Improving Implementation of Marketing Programs 517

Organizing for Marketing 519

The Evaluation Phase of the Strategic Marketing Process 522

The Marketing Evaluation Process 522

Evaluation Involves Marketing ROI, Metrics, and Dashboards 523

Evaluation Using Marketing Metrics and Marketing Dashboards at General Mills 523

Learning Objectives Review 526

Applying Marketing Knowledge 527

Building Your Marketing Plan 528

Video Case 19   General Mills Warm Delights™: Indulgent, Delicious, and Gooey! 528

20 Using Social Media and Mobile Marketing to Connect with Consumers 532

The Ultimate Marketing Machine . . . Is in Your Pocket! 532

Understanding Social Media 533

What Are Social Media? 533

Comparing Social and Traditional Media 535

A Look at Four Important Social Networks 536

Comparing Four Social Media 536

Facebook 537

Twitter 540

LinkedIn 541

YouTube 541

Marketing Matters: Mobile Marketing Discovers Video Bloggers 542

Integrating Social Media into Today's Marketing Strategies 543

Social Media and the Strategic Marketing Process 543

Selecting the Social Media 543

How Social Media Produce Sales 543

Measuring the Results of Social Media Programs 544

Social Media + Smartphones + Exotic Apps 546

The Convergence of Real and Digital Worlds 546

Mobile Marketing: Tightening Links to Marketing Actions 547

Social Media and Global Marketing 548

Learning Objectives Review 550

Applying Marketing Knowledge 551

Building Your Marketing Plan 551

Video Case 20 StuffDOT™, Inc.: Rewarding Users for Actively Shopping and Sharing! 552

Glossary GL-1

Chapter Notes CN-1

Name Index NI-1

Company/Product Index CI-1

Subject Index SI-1

PREFACE

Marketing utilizes a unique, innovative, and effective pedagogical approach developed by the authors through the integration of their combined classroom, college, and university experiences. The elements of this approach have been the foundation for each edition of *Marketing* and serve as the core of the text and its supplements as they evolve and adapt to changes in student learning styles, the growth of the marketing discipline, and the development of new instructional technologies. The distinctive features of the approach are illustrated below:

A high-engagement style

An easy-to-read, high-involvement, interactive writing style that engages students through active learning techniques, timely and interesting examples, and challenging applications.

A strong pedagogical framework

The use of Learning Objectives, Learning Reviews, key terms, boxed applications, and Learning Objectives Review summaries, along with supportive student supplements, appeals to a wide range of learning styles.

Personalized marketing

A vivid and accurate description of businesses, marketing professionals, and entrepreneurs—through cases, exercises, and testimonials—that allows students to personalize marketing and identify possible career interests and role models.

Marketing, Tenth Canadian Edition
Pedagogical Approach

Integrated technology

The use of powerful technical resources and learning solutions such as Connect and SmartBook.

Emphasis on marketing decision-making

The use of extended examples, cases, and videos involving people making marketing decisions, which helps students to easily relate to text concepts.

The goal of the tenth Canadian edition of *Marketing* is to create an exceptional experience for today's students and instructors of marketing. The development of *Marketing* was based on a rigorous process of assessment, and the outcome of the process is a text and package of learning tools that are based on experience, leadership, and innovation in marketing education.

CURRENT, STREAMLINED COVERAGE

The tenth Canadian edition of *Marketing* has been revised, updated, and packed with new examples of marketing in Canada and around the world. You'll find new or expanded coverage of topics such as marketing analytics, big data, the Internet of Things (IoT), sustainable marketing, social enterprise and benefits corporations, CROPing, brand community, intelligent marketing enterprise platforms, design thinking, crowdfunding, minimally viable product (MVP), service sweethearting, surge pricing, omnichannel marketing, programmatic ad purchasing, addressable television advertising, and time-based agendas. Social media marketing and mobile marketing are also emphasized throughout the text.

We also overhauled our examples, cases, and pedagogy. The tenth Canadian edition includes 19 new opening vignettes, 11 new Marketing Matters boxes, and 10 new Video Cases. The Using Marketing Dashboards feature exposes students to the measures that marketing professionals use to track and analyze marketing phenomena and performance. Finally, the end-of-chapter Building Your Marketing Plan feature provides students with guidance and instruction for developing their own marketing plan for a new business.

Detailed List of Changes

Chapter 1 – Marketing: Customer Value, Relationships, and Experiences Through Marketing

- Chapter 1 features a new opening vignette on the City of Hamilton and its marketing program. There is also a new definition of marketing, a new concept called customer value proposition, a new Marketing Matters box, and new material on social media.

Chapter 2 – Developing Successful Marketing Strategies

- The new opening vignette in Chapter 2 is about Ben & Jerry's. The chapter also includes a new Marketing Matters box; a new example of business portfolio analysis featuring Apple; new material on dashboards, metrics, marketing analytics, and big data; new material on CMOs; and a new end-of-chapter Video Case about IBM.

Chapter 3 – Scanning the Marketing Environment

- Chapter 3 features new opening vignette material on Facebook; a new Marketing Matters box; a new Making Responsible Decisions box; a new section on technology, including the Internet of Things and data analytics; new examples of environmental trends; new information on Millennials; and updated statistics on the Canadian and global marketplaces.

Chapter 4 – Ethics and Social Responsibility for Sustainable Marketing

- Chapter 4 has a new opening vignette on some of Canada's most ethically and socially responsible companies, new examples of social responsibility, a new discussion of sustainable marketing, new examples of green marketing, development on new concepts social enterprise and benefit corporations, and a new end-of-chapter Video Case about Toyota.

Chapter 5 – Consumer Behaviour

- Chapter 5 includes a new chapter opener that discusses a new concept called CROPing, an updated lifestyle section, a new Marketing Matters box, a new concept called brand community, a totally updated French Canadian subculture section, and a new section on South Asian Canadians as an emerging subculture.

Chapter 6 – Understanding Organizations as Customers

- Chapter 6 features a new chapter opener on Campus Living Centres, a new Marketing Matters box, updated literature throughout the chapter, as well as new examples of business-to-business marketing.

Chapter 7 – Reaching Global Markets

- Chapter 7 provides a new opening vignette on Dell in India, a new Marketing Matters box, updated statistics on world trade and Canadian trade data, a new concept called economic espionage, and material on the new Trans-Pacific Partnership (TPP) agreement. There is also a new end-of-chapter Video Case on Mary Kay in India.

Chapter 8 – Marketing Research: From Information to Action

- Chapter 8 includes a new opening vignette on using social media for marketing research, new material on novel research methods and tools, a new section on intelligent marketing enterprise platforms, and a new section on big data, data analytics, and data mining.

Chapter 9 – Market Segmentation, Targeting, and Positioning

- Chapter 9 provides a new opening vignette on segmenting the Canadian tourism market, new examples of targeting and positioning.

Chapter 10 – Developing New Products and Services

- Chapter 10 includes a new opening vignette on the ThothX Tower, a so-called space elevator; new examples of new products; a new discussion on product failure; new concepts such as design thinking, crowdfunding, and minimally viable products (MVPs); as well as a new end-of-chapter Video Case on X-1.

Chapter 11 – Managing Products and Brands

- Chapter 11 provides a new opening vignette on Canada's most trusted brands, updated examples in the section on the product life cycle, new Marketing Matters and Making Responsible Decision boxes, new material on picking a good brand name, a new example on sub-branding, and a new end-of-chapter Video Case on Secret deodorant.

Chapter 12 – Managing Services

- Chapter 12 features a new opening vignette on Airbnb, updated statistics on the services economy, a new section on services in the future, a new concept called service sweethearting, and a new end-of-chapter Video Case on the LA Galaxy.

Chapter 13 – Pricing Products and Services

- Chapter 13 contains a new opening vignette on Vizio, new material on the cost of marketing products, new material about competitors' prices and consumer awareness of such, a new example of estimating demand, new material on dynamic pricing, a new concept called surge pricing, and a new end-of-chapter Video Case on Carmex.

Chapter 14 – Managing Marketing Channels and Supply Chains

- Chapter 14 features an updated opening vignette on Callaway Golf as an example of a successful multichannel marketer, new material on Internet marketing channels, and a new concept called omnichannel marketing is discussed.

Chapter 15 – Retailing

- Chapter 15 opens with a new opening vignette on what is trending in Canadian retailing, featuring information about retailers such as Indochino, Kit and Ace, Starbucks Canada, and HBC. The chapter also features updated statistics related to global and Canadian retailing, a new section on trends shaping the retail landscape, new Marketing Matters and Making Responsible Decisions boxes, and a new end-of-chapter Video Case about the Mall of America.

Chapter 16 – Integrated Marketing Communications and Direct Marketing

- Chapter 16 includes a new opening vignette on Taco Bell, new Marketing Matters and Making Responsible Decisions boxes, new material on direct marketing and mobile marketing, and a new end-of-chapter Video Case discussing Taco Bell's IMC campaign.

Chapter 17 – Advertising, Sales Promotion, and Public Relations

- Chapter 17 offers a new opening vignette on virtual reality and advertising, new examples of advocacy ads, a new section on identifying a target audience, new examples of setting ad objectives, updated statistics on media spending, new concepts such as programmatic ad purchasing and addressable television advertising, updated material on online advertising, new data on ad complaints, and new Marketing Matters and Making Responsible Decisions boxes.

Chapter 18 – Personal Selling and Sales Management

- Chapter 18 includes a new opening vignette on today's sales professional, new material about personal selling and entrepreneurship, and updated literature on sales management.

Chapter 19 – Pulling It All Together: The Strategic Marketing Process

- Chapter 19 features a new opening vignette on marketing strategy at General Mills and an updated section on metrics in marketing planning. It also includes a new section on finding and using what works, a new section about disruptive innovation and long-range marketing planning, discussion of a new concept called time-based agendas, an updated section on the evolving role of chief marketing officers (CMOs), and a new section on digging beneath the numbers ("Hiring a Milkshake!")

Chapter 20 – Using Social Media and Mobile Marketing to Connect with Customers

- The title of Chapter 20 has been adapted to reflect the growing importance of mobile marketing. There is also a new opening vignette featuring mobile marketing. The chapter has been updated with the latest statistics on social media and mobile marketing in Canada, new examples of social media and mobile marketing, a new section on specialized social media such as Pinterest, and a new section about convergence. Finally, there is a new end-of-chapter Video Case featuring StuffDOT.

FEATURES

Chapter-opening vignettes introduce students to the concepts ahead in each chapter, using an exciting company (or companies) as an example. **Nineteen** vignettes are new to this edition, including new features about the City of Hamilton, Campus Living Centres, Airbnb, Dell in India, ThothX Tower, and Taco Bell.

Learning Objectives open each chapter to help students preview chapter content and study effectively.

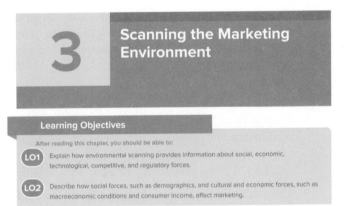

3 Scanning the Marketing Environment

Learning Objectives

After reading this chapter, you should be able to:

LO1 Explain how environmental scanning provides information about social, economic, technological, competitive, and regulatory forces.

LO2 Describe how social forces, such as demographics, and cultural and economic forces, such as macroeconomic conditions and consumer income, affect marketing.

Learning Review

1. What is strategy?
2. What is marketing accountability?
3. What are examples of a functional level in an organization?

Learning Reviews are checkpoints, found at the end of each major chapter section, that pose critical-thinking and memory-recall questions. These questions help students to reflect on the text and test their comprehension of the material before moving on.

Using Marketing Dashboards boxes highlight the increasing importance of metrics in marketing. Marketing dashboards graphically portray the measures that marketers use to track and analyze marketing phenomena and performance. Students will find commonly used measures applied by successful marketers throughout the text and will be exposed to their calculation, interpretation, and application.

USING MARKETING DASHBOARDS

Why Apple Stores May Be the Best Retailer

How effective is my retail format compared to other stores? How are my stores performing this year compared to last year? Information related to this question is often displayed in a marketing dashboard using two measures: (1) sales per square foot, and (2) same-store sales growth.

Your Challenge You have been assigned to evaluate the Apple Store retail format. The store's simple, inviting, and open atmosphere has been the topic of discussion among many retailers. Apple, however, is relatively new to the retailing business and many experts have been skeptical of the format. To allow an assessment of Apple Stores, use *sales per square foot* as an indicator of how effectively retail space is used to generate revenue and *same-store sales growth* to compare the increase in sales of stores that have been open for the same period of time. The calculations for these two indicators are:

MARKETING MATTERS

How Ethnic Canadian Buyers Shop!

Ethnic Canadians will double in size over the next 20 years, and marketers are going to have to understand how and why ethnic Canadians shop the way they do. Some marketers have already come to recognize the need to study the shopping behaviour of ethnic Canadians. For example, BrandSpark International studied the buying habits of more than 8,800 Canadians of Chinese, South Asian, and East Asian backgrounds, Canada's top ethnic groups. The study found that getting the biggest value for their money emerged as the most important factor in purchase decisions, and it revealed differences in the way that ethnic buyers rely on word of mouth and the Internet for shopping information. It also showed that ethnic Canadians are big consumers of high-tech gadgets, they're more likely to eat pre-made frozen meals or take-out, and they shop at Walmart more often than the average Canadian.

Marketing Matters boxes provide engaging, real-world examples of marketing applications in action to give students further insight into the practical world of marketing. The tenth Canadian edition features **11** new Marketing Matters boxes, including topics such as how ethnic Canadians shop; PRIZM5, a Canadian lifestyles psychographic system; the shopping bag of the future; and mobile marketing.

Making Responsible Decisions boxes focus on social responsibility, sustainability, and ethics, and provide examples of how companies approach these subjects in their marketing strategy. **New** boxes in the tenth Canadian edition cover topics such as female body image and marketing, and sustainable retailing.

MAKING RESPONSIBLE DECISIONS

Cross-Device Tracking and Consumer Privacy

According to privacy experts, advertisers looking to use cross-device tracking need to update their privacy practices to make users aware of it, as well as provide opportunities to opt out.

The technology to connect users' identities across their desktops and mobile devices is relatively new. Until recently, siloed mobile and desktop systems prevented marketers from using the same audience data across devices; desktop behavioural data, collected and applied with cookies, couldn't be used to target mobile ads, since it wasn't possible to identify the same user on mobile. But now companies such as Google, Facebook, and Adobe are offering cookie-free cross-device user identification, which allows marketers to connect audience profiles to users on whatever device they're on. That means a user logging in from home, at work, or on the go will be identified and targeted using the same data about their past behaviour and preferences.

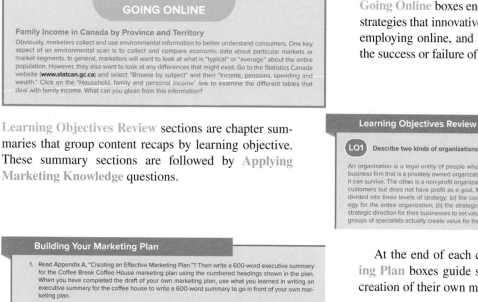

GOING ONLINE

Family Income in Canada by Province and Territory
Obviously, marketers collect and use environmental information to better understand consumers. One key aspect of an environmental scan is to collect and compare economic data about particular markets or market segments. In general, marketers will want to look at what is "typical" or "average" about the entire population. However, they also want to look at any differences that might exist. Go to the Statistics Canada website (**www.statcan.gc.ca**) and select "Browse by subject" and then "Income, pensions, spending and wealth." Click on the "Household, family and personal income" link to examine the different tables that deal with family income. What can you glean from this information?

Going Online boxes encourage students to explore digital strategies that innovative companies and organizations are employing online, and ask them to think critically about the success or failure of the company's efforts.

Learning Objectives Review sections are chapter summaries that group content recaps by learning objective. These summary sections are followed by **Applying Marketing Knowledge** questions.

Learning Objectives Review

LO1 Describe two kinds of organizations that exist and the three levels of strategy in them.

An organization is a legal entity of people who share a common mission. There are two kinds. One is a business firm that is a privately owned organization that serves its customers in order to earn a profit so that it can survive. The other is a non-profit organization that is a non-governmental organization that serves its customers but does not have profit as a goal. Most large business firms and non-profit organizations are divided into three levels of strategy: (a) the corporate level, where top management directs overall strategy for the entire organization; (b) the strategic business unit level, where managers set a more specific strategic direction for their businesses to set value-creating opportunities; and (c) the functional level, where groups of specialists actually create value for the organization.

Building Your Marketing Plan

1. Read Appendix A, "Creating an Effective Marketing Plan."? Then write a 600-word executive summary for the Coffee Break Coffee House marketing plan using the numbered headings shown in the plan. When you have completed the draft of your own marketing plan, use what you learned in writing an executive summary for the coffee house to write a 600-word summary to go in front of your own marketing plan.
2. Using Chapter 2 and Appendix A as guides, give focus to your marketing plan by (a) writing your mission statement in 25 words or less, (b) listing three non-financial goals and three financial goals, (c) writing your competitive advantage in 35 words or less, and (d) doing a SWOT analysis table.

At the end of each chapter, **Building Your Marketing Plan** boxes guide students through the step-by-step creation of their own marketing plan.

Each chapter concludes with a **Video Case** that provides an up-close look at a company example, reinforcing the chapter content while bringing the material to life. The video segments that accompany these written cases are available for viewing on *Connect*. IBM, GoPro, Mary Kay in India, Taco Bell, Carmex, Toyota, and Secret

Video Case 4

Toyota: Building Cleaner, Greener Cars
"Toyota's mission is to become the most respected and admired car company in North America," explains Jana Hartline, manager of environmental communications at Toyota. To accomplish this, Jana and her colleagues at Toyota are working toward a future where a wide range of innovative vehicles, fuel technologies, and partnerships converge to create an economically vibrant, mobile society in harmony with the environment. It's a challenge Jana finds exciting, and the result is cleaner, greener cars!

deodorant are just some of the exciting new Video Cases available with the tenth Canadian edition. Accompanying the Video Cases are updated questions, some of which require quantitative analysis.

MARKET LEADING TECHNOLOGY

Learn without Limits

McGraw-Hill Connect® is an award-winning digital teaching and learning platform that gives students the means to better connect with their coursework, with their instructors, and with the important concepts that they will need to know for success now and in the future.

With Connect, instructors can take advantage of McGraw-Hill's trusted content to seamlessly deliver assignments, quizzes, and tests online. McGraw-Hill Connect is a learning platform that continually adapts to each student, delivering precisely what they need, when they need it, so class time is more engaging and effective. Connect makes teaching and learning personal, easy, and proven.

Connect Key Features

SmartBook®

As the first and only adaptive reading experience, SmartBook is changing the way students read and learn. SmartBook creates a personalized reading experience by highlighting the most important concepts a student needs to learn at that moment. As a student engages with SmartBook, the reading experience continuously adapts by highlighting content based on what each student knows and doesn't know. This ensures that he or she is focused on the content needed to close specific knowledge gaps, while it simultaneously promotes long-term learning.

Connect Insight®

Connect Insight is Connect's new one-of-a-kind visual analytics dashboard—now available for instructors—that provides at-a-glance information regarding student performance, which is immediately actionable. By presenting assignment, assessment, and topical performance results together with a time metric that is easily visible for aggregate or individual results, Connect Insight gives instructors the ability to take a just-in-time approach to teaching and learning, which was never before available. Connect Insight presents data that help instructors improve class performance in a way that is efficient and effective.

Simple Assignment Management

With Connect, creating assignments is easier than ever, so instructors can spend more time teaching and less time managing. Instructors can:

- Assign SmartBook learning modules.
- Edit existing questions and create their own questions.
- Draw from a variety of text specific questions, resources, and test bank material to assign online.
- Streamline lesson planning, student progress reporting, and assignment grading to make classroom management more efficient than ever.

Smart Grading

When it comes to studying, time is precious. Connect helps students learn more efficiently by providing feedback and practice material when they need it, where they need it.

- Automatically score assignments, giving students immediate feedback on their work and comparisons with correct answers.
- Access and review each response; manually change grades or leave comments for students to review.
- Track individual student performance—by question, by assignment, or in relation to the class overall—with detailed grade reports.
- Reinforce classroom concepts with practice tests and instant quizzes.
- Integrate grade reports easily with learning management systems, including Blackboard, D2L, and Moodle.

Instructor Library

The Connect Instructor Library is a repository for additional resources to improve student engagement in and out of the class. It provides all the critical resources instructors need to build their course.

- Access instructor resources.
- View assignments and resources created for past sections.
- Post your own resources for students to use.

Instructor Resources

Crane Connect is a one-stop shop for instructor resources, including the following:

- **Instructor's Manual:** The Instructor's Manual contains learning objectives, key terms, detailed lecture notes, summaries of all boxed features, and answers to Learning Reviews and Applying Marketing Knowledge questions.
- **PowerPoint Presentations:** These robust presentations offer high-quality visuals that bring key marketing concepts to life.
- **Visually Enhanced Computerized Test Bank:** The Test Bank contains an extensive array of multiple choice and essay questions, Learning Objective, and Bloom's level of learning (knowledge, comprehension, or application). The Test Bank also offers a number of **visually enhanced questions** that include images and figures from the textbook. The computerized test bank allows instructors to create tests from book-specific items. It also offers a number of question types and allows instructors to add their own questions. It is available through a flexible and easy-to-use electronic testing program, with test items also available in Word format (rich text format).
- **Video Cases:** A unique series of 20 contemporary marketing cases, half of which are new for this edition. Each video corresponds with a chapter-specific topic and an end-of-chapter case in the text. This series is also available on DVD, and includes closed captioning.
- **Alternate Cases:** A wealth of additional cases provides even more opportunities to bring course content to life for students.
- **Video Case and Alternate Case Teaching Notes:** Helpful teaching suggestions and solutions for the Video Cases and alternate cases.
- **Brief Video Clips and Discussion Questions:** This resource is perfect for instructors who struggle to find time to play a longer video or Video Case in class. Instructors can access short (two to five minutes), engaging, and current video clips, as well as suggestions for encouraging class discussion around each clip.
- **Instructor Newsletter and Blog:** The Instructor Newsletter has been developed for adopters of *Marketing*. This newsletter is devoted to providing innovative resources to help improve student learning, offer timely marketing examples, and make class preparation easier. The newsletter includes links to video clips, synopses of articles with in-class discussion questions, teaching tips, and discussion of pedagogical features of *Marketing*. The newsletter is offered eight times during the academic year.
- **Instructor's Survival Kit (ISK):** Today's students are more likely to learn and be motivated by active, participative experiences than by classic classroom lecture and discussion. To illustrate marketing concepts and encourage student participation and collaboration, the Instructor's Survival Kit contains an In-Class Activities Guide. These activities have received extremely positive feedback from both instructors and students. In-class activities may relate to a specific Video Case or example from the tenth Canadian edition text.
- **Image Library:** A digital copy of each photo, illustration, and table from the textbook, which instructors can use to create customized PowerPoint slides or design compelling course websites.

Superior Learning Solutions and Support

The McGraw-Hill Education team is ready to help instructors assess and integrate any of our products, technology, and services into your course for optimal teaching and learning performance. Whether it's helping your students improve their grades, or putting your entire course online, the McGraw-Hill Education team is here to help you do it. Contact your Learning Solutions Consultant today to learn how to maximize all of McGraw-Hill Education's resources.

For more information, please visit us online: **http://www.mheducation.ca/he/solutions**

ACKNOWLEDGMENTS

To ensure continuous improvement of our product, we have utilized an extensive review and development process for each of our editions. Building on that history, the tenth Canadian edition development process included several phases of evaluation by a broad panel of instructors. Reviewers who were vital in helping us develop this edition include:

Ambika Badh, *McMaster University*

Michelle Clement, *Camosun College*

Lianne Foti, *University of Guelph*

E. Stephen Grant, *University of New Brunswick*

Dwight Heinrichs, *University of Regina*

Ingrid Mueller, *Seneca College*

Surjit Rai, *NAIT*

Kathleen Rodenburg, *University of Waterloo*

Mark Valvasori, *Mohawk College*

The preceding list demonstrates the amount of feedback and developmental input that went into this project; we are deeply grateful to the numerous people who have shared their ideas with us.

Thanks are due to John Shepherd of Kwantlen Polytechnic University for his contribution to the text (Appendix A). Many business people and organizations also provided substantial assistance in making available information that appears in the text and supplements.

Finally, we acknowledge the professional efforts of the McGraw-Hill Education Higher Education staff. Completion of this edition and its many supplements required the attention and commitment of many editorial, production, marketing, and research personnel. Thanks to Karen Fozard, Portfolio and Program Manager; Joy Armitage Taylor, Executive Marketing Manager; Janie Deneau, Supervising Editor; Mike Kelly, Copy Editor; and Derek Capitaine, Photo and Permissions Researcher. Finally, I really want to thank my Product Developer, Amy Rydzanicz, for her dedication, patience, professionalism, and good humour.

I am responsible for the Canadianization of this text, so any questions or concerns about the book should be directed to me. I would like to thank my co-authors for their input, encouragement, and continued support.

I want to thank my daughters for their love and support throughout the writing process. I particularly wish to thank my beautiful wife Kimberly for being my partner, my best friend, and my constant inspiration. I love you sweetheart!

Frederick G. Crane

1

Creating Customer Value, Relationships, and Experiences Through Marketing

Learning Objectives

After reading this chapter, you should be able to:

LO1 Define marketing and identify the requirements for successful marketing to occur.

LO2 Understand the breadth and depth of marketing.

LO3 Explain how marketing discovers and satisfies consumer needs and wants.

LO4 Distinguish between marketing mix elements and environmental forces.

LO5 Describe how a market orientation focuses on creating customer value, satisfaction, and customer relationships.

LO6 Explain why some organizations have transitioned from the market orientation era to the customer experience management era.

LO7 Understand the emergence of the social media marketing era.

LO8 Understand the meaning of ethics and social responsibility and how they relate to the individual, organizations, and society.

The Marketing of the City of Hamilton, Ontario

When you think about marketing, you probably do not think that a city could or should market itself. Well, many cities, counties, and countries do market themselves! One city that is engaging in a marketing program is the city of Hamilton, Ontario. It is aggressively marketing itself as a good place to live, work, and do business.

One of the main objectives of the marketing campaign is letting the world know that Hamilton is no longer Canada's Steel City. In fact, the city is aiming to shatter old stereotypes as it rebrands itself to highlight its newly diversified economy, says Michael Marini, coordinator of marketing of the City of Hamilton's Economic Development Division.

So Hamilton has turned to calling itself "the ambitious city," a moniker it once had in the early 1900s. "From a marketing perspective, we've been extremely aggressive," Marini says. He says the city has a growing culinary scene with "funky, cool eateries" popping up, many of which are helmed by chefs from Toronto. In fact, foodie tours have emerged as a major component of Hamilton's efforts to change perceptions about the city. The foodie tours have been successful in generating investment and foodie interest, and have garnered Hamilton a Marketing Canada Award from the Economic Developers Association of Canada. The foodie tours consist of stops at eateries, mostly in the rejuvenating downtown core, which is attracting increasing numbers of young professionals and empty nesters.

When thousands of manufacturing jobs went overseas or down south in the 1980s, Hamilton lost its swagger and its right to call itself ambitious, Marini says. But the swagger is back, he says. While steel is still a large part of the economy, the city is now ranked as Canada's most diversified economy by the Conference Board of Canada. That diversification has helped lower Hamilton's unemployment rate to 5.7 percent, below the national average of 7 percent.

Hamilton has seen "exponential economic growth" in the last five years, Marini says, with the city of about 520,000 increasingly known for its health care and scientific research industries. Refugees from the Greater Toronto

Area are also fuelling the growth of the city as they flee astronomical house prices and traffic jams. "A lot of people in the GTA are starting to look at Hamilton," says Marini. According to Marini, Torontonians who work in creative industries such as graphic design or web and app development and are getting hard hit by the city's rent and house prices are increasingly looking at Hamilton as a viable alternative in terms of prices and quality of life.

Some observers, like the *Huffington Post,* have taken to calling Hamilton Canada's answer to Brooklyn. To catch the interest of disgruntled Toronto suburbanites, the city released a YouTube video that urged them to "wake up from your commuting nightmare" and live, work, and play in downtown Hamilton. Meanwhile, the city is also using a print ad that asks: "You know what beats commuting to downtown Toronto every day? Having a life." And another print ad notes that studio space in downtown Hamilton is less than half the price of Toronto.

For the most part, however, marketing efforts for Hamilton have been online, with a YouTube video called "Hamilton — The Ambitious City" leading the way with more than 48,000 views. While many marketers may say "big deal, we do that in a day for some of our campaigns," you have to compare apples to apples, Marini notes. "When you look at economic development videos, you don't generally think of 50,000 views. You may get a couple hundred because, basically, you're selling your community to investors."

According to Marini, focusing the marketing effort online is cost-effective and provides the city with significant data. "That data really shows us where we have to focus our efforts—what cities, what countries, even what topics we need to be covering," adds Marini. When it comes to targeting international investment, analytics are very helpful in determining which countries are most interested in Hamilton and in what sectors. "We're starting to glean a lot of hard data, which helps us in the end make a sale or get an investment for the city."[1]

As this chapter opener illustrates, marketing affects all individuals, all organizations, all industries, all countries, and our natural environment. This text seeks not only to teach you marketing concepts but also to demonstrate marketing's many applications and how it affects our lives. This knowledge should make you a better consumer, enable you to be a more informed and responsible citizen, and even help you in your career.

In this chapter and those that follow, you will feel the excitement of marketing. You will be introduced to the dynamic changes that will affect all of us in the future, and you will also meet many men and women whose marketing creativity sometimes achieved brilliant, extraordinary results. And who knows? Somewhere in these pages you may even find a career in marketing. For example, perhaps your future may involve sales for a large corporation, conducting marketing research in a consulting company, preparing advertising plans in an advertising firm, or maybe even starting your own business! You can find plenty of marketing career options by reading the "Planning a Career in Marketing" Appendix available on *Connect*™.

LO1 WHAT MARKETING IS AND WHAT IT IS NOT

Right now, we want you to take your very first marketing test. We know you are probably saying, "What a way to start off the book!" But do not get too stressed out. There is just one question, and it is the only time that we will ever ask you "not" to think before you answer. Quickly and honestly, what is the first word that comes to your mind when you hear the word "marketing"?

We are going to make an educated guess and predict that most of you will answer "advertising," "selling," or "common sense." In our classes, we have asked thousands of other students this same question and have found these to be the most typical answers. But *marketing is not advertising.* Although advertising is one of the most visible aspects of marketing, it is but one small element of marketing. *Marketing is not selling.* In fact, many marketing experts believe that effective marketing can reduce the need for selling.

Marketing is not merely common sense. While good marketers are sensible, perceptive, and intuitive, these traits alone are not sufficient for making successful marketing decisions. Effective marketing requires intimate knowledge and understanding of consumers and the marketplace, which goes beyond simple common sense.

We are very much aware of the misconceptions about marketing, including many negative ones. But marketing is not hucksterism; it is not about selling unwanted things and taking the customer's money. Nor is marketing about manipulating, fooling, or tricking the customer.[2] Therefore, in order to appreciate marketing fully, you need to understand what it is and what it is not.

Marketing: Defined

The American Marketing Association represents individuals and organizations involved in the development and practice of marketing worldwide. It defines **marketing** as the activity, set of institutions, and processes for creating, communicating, delivering, and exchanging offerings that have value for customers, clients, partners, and society at large.[3] This definition stresses the need to deliver genuine value in the offerings of goods, services, and ideas marketed to customers. Also, notice that an organization's marketing activities should also create value for its partners and for society.

To serve both buyers and sellers, marketing seeks (1) to discover the needs and wants of prospective customers, and (2) to satisfy them. These prospective customers include both individuals buying for themselves or their households and organizations that buy for their own use (such as manufacturers) or for resale (such as wholesalers and retailers). You will also soon discover that marketing uses a number of terms and concepts that you'll have to know in order to truly understand marketing. For help, complete the Going Online exercise below.

GOING ONLINE

Understanding Marketing: Terms and Concepts

Marketing uses a number of terms and concepts that are often difficult to remember. But the American Marketing Association is a valuable source of information on marketing. In fact, on its website, the AMA actually has a comprehensive dictionary containing over 4,000 marketing terms and concepts.

Go to **www.marketingpower.com** (the AMA's official website) and look for the Marketing Dictionary in the site's Resources Channel. Search for key terms and concepts that are of interest to you. This exercise should prove invaluable to you as you attempt to gain a better understanding of the marketing discipline. There are also a number of provincial chapters of the AMA in Canada. You may also wish to check out their websites for the latest marketing news in Canada.

Requirements for Marketing to Occur

For marketing to occur, at least four factors are required: (1) two or more parties (individuals or organizations) with unsatisfied needs, (2) a desire and ability on their part to be satisfied, (3) a way for the parties to communicate, and (4) something to exchange.

Two or More Parties with Unsatisfied Needs

Suppose you have developed an unmet need—a desire for information about how computer and telecommunications are interacting to reshape the workplace—but you did not yet know that *ComputerWorld* magazine existed. Also unknown to you was that several copies of *ComputerWorld* were sitting on the magazine rack at your nearest bookstore, waiting to be purchased. This is an example of two parties with unmet needs: you, with a need for technology-related information, and your bookstore owner, needing someone to buy a copy of *ComputerWorld*.

Desire and Ability to Satisfy These Needs

Both you and the bookstore owner want to satisfy these unmet needs. Furthermore, you have the money to buy the item and the time to get to the bookstore. The store's owner has not only the desire to sell *ComputerWorld* but also the ability to do so, since it is stocked on the shelves.

A Way for the Parties to Communicate

The marketing transaction of buying a copy of *ComputerWorld* will never occur unless you know that the product exists and its location. Similarly, the store owner will not stock the magazine unless there is a market of potential buyers nearby. When you receive a free sample in the mail or see the magazine on display in the bookstore, this communications barrier between you (the buyer) and your bookstore (the seller) is overcome.

Something to Exchange

Marketing occurs when the transaction takes place and both the buyer and seller exchange something of value. In this case, you exchange your money for the bookstore's magazine. Both you and the bookstore have gained something and also given up something, but you are both better off because you have each satisfied your unmet needs. You have the opportunity to read *ComputerWorld* but you gave up some money; the store gave up the magazine but received money, which enables it to remain in business. This exchange process and, of course, the ethical and legal foundations of exchange are central to marketing.

LO2 The Breadth and Depth of Marketing

Marketing today affects every person and organization. To understand this, let us analyze (1) what a market is, (2) who markets, (3) what they market, (4) who buys and uses what is marketed, and (5) who benefits from these marketing activities.

What Is a Market?

A **market** is people with the desire and ability to buy a specific product. All markets ultimately are people. Even when we say a firm bought a photocopier, we mean one or several people in the firm decided to buy it. People who are aware of their unmet needs may have the desire to buy the product, but that alone is not sufficient. People must also have the ability to buy, that is, have the authority, time, and money. People may even "buy" an idea that results in an action, such as having their blood pressure checked or turning down their thermostats to save energy.

Who Markets?

Every organization markets! It is obvious that business firms involved in manufacturing (McCain Foods, General Motors of Canada, Ericsson Canada), retailing (Canadian Tire, Shoppers Drug Mart, Loblaws), and providing services (Canadian Broadcasting Corporation, Air Canada, Via Rail, Vancouver Canucks, Scotia **iTRADE.com**) market their offerings. Today, many other types of marketing are also popular. For example, non-profit organizations (Winnipeg Ballet, Canadian Red Cross, Canadian Museum of Civilization, Toronto Zoo) also engage in marketing.[4] Your college or university probably has a marketing program to attract students, faculty members, and donations. Places (cities, provinces, countries) often use marketing efforts to attract tourists, conventions, or businesses. Organizations associated with special events or causes use marketing to inform and influence a target audience. These marketing activities range from government agencies, such as WorkSafeBC encouraging young college and university students to keep safe in the workplace, to non-profit organizations, such as the Girl Guides of Canada and 4-H Clubs of Canada using marketing to attract new members and ABC Life Literacy Canada, a non-profit organization that inspires Canadians to increase their literary skills. Finally, individuals, such as politicians like Justin Trudeau, often use marketing to gain attention and voter preference.

Marketing is used by non-profit organizations, causes, and places.

What Is Marketed?

Goods, services, ideas, and experiences are marketed. *Goods* are physical objects, such as Crest toothpaste, Nikon cameras, or Apple computers, that satisfy consumer needs. *Services* are activities, deeds, or other basic intangibles, such as airline trips on WestJet airlines, financial advice from TD Waterhouse, or long-distance telephone calls offered by the Telus Group. *Ideas* are intangibles involving thoughts about actions or causes, such as donating to the Salvation Army or to the Trans Canada Trail project.

The use of idea marketing has grown significantly over the past three decades; in particular, idea marketing that focuses on enhancing social ends is a prevalent part of today's marketplace. This is referred to as social marketing. **Social marketing** is designed to influence the behaviour of individuals in which benefits accrue to those individuals or to society in general and not to the marketer.[5] Anti-smoking campaigns by Health Canada or the Canadian Cancer Society are examples of social marketing. Social marketing can be conducted by for-profit and non-profit organizations or by individuals. For example, the Heart and Stroke Foundation of Nova Scotia has a social marketing campaign encouraging Nova Scotians to walk in order to improve their health. Even your friend's attempt to influence you to eat a more healthy diet could be considered social marketing. And, as we discuss later in the chapter, many marketers are now engaged in creating and delivering experiences to customers. In fact, even companies that market traditional goods and services are also now engaging in the practice of customer experience management—focusing on ensuring that your shopping experience with them is positive and satisfying and goes beyond the mere act of acquiring a new good or service.

Who Buys and Uses What Is Marketed?

Both individuals and organizations buy and use goods and services that are marketed. **Ultimate consumers** are people—whether 80 years or 8 months old—who use the goods and services purchased for a household. In contrast, **organizational buyers** are units, such as manufacturers, retailers, or government agencies, that buy goods and services for their own use or for resale. Although the terms *consumers, buyers*, and *customers* are sometimes used for both ultimate consumers and organizations, there is no consistency on this. In this book, you will be able to tell from the example whether the buyers are ultimate consumers, organizations, or both.

Who Benefits?

In our free-enterprise society, there are three specific groups that benefit from effective marketing: consumers who buy, organizations that sell, and society as a whole. True competition among products and services in the marketplace ensures that we as Canadian consumers can find value from the best products, the lowest prices, or exceptional service. Providing choices leads to consumer satisfaction and the quality of life that we have come to expect from our Canadian economic system.

Organizations that provide need-satisfying products combined with effective marketing programs—for example, McDonald's Restaurants, Tim Hortons, IBM Canada, and Microsoft Canada—have blossomed. But competition creates problems for ineffective competitors, and hundreds of Canadian businesses fail every year. Effective marketing actions result in rewards for organizations that serve customers and in thousands of marketing jobs for individuals all across the country.

Finally, effective marketing benefits society. It enhances competition, which, in turn, both improves the quality of products and services and lowers their prices. This makes countries more competitive in world markets and provides jobs and a higher standard of living for their citizens.

The Diverse Factors Influencing Marketing Activities

Although an organization's marketing activity focuses on assessing and satisfying consumer needs, countless other people, groups, and forces interact to shape the nature of its activities (Figure 1–1). Foremost is the organization itself, whose mission and objectives determine what business it is in and what goals it seeks. Within the organization, organizational leaders are responsible for establishing these goals. And the marketing department works closely with a network of other departments and employees to help provide the customer-satisfying products required for the organization to survive and prosper.

Figure 1–1 also shows the key people, groups, and forces outside the organization that influence marketing activities. The marketing department is responsible for facilitating relationships, partnerships, and alliances with the organization's customers, its shareholders (or often representatives of groups served by a non-profit organization), its suppliers, and other organizations. Environmental forces, such as social, economic, technological, competitive, and regulatory factors, also shape an organization's marketing activities. Finally, an organization's marketing decisions are affected by society as a whole and, in turn, often have an important impact on society.

FIGURE 1–1

The Organization and Its Departments

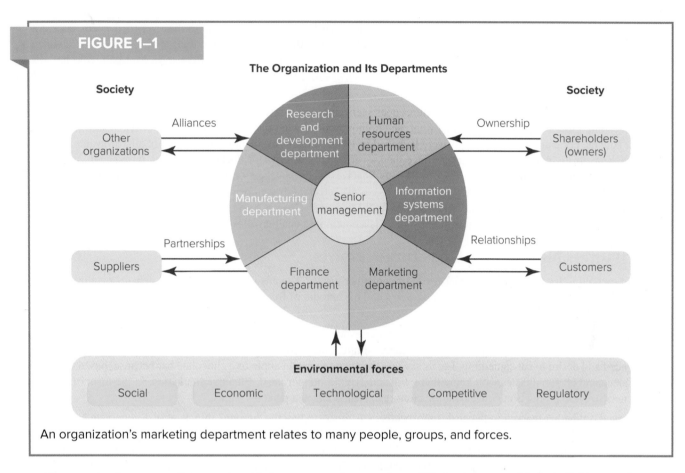

An organization's marketing department relates to many people, groups, and forces.

The organization must strike a continual balance among the sometimes differing interests of these individuals and groups. For example, it is not possible to simultaneously provide the lowest-priced and highest-quality products to customers and pay the highest prices to suppliers, highest wages to employees, and maximum dividends to shareholders.

Learning Review

1. What is marketing?
2. Marketing focuses on _____ and _____ prospective customers' needs and wants.
3. What four factors are needed for marketing to occur?

LO3   HOW MARKETING DISCOVERS AND SATISFIES CONSUMER NEEDS

The importance of discovering and satisfying consumer needs is so critical to understanding marketing that we look at each of these two steps in detail next.

Discovering Consumer Needs

The first objective in marketing is discovering the needs of prospective customers. Marketers often use customer surveys, concept tests, and other forms of marketing research (discussed in detail in Chapter 8) to better understand customer needs. Many firms also use "crowdsourcing" websites to solicit and evaluate ideas from customers. Still, discovering consumer needs is often difficult, and things can go wrong. For one thing, consumers may not always know or be able to describe what they need and want. And, as we will see later, in the case of high-technology or new-to-world products, consumers may have no idea about how they might benefit from such products. So, even listening to customers to discover their needs does not ensure marketing success. Market intelligence agency Mintel estimates that 33,000 new products are introduced worldwide each month. Yet research shows that most of those products fail or will fail in the long run. Robert M. McMath, who has studied over 110,000 of these new-product launches, has two key suggestions to marketers: (1) focus on what the customer benefit is, and (2) learn from past mistakes.[6]

The solution to preventing new product failures does seem embarrassingly obvious. First, find out what consumers need and want. Second, produce what they need and want, and do not produce what they do not need or want. This is far more difficult than it sounds. For example, Hot Pockets were launched in 1983. These convenient meat and cheese microwavable sandwiches became a favourite brand among students. Since then, over 80 varieties of Hot Pockets have been introduced, including Hot Pockets Pizza Snacks. However, in 2011, Hot Pockets Snackers were launched—bite-sized microwavable sandwiches in four flavours. But a none-too-serious showstopper arose: Excessive ice crystals can form on the product due to variations in freezer temperatures, and if this happens and the sandwich is thawed and refrozen before being microwaved, it does not taste very good.[7] So, meeting the needs and wants of consumers is a continuing challenge for firms around the globe.

Consumer Needs and Consumer Wants

Should marketing try to satisfy consumer needs or consumer wants? The answer is both! Heated debates rage over this question, with regard to the definitions of needs and wants and the amount of freedom given to prospective customers to make their own buying decisions.

A *need* occurs when a person feels physiologically deprived of basic necessities, such as food, clothing, and shelter. A *want* is a felt need that is shaped by a person's knowledge, culture, and personality. So, if you feel hungry, you have developed a basic need and desire to eat something. Let us say you then want to eat an apple or a chocolate bar because, based on your past experience and personal tastes, you know these will satisfy your hunger need. Effective marketing, in the form of creating an awareness of good products at convenient locations, can clearly shape a person's wants.

At issue is whether marketing persuades prospective customers to buy the "wrong" things—say, a chocolate bar rather than an apple to satisfy hunger pangs. Certainly, marketing tries to influence what we buy. A question then arises: At what point do we want government and society to step in to protect consumers? Most consumers would say they want government to protect us from harmful drugs and unsafe cars, but what about chocolate bars, cereals, and soft drinks? Another issue is whether marketing really makes us materialistic and desire things that we really can live without. Moreover, there is also debate about marketing's ability to influence us in terms of how we view ourselves and how we view others. Sometimes there are no clear-cut answers when it comes to the issue of what should be marketed, how it should be marketed, and importantly, to whom it should be marketed. Read the Making Responsible Decisions box, "Marketing and Female Body Dissatisfaction," which discusses how marketing may be responsible for female body dissatisfaction.[8] What do you think?

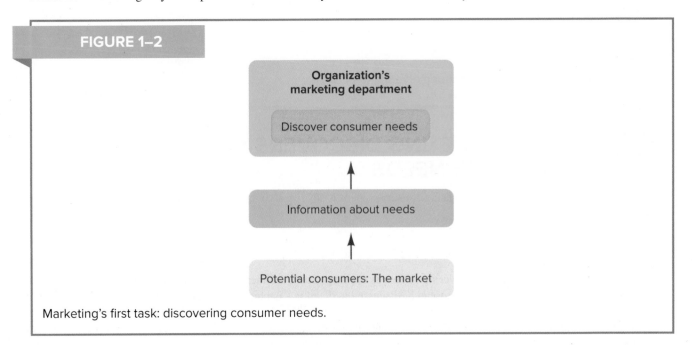

FIGURE 1–2

Marketing's first task: discovering consumer needs.

As shown in Figure 1–2, discovering needs involves looking carefully at prospective customers, whether they are children buying M&Ms, university or college students buying Apple iPads, or firms buying new laser printers. Principal activities of a firm's marketing department are to scrutinize its consumers carefully to understand what they need, to study industry trends, to examine competitors' products, and even to analyze the needs of a customer's customer.

Satisfying Consumer Needs

Marketing does not stop with the discovery of consumer needs. Because the organization obviously cannot satisfy all consumer needs, it must concentrate its efforts on certain needs of a specific group of potential consumers. This is the **target market**—one or more specific groups of potential consumers toward which an organization directs its marketing program.

MAKING RESPONSIBLE DECISIONS

Marketing and Female Body Dissatisfaction

Images of female bodies are everywhere, with women and girls—and their body parts—selling everything from food to cars. Popular film and television actresses are becoming younger, taller, and thinner. Women's magazines are full of articles urging that if you can just lose those last 20 pounds, you will have it all: the perfect marriage, loving children, great sex, and a rewarding career.

Many critics of marketing suggest marketers are playing a role in creating and imposing impossible standards of beauty on females. And critics say the motive is purely financial. They assert that by presenting a physical ideal that is extremely difficult to achieve and maintain, the cosmetic and diet industries are assured continual growth and profits. Marketers are also accused of making females insecure about their bodies and are thus making them more likely to buy beauty products, new clothes, and diet aids. In short, the argument is that marketers are fuelling female body dissatisfaction in order to sell products and services.

Research has shown that three-year-old girls prefer game pieces that depict thin people over those representing heavier ones and that by age seven, girls are able to identify something they would like to change about their appearance. These attitudes only get more powerful as girls get older. In one survey, nearly half of nine- to twelve-year-old girls said they wanted to be thinner and had either been on a diet or were aware of the concept of dieting. Other research links exposure to images of thin, young, air-brushed female bodies to depression, loss of self-esteem, and unhealthy eating habits in girls and young women. One study found that half of girls aged 16 to 21 said they would undergo surgery to improve their bodies. Another study found that girls who were unhappy with their bodies—whether they were genuinely overweight or not—were significantly more at risk for attempting suicide.

Media activist Jean Kilbourne argues that marketers and the media send messages that "ordinary" females are in need of adjustment and that the female body is an object to be perfected. The result is an alarming rise in female body dissatisfaction. Females internalize the so-called ideal stereotype presented to them by marketers and start judging themselves by that stereotype. Critics argue that the only reason this is happening is because marketers want to sell products and services and that they do this by making females anxious and unhappy about themselves. Advocates for women's rights suggest young females need to be educated about what marketers and the media are doing and to become empowered to challenge this assault on them and their bodies. What do you think about this issue?

LO4 The Four Ps: Controllable Marketing Mix Factors

Having selected the target market consumers, the firm must take steps to satisfy their needs. Someone in the organization's marketing department, often the marketing manager, must take action and develop a complete marketing program that creates, communicates, and delivers value to a target market. This happens through the use of a combination of four tools, often called the four Ps—a useful shorthand reference to them first published by Professor E. Jerome McCarthy:[9]

- *Product.* A good, service, or idea to satisfy the consumer's needs.

- *Price.* What is exchanged for the product.
- *Promotion.* A means of communication between the seller and buyer.
- *Place.* A means of getting the product into the consumer's hands.

We will define each of the four Ps more carefully later in the book, but for now, it is important to remember that they are the elements of the marketing mix, or simply the **marketing mix**. These are the marketing manager's controllable factors, the marketing actions of product, price, promotion, and place that he or she can take to create, communicate, and deliver value. The marketing mix elements are called controllable factors because they are under the control of the marketing department in an organization.

Designing an effective marketing mix also conveys to potential buyers a clear **customer value proposition**, which is a cluster of benefits that an organization promises customers to satisfy their needs. For example, Walmart's customer value proposition can be described as "helping people around the world save money and live better—anytime and anywhere." Michelin's customer value proposition can be summed up as "providing safety-conscious parents greater security in tires at a premium price."

The Uncontrollable, Environmental Forces

There are a host of factors largely beyond the control of the marketing department and its organization. These forces can be placed into five groups (as shown in Figure 1–1): social, economic, technological, competitive, and regulatory forces. Examples are what consumers themselves want and need, the state of the economy in terms of whether it is expanding or contracting, changing technology, actions that competitors take, and government restrictions. These are the **environmental forces** in a marketing decision, the uncontrollable factors involving social, economic, technological, competitive, and regulatory forces. These five forces may serve as accelerators or brakes on marketing, sometimes expanding an organization's marketing opportunities and other times restricting them. These five environmental forces are covered in Chapter 3.

Traditionally, many marketing executives have treated these environmental forces as rigid, absolute constraints that are entirely outside their influence. Accordingly, some executives simply fail to anticipate and respond to these environmental forces. But recent studies have shown that forward-looking, action-oriented firms can take advantage of changes in the marketing environment by aligning their organizations to capitalize on such changes by introducing new technologies or competitive breakthroughs.

But Wait, What About High-Technology or New-to-World Products?

The conventional marketing process of discovering and satisfying customer needs really works well in most cases. But it does not work so well with high-technology or new-to-world products.[10] Henry Ford, famous automobile pioneer, once said, "If I asked the customer what they really wanted, they'd have said a faster horse!" Basically, Ford is telling marketers that when you try to discover what customers want, they will often simply ask for better versions of existing products that they already buy from you. But this approach will not help marketers who wish to produce breakthrough innovations. In essence, conventional marketing focuses on fulfilling existing market needs and not on new market creation. High-technology or new-to-world products are radically different and sometimes beyond the imagination of the customers. Often, customers really do not recognize that they need or want such innovative products.

So marketers of high-technology or new-to-world products really have no market at the time of invention. But new inventions can and do create new markets and new industries. For example, the invention of the semiconductor created the computer industry in all its forms, while geneticists have created an entirely new biotechnology marketplace. Therefore, you should remember that if you wish to create something totally radical, existing customers using existing products are seldom going to be of any assistance to you. There may be no ready market for your invention, and you may never be successful in creating one. But if you do develop something that is better than all the existing technologies or products currently available, then you might become the next Henry Ford, or Bill Gates, or Steve Jobs!

The Marketing Program

Effective relationship marketing strategies help marketing managers discover what prospective customers need. They must translate this information into some concepts for products the firm might develop (Figure 1–3). These concepts must then be converted into a tangible **marketing program**—a plan that integrates the marketing mix to provide a good, service, or idea to prospective buyers. These prospects then react to the offering favourably (by buying) or unfavourably (by not buying), and the process is repeated. As shown in Figure 1–3, in an effective organization this process is continuous: Consumer needs trigger product concepts that are translated into actual products that stimulate further discovery of consumer needs.

FIGURE 1–3

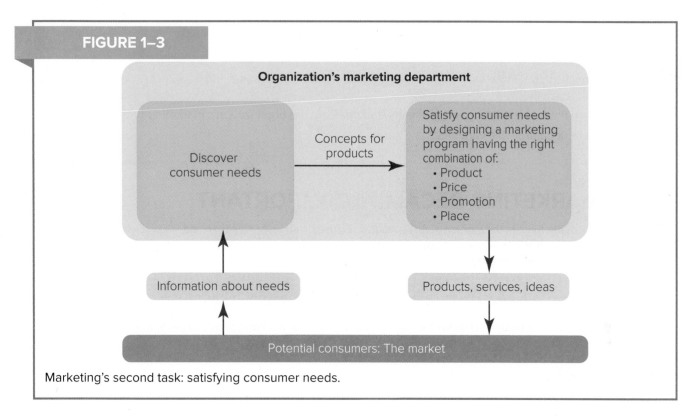

Marketing's second task: satisfying consumer needs.

A Marketing Program for the City of Hamilton

To see some specifics of an actual marketing program, let us return to the chapter opening example of the city of Hamilton and its efforts to attract residents, investors, and businesses to the city.[11] Figure 1–4 shows the basic features of the city's marketing program.

FIGURE 1–4

Mix Element	Specifics
Product	The City of Hamilton as a place to live, work, and do business.
Price	Varies: depends on residential housing prices and housing rentals; commercial leasing prices (cost per square metre); land and construction costs for residential, commercial, industrial, and institutional development; municipal taxes.
Promotion	Print advertising, website, public relations, social media including YouTube.
Place	The City of Hamilton.

Marketing program for the City of Hamilton.

4. An organization cannot satisfy the needs of all consumers, and so it must focus on one or more sub-groups, which are its _____.

5. What are the four marketing mix elements that make up the organization's marketing program?

6. What are uncontrollable variables?

HOW MARKETING BECAME SO IMPORTANT

Marketing is a driving force in the modern global economy. To understand why this is so and some related ethical aspects, let us look at (1) the evolution of businesses from the production era to the customer experience management era, and (2) ethics and social responsibility in marketing.

Evolution of North American Businesses

Many organizations have experienced distinct stages in the life of their firms. We can use Pillsbury, now part of General Mills, and General Electric as examples.

Production Era

Goods were scarce in the early years in North America, and so buyers were willing to accept virtually any goods that were produced and make do with them as best they could. The central notion was that products would sell themselves, and so the major concern of business firms was production, not marketing. Robert Keith, a Pillsbury president, described his company at this stage: "We are professional flour millers. . . . Our basic function is to mill quality flour."[12] As shown in Figure 1–5, this production era generally continued through the 1920s.

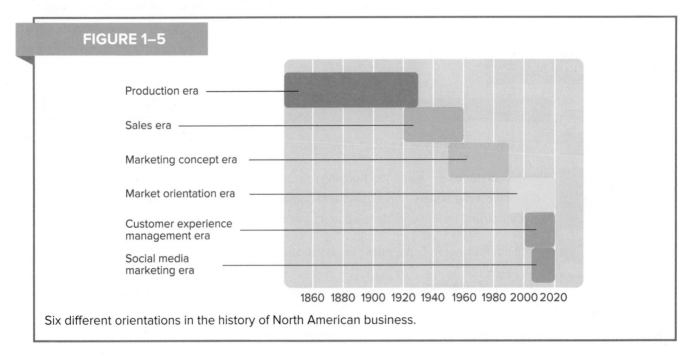

FIGURE 1–5

Production era

Sales era

Marketing concept era

Market orientation era

Customer experience management era

Social media marketing era

1860 1880 1900 1920 1940 1960 1980 2000 2020

Six different orientations in the history of North American business.

Sales Era

About that time, many firms discovered that they could produce more goods than their regular buyers could consume. Competition grew. The usual solution was to hire more salespeople to find new buyers. Pillsbury's philosophy at this stage was summed up simply by Keith: "We must hire salespersons to sell it [the flour] just as we hire accountants to keep our books." The role of the Pillsbury salesforce was simply to find consumers for the goods that the firm could produce best. This sales era continued into the 1950s for Pillsbury and into the 1960s for many other firms (see Figure 1–5).

Marketing Concept Era

In the 1960s, marketing became the motivating force among many firms. Then the policy became, "We are in the business of satisfying needs and wants of consumers." This is really a brief statement of what has come to be known as the **marketing concept**, which is the idea that an organization should strive to satisfy the needs of consumers, while also trying to achieve the organization's goals.

The statement of a firm's commitment to satisfying consumer wants and needs that probably launched the marketing concept appeared in a 1952 annual report of General Electric:[13] "The concept introduces . . . marketing . . . at the beginning rather than the end of the production cycle and integrates marketing into each phase of the business." This statement emphasizes that marketing ideas are fed into the production cycle from *after* an item is produced to *before* it is designed. Clearly, the marketing concept is a focus on the consumer. Unfortunately, many companies found that actually implementing the concept was very difficult.

LO5 Market Orientation Era

Many organizations transitioned from the marketing concept era to the market orientation era. Firms with a **market orientation** focus their efforts on (1) continuously collecting information about customers' needs and competitors' capabilities, (2) sharing this information throughout the organization, and (3) using the information to create value, ensure customer satisfaction, and develop customer relationships.

Customer value is defined as the unique combination of benefits received by the customer that include quality, price, convenience, on-time delivery, and both before-sale and after-sale service. As we point out in Chapter 5, Canadians are becoming increasingly value conscious, and Canadian companies are attempting to provide unique value that they alone can deliver to their targeted markets. This unique customer value can come in the form of best price, best product, best service, or as you will see later, the best customer experience.[14] For example, Walmart attempts to offer its customers the best price, Starbucks claims to offer its customers the best product, and Canadian Tire delivers value through exceptional customer service.

What type of value do these firms offer their customers? See the text.

(left): © Helen Sessions/Alamy Stock Photo; (centre): pio3/Shutterstock.com; (right): ValeStock/Shutterstock.com

When customers believe they have received good value, they tend to be satisfied with their providers. **Customer satisfaction** is the match between customer expectations of the product and the product's actual performance. This is an important measure of the ability of a firm to successfully meet the needs of the customer. If the product fails to meet the customer's expectations, the customer will be dissatisfied. If the product performance matches expectations, the customer is satisfied. If the performance exceeds the customer's expectations, the customer is likely to be highly satisfied. Recent research involving successful Canadian and American entrepreneurs revealed that customer satisfaction is an important ingredient for the long-term success of businesses. Moreover, this same research found that customer value and satisfaction are critical for an organization in order to develop ongoing customer relationships.[15]

Therefore, it is not surprising that organizations with a market orientation actually engage in **customer relationship management (CRM)**—the process of building and developing long-term relationships with customers by delivering customer value and satisfaction. CRM involves the use of relationship-centric strategies to optimize the long-term value of an organization's selected customers. Retaining customers over time, or managing the entire customer life cycle, is a cost-effective way for firms to grow in competitive markets. Organizations engaging in CRM understand the importance of the lifetime value of a customer, not just single transactions. **Customer lifetime value (CLV)** is the profit generated by the customer's purchase of an organization's product or service over the customer's lifetime. Kimberly-Clark, for example, reports that its retained customers buy about seven boxes of Kleenex per year and will spend over $1,400 on facial tissue over a lifetime. Meanwhile, Lexus estimates that a retained and satisfied customer is worth over $600,000 in lifetime sales.[16]

To be effective, CRM requires the involvement and commitment of managers and employees throughout the organization and the growing application of information technology. In fact, technology is a key CRM enabler. And with advances in information technology and changes in customer buying behaviour—specifically, online buying—the scope of CRM has been broadened to include **eCRM**—a web-centric, personalized approach to managing long-term customer relationships electronically.[17] Expenditures on CRM initiatives globally are expected to exceed $36 billion by 2017.[18]

An integral component of eCRM is interactive marketing. **Interactive marketing** involves two-way buyer–seller electronic communication in which the buyer can control the kind and amount of information received from the seller. For effective interactive marketing to occur, companies need to listen, understand, and respond to their customers' needs. Marketers must also treat customers as individuals and empower them to (1) influence the timing and extent of the buyer–seller interaction, and (2) have a say in the kind of products and services they buy, the information they receive, and, in some cases, even the prices they pay. Interactive marketing technology now allows for a level of customer interaction, individualization, and customer relationship management process to be carried out on a scale never before available. For example, Dove asked its customers to go online to create new ads for its Dove Cream Oil product and submit it to the company online for consideration. In this way, customers feel they are truly interacting with the company and co-participating in the type of messages the company will disseminate. Another example of interactive marketing was Sears Canada asking its customers to select the cover for its *Christmas Wish Book*. Canadians were invited to visit the Sears website and vote in an online poll for one of four potential covers for the book.

LO6   Customer Experience Management Era

Apple engages in CEM activities to retain customers for life.

Canadapanda/Shutterstock.com

Many experts have suggested that CRM initiatives are suffering because the focus has been on getting CRM technology in place while neglecting just how to build customer relationships.[19]

Many Canadian firms made heavy investments in CRM, including Bank of Montreal, Telus, Bell, Sears, Shoppers Drug Mart, and Staples. But they have discovered that good customer relationships really only result when companies offer their customers excellent experiences. So, CRM, with its information technology, information architecture and platforms, and other enabling processes, is necessary for customer relationship development but it is not sufficient. To be effective, CRM must include a **customer experience management (CEM)** strategy. CEM is managing the customers' interactions with the organization at all levels and at all touchpoints (direct and indirect contacts of the customer with an organization) so that the customer has a positive impression of the organization, is satisfied with the experience, and will remain loyal to the organization. In essence, it is about experience-based differentiation.

With more and more products and services becoming commoditized, most experts believe that, for the customer, it is the experience that counts, not the product or service per se. A recent study indicated that executives believed that improving customer experience was critical to the future growth of their companies. Yet, less than 25 percent of consumers believe organizations actually provide excellent customer experiences.[20] However, companies that do engage in CEM achieve double-digit revenue and profit growth compared to companies that do not.[21] These companies ensure that customers receive a positive, end-to-end experience with employees, websites, call centres, and even advertising. Companies that have invested heavily in CEM and have often ranked at best-in-class performers in CEM include Apple, Amazon, Zappos, Starbucks, and Disney.[22]

However, the transition to CEM also requires a new type of organization—a *customer-centric marketing organization (CCMO)*. In CCMO-based organizations, the customer is the focus and the company's brands, products and services, finances, leaders, and marketers are in tune and in time with the customers' needs, expectations, aspirations, and budgets.[23] Firms such as Apple, FedEx, Starbucks, and others have already made the shift to CCMO, resulting in these organizations delivering excellent customer experiences. Some organizations actually have "Chief Experience Officers" who oversee the creation and delivery of customer experiences. CEM has become so important that there is even an industry association, the Customer Service Institute of Canada (**www.csicanada.ca**), which has as its chief aim to advance the practice of CEM in Canada. For more insight into CEM, see the Marketing Matters box, "Lessons from the Leading Edge of Customer Experience Management."[24]

MARKETING MATTERS

Lessons from the Leading Edge of Customer Experience Management

Experts argue that customer experience management (CEM) has never been so important to an enterprise. Yet too few companies are creating effective CEM practices, and most companies do not view CEM as a strategic priority. Moreover, most companies are struggling to develop clear and consistent customer experience strategies, support, processes, and metrics across their organizations. Yet, leading-edge companies offer six key lessons for getting CEM right.

Lesson One: Create a Customer-Centric Culture

Some of the most effective customer experience management practices are those that help create an enterprise culture that is laser-focused on managing the customer experience. Perhaps not surprisingly, tying rewards to CEM performance is critical. As with most things, with CEM you get what you incentivize. Tying compensation to customer experience metrics creates a customer focus from top management down. And rewarding employees and executives based on customer experience results has been one of the biggest game changers for CEM in the past decade.

Lesson Two: Think Like the Customer

Customer experience can be impacted by a host of different people. Leading-edge companies in CEM make sure every employee understands who the customers are and what they want. Moreover, the actual voice of the customer is provided to each and every employee in the customer's exact words.

Lesson Three: Give the Business Control of Customer Experience

Making sure the business takes ownership of customer experience is critical to lasting CEM improvements. A coordinated approach to CEM—and one that is built from the ground up— is more likely to take root. One leading-edge company set up a centralized customer experience function as well as centres of customer excellence within each business group. Customer experience champions were also selected and not just at the vice president level but deeper into the organization.

Lesson Four: Tame Channels and Data

Systems integration, channel complexity, organizational structure, and data issues all make providing a consistent customer experience challenging for any company. However, leading-edge companies recognize multichannel management, including social media, as a strategic imperative. Additionally, these companies spend just as much time thinking about the customer's experience as they do corporate processes. One customer experience group accomplishes that by helping those in the business map the customer journey and by identifying customer personas. "Everyone is used to talking about things from his or her point of view," says the customer experience director. "But what's important is what it looks like from the customer standpoint."

Lesson Five: Embrace Analytics

The increase in the number of customer channels combined with the onslaught of structured and unstructured customer information is making CEM more difficult than ever. Yet, leading-edge companies are embracing new technologies and processes and are more effective than others in using analytics. Leading-edge companies also place more importance on a number of technologies for CEM including online surveys, marketing operations management, real-time decision-making tools, social media monitoring software, and content management systems. They recognize the importance of emerging analytics technologies, including systems that analyze online behaviour, social media sentiment, and text, as well as tools that can deliver real-time analysis of large data sets.

Lesson Six: Expand the Definition of Customer Experience Success

Measuring the impact of customer experience efforts is difficult—as evidenced by the trouble most companies have tying customer experience investments to business outcomes. The more traditional measure of customer success—customer satisfaction scores—is widely used in all companies. Leading-edge companies, however, use a wider range of metrics, often more effectively, to report on their customer experience management progress, including measures such as customer lifetime value, indirect traffic, social media sentiment, and upsell rates.

In the end, leading-edge companies are capitalizing on opportunities that come from every interaction they have with their customers over the duration of the relationship, and marketing analytics has now become critical to understanding and managing the CEM process.

LO7 Social Media Marketing Era

Some experts are suggesting that we are also in the midst of the emergence of a new era: the social media marketing era. In fact, some suggest that social media marketing is the biggest shift in the economy since the Industrial Revolution. There are really two distinct dimensions to **social media marketing**. First, social media marketing is about consumer-generated online-marketing efforts to promote brands and companies for which they are fans (or conversely, negatively promoting brands and companies for which they are non-fans). Second, social media marketing is the use by marketers of online tools and platforms to promote their brands or organizations. The most common tools or platforms used by both consumers and organizations are social networking sites (e.g., Facebook, LinkedIn, Google+, Twitter), blogs, wikis, podcasts, and other shared media sites, such as YouTube.

Social media is changing the way we live and the way we do business. To learn more, read the "Social Media Marketing Era" section of the text.

(top): © TP/Alamy Stock Photo; (bottom): The Twitter name, logo, Twitter T, Tweet, and Twitter blue bird are trademarks of Twitter, Inc.

It is the former dimension of social media marketing that is changing the rules of marketing and ushering in a new era of business. Social media creates a platform that empowers customers and provides them with an opportunity to communicate with an organization and with other customers. Social media marketing is creating a situation where consumers are no longer searching for products or services in traditional ways, but rather will find them via social media. In short, social media is transforming the way we live and the way organizations do business.[25] Social media experts argue that social media platforms such as Facebook connect hundreds of millions of people to each other via instant communication and that this is creating a socio-economic shift where online communities can build or destroy brands and can make traditional marketing obsolete.

To survive in this new social media world, social media experts suggest that organizations must understand, navigate, and adapt to this new landscape. These experts also suggest that social media can be used strategically in order to increase sales, cut marketing costs, and communicate more directly with their customers, and that the use of social media is essential for all businesses, large and small.[26] In fact, one of the signs of the importance of social media is the growth in **social CRM**—the use of social media to enable organizations to engage customers in collaborative conversations for mutually beneficial value. Social CRM spending, globally, exceeds over $1 billion.[27] Social media has become so important for marketers that we will discuss its role throughout the text, including its application in communicating with customers, marketing research, brand building, and marketing strategies. We also include an entire chapter on this topic (Chapter 20).

LO8 Ethics and Social Responsibility: Balancing the Interests of Different Groups

As organizations have changed their orientation, society's expectations of marketers have also changed. Today, the standards of marketing practice have shifted from an emphasis on producers' interests to consumers' interests. In addition, organizations are increasingly encouraged to consider the social and environmental consequences of their actions for all parties. Guidelines for ethical and socially responsible behaviour can help managers balance consumer, organizational, and societal interests.

Ethics

Many marketing issues are not specifically addressed by existing laws and regulations. Should information about a firm's customers be sold to other organizations? Should advertising by professional service providers, such as accountants and lawyers, be restricted? Should consumers be left on their own to assess the safety of a product? These questions may not involve strict legal issues but do raise some ethical questions. **Ethics** are the moral principles and values that govern the actions and decisions of an individual or group. Ethics serve as guidelines on how to act correctly and justly. In Chapter 4, we will discuss marketing ethics and how organizations must work to ensure that their employees not only live within the law but also practise ethical behaviour.

Social Responsibility

While many ethical issues involve only the buyer and seller, others involve society as a whole. For example, suppose you change the oil in your old Chevy yourself and dump the used oil on a corner of your backyard. Is this just a transaction between you and the oil manufacturer? Not quite! The used oil may contaminate the soil, and so society will bear a portion of the cost of your behaviour. This example illustrates the issue of social responsibility. **Social responsibility** means that individuals and organizations are part of a larger society and are accountable to that society for their actions (also see Chapter 4). In fact, some marketing experts stress the **societal marketing concept**, the view that an organization should discover and satisfy the needs of its consumers in a way that also provides for society's well-being.[28] Many organizations, such as Stratus Vineyards (an organic and sustainable winery in Ontario), have recognized they are an integral part of society and have committed to socially responsible behaviour, including sustainable business practices and green marketing.

The societal marketing concept is directly related to **macromarketing**, which looks at the aggregate flow of a nation's goods and services to benefit society.[29] Macromarketing addresses such broad issues as whether marketing costs too much, whether advertising is wasteful, and what resource scarcities and pollution side-effects result from the marketing system. Macromarketing issues are addressed in this book, but the main focus is on how an individual organization directs its marketing activities and allocates its resources to benefit its customers, referred to as **micromarketing**. An overview of this approach appears in Chapter 2. Because of the importance of ethical and social responsibility issues in marketing today, Chapter 4 focuses on these topics, while they are also highlighted throughout the book.

> ### Learning Review
>
> **7.** The match between customer expectations of the product and the product's actual performance is called _____.
>
> **8.** The process of building and developing long-term relationships with customers by delivering customer value and satisfaction is called _____.
>
> **9.** Some Canadian companies are now transitioning from the market orientation era to the _____ era.

Learning Objectives Review

Define marketing and identify the requirements for successful marketing to occur.

Marketing is the activity for creating, communicating, delivering, and exchanging offerings that benefit the organization, its stakeholders, and society at large. For marketing to occur, it is necessary to have (*a*) two or more parties with unmet needs, (*b*) a desire and ability to satisfy them, (*c*) communication between the parties, and (*d*) something to exchange.

Understand the breadth and depth of marketing.

Marketing affects every person and organization. Both for-profit and non-profit organizations perform marketing activities. They market products, services, ideas, and experiences that benefit consumers, organizations, and countries.

LO3   **Explain how marketing discovers and satisfies consumer needs and wants.**

The first objective in marketing is discovering the needs of prospective consumers. The second objective in marketing is satisfying the needs of targeted consumers. Because an organization cannot satisfy all consumer needs, it must concentrate its efforts on certain needs of a specific group of potential consumers or target market—one or more specific groups of potential consumers toward which an organization directs its marketing program. Having selected its target market, the organization then takes action to satisfy the customers' needs by developing a unique marketing program to appeal to that market.

LO4   **Distinguish between marketing mix elements and environmental forces.**

Four elements in a marketing program designed to satisfy customer needs are product, price, promotion, and place. These elements are called the marketing mix—the four Ps—or the controllable variables because they are under the general control of the marketing department within an organization. Designing an effective marketing mix also conveys to potential buyers a clear customer value proposition, which is a cluster of benefits that an organization promises customers to satisfy their needs. Environmental forces, also called uncontrollable variables, are largely beyond the organization's control. These include social, economic, technological, competitive, and regulatory forces.

Describe how a market orientation focuses on creating customer value, satisfaction, and customer relationships.

Organizations with a market orientation focus their efforts on (*a*) continuously collecting information about customers' needs and competitors' capabilities, (*b*) sharing this information throughout the organization, and (*c*) using the information to create value, ensure customer satisfaction, and develop customer relationships. Organizations with a market orientation engage in customer relationship management (CRM)—the process of building and developing long-term relationships with customers by delivering customer value and satisfaction. Organizations engaging CRM understand the importance of the customer lifetime value (CLV)—the profits generated by the customer's purchase of an organization's product or service over the customer's lifetime. The concept of eCRM—a web-centric, personalized approach to managing long-term customer relationships electronically, which includes interactive marketing—is changing the way buyers and sellers interact. Interactive marketing technology now allows for a level of customer interaction, individualization, and customer relationship management process to be carried out on a scale never before available.

LO6 **Explain why some organizations have transitioned from the market orientation era to the customer experience management era.**

Companies have found that CRM is necessary but not sufficient in building effective relationships with customers. Accordingly, many companies have transitioned from the market orientation era to the customer experience management (CEM) era—managing the customers' interactions with the organization at all levels and at all touchpoints so that the customer has a positive impression of the organization, is satisfied with the experience, and will remain loyal to the organization. This shift also requires a new type of organization called a customer-centric marketing organization (CCMO); some Canadian companies have already made this transition and are enjoying marketing success.

LO7 **Understand the emergence of the social media marketing era.**

The social media marketing era is ushering in a major structural change in our economy. Social media marketing has two distinct dimensions: (*a*) consumer-generated online-marketing efforts to promote brands and companies for which they are fans (or conversely, negatively promoting brands and companies for which they are non-fans), and (*b*) the use by marketers of online tools and platforms such as Facebook, LinkedIn, Google+, Twitter, and YouTube to promote their brands or organizations. Some suggest that social media marketing is creating a new form of economy called socialnomics where consumers will no longer search for products or services, but rather will find them via social media. To survive in this new social media world, organizations must understand, navigate, and adapt to this new landscape.

LO8 **Understand the meaning of ethics and social responsibility and how they relate to the individual, organizations, and society.**

Marketing managers must balance consumer, organizational, and societal interests. This involves issues of ethics and social responsibility. Ethics are the moral principles and values that govern the actions and decisions of an individual or group. Ethics serve as guidelines on how to act correctly and justly. Social responsibility means that individuals and organizations are part of a larger society and are accountable to that society for their actions. Some marketing experts stress the societal marketing concept, the view that an organization should discover and satisfy the needs of its consumers in a way that also provides for society's well-being, which includes sustainable business practices and green marketing.

Applying Marketing Knowledge

1. What value does the consumer receive by purchasing the following products or services? (*a*) Carnation Instant Breakfast, (*b*) Adidas running shoes, (*c*) Hertz Rent-A-Car, and (*d*) television home shopping programs.

2. Each of the four products, services, or programs in question 1 has substitutes. Respective examples are (*a*) a ham and egg breakfast, (*b*) regular tennis shoes, (*c*) taking a bus, and (*d*) a department store. What consumer value might these substitutes deliver instead of those mentioned in question 1?

3. What are the characteristics (e.g., age, income, education) of the target market customers for the following products or services? (a) *National Geographic* magazine, (b) *Wired* magazine, (c) Toronto Blue Jays baseball team, and (d) the Canadian Open golf tournament.

4. A university in a metropolitan area wishes to increase its evening-school offerings of business-related courses, such as marketing, accounting, finance, and management. Who are the target market customers (students) for these courses?

5. What actions involving the four marketing mix elements might be used to reach the target market in question 4?

6. What environmental forces (uncontrollable variables) must the university in question 4 consider in designing its marketing program?

7. Calculate the annual value of a specific purchase you make on a regular basis, for example, gasoline for your car. What would be the purchase value over a ten-year period? What does this tell you about the customer lifetime value concept?

8. Provide a recent example of a shopping experience where you were very satisfied and one where you were very dissatisfied with your purchase. Do you think the company was practising customer experience management? Why or not why? Explain why you were satisfied or dissatisfied with the experience. What impact will this experience have on your future purchases from that organization?

9. Have you had any experience talking about brands that you like or dislike using social media? What have you discussed and what has been the response from others?

Building Your Marketing Plan

If your instructor assigns a marketing plan for your class, don't make a face and complain about the work—for two special reasons. First, you will get insights into trying to actually "do marketing" that often go beyond what you can get by simply reading the textbook. Second, thousands of graduating students every year get a job by showing prospective employers a portfolio of samples of their written work from university or college—often a marketing plan. This can work for you.

The Building Your Marketing Plan section at the end of each chapter suggests ways to improve and focus your marketing plan. You will use the sample marketing plan in Appendix A (following Chapter 2) as a guide, and this section after each chapter will help you apply those Appendix A ideas to your own marketing plan.

The first step in writing a good marketing plan is to have a business or product/service that enthuses you and for which you can get detailed information, so you can avoid glittering generalities. We offer these additional bits of advice in selecting a topic:

Do pick a topic that has personal interest for you—a family business, a business or product/service you or a friend might want to launch, or a student organization needing marketing help.

Do not pick a topic that is so large it can't be covered adequately or so abstract it will lack specifics.

1. Now to get you started on your marketing plan, list four or five possible topics and compare these with the criteria your instructor suggests and those shown above. Think hard, because your decision will be with you all semester and may influence the quality of the resulting marketing plan you show to a prospective employer.

2. When you have selected your marketing plan topic, whether the plan is for an actual business, a possible business, or a student organization, write the "company description" in your plan, as shown in Appendix A.

Video Case 1

Chobani: Making Greek Yogurt a Household Name

"Everybody should be able to enjoy a real-good, simple yogurt. And that's what Chobani is," says Hamdi Ulukaya, founder and chief executive officer of Chobani, Inc., in summarizing his vision for the company.

As the winner of the 2013 Ernst & Young World Entrepreneur of the Year award, his words and success story carry great credibility.

The Idea

Hamdi Ulukaya moved to the United States in 1994 to learn English and to study business. He started a feta cheese company, Euphrates, when his visiting father complained about the quality of American feta cheese. In 2005, Kraft Foods closed its New Berlin, New York, plant that had been built in 1885. While tidying up his office, Ulukaya stumbled upon a postcard about the sale of the shuttered Kraft plant and tossed it. After sleeping on the decision, he fished it out of the wastebasket, visited the plant, and purchased it with the help of a U.S. Small Business Administration loan.

Ulukaya had no real experience in the business. He grew up milking sheep at his family's dairy in eastern Turkey and eating the thick, tangy yogurt of his homeland. Describing the regular yogurt he found on shelves, he has one comment: "Terrible!" In his view, it is too thin, too sweet, too fake. So he decided to produce what is known as "Greek yogurt"—an authentic strained version of yogurt, with a thick texture, high protein content, and with little or no fat. With the help of four former Kraft employees and Yogurt Master Mustafa Dogan, Hamdi worked 18 months to perfect the recipe for Chobani Greek Yogurt.

© Diane Bondareff/Invision for Chobani/AP Images

The very first cup for sale of Ulukaya's Greek yogurt appeared on the shelves of a small grocer in Long Island, New York, in 2007. The new product launch focused on the classic four Ps elements of marketing mix actions: product, price, place, and promotion.

Product Strategy

From the start, Ulukaya's Greek yogurt carried the brand name Chobani. There was no room for error, and the product strategy for the Chobani brand focused on the separate elements of (1) the product itself and (2) its packaging.

The Chobani product strategy stresses its authentic straining process that removes excess liquid whey. This results in a thicker, creamier yogurt that yields 13 to 18 g of protein per single-serve cup, depending on the flavour. Chobani is free of ingredients such as milk protein concentrate and animal-based thickeners, which some manufacturers add to make "Greek-style" yogurts.

Chobani uses three pounds of milk to make one pound of Chobani Greek Yogurt. Some other features that make Chobani Greek Yogurt "nothing but good"—to quote its tagline:

- Higher in protein than regular yogurts
- Made with real fruit and only natural ingredients
- Preservative-free
- No artificial flavours or artificial sweeteners
- Contains five live and active cultures, including three probiotics

Then, and still today, Ulukaya obsessed about Chobani's packaging of the original cups. In 2007, Ulukaya concluded that *not any cup* would do. He insisted on a European-style cup with a circular opening *exactly* 95 mm across. This made for a shorter, wider cup that was more visible on retailer's shelves. Also, instead of painted-on labels, Ulukaya chose shrink-on plastic sleeves that adhere to the cup and offer eye-popping colours.

"Our packaging people would say, 'You're making it all look different and why are you doing that?'" says Kyle O'Brien, executive vice president of sales. "If people pay attention to our cups—bright colours and all—we know we have won them, because what's inside the cup is different from anything else on the shelf."

Price Strategy

To keep control of their product, Ulukaya and O'Brien approached retailers directly rather than going through distributors. Prices were set high enough to recover Chobani's costs and give reasonable margins to retailers, but not so high that future rivals could undercut its price. Today, prices remain at about $1.29 for a single-serve cup.

Place Strategy

The decision of Ulukaya and O'Brien to get Chobani Greek Yogurt into the conventional yogurt aisle of traditional supermarkets—not on specialty shelves or in health food stores—proved to be sheer genius. So today, Chobani sees its Greek yogurt widely distributed in both conventional and mass supermarkets, club stores, and natural food stores. On the horizon: growing distribution in convenience and drug stores, as well as schools. Chobani is also focused on educating food service directors at schools about Greek yogurt's health benefits for school kids.

The Chobani growth staggers imagination. From its first order of 200 cases in 2007, 2013 sales grew to over 2 million cases a week. To increase capacity and bring new products to market faster, in 2012, Chobani opened a plant in Idaho that is nearly 1 million square feet in size. Built in just 326 days, it is the largest yogurt manufacturing facility in the world.

Along the way, Chobani faced a strange glitch: Demand for Chobani's Greek yogurt far surpassed supply, leading to unhappy retailers with no Chobani cups to sell. So Kyle O'Brien launched Operation Bear Hug. "Instead of hiding behind letters to retailers, we decided to communicate with them within 24 hours about the problem and what we proposed to do about it," says O'Brien. "So we found it critical to be very transparent and open with our communication at times like that."

Promotion Strategy

In its early years, Chobani had no money for traditional advertising, so it relied on word-of-mouth recommendations from enthusiastic customers. The brand harnessed consumer passion on social media channels early on and found that people loved the taste of Chobani once they tried it. So in 2010, Chobani kicked off its CHOmobile tour. A mobile vehicle with samples of Chobani yogurt visited events across the country, and consumers were encouraged to taste Greek yogurt for the first time. As Chobani grew, it launched new promotional activities tied to (1) traditional advertising, (2) social media, and (3) direct communications with customers.

In 2011, Chobani launched its first national advertising campaign: "Real Love Stories." The only problem: Apparently, it was *too* successful! The resulting additional consumer demand for Chobani Greek Yogurt exceeded its production capacity, leaving retailers unhappy because of complaining consumers. What did Chobani do then? It stopped the advertising campaign and sent in another Operation Bear Hug team to communicate with retailers. Since then, it has run other successful national advertising campaigns, and it was also a sponsor of the 2014 U.S. Olympic team.

"Social media is important to us because Chobani is a brand people love to discover and to share their discovery experience with others," says Nicki Briggs, Chobani's chief communications officer. She stresses the importance of the Chobani "high-touch model" that emphasizes positive communications with its customers. She points to its Customer Loyalty Team, which makes this happen.

Today, Chobani's Customer Loyalty Team receives about 7,000 inbound customer e-mails and phone calls a month and is able to make return phone calls to most of them. Consumers also get a handwritten note. "We launched our Go Real Chobani campaign in 2013, stressing that we're a *real* company making *real* products with *real* conversations with our consumers," says Briggs.

Besides Facebook, the company interacts with its consumers through Twitter, Pinterest, Instagram, Foursquare, and other social media platforms. Chobani Culture (**www.chobani.com/culture**) is an online resource with recipes, videos, and tips on how to use its Greek yogurt in favourite recipes.

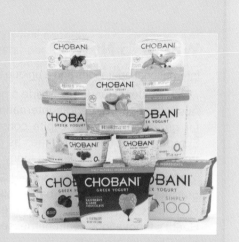

© Mike Hruby

Aggressive Innovation + Positive Social Change

Dannon, Yoplait, and PepsiCo were shocked by the success of Chobani Greek Yogurt. Each now offers its own competing Greek yogurt. With giant competitors like these, what can Chobani do? Chobani's focus: Innovate!—with creative, new Greek yogurt products!

These products emerge from Chobani's Innovation Team, which reports directly to Ulukaya and works closely with all other teams. "We are a separate group altogether, more like a Google Lab than a grocery products company, in terms of our extreme focus on innovation," says John Heath, senior vice president of innovation. "We're searching for ways to reach new market segments that have special motivations and needs," he adds.

Today, Chobani offers its hallmark Chobani® Greek Yogurt in single-serve and multi-serve sizes, while expanding its authentic strained Greek yogurt to new occasions and forms. Its recent new-product offerings include:

- *Chobani Bite*®. These 3.5-ounce four-packs reach the new "indulgent" segment of Chobani customers—those wanting a healthy afternoon or evening snack. Sample flavour: Raspberry with Dark Chocolate Chips.

- *Chobani Champions*® Tubes. Made for kids, the 2.25-ounce Tubes offer low-fat, blended Chobani flavours with fruit in grab-and-go packaging. Sample flavor: Jammin' Strawberry.

- *Chobani Flip*™. This 5.3-ounce, two-compartment package lets consumers bend or "flip" mix-ins such as granola or hazelnuts into the Chobani Greek Yogurt compartment. Sample flavour: Almond Coco Loco, a coconut low-fat yogurt paired with dark chocolate and sliced toasted almonds.

These new products illustrate the Innovation Team's focus on reaching consumers having special motivations or needs that John Heath described.

Chobani gives 10 percent of all profits to its Shepherd Gift Foundation to support people and organizations working for positive long-lasting change. The name comes from the "spirit of a shepherd," an expression in Turkey used to describe people who give without expecting anything in return. To date, the foundation has supported over 50 projects—from local ones to international famine relief efforts.

2 Developing Successful Marketing Strategies

Learning Objectives

After reading this chapter, you should be able to:

LO1 Describe two kinds of organizations that exist and the three levels of strategy in them.

LO2 Describe how core values, mission, organizational culture, business, and goals are important in organizations.

LO3 Discuss how an organization assesses where it is now and where it seeks to be.

LO4 Explain why managers are tracking strategic performance with marketing analytics, marketing dashboards, and marketing metrics.

LO5 Explain the three steps of the planning phase of the strategic marketing process.

LO6 Describe the elements of the implementation and evaluation phases of the strategic marketing process.

Making the World a Better Place, One Scoop at a Time!

Ben & Jerry's started in 1978 when longtime friends Ben Cohen and Jerry Greenfield opened an ice cream parlour in a renovated gas station. Buoyed with enthusiasm, $12,000 in borrowed and saved money, and ideas from a $5 correspondence course in ice cream making, Ben and Jerry were off and scooping. Their first flavour? Vanilla—because it's a universal best seller. Other flavours such as Chunky Monkey, Cherry Garcia, Peanut Butter Cup, and many others soon followed. The ice cream flavours weren't the only extraordinary thing about the company though. Ben and Jerry embraced a concept they called "linked prosperity," which encouraged the success of all constituents, including employees, suppliers, customers, and neighbours. They set out to achieve linked prosperity with a three-part mission statement:

- *Product mission.* To make, distribute, and sell the finest-quality all-natural ice cream.

- *Economic mission.* To operate the company for sustainable financial growth.

- *Social mission.* To operate the company in ways that make the world a better place.

© Rafael Ben-Ari/Alamy Stock Photo

The mission statement guided the entrepreneurs' decisions related to many aspects of the business, including purchasing practices, ingredient sourcing, manufacturing, and involvement in the community.[1]

Ben and Jerry's mission-driven approach led them to successfully implement many highly creative organizational and marketing strategies. Some examples include the following:

- *Fairtrade.* Ben & Jerry's believes that farmers who grow ingredients for their ice cream products (such as cocoa, coffee, and vanilla) should receive a fair price for their harvest. In return, Fairtrade farmers agree to use sustainable farming practices, implement fair working standards, and invest in local communities.

- *B-Corp Certification.* Ben & Jerry's was one of the first companies involved in the Benefit Corporation movement, which has developed a rigorous set of principles and standards on which to evaluate companies in terms of social and environmental performance, accountability, and transparency. The certification, provided by the non-profit organization B-Lab, indicates that Ben & Jerry's is using the power of business to solve social and environmental problems.

- *PartnerShop Program.* PartnerShops are Ben & Jerry's scoop shops that are independently owned and operated by community-based non-profit organizations. The shops employ youth and young adults who may face barriers to employment to help them build better lives.

As you can see, Ben & Jerry's has a strong link between its mission and its strategies. CEO Jostein Solheim explains that the purpose at Ben & Jerry's is "to be part of a global movement that makes changing the world seem fun and achievable."[2]

Today, Ben & Jerry's is owned by Unilever, which is the market leader in the global ice cream industry—one that is expected to reach $74 billion by 2018.[3] Ben & Jerry's operates in over two dozen countries, including coast-to-coast in Canada. While customers love Ben & Jerry's rich premium ice cream, many buy its products to support its social mission. As a testament to its success, Ben & Jerry's has over 7.5 million fans on Facebook—the most of any premium ice cream marketer! Ben & Jerry's Canada also has more than 1.5 million followers on Twitter (see **@BenJerryCanada**)!

This chapter describes how organizations set goals to provide an overall direction to their organizational and marketing strategies. The marketing department of an organization converts these strategies into plans that must be implemented and then evaluated so deviations can be exploited or corrected based on the marketing environment.

TODAY'S ORGANIZATIONS

In today's global competition, it is important to recognize (1) the kinds of organizations that exist, (2) what strategy is, and (3) how this strategy relates to the three levels found in many large organizations.

LO1 Kinds of Organizations

An *organization* is a legal entity of people who share a common mission. This mission motivates them to develop *offerings* (products, services, ideas, experiences) that create value for both the organization and its customers by satisfying customers' needs and wants.[4] Today's organizations can be divided into business firms and non-profit organizations. A *business firm* is a privately owned organization that serves its customers in order to earn a profit. Business firms must earn profits to survive. **Profit** is the money left after a business firm's total expenses are subtracted from its total revenue and is the reward for the risk it undertakes in marketing its offerings.

In contrast to business firms, a *non-profit organization* is a non-governmental organization that serves its customers but does not have profit as an organizational goal. Instead, its goals may be operational efficiency or client satisfaction. Regardless, it also must receive sufficient funds to continue operations. For simplicity, in the rest of the book we use the terms *firm, company, corporation,* and *organization* interchangeably to cover both business and non-profit operations.

Organizations that develop similar offerings, when grouped together, create an *industry*, such as the computer industry or the automobile industry. As a result, organizations make strategic decisions that reflect the dynamics of the industry to create a compelling and sustainable advantage for their offerings relative to those of competitors to achieve a superior level of performance.[5] The foundation of much of an organization's marketing strategy is having a clear understanding of the industry within which it competes.

What Is Strategy?

An organization has limited human, financial, technological, and other resources available to produce and market its offerings—it can't be all things to all people! Every organization must develop strategies to help focus and direct its efforts to accomplish its goals. However, the definition of strategy has been subject to debate among management and marketing theorists. For our purpose, **strategy** is an organization's long-term course of action designed to deliver a unique customer experience while achieving its goals.[6] Whether explicit or implicit, all organizations set a strategic direction. And marketing helps not only to set this direction but also to move the organization there.

Structure of Today's Organizations

Large organizations can be extremely complex. They usually consist of three organizational levels whose strategy is linked to marketing, as shown in Figure 2–1.

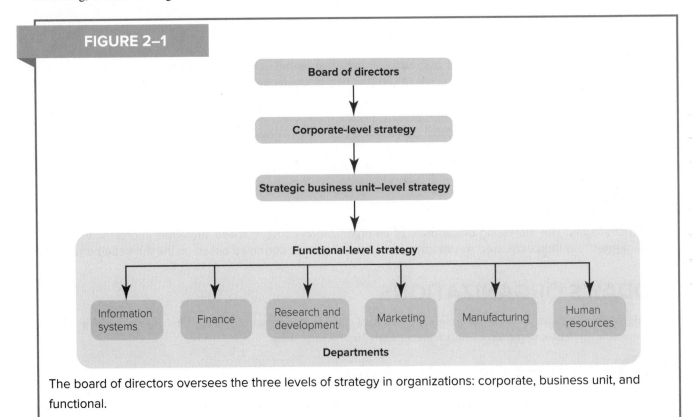

FIGURE 2–1

The board of directors oversees the three levels of strategy in organizations: corporate, business unit, and functional.

Corporate Level

The **corporate level** is where top management directs overall strategy for the entire organization. "Top management" usually means the board of directors and senior management officers with a variety of skills and experiences that are invaluable in establishing overall strategy.

The president or chief executive officer (CEO) is the highest-ranking officer in the organization and is usually a member of its board of directors. This person must possess leadership skills and expertise ranging from overseeing the organization's daily operations to spearheading strategy planning efforts that may determine its very survival.

In recent years, many large firms have changed the title of the head of marketing from vice president of marketing to chief marketing officer (CMO). These CMOs have an increasingly important role in top management because of their ability to think strategically. Most bring multi-industry backgrounds, cross-functional management expertise, analytical skills, and intuitive marketing insights to their job. These CMOs are increasingly called upon to be their organizations' "visionaries for the future" by staying in touch with consumers' needs and wants.[7] This responsibility comes with accountability, now called marketing accountability. The American Marketing Association (AMA) defines **marketing accountability** as *the responsibility for the systematic management of marketing resources and processes to achieve measurable gains in return on marketing investment and increased marketing efficiency, while maintaining quality and increasing the value of the corporation.*[8]

Strategic Business Unit Level

Some multimarket, multiproduct firms, such as Johnson & Johnson and General Electric, really manage a portfolio or group of businesses. Each group is called a **strategic business unit (SBU)**, which is a subsidiary, division, or unit of an organization that markets a set of related offerings to a clearly defined group of customers. At the **strategic business unit level**, managers set a more specific strategic direction for their businesses to exploit value-creating opportunities. For less complex firms with a single business focus, the corporate and business unit levels may merge.

Functional Level

Each strategic business unit has a **functional level**, where groups of specialists actually create value for the organization. The term *department* generally refers to these specialized functions, such as the marketing department or information systems department (Figure 2–1). At the functional level, the organization's strategic direction becomes more specific and focused. Just as there is a hierarchy of levels within organizations, there is also a hierarchy of strategic directions set by managers at each level.

A key role of the marketing department is to look outward, keeping the organization focused on creating customer value both for it and for customers. This is accomplished by listening to customers, developing and producing offerings, and implementing marketing program activities. In large organizations, marketing may be called on to assist managers at higher levels to assess environmental trends or aid in their strategic planning efforts.

When developing marketing programs for new offerings or for improving existing ones, an organization's senior management may form **cross-functional teams**. These consist of a small number of people from different departments who are mutually accountable to accomplish a task or a common set of performance goals. Sometimes these teams will have representatives from outside the organization, such as suppliers or customers, to assist them.

Learning Review

1. What is strategy?
2. What is marketing accountability?
3. What are examples of a functional level in an organization?

STRATEGY IN VISIONARY ORGANIZATIONS

Management experts stress that to be successful, today's organizations must be forward looking. They must both anticipate future events and respond quickly and effectively. This requires a visionary organization to specify its foundation (why does it exist?), set a direction (what will it do?), and formulate strategies (how will it do it?) as shown in Figure 2–2.[9]

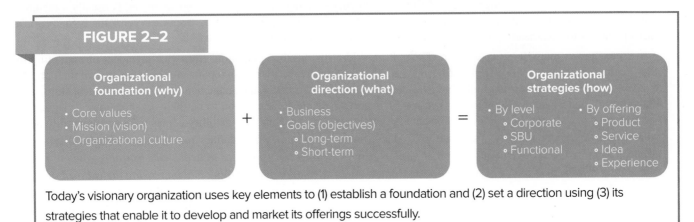

FIGURE 2–2

Organizational foundation (why)		Organizational direction (what)		Organizational strategies (how)

• Core values
• Mission (vision)
• Organizational culture
	+	• Business
		• Goals (objectives)
		  ○ Long-term
		  ○ Short-term
			=	• By level • By offering
				  ○ Corporate ○ Product
				  ○ SBU ○ Service
				  ○ Functional ○ Idea
				               ○ Experience

Today's visionary organization uses key elements to (1) establish a foundation and (2) set a direction using (3) its strategies that enable it to develop and market its offerings successfully.

Organizational Foundation: Why Does It Exist?

An organization's foundation is its philosophical reason for being—why it exists—and rarely changes.[10] Successful visionary organizations use this foundation to guide and inspire their employees through three elements: core values, mission, and organizational culture.

Core Values

An organization's **core values** are the fundamental, passionate, and enduring principles that guide its conduct over time.[11] A firm's founders or senior management develop these core values, which are consistent with their essential beliefs and character.[12] They capture the firm's heart and soul and serve to inspire and motivate its stakeholders—employees, shareholders, board of directors, suppliers, distributors, unions, government, local communities, and customers. Core values also are timeless and should not change due to short-term financial, operational, or marketing concerns. Finally, core values guide the organization's conduct. To be effective, an organization's core values must be communicated to and supported by its top management and employees; if not, they are just hollow words.[13]

Mission

By understanding its core values, an organization can take steps to define its **mission**, a statement of the organization's function in society, often identifying its customers, markets, products, and technologies. Today, often used interchangeably with *vision*, a mission statement should be clear, concise, meaningful, inspirational, and long-term.[14] This inspiration and focus appears in the mission of many organizations, including the following:

- *Canadian Red Cross.* To improve the lives of vulnerable people by mobilizing the power of humanity in Canada and around the world.

- *Tim Hortons.* Our guiding mission is to deliver superior quality products and services for our customers and communities through leadership, innovation and partnerships.

- *Canadian Tire.* To create sustainable growth by being a national champion and Canada's most trusted company. We will grow from our strengths—leveraging our brands, core capabilities, assets, and extraordinary people.

Each statement exhibits the qualities of a good mission: a clear, challenging, and compelling picture of an envisioned future.

Recently, organizations have added a social element to their mission statements to reflect an ideal that is morally right and worthwhile.[15] Stakeholders, particularly customers, employees, and now society, are asking organizations to be exceptional citizens by providing long-term value while solving society's problems.[16]

Organizational Culture

An organization must be connected with all of its stakeholders. Thus, an important corporate-level marketing function is communicating its core values and mission to them. Some organizations print these statements on cards or placards. Whether at the corporate, strategic business unit, or functional level, an **organizational culture** exists, which is a set of values, ideas, attitudes, and norms of behaviour that is learned and shared among the members of an organization.

Organizational Direction: What Will It Do?

As shown in Figure 2–2, the organization's foundation enables it to set a direction, in terms of (1) the "business it is in" and (2) its specific goals.

Business

A **business** describes the clear, broad, underlying industry or market sector of an organization's offering. To help define its business, an organization can start by looking at the set of organizations that sell similar offerings—those that are in direct competition with each other, such as "the automobile business" or "the personal computer business." The organization can then begin to answer the questions, "What do we do?" or "What business are we in?"

In the first half of the twentieth century, what "business" did railroads believe they were in? The text reveals their disastrous error.

© Digital Vision

To help us, Professor Theodore Levitt argues in his now-famous "Marketing Myopia" article that railroads in the first half of the twentieth century defined their business too narrowly, proclaiming, "We are in the railroad business!" This myopic focus caused these firms to lose sight of who their customers were and what they needed. Thus, railroads only saw other railroads as direct competitors and failed to develop strategies to compete with airlines, barges, pipelines, trucks, bus lines, and cars—offerings that carried both goods and people. As a result, many railroads eventually merged or went bankrupt. Railroads would probably have fared better if they had realized they were in "the transportation business."[17]

With today's increased global competition, many organizations are rethinking their **business model**, the strategies an organization develops to provide value to the customers it serves. Technological innovation is often a trigger for the business model change. Canadian newspapers, for example, are looking for a new business model as former subscribers get their news online. Other organizations have also seen their business models evolve. For example, Disney is no longer a theme park or movie business company; rather it is an entertainment business company, creating fun, fantasy, and experiences for its customers in a variety of ways. And bookstore retailers are rethinking their business models with the advent of e-book readers such as Amazon's Kindle and Apple's iPad.

Goals

Goals or objectives (terms used interchangeably in this textbook) are statements of an accomplishment of a task to be achieved, often by a specific time. Goals convert an organization's mission and business into long- and short-term performance targets to measure how well it is doing (see Figure 2–2).

Useful criteria for writing effective goals are given by the acronym SMART:

- **S**pecific. Be a precise description of what is to be achieved
- **M**easurable. Be a quantitative value to show attainment
- **A**ttainable. Be achievable, but challenging
- **R**elevant. Be pertinent to the organization's mission
- **T**ime-based. Have a deadline for completion

Business firms can pursue several different types of goals:

- *Profit*. Most firms seeks to maximize long-run profit, achieving as high a financial return on their investment (ROI) as possible.
- *Sales (dollars or units)*. If profits are acceptable, a firm may elect to maintain or increase its sales level, even though profitability may not be maximized. Canadian Tire's goal over the next five years is to increase top-line growth (sales) as well as improve its profitability.
- *Market share*. A firm may choose to maintain or increase its market share, sometimes at the expense of greater profits if industry status or prestige is at stake. **Market share** is the ratio of sales revenue of the firm to the total sales revenue of all firms in the industry, including the firm itself.
- *Quality*. A firm may target the highest-quality products or services in its industry, as 3M does with its Six Sigma program; Loblaws' goal is to offer customers high-quality food products and a quality shopping experience.
- *Customer satisfaction*. Customers are the reasons the organization exists, and so their satisfaction is of vital importance. At IBM Canada, based in Markham, Ontario, customer satisfaction is tracked just the same as financial revenue figures. At Maritime Life Assurance Company in Halifax, Nova Scotia, yearly bonuses paid to employees are based on customer satisfaction data.
- *Employee welfare*. A firm may recognize the critical importance of its employees by having an explicit goal stating its commitment to provide good employment opportunities and working conditions. For example, Telus has a highly accessible head office in downtown Vancouver and allows many employees to work from home. Shaw Communications has profit-sharing incentives, new parent-support initiatives, and generous pension plans. And Great Little Box Company has a head office that features a fully equipped on-site fitness facility, outdoor sand volleyball court, book exchange library, outdoor gazebo, and rooftop deck. It also supports employees who are new parents by offering flexible work options, and provides university and college tuition subsidies to employees and scholarships for children of employees.
- *Social responsibility*. A firm may seek to balance the conflicting goals of stakeholders to promote their overall welfare, even at the expense of profits. Firms marketing on a global basis are often confronted with the notion of being "good global citizens." The Making Responsible Decisions box, "The Global Dilemma: How to Achieve Sustainable Development," deals with the concept of sustainable development, an issue relevant to global marketers.[18]

MAKING RESPONSIBLE DECISIONS

The Global Dilemma: How to Achieve Sustainable Development

Corporate executives and world leaders are increasingly asked to address the issue of "sustainable development." This term was formally defined in a 1987 United Nations report as meeting present needs "without compromising the ability of future generations to meet their own needs." What often happens is the achievement of profits for a firm and economic development for a country by adding jobs in highly polluting industries, thereby pushing cleanup actions into the future.

Eastern Europe and the nations of the former Soviet Union provide an example. Tragically, poisoned air and dead rivers are the legacies of seven decades of communist rule. With more than a third of the households of many of these nations below the poverty level, should the immediate goal be a cleaner environment or more food, clothing, housing, and consumer goods? What should the heads of these governments do? What should Western firms trying to enter these new, growing markets do? What will be the impact on future generations?

3M developed an innovative program called Pollution Prevention Pays (3P) to reduce harmful environmental impacts, making a profit doing so. 3M estimates that the 3P program has eliminated more than 3.5 million pounds of pollution and saved the company $1.5 billion. 3M has also adopted a life cycle management (LCM) approach to new and existing products. This holistic approach encompasses the whole product supply chain, from raw materials through manufacturing to disposal and recycling, in order to minimize the energy consumption and the overall environmental footprint of products. Finally, 3M Canada has been recognized as one of the Top 50 Socially Responsible Corporations in Canada.

Should the environment or economic growth come first? What are the societal trade-offs? Will profit-making firms adopt and implement a 3P kind of program?

Many Canadian non-profit organizations also have goals, such as to serve consumers as efficiently as possible at the least cost. Examples include museums, such as the Montreal Museum of Fine Arts; symphony orchestras, such as the Edmonton Symphony Orchestra; hospitals, such as Saint Joseph's Hospital in Hamilton, Ontario; and research institutes, such as the Conference Board of Canada and the Fraser Institute in Vancouver.

Although technically not falling under the definition of "non-profit organization," government agencies also perform marketing activities in trying to achieve their goal of serving the public good. For example, Innovation, Science and Economic Development Canada (formerly, Industry Canada) is a federal government department responsible for fostering a competitive, knowledge-based Canadian economy. The department works with Canadians in all parts of the country and throughout the economy to improve conditions for investment, improve Canada's innovation performance, increase Canada's share of global trade, and build a fair, efficient, and competitive marketplace. Some of their marketing initiatives include promoting investment and trade, promoting tourism, and facilitating small business development.[19]

Organizational Strategies: How Will It Do It?

As shown in Figure 2–2, the organizational foundation sets the "why" of organizations and organizational direction sets the "what." To convert these into actual results, the organizational strategies are concerned with the "how." These organizational strategies vary in at least two ways, partly depending on the level in the organization and the offerings it provides customers.

Variation by Level

Moving down an organization involves creating increasingly specific, detailed strategies and plans. For example, at the corporate level, top management may struggle with writing a meaningful mission statement, while at the functional level the issue may involve whether Joan or John makes a sales call tomorrow.

Variation by Offering

Organizational strategies also vary by the organization's offering. The strategy will be far different when marketing a very tangible physical product (a heart pacemaker), a service (a WestJet flight), an idea (donation to the Canadian Red Cross), or an experience (bungee jumping at WildPlay Element Parks).

Most organizations develop a marketing plan as a part of their strategic marketing planning efforts. A **marketing plan** is a road map for the marketing actions of an organization for a specified future time period, such as one year or five years. The planning phase of the strategic marketing process (discussed later) usually results in a marketing plan that directs the marketing actions of an organization. In fact, a marketing plan is extremely important for a new venture and you should keep that in mind should you decided to become an entrepreneur someday.[20] Appendix A at the end of this chapter provides guidelines for writing a marketing plan.

> ### Learning Review
>
> **4.** What is the meaning of an organization's mission?
> **5.** What is the difference between an organization's "business" and its "goals"?

LO3   SETTING STRATEGIC DIRECTIONS

Setting strategic directions involves answering two other difficult questions: (1) Where are we now? (2) Where do we want to go?

A Look Around: Where Are We Now?

Asking an organization where it is at the present time involves identifying its competencies, customers, and competitors. More detailed approaches of assessing "where are we now?" include both SWOT analysis, discussed later in this chapter, and environmental scanning (Chapter 3).

Competencies

Senior managers of an organization must ask a critical question: "What do we do best?" The answer involves a frank assessment of the organization's core **competencies**, which are its special capabilities, including the skills, technologies, and resources that distinguish it from other organizations and that provide value to its customers. Exploiting these competencies can lead to success, particularly if other organizations cannot copy them.[21] Competencies should be distinctive enough to provide a **competitive advantage**, a unique strength relative to competitors that is often based on quality, time, cost, innovation, customer intimacy, or customer experience management.[22]

For example, if 3M has a goal of generating a specific portion of its sales from new products, it must have a supporting competency in research and development and new-product marketing. Canadian Tire believes one of its competitive advantages is its ability to stay close to the customer (customer intimacy). It is able to do so, in part, because of its strategic retail locations. In fact, 92 percent of the Canadian population lives within 15 minutes of a Canadian Tire store, and more than 40 percent of Canadian adults shop there every week. Once the customer is in the store, Canadian Tire associates attempt to provide outstanding customer experiences.

Another strategy is to develop a competency in producing high-quality products. **Quality** here means those features and characteristics of a product that influence its ability to satisfy customer needs. Firms often try to improve quality through benchmarking—discovering how others do something better than your own firm so that you can imitate or leapfrog the competition. **Benchmarking** can also involve studying operations in completely different businesses and applying this new knowledge to your own business. And, as we saw in Chapter 1, developing a competency to deliver an excellent customer experience is now an extremely important mission for many firms competing in the new customer experience management economy.

More and more often, many Canadian companies are using innovation as a competitive advantage to win in the marketplace. This is particularly true of entrepreneurial firms. For example, Lululemon Athletica Inc. has become a major success story as a result of introducing a whole new category of innovative leisure wear, its yoga-inspired athletic apparel; AbeBooks revolutionized bookselling with its online book marketplace where millions of books can be purchased from thousands of booksellers around the world.[23] Another example of winning with innovation is Saltworks Technologies of British Columbia. It developed an innovative technology that turns salt water and waste water into safe drinking water. And it is important to remember that innovation does not have to involve new products or new technologies, but simply a new way of doing business. Just ask Jim Bodden. Bodden, also from British Columbia, is the founder of Wow-1Day! Painting Inc. Instead of the prevailing model where paint contractors use small crews to paint a typical house over several days, Bodden uses larger crews and gets the job done in one day, saving the customer time and frustration![24]

Customers

A sound strategic direction is set by knowing in great detail exactly who an organization's customers and prospective customers are and the type of products and services (value) they are seeking. Moreover, where, how, and in what form they want this value delivered must also be known. Without such intimate knowledge, an organization's strategic direction may be misaligned and finite corporate resources wasted. In order to stay close to their customers and to understand their needs, every employee at R.C. Purdy's Chocolates of Vancouver actually serves customers.

Competitors

In today's globalized economy, a given organization is likely to face a complex array of competitors. Moreover, the distinctions among competitors are becoming increasingly blurred. Therefore, successful organizations continuously assess both who the competitors are and how they are behaving in order to respond with their own competitive strategies, including how they differentiate themselves from such competitors.

Growth Strategies: Where Do We Want to Go?

Knowing where the organization is at the present time enables managers to set a direction for the firm and start to allocate resources to move toward that direction. Two techniques to aid in these decisions are (1) business portfolio analysis and (2) market–product analysis.

Business Portfolio Analysis

Successful organizations have a portfolio or range of offerings (products and services) that possess different growth rates and market shares within the industry in which they operate. The Boston Consulting Group (BCG), an internationally known management consulting firm, has developed business portfolio analysis. It is a technique that managers use to quantify performance measures and growth targets to analyze their firms' SBUs as though they were a collection of separate investments.[25] The purpose of this tool is to determine which SBU or offering generates cash and which one requires cash to fund the organization's growth opportunities. As described in the Marketing Matters box, let's assume you are filling the shoes of Apple CEO Tim Cook. Based on your knowledge of Apple products, you are currently conducting a quick analysis of four major Apple SBUs through 2018. Try to rank them from highest to lowest in terms of percentage growth in expected unit sales. We will introduce you to business portfolio analysis as we look at the possible future of the four Apple SBUs.

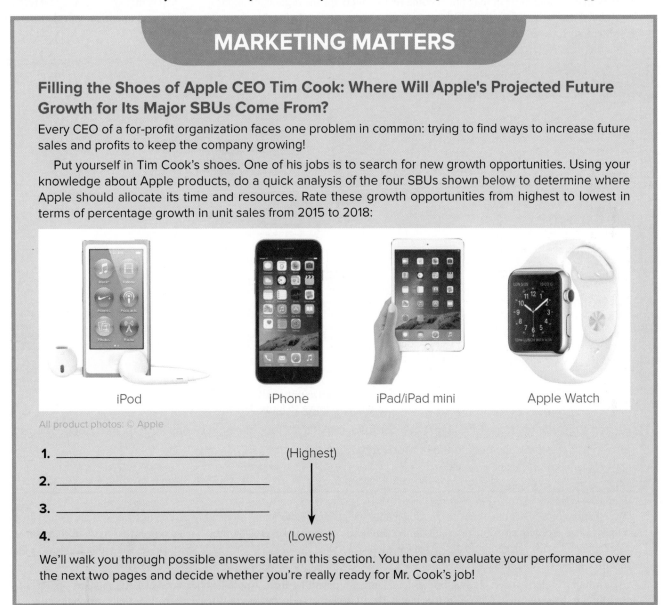

MARKETING MATTERS

Filling the Shoes of Apple CEO Tim Cook: Where Will Apple's Projected Future Growth for Its Major SBUs Come From?

Every CEO of a for-profit organization faces one problem in common: trying to find ways to increase future sales and profits to keep the company growing!

Put yourself in Tim Cook's shoes. One of his jobs is to search for new growth opportunities. Using your knowledge about Apple products, do a quick analysis of the four SBUs shown below to determine where Apple should allocate its time and resources. Rate these growth opportunities from highest to lowest in terms of percentage growth in unit sales from 2015 to 2018:

iPod   iPhone   iPad/iPad mini   Apple Watch

All product photos: © Apple

1. _____ (Highest)

2. _____

3. _____

4. _____ (Lowest)

We'll walk you through possible answers later in this section. You then can evaluate your performance over the next two pages and decide whether you're really ready for Mr. Cook's job!

The BCG business portfolio analysis requires an organization to locate the position of each of its SBUs on a growth-share matrix (see Figure 2–3). The vertical axis is the market growth rate, which is the annual rate of growth of the SBU's industry. The horizontal axis is the relative market share, defined as the sales of the SBU divided by the sales of the largest firm in the industry. A relative market share of 10 × (at the left end of the scale) means that the SBU has 10 times the share of its largest competitor, whereas a share of 0.1 × (at the right end of the scale) means it has only 10 percent of the share of its largest competitor. The BCG has given specific names and descriptions to the four resulting quadrants in its growth-share matrix based on the amount of cash they generate for or require from the organization:

1. Question marks are SBUs with a low share of high-growth markets. They require large injections of cash just to maintain their market share, much less increase it. The name implies management's dilemma for these SBUs: choosing the right ones to invest in and phasing out the rest.

2. Stars are SBUs with a high share of high-growth markets that may need extra cash to finance their own rapid future growth. When their growth slows, they are likely to become cash cows.

3. Cash cows are SBUs that generate large amounts of cash, far more than they can use. They have dominant shares of slow-growth markets and provide cash to cover the organization's overhead and to invest in other SBUs.

4. Dogs are SBUs with low shares of slow-growth markets. Although they may generate enough cash to sustain themselves, they may no longer be or may not become real winners for the organization. Dropping SBUs that are dogs may be required if they consume more cash than they generate, except when relationships with other SBUs, competitive considerations, or potential strategic alliances exist.[26]

FIGURE 2–3

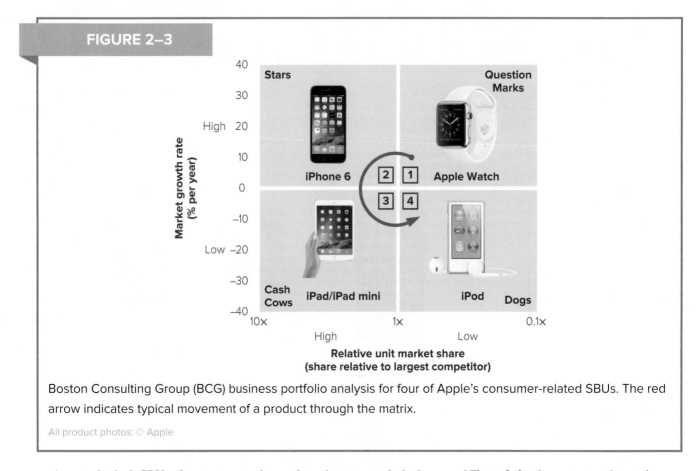

Boston Consulting Group (BCG) business portfolio analysis for four of Apple's consumer-related SBUs. The red arrow indicates typical movement of a product through the matrix.

All product photos: © Apple

An organization's SBUs often start as question marks and go counterclockwise around Figure 2–3 to become stars, then cash cows, and finally dogs. Because an organization has limited influence on the market growth rate, its main objective is to try to change its relative dollar or unit market share. To do this, management decides what strategic role each SBU should have in the future and either injects cash into or removes cash from it.

According to Interbrand, a leading brand management consulting firm, Apple has been consistently cited as one of the top global brands over the past decade in its annual Best Global Brands survey.[27] What has made Apple so iconic is not only its revolutionary products but also its commitment to infusing the "human touch" with its technology such that its customers connect with the brand on both a cognitive and an emotional level. The late Steve Jobs was instrumental in creating Apple's organizational culture and core values that will continue to guide its future.[28]

Using the BCG business portfolio analysis framework, Figure 2–3 shows that the Apple picture might look this way from 2015 to 2018 for four of its SBUs:[29]

1. *Apple Watch (wearable technology).* Apple entered the wearable technology market in April 2015 with its version of a smart watch, the Apple Watch. The watch competes with Samsung, Pebble, and Motorola watches and a wide range of other wearable technologies such as Fitbit and Jawbone fitness trackers. The market grew at a rate of more than 100 percent in 2015, and Apple Watch sales were substantial despite a relatively high price and short battery life. The Apple watch enters the market as a question mark and awaits consumers' response.[30]

2. *iPhone (smartphones).* Apple launched its revolutionary iPhone smartphone in 2007. iPhone unit sales skyrocketed, and Apple's U.S. market share has grown to 47.7 percent, exceeding the market share of its largest competitor, Samsung. The smartphone market is expected to grow at an annual rate of 9.8 percent through 2018 due to growth in China and falling prices. High market share and high growth suggest that Apple's iPhone is a star.[31]

3. *iPad/iPad mini (tablets).* Launched in 2010, iPad unit sales reached 40 percent market share by 2013—leading both Samsung's Galaxy (18 percent) and Amazon's Kindle (4 percent). Tablet sales are increasing, although the rate of growth is plummeting as consumers are substituting big-screen smartphones, or "phablets" for tablets. For Apple, its iPad SBU is a cash cow (high market share in a low-growth market).[32]

4. *iPod (music players).* Apple entered the music player market with its iPod device in 2001. The product became a cultural icon, selling more that 50 million units annually until 2010 when the iPhone integrated a music player. Since 2010 sales have been declining dramatically, and in October 2014, Apple announced that it was discontinuing the iPod classic. Today Apple still sells three iPod product lines—the nano, the shuffle, and the touch—although declining sales and discontinued products suggest that this SBU is entering the dog category.[33]

So, how did you—as Tim Cook—rank the growth opportunity for each of the four SBUs? The Apple Watch represents the highest unit growth rate at more than 100 percent. The iPhone SBU is likely to continue growing at almost 10 percent, while the iPad SBU is experiencing a declining growth rate. Despite the difference in growth rates, the iPhone and iPad product lines together accounted for 72 percent of Apple's revenues in 2014. These revenues are used to pursue growth opportunities such as the Apple Watch, a next-generation phone, and a huge 13-inch iPad. Finally, no growth and the discontinuation of the iPod classic may signal the beginning of the end for Apple's iPod.[34]

The primary strength of business portfolio analysis lies in forcing a firm to place each of its SBUs in the growth-share matrix, which in turn suggests which SBUs will be cash producers and cash users in the future. Weaknesses of this analysis arise from the difficulty in (1) getting the needed information and (2) incorporating competitive data into business portfolio analysis.[35]

Market–Product Analysis

An alternative to business portfolio analysis, and one favoured by many marketers, is the use of market–product analysis. With this approach, firms view growth opportunities in terms of markets and products. Let us think of it this way: For any product, there is both a current market (consisting of existing customers) and a new market (consisting of potential customers). And for any market, there is a current product (what they are now using) and a new product (something they might use if it were developed). These four market–product strategies are shown in Figure 2–4.[36]

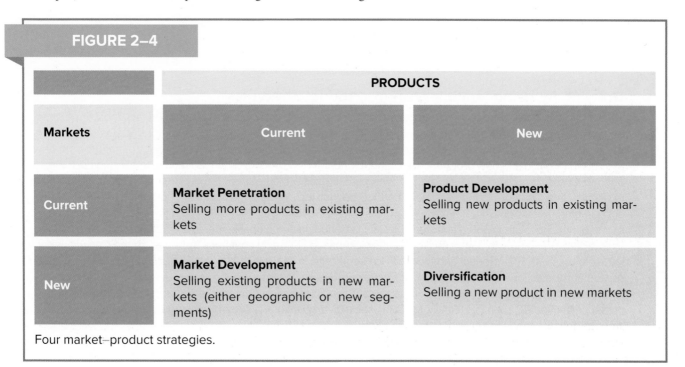

FIGURE 2–4

	PRODUCTS	
Markets	Current	New
Current	**Market Penetration** Selling more products in existing markets	**Product Development** Selling new products in existing markets
New	**Market Development** Selling existing products in new markets (either geographic or new segments)	**Diversification** Selling a new product in new markets

Four market–product strategies.

For example, a firm can try to use *market penetration*—a marketing strategy of increasing sales of present products in existing markets. There is no change in either the basic product line or the market served, but increased sales are possible—either by selling more products (through better promotion or distribution) *or* by selling the same amount of product at a higher price to its existing customers. For example, Fédération des producteurs de lait du Québec promotes the consumption of two glasses of milk daily in order to increase their market penetration in the beverage market in Quebec.[37]

Market development is a marketing strategy of selling existing products to new markets. This could be new geographic markets, such as opening a new Tim Hortons location where no outlet currently exists, or selling to a new market segment that currently does not consume your product. For example, a firm that sells mainly to women, such as Weight Watchers, now sells to the overweight male market.

Product development is a marketing strategy of selling new products to existing markets. For example, Second Cup now offers a line of fruit smoothies to its customers in addition to its traditional coffee and tea offerings.[38]

Diversification is a marketing strategy of developing new products and selling them in new markets. This is the riskiest growth strategy because the organization cannot use its expertise with current products or knowledge of its existing markets. There are, however, varying degrees of diversification: related diversification and unrelated diversification. *Related diversification* occurs when new products and new markets have something in common with the firm's existing operations. For example, McDonald's Canada could buy out and operate Red Lobster restaurants. In this case, it remains in the restaurant industry, just a different sector of it. *Unrelated diversification* means the new products and new markets have nothing in common with existing operations. In this case, McDonald's Canada might diversify into completely new business areas, such as financial services. To see how some firms grow using multiple market–product strategies, read the accompanying Marketing Matters box, "Growing by Using Multiple Market–Product Strategies."[39]

To see how two Canadian organizations, the Fédération des producteurs de lait du Québec and Second Cup, effectively used market–product strategies, read the text.

Federation des producteurs de lait du Quebec\ Agency: BBDO Montreal

---

MARKETING MATTERS

Growing by Using Multiple Market–Product Strategies

Most firms do not rely solely on a single growth path, or on one market–product strategy. In fact, most firms simultaneously pursue multiple growth paths, or multiple market–product strategies. For example, Stratus Vineyards is using market penetration to enter the Canadian wine market. It is also using market development (growing new markets in the U.S.) and new product development (offering new products such as icewine to existing customers). Second Cup also pursues a multi-prong growth path. It uses a market penetration strategy, allowing customers to use its Café Card (pre-loaded payment card) to pay for their orders, thus providing greater convenience and encouraging greater consumption by existing customers. Second Cup also offers new in-store products, such as its line of hot chocolate in 350 g canisters. McCain, a Canadian and global leader in the frozen food category, also uses a multi-prong growth path. The New Brunswick–based company continues to penetrate the Canadian market, both the consumer product and food service segments. In fact, it is the largest french fry provider to the food service and institutional market segment. It also grows by constantly launching new products to meet the changing needs of its customers. The company also continues to develop new markets (market development) with a presence in over 100 countries. Finally, McCain uses a diversification strategy, branching out from the frozen foods category into the ready-to-serve beverage market.

One of the reasons why firms do not or cannot rely on a single growth path or one market–product strategy is because that single strategy may, eventually, lead to stalled growth. For example, some firms work on market penetration as their initial primary growth strategy. But, if successful, sometimes additional penetration is not possible or might be cost prohibitive. Heinz Canada, for instance, has 90 percent share of the jarred baby food market in Canada and cannot cost-effectively increase its market penetration. Therefore, the company focuses on maintaining this penetration while developing new products and new markets. Ultimately, successful firms understand the importance of using multiple market–product strategies in order to sustain their growth.

LO4 Tracking Strategic Performance with Marketing Analytics, Marketing Dashboards, and Marketing Metrics

Although marketing managers can set strategic direction for their organizations, how do they know if they are making progress in getting there? A popular adage attributed to the management and statistics visionary, W. Edwards Deming, says, "You can't manage what you don't measure." One answer to this problem is the growing field of data analytics, or big data, which enables data-driven decisions by collecting data and presenting it in a visual format such as a marketing dashboard.

Car Dashboards and Marketing Dashboards

A **marketing dashboard** is the visual computer display of the essential information related to achieving a marketing objective.[40] Often, active hyperlinks provide further detail. An example is when a chief marketing officer (CMO) wants to see hourly what effect a new TV advertising campaign has on a product's sales.

The idea of a marketing dashboard really comes from the display of information found on a car's dashboard. On a car's dashboard, we glance at the fuel gauge and take action when our gas is getting low. With a marketing dashboard, a marketing manager glances at a graph or table and makes a decision whether to take action, or often to do more analysis to understand the problem better.[41]

Dashboards, Metrics, and Plans

The marketing dashboard of Sonatica, a hypothetical hardware and software firm (pictured below) shows graphic displays of key performance indicators linked to its product lines. Each display in a marketing dashboard shows a **marketing metric**, which is a measure of the quantitative value or trend of a marketing activity or result.[42] The choice of which marketing metrics to display is critical for a busy marketing manager, who can be overwhelmed with irrelevant data.[43]

Today's marketers use data visualization, which presents information about an organization's marketing metrics graphically so that marketers can quickly (1) spot deviations from plans and (2) take corrective actions.[44] The Sonatica marketing dashboard uses data visualization tools like graphs to provide a snapshot of how parts of the business are performing:

- *Website Traffic Sources.* The colour-coded perimeter of the pie chart shows the three main sources of website traffic (referral sites at 47 percent, search engines at 37 percent, and direct traffic at 16 percent), with each of eight specific sources represented as one slice in the pie. Of the 47 percent of traffic coming from referral sites, the horizontal *bullet graphs* to the right show that Sonatica's Facebook visits comprise 15 percent of total website traffic, up from a month ago (as shown by the vertical line).

- *Sales Performance by SBU.* The *spark lines* (the wavy lines in the far left column) show the 13-month trends of Sonatica's strategic business units (SBUs). For example, the trends in electronics and peripherals are generally up, causing their sales to exceed their year-to-date (YTD) targets. Conversely, both software and hardware sales failed to meet YTD targets, a problem quickly noted by a marketing manager seeing the red "warning" circles in their rows at the far right. This suggests immediate corrective actions for the software and hardware SBUs.

A three-step "challenge-findings-action" format is utilized for the Using Marketing Dashboards boxes featured throughout the textbook. This format stresses the importance of using marketing dashboards and the metrics contained within them to measure or evaluate marketing strategies and marketing program actions. You will have an opportunity to use a marketing dashboard in this chapter for a snack company you started after your graduation (see the Using Marketing Dashboards box below).

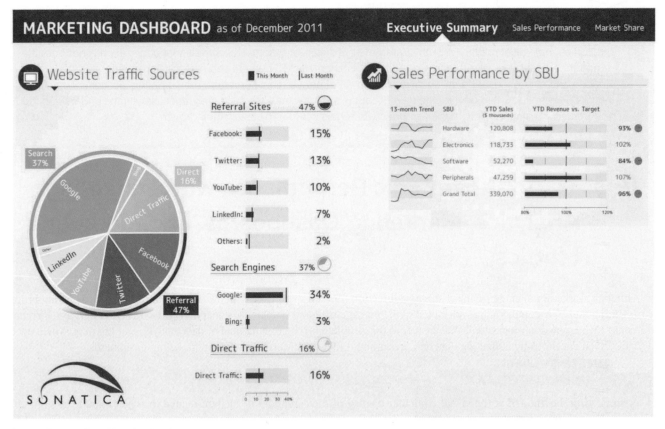

Source: Dundas Data Visualization, Inc.

An effective marketing dashboard like this one helps managers assess a business situation at a glance.

USING MARKETING DASHBOARDS

Which Provinces Are Underperforming?

Three years ago, you started your own company to sell a snack that includes a top-secret ingredient you discovered while travelling in the Amazon after graduation. The snack is really delicious and adds IQ and strength with every bite!

Your Challenge   The snack is sold in all ten provinces. Your goal is 10 percent growth annually. You want to get 2017 off to a fast start. You want to act quickly to solve any sales problems. You know that pockets of sales stagnation or decline (0 percent or negative growth) are offset by growth markets with greater than 10 percent growth.

Studying a table of sales and percent change versus a year ago in each of the ten provinces would work but would be very time consuming. A good graphic is better. You choose the following marketing metric, where "sales"? is measured in units:

$$\text{Annual \% Sales Change} = \frac{(2017 \text{ Sales} - 2016 \text{ Sales} \times 100)}{2016 \text{ Sales}}$$

You want to act quickly to improve sales. In your map, growth that is greater than 10 percent is GREEN, 0 to 10 percent growth is ORANGE, and decline is RED. Notice that you (1) picked a metric and (2) made your own rules that GREEN is good, ORANGE is bad, and RED is very bad.

Your Findings   At a glance you see that sales growth in Atlantic Canada and Alberta is weaker than the 10 percent target, and sales are declining in other provinces, too.

Your Action   Marketing is often about grappling with sales shortfalls. You'll need to start by trying to identify and correct the problems in the provinces that are underperforming—in this case, Atlantic Canada and Alberta are declining, and sales are weaker than what you want in Saskatchewan and Manitoba.

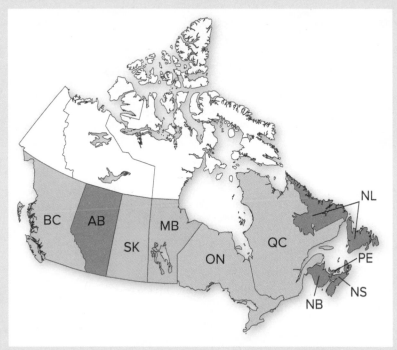

You'll want to do the marketing research to see if the problem starts with (1) an external factor, such as changing consumer tastes, or (2) an internal factor, such as a breakdown in your distribution system.

Learning Review

6. What is business portfolio analysis?
7. What are the four market–product strategies?
8. What is a marketing dashboard?

LO5   THE STRATEGIC MARKETING PROCESS

After the organization assesses where it is at and where it wants to go, other questions emerge:

1. How do we allocate our resources to get where we want to go?
2. How do we convert our plan to actions?
3. How do our results compare with our plans, and do deviations require new plans?

This same approach is used in the **strategic marketing process**, whereby an organization allocates its marketing mix resources to reach its target markets. This process is divided into three phases: planning, implementation, and evaluation (Figure 2–5).

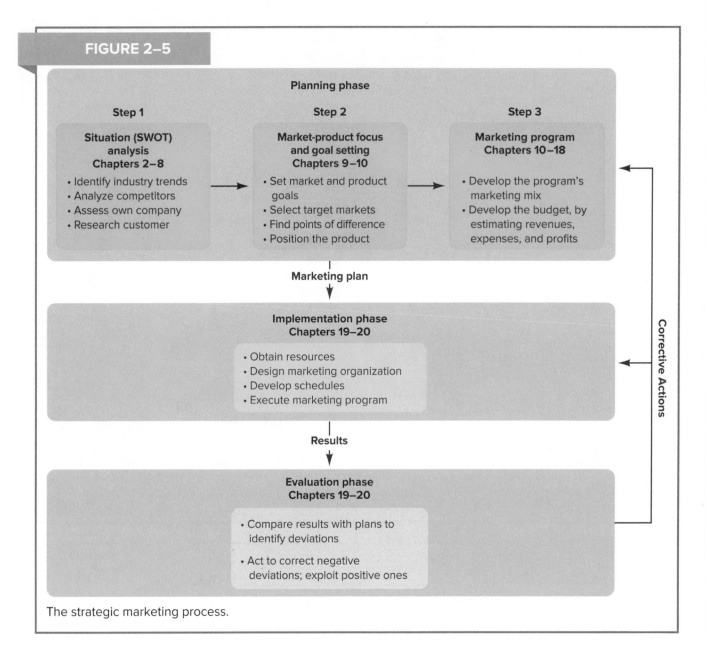

FIGURE 2–5

The strategic marketing process.

Strategic Marketing Process: The Planning Phase

As shown in Figure 2–5, the planning phase of the strategic marketing process consists of the three steps shown at the top of the figure: (1) situation (SWOT) analysis, (2) market–product focus and goal setting, and (3) the marketing program. Let us use the recent marketing planning experiences of several companies to look at each of these steps.

Figure 2–5 also shows how the strategic marketing process integrates the chapters in this book. Chapters 2 through 8 provide the information for the situation (SWOT) analysis, step 1 of the planning phase. Step 2, developing a market–product focus and goals for the product, is covered in Chapters 9 and 10. The elements of the marketing program in step 3—the 4 Ps—are discussed in Chapters 10 through 18. The book concludes with Chapter 19, which ties together the planning, implementation, and evaluation phases of the strategic marketing process, and Chapter 20, which covers social media and how marketers need to integrate social media into their strategic marketing process.

Step 1: Situation (SWOT) Analysis

The essence of **situation analysis** is taking stock of where the firm or product has been recently, where it is now, and where it is headed in terms of the organization's plans and the external factors and trends affecting it. The situation analysis box in Figure 2–5 is the first of the three steps in the planning phase.

An effective shorthand summary of the situation analysis is a **SWOT analysis**, an acronym describing an organization's appraisal of its internal **S**trengths and **W**eaknesses and its external **O**pportunities and **T**hreats. Both the situation and SWOT analyses can be done at the level of the entire organization, the business unit, the product line, or the specific product. As an analysis moves from the level of the entire organization to the specific product, it, of course, gets far more detailed. For small firms or those with basically a single product line, an analysis at the firm or product level is really the same thing.

The SWOT analysis is based on an exhaustive study of the four areas shown in step 1 of the planning phase of the strategic marketing process (see Figure 2–5). Knowledge of these areas forms the foundation on which the firm builds its marketing program:

- Identifying trends in the firm's industry
- Analyzing the firm's competitors
- Assessing the firm itself
- Researching the firm's present and prospective customers

Let us assume that you are responsible for growing the Ben & Jerry's ice cream brand in Canada. This product is widely available in the United States and many other countries but has only limited market coverage via its franchised Scoop Shops in Canada; in fact, the scoop stores can be currently found only in Ontario, Quebec, Alberta, and British Columbia. But the good news is that the brand is also available through supermarkets and grocery stores in Canada. Given your task, the first thing you might want to do is a SWOT analysis. One is completed for you and shown in Figure 2–6. Note that your SWOT table has four cells formed by the combination of internal versus external factors (the rows) and favourable versus unfavourable factors (the columns) that summarize Ben & Jerry's strengths, weaknesses, opportunities, and threats. This SWOT analysis can identify opportunities to grow the brand as well as possibly eliminate Ben & Jerry's flavours that will not meet Canadian customers' tastes. Those that do not will wind up in the "Flavor Graveyard." Go to the Going Online box and check it out!

A SWOT analysis helps a firm identify the strategy-related factors in these four cells that can have a major effect on the firm. The goal is not simply to develop the SWOT analysis but to translate the results of the analysis into specific actions to help the firm grow and succeed. The ultimate goal is to identify the *critical* factors affecting the firm and then build on vital strengths, correct glaring weaknesses, exploit significant opportunities, and avoid disaster-laden threats. That is a big order.

The Ben and Jerry's SWOT analysis in Figure 2–6 can be the basis for these kinds of specific actions. An action in each of the four cells might be the following:

- *Build on a strength.* Find specific efficiencies in distribution with Unilever's (the parent company of Ben & Jerry's) existing ice cream brands.

- *Correct a weakness.* Recruit experienced managers from other consumer product firms to help stimulate growth in the supermarket segment. Locate bright, assertive Canadian entrepreneurs who wish to own their own business and would do well operating a Ben & Jerry's Scoop Shop.

- *Exploit an opportunity.* Develop a new line of low-fat frozen yogurts to respond to consumer health concerns.

- *Avoid a disaster-laden threat.* Focus on physical markets only where there is high consumer discretionary income and desire for a premium ice cream product.

Step 2: Market–Product Focus and Goal Setting

Determining which products will be directed toward which customers (step 2 of the planning phase in Figure 2–5) is essential for developing an effective marketing program (step 3). This decision is often based on **market segmentation**, which involves aggregating prospective buyers into groups, or segments, that (1) have common needs and (2) will respond similarly to a marketing action. This enables an organization to focus specific marketing programs on its target market segments. The match between products and segments is often related to **points of difference**, or those characteristics of a product that make it superior to competitive substitutes. Goal setting involves specifying measurable marketing objectives to be achieved. So step 2 in the planning phase of the strategic marketing process—deciding which products will be directed toward which customers—is the foundation for step 3, developing the marketing program.

FIGURE 2–6

Location of Factor	TYPE OF FACTOR	
	Favourable	**Unfavourable**
Internal	**Strengths** • Prestigious brand name • Major share of the superpremium ice cream market • Can complement Unilever's existing ice cream brands	**Weaknesses** • Danger that B&J's social responsibility actions may add costs, reduce focus on core business • Need for experienced managers to help growth • Flat sales and profits in recent years
External	**Opportunities** • Growing demand for quality ice cream • Increasing demand for frozen yogurt and other low-fat desserts • Success of many firms in extending successful brand in one product category to others	**Threats** • Consumer concern about fatty desserts; B&J customers are the type who read new nutritional labels • Competes with Haagen-Dazs brand • Downturn in Canadian economy

Ben & Jerry's: a SWOT analysis to get it growing in Canada.

GOING ONLINE

Ben & Jerry's Flavours: From Chocolate Fudge Brownie Ice Cream and One Sweet Whirled Novelty Bars to . . . the Flavor Graveyard

Ben & Jerry's markets its flavours of ice cream, frozen yogurt, sorbet, and novelty bars in response to both consumer—ahem!—tastes and important causes it supports, a practice continued even after being sold to Unilever in 2000. For more than a decade, the brownies for Ben & Jerry's popular Chocolate Fudge Brownie ice cream have been supplied by Greyston Bakery, a non-profit organization that trains, employs, and houses low-income people in the area. Recently, Ben & Jerry's teamed up with the award-winning Dave Matthews Band and **SaveOurEnvironment.org** to fight global warming by creating the One Sweet Whirled ice cream flavour in pints and novelty bars. But not all flavours last. The ones that don't survive wind up in Ben & Jerry's "Flavor Graveyard." To see Ben & Jerry's current flavours as well as those "dearly departed flavours" in the Flavor Graveyard, visit **www.benjerry.com/flavors/flavor-graveyard**. Which flavours have been "laid to rest"?

LO5 Step 3: Marketing Program

Activities in step 2 tell the marketing manager which customers to target and which customer needs the firm's product offerings can satisfy—the *who* and *what* aspects of the strategic marketing process. The *how* aspect—step 3 in the planning phase—involves developing the program's marketing mix and its budget. Figure 2–7 shows components of each marketing mix element that are combined to provide a cohesive marketing program.

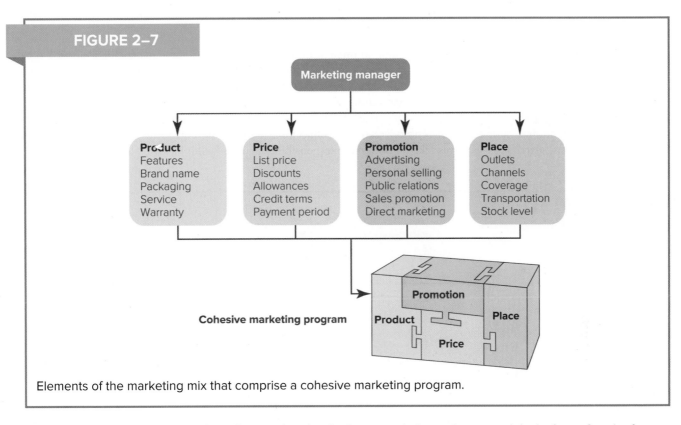

FIGURE 2–7

Elements of the marketing mix that comprise a cohesive marketing program.

Putting this marketing program into effect requires that the firm commit time and money to it in the form of a sales forecast and budget that must be approved by top management.

Learning Review

9. What is the difference between a strength and an opportunity in a SWOT analysis?

10. What is market segmentation?

11. What are points of difference, and why are they important?

LO6 Strategic Marketing Process: The Implementation Phase

As shown in Figure 2–5, the result of the tens or hundreds of hours spent in the planning phase of the strategic marketing process is the firm's marketing plan. Implementation, the second phase of the strategic marketing process, involves carrying out the marketing plan that emerges from the planning phase. If the firm cannot put the marketing plan into effect—in the implementation phase—the planning phase was a waste of time. Figure 2–5 also shows the four components of the implementation phase: (1) obtaining resources, (2) designing the marketing organization, (3) developing schedules, and (4) actually executing the marketing program designed in the planning phase.

Obtaining Resources

As you have discovered, most companies have numerous options for growth. But such growth requires an investment. Corporate leadership within an organization determines the best options for growth and how they should be funded. For example, car2go, a one-way car-sharing service, wants to obtain greater market penetration in Canada, which will require brand building, brand management, member experience management, and consumer insight work. Amber Quist, chief marketing officer for car2go, will be responsible for these activities and she will have to obtain the resources to do so, both financial and human resources.[45]

Designing the Marketing Organization

A marketing program needs a marketing organization to implement it. Figure 2–8 shows the organization chart of a typical manufacturing firm, giving some details of the marketing department's structure. Four managers of marketing activities are shown to report to the vice president of marketing. Several regional sales managers and an international sales manager may report to the manager of sales. This marketing organization, as a part of the corporate team, is responsible for converting marketing plans to reality. As we saw in Chapter 1, many organizations are placing more emphasis on their marketing organization as they attempt to become more customer-centric, creating customer-centric marketing organizations (CCMOs). In CCMO-based organizations, marketing executives take on even more responsibility and leadership in terms of crafting the organization's growth.[46]

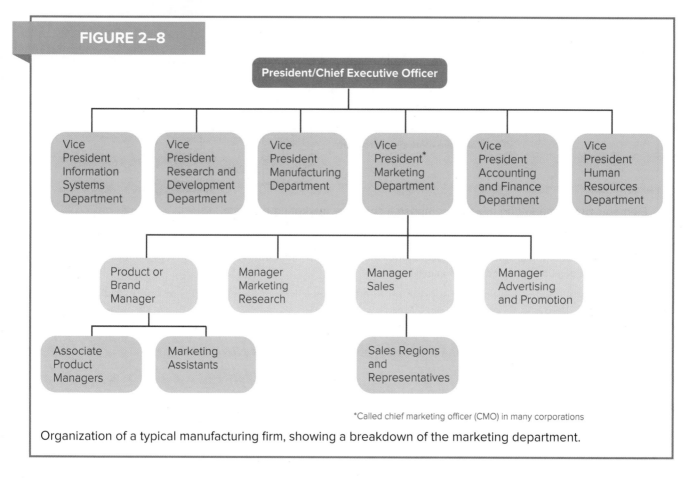

FIGURE 2–8

*Called chief marketing officer (CMO) in many corporations

Organization of a typical manufacturing firm, showing a breakdown of the marketing department.

Developing Schedules

Effective implementation requires developing appropriate schedules and determining specific deadlines for the creation and execution of marketing activities. For example, ads to be run during a Super Bowl take several months of planning in order to ensure that they are ready to air on television during the game. Marketers also have to make the ad space purchase before the network deadline; otherwise, the ads will not run.

Executing the Marketing Program

Marketing plans are meaningless pieces of paper without effective execution of those plans. This effective execution requires attention to detail for both marketing strategies and marketing tactics. A **marketing strategy** is the means by which a marketing goal is to be achieved, usually characterized by a specified target market and a marketing program to reach it. Although the term *marketing strategy* is often used loosely, it implies both the end sought (target market) and the means to achieve it (marketing program). For example, at Mars Incorporated, the company targets health-conscious females by advertising its 3 MUSKETEERS® Bar which has "45 percent less fat than average of the leading chocolate brands." It uses clever television ads to promote this product benefit and is achieving good sales results using this strategy.[47]

To implement a marketing program successfully, hundreds of detailed decisions are often required. These decisions, called **marketing tactics**, are detailed day-to-day operational decisions essential to the overall success of marketing strategies. At many Canadian companies, this might involve writing ads, setting prices, training salespeople, and working with channel members to ensure successful execution of the marketing program.

Marketing strategies and marketing tactics shade into each other. Effective marketing program implementation requires excruciating concern for both.

Strategic Marketing Process: The Evaluation Phase

The evaluation phase of the strategic marketing process seeks to keep the marketing program moving in the direction set for it (see Figure 2–5). Accomplishing this requires the marketing manager (1) to compare the results of the marketing program with the goals in the written plans to identify deviations, and (2) to act on these deviations—correcting negative deviations and exploiting positive ones. For example, sometimes the marketing program falls short of its goals. When this occurs, managers need to take corrective actions. This is called *correcting a negative deviation*. But when actual results are far better than the plan called for, creative managers find ways to exploit the situation. This is called *exploiting a positive deviation*.

There are numerous tools available to the marketer in the evaluation phase of the marketing process in order to assess properly the success or failure of marketing programs, including marketing ROI, marketing dashboards, and marketing metrics. These will be discussed in greater detail in Chapter 19.

Learning Review

12. What is the implementation phase of the strategic marketing process?

13. How do the goals set for a marketing program in the planning phase relate to the evaluation phase of the strategic marketing process?

Learning Objectives Review

 Describe two kinds of organizations that exist and the three levels of strategy in them.

An organization is a legal entity of people who share a common mission. There are two kinds. One is a business firm that is a privately owned organization that serves its customers in order to earn a profit so that it can survive. The other is a non-profit organization that is a non-governmental organization that serves its customers but does not have profit as a goal. Most large business firms and non-profit organizations are divided into three levels of strategy: (a) the corporate level, where top management directs overall strategy for the entire organization; (b) the strategic business unit level, where managers set a more specific strategic direction for their businesses to set value-creating opportunities; and (c) the functional level, where groups of specialists actually create value for the organization.

 Describe how core values, mission, organizational culture, business, and goals are important in organizations.

Organizations exist to accomplish something for someone. To give organizations direction and focus, they continuously assess their core values, mission, organizational culture, business, and goals. Today's organizations specify their foundation, set a direction, and formulate strategies—"why,"? "what,"? and "how"? factors, respectively. Core values are the organization's fundamental, passionate, and enduring principles that guide its conduct over time—what Enron forgot when it lost sight of its responsibilities to its stakeholders. The organization's mission is a statement of its function in society, often identifying its customers, markets, products, and technologies. Organizational culture is a set of values, ideas, attitudes, and norms of behaviour that is learned and shared among the members of an organization. To answer the question, "What business are we in?"? an organization defines its "business"?—the clear, broad, underlying industry category or market sector of its offering. Finally, the organization's goals (or objectives) are statements of an accomplishment of a task to be achieved, often by a specific time.

 Discuss how an organization assesses where it is now and where it seeks to be.

Managers of an organization ask two key questions to set a strategic direction. The first question, "Where are we now?"? requires an organization to (a) re-evaluate its competencies to ensure that its special capabilities still provide a competitive advantage; (b) assess its present and prospective customers to ensure they have a satisfying customer experience, the central goal of marketing today; and (c) analyze its current and potential competitors from a global perspective to determine whether it needs to redefine its business.

The second question, "Where do we want to go?"? requires an organization to set a specific direction and allocate resources to move it in that direction. Business portfolio analysis and market–product analysis are two useful techniques to do this.

LO4 **Explain why managers are tracking strategic performance with marketing analytics, marketing dashboards, and marketing metrics.**

Marketing managers can track strategic performance with the use of marketing analytics or big data. Marketing analytics or big data enables data-driven decisions, which can be gleaned from a marketing dashboard—the visual computer display of the essential information related to achieving a marketing objective. This information consists of key performance measures of a product category, such as sales or market share, and is known as a marketing metric, which is a measure of the quantitative value or trend of a marketing activity or result. Most organizations tie their marketing metrics to the quantitative objectives established in their marketing plan, which is a road map for the marketing activities of an organization for a specified future time period, such as one year or five years.

 Explain the three steps of the planning phase of the strategic marketing process.

An organization uses the strategic marketing process to allocate its marketing mix resources to reach its target markets. This process is divided into three phases: planning, implementation, and evaluation. The planning phase consists of three steps: (*a*) a situation (SWOT) analysis, which involves taking stock of where the firm or product has been recently, where it is now, and where it is headed, an assessment that focuses on the organization's internal strengths and weaknesses, as well as external opportunities and threats; (*b*) a market–product focus through market segmentation and goal setting, which in part requires creating points of difference—those characteristics of a product that make it superior to competitive substitutes; and (*c*) a marketing program that specifies the budget and activities (marketing strategies and tactics) for each marketing mix element.

LO6 **Describe the elements of the implementation and evaluation phases of the strategic marketing process.**

The implementation phase of the strategic marketing process carries out the marketing plan that emerges from the planning phase. It has four key elements: (*a*) obtaining resources; (*b*) designing the marketing organization to perform product management, marketing research, sales, and advertising and promotion activities; (*c*) developing schedules to identify the tasks that need to be done, the time that is allocated to each one, the people responsible for each task, and the deadline for each task's accomplishment; and (*d*) executing the marketing strategies, which are the means by which marketing goals are to be achieved, and their associated marketing tactics, which are the detailed day-to-day operational decisions essential to the overall success of a firm's marketing strategies

The evaluation phase of the strategic marketing process seeks to keep the marketing program moving in the direction that was established in the marketing plan. This requires the marketing manager to compare the results from the marketing program with the marketing plan's goals to (*a*) identify deviations and (*b*) take corrective actions to exploit positive deviations or correct negative ones.

Applying Marketing Knowledge

1. (*a*) Explain what a mission statement is. (*b*) Explain how it gives a strategic direction to its organization. (*c*) Create a mission statement for your own career.

2. What competencies best describe (*a*) your college or university, (*b*) your favourite restaurant, and (*c*) the company that manufactures the computer you own or use most often?

3. Assume you were starting a new business. In terms of competition, how would you differentiate your business from your competition?

4. Why does a product often start as a question mark and then move counter-clockwise around BCG's growth-share matrix shown in Figure 2–3?

5. Many Canadian universities have traditionally offered an undergraduate degree in liberal arts (the product) to full-time 18- to 22-year-old students (the market). How might such an institution use the four market–product expansion strategies shown in Figure 2–4 to compete in the twenty-first century?

6. What is the main result of each of the three phases of the strategic marketing process: (a) planning, (b) implementation, and (c) evaluation?

7. Select one strength, one weakness, one opportunity, and one threat from the SWOT analysis for Ben & Jerry's shown in Figure 2–6, and suggest a specific possible action that Unilever might take to exploit or address each one.

8. The goal-setting step in the planning phase of the strategic marketing process sets quantified objectives for use in the evaluation phase. What actions are suggested for a marketing manager if measured results are below objectives? Above objectives?

Building Your Marketing Plan

1. Read Appendix A, "Creating an Effective Marketing Plan."? Then write a 600-word executive summary for the Coffee Break Coffee House marketing plan using the numbered headings shown in the plan. When you have completed the draft of your own marketing plan, use what you learned in writing an executive summary for the coffee house to write a 600-word summary to go in front of your own marketing plan.

2. Using Chapter 2 and Appendix A as guides, give focus to your marketing plan by (a) writing your mission statement in 25 words or less, (b) listing three non-financial goals and three financial goals, (c) writing your competitive advantage in 35 words or less, and (d) doing a SWOT analysis table.

Video Case 2

IBM: Using Strategy to Build a "Smarter Planet"

"'Smarter Planet' is not an advertising campaign, it's not even a marketing campaign, it is a business strategy," explains Ann Rubin, vice president of advertising at IBM.

The "Smarter Planet" strategy is based on the idea that the next major revolution in the global marketplace will be the instrumentation and integration of the world's processes and infrastructures, generating unprecedented amounts of data. The data captured and analyzed in industries such as banking, energy, health care, and retailing will allow IBM to help businesses be more efficient, productive, and responsive.

The Company

Founded in 1911, IBM has a history of innovation and focus on customers. The blue covers on its computers, blue letters in the IBM logo, and dark blue suits worn by IBM salespeople led to the now popular company nickname, "Big Blue." Today, it has over 380,000 employees in more than 170 countries. Forbes magazine ranks IBM as the fifth-most valuable brand in the world. The company is a leading developer of new business technologies, receiving more than 5,000 patents each year. Some of its well-known inventions include the automated teller machine (ATM), the hard disk drive, the magnetic stripe card, relational databases, and the Universal Product Code (UPC). In addition, IBM recently gained attention for its artificial intelligence program called Watson, which challenged two *Jeopardy!* game show champions and won! According to Virginia Rometty, the current CEO of IBM, "IBM is an innovation company."

Values, Mission, and Strategy

Recently, IBM initiated a project to facilitate online discussions of key business issues among 50,000 employees to identify common themes and perspectives. According to Sam Palmisano, former CEO of IBM, "We needed to affirm IBM's reason for being, what sets the company apart, and what should drive our actions as individual IBMers." The results were three underlying values of IBM's business practices: (1) dedication to every client's success, (2) innovation that matters—for our company and for the world, and (3) trust and personal responsibility in all relationships. These values now come to life at IBM in its "policies, procedures, and daily operations," explains Palmisano.

© Peter Probst/Alamy Stock Photo

IBM's core values also help to define its mission, or its general function in society. In clear, concise, inspirational language, IBM's mission statement is:

- At IBM, we strive to lead in the invention, development and manufacture of the industry's most advanced information technologies, including computer systems, software, storage systems, and microelectronics.

- We translate these advanced technologies into value for our customers through our professional solutions, services, and consulting businesses worldwide.

The mission, and the values it represents, helps define the organizational culture at IBM. Executives, managers, and all employees create the culture through the strategies they select and the detailed plans for accomplishing them. IBM's strategies are based on its assessment of fundamental changes in the business environment. First, IBM sees global changes such as fewer trade barriers, the growth of developing economies, and increasing access to the World Wide Web. These changes necessitate a new type of corporation that IBM calls the "globally integrated enterprise." Second, IBM foresees a new model of computing that includes computational capability in phones, cameras, cars, and other appliances and allows economic, social, and physical systems to be connected. This connectivity creates a "smarter planet." Finally, IBM predicts a growing demand for technological solutions that help organizations measure and achieve specific outcomes.

As a result, IBM began to shift from commodity-based businesses such as PCs and hard disk drives, to "customizable" businesses such as software and services. The change in IBM was so substantial that it has described its plan in a document called the *2015 Road Map*. The map describes four strategic opportunities: (1) growth markets such as China, India, Brazil, and Africa; (2) business analytics and optimization; (3) cloud and smarter computing; and (4) the connected, "smarter" planet. These opportunities suggest a strategy that delivers value through business and IT innovation to selected industries with an integrated enterprise. The overarching strategy that highlights IBM's capabilities is called "Building a Smarter Planet."

Building a Smarter Planet

The Smarter Planet initiative is designed for clients who value IBM's industry and process expertise, systems integration capability, and research capacity. A smarter planet, while global by definition, happens on the industry level. It is driven by forward-thinking organizations that share a common outlook: They see change as an opportunity, and they act on possibilities, not just react to problems.

John Kennedy, vice president of marketing, explains, "'A Smarter Planet' actually surfaced from observing what was happening in our clients. They were looking to take the vast amount of data that was being generated inside their companies and looking to better understand it." To IBM, "smart" solutions have three characteristics. They are instrumented, they are intelligent, and they are interconnected. Millions of digital devices, now connected through the Internet, produce data that can be turned into knowledge through advanced computational power. IBM believes that this knowledge can help reduce costs, cut waste, improve efficiency, and increase productivity for companies, industries, and cities.

Since introducing the Smarter Planet strategy, IBM has collaborated with more than 600 organizations around the globe. The success of the strategy is evident in the broad range of industries where "smart" solutions are being implemented. They include banking; communications; electronics, automotive, and aerospace; energy and utilities; government; health care; insurance; oil and gas; retailing; and transportation. Each industry has reported a variety of applications.

In a study of 439 cities, for example, smart solutions such as ramp metering, signal coordination, and accident management reduced travel delays by more than 700,000 hours annually, saving each city $15 million. A study by the U.S. Department of Energy found that consumers with smart electric meters cut their power usage and saved 10 percent on their power bills. Retailers who implemented smart systems to analyze buying behaviour, merchandise assortment, and demand were able to cut supply chain costs by 30 percent, reduce inventory levels by 25 percent, and increase sales by 10 percent.

© IBM Corporation

The Building a Smarter Planet Marketing Plan

Marketing and communications professionals at IBM have developed the marketing plan for IBM's Smarter Planet strategy. The general goal is to describe the company's view of the next era of information technology and its impact on business and society. The execution of the plan includes messaging from IBM leaders, an advertising campaign, an Internet presence, and public relations communications. In addition, IBM measures and tracks the performance of the marketing activities.

The importance of the Smarter Planet strategy was first communicated through a message from the top. Palmisano prepared a "Letter from the Chairman" for the annual report. His message was a powerful statement. Smarter Planet, according to Palmisano, "is not a metaphor. It describes the infusion of intelligence into the way the world actually works."

IBM also used a print and television advertising campaign to add detail to the general message. The ads focused on the ability to improve the world now, with IBM's help. "I think what's different about Smarter Planet," says Ann Rubin, "is that it was not inward facing, it was looking out at what the world needed. We felt like we could go out there and influence the world for the better."

IBM recently celebrated its 100th anniversary! Its record of success is testimony to the resilience of a business model that encourages long-term strategies that can say "Welcome to a Smarter Planet."[48]

QUESTIONS

1. What is IBM's Smarter Planet business strategy? How does this strategy relate to IBM's mission and values?

2. Conduct a SWOT analysis for IBM's Smarter Planet initiative. What are the relevant trends to consider for the next three to five years?

3. How can IBM communicate its strategy to companies, cities, and governments?

4. What are the benefits of the Smarter Planet initiative to (*a*) society and (*b*) IBM?

5. How should IBM measure the results of the Smarter Planet strategy?

Case: This case was written by Steven Hartley. Sources: Jessi Hempel, "IBM's Super Second Act," *Fortune*, March 21, 2011, pp. 114–24; Bruce Upbin, "IBM Plays Jeopardy!" *Forbes*, January 17, 2011, pp. 36–37; Kurt Badenhausen, "The World's Most Valuable Brands," *Forbes*, May 13, 2015; Jeffrey M. O'Brien, "IBM's Grand Plan to Save the Planet," *Fortune*, May 4, 2009, pp. 84–91; IBM *2009 Annual Report*; IBM *2010 Annual Report*; Samuel J. Palmisano, "Our Values at Work on Being an IBMer," IBM website, see http://www.ibm.com/ibm/values/us; and "Welcome to the Decade of Smart," IBM website, http://www.ibm.com/smarterplanet/us/en/events/sustainable*development/12jan2010/files/palmisano* decadeofsmart-12jan2010.pdf.

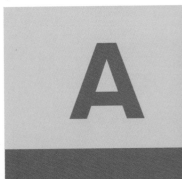

Appendix
Creating an Effective
Marketing Plan

"New ideas are a dime a dozen," observes Arthur R. Kydd, "and so are new products and new technologies." Kydd should know. As chief executive officer of St. Croix Venture Partners, he and his firm have provided the seed money and venture capital to launch more than 60 start-up firms in the last 25 years. Today, those firms have more than 5,000 employees. Kydd elaborates:

> I get 200 to 300 marketing and business plans a year to look at, and St. Croix provides start-up financing for only two or three. What sets a potentially successful idea, product, or technology apart from all the rest is markets and marketing. If you have a real product with a distinctive point of difference that satisfies the needs of customers, you may have a winner. And you get a real feel for this in a well-written marketing or business plan.[1]

This appendix (1) describes what marketing and business plans are, including the purposes and guidelines in writing effective plans, and (2) provides a sample marketing plan.

MARKETING PLANS AND BUSINESS PLANS

After explaining the meanings, purposes, and audiences of marketing plans and business plans, this section describes some writing guidelines for them and what external funders often look for in successful plans.

Meanings, Purposes, and Audiences

A *marketing plan* is a road map for the marketing activities of an organization for a specified future period of time, such as one year or five years.[2] It is important to note that no single generic marketing plan applies to all organizations and all situations. Rather, the specific format for a marketing plan for an organization depends on the following:

- *The target audience and purpose.* Elements included in a particular marketing plan depend heavily on (1) who the audience is, and (2) what its purpose is. A marketing plan for an internal audience seeks to point the direction for future marketing activities and is sent to all individuals in the organization who must implement the plan or who will be affected by it. If the plan is directed to an external audience, such as friends, banks, venture capitalists, or potential investors, for the purpose of raising capital, it has the additional function of being an important sales document. In this case, it contains elements such as the strategic plan/focus, organization, structure, and biographies of key personnel that would rarely appear in an internal marketing plan. Also, the financial information is far more detailed when the plan is used to raise outside capital. The elements of a marketing plan for each of these two audiences are compared in Figure A–1.

- *The kind and complexity of the organization.* A small neighbourhood restaurant has a somewhat different marketing plan from that of Nestlé, which serves international markets. The restaurant's plan would be relatively simple and directed at serving customers in a local market. In Nestlé's case, because there is a hierarchy of marketing plans, various levels of detail would be used—such as the entire organization, the business unit, or the product/product line.

- *The industry.* Both the restaurant that serves a local market and Medtronic that sells heart pacemakers globally analyze competition. Not only are their geographic thrusts far different, but the complexities of their offerings and hence the time periods likely to be covered by their plans also differ. A one-year marketing plan may be adequate for the restaurant, but Medtronic may need a five-year planning horizon because product-development cycles for complex, new medical devices may be three or four years.

FIGURE A–1

Element of the plan	Marketing plan		Business plan	
	For internal audience (to direct the firm)	For external audience (to raise capital)	For internal audience (to direct the firm)	For external audience (to raise capital)
1. Executive summary	✓	✓	✓	✓
2. Description of company		✓		✓
3. Strategic plan/focus		✓		✓
4. Situation analysis	✓	✓	✓	✓
5. Market-product focus	✓	✓	✓	✓
6. Marketing program strategy and tactics	✓	✓	✓	✓
7. R&D and operations program			✓	✓
8. Financial projections	✓	✓	✓	✓
9. Organization structure		✓		✓
10. Implementation plan	✓	✓	✓	✓
11. Evaluation	✓		✓	
Appendix A: Biographies of key personnel		✓		✓
Appendix B, etc.: Details on other topics	✓	✓	✓	✓

Elements in typical marketing and business plans targeted at different audiences.

In contrast to a marketing plan, a *business plan* is a road map for the entire organization for a specified future period of time, such as one year or five years.[3] A key difference between a marketing plan and a business plan is that the business plan contains details on the research and development (R&D), operations, and manufacturing activities of the organization. Even for a manufacturing business, the marketing plan is probably 60 or 70 percent of the entire business plan. For such businesses as a small restaurant or an auto repair shop, marketing and business plans are virtually identical. The elements of a business plan typically targeted at internal and external audiences appear in the two right-hand columns in Figure A–1.

The Most-Asked Questions by Outside Audiences

Lenders and prospective investors reading a business or marketing plan that is used to seek new capital are probably the toughest audiences to satisfy. Their most-asked questions include the following:

1. Is the business or marketing idea valid?

2. Is there something unique or distinctive about the product or service that separates it from substitutes and competitors?

3. Is there a clear market for the product or service?

4. Are the financial projections realistic and healthy?

5. Are the key management and technical personnel capable, and do they have a track record in the industry in which they must compete?

6. Does the plan clearly describe how those providing capital will get their money back and make a profit?

Rhonda M. Abrams, author of *The Successful Business Plan*, observes that "within the first five minutes of reading your ... plan, readers must perceive that the answers to these questions are favourable."[4] While her comments apply to plans seeking to raise capital, the first five questions just listed apply equally well to plans for internal audiences.

Writing and Style Suggestions

There are no magic one-size-fits-all guidelines for writing successful marketing and business plans. Still, the following writing and style guidelines generally apply:[5]

- Use a direct, professional writing style. Use appropriate business terms without jargon. Present and future tenses with active voice ("I will write an effective marketing plan.") are generally better than past tense and passive voice ("An effective marketing plan was written by me.").
- Be positive and specific to convey potential success. At the same time, avoid superlatives ("terrific," "wonderful"). Specifics are better than glittering generalities. Use numbers for impact, justifying projections with reasonable quantitative assumptions, where possible.
- Use bullet points for succinctness and emphasis. As with the list you are reading, bullets enable key points to be highlighted effectively.
- Use A-level (the first level) and B-level (the second level) headings under the numbered section headings to help readers make easy transitions from one topic to another. This also forces the writer to organize the plan more carefully. Use these headings liberally, at least one every 200 to 300 words.
- Use visuals, where appropriate. Photos, illustrations, graphs, and charts enable massive amounts of information to be presented succinctly.
- Aim for a plan 15 to 35 pages in length, not including financial projections and appendixes. An uncomplicated small business may require only 15 pages, while a high-technology start-up may require more than 35 pages.
- Use care in layout, design, and presentation. Laser printers give a more professional look than do ink-jet printers. Use 11- or 12-point type (you are now reading 10.5-point type) in the text. Use a serif type (with "feet," like that you are reading now) in the text because it is easier to read, and sans serif (without "feet") in graphs and charts, as in Figure A–1. A bound report with an attractive cover and clear title page adds professionalism.

These guidelines are used, where possible, in the sample marketing plan that follows.

SAMPLE FIVE-YEAR MARKETING PLAN FOR COFFEE BREAK COFFEE HOUSE

To help interpret the marketing plan for Coffee Break Coffee House that follows, we suggest some guidelines.

Interpreting the Marketing Plan

The sample marketing plan for Coffee Break, a specialty coffee house on Kwantlen Polytechnic University's Surrey campus, was written by Professor John Shepherd of Kwantlen Polytechnic University. The invaluable assistance provided by Aina Adashynski, Belinda Kaplan, Catherine Wilkinson, and Connie Shepherd during the preparation of the plan is greatly appreciated.

Notes in the margins next to the plan fall into two categories:

1. *Substantive notes* are shaded blue and elaborate on the significance of an element in the marketing plan and are keyed to chapter references in this text.

2. *Writing style, format, and layout notes* are shaded in pink and explain the editorial or visual rationale for the element.

A Closing Word of Encouragement

Writing an effective marketing plan is hard—but challenging and satisfying—work. However, dozens of the authors' students have used effective marketing plans they wrote for class in their interviewing portfolio to show prospective employers what they could do and to help them get their first job.

> Blue boxes explain the significance of marketing plan elements.

> Orange boxes give writing style, format, and layout guidelines.

Marketing Plan
Coffee Break Coffee House

A-1

Table of Contents

A-2

1. Executive Summary

The following plan outlines the marketing strategy and tactics for *Coffee Break*, a specialty coffee house opening on *Kwantlen Polytechnic University*'s Surrey campus in autumn 2017. Located in a residential area, the Surrey campus has two existing restaurants: a cafeteria and a student association café. There are several additional restaurants within easy walking distance.

A–1

The Table of Contents provides quick access to the topics in the plan, usually organized by section and subsection headings.

A–2

Seen by many experts as the single most important element in the plan, the Executive Summary "sells" the plan to readers through its clarity and brevity.

Coffee Break will target a combined student and staff population of 11,000 with a take-out coffee counter and coffee house. *Coffee Break* will have four distinguishing features: a coffee take-out counter, a comfortable atmosphere created by a skilled serving team, excellent beverages, and the use of on-campus promotional activities to build awareness and a steady clientele.

In addition to securing a suitable location, *Coffee Break* must expand the campus food services market by attracting student beverage purchases now spent in local restaurants. Unless campus amenities, such as *Coffee Break*, can provide reasons for students to remain on campus after hours, the market is inherently limited by the number of days that classes are in session each year.

2. Company Description A-3

Coffee Break is opening a 60-seat coffee house adjacent to the central courtyard of the *Kwantlen Polytechnic University*'s Surrey campus. The coffee house will target the 10,000 students, 900 staff, and visitors of the campus with a selection of specialty coffees, teas, beverages, and healthy snacks.

A–3

The Company Description highlights the recent history of the organization.

Kwantlen Polytechnic University has a student population of 17,000 spread over four campuses that service the growing municipalities of Surrey, Langley, Delta, and Richmond. The main *Kwantlen* campus is near the western boundary of Surrey, a municipality of 400,000 people located southeast of the City of Vancouver. Originally a college, *Kwantlen Polytechnic* has grown rapidly over the past 20 years and is now a university.

Coffee Break will be known for its warm, inviting atmosphere, a fun place for students between 18 and 25 years of age to relax and meet with friends. A coffee take-out counter at the front will focus on fast turnaround times for students and staff who desire a quick coffee or a snack between classes.

The café will offer a wide selection of coffees, teas, and other refreshments, along with light food items such as wraps, pastries, and vegetarian dishes. *Coffee Break* will focus on providing quality coffee and superior customer service. The restaurant's menu prices will match those of its on-campus competitors.

The interior of the coffee house will resemble a neighbourhood pub with lots of wood and a youthful spin. Features will include comfortable chairs of a variety of types, an outside view of the campus courtyard, and the aroma of fine coffee. Warm colours, local art, evening entertainment, theme nights, and light background music will create a fun, enjoyable atmosphere.

Customer service will be emphasized. Serving staff will be hired based on their warm, friendly personalities and carefully trained in the arts of service and fine coffee. Staff will be recognized for outstanding performance and every effort will be made for them to feel an integral part of the team.

Coffee Break's focus on atmosphere, service, fine coffee, and ongoing promotional activities will expand the size of the food-services pie on campus by giving students another reason to linger on campus after class. This plan describes how *Coffee Break* can establish a leading position on the Surrey campus and develops a business model that can be franchised to other medium-sized college and university campuses.

A-4

3. Strategic Focus and Plan

Core Values

The core values of *Coffee Break* are as follows:

1. To respect our customers and fellow workers.
2. A commitment to providing our customers with a superior quality product, delivered with a smile.

A-5

Mission

The mission of *Coffee Break* is to create a social place where people leave their worries at the door, enjoy the best coffee on campus, and meet fellow students in a relaxed atmosphere.

Non-Financial Objectives [A-6]

1. To open the first *Coffee Break* restaurant in August 2017.
2. To become known as the best student employer on campus.
3. To become the place for students to relax and meet with friends on campus.
4. To open three *Coffee Break* restaurants at other western Canadian colleges or universities within five years.

A-7

Financial Objectives

1. To reach the break-even point for the *Kwantlen* coffee house by the end of its first year of operations (e.g., $230,000 in annual sales).
2. To achieve the revenue target of $300,000 and an operating profit of $46,500 during the 2018-2019 fiscal year.
3. To finance future expansion using internally generated funds.

Competencies and Competitive Advantage

The core competency of *Coffee Break* is its management's expertise and focus in the unique needs of the post-secondary market. This capability will enable the business to create a student-centred atmosphere, where learners can drink a good cup of coffee or other beverage in a friendly, youth-focused atmosphere.

Management will achieve service and product excellence by carefully selecting the staff, conducting ongoing staff training, providing leadership by example, and creating a supportive environment where employees feel valued.

A-8

4. SWOT and Market Analysis

SWOT Analysis

The SWOT analysis is summarized in Figure 1, showing the internal and external factors that could affect the restaurant's competitive success.

A–4

The Strategic Focus and Plan sets the strategic direction for the entire organization, a direction with which proposed actions of the marketing plan must be consistent. This section is not included in all marketing plans. See Chapter 2.

A–5

The qualitative Mission Statement focuses the activities of Coffee Break for the stakeholder groups to be served. See Chapter 2.

A–6

The Objectives sections set both the non-financial and financial targets—where possible in quantitative terms—against which the company's performance will be measured. See Chapter 2.

A–7

Lists use parallel construction to improve readability—in this case a series of infinitives starting with "To .-.-."

A–8

The SWOT Analysis identifies strengths, weaknesses, opportunities, and threats to provide a solid foundation as a springboard to identify subsequent actions in the marketing plan. See Chapter 2.

A–9

Each long table, graph, or photo is given a figure number and title. It then appears as soon as possible after the first reference in the text, accommodating necessary page breaks. Short tables or graphs that are less than 3 cm are often inserted in the text without figure numbers because they do not cause serious problems with page breaks.

A-9

FIGURE 1: *Coffee Break* SWOT Analysis

Internal Factors	Strengths	Weaknesses
Management	Experienced and entrepreneurial management	Competitive market for qualified and experienced staff.
Offering	Quality coffee, good service, and a student-friendly atmosphere.	Wide range of nearby specialty coffee and fast food restaurants.
Marketing	Low-cost promotional activities targeted to each market segment.	A limited marketing budget.
Human Resources	Practices that attract and retain quality serving staff.	A highly competitive job market for quality service staff.
Manufacturing	Partnerships with post-secondary culinary arts programs.	Limited access to experienced and talented chefs.
Product Development	Partnerships with post-secondary culinary arts programs.	Limited in-house capacity for new menu item development.
A-10 **External Factors**	Opportunities	Threats
A–10 Effective tables seek to summarize a large amount of information in a short amount of space.		
Consumer/Social	Significant, underserved customer demographic. Retail location key.	Price sensitive and seasonal market.
Competition	Limited on-campus competition.	Wide range of specialty coffee and fast food restaurants within walking distance.

Technological	No fundamental changes expected.	Product and process innovations by specialty coffee and fast food chains.
Socio-demographic	Continued population growth expected in the Kwantlen service area.	Disposable income of students affected by availability of work and tuition fees.
Legal/Regulatory	Health regulations benefit well-managed operations.	Few barriers for entry.

A-11

In the company's favour are internal factors such as the strength of the concept, detailed planning, and a management team with restaurant experience. Favourable external factors include a growing population base in *Kwantlen*'s service area and limited on-campus competition.

Coffee Break faces adverse factors, both internally and externally. Business start-ups are risky propositions, particularly in the food-services sector. Securing a good on-campus location near high pedestrian areas is crucial. Staffing the coffee house with qualified service and food preparation staff will be a challenge.

A-12

Industry Analysis

Coffee is the second-largest commodity in the world in market value. Discovered in Ethiopia, the coffee plant was first chewed as a stimulant. Coffee houses spread to Europe in the 1600s and became popular meeting places for people of all social classes. Both Lloyds of London and the London Stock Exchange started in coffee houses.

A-13

Coffee farming is labour intensive, as 4,000 handpicked beans are needed to produce a pound of the coffee. The best coffees use beans from the *arabica* plant, which is grown in the tropics at altitudes around 1,500 metres. The plant is delicate, requiring a steady temperature year-round and tender loving care. Coffees are judged by their aroma, body, acidity, and flavour.

A-13

Over the past 30 years, specialty coffee houses have transformed the industry. According to Barney McKenzie, cofounder of Vancouver-based *Bean Around the World*, the specialty coffee boom should have peaked around 1997.

However, social trends such as less tolerance for alcohol as a social lubricant, a focus on a healthier lifestyle, and a greater sophistication among consumers have transformed specialty coffee houses into a mainstream product. Nearly 20 percent of adults drink a cup of specialty coffee each day, and the market for specialty coffees experienced sales growth of 5 to 10 percent per year until the 2008 recession.

A–11

The text discussion of Figure 1 (the SWOT Analysis table) elaborates on its more important elements. This "walks" the reader through the information from the vantage of the plan's writer. In brief plans, this accompanying discussion is sometimes omitted, but is generally desirable to give the reader an understanding of what the company sees as the critical SWOT elements.

A–12

The Industry Analysis section provides the backdrop for the subsequent, more detailed analysis of competition, the company, and the company's customers. Without an in-depth understanding of the industry, the remaining analysis may be misdirected. See Chapter 2.

A–13

Even though relatively brief, this in-depth treatment of the coffee industry demonstrates to the plan's readers the company's understanding of the industry in which it competes. It gives both external and internal readers confidence that the company thoroughly understands its own industry.

Speciality coffee retailers were hit hard by the recent recession. For example, the *Starbucks* chain has shut down over a thousand stores since July 2008. Moreover, fast food chains, such as *McDonald's*, are moving aggressively into the market with new offerings and multi-million dollar advertising budgets.

While coffee houses still sell 49 percent of specialty coffee servings , hamburger chains sell 11 percent and doughnut chains were 19 percent. The dividing line both in quality and in price is blurring between traditional and specialty brands. According to *Leaky Bucket Report, Starbucks* faces a "price-value problem" and "credible threats from *McDonald's* and *Dunkin' Donuts*."

While coffee is the most popular beverage, it is facing competition from energy drinks. Stimulant energy drinks such as *Red Bull* have been growing by double-digits per year. Energy drinks target consumers under 30 with active lifestyles and a desire for an energy kick.

Energy drinks and teas have become attractive substitutes to coffee among younger people. According to a *Restaurants and Institutions* article, Generation Y is more adventuresome in their tea preferences, drinking more green tea, herbal teas, and chai than other age groups.

Greater Vancouver Specialty Coffee Retail Market

Greater Vancouver has a sophisticated and highly competitive coffee market. The Yellow Pages, listed more than 220 coffee houses and coffee specialty bars with City of Vancouver addresses. Roughly 100 of these retailers were independents and the remainder were chain operations.

The largest player is *Starbucks,* followed by *Blenz Coffee, Tim Hortons* and several smaller chains. Regional chains include *Blenz Coffee, Bean Around the World,* and *Caffè Artigiano.*

Surrey Specialty Coffee Retail Market

In comparison, the City of Surrey, with roughly 70 percent of the City of Vancouver's population, has over 50 restaurants listed under the Coffee Houses & Specialty Bars, and Coffee – Retail categories of the Yellow Pages. The majority of listings are either *Starbucks*or *Tim Hortons*. There are two local chains: *Java Hut* and *Esquires Coffee*. The remaining 15 listings are single-store operations.

The different number of coffee houses servicing the Vancouver and Surrey markets is hard to explain. Median family and individual incomes are similar, though there are a larger number of low-income households in Surrey. Vancouver is more urbanized than Surrey, which has several town centres embedded in suburban sprawl.

According to a recent Census, the provincial electoral district that surrounds *Kwantlen Polytechnic University*'s Surrey campus is largely composed of visible minorities and recent immigrants. The largest ethnic group are South Asians followed by residents of European descent. This ethnic mix may be significant as India is a tea region. Five times more tea than coffee is consumed per capita in India.

A-14

Competitive Analysis—On-Campus Restaurants

The *Chartwells College & University Dining Division* of the Compass Group used to hold the food-services contract at the *Kwantlen* campuses. But now Sodexo Canada holds the institutional food-services contract.

A–14

As with the Industry Analysis, the Competitive Analysis demonstrates that the company has a realistic understanding of who its major competitors are and what their marketing strategies are. Again, a realistic assessment gives confidence to both internal and external readers that subsequent marketing actions in the plan rest on a solid foundation. See Chapters 2, 3, 8, and 9.

The facility is a standard college cafeteria with plastic seating and is overdue for a renovation. *Starbucks* specialty coffees were added to the menu with a wide range of lattes, iced coffees, cappuccinos, and espresso drinks available on request. Demand for the 50 to 60 specialty brews steadily grew during the autumn semester. Coffee is the most popular hot beverage. Tea is much less popular. The cafeteria also provides a selection of breakfast items, along with soups, burgers and fries, daily entree features, chili, wraps, sandwiches, pizzas, pastries, muffins, and pre-packaged salads.

According to Belinda Kaplan, manager of food services, most coffee is sold during the following times: 9 to 10 a.m., 11 a.m. to 1 p.m., and 5 to 6:30 p.m. The busiest days in cafeteria are Monday through Thursday. Friday is the slowest weekday, and Saturdays are very slow. The cafeteria is open from 7 a.m. to 9 p.m., Monday to Thursday, and for reduced hours on Friday and Saturday.

The *GrassRoots Café* is operated by the *Kwantlen Student Association (KSA)* on the Surrey campus. The student association is located in part of a campus building that includes student offices, a café, and a fitness centre.

GrassRoots offers a trendier food menu, including wraps, burgers, pasta, stir-fry, soups, salads, bagels, a line of vegetarian items, muffins, and dessert items. The prices of its menu items are similar to those in the cafeteria, mainly in the $5 to $7 range.

The café has a pleasant atmosphere, with students at the front counter, who may connect better with the students than the older staff in the cafeteria. *GrassRoots Café* is open from 8 a.m. to 8 p.m., Monday to Thursday, and until 5 p.m. on Friday. The sit-ting area contains a mixture of couches, bar stools, and chairs surrounding round and rectangular tables. A big-screen TV at one end of the room is used for movie nights, and an open mike is available. While the KSA received a liquor licence in 2012, it has not emphasized that aspect of the business. According to Catherine Wilkinson, the KSA commercial services manager, most coffee sales are made before and between classes. The majority of coffee sales occur during the following times: 9:30 to 10:30 a.m., 11:30 a.m. to 1:00 p.m., 1:45 to 2:15 p.m., and 5:30 to 6:30 p.m. Coffee sales average $500 per weekday.

Sales volume is highly seasonal. Daily sales during the summer semester are roughly a quarter of those during the autumn and spring semesters. According to a recent edition of the student newspaper, the budget for the *Grassroots Café* is $286,000 in annual sales.

The *GrassRoots Café* relies heavily on word of mouth among students and discount coupons for faculty and staff. KSA is actively involved in student orientation at the beginning of each semester. The cafeteria doesn't actively promote its services.

Both campus restaurants would benefit from improved signage, as they are not visible from the central courtyard. The university cafeteria is on the second floor of a building and *GrassRoots Café* at the edge of the campus. Both restaurants have ample floor space—1,400 square feet for the café and 3,200 for the cafeteria. However, limited food preparation and storage space are a challenge for the *GrassRoots Café*. A visit to both restaurants on a Tuesday, at 11 a.m., revealed comparable traffic at their front counters and a similar number of people seated.

A-15

Competitive Analysis—Off-Campus Restaurants

Kwantlen's Surrey campus is located on 72nd Avenue, near Surrey's Newton Town Centre. According to the City of Surrey, the avenue is a busy street with a daily traffic count (in both directions for a typical weekday) of 30,000 vehicles.

Direct competition for *GrassRoots Café* and the cafeteria are five pizza and ethnic restaurants (e.g., *Urban Masala, Great Pizza, Gulberg Restaurant, Ocean Park Pizza*, and *Yellow Chilli Restaurant*) adjacent to the Surrey campus. The menu items at these restaurants are significantly cheaper than those found on campus.

> **A–15**
>
> These two sections use a "block" style and do *not* indent each paragraph, although an extra space separates each paragraph. Compare this page with the previous page, which has indented paragraphs. Most readers find that indented paragraphs in market plans and long reports are easier to follow.

Kwantlen students frequently meet off campus at *Tim Hortons, Starbucks*, or *KFC*, a short drive away in the Strawberry Hill Shopping Mall. *Tim Hortons* is a doughnut shop, with a dedicated clientele who line up each morning for their coffee at the take-out window. *Tim Hortons* caters to people interested in a coffee, snack, or light meal. Given its relatively inexpensive menu and adequate seating, it is popular among the students.

The nearest *Starbucks* is attached to a *Chapters* bookstore in the Strawberry Hill Shopping Mall. The coffee house has limited seating but a better selection of specialty coffee and teas. A larger Starbucks is slightly farther away on Scott Road.

A-15

Customer Analysis—Canadian and U.S. Markets

According to *a Canadian Coffee Drinking Study*, coffee was Canada's most popular beverage with 63 percent of adults drinking coffee on a daily basis. The average Canadian coffee drinker consumed 2.6 cups a day. Men and women were equally likely to drink coffee.

Most coffee was consumed earlier in the day, half during breakfast and an additional 16 percent during the morning hours. People drank a further 9 percent during lunches, 10 percent in the afternoons, 8 percent during supper, and 7 percent in evening hours.

Coffee was consumed by Canadians at home (66 percent), at work (12 percent), at eateries (16 percent), and at institutions such as public libraries (5 percent). Roughly half of Canadians drank a specialty coffee during the year and 6 percent drank such brews on a daily basis. Canadians reported drinking iced coffee (24 percent) and cappuccinos (32 percent) during that year. According to the *US National Coffee Association's Annual Coffee Study*, 17 percent of adult Americans drank gourmet coffee on a daily basis. Americans in the 18-to-24 age group were "the fastest-growing segment of coffee drinkers" according to the report, drinking an average of 3.2 cups a day.

An article in *Automatic Merchandiser* suggests that coffee drinkers in the 18-to-34 age group are more likely to visit coffee houses and less likely to prepare coffee at home. It suggested that the message of marketers should stress the "coffee house experience" and "energy boost" among younger consumers.

Another article in *Dairy Foods* explored the young adult market, stating that many young people do not use either ground or instant coffee. This age group is driving the markets for coffee beverages (such as coffee-milk beverages), organic coffees, and ethical coffees. These consumers are more likely to drink iced coffee, lattes, flavoured coffees, espressos, or cappuccinos than other age groups.

A personal conversation with a counter person at a nearby *Starbucks* store suggested that lattes (i.e., coffees or other beverages with hot milk) are very popular for women during the winter months, though they are considered "girlie drinks" by men. Blended ice drinks are very popular among both men and women during the summer months.
A-16

Customer Analysis—Campus Market

The coffee house's primary market will be students at the Surrey campus of *Kwantlen Polytechnic University*. Surrey lacks a central downtown core and its businesses are spread among six different townships. As a result, most students either drive or catch a ride to the Surrey campus each day.

> **A–16**
>
> Satisfying customers and providing genuine value to them is why organizations exist in a market economy. This section addresses the question of "Who are the customers for Coffee Break?" citing relevant survey data. See Chapters 5, 6, 7, 8, and 9.

The student registrations at the campus for the 2016-2017 academic year were over 10,000, a figure that has grown 5 percent over the past three years. Student numbers are highly seasonal, with peak figures during the September to April semesters. Student enrollments for the summer semester are roughly one-third of enrollments during the regular academic year.

According to the *Fall Registration Survey*, one-third of the students are new to *Kwantlen* each autumn, highlighting the need for regular promotional activities. Primary residence figures illustrate that 79 percent of *Kwantlen* students live within the university's service area, which includes the cities of Surrey, Langley, Delta, and Richmond. Less than 5 percent of the student population are international students. The age profile of the student body is heavily weighted to recent high school graduates, with 48 percent of students between 18 and 21 years of age.
A-17

The registration survey asked the students why they selected the institution. The most common reasons were selection of programs, affordable tuition, proximity to home, and program reputation. Most students were either preparing for a specific occupation (51 percent) or planning to transfer to another college or university (31 percent).

> **A–17**
>
> This section demonstrates the company's insights into major trends that have a potentially large impact.

Unfortunately, the survey reported on the student population as a whole. No figures were available for the Surrey campus. Limited funds and lack of free time are issues facing *Kwantlen* students. Many of the students are employed part-time while attending the university—48 percent reported working 10 to 29 hours a week and 14 percent in excess of 30 hours.

FIGURE 2: Kwantlen Student Age Profile, 2016-2017

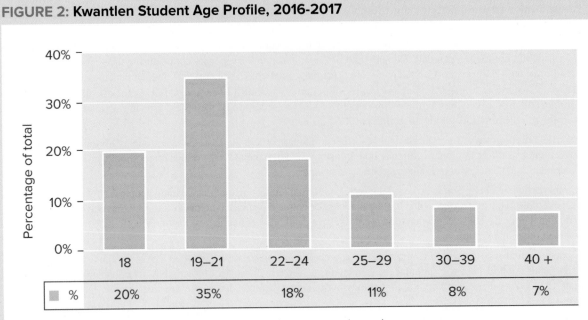

| % | 20% | 35% | 18% | 11% | 8% | 7% |

Age groups (years)

The major ethnic groups at *Kwantlen* are Caucasian (47 percent), East Asian (19 percent), South Asian (18 percent), Southeast Asian (6 percent), and other (10 percent). As many South Asians live in the City of Surrey, their percentage of the Surrey campus student population is higher than indicated by the figures above.

A*ny industry* study stressed the importance of a social space in the lives of post-secondary students. Eighty percent of students reported their favourite social place as off campus, mainly in coffee shops and restaurants. These places help students find companionship, relax, and adjust to academic life. Over 70 percent of university students visit their social place at least once a week and nearly a quarter visit daily. Important features for favoured social places are location, atmosphere, and the opportunity to meet other students.

A secondary market for *Coffee Break* is the staff and faculty of *Kwantlen Polytechnic University*. There were 1,600 *Kwantlen* employees, of which, 56 percent reported Surrey as their primary campus, suggesting a head count of 900 at that location.

While faculty (40 percent of total staff) workloads are often spread over multiple campuses, support staff and administration are typically stationed at a specific campus. Eighty-five percent of employees had worked at *Kwantlen* for over 2 years and 44 percent for more than 10 years. Given the long service of many *Kwantlen* employees, many are nearing retirement. For example, 29 percent of faculty, 19 percent of staff, and 23 percent of administration employees are 55 years of age or older.

Market Potential

The combined daily sales of the two existing restaurants are probably in the range of $5,000 per weekday, from September to April, when the institution's classes are in session. A ballpark estimate of coffee sales is in the range of 25 percent of total food and beverage sales, perhaps $1,250 per day.

If a conservative estimate is made, based on 25 percent of people on campus buying one cup a day at $2.00 per cup, this results in an estimate of $5,000 in potential daily coffee sales. Clearly, there must be a lot of leakage of food-services sales to nearby restaurants. Based on this estimate and the number of school days per year, a total market potential of $800,000 of annual coffee sales appears reasonable.

A-18

5. Market–Product Focus and Goal Setting

This section outlines the marketing objectives for *Coffee Break*, the target markets, points of difference, and restaurant positioning.

A-18

Marketing and Product Objectives

One-Year Marketing Objectives

- To create awareness of the *Coffee Break* concept on campus among 80 percent of students, staff and faculty.
- To stimulate trial and repeat purchases by 40 percent of consumers in all target market segments.
- To become recognized among *Kwantlen* students and staff for its prompt and friendly service and the best coffee on campus.
- To be the most popular place on campus for students to relax and meet with friends.

A-19

Five-Year Marketing Objectives

- To become known as the employer of choice at all college and university campuses where *Coffee Break* has operations.
- To establish coffee houses in three other medium-sized colleges or universities in Western Canada.

A-20

Marketing and Product Objectives

Coffee Break's primary market is the 10,000 students enrolled in courses at the Surrey campus between September and April. One-third as many students are enrolled during the summer semester. The take-out window will service students looking for a quick coffee or snack between classes. The coffee house will serve students looking for a place to socialize, eat light meals, or do school work.

The venture's secondary market is the 900 employees working at the Surrey campus. Roughly 40 percent are faculty, who spend little time on campus when classes are not in session. The remaining 60 percent of support staff and administrators have a fairly regular work week on campus. A warm, inviting atmosphere should attract employees looking for a place to relax and socialize with colleagues. Employees could become a steady clientele of a take-out coffee counter if the service was prompt, the location was convenient, and the price was right.

Finally, depending on the exact location of the coffee house, a tertiary market could be the high school students and staff of the 1,500-student Princess Margaret Secondary School, a few hundred metres east of the campus, along 72nd Avenue. Partnerships between the two institutions, such as an enrichment program, already result in some mixing of the student populations.

A-18

Size of headings should give a professional look to the report and not overwhelm the reader. These two headings are too large.

A–19

As noted in Chapter 10, the chances of success for a new product are significantly increased if objectives are set for the product itself and if target market segments are identified for it. This section makes these explicit for Coffee Break. The objectives also serve as the planned targets against which marketing activities are measured in program implementation and evaluation.

A–20

This section identifies the specific niches or target markets toward which the company's products are directed. When appropriate and when space permits, this section often includes a market–product grid. See Chapter 9.

A-21

Points of Difference

Coffee Break will have three distinguishing characteristics.

1. A comfortable, youth-oriented atmosphere created by serving teams with a "can do" attitude, regular entertainment, and a warm decor.

2. Hot and cold beverages prepared by staff with a passion for excellence.

3. The skillful use of advertising, promotions, and publicity to establish a brand identity, create a sense of excitement, and target specific market segments.

A-22

Positioning

Coffee Break is positioned in the middle of the specialty coffee spectrum in pricing and product quality. The restaurant's differentiation will be its student-focused atmosphere and friendly well-trained staff. *Coffee Break* will raise the competitive bar for customer service and beverage quality on campus.

A–21

An organization cannot grow by offering only "me-too" products or services. The greatest single factor in a new product's or service's failure is the lack of significant "points of difference" that set it apart from competitors' substitutes. This section makes these points of difference explicit. See Chapter 10.

A–22

A positioning strategy helps communicate the company's unique points of difference of its products to prospective customers in a simple, clear way. This section describes this positioning. See Chapters 9 and 10.

A–23

Everything that has gone before in the marketing plan sets the stage for the marketing mix actions—the 4 Ps—covered in the marketing program. See Chapters 10 through 20.

A–24

To improve readability, each numbered section usually starts on a new page. (This is not always done in this plan to save space.)

A-23 A-24

6. Marketing Program

Coffee Break must reduce the leakage of student spending on food in off-campus restaurants and counter competitive reactions from the two existing restaurants.

More fundamentally, *Coffee Break* must collaboratively work with university administration and other partners to provide students and staff with more reasons to stay on campus after class. Otherwise, *Coffee Break* market will be limited to the 150 days when classes are in session between September to April and a summer session of 60 days.

A-25

Product Strategy

The retailing concept is based on *The Beanery Coffee House*, a 60-seat specialty coffee house on the UBC campus. *The Beanery* is like a two-storey house of about 2,000 square feet. Spread among several rooms are sofas, places to study, computers, a piano, a pool table, and a television, a relaxing environment like someone's home. *The Beanery* offers a variety of beverages, sandwiches, wraps, salads, and light snacks.

An industry study summarized the design elements that create a warm atmosphere for students. Features include comfortable chairs, furniture that students can rearrange, wood furniture, an outside view, and pleasant food smells. The layout should allow students to rearrange the furniture to create "temporary territories." Students like to "anchor themselves against walls" and look outside to people watch.

Coffee Break will provide a variety of seating, ranging from bar stools to sofas to places to spread out and do homework. Lighting will be adequate in study areas so that students can read and use their computers. Tables that are square or rectangular are easier to assemble for group projects and socializing.

The aroma of baked goods and coffee is important in creating a coffee house atmosphere. Coffee shops vent smells into the seating areas and outside to draw people in. A "soft and cozy atmosphere" can be created by using soft lighting and through the colour and texture of the flooring, walls, and furnishings. Amenities such as a pool table, dart boards, a book/magazine exchange, local art, and background music help create the right atmosphere and acoustic privacy for conversations.

Coffee Break will add to its menu a limited selection of South Asian cuisine and attempt to recruit servicing staff fluent in the major Indian dialects.

A-26

Price Strategy

The strategy of *Coffee Break* is to match the prices of on-campus restaurants and to offer similar prices as specialty coffee shops such as *Starbucks* (see Figure 3). The goal is to avoid price competition with existing on-campus restaurants.

A–25

This section describes in detail key elements of the company's product strategy. See Chapters 10, 11, and 12.

A–26

The Price Strategy section makes the company's price point very clear, along with its price position relative to potential substitutes. When appropriate and when space permits, this section might contain a break-even analysis. See Chapter 13.

FIGURE 3: **Price Ranges for Coffee near Campus**

Beverages	Cafeteria	GrassRoots	Tim Hortons	Starbucks	McDonald's
Regular Coffee	$1.75–$2.20	$1.75–$2.50	$1.16–$1.67	$1.65–$2.10	$1.19–$1.59
Tea	$1.40	$1.50	$1.16–$1.67	$1.85–$2.45	$1.19
Flavoured and Specialty Coffees	$2.45–$3.75	$3.75–$4.75	$1.47–$2.32	$3.50–$5.00	–
Iced Coffees	$2.70–$4.45	$4.75	$1.89–$3.09	$3.45–$4.55	$1.59–$1.99
Espresso or Americano	$2.15–$3.10	$1.75–$2.50	$1.19–$1.59	$1.60–$2.05	–
Cappuccino	$3.10–$4.10	–	$2.04–$3.14	$3.05–$4.05	–

GrassRoots Café will distribute discount coupons to *Kwantlen* staff and will not charge for coffee refills. *Coffee Break* will provide similar incentives.

A-27

Promotion Strategy

Print Material. The plan is designed to create local awareness and build a consistent identity among the university community. Print materials, menus, and signage will have the same style of lettering. A logo (two people with an arm on each others' shoulder) and a common theme—**where good friends gather**—will be used. Standard templates for menus, print advertisements, and brochures will be prepared.

Publicity. Prior to opening, interviews are planned with the editorial staffs of campus newspapers such as the *Kwantlen Chronicle* and *The Runner*. Management will seek interviews with reporters from local community newspapers.

Grand Opening. After a few weeks of limited hours and staff training at the end of summer, the Grand Opening is scheduled for September 2017. *Coffee Break* will partner with a suitable charity such as *SPCA* to use the Grand Opening as a fundraising event. A local radio station could co-sponsor the fundraiser, supplying live broadcasting on location during the event.

Advertisements. A small advertisement will be placed in each edition of the two *Kwantlen* newspapers, *Kwantlen Chronicle* and *The Runner*.

A-28

Student Orientation. Student orientations are held in September and January each year for new students. *Coffee Break* will staff a table and hand out student discount coupons at the beginning of each semester. Staff coupons will be distributed twice each year.

Sponsorships. A small budget will be available to sponsor sports teams and campus events.

Coffees of the World. *Coffee Break* will bring in specialty coffees, hold coffee tasting events, and create a coffee passport program, where a patron receives a stamp whenever a coffee from another country is consumed. Patrons with enough stamps receive a certificate.

Entertainment, Coffee Workshops, and Theme Nights. *Kwantlen* marketing students could help organize special events and promotions to gain applied work experience. Events could include coffee appreciation workshops, entertainment from local musicians, and cultural events organized by local ethnic groups.

Fantasy Getaways. Two fantasy getaway events are planned for the first year during the dreary winter months—*Amazon Adventure* and *African Escape*. *Amazon Adventure* would involve a special tasting of coffees from South America. *Coffee Break* staff, through the local consulate, will invite local Brazilian groups to display their traditional dances, music, and cuisine.

A-29

Place (Distribution) Strategy

The location of the coffee house is vital, particularly for the coffee take-out window. The ideal location is on the ground floor of one the buildings facing the central courtyard. Successful specialty coffee houses are typically located in high pedestrian traffic areas, allowing people to people watch. Outside tables allow people to take advantage of sunny days, an attractive amenity during the summer months.

Securing such a location will not be easy, given the space constraints on campus and the alternative uses for such locations such as campus bookstores, etc. However, given the desire of the university administration to improve on-campus facilities and amenities, an acceptable location might be found.

A–27

Elements of the Promotion Strategy are highlighted in terms of the key promotional activities the company is emphasizing. For space reasons, the company's online strategies are not shown in the plan. See Chapters 16, 17, and 18.

A–28

The higher-level "A heading" of Promotion Strategy above has a more dominant typeface and position than the lower-level "B heading" of Student Orientation. These headings introduce the reader to the sequence and level of topics covered. The organization of this textbook uses this kind of structure and headings.

A–29

The Place Strategy is described here. See Chapters 14 and 15.

If adequate retail space is not available on campus, a market likely exists for an express coffee take-out service, much like the express Tim Hortons outlet at the Vancouver International Airport. The retail space for take-out coffee counter should be easier to lease and less costly to operate than a full coffee house.

A-30

7. Sales Forecast

The sales forecast of $300,000 during year one is based on $1,500 per day during the academic year and one-third that figure during the summer semester. Sales are split between coffee sales and other beverages, snack, and light meal menu items.

Cost of goods sold is budgeted at 32.5 percent of sales, rent at $3,500 per month, and other costs at $2,000 per month, including marketing costs. Schedules showing breakdowns of start-up costs, along with pro-forma income statements (see Figure 4), balance sheets, and monthly cash flow forecasts are found in the financials section of the business plan.

> **A–30**
>
> All the marketing mix decisions covered in the just-described marketing program have both revenue and expense effects. These are summarized in this section of the marketing plan. See Appendix B.

FIGURE 4: *Coffee Break* Pro-forma Income Statement (year ended August 31, 2018)

Revenues and Expenses	Budget	
Revenues	$300,000	
Cost of Sales	97,500	
Gross Profit	202,500	
Employee Wages and Benefits	90,000	
Rent and Common Area Costs	42,000	
Other Operating Expenses	24,000	
Total Operating Expenses		156,000
Operating Profit		46,500

> **A–31**
>
> The financial projections are often based on judgment forecasts. Gross revenue and then operating profit—critical to the coffee house's survival—are also projected. Often, multiple forecasts using different forecast scenarios are included in the appendix to the plan.

A-31

As most operating expenses are fixed costs and cost of goods sold is a variable cost, the estimated break-even point of *Coffee Break* is:

$$\text{Break-even point}(\$ \text{ sales}) \ = \ \text{Fixed costs} / (1 - \% \text{ variable costs})$$

$$= \ \$156,000 / (1 - 32.5\%) = \$231,000 \quad \text{in annual sales}$$

While this sales amount suggests a comfortable safety margin, there is a tendency for new ventures to underestimate costs. A common rule of thumb used in the specialty coffee industry is a break-even point of ten times the commercial rent payment. This ballpark figure suggests that *Coffee Break* will break even on $300,000 of sales.

A-32

8. Implementation Plan

Marketing Organization

The manager of the coffee house will have overall responsibility for all marketing and promotional activities.

> **A–32**
>
> The Implementation Plan shows how the company will turn plans into results. Action-item lists are often used to set deadlines and assign responsibilities for the many tactical marketing decisions needed to enter a new market. See Chapter 19.

As additional coffee houses are added to the chain, a group management position will be created to develop and oversee the implementation of chain-wide marketing program activities. The division of marketing responsibilities between the individual coffee house managers and the group manager will be specified in their job descriptions. Separate annual budgets for local and group-wide marketing activities will be prepared by managers each year.

Marketing Budget

The marketing budget for 2017-2018 is outlined in Figure 5.

FIGURE 5: *Coffee Break* Marketing Budget (year ended August 31, 2018)

Marketing Costs	Budget
Advertising – Campus Newspapers	$500
Give-Away Items – Certificates, Small Prizes, etc.	500
Grand Opening Celebration	2,500
Entertainment, Theme Nights, etc.	2,000
Printing – Posters, Coupons, Promotional Materials, etc.	500
Sponsorships	500
Marketing Budget – Year One	**$6,500**

Marketing Activities Plan

Marketing activities will support the two-phase opening of the first *Coffee Break* outlet. The take-out window will open during the late summer before students arrive on campus. After staff training is complete, the Grand Opening of the coffee house is planned for the second week of September 2017.

A more detailed implementation plan for marketing and promotional activities, during year one, can be found in Figure 6.

A-33

9. Evaluation Phase

Annual budgets will be prepared for *Coffee Break*. Actual sales and expenses will be compared to budgeted figures and variances investigated. Weekly sales by category will be tracked and the results of each promotional activity evaluated.

> **A–33**
>
> The essence of the Evaluation Phase is comparing actual sales with the targeted values set in the plan and taking appropriate actions. See Chapter 19.

For each institution, *Coffee Break* will create an advisory board composed of students, faculty, and staff members. Each group will meet with *Coffee Break* staff on a monthly basis, over coffee, to identify problem areas and to evaluate how well the restaurant is meeting the needs of the campus community.

FIGURE 6: *Coffee Break* Marketing Activities Plan (year ended August 31, 2018)

When	Who	What
August 2017	Manager	Limited hours – coffee take-out window Distribution of staff coupons
September 2017	Manager	Student orientation week activities Grand Opening (second week of classes)
October 2017	Manager and staff	Tastes of the World (coffee and biscotti)
November 2017	Manager and staff	Tastes of the World (coffees and biscotti) Fantasy getaway – Amazon Adventure
December 2017	Manager and staff	Tastes of the World (coffee and biscotti) End of Classes Party
January 2018	Manager and staff	Tastes of the World (coffee and biscotti) Fantasy getaway – African Escape
February 2018	Manager and staff	Student orientation week activities Tastes of the World (coffees and biscotti) Valentine's Day Coffee and Chocolate
March 2018	Manager and staff	Tastes of the World (coffees and biscotti)
April 2018	Manager and staff	Tastes of the World (coffees and biscotti) End of Classes Party
May 2018	Manager and staff	Limited hours of operation Tastes of the World (coffee and biscotti)
June to August	Manager	Limited hours of operation Planning for the upcoming year

3

Scanning the Marketing Environment

Learning Objectives

After reading this chapter, you should be able to:

LO1 Explain how environmental scanning provides information about social, economic, technological, competitive, and regulatory forces.

LO2 Describe how social forces, such as demographics, and cultural and economic forces, such as macroeconomic conditions and consumer income, affect marketing.

LO3 Describe how technological changes are impacting marketers and customers.

LO4 Discuss the forms of competition that exist in a market, key components of competition, and the impact of small businesses as competitors.

LO5 Explain the major legislation that ensures competition and protects consumers in Canada.

Is "Connecting the World" an Ambitious Vision? Not If You Are Facebook!

In 2004 Mark Zuckerberg started Facebook in his Harvard dorm room. His vision was not just to be a company, but to connect everyone in the world. Today, with 1.4 billion active users, or one-fifth of the world's population, Facebook is well on its way to accomplishing that vision! Facebook's incredible success is the result of many things, including its ability to observe and adapt to a rapidly changing marketing environment. Let's take a look at the environmental forces that influence Facebook:

- Social forces are changing as people look for new ways to communicate, obtain information, and offer opinions. Simple online interactions that began on desktops have migrated to mobile devices and now include communication with photos, group and video chats, and instant messaging.

- Economic forces also influence the demand for Facebook as the cost of smartphones and wireless connectivity declines and Internet access expands throughout the globe, making social networking increasingly affordable to more and more people.

- Technological advances in software integration, server speed, and data storage are making Facebook increasingly fast and convenient. New enhancements such as photo editing and an app development kit also increase the use of Facebook.

- Competitive forces, such as the rivalry with Google, Twitter, and Snapchat; the ability of users to easily switch platforms; and the constant threat of new social networks targeted at specific interest groups, encourage rapid expansion.
- Legal and regulatory forces also influence the growth of Facebook. The company obtains trademark and patent rights to its name and many of its features, and it provides guidelines for a variety of topics such as privacy, data protection, protection of minors, and taxation. Zuckerberg's rapid responses to changes in the environment and his willingness to try new things has resulted in the world's largest social network—one that is quickly connecting the world.

© dolphfyn/Alamy Stock Photo

Facebook in the Future

Facebook's challenge now is to keep growing by continuing to respond to changes in the marketing environment. As Zuckerberg explains, Facebook needs to "think about the next big things that we want to do." For example, Zuckerberg wants Facebook to become more intuitive, and to help users answer questions and solve problems. Another change may be related to Facebook's requirement that users log in with their own names. In some parts of the world where Facebook hopes to expand, anonymity encourages users to speak freely. In addition, Facebook is currently testing large drones that are powered by solar panels to hover above remote communities and transmit Internet signals. Facebook also purchased virtual reality headset company Oculus VR for $2 billion in anticipation of consumer interest in 3-D communication. Finally, Facebook created a new division of the company called Creative Labs, which is charged with trying to predict the future and developing Facebook's future products![1] Chapter 20 provides additional discussion on social networks and social media.

Many businesses operate in environments where important forces change. Anticipating and responding to changes often means the difference between marketing success and failure. This chapter describes how the marketing environment has changed in the past and how it is likely to change in the future.

LO1   THE IMPORTANCE OF ENVIRONMENTAL SCANNING

Changes in the marketing environment are a source of opportunities and threats to be managed. The process of continually acquiring information on events occurring outside the organization to identify and interpret potential trends is called **environmental scanning**. Environmental scanning is critically important to marketers who wish to ensure that they remain aligned with the evolving marketplace. Companies that fail to engage in environmental scanning do so at their peril and perhaps truncate their future growth.

Tracking Environmental Trends

Environmental trends typically arise from five sources: social, economic, technological, competitive, and regulatory forces. As shown in Figure 3–1 and described later in this chapter, these forces affect the marketing activities of a firm in numerous ways. To illustrate how environmental scanning is used, consider the following trends:

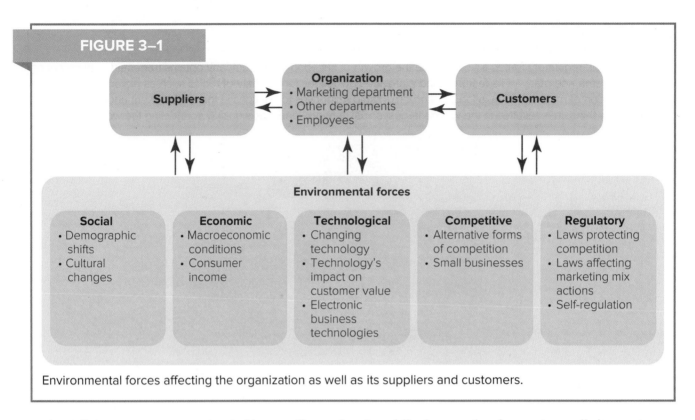

FIGURE 3–1

Environmental forces affecting the organization as well as its suppliers and customers.

According to a consumer report, out-of-home coffee servings have fallen by more than 3 percent annually in recent years. The report blames the decline mostly on the rising popularity of in-home, single-serve coffee machines like the Keurig, sales of which now rival traditional drip brewers. Research from Nielsen estimates one-third of Canadian households now have single-cup brew machines like Keurig and Tassimo. Boomers remain the biggest consumers of hot brewed coffee at 37 percent, while millennials increased their consumption by 6 percent.[2] At the same time, tea consumption also continues to increase, with Canadians consuming 10 billion cups of tea or 83 litres per capita annually.[3]

Will the reported healthful benefits of drinking specialty teas lead to increased tea consumption in Canada?

John A. Rizzo/Getty Images

What types of businesses are likely to be influenced by these trends? What future would you predict for coffee and tea? First, you may have concluded that these changes in coffee consumption are likely to influence coffee and tea manufacturers, coffee shops, tea shops, and supermarkets. If so, you are correct. Coffee manufacturers are offering new flavours and seasonal blends, coffee shops such as Starbucks are testing a delivery service and new flavours such as S'mores Frappuccino, and supermarkets are adding boutiques and gourmet brands of coffee and specialty teas, including more tea in single-serving pods. Predicting the future of coffee and tea requires assumptions about the number of years the trends will continue and their rate of increase or decline.

This example of the trend in coffee and tea consumption illustrates how successful scanning works: identifying trends, understanding the reasons behind the trends, and taking action to respond to such trends.

An Environmental Scan of Canada

What other trends might affect marketing in the future? A firm conducting an environmental scan of the marketplace might uncover key trends, such as those listed in Figure 3–2 for each of the five environmental forces.[4] Although the list of trends is far from complete, it reveals the breadth of an environmental scan—from the growing diversity of the Canadian population, to the shift to the experience economy, to the increasing use of new technologies. These trends affect consumers and the businesses and organizations that serve them. Such trends are covered as the five environmental forces are described in the following pages.

FIGURE 3–2

ENVIRONMENTAL FORCE	TREND IDENTIFIED BY AN ENVIRONMENTAL SCAN
Social	• Binge-watching is becoming a common way for consumers to view television programming. • Video bloggers (vloggers) are growing in popularity and influence. • Consumers are placing a growing emphasis on personalized consideration lists (friend recommendations).
Economic	• Shift to the experience economy. • Companies focusing on cost control and cost-cutting as sales slow in emerging markets and competition increases in mature countries.
Technological	• Connectivity and mobility have combined to increase the use of mobile and wearable devices and to create connected cars, homes, and airplanes. • Addressable TV (IPTV) will soon allow advertising targeted to individual households based on their characteristics. • Social media such as Facebook and Twitter are adding new features such as a "Buy" button to allow marketers to sell directly to users. • The emergence of CAMS—Cloud, Analytics, Mobile, and Social.
Competitive	• Established industries such as banking, insurance, and retailing will be challenged by new competitors such as peer-to-peer lenders, self-insurance groups, and direct-to-consumer food producers. • Companies will increase their use of data and data analytics to compete with personalized products, promotion, and pricing. • Competitors are moving away from loyalty programs based only on points toward rewards, cash, and promotions.
Regulatory	• Privacy guidelines must find a balance to accommodate millennial consumers who do not mind their mobile devices being tracked if they receive timely and relevant advertising. • Net neutrality—that all Internet traffic should receive equal access and speed—is a growing issue for consumers, companies, content creators, and marketers. • Stricter requirements regarding promotions, disclosures, and substantiation studies.

An environmental scan of Canada's marketplace.

LO2   SOCIAL FORCES

The **social forces** of the environment include the demographic characteristics of the population and its values. Changes in these forces can have a dramatic impact on marketing strategy.

Demographics

Demographics is the study of the characteristics of a human population. These characteristics include population size, growth rate, gender, marital status, ethnicity, income, and so forth. Several organizations, such as the United Nations, monitor the world population profile, while other organizations, such as Statistics Canada, provide information on the Canadian population.

The World Population at a Glance

The most recent estimates indicate that there are over 7.3 billion people in the world today and that the population is likely to grow to 9.7 billion by 2050. While this growth has led to the term *population explosion*, the increases have not occurred worldwide—they are primarily in the developing countries of Africa, Asia, and Latin America. In fact, India is predicted to have the world's largest population in 2050 with over 1.7 billion people, and China will be a close second with 1.3 billion people. Moreover, as Figure 3–3 reveals, just ten countries will account for almost 55 percent of the world's population by 2050.[5]

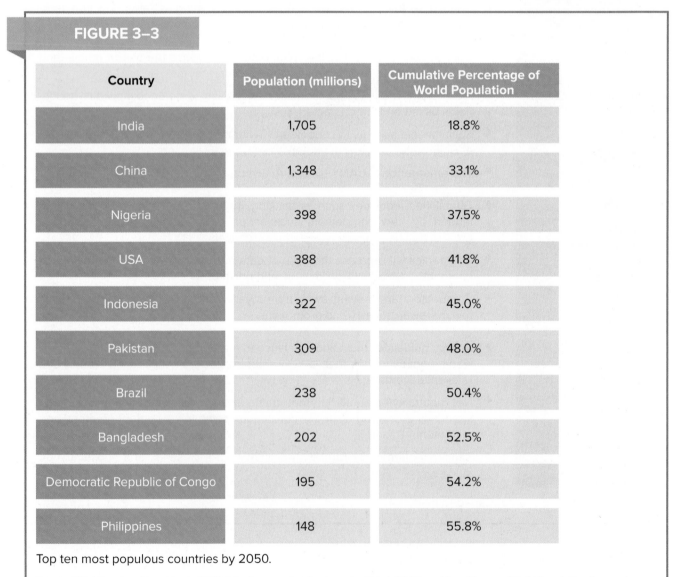

FIGURE 3–3

Country	Population (millions)	Cumulative Percentage of World Population
India	1,705	18.8%
China	1,348	33.1%
Nigeria	398	37.5%
USA	388	41.8%
Indonesia	322	45.0%
Pakistan	309	48.0%
Brazil	238	50.4%
Bangladesh	202	52.5%
Democratic Republic of Congo	195	54.2%
Philippines	148	55.8%

Top ten most populous countries by 2050.

Source: Most Populous Countries in 2050; http://geography.about.com/od/lists/a/2050pop.htm. Also see *World Population Prospects: The 2012 Revision*, United Nations, New York. Source: *CIA World Factbook*, 2007.

Another important global trend is the shifting age structure of the world population. It is expected that the number of people older than 65 will more than double in the coming decades, while the number of youth will grow at a much lower rate. Again, the magnitude of this trend varies by region, and the developed countries, such as Canada, are expected to face a high growth rate of the elderly age group. For example, by 2050, over 30 percent of the Canadian population will be 60 years of age or older.[6] Global income levels and living standards have also been increasing, although the averages across countries are very different. Per capita income (as per gross domestic product in US dollars), for example, ranges from $102,000 in Norway to $52,000 in Canada to under $500 in Ethiopia.

For marketers, such trends have many implications. Obviously, the relative size of such countries as India and China will mean they represent huge markets for many product categories. Elderly populations in the developed countries are likely to save less and begin spending their funds on health care, travel, and other retirement-related products and services. Economic progress in the developing countries will lead to growth in entrepreneurship; new markets for infrastructure related to manufacturing, communication, and distribution; and the growth of exports.

The Canadian Population

Studies of the demographic characteristics of the Canadian population suggest several important trends. The Canadian population is over 35 million and is expected to grow to 44 million by 2050.[7] But it is a population that is growing older and more ethnically diverse. The median age will rise from 40 years of age to almost 45 years of age by 2050.[8] With Canada's declining birth rate, the principal source of growth in the Canadian population will be from immigration, which will add even more diversity to the Canadian population. If current trends in life expectancy, birth rates, and immigration continue, niche markets based on age, life stage, family structure, geographic location, and ethnicity will become increasingly important.

Generational Cohorts

A major reason for the greying of Canada is that the **baby boomers**—the generation of those born between 1946 and 1964—are growing older. Currently, 30 percent of the Canadian population are baby boomers.[9] As the baby boomers have aged, their participation in the workforce and their earnings have increased, making them an important consumer market. Companies that target boomers will need to respond to their interests in health, fitness, retirement housing, financial planning, and appearance. Frito-Lay, for example, attracts baby boomers with its Lay's Kettle Cooked potato chips, which have 40 percent less fat than regular potato chips. Similarly, Prudential offers a retirement plan and Olay offers anti-aging and restoration products for this age group. Baby boomers are also called the "sandwich generation" because they often find themselves balancing obligations to their parents and their children.

Courtesy of Frito-Lay North America, Inc.

The baby boom cohort is followed by **Generation X**, which includes the population of those born between 1965 and 1976. This group represents about 15 percent of the Canadian population. This period is also known as the "baby bust" because the number of children born each year declined during that period. This generation of consumers is self-reliant, entrepreneurial, supportive of ethnic diversity, and better educated than any previous generation. Generation Xers are not prone to extravagance and are likely to pursue lifestyles that are a blend of caution, pragmatism, and traditionalism.

In terms of net worth, Generation X is the first generation to have less than the previous generation. As baby boomers move toward retirement, however, Generation X is becoming a dominant force in many markets. Generation X, for example, spends more on food, housing, apparel, and entertainment than other generations. In addition, this generation is on the Internet more than any other generation and also leads in terms of online spending. Surveys of Generation X consumers indicate they want online customer support; websites that are comprehensive, professional, and interactive; and advertising that is authentic, family-oriented, and unique. Generation X is also replacing baby boomers as the largest segment of business travellers. In response, many airlines are offering these travellers in-flight Wi-Fi, entertainment on demand, and personal powerports.[10]

The generational cohort labelled **Generation Y (Millennials)** includes those born between 1977 and 1994. This was a period of increasing births, which resulted from baby boomers having children, and is often referred to as the "echo-boom" or "baby boomlet." However, members of this group prefer to be called Millennials. Moreover, various experts use different starting and ending birth years for this important generational group, often depending on the country. For example, in Canada, 1983 is often thought to be the starting birth year for the group while the late 1990s is considered the ending birth years for this group.

Currently, Gen Y makes up over 25 percent of the Canadian population, making them a very important consumer group. Generation Y exerts influence on music, sports, computers, video games, and all forms of communication and networking. Generation Y members are interested in distinctive, memorable, and personal experiences and are very adept at managing their lives to create a work–life balance. They are strong-willed, passionate about the environment, and optimistic. They are also heavy users of social media but want to interact with companies on social media who they perceive as sincere and authentic.[11]

Because the members of each generation are distinctive in their attitudes and consumer behaviour, marketers have been studying the many groups or cohorts that make up the marketplace and have developed *generational marketing* programs for them.

The Canadian Family

The types of families in Canada are changing in both size and structure. The average family size in Canada is about three persons. In 1971, one in three Canadian families consisted of the once-typical scenario of a husband working outside the home, with a wife inside the home with their children. Today, only one in seven families falls into this category. The dual-income family is the norm in Canada. Additionally, the traditional mom, dad, and kids household makes up just a quarter of all Canadian households. Instead, the family that gathers around the kitchen table is increasingly likely to be a common-law couple, same-sex couple, or someone simply sitting there alone since more and more Canadians are now living alone.

About 50 percent of all first marriages in Canada end in divorce. Thus, the single-parent family is also becoming more typical and is more socially acceptable. But the majority of divorced people eventually remarry, giving rise to the **blended family**, one formed by the merging into a single family of two previously separated units. Today, many Canadians are finding themselves as a step-parent, step-child, step-sibling, or some other member of a blended family. In fact, Hallmark Cards specially designs cards and verses for such blended families. But many people do not remarry, and single-parent families now represent almost 20 percent of all family units in Canada.

Population Shifts

Since the mid-1970s, there has been a major shift in the Canadian population from rural to urban areas. In fact, more than 80 percent of Canadians are urban dwellers. Most Canadians live in **census metropolitan areas (CMAs)**, geographic labour markets having a population of 100,000 persons or more. Over 50 percent of the Canadian population lives in just the top ten CMAs, cities that include Toronto, Montreal, Vancouver, Calgary, Ottawa-Gatineau, Edmonton, and Quebec City. With the concentration of the population in or near the CMAs and key urban regions, marketers can reach large segments of the Canadian population efficiently and effectively.

Companies like Air Canada have recognized the growing ethnic diversity in Canada.

Reproduced with the permission of Air Canada.

Ethnic Diversity

While we often think of Canada as consisting of French and English Canadians, close to three out of ten Canadians are of neither French nor British descent. While the majority of the non-British, non-French populations are of European descent, there has been a major growth in other ethnic groups and visible minorities in Canada. In fact, more than 100 different ethnic groups are represented in Canada. And close to 70 percent of all immigrants to Canada are now classified as visible minorities, primarily people from China, Southeast Asia, Africa, and India. Visible minorities are projected to represent almost 30 percent of the Canadian population by 2031. The largest groups will be South Asians, Chinese, and blacks.[12]

Additionally, more than one out of every three newcomers who arrive in Canada will settle in one of our three largest cities: Toronto, Vancouver, or Montreal. The result? Statistics Canada forecasts that 63 percent of the population in Toronto, 59 percent in Vancouver, and 31 percent in Montreal will belong to a visible minority group by 2031.[13]

Marketers have recognized the growing ethnic diversity in Canada and have developed **ethnic marketing** (sometimes called *multicultural marketing*) programs, which are combinations of the marketing mix that reflect the unique attitudes, race or ancestry, communication preferences, and lifestyles of ethnic Canadians. For example, TD Canada Trust has obtained the largest share of the ethnic market in the financial services sector by targeting ethnic groups through community events and in-branch promotions. And Scotiabank also targets to ethnic markets through community involvement and sponsorships.

Many other Canadian companies also engage in ethnic marketing, including Walmart, Sears Canada, IKEA, and The Brick. For example, Walmart leverages a variety of digital and social media to engage its multicultural customers.[14] More and more often, Canadian companies are recognizing the need to better understand how and why ethnic Canadians shop (see the Marketing Matters box, "How Ethnic Canadian Buyers Shop!").[15]

MARKETING MATTERS

How Ethnic Canadian Buyers Shop!

Ethnic Canadians will double in size over the next 20 years, and marketers are going to have to understand how and why ethnic Canadians shop the way they do. Some marketers have already come to recognize the need to study the shopping behaviour of ethnic Canadians. For example, BrandSpark International studied the buying habits of more than 8,800 Canadians of Chinese, South Asian, and East Asian backgrounds, Canada's top ethnic groups. The study found that getting the biggest value for their money emerged as the most important factor in purchase decisions, and it revealed differences in the way that ethnic buyers rely on word of mouth and the Internet for shopping information. It also showed that ethnic Canadians are big consumers of high-tech gadgets, they're more likely to eat pre-made frozen meals or take-out, and they shop at Walmart more often than the average Canadian.

Price was the most important factor influencing a purchase for the ethnic Canadian, according to the study. For example, 72 percent of East Asian Canadians cited it as their most important criterion when it comes to food shopping, along with 68 percent of Chinese Canadians and 66 percent of South Asian Canadians, compared with 62 percent of Canadians overall. The survey also revealed a rift between individual ethnic groups on the question of brand-name love. Despite their stated concern for getting a good deal, South Asians and East Asians are far more likely to also say they'll choose their favourite brands regardless of the price—21 percent and 17 percent, respectively. Only 10 percent of Chinese Canadians and Canadians overall placed the same importance on brand names.

The study also showed that consumers from those ethnic groups rely heavily on word of mouth. They also use the Internet slightly differently, relying on web searches more than Canadians overall do for nutritional information. They are also more likely to shop at Walmart, especially if they're South Asian or East Asian, than Canadians overall. In terms of buying choices, there is a big difference in ethnic consumers' view of ready-made food: 54 percent of Chinese respondents said they had picked up a ready-to-eat meal for dinner from the grocery store in the past week; 48 percent of South Asians and 46 percent of East Asians said the same. Only 32 percent of Canadians overall did so. Finally, Canadians from all three ethnic groups are significantly more likely to be ahead of the curve on tablet and smartphone ownership than Canadians overall.

Culture

A second social force, **culture**, incorporates the set of values, ideas, and attitudes that are learned and shared among the members of a group. Because many elements of culture influence consumer buying patterns, monitoring national and global cultural trends is important in marketing. Cross-cultural analysis needed for global marketing is discussed in Chapter 7. Some noteworthy cultural trends in Canada are discussed here.

Changing Attitudes and Values

In recent years, Canadians have experienced notable cultural changes that have affected consumer attitudes and values. Attitudes toward work, lifestyles, and consumption are evolving. For example, more than 60 percent of Canadian women work outside the home. In fact, women now make up close to half of the Canadian labour force. But with more working women, the number of tasks to do is expanding, while the time available to do them is shrinking. This has led to the phenomenon of time poverty. Therefore, many Canadian consumers, particularly working women, are living harried lives and want to do business with companies that can offer them greater convenience. Many businesses are responding by offering express lanes of checkouts, longer store hours, drive-through windows, delivery services, and electronic shopping. Sobeys Inc., a major supermarket, offers its time-pressed shoppers the convenience of one-stop shopping, including groceries, in-store pharmacies, wellness centres, and banking services. The Hudson's Bay Company offers its customers the option of shopping in its retail stores or on the Internet via its online store at **HBC.com**. Esso allows customers to pay for their purchases with its electronic "Speedpass" payment system.

Companies are also creating new products to meet the convenience imperative demanded by consumers. From soup to desserts, products now come in hands-free versions for easier consumption. The concept of "dashboard dining" is now a major trend in the food industry with car-friendly products and packaging popping up everywhere.

Many Canadians are changing their attitudes toward health. Fitness activity and sports participation are on the rise. Many Canadians are also changing their eating habits. For example, Statistics Canada reports that Canadians have shifted toward a diet that includes more fruits and vegetables, cereal products, and nuts and beans. Poultry consumption is up, while beef and pork consumption has declined. Canadians are also drinking healthier beverages, including bottled water and juices and less alcohol and soft drinks.[16]

Health-conscious Canadians are also buying more health supplements and medical self-diagnostic kits. For example, sales of multivitamins and calcium supplements are soaring, and brands such as Centrum, Shoppers Drug Mart's Life brand, and Roots Canada's vitamin lines are enjoying growth. LifeScan Canada is also doing well with its self-testing kits that can monitor cholesterol or test for colorectal cancer.

However, while some Canadians are trying to be healthier, the medical community suggests that obesity is becoming a major public health threat. In fact, obesity in Canada is reaching epidemic proportions and is even showing up in young children. Some firms are responding to this trend by marketing plus-sized clothing. In fact, Canadian retailers report clothing sales to larger women are growing faster than the overall rate.

Canadians are spending more of their dining-out budget at ethnic restaurants.

Another change in the attitudes of Canadians is the trend toward **value consciousness**—the concern for obtaining the best quality, features, and performance of a product or service for a given price. Innovative marketers have responded to this new orientation in numerous ways. Holiday Inn Worldwide offers customers Holiday Inn Express hotels, which feature comfortable accommodations with room rates lower the traditional Holiday Inns. Sobeys Inc., one of Canada's top food retailers, offers customers its Signal brand of products, which is a private-label, value-based line. Canada's major banks offer lower-interest credit cards, some with value-added enhancements, such as frequent flyer programs and cash-back offers. Even Canada's sports, restaurant, and entertainment industries are appealing to the value-conscious customer. A tangible sign of growing value consciousness in Canada is the rise in popularity of online couponing companies such as Groupon.

Another emerging consumer trend is *eco-consciousness* or *going green*. Many Canadians are more sensitive about the impact their consumption has on their natural environment, and they make their buying decisions accordingly. This may mean buying more environmentally safe or more environmentally friendly products, buying products that can be reused or recycled, or actually reducing consumption altogether. The Hotel Association of Canada, for instance, says six in ten Canadians look for an environmentally friendly hotel as part of their travel plans. The concern for the environment is also presenting itself with the growth in sales of hybrid and electric cars and Canadian companies attempting to reduce their carbon footprints.

Responding to consumer demand for value, Sobeys offers a value-based line of products that come with a low-price guarantee.

This trend toward eco-consciousness has opened up numerous opportunities for creative businesspeople, who are called *ecopreneurs,* entrepreneurs who see business opportunities through an environmental lens. The Ontario-based winery Stratus Vineyards began with this perspective and has found customers who appreciate this philosophy and buy its products. Another example of an eco-based business is Vancouver-based Earthcycle Packaging. It has created an eco-friendly package made from a renewable resource called palm fibre, which composts in less than 90 days and provides a healthy contribution to soil.

Finally, another important trend is that Canadians are becoming more experiential. As the chapter opener points out, Canadians are willing to try new things and are seeking new experiences. For example, spending on foreign travel is up, and spending on entertainment and dining outside the home is also up, in particular, spending on ethnic foods. Canadians looking to spice up their lives are flocking to a new generation of ethnic restaurants. Spending on Chinese, Japanese, and Greek food has increased dramatically. Food chains such as Manchu Wok, Edo Japan, and Mr. Greek have all reported major jumps in revenue.[17] This trend is consistent with discussions in previous chapters of this text regarding the emerging customer experience era.

Learning Review

1. Describe three generational cohorts.

2. Why are many companies developing multicultural marketing programs?

3. What is a census metropolitan area?

ECONOMIC FORCES

The second component of the environmental scan, the **economy**, pertains to the income, expenditures, and resources that affect the cost of running a business and household. We will consider two aspects of these economic forces: a macroeconomic view of the marketplace and a microeconomic perspective of consumer income.

Macroeconomic Conditions

Of particular concern at the macroeconomic level is the inflationary or recessionary state of the economy, whether actual or perceived by consumers or businesses. In an inflationary economy, the cost to produce and buy products and services escalates as prices increase. From a marketing standpoint, if prices rise faster than consumer incomes do, the number of items consumers can buy decreases. Whereas inflation is a period of price increases, recession is a time of slow economic activity. Businesses decrease production, unemployment rises, and many consumers have less money to spend. The Conference Board of Canada's report, *Canadian Outlook Long-Term Economic Forecast* (through the year 2030), indicates modest economic growth, stable inflation, strong commodity prices, and a strong Canadian dollar.

Assessing consumer expectations of an inflationary and recessionary economy is an important element of environmental scanning. Consumer spending, which accounts for two-thirds of Canadian economic activity, is affected by expectations of the future. Surveys of consumer expectations are tracked over time by researchers, who ask such questions as "Do you expect to be better off or worse off financially a year from now?" Surveyors record the share of positive and negative responses to this question and related ones to develop an index, sometimes called a consumer confidence or consumer sentiment index. The higher the index, the more favourable are consumer expectations. Many firms evaluate such indexes in order to plan production levels. Chrysler LLC, for example, uses such indexes to plan its automobile production levels in order to avoid overproducing cars during a recessionary economy.

Consumer Income

The microeconomic trends in terms of consumer income are also important issues for marketers. Having a product that meets the needs of consumers may be of little value if they are unable to purchase it. A consumer's ability to buy is related to income, which consists of gross, disposable, and discretionary components.

Gross Income

The total amount of money made in one year by a person, household, or family unit is referred to as **gross income**. Average gross family income in Canada is slightly over $72,000. But family income in Canada varies by province as well as by the education level and profession of the head(s) of the family. For example, the majority of families earning above the average income of $72,000 are headed by university graduates. Average gross family income also varies by province and territory. Do the Going Online exercise, "Family Income in Canada by Province and Territory," to learn about family income in Canada.

GOING ONLINE

Family Income in Canada by Province and Territory

Obviously, marketers collect and use environmental information to better understand consumers. One key aspect of an environmental scan is to collect and compare economic data about particular markets or market segments. In general, marketers will want to look at what is "typical" or "average" about the entire population. However, they also want to look at any differences that might exist. Go to the Statistics Canada website (**www.statcan.gc.ca**) and select "Browse by subject" and then "Income, pensions, spending and wealth." Click on the "Household, family and personal income" link to examine the different tables that deal with family income. What can you glean from this information?

Disposable Income

The second income component, **disposable income**, is the money a consumer has left after paying taxes to use for such necessities as food, shelter, clothing, and transportation. Thus, if taxes rise at a faster rate than does disposable income, consumers must economize. The average Canadian household saw about 20 percent of their expenditures go to personal income tax, while shelter (28 percent), transportation (21 percent), food (14 percent), and clothing (6 percent) accounted for almost 70 percent of total household expenditures. However, the proportion of income spent on necessities varies by household income level and even by province. For example, the highest average spending on goods and services occurred in households in Alberta.[18]

Discretionary Income

The third component of income is **discretionary income**, the money that remains after paying for taxes and necessities. Discretionary income is used for luxury items, such as vacations at a Four Seasons resort. An obvious problem in defining discretionary versus disposable income is determining whether something is a luxury or a necessity. Observation can be a way to make this determination; if a family has Royal Doulton china, Rolex watches, and Lexus automobiles, one could assume that they have, or had, discretionary income. Still, it is important to note that a product defined as a necessity by one individual may be viewed as a luxury by another. For example, some Canadians view a microwave oven as a necessity, while others see it as a luxury item.

(LO3) TECHNOLOGICAL FORCES

Our society is in a period of dramatic technological change. **Technology**, the third environmental force, refers to inventions or innovations from applied science or engineering research. Each new wave of technological innovation can replace existing products, services, and companies.

Technological change is difficult to predict, but some of the more dramatic technological innovation occurring now include the following:

- Connectivity will grow to include all customers, homes, vehicles, appliances, and mobile devices to create the "Internet of Things."
- Computers will develop all five senses to create intelligent data collection and personalized predictive capabilities.
- Green technologies such as smart grid electricity services, online energy management, and consumer-generated energy (e.g., home solar systems) will gain widespread acceptance among consumers.
- 3D technologies will move from movie theatres and televisions to many new and useful applications.

Some of these trends in technology are already being realized in today's marketplace. Oral-B toothbrushes, for example, now connect to your smartphone to provide real-time feedback on your brushing. MindMeld uses speech recognition to listen to your phone calls and pull up search data related to your conversations. Amazon recently introduced its 3D Printing Store, which offers jewellery, home decor, and tech accessories in customizable 3D options. Other technologies such as the Texture app, Tesla's electric cars, and Apple Pay are likely to replace or become substitutes for existing products and services such as paper versions of magazines, gasoline-powered vehicles, and plastic credit cards and money, respectively.

Other new technologies are also dramatically changing marketing practices and forever altering the way consumers shop and what they buy. Business experts agree that new technologies are enabling marketers and, more importantly, are empowering customers.

Technology Enables Data Analytics

Technology has also had a dramatic impact on the operations of marketing organizations. First, the development of online capabilities created the **marketspace**, an information- and communication-based electronic exchange environment occupied by sophisticated computer and telecommunication technologies and digital offerings. Second, these capabilities led to **electronic commerce** (e-commerce), or the activities that use electronic communication in the inventory, promotion, distribution, purchase, and exchange of products and services. Internet-based technology also allows companies to create *intranets* to communicate within the organization, and *extranets* to communicate with suppliers, distributors, and other partners such as advertising agencies. Today, technologies have advanced to allow computer chips to be placed in almost anything and to be connected to a network almost anywhere. This network of products embedded with connectivity-enabled electronics has come to be known as the **Internet of Things (IoT)**. The information generated by the Internet of Things has led to an explosion in interest in advanced analytics that can predict consumer preferences and behaviour. A recent survey showed that 50 percent of managers around the globe thought that improving information and analytics was a top priority. Some experts suggest that the use of analytics is associated with success in the marketplace. Firms that have grown their revenues through analytical insights include Netflix, Google, Amazon, Dell, and eBay.[19]

COMPETITIVE FORCES

The fourth component of the environmental scan, **competition**, refers to the alternative firms that could provide a product to satisfy a specific market's needs. There are various forms of competition, and each company must consider its present and potential competitors in designing its marketing strategy.

LO4 Alternative Forms of Competition

There are four basic forms of competition that form a continuum from pure competition to monopolistic competition to oligopoly to pure monopoly. Chapter 13 contains further discussions on pricing practices under these four forms of competition.

At one end of the continuum is *pure competition,* in which every company has a similar product. Companies that deal in commodities common to agribusiness (for example, wheat, rice, and grain) often are in a pure competition position, in which distribution (in the sense of shipping products) is important but other elements of marketing have little impact.

In the second point on the continuum, *monopolistic competition,* many sellers compete with their products on a substitutable basis. For example, if the price of coffee rises too much, consumers may switch to tea. Coupons or sales are frequently used marketing tactics.

Oligopoly, a common industry structure, occurs when a few companies control the majority of industry sales. Because there are few sellers in an oligopolistic situation, price competition among firms is not desirable because it would lead to reduced revenue for all producers. Instead, nonprice competition is common, which means competing on other dimensions of the marketing mix, such as product quality, distribution, and/or promotion. Canada is sometimes referred to by some economists as the "land of oligopoly" because it has several major industries that can be considered oligopolistic, including the airline industry and the banking industry.

The final point on the continuum, *monopoly,* occurs when only one firm sells the product or service. It has been common for producers of goods and services considered essential to a community: water, electricity, or telephone service. Typically, marketing plays a small role in a monopolistic setting because it is regulated by a province or the federal government. Government control usually seeks to ensure price protection for the buyer.

Components of Competition

In developing a marketing program, companies must consider the factors that drive competition: entry, bargaining power of buyers and suppliers, existing rivalries, and substitution possibilities.[20] Scanning the environment requires a look at all of them. These factors relate to a firm's marketing mix decisions and may be used to create a barrier to entry, increase brand awareness, or intensify a fight for market share. Read the accompanying Using Marketing Dashboards box for ideas about assessing the components of competition.[21]

USING MARKETING DASHBOARDS

Assessing Competition Is a Key to Success

To include competition in your marketing dashboard, you need to assess the components of competition. For example, the probability of a new competitor entering a market can be assessed on a scale from 0 to 100 percent. The power or influence of a buyer or supplier declines as the number of buyers and suppliers in the same product category increases. As the number of similar firms or substitute products increases, the competitiveness of an industry increases. The combination of these measurements will allow you to make an overall assessment of competitors and their likely actions.

Your Challenge You are responsible for price recommendations for an existing product that has been very successful during the past year. In general, you believe that there is a strong relationship between price and sales, and that a reduction in price would lead to an increase in sales. That is:

Sales Increase (%) = Price Reduction (%) × Ratio of Sales Increase to Price Reduction

Your goal is to increase sales by 10 percent.

Your Findings After studying the prices of similar products and their sales, you estimate that a 1 percent decrease in price will lead to a 4 percent increase in sales. This calculation, however, ignores the likely reaction of competitors. That is, when a firm lowers its price, competitors may reduce price also, changing the ratio of sales increase to price reduction for the product. Based on your assessment of the components of competition, you estimate that competitors will meet half of your price reduction.

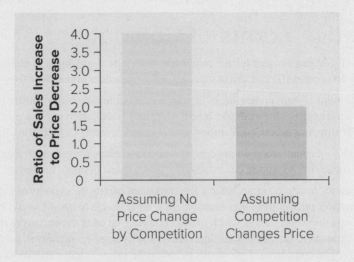

Your Action The information about competition allows you to adjust your estimates. Because competitors will meet half of your price reduction, the increase in sales will probably be about half of your original estimate. So, the ratio of sales increase to price reduction will change from 4-to-1 to 2-to-1. To achieve the 10 percent increase in sales, you estimate that a 5 percent price reduction is needed (5% × 2/1).

This use of marketing metrics shows how assessment of competition can allow higher precision in the actions taken by marketing managers.

Note: The ratio of the unit amount of increase in sales for each unit decrease in price is often referred to as price elasticity, and is discussed in Chapter 13.

Entry

In considering the competition, a firm must assess the likelihood of new entrants. Additional producers increase industry capacity and tend to lower prices. A company scanning its environment must consider the possible **barriers to entry** for other firms, which are business practices or conditions that make it difficult for new firms to enter a market. Barriers to entry can be in the form of capital requirements, advertising expenditures, product identity, distribution access, or switching costs. The higher the expense of the barrier, the more likely it will deter new entrants.

Power of Buyers and Suppliers

A competitive analysis must consider the power of buyers and suppliers. Powerful buyers exist when they are few in number, there are low switching costs, or the product represents a significant share of the buyer's total costs. This last factor leads the buyer to exert significant pressure for price competition. A supplier gains power when the product is critical to the buyer and when it has built up the switching costs.

Existing Competitors and Substitutes

Competitive pressures among existing firms depend on the rate of industry growth. In slow-growth settings, competition is more heated for any possible gains in market share. High fixed costs also create competitive pressures for firms to fill production capacity. For example, airlines offer discounts for making early reservations and charge penalties for changes or cancellations in an effort to fill seats, which represent a high fixed cost.

Small Businesses as Competitors

While large companies provide familiar examples of the forms and components of competition, small businesses make up the majority of the competitive landscape for most businesses. In fact, in Canada there are over 2.7 million small- and medium-sized enterprises (SMEs), and they generate half of the country's total gross domestic product (GDP), employ six out of ten Canadians, and create the bulk of all new jobs. Economic growth in Canada is largely tied to the activities of SMEs, and entrepreneurs who start new businesses provide new competition for existing large companies. A small business is a firm that has fewer than 100 employees while a medium-sized business has more than 100 but less than 500 employees. Currently, 98 percent of all businesses in Canada are small businesses. Moreover, SMEs not only play a significant role in our economy but also are a significant source of innovation, including new products, new services, and new technologies. SMEs participate in every sector but are dominant players in several key areas including retail, construction, professional services, accommodation, and food service. It is very likely that your first marketing job may be working with an SME, or perhaps with a *micro-enterprise* (firm with fewer than five employees). It is also entirely possible that you may become a self-employed entrepreneur and find yourself competing against a range of competitors of all sizes, both here and globally. For example, right now more than 1 million Canadian women are self-employed! Moreover, a recent study found that 40 percent of Canadians indicated that starting their own company would be the most rewarding career for them. If this is in your future, marketing will play a critical role in the success of your new venture.[22]

Pure-Play Online Competitors

While many traditional companies (bricks and mortar) also have a presence in the new marketspace or online world, there are a host of companies that exist only in this new space: pure-play online competitors. Many of these competitors are also small, entrepreneurial start-ups that target specialized or niche markets.

4. What is the difference between a consumer's disposable income and discretionary income?

5. How does technology impact customer value?

6. In pure competition, there are a _____ number of sellers.

LO5 REGULATORY FORCES

For any organization, the marketing and broader business decisions are constrained, directed, and influenced by regulatory forces. **Regulation** consists of restrictions that provincial and federal laws place on business with respect to the conduct of its activities. Regulation exists to protect companies as well as consumers. Much of the regulation from the federal and provincial levels has been passed to ensure competition and fair business practices. For consumers, the focus of legislation is to protect them from unfair trade practices and ensure their safety.

Protecting Competition and Consumers

Legislation and regulations exist in Canada at all three levels of government—federal, provincial, and municipal—to protect and encourage a competitive environment, which is deemed desirable because it permits the consumer to determine which competitor will succeed and which will fail.

The *Competition Act*

The key legislation designed to protect competition and consumers in Canada is the *Competition Act*. The purpose of the *Competition Act* is:

> to maintain and encourage competition in Canada in order to promote the efficiency and adaptability of the Canadian economy, in order to expand opportunities for Canadian participation in world markets while at the same time recognizing the role of foreign competition in Canada, in order to ensure that small- and medium-sized enterprises have an equitable opportunity to participate in the Canadian economy and in order to provide consumers with competitive prices and product choices.[23]

In essence, the ***Competition Act*** is designed to protect and to balance the interests of competitors and consumers. The Competition Bureau, which is part of Industry Canada, is responsible for administering and enforcing the provisions of the *Competition Act*. The *Competition Act* contains both criminal and non-criminal provisions.

Criminal offences under Part VI of the *Competition Act* include conspiracy (e.g., price fixing), bid rigging, discriminatory and predatory pricing, price maintenance, and misleading or deceptive marketing practices, such as double ticketing or bait-and-switch selling.

Non-criminal reviewable matters under Part VIII of the *Competition Act* include mergers, abuse of dominant position, refusal to deal, consignment selling, exclusive dealing, tied selling, market restriction, and delivered pricing. The director of the Competition Bureau refers these matters to the Competition Tribunal under non-criminal law standards. The tribunal was established when the *Competition Act* took effect, and is governed by the *Competition Tribunal Act*. The tribunal adjudicates all reviewable matters under the *Competition Act*.

Industry Canada is responsible for most of the legislation affecting business practices in Canada. Figure 3–4 lists the more significant federal legislation that protects competition and consumers in Canada. Marketers must also be cognizant of the fact that in addition to federal laws and regulations, there are many more at the provincial level. Many provinces have their own departments of consumer affairs in order to administer any such legislation and regulations enacted on the provincial government level.

However, the laws and regulations at the provincial level tend to vary from province to province. Therefore, a marketer may find it necessary to adapt some aspect of the marketing mix or some broader business practice, depending on the province. For example, in Quebec, there are specific laws dealing with store signage, packaging, and labelling. Additionally, advertising directed toward children is prohibited in Quebec. Many provinces, including Quebec, also have consumer protection acts and/or business or trade practices acts.

FIGURE 3-4

Bank Cost Borrowing Act	Hazardous Products Act
Bankruptcy Act	Income Tax Act
Bills of Exchange Act	Industrial Design Act
Board of Trade Act	The Interest Act
Broadcasting Act	Maple Products Industry Act
C-28 Anti-Spam Legislation (CASL)	Motor Vehicle Safety Act
Canada Agricultural Products Standards Act	Official Languages Act
Canada Cooperative Association Act	Patent Act
Canada Corporations Act	Personal Information Protection and Electronic Documents Act
Canada Dairy Products Act	Precious Metals Marketing Act
Canadian Human Rights Act	Privacy Act
Competition Act	Small Loans Act
Consumer Packaging and Labelling Act	Standards Council of Canada Act
Copyright Act	Textile Labelling Act
Criminal Code	Timber Marketing Act
Department of Consumer and Corporate Affairs Act	Trade-marks Act
Electricity Inspection Act and Gas Inspection Act	True Labelling Act
Electronic Commerce Protection Act	Weights and Measures Act
Fish Inspection Act	Winding-up Act
Food and Drugs Act	

> Major federal legislation designed to protect competition and consumers.

Self-Regulation

The government has provided much legislation to create a competitive business climate and protect the consumer. An alternative to government control is **self-regulation**, where an industry attempts to police itself. The Canadian Broadcasting Association, whose members include major television networks and radio stations across the country, has a code of ethics that helps govern the conduct of its members in terms of protecting the consumer against deceptive trade practices, such as misleading advertising. Similarly, the Advertising Standards Council, the self-regulatory arm of the Canadian Advertising Foundation, has established the Canadian Code of Advertising Standards for its members to follow. The members of this organization consist of major advertising agencies that are responsible for allocating the bulk of advertising dollars in Canada. The Canadian Radio-television and Telecommunications Commission (CRTC), the federal agency responsible for licensing and regulating broadcasting in Canada, is in favour of greater industry self-regulation.

The Canadian Marketing Association, whose members represent 80 percent of direct-marketing sales in Canada, has mandated that its members comply with the consumer's right to privacy and honour consumers who request not to be contacted by telephone or mail for selling purposes. Critics argue that telemarketers in Canada demonstrate what is wrong with self-regulation efforts—noncompliance by members and enforcement.

Another well-known self-regulatory group is the Better Business Bureau (BBB). This organization is a voluntary alliance of companies whose goal is to help maintain fair business practices. Although the BBB has no legal power, it does try to use "moral suasion" to get members to comply with its regulations.

Consumerism

Regulation by government and self-regulation by industry help in protecting the consumer in the marketplace. But the consumer can also play a direct and active role. **Consumerism** is a movement to increase the influence, power, and rights of consumers in dealing with institutions. Modern consumerism in Canada and the United States really began in the 1960s. U.S. President John F. Kennedy, in a speech entitled "Consumer Bill of Rights," outlined four basic consumer rights: (1) the right to safety, (2) the right to be informed, (3) the right to choose, and (4) the right to be heard. Although not passed as laws, these proclaimed rights serve as the basis for modern consumerism. Shortly after President Kennedy's Consumer Bill of Rights was unveiled in the United States, the Canadian government formed the Department of Consumer and Corporate Affairs, making it the agency responsible for protecting consumers and regulating corporate activities.

Canada also has many independent consumer organizations that advance the cause of consumerism. The Consumers Association of Canada (CAC) is the largest consumer group working on behalf of the Canadian consumer. The CAC serves as a channel for supplying consumers' views to government and industry, providing consumer information, and studying consumer problems and presenting recommended solutions to those problems. In addition to ensuring that the four original consumer rights are protected, the consumer movement also includes consumer demands for environmentally safe products and ethical and socially responsible business practices, including the right to privacy.

The *Privacy Act (PA)* and *Personal Information Protection and Electronic Documents Act (PIPEDA)* were enacted by the federal government to protect Canadian citizens' privacy and to ensure that information on individuals is collected, used, and disclosed legally and ethically. In order to protect consumers' privacy and ensure their security, the Canadian government has also enacted Internet and wireless spam legislation. Still, privacy experts suggest that new emerging technologies are creating new concerns about consumer privacy and marketers, not just legislation, must be part of solution with regard to protecting consumer privacy.[24] One new technology that is raising privacy concerns is a cross-device tracking technology. You can read more about this in the Making Responsible Decisions box.[25]

MAKING RESPONSIBLE DECISIONS

Cross-Device Tracking and Consumer Privacy

According to privacy experts, advertisers looking to use cross-device tracking need to update their privacy practices to make users aware of it, as well as provide opportunities to opt out.

The technology to connect users' identities across their desktops and mobile devices is relatively new. Until recently, siloed mobile and desktop systems prevented marketers from using the same audience data across devices; desktop behavioural data, collected and applied with cookies, couldn't be used to target mobile ads, since it wasn't possible to identify the same user on mobile. But now companies such as Google, Facebook, and Adobe are offering cookie-free cross-device user identification, which allows marketers to connect audience profiles to users on whatever device they're on. That means a user logging in from home, at work, or on the go will be identified and targeted using the same data about their past behaviour and preferences.

But privacy experts are concerned that cross-device tracking may not be transparent to users, and if it involves device fingerprinting, users may not have any choice—and choice, according to privacy experts, is a key privacy practice. It is suggested that consumers likely have not realized that their behaviour on mobile apps, for example, can impact their desktop permissions, and vice versa. Consumers are more likely to assume that their mobile and desktop experiences are separate, and they expect the privacy decisions they make in those environments are limited to those environments. For example, if a user gives an app permission to collect their location data, the user likely does not take that to mean the developer can collect and use location data the next time the same user logs in from a work computer. Thus, marketers need to be careful with cross-device tracking.

While some cross-device technologies use user log-ins to identify users on multiple devices (called "deterministic" tracking), many marketers use probabilistic tracking, which uses behavioural signals and predictive algorithms to assess the probability that user on device A is the same as user on device B. The problem arises when the technology attempts to apply users' opt-out choices probabilistically. When one is using a probabilistic cross-device methodology—in other words, it's not based on a log-in—the opt-in that you utilize in that context needs to be persistent, and apply across all the devices that the user is using. In other words, it has to work across [a consumer's] laptop, smartphone, tablet, and desktop. Privacy experts argue that accidentally violating opt-outs by making the wrong guess about a user's identity is a no-fly zone. Finally, privacy experts argue for a practice called "notice in time," where the marketer informs the user before collecting any data they wouldn't reasonably expect. For example, if you're collecting precise geographic information, but you're not a map service and the user would not expect you to do so, it's important to give the user direct notice, and not attempt to hide it.

What you do you think about this cross-device tracking as it pertains to your privacy?

Learning Review

7. The _____ Act is the most important legislation designed to protect competition and consumers in Canada.

8. An alternative to legislation protecting competition and consumers is self-_____.

9. What is consumerism?

Learning Objectives Review

 Explain how environmental scanning provides information about social, economic, technological, competitive, and regulatory forces.

Many businesses operate in environments where important forces change. Environmental scanning is the process of acquiring information about these changes to allow marketers to identify and interpret trends. There are five environmental forces that businesses must monitor: social, economic, technological, competitive, and regulatory. By identifying trends related to each of these forces, businesses can develop and maintain successful marketing programs. Several trends that most businesses are monitoring include the growing diversity of the Canadian population, the increasing use of electronic information and communication technologies, and new legislation related to consumer privacy.

LO2 **Describe how social forces, such as demographics, and cultural and economic forces, such as macroeconomic conditions and consumer income, affect marketing.**

Demographic information helps describe the world population; the Canadian population; generational cohorts, such as baby boomers, Generation X, and Generation Y; the structure of the Canadian family; and ethnic diversity. Ethnic diversity, for example, has led to ethnic marketing programs in Canada. Cultural trends in Canada indicate that many individuals are suffering from time poverty and are more interested in health and fitness. Still, obesity persists and is a public health problem. Economic forces include the strong relationship between consumers' expectations about the economy and their spending habits.

LO3 **Describe how technological changes are impacting marketers and customers.**

New technologies have dramatically changed marketing practices and have altered the way consumers shop and what they buy. Today, technologies have advanced to allow computer chips to be placed in almost anything and to be connected to a network almost anywhere. This network of products embedded with connectivity-enabled electronics has come to be known as the Internet of Things (IoT). The information generated by the Internet of Things has led to an explosion in interest in advanced analytics that can predict consumer preferences and behaviour.

 Discuss the forms of competition that exist in a market, key components of competition, and the impact of small businesses as competitors.

There are four forms of competition: pure competition, monopolistic competition, oligopoly, and monopoly. The key components of competition include the likelihood of new competitors, the power of buyers and suppliers, and the presence of competitors and possible substitutes. While large companies are often used as examples of marketplace competitors, there are over two million small- and medium-sized enterprises in Canada that have a significant impact on the economy and the competitive landscape. Also, traditional marketers must now contend with new pure-play online competition.

 Explain the major legislation that ensures competition and protects consumers in Canada.

Regulation exists to protect competition and consumers. The key legislation in Canada that ensures a competitive marketplace and consumer protection is the *Competition Act.* Self-regulation through such organizations as the Canadian Marketing Association and the Better Business Bureau provides an alternative to federal and provincial regulations.

Applying Marketing Knowledge

1. For many years, Gerber has manufactured baby food in small, single-serving containers. In conducting an environmental scan, identify three trends or factors that might significantly affect this company's future business, and then propose how Gerber might respond to these changes.

2. Describe the new features you would add to an automobile designed for an aging baby boomer. In what magazines would you advertise to appeal to this target market?

3. How have social media tools such as Facebook and MySpace changed the way that companies market? How has social media changed how you shop and buy?

4. Historically, a couple of large firms dominated the Canadian brewing industry (Labatt and Molson). But now, these companies face competition from many regional brands and micro-breweries. In terms of the continuum of competition, how would you explain this change?

5. What role does marketing play now in the deregulated Canadian airline industry? What elements of the marketing mix are more or less important now?

6. The Johnson Company manufactures buttons and pins with slogans and designs. These pins are inexpensive to produce and are sold in retail outlets, such as discount stores, hobby shops, and bookstores. Little equipment is needed for a new competitor to enter the market. What strategies should Johnson consider to create effective barriers to entry?

7. Today's consumer is more value-conscious. How could a retail home improvement centre sell the same products but still offer the consumer greater perceived value? What specific things could the retailer do?

Building Your Marketing Plan

Your marketing plan will include a situation analysis based on internal and external factors that are likely to affect your marketing program.

1. To summarize information about external factors, create a table similar to Figure 3–2 and identify three trends related to each of the five forces (social, economic, technological, competitive, and regulatory) that relate to your product or service.

2. When your table is completed, describe how each of the trends represents an opportunity or a threat for your business.

Video Case 3

Geek Squad: A New Business for a New Environment

"As long as there's innovation there is going to be new kinds of chaos," explains Robert Stephens, founder of the technology support company Geek Squad. The chaos Stephens is referring to is the difficulty we have all experienced trying to keep up with the many changes in our environment, particularly those related to computers, technology, software, communication, and entertainment. Generally, consumers have found it difficult to install, operate, and use many of the electronic products available today. "It takes time to read the manuals," Stephens says. "I'm going to save you that time because I stay home on Saturday nights and read them for you!"

The Company

The Geek Squad story begins when Stephens, a native of Chicago, passed up an Art Institute scholarship to pursue a degree in computer science. While Stephens was a computer science student he took a job fixing computers for a research laboratory, and he also started consulting. He could repair televisions, computers, and a variety of other items, although he decided to focus on computers. His experiences as a consultant led him to realize that most people needed help with technology and that they saw value in a service whose employees would show up at a specified time, be friendly, use understandable language, and solve the problem. So, with just $200, Stephens formed Geek Squad in 1994.

© Tim Boyle/Getty Images

Geek Squad set out to provide timely and effective help with all computing needs regardless of the make, model, or place of purchase. Geek Squad employees were called "agents" and wore uniforms consisting of black pants or skirts, black shoes, white shirts, black clip-on ties, a badge, and a black jacket with a Geek Squad logo to create a "humble" attitude that was not threatening to customers. Agents drove black-and-white Volkswagen Beetles, or Geekmobiles, with a logo on the door, and charged fixed prices for services, regardless of how much time was required to provide the service. The "house call" services ranged from installing networks, to debugging a computer, to setting up an entertainment system, and cost from $100 to $300. "We're like 'Dragnet'; we show up at people's homes and help," Stephens says. "We're also like *Ghostbusters* and there's a pseudogovernment feel to it like *Men in Black*."

The Changing Environment

Many changes in the environment occurred to create the need for Geek Squad's services. Future changes are also likely to change the way Geek Squad operates. An environmental scan helps illustrate the changes.

The most obvious changes may be related to technology. Wireless broadband technology, high-definition televisions, products with Internet interfaces, and a general trend toward computers, smartphones, entertainment systems, and even appliances being interconnected are just a few examples of new products and applications for consumers to learn about. There are also technology-related problems such as viruses, spyware, lost data, and "crashed" or inoperable computers. New technologies have also created a demand for new types of maintenance such as password management, operating system updates, disk cleanup, and "defragging."

Another environmental change that contributes to the popularity of Geek Squad is the change in social factors such as demographics and culture. In the past many electronics manufacturers and retailers focused primarily on men. Women, however, are becoming increasingly interested in personal computing and home entertainment and, according to the Consumer Electronics Association, are likely to outspend men in the near future. Best Buy's consumer research indicates that women expect personal service during the purchase as well as during the installation after the purchase—exactly the service Geek Squad is designed to provide. Our culture is also embracing the Geek Squad concept. For example, in the recently discontinued television series *Chuck* (2007–2012), one of the characters worked for the "Nerd Herd" at "Buy More" and drove a car like a Geekmobile on service calls!

© Tim Boyle/Getty Images.

Competition, economics, and the regulatory environment have also had a big influence on Geek Squad. As discount stores such as Walmart and PC makers such as Dell began to compete with Best Buy, new services such as in-home installation were needed to create value for customers. Now, just as change in competition created an opportunity for Geek Squad, it is also leading to another level of competition as Staples has introduced EasyTech services and Office Depot has introduced Tech Depot services. The economic situation for electronics continues to improve as prices decline and demand increases. Consumers purchased 2 million 3D TVs in 2010, and sales of all consumer electronics exceeded $180 billion. Finally, the regulatory environment continues to change with respect to the electronic transfer of copyrighted materials such as music and movies and software. Geek Squad must monitor the changes to ensure that its services comply with relevant laws.

The Future for Geek Squad

The combination of many positive environmental factors helps explain the extraordinary success of Geek Squad. Today, it repairs more than 3,000 PCs a day and generates more than $2 billion in revenue. Because Geek Squad services have a high profit margin they contribute to the overall performance of Best Buy, and they help generate traffic in the store and create store loyalty. To continue to grow, however, Geek Squad will need to continue to scan the environment and try new approaches to creating customer value.

One possible new approach is to create new partnerships. Geek Squad and Ford, for example, have developed a partnership to help consumers install in-car communication systems. In the future, Best Buy will offer 240-volt home charging stations for Ford's electric vehicle, the Focus. Geek Squad will offer electrical audits and residential installations for the car owners. Geek Squad is also using new technology to improve. Agents now use a smartphone to access updated schedules, log in their hours, and run diagnostics tests on clients' equipment. Best Buy is also testing a "Solutions Central" desk, similar to the Genius Bar concept in Apple stores, and staffing it with Geek Squad agents. Finally, to attract the best possible employees, Geek Squad and Best Buy are trying a "results-only work environment" that has no fixed schedules and no mandatory meetings. By encouraging employees to make their own work–life decisions, the Geek Squad hopes to keep morale and productivity high.

Other changes and opportunities are certain to appear soon. However, despite the success of the Geek Squad and the potential for additional growth, Robert Stephens is modest and claims, "Geeks may inherit the Earth, but they have no desire to rule it!"

QUESTIONS

1. What are the key environmental forces that created an opportunity for Robert Stephens to start the Geek Squad?

2. What changes in the purchasing patterns of (*a*) all consumers and (*b*) women made the acquisition of Geek Squad particularly important for Best Buy?

3. Based on the case information and what you know about consumer electronics, conduct an environmental scan for Geek Squad to identify key trends. For each of the five environmental forces (social, economic, technological, competitive, and regulatory), identify trends likely to influence Geek Squad in the near future.

4. What promotional activities would you recommend to encourage consumers who currently use independent installers to switch to Geek Squad?

Case: This case was written by Steven Hartley. Sources: Thomas Lee, "Best Buy Stakes Big Share of Its Future on Geek Squad," *San Jose Mercury News*, August 7, 2012; Natalie Zmuda, "Best Buy Gets Back in the Game with New Tagline," *Advertising Age*, June 25, 2012, p. 4; "Best Buy Continues to Diversify by Selling Geek Squad Services," *Trefis*, October 9, 2012; Mike Snider and Edward C. Baig, "Companies Foresee Record Electronics Sales This Year," *USA Today*, January 10, 2011, p. 8A; "3D TV Surpasses HD Sales Success," *Broadcast*, February 25, 2011; "Ford Working with Best Buy to Offer Focus Electric Charging Station Sales and Support,"*ENP Newswire*, January 10, 2011; Mary Ellen Lloyd, "Camp Teaches Power of Geekdom," *The Wall Street Journal*, July 11, 2007; Dean Foust, Michael Mandel, Frederick F. Jespersen, and David Henry, "The BusinessWeek 50—The Best Performers," *BusinessWeek*, March 26, 2007, p. 58; Jessica E. Vascellaro, "What's a Cellphone For? Businesses Are Finding All Sorts of New Uses for Mobile Devices," *The Wall Street Journal*, March 26, 2007, p. R5; Cade Metz, "Just How Stupid Are You? Geek Squad War Stories," *PC Magazine*, February 1, 2006; Brad Stone, "Lore of the Geek Squad," *Newsweek*, February 20, 2006, p. 44; Michelle Conlin, "Smashing the Clock,"*BusinessWeek*, December 11, 2006, p. 60; "Best Buy: How to Break Out of Commodity Hell,"*BusinessWeek*, March 27, 2006, p. 76; Pallavi Gogoi, "Meet Jane Geek," *BusinessWeek*,November 28, 2005, p. 94; Desiree J. Hanford, "Geek Squad Is Popular at Best Buy," *The Wall Street Journal*, December 14, 2005, p. 1; Michelle Higgins, "Getting Your Own IT Department," *The Wall Street Journal*, May 20, 2004, p. D1; and information contained on the Geek Squad website (www.geeksquad.com).

4 Ethics and Social Responsibility for Sustainable Marketing

Learning Objectives

After reading this chapter, you should be able to:

LO1 Explain the differences between legal and ethical behaviour in marketing.

LO2 Identify factors that influence ethical and unethical behaviour in marketing.

LO3 Describe the different concepts of social responsibility.

LO4 Recognize unethical and socially irresponsible consumer behaviour.

Introducing Some of Canada's Most Ethical and Socially Responsible Companies

Many Canadian companies are consistently ranked among the most ethical and socially responsible in the world by several organizations that prepare such rankings using multiple methodologies. This section introduces a few of those Canadian companies. B.C.-based Vancity, a financial co-operative and Canada's largest community credit union, is heavily invested in the environment and is set up as a "values based" company. It is also considered one of Canada's greenest employers. For example, it has a corporate target to ensure no less than 70 percent of office waste is recycled, and it offers green financial products, including financing rewards for green home renovations and discounted loans for the purchase of fuel-efficient hybrid and electric cars.

Encana Corporation is an oil and gas company headquartered in Calgary, Alberta. It is recognized as a leading North American company in its field but it also operates in an environmentally and socially responsible manner. Environmental, social, and governance (ES&G) issues are central to its business. Its ES&G focus is guided by its business code of conduct ("the Code"), which communicates its expectations and obligations to the environment, the communities in which it operates, and its people. Every year the company produces a sustainability report that it makes available to its stakeholders and the general public.

PepsiCo Beverages Canada is another company recognized for its ethical and socially responsible conduct. For example, PepsiCo focuses its environmental sustainability efforts on water, energy, and packaging. It has reduced water usage at its manufacturing plants by 40 percent. It was also the first manufacturer in Canada to introduce all-electric, zero-emissions, green-powered delivery trucks. Richard Glover, president at PepsiCo Beverages Canada, describes the company as "committed to achieving business and financial success while leaving a positive imprint on society—delivering what we call 'performance with purpose.' It's at the heart of every aspect of our business."

TRIPLE-BOTTOM-LINE: PEOPLE, PLANET, PROFIT

© Stocktrek Images, Inc./Alamy Stock Photo

Another Canadian company also ranked highly for its ethical and socially responsible conduct is ENMAX Corporation. It is a vertically integrated utility that generates and distributes electricity, natural gas, renewable energy, and value-added services to customers in Alberta. It is also a wholly owned subsidiary of the City of Calgary. The company fully integrates the concept of corporate responsibility (CR) into its entire operations. Its CR is demonstrated through its commitment to reducing carbon dioxide emissions, making greater use of renewable energy, investing in and involving the community, promoting employee safety, and delivering exemplary customer experiences.

Finally, Telus created a sustainability office as part of its commitment to being a responsible corporation. According to Andrea Goertz, the company's chief sustainability officer, "We believe that the health of our communities, our customers, and our team is tied to the health of our planet. Sustainability is a holistic mindset that guides every decision we make and challenges us to innovate." The company has been named to the Dow Jones Sustainability North America Index 14 years in a row. It also signed on to the Catalyst Accord, a pledge by major Canadian corporations to increase the proportion of their board seats held by women to 25 percent by 2017. Telus is also known for its strict animal-advertising code that requires it work only with reputable owners, accredited zoos, and sanctuaries when filming animals for its advertisements. Telus also requires that a professional advocacy representative oversee the ethical treatment of animals during its productions. Finally, Telus's data centres in Rimouski, Quebec, and Kamloops, British Columbia, are built to LEED gold standards and consume 80 percent less power than a typical data centre of the same size.[1]

This chapter focuses on ethics and social responsibility in marketing. You will see that some Canadian companies recognize that while ethically and socially responsible behaviour often comes with a price tag, the price for unethical and socially irresponsible behaviour is often much higher. In essence, in this marketplace, companies can "do well by doing good."

NATURE AND SIGNIFICANCE OF MARKETING ETHICS

As defined in Chapter 1, *ethics* are the moral principles and values that govern the actions and decisions of an individual or group.[2] Simply put, ethics serve as guidelines on how to act correctly and justly when faced with moral dilemmas. For marketing managers, ethics concern the application of moral principles and values to marketing decision-making.

LO1 Ethical/Legal Framework in Marketing

A good starting point for understanding the nature and significance of ethics is the distinction between legality and ethicality of marketing decisions. Figure 4–1 helps you visualize the relationship between laws and ethics.[3] While ethics deal with personal and moral principles and values, **laws** are society's values and standards that are enforceable in the courts.[4]

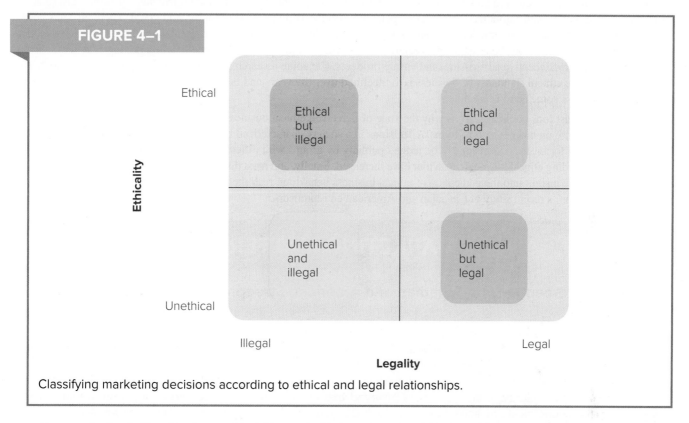

FIGURE 4–1

Classifying marketing decisions according to ethical and legal relationships.

In general, what is illegal is also unethical. For example, deceptive advertising is illegal. It is also unethical because it conflicts with the moral principles of honesty and fairness. But not all unethical conduct is illegal. For instance, price gouging is usually not illegal but is often viewed as unethical. Marketing managers often find themselves in many situations where they must make judgments in defining ethical and legal boundaries. For some, the distinction between ethics and laws can sometimes lead to the rationalization that if a behaviour is within legal limits, then it is not really unethical. For example, in a recent survey, more than 5 percent of Canadian entrepreneurs and corporate managers felt it was okay to knowingly overcharge a customer for products or services.[5] How would you have answered this question? Do you feel it is okay to knowingly overcharge customers for products or services?

Now consider the following situations. After reading each, assign it to the cell in Figure 4–1 that you think best fits the situation along the ethical–legal continuum.

1. Several companies meet and agree to bid rigging for sealed tendered government contract work. Bid rigging is illegal under the *Competition Act* because it eliminates free and open competition.

2. A company uses a technique called "slugging," or selling under the guise of research. Once prospective customers agree to take part in the research, the salespeople switch to their sales pitch.

3. A real estate agent sells a high-rise condo unit to a customer, primarily because the customer loves the city view from the condo windows. The agent knows that in one year another high-rise will be built, effectively blocking the view so important to the customer. The agent decides not to give that information to the customer.

4. A company interviews a very qualified female for a business sales position. She is more qualified than any males who have been interviewed. However, the company knows that some male purchasing agents prefer to deal with a male salesperson, and so they hire a less qualified male applicant.

Do these situations fit neatly into Figure 4–1 as clearly defined ethical and legal or unethical and illegal? Some probably do not. As you read further in this chapter, you will be asked to consider other ethical dilemmas.

Current Perceptions of Ethical Behaviour

There has been much discussion about the possible deterioration of personal morality and ethical standards on a global scale. The news media offer well-publicized examples of personal dishonesty, hypocrisy, cheating, and greed. There also has been a public outcry about the ethical practices of businesspeople, and public cynicism about the ethical practices of business leaders and their organizations is on the rise.[6] In particular, there is widespread concern over unethical marketing practices, such as price fixing, bribery, deceptive advertising, and unsafe products. Canadian research also shows that most business students surveyed feel that the ethical standards of business have declined over the years and believe the situation is not likely to improve in the future unless some actions are taken.[7]

There are at least four possible reasons why the state of perceived ethical business conduct is at its present level. First, there is increased pressure on businesspeople to make decisions in a society characterized by diverse value systems. Second, there is a growing tendency for business decisions to be judged publicly by groups with different values and interests. Third, the public's expectations regarding ethical business behaviour have increased. Finally, and most disturbing, ethical business conduct may have declined. For some insight into the perception of ethical business behaviour, read the Marketing Matters box (below), which discusses findings from a recent study of Canadian and American entrepreneurs.[8]

MARKETING MATTERS

Ethical Perceptions of Canadian and American Entrepreneurs: A Cross-Cultural Study

A recent study examined the ethical perceptions of Canadian and American entrepreneurs. Overall, there was a great deal of consensus between the groups regarding their perceptions of the behaviours and/or practices posed in the item statements used in the study. In fact, there were no statistically significant differences between Canadian or American entrepreneurs on 12 of the 17 statements. Moreover, the overwhelming majority of entrepreneurs believed that most of the item statements posed in the survey were clearly unethical practices. For example, 100 percent of both Canadian and American entrepreneurs considered blaming errors on innocent co-workers as unethical. Additionally, almost all the Canadian and American entrepreneurs perceived claiming credit for a co-worker's work, falsifying reports, and exaggerating the company's financial performance as unethical practices. About 97 percent of all entrepreneurs, Canadian and American, also believed that overstating expense accounts was an unethical practice, while more than 97 percent of respondents in both groups believed that divulging confidential information on customers was unethical. About 95 percent of respondents in both groups also believed that knowingly overcharging customers and using company supplies for personal use were unethical practices.

However, not disclosing product defects to customers was considered ethical by at least 10 percent of both Canadian and American entrepreneurs. Additionally, 10 percent of Canadian and American entrepreneurs believed that purchasing and selling shares using insider information was ethical, despite it being both an unethical and illegal practice.

There were also some statistically significant differences in responses, to certain survey item statements, between Canadian and American entrepreneurs. For example, American entrepreneurs were more likely to agree that using company services for personal use was ethical, compared to Canadian entrepreneurs. American entrepreneurs were also more likely than Canadian entrepreneurs to believe that doing personal business on company time, taking extra personal time or breaks at work, and taking longer than necessary to do a job were ethical. Finally, American entrepreneurs were more likely to believe that exaggerating the performance of the company's products or services to customers and unfairly criticizing competitors' products were ethical practices, compared to Canadian entrepreneurs.

Still, overall, the study found very high ethical attitudes for both Canadian and American entrepreneurs, and this is a positive sign given the emergence of our new entrepreneurial society. Importantly, the research does appear to point out that contrary to the negative portrayal of businesspeople in the media, entrepreneurs, at least, appear to exhibit a high level of ethical awareness and ethical concern, with very few exceptions. Thus, given the high ethical attitudes of the entrepreneurs in this study, it does seem possible that the entrepreneur can set an elevated ethical tone for this new entrepreneurial business society. What do you think about the findings of this study? Are you encouraged by the results?

Learning Review

1. What are ethics?
2. What are laws?

UNDERSTANDING ETHICAL MARKETING BEHAVIOUR

Researchers have identified numerous factors that influence ethical marketing behaviour.[9] Figure 4–2 presents a framework that shows these factors and their relationships.

FIGURE 4–2

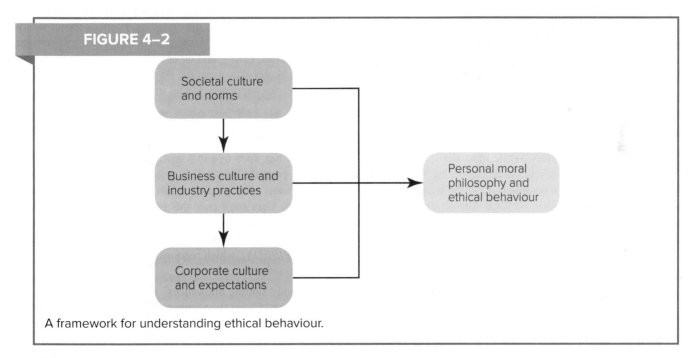

A framework for understanding ethical behaviour.

LO2 Societal Culture and Norms

As described in Chapter 3, culture incorporates the set of values, ideas, and attitudes that are learned and shared among members of a group. Culture also serves as a socializing force that dictates what is morally right and just. This means that moral standards are relative to particular societies. These standards often reflect the laws and regulations that affect social and economic behaviour, which can create moral dilemmas.[10] For example, restraining trade, price fixing, deceiving buyers, or marketing unsafe products are behaviours that are considered morally wrong in Canada. Furthermore, the unauthorized use of intellectual property, such as another's ideas, copyright, trademark, or patent, is also considered both illegal and unethical in Canada.

Outside Canada, however, is another story.[11] Unauthorized use of copyrights, trademarks, and patents is routine in some countries, such as China, Mexico, and Korea, and costs the authorized owners billions of dollars annually. In Korea, for

Desjardins also assists customers who have run into severe financial difficulty and who are often excluded from conventional credit networks. It offers free budget advisory services and "tide-over" loans of up to $500 that can be paid back without interest over 24 months. Small businesses can tap into microcredit, and homeowners can take out green mortgage loans to pay for energy-efficiency retrofits. For customers who purchase fuel-efficient vehicles, such as hybrid-electrics, Desjardins offers discounts of between 10 and 15 percent on auto insurance premiums. It also offers low-cost home insurance to low-income earners. It also offers a line of socially responsible mutual funds that have seen significant growth.

Other aspects of CSR being pursued by the company include the differentials between CEO compensation and average employee pay. Desjardins also links its executive compensation to the achievement of sustainability-related performance targets and growing the proportion of women on its board of directors, which currently stands at nearly 50 percent. According to Chief Executive Officer Monique Leroux, "If you read our mission, it's a very special mission. It's really to contribute to improve the economic and social well-being of people and communities. It's not just a question of making money. And that philosophy—although we are not perfect—is spread throughout our network."

What do you think about Desjardins and its CSR efforts? Would this be the type of company you would like to work for?

Canada is also seeing growth in the form of a new type of business called a social enterprise. A **social enterprise** is an organization that applies business strategies to maximize improvements in human and environmental well-being as well as social impact, rather than profits for external shareholders.

An emerging type of social enterprise is the *benefit corporation* (or B Corp) that is structured to create environmental and social benefits. For example, a Canadian B Corp is Oliberté, a premium leather goods company that sustainably sources its materials from and manufactures in Africa to create pathways out of poverty.

ECOLOGO

PRODUCT CERTIFIED FOR REDUCED ENVIRONMENTAL IMPACT. VIEW SPECIFIC ATTRIBUTES EVALUATED: UL.COM/EL

UL XXXX

for illustrative purposes only

Used by permission of ECOLOGO.

You should be mindful, however, that there are many critics who suggest that some companies simply claim to engage in sustainable marketing and societally responsible practices. One practice that is under scrutiny is green marketing. Some environmentalists, for example, suggest some companies are simply *greenwashers*. **Greenwashing**, a modification of the term whitewashing, is defined as disinformation disseminated by an organization so as to present an environmentally responsible public image. Greenwashing is considered a deceptive marketing practice, but its prevalence is hotly debated. However, most experts agree that it does exist, and therefore, it can be difficult for the consumer to determine which companies are really green and which are not. Some suggest that greenwashing is common in food marketing where claims of environmental friendliness or sustainable agricultural practices can attract consumers to the products being offered. In order to combat greenwashing and to help Canadians make informed choices of genuinely environmentally preferable products and services, the Canadian government developed ECOLOGO, an eco-labelling certification program. ECOLOGO-certified products, services and packaging are certified for reduced environmental impact. ECOLOGO certifications are voluntary, multi-attribute, life-cycle-based environmental certifications that indicate a product has undergone rigorous scientific testing, exhaustive auditing, or both, to prove its compliance with stringent, third-party, environmental performance standards. There are currently over 75 categories under the ECOLOGO program, now part of UL (Underwriters Laboratories), and over 10,000 certified ECOLOGO products and services.[35] You can find the list of participating companies for each product category on UL's website under the sustainable product guide (**www.ul.com/spg**).

Turning the Table: Consumer Ethics and Social Responsibility

Consumers also have an obligation to act ethically and responsibly in the exchange process and in the use and disposition of products. Unfortunately, consumer behaviour is sometimes spotty on both counts.

Unethical practices of consumers are a serious concern to marketers.[36] These practices include filing warranty claims after the claim period; misredeeming coupons; making fraudulent returns of merchandise; providing inaccurate information on credit applications; tampering with utility meters; tapping cable TV lines; illegally downloading music, movies, and software from the Internet; and submitting phony insurance claims. Some consumers routinely redeem coupons for unpurchased products or use coupons destined for other products. And retailers lose billions of dollars yearly from shoplifting.

Consumer purchase, use, and disposition of environmentally sensitive products relate to consumer social responsibility. Research indicates that almost 80 percent of Canadians believe companies should operate in an environmentally responsible way and 70 percent believe there are great benefits to locally sourced goods. But just 12 percent of Canadians say they would pay more for environmentally friendly products! Thus, it seems Canadians might be more concerned about their own personal financial environment situation than the actual ecological environment.[37] Another recent study found that Canadians considered themselves environmentally friendly, engaged in recycling, and were likely to buy pre-owned goods; overall, Canadians ranked 16th out of 17 countries when it came to overall sustainable behaviour.[38]

Many marketers suggest that consumers must become more educated when it comes to environmentally conscious behaviour. As noted earlier, eco-labelling is one way to accomplish this. Additionally, other educational efforts are being implemented. For example, *Corporate Knights* has prepared numerous reports for consumers to inform individuals and encourage green behaviour. These guides include advice on how to choose and use environmentally friendly products, as well as recommended choices in various product categories such as automobiles, appliances, and consumer packaged goods.[39] It is also important for consumers to be proactive and to conduct their own research concerning the credibility of companies that make green or sustainable development claims.

In the end, both marketers and consumers are responsible and accountable for ethical and socially responsible behaviour.

Learning Review

6. What is meant by social responsibility?
7. Marketing efforts to produce, promote, and reclaim environmentally sensitive products are called _____.
8. What is a social audit?

Learning Objectives Review

 Explain the differences between legal and ethical behaviour in marketing.

A good starting point for understanding the nature and significance of ethics is the distinction between legality and ethicality of marketing decisions. Whereas ethics deal with personal moral principles and values, laws are society's values and standards that are enforceable in the courts. This distinction can lead to the rationalization that if a behaviour is within reasonable ethical and legal limits, then it is not really illegal or unethical. Judgment plays a large role in defining ethical and legal boundaries in marketing. Ethical dilemmas arise when acts or situations are not clearly ethical and legal or unethical and illegal.

LO2 **Identify factors that influence ethical and unethical behaviour in marketing.**

Four factors influence ethical marketing behaviour. First, societal culture and norms serve as socializing forces that dictate what is morally right and just. Second, business culture and industry practices affect ethical conduct both in the exchange relationships between buyers and sellers and the competitive behaviour among sellers. Third, corporate culture and expectations are often defined by corporate ethics codes and the ethical behaviour of top management and co-workers. Finally, an individual's personal moral philosophy, such as moral idealism or utilitarianism, will dictate ethical choices. Ultimately, ethical behaviour rests with the individual, but the consequences affect many.

LO3 **Describe the different concepts of social responsibility.**

Social responsibility means that individuals and organizations are part of a larger society and are accountable to that society for their actions. In a corporate behaviour context, social responsibility is called corporate social responsibility (CSR). There are three concepts of social responsibility. First, profit responsibility holds that companies have a simple duty: to maximize profits for their owners or shareholders. Second, stakeholder responsibility focuses on the obligations an organization has to those who can effect the achievement of its objectives. Those constituencies include consumers, employees, suppliers, and distributors. Finally, societal responsibility focuses on obligations that organizations have to the preservation of the ecological environment and the general public, including placing an emphasis on the triple-bottom-line and engaging in green marketing and sustainable development activities. Companies are placing greater emphasis on sustainable marketing as well as other societally responsible activities and are reaping the rewards of positive word of mouth from their consumers and favourable financial performance. However, they must do more to make consumers aware of their corporate social responsibility initiatives.

 Recognize unethical and socially irresponsible consumer behaviour.

Consumers, like marketers, have an obligation to act ethically and responsibly in the exchange process and in the use and disposition of products. Unfortunately, consumer behaviour is sometimes spotty on both counts. Unethical consumer behaviour includes filing warranty claims after the claim period; misredeeming coupons; pirating music, movies, and software from the Internet; and submitting phony insurance claims, among other behaviours. Consumer purchase, use, and disposition of environmentally sensitive products relate to consumer social responsibility. Even though consumers are sensitive to ecological issues, they may be unwilling to sacrifice convictions and pay potentially higher prices to protect the environment, and may lack the knowledge to make informed decisions dealing with the purchase, use, and disposition of products. Greater consumer education about environmentally conscious behaviour is required.

Applying Marketing Knowledge

1. What concepts of moral philosophy and social responsibility are applicable to the practices of ethically and socially responsible Canadian companies described in the introduction to this chapter? Why?

2. Where would the following situations fit in Figure 4–1? (a) Exaggerating the performance of a product to get a sale, and (b) selling a used automobile knowing it had a major mechanical problem and not telling the buyer.

3. A recent survey of Canadian business students asked, "Is calling your office pretending to be sick in order to take the day off ethical or unethical behaviour?" How would you respond to this question?

4. Compare and contrast moral idealism and utilitarianism as alternative personal moral philosophies.

5. How would you evaluate Milton Friedman's view of the social responsibility of a firm?

6. The text lists several unethical practices of consumers. Can you name others? Why do you think consumers engage in unethical conduct?

7. Cause marketing programs have become popular. Describe two such programs that you are familiar with.

Building Your Marketing Plan

Consider these potential stakeholders that may be affected in some way by the marketing plan on which you are working: shareholders (if any), suppliers, employees, customers, and society in general. For each group of stakeholders:

1. Identify what, if any, ethical and social responsibility issues might arise.

2. Describe, in one or two sentences, how your marketing plan addresses each potential issue.

Video Case 4

Toyota: Building Cleaner, Greener Cars

"Toyota's mission is to become the most respected and admired car company in North America," explains Jana Hartline, manager of environmental communications at Toyota. To accomplish this, Jana and her colleagues at Toyota are working toward a future where a wide range of innovative vehicles, fuel technologies, and partnerships converge to create an economically vibrant, mobile society in harmony with the environment. It's a challenge Jana finds exciting, and the result is cleaner, greener cars!

The Company

Kiichiro Toyoda began research on gasoline-powered engines in 1930. By 1935 he had developed passenger car prototypes, and in 1957 he introduced the "Toyopet" in the United States. The Toyopet was not successful and was discontinued. In 1965, however, the Corona was introduced, and it was followed by the Corolla in 1968. The Corolla went on to become the best-selling passenger car in the world, with 27 million purchased in more than 140 countries! The popularity of Toyota's automobiles continued to grow in the United States, and in 1975 it surpassed Volkswagen to become the number one import brand. In 1998 Toyota launched its first full-sized pickup, the Toyota Tundra. Toyota also expanded its product line by adding the Lexus brand, which became known for its exceptional quality and customer service. By 2000,

Lexus was one of the best-selling luxury brands in the United States, competing with both Mercedes-Benz and BMW. Toyota also introduced the Scion brand of moderately priced vehicles for the youth market. The company opened a national sales headquarters in Torrance, California, and also opened manufacturing facilities so it could produce cars in the United States. By 2012 Toyota had the capacity to build 2.2 million cars and trucks and 1.45 million engines in 15 plants across North America. Toyota's sales and distribution organization includes 1,500 Toyota, Lexus, and Scion dealers. Toyota's marketing organization has led to many memorable marketing campaigns. Some of its early taglines included "You Asked For It, You Got It!" and "Oh What a Feeling!" which included the "Toyota Jump." The Lexus tagline, "The Relentless Pursuit of Perfection," is still in use today, while Toyota's ads now exclaim, "Let's Go Places." Today, Toyota is the world's largest automobile manufacturer. The company is ranked the tenth-largest corporation by *Fortune* magazine. The company's core principle is "to contribute to society and the economy by producing high-quality products and services." Its success is often attributed to a business philosophy referred to as "The Toyota Way."

The Toyota Way

The Toyota Way is a business philosophy used to (1) improve processes and products, (2) build trust, and (3) empower individuals and teams. There are two values that act as pillars of the Toyota Way. They are continuous improvement and respect for people. These values are evident in five business practices:

- Challenge: To build a long-term vision and meet challenges with courage and creativity.
- *Kaizen:* To continuously improve business operations, always striving for innovation and evolution.
- *Genchi Genbutsu:* To always go to the source to find the facts and make correct decisions; to build consensus and expeditiously achieve goals.
- Respect: To respect others and the environment, to build trust, and to take responsibility.
- Teamwork: To stimulate personal and professional growth, and maximize individual and team performance.

In fact, according to Jana Hartline, the two values are "integrated into everything that we do on a daily basis," creating "a unique corporate environment." As the company has grown it has also sought a larger role in society. For example, Toyota created the Toyota USA Foundation with a $10 million endowment and a mission to make Toyota a leading corporate citizen. The foundation supports programs focused on the environment, education, and safety that help strengthen communities. Since 1991 Toyota has contributed over $500 million to philanthropic programs in the United States. Combining the Toyota Way with its corporate philanthropy has been very successful. Toyota believes that the foundation of its success involves a constant spirit of challenge and enthusiasm for new ideas. For example, Toyota's environmental vision includes the concept of sustainable mobility.

© Toyota

Environmental Vision and the Prius

To make its environmental vision actionable, Toyota developed a five-year Environmental Action Plan. The plan is structured around five key areas:

- Energy and climate change
- Recycling and resource management
- Air quality
- Environmental management
- Cooperation with society

For each area Toyota creates goals and measurable targets based on a life-cycle view of vehicles: from design, to manufacturing, to sales and distribution, to use, and finally to how the vehicle is recycled at end-of-life. One of its top goals has been to develop advanced vehicle technologies to complement traditional automobile technologies. Ed LaRocque, national manager of vehicle marketing, describes how Toyota started one of these initiatives:

In the early 90s Toyota developed what we called the G21 vision. The goal of the G21 plan was to bring a vehicle to market that represented a great value, and had great environmental benefits, not just in Japan but globally.

The concept was eventually introduced as the Prius, a hybrid vehicle with a gasoline engine and an electric motor combination called the Hybrid Synergy Drive. The car received a U.S. EPA-estimated mileage rating of 50 mpg (4.7 L/100km). Initially the Prius was attractive to very eco-conscious consumers, but it met with some resistance from the press and the general population. The cars were fuel-efficient, but they were not attractive. Since the first introduction, Toyota has made changes and introduced two new generations of the Prius to help it become the world's most-popular hybrid, selling more than three million of the vehicles. Toyota's development of new technologies such as the Hybrid Synergy Drive helped it recognize the implications for the entire mobility system. A strategy for sustainable mobility affects not only new technologies and vehicles, but also new energy sources, new transportation systems, and the many partnerships of involved stakeholders. Advertising for the Prius emphasizes this point, claiming the car provides "Harmony between man, nature, and machine." In the long term, however, this strategy will not be successful if consumers are not aware of or knowledgeable about advanced technologies. To increase awareness and knowledge Toyota specified the development of partnerships as a goal.

Strategic Partnerships

Toyota believes that partnerships with relevant organizations help increase awareness of its technologies and products. These programs are designed to educate people so they can reduce their environmental footprint. One of these programs, for example, is Together Green—a $20 million, five-year alliance with Audubon to fund projects, train leaders, and offer volunteer opportunities. Similarly, Toyota has partnered with the World Wildlife Fund to establish hybrid energy systems, oil recycling programs, and renewable energy outreach campaigns. The exposure from these programs is often much more effective than other communication options. Mary Nickerson, national manager of advanced technology, explains, "We [have] used partnerships with the Lung Association, with the Electric Drive Transportation Association, Environmental Media Association, and the national parks to help touch many more millions of people than we ever could have done with a traditional advertising campaign." Toyota recently announced a grant of $5 million and 25 Toyota vehicles in support of U.S. National Parks. Parks included in this grant and other Toyota partnerships are Yellowstone National Park, Great Smoky Mountains National Park, Everglades National Park, Yosemite National Park, the Grand Canyon, the Santa Monica National Recreation Area, and the Golden Gate Bridge Foundation. The national parks partnership offers an opportunity to enhance the experiences of visitors through education and hybrid vehicle use (park employees use the donated Toyota vehicles to reduce noise and emissions in the parks).

Generally, the goal of the national parks partnership program is to make a personal connection with park visitors about Toyota's hybrid vehicles when they are in a natural setting in which they are receptive to receiving a message about sustainable mobility. The message implies important links:

"Green" Vehicles > Cleaner Air > Preservation of Parks

In addition, Toyota believes that the programs have other benefits, including the following:

- Strengthening Toyota's image as an environmental leader among automakers.
- Communicating a message of environmental stewardship.
- Building awareness of the Prius and other Toyota hybrids.
- Educating park visitors on the benefits of advanced vehicle technology.

Research by Toyota indicates that the program is working. A recent corporate image study indicated that among four leading automakers (Toyota, Honda, Ford, and GM), Toyota was rated highest on dimensions such as "Leader in High MPG," "Leader in Technology Development," "Environmentally Friendly Vehicles," and "Wins Environmental Awards."

The Future

Figure 1 shows the results of a survey of consumer interests and consumer response to the question, "Who should take the lead in addressing environmental issues?" The results suggest that in the future consumers will expect businesses to be proactive about the environment and sustainability.

FIGURE 1

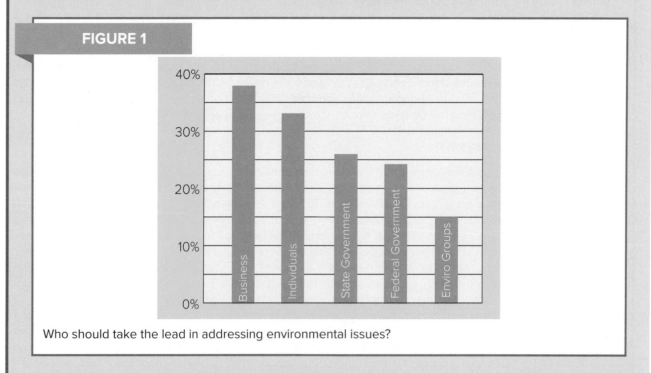

Who should take the lead in addressing environmental issues?

For Toyota, a focus on sustainability will mean considering the environmental, social, and economic consequences of the auto business and continuously working to reduce the negative and increase the positive impacts of its activities and decisions. The increasing importance of sustainability will challenge Toyota to look at these impacts from all stages of the vehicle life cycle. It will also encourage Toyota's managers to consider the opinions of many stakeholders such as consumers, regulators, local communities, and non-governmental organizations. The recent concerns about Toyota vehicle product quality, which led to the recall of 16 million vehicles, have hurt Toyota's reputation. In the future, all activities, including the partnership strategy and the national parks program, will determine if Toyota can become "the most respected car company in the world."[40]

QUESTIONS

1. How does Toyota's approach to social responsibility relate to the three concepts of social responsibility described in the text (profit responsibility, stakeholder responsibility, and societal responsibility)?

2. How does Toyota's view of sustainable mobility contribute to the company's overall mission?

3. Has Toyota's National Parks project been a success? What indicators suggest that the project has had an impact?

4. What future activities would you suggest for Toyota as it strives to improve its reputation?

Case: This case was written by Steven Hartley. Sources: "Global 500: The World's Largest Corporations," *Fortune*, July 23, 2012, p. F-1; "2010 North America Environmental Report," Toyota Motor North America, Inc., p. 1; "Toyota's Mobile Hybrid Tour and The Power of Partnership," Presentation by Mary Nickerson, National Marketing Manager, Toyota Motor sales, U.S.A., Inc.; Toyota website, http://www.toyota.com/sitemap.html, accessed July 6, 2013; "Lexus Seeks to Regain Luxury Crown with New Advertisement," AutoShopper.com, June 28, 2013; Tim Higgins, "Luxury Cars Are Neck and Neck in the U.S.," *Bloomberg Businessweek*, October 18, 2010, p. 26; Lucy Tobin, "Recall Tarnishes Toyota's Reputation," *The Evening Standard*, July 3, 2013, p. 45; and Mark Rechtin, "Toyota Reputation Starts to Recover," *Advertising Age*, January 24, 2011, p. 34.

5 Consumer Behaviour

Learning Objectives

After reading this chapter, you should be able to:

LO1 Describe the stages in the consumer purchase decision process.

LO2 Distinguish among three variations of the consumer purchase decision process: routine, limited, and extended problem solving.

LO3 Identify the major psychological influences on consumer behaviour.

LO4 Identify the major socio-cultural influences on consumer behaviour.

Enlightened Carmakers Know What Custom(h)ers Value

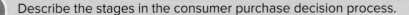

Who makes more than 50 percent of new-car buying decisions? Who influences over 80 percent of new-car buying decisions? Women. Yes, women. Women are a driving force in the Canadian automobile industry. Enlightened carmakers have hired women designers, engineers, and marketing executives to better understand and satisfy this valuable car buyer and influencer. What have they learned? While car price and quality are important, women and men think and feel differently about car features and key elements of the new-car buying decision process and experience.

- *The sense of styling.* Women and men care about styling. For men, styling is more about a car's exterior lines and accents or "curb appeal." Women are more interested in interior design and finishes. Designs that fit their proportions, provide good visibility, offer ample storage space, and make for effortless parking are particularly important.

- *The need for speed.* Both sexes want speed, but for different reasons. Men think about how many seconds it takes to get from zero to 100 kilometres per hour. Women want to feel secure that the car has enough acceleration to outrun an 18-wheeler trying to pass them on a freeway entrance ramp.

- *The substance of safety.* Safety for men is about features that help avoid an accident, such as antilock brakes and responsive steering. For women, safety is about features that help to survive an accident. These features include passenger airbags and reinforced side panels.

- *The shopping experience.* The new-car buying experience differs between men and women in important ways. Generally, men decide up front what car they want and set out alone to find it. By contrast, women approach it as an intelligence-gathering expedition. Referred to as CROPing, women shoppers look for **CR**edible **OP**inions. They actively seek information and postpone a purchase decision until all options have been evaluated. Women, more frequently than men, visit auto-buying websites, read car-comparison articles, and scan car advertisements. Still, recommendations of friends and relatives matter most to women. Women typically shop three dealerships before making a purchase decision—one more than men.

© Blend Images/Getty Images

Carmakers have learned that women, more than men, dislike the car-buying experience—specifically, the experience of dealing with car salespeople. In contrast to many male car buyers, women do not typically revel in the gamesmanship of car buying. "Men get all excited about going out to buy a car and talk about how they're going to one-up the salesman and get a great deal," said Anne Fleming, president of **www.women-drivers.com**, a consumer ratings site. "I've never heard or seen any comments from women like that." In particular, women dread the price negotiations that are often involved in buying a new car. Not surprisingly, about half of women car buyers take a man with them to finalize the terms of sale.[1]

This chapter examines **consumer behaviour**, the actions that a person takes in purchasing and using products and services, including the mental and social processes that precede and follow these actions. This chapter shows how the behavioural sciences help answer such questions as why people choose one product or brand over another, how they make these choices, and how companies use this knowledge to provide value to consumers.

LO1 CONSUMER PURCHASE DECISION PROCESS

Behind the visible act of making a purchase lies an important decision process that must be investigated. The stages that a buyer passes through in making choices about which products and services to buy is the **purchase decision process**. This process has the five stages shown in Figure 5–1: (1) problem recognition, (2) information search, (3) alternative evaluation, (4) purchase decision, and (5) post-purchase behaviour.

Problem Recognition

Problem recognition, the initial step in the purchase decision, is perceiving a difference between a person's ideal and actual situations that is big enough to trigger a decision.[2] This can be as simple as finding an empty milk carton in the refrigerator; noting, as a first-year university student, that your high school clothes are not in the style that other students are wearing; or realizing that your notebook computer may not be working properly.

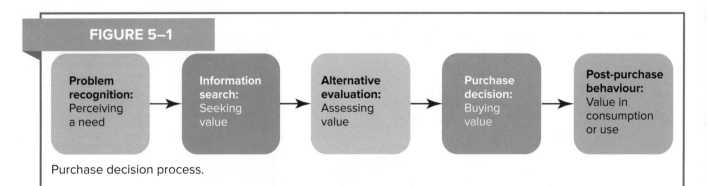

FIGURE 5–1

| Problem recognition: Perceiving a need | → | Information search: Seeking value | → | Alternative evaluation: Assessing value | → | Purchase decision: Buying value | → | Post-purchase behaviour: Value in consumption or use |

Purchase decision process.

In marketing, advertisements or salespeople can activate a consumer's decision process by showing the shortcomings of competing (or currently owned) products. For instance, an advertisement for a new generation smartphone could stimulate problem recognition because it emphasizes "maximum use from one device."

Information Search

After recognizing a problem, a consumer begins to search for information, the next stage in the purchase decision process. First, you may scan your memory for previous experiences with products or brands.[3] This action is called *internal search.* For frequently purchased products, such as shampoo and conditioner, this may be enough. Or a consumer may undertake an *external search* for information.[4] This is especially needed when past experience or knowledge is insufficient, the risk of making a wrong purchase decision is high, and the cost of gathering information is low. The primary sources of external information are (1) *personal sources,* such as relatives and friends whom the consumer trusts; (2) *public sources,* including various product-rating organizations, such as *Consumer Reports,* government agencies, and TV "consumer programs"; and (3) *marketer-dominated sources,* such as information from sellers that includes advertising, company websites, salespeople, and point-of-purchase displays in stores.

Suppose you are considering buying a new smartphone. You will probably tap several information sources: friends and relatives, smartphone advertisements, brand and company websites, and stores carrying these phones (for demonstrations). You might also study a comparable evaluation of various smartphones as found in *Consumer Reports,* found either in hard copy or online. In fact, online information search has become very popular, with recent research indicating that 65 percent of Canadians research products online.[5] Also, as you have already learned from previous chapters, more and more often, consumers are relying on social media for information on products, services, and brands, and paying very close attention to what others are saying about various brands on these social media sites.

Alternative Evaluation

The information search stage clarifies the problem for the consumer by (1) yielding brand names, (2) suggesting criteria to use to judge the various brands, and (3) developing consumer value perceptions. The brands that you become aware of during your search become part of your *awareness set.* The criteria you consider when evaluating smartphones are called **evaluative criteria**—factors that represent both the objective attributes of a brand (such as display screen) and the subjective ones (such as brand prestige) you use to compare different products and brands.[6] Only the brands that meet your criteria become part of your evoked set, or **consideration set**—the group of brands that a consumer would consider acceptable from among all the brands of which he or she is aware.[7] For example, your consideration set might consist of Apple iPhone, LG, Samsung, and HTC.

Consumers often have several criteria for evaluating brands. Knowing this, companies seek to identify the most important evaluative criteria that consumers use when judging brands and often display these criteria in advertisements. The goal is to create in the consumer's mind the best brand or best value for the money sought by him or her and other consumers. For example, if you were buying a new smartphone, your selection criteria might consist of price, display screen quality, speed of web browsing, ease of use, or some combination of these and other criteria. Companies developing smartphones would have to demonstrate to you that their brands meet your criteria and do so better than do the competitors.

Purchase Decision

Having examined the alternatives in the consideration set, you are almost ready to make a purchase decision. Two choices remain: (1) from whom to buy and (2) when to buy. For a product like a smartphone, the information search process probably involves visiting retail stores, seeing different brands in catalogues, and viewing a smartphone on a seller's website. The choice of which seller to buy from will depend on such considerations as the terms of sale, past experience buying from the seller, and the return policy. Often, a purchase decision involves a simultaneous evaluation of both product attributes and seller characteristics. For example, you might choose the second-most preferred brand of smartphone at a store with a liberal refund and return policy versus the most preferred brand at a store with more conservative policies. More and more often, Canadians are actually using their smartphones in-store to look up information—including product reviews—and this is influencing on the spot whether to make the purchase then and there or to keep looking.

Deciding when to buy is frequently determined by a number of factors. For instance, you might buy sooner if one of your preferred brands is on sale or its manufacturer offers a rebate. Other factors, such as the store atmosphere, pleasantness of the shopping experience, salesperson persuasiveness, time pressure, and financial circumstances, could also affect whether a purchase decision is made or postponed.[8]

Post-purchase Behaviour

After buying a product, the consumer compares it with his or her expectations and is either satisfied or dissatisfied. If the consumer is dissatisfied, marketers must decide whether the product was deficient or consumer expectations were too high. Product deficiency may require a design change; if expectations are too high, perhaps the company's advertising or the salesperson oversold the product's features and benefits.

Sensitivity to a customer's consumption or use experience is extremely important in a consumer's value perception. For example, research indicates that satisfaction or dissatisfaction does affect consumer value perceptions.[9]

A satisfactory or unsatisfactory consumption or use experience is an important factor in post-purchase behaviour. Marketer attention to this stage can pay huge dividends, as described in the text.

Furthermore, studies show that satisfaction or dissatisfaction affects consumer communications and repeat-purchase behaviour. Satisfied buyers tell three other people about their experiences. Dissatisfied buyers complain to nine people.[10] Satisfied buyers also tend to buy from the same seller each time a purchase occasion arises. The financial impact of repeat-purchase behaviour is significant.[11] Accordingly, such firms as General Electric (GE), Johnson & Johnson, Coca-Cola, and British Airways focus attention on post-purchase behaviour to maximize customer satisfaction and retention. These firms, among many others, provide toll-free telephone numbers, offer liberalized return and refund policies, and engage in staff training to handle complaints, answer questions, and record suggestions. Many forward-thinking firms are also monitoring what is being said about their brands on social media sites in order to gauge customer satisfaction.

Often, a consumer is faced with two or more highly attractive alternatives, such as an Apple iPhone or a Samsung smartphone. If you choose the iPhone, you may think, "Should I have purchased the Samsung?" This feeling of post-purchase psychological tension or anxiety is called **cognitive dissonance**. To alleviate it, consumers often attempt to applaud themselves for making the right choice. So, after your purchase, you may seek information to confirm your choice by asking friends such questions as, "Don't you like my new iPhone?" or by reading ads of the brand you chose. You might even look for negative features about the brand you did not buy and decide that that brand was not right for you. Firms often use ads or follow-up calls from salespeople in this post-purchase stage to assure buyers that they made the right decision. For many years, Buick ran an advertising campaign with the message, "Aren't you really glad you bought a Buick?"

LO2 Involvement and Problem-Solving Variations

Sometimes, consumers do not engage in the five-stage purchase decision process. Instead, they skip or minimize one or more stages, depending on the level of **involvement**, the personal, social, and economic significance of the purchase to the consumer.[12] High-involvement purchase occasions typically have at least one of three characteristics: The item to be purchased (1) is expensive, (2) can have serious personal consequences, or (3) could reflect on one's social image. For these occasions, consumers engage in extensive information search, consider many product attributes and brands, form attitudes, and participate in word-of-mouth communication. Low-involvement purchases, such as toothpaste and soap, are barely involving to most of us, but audio and video systems and automobiles are very involving. There are three general variations in the consumer purchase decision process based on consumer involvement and product knowledge. Figure 5–2 shows some of the important differences between the three problem-solving variations.[13]

FIGURE 5–2

CHARACTERISTICS OF THE CONSUMER PURCHASE DECISION PROCESS	HIGH ◄ CONSUMER INVOLVEMENT ► LOW		
	EXTENDED PROBLEM SOLVING	LIMITED PROBLEM SOLVING	ROUTINE PROBLEM SOLVING
Number of brands examined	Many	Several	One
Number of sellers considered	Many	Several	Few
Number of product attributes evaluated	Many	Moderate	One
Number of external information sources used	Many	Few	None
Time spent searching	Considerable	Little	Minimal

Comparison of problem-solving variations.

Extended Problem Solving

In extended problem solving, each of the five stages of the consumer purchase decision process is used in the purchase, including considerable time and effort on external information search and in identifying and evaluating alternatives. Several brands are in the consideration set, and these brands are evaluated on many attributes. Extended problem solving exists in high-involvement purchase situations for such items as automobiles and elaborate audio systems.

Limited Problem Solving

In limited problem solving, consumers typically seek some information or rely on a friend to help them evaluate alternatives. In general, several brands might be evaluated using a moderate number of different criteria. You might use limited problem solving in choosing a toaster, a restaurant for lunch, and other purchase situations in which you have little time or effort to spend.

Routine Problem Solving

For such products as table salt and milk, consumers recognize a problem, make a decision, and spend little effort seeking external information and evaluating alternatives. The purchase process for such items is virtually a habit and typifies low-involvement decision making. Routine problem solving is typically the case for low-priced, frequently purchased products.

Involvement and Marketing Strategy

Low and high consumer involvement has important implications for marketing strategy. If a company markets a low-involvement product and its brand is a market leader, attention is placed on (1) maintaining product quality, (2) avoiding stock-out situations so that buyers do not substitute a competing brand, and (3) advertising messages that reinforce a consumer's knowledge or assure buyers they made the right choice. Market challengers have a different task. They must break buying habits and use free samples, coupons, and rebates to encourage trial of their brand. Advertising messages will focus on getting their brand into a consumer's consideration set. For example, Campbell's V8 vegetable juice advertising message—"I could have had a V8!"—is targeted at consumers who routinely purchase fruit juices and soft drinks. Challengers can also link their brand attributes with high-involvement issues. For example, Post Cereal does this by linking consumption of its whole grain cereal with improved heart health and protection against major diseases.

Marketers of high-involvement products know that their consumers constantly seek process information about objective and subjective brand attributes, form evaluative criteria, rate product attributes of various brands, and combine these ratings for an overall brand evaluation—like that described in the smartphone purchase decision. Market leaders supply consumers with product information through advertising and personal selling and use social media to create online experiences for their company and/or brand. Market challengers capitalize on this behaviour through comparative advertising that focuses on existing product attributes and often introduce novel evaluative criteria for judging competing brands. Challengers also benefit from Internet search engines such as Google and Bing that assist buyers of high-involvement products.

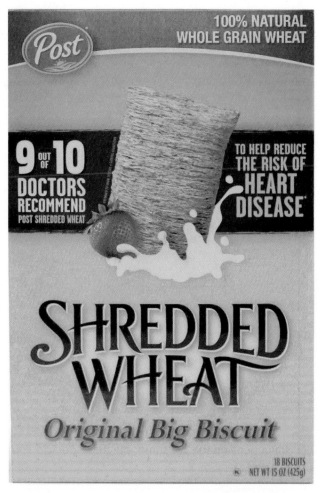

What does this ad for Post Cereal have to do with consumer involvement? Read the text to find out.

Situational Influences

Often the purchase situation will affect the purchase decision process. Five **situational influences** have an impact on your purchase decision process: (1) the purchase task, (2) social surroundings, (3) physical surroundings, (4) temporal effects, and (5) antecedent states.[14] The purchase task is the reason for engaging in the decision in the first place. Information searching and evaluating alternatives may differ, depending on whether the purchase is a gift, which often involves social visibility, or for the buyer's own use. Social surroundings, including the other people present when a purchase decision is made, may also affect what is purchased. Physical surroundings, such as decor, music, and crowding in retail stores, may alter how purchase decisions are made. Temporal effects, such as time of day or the amount of time available, will influence where consumers have breakfast and lunch and what is ordered. Finally, antecedent states, which include the consumer's mood or the amount of cash on hand, can influence purchase behaviour and choice. For example, consumers with credit cards purchase more than those with cash!

Figure 5–3 shows the many influences that affect the consumer purchase decision process. The decision to buy a product also involves important psychological and socio-cultural influences, the two important topics discussed in the remainder of this chapter. Marketing mix influences are described in Chapters 10 through 18.

FIGURE 5–3

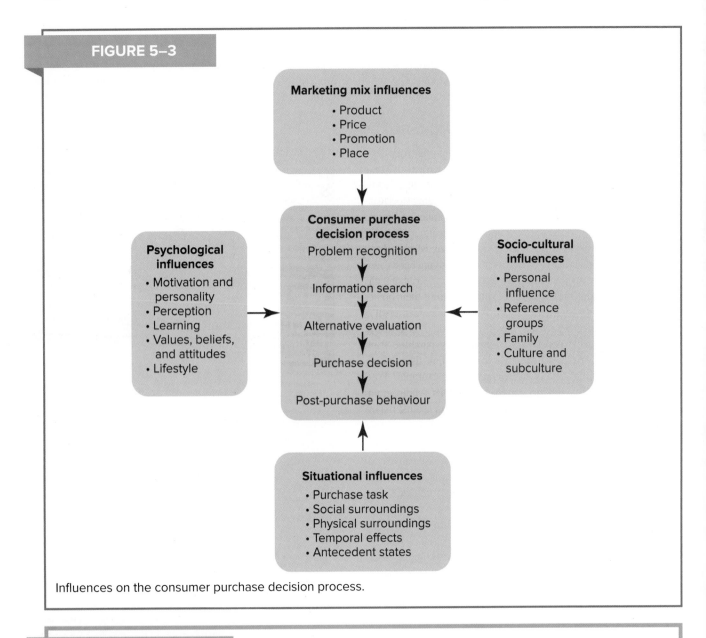

Influences on the consumer purchase decision process.

Learning Review

1. What is the first stage in the consumer purchase decision process?
2. The brands that a consumer considers buying out of the set of brands in a product class of which the consumer is aware is called the _____.
3. What is the term for post-purchase anxiety?

PSYCHOLOGICAL INFLUENCES ON CONSUMER BEHAVIOUR

Psychology helps marketers understand why and how consumers behave as they do. In particular, such concepts as motivation and personality; perception; learning; values, beliefs, and attitudes; and lifestyle are useful for interpreting buying processes and directing marketing efforts.

Motivation and Personality

Motivation and personality are two familiar psychological concepts that have specific meanings and marketing implications. They are both used frequently to describe why people do some things and not others.

Motivation

Motivation is the energizing force that causes behaviour that satisfies a need. Because consumer needs are the focus of the marketing concept, marketers try to arouse these needs.

An individual's needs are boundless. People possess physiological needs for such basics as water, sex, and food. They also have learned needs, including esteem, achievement, and affection. Psychologists point out that these needs are hierarchical; that is, once physiological needs are met, people seek to satisfy their learned needs. Figure 5–4 shows one need hierarchy and classification scheme that contains five need classes.[15] *Physiological needs* are basic to survival and must be satisfied first. A Burger King advertisement featuring a juicy hamburger attempts to activate the need for food. *Safety needs* involve self-preservation and physical well-being. Smoke detector and burglar alarm manufacturers focus on these needs. *Social needs* are concerned with love and friendship. Dating services and fragrance companies try to arouse these needs. *Personal needs* are represented by the need for achievement, status, prestige, and self-respect. The American Express Gold Card and Harry Rosen men's wear appeal to these needs. Sometimes, firms try to arouse multiple needs to stimulate problem recognition. For example, Michelin combines security with parental love to promote tire replacement. *Self-actualization needs* involve personal fulfillment, such as completing your degree.

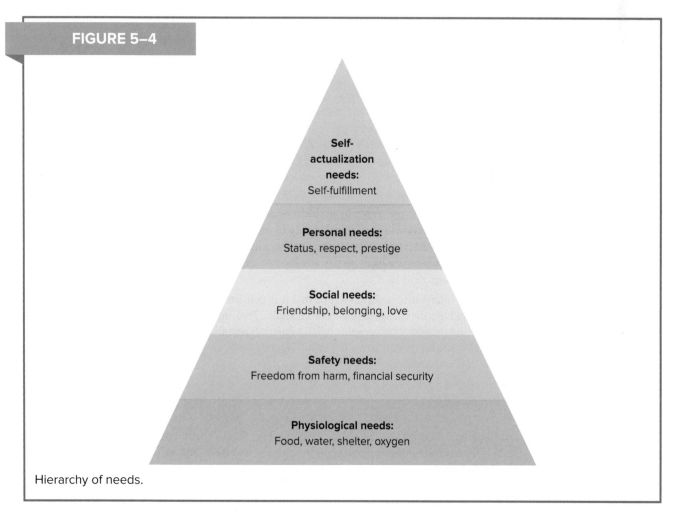

FIGURE 5–4

Hierarchy of needs.

Personality

Personality refers to a person's consistent behaviours or responses to recurring situations. Although numerous personality theories exist, most identify key traits—enduring characteristics within a person or in his or her relationships with others. Such traits include assertiveness, extroversion, compliance, dominance, and aggression, among others. Research suggests that compliant people prefer known brand names and use more mouthwash and toilet soaps. In contrast, aggressive types use razors, not electric shavers, apply more cologne and after-shave lotions, and purchase signature goods, such as Birks' jewellery in its famous blue box, or clothing and accessories from Gucci, Yves St. Laurent, and Donna Karan, all as indicators of status.[16] Cross-cultural analysis also suggests that residents of different countries have a **national character**, or a distinct set of personality characteristics common among people of a country or society.[17] For example, Canadians are more deliberate and cautious about purchasing anything without examining it.

These personality characteristics are often revealed in a person's **self-concept**, which is the way people see themselves and the way they believe others see them. Marketers recognize that people have an actual self-concept and an ideal self-concept. The *actual self* refers to how people actually see themselves. The *ideal self* describes how people would like to see themselves. These two self "images" are reflected in the products and brands a person buys, including automobiles, home appliances and furnishings, magazines, clothing, grooming products, and leisure products, and, frequently, in the stores a person shops. The importance of self-concept is summed up by a senior executive at Lenovo, a global supplier of notebook computers: "The notebook market is getting more like cars. The car you drive reflects you, and notebooks are becoming a form of self-expression as well."[18]

Perception

One person sees a Cadillac as a mark of achievement; another sees it as ostentatious. This is the result of **perception**—the process by which an individual selects, organizes, and interprets information to create a meaningful picture of the world.

Selective Perception

Because the average consumer operates in a complex environment, the human brain attempts to organize and interpret information through a filtering process called *selective perception*. The four stages of selective perception are selective exposure, selective attention, selective comprehension, and selective retention. First, consumers are not exposed to all information or messages in the marketplace. In other words, there is *selective exposure*. For example, you may watch CTV, but not CBC television. In doing so, you do not expose yourself to any information broadcast on the CBC network. Because of selective exposure, marketers must work to determine where consumers are most likely to be exposed to information.

But even if a consumer is exposed to a message, either by accident or design, the consumer may not attend to that message. In general, with *selective attention,* consumers will pay attention only to messages that are consistent with their attitudes and beliefs and will ignore those that are inconsistent. Consumers are also more likely to attend to messages when they are relevant or of interest to them. For example, consumers are likely to pay attention to an ad about a product they just bought or to an ad for a product they are interested in buying.

Selective comprehension involves interpreting information so that it is consistent with one's attitudes and beliefs. A marketer's failure to understand this can have disastrous results. For example, Toro introduced a small, lightweight snowblower called the Snow Pup. Even though the product worked, sales failed to meet expectations. Why? Toro later found out that consumers perceived the name to mean that Snow Pup was a toy or too light to do any serious snow removal. When the product was renamed Snow Master, sales increased sharply.[19]

Selective retention means that consumers do not remember all the information they see, read, or hear, even minutes after exposure to it. This affects the internal and external information search stage of the purchase decision process. This is why furniture and automobile retailers often give consumers product brochures to take home after they leave the showroom.

Because perception plays such an important role in consumer behaviour, it is not surprising that the topic of subliminal perception is a popular item for discussion. **Subliminal perception** means that you see or hear messages without being aware of them. The presence and effect of subliminal perception on behaviour is a hotly debated issue, with more popular appeal than scientific support. Indeed, evidence suggests that such messages have limited effects on behaviour.[20] If these messages did influence behaviour, would their use be an ethical practice? (See the accompanying Making Responsible Decisions box, "The Ethics of Subliminal Messages.")[21]

MAKING RESPONSIBLE DECISIONS

The Ethics of Subliminal Messages

For almost 50 years, the topic of subliminal perception and the presence of subliminal messages embedded in commercial communications has sparked debate. To some, the concept of subliminal messages is a hoax. To others, the possibility of people being influenced without their knowledge is either an exciting or a frightening concept. Many experts suggest that the use of subliminal messages by marketers, effective or not, is deceptive and unethical.

But there are marketers who occasionally pursue opportunities to create these messages. For example, a book by August Bullock, *The Secret Sales Pitch: An Overview of Subliminal Advertising,* is devoted to this topic. Bullock identifies images and advertisements that he claims contain subliminal messages, and describes techniques that can be used for conveying these messages.

Do you believe that attempts to implant subliminal messages in electronic and print media are a deceptive practice and unethical, regardless of their intent?

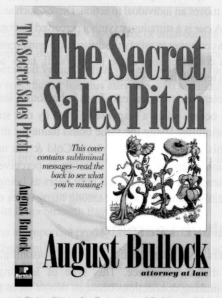

The Secret Sales Pitch: An Overview of Subliminal Advertising.

Perceived Risk

Perception plays a major role in the perceived risk in purchasing a product or service. **Perceived risk** represents the anxieties felt because the consumer cannot anticipate the outcomes of a purchase but believes that there may be negative consequences. Examples of possible negative consequences are the size of the financial outlay required to buy the product (Can I afford $200 for those skis?), the risk of physical harm (Is bungee jumping safe?), and the performance of the product (Will the hair colouring work?). A more abstract form is psychosocial (What will my friends say if I wear that sweater?). Perceived risk affects information search because the greater the perceived risk, the more extensive the external search phase is likely to be.

Recognizing the importance of perceived risk, companies develop strategies to reduce the consumer's risk and encourage purchases. These strategies and examples of firms using them include the following:

- *Obtaining seals of approval.* Canadian Standards Association (CSA) seal or the Good Housekeeping seal for Fresh Step Crystals cat litter.
- *Securing endorsements from influential people.* Athletes promoting milk consumption.
- *Providing free trials of the product.* Sample packages of General Mills Cheerios Snack Mix or Mary Kay's Velocity fragrance.
- *Giving extensive usage instructions.* Clairol Haircolouring.
- *Providing warranties and guarantees.* Kia Motors' 5-year, 100,000-kilometre warranty.

Learning

Much consumer behaviour is learned. Consumers learn which sources to use for information about products and services, which evaluative criteria to use when assessing alternatives, and, more generally, how to make purchase decisions. **Learning** refers to those behaviours that result from (1) repeated experience, and (2) thinking.

FIGURE 5–5

Working-class old and young industrial towns and cities

Located in industrial towns and cities across southern Ontario, Lunch at Tim's consists of high school–educated, blue-collar workers living in older homes and small apartment buildings. They're the kind of tight-knit communities where residents like to socialize at local eateries. Few clusters rank higher in the popularity of pizza parlours, Chinese restaurants, and doughnut shops. Residents also like to wind down after work by watching TV, playing video games, and going snowboarding. They'll occasionally splurge on a visit to a casino, but these working-class folks are more concerned about hanging on to their paycheques than gambling them away. As they put it: "I am willing to work at a boring job as long as the pay is good."

63

Lunch at Tim's

U6 Urban Downscale

Average household income $67,248

About 3 percent of total Canadian households

Example of PRIZM5 Psychographic Segments

MARKETING MATTERS

Understanding a Canadian Lifestyle Segment from PRIZM5—Lunch at Tim's

PRIZM5 is a home-grown Canadian lifestyle system that classifies Canadian neighbourhoods into 68 lifestyle types. One lifestyle segment is called "Lunch at Tim's." Lunch at Tim's consists of singles and solo-parent families living in older single-detached homes, semis, and duplexes in dense, industrial neighbourhoods scattered across second-tier Canadian cities. This segment accounts for a little over 3 percent of total Canadian households. They're the kind of tight-knit communities where residents enjoy socializing at local eateries like Tim Hortons—as well as coffee shops, burger joints, delis, and fish-and-chips restaurants. Lunch at Tim's has above-average rates for residents who are single, divorced, separated, or widowed; half of the adults in these neighbourhoods are unattached. Despite relatively low education levels and downscale incomes, more than two-thirds of households own their homes—most of which were built before 1980. Residents enjoy quieter pastimes, and have high rates for knitting, fishing, and going to the movies. When the mood strikes, they might play a friendly game of football or splurge on tickets to a country music concert or a craft or bridal show. They like to gamble with regular excursions to casinos and the closer-to-home thrill of buying lottery tickets.

In the marketplace, members of Lunch at Tim's are big bargain hunters. They shop for bargains at Walmart and Payless Shoe Source, and they note that while price is important, they have their favourite brands and like to look their best. Given their wide range of ages, they're interested in varied media. They like to watch sports on TV, including CFL games and auto races. They tune in to rock music and new country on the radio. And they pick up magazines like *Maclean's*, *Canadian Geographic*, and *Canadian Health and Lifestyle*. Without deep pockets, they spend a fair amount of time at home with digital media, going online to play games, listening to music, participating in online forums, and checking out dating websites. Many express a need to escape, which typically means a domestic vacation or a stay in a campground or RV park.

The residents of Lunch at Tim's express difficulty trying to adapt to the fast-paced change of modern life (aversion to complexity). And with their very low enthusiasm for technology, don't expect them to turn to their smartphones—if they even have one—to help them navigate the complex world. Scoring high on fatalism and anomie/aimlessness, they feel that their lives are out of control and detached from the world, despite exhibiting a remarkable personal optimism for their future. As consumers, these Canadians are a tough sell, expressing a skepticism of advertising. But they will open their wallets if they see that one-of-a-kind product (buying on impulse).

How could marketers use this information to better market to this Lunch at Tim's group?

Learning Review

4. The problem with the Toro Snow Pup was an example of selective _____.
5. What three attitude-change approaches are most common?
6. What does lifestyle mean?

SOCIO-CULTURAL INFLUENCES ON CONSUMER BEHAVIOUR

Socio-cultural influences, which evolve from a consumer's formal and informal relationships with other people, also exert a significant impact on consumer behaviour. These involve personal influence, reference groups, family, social class, culture, and subculture.

Personal Influence

A consumer's purchases are often influenced by the views, opinions, or behaviours of others. Two aspects of personal influence are important to marketing: opinion leadership and word-of-mouth activity.

Opinion Leadership

Individuals who exert direct or indirect social influence over others are called **opinion leaders**. Opinion leaders are considered to be knowledgeable about users of particular products and services, and so their opinions influence others' choices. Opinion leadership is widespread in the purchase of cars and trucks, clothing and accessories, club membership, consumer electronics, vacation locations, and financial investments.

About 10 percent of adults are considered opinion leaders.[26] Identifying, reaching, and influencing opinion leaders is a major challenge for companies. Some firms use sports figures or celebrities as spokespersons to represent their products; for example, Sidney Crosby endorses Reebok, Gatorade, and Dempster's Bread. Others promote their products in those media believed to reach opinion leaders. Still others use more direct approaches, such as actually inviting people deemed opinion leaders to try their products and services or providing such products and services for free to the opinion leaders in the hope that they will influence others to purchase.

Word of Mouth

The influencing of people during conversations is called **word of mouth**. Word of mouth is the most powerful and authentic information source for consumers because it typically involves family and friends viewed as trustworthy. Canadian research illustrates this well with two-thirds of Canadians stating that recommendations from family and friends have the greatest influence on them when they go shopping.[27] For services, word of mouth plays an even stronger role, with 70 percent of Canadians saying that they used word of mouth when selecting a bank, and 95 percent relied on word of mouth when choosing a physician.[28]

The power of personal influence has prompted firms to promote positive word of mouth and to retard negative word of mouth. For instance, "teaser" advertising campaigns are run in advance of new-product introductions to stimulate conversations. Other techniques, such as advertising slogans, music, and humour, also heighten positive word of mouth. Many commercials shown during the Grey Cup or Super Bowl games, for instance, are created expressly to initiate conversations about the advertisements and featured product or service the next day.

Increasingly, companies are working hard to stimulate positive consumer word of mouth about their products or services. This is called **buzz marketing**—popularity created by consumer word of mouth. The use of buzz marketing is becoming increasingly popular with Canadian marketers. In fact, according to the Canadian Marketing Association, buzz marketing is now closely linked to business and brand growth.[29]

The online version of word of mouth is often called **viral marketing**, which involves the use of messages "infectious" enough that consumers wish to pass them along to others through online communications. This includes forums, social networks, chat rooms, bulletin boards, blogs, message board threads, instant messages, and e-mails. Many Canadian marketers actively encourage viral marketing and/or also generate marketer-initiated messages designed to go "viral." This might include compelling website content that consumers will want to share with others. And, of course, marketers are monitoring what is going viral to order to determine who is saying what and to whom. One trend that seems to be emerging is online product reviews being written by ethnic Canadians. In fact, recent immigrants to Canada are the most likely to create viral buzz online about their purchases. For example, Asian Canadians tend to be the first to trumpet or trash a new product by writing online reviews.

On the other hand, rumours about Kmart (snake eggs in clothing), McDonald's (worms in hamburgers), Corona Extra beer (contaminated beer), and Snickers candy bars in Russia (a cause of diabetes) have resulted in negative word of mouth, none of which was based on fact. Overcoming or neutralizing negative word of mouth, especially electronic or Internet-based word of mouth, is difficult and costly. Marketers have found that supplying factual information, providing toll-free numbers for consumers to call the company, giving appropriate product demonstrations, and monitoring and responding to word-of-mouth activity on the Internet have proven helpful.

Reference Groups

Reference groups are people to whom an individual looks as a basis for self-appraisal or as a source of personal standards. Reference groups affect consumer purchases because they influence the information, attitudes, and aspiration levels that help set a consumer's standards. For example, one of the first questions one asks others when planning to attend a social occasion is, "What are you going to wear?" Reference groups have an important influence on the purchase of luxury products but not of necessities—reference groups exert a strong influence on the brand chosen when its use or consumption is highly visible to others.

Consumers have many reference groups, but three groups have clear marketing implications. A *membership group* is one to which a person actually belongs, including fraternities and sororities, social clubs, and the family. Such groups are easily identifiable and are targeted by firms selling insurance, insignia products, and charter vacations.

Associative reference groups can also form around a brand, as is the case with clubs like the HOG (Harley Owners Group), which is made up of Harley-Davidson fans. A **brand community** is a specialized group of consumers with a structured set of relationships involving a particular brand, fellow customers of that brand, and the product in use. A consumer who is a member of a brand community thinks about brand names (e.g., Harley-Davidson), the product category (e.g., motorcycles), other customers who use the brand (e.g., HOG members), and the marketer that makes and promotes the brand.

An *aspiration group* is one that a person wishes to be a member of or wishes to be identified with, such as a professional society. Firms frequently rely on spokespeople or settings associated with their target market's aspiration group in their advertising. A *dissociative group* is one that a person wishes to maintain a distance from because of differences in values or behaviours.

Family Influence

Family influences on consumer behaviour result from three sources: consumer socialization, passage through the family life cycle, and decision making within the family or household.

Consumer Socialization

The process by which people acquire the skills, knowledge, and attitudes necessary to function as consumers is **consumer socialization**.[30] Children learn how to purchase (1) by interacting with adults in purchase situations, and (2) through their own purchasing and product usage experiences. Research shows that children evidence brand preferences at age two, and these preferences often last a lifetime.[31] As discussed in Chapter 1, this leads many companies to target children at a very young age in the hopes of developing customers for life.

Family Life Cycle

Consumers act and purchase differently as they go through life. The **family life cycle** concept describes the distinct phases that a family progresses through, from formation to retirement, each phase bringing with it identifiable purchasing behaviours.[32] Figure 5–6 illustrates the traditional progression as well as contemporary variations of the family life cycle. Today, the traditional family—married couples with children younger than 18 years—constitutes less than one-third of all households. The remaining households include single parents; unmarried couples; divorced, never-married, or widowed individuals; and older married couples whose children no longer live at home.

Young singles' buying preferences are for non-durable items, including prepared foods, clothing, personal care products, and entertainment. They represent a target market for recreational travel, automobile, and consumer electronics firms. Young married couples without children are typically more affluent than young singles because usually both spouses are employed. These couples exhibit preferences for furniture, housewares, and gift items for each other. Young marrieds with children are driven by the needs of their children. They make up a sizable market for life insurance, various children's products, and home furnishings. Single parents with children are the least financially secure of households with children. Their buying preferences are affected by a limited economic status and tend toward convenience foods, child care services, and personal care items.

FIGURE 5–6

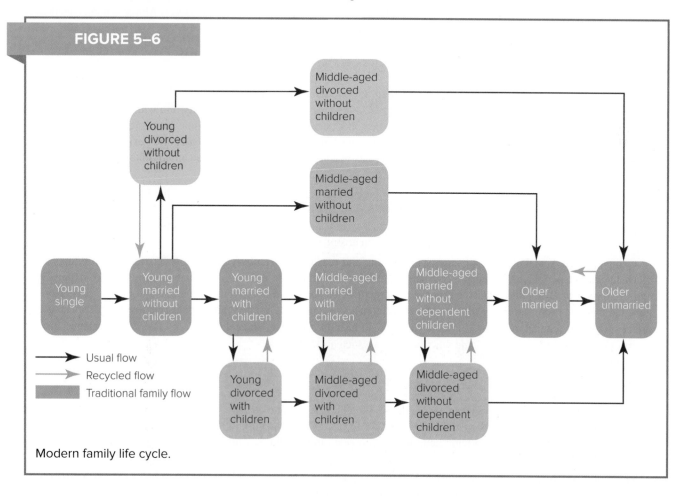

Modern family life cycle.

Middle-aged married couples with children are typically better off financially than their younger counterparts. They are a significant market for leisure products and home improvement items. Middle-aged couples without children typically have a large amount of discretionary income. These couples buy better home furnishings, status automobiles, and financial services. Persons in the last two phases—older married and older unmarried—make up a sizable market for prescription drugs, medical services, vacation trips, and gifts for younger relatives.

Family Decision Making

A third influence in the decision-making process occurs within the family.[33] Two decision-making styles exist: spouse-dominant and joint decision making. With a joint decision-making style, most decisions are made by both husband and wife. Spouse-dominant decisions are those for which either the husband or the wife is responsible. Research indicates that wives tend to have the most say when purchasing groceries, children's toys, clothing, and medicines. Husbands tend to be more influential in home and car maintenance purchases. Joint decision making is common for cars, vacations, houses, home appliances and electronics, and medical care. As a rule, joint decision making increases with the education of the spouses.

Roles of individual family members in the purchase process are another element of family decision making. Five roles exist: (1) information gatherer, (2) influencer, (3) decision maker, (4) purchaser, and (5) user. Family members assume different roles for different products and services. This knowledge is important to firms. For example, many wives either influence or make outright purchases of men's clothing. Knowing this, Haggar Clothing, a men's wear marketer, advertises in women's magazines, such as *Vanity Fair* and *Redbook*. Even though women are often the grocery decision maker, they are not necessarily the purchaser. More than 40 percent of all food-shopping dollars are spent by male customers. Increasingly, preteens and teenagers are the information gatherers, influencers, decision makers, and purchasers of products and services for the family, given the prevalence of working parents and single-parent households. Children under 12 directly influence billions of dollars in annual family purchases. Teenagers also influence billions of dollars in annual family purchases and spend millions of dollars of their own money annually. These figures help explain why, for example, Nabisco, Johnson & Johnson, Apple, Kellogg, P&G, Sony, and Oscar Mayer, among countless other companies, spend close to billions annually in media that reach preteens and teens.

Social Class

A more subtle influence on consumer behaviour than direct contact with others is the social class to which people belong. **Social class** may be defined as the relatively permanent, homogeneous divisions in a society into which people sharing similar values, interests, and behaviour can be grouped. A person's occupation, source of income (not level of income), and education determine his or her social class. Generally speaking, three major social class categories exist—upper, middle, and lower—with subcategories within each. This structure has been observed in Canada, the United States, the United Kingdom, Western Europe, and Latin America.[34]

To some degree, persons within social classes exhibit common attitudes, lifestyles, and buying behaviours. Compared with the middle classes, people in the lower classes have a more short-term time orientation, are more emotional than rational in their reasoning, think in concrete rather than abstract terms, and see fewer personal opportunities. Members of the upper classes focus on achievements and the future and think in abstract or symbolic terms.

Companies use social class as a basis for identifying and reaching particularly good prospects for their products and services. In general, people in the upper classes are targeted by companies for such items as financial investments, expensive cars, and evening wear. The middle classes represent a target market for home improvement centres, automobile parts stores, and personal hygiene products. Firms also recognize differences in media preferences among classes: lower and working classes prefer sports and scandal magazines; middle classes read fashion, romance, and celebrity (e.g., *People*) magazines; and upper classes tend to read literary, travel, and news magazines, such as *Maclean's*.

Culture and Subculture

As described in Chapter 3, culture incorporates the set of values, ideas, and attitudes that are learned and shared among members of a group. This we often refer to as, say, Canadian culture, American culture, British culture, or Japanese culture. (Cultural underpinnings of Canadian buying patterns are described in Chapter 3, while Chapter 7 explores the role of culture in global marketing.)

Subgroups within the larger, or national, culture with unique values, ideas, and attitudes are referred to as **subcultures**. Subcultures can be identified by age (e.g., baby boomers versus Generation X), geography (e.g., Western Canadian versus Atlantic Canadian), and ethnicity. Here, we focus on ethnic subcultures.

An *ethnic subculture* is a segment of a larger society whose members are thought, by themselves and/or by others, to have a common origin and to participate in shared activities believed to be culturally significant. Common traits, such as customs, language, religion, and values, hold ethnic subcultures together.

Canada has traditionally thought of itself as a cultural mosaic, a pluralist society, rather than a melting pot. In this case, ethnic groups did not necessarily join the mainstream culture. This was referred to as the *salad bowl phenomenon,* where a pot-pourri of people mix but do not blend. However, new Canadian research indicates that Canada's ethnic population is becoming integrated into the cultural mainstream in a single generation. This has implications for marketers wanting to appeal to ethnic Canadians and for ethnic media attempting to reach ethnic groups. Assimilation means a possible loss of ethnic markets.[35]

French-Canadian Subculture

There are over seven million French-speaking Canadians, about 25 percent of the total Canadian population. The overwhelming majority of French Canadians live in Quebec. Some experts have argued that in recent decades, French Canadians in Quebec have become more aligned with the brand preferences and purchase decisions of consumers in the rest of Canada. However, real significant differences persist.[36] So what distinguishes the Quebec market from the rest of the country? Well, first, experts suggest what makes French Quebec different often has less to do with language and more to do with socio-demographic, lifestyle, and cultural differences that drive consumption decisions.[37] For example, PRIZM5, the psychographic system mentioned earlier in this chapter, has found that French-speaking Quebecers are very different from other Canadians in terms of lifestyle. In fact, 16 of the 68 segments or clusters in the PRIZM5 system are distinctly Quebecois. Moreover, because of the distinct differences, Environics has created PRIZM5 QC, which captures and illustrates these differences. PRIZM5 QC categorizes francophone segments by urbanity with 28 urban, 15 suburban, 6 exurban, 6 rural, and 3 town segments.

Other research has also confirmed that French Canadians are different culturally from other Canadians. For example, a recent study identified five cultural "connectors" it says Quebecers identify with more strongly than other Canadians—attitudes that marketers can leverage.[38]

1. *Living in the moment.* The old adage "live for today, for tomorrow may never come" is embraced by Quebecers. They seize the day and give less thought to the future.

2. *Chez nous.* Quebecers' sense of place is central to their identity. They're closer to home, to the land, and to people like them. They'll enthusiastically support all that reinforces their local pride.

3. *Joyful living.* It's the proverbial *joie de vivre* that compels Quebecers to seek pleasure in all aspects of their lives. Quebecers typically take this joyful approach to life to more intense levels than other Canadians. They want to live experiences more fully, and they are more adventurous.

4. *All about me.* Quebecers look after number one. This makes them ask "what's in it for me." It's a trait that may make them appear self-centred at times, but it's also what makes them relentless at getting what they want. For example, they give less to charities than other Canadians, but they give to causes that are close to them, locally.

5. *Life, uncomplicated.* Citizens of *la belle province* want to keep things simple, short, and sweet to help reduce complexity in their lives. They seek simplicity in everything and will reward those who deliver simpler solutions.

So, what does this mean for marketers? Well, many marketers will have to adapt their marketing strategy and messaging for the Quebec market. They must communicate so that the messaging resonates more effectively with the French-Canadian consumer. Importantly, marketers should leverage at least one of the five connectors in their marketing campaigns.[39]

In the end, to be successful in marketing to French Canadians living in Quebec, marketers must be sensitive to the wants and needs of Quebecois consumers and appreciate the inherent differences between them and other Canadians. In addition to lifestyle and cultural differences, there are also other issues that marketers must address. Commercial advertising to children is prohibited, and there are greater restrictions on alcohol advertisements. Provincial regulations require that labels and packages be in both French and English, while store-front signage may be only in French.

Acadian Subculture

Many Canadians assume that French Canadians are basically the same. Even though the majority of French-speaking Canadians reside in Quebec, another special group of French-speaking Canadians live outside of Quebec. These people are the Acadians, most of whom live in New Brunswick and are proud of their distinctive heritage. The Acadians are often referred to as the "forgotten French market."

Acadians are different from French Quebecers in many ways. In terms of consumption, Acadians are very fashion-oriented and tend to dine out more often than their French counterparts in Quebec. Acadians are very price-conscious. They also prefer companies that speak to them in their language, which is slightly different from French Quebecois.

South-Asian Canadian and Chinese-Canadian Subcultures

The South-Asian Canadian (immigrants from India, Pakistan, Bangladesh, Sri Lanka, and Nepal) and Chinese-Canadian (immigrants from Hong Kong, mainland China, and Taiwan) markets currently represent almost 10 percent of Canada's population—10 percent of total Canadian household expenditures—and are the fastest-growing subcultures in Canada. These ethnic groups are largely concentrated in Ontario, British Columbia, and Alberta, particularly in cities such as Toronto and Vancouver.[40]

South-Asian Canadians are moderate television watchers, often watching multicultural stations; light radio listeners; and moderate to heavy Internet users and social networkers. They are also heavy users of tablets and smartphones. Chinese-Canadian consumers are relatively young, educated, and affluent. They tend to spend their money on homes and home furnishings, automobiles, kids' education, investments, high-tech gadgets, travelling, and gifts. They like to do business within their own communities and prefer media in their own languages. They have strong allegiance to brands and are very family-oriented. Because they live in close-knit communities, word of mouth is extremely important to them. They also place great value on business success and financial stability.[41]

However, like other Canadians, South-Asian Canadians and Chinese Canadians are not monolithic groups and can be segmented based on socio-demographics as well as lifestyles. Many Canadian firms have recognized the importance of these emerging ethnic markets and are successfully marketing to them, including Rogers Communications, Western Union, and BMW. Additionally, Canadian media outlets are responding to these subcultures. For example, Global News has a Mandarin-language evening newscast in Calgary and Vancouver, the *Vancouver Sun* has a Chinese-language website, and the *Epoch Times* newspaper publishes in Mandarin.

Other Ethnic Subcultures

Many other ethnic Canadians can be found in large metropolitan centres or clustered in certain geographic areas. For example, large numbers of South Asian Canadians (from countries including India and Pakistan) and Southeast Asians (from countries including Korea, Philippines, and Vietnam) can be found in Toronto, Montreal, Calgary, and Vancouver. Kitchener-Waterloo has a large German-Canadian population, Winnipeg is home to many Ukrainian Canadians, and Toronto has a large number of Italian Canadians. Marketers must appreciate the fact that these ethnic Canadians may carry with them distinctive social and cultural behaviours that might affect their buying patterns. Subcultural research and sensitivity can aid organizations in developing effective marketing strategies designed to appeal to these groups.

Learning Review

7. What are the two primary forms of personal influence?

8. Which types of reference groups are marketers concerned with?

9. What is an ethnic subculture?

Learning Objectives Review

LO1 Describe the stages in the consumer purchase decision process.

The consumer purchase decision process consists of five stages. They are problem recognition, information search, alternative evaluation, purchase decision, and post-purchase behaviour. Problem recognition is perceiving a difference between a person's ideal and actual situation that is big enough to trigger a decision. Information search involves remembering previous purchase experiences (internal search) and external search behaviour, such as seeking information from other sources. Alternative evaluation clarifies the problem for the consumer by (*a*) yielding brand names that might meet the criteria, (*b*) suggesting the evaluative criteria to use for the purchase, and (*c*) developing consumer value perceptions. The purchase decision involves the choice of an alternative, including from whom to buy and when to buy. Post-purchase behaviour involves the comparison of the chosen alternative with a consumer's expectations, which leads to satisfaction or dissatisfaction and subsequent purchase behaviour.

LO2 Distinguish among three variations of the consumer purchase decision process: routine, limited, and extended problem solving.

Consumers do not always engage in the five-stage purchase decision process. Instead, they skip or minimize one or more stages depending on the level of involvement—the personal, social, and economic significance of the purchase. For low-involvement purchase occasions, consumers engage in routine problem solving. They recognize a problem, make a decision, and spend little effort seeking external information and evaluating alternatives. For high-involvement purchase occasions, each of the five stages of the consumer purchase decision process is used, including considerable time and effort on external information search and in identifying and evaluating alternatives. With limited problem solving, consumers typically seek some information or rely on a friend to help them evaluate alternatives.

LO3 Identify the major psychological influences on consumer behaviour.

Psychology helps marketers understand why and how consumers behave as they do. In particular, psychological concepts, such as motivation and personality; perception; learning; values, beliefs, and attitudes; and lifestyle are useful for interpreting buying processes. Motivation is the energizing force that stimulates behaviour to satisfy a need. Personality refers to a person's consistent behaviours or responses to recurring situations. Perception is the process by which an individual selects, organizes, and interprets information to create a meaningful picture of the world. Consumers filter information through selective attention, selective exposure, selective comprehension, and selective retention.

Much consumer behaviour is learned. Learning refers to those behaviours that result from (*a*) repeated experience, and (*b*) reasoning. Brand loyalty results from learning. Values, beliefs, and attitudes are also learned and influence how consumers evaluate products, services, and brands. A more general concept is lifestyle. Lifestyle, also called psychographics, combines psychology and demographics and focuses on how people spend their time and resources, what they consider important in their environment, and what they think of themselves and the world around them.

LO4 Identify the major socio-cultural influences on consumer behaviour.

Socio-cultural influences, which evolve from a consumer's formal and informal relationships with other people, also affect consumer behaviour. These involve personal influence, reference groups, the family, social class, culture, and subculture. Opinion leadership and word-of-mouth behaviour are two major sources of personal influence on consumer behaviour. Reference groups are people to whom an individual looks as a basis for self-approval or as source of personal standards. Family influences on consumer behaviour result from three sources: consumer socialization, passage through the family life cycle, and decision making within the family or household. A more subtle influence on consumer behaviour than direct contact with others is the social class to which people belong. Persons within social classes tend to exhibit common values, attitudes, beliefs, lifestyles, and buying behaviours. Finally, a person's culture and subculture have been shown to influence product preferences and buying patterns.

Applying Marketing Knowledge

1. Outline the consumer purchase decision process you used to select your college or university. Discuss your perceived problem, information sources used, awareness set, evaluative criteria, consideration set, and how happy you are with your decision.

2. Suppose research at Panasonic reveals that prospective buyers are anxious about buying expensive high-definition television sets. What strategies might you recommend to the company to reduce consumer anxiety?

3. A Porsche salesperson was taking orders on new cars because he was unable to satisfy the demand with the limited number of cars in the showroom and lot. Several persons had backed out of the contract within two weeks of signing the order. What explanation can you give for this behaviour, and what remedies would you recommend?

4. Which social class would you associate with each of the following items or actions: (*a*) tennis club membership, (*b*) an arrangement of plastic flowers in the kitchen, (*c*) *True Romance* magazine, (*d*) *Maclean's* magazine, (*e*) formally dressing for dinner frequently, and (*f*) being a member of a bowling team?

5. Assign one or more levels of the hierarchy of needs and the motives described in Figure 5–4 to the following products: (*a*) life insurance, (*b*) cosmetics, (*c*) the *Financial Post,* and (*d*) hamburgers.

6. With which stage in the family life cycle would the purchase of the following products and services be most closely identified: (*a*) bedroom furniture, (*b*) life insurance, (*c*) a Caribbean cruise, (*d*) a house mortgage, and (*e*) children's toys?

7. "The greater the perceived risk in a purchase situation, the more likely that cognitive dissonance will result." Does this statement have any basis given the discussion in the text? Why?

8. In terms of social media, Canadians fall into one of three categories: producers of content, followers of content, and non-users. What category do you fall into? And what are the implications to marketers trying to reach you via social media?

Building Your Marketing Plan

To do a consumer analysis of the product—the good, service, idea, or experience—in your marketing plan:

1. Identify the consumers who are most likely to buy your product—the primary target market—in terms of (*a*) their demographic characteristics and (*b*) any other kinds of characteristics you believe are important.

2. Describe (a) the main points of difference of your product for this group and (b) what problem it helps solve for the consumer, in terms of the first stage in the consumer purchase decision process in Figure 5–1.

3. Identify the one or two key influences for each of the four outside boxes in Figure 5–3: (a) marketing mix, (b) psychological, (c) socio-cultural, and (d) situational influences.

This consumer analysis will provide the foundation for the marketing mix actions you develop later in your plan.

Video Case 5

Groupon: Helping Consumers with Purchase Decisions

University of Chicago graduate student Andrew Mason was in a rut. "There's so much to do in Chicago," he explains, "but I found myself going to the same movie theatres and restaurants."

To help people like him try new places, Mason started a website that offered coupons to large groups. He reasoned that people would try something new if the price was low enough, and that businesses would offer low prices if they knew they could sell a large quantity. The result was Groupon, a company that offers "group coupons" in deal-of-the-day offerings for local or national businesses. Consumers love the concept, buying everything from restaurant certificates, to yoga lessons, to tickets to a museum exhibit. "We think the Internet has the potential to change the way people discover and buy from local businesses," says Mason.

The Company and Groupon Concept

Mason started with a website called ThePoint.org, which was designed to organize campaigns, protests, boycotts, and fundraising drives for important social issues. Though it was not successful, ThePoint provided the concept of making offers that are only carried out if enough people commit to participate in them. With that idea, Mason launched Groupon in October 2008 with a two-pizzas-for-the-price-of-one offer at the Motel Bar, located in the same building where ThePoint rented space. The concept quickly grew in Chicago, and Groupon expanded into other U.S. cities, and then into other countries. Today, Groupon is available in 375 American cities and 40 countries, and its subscriber base has grown from 400 in 2008 to 60 million today. According to *Forbes* magazine, Groupon is the fastest-growing company in history.

Part of Groupon's success is the simplicity of its business model—offer subscribers at least one deal in their city each day. The unique aspect of the concept is that a certain number of people need to buy into the offer before the coupon discount is valid. Approximately 95 percent of Groupon offers "tip," or reach the number of buyers required by the merchant. Once the minimum number is met, Groupon and the merchant split the revenue. For example, a yoga studio might offer a $100 membership for $50 if 200 people participate in the offer. Once 200 consumers have indicated interest, the deal "tips" and Groupon and the yoga studio each receive 50 percent of the revenue. Everyone wins. Consumers receive an exceptional value, the merchant obtains new customers without any advertising cost, and Groupon generates revenue for creating value in the marketplace.

Many of the deals have generated extraordinary demand. The Joffrey Ballet, for example, sold 2,338 season subscriptions, doubling its subscriber base in one day! Similarly, consumers purchased 445,000 Groupons offering $50 worth of merchandise for $25 at the Gap, and 6,561 tickets to a King Tut exhibit in

New York's Times Square for half price at $18 apiece. The most popular offering so far was a $25 ticket for an architectural boat tour in Chicago for $12. Groupon sold 19,822 tickets in eight hours! The company's attention to customer satisfaction ensures success stories like these. "We have a policy called 'The Groupon Promise' that any customer can return a Groupon, no questions asked—even if they used it—if they feel like Groupon has let them down," explains Mason. Groupon's success has attracted many more merchants than it can accommodate. In fact, only about 12 percent of all merchants that contact Groupon are selected to offer a deal.

In addition to the deal-of-the-day offerings, Groupon has several other services. First, it is testing a concept called Groupon Stores, which allows merchants to create their own deals and send them out to their own audience. This allows more merchants to participate on a regular basis. Second, the company has recently introduced a mobile service called Groupon Now. To use the service, consumers log in to the app on their smartphone and select one of two options: "I'm Hungry" or "I'm Bored." The phone then transmits its location to the Groupon servers and displays a list of nearby deals at restaurants or entertainment venues. The Groupon Now offerings represent a combination of Yellow Pages advertising and newspaper coupons for price-conscious consumers.

© Daniel Ackerl Bloomberg via Getty Images

Groupon's growth is evident in some amazing numbers. The company now sends more than 900 deals each day, occupies six floors of the former Montgomery Ward headquarters in Chicago, and employs more than 5,900 people. In addition, Groupon has created a market of consumer deal hunters and an industry of more than 500 competitive deal services. The competitors include LevelUp, Tippr, Bloomspot, Scoutmob, BuyWithMe, Yelp, and OpenTable. In addition, Google Offers, Facebook Deals, Yahoo! Deals, and Amazon's LivingSocial have all recently launched deal services.

Using Coupons to Influence Consumers' Buying Behaviour

"Part of the reason that Groupon has grown as quickly as it has is because we really understand consumer behaviour," explains Julie Mossler, public relations and consumer marketing manager at Groupon. Generally, Groupon consumers follow the same purchase decision process common to many consumer purchases. The first stage, problem recognition, may be triggered by an e-mail or an appointment to have lunch with friends. Groupon deal-of-the-day e-mail messages, for example, often present consumers with an opportunity to do something they wouldn't ordinarily do—take sky-diving lessons or subscribe to the ballet. Groupon Now presents real-time offers on smartphone apps in response to an immediate need in a specific location. While the two types of offers generate different types of purchases, they both begin the purchase process.

The second stage, information search, may simply be a review of previous experiences with the merchant making the offer, online comparisons with competitors, or discussions with friends on Facebook or Twitter. In fact, the collective buying aspect of Groupon encourages subscribers to share promotions with family and friends to increase the chances of reaching the required number of buyers.

In the alternative evaluation stage, many Groupon customers focus on price as the most important evaluative criteria, although other aspects such as quantity or time restrictions may be considered. The Groupon Now offers, for example, may only be valid on specific days or during short windows of time. Piece Brewery & Pizzeria in Chicago used Groupon Now to sell a $30 coupon for $20 valid only during its slow periods—11 a.m. to 3 p.m. Tuesday through Thursday.

The fourth stage, the purchase decision, is made online and then confirmed when the deals tip. Bo Hurd, national sales manager at Groupon, believes that the purchase stage is unique for Groupon users. He explains, "The fact that [consumers] have put money on the line . . . is driving them from the online piece, to the computers . . . to do something, to try something." Finally, post-purchase, consumers compare their experience with their expectations to determine if they are satisfied or dissatisfied.

Psychological, socio-cultural, and situational factors also influence Groupon users' purchase behaviour. The recession has increased the importance of personal values such as thriftiness, so deal-prone people who were attracted to websites such as Gilt in fashion and Woot in consumer electronics are also attracted to Groupon. The typical Groupon user is an 18- to 34-year-old woman with an average income of about $70,000. This is significant because this group's affinity to social media enables the use of Groupon, which depends on e-mail and smartphone apps to reach its customers. Specific situations such as planning entertainment activities, finding a close restaurant for lunch, or buying a gift are also common to Groupon users. As Groupon has learned more about its subscribers, it has begun personalizing the deals they see. The company uses variables such as gender, location of residence or office, and buying history to match deals with the customers. This process provides offers that are more likely to be of interest to consumers and allows Groupon to serve more merchants.

© Iain Masterton/Alamy Stock Photo

Groupon Challenges

As popular as Groupon has become, it does face three challenges. The first challenge is related to the use of coupons. Some consumers buy the coupons but never use them, eventually leaving them dissatisfied and unlikely to use Groupon again. Some consumers use the coupons but do not become regular customers. Because of the deep discounts used to sell the Groupons, most of the deals are not profitable for the merchants, so they are dissatisfied if the Groupon users do not make repeat purchases. David Perlman, owner of the Essex restaurant in New York City, for example, offered deals on Groupon and OpenTable, selling 1,500 and 1,000 coupons, respectively. Now he is comparing the diners each deal brought in to determine which group has generated more repeat customers. Some merchants are also concerned that frequent discounting could discourage customers from ever making purchases without a discount.

Another challenge facing Groupon is managing its growth. The company has expanded into Europe, Latin America, Asia, and Russia by acquiring local daily deal services. For example, in Europe it purchased CityDeal, in Russia it purchased Darberry, and in Japan it purchased Qpod. It also acquired sites with customer bases in Hong Kong, Singapore, Taiwan, and the Philippines. As a result, Groupon currently has more subscribers abroad than in the U.S., although more deals are still sold in the U.S. As Groupon continues to grow, it anticipates that it must develop a comprehensive understanding of the differences in international buying behaviours.

Finally, Groupon faces an extraordinary level of competition. Part of the problem is that the daily deal technology is not very sophisticated and the model is easy to copy. Manufacturers, large retailers, and small businesses are all trying the concept. ConAgra has offered a group coupon deal for its Healthy Choice brand through a Facebook app, Walmart launched its own deals app called Crowdsaver, and some businesses use recently developed plug-and-play software that helps build deals into their websites. Mason hopes that Groupon Now is one answer to this challenge because it is much more difficult to replicate. "We have always been thinking about how to solve these fundamental problems of our model. We have known since very early on that some form of real-time deal optimization is where this had to go," he explains.

Groupon's success is the result of a simple and effective business model and an insightful understanding of consumer behaviour. In the future, Groupon's strategies will require continued attention to understanding consumers around the globe. Mossler explains, "Groupon has been heralded as the fastest-growing company of all time, and the reason for that is because we have solved this unsolvable problem, which is how do you engage with local customers. The model really works anywhere as long as you adapt for local communities."

QUESTIONS

1. How has an understanding of consumer behaviour helped Groupon grow from 400 subscribers in Chicago in 2008 to 60 million subscribers in 40 countries today?

2. What is the Groupon Promise? How does the Groupon Promise affect a consumer's perceived risk and cognitive dissonance?

3. Describe the five-stage purchase decision process for a typical Groupon user.

4. What are possible psychological and sociological influences on the Groupon consumer purchase decision process?

5. What challenges does Groupon face in the future? What actions would you recommend related to each challenge?

Case: This case was written by Steven Hartley. Sources: Bari Weiss, "The Journal Interview with Andrew Mason: Groupon's $6 Billion Gambler," *Wall Street Journal*, December 20, 2010, p. 12; Brad Stone and Douglas MacMillan, "Are Four Words Worth $25 Billion?" *Bloomberg Businessweek*, March 21, 2011, pp. 70–75; Brendan Coffey, "What's the Deal?" *Forbes*, April 25, 2011, pp. 20–22; Brad Stone and Douglas MacMillan, "Groupon's $6 Billion Snub," *Bloomberg Businessweek*, December 13, 2010, pp. 6–7; Christopher Steiner, "Meet the Fastest Growing Company Ever," *Forbes*, August 30, 2010; Rupal Parekh, "Groupon," *Advertising Age*, November 15, 2010, p. 20; "10 Big Stories for the Week," *Advertising Age*, December 13, 2010, pp. 12–13; Jessi Hempel, "Social Media Meets Retailing," *Fortune*, March 22, 2010, p. 30; Kunur Patel, "Suddenly, Everyone Wants to Be Groupon," *Advertising Age*, November 1, 2010, p. 1; and Brad Stone, "Coupon Deathmatch, Party of Two?" *Bloomberg Businessweek*, October 4, 2010, pp. 37–38.

6

Understanding Organizations as Customers

Learning Objectives

After reading this chapter, you should be able to:

LO1 Distinguish among industrial, reseller, and government organizational markets.

LO2 Describe the key characteristics of organizational buying that make it different from consumer buying.

LO3 Explain how buying centres and buying situations influence organizational purchasing.

LO4 Recognize the importance and nature of online buying in industrial, reseller, and government organizational markets.

A New Solution to Student Housing

Ever think about who plans, designs, builds, and manages your college or university's student housing? Often it is your college and university itself. However, more frequently, colleges and universities are turning to outside service providers to complete these tasks. When they do, this is considered a business-to-business (B2B) transaction. In this case, it is an organization that is a customer and making a purchase. One of the largest owners and operators of student housing in Canada is Toronto-based Campus Living Centres. It partners with dozens of colleges and universities and currently manages over 20,000 student beds!

Basically, Campus Living Centres offers four basic types of products or services to Canadian colleges and universities: (1) building and financing new residences, (2) managing existing residences, (3) providing student life programs and services, and (4) offering property management services. Campus Living Centres offers colleges and universities a single source solution when it comes to building and financing new residences, including the design, build, financing, and operation of the new residences. Research has shown that student housing is an important recruitment and retention tool, and Campus Living Centres builds facilities designed to appeal to students. The company also manages existing residences with a proven management model that improves the financial performance of residence operations while not compromising the student experience. The company has demonstrated business cases where its management model ensures student safety and security, improves student retention rates, and reduces purchasing and operating costs.

Campus Living Centres also offers colleges and universities student life programs and services, including community-building programs, student outreach and support services, student leadership programs, staff training, residence recruitment, and research and assessment. Finally, the company offers off-campus student housing property management. Here, colleges and universities contract Campus Living Centres to operate these facilities and to take responsibility for student occupancy, revenue, costs, student safety, and property maintenance.

© Arcaid Images/Alamy Stock Photo

In short, many colleges and universities continue to handle student housing on their own, including building, managing, and maintaining these facilities. On the other hand, many other colleges and universities are making the decisionM to allow companies like Campus Living Centres to assume the responsibility to build, manage, and maintain both on-campus and off-campus housing. The key to convincing colleges and universities to contract out the responsibility for student housing is for firms like Campus Living Centres to make a compelling business case that its "customers"—in this case, these academic organizations—are better off, in the end, financially and operationally to do so.[1]

This chapter focuses on organizational buying, including types of organizational buyers; key characteristics of organizational buying, including online buying; some typical buying situations; unique aspects of the organizational buying process compared with the consumer purchase process; and some typical buying procedures and decisions made by organizations as customers.

LO1 THE NATURE AND SIZE OF ORGANIZATIONAL MARKETS

Business marketing is the marketing of goods and services to companies, governments, and not-for-profit organizations for use in the creation of goods and services that they can produce and market to others. This is also sometimes referred to as *business-to-business*, or *B2B, marketing*. Because many Canadian business school graduates take jobs in firms that engage in business marketing, it is important to understand the fundamental characteristics of organizational buyers and their buying behaviour.

As introduced in Chapter 1, *organizational buyers* are those manufacturers, retailers, and government agencies that buy goods and services for their own use or for resale. For example, all these organizations buy computers and telephone services for their own use. However, manufacturers buy raw materials and parts that they reprocess into the finished goods they sell, whereas retailers resell goods they buy without reprocessing them. Organizational buyers include all the buyers in a nation, except the ultimate consumers. These organizational buyers purchase and lease tremendous volumes of capital equipment, raw materials, manufactured parts, supplies, and business services. In fact, because they often buy raw materials and parts, process them, and sell the upgraded product several times before it is purchased by the final organizational buyer or ultimate consumer, the aggregate purchases of organizational buyers in a year are far greater than those of ultimate consumers.

Organizational buyers are divided into three markets: (1) industrial, (2) reseller, and (3) government markets.

Industrial Markets

There are thousands of firms in the industrial, or business, market in Canada. **Industrial firms**, in some way, reprocess a good or service they buy before selling it again to the next buyer. This is certainly true of a steel mill that converts iron ore into steel. It is also true (if you stretch your imagination) of a firm selling services, such as a bank that takes money from its depositors, reprocesses it, and "sells" it as loans to its commercial borrowers.

There has been a marked shift in the scope and nature of the industrial marketplace. Service industries are growing; they currently make the greatest contribution to Canada's gross domestic product (GDP). Because of the importance of service firms, service marketing is discussed in detail in Chapter 12. Industrial firms and primary industries currently account for about 20 percent of Canada's GDP. Nevertheless, primary industries (e.g., farming, mining, fishing, and forestry) and the manufacturing sector are important components of Canada's economy. There are over 50,000 manufacturers in Canada whose estimated value of shipments is over $600 billion. For an understanding of the role of manufacturing in the Canadian economy, and the emergence of a new leader in the manufacturing sector in Canada, read the accompanying Marketing Matters box, "Some Facts about Canada's Manufacturing Industry."[2]

MARKETING MATTERS

Some Facts about Canada's Manufacturing Industry

While Canada has been transitioned to a services-based economy, the manufacturing sector still plays an important role in the national economy. According to the Canadian Manufacturers & Exporters (CME-MEC) trade association and the Canadian Manufacturing Coalition, manufacturing employs over 1.7 million Canadians directly, and another 2 million more depend on the sector for their livelihood. Directly, manufacturing accounts for over $170 billion in gross domestic product, or roughly 11 percent of total Canadian GDP. But when spin-offs are included, such as the purchases of goods and services in Canada, manufacturers drive 55 percent of the economy. Every $1 of manufacturing in Canada generates $3 in total economic activity. Pay in the manufacturing sector is also above the national average. And more manufacturers have employee-training programs than any other sector of the economy. Over 60 percent of all goods manufactured in Canada are exported, and manufactured products account for the bulk of Canada's merchandise exports. Manufacturers also perform close to 50 percent of private-sector research and development (R&D) in Canada. The leading sectors in manufacturing in Canada are food, motor vehicles and parts, coal and petroleum, and chemical products.

However, in order to continue to grow in the future, the manufacturing sector has to make improvements when it comes to investing in lean manufacturing, developing differentiated products, and broadening its reach in global markets. Additionally, research shows a significant skills gap in the field of manufacturing management. Therefore, the Canadian Manufacturers & Exporters has rolled out a new manufacturing management certificate (MMC) program that is delivered online and in partnership with Athabasca University. The program is designed to provide the necessary applied skills training to develop and nurture new managers and supervisors from within existing manufacturing operations.

Reseller Markets

Wholesalers and retailers that buy physical products and sell them again without any reprocessing are **resellers**. Over 200,000 retailers and over 65,000 wholesalers are currently operating in Canada. Some of the largest retailers in Canada include Canadian Tire, Walmart, and Costco. Some major wholesalers are Cargill, Medis Health, and Federated Co-Operatives. These companies participate in B2B marketing. In later chapters, we see how manufacturers use wholesalers and retailers in their distribution ("place") strategies as channels through which their products reach ultimate consumers. In this chapter, we look at resellers mainly as organizational buyers in terms of (1) how they make their own buying decisions, and (2) which products they choose to carry.

Government Markets

Government units are the federal, provincial, and local agencies that buy goods and services for the constituents they serve. Their annual purchases vary in size from billions of dollars for a federal department, such as National Defence, to millions or thousands of dollars for a local university or school. The bulk of the buying at the federal government level is done by Service Canada. Most provincial governments have a government services department that does the buying on the provincial level. Hundreds of government departments, including agencies and Crown corporations, such as CBC, VIA Rail, and the Royal Canadian Mint, must purchase goods and services to operate. The federal government is a large organizational consumer, making total purchases of goods and services amounting to over $270 billion annually.[3]

Global Organizational Markets

Industrial, reseller, and government markets also exist on a global scale. In fact, many of Canada's top exporters, including Bombardier, Canadian Pacific, DuPont Canada, Maple Leaf Foods, and Pratt & Whitney, focus on organizational customers, not ultimate consumers.

Most world trade involves manufacturers, resellers, and government agencies buying goods and services for their own use or for resale to others. The exchange relationships often involve numerous transactions spanning the globe. For example, Honeywell's Micro Switch Division sells its fibre-optic technology and products to manufacturers of data communication systems worldwide, through electronic component resellers in more than 20 countries, and directly to national governments in Europe and elsewhere. Europe's Airbus Industrie, the world's largest aircraft manufacturer, sells its passenger airplanes to Air Canada, which flies Canadian businesspeople to Asia. Ontario-based Inco, one of the world's largest nickel producers, is a global business participant, marketing its products to customers around the world. In fact, it exports 90 percent of its products to global organizational markets.

MEASURING DOMESTIC AND GLOBAL INDUSTRIAL, RESELLER, AND GOVERNMENT MARKETS

The measurement of industrial, reseller, and government markets is an important step for a firm interested in gauging the scope and size of one, two, or all three of these markets in Canada and around the world. The North American Free Trade Agreement (NAFTA) partners—Canada, Mexico, and the United States—now have a common system for measuring economic activities in organizational markets. It is called the *North American Industry Classification System (NAICS).*[4]

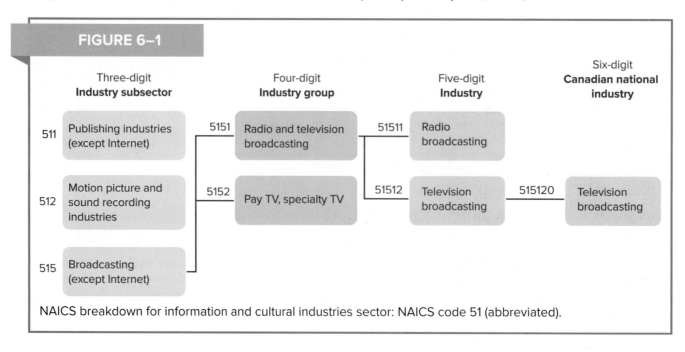

FIGURE 6–1

NAICS breakdown for information and cultural industries sector: NAICS code 51 (abbreviated).

The NAICS divides the economy into sectors using a six-digit coded system. The first two digits designate sectors, the third digit designates subsectors, the fourth digit designates industry groups, and the fifth digit designates industries. The sixth digit is used to designate national industries. NAICS in Canada consists of 20 sectors, 102 subsectors, 323 industry groups, 711 industries, and 922 national industries. Figure 6–1 illustrates how the NAICS works, with an abbreviated breakdown for the Canadian information and cultural industries sector (code 51).

The NAICS allows marketers to examine organizational markets in terms of size and growth as well as to identify customers and competition. However, there are some limitations with the system. For example, with the NAICS, each organization is assigned one code based on its principal economic activity. So, large firms that engage in many different activities are still assigned only one code. Hence, there will be a few large and complex enterprises whose activities may be spread over the different sectors in such a way that classifying them to one sector might misrepresent the range of their activities. Also, five-digit national industry codes are not available for all three countries because the respective governments will not reveal data when too few organizations exist in a category.

U.S. Census Bureau

Learning Review

1. What are the three main types of organizational buyers?

2. What is the North American Industry Classification System (NAICS)?

LO2   CHARACTERISTICS OF ORGANIZATIONAL BUYING

Organizations are different from individuals, and so buying for an organization is different from buying for yourself or your family.[5] True, in both cases, the objective in making the purchase is to solve the buyer's problem—to satisfy a need or want. But unique objectives and policies of an organization put special constraints on how it makes buying decisions. Understanding the characteristics of organizational buying is essential in designing effective marketing programs to reach these buyers.

Organizational buying behaviour is the decision-making process that organizations use to establish the need for products and services, and to identify, evaluate, and choose among alternative brands and suppliers. Key characteristics of organizational buying behaviour are listed in Figure 6–2 and discussed next.[6]

Demand Characteristics

Consumer demand for products and services is affected by their price and availability and by consumers' personal tastes and discretionary income. By comparison, demand for business products and services is derived. **Derived demand** means that the demand for business products and services is driven by, or derived from, demand for consumer products and services. For example, the demand for MacMillan Bloedel's pulp and paper products is based on consumer demand for newspapers, Pizza Pizza's "keep warm" pizza-to-go boxes, Federal Express packages, and disposable diapers. Derived demand is often based on expectations of future consumer demand. For instance, Whirlpool purchases parts for its washers and dryers in anticipation of consumer demand, which is affected by the replacement cycle for these products and by consumer income.

Ultimately, most demand is derived from consumer demand, the exception being demand derived from government purchases. Therefore, because of the importance of the concept of derived demand, business marketers are always paying close attention to consumer demand forecasts and reports.[7]

Size of the Order or Purchase

The size of the purchase involved in organizational buying is typically much larger than that in consumer buying. The dollar value of a single purchase made by an organization often runs into the thousands or millions of dollars. For example, the Boeing Company, the world's largest aerospace company, charges about $96 million for its "average" Boeing 737 commercial jetliner, $327 million for its Boeing 777, and $257 million for the Boeing 787.[8] With so much money at stake, most organizations place constraints on their buyers in the form of purchasing policies or procedures. Buyers must often get competitive bids from at least three prospective suppliers when the order is above a specific amount, such as $5,000. When the order is above an even higher amount, such as $50,000, it may require the review and approval of a vice president or even the president of the company. Knowing how order size affects buying practices is important in determining who will participate in the purchase decision, who will make the final decision, and the length of time that will be required to arrive at a purchase agreement.

FIGURE 6–2

CHARACTERISTICS	DIMENSIONS
Market characteristics	• Demand for industrial products and services is derived. • Few customers typically exist, and their purchase orders are large.
Product or service characteristics	• Products or services are technical in nature and purchased on the basis of specifications. • Many of the goods purchased are raw and semifinished. • Heavy emphasis is placed on delivery time, technical assistance, and postsale service.
Buying process characteristics	• Technically qualified and professional buyers follow established purchasing policies and procedures. • Buying objectives and criteria are typically spelled out, as are procedures for evaluating sellers and their products or services. • There are multiple buying influences, and multiple parties participate in purchase decisions. • There are reciprocal arrangements, and negotiation between buyers and sellers is commonplace. • Online buying over the Internet is widespread.
Marketing mix characteristics	• Direct selling to organizational buyers is the rule, and distribution is very important. • Advertising and other forms of promotion are technical in nature. • Price is often negotiated, evaluated as part of broader seller and product or service qualities, and frequently affected by quantity discounts.

Key characteristics of organizational buying behaviour.

Number of Potential Buyers

Firms selling consumer products or services often try to reach thousands or millions of individuals or households. For example, your local supermarket or bank probably serves thousands of people, and Kellogg's Canada tries to reach more than 10 million Canadian households with its breakfast cereals and probably succeeds in selling to a third or half of these in any given year. In contrast, firms selling to organizations are often restricted to far fewer buyers. Bombardier can sell its business jets to a few thousand organizations throughout the world, and B. F. Goodrich sells its original equipment tires to fewer than 10 car manufacturers.

Organizational Buying Objectives

Organizations buy products and services for one main reason: to help them achieve their objectives. For business firms, the buying objective is usually to increase profits through reducing costs or increasing revenues. Mac's buys automated inventory systems to increase the number of products that can be sold through its convenience stores and to keep them fresh. Nissan

Motor Company switched its advertising agency because it expects the new agency to devise a more effective ad campaign to help it sell more cars and increase revenues. To improve executive decision making, many firms buy advanced computer systems to process data. The objectives of non-profit firms and government agencies are usually to meet the needs of the groups they serve. Thus, a hospital buys a high-technology diagnostic device to serve its patients better. Understanding buying objectives is a necessary first step in marketing to organizations. Recognizing the high costs of energy, Sylvania promotes to prospective buyers cost savings and increased profits made possible by its fluorescent and halogen lights. Many companies today have broadened their buying objectives to include environmental considerations. For example, the Home Depot no longer purchases lumber from companies that harvest timber from the world's endangered forests.[9] Successful business marketers recognize that understanding buying objectives is a necessary first step in marketing to organizations.

Organizational Buying Criteria

In making a purchase, the buying organization must weigh key buying criteria that apply to the potential supplier and what it wants to sell. **Organizational buying criteria** are the objective attributes of the supplier's products and services and the capabilities of the supplier itself. These criteria serve the same purpose as the evaluative criteria used by consumers and described in Chapter 5. Seven of the most commonly used criteria are (1) price, (2) ability to meet the quality specifications required for the item, (3) ability to meet required delivery schedules, (4) technical capability, (5) warranties and claim policies in the event of poor performance, (6) past performance on previous contracts, and (7) production facilities and capacity.[10] Suppliers that meet or exceed these criteria create customer value.

Organizational buyers who purchase products and services in a global marketplace often supplement their buying criteria with supplier ISO 9000 certification. **ISO 9000 standards**, developed by the International Standards Organization (ISO) in Geneva, Switzerland, refer to standards for registration and certification of a manufacturer's quality management and assurance system based on an on-site audit of practices and procedures. ISO certification is administered in Canada by SCC (Standards Council of Canada: **www.scc.ca**). Many Canadian companies that market globally have achieved this certification.[11]

Many organizational buyers today are transforming their buying criteria into specific requirements that are communicated to prospective suppliers. This practice, called **supplier development**, involves the deliberate effort by organizational buyers to build relationships that shape suppliers' products, services, and capabilities to fit a buyer's needs and those of its customers.[12] For example, consider Deere & Company, the maker of John Deere farm, construction, and lawn-care equipment. Deere employs 94 supplier-development engineers who work full-time with the company's suppliers to improve their efficiency and quality and reduce their costs. According to a Deere senior executive, "Their quality, delivery, and costs are, after all, our quality, delivery, and costs."[13] Harley-Davidson also emphasizes supplier collaboration in its product design.[14]

With many Canadian manufacturers using a "just-in-time" (JIT) inventory system that reduces the inventory of production parts to those to be used within hours or days, on-time delivery is becoming an even more important buying criterion and, in some instances, a requirement. Caterpillar trains its key suppliers at its Quality Institute in JIT inventory systems and conducts supplier seminars on how to diagnose, correct, and implement continuous quality improvement programs. The just-in-time inventory system is discussed further in Chapter 14.

Buyer–Seller Relationships and Supply Partnerships

Another distinction between organizational and consumer buying behaviour lies in the nature of the relationship between organizational buyers and suppliers. Specifically, organizational buying is more likely to involve complex negotiations concerning delivery schedules, price, technical specifications, warranties, and claim policies. These negotiations also can last for an extended period of time. This was the case when the Lawrence Livermore National Laboratory acquired an IBM Sequoia supercomputer at a cost of about $250 million. In terms of processing speed, the amount of data that the Sequoia can process in one hour is equivalent to what 6.7 billion people would be able to calculate (using calculators)—if they had 320 years to do their work![15]

Reciprocal arrangements also exist in organizational buying. **Reciprocity** is a business buying practice in which two organizations agree to purchase each other's products and services. Industry Canada frowns on reciprocal buying because it restricts the normal operation of the free market. However, the practice exists and can limit the flexibility of organizational buyers in choosing alternative suppliers.

Long-term relationships are also prevalent.[16] For example, Kraft announced it would spend $1.7 billion over seven years for global information technology services from Electronic Data Systems. Hewlett-Packard engaged in a 10-year, $3 billion contract to manage Procter & Gamble's information technology in 160 countries.[17]

In some cases, buyer–seller relationships develop into supply partnerships.[18] A **supply partnership** exists when a buyer and its supplier adopt mutually beneficial objectives, policies, and procedures for the purpose of lowering the cost and/or increasing the value of products and services delivered to the ultimate consumer. Intel, the world's largest manufacturer of microprocessors and the "computer inside" most personal computers, is a case in point. Intel supports its suppliers by offering them quality management programs and by investing in supplier equipment that produces fewer product defects and boosts supplier productivity. Suppliers, in turn, provide Intel with consistently high-quality products at a lower cost for its customers, the makers of personal computers, and finally you, the ultimate customer. Retailers, too, are forging partnerships with their suppliers. Walmart has such a relationship with Procter & Gamble for ordering and replenishing P&G's products in their stores. By using computerized cash register scanning equipment and direct electronic linkages to P&G, these retailers can tell P&G what merchandise is needed, along with how much, when, and to which store to deliver it on a daily basis. Because supply partnerships also involve the physical distribution of goods, they are again discussed in Chapter 14 in the context of supply chains.

Supply partnerships often include provisions for what is called *sustainable procurement*. This buying practice is described in the accompanying Making Responsible Decisions box.[19]

MAKING RESPONSIBLE DECISIONS

Sustainable Procurement for Sustainable Growth

Manufacturers, retailers, wholesalers, and government agencies are increasingly sensitive to how their buying decisions affect the environment. Concerns about the depletion of natural resources; air, water, and soil pollution; and the social consequences of economic activity have given rise to the concept of sustainable procurement. Sustainable procurement aims to integrate environmental considerations into all stages of an organization's buying process with the goal of reducing the impact on human health and the physical environment.

Jewel Samad/AFP/Getty Images

Starbucks is a pioneer and global leader in sustainable procurement. The company's attention to quality coffee extends to its coffee growers located in more than 20 countries. This means that Starbucks pays coffee farmers a fair price for the beans, that the coffee is grown in an ecologically sound manner, and that Starbucks invests in the farming communities where its coffees are produced. In this way, Starbucks focuses on the sustainable growth of its suppliers.

LO3   The Buying Centre: A Cross-Functional Group

For routine purchases with a small dollar value, a single buyer or purchasing manager often makes the purchase decision alone. In many instances, however, several people in the organization participate in the buying process. The individuals in this group, called a **buying centre**, share common goals, risks, and knowledge important to a purchase decision. For most large multistore chain resellers, such as Best Buy, Lowe's, and Walmart, the buying centre is highly formalized and is called a *buying committee*. However, most industrial firms or government units use informal groups of people or call meetings to arrive at buying decisions.

The importance of the buying centre requires that a firm marketing to many business firms and government units understand the structure, technical and business functions, and behaviour of these groups. Four questions provide guidance in understanding the buying centre in these organizations:[20]

1. Which individuals are in the buying centre for the product or service?

2. What is the relative influence of each member of the group?

3. What are the buying criteria of each member?

4. How does each member of the group perceive our firm, our products and services, and our salespeople?

Answers to these questions are difficult to come by, particularly when dealing with industrial firms, resellers, and governments outside Canada.[21] For example, Canadian firms are often frustrated by the fact that Japanese buyers "ask a thousand questions" but give few answers, sometimes rely on third-party individuals to convey views on proposals, are prone to not "talk business," and often say yes to be courteous when they mean no. Firms in the global chemical industry recognize that production engineering personnel have a great deal of influence in Hungarian buying groups, while purchasing agents in the Canadian chemical industry have relatively more influence in buying decisions.

Selling to the buying centre where buying decisions are made.

Stockbyte/Getty Images

People in the Buying Centre

The composition of the buying centre in a given organization depends on the specific item being bought. Although a buyer or purchasing manager is almost always a member of the buying centre, individuals from other functional areas are included, depending on what is to be purchased. In buying a million-dollar machine tool, the president (because of the size of the purchase) and the production vice-president or manager would probably be members. For key components to be incorporated in a final manufactured product, a cross-functional group of individuals from research and development (R&D), engineering, and quality control are likely to be added. For new word-processing equipment, experienced secretaries who will use the equipment would be members. Still, a major question in penetrating the buying centre is finding and reaching the people who will initiate, influence, and actually make the buying decision.

Roles in the Buying Centre

Researchers have identified five specific roles that an individual in a buying centre can play.[22] In some purchases, the same person may perform two or more of these roles.

- *Users* are the people in the organization who actually use the product or service, such as a nurse who will use a new PDA medical device.
- *Influencers* affect the buying decision, usually by helping define the specifications for what is bought. The information systems manager would be a key influencer in the purchase of new computer servers.
- *Buyers* have formal authority and responsibility to select the supplier and negotiate the terms of the contract. The purchasing manager probably would perform this role in the purchase of the new servers.
- *Deciders* have the formal or informal power to select or approve the supplier that receives the contract. Whereas in routine orders the decider is usually the buyer or purchasing manager, in important technical purchases, it is more likely to be someone from R&D, engineering, or quality control. The decider for a key component being incorporated in a final manufactured product might be any of these three people.
- *Gatekeepers* control the flow of information in the buying centre. Purchasing personnel, technical experts, and administrative assistants can all keep salespeople or information from reaching people performing the other four roles.

Buying Situations and the Buying Centre

The number of people in the buying centre largely depends on the specific buying situation. Researchers who have studied organizational buying identify three types of buying situations, called **buy classes**. These buy classes vary from the routine reorder, or *straight rebuy,* to the completely new purchase, termed *new buy*. In between these extremes is the *modified rebuy*. Some examples will clarify the differences.[23]

- *New buy.* Here, the organization is a first-time buyer of the product or service. This involves greater potential risks in the purchase, and so the buying centre is enlarged to include all those who have a stake in the new buy. Procter & Gamble's purchase of a multi-million dollar fibre-optic network to link its corporate offices from Corning, Inc. represents a new buy.[24]
- *Modified rebuy.* In this buying situation, the users, influencers, or deciders in the buying centre want to change the product specifications, price, delivery schedule, or supplier. Although the item purchased is largely the same as with the straight rebuy, the changes usually necessitate enlarging the buying centre to include people outside the purchasing department.

- *Straight rebuy.* Here, the buyer or purchasing manager reorders an existing product or service from the list of acceptable suppliers, probably without even checking with users or influencers from the engineering, production, or quality control departments. Office supplies and maintenance services are usually obtained as straight rebuys.

Figure 6–3 summarizes how buy classes affect buying centre tendencies in different ways.[25]

FIGURE 6–3

BUYING CENTRE DIMENSION	NEW BUY	MODIFIED REBUY	STRAIGHT REBUY
People involved	Many	Two to three	One
Decision time	Long	Moderate	Short
Problem definition	Uncertain	Minor modifications	Well-defined
Buying objective	Good solution	Low-price supplier	Low-price supplier
Suppliers considered	New/present	Present	Present
Buying influence	Technical/operating personnel	Purchasing agent and others	Purchasing agent

How the buying situation affects buying centre behaviour.

The marketing strategies of sellers facing each of these three buying situations can vary greatly because the importance of personnel from functional areas, such as purchasing, engineering, production, and R&D, often varies with (1) the type of buying situation, and (2) the stage of the purchasing process.[26] If it is a new buy for the manufacturer, you should be prepared to act as a consultant to the buyer, work with technical personnel, and expect a long time for a buying decision to be reached. However, if the manufacturer has bought the component part from you before (a straight or modified rebuy), you might emphasize a competitive price and a reliable supply in meetings with the purchasing agent.

Learning Review

3. What one department is almost always represented by a person in the buying centre?
4. What are the three types of buying situations or buy classes?

CHARTING THE ORGANIZATIONAL BUYING PROCESS

Organizational buyers, like consumers, engage in a decision process when selecting products and services. As defined earlier in this chapter, organizational buying behaviour is the decision-making process that organizations use to establish the need for products and services, and to identify, evaluate, and choose among alternative brands and suppliers. There are important similarities and differences between the two decision-making processes. To better understand the nature of organizational buying behaviour, we first compare it with consumer buying behaviour and then describe an actual organizational purchase in detail.

Stages in the Organizational Buying Process

As shown in Figure 6–4 (and covered in Chapter 5), the five stages a student might use in buying a smartphone also apply to organizational purchases. However, comparing the two right-hand columns in Figure 6–4 reveals some key differences. For example, when a smartphone manufacturer buys earbud headsets for its units from a supplier, more individuals are involved, supplier capability becomes more important, and the post-purchase evaluation behaviour is more formalized.

FIGURE 6–4

STAGE IN THE BUYING DECISION PROCESS	CONSUMER PURCHASE: SMARTPHONE FOR A STUDENT	ORGANIZATIONAL PURCHASE: EARBUD HEADSET FOR A SMARTPHONE
Problem recognition	Student doesn't like the features of the smartphone now owned and desires a new one.	Marketing research and sales departments observe that competitors are improving the earbud headsets for their smartphones. The firm decides to improve the earbud headsets on its own new models, which will be purchased from an outside supplier.
Information search	Student uses personal past experience and that of friends, ads, the Internet, and *Consumer Reports* to collect information and uncover alternatives.	Design and production engineers draft specifications for earbud headsets. The purchasing department identifies suppliers of earbud headsets.
Alternative evaluation	Alternative smartphones are evaluated on the basis of important attributes desired in a phone, and several stores are visited.	Purchasing and engineering personnel visit with suppliers and assess (1) facilities, (2) capacity, (3) quality control, and (4) financial status. They drop any suppliers not satisfactory on these attributes.
Purchase decision	A specific brand of smartphone is selected, the price is paid, and the student leaves the store.	They use (1) quality, (2) price, (3) delivery, and (4) technical capability as key buying criteria to select a supplier. Then they negotiate terms and award a contract.
Post-purchase behaviour	Student reevaluates the purchase decision and may return the phone to the store if it is unsatisfactory.	They evaluate suppliers using a formal vendor rating system and notify a supplier if the earbud headsets do not meet their quality standard. If the problem is not corrected, they drop the firm as a future supplier.

Comparing the stages in consumer and organizational purchases.

The earbud-headset buying decision process is typical of the steps made by organizational buyers. Let us now examine in detail the decision-making process for a more complex product—machine vision systems.

Buying a Machine Vision System

Machine vision is widely regarded as one of the keys to the factory of the future. The chief elements of a machine vision system are its optics, light source, camera, video processor, and computer software. Vision systems are mainly used for product inspection. They are also becoming important as one of the chief elements in the information feedback loop of systems that control manufacturing processes.

Vision systems, selling for around $50,000 to $300,000, are mostly sold to original equipment manufacturers (OEMs) who incorporate them in still larger industrial automation systems that sell for millions of dollars.

Finding productive applications for machine vision involves the constant search for technology and designs that satisfy user needs. The buying process for machine vision components and assemblies is frequently a new buy because many machine vision systems contain elements that require some custom design. Let us track five purchasing stages that a company, such as the Industrial Automation Division of Siemens, a large German industrial firm, would follow when purchasing components and assemblies for the machine vision systems it produces and installs.

Problem Recognition

Sales engineers constantly canvass industrial automation equipment users, such as Ford Motor Company, Grumman Aircraft, and many Asian and European firms, for leads on upcoming industrial automation projects. They also keep these firms current on Siemens' technology, products, and services. When a firm needing machine vision capability identifies a project that would benefit from Siemens' expertise, company engineers typically work with the firm to determine the kind of system required to meet the customer's need.

After a contract is won, project personnel must often make a **make-buy decision**—an evaluation of whether components and assemblies will be purchased from outside suppliers or built by the company itself. (Siemens produces many components and assemblies.) When these items are to be purchased from outside suppliers, the company engages in a thorough supplier search and evaluation process.

Information Search

Such companies as Siemens employ a sophisticated process for identifying outside suppliers of components and assemblies. For standard items, such as connectors, printed circuit boards, and components—for example, resistors and capacitors—the purchasing agent consults the company's purchasing databank, which contains information on hundreds of suppliers and thousands of products. All products in the databank have been pre-negotiated as to price, quality, and delivery time, and many have been assessed using **value analysis**—a systematic appraisal of the design, quality, and performance of a product to reduce purchasing costs.

For one-of-a-kind components or assemblies, such as new optics, cameras, and light sources, the company relies on its engineers to keep current on new developments in product technology. This information is often found in technical journals and industry magazines or at international trade shows where suppliers display their most recent innovations. In some instances, supplier representatives might be asked to make presentations to the buying centre at Siemens. Such a group often consists of a project engineer; several design, system, and manufacturing engineers; and a purchasing agent.

Alternative Evaluation

The main buying criteria that are used to select suppliers include product performance, supplier's technical support, and ease of use. Price is not a top criterion. Typically, two or three suppliers for each standard component and assembly are identified from a **bidders' list**—a list of firms believed to be qualified to supply a given item. This list is generated from the company's purchasing databank as well as from engineering inputs. Specific items that are unique or one-of-a-kind may be obtained from a single supplier after careful evaluation by the buying centre.

Firms selected from the bidders' list are sent a quotation request from the purchasing agent, describing the desired quantity, delivery date(s), and specifications of the components or assemblies. Suppliers are expected to respond within 30 days.

Purchase Decision

Unlike the short purchase stage in a consumer purchase, the period from supplier selection to order placement to product delivery can take several weeks or even months. Even after bids for components and assemblies are submitted, further negotiation concerning price, performance, and delivery terms is likely. Sometimes, conditions related to warranties, indemnities, and payment schedules have to be agreed on. The purchase decision is further complicated by the fact that two or more suppliers of the same item might be awarded contracts. This practice can occur when large orders are requested. Furthermore, suppliers who are not chosen are informed why their bids were not selected.

Post-purchase Behaviour

As in the consumer purchase decision process, post-purchase evaluation occurs in the organizational purchase decision process, but it is formalized and often more sophisticated. All items purchased are examined in a formal product-acceptance process. The performance of the supplier is also monitored and recorded. Performance on past contracts determines a supplier's chances of being asked to bid on future purchases, and poor performance may result in a supplier's name being dropped from the bidders' list.

The preceding example of an organizational purchase suggests four lessons for marketers to increase their chances of selling products and services to organizations. Firms selling to organizations must (1) understand the organization's needs, (2) get on the right bidders' list, (3) find the right people in the buying centre, and (4) provide value to the organizational buyer.

Learning Review

5. What is a make-buy decision?

6. What is a bidders' list?

LO4   ONLINE BUYING IN ORGANIZATIONAL MARKETS

Organizational buying behaviour and business marketing continues to evolve with the application of *information communication technologies (ICTs),* including the Internet. Organizations dwarf consumers in terms of both online transactions made and purchase volume.[27] In fact, organizational buyers account for about 80 percent of the total worldwide dollar value of all online transactions.

Prominence of Online Buying in Organizational Markets

Online buying in organizational markets is prominent for three major reasons.[28] First, organizational buyers depend heavily on timely supplier information that describes product availability, technical specifications, application uses, price, and delivery schedules. This information can be conveyed quickly via Internet technology. Second, this technology has been shown to reduce buyer order processing costs substantially. At General Electric, online buying has cut the cost of a transaction from $50 to $100 per purchase to about $5. Third, business marketers have found that online technology can reduce marketing costs, particularly sales and advertising expense, and broaden their potential customer base for many types of products and services. For these reasons, online buying is popular in all three kinds of organizational markets. For example, airlines order more than $400 million in spare parts from the Boeing website each year.

Customers of Provigo, a large Canadian food wholesaler, can buy online, while provincial and municipal governments across Canada also engage in online purchasing. Online buying can assume many forms. Organizational buyers can purchase directly from suppliers. For instance, a buyer might acquire a dozen desktop photocopiers from **Xerox.ca**. This same buyer might purchase office furniture and supplies online through a reseller, such as Staples at **Staples.ca**. Increasingly, organizational buyers and business marketers are using e-marketplaces and online auctions to purchase and sell products and services.

E-marketplaces: Virtual Organizational Markets

A significant development in organizational buying has been the creation of online trading communities, called **e-marketplaces**, that bring together buyers and supplier organizations. These online communities go by a variety of names, including B2B exchanges and e-hubs, and make possible the real-time exchange of information, money, products, and services.

E-marketplaces can be independent trading communities or private exchanges.[29] Independent e-marketplaces act as a neutral third party and provide an Internet-technology trading platform and a centralized market that enable exchanges between buyers and sellers. They charge a fee for their services and exist in settings that have one or more of the following features: (1) thousands of geographically dispersed buyers and sellers, (2) volatile prices caused by demand and supply fluctuations, (3) time sensitivity due to perishable offerings and changing technologies, and (4) easily comparable offerings between a variety of suppliers. Well-known independent e-marketplaces include PlasticsNet (plastics), Ariba (industrial parts, raw material, and commodities), and **FarmTrade.com** (agricultural products). Small business buyers and sellers, in particular, benefit from independent e-marketplaces. These e-marketplaces offer them an economical way to expand their customer base and reduce the cost of products and services. eBay launched eBayBusiness to serve the small businesses market in Canada and the United States. You can learn about how B2B exchanges work and about eBayBusiness by doing the Going Online exercise, "eBay Means Business, Too."[30]

GOING ONLINE

eBay Means Business, Too

eBay, Inc., is a true Internet phenomenon. By any measure, it is the predominant person-to-person trading community in the world.

But eBay also has a trading platform for the millions of small businesses in Canada, the United States, and around the world. When you go to eBay's site (**www.ebay.com** or **www.ebay.ca**), you can select a category called Business & Industrial. Business buyers and sellers are enabled to buy and sell on this platform. Business transactions currently exceed over $2 billion annually.

grzegorz knec/Alamy Stock Photo

eBay is always updating its business and industry categories. Check it out. What types of industries are most prominent? Are products for all three kinds of organizational markets—industrial, reseller, and government—available?

Large companies tend to favour private exchanges that link them with their network of qualified suppliers and customers. Private exchanges focus on streamlining a company's purchase transactions with its suppliers and customers. Like independent e-marketplaces, they provide a technology trading platform and central market for buyer–seller interactions. They are not a neutral third party, however, but represent the interests of their owners. For example, Agentrics is an international business-to-business private exchange. It connects more than 250 retail customers with 80,000 suppliers. Its members include Best Buy, Campbell Soup, Costco, and Target. The Global Healthcare Exchange and its Canadian counterpart, GHX Canada, engage in the buying and selling of health care products for 3,900 hospitals and more than 300 health care suppliers, such as Abbott Laboratories, GE Medical Systems, Johnson & Johnson, and McKesson Corporation.

Online Auctions in Organizational Markets

Online auctions have grown in popularity among organizational buyers and business marketers. Many e-marketplaces offer this service. Two general types of auctions are common: (1) a traditional auction, and (2) a reverse auction.[31] Figure 6–5 shows how buyer and seller participants and price behaviour differ by type of auction. Let us look at each auction type more closely to understand the implications of each for buyers and sellers.

In a **traditional auction**, a seller puts an item up for sale and would-be buyers are invited to bid in competition with each other. As more would-be buyers become involved, there is an upward pressure on bid prices. Why? Bidding is sequential.

Prospective buyers observe the bids of others and decide whether to increase the bid price. The auction ends when a single bidder remains and "wins" the item with its highest price. For example, eBayBusiness uses a traditional auction. Traditional auctions are also used to dispose of excess merchandise. For example, Dell Inc. sells surplus, refurbished, or closeout computer merchandise at its **dellauction.com** website.

A reverse auction works in the opposite direction from a traditional auction. In a **reverse auction**, a buyer communicates a need for a product or service, and would-be suppliers are invited to bid in competition with each other. As more would-be suppliers become involved, there is a downward pressure on bid prices for the buyer's business. Why? Like traditional auctions, bidding is sequential, and prospective suppliers observe the bids of others and decide whether to decrease the bid price. The auction ends when a single bidder remains and "wins" the business with its lowest price. Reverse auctions benefit organizational buyers by reducing the cost of their purchases. As an example, United Technologies Corporation estimates that it has saved $600 million on the purchase of $6 billion in supplies using online reverse auctions.[32]

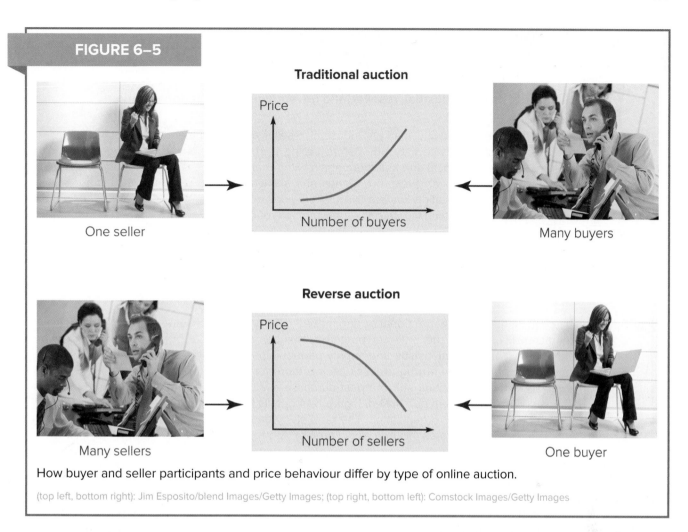

FIGURE 6–5

Traditional auction

One seller → Price / Number of buyers ← Many buyers

Reverse auction

Many sellers → Price / Number of sellers ← One buyer

How buyer and seller participants and price behaviour differ by type of online auction.

(top left, bottom right): Jim Esposito/blend Images/Getty Images; (top right, bottom left): Comstock Images/Getty Images

Clearly, buyers welcome the lower prices generated by reverse auctions. Some suppliers also favour reverse auctions because they give them a chance to capture business that they might not have otherwise had because of a long-standing purchase relationship between the buyer and another supplier. On the other hand, suppliers say that reverse auctions put too much emphasis on prices, discourage consideration of other important buying criteria, and threaten supply partnership opportunities.[33]

Learning Review

7. What are e-marketplaces?
8. In general, which type of online auction creates upward pressure on bid prices, and which type creates downward pressure on bid prices?

Learning Objectives Review

LO1 **Distinguish among industrial, reseller, and government organizational markets.**

There are three different organizational markets: industrial, reseller, and government. Industrial firms, in some way, reprocess a product or service they buy before selling it to the next buyer. Resellers—wholesalers and retailers—buy physical products and sell them again without any reprocessing. Government agencies, at the federal, provincial, and local levels, buy goods and services for the constituents they serve. The North American Industry Classification System (NAICS) provides common industry definitions for Canada, Mexico, and the United States, which facilitate the measurement of economic activity for these three organizational markets.

LO2 **Describe the key characteristics of organizational buying that make it different from consumer buying.**

Seven major characteristics of organizational buying make it different from consumer buying. These include demand characteristics, size of the order or purchase, number of potential buyers, buying objectives, buying criteria, buyer–seller relationships and supply partnerships, and multiple buying influences within organizations. The organizational buying process itself is more formalized, more individuals are involved, supplier capability is more important, and the post-purchase evaluation behaviour often includes performance of the supplier and the item purchased. Figure 6–4 details how the purchase decision process differs between a consumer and an organization. The case study describing the purchase of machine vision systems by a business firm illustrates this process in greater depth.

LO3 **Explain how buying centres and buying situations influence organizational purchasing.**

Buying centres and buying situations have an important influence on organizational purchasing. A buying centre consists of a group of individuals who share common goals, risks, and knowledge important to a purchase decision. A buyer or purchasing manager is almost always a member of a buying centre. However, other individuals may affect organizational purchasing due to their unique roles in a purchase decision. Five specific roles that a person may play in a buying centre include user, influencer, buyer, decider, and gatekeeper. The specific buying situation will influence the number of people and the different roles played in a buying centre. For a routine reorder of an item—a straight rebuy situation—a purchasing manager or buyer will typically act alone in making a purchasing decision. When an organization is a first-time purchaser of a product or service—a new buy situation—a buying centre is enlarged and all five roles in a buying centre often emerge. A modified rebuy buying situation lies between these two extremes. Figure 6–3 offers additional insights into how buying centres and buying situations influence organization purchasing.

LO4 **Recognize the importance and nature of online buying in industrial, reseller, and government organizational markets.**

Organizations dwarf consumers in terms of online transactions made and purchase volume. Online buying in organizational markets is popular for three reasons. First, organizational buyers depend on timely supplier information that describes product availability, technical specifications, application uses, price, and delivery schedules. This information can be conveyed quickly via Internet technology. Second, this technology substantially reduces buyer order processing costs. Third, business marketers have found that Internet technology can reduce marketing costs, particularly sales and advertising expense, and broaden their customer base. Two developments in online buying have been the creation of e-marketplaces and online auctions. E-marketplaces provide a technology trading platform and a centralized market for buyer–seller transactions and make possible the real-time exchange of information, money, products, and services. These e-marketplaces can be independent trading communities or private exchanges. Online traditional and reverse auctions represent a second major development. With traditional auctions, the highest-priced bidder "wins." Conversely, the lowest-priced bidder "wins" with reverse auctions.

Applying Marketing Knowledge

1. Describe the major differences among industrial firms, resellers, and government units in Canada.

2. Explain how the North American Industry Classification System (NAICS) might be helpful in understanding industrial, reseller, and government markets, and discuss the limitations inherent in this system.

3. List and discuss the key characteristics of organizational buying that make it different from consumer buying.

4. What is a buying centre? Describe the roles assumed by people in a buying centre and what useful questions should be raised to guide any analysis of the structure and behaviour of a buying centre.

5. Effective marketing is of increasing importance in today's competitive environment. How can firms more effectively market to organizations?

6. A firm that is marketing multimillion-dollar wastewater treatment systems to cities has been unable to sell a new type of system. To date, the firm's marketing efforts have been directed to city purchasing departments to be included on approved bidders' lists. Talks with city-employed personnel have indicated that the new system is very different from current systems, and therefore, city sanitary and sewer department engineers, directors of these two departments, and city council members are unfamiliar with the workings of the system. Consulting engineers, hired by cities to work on the engineering and design features of these systems and paid on a percentage of system cost, are also reluctant to favour the new system. (*a*) What roles do the various individuals play in the purchase process for a wastewater treatment system? (*b*) How could the firm improve the marketing effort behind the new system?

Building Your Marketing Plan

Your marketing plan may need an estimate of the size of the market potential or industry potential (see Chapter 9) for a particular market–product in which you compete. Use these steps:

1. Define the market–product precisely, such as ice cream manufacturing.

2. Visit the Industry Canada site at **www.ic.gc.ca/cis-sic/cis-sic.nsf/IDE/cis-sic31152defe.html** and search for your market–product. For example, if you search for ice cream manufacturing, you can select "Ice Cream and Frozen Dessert Manufacturing."

3. On the left-hand side, you will see a menu that you can use to access information on ice cream manufacturing (e.g., click on "Performance" and you will find "Net Revenues").

4. Check out the type of data available there that will allow you to assess the market potential for an ice cream manufacturing business.

Trek: Building Better Bikes through Organizational Buying

"Let me tell you a little bit about the history of Trek," says Mark Joslyn, vice president of human resources at Trek Bicycle Corporation. "It's a fantastic story," he continues proudly, "It's a story about a business that started in response to a market opportunity." That opportunity was to build bicycles with the highest-quality frames. In fact, Trek's mission was simple: "Build the best bikes in the world." To do this, Trek needed to find the best raw materials from the best vendors. Michael Leighton, a Trek product manager, explains, "Our relationship with our vendors is incredibly important, and one of our recipes for success!"

The Company

Trek Bicycle was founded in 1976 by Richard Burke and Bevill Hogg. With just five employees, Trek began manufacturing bicycles in a Wisconsin barn. From the beginning, it targeted the high-quality, prestige segment of the bicycle market, using only the best materials and components for their bicycles. The first year, it manufactured 900 custom-made bicycles, which sold quickly. Soon, Trek exceeded its manufacturing capacity. It built a new 26,000-square-foot factory and corporate headquarters to help meet growing demand.

Courtesy Trek Bicycle Corporation

Trek's focus on quality meant that it was very sensitive to the materials used to manufacture the bicycles. The first models, for example, used hand-brazed steel for the frames. Then, borrowing ideas from the aerospace industry, Trek soon began making frames out of bonded aluminum. Following on the success of its aluminum bicycles, Trek began manufacturing bicycles out of carbon fibre. The idea was to be "at the front of technology," explains Joslyn.

The company also expanded its product line. Its first bikes were designed to compete directly with Japanese and Italian bicycles, and included road-racing models. In 1983, Trek manufactured its first mountain bike. In 1990, Trek developed a new category of bicycle—called a multitrack—that combined the speed of road bikes with the ruggedness of mountain bikes. The company also began manufacturing children's bikes, tandem bikes, BMX bikes, and models used by police departments and the U.S. Secret Service. In addition, it added a line of cycling apparel called Trek Wear and cycling accessories such as helmets. Recently, Trek also undertook an Eco Design initiative to build bicycles and parts that are "green" in terms of the environmental impact of manufacturing them, how long they last, and how they can be recycled. To accommodate these production demands, Trek expanded its facilities two more times.

In 1997, Trek became a sponsor of American cyclist Lance Armstrong. In 1999, riding a Trek bicycle, Armstrong won his first Tour de France racing competition, and subsequently went on to win the race in seven consecutive years. As Trek's popularity increased, it began to expand outside of the U.S. For example, the company acquired a Swiss bicycle company called Villiger and the oldest bicycle company in Germany, Diamant. It also expanded into China, opening two stores and signing deals with 20 Chinese distributors.

Today, Trek is one of the leading manufacturers of bicycles and cycling products with more than $600 million in sales and 2,000 employees. Trek's products are now marketed through 1,700 dealers in

North America and wholly owned subsidiaries in seven countries, and through distributors in 80 other countries. Its brands include Trek, Gary Fisher, Bontrager, and Klein. As a global company, Trek's mission has evolved also, and today the mission is to "help the world use the bicycle as a simple solution to complex problems." Trek employees believe that the bicycle is the most efficient form of human transportation and that it can combat climate change, ease urban congestion, and build human fitness. Their motto: "We believe in bikes." Mark Joslyn explains:

> In the world today, we are faced with a number of challenges. We are faced with congestion, issues with mobility, issues with the environment, and quite frankly, issues with health. We believe that the bicycle is a simple solution to all of those things. We are clearly an alternative to other forms of transportation and that's evident in the way that people are embracing cycling not just for recreation but also for transportation. And more and more, particularly in the United States, we are seeing people move to the bike as a way to get around and get to the places they need to ultimately get their life done.

Organizational Buying at Trek

Trek's success at accomplishing its mission is the result of many important business practices, including its organizational buying process. The process begins when managers specify types of materials such as carbon fibre, component parts such as wheels and shifters, and finishing materials such as paint and decals needed to produce a Trek product. In addition, it specifies quality requirements, sizing standards, and likely delivery schedules. According to Leighton, once the requirements are known, the next step is to "go to our buying centre and say 'can you help us find this piece?'"

The buying centre is the group of individuals who are responsible for finding the best suppliers and vendors for the organization's purchases. At Trek, the buying centre consists of a purchasing manager, buyers who identify domestic and international sources of materials and components, and representatives from research and development, production, and quality control. The communication between the product managers and the buying centre is important. "I work very closely with our buying centres to ensure that we're partnering with vendors who can supply reliable quality, and they are actually the ones who, with our quality control team, go in and say 'Yes, this vendor is building product to the quality that meets Trek's standards.' They also negotiate the pricing. Our buying centre domestically is a relatively small team of people and they are focused on specific components."

When potential suppliers are identified, they are evaluated on four criteria—quality, delivery capabilities, price, and environmental impact of their production process. This allows Trek to compare alternative suppliers and to select the best match for Trek and its customers. Once a business is selected as a Trek supplier, it is continuously evaluated on elements of the four criteria. For example, current suppliers might receive scores on the number of defects in a large quantity of supplies, whether just-in-time orders made their deadlines, if target prices were maintained, and if recycled packaging was used. At Trek, the tool that is used to record information about potential and existing suppliers is called a "white paper." Michael Leighton describes how they work: "Our buying centre is tasked with developing what we call white papers. It's a sheet that managers can look at that shows issues and benefits related to working with these people." Every effort is made to develop long-term relationships with suppliers so that they become partners with Trek. These partnerships mean that Trek's success also contributes to the partner's success.

Courtesy Trek Bicycle Corporation

Trek's product managers and the buying centre are involved in three types of organizational purchases. First, new buys are purchases that are made for the first time. Second, modified rebuys involve changing some aspect of a previously ordered product. Finally, straight rebuys are reorders of existing products from the list of acceptable suppliers. Leighton offers examples of each type of purchase at Trek:

> So, [for] a new buy, we work with our buying centres to find new products, something we've never done before, whether it's a new saddle with a new material or a new technology that goes into the frame that damps vibration or gives a better ride. Another case might be electric bikes—maybe we are putting a motor in a bike, that's a new thing, so our buying centre will help us go find those vendors. A modified rebuy is basically a saddle with a little bit different material, but we are sharing some components of it, so the existing components of the saddle [are the same] . . . the cover is new, so it's a little bit different, but it's just the evolution of the product. A straight rebuy is looking at our strategic vision for the component further on down the line where we are just buying the same component and the volume goes up. We look at how we can make this a better business, can save some money, or can make it more worth our while to keep buying the same product rather than buying something new.

While each of the types of purchases may occur frequently at Trek, the criteria that are used to select or evaluate a vendor may vary by the type of purchase and the type of product, making the buying process a dynamic challenge for managers.

Eco-Buying and the Future at Trek

One of Trek's criteria for evaluating existing and potential vendors is their environmental impact. Joslyn says it well: "We evaluate our vendors on many criteria, including, increasingly, the elements that we would consider to be the 'green' part of their offering." For example, Trek recently selected a supplier that (1) owned a quarry for extracting material, (2) used its own manufacturing facilities, and (3) used natural gas instead of coal in its production process. This was appealing to Trek because it suggested that the supplier had a "thorough understanding" of the impact of the product on the environment from start to finish.

Trek's organizational buying reflects the growing importance of its "Eco" perspective. Its bikes are becoming "smarter" as it adds electric-assist components to help them become a practical transportation alternative. Its bikes are also becoming "greener" as more low-impact materials and components are used and as packaging size and weight are reduced. Trek is also addressing the issue of recycling by building the bikes to last longer, using its dealers to help recycle tires and tubes, and funding a non-profit organization called Dream Bikes to teach youth to fix and repair donated bikes.

In addition to changing bikes and the way it makes them, Trek faces several other challenges as it strives to improve its organizational buying process. For example, the growing number of suppliers and vendors necessitates constant, coordinated, and real-time communication to ensure that all components are available when they are needed. In addition, changes in consumer interests and in economic conditions mean that Trek must anticipate fluctuations in demand and make appropriate changes in order sizes and delivery dates. As Mark Joslyn explains, "Everything we do all the time can and should be improved. So, the search for ideas inside of our business and outside of our business, always looking for ways that we can improve and bring new technology and new solutions to the marketplace, is just a core of who we are."

QUESTIONS

1. What is the role of the buying centre at Trek? Who is likely to comprise the buying centre in the decision to select a new supplier at Trek?

2. What selection criteria does Trek utilize when it selects a new supplier or evaluates an existing supplier?

3. How has Trek's interest in the environmental impact of its business influenced its organizational buying process?

4. Provide an example of each of the three buying situations—straight rebuy, modified rebuy, and new buy—at Trek.

Case: This case was written by Steven Hartley. Sources: "Trek Bicycle Corporation," Hoovers, 2011; "Alliance Data Signs Long-Term Extension Agreement with Trek Bicycle Corporation," *PR Newswire*, November 22, 2010; Lou Massante, "Trek Bicycle Buys Villiger, A Leader in the Swiss Market," *Bicycle Retailer & Industry News*, January 1, 2003, p. 10; "Trek Bicycle Corporation," Wikipedia, accessed September 4, 2011; and Trek website, www.trekbikes.com/us/en/company/believe, accessed September 4, 2011.

7

Reaching Global Markets

Learning Objectives

After reading this chapter, you should be able to:

LO1 Describe the scope and nature of world trade from a global perspective and its implications for Canada.

LO2 Identify the major trends that have influenced the landscape of global marketing in the past decade.

LO3 Identify the environmental factors that shape global marketing efforts.

LO4 Name and describe the alternative approaches companies use to enter global markets.

LO5 Explain the distinction between standardization and customization when companies craft worldwide marketing programs.

Building a $2.5 Billion Business in India the Dell Inc. Way

Why did Dell Inc. embark on a bold global growth initiative in 2007? In the words of Steve Felice, former president of Dell Asia-Pacific and Japan, "Our success was going to be largely dependent on our ability to expand globally." Dell's global initiative focused on emerging economies in Asia, Africa, and Latin America. Compared with mature economies in North America and Western Europe, emerging economies offered significant growth potential, according to Michael Dell, Dell's founder and chief executive officer. And Dell's global strategy has proven successful. India is a major growth market for Dell Inc. and now posts annual sales of $2.5 billion. Dell employs some 25,000 people in India, which represents about one-fourth of its global workforce. Dell's global initiative was bold in its departure from prior product-development practices. Prior to its global initiative, Dell designed products for global requirements and distributed the same product globally. The company now routinely designs low-cost notebook, tablet, laptop, and desktop personal computers for customers in China, India, and other emerging economies. Dell's global initiative also required many changes in its signature direct sales, service, and distribution strategy. The company built its U.S. business with telephone- and Internet-based sales—without retailers. However, in emerging economies and India, customers prefer to see, touch, and use a personal computer before they buy. In response, Dell uses individual sales affiliates who reach out to customers in person and give them a firsthand product experience at their doorstep. At the same time, Dell joined hands with Indian chain retailers such as Croma and eZone for a shop-in-a-shop counter for its products. Dell backs this hybrid retail model by offering extended onsite service (technicians who visit individuals' homes) in over 650 cities to both retail and small business customers. Dell also opened Dell exclusive stores in 2008. According to a company spokesperson, "The exclusive Dell store is a step towards enhancing the overall purchase experience for consumers in India. We have rapidly increased our presence in the consumer market here with new products and by expanding our reach. With the launch of Dell exclusive stores, we offer our customers the touch and feel for Dell-branded products within a unique shopping experience." Each Dell-exclusive store offers the advantages of Dell's direct-purchasing model with the additional benefit of retail availability—allowing customers to browse, touch, and feel the product. Dell's approach makes it possible for customers to see the products on the retail shelves and then place an order for the preferred model with the choice to customize the looks and configuration of the unit. By 2015, Dell had 400 exclusive stores in India.

© Indian Photo Agency (InPA)

Dell's global initiative also involved a new advertising campaign, with Dell opting for real-life successful entrepreneurs in India to endorse its products. The "Take Your Own Path" advertising campaign has proven to be highly effective. Dell's success in India illustrates the importance of understanding global customers and reaching them by adapting to their specific needs and preferences.[1]

This chapter describes today's complex and dynamic global marketing environment. It begins by describing the dynamics of world trade and major trends that have influenced the landscape of global marketing. Attention is then focused on prominent cultural, economic, and political-regulatory factors that present both an opportunity and a challenge for global marketers. Four major global market entry strategies are then detailed, including the advantages and disadvantages of each. Finally, the task of designing, implementing, and evaluating worldwide marketing programs for companies such as Dell Inc. is described.

LO1   DYNAMICS OF WORLD TRADE

The dollar value of world trade has more than doubled in the past decade and will exceed $25 trillion by 2020. Manufactured goods and commodities account for about 75 percent of world trade. Service industries, including telecommunications, transportation, insurance, education, banking, and tourism, represent the other 25 percent of world trade.[2]

World Trade

All nations and regions of the world do not participate equally in world trade. World trade flows reflect interdependencies among industries, countries, and regions. These flows manifest themselves in country, company, industry, and regional exports and imports. The dynamics of world trade are evolving. For example, China is now the biggest country measured by world trade and Asia has now surpassed Western Europe as the largest region measured by world trade.

Growing Prevalence of Economic Espionage

The borderless economic world also has a dark side— economic espionage. As you read in Chapter 4, *economic espionage* is the clandestine collection of trade secrets or proprietary information about a company's competitors. This practice is common in high-technology industries such as electronics, specialty chemicals, industrial equipment, aerospace, and pharmaceuticals, where technical know-how and trade secrets separate global industry leaders from followers. It is estimated that economic espionage costs global companies hundreds of billions of dollars a year in lost sales. In many cases, the economic espionage is state-sponsored, with the intelligence services of some two dozen nations routinely attempt to steal information about research and development efforts, manufacturing and marketing plans, and customer lists of major global companies. This state-sponsored economic espionage is becoming more common in our highly competitive global economy. For example, Brazil was caught spying on Bombardier because the country produces a competitive aircraft. Canada admits that it targets countries engaged in economic espionage against us, including Russia and China.

> **Learning Review**
>
> 3. What is protectionism?
> 4. Among which countries was the North American Free Trade Agreement designed to promote free trade?
> 5. What is the difference between a multidomestic marketing strategy and a global marketing strategy?

 A GLOBAL ENVIRONMENTAL SCAN

Global companies conduct continuing environmental scans of the five sets of environmental forces described in Chapter 3 (Figure 3–1: social, economic, technological, competitive, and regulatory forces). This section focuses on three kinds of uncontrollable environmental variables—cultural, economic, and political-regulatory—that affect global marketing practices in strikingly different ways from those in domestic markets.

Cultural Diversity

Marketers must be sensitive to the cultural underpinnings of different societies if they are to initiate and consummate mutually beneficial exchange relationships with global consumers. A necessary step in this process is **cross-cultural analysis**, which involves the study of similarities and differences among consumers in two or more nations or societies.[19] A thorough cross-cultural analysis involves an understanding of and an appreciation for the values, customs, symbols, and languages of other societies.

Values

As defined in Chapter 5, *values* are personally or socially preferable modes of conduct or states of existence that are enduring. Understanding and working with these aspects of a society's values are important factors in global marketing. For example,

- McDonald's does not sell beef hamburgers in its restaurants in India because the cow is considered sacred by almost 85 percent of the population. Instead, McDonald's sells the McMaharajah: two all-mutton patties, special sauce, lettuce, cheese, pickles, and onions on a sesame-seed bun.
- Germans have not been overly receptive to the use of credit cards, such as Visa or MasterCard, and installment debt to purchase goods and services. Indeed, the German word *Schuld* is the same for debt as well as for guilt.

These examples illustrate how cultural values can influence behaviour in different societies. Cultural values become apparent in the personal values of individuals that affect their attitudes and beliefs and the importance assigned to specific behaviours and attributes of goods and services. These personal values affect consumption-specific values, such as the use of installment debt by Germans, and product-specific values, such as the importance assigned to credit card interest rates.

Customs

Customs are the norms and expectations about the way people do things in a specific country. Clearly, customs can vary significantly from country to country. For example, 3M Company executives were perplexed when the company's Scotch-Brite floor-cleaning product initially produced lukewarm sales in the Philippines. When a Filipino employee explained that consumers there customarily clean floors by pushing coconut shells around with their feet, 3M changed the shape of the pad to a foot, and sales soared! Some other customs are unusual to Canadians. Consider, for example, that in France, men use more than twice the number of cosmetics than women do and that Japanese women give Japanese men chocolates on Valentine's Day.

Customs also relate to the nonverbal behaviour of individuals in different cultural settings. For example, in many European countries, it is considered impolite not to have both hands on the table in business meetings. A simple gesture in a commercial, such as pointing a finger, is perfectly acceptable in Western culture, but is perceived as an insult in Middle and Far Eastern countries. Direct eye contact is viewed positively in North and Latin America but negatively in Japan. Casual touching is also inappropriate in Japan, while men hold hands in Middle Eastern countries as a sign of friendship. Business executives in Japan like to hold their opinions, listen longer, and pause before responding in meetings. Sometimes, the silence is misread by North American executives as lack of response.[20]

Cultural Symbols

Cultural symbols are things that represent ideas and concepts. Symbols or symbolism play an important role in cross-cultural analysis because different cultures ascribe different meanings to things. So important is the role of symbols that a field of study, called **semiotics**, has emerged that examines the correspondence between symbols and their role in the assignment of meaning for people. By adroitly using cultural symbols, global marketers can tie positive symbolism to their products and services to enhance their attractiveness to consumers. However, improper use of symbols can spell disaster. A culturally sensitive global marketer will know that.[21]

What cultural lesson did Coca-Cola executives learn when they used the Parthenon in a global advertising campaign?

© Bruno Cossa/SOPA/Corbis

- North Americans are superstitious about the number 13, and Japanese feel the same way about the number 4. *Shi,* the Japanese word for four, is also the word for death. Knowing this, Tiffany & Company sells its fine glassware and china in sets of five, not four, in Japan.

- "Thumbs-up" is a positive sign in Canada. However, in Russia and Poland, this gesture has an offensive meaning when the palm of the hand is shown, as AT&T learned. The company reversed the gesture depicted in ads, showing the back of the hand, not the palm.

Cultural symbols evoke deep feelings. Consider how executives at Coca-Cola Company's Italian office learned this lesson. In a series of advertisements directed at Italian vacationers, the Eiffel Tower, the Empire State Building, and the Tower of Pisa were turned into the familiar Coca-Cola bottle. However, when the white marble columns in the Parthenon that crowns Athens' Acropolis were turned into Coca-Cola bottles, the Greeks were outraged. Greeks refer to the Acropolis as the "holy rock," and a government official said the Parthenon is an "international symbol of excellence" and that "whoever insults the Parthenon insults international culture." Coca-Cola apologized for the ad.[22]

Global markets are also sensitive to the fact that the "country of origin or manufacture" of products and services can symbolize superior or poor quality in some countries. For example, Russian consumers believe products made in Japan and Germany are superior in quality to products from North America and the United Kingdom. Japanese consumers believe Japanese products are superior to those made in Europe and North America. However, recently, Canadian firms marketing in Japan have discovered that Japanese like the "Canadian-ness" of products, and so brands and labels that say "Canada" add cachet for Japanese consumers.[23]

The Mini is marketed in many countries using many languages, such as English and Italian. The Italian translation is "Stop Looking at My Rear."

(both): MINI USA

Language

Global marketers should know not only the native tongues of countries in which they market their products and services but also the nuances and idioms of a language. Even though about 100 official languages exist in the world, anthropologists estimate that at least 3,000 different languages are spoken. There are 20 official languages spoken in the European Union, and Canada has two official languages (English and French). Seventeen major languages are spoken in India alone.

English, French, and Spanish are the principal languages used in global diplomacy and commerce. However, the best language to communicate with consumers is their own, as any seasoned global marketer will attest to. Unintended meanings of brand names and messages have ranged from the absurd to the obscene:

- When the advertising agency responsible for launching Procter & Gamble's successful Pert shampoo in Canada realized that the name means "lost" in French, it substituted the brand name Pret, which means "ready."

- In Italy, Cadbury Schweppes, the world's third-largest soft drink manufacturer, realized that its Schweppes Tonic Water brand had to be renamed Schweppes Tonica because "il water" turned out to be an idiom for bathroom.

- The Vicks brand name common in North America is German slang for sexual intimacy; therefore, Vicks is called Wicks in Germany.

Experienced global marketers use **back translation**, where a translated word or phrase is retranslated into the original language by a different interpreter to catch errors. For example, IBM's first Japanese translation of its "Solutions for a small planet" advertising message yielded "Answers that make people smaller." The error was caught and corrected. Nevertheless, unintended translations can produce favourable results. Consider Kit Kat bars marketed by Nestle worldwide. Kit Kat is pronounced "kitto katsu" in Japanese, which roughly translates to "I hope you win." Japanese teens eat Kit Kat bars for good luck, particularly when taking crucial school exams.

The use of language in global marketing is assuming greater importance in an increasingly networked and borderless economic world. For example, Oracle Corporation, a leading worldwide supplier of software, now markets its products by language groups instead of through 145 country-specific efforts. The French group markets to France, Belgium, Switzerland, and Canada. A Spanish-language group oversees Spain and Latin America. Eight other language groups—English, Japanese, Korean, Chinese, Portuguese, Italian, Dutch, and German—cover Oracle's top revenue-producing countries.[24]

Cultural Ethnocentricity

The tendency for people to view their own values, customs, symbols, and language favourably is well known. However, the belief that aspects of one's culture are superior to another's is called *cultural ethnocentricity* and is a sure impediment to successful global marketing.

An outgrowth of cultural ethnocentricity exists in the purchase and use of goods and services produced outside of a country. Global marketers are acutely aware that certain groups within countries disfavour imported products, not on the basis of price, features, or performance, but purely because of their foreign origin. **Consumer ethnocentrism** is the tendency to believe that it is inappropriate, indeed immoral, to purchase foreign-made products.[25] Ethnocentric consumers believe that buying imported products is wrong because such purchases are unpatriotic, harm domestic industries, and cause domestic unemployment.[26]

Economic Considerations

Global marketing is also affected by economic considerations. Therefore, a scan of the global marketplace should include (1) a comparative analysis of the economic development in different countries, (2) an assessment of the economic infrastructure in these countries, (3) measurement of consumer income in different countries, and (4) recognition of a country's currency exchange rates.

Stage of Economic Development

There are about 200 independent countries in the world today, each of which is at a slightly different point in terms of its stage of economic development. However, they can be classified into two major groupings that will help the global marketer better understand their needs:

- *Developed* countries have somewhat mixed economies. Private enterprise dominates, although they have substantial public sectors as well. Canada, the United States, Japan, and most of Western Europe can be considered developed.

- *Developing* countries are in the process of moving from an agricultural to an industrial economy. There are two subgroups within the developing category: (1) those that have already made the move, and (2) those that remain locked in a preindustrial economy. Such countries as Brazil, China, India, Poland, Hungary, Israel, Venezuela, Singapore, and South Africa fall into the first group. In the second group are Afghanistan, Sri Lanka, Tanzania, and Chad, where living standards are low and improvement will be slow.

About 86 percent of the world's population of roughly 7 billion people reside in developing countries and have only one-fifth of the total world income. Four billion of these people live on less than $2 per day. In global marketing terms, they are viewed as being at the **bottom of the pyramid**, which is the largest, but poorest socio-economic group of people in the world.[27]

Today, global companies are choosing to serve people at the bottom of the pyramid by being responsive to their conditions and needs. Motorola is an example. The company developed a low-cost cellphone with battery life as long as 500 hours for rural villagers without regular electricity and an extra-loud volume for use in noisy markets. Motorola's cellphone, a no-frills design, is priced at $40, has a standby time of two weeks, and conforms to local language and customs. Motorola has been successfully selling this cellphone design in rural areas across China, India, and Turkey. Still, the task facing global marketers is not easy. A country's stage of economic development affects and is affected by other economic factors, as described next.

Economic Infrastructure

The *economic infrastructure*—a country's communications, transportation, financial, and distribution systems—is a critical consideration in determining whether to try to market to a country's consumers and organizations. Parts of the infrastructure that North Americans or Western Europeans take for granted can be huge problems elsewhere—not only in the developing nations but also in Eastern Europe, the Indian subcontinent, and China, where such an infrastructure is assumed to be in place. Consider, for instance, the transportation and distribution systems in these countries. Two-lane roads that limit average speeds to 55 or 65 kilometres per hour are commonplace—and a nightmare for firms requiring prompt truck delivery. In China, the bicycle is the preferred mode of transportation. This is understandable because China has few navigable roads outside its major cities, where 80 percent of the population lives. In India, Coca-Cola uses large tricycles to distribute cases of Coke along narrow streets in many cities. Wholesale and retail institutions tend to be small and are operated by new owner-managers still learning the ways of a free market system.

The communications infrastructures in these countries also differ. This infrastructure includes telecommunications systems and networks in use, such as Internet, telephones, cable television, broadcast radio and television, computers, satellites, and wireless telephones. In general, the communications infrastructure in many developing countries is limited or antiquated compared with that of the developed countries.

Even the financial and legal systems can cause problems. Formal operating procedures among financial institutions and private properties did not exist under communism and are still limited. As a consequence, it is estimated that two-thirds of the commercial transactions in Russia involve nonmonetary forms of payment. The legal red tape involved in obtaining title to buildings and land for manufacturing, wholesaling, and retailing operations also has been a huge problem. Nevertheless, the Coca-Cola Company invested $750 million from 1991 through 1998 to build bottling and distribution facilities in Russia, PepsiCo. has invested $1.5 billion in transportation and manufacturing systems in China and India since 2010, Allied Lyons spent $30 million to build a plant to make Baskin-Robbins ice cream, and Mars opened a $200 million candy factory outside Moscow.[28]

Consumer Income and Purchasing Power

A global marketer selling consumer goods must also consider what the average per-capita or household income is among a country's consumers and how the income is distributed to determine a nation's purchasing power. Per-capita income varies greatly between nations. Average yearly per-capita income in EU countries is more than $30,000 and is less than $300 in some developing countries, such as Vietnam. A country's income distribution is important because it gives a more reliable picture of a country's purchasing power. Generally speaking, as the proportion of middle-income-class households in a country increases, the greater a nation's purchasing power tends to be. In established market economies, such as those in North America and Western Europe, 65 percent of households have an annual purchasing capability of $20,000 or more. In comparison, 75 percent of households in the developing countries of Sub-Saharan Africa have an annual purchasing power of less than $5,000.[29]

Seasoned global marketers recognize that people in the developing countries often have government subsidies for food, housing, and health care that supplement their income. Accordingly, people with seemingly low incomes are potentially promising customers for a variety of products. For example, a consumer in South Asia earning the equivalent of $250 per year can afford Gillette razors. When that consumer's income rises to $1,000, a Sony television becomes affordable, and a new Volkswagen or Nissan can be bought with an annual income of $10,000. In the developing countries of Eastern Europe, a $1,000 annual income makes a refrigerator affordable, and $2,000 brings an automatic washer within reach.

Efforts to raise household incomes in developing countries are evident in the growing popularity of microfinance. **Microfinance** is the practice of offering small, collateral-free loans to individuals who otherwise would not have access to the capital necessary to begin small businesses or other income-generating activities. An example of microfinance is found in Hindustan Lever's initiative in India. The company realized it could not sell to the rural poor in India unless it found ways to distribute its products such as soap, shampoos, and laundry detergents. Lever provided startup loans to women to buy stocks of products to sell to local villagers. Today, thousands of women entrepreneurs sell Lever products in 100,000 villages in India and account for about 15 percent of the company's rural sales in that country. Equally important, these women now have a source of income, whereas before they had nothing.[30]

Income growth in the developing countries of Asia, Latin America, and Eastern Europe is expected to stimulate world trade. The number of consumers in these countries earning the equivalent of $10,000 per year is expected to surpass the number of consumers in North America, Japan, and Western Europe combined by 2015. In essence, much of the world population is achieving "middle-class status" and for this reason, developing countries now represent a significant marketing opportunity for global companies.

Currency Exchange Rates

Fluctuations in exchange rates among the world's currencies are of critical importance in global marketing. Such fluctuations affect everyone—from international tourists to global companies.

A **currency exchange rate** is the price of one country's currency expressed in terms of another country's currency, such as the Canadian dollar expressed in Japanese yen or Swiss francs. Failure to consider exchange rates when pricing products for global markets can have dire consequences.

Exchange-rate fluctuations have a direct impact on the sales and profits made by global companies. When foreign currencies can buy more Canadian dollars, for example, Canadian products are less expensive for foreign customers. Short-term fluctuations, however, can have a significant effect on the profits of global companies. Hewlett-Packard gained nearly a half-million dollars of additional profit through exchange rate fluctuation in one year. On the other hand, Honda lost over $400 million on its European operations due to currency swings in the Japanese yen compared with the euro and the British pound. Severe and protracted fluctuations in a country's currency can affect trade as well. For example, Procter & Gamble briefly suspended product shipments to Turkey, one of its largest export markets, because of instability of the Turkish currency.

Political-Regulatory Climate

The political and regulatory climate for marketing in a country or region of the world lies not only in identifying the current climate but also in determining how long a favourable or unfavourable climate will last. An assessment of a country or regional political-regulatory climate includes an analysis of its political stability and trade regulations.

Political Stability

Trade among nations or regions depends on political stability. Billions of dollars have been lost in the Middle East and Africa as a result of internal political strife and war. Such losses encourage careful selection of politically stable countries and regions of the world for trade.

Political stability in a country is affected by numerous factors, including a government's orientation toward foreign companies and trade with other countries. These factors combine to create a political climate that is favourable or unfavourable for marketing and financial investment in a country or region of the world. Marketing managers monitor political stability using a variety of measures and often track country risk ratings supplied by such agencies as the PRS Group. Visit the PRS Group website shown in the accompanying Going Online box, "Checking a Country's Political Risk Rating," to see the most recent political risk ratings for countries.

GOING ONLINE

Checking a Country's Political Risk Rating

The political climate in every country is regularly changing. Governments can make new laws or enforce existing policies differently. Numerous consulting firms prepare political risk analyses that incorporate a variety of variables, such as the risk of internal turmoil, external conflict, government restrictions on company operations, and tariff and non-tariff trade barriers.

The PRS Group maintains multiple databases of country-specific information and projections, including country political risk ratings. These ratings can be accessed at **www.prsgroup.com**. Click "Products" and then "Free Samples" (you will need to give your name and e-mail address to obtain the table). Which three countries have the highest rating (lowest risk), and which three have the lowest rating (highest risk)? Which countries have risk ratings closest to Canada?

The **PRS** Group

Courtesy of The PRS Group, Inc.

Trade Regulations

Countries have a variety of rules that govern business practices within their borders. These rules often serve as trade barriers.[31] For example, Japan has some 11,000 trade regulations. Japanese car safety rules effectively require all automobile replacement parts to be Japanese and not North American or European; public health rules make it illegal to sell aspirin or cold medicine without a pharmacist present. The Malaysian government has advertising regulations stating that "advertisements must not project or promote an excessively aspirational lifestyle," Greece bans toy advertising, and Sweden outlaws all advertisements to children. Until recently, the EU banned Canadian icewine from its markets because the icewine's alcohol content was beyond accepted levels.

Trade regulations also appear in free trade agreements among countries. European Union nations abide by some 10,000 rules that specify how goods are to be made and marketed. For instance, the rules for a washing machine's electrical system are detailed on more than 100 typed pages. There are also regulations related to contacting consumers via telephone, fax, and e-mail without their prior consent. The European Union's ISO 9000 quality standards, though not a trade regulation, have the same effect on business practice. These standards, described in Chapter 6, involve registration and certification of a manufacturer's quality management and quality assurance system. Many European companies require suppliers to be ISO 9000 certified as a condition of doing business with them. Certified companies have undergone an on-site audit that includes an inspection of its facilities to ensure that documented quality control procedures are in place and that all employees understand and follow them.

6. Semiotics involves the study of_____.

7. When foreign currencies can buy more U.S. dollars, are American products more or less expensive for a foreign consumer?

(LO4) COMPARING GLOBAL MARKET ENTRY STRATEGIES

Once a company has decided to enter the global marketplace, it must select a means of market entry. Four general options exist: (1) exporting, (2) licensing, (3) joint venture, and (4) direct investment.[32] As Figure 7–5 demonstrates, the amount of financial commitment, risk, marketing control, and profit potential increases as the firm moves from exporting to direct investment.

FIGURE 7–5

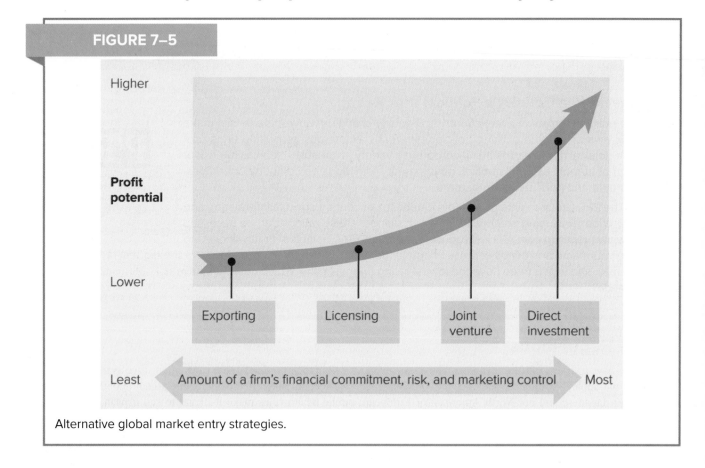

Alternative global market entry strategies.

Exporting

Exporting is producing goods in one country and selling them in another country. This entry option allows a company to make the least number of changes in terms of its product, its organization, and even its corporate goals. Host countries usually do not like this practice because it provides less local employment than under alternative means of entry.

Indirect exporting is when a firm sells its domestically produced goods in a foreign country through an intermediary. It involves the least amount of commitment and risk but will probably return the least profit. This kind of exporting is ideal for the company that has no overseas contacts but wants to market abroad. The intermediary is often a distributor that has the marketing know-how and the resources necessary for the effort to succeed.

Direct exporting occurs when a firm sells its domestically produced goods in a foreign country without intermediaries. Most companies become involved in direct exporting when they believe their volume of sales will be sufficiently large and easy to obtain that they do not require intermediaries. For example, the exporter may be approached by foreign buyers that are willing to contract for a large volume of purchases. Direct exporting involves more risk than indirect exporting for the company but also opens the door to increased profits.

Novartis Consumer Health Canada markets its cough remedy product, Buckley Mixture, using an indirect exporting strategy in the Australian market and a direct exporting strategy for the United States market. Reif Estate Winery in Niagara-on-the-Lake, Ontario, and Andrés Wines of Grimsby, Ontario, both engage in exporting their Canadian wines to the European Union as well as other foreign markets, where sales have grown significantly.

Licensing

Under **licensing**, a company offers the right to a trademark, patent, trade secret, or other similarly valued items of intellectual property in return for a royalty or a fee. In international marketing, the advantages to the company granting the licence are low risk and a capital-free entry into a foreign country. The licensee gains information that allows it to start with a competitive advantage, and the foreign country gains employment by having the product manufactured locally.

There are some serious drawbacks to this mode of entry, however. The licensor forgoes control of its product and reduces the potential profits gained from it. In addition, while the relationship lasts, the licensor may be creating its own competition. Some licensees are able to modify the product somehow and enter the market with product and marketing knowledge gained at the expense of the company that got them started. To offset this disadvantage, many companies strive to stay innovative so that the licensee remains dependent on them for improvements and successful operation. Finally, should the licensee prove to be a poor choice, the name or reputation of the company may be harmed.

McDonald's uses franchising as a market-entry strategy, and more than 60 percent of the company's sales come from foreign operations. Note that the golden arches appear prominently—one aspect of its global brand promise.

China/Alamy Stock Photo

Two variations of licensing, *contract manufacturing* and *contract assembly,* represent alternative ways to produce a product within the foreign country. With contract manufacturing, a Canadian company may contract with a foreign firm to manufacture products according to stated specifications. The product is then sold in the foreign country or exported back to Canada. With contract assembly, the Canadian company may contract with a foreign firm to assemble (not manufacture) parts and components that have been shipped to that country. In both cases, the advantage to the foreign country is the employment of its people, and the Canadian firm benefits from the lower wage rates in the foreign country. Contract manufacturing and assembly in the developing countries had sparked controversy in the toy, textile, and apparel industries, where poor working conditions, low pay, and child labour practices have been documented. However, this practice has been an economic boon to many developing countries. For example, Taiwan makes more than half of the world's notebook computers, contracting for Dell and IBM, and this has generated personal income and employment for the Taiwanese people.

A third variation of licensing is *franchising.* Franchising is one of the fastest-growing market entry strategies. Franchises include soft-drink, motel, retailing, fast-food, and car rental operations, as well as a variety of business services. McDonald's is a premier global franchiser: More than 70 percent of the company's stores are franchised, and over 60 percent of the company's sales come from foreign operations.[33]

Joint Venture

When a foreign country and a local firm invest together to create a local business, it is called a **joint venture**. These two companies share ownership, control, and profits of the new company. Investment may be made by having either of the companies buy shares in the other or by creating a third and separate entity. This was done by Caterpillar, Inc., the world's largest manufacturer of earth-moving and construction equipment, when it created NEVAMASH with its joint-venture partner, Kirovsky Zvod, a large Russian manufacturer of heavy equipment.

The advantages of this option are twofold. First, one company may not have the necessary financial, physical, or managerial resources to enter a foreign market alone. Ford and Volkswagen formed a joint venture to make four-wheel-drive vehicles in Portugal. Second, a government may require or strongly encourage a joint venture before it allows a foreign company to enter its market. This is the case in China. Today, more than 50,000 Chinese–foreign joint ventures operate in China.[34]

The disadvantages arise when the two companies disagree about policies or courses of action for their joint venture or when governmental bureaucracy bogs down the effort. For example, Canadian firms often prefer to reinvest earnings gained, whereas some foreign companies may want to spend those earnings. Or a Canadian firm may want to return profits earned to Canada, while the local firm or its government may oppose this—the problem now faced by many potential joint ventures in Eastern Europe, Russia, Latin America, and South Asia.

Direct Investment

The biggest commitment a company can make when entering the global market is **direct investment**, which entails a domestic firm actually investing in and owning a foreign subsidiary or division. Examples of direct investment are Toyota's automobile plant in Ontario and Hyundai's plant in Quebec. Many Canadian-based companies are also switching to this mode of entry. Alcan Aluminium built a recycling plant in Worrington, England, and Ganong Brothers owns a plant that manufactures chocolates in Thailand. And New Brunswick–based McCain Foods, a global leader in the frozen-food industry has 55 production facilities on six continents. It is the world's largest processor of frozen french fries, producing, in fact, one-third of all frozen french fries in the world.

For many firms, direct investment often follows one of the other three market entry strategies. For example, Ernst & Young, an international accounting and management consulting firm, entered Hungary first by establishing a joint venture with a local company. Ernst & Young later acquired the company, making it a subsidiary with headquarters in Budapest. Following the success of its European and Asian exporting strategy, Harley-Davidson now operates wholly owned subsidiaries in Germany, Italy, and Japan.

The advantages to direct investment include cost savings, better understanding of local market conditions, and fewer local restrictions. Firms entering foreign markets using direct investment believe that these advantages outweigh the financial commitments and risks involved.

Learning Review

8. What mode of entry could a company follow if it has no previous experience in global marketing?

9. How does licensing differ from a joint venture?

LO5 CRAFTING A WORLDWIDE MARKETING PROGRAM

The choice of a market entry strategy is a necessary first step for a marketer when joining the community of global companies. The next step involves the challenging task of designing, implementing, and evaluating marketing programs worldwide.

Successful global marketers standardize global marketing programs whenever possible and customize them wherever necessary. The extent of standardization and customization is often rooted in a careful global environment scan supplemented with judgment based on experience and marketing research.

Product and Promotion Strategies

Global companies have five strategies for matching products and their promotion efforts to global markets. As Figure 7–6 shows, the strategies focus on whether a company extends or adapts its product and promotion message for consumers in different countries and cultures.

A product may be sold globally in one of three ways: (1) in the same form as in its home market, (2) with some adaptations, or (3) as a totally new product:[35]

FIGURE 7–6

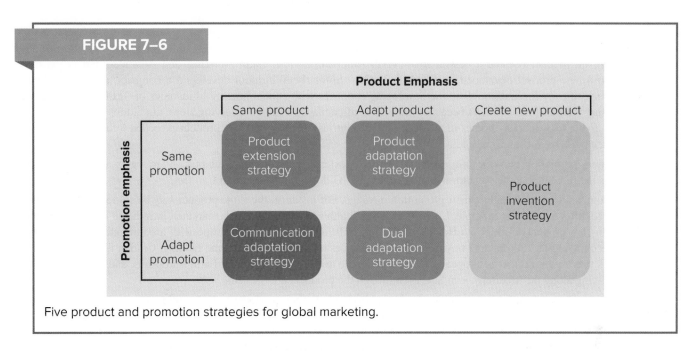

Five product and promotion strategies for global marketing.

1. *Product extension.* Selling virtually the same product in other countries is a product extension strategy. It works well for such products as Coca-Cola, McCain frozen french fries, Gillette razors, Wrigley's gum, Levi's jeans, Sony consumer electronics, Harley-Davidson motorcycles, and Apple smartphones. As a general rule, product extension seems to work best when the consumer market target for the product is alike across countries and cultures—that is, consumers share the same desires, needs, and uses for the product.

2. *Product adaptation.* Changing a product in some way to make it more appropriate for a country's climate or consumer preferences is a product adaptation strategy. Gerber baby food comes in different varieties in different countries. Vegetable and Rabbit Meat is a favourite in Poland. Freeze-Dried Sardines and Rice is popular in Japan. Maybelline's makeup is formulaically adapted in labs to suit local skin types and weather across the globe, including an Asia-specific mascara that does not run during the rainy season.

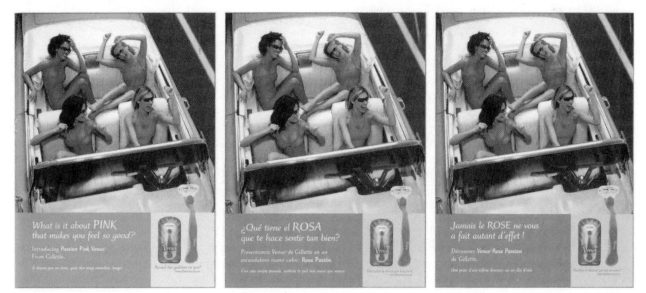

Gillette delivers the same global message whenever possible, as shown in the Gillette for Women Venus ads from Canada, Mexico, and France.

(all): Procter & Gamble

3. *Product invention.* Alternatively, companies can invent totally new products designed to satisfy common needs across countries. Black & Decker did this with its Snake Light Flexible Flashlight. Created to address a global need for portable lighting, the product became a bestseller in North America, Europe, Latin America, and Australia, and is the most successful new product developed by Black & Decker. Similarly, Whirlpool developed a compact, automatic clothes washer specifically for households in the developing countries with annual household incomes of $2,000. Called Ideale, the washer features bright colours because washers are often placed in a home's living areas, not hidden in laundry rooms (which do not exist in many homes in the developing countries). Demand for this product exceeded forecasts when it was introduced in Brazil, China, and India.

An identical promotion message is used for the product extension and product adaptation strategies around the world. Gillette uses the same global message for its men's toiletries: "Gillette, the Best a Man Can Get."

Global companies may also adapt their promotion message. For instance, the same product may be sold in many countries but advertised differently. As an example, L'Oréal, a French health and beauty products marketer, introduced its Golden Beauty brand of sun-care products through its Helena Rubenstein subsidiary in Western Europe with a communication adaptation strategy. Recognizing the cultural and buying motive differences related to skin care and tanning, Golden Beauty advertising features dark tanning for northern Europeans, skin protection to avoid wrinkles among Latin Europeans, and beautiful skin for Europeans living along the Mediterranean Sea, even though the products are the same.

Other companies use a dual adaptation strategy by modifying both their products and promotion messages. Nestlé does this with Nescafé coffee. Nescafé is marketed using different coffee blends and promotional campaigns to match consumer preferences in different countries. For example, Nescafé, the world's largest brand of coffee, generally emphasizes the taste, aroma, and warmth of shared moments in its advertising around the world. However, Nescafé is advertised in Thailand as a way to relax from the pressures of daily life.

These examples illustrate the simple rule applied by global companies: Standardize product and promotion strategies whenever possible and customize them wherever necessary. This is the art of global marketing.[36] Part of the standardization and customization discussion must now also involve the use of social media in a global context. To read more about this important consideration, read the Marketing Matters box, "Global Marketing and Social Media."[37]

MARKETING MATTERS

Global Marketing and Social Media

A study from Simon Fraser University suggests global marketers must consider how to effectively use social media in a global context. A major conclusion reached by reseachers Leyland Pitt, Kirk Plangger, Daniel Shapiro, and Pierre Berthon is that a "one-size-fits-all" or standardized approach to social media will not work across countries. For example, they discovered that not all countries share the same preferences for specific social media channels. They suggest that there is evidence of a relationship between cultural norms and values and the relative interest in a social media site across different countries. Using data from Google searches, they showed that relative interest in particular social media differs markedly across countries. For instance, Facebook and LinkedIn are very popular in the United States, India, and South Africa, but are less popular in Japan, where consumers prefer homegrown venues such as GREE in addition to Twitter. Thus, the researchers state that companies operating in global markets "will need to customize the social media aspects of its global marketing strategy to fit and accommodate national differences."

To help global marketing strategists, the researchers offer five axioms for effectively incorporating social media into global marketing programs:

1. Social media is a function of the technology, culture, and government of a particular country.

2. In the age of social media, local events seldom remain local.

3. In the age of social media, general issues seldom remain general; that is, macro issues tend to be re-interpreted locally.

4. The actions and creations of creative consumers (those who create content on social media) tend to be a function of the technology, culture, and government of a particular country.

5. Technology tends to be historically dependent; that is, technologies in different countries evolve along unique trajectories due to inertia rather than because they are the optimal solution.

The researchers suggest that global marketers need to continually stay up to date on technology, customers, and social media when operating in global markets. They also argue that it is important to truly engage customers—in the right way, using the technology wisely and informing senior leadership about the opportunities to use social media in global settings.

Distribution Strategy

Distribution is of critical importance in global marketing. The availability and quality of retailers and wholesalers, as well as transportation, communication, and warehousing facilities, are often determined by a country's stage of economic development. Figure 7–7 outlines the channel through which a product manufactured in one country must travel to reach its destination in another country. The first step involves the seller; its headquarters is the starting point and is responsible for the successful distribution to the ultimate consumer. The next step is the channel between two nations, moving the product from one country to another. Intermediaries that can handle this responsibility include resident buyers in a foreign country, independent merchant wholesalers who buy and sell the product, or agents who bring buyers and sellers together.

Once the product is in the foreign nation, that country's distribution channels take over.[38] These channels can be very long or surprisingly short depending on the product line. In Japan, fresh fish go through three intermediaries before getting to a retail outlet. Conversely, shoes go through only one intermediary. In other cases, the channel does not even involve the host country. Procter & Gamble sells its soap door to door in the Philippines because there are no other alternatives in many parts of that country. The sophistication of a country's distribution channels increase as its economic infrastructure develops. Supermarkets facilitate selling products in many nations, but they are not popular or available in many others where culture and lack of refrigeration dictate shopping on a daily rather than a weekly basis. For example, when Coke and Pepsi entered China, both had to create direct-distribution channels, investing in refrigerator units for small retailers.

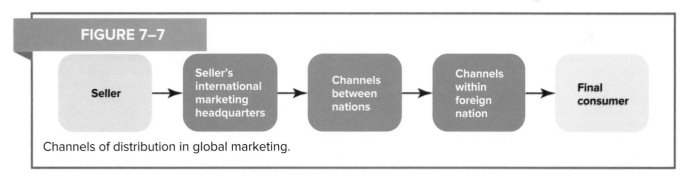

FIGURE 7–7

Channels of distribution in global marketing.

Pricing Strategy

Global companies also face many challenges in determining a pricing strategy as part of their worldwide marketing effort. Individual countries, even those with free trade agreements, may impose considerable competitive, political, and legal constraints on the pricing latitude of global companies. For example, antitrust authorities in Germany limited Walmart from selling some items below cost to lure shoppers. Without this practice, Walmart was unable to compete against German discount stores. This, and other factors, led Walmart to leave Germany.[39] Of course, economic factors, such as the costs of production, selling, and tariffs, plus transportation and storage costs, also affect global pricing decisions.

Pricing too low or too high can have dire consequences. When prices appear too low in one country, companies can be charged with dumping, a practice subject to severe penalties and fines. **Dumping** is when a firm sells a product in a foreign country below its domestic price or below its actual cost. This is often done to build a company's share of the market by pricing at a competitive level. Another reason is that the products being sold may be surplus or cannot be sold domestically and, therefore, are already a burden to the company. The firm may be glad to sell them at almost any price.

When companies price their products very high in some countries but competitively in others, they face a grey-market problem. A **grey market**, also called *parallel importing,* is a situation where products are sold through unauthorized channels of distribution. A grey market comes about when individuals buy products in a lower-priced country from a manufacturer's authorized retailer, ship them to higher-priced countries, and then sell them below the manufacturer's suggested retail price through unauthorized retailers. Many well-known products have been sold through grey markets, including Olympus cameras, Seiko watches, Chanel perfume, and Mercedes-Benz cars.

Learning Review

10. Products may be sold globally in three ways. What are they?

11. What is dumping?

Learning Objectives Review

LO1

Describe the scope and nature of world trade from a global perspective and its implications for Canada.

A global perspective on world trade views exports and imports as complementary economic flows: A country's imports affect its exports, and exports affect its imports. World trade flowing to and from Canada reflects demand and supply interdependencies for goods among nations and industries. Canada is a trading nation and currently maintains a surplus in its balance of trade. The largest importers of Canadian goods and services are the United States, Japan, and the EU.

LO2

Identify the major trends that have influenced the landscape of global marketing in the past decade.

Four major trends have influenced the landscape of global marketing. First, there has been a gradual decline of economic protectionism by individual countries, leading to a reduction in tariffs and quotas. Second, there is growing economic integration and free trade among nations, reflected in the creation of the European Union and the North American Free Trade Agreement. Third, there is increased global competition among global companies for global consumers, resulting in firms adopting global marketing strategies and promoting global brands. And finally, a networked global marketspace has emerged using Internet technology as a tool for exchanging goods, services, and information on a global scale.

LO3

Identify the environmental factors that shape global marketing efforts.

Three major environmental factors shape global marketing efforts. First, there are cultural factors, including values, customs, cultural symbols, and language. Economic factors also shape global marketing efforts. These include a country's stage of economic development and economic infrastructure, consumer income and purchasing power, and currency exchange rates. Finally, political-regulatory factors in a country or region of the world create a favourable or unfavourable climate for global marketing efforts.

LO4

Name and describe the alternative approaches companies use to enter global markets.

Companies have four alternative approaches for entering global markets. These are exporting, licensing, joint venture, and direct investment. Exporting involves producing goods in one country and selling them in another country. Under licensing, a company offers the right to a trademark, patent, trade secret, or similarly valued items of intellectual property in return for a royalty or fee. In a joint venture, a foreign company and a local firm invest together to create a local business. Direct investment entails a domestic firm actually investing in and owning a foreign subsidiary or division.

LO5

Explain the distinction between standardization and customization when companies craft worldwide marketing programs.

Companies distinguish between standardization and customization when crafting worldwide marketing programs. Standardization means that all elements of the marketing program are the same across countries and cultures. Customization means that one or more elements of the marketing program are adapted to meet the needs or preferences of consumers in a particular country or culture. Global marketers apply a simple rule when crafting worldwide marketing programs: standardize marketing programs whenever possible and customize them wherever necessary.

Applying Marketing Knowledge

1. What is meant by this statement: "Quotas are a hidden tax on consumers, whereas tariffs are a more obvious one"?

2. Is the trade feedback effect described in the text a long-run or short-run view on world trade flows? Explain your answer.

3. Because English is the official language in Australia, some Canadian global companies might select it as an easy market to enter. Others believe that this similarity in language could make it harder to enter that market successfully. Who is right? Why?

4. How successful would a television commercial in Japan be if it featured a husband surprising his wife in her dressing area on Valentine's Day with a small box of chocolates containing four candies? Why?

5. As a novice in global marketing, which alternative for global market entry strategy would you be likely to start with? Why? What other alternatives do you have for a global market entry?

6. Coca-Cola is sold worldwide. In some countries, Coca-Cola owns the bottling facilities; in others, it has signed contracts with licensees or relies on joint ventures. When selecting a licensee in each country, what factors should Coca-Cola consider?

7. If a global company wished to leverage social media as part of its global marketing strategy, what guidelines or recommendations would you give to that firm?

Building Your Marketing Plan

Does your marketing plan involve reaching global customers outside of Canada? If the answer is no, read no further and do not include a global element in your plan. If the answer is yes, try to identify the following:

1. What features of your product are especially important to potential customers.

2. In which countries these potential customers live.

3. Special marketing issues that are involved in trying to reach them.

Answers to these questions will help in developing more detailed marketing mix strategies described in later chapters.

Video Case 7

Mary Kay, Inc.: Building a Brand in India

Sheryl Adkins-Green couldn't ask for a better assignment. As the newly appointed vice president of brand development at Mary Kay, Inc., she is responsible for development of the product portfolio around the world, including global initiatives and products specifically formulated for global markets. She is enthusiastic about her position, noting that, "There is tremendous opportunity for growth. Even in these economic times, women still want to pamper themselves, and to look good is to feel good." Getting up to speed on her new company and her new position topped her short-term agenda. She was specifically interested in the company's efforts to date to build the Mary Kay brand in India.

The Mary Kay Way

Mary Kay Ash founded Mary Kay Cosmetics in 1963 with her life savings of $5,000 and the support of her 20-year-old son, Richard Rogers, who currently serves as executive chairman of Mary Kay, Inc. Mary Kay, Inc., is one of the largest direct sellers of skin care and colour cosmetics in the world with more than $2.5 billion in annual sales. Mary Kay brand products are sold in more than 35 markets on five continents. The United States, China, Russia, and Mexico are the top four markets served by the company. The company's global independent sales force exceeds 2 million. About 65 percent of the company's independent sales representatives reside outside the United States. Mary Kay Ash's founding principles were simple and time-tested, and remain a fundamental company business philosophy. She adopted the Golden Rule as her guiding principle, determining the best course of action in virtually any situation could be easily discerned by "doing unto others as you would have them do unto you." She also steadfastly believed that life's priorities should be kept in their proper order, which to her meant "God first, family second, and career third." Her work ethic, approach to business, and success have resulted in numerous awards and recognitions, including, but not limited to, the Horatio Alger American Citizen Award, recognition as one of "America's 25 Most Influential Women," and induction into the National Business Hall of Fame. Mary Kay, Inc., engages in the development, manufacture, and packaging of skin care, makeup, spa and body, and fragrance products for men and women. It offers anti-aging, cleanser, moisturizer, lip and eye care, body care, and sun care products. Overall, the company produces more than 200 premium products in its state-of-the-art manufacturing facilities in Dallas, Texas, and Hangzhou, China. The company's approach to direct selling employs the "party plan," whereby independent sales representatives host parties to demonstrate or sell products to consumers.

Growth Opportunities in Asia-Pacific Markets

Asia-Pacific markets represent major growth opportunities for Mary Kay, Inc. These markets for Mary Kay, Inc., include Australia, China, Hong Kong, India, Korea, Malaysia, New Zealand, the Philippines, Singapore, and Taiwan. China accounts for the largest sales revenue outside the United States, representing about 25 percent of annual Mary Kay, Inc., worldwide sales. The company entered China in 1995 and currently has some 200,000 independent sales representatives or "beauty consultants" in that country. Part of Mary Kay's success in China has been attributed to the company's message of female empowerment and femininity, which has resonated in China, a country where young women have few opportunities to start their own business. Speaking about the corporate philosophy at Mary Kay, Inc., KK Chua, president of Mary Kay's Asia-Pacific operation, said, "Mary Kay's corporate objective is not only to create a market, selling skin care and cosmetics; it's all about enriching women's lives by helping women reach their full potential, find their inner beauty and discover how truly great they are." This view is echoed by Sheryl Adkins-Green, who notes that the Mary Kay brand has "transformational and aspirational" associations for users and beauty consultants alike. Mary Kay, Inc., learned that adjustments to its product line and message for women were necessary in some Asia-Pacific markets. In China, for example, the order of life's priorities—"God first, family second, and career third"—has been modified to "Faith first, family second, and career third." Also, Chinese women aren't heavy users of makeup. Therefore, the featured products include skin cream, anti-aging cream, and whitening creams. As a generalization, whitening products are popular among women in China, India, Korea, and the Philippines, where lighter skin is associated with beauty, class, and privilege.

Mary Kay India

Mary Kay, Inc., senior management believed that India represented a growth opportunity for three reasons. First, the Indian upper and consuming classes were growing and were expected to total over 500 million individuals. Second, the population was overwhelmingly young and optimistic. This youthful population continues to push consumerism as the line between luxury and basic items continues to blur. Third, a growing number of working women have given a boost to sales of cosmetics, skin care, and fragrances in India's urban areas, where 70 percent of the country's middle-class women reside. Senior management also believed that India's socio-economic characteristics in 2007 were similar in many ways to China's in 1995, when the company entered that market (see Figure 1). The Mary Kay culture was viewed as a good fit with the Indian culture, which would benefit the company's venture into this market. For example, industry research has shown that continuing modernization of the country has led to changing aspirations. As a result, the need to be good looking, well-groomed, and stylish has taken on a newfound importance. Mary Kay initiated operations in India in September 2007 with a full marketing launch in early 2008. The initial launch was in Delhi, the nation's capital and the second-most populated metropolis in India, and Mumbai, the nation's most heavily populated metropolis. Delhi, with per capita income of US$1,420, and Mumbai, with per capita income of US$2,850, were among the wealthiest metropolitan areas in India.

FIGURE 1

	India 2007	China 1995
Population (million)	1,136	1,198
Population age distribution (0–24; 25–49; 50+)	52%, 33%, 15%	43%, 39%, 18%
Urban population	29.2%	29.0%
Population/square mile	990	332
Gross domestic product (US$ billion)	3,113	728
Per capita income (US$)	950	399
Direct selling sales percent of total cosmetics/skin care sales	3.3%	3.0%

Social and economic statistics for India in 2007 and China in 1995.

According to Rhonda Shasteen, chief marketing officer at Mary Kay, Inc., "For Mary Kay to be successful in India, the company had to build a brand, build a sales force, and build an effective supply chain to service the sales force."

Building a Brand

Mary Kay, Inc., executives believed that brand building in India needed to involve media advertising; literature describing the Mary Kay culture, the Mary Kay story, and the company's image; and educational material for Mary Kay independent sales representatives. In addition, Mary Kay, Inc., became the cosmetics partner of the Miss India Worldwide Pageant 2008. At this event, Mary Kay Miss Beautiful Skin 2008 was crowned.

Brand building in India also involved product mix and pricing. Four guidelines were followed:

1. Keep the offering simple and skin care focused for the new Indian sales force and for a new operation.
2. Open with accessibly priced basic skin care products in relation to the competition in order to establish Mary Kay product quality and value.
3. Avoid opening with products that would phase out shortly after launch.
4. Address the key product categories of skin care, body care, and colour based on current market information.

Brand pricing focused on offering accessibly priced basic skin care to the average middle-class Indian consumer between the ages of 25 and 54. This strategy, called "mass-tige pricing," resulted in product price points that were above mass but below prestige competitive product prices. Following an initial emphasis on offering high-quality, high-value products, Mary Kay introduced more technologically advanced products that commanded higher price points.

For example, in March 2009, the company introduced the Mary Kay MelaCEP Whitening System, consisting of seven products, which was specifically formulated for Asian skin. This system was ". . . priced on the lower price end of the prestige category with a great value for money equation," said Hina Nagarajan, country manager for Mary Kay India.

Building a Sales Force

According to Adkins-Green, "Mary Kay's most powerful marketing vehicle is the direct-selling organization," which is a key component of the brand's marketing strategy. Mary Kay relied on its global leadership development program directors and national sales directors, as well as the Mary Kay sales education staff from the United States and Canada for the initial recruitment and training of independent sales representatives in India. New independent sales representatives received two to three days of intensive training and a starter kit that included not only products but also information pertaining to product demonstrations, sales presentations, professional demeanour, the company's history and culture, and team building. "Culture

Courtesy of Mary Kay, Inc.

training is very important to Mary Kay (independent sales representatives) because they are going to be the messengers of Mary Kay," said Hina Nagarajan. "As a direct-selling company that offers products sold person-to-person, we recognize that there's a personal relationship between consultant and client with every sale," added Rhonda Shasteen. By late 2009, there were some 4,000 independent sales representatives in India, present in some 200 cities mostly in the northern, western, and northeastern regions of the country.

Creating a Supply Chain

Mary Kay India imported products into India from China, Korea, and the United States. Products were shipped to regional distribution centres in Delhi and Mumbai, India, where the Mary Kay Beauty Center was located. Beauty centres serve as order pickup points for the independent sales representatives. Mary Kay beauty consultants purchased products from the company and, in turn, sold them to consumers.

Looking Ahead

Mary Kay, Inc., plans to invest around $20 million in the next five years on product development, company infrastructure, and building its brand in India. "There is a tremendous opportunity for growth," says Sheryl Adkins-Green. India represents a particularly attractive opportunity. Developing the brand and brand portfolio and specifically formulating products for Indian consumers will require her attention to brand positioning and brand equity.

QUESTIONS

1. Is Mary Kay an international firm, a multinational firm, or a transnational firm based on its marketing strategy? Why?

2. What global market-entry strategy did Mary Kay use when it entered India?

3. Is Mary Kay a global brand? Why or why not?

Case: This case was prepared by Roger A. Kerin based on company interviews.

8 Marketing Research: From Information to Action

Learning Objectives

After reading this chapter, you should be able to:

LO1 Know what marketing research is.

LO2 Explain the different types of marketing research.

LO3 Understand the stages in the marketing research process.

LO4 Explain the use of secondary data, surveys, experiments, and observation in marketing research.

LO5 Explain how an intelligent marketing enterprise platform can trigger marketing actions.

Using Social Media for Marketing Research

Many companies have realized that social media can be used for conducting very insightful and cost-effective marketing research. Experts offer some advice as to the ways social media can be used to conduct marketing research and the best ways to do so.

1. *Social media can be used to listen to customers.* Observing and analyzing how customers speak about products or services can ensure there is alignment with the marketing message and what customers really care about. Learning the language of customers allows for more effective communication.

2. *Social media can be used to monitor competitors.* Social media allows companies to monitor competitors closely, especially how they engage customers. Monitoring competitors' pages and feeds unveils the offers being made to customers and what customers are saying about competitors.

3. *Social media can be used to track trends.* Marketers can track significant trends through various social media platforms. For example, Twitter allows you to find trending topics by monitoring hashtags or mentions. The tracking of trends provides real-time insights, such as the ability to receive notifications when customers use certain terms.

4. *Social media can be used in real time for quick research.* Traditional market-research methods, such as surveys or study groups, can take months to plan, form, and execute. With social media, research can be conducted in a matter of minutes or hours. This makes it possible to use market research to follow increasingly specific aspects of marketing efforts. From product launches to follow-up marketing, each part of a marketing plan can be analyzed independently for improved results.

10 FACE/Shutterstock.com

5. *Social media can broaden the scope of marketing research.* Over 90 percent of people who access the Internet utilize social media. This makes it possible to conduct market research with an audience that is many times larger than nearly any other marketing or media source can provide. The casual nature and easy access of social media also helps to promote user interaction, engagement, and participation. This improves the chances of obtaining useful, accurate, and honest data from your efforts.

6. *Social media allows marketers to engage customers instead of simply asking questions.* One of the biggest weaknesses to most marketing research methods is that they are driven by questions. To obtain the proper information, you must first know what to ask. At the same time, simply rewording a question can result in drastically different answers. This means that marketing research is only as good as the questions. With the broad scope and interactive nature of social media, information is gained through interaction and observation. Instead of leading the discussions, marketers can simply observe or join in as an equal. This can result in a variety of answers and discoveries that might have remained hidden using other research methods.

7. *Social media can deliver cost-effective research.* In most cases, utilizing social media for marketing research is simply a matter of investing time. Free tools exist for nearly every social media platform to help gather information and use it to derive useful information. When compared to focus groups and surveys, the cost difference can be staggering. Through user engagement and discussion, your social media research also serves as advertising, brand building, network building, and lead generation, and offers numerous other improvements for a company or its brand.

When planned and implemented properly, few marketing research tools offer the cost efficiency and overall benefit of social media research. From reduced costs and real-time access to information, to the ability to uncover hidden trends and improve marketing actions, social media offers powerful ways to optimize the marketing research efforts of any business. Best of all, social media research offers numerous ways to interact with customers and build the business. Conducting research is as simple as signing up for a social media service, such as LinkedIn or Twitter, and utilizing their built-in search features. Within minutes, a business can start analyzing trends, improving marketing strategies, and working toward better achievement of marketing goals.[1]

This chapter examines the concept of marketing research and its link to successful marketing decision-making.

(LO1) WHAT IS MARKETING RESEARCH?

Marketing research is the process of defining a marketing problem or opportunity, systematically collecting and analyzing information, and recommending actions to improve an organization's marketing activities.[2] Broadly speaking, assessing the needs and wants of consumers and providing information to help design an organization's marketing program to satisfy them is the principal role that marketing research performs. This means that marketing research attempts to identify and define both marketing problems and opportunities and to generate and evaluate marketing actions. Although marketing research can provide few answers with complete assurance, it can reduce risk and uncertainty to increase the likelihood of the success of marketing decisions. It is a great help to the marketing managers who must make final decisions. Conducted properly, marketing research can solve most marketing-related problems that an executive might have. However, marketing research should not be designed to simply replace an executive's good sense, experience, or intuition but rather should be used in conjunction with those skills and as a way of taking out some of the guesswork in the marketing decision-making process.

LO2 TYPES OF MARKETING RESEARCH

To understand the variety of research activity, it is helpful to categorize different types of marketing research. Marketing research is often classified on the basis of either technique or function. Surveys, experiments, and observation are a few research techniques with which you may be familiar. However, categorizing research by its purpose or function shows how the nature of the marketing problem influences the choice of research techniques. The nature of the problem will determine whether the research is (1) exploratory, (2) descriptive, or (3) causal.

Exploratory Research

Exploratory research is preliminary research conducted to clarify the scope and nature of the marketing problem. It is generally carried out to provide the researcher with a better understanding of the dimensions of the problem. Exploratory research is often conducted with the expectation that subsequent and more conclusive research will follow.

For example, the Dairy Farmers of Canada, an association representing dairy producers in the country, wanted to discover why milk consumption was declining in Canada. They conducted a search of existing literature on milk consumption, talked to experts in the field, and even conducted preliminary interviews with consumers to get ideas about why consumers were drinking less milk. This exploratory research helped the association to crystallize the problem and identify issues for more detailed follow-up research. We examine exploratory research as an integral component of the basic marketing research process later in this chapter.

Descriptive Research

Descriptive research is research designed to describe the basic characteristics of a given population or to profile particular marketing situations. Unlike exploratory research, with descriptive research, the researcher has a general understanding of the marketing problem and is seeking conclusive data that answer the questions necessary to determine a particular course of action. Examples of descriptive research would include profiling product purchasers (e.g., the Canadian shopper at the health food store), describing the size and characteristics of markets (e.g., the Canadian pizza restaurant market), detailing product usage patterns (e.g., ATM usage by Canadian bank customers), or outlining consumer attitudes toward particular brands (e.g., Canadian attitudes toward national, private, and generic brands).

The Dairy Farmers of Canada conducted three types of marketing research in an effort to solve the problem of decline in milk consumption. For details, read the text.

Used by permission of kbs+ montreal. Artwork by Paul Abraham.

Magazines, radio stations, and television stations almost always do descriptive research to identify the characteristics of their audiences in order to present them to prospective advertisers. As a follow-up to its exploratory research, the Dairy Farmers of Canada conducted descriptive research to determine the demographic characteristics of milk consumers, current usage patterns, and consumer attitudes toward milk consumption.

Causal Research

Causal research is research designed to identify cause-and-effect relationships among variables. In general, exploratory and descriptive research normally precede causal research. With causal research, there is typically an expectation about the relationship to be explained, such as predicting the influence of a price change on product demand. In general, researchers attempt to establish that one event (e.g., a price change) will produce another event (e.g., a change in demand). Typical causal research studies examine the effect of advertising on sales, the relationship between price and perceived quality of a product, and the impact of a new package on product sales. When the Dairy Farmers of Canada conducted its descriptive research on milk consumers, it discovered that many believed milk was too fattening and too high in cholesterol. The association felt that these beliefs might be related to the overall decline in milk consumption in Canada. To test this assumption, the association ran a television advertising campaign to demonstrate that milk was a healthful product and essential to a person's diet. In its tracking studies, it found that the ad campaign did change consumer attitudes toward milk, which, in turn, was causally related to a subsequent increase in milk consumption. We refer to causal research later in this chapter when we deal with experiments as a basic research technique.

LO3 THE MARKETING RESEARCH PROCESS

Marketing research should always be conducted on the basis of the *scientific method*, a process of systematically collecting, organizing, and analyzing data in an unbiased, objective manner. Marketing research must meet two basic principles of the scientific method—reliability and validity. *Reliability* refers to the ability to replicate research results under identical environmental conditions. In other words, if a research project were to be conducted for the second, third, or fourth time, the results should be the same. Marketers need to have reliable information to make effective decisions. If the results of a study are not reliable, the research can do more harm than no research at all. *Validity* involves the notion of whether the research measured what was intended to be measured. In other words, does the research tell marketers what they need to know? You should keep the concepts of reliability and validity in mind as we discuss the marketing research process.

Figure 8–1 outlines the basic marketing research process. The figure is perhaps an oversimplification of the process, as marketing research does not always follow such a neat and ordered sequence of activities. However, all marketing research consists of four basic stages: (1) defining the problem, (2) determining the research design, (3) collecting and analyzing data, and (4) drawing conclusions and preparing a report.

FIGURE 8–1

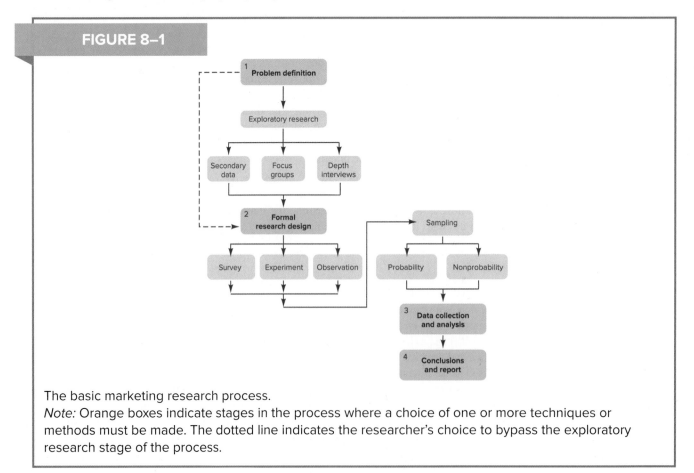

The basic marketing research process.
Note: Orange boxes indicate stages in the process where a choice of one or more techniques or methods must be made. The dotted line indicates the researcher's choice to bypass the exploratory research stage of the process.

In reviewing Figure 8–1, you can see that the researcher has a number of decisions and choices to make during the stages of the process. For example, the orange boxes in Figure 8–1 indicate stages in the process where a choice of one or more techniques or methods must be made. The dotted line indicates the researcher's choice to bypass the exploratory research stage of the process.

Learning Review

3. What are reliability and validity?

4. What are the four basic stages in the marketing research process?

LO4 PROBLEM DEFINITION

The first step in the marketing research process is to properly define the scope and nature of the marketing problem to be investigated. In general, the term *problem* suggests that something has gone wrong. In reality, to the marketing researcher, the word *problem* may also mean something to explore or an opportunity to define, or a current marketing situation to monitor or evaluate. Sometimes, the problem is obvious, but in other cases, the problem may be more difficult to identify and define. In either case, the marketing researcher must fully understand and properly identify the problem at hand.

The marketing research process is often initiated by the marketing manager, who will approach the marketing researcher with a problem that requires information for decision making. For example, suppose you were the marketing manager for cranberry juice at Ocean Spray. You want to know if Asian consumers who have never heard of cranberries would buy cranberry juice. You also have other problems. The word "cranberry" is not part of any foreign language, and so you would have to find a name for it and its juice. Also, if you are going to take the product to Asia, you have to find a way to encourage consumers there to try the new product.[3] The marketing researcher has to fully understand these problems. The researcher must also remember that the best place to begin a research project is at the end. In other words, the researcher must know what is to be accomplished through the research process. In this case, as the marketing manager, what you really want to know is: Is there a market opportunity in Asia for cranberry juice? If so, how can it be exploited?

Proper problem definition is critical, because research based on incorrect problem definition will be a waste of resources. Good marketing researchers adhere to the old adage "a problem well defined is a problem half-solved." If the research problem is clear, the chances of collecting the necessary information to solve the problem are increased.

Exploratory Research

Your colleague, the marketing researcher at Ocean Spray, has to make a decision early on in the marketing research process. Should exploratory research be conducted in an attempt to help answer the question of whether a market opportunity for cranberry juice exists in Asia? As we note earlier in the chapter, exploratory research is preliminary research conducted to clarify the scope and nature of the marketing problem. In general, it is designed to provide the researcher with a better understanding of the dimensions of the problem and is often conducted with the expectation that subsequent and more conclusive research may follow.

Most researchers will usually conduct some basic exploratory research during the early stage of the research process. The extent of the exploratory research will depend on the magnitude of the problem as well as its complexity. If the researcher decides to conduct exploratory research, he or she has four basic techniques to choose from: (1) secondary data analysis, (2) focus groups, (3) depth interviews, and (4) other tools.

Secondary Data

Exploratory research almost always involves the use of **secondary data** (or historical data)—data previously collected and assembled for some project other than the one at hand. **Primary data**, on the other hand, are data gathered and assembled specifically for the project at hand. As a rule, researchers gather secondary data before collecting primary data. In general, secondary data can be obtained more quickly and at a lower cost compared with primary data. For example, many of you that have a question simply use Google to search for answers and you often locate many existing sources of information that might answer your question. However, there can be problems with secondary data. The required information may not exist, and if it does, it may not be current or particularly pertinent to the problem at hand. Still, most researchers agree that investigating secondary data sources can save researchers from "reinventing the wheel."

Researchers examine secondary data both inside and outside the organization. Internal secondary data include financial statements, research reports, customer letters, and customer lists. What did your colleague in marketing research at Ocean Spray discover during the secondary data search efforts? She discovered that Ocean Spray did attempt to introduce a bland cranberry juice in Japan—named "Cranby"—but the attempt fizzled, and the product was pulled off the market. As a marketing manager, this information does provide some background, but you still have more questions than answers about the possible marketing opportunity in Asia.

Sources of external secondary data can be wide and varied. One key Canadian source of marketing data is Statistics Canada (**www.statcan.gc.ca**). This federal government agency provides census data as well as numerous other reports on Canadian households and businesses, most of which are available through its searchable online database.

In addition to Statistics Canada, there are numerous other sources of secondary data, including business directories, business periodicals, newspapers, magazines, and trade associations. Finally, there are many online databanks that provide specialized data services. Figure 8–2 provides some key sources of secondary data.

One emerging type of secondary data that is available to marketers is called *single source data.* This is integrated information from multiple sources that allows marketers to examine customers' household demographics and lifestyles, product purchases, media habits, and responses to sales promotions, such as coupons and free samples. For example, if you have a loyalty card with a particular retailer, your purchase data is captured by the checkout scanner and can be archived in a marketing information system where it can be examined along with your personal information to determine how the company can better market its product or services. If you purchase online, your purchase data is also captured and stored along with your personal information. This information can then be used to tailor offerings to you based on your past purchase behaviour. We will discuss the use of integrated data when we examine intelligent marketing enterprise platforms later in this chapter.

Getting back to our marketing researcher at Ocean Spray and the cranberry juice in Asia question, she discovers some external secondary data, specifically a study on Taiwan consumers that shows increased consumption of juice beverages. Still, the study is not specific to cranberry juice and is about four years old. As marketing manager, you realize you still have a high degree of uncertainty about the possible marketing opportunity in Asia. So you ask your colleague in marketing research to continue the exploratory stage of the marketing process.

Focus Groups

A very popular exploratory research technique designed to obtain primary data is the use of focus groups. **Focus groups** are informal interview sessions in which six to ten persons, relevant to the research project, are brought together in a room with a moderator to discuss topics surrounding the marketing research problem. The moderator poses questions and encourages the individuals to answer in their own words and to discuss the issues with each other. Often, the focus-group sessions are watched by observers through one-way mirrors, and/or the sessions are videotaped. (Of course, participants should be informed they are being observed and/or taped.)

Should Ocean Spray introduce cranberry juice in Asia when consumers there have never heard of cranberries? See the text.

Many companies are also conducting online focus groups where participants and the moderator interact in an online setting. Companies can present online participants with audio or video material for respondent evaluation, and even present them with virtual product concepts to evaluate. Focus group sessions often provide the marketer with valuable information for decision making or can uncover other issues that should be researched in a more quantitative fashion.[4]

FIGURE 8–2

Selected Statistics and Trade Sources	Canadian Trade Index (**www.ctidirectory.com**) Conference Board of Canada (**www.conferenceboard.ca**) *Financial Post*'s Canadian Demographics: Key census data at the municipal level Fraser's Canadian Trade Directory (**www.frasers.com**) Innovation, Science and Economic Development Canada website (**www.ic.gc.ca**): Includes Canadian Company Capabilities, online directory, Canadian Patent Database, Canadian Trademark Database Scott's Directories (**www.scottsinfo.com**) Statistics Canada (**www.statcan.gc.ca**): Online database, including census data, plus guidebooks such as the *Market Research Handbook*
Marketing Journals	*Canadian Journal of Marketing Research* *Journal of Advertising* *Journal of Consumer Research* *Journal of Marketing* *Journal of Marketing Research* *Journal of Retailing*
Business/Trade Magazines	*Advertising Age* *American Demographics* *Business Week* *Canadian Business* *Forbes* *Fortune* *Harvard Business Review* *The Globe and Mail Report on Business* *Marketing Magazine* *Marketing News* *Profit Magazine* *Progressive Grocer* *Sales and Marketing Management* *Small Business Canada Magazine* *Strategy Magazine*
Other Sources (Including Online Databases)	ABI Inform / Proquest (**www.proquest.com**) AC Nielsen Canada (**www.acnielsen.ca**) Blue Book of Canadian Business (**www.cbr.ca**) Dialog (**www.dialog.com**) Dun & Bradstreet Canada (**www.dnb.ca**) Hoover's (**www.hoovers.com**) Interactive Advertising Bureau of Canada (**www.iabcanada.com**) LexisNexis (**www.lexis-nexis.com**)

Sources of secondary data.

For example, Canada's military ran focus groups in cities across Canada to find out what images should appear in the Army's next recruitment campaign. The research revealed that prospective recruits, particularly young men 18 to 24 years of age, wanted more reality in military ads. Importantly, they wanted to see action rather than a soft pitch about career opportunities. As a result of the focus groups, the ad program called "Fight" was developed. The centrepiece was two stark 60-second TV spots. In one, soldiers rescue flood victims in Manitoba. In the other, tanks patrol war-torn streets, a nail bomb explodes, and soldiers do battle in Afghanistan. Both end with the superimposed tag line: "Fight fear, fight distress, fight chaos. . . Fight with the Canadian Forces." The ads clearly struck a nerve. The number of applicants rose 40 percent to 40,000, and Canadian Forces signed up 12,862 full-time and reserve members—about 400 more than the target.[5]

Depth Interviews

Another exploratory research technique used to obtain primary data involves the use of depth interviews. **Depth interviews** are detailed individual interviews with people relevant to a research project. The researcher questions the individual at length in a free-flowing conversational style to obtain information that may help solve the marketing problem being investigated. Sometimes these interviews can take a few hours, and they are often recorded on audio or video.

Hamburger Helper did not fare too well with consumers when General Mills first introduced it. Initial instructions called for cooking separately a half-pound of hamburger, which was later mixed with the noodles. Depth interviews revealed that consumers did not think the recipe called for enough meat and that they did not want the hassle of cooking in two different pots. So the Hamburger Helper product manager changed the recipe to call for a full pound of meat and to allow users to prepare the meal in one dish; this converted a potential failure into a success.

Other Tools

Researchers have also become creative in devising other exploratory research techniques. For example, finding "the next big thing" for consumers has become the obsession in many industries. In order to unearth the next big thing, marketing researchers have developed some unusual techniques, sometimes referred to as "fuzzy front-end" methods. These techniques are designed to identify elusive consumer tastes or trends far before typical consumers have themselves recognized them. For example, having consumers take a photo of themselves every time they snack resulted in General Mills' Homestyle Pop Secret popcorn, which delivers the real butter and bursts of salt in microwave popcorn that consumers thought they could only get from the stovetop variety.[6] Other tools are also being used to try to identify trends and/or capture customer insight. For example, Teenage Research Unlimited had teenagers complete a drawing to help discover what teenagers like, wear, listen to, and read.[7] Another company, Trend Hunter, is a firm that seeks to anticipate and track "the evolution of cool." Trend hunting (or watching) is the practice of identifying "emerging shifts in social behaviour," which are driven by changes in pop culture that can lead to new products. Trend Hunter has identified about 250,000 cutting-edge ideas through its global network of 155,000 members, and features these new ideas on its daily Trend Hunter TV broadcast via its YouTube channel (**Trend Hunter TV**).[8]

Finally, exploratory customer insights are also being captured via social media. For example, the "voice of customer" is being gleaned via *social listening*—monitoring what customers are talking about on social media. Also, as noted in the chapter opener, researchers are using social media is a variety of novel ways, including monitoring competition and tracking trends.

> ### Learning Review
>
> **5.** What are secondary data?
> **6.** What are focus groups?

FORMAL RESEARCH DESIGN

After identifying and clarifying the marketing problem, with or without exploratory research, the researcher must determine the basic framework for finding a solution to the problem. At the formal research design stage, the researcher produces a plan that outlines the method and procedures for collecting and analyzing the required information. The plan includes the objectives of the research, the sources of information to be used, the research methods (e.g., survey, experiment), the sampling plan, and the schedule and cost of the research.

In selecting basic research methods, the researcher must make decisions. In general, the objectives of the research, available data sources, nature of the information required, and timing and cost considerations will determine which research method will be chosen. The basic methods the researcher can choose for descriptive and causal research include (1) survey, (2) experiment, and (3) observation.

Survey

The most common research method of generating new or primary data is the use of surveys. A **survey** is a research technique used to generate data by asking people questions and recording their responses on a questionnaire. Surveys can be conducted by personal interview (face-to-face), by mail, by telephone, or online. In choosing these alternatives, the marketing researcher has to make important trade-offs (as shown in Figure 8–3) in order to balance, for instance, cost against the expected quality of information obtained. For example, personal interview (face-to-face) surveys have the major advantage of enabling the interviewer to be flexible in asking probing questions or getting reactions to visual materials, but they are very costly to conduct. Mail surveys are usually biased because those likely to respond have had especially positive or negative experiences with a given product, service, or brand. While telephone surveys allow flexibility, they are increasingly difficult to complete because respondents may hang up on the interviewer. Also, with many unlisted telephone numbers, it is becoming increasingly more difficult to obtain representative samples. Online surveys are somewhat restrictive in that they are limited to respondents having the technology.[9] Still, as Internet penetration grows, so too will the use of online surveys. Some of you are probably already familiar with popular online survey sites such as Zoomerang or Survey Monkey.

FIGURE 8–3

Basis of Comparison	Mail Surveys	Telephone Surveys	Personal Interview	Online Surveys
Cost per completed survey	Not very expensive	Moderately expensive	Most expensive	Very inexpensive
Ability to probe and ask complex questions	Little to none	Some—interviewer can probe and elaborate	Much—interviewer is face-to-face	Depends—can go back and ask respondent to clarify responses
Opportunity for interviewer to bias results	None	Some—because of voice and gender	Significant—voice, appearance, gender present	Little—if done correctly
Anonymity given to respondent	Complete—unless coded instrument is used	Some—because of telephone contact	Little—because of face-to-face contact	Some—e-mail and/or user name may be known
Response rate	Poor or fair	Fair—refusal rates are increasing	Good	Very good—if done correctly
Speed of data collection	Poor	Good	Good	Very good

Comparing mail, telephone, personal, and online surveys.

The high cost of reaching respondents in their homes through personal interview surveys has led to an increase in the use of *mall intercept interviews,* which are personal interviews of consumers at shopping centres. These face-to-face interviews reduce the cost of personal visits to consumers in their homes while providing flexibility to show respondents visual cues, such as ads or actual product samples. However, a critical disadvantage of mall intercept interviews is that the people selected for the interviews may not be representative of the consumers targeted for the interviews, causing possible bias in results.

Sometimes, marketers will survey over time the same sample of people, commonly known as a survey *panel.* A panel can consist of a sample of consumers, stores, or experts, from which researchers can take a series of measurements. For example, a consumer's switch from one brand of breakfast cereal to another can be measured with panel data. The use of panels is becoming more popular with marketers as they attempt to obtain ongoing information about their constituents. Panel data are often incorporated into marketing information systems, which are discussed later in the chapter. More and more often, marketers are using online panels to provide immediate access to their consumers as well as real-time feedback. For example, the NDP Group has an online panel that consists of nearly 2 million individuals worldwide and it uses the panel to collect data about consumer purchases.

When marketers decide to use surveys to ask questions, they assume that (1) the right questions are being asked, (2) people will understand the questions being asked, (3) people know the answers to the questions, (4) people will answer the questions truthfully, and (5) the researchers themselves will understand the answers provided. Marketers must concern themselves not only with asking the right questions but also with how to word those questions properly. Proper phrasing of a question is vital to uncovering useful marketing information.

Wendy's spent over two years remaking its 42-year-old burger. The result: Dave's Hot 'N Juicy, named after Wendy's founder Dave Thomas. See Figure 8–5 for some questions that Wendy's asked consumers in a survey to discover their fast-food preferences, behaviours, and demographics.

Wendy's International, LLC

Figure 8–4 shows typical problems to guard against in wording questions to obtain meaningful answers from respondents. For example, in the question about whether you eat at fast-food restaurants regularly, the word "regularly" is ambiguous. Two people might answer "yes" to the question, but one might mean "once a day" while the other means "once or twice a year." Both answers appear as "yes" to the researcher who tabulates them, but they suggest that dramatically different marketing actions be directed to each of these two prospective consumers. Therefore, it is essential that marketing research questions be worded precisely so that all respondents interpret the same question similarly. Marketing researchers must also take great care not to use "leading" questions (wording questions in a way to ensure a particular response), which can lead to a very distorted picture of the respondents' actual feelings or opinions.

In Figure 8–5, we can see the number of different formats that questions can take in a survey instrument. The questions presented are taken from a Wendy's survey that assessed fast-food preferences among present and prospective consumers. Question 1 is an example of an *open-end question,* which the respondent can answer in his or her own words. In contrast, questions in which the respondent simply checks an answer are *closed-end* or *fixed alternative questions.* Question 2 is an example of the simplest fixed alternative question, a *dichotomous question* that allows only a "yes" or "no" answer. A fixed alternative question with three or more choices uses a scale. Question 5 is an example of a question that uses a *semantic differential scale,* a five-point scale in which the opposite ends have one- or two-word adjectives that have opposite meanings. For example, depending on how clean the respondent believes that Wendy's is, he or she would check the left-hand space on the scale, the right-hand space, or one of the three intervening points. Question 6 uses a *Likert scale,* in which the respondent is asked to indicate the extent to which he or she agrees or disagrees with a statement.

The questionnaire in Figure 8–5 is an excerpt of a precisely worded survey that provides valuable information to the marketing researcher at Wendy's. Questions 1 to 8 inform the researcher about the likes and dislikes in eating out, frequency of eating out at fast-food restaurants generally and at Wendy's specifically, and sources of information used in making decisions about fast-food restaurants. Question 9 gives details about the personal or household characteristics, which can be used in trying to segment the fast-food market, a topic discussed in Chapter 9.

Surveys of distributors—retailers and wholesalers in the marketing channel—are also very important for manufacturers. A reason given for the success of many Japanese consumer products in Canada, such as Toyota automobiles, is the emphasis that Japanese marketers place on obtaining accurate information from their distributors.

New technologies, including the Internet, have revolutionized the traditional concept of surveys. In addition to online research, marketers can survey respondents via electronic kiosks in shopping centres. Respondents read questions on-screen and key their answers into a computer with a touch screen. Marketers can also utilize fully automated telephone systems to conduct surveys. An automated voice questions respondents over the telephone, who then key in their replies on a touch-tone telephone. Marketers are also using wireless phones to send text surveys, and even conducting surveys via iPods and other handheld wireless devices.

FIGURE 8–4

PROBLEM	SAMPLE QUESTION	EXPLANATION
Leading question	Why do you like Wendy's fresh meat hamburgers better than those of competitors?	Consumer is led to make statements favouring Wendy's hamburgers.
Ambiguous question	Do you eat at fast-food restaurants regularly? □ Yes □ No	What is meant by the word *regularly*—once a day, once a month, or what?
Unanswerable question	What was the occasion for your eating your first hamburger?	Who can remember the answer? Does it matter?
Two questions in one	Do you eat Wendy's hamburgers and chili? □ Yes □ No	How do you answer if you eat Wendy's hamburgers but not chili?
Non-exhaustive question	Where do you live? □ At home □ In dormitory	What do you check if you live in an apartment?
Non–mutually exclusive answers	What is your age? □ Under 20 □ 20–40 □ 40 and over	What answer does a 40-year-old check?

Typical problems in wording questions.

Experiment

Another method that can be used by marketing researchers to generate primary data is the experiment. Marketing experiments offer the potential for establishing cause-and-effect relationships (causal research). An **experiment** involves the manipulation of an independent variable (cause) and the measurement of its effect on the dependent variable (effect) under controlled conditions.

In marketing experiments, the independent variables are often one or more of the marketing mix variables—sometimes called the marketing *drivers*—such as product features, price, or promotion used. An ideal dependent variable usually is a change in purchases by an individual, household, or entire organization. If actual purchases cannot be used as a dependent variable, factors that are believed to be highly related to purchases, such as preferences in a taste test or intentions to buy, are used.

Experiments can be conducted in the field or in a laboratory. In *field experiments*, the research is conducted in the real world, such as in a store, in a bank, or on the street, wherever the behaviour being studied occurs naturally. Field experiments can be expensive but are a good way to determine people's reactions to changes in the elements of the marketing mix. Test marketing is probably the most common form of field experiments. For example, suppose you wanted to know if Asian consumers would buy cranberry juice when they had never tasted cranberries? Perhaps your marketing research colleague might recommend taste tests in Asia to gauge consumers' responses to the product. In fact, many food companies use test marketing. Walmart, for instance, opened three experimental stand-alone supercentres to gauge consumer acceptance before deciding to open others. Today, Walmart operates over 1,000 supercentres around the world.

Because marketers cannot control all the conditions in the field, they sometimes turn to a laboratory setting. Laboratories are not the real world but do offer highly controlled environments. Unlike in the field, the marketer has control over all the factors that may impact the behaviour under investigation.

For example, in a field experiment, the marketer may wish to examine the impact of a price reduction on the sales of a particular product. The competition, however, may see the price reduction and offer its own price deal, thus interfering with the possible results of the field experiment. This does not occur in a laboratory setting. Many companies are using laboratory settings where they can control

FIGURE 8–5

1. What things are most important to you when you decide to eat out at a fast-food restaurant?

_____

_____

_____

2. Have you eaten at a fast-food restaurant in the past month?

◯ Yes   ◯ No

3. If you answered yes to question 2, how often do you eat at a fast-food restaurant?

◯ Once a week or more   ◯ 2 to 3 times a month   ◯ Once a month or less

4. How important is it to you that a fast-food restaurant satisfies you on the following characteristics?
[Check the response that describes your feelings for each characteristic listed.]

Characteristic	Very Important	Somewhat Important	Important	Unimportant	Somewhat Unimportant	Very Unimportant
· Taste of food	◯	◯	◯	◯	◯	◯
· Cleanliness	◯	◯	◯	◯	◯	◯
· Price	◯	◯	◯	◯	◯	◯
· Variety of menu	◯	◯	◯	◯	◯	◯

5. For each of the characteristics listed below check the space on the scale that describes how you feel about Wendy's. Mark an X on only one of the five spaces for each characteristic listed.

Characteristic		Check the space that describes the degree to which Wendy' is . . .					
· Taste of food	Tasty	____	____	____	____	____	Not Tasty
· Cleanliness	Clean	____	____	____	____	____	Dirty
· Price	Inexpensive	____	____	____	____	____	Expensive
· Variety of menu	Broad	____	____	____	____	____	Narrow

6. Check the response that describes your agreement or disagreement with each statement listed below:

Statement	Strongly Agree	Agree	Don't Know	Disagree	Strongly Disagree
· Adults like to take their families to fast-food restaurants	◯	◯	◯	◯	◯
· Our children have a say in where the family chooses to eat	◯	◯	◯	◯	◯

7. How important are each of the following sources of information to you when selecting a fast-food restaurant at which to eat? [Check one response for each source listed.]

Source of Information	Very Important	Somewhat Important	Not at all Important
· Television	◯	◯	◯
· Newspapers	◯	◯	◯
· Radio	◯	◯	◯
· Billboards	◯	◯	◯
· Internet	◯	◯	◯
· Social networks	◯	◯	◯

8. How often do you eat out at each of the following fast-food restaurants? [Check one response for each restaurant listed.]

Restaurant	Once a week or more	2 to 3 Times a month	Once a month or less
· Burger King	◯	◯	◯
· McDonald's	◯	◯	◯
· Wendy's	◯	◯	◯

9. As head of the household, please answer the following questions about you and your household.
[Check only one response for each question.]

a. What is your gender?   ◯ Male   ◯ Female

b. What is your marital status?   ◯ Single   ◯ Married   ◯ Other (widowed, divorced, etc.)

c. How many children under age 18 live in your home?   ◯ 0   ◯ 1   ◯ 2   ◯ 3 or more

d. What is your age?   ◯ Under 25   ◯ 25–44   ◯ 45 or older

e. What is your total annual individual or household income?
    ◯ Less than $15,000   ◯ $15,000–$49,000   ◯ Over $49,000

To obtain the most valuable information from consumers, the Wendy's survey utilizes nine different kinds of questions, which are discussed in the text.

conditions but can do so in a real-world fashion, such as simulated super-markets. Here, they can experiment with changes in aisle displays, packaging changes, or other variables that may affect buyer behaviour without the fear of other extraneous factors influencing the results.

Today, the Internet, including social media, as discussed in the chapter opener, has also opened up opportunities to do creative online market testing of products, packaging, advertising, and so on. For example, Coca-Cola used online research to test consumer responses to proposed new Fruitopia flavours, and Breyers asked for consumer feedback on proposed new ice cream flavours. Ipsos Canada, a major Canadian research firm, argues that online market testing can be fast and very effective. Using online technology, Ipsos assists their clients by conducting virtual reality testing of product concepts where consumers can view the products online, click on features, and rank preferences. With online panels, companies also have the added advantage of ready-made beta-test samples for new concepts, products, and services. In fact, you recently used an online panel to test your current format of your super snack bar against a proposed new format, and the results are shown in the Using Marketing Dashboard box, "Making Sense of Online Panel Results." What conclusions can you draw from the results?

How might Walmart have done early marketing research to help develop its supercentres, which have achieved international success? For its unusual research, see the text.

Cancun Chu/Getty Images

Observation

Another basic research method used to obtain primary data is observation. In general, **observation** involves watching, either mechanically or in person, how people behave. In some circumstances, the speed of events or the number of events being observed make mechanical or electronic observation more appropriate than personal observation. Retailers, for example, can use electronic cameras to count the number of customers entering or leaving a store.

A classic form of mechanical observation is Nielsen Media Research's *people meter,* which is a box attached to television sets, cable boxes, and satellite dishes in selected households in Canada and the United States in order to determine the size of audiences watching television programs delivered by the networks. When a household member watches TV, he or she is supposed to push a button on a remote and push it again when viewing stops. The information is transmitted and analyzed by Nielsen in order to measure who in the household is watching what program on every TV set owned.

This information is used to calculate ratings for each TV program, which, in turn, is used to set advertising rates for such programs. But people meters have limitations—as with all observations collected mechanically. Critics do not believe the devices accurately measure who is watching a given TV program or what is actually watched. Moreover, traditional people meters cannot measure large segments of the population that watch TV programs at parties, hotels, or sports bars. To solve this problem, a *portable people meter (PPM)* was developed by BBM Canada. This device, which is the size of a pager, is carried by consumers and automatically detects audible codes in TV programming at both in-home and outside venues. Each night, participants place the meter into a base station, which then transmits the data for analysis.[10]

USING MARKETING DASHBOARDS

Making Sense of Online Panel Results

While you are happy with the results of sales overall with your new super snack bar, your R&D and food science group within the company have developed a new bar format that they feel might better appeal to your current user group. The existing bar format looks like a dark-chocolate bar with a smooth, pressed, and tabbed (easy to break in pieces) appearance. But some of your people think a new format, a light, granular-looking (similar to granola), non-tabbed appearance, may have appeal with current users. So you present both formats to your online panel. You ask them to rate the two formats on several attributes known to be important to the buyers and then ask if they have a preference for one format over the other. Below are the results.

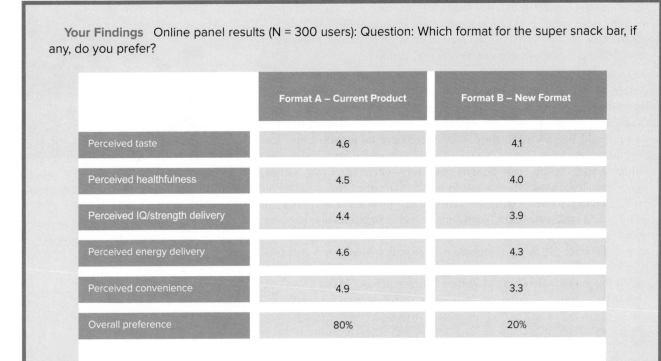

Your Findings   Online panel results (N = 300 users): Question: Which format for the super snack bar, if any, do you prefer?

	Format A – Current Product	Format B – New Format
Perceived taste	4.6	4.1
Perceived healthfulness	4.5	4.0
Perceived IQ/strength delivery	4.4	3.9
Perceived energy delivery	4.6	4.3
Perceived convenience	4.9	3.3
Overall preference	80%	20%

Scale: 1–5 (1 = very unlikely to deliver on this attribute, 5 = very likely to deliver on this attribute)

Your Action   It is clear that your current users prefer the current format of your super snack bar (80 percent versus 20 percent), and all users expressed a strong preference one way or another. It is also clear that the current format is also ranked higher on all attributes compared to the new format. The perceived convenience score difference between the two formats is particularly large. Thus, it appears the current tabbed format is strongly preferred. Yet, there is a distinctive 20 percent of your panel that has expressed a preference for the proposed new format. You have to consider whether to add this new format (a new offering, line-extension), which means new production issues and securing channel members' cooperation to handle a new SKU (stock-keeping unit). You have to consider whether introducing the new format (while retaining the existing format) will improve your top-line revenue numbers as well as your bottom-line profitability.

Nielsen also uses an electronic meter to record Internet user behaviour. These data are collected by tracking the actual mouse clicks made by users as they surf the Internet via a meter installed on their home or work computers. Nielsen has been able to identify the websites that have the largest audiences, the top advertising banners viewed, the top Internet advertisers, and global Internet usage for selected countries. Nielsen has also implemented a new measurement program called *Anytime Anywhere Media Measurement (A2/M2),* which measures all types of viewing behaviour from a variety of devices and sources such as DVR (digital video recorder), VOD (video on demand), and Internet-delivered TV shows on computers via iTunes, streaming media, smartphones, etc.

Watching consumers in person or by videotaping them are other observational approaches used to collect primary data. For example, Procter & Gamble watched women do their laundry, clean the floor, put on makeup, and so on, because 80 percent of the customers who buy its products are women! Gillette marketing researchers actually videotaped consumers brushing their teeth in their own bathrooms to find out how they really brush—not just how they say they brush. The result: Gillette's new Oral-B CrossAction toothbrush that is supposed to do a better job![11]

A specialized observational approach is **ethnographic research**, in which anthropologists and other trained observers seek to discover subtle emotional reactions as consumers encounter products in their "natural use environments," such as in homes, cars, or hotels. For example, Office Max used this anthropological method to observe how its shoppers interacted with its stores. The result: Office Max moved products that consumers bought in tandem closer together, thus increasing sales. Kraft launched Deli Creations, which are sandwiches made with its Oscar Meyer meats, Kraft cheeses, and Grey Poupon mustard, after spending several months with consumers in their kitchens. Kraft discovered that consumers wanted complete, ready-to-serve meals that are easy to prepare—and it had the products to create them.[12]

Finally, before Moen Inc. put its new massaging shower head, the Revolution, on the market, it wanted to find out what consumers thought about the new product design. But Moen did not want to just give consumers the shower head and later ask them if they liked it or not. The company wanted to see the consumers actually using the product . . . in the shower. So it hired QualiData Research Inc. to do some ethnographic research. QualiData enlisted 20 nudists as their volunteers and paid them $250 each to answer questions about their lifestyles, and to allow QualiData to install a tiny video camera in the shower of each volunteer in order to watch them use the new shower head. As a result of the research, the product was redesigned and has become a major new product success for Moen.[13]

How do you do marketing research on something like toothbrushes? For some creative answers, see the text.

Thomas J. Peterson/Alamy Stock Photo

Another creative approach to obtaining observational data is the hiring of *mystery shoppers.* Companies hire people to pose as real customers and have them go through an exchange process and record their observations in detailed reports. For example, a mystery shopper might be paid to travel to a vacation resort, eat at restaurants, play golf, open up bank accounts, test-drive new cars at auto dealers, or shop for groceries or clothes. The information they provide based on their observations often gives marketers unique insight that cannot be obtained any other way. Plus, more and more often this information is being collected via mobile technology and passed along in real time. By the way, there are Canadian mystery shopping companies, just in case you want a job like this!

Personal observation is both useful and flexible, but it can be costly and unreliable, especially when different observers report different conclusions in watching the same activities. Also, although observation can reveal what people do, it cannot determine why they do it, such as why they are buying or not buying a product. To determine why consumers behave as they do, marketing researchers must talk with consumers and record their responses. This is usually accomplished through the use of surveys.

Many marketers, however, feel that traditional marketing research methods do not go far enough in really understanding consumers. And, as previous chapters have pointed out, understanding the customer's experience with products and brands has become more important for marketers. Therefore, marketers are developing new and innovative ways to conduct research that goes a little deeper. One new concept is known as *neuromarketing,* which measures brain activity to discover how consumers respond to brands and advertising. For a peek at this new method, read the accompanying Marketing Matters box that discusses neuromarketing and whether it might become the holy grail of marketing research.[14]

MARKETING MATTERS

Neuromarketing: The Holy Grail of Marketing Research?

Thirty men and women study a sporty silver test model of a new Hyundai. They are asked to stare at specific parts of the vehicle, including the bumper, the windshield, and the tires. Electrode-studded caps on their heads capture the electrical activity in their brains as they view the car for an hour. That information is recorded in a hard drive each person wears on a belt. Their brain activity is supposed to show preferences that could lead to purchasing decisions. "We want to know what consumers think about a car before we start manufacturing thousands of them," says Dean Macko, manager of brand strategy at Hyundai Motors. Macko expects the carmaker will tweak the exterior based on the electroencephalograph reports, which track activity in all parts of the brain.

Neuromarketing, or brain-wave marketing, is becoming popular as a marketing research tool. Using EEGs and/or MRIs to track electrical activity and blood flow in consumers' brains is thought to guide marketers to develop the right products, right brands, and right ads to boost sales. For example, executives at PepsiCo's Frito-Lay unit use neuromarketing to test commercials, products, and packaging. According to Frito-Lay chief marketing officer Ann Mukherjee, brain-imaging tests can be more accurate than focus groups. Frito-Lay brain-tested a commercial that traditional focus groups panned. The spot for Cheetos featured a woman taking revenge on someone in a laundromat by putting the orange snack food in a dryer full of white clothes. Participants said they didn't like the prank, probably because they didn't want to look too mean-spirited to other focus group members. But EEG tests showed brain activity that suggested women loved the ad. The snack-food marketer then started airing the prank ad. Yahoo has a 60-second television commercial that features happy, dancing people around the world. Before spending the money to air the ad on prime-time and cable TV, as well as online, Yahoo ran it by EEG-cap-wearing consumers. The brain waves showed stimulation in the limbic system and frontal cortices of their brains, where memory and emotional thought occurs. The ad, which was part of Yahoo's recent $100 million branding campaign, was rolled out to bring more users to the search engine. A few years ago, the cost of renting brain-imaging machines kept many marketers from dabbling in neuromarketing. Today, there are several companies offering EEG and MRI testing devices and thus the costs have come down significantly. A marketer can hook 30 consumers up to an EEG device for $50,000. An MRI trial with 20 people would cost more like $40,000.

However, there are skeptics of neuromarketing. For example, Craig Bennett, a neuroscientist, wrote a report about running a dead Atlantic salmon through an MRI machine. The result showed signals of brain activity similar to the ones neuromarketers see when testing commercials on consumers. "You could say the salmon liked one brand of peanut butter over another brand," says Bennett. "But it was dead." So, the question is: Will neuromarketing become the holy grail of marketing research?

Is There an Optimal Research Design?

In short, there is no optimal research design. A researcher may choose among a variety of alternative methods for solving a particular marketing problem. A good marketing researcher understands that there is likely to be more than one way to tackle a problem. The ability to select the most appropriate research design develops with experience. Inexperienced researchers often embrace the survey method as the best design because they are most familiar with this method. More experienced researchers, on the other hand, recognize the value of other methods and can often put together creative research designs that can solve marketing problems more quickly and less expensively. Experienced researchers often note that the proper definition of marketing plays a central role in determining the most appropriate research design.

Sampling

Although sampling is an inherent component of the research design stage, it is a distinctive aspect of the research process. The researcher's sampling plan indicates who is to be sampled, how large a sample is needed, and how the sampling units will be selected. Rarely does a research project involve a complete census of every person in the research population. This is because of the time and cost involved in conducting a census. Thus, sampling is used. **Sampling** is the process of gathering data from a subset of the total population rather than from all members (census) of that particular population. A *sample,* then, is a subset from a larger population.

If proper statistical procedures are followed, a researcher does not need to select every member in a population, because a properly selected sample should be representative of the population as a whole. However, errors can and do occur in sampling, and the reliability of the data obtained through sampling can sometimes become an issue. Thus, the first and most critical sampling question for researchers to ask is: Who is to be sampled?

Another key question concerns the sample size: How big should the sample be? As mentioned, it is usually unrealistic to expect a census of the research population be conducted. In general, larger samples are more precise than smaller ones, but proper sampling can allow a smaller subset of the total population to provide a reliable measure of the whole.

The final question in the sampling plan concerns how to select the sampling units. There are two basic sampling techniques: probability and nonprobability sampling. **Probability sampling** involves precise rules to select the sample such that each element of the population has a specific known chance of being selected. For example, if your university wants to know how last year's 1,000 graduates are doing, it can put their names in a bowl and randomly select 100 names of graduates to contact. The chance of being selected—100/1000 or 0.10—is known in advance, and all graduates have an equal chance of being contacted. This procedure helps select a sample (100 graduates) that should be representative of the entire population (the 1,000 graduates) and allows conclusions to be drawn about the entire population.

Nonprobability sampling involves the use of arbitrary judgment by the marketing researcher to select the sample so that the chance of selecting a particular element of the population is either unknown or zero. If your university decided to talk to 100 of last year's graduates but only those who lived closest to the university, many class members would be arbitrarily eliminated. This has introduced a bias, or possible lack of representativeness, which may make it dangerous to draw conclusions about the entire population of the graduating class. Nonprobability samples are often used when time and budgets are limited and are most often used for exploratory research purposes. In general, marketing researchers use data from such samples with caution.

Learning Review

7. What is a survey?

8. Which research method offers the potential for establishing cause-and-effect relationship?

9. What is sampling?

DATA COLLECTION AND ANALYSIS

Once the research design has been formalized, the process of gathering or collecting data begins. Sometimes referred to as *fieldwork,* data collection at this stage of the research process includes all the activities that the researcher (and staff) undertakes to obtain data from the identified sources or respondents. Because there are several research methods that could be used by the researcher, this means there may be multiple ways to collect the data. For example, with the survey method, data may be collected by telephone, mail, or personal interview.

However the data are collected, it is important to minimize errors in the process. Most research experts agree that the data collection stage of the research process is one of the major sources of error in marketing research. Some of the errors that occur are a result of a variety of problems ranging from failure to select the right respondents to incorrect recording of observations. Competent and well-trained researchers inside the organization or those employed by outside research companies can go a long way in ensuring proper data collection.

The next step for the marketing researcher is data analysis. Mark Twain once observed, "Collecting data is like collecting garbage. You've got to know what you're going to do with the stuff before you collect it." In essence, the marketing researcher must know *why* the data are being collected and *how* to analyze them effectively in order for the data to have any value in decision making.

The level of analysis conducted on the data depends on the nature of the research and the information needed to provide a solution to the marketing problem. For survey data, frequency analysis is completed—calculating the responses question by question. The researcher may then wish to identify patterns in the data or examine how data pertaining to some questions may relate to data obtained from asking other questions. Probably the most widely used technique for organizing and analyzing marketing data is cross-tabulation. This method is particularly useful for market segmentation analysis.

CONCLUSIONS AND REPORT

At this stage of the process, the marketing researcher, often in conjunction with marketing management, must review the analysis and ask: What does this information tell us? A critical aspect of the marketing researcher's job is to interpret the information and make conclusions with regard to managerial decision making. The researcher must prepare a report to communicate the research findings. Included in this report should be suggestions for actions that might be taken by the organization to solve the marketing problem.

The researcher must be careful not to overwhelm management with technical terminology. Rather, the report should highlight the important results and conclusions in a clear and concise manner. Ultimately, the marketing researcher and management must work closely together to ensure proper interpretation of the research results. In addition, management must make a commitment to act—to make decisions based on the research and their good judgment and knowledge of the situation. In other words, someone must "make something happen" to see that a solution to the marketing problem gets implemented. Failure to act on the research findings creates an appearance that the marketing research effort is of little value. Finally, once implemented, the proposed solution should be monitored to ensure that intended results do occur.

ETHICAL ISSUES IN THE MARKETING RESEARCH PROCESS

According to the Marketing Research and Intelligence Association (MRIA), Canada's national association for professional marketing researchers, nine out of ten Canadians support marketing and survey research and believe that it serves a valuable societal purpose. However, unethical practices by some individual organizations are threatening the goodwill that Canadians have toward research.[15] Ethical issues can arise in the marketing researchers' relationships with all parties involved in the research process, including the respondents, the general public, their organizations, and/or clients. Professional marketing researchers must make ethical decisions regarding the collecting, using, and reporting of research data. Examples of unethical behaviour include failure to report problems with research results because of incomplete data, reporting only favourable results, using deception to collect information, and breaching the confidentiality of respondents.[16] Many companies are also collecting clickstream data when consumers go online, and sometimes these data are used for marketing purposes without the knowledge and consent of the consumer. The MRIA has developed formal ethical standards, guidelines, and policies for all its members to adhere to with regard to all aspects of marketing research. An example of the organization's efforts to respect respondent's time and privacy, and to honour their societal contribution by providing feedback to marketing researchers, is the world's first charter of respondent rights as outlined in the Making Responsible Decisions box, "A Charter of Respondent Rights."[17]

MAKING RESPONSIBLE DECISIONS

A Charter of Respondent Rights

The Marketing Research and Intelligence Association (MRIA), Canada's national association for professional marketing researchers, has developed the world's first Charter of Respondent Rights. The MRIA states that Canadians who participate in research by providing their opinions to researchers should be respected in terms of their time and their privacy. The Charter sets out nine rights of respondents, and all MRIA members must adhere to this Charter and its nine article components. The MRIA believes this Charter (reprinted below) will help protect the relationship between researchers and the general public.

Charter of Respondent Rights Your participation in legitimate marketing, social or public opinion research is very important to us. We value your honest feedback and your time. Your opinions help companies develop new products, make existing ones better, and improve customer service. Your views also assist government and non-profit organizations in advancing laws and policies that are in the public interest.

Our relationship with you is based on respect, trust and goodwill. When you participate in research conducted by our firm, or by any other corporate member of the Marketing Research and Intelligence Association (MRIA), you can be assured that:

Article 1 You will always be told the first name of the person contracting you, the research company's name and the nature of the study.

Article 2 You can verify that the research you have been invited to participate in is legitimate in one of two ways. You can either obtain a registration number and the MRIA's toll-free telephone number for any research registered with MRIA's Research Registration System or you can obtain the contact information of the research director who is conducting the study.

Article 3 You will not be sold anything or asked for money.

Article 4 Your privacy and the privacy of your answers will be respected and strictly preserved in accordance with the organization's privacy policy and applicable federal and provincial laws.

Article 5 You will be contacted at reasonable times, but it the time is inconvenient, you may ask to be re-contacted at a more convenient time.

Article 6 You are entitled to know the approximate duration of the interview.

Article 7 Your decision to participate in a study, answer specific questions, or discontinue your participation will be respected without question.

Article 8 You will be informed in advance if the interview will be recorded and the intended use of the recording. You may choose not to proceed with the interview if you do not want it to be recorded.

Article 9 You are assured that the highest standards of professional conduct will be upheld throughout all stages of the study.

LO5 USING AN INTELLIGENT MARKETING ENTERPRISE PLATFORM TO TRIGGER MARKETING ACTIONS

Today, businesses can obtain data from many sources, such as barcode scanners at checkout counters, online tracking software on computers and tablets, and usage histories on your telephone. In fact, the growth of the Internet of Things now allows data collection from almost any device a consumer might use. Marketing managers must use the combination of data, technology, and analytics to convert the data into useful information that will answer marketing questions and lead to effective marketing actions. Organizations that accomplish this successfully are often referred to as an *intelligent enterprise*.[18]

As shown in Figure 8–6, the elements of an intelligent marketing enterprise platform interact to facilitate the work of the marketing researcher. The top half of the figure shows how big data is created through a sophisticated communication network that collects data from internal and external sources. These data are stored, organized, and managed in databases. Collectively, these databases form a data warehouse. Data storage (and computing) may also take place in "the cloud," which is simply a collection of servers accessed through an Internet connection. As shown at the bottom of Figure 8–6, data analytics consists of several elements. Marketers use computers to specify important marketing queries or questions and to access the databases in the warehouse (or the cloud). Analytical tools are used to organize and manipulate the data to identify any managerial insights that may exist. The results are then presented using tables and graphics for easier interpretation. When accessing a database, marketers can use sensitivity analysis to ask "what if" questions to determine how hypothetical changes in product or brand drivers—the factors that influence the buying decisions of a household or organization—can affect sales. Traditional marketing research typically involves identifying possible drivers and then collecting data. For example, we might collect data to test the hypothesis that increasing couponing (the driver) during spring will increase trials by first-time buyers (the result).

Big Data and Data Analytics

Big data is a vague term generally used to describe large amounts of data collected from a variety of sources and analyzed with an increasingly sophisticated set of technologies. *Information technology* includes all of the computing resources that collect, store, and analyze the data. Marketing researchers have observed that today we live in an era of data deluge. The challenge facing managers is not data collection or even storage but how to efficiently transform the huge amount of data into useful information. This transformation is accomplished through the use of data analytics. A wide variety of analytical tools is available for people who are often referred to as *data scientists*. Their work is also creating a new field of marketing research that focuses on data visualization, or the presentation of the results of the analysis.

Data Mining

In contrast, **data mining** is the extraction of hidden predictive information from large databases to find statistical links between consumer purchasing patterns and marketing actions. Some of these are common sense: Since many consumers buy peanut butter and grape jelly together, why not run a joint promotion featuring Skippy peanut butter and Welch's grape jelly? But would you have expected that men buying diapers in the evening sometimes buy a six-pack of beer as well? Supermarkets discovered this when they mined checkout data from scanners. So they placed diapers and beer near each other, then placed potato chips between them, and increased sales on all three items! Now, data mining is even more robust with the advent of RFID (radio frequency identification) technology where "smart tags" are placed on the diapers and beer to tell whether they end up in the same shopping bag.

Still, success in data mining ultimately depends on humans—the marketing managers and researchers—and their judgments in how to select, analyze, and interpret the information. Additionally, new techniques and methods are always emerging, and marketing researchers must keep abreast of such developments. For example, data mining related to the Internet and social media is exploding. This information is obtained via cookies, Facebook pages, Twitter accounts, and Google Ad Preferences. This form of data mining is leading to one-to-one personalization and targeting of individual consumers. So be aware of that when you visit a website; someone might be collecting data about you.[19] The MRIA provides the latest news in marketing research on its website. Check out the accompanying Going Online box, "The Latest News in Marketing Research," to keep yourself up to date on the latest developments.

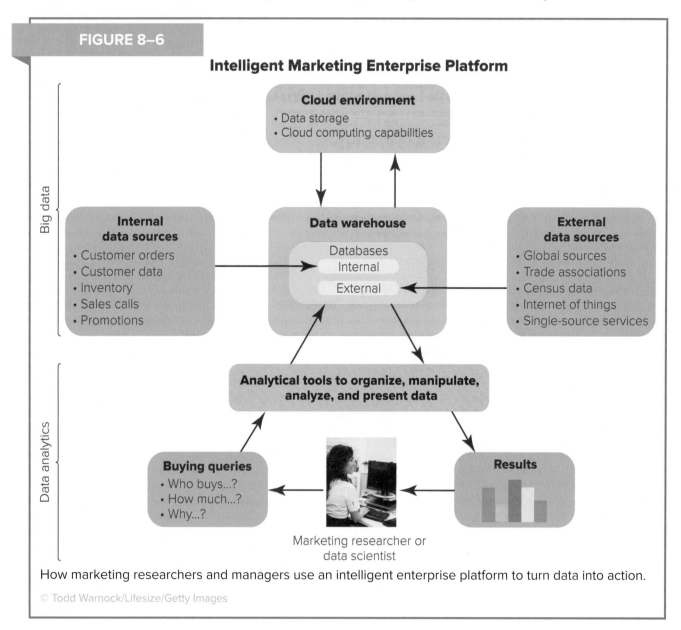

FIGURE 8–6

Intelligent Marketing Enterprise Platform

Big data

Cloud environment
- Data storage
- Cloud computing capabilities

Internal data sources
- Customer orders
- Customer data
- Inventory
- Sales calls
- Promotions

Data warehouse
Databases
Internal
External

External data sources
- Global sources
- Trade associations
- Census data
- Internet of things
- Single-source services

Data analytics

Analytical tools to organize, manipulate, analyze, and present data

Buying queries
- Who buys...?
- How much...?
- Why...?

Marketing researcher or data scientist

Results

How marketing researchers and managers use an intelligent enterprise platform to turn data into action.

© Todd Warnock/Lifesize/Getty Images

GOING ONLINE

The Latest News in Marketing Research

Go to the Marketing Research and Intelligence Association's website to check out all the latest news in marketing research (**www.mria-arim.ca**). On the site, you will find a link for the latest news.

Learning Review

10. What is an intelligent marketing enterprise platform?

11. What is data mining?

Learning Objectives Review

 Know what marketing research is.

Marketing research is the process of defining a marketing problem or opportunity, systematically collecting and analyzing information, and recommending actions to improve an organization's marketing activities. Marketing research is used by executives to aid in the decision-making process.

LO2 **Explain the different types of marketing research.**

There are three basic types of marketing research: (*1*) exploratory research, which is preliminary research conducted to clarify the scope and nature of the marketing problem; (*2*) descriptive research, which is research designed to describe basic characteristics of a given population or to profile particular marketing situations; and (*3*) causal research, which is research designed to identify cause-and-effect relationships among variables.

LO3 **Understand the stages in the marketing research process.**

The four basic stages in the marketing research process generally are: (*1*) defining the problem, (*2*) determining the research design, (*3*) collecting and analyzing data, and (*4*) drawing conclusions and preparing a report. The first stage—problem definition—is critical, because research based on incorrect problem definition will be a waste of resources. At the research design stage, the researcher produces a plan that outlines the methods and procedures for collecting and analyzing the required information. The plan includes the objectives of the research, the sources of information to be used, the research methods, the sampling plan, and the schedule and cost of the research.

LO4 **Explain the use of secondary data, surveys, experiments, and observation in marketing research.**

The marketing research can utilize secondary data—data previously collected and assembled for some other project than the one at hand. These data consist of information from both inside and outside the organization that may provide some insight into the marketing problem and its solution. If it does not, the marketing researcher may turn to the collecting of primary data—new data gathered and assembled specifically for the project—which can be obtained via surveys, experiments, and observation. A survey generates data by asking people questions and recording their responses on a questionnaire. An experiment involves the manipulation of an independent variable (e.g., price) and measuring its effect on the dependent variable (e.g., purchase behaviour). Observation involves watching, either mechanically or in person, how people actually behave. Research is being conducted more and more often via the Internet (online research) because it can be cheaper, faster, and better. And researchers are also using more creative approaches to research, including ethnographic research and neuromarketing research.

 Explain how an intelligent marketing enterprise platform can trigger marketing actions.

Today's marketing managers are often overloaded with data—from internal data to that provided on, say, TV viewing habits or grocery purchases from the scanner data at checkout counters. This can involve millions of bits of new information in a week or a month. An intelligent marketing enterprise platform enables marketing researchers and managers to turn data into marketing actions. Basically, the information technology that is part of the intelligent enterprise platform allows massive amounts of marketing data to be stored, accessed, and processed. The resulting databases (big data) can be analyzed (data analytics) or can be queried using data mining to find statistical relationships useful for marketing decisions and actions.

Applying Marketing Knowledge

1. Is it possible to make effective marketing decisions without marketing research?

2. Why is the problem definition stage of the marketing research process probably the most important stage?

3. You plan to open an ice cream shop in your town. What type of exploratory research would you conduct to help determine its feasibility? You find the exploratory research does not answer all your questions. You decide to do a survey to determine whether you should open the shop. What kind of questions will you ask? Whom do you ask?

4. Suppose you are trying to determine the top three favourite department stores in your area. You show customers at a shopping mall a list of department stores and ask them to rank their three favourite stores from 1 to 3 (with 1 being the favourite). What problems can occur with the survey?

5. Your university bookstore wants to find out students' opinions about the store's merchandise, prices, and customer service. What type of marketing research would you recommend to the store?

6. You are a marketing researcher observing what people do when selecting bread in a supermarket. You are behind a one-way mirror, and the customers do not know they are being observed. During the course of the day, you observe several people shoplifting a smaller snack product near the bread section. You know personally two of the shoplifters you see. What are the ethical problems you face in this situation?

7. You plan to open a new rent-a-car business. You have drafted a survey you want to distribute to airline passengers. The survey will be left at the airports, and respondents will mail the surveys back in a prepaid envelope. Some of the questions you plan to use are shown below. Use Figure 8–4 to (a) identify the problem with each question, and (b) correct it. (Note: Some questions may have more than one problem.)

   a. Do you own your own car or usually rent one?

       □ Yes □ No

   b. What is your age?

       □ 21–30 □ 30–40 □ 41–50 □ 50+

   c. How much did you spend on rental cars last year?

       □ $100 or less □ $101–$400 □ $401–$800 □ $800–$1,000 □ $1,000 or more

   d. What is a good daily rental car rate? _____

8. Suppose the government of British Columbia hired you to develop a new tourism ad campaign for the province. You have developed two ad concepts. But you need to test customer response to the ads online. How would you go about the testing? And what would you measure?

Building Your Marketing Plan

To help you collect the most useful data for your marketing plan, develop a three-column table:

1. In column 1, list the information you would ideally like to have to fill holes in your marketing plan.

2. In column 2, identify the source for each bit of information in column 1, such as a Web search, talking to prospective customers, looking at internal data, and so forth.

3. In column 3, set a priority on information you will have time to spend collecting by ranking them: 1 = most important, 2 = next most important, and so forth.

Video Case 8

Carmex®: Leveraging Facebook for Marketing Research

"What makes social media 'social' is its give and take," says Jeff Gerst of Bolin Marketing, who manages the Carmex® social media properties. By "give," Gerst is referring to the feedback messages that consumers send on social media; "take" is what they receive, such as news and coupons. "For Carmex, Facebook isn't just a way to share coupons or the latest product news, but it is also a marketing research resource. We have instantaneous access to the opinions of our consumers."

"While some people think of social media as 'free,' that is not true. However, almost everything in social media can be faster and cheaper than in the offline world," adds Dane Hartzell, general manager of Bolin Digital. "Many platforms have been prebuilt and we marketers only need to modify them slightly."

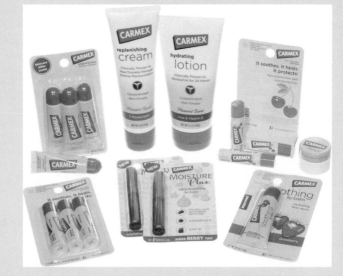

Carmex and Its Product Line

Although Carmex has been making lip balm since 1937, only in the last five years has it made serious efforts to stress growth and become more competitive. For example, Carmex has:

- Extended its core line of lip balm products into new flavours and varieties.

- Expanded into nearly 40 international markets.

- Developed the Carmex Moisture Plus line of premium lip balms for women.

- Launched a line of skin care products, its first venture outside of lip care.

Carmex has used social media tools in developing all of these initiatives, but the focus of this case is how Carmex might use Facebook marketing research to grow its lip balm varieties in North America.

Facebook Marketing Research: Two Key Metrics

"We have three potential new flavours and we can only put two into quantitative testing," explains Jeff Gerst to his Carmex marketing team. "So we have two goals in doing marketing research on this. Our first goal is to use Facebook to help us determine which two flavours we should move forward with. The second goal is to drive our Facebook metrics."

The two key Facebook metrics that the Carmex marketing team has chosen to help narrow the flavour choices from three to two are "likes" and "engagement." "Likes" are the number of new "likers" to the brand's Facebook page. This metric measures the size of the brand's Facebook audience. In contrast, "engagement" measures how active its Facebook audience is with Carmex. Any time a liker posts a comment on the Carmex Facebook wall, likes its status, or replies to one of its posts, the engagement level increases.

The easiest way for Carmex to grow the number of "likes" on its Facebook page is through contests and promotions. If it gives away prizes, people will be drawn to its site and its likes will increase. However, these people may not actually be fans of the Carmex product, so at the end of the promotion, they may "unlike" Carmex or they may remain fans but not engage with the Carmex page at all. The people who were already on the page were there because they like Carmex and are engaged.

"One of the biggest challenges facing Facebook community managers for brands is how to grow your likes without hurting the level of engagement that takes place on your page," says Holly Matson, senior manager of community strategy at Bolin Marketing.

"Depending on how we go about conducting the research," Gerst adds, "we can drive engagement with our existing Facebook community, we can use this as an opportunity to grow our Facebook community or, potentially, we could do both."

The benefits of this Carmex Facebook strategy are twofold: (1) narrowing the number of flavours to be researched from three to two, and (2) enhancing the connections with the Carmex Facebook community. Narrowing the flavour choices reduces the cost of the marketing research substantially. So Carmex can reduce expected costs while simultaneously linking better to consumers on its Facebook page.

How the Metrics Might Be Used

Carmex's Facebook activity can benefit (1) by using a poll to increase engagement, (2) by launching a contest to increase the number of likers, and (3) by trying to increase both engagement and likers through combining a poll with a contest.

The "Engagement" Strategy: Use a Poll

Let's look at two ways to use the engagement strategy showing actual Facebook screens. First, Carmex can post a somewhat open-ended question on its Facebook wall, such as, "Which Carmex lip balm flavour would you most like to see next: Watermelon, Green Apple, or Peach Mango?" (Figure 1). However, consumers are less likely to respond to a question if they have to type in a response and have their name attached to it.

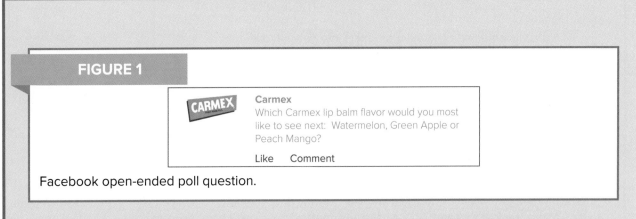

FIGURE 1

Facebook open-ended poll question.

Alternatively, Carmex can post the same question on its wall as a fixed-alternative poll question (Figure 2). Then, consumers need only to click on a flavour to vote for their favourite; this is quick and anonymous, and will drive more people to vote, where more votes mean more engagement. As consumers reply to the poll question, the results are measured in real time. Within five minutes, Carmex will have several dozen votes; by the end of a business day, Carmex can very easily have over 500 responses.

In this scenario, the consumers are content because they are able to engage with a brand they like and have their opinions heard. Carmex is content because it has engaged hundreds of its fans on its Facebook page, and it gains results that, while not statistically valid, are directionally very helpful in deciding which flavours to put into testing. This scenario gets an answer quickly and drives fan engagement with existing fans but does not drive new likers to the Carmex Facebook page.

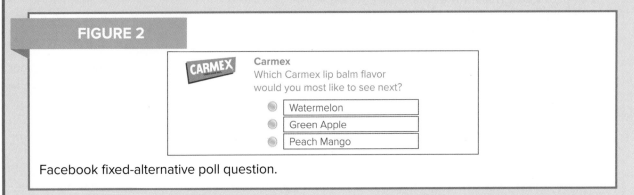

FIGURE 2

Facebook fixed-alternative poll question.

The "Likes" Strategy: Use a Contest

If Carmex wants to grow the size of its Facebook community, which means the number of its brand page "likes," it can adopt a different strategy. Carmex can announce a contest where if consumers "like" Carmex on Facebook and share a comment, they will be entered to win three limited-edition flavours. The chance to win limited-edition flavours is exciting to Carmex enthusiasts, and a contest like this will draw new consumers to the page. Carmex can ask the winners to review the limited edition flavours and see if there is a consensus on which flavours should move on to quantitative testing. Setting up a contest, developing official rules, promoting the contest through Facebook ads, and fulfilling a contest can be costly and time-consuming.

The Combined Strategy: Use Poll and Contest

Carmex can also choose to layer these two strategies into a combined strategy where it runs the limited-edition flavour contest to promote new likes and meanwhile posts the poll question on its Facebook wall to drive engagement.

Reaching a Decision

Figure 3 shows the potential results from the three Facebook strategies being considered—the poll only, the contest only, or both strategies together. Assume that the Carmex marketing team has sought your help in selecting a strategy and needs your answers to the questions below.

FIGURE 3

FACEBOOK STRATEGY	POTENTIAL IMPACT ON...		
	Increased "Engagement"	Increased "Likes"	Cost
Poll Only	High	Low	Low
Contest Only	Low	High	Moderate
Poll + Contest	High	High	Moderate to High

■ Favourable   □ Neutral   ■ Unfavourable

Potential results from three possible Facebook strategies.

QUESTIONS

1. What are the advantages and disadvantages for the Carmex marketing team in collecting data to narrow the flavour choices from three to two using (*a*) an online survey of a cross-section of Internet households or (*b*) an online survey of Carmex Facebook likers?

2. (*a*) On a Facebook brand page, what are "engagement" and "likes" really measuring? (*b*) For Carmex, which is more important and why?

3. (*a*) What evokes consumers' "engagement" on a brand page on Facebook? (*b*) What attracts consumers to "like" a brand page on Facebook?

4. (*a*) What are the advantages of using a fixed-alternative poll question on Facebook? (*b*) When do you think it would be better to use an open-ended question?

5. (*a*) If you had a limited budget and two weeks to decide which two flavours to put into quantitative testing, would you choose a "poll only" or a "contest only" strategy? Why? (*b*) If you had a sizable budget and two months to make the same decision, which scenario would you choose? Why?

Case: This case was written by Jeff Gerst of Bolin Marketing.

9

Market Segmentation, Targeting, and Positioning

Learning Objectives

After reading this chapter, you should be able to:

LO1 Explain what market segmentation is and when to use it.

LO2 Identify the five steps involved in segmenting and targeting markets.

LO3 Recognize the different factors used to segment consumer and organizational (business) markets.

LO4 Know how to develop a market–product grid to identify a target market and recommend resulting actions.

LO5 Explain how marketing managers position products in the marketplace.

LO6 Describe three approaches to developing a sales forecast for a company.

Segmenting the Tourism Market

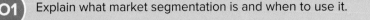

Tourism is an important industry in Canada. The Canadian Tourism Commission (CTC) recently developed something called the *explorer quotient* (EQ) to help small- and medium-sized businesses (SMEs) in the tourism sector to better focus product development, marketing, and sales efforts on the "best" tourism customers. The CTC's marketing research revealed that different types of tourists seek out different types of travel experiences. Accordingly, the CTC "segmented" tourists into different groups called explorer types based on particular characteristics stemming from social and travel values, travel motivations, and behaviours. Then, the CTC selected Canada's best explorer-type prospects based on their affinity for the Canada "Keep Exploring" brand, as well as for love of travel, potential for being high-yield customers, and propensity for word-of-mouth advocacy. This resulted in the selection of specific target types in each of the CTC's primary geographic markets. The objective was to help businesses target the right customer with the right offer and the right message.

The CTC found three very specific and important explorer segments for the Canadian market: Free Spirits, Cultural Explorers, and Authentic Experiencers. These three segments account for almost 35 percent of the total global tourist market and are the ones most likely to consider Canada as a tourist destination. *Free Spirits* are highly social and open-minded. Their enthusiasm for life extends to their outlook on travel. Experimental and adventurous, they indulge in high-end experiences that are shared with others. The Free Spirit is the traveller's traveller—they seem to love everything about travel and, as in life, they embrace the experiences it offers with arms wide open. A Free Spirit will seek hedonistic rejuvenation, viewing vacation is a time to be carefree, to indulge, and to enjoy a spa, nightlife, and great cuisine and other opportunities for a little pampering. They are most likely to want to view the Northern and Southern lights, engage in mountain and glacier viewing, stay at a waterfront resort, visit well-known natural wonders, go to aquariums and zoos, and view wildlife.

© David Buzzard/Alamy Stock Photo

Cultural Explorers are defined by their love of constant travel and continuous opportunities to embrace, discover, and immerse themselves in the culture, people, and settings of the places they visit. The Cultural Explorer is an avid traveller who values learning and discovery while travelling. They don't want to feel like a "tourist," preferring just to blend in and have the most authentic experience possible rather than being confined to group tours and schedules. They love to learn about and absorb themselves in the ancient history as well as the modern cultures of the places they visit. They will choose destinations that provide opportunities to experience natural beauty. For them, travel is a journey, not the destination. Cultural Explorers are more likely than other travellers to be interested in visiting heritage sites, interacting with the locals, visiting national parks, visiting well-known natural wonders, attending festivals and events, dining at restaurants offering local ingredients, and engaging in wildlife viewing.

Authentic Experiencers are typically understated travellers looking for authentic, tangible engagement with destinations they seek, with a particular interest in understanding the history of the places they visit. Travel is not their only interest in life, but they certainly appreciate it when they go. They prefer to do their own thing while at a destination, having control over what they see and when they see it. An Authentic Experiencer will avoid hedonistic rejuvenation and will not shy away from living like the locals do. Authentic Experiencers are more likely than other travellers to be interested in attending exhibits, viewing architecture, and visiting historic sites. They are also interested in nature observation, sightseeing, shopping, and dining, as well as participating in hands-on learning activities.

This example illustrates the essence and importance of successful market segmentation. In this chapter, we will discuss more fully why markets need to be segmented, the steps used in segmenting markets, the process of selecting target segment(s), and how to position a product or service offering effectively in the marketplace. We will then discuss forecasting sales for given segments or targets.

 ## WHY SEGMENT MARKETS?

One of the oldest stories about the need for market segmentation comes from the early automobile industry. Henry Ford developed his Model T, a car he felt would satisfy the needs of everyone. Ford said, "They can have it in any colour, as long as it's black." His strategy was simple: focus on the economies of scale created by mass production. Ford's strategy was also known as a mass marketing strategy. In contrast, General Motors began producing different models of cars, each available in different colours, designed to appeal to the preferences of different consumers. This strategy enabled GM to surpass Ford and become the leading automaker. In short, most companies segment markets because of an almost unassailable premise: People are different, and people who are different are likely to have different needs and wants. Accordingly, smart marketers segment markets so that they can respond more effectively to the specific needs and wants of groups of potential buyers and thus increase sales and profits. Not-for-profit organizations also segment the clients they serve to satisfy client needs more effectively while achieving the organization's goals. Let's now talk in more detail about (1) what market segmentation is, and (2) when it is necessary to segment markets.

What Market Segmentation Means

The fact that people are different is not necessarily a comfortable notion for marketers. In fact, it would be easier for marketers if people were all the same. But they are not. So, market segmentation involves aggregating prospective buyers into groups that

(1) have common needs, and (2) will respond similarly to a marketing action. **Market segments** are the relatively homogeneous groups of prospective buyers that result from the market segmentation process. Each market segment consists of people who are relatively similar to each other in terms of their consumption behaviour.

The existence of different market segments has caused firms to use a marketing strategy of **product differentiation**. This strategy involves a firm using different marketing mix activities, such as product features and advertising, to help consumers perceive the product as being different from and better than competing products. The perceived differences may involve physical features or nonphysical ones, such as image or price.

Segmentation: Linking Needs to Actions

The process of segmenting a market and selecting specific segments as targets is the link between the various buyers' needs and the organization's marketing program (Figure 9–1). Market segmentation is only a means to an end: to lead to tangible marketing actions that can increase sales and profitability.

FIGURE 9–1

Market segmentation—linking market needs to an organization's marketing program.

Market segmentation first stresses the importance of grouping people or organizations in a market according to the similarity of their needs and the benefits they are looking for in making a purchase. Second, such needs and benefits must be related to specific marketing actions that the organization can take. These actions may involve separate products or other aspects of the marketing mix, such as price, advertising, or distribution strategies.

Using Market–Product Grids

A **market–product grid** is a framework to relate the market segments of potential buyers to products offered or potential marketing actions by the firm. The market–product grid in Figure 9–2 shows different market segments for bed pillows. The market segments appear in the horizontal rows while the product offerings appear in the vertical columns. Also, notice in this market–product grid analysis that the estimated market size of each sleeper segment is also provided. This provides the bed pillow manufacturers an indication of the relative attractiveness of given segments and an idea about the type and amount of pillows that should be produced to cater to those segments.

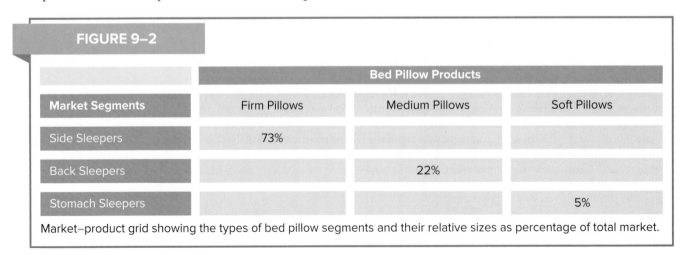

FIGURE 9–2

Market Segments	Bed Pillow Products		
	Firm Pillows	Medium Pillows	Soft Pillows
Side Sleepers	73%		
Back Sleepers		22%	
Stomach Sleepers			5%

Market–product grid showing the types of bed pillow segments and their relative sizes as percentage of total market.

When to Segment Markets

A business firm goes to the trouble and expense of segmenting its markets when it expects that this will increase its sales, profit, and return on investment. When expenses are greater than the potentially increased sales from segmentation, a firm should not attempt to segment its market. However, three specific situations that illustrate effective use of market segmentation are the cases of (1) one product and multiple market segments, (2) multiple products and multiple market segments, and (3) "segments of one," or mass customization.

One Product and Multiple Market Segments

When a firm produces only a single product or service and attempts to sell it to two or more market segments, it avoids the extra costs of developing and producing additional versions of the product, which often entail extremely high research, engineering, and manufacturing expenses. In this case, the incremental costs of taking the product into new market segments are typically those of a separate promotional campaign or a new channel of distribution. Although these expenses can be high, they are rarely as large as those for developing an entirely new product.

Movies, magazines, and books are single products frequently directed to two or more distinct market segments. Movie companies often run different TV commercials or magazine ads featuring different aspects of a newly released film (love, or drama, or spectacular scenery) that are targeted to different market segments. Many Canadian magazines produce separate editions usually targeting unique geographic and demographic segments using a special mix of editorial content and advertisements. *Maclean's* produces 15 different editions, and *Reader's Digest* produces nine.

Although multiple TV commercials for movies and separate covers or advertisements for magazines or books are expensive, they are minor compared with the costs of producing an entirely new movie, magazine, or book for another market segment.

Multiple Products and Multiple Market Segments

Ford's different lines of cars, SUVs, and pickup trucks are each targeted at a different type of customer—examples of multiple products aimed at multiple market segments. Producing these different vehicles is clearly more expensive than producing only a single vehicle. But this strategy is very effective *if* it meets customers' needs better, doesn't reduce quality or increase price, and adds to Ford's sales revenues and profits.

Unfortunately, this product differentiation strategy in the auto industry has a huge potential downside: The proliferation of different models and options can reduce quality and raise prices—especially in relation to foreign imports. Perhaps the extreme was in 1982, when the Ford Thunderbird had thousands of options compared with 32 (including colours) on the 1982 Honda Accord.

Three decades later, Ford is relearning its models and options lessons. Its current successful turnaround is partly related to a reduction in the number of frames, engines, and brands offered. As a result, Ford has reduced its number of models from 97 to 36 and sold off the Jaguar, Land Rover, and Volvo brands. Although there are fewer choices, Ford's simplified product line provides two benefits to consumers: (1) lower prices through producing a higher volume of fewer models, and (2) higher quality because of the ability to debug fewer basic designs.

Segments of One: Mass Customization

Canadian marketers are rediscovering today what their ancestors running the corner general store knew a century ago: Every customer is unique, has unique wants and needs, and desires special tender loving care or a particular customer experience from the marketer. Economies of scale in manufacturing and marketing during the past century made mass-produced goods so affordable that most customers were willing to compromise their individual tastes and settle for standardized products. Today's Internet environment, coupled with flexible manufacturing and marketing processes, have made *mass customization* possible, that is, tailoring goods or services to the tastes of individual customers on a high-volume scale. For example, Mars, Inc. can personalize your M&M'S® candies with your photo or a personal message.

Mass customization is the next step beyond *build-to-order (BTO)*, manufacturing a product only when there is an order from a customer. Apple uses BTO systems that trim work-in-progress inventories and shorten delivery times to customers. To do this, Apple restricts its computer manufacturing line to only a few basic models that can be assembled in four minutes. This gives customers a good choice with quick delivery. But even this system falls a bit short of total mass customization because customers do not have an unlimited number of features from which to choose.

But there are companies that will completely customize products or services for you, individually, on a much smaller scale. For example, you can go online right now and order custom M&M'S® candies especially made for you, including even having your name and photo of yourself printed on the candy, and have them delivered right to your door. This is often called *ultra-customization.* Ultra-customization allows you to hand-pick your entertainment packages, personalize your next vacation, design your own clothes, customize your website, and choose exactly the information you want to be exposed to, including receiving customized newsletters and magazines. By Terry is a company that caters to the very affluent consumer who desires complete personalization. This Paris-based boutique will use your DNA and planetary alignment to customize your very own lipstick. The lipstick is designed and created solely for you. But it will cost you US$1,200.[1] Talk about segments of one!

The Segmentation Trade-Off: Synergies versus Cannibalization

The key to successful product differentiation and market segmentation strategies is finding the ideal balance between satisfying a customer's individual wants and achieving *organizational synergy,* the increased customer value achieved through performing organizational functions such as marketing or manufacturing more efficiently. The "increased customer value" can take many forms: more products, improved quality on existing products, lower prices, easier access to products through improved distribution, and so on. So the ultimate criterion for an organization's marketing success is that customers should be better off as a result of the increased synergies.

The organization should also achieve increased revenues and profits from the product differentiation and market segmentation strategies it uses. When the increased customer value involves adding new products or a new chain of stores, the product differentiation–market segmentation trade-off raises a critical issue: Are the new products or new chain simply stealing customers and sales from the older, existing ones? This is known as *cannibalization.*

Marketers increasingly emphasize a two-tier, "Tiffany/Walmart" strategy. Many firms now offer different variations of the same basic offering to high-end and low-end segments. Gap's Banana Republic chain sells blue jeans for $58, whereas its Old Navy stores sell a slightly different version for $22.

Unfortunately, the lines between customer segments can often blur and lead to problems, such as the Ann Taylor flagship store competing with its LOFT outlets. The flagship Ann Taylor chain targets "successful, relatively affluent, fashion-conscious women" while its sister Ann Taylor LOFT chain targets "value-conscious women who want a casual lifestyle at work and home." The LOFT stores wound up stealing sales from the Ann Taylor chain.

Walmart is now building 30 to 40 new stores to test the concept of putting small stores in large cities. These will be one-third the size of its supercentres and will sell groceries. They are intended to compete with the dollar chains and bare-bones outlets that are stealing Walmart customers and causing lagging sales. Will its own Tiffany/Walmart strategy prove successful or simply be another case of cannibalization?

Learning Review

1. Market segmentation involves aggregating prospective buyers into groups that have two key characteristics. What are they?

2. When should a firm segment its markets?

(LO2) STEPS IN SEGMENTING AND TARGETING MARKETS

The process of segmenting a market and then selecting and reaching the target segments is divided into the five steps discussed in this section, as shown in Figure 9–3. Segmenting a market is not an exact science—it requires large doses of common sense and managerial judgment.[2]

FIGURE 9–3

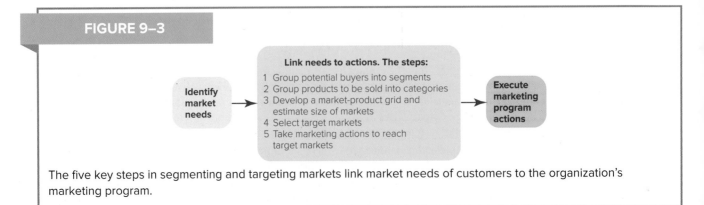

Identify market needs

Link needs to actions. The steps:
1 Group potential buyers into segments
2 Group products to be sold into categories
3 Develop a market-product grid and estimate size of markets
4 Select target markets
5 Take marketing actions to reach target markets

Execute marketing program actions

The five key steps in segmenting and targeting markets link market needs of customers to the organization's marketing program.

So, now let us have you put on your entrepreneur's hat to use the market segmentation process to choose target markets and take useful marketing actions. Suppose that you own a Wendy's fast-food restaurant next to a large urban university that offers both day and evening classes. Your restaurant specializes in the Wendy's basics: hamburgers, french fries, Frosty desserts, and chili. Even though you are part of a chain and have some restrictions on menu and decor, you are free to set your hours of business and to undertake local advertising. How can market segmentation help?

Step 1: Group Potential Buyers into Segments

It is not always a good idea to segment a market. Grouping potential buyers into meaningful segments involves meeting some specific criteria that answer the questions: "Would segmentation be worth doing?" and "Is it possible?" If so, the next step is to find specific variables that can be used to create the various segments.

LO3 Criteria to Use in Forming the Segments

A marketing manager should develop market segments that meet five main criteria:

- *Potential for increased profit.* The best segmentation approach is the one that maximizes the opportunity for future profit and return on investment (ROI). If this potential is maximized without segmentation, do not segment. For not-for-profit organizations, the criterion is the potential for serving client users more effectively.
- *Similarity of needs of potential buyers within a segment.* Potential buyers within a segment should be similar in terms of a marketing action, such as product features sought or advertising media used.
- *Difference of needs of buyers among segments.* If the needs of the various segments are not very different, combine them into fewer segments. A different segment usually requires a different marketing action, which, in turn, means greater costs. If increased sales do not offset extra costs, combine segments and reduce the number of marketing actions.
- *Potential of a marketing action to reach a segment.* Reaching a segment requires a simple but effective marketing action. If no such action exists, do not segment.
- *Simplicity and cost of assigning potential buyers to segments.* A marketing manager must be able to put a market segmentation plan into effect. This means being able to recognize the characteristics of potential buyers and then assigning them to a segment without encountering excessive costs.

Ways to Segment Consumer Markets

Figure 9–4 shows the main dimensions used to segment Canadian consumer markets. These include geographic, demographic, psychographic, and behavioural segmentation. By examining Figure 9–4, you can also see that a number of variables can be used within each dimension for segmentation purposes. What you should remember is that segmenting markets is not a pure science—it requires large doses of common sense and managerial judgment. A marketer may have to use several dimensions and multiple variables within each dimension to form proper market segments. Let us take a look at how some marketers might segment consumer markets using the information in Figure 9–4.

- *Geographic segmentation.* Using geographic segmentation, a marketer segments based on where consumers live. Geographic variables, such as countries, regions, provinces, counties, cities, or even neighbourhoods, could be used. Marketers often find that Canadians differ in terms of needs or preferences based on the region in which they live. This is a form of geographic segmentation. For example, Colgate-Palmolive markets Arctic Power, its cold-water detergent, on an energy-cost-saving dimension in Quebec, but as a clothes saver (cold-water washing is easier on clothes) in Western Canada.
- *Demographic segmentation.* One of the most common ways to segment consumer markets is to use demographic segmentation, or segmenting a market based on population characteristics. This approach segments consumers according to such variables as age, gender, income, education, occupation, and so forth. Cyanamid Canada Inc. uses age as a segmentation variable, producing and marketing its vitamins to various age groups, including children, young adults, and older Canadians. Centrum Select, for instance, is specifically designed for adults over 50. Trimark Investments of Ontario segments the financial services market by gender, targeting males and females with different products and different advertising campaigns. General Electric uses family size as a segmentation variable, targeting smaller families with compact microwaves and larger families with extra-large refrigerators. You should note, however, that a single demographic variable may not be sufficient in understanding and segmenting a given market.[3] Thus, many marketers combine a number of demographic variables that might clearly distinguish one segment from another. For example, cosmetics companies, such as Clinique, combine gender, income, and occupation in order to examine market segments for different lines of cosmetic products.
- *Psychographic segmentation.* Marketers use psychographic segmentation when they segment markets according to personality or lifestyle. It has been found that people who share the same demographic characteristics can have very different psychographic profiles. As we saw in Chapter 5, personality traits have been linked to product preferences and brand choice.

In addition, a person's lifestyle (his or her activities, interests, and opinions) also affects the types of products, the brands of products, and how they may be purchased. Remember the PRIZM5 lifestyle segments or clusters from Chapter 5? Well, for example, the Grads & Pads segment consists of young midscale urban singles with liberal lifestyles. They are night owls and like to frequent bars. Other segments in PRIZM5 include Fresh Air Families, Our Time, and Pets & PCs.[4]

FIGURE 9–4

Main Dimensions	Variables	Typical Breakdown
Geographic segmentation	Region	Atlantic, Quebec, Ontario, Prairies, British Columbia
	City or census metropolitan area (CMA) size	Under 5,000; 5,000–19,999; 20,000–49,999; 50,000–99,999; 100,000–249,999; 250,000–499,999; 500,000–999,999; 1,000,000–3,999,999; 4,000,000 +
	Density	Urban; suburban; rural
	Climate	East; West
Demographic segmentation	Age	Infant; under 6; 6–11; 12–17; 18–24; 25–34; 35–49; 50–64; 65+
	Gender	Male; female
	Family size	1–2; 3–4; 5+
	Life stage	Infant; preschool; child; youth; collegiate; adult; senior
	Birth era	Baby Boomer (1946–1964); Generation X (1965–1976); Baby Boomlet/Generation Y (1977–1994)
	Marital status	Never married; married; separated; divorced; widowed
	Income	Under $10,000; $10,000–$19,999; $20,000–$29,999; $30,000–$39,999; $40,000–$54,999; $55,000–$74,999; $75,000+
	Occupation	Professional; managerial; clerical; sales; labourers; students; retired; housewives; unemployed
	Education	Grade school or less; some high school; high school graduate; some university; university graduate
	Race	White; Black; Asian; Native; other
	Home ownership	Own home; rent home
Psychographic segmentation	Personality	Gregarious; compulsive; extroverted; introverted
	Lifestyle (PRIZM C2)	Cosmopolitan Elite; Suburban Gentry; Grads & Pads; Les Chics; Lunch at Tim's; and so on
Behavioural segmentation	Benefits sought	Quality; service; low price
	Usage rate	Light user; medium user; heavy user
	User status	Non-user; ex-user; prospect; first-time user; regular user
	Loyalty status	None; medium; strong

Segmentation variables and breakdowns for Canadian consumer markets.

• *Behavioural segmentation.* When marketers use consumers' behaviour with or toward a product to segment the market, they are using behavioural segmentation. A powerful form of behavioural segmentation is to divide the market according to the benefits consumers seek from a product category. Using *benefits sought,* the marketer examines the major benefits consumers look for in the product category, the kinds of consumers who look for each benefit, and the major brands that deliver each benefit. For example, Telus Mobility and Bell Mobility both market their wireless communications products and services to young adults under 24 years of age who want smartphones as their mobile communications platform. On the other hand, Rogers Wireless targets CEOs of large businesses who want to improve employee productivity through the use of wireless technology. Another example is Schick marketing its Intuition razor to Canadian women who seek the convenience benefit of a one-step lather-and-shave design while it also markets its Quattro to women who want the benefit of a truly long-lasting shave. Finally, in a recent study of tourists visiting New Brunswick, it was found that those tourists could be segmented using a benefits sought approach and they were sorted into three distinctive groups: outdoor lovers, active explorers and cultural shoppers, each group being significantly different based on benefit-related variables being sought.[5]

Another behavioural segmentation variable often used by marketers is **usage rate**—quantity consumed or patronage during a specific period, which varies significantly among different customer groups. Air Canada, for example, focuses on usage rate for its frequent-flyer program, which is designed to encourage passengers to use its airline repeatedly. Usage rate is sometimes referred to in terms of the **80/20 rule**, a concept that suggests that 80 percent of a firm's sales are obtained from 20 percent of its customers. The percentages in the 80/20 rule are not really fixed; rather, the rule suggests that a small fraction of customers provide a large fraction of sales. For example, Air Canada pays special attention to the business travel segment that comprises only 20 percent of the airline seats but 40 percent of overall revenues.

Research shows that the fast-food market can also be segmented into light, medium, or heavy users. For every $1 spent by a light user in a fast-food restaurant, each heavy user spends about $5.[6] This is the reason for the emphasis in almost all marketing strategies on effective ways to reach heavy users of products and services. Thus, as a Wendy's restaurant owner, you want to keep the heavy-user segment constantly in mind. With advances in information technology, including data mining tools, marketers are now able to conduct detailed segmentation studies. Additionally, with the advent of social media, many marketers are interested in segmenting the users of social media. For some insight into how some social media user segments, read the Marketing Matters box, "Segmenting the Social Media User."[7]

Wireless communications providers target young adults seeking specific benefits from wireless technology, specifically smartphones that provide mobile communications platforms.

© Alex Segre/Alamy Stock Photo

MARKETING MATTERS

Segmenting the Social Media User

With the growth of social media usage in Canada, many marketers are interested in understanding these users, including if it is possible to segment such users into meaningful groups. One Canadian proprietary online market survey conducted by Zinc Research identified five key social media segments to help marketers better understand who is using social media and how best to connect and engage with them. Data was collected from a variety of social media platforms including Facebook (by far, the favourite destination of Canadians), LinkedIn, Twitter, and others.

The study identified five types of social media users and organized them into five distinct behavioural segments:

- *Online/Real time* (heavy users): 6 percent of users

- *Suits & Strategy* (business users): 5 percent of users

- *3Cs - Chat, Chill and Connect* (socializers): 14 percent of users

- *Friend & Family Circles* (Facebook friends): 24 percent of users

- *Samplers & Lurkers* (casual users): 29 percent of users

Let's take a look at some of these segments. The Online/Real time segment is the heaviest user group, spending 20 hours a week on social media sites. They are more likely to be younger, college-educated males and are members of Facebook, Twitter, and LinkedIn. Social media is important to them for sharing ideas and being part of a community. They tend to get their news and information online. The Suits & Strategy segment consists primarily of business users. They tend to be younger, college-educated males and big users of LinkedIn. Social media is important to them for promoting and developing their businesses and careers. They also tend to get their news and information online. The 3Cs segment consists primarily of females with a mean age of 42. This group tends to use Facebook. Social media is important to them for playing online games, sharing ideas, and being part of a community.

Environics has also segmented Canadian social media users into three distinctive groups: producers of content, followers of content, and non-users. The producers of content segment consists of young, upwardly mobile immigrants and young, ethnic, urban singles. They tend to be heavy users of LinkedIn and value social media for boosting their professional status. The social media followers segment tends to be older, more affluent suburbanites with established families, especially those living in Toronto and Montreal. They tend to be discriminating buyers and are brand-conscious. Finally, the non-users of social media segment includes a wide-ranging group of older, exurban households and upper-middle-class town couples and families who tend to be risk-averse and are content to keep to themselves.

Variables to Use in Forming Segments for Wendy's

Now, in determining one or two variables to segment the market for your Wendy's restaurant, very broadly, we find two main markets: students and nonstudents. To segment the students, we could try a variety of demographic variables, such as age, gender, year in school, or university major, or psychographic variables, such as personality or lifestyle. But none of these variables really meets the five criteria listed previously—particularly the fourth criterion: leading to a feasible marketing action to reach the various segments. Four student segments that *do* meet these criteria include the following:

- Students living in dormitories (residence halls, fraternity houses)
- Students living near the university in apartments
- Day commuter students living outside the area
- Night commuter students living outside the area

These segmentation variables are really a combination of where the student lives and the time he or she is on campus (and near your restaurant). For nonstudents who might be customers, similar variables might be used:

- Faculty and staff members at the university
- People who live in the area but are not connected with the university
- People who work in the area but are not connected with the university

Ways to Segment Organizational (Business) Markets

Variables for segmenting organizational (business) markets are shown in Figure 9–5. A product manager at Xerox responsible for its new line of multifunction (MFP) colour printers might use a number of the following segmentation variables:

- *Geographic segmentation.* The product manager might segment on the basis of region or actual location of the potential customer. Firms located in a census metropolitan area (CMA) might receive a personal sales call, whereas those outside the CMA might be contacted by phone.
- *Demographic segmentation.* Firms might be categorized by the North American Industry Classification System (NAICS). Manufacturers, for example, with global customers might have different printing needs than do retailers or lawyers serving local customers.
- *Behavioural segmentation.* The market might also be segmented on the basis of benefits sought. Xerox may decide to focus on firms looking for quality product and good customer service as opposed to those looking for simply low prices. The product manager might also segment the market on the basis of usage rate, recognizing that larger, more globally oriented firms are more likely to be heavy users.

Xerox® WorkCentre®
7755 / 7765 / 7775
Multifunction System
Exceptionally efficient.
Extra secure.
Extremely easy.   xerox

What variables might Xerox use to segment the organizational markets for its answer to colour copying problems? For the possible answer and related marketing actions, see the text.

Some experts have combined geographic, demographic, and behavioural segmentation variables used in segmenting organizational (business) markets to produce a segmentation concept known as firmographics. *Firmographics* involves both organizational or business characteristics—such as location, size of firm, industry category, corporate activities, business objectives, and buying objectives—and characteristics of the composition of the organization—such as the income distribution of employees, age, gender, and education of the workforce. Organizations with distinguishing firmographics are then grouped into market segments.[8]

FIGURE 9–5

Main Dimensions	Variables	Typical Breakdowns
Geographic segmentation	Region Location	Atlantic, Quebec, Ontario, Prairies, British Columbia In CMA; not in CMA
Demographic segmentation	NAICS code Number of employees Annual sales volume	2-digit: section; 3-digit: subsection; 4-digit: Industry Group 1–19; 20–99; 100–249; 250+ Less than $1 million; $1–10 million; $10–100 million; over $100 million
Behavioural segmentation	Benefits sought Usage rate User status Loyalty status Purchase method Type of buy	Quality; customer service; low price Light user; medium user; heavy user Non-user; ex-user; prospect; first-time user; regular user None; medium; strong Centralized; decentralized; individual; group New buy; modified rebuy; straight rebuy

Dimensions used to segment Canadian organizational markets.

Step 2: Group Products to Be Sold into Categories

As important as grouping customers into segments is finding a means of grouping the products you are selling into meaningful categories. If the firm has only one product or service, this is not a problem, but when it has dozens or hundreds, these must be grouped in some way so that buyers can relate to them. This is why department stores and supermarkets are organized into product groups, with the departments or aisles containing related merchandise. Likewise, manufacturers have product lines that are the groupings they use in the catalogues sent to customers.

What are the groupings for your Wendy's restaurant? It could be the item purchased, such as a Frosty, chili, hamburgers, and french fries, but this is where judgment—the qualitative aspect of marketing—comes in. Students really buy an eating experience, or a meal that satisfies a need at a particular time of day, and so the product grouping can be defined by meal or time of day such as breakfast, lunch, between-meal snack, dinner, and after-dinner snack. These groupings are more closely related to the way purchases are actually made and permit you to market the entire meal, not just your french fries or Frosty. To examine how Apple Inc. grouped its products to be sold into specific categories over its 30-year history, see the Going Online exercise below.

GOING ONLINE

Apple Inc. Product Groupings

In its 30-year history, Apple Inc. has developed hundreds of products. Visit **www.apple-history.com**, look for "by family" (for family of products) on the right-hand side and hit the Family tab. There you will see Apple's approach to grouping its products from computers to its iPad line.

LO4 ## Step 3: Develop a Market–Product Grid and Estimate Size of Markets

As you recall from earlier in the chapter, a key step in the segmentation process is developing a market–product grid: labelling the markets (or horizontal rows) and products (or vertical columns), as shown in Figure 9–6. In addition, the size of the market in each cell, or the market–product combination, must be estimated. For your restaurant, this involves estimating the number of, or sales revenue obtained from, each kind of meal that can reasonably be expected to be sold to each market segment. This is a form of the usage rate analysis discussed earlier in the chapter.

FIGURE 9–6

MARKETS		PRODUCTS: MEALS				
		BREAKFAST	LUNCH	BETWEEN-MEAL SNACK	DINNER	AFTER-DINNER SNACK
STUDENT	Dormitory	0	1	3	0	3
	Apartment	1	3	3	1	1
	Day commuter	0	3	2	1	0
	Night commuter	0	0	1	3	2
NONSTUDENT	Faculty or staff	0	3	1	1	0
	Live in area	0	1	2	2	1
	Work in area	1	3	0	1	0

Key: 3 = Large market; 2 = Medium market; 1 = Small market; 0 = No market.

Selecting a target market for your fast-food restaurant next to an urban university (target market is shaded).

The market sizes in Figure 9–6 may be simple "guesstimates" if you do not have time for formal marketing research (as discussed in Chapter 8). But even such crude estimates of the size of specific markets using a market–product grid are far better than the usual estimates of the entire market. Estimating the size of given market segments is very helpful when completing Step 4 of the segmentation process: determining which target markets to select.

Step 4: Select Target Markets

A firm must take care to choose its target market segments carefully. If it chooses too narrow a group of segments, it may fail to reach the volume of sales and profits it needs. If it selects too broad a group of segments, it may spread its marketing efforts so thin that the extra expenses more than offset the increased sales and profits.

Criteria to Use in Choosing the Target Segments

Two different kinds of criteria are present in the market segmentation process: (1) those to use in dividing the market into segments (discussed earlier), and (2) those to use in actually choosing the target segments. Even experienced marketing executives often confuse these two different sets of criteria. The five criteria to use in actually selecting the target segments apply to your Wendy's restaurant in this way:

- *Market size.* The estimated size of the market in the segment is an important factor in deciding whether it is worth going after. There is really no market for breakfasts among campus students (see Figure 9–6), so why devote any marketing effort toward reaching a small or non-existent market?

- *Expected growth.* Although the size of the market in a segment may be small now, perhaps it is growing significantly or is expected to grow in the future. For example, the segment using drive-through ordering is growing three times faster than the eat-inside segment. So having a fast-service drive-through facility may be critical for your restaurant's success.

- *Competitive position.* Is there a lot of competition in the segment now or is there likely to be in the future? The less the competition, the more attractive the segment is. For example, if the university cafeterias announce a new policy of "no meals on weekends," this segment is suddenly more promising for your restaurant.

- *Cost of reaching the segment.* A segment that is inaccessible to a firm's marketing actions should not be pursued. For example, the few nonstudents who live in the area may not be economically reachable with ads in newspapers or other media. As a result, do not waste money trying to advertise to them.

- *Compatibility with the organization's objectives and resources.* If your restaurant does not have the cooking equipment to make breakfasts and has a policy against spending more money on restaurant equipment, then do not try to reach the breakfast segment.

How can Wendy's target different market segments, such as drive-through customers, with different advertising programs? For the answer, see the text and Figure 9–7.

Wendy's International, LLC

As is often the case in marketing decisions, a particular segment may appear attractive according to some criteria and very unattractive according to others.

Choose the Segments

Ultimately, a marketing executive has to use these criteria to choose the segments for special marketing efforts. As shown in Figure 9–6, let us assume you have written off the breakfast market for two reasons: too small market size and incompatibility with your objectives and resources. In terms of competitive position and cost of reaching the segment, you choose to focus on the four student segments and not the three nonstudent segments (although you are certainly not going to turn away business from the nonstudent segments). This combination of market–product segments—your target market—is shaded in Figure 9–6. In some cases, after selecting target markets, a firm may discover some segments may be too costly or unprofitable to serve. This may lead to de-selection of certain customers or segments, as the Making Responsible Decisions box, "De-selection of Customers or Customer Segments," points out.

MAKING RESPONSIBLE DECISIONS

De-selection of Customers or Customer Segments

Obviously, every organization has a right to determine the customer segments it wants to serve. And no one will dispute that organizations can do so as long as they are not discriminating against customers on the basis of race, ethnicity, or gender. However, as you have learned in this chapter, not all customers have the same value to an organization. In fact, in a world of high-technology and sophisticated segmentation analysis, many organizations are now able to discern the true costs and bottom-line value of individual consumers and/or given customer segments.

In most cases, good segmentation analysis reveals these hard numbers to show the real costs and contribution margins of certain customers. When this information is presented to executives, they may have to make some tough decisions. In some cases, it might mean to de-market or de-select certain customers. In other words, a firm might "fire" or quit the customer or invoke such practices as charging additional fees or restricting access to certain customer service levels, which might force some customers to find another alternative to do business with.

One bank, for example, determined through detailed segmentation analysis that certain customers were clearly less profitable, or even unprofitable, to serve compared with others. They started to charge a fee to those high-cost, low-profit customers if they used a teller at a branch or if they phoned a call centre for customer assistance. Many of these customers, upon finding charges of $2 per contact, decided to leave the bank, which is exactly what the bank intended. Others simply complained about unfair treatment and sought to have those fees removed from their statements. Another financial services company, finding that only their business-to-business (B2B) segment was highly profitable, simply stopped serving the business-to-consumer (B2C) market segment and informed those customers that they were exiting the B2C segment of the market, thus forcing this segment to find a new provider.

What do you think about the de-selection of customers or customer segments? Does a company have the right to de-select customers after segmentation analysis reveals that these customers are more costly to serve and/or contribute less to the profitability of the organization compared with other customers? If so, who will serve these customers?

Step 5: Take Marketing Actions to Reach Target Markets

The purpose of developing a market–product grid is to trigger marketing actions to increase revenues and profits. This means that someone must develop and execute an action plan.

Your Wendy's Segmentation Strategy

With your Wendy's restaurant, you have already reached one significant decision: There is a limited market for breakfast, and so you will not open for business until 10:30 a.m. In fact, Wendy's first attempt at a breakfast menu was a disaster and was discontinued in 1986. Wendy's evaluates possible new menu items continuously, to compete not only with McDonald's and Burger King but also with a complex array of supermarkets, convenience stores, and gas stations that sell reheatable packaged foods as well as new "easy-lunch" products.

Another essential decision is where and what meals to advertise to reach specific market segments. An ad in the student newspaper could reach all the student segments, but you might consider this "shotgun approach" too expensive and want a more focused "rifle approach" to reach smaller segments. If you choose three segments for special actions (Figure 9–7), advertising actions to reach them might include the following:

- *Day commuters* (an entire market segment). Run ads inside commuter buses and put flyers under the windshield wipers of cars in parking lots used by day commuters. These ads and flyers promote all the meals at your restaurant to a single segment of students—a horizontal cut through the market–product grid.

- *Between-meals snacks* (directed to all four student markets). To promote eating during this downtime for your restaurant, offer "Ten percent off all purchases between 2 and 4:30 p.m. during the winter term." This ad promotes a single meal to all four student segments—a vertical cut through the market–product grid.

- *Dinners to night commuters*. The most focused of all three campaigns, this ad promotes a single meal to a single student segment. The campaign might consist of a windshield flyer offering a free Frosty with a coupon when the customer buys a drive-through meal between 5 and 7 p.m.

Depending on how your advertising actions work, you can repeat, modify, or drop them and design new campaigns for other segments you feel are worth the effort. This example of advertising your Wendy's restaurant is just a small part of a complete marketing program using all the elements of the marketing mix. In other words, other changes in your marketing mix elements may be required to appeal to particular segments. For the night commuter, for example, having a late-night drive-through window that is open past 11 p.m. would be an important marketing mix decision.

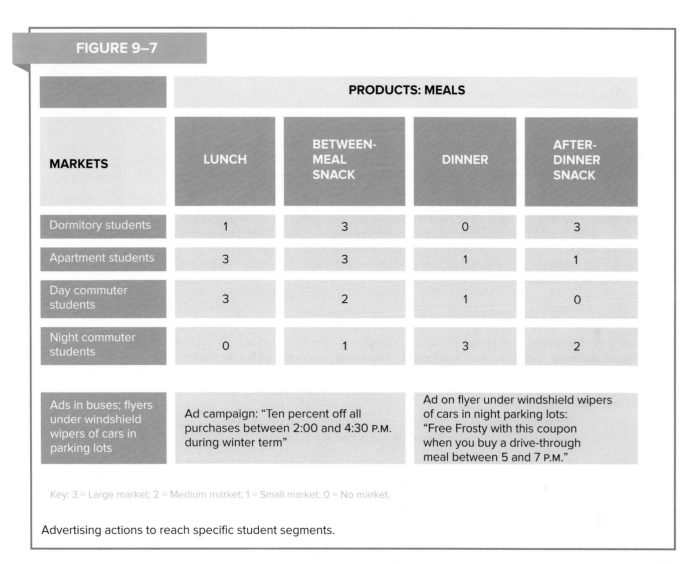

FIGURE 9–7

MARKETS	PRODUCTS: MEALS			
	LUNCH	BETWEEN-MEAL SNACK	DINNER	AFTER-DINNER SNACK
Dormitory students	1	3	0	3
Apartment students	3	3	1	1
Day commuter students	3	2	1	0
Night commuter students	0	1	3	2
Ads in buses; flyers under windshield wipers of cars in parking lots	Ad campaign: "Ten percent off all purchases between 2:00 and 4:30 P.M. during winter term"		Ad on flyer under windshield wipers of cars in night parking lots: "Free Frosty with this coupon when you buy a drive-through meal between 5 and 7 P.M."	

Key: 3 = Large market; 2 = Medium market; 1 = Small market; 0 = No market.

Advertising actions to reach specific student segments.

Learning Review

3. What are some criteria used to decide which segments to choose for targets?
4. In a market–product grid, what factor is estimated or measured for each of the cells?

LO5 POSITIONING THE PRODUCT

When a company introduces a new product, a decision critical to its long-term success is how prospective buyers view it in relation to those products offered by its competitors. **Product positioning** refers to the place an offering occupies in consumers' minds on important attributes relative to competitive products. In contrast, **product repositioning** involves *changing* the place an offering occupies in a consumer's mind relative to competitive products.

Two Approaches to Product Positioning

There are two main approaches to positioning a new product in the market. *Head-to-head positioning* involves competing directly with competitors on similar product attributes in the same target market. Using this strategy, Dollar competes directly with Avis and Hertz. *Differentiation positioning* involves seeking a less competitive, smaller market niche in which to locate a brand, usually stressing the unique aspects of the product. For example, the irreverent Canadian underwear company, Ginch Gonch, does not compete head-to-head against the larger players in the mainstream underwear market. Instead, it markets its brands (brands that cannot be mentioned in this text) to a niche market of upwardly mobile 18- to 40-year-old men and women who are not afraid to show their underwear.[9]

Similarly, Leading Brands of Vancouver avoids competing against bigger national brands by positioning its unique TrueBlue blueberry drink to the health-conscious consumer.[10] Finally, Burlington, Ontario–based Shian Naturals Health & Beauty Products produces a line of high-quality, all-natural, unscented skin, hair, and body care products that are designed for people who have allergies, or sensitivities, to synthetic fragrances, dyes, or other potential toxins found in most name-brand personal care products. The products are designed for environmentally conscious and health-conscious Canadians who wish to, or need to, make healthier lifestyle choices about what they put on, and in, their bodies. In keeping with their niche play, Shian Naturals products are sold only in independently owned and operated drug stores, pharmacies, health food stores, and health-related clinics.[11] Companies also follow a differentiation positioning strategy among brands within their own product line to try to minimize cannibalization of a brand's sales or shares.

Competing based on differentiation positioning with high-quality products in niche markets.

Courtesy of Leading Brands, Inc.

Writing a Positioning Statement

Marketing managers often convert their positioning ideas for an offering into a succinct written positioning statement. The positioning statement is used not only internally within the marketing department but also for others, outside it, such as research companies and marketing communications firms working for the company.[12] Here is the Volvo positioning statement for the North American market:

> For upscale families who desire a carefree driving experience, Volvo is a premium-priced automobile that offers the upmost in safety and dependability.

This focuses Volvo's North American marketing strategy and has led to adding side-door airbags for its cars. Also, Volvo advertising almost always mention safety and dependability, as seen in its "Volvo for life" campaign.

Product Positioning Using Perceptual Maps

A key to positioning a product or brand effectively is discovering the perceptions of its potential customers. In determining its positioning in the hearts or minds of customers, companies take four steps:

1. Identify the important attributes for a product or brand class.

2. Discover how target customers rate competing products or brands with respect to these attributes.

3. Discover where the company's product or brand is on these attributes in the hearts or minds of potential customers.

4. If necessary, reposition the company's product or brand in the hearts or minds of potential customers.

From these data, it is possible to develop a **perceptual map**, a means of displaying or graphing in two dimensions the location of products or brands in the hearts or minds of consumers to enable a manager to see how consumers perceive competing products or brands, as well as its own product or brand.

Repositioning Chocolate Milk for Adults

Figure 9–8 shows the positions that consumer beverages might occupy in the minds of adults. Note that even these positions vary from one consumer to another. But for simplicity, let's assume these are the typical positions on the beverage perceptual map of adults.

Dairies, struggling to increase milk sales, hit on a wild idea: Target adults by positioning chocolate milk to the location of the star shown in the perceptual map in Figure 9–9, the position of letter "B" in Figure 9–8. Their arguments are nutritionally powerful. For women, chocolate milk provides calcium, critically important in female diets. And dieters get a more filling, nutritious beverage than with a soft drink for about the same calories.[13] The result: Chocolate milk sales increased dramatically, much of it because of adult consumption.[14] Part of this is due to giving chocolate milk "nutritional respectability" for adults, but another part is due to the innovative packaging that enables many new chocolate milk containers to fit in a car's cup holders.

FIGURE 9–8

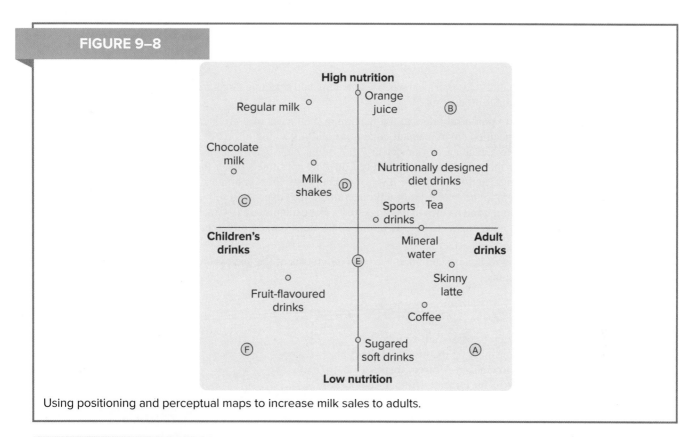

Using positioning and perceptual maps to increase milk sales to adults.

FIGURE 9–9

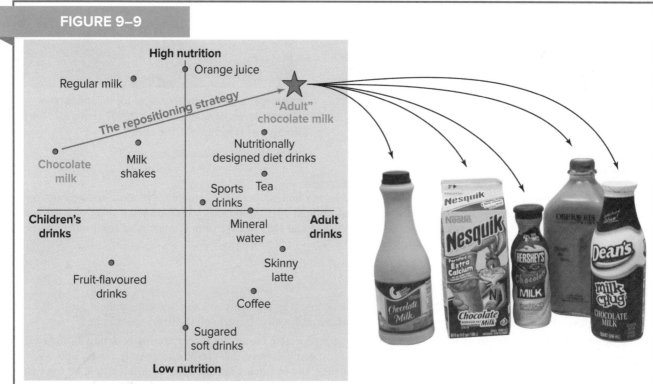

The strategy that dairies are using to reposition chocolate milk to reach adults: Have adults view chocolate milk both as more nutritional and "more adult."

LO6　SALES FORECASTING TECHNIQUES

Forecasting or estimating potential sales is critical when segmenting and selecting target markets. Good sales forecasts are also important for a firm as it schedules production.[15]

The term **market (industry) potential** refers to the maximum total sales of a product by all firms to a segment during a specified time period under specified environmental conditions and marketing efforts of the firms. For example, the market potential for cake mix sales to Canadian consumers in 2017 might be 1.5 million cases—what Pillsbury, Betty Crocker, Duncan Hines, and other cake mix producers would sell to Canadian consumers under the assumptions that (1) past patterns of dessert consumption continue, and (2) the same level of promotional effort continues relative to other desserts. The term **sales (company) forecast** refers to the total sales of a product that a firm expects to sell during a specified time period under specified environmental conditions and its own marketing efforts. For example, Betty Crocker might develop a sales forecast of 500,000 cases of cake mix for consumers in 2017, assuming consumers' dessert preferences remain constant and competitors do not change prices.

Three main sales forecasting techniques are often used: (1) judgments of the decision maker, (2) surveys of knowledgeable groups, and (3) statistical methods.

Judgments of the Decision Maker

Probably 99 percent of all sales forecasts are simply the judgment of the person who must act on the results of the forecast—the individual decision maker. A **direct forecast** involves estimating the value to be forecast without any intervening steps. Examples appear daily: How many quarts of milk should I buy? How much money should I get out of the ATM?

You probably get the same cash withdrawal most times you use the ATM. But if you need to withdraw more than the usual amount, you would probably take some intervening steps (such as counting the cash in your pocket or estimating what you will need for special events this week) to obtain your direct forecast.

A **lost-horse forecast** involves making a forecast using the last known value and modifying it according to positive or negative factors expected in the future. The technique gets its name from how you would find a lost horse: go to where it was last seen, put yourself in its shoes, consider those factors that could affect where you might go (to the

How might a marketing manager for Wilson tennis racquets forecast sales through 2019? Use a lost-horse forecast, as described in the text.

Andrei Tudoran/Shutterstock.com

pond if you are thirsty, the hay field if you are hungry, and so on), and go there. For example, a product manager for Wilson's tennis racquets in 2016 who needed to make a sales forecast through 2019 would start with the known value of 2015 sales and list the positive factors (more tennis courts, more TV publicity) and the negative ones (competition from other sports, high prices of graphite and ceramic racquets) to arrive at the final series of annual sales forecasts.

Surveys of Knowledgeable Groups

If you wonder what your firm's sales will be next year, ask people who are likely to know something about future sales. Two common groups that are surveyed to develop sales forecasts are prospective buyers and the firm's salesforce.

A **survey of buyers' intentions forecast** involves asking prospective customers if they are likely to buy a product during some future time period. For industrial products with few prospective buyers, this can be effective. There are only a few hundred customers in the entire world for Boeing's largest airplanes, and so Boeing surveys them to develop its sales forecasts and production schedules.

A **salesforce survey forecast** involves asking a firm's salespeople to estimate sales during a coming period. Because these people are in contact with customers and are likely to know what customers like and dislike, there is logic to this approach. However, salespeople can be unreliable forecasters—painting too rosy a picture if they are enthusiastic about a new product and too grim a forecast if their sales quota and future compensation are based on it.

Statistical Methods

The best-known statistical method of forecasting is **trend extrapolation**, which involves extending a pattern observed in past data into the future. When the pattern is described with a straight line, it is **linear trend extrapolation**. Suppose that in early 2000 you were a sales forecaster for the Acme Corporation and had actual sales running from 1988 to 1999 (Figure 9–10). Using linear trend extrapolation, you draw a line to fit the past data and project it into the future to give the forecast values shown for 2000 to 2012.

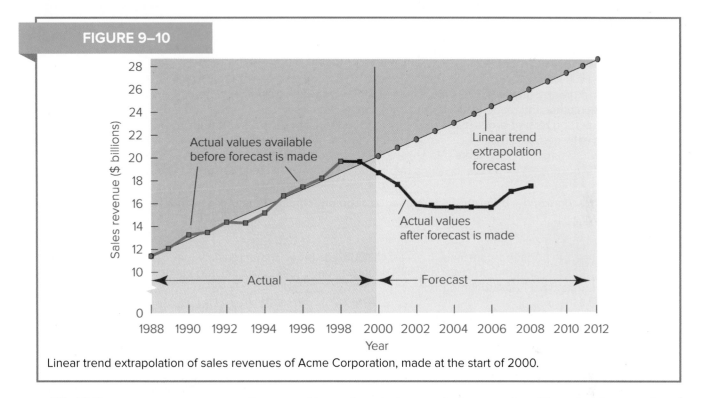

FIGURE 9–10

Linear trend extrapolation of sales revenues of Acme Corporation, made at the start of 2000.

If in 2008 you want to compare your forecasts with actual results, you are in for a surprise—illustrating the strength and weakness of trend extrapolation. Trend extrapolation assumes that the underlying relationships in the past will continue into the future, which is the basis of the method's key strength: simplicity. If this assumption proves correct, you have an accurate forecast. However, if this proves wrong, the forecast is likely to be wrong. In this case, your forecasts from 2001 through 2008 were too high, as shown in Figure 9–10, largely because of fierce competition.

Learning Review

5. Why do marketers use perceptual maps in product positioning decisions?
6. What are the three kinds of sales forecasting techniques?
7. How do you make a lost-horse forecast?

Learning Objectives Review

 Explain what market segmentation is and when to use it.

Market segmentation involves aggregating prospective buyers into groups that (*a*) have common needs, and (*b*) will respond similarly to a marketing action. Organizations go to the trouble and expense of segmenting their markets when it increases their sales, profits, and ability to serve customers better.

 Identify the five steps involved in segmenting and targeting markets.

Step 1 is to group potential buyers into segments. Buyers within a segment should have similar characteristics to each other and respond similarly to marketing actions, such as a new product or a lower price. Step 2 involves putting related products to be sold into groups. In step 3, organizations develop a market–product grid with estimated size of markets in each of the market–product cells of the resulting table. Step 4 involves selecting the target market segments on which the organization should focus. Step 5 involves taking marketing mix actions—often in the form of a marketing program—to reach the target market segments.

 Recognize the different factors used to segment consumer and organizational (business) markets.

Factors used to segment consumer markets include customer characteristics (geographic, demographic, psychographic, and behavioural variables). Organizational markets use related variables, often combining them to create what is called firmographics.

LO4 **Know how to develop a market–product grid to identify a target market and recommend resulting actions.**

Organizations use five key criteria to segment markets, whose groupings appear in the rows of the market–product grid. Groups of related products appear in the columns. After estimating the size of market in each cell in the grid, they select the target market segments on which to focus. They then identify marketing mix actions—often in a marketing program—to reach the target market most efficiently.

 Explain how marketing managers position products in the marketplace.

Marketing managers often locate competing products on two-dimensional perceptual maps to visualize the products in the hearts or minds of consumers. They then try to position new products or reposition existing products in this space to attain the maximum sales and profits.

LO6 **Describe three approaches to developing a sales forecast for a company.**

One approach uses subjective judgments of the decision maker, such as direct or lost-horse forecasts. Surveying knowledgeable groups is a second method. It involves obtaining such information as the intentions of potential buyers or estimates of the salesforce. Statistical methods involving extending a pattern observed in past data into the future is a third example. The best-known example is linear trend extrapolation.

Applying Marketing Knowledge

1. What variables might be used to segment these consumer markets: (*a*) lawn mowers, (*b*) frozen dinners, (*c*) dry breakfast cereals, and (*d*) soft drinks?

2. What variables might be used to segment these industrial markets: (*a*) industrial sweepers, (*b*) photocopiers, (*c*) computerized production control systems, and (*d*) car rental agencies?

3. In Figure 9–6, the dormitory market segment includes students living in university-owned residence halls, sororities, and fraternities. What market needs are common to these students that justify combining them into a single segment in studying the market for your Wendy's restaurant?

4. You may disagree with the estimates of market size given for the rows in the market–product grid in Figure 9–6. Estimate the market size, and give a brief justification for these market segments: (*a*) dormitory students, (*b*) day commuters, and (*c*) people who work in the area.

5. Suppose you want to increase revenues for your fast-food restaurant even further. Referring to Figure 9–7, what advertising actions might you take to increase revenues from (*a*) dormitory students, (*b*) dinners, and (*c*) after-dinner snacks from night commuters?

6. Find examples of some good positioning statements used by successful Canadian companies. Why would you deem the ones you have located as being "good" examples?

7. For which of the following variables would linear trend extrapolation be more accurate: (*a*) annual population of Canada, or (*b*) annual sales of cars produced in Canada by General Motors? Why?

Building Your Marketing Plan

Your marketing plan (*a*) needs a market–product grid to focus your marketing efforts, and (*b*) leads to a forecast of sales for the company. Use these steps:

1. Define the market segments (the rows of your grid) using the factors in Figures 9–4 or 9–5. Also, see Figure 9–2 for how to form the market–product grid.

2. Define the groupings of related products (the columns in your grid).

3. Form your grid and estimate the size for the market in each market–product cell.

4. Select the target market segments on which to focus your marketing program efforts.

5. Use the information and the lost-horse forecasting technique to make a sales forecast (company forecast).

6. Also, take an initial shot at crafting your positioning statement.

Video Case 9

Prince Sports, Inc.: Tennis Racquets for Every Segment

"Over the last decade we've seen a dramatic change in the media to reach consumers," says Linda Glassel, vice president of sports marketing and brand image of Prince Sports, Inc.

Prince Sports in Today's Changing World

"Today—particularly in reaching younger consumers—we're now focusing so much more on social marketing and social networks, be it Facebook, Twitter, MySpace, and internationally with Hi5, Bebo, and Orkut," she adds.

Linda Glassel's comments are a snapshot look at what Prince Sports faces in the changing world of tennis in the 2010s.

Prince Sports is a racquet sports company whose portfolio of brands includes Prince (tennis, squash, and badminton), Ektelon (racquetball), and Viking (platform/paddle tennis). Its complete line of tennis products alone is astounding: more than 150 racquet models, more than 50 tennis strings, over 50 footwear models, and countless types of bags, apparel, and other accessories.

Prince prides itself on its history of innovation in tennis—including inventing the first "oversize" and "long-body" racquets, the first "synthetic gut" tennis string, and the first "Natural Foot Shape" tennis shoe. Its challenge today is to continue to innovate to meet the needs of all levels of tennis players.

"One favourable thing for Prince these days is the dramatic growth in tennis participation—higher than it's been in many years," says Nick Skally, senior marketing manager. A recent study by the Sporting Goods Manufacturers Association confirms this point: Tennis participation in the U.S. was up 43 percent from 2000 to 2008—the fastest-growing traditional individual sport in the country.

Taming Technology to Meet Players' Needs

Every tennis player wants the same thing: to play better. But tennis players don't all have the same skills, or the same ability to swing a racquet fast. So adult tennis players fall very broadly into three groups, each with special needs:

- *Those with shorter, slower strokes.* They want maximum power in a lightweight frame.
- *Those with moderate to full strokes.* They want the perfect blend of power and control.
- *Those with longer, faster strokes.* They want greater control with less power.

To satisfy all these needs in one racquet is a big order.

"When we design tennis racquets, it involves an extensive amount of market research on players at all levels," explains Tyler Herring, global business director for Performance Tennis Racquets. In 2005, Prince's research led it to introduce its breakthrough O^3 technology. "Our O^3 technology solved an inherent contradiction between racquet speed and sweet spot," he says. Never before had a racquet been designed that simultaneously delivers faster racquet speed with a dramatically increased "sweet spot." The "sweet spot" in a racquet is the middle of the frame that gives the most power and consistency when hitting. In 2009, Prince introduced their latest evolution of the O^3 platform called EXO^3. Its patented design suspends the string bed from the racquet frame—thereby increasing the sweet spot by up to 83 percent while reducing frame vibration up to 50 percent.

Segmenting the Tennis Market

"The three primary market segments for our tennis racquets are our performance line, our recreational line, and our junior line," says Herring. He explains that within each of these segments Prince makes difficult design trade-offs to balance (1) the price a player is willing to pay, (2) what playing features (speed versus spin, sweet spot versus control, and so on) they want, and (3) what technology can be built into the racquet for the price point.

Within each of these three primary market segments, there are at least two sub-segments—sometimes overlapping! Figure 1 gives an overview of Prince's market segmentation strategy and identifies sample racquet models. The three right-hand columns show the design variations of length, unstrung weight, and head size. The table shows the complexities Prince faces in converting its technology into a racquet with physical features that satisfy players' needs.

FIGURE 1

MARKET SEGMENTS				PRODUCT FEATURES IN RACQUET		
Main Segments	Sub-Segments	Segment Characteristics (Skill Level, Age)	Brand Name	Length (Inches)	Unstrung Weight (Ounces)	Head Size (Sq. In.)
Performance	Precision	For touring professional players wanting great feel, control, and spin	EXO^3 Ignite 95	27.0	11.8	95
	Thunder	For competitive players wanting a bigger sweet spot and added power	EXO^3 Red 95	27.25	9.9	105
Recreational	Small head size	Players looking for a forgiving racquet with added control	AirO Lightning MP	27.0	9.9	100
	Larger head size	Players looking for a larger sweet spot and added power	AirO Maria Lite OS	27.0	9.7	110
Junior	More experienced young players	Ages 8 to 15; somewhat shorter and lighter racquets than high school adult players	AirO Team Maria 23	23.0	8.1	100
	Beginner	Ages 5 to 11; much shorter and lighter racquets; tennis balls with 50% to 75% less speed for young beginners	Air Team Maria 19	19.0	7.1	82

Prince targets racquets at specific market segments.

Distribution and Promotion Strategies

"Prince has a number of different distribution channels—from mass merchants like Walmart and Target, to sporting goods chains, to smaller specialty tennis shops," says Nick Skally. For the large chains, Prince contributes co-op advertising for their in-store circulars, point-of-purchase displays, in-store signage, consumer brochures, and even "space planograms" to help the retailer plan the layout of Prince products in their tennis area. Prince aids for small tennis specialty shops include a supply of demo racquets, detailed catalogues, posters, racquet and string guides, merchandising fixtures, and hardware, such as racquet hooks and footwear shelves, in addition to other items. Prince also provides these shops with "player standees," which are corregated life-size cutouts of professional tennis players.

Prince reaches tennis players directly through its website (**www.princetennis.com**), which gives product information, tennis tips, and the latest tennis news. Besides using social networks like Facebook and Twitter, Prince runs ads in regional and national tennis publications, and develops advertising campaigns for online sites and broadcast outlets.

In addition to its in-store activities, advertising, and online marketing, Prince invests heavily in its Teaching Pro program. These sponsored teaching pros receive all the latest product information, demo racquets, and equipment from Prince, so they can truly be Prince ambassadors in their community. Aside from their regular lessons, instructors and teaching professionals hold local "Prince Demo events" to give potential customers a hands-on opportunity to see and try various Prince racquets, strings, and grips.

© Consumer Trends/
Alamy Stock Photo

Prince also sponsors over 100 professional tennis players who appear in marquee events such as the four Grand Slam tournaments (Wimbledon and the Australian, French, and U.S. Opens). TV viewers can watch Russia's Maria Sharapova walk onto a tennis court carrying a Prince racquet bag or France's Gael Monfils hit a service ace using his Prince racquet.

Where is Prince headed in the 2010s? "As a marketer, one of the biggest challenges is staying ahead of the curve," says Glassel. And she stresses, "It's learning, it's studying, it's talking to people who understand where the market is going."

QUESTIONS

1. In the 2010s, what trends in the environmental forces (social, economic, technological, competitive, and regulatory) (*a*) work for and (*b*) work against success for Prince Sports in the tennis industry?

2. Because sales of Prince Sports in tennis-related products depends heavily on growth of the tennis industry, what marketing activities might it use in North America to promote tennis playing?

3. What promotional activities might Prince use to reach (*a*) recreational players and (*b*) junior players?

4. What might Prince do to help it gain distribution and sales in (*a*) mass merchandisers like Target and Walmart and (*b*) specialty tennis shops?

5. In reaching global markets outside North America, (*a*) what are some criteria that Prince should use to select countries in which to market aggressively, (*b*) what three or four countries meet these criteria best, and (*c*) what are some marketing actions Prince might use to reach these markets?

Case: This case was written by William Rudelius and is based on personal interviews with Linda Glassel, Tyler Herring, and Nick Skally.

10

Developing New Products and Services

Learning Objectives

After reading this chapter, you should be able to:

LO1 Recognize the various terms that pertain to products and services.

LO2 Identify the ways in which consumer and business goods and services can be classified.

LO3 Explain the implications of alternative ways of viewing "newness" in new products and services.

LO4 Describe the factors contributing to a product's or service's failure.

LO5 Explain the purposes of each step of the new-product process.

The Space Elevator Is No Longer Science Fiction

A Canadian space firm is one step closer to revolutionizing space travel with a simple idea—instead of taking a rocket ship, why not take a giant elevator into space? Thoth Technology Inc has been granted both U.S. and U.K. patents for a space elevator designed to take astronauts up into the stratosphere so that they can then be propelled into space.

The company said the tower, named the ThothX Tower, will be an inflatable, free-standing structure complete with an electrical elevator that will reach 20 km (12.5 miles) above the Earth.

"Astronauts would ascend to 20 km by electrical elevator. From the top of the tower, space planes will launch in a single stage to orbit, returning to the top of the tower for refuelling and reflight," according to Brendan Quine, the tower's inventor. Traditionally, regions above 50km (31 miles) in altitude can be reached only by rocket ships, where mass is expelled at a high velocity to achieve thrust in the opposite direction. Quine suggests that rocketry is "extremely inefficient" and that a space elevator would take less energy. In contrast, by using an elevator system, "the work done is significantly less as no expulsion mass must be carried to do work against gravity, and lower ascent speeds in the lower atmosphere can virtually eliminate atmospheric drag."

This new innovation can help overcome the greatest limitation on space travel, which is the cost of getting to space. The tower could change space travel because professional rockets are very energy-intensive and not very environmentally friendly. The elevator cars can also be powered electrically or inductively, eliminating the need to carry fuel. The technology offers a way to access space through reusable hardware, and will save more than 30 percent of the fuel of a conventional rocket.

When a traditional rocket ship launches from Earth, it flies vertically about 15 to 25 km (9–15 miles) before hitting drop-off stages, when sections of the rocket drop back to Earth, usually falling into the ocean. During the final stage, when it enters space, it is flying horizontally. The ThothX Tower will eliminate the need for the vertical flight and drop-off stages, which are very energy-intensive. With the ThothX Tower, one ascends electrically, which removes the whole vertical-launch phase. Then you get into a space plane, which is like a passenger jet, and take off horizontally.

An elevator to space has been a longstanding idea as an alternative to rocket ships, but it has always been believed to be unfeasible because no known material can support itself at such a height. Thoth's design sidesteps this problem by building the elevator to 20 km so that it sits within the stratosphere rather than all the way in the geostationary orbit, where satellites fly.

The tower, pneumatically pressurized and actively guided over its base, could also be used for wind-energy generation and communications, according to Thoth Technology. The tower would also be open to tourists, providing a way for people to experience space-like conditions without losing gravity. Thoth's president and CEO, Caroline Roberts, suggests that space travel, coupled with self-landing rocket technologies being developed by other companies, will bring a new era of space transportation.[1]

The life of an organization depends on how it conceives, produces, and markets new products and/or services, the topic of this chapter. In Chapter 11, we will discuss the process of managing products, services, and brands.

 THE VARIATIONS OF PRODUCTS

We define a **product** as a good, service, or idea consisting of a bundle of tangible and intangible attributes that satisfies consumers and is received in exchange for money or some other unit of value. Tangible attributes include physical characteristics such as colour or sweetness, and intangible attributes include becoming healthier or wealthier. Hence, a product may be the breakfast cereal you eat, the accountant who fills out your tax return, or quitting smoking.

A product varies in terms of whether it is a consumer or business good. For most organizations, the product decision is not made in isolation because companies often offer a range of products. To better appreciate the product decision, let us first define some terms pertaining to products.

Product Line and Product Mix

A **product line** is a group of products that are closely related because they satisfy a class of needs, are used together, are sold to the same customer group, are distributed through the same type of outlets, or fall within a given price range. Nike's product lines are athletic shoes and clothing; the Toronto Hospital for Sick Children's product lines consist of in-patient hospital care, outpatient physician services, and medical research. Each product line has its own marketing strategy.

Within each product line is the *product item,* a specific product as noted by a unique brand, size, or price. For example, Downy softener for clothes comes in 360-mL and 700-mL sizes; each size is considered a separate item and assigned a distinct ordering code, or *stock-keeping unit (SKU),* which is a unique identification number that defines an item for ordering or inventory purposes.

The third way to look at products is by the **product mix**, or the number of product lines offered by a company. Cray, Inc. has a small product mix of four supercomputer lines that are sold mostly to governments and large businesses. Fortune Brands, however, has a large product mix that includes many product lines, including home security products (Master Lock padlocks) and plumbing products (Moen faucets).

Classifying Products

Both the federal government and companies classify products, but for different purposes. The government's classification method helps it collect information on industrial activity. Companies classify products to help develop similar marketing strategies for the wide range of products offered. Two major ways to classify products are by type of user and degree of product tangibility.

Type of User

A major type of product classification is based on the type of user. **Consumer goods** are products purchased by the ultimate consumer, whereas **business goods** (also called *B2B goods, industrial goods,* or *organizational goods*) are products that assist directly or indirectly in providing products for resale.

There are difficulties, however, with this classification because some products can be considered both consumer and business items. An Apple computer can be sold to consumers for personal use or to business firms for office use. Each classification results in different marketing actions. Viewed as a consumer product, the Apple computer would be sold through computer stores or directly from the company website. As a business product, the HP computer might be sold by a salesperson offering discounts for multiple purchases.

Degree of Tangibility

Classification by degree of tangibility divides products into one of three categories. First is a *nondurable good,* an item consumed in one or a few uses, such as food products and fuel. A *durable good* is one that usually lasts over an extended number of uses, such as appliances, automobiles, and stereo equipment. *Services* are defined as activities, deeds, or other basic intangibles offered for sale to consumers in exchange for money or something else of value. According to this classification, government data indicate that Canada has a service economy, the reason for a separate chapter (Chapter 12) on the topic.

This classification method also provides direction for marketing actions. For nondurable products like Wrigley's gum, inexpensive and purchased frequently, consumer advertising and wide distribution in retail outlets is essential. Durable products such as cars, however, generally cost more than nondurable goods and last longer, so personal selling is an important marketing activity in answering consumer questions and concerns. Because services are intangible, special marketing effort is usually needed to communicate their benefits to potential buyers.

LO2   CLASSIFYING CONSUMER AND BUSINESS GOODS

Because the buyer is the key to marketing, consumer and business product classifications are discussed in greater detail.

Classification of Consumer Goods

Convenience, shopping, specialty, and unsought products are the four types of consumer goods. They differ in terms of (1) effort the consumer expends on the decision, (2) attributes used in purchase, and (3) frequency of purchase.

Convenience goods are items that the consumer purchases frequently, conveniently, and with a minimum of shopping effort. **Shopping goods** are items for which the consumer compares several alternatives on criteria, such as price, quality, or style. **Specialty goods** are items, such as Tiffany sterling silver, that a consumer makes a special effort to search out and buy. **Unsought goods** are items that the consumer either does not know about or knows about but does not initially want. Figure 10–1 shows how the classification of a consumer product into one of these four types results in different aspects of the marketing mix being stressed. Different degrees of brand loyalty and amounts of shopping effort are displayed by the consumer for a product in each of the four classes.

FIGURE 10–1

BASIS OF COMPARISON	TYPE OF CONSUMER PRODUCT			
	CONVENIENCE PRODUCT	**SHOPPING PRODUCT**	**SPECIALTY PRODUCT**	**UNSOUGHT PRODUCT**
Product	Toothpaste, cake mix, hand soap, ABM cash withdrawal	Cameras, TVs, briefcases, airline tickets	Rolls-Royce cars, Rolex watches, heart surgery	Burial insurance, thesaurus
Price	Relatively inexpensive	Fairly expensive	Usually very expensive	Varies
Place (distribution)	Widespread; many outlets	Large number of selective outlets	Very limited	Often limited
Promotion	Price, availability, and awareness stressed	Differentiation from competitors stressed	Uniqueness of brand and status stressed	Awareness is essential
Brand loyalty of consumers	Aware of brand but will accept substitutes	Prefer specific brands but will accept substitutes	Very brand loyal; will not accept substitutes	Will accept substitutes
Purchase behaviour of consumers	Frequent purchases; little time and effort spent shopping	Infrequent purchases; needs much comparison shopping time	Infrequent purchases; needs extensive search and decision time	Very infrequent purchases; some comparison shopping

Classification of consumer goods.

The manner in which a consumer good is classified depends on the individual. One person may view a camera as a shopping good and visit several stores before deciding on a brand, whereas a friend may view cameras as a specialty good and will only buy a Nikon.

Classification of Business Goods

A major characteristic of business goods is that their sales are often the result of *derived demand;* that is, sales of business goods frequently result (or are derived) from the sale of consumer goods. For example, if consumer demand for Ford cars (a consumer product) increases, the company may increase its demand for paint-spraying equipment (a business good). Business goods may be classified as production or support goods.

Production Goods

Items used in the manufacturing process that become part of the final product are **production goods**. These include raw materials, such as grain or lumber, as well as component parts. For example, a company that manufactures door hinges used by GM in its car doors is producing a component part. As noted in Chapter 6, the marketing of production goods is based on such factors as price, quality, delivery, and service. Marketers of these products tend to sell directly to business users.

Support Goods

The second class of business goods is **support goods**, which are items used to assist in producing other goods and services. Support goods include installations, accessory equipment, supplies, and services.

- *Installations* consist of buildings and fixed equipment. Because a significant amount of capital is required to *purchase* installations, the business buyer deals directly with construction companies and manufacturers through sales representatives. The pricing of installations is often by competitive bidding.

- *Accessory equipment* includes tools and office equipment and is usually purchased in small-order sizes by buyers. As a result, instead of dealing directly with buyers, sellers of business accessories use distributors to contact a large number of buyers.

- *Supplies* are similar to consumer convenience goods and consist of such products as stationery, paper clips, and brooms. These are purchased with little effort, using the straight rebuy decision sequence discussed in Chapter 6. Price and delivery are key factors considered by the buyers of supplies.

- *Services* are intangible activities to assist the business buyer. This category can include maintenance and repair services and advisory services, such as tax or legal counsel, where the seller's reputation is critical.

Specialty goods, such as Raymond Weil watches, require distinct marketing programs to reach narrow target markets.

Courtesy of Raymond Weil

Learning Review

1. Explain the difference between product mix and product line.
2. What are the four main types of consumer goods?
3. To which type of good (business or consumer) does the term derived demand generally apply?

LO3   WHAT IS A NEW PRODUCT?

The term *new* is difficult to define. Is Sony's PlayStation 4 *new* when there was a PlayStation 3? Is Nintendo's Wii U a *new* product given the company had many previous video game consoles in the past? Or is Microsoft's Xbox *new* when Microsoft has not been a big player in video games before? What does *new* mean for new-product marketing? Newness from several points of view and some marketing implications of this newness are discussed below.

Newness Compared with Existing Products

If a product is functionally different from existing products, it can be defined as new. Sometimes this newness is revolutionary and creates a whole new industry, as in the case of the Apple II computer. At other times, additional features are added to an existing product to try to make it appeal to more customers. And as microprocessors now appear not only in computers and smartphones but also in countless applications in vehicles and appliances, consumers' lives get far more complicated. In fact, this proliferation of extra features—sometimes called "feature bloat"—can often overwhelm consumers.[2] Thus, while adding more features seems like a no-brainer, the feature bloat can lead to mind-boggling complexity for the consumer. As we will see later in the chapter, this is why "less is more"—taking features out of a product—can be a new-product success strategy.

Newness in Legal Terms

Industry Canada, the federal government's department that regulates business practices, has determined that a product can be called "new" for only up to 12 months.

Newness from the Company's Perspective

Successful companies are starting to view newness and innovation in their products at three levels. At the lowest level, which usually involves the least risk, is a product line extension. This is an incremental improvement of an existing product for the company, such as PepsiCo Canada's new Pepsi Ginger Cola that is made with real ginger. At the next level is a significant jump in innovation or technology, such as a cellphone manufacturer offering new smartphones. The third level is true innovation, a truly revolutionary new product, like Apple's Apple II computer or its iPad. Effective new-product programs in large firms deal at all three levels.

Newness from the Consumer's Perspective

A fourth way to define new products is in terms of their effects on consumption. This approach classifies new products according to the degree of learning required by the consumer, as shown in Figure 10–2.

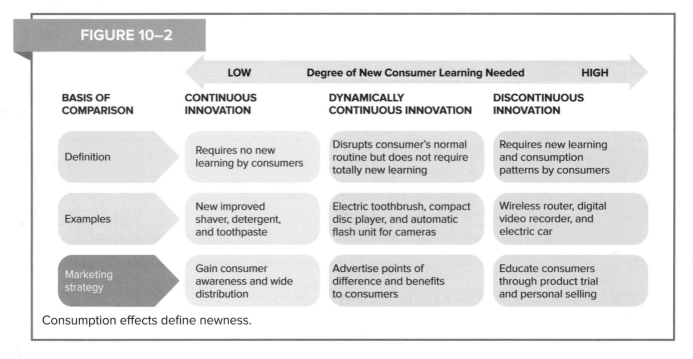

FIGURE 10–2

BASIS OF COMPARISON	LOW ← Degree of New Consumer Learning Needed → HIGH		
	CONTINUOUS INNOVATION	**DYNAMICALLY CONTINUOUS INNOVATION**	**DISCONTINUOUS INNOVATION**
Definition	Requires no new learning by consumers	Disrupts consumer's normal routine but does not require totally new learning	Requires new learning and consumption patterns by consumers
Examples	New improved shaver, detergent, and toothpaste	Electric toothbrush, compact disc player, and automatic flash unit for cameras	Wireless router, digital video recorder, and electric car
Marketing strategy	Gain consumer awareness and wide distribution	Advertise points of difference and benefits to consumers	Educate consumers through product trial and personal selling

Consumption effects define newness.

With *continuous innovation,* no new behaviours must be learned. Toothpaste manufacturers can add new attributes or features like "whitens teeth" or "removes plaque," as when they introduce a new or improved product. But the extra features in the new toothpaste do not require buyers to learn new tooth-brushing behaviours, so it is a continuous innovation. The benefit of this simple innovation is that effective marketing mainly depends on generating awareness and not completely re-educating customers.

With *dynamically continuous innovation,* only minor changes in behaviour are required. Heinz launched its EZ Squirt Ketchup in an array of unlikely hues—from green and orange to pink and teal—with kid-friendly squeeze bottles and nozzles. Encouraging kids to write their names on hot dogs or draw dinosaurs on burgers as they use this new product requires only minor behavioural changes. So the marketing strategy is to educate prospective buyers on the product's benefits, advantages, and proper use.

A *discontinuous innovation* involves making the consumer learn entirely new consumption patterns in order to use the product. Hence, marketing efforts for discontinuous innovations involve educating consumers on both the benefits and proper use of the innovative product—activities that can cost millions of dollars. For example, consider e-book devices such as Kindle by Amazon. These devices are changing the way we read! For example, the Kindle is a software and hardware platform that requires you to learn how to use this technology, whether you buy the Kindle reader device or have the content sent to your iPhone. Really interesting is that the e-books on Kindle are licensed for use, not purchased. Thus, unlike paper books, you do not really own your e-books. Amazon is investing very heavily on advertisements to show you how the Kindle works and how you benefit from its use over traditional books. Millions of Kindle units have already been sold.

For how the kind of innovation present in this ketchup bottle and the innovation present in the Amazon Kindle affects marketing strategy, see the text.

WHAT ARE NEW SERVICES?

Many services-marketing experts suggest that creating and delivering new services is much more difficult than creating new tangible products. Furthermore, new services differ from product innovations in several important ways. First, for labour-intensive, interactive services, the actual providers (the service delivery staff) are part of the customer experience and thus are part of the innovation. Second, many services require the physical presence of the customer, which demands local decentralized production of the service. Third, new services usually do not have a tangible product to carry a brand name. The new-service development process is also difficult to map out for the service company and often difficult for the service customer to observe.

Services-marketing experts generally agree that there is a hierarchy of new-service categories that is somewhat similar to the continuous, dynamically continuous, and discontinuous innovation continuum discussed previously for physical products. There are seven categories of new services in this hierarchy, ranging from major innovations to simple style changes.[3]

1. *Major service innovations* are new core products for markets that have not been previously defined. These services include both new-service offerings and radical new processes. For example, FedEx's overnight express delivery, CNN's 24/7 global news service, and eBay's online auction services would be examples of major service innovations.

2. *Major process innovations* consist of innovative new processes to deliver existing core services in new ways with greater value enhancement to the customer. An example would be a Canadian university or college offering a totally online MBA program where you never have to visit the campus to complete your degree.

3. *Service-line extensions* are additions to existing lines of services. For example, many Canadian banks now offer their customers insurance offerings.

4. *Process-line extensions* are less innovative than major process innovations, but are new ways of delivering existing services so that they offer greater convenience or a different experience to the customer. A common example is a bank offering telephone or Internet banking.

5. *Supplementary-service innovations* take the form of adding new elements to the core service or improving existing supplementary services that accompany the core service. FedEx Office, for example, offers high-speed Internet access at its locations for its customers. Another example would be a hospital that adds valet parking when you visit a family member who is being treated there.

6. *Basic service improvements* are the most common type of new-service innovation. This involves modest changes in the performance of the current service, like serving customers quicker.

7. *Style changes* are the simplest type of new-service innovation and require no change in the service core or service process. Examples would be new uniforms for service personnel, new colour schemes for the service facilities, or way scripts for employees to use when servicing customers.

Most services companies, like their counterpart product-based companies, focus on creating only incremental improvements (continuous innovation) to their current core offerings. But the few service firms that focus on breakthrough or truly disruptive innovations can create entirely new markets or can dramatically reshape existing markets so that they can enjoy the benefits of unforeseen profits for a considerable length of time.[4] Can you say Google?

 ## WHY NEW PRODUCTS OR SERVICES SUCCEED OR FAIL

We all know of giant product or service success stories, such as Apple's iPhone and Google. Yet thousands of product failures that occur every year cost Canadian businesses millions of dollars. Research suggests that it takes about 3,000 raw unwritten ideas to produce a single commercially successful new product.[5] To learn marketing lessons and convert potential failures to successes, we can analyze why new products fail and then study several failures in detail. As we go through the new-product process later in the chapter, we can identify ways such failures might have been avoided—admitting, of course, that hindsight is clearer than foresight.

Marketing Reasons for New-Product Failures

Both marketing and non-marketing factors contribute to new-product failures. Using the research results from several studies on new-product success and failure, we can identify critical marketing factors—which sometimes overlap—that often separate new-product winners and losers.[6]

1. *Insignificant "point of difference."* Research shows that a distinctive "point of difference" is the single most important factor for a new product to defeat competitive ones—that is, having superior characteristics that deliver unique benefits to the user. For example, General Mills introduced "Fingos," a sweetened cereal flake about the size of a corn chip. Consumers were supposed to snack on them dry, but they did not.[7] The point of difference was not important enough to get consumers to give up eating competing snacks, such as popcorn, potato chips, or Cheerios from the box, late at night.

2. *Incomplete market and product definition before product development starts.* Ideally, a new product needs a precise **protocol**, a statement that, before product development begins, identifies (1) a well-defined target market; (2) specific customers' needs, wants, and preferences; and (3) what the product will be and do to satisfy consumers. Without this precision, loads of money disappears as research and development (R&D) tries to design a vague product for a phantom market. Apple Computer's hand-sized Newton computer, which intended to help keep the user organized, fizzled badly because no clear protocol existed.

3. *Not satisfying customer needs on critical factors.* Overlapping somewhat with point 1, this factor stresses that problems on one or two critical factors can kill the product, even though the general quality is high. For example, the Japanese, like the British, drive on the left side of the road. Until 1996, North American car makers sent Japan few right-hand-drive cars—unlike German car makers, which exported right-hand-drive models in several of their brands.

4. *Bad timing.* The product is introduced too soon, too late, or at a time when consumer tastes are shifting dramatically. Bad timing gives new-product managers nightmares. Microsoft, for example, introduced its Zune player a few years after Apple launched its iPod and was considered by many as a little late to the party.

5. *Poor product quality.* This factor often results when a product is not thoroughly tested. The costs to the organization for poor quality can be staggering and may include labour, materials, and other expenses to fix the problem—not to mention the lost sales, profits, and market share that usually result. With a $500 million promotional budget, Microsoft launched its Windows Vista to replace Windows XP. But the Vista software had so many quality problems even Microsoft's most loyal users revolted.

6. *Poor execution of the marketing mix (brand name, package, price, promotion, distribution).* Coca-Cola thought its Minute Maid Squeeze-Fresh frozen orange juice concentrate in a squeeze bottle was a hit. The idea was that consumers could make one glass of juice at a time, and the concentrate stayed fresh in the refrigerator for more than a month. After two test markets, the product was finished. Consumers loved the idea, but the product was messy to use, and the advertising and packaging did not educate them effectively on how much concentrate to mix.

7. *Too little market attractiveness.* Market attractiveness refers to the ideal situation every new-product manager looks for: a large target market with high growth and real buyer need. But often, when looking for ideal market niches, the target market is too small and too competitive to warrant the research and development (R&D), production, and marketing expenses necessary to reach it. In the early 1990s, Kodak discontinued its Ultralife lithium battery. With its 10-year shelf life, the battery was touted as lasting twice as long as an alkaline battery. Yet, the product was available only in the 9-volt size, which accounts for less than 10 percent of the batteries sold in North America.

Simple marketing research should have revealed the problems in these new-product disasters. Developing successful new products may sometimes involve luck, but more often it involves a product that really meets a need and has significant points of difference over competitive products.

What Were They Thinking? Organizational Problems in New-Product Failure

Besides the marketing reasons for new-product success and failure given above, a number of other organizational problems can cause disasters. Key ones—some that overlap—include the following:

1. *Not really listening to the "voice of the consumer."* Product managers may believe they "know better" than their customers or feel they "can't afford" the valuable marketing research that could uncover problems.

2. *Skipping steps in the new-product process.* Though details may vary, the seven-step new-product process discussed in the next section is a sequence used in some form by most large organizations. Skipping a step often leads to disaster, the reason that many firms have a "gate" or "milestone" to ensure that one step is completed satisfactorily before going to the next step.[8]

3. *Pushing a poorly conceived product into the market to generate quick revenue.* Today's marketing managers are under incredible pressure from top management to meet quarterly revenue targets. Often, this focus on speed also results in overlooking the network of services needed to support the physical product.[9]

4. *"Groupthink" in task force and committee meetings.* Someone in the new-product planning meeting knows or suspects the product concept is a dumb idea. But that person is afraid to speak up for fear of being cast as a "negative thinker" and "not a team player" and then being ostracized from real participation in the group. And a strong public commitment to a new product by its key advocate may make it difficult to kill the product even when the new negative information comes to light.[10]

5. *Not learning critical takeaway lessons from past failures.* The easiest lessons are from "intelligent failures"—ones that happen early in the new-product process so that they are less expensive and that immediately give better understanding of customers' wants and needs.[11]

Helen Greiner, co-founder and chairman of iRobot, talks about lessons she learned from a key product failure. iRobot manufactures a variety of robots—from the Scooba floor washer to the PackBot bomb-disposal robot. Her lessons came from the Ariel, an amphibious mine-clearing robot that was the most advanced walking robot in the world at the time. Helen Greiner notes Ariel didn't satisfy the user's needs because "it couldn't walk far enough, it couldn't carry the payload it would need to carry, and it was too complex." The result: The failure shifted iRobot's focus from "innovation for innovation's sake" to "building practical and affordable robots that help people."[12]

While we have talked a lot about new product and new service failure—which is the norm and not the exception, there are some Canadian success stories you should be aware of. Read the Marketing Matters box, "Some Canadian Innovation Success Stories," which discusses several innovation success stories and why these innovators have succeeded.[13]

MARKETING MATTERS

Some Canadian Innovation Success Stories

Canadians have an impressive history of invention and innovation. This includes pablum, kerosene, the electron microscope, five-pin bowling, Marquis wheat, the self-propelled combine harvester, the snowmobile, insulin, the first mobile blood bank, and the use of cobalt for treating cancer. And while you have read about new product and new service failures—which are the norm—it is nice to see some modern-day Canadian innovators defy the odds and succeed with innovative products and services. They are successful because, among other things, their innovations have significant points of differences; they compete in large attractive markets, and are of high quality. For example, take Geoffrey Auchinleck of Vancouver, who developed and commercialized BloodTrack® Blood Transfusion Management System. The system tracks and controls the movement and transfusion of blood all the way from the blood bank to the patient's vein using barcodes and mobile computers. It is widely adopted including at over 180 large hospitals around the globe. Or consider Geoff Gyles and Kerry Green, founders of Wolf Trax DDP Micronutrient Technology in Winnipeg. They are improving the world of agriculture with their patented fertilizer coating technology that delivers better and more efficient micronutrients that farmers are demanding. This technology is currently being used in more than a dozen countries.

Two other innovators are Dr. Roger Lecomte and Dr. Réjean Fontaine of Sherbrooke, Quebec. These two University of Sherbrooke professors and innovators developed one of the most important diagnostic tools for research centres and hospitals, the LabPET^{TM} – Digital PET Scanner, a diagnostic tool essential for molecular imaging. Their innovation is being used in over 40 of the world's largest research labs and universities. And then there is Ben Sparrow and Joshua Zoshi, co-founders of Vancouver-based Saltworks. These innovators found a way to turn saltwater and wastewater into potable water. One in six people on the planet do not have access to fresh water, so there is a huge demand for this patented technology, called Thermo-Ionic technology, a low-cost and more effective desalination solution. Then there is Terry Bigsby of Lumby, British Columbia, the founder of Aspenware®. He found a use for readily available, totally compostable, renewable, and cheap wood like aspen and birch. His laminated compostable utensils made from this wood are now sold all across Canada.

Finally, female entrepreneur Susan Niczowski identified a need for specialty gourmet salads in the deli section of food stores. She founded Summer Fresh Salads, in Vaughan, Ontario. Her company is now the leading North American supplier of prepared foods to the retail and food service sectors, including supermarkets, restaurants, retail stores, and caterers. The company produces healthy and nutritious gourmet salads, dips, and appetizers—all via a "just-in-time fresh production" process. Her products are a big hit with customers with a busy lifestyle who still want "summer fresh."

How Marketing Dashboards Can Reduce New-Product Failures

The Using Marketing Dashboards box shows how marketers measure actual market performance versus the goals set in new-product planning. A new-product success in the marketplace is hardly guaranteed by it being ready to ship from the factory loading dock. The marketing manager responsible tracks its sales and acceptance in the marketplace to see what's working and what's not in the marketing mix actions for the product. Is the product getting on the retailers' shelves okay? Is the price right? Is the advertising effective?

USING MARKETING DASHBOARDS

Monitoring Your New-Product Launch

The goal of new-product introductions is to increase sales. Because sales expectations for new products are usually optimistic, they often are monitored on a month-by-month basis.

Your Challenge As the CEO, you carefully track the results of new-product launches. The dashboard figures show actual monthly results (blue line) matched up to goals (red line).

Let's say your total potential market contains 100 million (MM) households. In terms of new households buying, your new Super Snack Bar is purchased by 5 million households (HH) in the first month, 4 million in the second month, and 3 million in the third month.

$$\text{Triers} = ((5\text{MM} + 4\text{MM} + 3\text{MM})/100\text{MM}) \times 100 = 12\%$$

of HH have tried the new bar in the first three months.

Repeaters in first month: (1MM/5MM) = 20% of triers repeated. In the second month, a total of 2MM HH bought again. This is divided into the triers in the first two months (5MM + 4MM).

$$\text{Repeat} = \left[\frac{2\text{MM bought again}}{\text{All who bought to date}}[5\text{MM} + 4\text{MM}]\right] \times 100 = 22\%$$

Your Findings The top figure shows the number of households trying the new flavour (blue line), which is far below the red goal line. To make matters worse, consumers are not repeating to the level of the goal set in the bottom figure. Do you get the sense that this might be a sales train wreck?

Your Action There could be three different problems. (1) Why are fewer people trying the flavour than expected? This will trace to a marketing, sales, and communication issue. (2) Why are those who bought it not buying it again? This could be a distribution problem (it's not in stock) or it could be a product or packaging problem. (3) Lastly, it is possible that the product is doing fine, and the goals are unrealistic. You decide to tackle the third issue first. You ask the marketing research team for the details on other new-product introductions and make a careful comparison of the assumptions behind the red goals for your new product versus the actual performance of your past new-product launches.

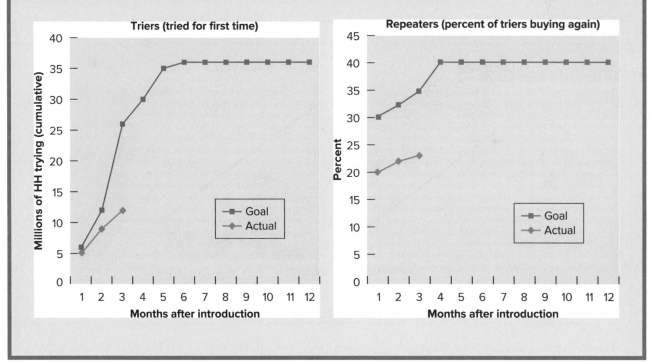

Learning Review

4. From a consumer's viewpoint, what kind of innovation would an improved electric toothbrush be?

5. What does "insignificant point of difference" mean as a reason for new-product failure?

THE NEW-PRODUCT PROCESS

Such companies as General Electric, Sony, and Procter & Gamble take a sequence of steps or stages (sometimes called "gates") before their products are ready for market. Figure 10–3 shows the seven stages of the **new-product process**, the stages a firm uses to identify business opportunities and convert them to a saleable good or service. This sequence begins with new-product strategy development and ends with commercialization.

Stage 1: New-Product Strategy Development

New-product strategy development is the first stage of the new-product process. It provides the necessary focus, structure, approach, and guidelines for pursuing innovation. At this stage, a company typically determines the type of innovation it wishes to pursue (its focus). For example, does it wish to only inch out with incremental innovation or attempt to leap out with breakthrough or discontinuous innovation? It might also pre-determine the exact role new products will play in terms of the company's overall growth strategy. In other words, how much overall cost and profitability should new products or new services contribute to the company?

Many companies also develop specific structures, approaches, and guidelines for new-product strategy. For example, many companies utilize *cross-functional teams,* a small number of people from different departments in an organization who are mutually accountable to a common set of performance goals. At 3M, teams of individuals from R&D, marketing, sales, manufacturing, and finance work simultaneously together in a collaborative environment on new-product and market opportunities. In the past, 3M often utilized these department people in sequence—resulting in R&D designing new products that the manufacturing department could not produce economically and that the marketing department could not sell.

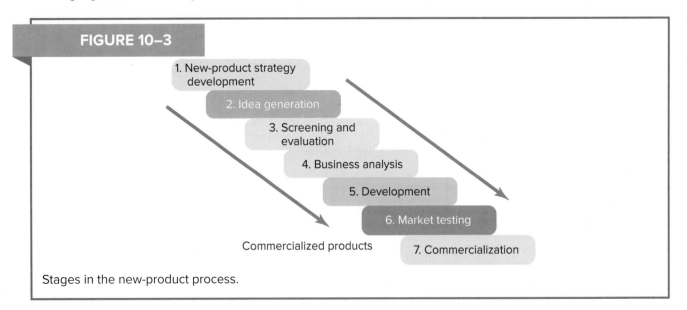

FIGURE 10–3

1. New-product strategy development
2. Idea generation
3. Screening and evaluation
4. Business analysis
5. Development
6. Market testing
7. Commercialization

Commercialized products

Stages in the new-product process.

Many companies also use Six Sigma protocols as part of their new-product strategy. **Six Sigma** is a means to "delight the customer" by achieving quality through a highly disciplined process that focuses on developing and delivering near-perfect products and services. "Near perfect" here means being 99.9997 percent perfect, or allowing 3.4 defects per million products produced or transactions processed—getting as close as possible to "zero defects." Six Sigma's success lies in determining what variables impact the results, measuring them, and making decisions based on data, not gut feeling.[14]

Finally, many companies now identify and involve lead users as an inherent part of their new-product strategy development process. In consumer markets, *lead users* are a small group of potential product or service users who desire new products or services before the general market recognizes this need. These lead users, if identified properly, can provide valuable information and assistance early in the new-product process in order to properly shape the nature and scope of what is actually to be created or produced. In business markets, *lead users* are buying organizations that are consistently early adopters of new products or services. Like lead users in consumer markets, these adopters can help shape a company's new-product strategy as well as influence the adoption of the newly developed products, services, or technologies. Collaboration or co-participation of lead users in the new-product strategy development process has helped many companies improve the success rate of their new product and services introductions.[15]

Stage 2: Idea Generation

Perhaps one of the most difficult stages of the new-product process is the **idea generation** stage—developing a pool of concepts as candidates for new products. The idea should be made as concrete as possible before moving to the next stage of the new-product process.[16] New-product ideas can be generated by consumers, particularly lead users; suppliers; employees; basic R&D; and competitors. Also, there are other "outsiders": universities, investors, and small technology firms that can contribute at this stage of the process. In fact, many companies have discovered their own organizations are not generating enough useful new-product ideas. This has led to the concept of *open innovation,* in which organizations find and execute creative new-product ideas by developing strategic relationships with outside individuals and organizations.

Customer and Supplier Suggestions

Many researchers suggest that one of the greatest sources of new product or service ideas is the customer. Lead users, in particular, can play a vital role in providing companies with suggestions or ideas about what they need in terms of new products and services as well as how the new products and services should meet those needs.[17] But it is also important for companies to consider what their non-customers may want in terms of new products or services. If these customers are not buying the company's current products or services, there must be a good reason, and perhaps a new innovation might help. Examining customer complaints is another tactic that can lead to new product or service concepts. Many companies actively encourage complaints from customers and then use the complaints as a source of inspiration to innovate. Many companies also engage suppliers to provide ideas for new products or services. A novel approach to idea generation is called *crowdsourcing.* Crowdsourcing involves generating insights leading to actions based on massive numbers of people's ideas. It requires a precise question to focus the idea-generation process. Dell, for example, used crowdsourcing to develop an online site to generate 13,464 ideas for new product and website and marketing improvements, of which 402 were implemented.[18] Today, R&D and marketing teams can easily generate thousands of ideas using crowdsourcing, often through the use of social media and/or the companies' websites.

Employee and Co-worker Suggestions

Many companies think that new product or service ideas come from a few big brains: an inspired founder, an eccentric inventor, or a visionary boss. But every employee or co-worker can contribute new product or service ideas. Some companies, for example, now put their employees through "idea creation and idea management" training programs. Others actively encourage employee suggestions by offering monetary rewards for each successful new product or service launched.[19] Kathryn From, former CEO of Bravado! Designs, a Toronto-based company that manufactures and markets maternity and nursing bras, actively solicited ideas and feedback from all her employees. This included the front-line personnel, such as the people who answer the telephones and talk to customers. She also had regular meetings with employees away from the office to discuss new ideas.[20]

Research and Development Laboratories

Another source of new products is a firm's basic research and development laboratories. Apple's sleek iPad, iPhone, and Apple Watch came out of its Apple Industrial Design Group, which is driven by the obsessive concerns for cutting-edge industrial design in all the company's products. Interestingly enough, recent Canadian research found that Canadian consumers believe that research and development is the key for new product innovation.[21]

An IDEO innovation: A five-section, single-serve package for salads. Visit IDEO's website (**www.ideo.com**) to view its recent innovations.

Courtesy of IDEO, **www.ideo.com/ work/gourmet-cafe-salad-packaging**

Professional R&D and innovation laboratories that are outside the walls of large corporations are sources of open innovation and can provide new-product ideas. IDEO, for example, is a world-class new-product development firm. IDEO designs include the Apple mouse and the Crest Neat Squeeze toothpaste dispenser. IDEO uses "design thinking," which involves incorporating human behaviour as well as building upon the ideas of others in the innovation-design process. Ideation sessions conducted at IDEO can generate 100 new ideas in an hour. IDEO's "shop-a-long" visits with client firms let a client's managers experience firsthand what their customers do. A sample recommendation from a shop-a-long visit with managers from a health care organization came from actually playing the part of a patient. The recommendation was to make examining rooms larger to enable the nervous patient to have a friend or relative in the room while waiting for the doctor.[22]

Recently, Fresh Express asked IDEO to design an innovative single-serve package for salads. IDEO's solution: a five-section package—one large section for the salad greens and four smaller ones for proteins, dressings, and so on—with each section sealed in plastic.

Competitive Products

New-product ideas can also be found by analyzing the competition. A six-person intelligence team from the Marriott Corporation spent six months travelling around the United States staying at economy hotels. The team assessed the competition's strengths and weaknesses on everything from the soundproof qualities of the rooms to the softness of the towels. Marriott then budgeted $500 million for a new economy hotel chain, Fairfield Inns.

Universities, Inventors, and Small Technology Firms

Many firms look for outside visionaries that have inventions or innovative ideas that can become new products. Some sources of this open innovation strategy include the following:

- *Universities.* Many universities have technology transfer centres that often partner with business firms to commercialize faculty inventions.
- *Inventors.* Many lone inventors and entrepreneurs develop brilliant new-product ideas.
- *Small technology firms.* Small technology firms and even small, non-traditional firms in adjacent industries can provide innovative solutions and partner with larger firms to commercialize these solutions.

Great ideas can come from almost anywhere—if one can only recognize them. For example, young female entrepreneur Courtney Jeffries did just that. She observed that most females do not sit directly on public toilet seats—instead, they "hover." Based on her observations, she founded Happy Cheeks, a company that makes products that give consumers peace of mind when using public toilets. They include toilet seat cleaners and disposable toilet covers—all portable, convenient, and effective. With her "no more fear for your rear" mantra, her company is a commercial success story.[23]

However, early-stage financing is almost always a problem for inventors and those starting a new business. *Crowdfunding* is a way to gather an online community of supporters to financially rally around a specific project that is unlikely to get resources from traditional sources such as banks or venture capital firms. For example, **Kickstarter.com** raised $1.2 million for start-up SmartThings to introduce a product that allows users to monitor their homes by remote control. But its biggest crowdfunding project was for the Pebble Time digital smartwatch with iPhone and Android smartphone integration: Almost 70,000 backers contributed over $10 million to develop this amazing product, which initially sold for $150! If you want to donate to crowdfunding projects, that's fine, too: The average Kickstarter donor gives $25.[24]

Stage 3: Screening and Evaluation

Screening and evaluation is the stage of the new-product process that involves internal and external evaluations of the new-product ideas to eliminate those that warrant no further effort.

Internal Approach

Internally, the firm evaluates the technical feasibility of the proposal and whether the idea meets the objectives defined in the new-product strategy development step or stage. For example, 3M scientists develop many world-class innovations in the company's labs. A recent innovation was its micro-replication technology, one that has 3,000 tiny gripping "fingers" per square inch. An internal assessment showed 3M that this technology could be used to improve the gripping of golf or work gloves.

Organizations that develop service-dominated offerings need to ensure that employees have the commitment and skills to meet customer expectations and sustain customer loyalty, an important criterion in screening a new-service idea. Marketers must consider employees' interactions with customers so that the new services are consistently delivered and experienced, clearly differentiated from other service offerings, and relevant and valuable to the target market. Ultimately, as was pointed out in Chapter 1, it is all about customer experience management (CEM).

External Approach

Concept tests are external evaluations that consist of preliminary testing of the new-product idea (rather than the actual, final product) with consumers. Generally, these tests are more useful with minor modifications of existing products than with new, innovative products that are not familiar to consumers. Concept tests usually rely on written descriptions of the product but may be augmented with sketches, mockups, or promotional literature. With food products, consumers may actually be asked to taste-test the products. Several key questions are asked during concept testing: How does the customer perceive the product? Who would buy it? How would it be used? Frito-Lay, for example, spent a year interviewing 10,000 consumers about the concept of a new multigrain snack chip before introducing its highly successful Sun Chips. Many companies also leverage the power of the Internet to conduct online concept tests. As we saw in Chapter 8, the Internet has enabled this type of research to be conducted quickly, inexpensively, and accurately. For example, Ipsos Canada, a major marketing research firm, offers its clients online concept testing to determine whether a new product or service can be successful. The company combines online interviewing, rich visuals of the concepts, and discrete choice modelling to test concepts and products effectively. In many cases, the concepts can be altered in real-time based on consumer feedback and then re-tested.[25]

The use of online concept tests: an external evaluation method for new-product ideas.

Learning Review

6. What is the first stage in the new-product process?
7. What are the main sources of new-product ideas?
8. What is the difference between internal and external screening and evaluation approaches used by a firm in the new-product process?

Stage 4: Business Analysis

Business analysis is the stage of the new-product process that involves specifying the product features and marketing strategy and making financial projections needed to commercialize a product. This is the last checkpoint before significant capital is invested in creating a *prototype*, a full-scale operating model of the product under development. The business analysis stage assesses the total "business fit" of the proposed new product with the company's mission and objectives, from whether the product can be economically developed and manufactured to the marketing strategy needed to have it succeed in the marketplace.

This process requires not only detailed financial projections but also assessments of the marketing and product synergies related to the company's existing operations. Will the new product require a lot of new machinery to produce it or can it be produced using the unused capacity of existing machines? Will the new product cannibalize sales of existing products or will it increase revenue by reaching new market segments? Can the new product be protected with a patent or copyright? Financial projections of expected profits require estimates of expected prices per unit and units sold, as well as detailed estimates of the costs of R&D, production, and marketing.

For services, business analysis involves using capacity management to find ways to match the availability of the service offering to when it is needed. For example, airlines and mobile phone service providers use off-peak pricing to charge different prices during different times of the day or during different days of the week to help match the supply and demand for their services.

Stage 5: Development

Product ideas that survive the business analysis proceed to actual **development**, the stage of the new-product process that involves turning the idea on paper into a prototype. This results in a demonstrable, producible product in hand, which involves not only manufacturing the products but also performing laboratory and consumer tests to ensure it meets the standards set for it in the protocol.

In essence, the goal is to achieve what is called a *minimally viable product*, or MVP, that could be manufactured at a reasonable cost with the required quality.[26]

This is not always an easy task. For example, Google's driverless car was designed and built by a team of 15 engineers and with a fleet of 10 vehicles as the test models, among them the Toyota Prius and the Lexus RX 450. In early 2015, the Google team announced its cars had completed over 700,000 miles of accident-free, "autonomous driving." These miles were "driven" by a driver with an unblemished driving record behind the wheel and a Google engineer in the passenger seat. A spinning, roof-mounted laser range finder and sophisticated software negotiated steep hairpin turns and performed well in busy commuter traffic. Where is Google's driverless car headed? Google has no plans to commercialize the vehicle itself but wants to market the technology to auto manufacturers. But it is clear Google will need to invest tens of millions of dollars into additional development and testing (see Stage 6 below) before anyone can buy a driverless car—typical of high-technology devices.

The Google driverless car, an example of a minimally viable product, or MVP. Read the text.

© Rex Features/AP Images

For services, improving the delivery of customer service is critical. This involves analyzing the entire sequence of steps or "service encounters" to improve the interactions between consumers and the service provider. High-contact services such as hotels, car rental agencies, and web providers use this approach to serve customers better. That white, plain-vanilla Google home page may look like it was designed by a child. But it took a lot of work to get exactly the right "feel" for Google's millions of users.[27]

Stage 6: Market Testing

The **market testing** stage of the new-product process involves exposing actual products to prospective consumers under realistic purchase conditions to see if they will buy. If the budget permits, consumer packaged goods firms do this by *test marketing,* which involves offering a product for sale on a limited basis in a defined area for a specific time period. The three main kinds of test markets are (1) standard, (2) controlled, and (3) simulated.[28] Because standard test markets are so time-consuming and expensive and can alert competitors to a firm's plans, some firms skip test markets entirely or use controlled or simulated test markets.

Standard Test Markets

In a *standard test market,* a company develops a product and then attempts to sell it through normal distribution channels in a number of test-market cities. Cities selected as test markets must be demographically representative of markets targeted for the new product, have cable TV systems that can deliver different ads to different homes, and have retailers with checkout counter scanners to measure sales results. A distinguishing feature of a standard test market is that the producer sells the product to distributors, wholesalers, and retailers, just as it would do for other products.

Controlled Test Markets

A *controlled test market* involves contracting the entire test program to an outside service. The service pays retailers for shelf space and can therefore guarantee a specified percentage of the test product's potential distribution volume. SymphonyIRI Group is a leader in supplying controlled test markets. Its BehaviorScan service uses five demographically representative cities to track sales made to a panel of households. In some cases, the effectiveness of different TV commercials and other direct-to-consumer promotions can be measured.

Simulated Test Markets

To save time and money, companies often turn to *simulated (or laboratory) test markets (STM),* a technique that replicates a full-scale test market to a limited degree. STMs are often run in shopping malls, where consumers are questioned to identify who uses the product class being tested. Next, qualified participants are shown the product or the product concept and are asked about usage, reasons for purchase, and important product attributes. They then see the company's ads for the test product along with those of competitors. Finally, participants are given money to decide to buy or not buy the firm's or the competitors' product from a real or simulated store environment.

When Test Markets Don't Work

Not all products can use test marketing. Test marketing a service is very difficult because it is intangible and consumers can't see what they are buying. For example, how do you test market a new building for an art museum? Similarly, test markets for expensive consumer products such as cars or costly industrial products such as jet engines are impractical. For these products, reactions of potential buyers to mockups or one-of-a-kind prototypes are all that is feasible.

When traditional test marketing is difficult and costly, some firms turn to *virtual reality test marketing* using the power of technology, including the Internet. Several consulting companies have developed the capabilities that enable them to test market their clients' products in virtual space, or in virtual reality (VR). For example, researchers are able to create virtual markets and test how well the new products perform in those markets. A variety of simulated market environments can be created, including grocery stores and auto showrooms. It is even possible to create individually simulated store shelves. Virtual reality market testing can be less expensive and more flexible, and can radically decrease time to market compared to real market testing. However, virtual reality is just that, virtual or a simulation, and is not the real thing, and this may be a limitation in that virtual reality markets may not be analogous to what will actually happen in a real test market.

Stage 7: Commercialization

Finally, the product is brought to the point of **commercialization** —the stage of the new-product process that involves positioning and launching a new product in full-scale production and sales. Companies proceed very carefully at the commercialization stage because this is the most expensive stage for most new products, especially consumer products. If competitors introduce a product that leapfrogs the firm's own new product, or if cannibalization of its own existing products looks significant, the firm may halt the new-product launch permanently.[29] Large companies often use regional rollouts, introducing the product sequentially into certain geographical areas to allow production levels and marketing activities to build up gradually in order to minimize the risk of new-product failure. Grocery product manufacturers and some telecommunications service providers are two examples of firms that use this strategy.

Grocery product manufacturers, in fact, are also exposed to other special commercialization problems. Because shelf space is so limited, many supermarkets require a **slotting fee** for new products, a payment a manufacturer makes to place a new item on a retailer's shelf. This can run to several million dollars for a single product. But there is yet another potential expense. If a new grocery product does not achieve a predetermined sales target, some retailers require a **failure fee**, a penalty payment a manufacturer makes to compensate a retailer for failed sales from its valuable shelf space. These costly slotting fees and failure fees are further examples of why large grocery product manufacturers use regional rollouts.

In recent years, companies have been trying to move very quickly from the idea generation or product concept stage to the commercialization stage of the new-product process. This is because speed, or *time to market (TtM),* has been found to be correlated to new-product success. Recent studies, for example, have shown that high-tech products coming to market on time are far more profitable than those arriving late. So some companies—such as Sony, Honda, BMW, 3M, and Hewlett-Packard—have overlapped the sequence of stages described in this chapter.

With this approach, termed *parallel development,* cross-functional team members, who conduct the simultaneous development of both the product and the product process, stay with the product from concept to production. This has enabled Hewlett-Packard (HP) to reduce the development time for notebook computers from 12 to 7 months.[30] In software development, *fast prototyping* uses a "do it, try it, fix it" approach—encouraging continuous improvements after the initial design. To speed up time to market, many large companies are building "fences" around their new product teams to keep them from getting bogged down in red tape.[31]

Figure 10–4 identifies the purpose of each stage of the new-product process and the kinds of marketing information and methods used. The third column of the figure also suggests information that might help avoid some new-product failures. Although using the new-product process does not guarantee the success of products, it does increase a firm's success rate.[32]

FIGURE 10–4

	TEXT	
STAGE OF PROCESS	**PURPOSE OF STAGE**	**MARKETING INFORMATION AND METHODS USED**
New-product strategy development	Identify focus, structure, approach, and guidelines for innovation	Company objectives; use of cross-functional teams, Six Sigma, and lead users
Idea generation	Develop concepts for possible products	Ideas from employees and co-workers, consumers, R&D, and competitors; methods of brainstorming and focus groups
Screening and evaluation	Separate good product ideas from bad ones inexpensively	Screening criteria, concept tests, and weighted point systems
Business analysis	Identify the product's features and its marketing strategy, and make financial projections	Product's key features, anticipated marketing mix strategy; economic, marketing, production, legal, and profitability analyses
Development	Create the prototype product, and test it in the laboratory and on consumers	Laboratory and consumer tests on product prototypes
Market testing	Test product and marketing strategy in the marketplace on a limited scale	Test markets, simulated test markets (STMs), virtual reality market testing
Commercialization	Position and offer product in the marketplace	Perceptual maps, product positioning, regional rollouts

Marketing information and methods used in the new-product process.

Learning Review

9. How does the development stage of the new-product process involve testing the product inside and outside the firm?

10. What is a test market?

11. What is commercialization of a new product?

Learning Objectives Review

 Recognize the various terms that pertain to products and services.

A product is a good, service, or idea consisting of a bundle of tangible and intangible attributes that satisfies consumers and is received in exchange for money or some other unit of value. Firms can offer a range of products, which involve decisions regarding the product item, product line, and product mix.

LO2 **Identify the ways in which consumer and business goods and services can be classified.**

Products can be classified by type of user and tangibility. By user, the major distinctions are consumer goods, which are products purchased by the ultimate consumer, and business goods, which are products that assist in providing other products for resale. By degree of tangibility, products may be classified as (*a*) nondurable goods, which are consumed in one or a few uses; (*b*) durable goods, which are items that usually last over an extended number of uses; or (*c*) services, which are activities, deeds, or other basic intangibles offered for sale. Consumer goods can further be broken down on the basis of the effort involved in the purchase decision process, marketing mix attributes used in the purchase, and the frequency of purchase: (*a*) convenience goods are items that consumers purchase frequently and with a minimum of shopping effort; (*b*) shopping goods are items for which consumers compare several alternatives on selected criteria; (*c*) specialty goods are items that consumers make special efforts to seek out and buy; and (*d*) unsought goods are items that consumers do not either know about or initially want. Business goods can further be broken down into (*a*) production goods, which are items used in the manufacturing process that become part of the final product, such as raw materials or component parts; and (*b*) support goods, which are items used to assist in producing other goods and services and include installations, accessory equipment, supplies, and services.

LO3 **Explain the implications of alternative ways of viewing "newness" in new products and services.**

A product may be defined as "new" if it (*a*) is functionally different from the firm's existing products; (*b*) falls within the Industry Canada definition; (*c*) is a product line extension, a significant innovation, or a revolutionary new product; or (*d*) affects the degree of learning that consumers must engage in to use the product. With a continuous innovation, no new behaviours must be learned. With a dynamically continuous innovation, only minor behavioural changes are needed. With a discontinuous innovation, consumers must learn entirely new consumption patterns. New services can be defined similarly from major service innovations to simple style changes.

 Describe the factors contributing to a product's or service's failure.

A new product often fails for these marketing reasons: (*a*) insignificant points of difference, (*b*) incomplete market and product definition before product development begins, (*c*) too little market attractiveness, (*d*) poor execution of the marketing mix, (*e*) poor product quality on critical factors, (*f*) bad timing, and (*g*) no economical access to buyers.

 Explain the purposes of each step of the new-product process.

The new-product process consists of seven stages a firm uses to develop a saleable good or service. (*1*) New-product strategy development involves defining the role for the new product within the firm's overall objectives. (*2*) Idea generation involves developing a pool of concepts from consumers, employees, basic R&D, and competitors to serve as candidates for new products. (*3*) Screening and evaluation involve evaluating new-product ideas to eliminate those that are not feasible from a technical or consumer perspective. (*4*) Business analysis involves defining the features of the new product, developing the marketing strategy and marketing program to introduce it, and making a financial forecast. (*5*) Development involves not only producing a prototype product but also testing it in the laboratory and on consumers to see that it meets the standards set for it. (*6*) Market testing involves exposing actual products (or virtual products) to prospective consumers under realistic (or virtual reality) purchasing conditions to see if they will buy the product. (*7*) Commercialization involves positioning and launching a product in full-scale production and sales with a specific marketing program.

Applying Marketing Knowledge

1. Products can be classified as either consumer or business goods. How would you classify the following products: (*a*) Johnson's baby shampoo, (*b*) a Black & Decker two-speed drill, and (*c*) an arc welder?

2. Are such products as Nature Valley granola bars and Eddie Bauer hiking boots convenience, shopping, specialty, or unsought goods?

3. Based on your answer to question 2, how would the marketing actions differ for each product and the classification to which you assigned it?

4. In terms of the behavioural effect on consumers, how would a PC, such as an Apple iMac be classified? In light of this classification, what actions would you suggest to the manufacturers of these products to increase their sales in the market?

5. Several alternative definitions were presented for a new product. How would a company's marketing strategy be affected if it used (*a*) the legal definition, or (*b*) a behavioural definition?

6. What methods would you suggest to assess the potential commercial success for the following new products: (*a*) a new, improved ketchup, (*b*) a three-dimensional television system that took the company ten years to develop, and (*c*) a new children's toy on which the company holds a patent?

7. Concept testing is an important step in the new-product process. Outline the concept tests for (*a*) an electrically powered car, and (*b*) a new loan payment system for automobiles that is based on a variable interest rate. What are the differences in developing concept tests for products as opposed to services?

8. In this chapter, you read about a young female entrepreneur, Courtney Jeffries, who observed a problem and crafted a new-product solution. Visit her website, **www.myhappycheeks.com**, and read her story. Then, go into the marketplace and observe and talk with some consumers. Uncover some problems these consumers may have and come up with some new products or new services to solve those problems. Report out to your professor.

Building Your Marketing Plan

In fine-tuning the product/service strategy for your marketing plan, do these two things:

1. Develop a simple three-column table in which (a) market segments of potential customers are in the first column, and (b) the one of two key points of difference of the product/service to satisfy the segment's needs are in the second column.

2. In the third column of your table, write ideas for specific new products/services for your business in each of the rows in your table.

Video Case 10

X-1: Breaking the Barriers of Sound with New-Product Development

X-1 started as a simple idea for a business school project and has quickly grown to become the foremost leader in waterproof, sweatproof, and weatherproof audio equipment for athletes. Many factors contribute to the success of X-1, "but new product development is the engine that drives it all," explains CEO Carl Thomas.

If you are a swimmer, runner, snowboarder, surfer, triathlete, climber, bicyclist, or any kind of sports enthusiast who enjoys music while you exercise, chances are you've seen X-1's products. The first product, a waterproof case for iPods, served as the starting point for a new-product development process that has added headphones, earbuds, cases, armbands, and accessories—an entire product line of audio solutions—to the company's offerings.

The commitment to new products has been so successful that the company now holds eight patents on its technology and was recognized by *Inc.* magazine as one of the top 500 fastest-growing companies in the United States. It is not surprising, then, to hear Thomas explain that marketing and new-product development "is a very key function for any company, but it's especially important for us."

The Company

X-1 has a fascinating history. Its founders were scuba divers who wanted to listen to music while they were diving, so they investigated how to use electronic devices and speakers underwater. The waterproof case they developed functioned to depths of 300 feet and led to a U.S. patent for a "waterproof enclosure for an audio device." At the same time, they were enrolled in a business school course that required the development of a business plan. They wrote the plan for their new technology, called their company Diver Entertainment, and began shipping products to other scuba divers.

It soon became obvious that the concept of waterproof audio equipment would appeal to many applications other than scuba diving. The company began developing waterproof headphones, changed its name to H2O Audio, and adopted the advertising tagline "Your Sport, Your Music." Swimmers, surfers, and triathletes were obvious potential customers, so Olympic swimmers Natalie Coughlin and Michael Phelps, professional surfer Laird Hamilton, and triathletes Greg and Laura Bennett were signed as official H2O Audio Ambassadors. The popularity of the brand grew rapidly as athletes in each of the sports learned about and tried the new products.

The success of H2O Audio products with aquatic athletes led the company to look for the next opportunity for growth. The obvious step was to expand to other sports and to attract athletes such as runners, kayakers, snowboarders, climbers, and weightlifters. In fact, H2O Audio soon came to realize that its market could be all athletes regardless of their sport.

So, what brands are most trusted by category? Well, for sunscreen, it is Coppertone; for vitamins, it is Centrum; for condoms, it is Trojan; for cheese, it is Kraft; for ketchup, it is Heinz; for yogurt, it is Danone; for bar soap, it is Dove; for baking, it is Robin Hood; for laundry detergent, it is Tide; and for beer, it is Molson. By the way, consumers also revealed the retail store brands they most trusted, and they included, among others, Tim Hortons, Canadian Tire, Shoppers Drug Mart, Carter's, Hudson's Bay, and The Brick.[1]

This chapter will discuss the importance of managing products and brands and how marketing executives take actions to ensure the success of their products and brands.

 ## PRODUCT LIFE CYCLE

Products, like people, have been viewed as having a life cycle. The concept of the **product life cycle** describes the stages a new product goes through in the marketplace: introduction, growth, maturity, and decline (Figure 11–1).[2] There are two curves shown in this figure: total industry sales revenue and total industry profit, which represent the sum of sales revenue and profit of all firms producing the product. The reasons for the changes in each curve and the marketing decisions involved are discussed on the following pages.

Introduction Stage

The *introduction* stage of the product life cycle occurs when a product is first introduced to its intended target market. During this period, sales grow slowly and profit is minimal. The lack of profit is often the result of large investment costs in product development, such as the millions of dollars spent by Gillette to develop and launch the Gillette Fusion razor shaving system. The marketing objective for the company at this stage is to create consumer awareness and stimulate *trial*—the initial purchase of a product by a consumer.

Companies often spend heavily on advertising and other promotion tools to build awareness and stimulate product trial among consumers in the introductory stage. For example, Gillette budgeted millions in advertising alone to introduce the Fusion to male shavers. The result? Over 60 percent of male shavers became aware of the new razor within six months and 26 percent tried the product.[3] However, advertising and promotion expenditures are often made to stimulate *primary demand,* or desire for the product class, rather than for a specific brand, as there are few competitors with the same product. As more competitors introduce their own products and the product progresses along its life cycle, company attention is focused on creating *selective demand,* or demand for a specific brand.

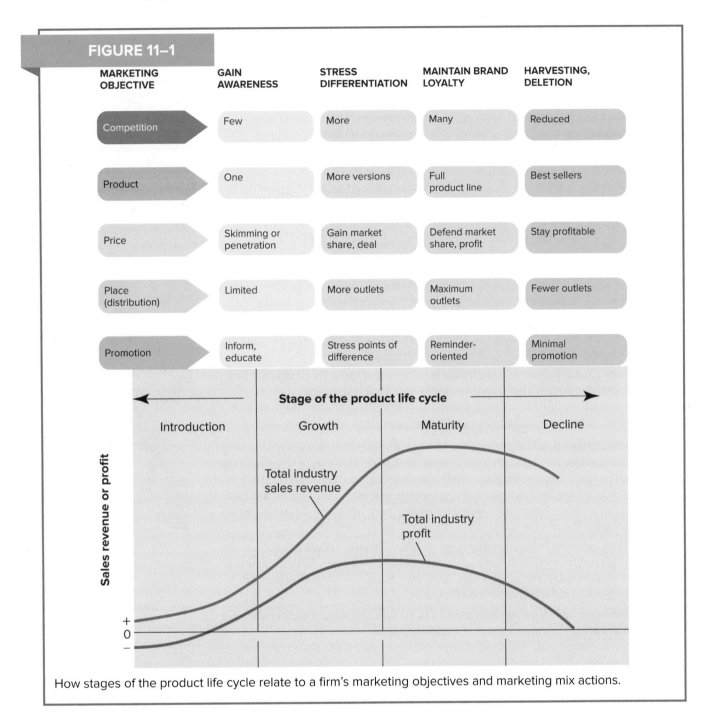

How stages of the product life cycle relate to a firm's marketing objectives and marketing mix actions.

Other marketing mix variables also are important at this stage. Gaining distribution can be a challenge because channel intermediaries may be hesitant to carry a new product. Moreover, in this stage, a company often restricts the number of variations of the product to ensure control of product quality. For example, Gatorade originally came in only one flavour. During introduction, pricing can be either high or low. A high initial price may be used as part of a *skimming* strategy to help the company recover the costs of development as well as capitalize on the price insensitivity of early buyers. 3M is a master of this strategy. According to a 3M manager, "We hit fast, price high, and get the heck out when the me-too products pour in."[4] High prices also tend to attract competitors more eager to enter the market because they see the opportunity for profit. To discourage competitive entry, a company can price low, referred to as *penetration pricing*. This pricing strategy also helps build unit volume, but a company must closely monitor costs. These and other pricing techniques are covered in depth in Chapter 13.

Several product classes are in the introductory stage of the product life cycle. These include space tourism and hydrogen cars.

Growth Stage

The second stage of the product life cycle, *growth,* is characterized by rapid increases in sales. It is in this stage that competitors appear. The result of more competitors and more aggressive pricing is that profit usually peaks during the growth stage. At this stage, the emphasis of advertising shifts to stimulating selective demand, in which product benefits are compared with those of competitors' offerings for the purpose of gaining market share.

Product sales in the growth stage grow at an increasing rate because of new people trying or using the product and a growing proportion of *repeat purchasers*—people who tried the product, were satisfied, and bought again. For the Gillette Fusion razor, over 60 percent of men who tried the razor adopted the product permanently. For successful products, the ratio of repeat to trial purchases grows as a product moves through the life cycle.

Changes start to appear in the product during the growth stage. To help differentiate a company's brand from those of its competitors, an improved version is created or new features are added to the original design, and product proliferation occurs.

In the growth stage, it is important to gain as much distribution for the product as possible. In the retail store, for example, this often means that competing companies fight for display and shelf space.

Numerous product classes or industries are in the growth stage of the product life cycle. Examples include e-book readers and other tablet devices such as the iPad.

Space tourism and hydrogen cars are in the introductory stage of the product life cycle.

© Reed Saxon/AP Photo/The Canadian Press

Maturity Stage

The third stage, *maturity,* is characterized by a slowing of total industry sales or product class revenue. Also, marginal competitors begin to leave the market. Most consumers who would buy the product are either repeat purchasers of the item or have tried and abandoned it. Sales increase at a decreasing rate in the maturity stage as fewer new buyers enter the market. Profit declines because there is fierce price competition among many sellers and the cost of gaining new buyers at this stage increases.

Marketing attention in the maturity stage is often directed toward holding market share through further product differentiation and finding new buyers. Still, a major consideration in a company's strategy in this stage is to reduce overall marketing costs by improving promotional and distribution efficiency.

Numerous product classes and industries are in the maturity stage of their product life cycle. These include soft drinks and pre-sweetened cereals.

E-book readers are in the growth stage of the product life cycle.

© Alex Segre/Alamy Stock Photo

Decline Stage

The *decline* stage occurs when sales and profits begin to drop. Frequently, a product enters this stage not because of any wrong strategy on the part of the company but because of environmental changes. Technological innovation often precedes the decline stage as newer technologies replace older technologies. For example, digital music players pushed compact discs into decline in the recorded music industry. Numerous product classes or industries are in the decline stage of their product life cycle. Two key examples include analogue TVs and desktop personal computers.

Products in the decline stage tend to consume a disproportionate share of management time and financial resources relative to their potential future worth. A company will follow one of two strategies to handle a declining product: deletion or harvesting.

Deletion

Product *deletion,* or dropping a product from a company's product line, is the most drastic strategy for a declining product. Because a residual core of consumers still consume or use a product even in the decline stage, product elimination decisions are not taken lightly. For example, Sanford continues to sell its Liquid Paper correction fluid for use in typewriters, even in the era of word-processing equipment.

Harvesting

A second strategy, *harvesting,* occurs when a company retains the product but reduces marketing support costs. The product continues to be offered, but salespeople do not allocate time in selling nor are advertising dollars spent. The purpose of harvesting is to maintain the ability to meet customer requests. Coca-Cola, for instance, still sells Tab, its first diet cola, to a small group of die-hard fans. According to Coke's CEO, "It shows you care. We want to make sure those who want Tab get Tab."[5]

Four Dimensions of the Product Life Cycle

Some important aspects of product life cycles are (1) their length, (2) the shape of their curves, (3) how they vary with different levels of the products, and (4) the rate at which consumers adopt products.

Length of the Product Life Cycle

There is no exact time that a product takes to move through its life cycle. As a rule, consumer products have shorter life cycles than do business products. For example, many consumer food products, such as Frito-Lay's Baked Lay's potato chips, move from the introduction stage to maturity in 18 months. The availability of mass communication vehicles informs consumers faster and shortens life cycles. Also, the rate of technological change tends to shorten product life cycles as new-product innovation replaces existing products.

The Shape of the Product Life Cycle

The product life-cycle curve shown in Figure 11–1 is the *generalized life cycle,* but not all products have the same shape to their curve. In fact, there are several different life-cycle curves, each type suggesting different marketing strategies. Figure 11–2 shows the shape of life-cycle curves for four different types of products: high-learning, low-learning, fashion, and fad products.

FIGURE 11–2

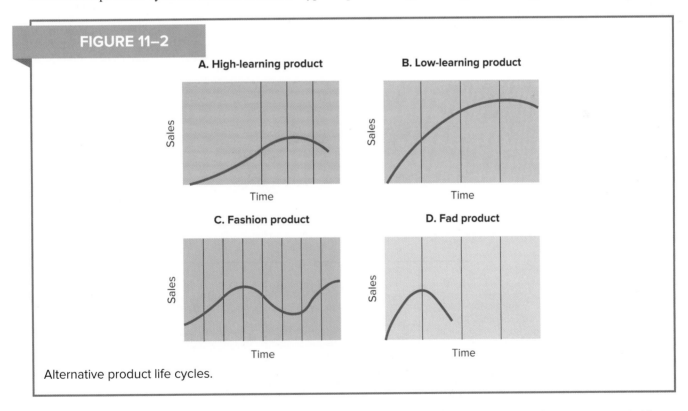

Alternative product life cycles.

A *high-learning product* is one for which significant education of the customer is required and there is an extended introductory period (Figure 11–2A). It may surprise you, but personal computers had this type of life-cycle curve in the 1980s because consumers had to understand the benefits of purchasing the product or be educated in a new way of performing a familiar task. Convection ovens also necessitated that the consumer learn a new way of cooking and alter familiar recipes. As a result, these ovens spent years in the introductory period.

In contrast, for a *low-learning product,* sales begin immediately because little learning is required by the consumer, and the benefits of purchase are readily understood (Figure 11–2B). This product often can be easily imitated by competitors, and so the marketing strategy is to broaden distribution quickly. In this way, as competitors rapidly enter, most retail outlets already have the innovator's product. It is also important to have the manufacturing capacity to meet demand. A recent example of a successful low-learning product is Gillette's Fusion razor. This product achieved $1 billion in worldwide sales in less than three years.[6]

A *fashion product* (Figure 11–2C), such as hemline lengths on skirts or lapel widths on sports jackets, is introduced, declines, and then seems to return. Life cycles for fashion products most often appear in women's and men's clothing styles. The length of the cycles may be years or decades.

A *fad* experiences rapid sales on introduction and then an equally rapid decline (Figure 11–2D). These products are typically novelties and have a short life cycle.

The Product Level: Class and Form

The product life cycle shown in Figure 11–1 is a total industry or product class sales curve. Yet, in managing a product, it is important to often distinguish among the multiple life cycles (class and form) that may exist. **Product class** refers to the entire product category or industry, such as video game consoles and software. **Product form** pertains to variations within the class. For video games, product form exists in the computing capability of game consoles or the portability of the machines such as Sony's PSP, Nintendo's Wii, and Microsoft's Xbox. Game consoles and software have life cycles of their own. They typically move from the introduction stage to maturity in five years.

The Life Cycle and Consumers

The life cycle of a product depends on sales to consumers. Not all consumers rush to buy a product in the introductory stage, and the shapes of the life-cycle curves indicate that most sales occur after the product has been on the market for some time. In essence, a product diffuses, or spreads, through the population, a concept called the *diffusion of innovation.*[7]

Some people are attracted to a product early, while others buy it only after they see their friends with the item. Figure 11–3 shows the consumer population divided into five categories of product adopters based on when they adopt a new product. Brief

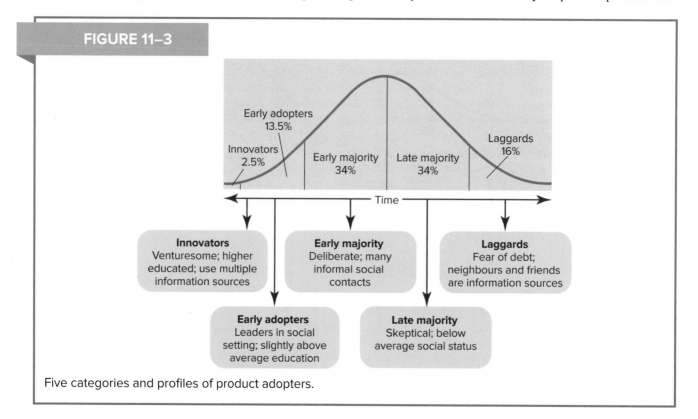

FIGURE 11–3

Five categories and profiles of product adopters.

profiles accompany each category. For any product to be successful, it must be purchased by innovators and early adopters. This is why manufacturers of new pharmaceuticals try to gain adoption by leading hospitals, clinics, and physicians that are widely respected in the medical field. Once accepted by innovators and early adopters, the adoption of new products moves on to the early majority, late majority, and laggard categories.

Several factors affect whether a consumer will adopt a new product. Common reasons for resisting a product in the introduction stage are usage barriers (the product is not compatible with existing habits), value barriers (the product provides no incentive to change), risk barriers (physical, economic, or social), and psychological barriers (cultural differences or image).[8]

Companies attempt to overcome these barriers in numerous ways. They provide warranties, money-back guarantees, extensive usage instructions, demonstrations, and free samples to stimulate initial trial of new products. For example, software developers offer demonstrations downloaded from the Internet while cosmetics consumers browse through the Embrace Your Face site at **www.covergirl.com** to find out how certain makeup products will look. Free samples are one of the most popular means to gain consumer trial. For example, some Ontario winemakers from the Niagara region believe that sampling (via taste testing) is critical in order for a new wine product to be successful in the crowded and competitive Canadian market.[9]

Learning Review

1. Advertising plays a major role in the _____ stage of the product life cycle, and _____ plays a major role in maturity.
2. How do high-learning and low-learning products differ?
3. What does the life cycle for a fashion product look like?

LO2 MANAGING THE PRODUCT LIFE CYCLE

An important task for a firm is to manage its products through the successive stages of their life cycles. This section discusses the role of the product manager, who is usually responsible for this, and analyzes three ways to manage a product through its life cycle: modifying the product, modifying the market, and repositioning the product.

Role of a Product Manager

The product manager (sometimes called *brand manager*) manages the marketing efforts for a close-knit family of products or brands.[10] Introduced by Procter & Gamble (P&G) in 1928, the product manager–style of marketing organization is used by consumer goods firms, such as General Mills and PepsiCo, and by business firms, such as Intel and Hewlett-Packard. All product managers are responsible for managing existing products through the stages of the life cycle, and some are also responsible for developing new products. Product managers' marketing responsibilities include developing and executing a marketing program for the product line described in an annual marketing plan and approving ad copy, media selection, and package design.

Product managers also engage in extensive data analysis related to their products and brands. Sales, market share, and profit trends are closely monitored. Managers often supplement these data with two measures: (1) a category development index (CDI), and (2) a brand development index (BDI). These indexes help to identify strong and weak market segments (usually demographic or geographic segments) for specific consumer products and brands and provide direction for marketing efforts. The calculation, visual display, and interpretation of these two indexes for Hawaiian Punch are described in the Using Marketing Dashboards box, "Knowing Your CDI and BDI."

Modifying the Product

Product modification involves altering a product's characteristics, such as its quality, performance, appearance, features, or package, to try to increase and extend the product's sales. Wrinkle-free and stain-resistant clothing made possible by nanotechnology has revolutionized the men's and women's apparel business and stimulated industry sales of casual pants, shirts, and blouses. A common approach to product modification to increase a product's value to consumers is called *product bundling*—the sale of two or more separate products in one package. For example, Microsoft Office is sold as a bundle of computer software, including Word, Excel, and PowerPoint.

New features, ingredients, packages, or scents can be used to change a product's characteristics and give the sense of a revised product. Procter & Gamble revamped Pantene shampoo and conditioner with a new vitamin formula and relaunched the brand with a multimillion-dollar advertising and promotion campaign. The result? Pantene, a brand first introduced in the 1940s, is now a top-selling brand. Finally, Heinz Canada has modified its original red ketchup and now offers a light version, a reduced-sugar version, and an organic version of its product.

Modifying the Market

With **market modification** strategies, a company tries to find new customers, increase a product's use among existing customers, or create new-use situations.

Finding New Users

Produce companies have begun marketing and packaging prunes as "dried plums" for the purposes of attracting younger buyers. Ocean Spray offers sweetened dried cranberries, called Craisins, as a healthy snack for younger consumers. Harley-Davidson tailored its marketing program to encourage women to take up cycling, thus doubling the number of potential customers for its motorcycles.

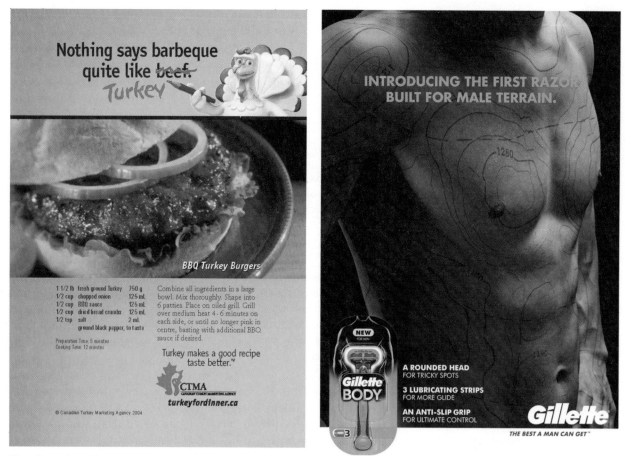

The Canadian Turkey Marketing Agency is modifying the market for turkey by advocating that Canadians eat turkey as an everyday meal and not just for special occasions.

Courtesy of Canadian Turkey Marketing Agency c.o.b. Turkey Farmers of Canada

Gillette created a new-use situation called "manscraping."

Procter & Gamble

Increasing Use

Promoting more frequent usage has been a strategy of Campbell Soup Company. Because soup consumption rises in the winter and declines during the summer, the company now advertises more heavily in warm months to encourage consumers to think of soup as more than a cold-weather food. Similarly, orange juice producers advocate drinking orange juice throughout the day rather than for breakfast only. And the Canadian Turkey Marketing Agency tells Canadians that turkey meat is a good option for everyday meals, not just for Thanksgiving and Christmas.

Creating New-Use Situations

Finding new uses for an existing product has been the strategy behind Gillette, the world leader for men's shaving products. The company now markets its Gillette Body line of razors, blades, and shaving gels for "manscaping"—the art of shaving body hair in areas below the neckline—that represents a new use situation. Also, Mars, Inc. suggests a new-use situation when it markets its M&M's candy as a replacement for chocolate chips in baked goods.

Repositioning the Product

Often, a company decides to reposition its product or product line in an attempt to bolster sales. **Product repositioning** is changing the place a product occupies in a consumer's mind relative to competing products. A firm can reposition a product by changing one or more of the four marketing mix elements. Four factors that trigger a repositioning action are discussed next.

Reacting to a Competitor's Position

One reason to reposition a product is that a competitor's entrenched position is adversely affecting sales and market share. New Balance, Inc. successfully repositioned its athletic shoes to focus on fit and comfort rather than competing head-on against Nike and Reebok on fashion and sport. The company offers an expansive range of shoe widths with the message, "N is for fit," and it networks with podiatrists, not sport celebrities.[11]

USING MARKETING DASHBOARDS

Knowing Your CDI and BDI

Where are sales for my product category and brand strongest and weakest? Data related to this question are often displayed in a marketing dashboard using two indexes: (1) a category development index (CDI), and (2) a brand development index (BDI).

Your Challenge   You have joined the marketing team for Hawaiian Punch, the number-one fruit punch drink sold in the market. The brand has been marketed to mothers with children under 12 years old. The majority of Hawaiian Punch sales are in gallon and two-litre bottles. Your assignment is to examine the brand's performance and identify growth opportunities for the Hawaiian Punch brand among households that consume prepared fruit drinks (the product category).

Your marketing dashboard displays a category development index and a brand development index provided by a syndicated marketing research firm. Each index is based on the calculations below:

$$\text{Category Development Index (CDI)} = \frac{\text{Percent of a Product Category's Total Market Sales in a Market Segment}}{\text{Percent of the Total Market Population in a Market Segment}} \times 100$$

$$\text{Brand Development Index (BDI)} = \frac{\text{Percent of a Brand's Total Market Sales in a Market Segment}}{\text{Percent of the Total Market Population in a Market Segment}} \times 100$$

A CDI over 100 indicates above-average product-category purchases by a market segment. A number under 100 indicates below-average purchases. A BDI over 100 indicates a strong brand position in a segment; a number under 100 indicates a weak brand position.

You are interested in CDI and BDI displays for four household segments that consume prepared fruit drinks: (1) households without children; (2) households with children 6 and under; (3) households with children 7 to 12; and (4) households with children 13 to 18.

Your Findings The BDI and CDI measures displayed below show that Hawaiian Punch is consumed by households with children, and particularly households with children 12 and under. The Hawaiian Punch BDI is over 100 for both segments—not surprising because the brand is marketed to these segments. Households with children 13 to 18 years old evidence high fruit drink consumption with a CDI over 100. But Hawaiian Punch is relatively weak in this segment with a BDI under 100.

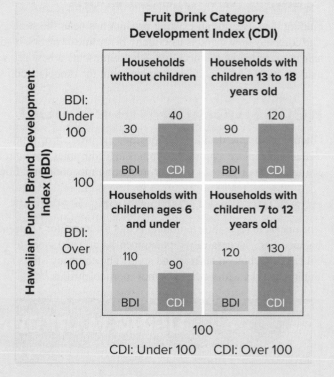

Fruit Drink Category Development Index (CDI)

Your Action An opportunity for Hawaiian Punch exists among households with children 13 to 18 years old—teenagers. You might propose that Hawaiian Punch be repositioned for teens. In addition, you might recommend that Hawaiian Punch be packaged in single-serve cans or bottles to attract this segment, much like soft drinks. Teens might also be targeted for advertising and promotions.

Reaching a New Market

When Unilever introduced iced tea in the United Kingdom in the mid-1990s, sales were disappointing. British consumers viewed it as leftover hot tea, not suitable for drinking. The company made its tea carbonated and repositioned it as a cold soft drink to compete as a carbonated beverage, and sales improved. Johnson & Johnson effectively repositioned St. Joseph Aspirin from one for infants to an adult low-strength aspirin to reduce the risk of heart problems or strokes.[12]

Catching a Rising Trend

Changing consumer trends can also lead to repositioning. Growing consumer interest in foods that offer health and dietary benefits is an example, and many products have been repositioned to capitalize on this trend. Quaker Oats makes the claim that oatmeal, as part of a low-saturated-fat, low-cholesterol diet, may reduce the risk of heart disease. Calcium-enriched products, such as Uncle Ben's Calcium Plus rice, emphasize healthy bone structure for children and adults. Weight-conscious consumers have embraced low-fat diets in growing numbers. Today, every major consumer food and beverage company in Canada offers and advertises reduced-fat versions of its products.[13]

Changing the Value Offered

In repositioning a product, a company can decide to change the value it offers buyers and trade up or down. **Trading up** involves adding value to the product (or line) through additional features or higher-quality materials. Michelin has done this with its "run-flat" tire, which can keep going up to 70 kilometres after suffering total air loss. Dog food manufacturers, such as Ralston Purina, also have traded up by offering super-premium foods based on "life-stage nutrition." Mass merchandisers, such as Target and Hudson's Bay, can trade up by adding designer clothes sections to their stores.

Trading down involves reducing the number of features, quality, or price. For example, airlines have added more seats, thus reducing leg room, and eliminated extras, such as snack service and food portions. Trading down often exists when companies engage in **downsizing**—reducing the content of packages without changing package size and maintaining or increasing the package price. Firms have been criticized for this practice, as described in the accompanying Making Responsible Decisions box, "Consumer Economics of Downsizing: Get Less, Pay More."[14]

MAKING RESPONSIBLE DECISIONS

Consumer Economics of Downsizing: Get Less, Pay More

For more than 30 years, Starkist put 185 g of tuna into its regular-sized can. Today, Starkist puts 175 g ounces of tuna into its can but charges the same price. Frito-Lay (Doritos and Lay's snack chips), PepsiCo (Tropicana orange juice), and HáagenDazs (ice cream) have whittled away at package contents 5 to 10 percent while maintaining their products' package size, dimensions, and prices. Procter & Gamble recently kept its retail price on its jumbo pack of Pampers and Luvs diapers, but reduced the number of diapers per pack from 140 to 132. Similarly, Unilever reduced the number of Popsicles in each package from 24 to 20 without changing the package price. GeorgiaPacific reduced the content of its Brawny paper towel six-roll pack by 20 percent without lowering the price.

Consumer advocates charge that downsizing the content of packages while maintaining prices is a subtle and unannounced way of taking advantage of consumer buying habits. They also say downsizing is a price increase in disguise and a deceptive, but legal, practice. Some manufacturers argue that this practice is a way of keeping prices from rising beyond psychological barriers for their products. Other manufacturers say prices are set by individual stores, not by them.

Is downsizing an unethical practice if manufacturers do not inform consumers that the package contents are less than they were previously?

Learning Review

4. How does a product manager help manage a product's life cycle?
5. What does "creating new-use situations" mean in managing a product's life cycle?
6. Explain the difference between trading up and trading down in repositioning.

LO3   BRANDING AND BRAND MANAGEMENT

According to a study by the Canadian Marketing Association, building and managing brands is critically important for marketers but also very difficult in a complex marketplace environment. The study suggests several environmental forces are impacting on just how Canadian marketers can effectively build and manage brands. These forces include the empowered consumer, new media such as social media and new technologies, increased pressure to demonstrate a return on investment, the importance of changing demographics, ethics in business, organizational change, and globalization. The Canadian Marketing

Association cites the empowered consumer as having the most critical impact on marketers and their branding strategies.[15] As you have already learned, in this new marketing era of customer experience management, marketers must focus on creating brands that can deliver the experiences that the customer is now demanding. In short, the goal is to create and deliver positive experiences with the brand in order to ensure customer satisfaction and strong customer loyalty to the brand. The basic starting point is the decision by the marketer to actually create a brand.

Branding is an activity in which an organization uses a name, phrase, design, symbols, or combination of these to identify its products and distinguish them from those of competitors. A **brand name** is any word, *device* (design, sound, shape, or colour), or combination of these used to distinguish a seller's goods or services. Some brand names can be spoken, such as Gatorade or Bauer. Other brand names cannot be spoken, such as the white (the *logotype* or *logo*) that Apple Inc. puts on its products and in its ads. A **trade name** is a commercial, legal name under which a company does business. The Campbell Soup Company is the trade name of that firm.

A **trademark** identifies that a firm has legally registered its brand name or trade name so that the firm has its exclusive use, thereby preventing others from using it. In Canada, trademarks are registered under the *Trademarks Act* with Industry Canada. A well-known trademark can help a company advertise its offerings to customers and develop their brand loyalty.

Because a good trademark can help sell a product, *product counterfeiting,* which involves low-cost copies of popular brands not manufactured by the original producer, has been a growing problem. Counterfeit products can steal sales from the original manufacturer or hurt the company's reputation.

For example, Canada Goose (CG) was experiencing an increase in counterfeit outerwear. To combat the problem, Canada Goose has developed hologram labels that can be found on the inside of CG jackets and accessories as proof of authenticity. The hologram features images and elements that can be seen from different angles. It is very complex and makes it difficult for counterfeiters to reproduce.

Canada Goose uses technology to prevent counterfeiting. Read the text to find out more.

Used by permission of Canada Goose Inc.

Consumers may benefit most from branding. Recognizing competing products by distinct trademarks allows them to be more efficient shoppers. Consumers can recognize and avoid products with which they are dissatisfied while becoming loyal to other, more satisfying brands. As discussed in Chapter 5, brand loyalty often eases consumers' decision making by eliminating the need for an external search. Until it was brought under the Shaw Communications umbrella in the early 2010s, GlobalTV was the single television network brand of the CanWest Global System, which made it easier for viewers to identify the network's stations and to find the schedule they have.

Brand Personality and Brand Equity

Product managers recognize that brands offer more than product identification and a means to distinguish their products from competitors. Successful and established brands take on a **brand personality**, a set of human characteristics associated with a brand name.[16] Research shows that consumers often assign personality qualities to products—traditional, romantic, rugged, sophisticated, rebellious—and choose brands that are consistent with their own or desired self-image. Marketers can and do imbue a brand with a personality through advertising that depicts a certain user or usage situation and conveys certain emotions or feelings to be associated with the brand. For example, the personality traits associated with Coca-Cola are *real* and *cool*; with Pepsi, *young, exciting,* and *hip*; and with Dr. Pepper, *nonconforming, unique,* and *fun*. The traits often linked to Harley-Davidson are *masculinity, defiance,* and *rugged individualism*.

Brand name importance to a company has led to a concept called **brand equity**, the added value that a given brand name gives to a product beyond the functional benefits provided. This value has two distinct advantages. First, brand equity provides a competitive advantage, such as the Sunkist label, which implies quality fruit, and the Disney name, which defines children's entertainment. A second advantage is that consumers are often willing to pay a higher price for a product with brand equity. Brand equity, in this instance, is represented by the premium that a consumer will pay for one brand over another when the functional benefits provided are identical. Intel microchips, Bose audio systems, Duracell batteries, Microsoft computer software, and Louis Vuitton luggage all enjoy a price premium arising from brand equity.

Creating Brand Equity

Brand equity does not just happen. It is carefully crafted and nurtured by marketing programs that forge strong, favourable, and unique consumer associations and experiences with a brand. Brand equity resides in the minds of consumers and results from what they have learned, felt, seen, and heard about a brand over time. Marketers recognize that brand equity is not easily or quickly achieved. Rather, it arises from a sequential building process consisting of four steps (Figure 11–4).[17]

- The first step is to develop positive brand awareness and an association of the brand in consumers' minds with a product class or need to give the brand an identity. Gatorade and Kleenex have done this in the sports drink and facial tissue product classes, respectively.

- Next, a marketer must establish a brand's meaning in the minds of consumers. Meaning arises from what a brand stands for and has two dimensions—a functional, performance-related dimension and an abstract, imagery-related dimension. Nike has done this through continuous product development and improvement, and its links to peak athletic performance in its integrated marketing communications program.

- The third step is to elicit the proper consumer responses to a brand's identity and meaning. Here, attention is placed on how consumers think and feel about a brand. Thinking focuses on a brand's perceived quality, credibility, and superiority relative to other brands. Feeling relates to the consumer's emotional reaction to a brand. Michelin elicits both responses for its tires. Not only is Michelin thought of as a credible and superior-quality brand, but consumers also acknowledge a warm and secure feeling of safety, comfort, and self-assurance without worry or concern about the brand.

- The final, and most difficult, step is to create a consumer–brand resonance evident in an intense, active loyalty relationship between consumers and the brand. A deep psychological bond characterizes consumer–brand resonance and the personal identification that consumers have with the brand. Examples of brands that have achieved this status include Harley-Davidson, Apple, and eBay.

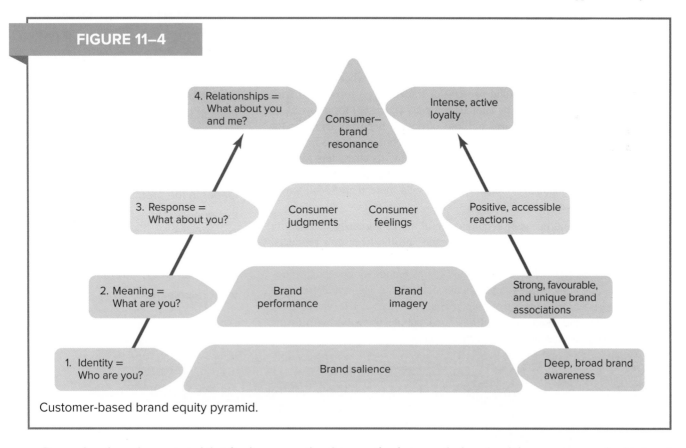

FIGURE 11–4

4. Relationships = What about you and me?

Consumer–brand resonance

Intense, active loyalty

3. Response = What about you?

Consumer judgments   Consumer feelings

Positive, accessible reactions

2. Meaning = What are you?

Brand performance   Brand imagery

Strong, favourable, and unique brand associations

1. Identity = Who are you?

Brand salience

Deep, broad brand awareness

Customer-based brand equity pyramid.

Researchers have demonstrated that forging an emotional connection between the brand and the consumer can lead to brand differentiation, consumer loyalty, and evangelical promotion of the brand. This is particularly true for service brands.[18] The intangible nature of services often makes brand building more difficult. But like their product counterparts, marketers of services also need to actively build their brand names and to create brand equity. Whether they market financial services or sports entertainment, the goal is the same—connect with customers, engage them, offer a positive experience, and encourage them to become "brand ambassadors," a term that refers to people who will spread the word about the brand. In fact, people who trust the brands they buy will recommend those brands to others. Recent Canadian research on entrepreneurial start-ups also suggests that building the brand is a key imperative for new-venture success. In crowded and competitive markets, the entrepreneur must be able to develop a brand that resonates with the consumer and encourage that consumer to talk about the brand.[19] Additionally, other Canadian research on existing small businesses found that almost 85 percent of small business owners believe branding is important to business success.[20] Of course, any size business today must also accept the fact that brands can be brought to life or be killed on social media, almost overnight. Researchers suggest that Canadians are interested in engaging with brands on social media, but only if the communication with the brands resonates with them. The key, according to researchers, is to create authenticity through the humanization of the brand—in other words, "brand as friend." Brands that engage consumers at a human level are likely to build a foundation for a trusted and long-term relationship.[21]

Valuing Brand Equity

Brand equity also provides a financial advantage for the brand owner. Successful, established brand names, such as Google, Nike, Gatorade, and Apple, have an economic value in the sense that they are intangible assets. Unlike physical assets that depreciate with time and use, brands can actually appreciate in value when marketed effectively. However, brands can also lose value when they are not managed properly. Attaching monetary value to brands can often be complicated, and there is little agreement among experts concerning the optimal way to calculate brand equity. Therefore, marketers often use a variety of direct and indirect measures to determine the equity of a brand, including communication investment in the brand and customer loyalty to the brand. Read the accompanying Marketing Matters box, "Top Global and Top Canadian Brands," to find out about the top global brands and the top Canadian brands in the marketplace today.[22]

Financially lucrative brand licensing opportunities can also arise from brand equity. **Brand licensing** is a contractual agreement whereby one company (licensor) allows its brand name(s) or trademark(s) to be used with products or services offered by another company (licensee) for a royalty or fee. For example, Playboy earns millions of dollars licensing its name for merchandise ranging from wallpaper in Europe to cooking classes in Brazil. Disney makes billions of dollars each year licensing its characters for children's toys, apparel, and games. Licensing fees for Winnie the Pooh alone exceed $3 billion annually. General Motors sells more than $2 billion in licensed products each year.[23]

Successful brand licensing requires careful marketing analysis to assure a proper match between the licensor's brand and the licensee's products. World-renowned designer Ralph Lauren earns over $140 million each year by licensing his Ralph Lauren, Polo, and Chaps brands for dozens of products, including paint by Sherwin-Williams, furniture by Henredon, footwear by Rockport, and fragrances by Cosmair. Such mistakes as Kleenex diapers, Bic perfume, and Domino's fruit-flavoured bubble gum represent a few examples of poor matches and licensing failures.

Ralph Lauren has a long-term licensing agreement with Luxottica Group, S.P.A. of Milan for the design, production, and worldwide distribution of prescription frames and sunglasses under the Ralph Lauren brand. The agreement is an ideal fit for both companies. Ralph Lauren is a leader in the design, marketing, and distribution of premium lifestyle products. Luxottica is the global leader in the premium and luxury eyewear sector.

Luxottica Group, S.P.A.
www.luxottica.com
Ralph Lauren Corporation
www.ralphlauren.com

MARKETING MATTERS

Top Global and Top Canadian Brands

Interbrand is the world's largest brand consultancy firm. The firm conducts studies to determine the best brands around the globe, including Canada. To make this assessment, Interbrand measures (1) the financial performance of the brand, (2) the role the brand plays in the purchase decision process (i.e., how important the brand is when buying), and (3) the strength of the brand (i.e., the ability to create brand loyalty). Interbrand argues that the best brands influence customer choice, create loyalty, and lower the cost of financing. Importantly, they have a presence in people's lives and live the key moments in those lives. The top ten global brands in 2015 were (1) Apple, (2) Google, (3) Coca-Cola, (4) Microsoft, (5) IBM, (6) Toyota, (7) Samsung, (8) GE, (9) McDonald's, and (10) Amazon.

The top ten brands in Canada in 2014, according to Interbrand, were (1) TD, (2) RBC, (3) Thomson Reuters, (4) Scotiabank, (5) Tim Hortons, (6) Bell, (7) Shoppers Drug Mart, (8) Rogers, (9) Lululemon, and (10) Telus.

According to Interbrand, today's most successful brands—the ones with the most presence in a person's life—are designed to live in moments, even as they scale, try new things, and push boundaries. They often stand out by blending in, because people measure the entire experience by how much it adds to their lives and how little it disrupts it. They empathize with an individual's priorities, figuring out how to meet people exactly where they are, and when they want it, and tailor it to how people move through their worlds. It's why we hold brands to such high expectations—for better choices, richer experiences, meaningful narratives, one-on-one attention, new form factors. As data and technology have helped optimize every experience, as GAFA brands (Google, Apple, Facebook, and Amazon) have changed the definition of service and connectivity, as people have gained access to greater and more nuanced choices, our expectations have been fundamentally retrained. Brands are now expected to move at the speed of people's demands—at the speed of their lives.

Picking a Good Brand Name

We take such brand names as Red Bull, iPod, and Adidas for granted, but it is often a difficult and expensive process to choose a good name. Companies will spend between $25,000 and $100,000 to identify and test a new brand name. For instance, Intel spent $45,000 for the Pentium name given to its family of microchips. There are six criteria mentioned most often when selecting a good brand name:[24]

- The name should suggest the product benefits. For example, Accutron (watches), Easy Off (oven cleaner), Glass Plus (glass cleaner), Cling-Free (antistatic cloth for drying clothes), PowerBook (laptop computer), and Tidy Bowl (toilet bowl cleaner) all clearly describe the benefits of purchasing the product.

- The name should be memorable, distinctive, and positive. In the auto industry, when a competitor has a memorable name, others quickly imitate. When Ford named a car Mustang, others soon followed with Pintos, Colts, and Broncos. The Thunderbird name led to Phoenix, Eagle, Sunbird, and Firebird.

- The name should fit the company or product image. Sharp is a name that can apply to audio and video equipment. Excedrin, Anacin, and Nuprin are scientific-sounding names, good for an analgesic. Eveready, Duracell, and DieHard suggest reliability and longevity. However, naming a personal computer PCjr, as IBM did with its first computer for home use, fit neither the company nor the product. PCjr sounded like a toy and stalled IBM's initial entry into the home-use market.

- The name should have no legal or regulatory restrictions. Legal restrictions produce trademark infringement suits, and regulatory restrictions can arise through improper use of words. Increasingly, brand names need a corresponding address on the Internet. This further complicates name selection because millions of domain names are already registered.

- The name should be simple (such as Bold laundry detergent, Sure deodorant, and Bic pens) and should have emotional appeal (such as Joy and Obsession perfumes).

- The name should have favourable phonetic and semantic associations in other languages. In the development of names for international use, having a non-meaningful brand name has been considered a benefit. A name such as Exxon does not have any prior impressions or undesirable images among a diverse world population of different languages and cultures. The 7UP name is another matter. In Shanghai, China, the phrase means "death through drinking" in the local dialect. Sales have suffered as a result.

Do you have an idea for a brand name? If you do, find out whether the name has been registered with Industry Canada's trademark division. Visit its website, described in the Going Online box, "Have an Idea for a Brand or Trade Name? Check It Out!"

Branding Strategies

Companies can employ several different branding strategies, including multiproduct branding, multibranding, private branding, or mixed branding (Figure 11–5).

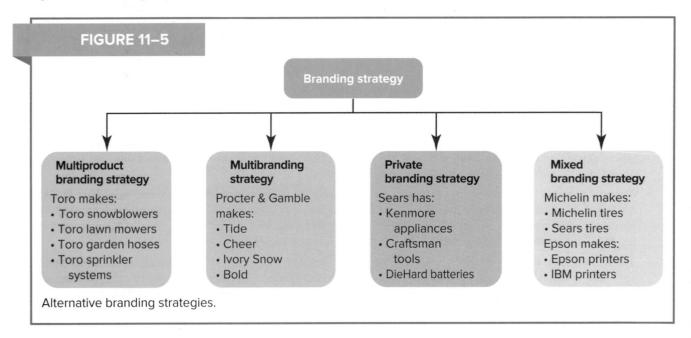

FIGURE 11–5

Alternative branding strategies.

Multiproduct Branding

With **multiproduct branding**, a company uses one name for all its products in a product class. This approach is sometimes called *family branding,* or *corporate branding* when the company's trade name is used. For example, General Electric, Gerber, Samsung, and Sony engage in corporate branding—the company's trade name and brand name are identical. Church & Dwight employs the Arm & Hammer family brand name for all its products featuring baking soda as the primary ingredient.

There are several advantages to multiproduct branding. Capitalizing again on brand equity, consumers who have a good experience with the product will transfer this favourable attitude to other items in the product class with the same name. Therefore, this brand strategy makes possible *product line extensions,* the practice of using a current brand name to enter a new market segment in its product class. Campbell Soup Company effectively employs a multiproduct branding strategy with soup line extensions. It offers regular Campbell's soup, home-cooking style, and chunky varieties, as well as more than 100 soup flavours. This strategy can also result in lower advertising and promotion costs because the same name is used on all products, thus raising the level of brand awareness. A risk with line extensions is that sales of an extension may come at the expense of other items in the company's product line. Therefore, line extensions work best when they provide incremental company revenue by taking sales away from competing brands or attracting new buyers.

Some companies employ *sub-branding,* which combines a corporate or family brand with a new brand. Consider American Express. It has applied subbranding with its American Express Green, Gold, Platinum, Optima Blue, and Centurion charge cards, with unique service offerings for each. Similarly, Porsche successfully markets its higher-end Porsche Carrera and its lower-end Porsche Boxster.

A strong brand equity also allows for *brand extension,* the practice of using a current brand name to enter a completely different product class. For instance, the equity in the Tylenol name as a trusted pain reliever allowed Johnson & Johnson to successfully extend this name to Tylenol Cold & Flu and Tylenol PM, a sleep aid. Honda's established name for motor vehicles has extended easily to snowblowers, lawn mowers, marine engines, and snowmobiles.

However, there is a risk with brand extensions. Too many uses for one brand name can dilute the meaning of a brand for consumers. Marketing experts claim this has happened to the Arm & Hammer brand given its use for toothpaste, laundry detergent, gum, cat litter, air freshener, carpet deodorizer, and antiperspirant.[25]

A variation on brand extensions is the practice of **co-branding**, the pairing of two or more recognized brands on a single product or service.[26] Co-branding benefits firms by allowing them to enter new product classes, capitalize on an already established brand name in a product class, or reach new market segments. Co-branding is particularly popular in the service sector where two or more service companies often bundle their offerings together. For example, Petro-Canada and A&W co-brand; Holiday Inn and Pizza Hut Express co-brand; Renaissance Hotels co-brands with Bath & Body Works; and WestJet and Bell also co-brand in delivering an in-flight experience to WestJet guests.

Multibranding

Alternatively, a company can engage in **multibranding**, which involves giving each product a distinct name. Multibranding is a useful strategy when each brand is intended for a different market segment. P&G makes Camay soap for those concerned about soft skin and Safeguard for those who want deodorant protection. Black & Decker markets its line of tools for the household do-it-yourselfer segment with the Black & Decker name but uses the DeWalt name for its professional tool line. Disney uses the Miramax and Touchstone Pictures names for films directed at adults and its Disney name for children's films.

Multibranding is applied in a variety of ways. Some companies array their brands on the basis of price–quality segments.[27] Marriott International offers 14 hotel and resort brands, each suited for a particular traveller experience and budget. To illustrate, Marriott Marquis hotels and Vacation Clubs offer luxury amenities at a premium price. Marriott and Renaissance hotels offer medium- to high-priced accommodations. Courtyard hotels and TownePlace Suites appeal to economy-minded travellers, whereas the Fairfield Inn is for those on a very low travel budget. Other multibrand companies introduce new product brands as defensive moves to counteract competition. Called *fighting brands,* their chief purpose is to confront competitor brands. For instance, Frito-Lay introduced Santitas-brand tortilla chip to go head-to-head against regional tortilla chip brands that were biting into the sales of its flagship Doritos- and Tostitos-brand tortilla chips. Mattel launched its Flava brand of hip-hop fashion dolls in response to the popularity of Bratz brand dolls sold by MGA Entertainment, which were attracting the 8- to 12-year-old girl segment of Barbie brand sales.

Compared with the multiproduct approach, promotional costs tend to be higher with multibranding. The company must generate awareness among consumers and retailers for each new brand name without the benefit of any previous impressions. The advantages of this approach are that each brand is unique to each market segment, and there is no risk that one product's failure will affect other products in the line. Nevertheless, some large multibrand firms have found that the complexity and expense of implementing this strategy can outweigh the benefits. For example, Procter & Gamble recently announced that it would prune 100 of its brands through product deletion and sales to other companies.[28]

Private Branding

A company uses **private branding**, often called *private labelling* or *reseller branding,* when it manufactures products but sells them under the brand name of a wholesaler or retailer. Radio Shack and Sears are large retailers that have their own brand names. Other examples of private branding are Loblaws' very successful President's Choice private brand as well as Sobeys' Smart Choice brand and Shoppers Drug Mart's Life brand.

Black & Decker uses a multibranding strategy to reach different market segments. Black & Decker markets its line of tools for the do-it-yourselfer market with the Black & Decker name but uses the DeWalt name for its professional tool line.

Black & Decker

www.blackanddecker.com

(left): Courtesy of Black & Decker Corporation; (right): Courtesy of DeWalt Industrial Tool Company

Private branding is popular because it typically produces high profits for manufacturers and resellers. Consumers also buy these private brands with regularity. For example, more than 90 percent of Canadians have purchased private brands in the past year and more than 60 percent believe private or store brands are good value for money. Trust in private brands is strongest in the food and beverage category, with more than 50 percent of Canadians regularly purchasing store brand dry food, frozen vegetables, and bottled water.[29]

Cohort Brand Management

A recent innovation in brand management is the concept of **cohort brand management**—the bundling of one company's multiple brands into a single marketing effort aimed at a common consumer group. It is a collective approach to marketing in contrast to the traditional individualistic brand management approach. Cohort brand management is typically done through online marketing. For example, Procter & Gamble uses cohort brand management via its website, **HomeMadeSimple.com**. The site offers an online guide to home and lifestyle issues while promoting several P&G brands, including Mr. Clean, Swiffer, and Febreze.

Mixed Branding

A fourth branding strategy is **mixed branding**, where a firm markets products under its own name(s) and that of a reseller because the segment attracted to the reseller is different from its own market. Beauty and fragrance marketer Elizabeth Arden is a case in point. The company sells its Elizabeth Arden brand through department stores and a line of skincare products at Walmart with the "skinsimple" brand name. Companies such as Del Monte, Whirlpool, and Dial produce private brands of pet foods, home appliances, and soap, respectively.

Emerging Branding Concepts

There are some new emerging concepts when it comes to branding. One is referred to as a *social benefit brand.* Social benefit brands are brands that have a special added value in terms of their core environmental or social benefits that they provide to the customer. Social benefit brands are not to be confused with the concept of the social branding process where established brands simply attempt to promote their brands via social media—in other words, brands that are going social. Some social benefit brands focus on environmental sustainability and are sometimes called *green brands.* Other social benefit brands focus on a variety of non-ecological social benefits like solving particular societal problems such as poverty. For example, the TOMS brand markets shoes and eyewear. However, it is a social benefit brand because when the company sells a pair of shoes, another pair of shoes is given to an impoverished child, and when eyewear is sold, part of the profit is used to save or restore the eyesight for people in developing countries. With the growth in social entrepreneurship—where entrepreneurs start ventures designed to solve societal problems—we are likely to see more social benefit brands that are designed to appeal to consumers with heightened levels of social consciousness.

LO4 PACKAGING AND LABELLING

The **packaging** component of a product refers to any container in which it is offered for sale and on which label information is conveyed. A **label** is an integral part of the package and typically identifies the product or brand, who made it, where and when it was made, how it is to be used, and package contents and ingredients. To a great extent, the customer's first exposure to a product is the package and label, and both are an expensive and important part of marketing strategy. For Pez Candy, Inc., the character-head-on-a-stick plastic container that dispenses a miniature brick candy is the central element of its marketing strategy, as described in the accompanying Marketing Matters box, "Creating Customer Value through Packaging: Pez Heads Dispense More Than Candy."[30]

MARKETING MATTERS

Creating Customer Value through Packaging: Pez Heads Dispense More Than Candy

Customer value can assume numerous forms. Pez Candy, Inc. (**www.pez.com**) manifests its customer value in some 450 Pez character candy dispensers. Each refillable dispenser ejects tasty candy tablets in a variety of flavours that delight preteens and teens alike in more than 60 countries.

Pez was formulated in 1927 by Austrian food mogul Edward Haas III and successfully sold in Europe as an adult breath mint. Pez, which comes from the German word for peppermint, *Pfefferminz,* was originally packaged in a hygienic, headless plastic dispenser. Pez first appeared in North America in 1953 with a headless dispenser marketed to adults. After conducting extensive marketing research, Pez was repositioned with fruit flavours, repackaged with licensed character heads on top of the dispenser, and remarketed as a children's product in the mid-1950s. Since then, most top-level licensed characters and hundreds of other characters have become Pez heads. Consumers eat more than three billion Pez tablets annually, and company sales growth exceeds that of the candy industry as a whole.

The unique Pez package dispenses a "use experience" for its customers beyond the candy itself—namely, fun. And fun translates into a 98 percent awareness level for Pez among teenagers and 89 percent among mothers with children. Pez has not advertised its product for years. With that kind of awareness, who needs advertising?

Creating Customer Value through Packaging and Labelling

Today's packaging and labelling cost Canadian companies billions of dollars, and an estimated 15 cents of every dollar spent by a consumer goes to packaging.[31] Despite the cost, packaging and labelling are essential because both provide important benefits for the manufacturer, retailer, and ultimate consumer. Packaging and labelling can also provide a competitive advantage.

Communication Benefits

A major benefit of packaging is the label information on it conveyed to the consumer, such as directions on how to use the product and the composition of the product, which is needed to satisfy legal requirements of product disclosure. This is particularly important in light of federal legislation requiring the listing of product ingredients on the product's package. Many packaged foods contain informative recipes to promote usage of the product. Campbell Soup estimates that the green bean casserole recipe on its cream of mushroom soup can accounts for $20 million in soup sales each year.[32] Other information consists of seals and symbols, either government-required or commercial seals of approval (such as the Good Housekeeping seal or the CSA seal).

Which chip stacks up better? Frito-Lay's recent introduction of Lay's Stax potato crisps to compete against Procter & Gamble's Pringles illustrates the role of packaging in product and brand management.
Lay's Stax www.fritolay.com
Pringles www.pringles.com

© Mike Hruby

Functional Benefits

Packaging often plays an important functional role, such as storage, convenience, protection, or product quality. Storing food containers is one example, and beverage companies have developed lighter and easier ways to stack products on shelves and in refrigerators. Examples include Coca-Cola beverage packs designed to fit neatly into refrigerator shelves and Ocean Spray Cranberries' rectangular juice bottles that allow ten units per package versus eight of its former round bottles.[33]

The convenience dimension of packaging is becoming increasingly important. Kraft Miracle Whip salad dressing, Heinz ketchup, and Skippy Squeez'It peanut butter are sold in squeeze bottles; microwave popcorn has been a major market success; and Cloverleaf tuna and Folgers coffee are packaged in single-serving portions. Nabisco offers portion-control package sizes for the convenience of weight-conscious consumers. It offers 100-calorie packs of Oreos, Cheese Nips, and other products in individual pouches.

Consumer protection has become an important function of packaging, including the development of tamper-resistant containers. Today, companies commonly use safety seals or pop-tops that reveal previous opening. Nevertheless, no package is truly tamper resistant. There are now laws that provide for prison and fines for package tampering. Consumer protection through labelling also exists in "open dating," which states the expected shelf life of the product.

Functional features of packaging also can affect product quality. Procter & Gamble's Pringles, with its cylindrical packaging, offers uniform chips, minimal breakage, and, for some con-

The distinctive design of Celestial Seasonings tea boxes reinforces the brand's positioning as a New Age, natural herbal tea.

© 2001 Susan G. Holtz

sumers, better value for the money than flex-bag packages for chips. Not to be outdone, Frito-Lay, the world's leading producer of snack chips decided to "stand up" to Pringles with its line of Lay's Stax potato crisps.[34] The consumers will be the final judge of which chip stacks up better. Finally, Molson Canadian introduced a new vented end can for Molson Canadian and Coors Light that has a second opening to help consumers achieve a smoother pour! To activate the "dual aperture" technology, drinkers need only turn the tab and pop it a second time, and the can will let in air for a more consistent, less heady pour.[35]

Perceptual Benefits

A third component of packaging and labelling is the perception created in the consumer's mind. Package and label shape, colour, and graphics distinguish one brand from another, convey a brand's positioning, and build brand equity. In fact, packaging and labelling have been shown to enhance brand recognition and facilitate the formation of strong, favourable, and unique brand associations.[36] This logic applies to Celestial Seasonings' packaging and labelling, which uses delicate illustrations, soft and warm colours, and quotations about life to reinforce the brand's positioning as a New Age, natural herbal tea.

Successful marketers recognize that changes in packages and labels can update and uphold a brand's image in the customer's mind. Just Born Inc., a candy manufacturer of such brands as Jolly Joes and Mike and Ike Treats is a case in point. For many years, the brands were sold in old-fashioned black and white packages, but when the packaging was changed to four-colour, with animated grape and cherry characters, sales increased 25 percent. Coca-Cola brought back its famous and universally recognized contoured bottle shape to further differentiate itself from competitors.

Can you name this soft drink brand?

Because labels list a product's source, brands competing in the global marketplace can benefit from "country of origin or manufacture" perceptions as described in Chapter 7. Consumers tend to have stereotypes about country–product pairings that they judge "best"—English tea, French perfume, Italian leather, and Japanese electronics—which can affect a brand's image. Increasingly, Chinese firms are adopting the English language and Roman alphabet for their brands' labels. This is being done because of the perception in many Asian countries that "things Western are good," even if consumers do not understand the meaning of the English words![37]

Contemporary Packaging and Labelling Challenges

Package and label designers face four challenges. They are (1) the continuing need to connect with customers; (2) environmental concerns; (3) health, safety, and security issues; and (4) cost reduction.

Connecting with Customers

Packages and labels must be continually updated to connect with customers. The challenge lies in creating aesthetic and functional design features that attract customer attention and deliver customer value in their use. If done right, the rewards can be huge.[38]

For example, the marketing team responsible for Kleenex tissues converted its standard rectangular box into an oval shape with colourful seasonal graphics. Sales soared with this aesthetic change in packaging. After months of in-home research, Kraft product managers discovered that consumers often transferred Chips Ahoy! cookies to jars for easy access and to avoid staleness. The company solved both problems by creating a patented resealable opening on the top of the bag. The result? Sales of the new package doubled that of the old package with the addition of this functional feature.

Environmental Concerns

Because of widespread worldwide concern about the growth of solid waste and the shortage of viable landfill sites, the amount, composition, and disposal of packaging material continues to receive much attention. Recycling packaging material is a major thrust.[39] Procter & Gamble now uses recycled cardboard in over 70 percent of its paper packaging and is packaging its detergents in jugs that contain 25 percent recycled plastic. Spic and Span liquid cleaner is packaged in 100 percent recycled material. Other firms, such as Walmart, are emphasizing the use of less packaging material. The company is working with its 600,000 global suppliers to reduce overall packaging and shipping material by 5 percent.

European countries have been trendsetters concerning packaging guidelines and environmental sensitivity. Many of these guidelines now exist in provisions governing trade to and within the European Union. In Germany, 80 percent of packaging material must be collected, and 80 percent of this amount must be recycled or reused to reduce solid waste in landfills. Canadian firms marketing in Europe have responded to these guidelines and ultimately benefited Canadian consumers.

Health, Safety, and Security Issues

A third challenge involves the growing health, safety, and security concerns of packaging materials. Today, most Canadian and European consumers believe companies should make sure products and their packages are safe and secure, regardless of the cost, and companies are responding in numerous ways. Most butane lighters sold today, like those made by Scripto, contain a child-resistant safety latch to prevent misuse and accidental fire. Child-proof caps on pharmaceutical products and household cleaners and sealed lids on food packages are now common. New packaging technology and materials that extend a product's *shelf life* (the time a product can be stored) and prevent spoilage continue to be developed with special applications for developing countries.

Cost Reduction

About 80 percent of packaging material used in the world consists of paper, plastics, and glass. As the cost of these materials rises, companies are constantly challenged to find innovative ways to cut packaging costs while delivering value to their customers. Many food and personal care companies have replaced bottles and cans with sealed plastic or foil pouches. Pouches cut packaging costs by 10 to 15 percent.[40]

PRODUCT WARRANTY

A final component for product consideration is the **warranty**, which is a statement indicating the liability of the manufacturer for product deficiencies. There are various degrees of product warranties with different implications for manufacturers and customers.

Some companies offer *express warranties,* which are written statements of liabilities. In recent years, government has required greater disclosure on express warranties to indicate whether the warranty is a limited-coverage or full-coverage alternative. A *limited-coverage warranty* specifically states the bounds of coverage and, more importantly, areas of non-coverage, whereas a *full warranty* has no limits of non-coverage. Cadillac is a company that boldly touts its warranty coverage. Also, in an effort to improve its image with Canadian consumers, Hyundai offers what it claims to be the best automobile warranty in the industry.

With greater frequency, manufacturers are being held to *implied warranties,* which assign responsibility for product deficiencies to the manufacturer. Studies show that warranties are important and affect a consumer's product evaluation. Brands that have limited warranties tend to receive less positive evaluations compared with full-warranty items.[41]

Warranties are important in light of increasing product liability claims. In the early part of the twentieth century, the courts protected companies, but the trend now is toward "strict liability" rulings, where a manufacturer is liable for any product defect, whether it followed reasonable research standards or not. This issue is hotly contested by companies and consumer advocates.

Warranties represent much more to the buyer than just protection from negative consequences—they can hold a significant marketing advantage for the producer. Sears has built a strong reputation for its Craftsman tool line with a simple warranty: If you break a tool, it is replaced with no questions asked. Zippo has an equally simple guarantee: "If it ever fails, we'll fix it for free."

Learning Review

7. How does a generic brand differ from a private brand?

8. Explain the role of packaging in terms of perception.

9. What is the difference between an expressed warranty and an implied warranty?

Learning Objectives Review

LO1   Explain the product life cycle.

The product life cycle describes the stages a new product goes through in the marketplace: introduction, growth, maturity, and decline. Product sales growth and profitability differ at each stage, and marketing managers have marketing objectives and marketing mix strategies unique to each stage based on consumer behaviour and competitive factors. In the introductory stage, the need is to establish primary demand, whereas the growth stage requires selective demand strategies. In the maturity stage, the need is to maintain market share; the decline stage necessitates a deletion or harvesting strategy. Some important aspects of product life cycles are (*a*) their length, (*b*) the shape of the sales curve, (*c*) how they vary by product classes and forms, and (*d*) the rate at which consumers adopt products.

LO2   Identify ways that marketing executives manage a product's life cycle.

Marketing executives manage a product's life cycle in three ways. First, they can modify the product itself by altering its characteristics, such as product quality, performance, or appearance. Second, they can modify the market by finding new customers for the product, increasing a product's use among existing customers, or creating new-use situations for the product. Finally, they can reposition the product using any one or a combination of marketing mix elements. Four factors trigger a repositioning action. They include reacting to a competitor's position, reaching a new market, catching a rising trend, and changing the value offered to consumers.

LO3   Recognize the importance of branding and alternative branding strategies.

A basic decision in marketing products is branding, in which an organization uses a name, phrase, design, symbols, or a combination of these to identify its products and distinguish them from those of its competitors. Product managers recognize that brands offer more than product identification and a means to distinguish their products from competitors. Successful and established brands take on a brand personality and acquire brand equity—the added value a given brand name gives to a product beyond the functional benefits provided—that is crafted and nurtured by marketing programs that forge strong, favourable, and unique consumer associations with a brand. A good brand name should suggest the product benefits, be memorable, fit the company or product image, be free of legal restrictions, and be simple and emotive. Companies can and do employ several different branding strategies. With multiproduct branding, a company uses one name for all its products in a product class. A multibranding strategy involves giving each product a distinct name. A company uses private branding when it manufactures products but sells them under the brand name of a wholesaler or retailer. A company can also employ mixed branding, where it markets products under its own name(s) and that of a reseller. A recent trend in brand management is cohort brand management, or the bundling of multiple brands into a single marketing effort aimed at a common consumer group. Finally, emerging brand concepts also include social benefit brands and green brands.

LO4   Describe the role of packaging, labelling, and warranties in the marketing of a product.

Packaging, labelling, and warranties play numerous roles in the marketing of a product. The packaging component of a product refers to any container in which it is offered for sale and on which label information is conveyed. Manufacturers, retailers, and consumers acknowledge that packaging and labelling provide communication, functional, and perceptual benefits. Contemporary packaging and labelling challenges include (*a*) the continuing need to connect with customers; (*b*) environmental concerns; (*c*) health, safety, and security issues; and (*d*) cost reduction. Warranties indicate the liability of the manufacturer for product deficiencies and are an important element of product and brand management.

Applying Marketing Knowledge

1. Listed here are four different products in various stages of the product life cycle. What marketing strategies would you suggest to these companies: (*a*) Canon digital cameras—maturity stage; (*b*) Panasonic high-definition televisions—growth stage; (*c*) handheld manual can openers—decline stage; and (*d*) BMW hydrogen-fuelled cars—introduction stage?

2. It has often been suggested that products are intentionally made to break down or wear out. Is this strategy a planned product modification approach?

3. The product manager of GE is reviewing the penetration of trash compactors in Canadian homes. After more than two decades in existence, this product is in relatively few homes. What problems can account for this poor acceptance? What is the shape of the trash compactor life cycle?

4. For years, Ferrari has been known as the manufacturer of expensive luxury automobiles. The company plans to attract the major segment of the car-buying market of those who purchase medium-priced automobiles. As Ferrari considers this trading-down strategy, what branding strategy would you recommend? What are the trade-offs to consider with your strategy?

5. The nature of product warranties has changed as the federal court system reassesses the meaning of warranties. How does the regulatory trend toward warranties affect product development?

6. Suppose that you were launching a new service venture, perhaps a marketing consulting company that would cater to small and medium-size Canadian companies. Determine your brand promise (what the brand will do for the customer), create a name, and describe how you communicate the brand and how you would deliver on your brand promise.

7. What are your thoughts on social benefit brands? Would you buy from companies that have social benefit brands? Why or why not?

Building Your Marketing Plan

For the product offering in your marketing plan:

1. Identify (*a*) its stage in the product life cycle and (*b*) key marketing mix actions that might be appropriate, as shown in Figure 11–1.
2. Develop (*a*) branding and (*b*) packaging strategies, if appropriate for your offering.

P&G's Secret Deodorant: Finding Inspiration in Perspiration

How do you revitalize a 50-plus-year-old brand? By focusing the brand's marketing efforts on its core purpose—a purpose that is both benefit-driven and inspirational—and using that purpose to build essential one-to-one personal connections with consumers.

Procter & Gamble's (P&G's) Secret brand, launched in 1956, has dominated the women's antiperspirant deodorant category for many years. Secret maintains its leadership position as one of many products in what is typically considered a low-involvement product category. Underarm deodorant isn't traditionally the type of product consumers think about engaging with in an ongoing, meaningful way. However, Secret has demonstrated that delivering the product benefit is important to establish trust and build engagement. This type of engagement often results in amplifying the brand's marketing investment, or paid media. Since 2009, Secret's purpose has been at the centre of its marketing efforts, resulting in tremendous growth and brand advocacy among consumers.

Product Background

Secret was the first deodorant marketed exclusively to women. In the 1960s and 1970s, Secret's growth was supported by a recurring series of ads featuring a husband and wife dealing with issues of the day, such as having children and returning to work afterward. "It was all about empowering women to make the right choices for themselves and to embrace those choices fearlessly," according to Kevin Hochman, marketing director for skin and personal care at P&G North America at the time.

However, in 2004 and 2005, brand executives felt the theme was getting dated, so Secret backed off from that positioning. "We walked away," Hochman says. "We thought, women are empowered, and maybe this isn't so relevant. That was a mistake. Of course the idea was still relevant; we just hadn't modernized it in a contemporary way." Secret made a deliberate decision to go back to its roots.

The Road to Purpose

Secret started to experience slower growth in 2008 due to a down economy. The launch of a super-premium line of antiperspirant, Secret Clinical Strength, helped increase sales and market share, but competitors soon followed suit with similar products. Meanwhile, top P&G management began infusing the idea of purpose-driven marketing throughout the organization. The company-wide vision focused on building brands through lifelong, one-to-one personal connections that ultimately build relationships and fulfill the company's purpose to "touch and improve more lives of more consumers more completely." With this in mind, Secret brand management realized it needed to get clear on defining who Secret was, why Secret existed, and what Secret's purpose was. The brand needed a reason for its consumers to care and wanted to give them a reason to share.

Through the leadership and efforts of its senior brand management and partner agencies, including MEplusYOU (formerly imc2), Leo Burnett Co., SMG, Marina Maher Communications, and consultancy group BrightHouse, the Secret brand team began to establish the brand's purpose and convey it across all marketing touch points in ways that resonated with target consumers' core values and beliefs. "It becomes about more than selling deodorant, or promoting functional benefits, and more about rallying around something higher-order," says Hochman.

The Secret team started by defining the brand's core beliefs: "We believe in the equality of the genders and that all people should be able to pursue their goals without fear. We believe that by acting courageously, supporting others, empathizing with their challenges, and finding innovative solutions, we can help

In the summer of 2011, Secret and Apple joined forces to create an iAd experience that tackled the issue for girls on the device that's most personal—their iPhone. The ignition received unusually high engagement levels and led to many "firsts" for Secret:

- First brand to create and share customized wallpapers via iPhone and iPod touch devices, which led to an "average time spent" rate that was 16 percent higher than average.

- First brand to use transition banners on the iAd Network, which resulted in exceeding benchmarks for banner "tap-through rates" (50 percent higher than average for iAd).

- First brand to drive donations for a cause through the iAd, which resulted in donations to PACER's National Bullying Prevention Center.

In the first 10 days after launch, 23,000 consumers engaged with the Secret iAd, with more than eight page views per visit and an average of 80 seconds spent on the ad.

What's Next for Secret

Secret executives saw success behind the purpose activation the year after it was established, but they noticed it wasn't truly part of the brand's DNA or fully integrated into every marketing element. "[At first] we had a lot of grandiose ideas, but they added layers to our existing plan. Dollars were tight, and the purpose ideas started getting cut. Old Spice was ahead of us, and I wondered what they were doing differently," says Hochman. "By [working with our agency partners], we finally were able to ensure that [the ignitions] weren't just elements of our plans; they WERE our plan," Hochman says. "The way the Secret team operates now compared with four years ago—it's like day and night."

Hochman says the brand has more ideas that include educating, generating awareness, and empowering people to take meaningful action. Secret is recognized as being best in its class, something the brand is happy to tout. "But [success] isn't a Secret-only thing . . . it's a priority for all of our brands. And when people are living the brand, they're more excited to come to work. It's much more enabling and inspiring," Hochman says. And to continue in this success,

Hochman suggests remembering that a brand's purpose is inextricably linked to the overall plan, it pervades everything about the business—including team culture—and it's in the company's roots. Hochman emphasizes the importance of transparency, something he believes Secret will continue to win out on in the future. "Today, information is free and plentiful. If there's a lack of sincerity, consumers know it."

QUESTIONS

1. What is purpose-driven marketing from a product and brand management perspective at Procter & Gamble?

2. How does purpose-driven marketing for Secret deodorant relate to the hierarchy of needs concept detailed in Chapter 5?

3. What dimensions of the consumer-based brand equity pyramid have the Secret brand team focused on with its Let Her Jump and Mean Stinks ignitions?

Case: This case was prepared by Jana Boone. Used with permission.

Managing Services

Learning Objectives

After reading this chapter, you should be able to:

LO1 Describe four unique elements of services.

LO2 Explain the service continuum.

LO3 Understand how consumers purchase services.

LO4 Develop a customer contact audit to understand the service purchasing process.

LO5 Understand how customers evaluate the services they have purchased.

LO6 Explain the special nature of the marketing mix for services: the seven Ps of services marketing.

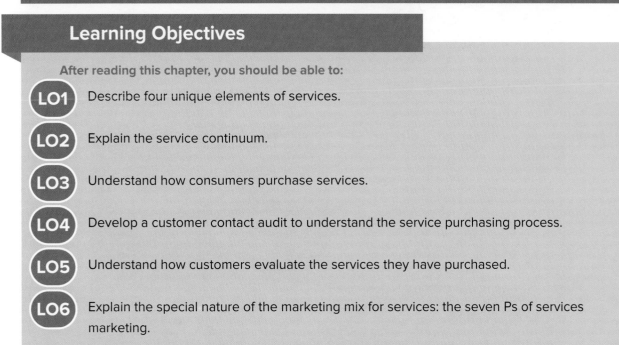

Airbnb Redefines Services—and the Economy!

"We were just trying to solve our own problem," explains Brian Chesky, who started the first "sharing economy" business with co-founder Joe Gebbia. Their problem was to make pocket cash. They didn't have anything except space in their apartment, so they created a website called **Airbedandbreakfast.com** to advertise floor space where people could temporarily sleep on air mattresses while attending a nearby conference. The idea was so successful they shortened the name to **Airbnb.com** and expanded the business to include many other kinds of spaces such as houses, villas, and even boats.

Initially, they focused on large events such as national conventions where hotels were sold out. Airbnb offered to help visitors "Find a place to stay" by enabling them to rent from people who were willing to share their spaces. In exchange for providing the service, Airbnb charged the renter 3 percent and the traveller 6 to 12 percent. Demand for the service increased rapidly, and soon an average of 425,000 people were staying in an Airbnb listing each night. Today, Airbnb has more than a million listings available in 34,000 cities and 190 countries. In addition, *Forbes* estimates that Chesky and Gebbia are now worth $1.5 billion each, and Airbnb was recently designated Company of the Year by *Inc.* magazine.[1]

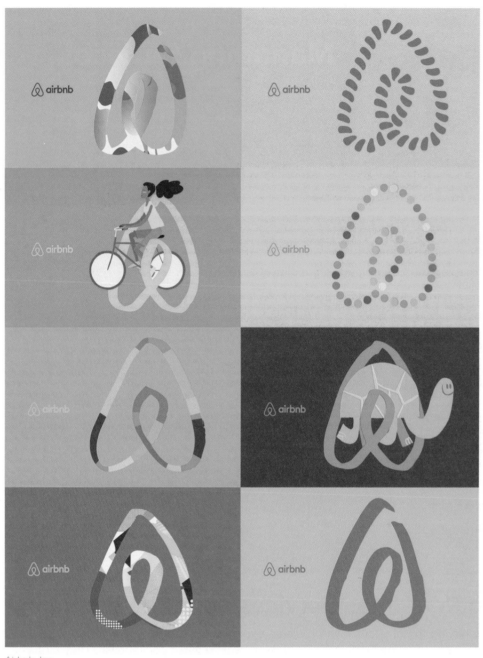

Airbnb, Inc.

Airbnb was the genesis for what has come to be known as the sharing economy. It turns out that peer-to-peer sharing, or collaborative consumption, is a perfect match with the changes in consumer attitudes about ownership. Millennials typically don't buy newspapers, DVDs, or CDs; instead they find news on Facebook, stream movies from Hulu, and subscribe to music on Pandora. They are much more likely to borrow, rent, and share than previous generations of consumers. As a result, many new services are being offered to accommodate these attitudes. Uber and Lyft now offer peer-to-peer ride sharing (similar to a taxi), while Turo (formerly known as RelayRides) and Getaround offer peer-to-peer car sharing (similar to a car rental). Parking Panda allows drivers to find homeowners who want to rent extra space in their driveway, and DogVacay helps pet owners find friendly places for canines to stay for a day. Rentoid and Spinlister help people rent products, tools, and bicycles rather than purchase them. Similarly, TaskRabbit allows users to outsource small jobs and tasks to people in their neighbourhood. There are even sharing sites that encourage free exchanges, such as **Couchsurfing.com**, which is a network of volunteers who offer free hospitality, advice, and accommodation to international travellers.

Experts estimate that hundreds of new peer-to-peer sharing services are now in operation and that the revenue generated by the sharing economy exceeds $15 billion annually. Neil Turner, the founder and CEO of adverCar, a service that allows drivers to rent advertising space on their cars, suggests that "this is the way of the future." As we move from a perspective based on ownership to this new approach based on sharing and renting, traditional businesses will need to make changes. Avis Budget Group, for example, recently paid $500 million for Zipcar, while General Motors invested in Turo, and Home Depot has introduced product rental in about half of its stores.[2]

In this chapter, we discuss how services differ from traditional products (goods), how services consumers make purchase decisions, and the important aspects of developing and managing the marketing mix for services in order to create and deliver exceptional customer experiences.

THE SERVICE ECONOMY

As defined in Chapter 1, **services** are activities, deeds, or other basic intangibles offered for sale to consumers in exchange for money or something else of value. One services-marketing expert suggests that services permeate every aspect of our lives.[3] We use transportation services, such as Via Rail, Air Canada, and Uber, when we travel. We use restaurant services, such as McDonald's, to feed us, and hotels, such as the Four Seasons, to put a roof over our heads when we are away from home. When we are at home, we rely on electricity providers, such as Ontario Power Generation, to keep the lights on, and telephone services from Bell Canada to keep in touch with family. We also use Sympatico to keep us connected to the Internet and use Molly Maid to keep our houses clean.

At work, we rely on Canada Post to deliver our mail, and Fedex to get our urgent documents to their destinations overnight. And we use ServiceMaster to keep our offices clean and Intercon Security services to keep them safe. Our employers use public relations firms, such as Edelman Public Relations, and advertising agencies, such as Cossette Communications, to maintain their corporate images, while we use the services of First Choice Haircutters to maintain our personal appearances. We use colleges and universities to improve our minds, and online employment services, such as Workopolis, to find us better jobs. We use financial institutions, such as Scotiabank, to safeguard our money, and we buy peace of mind with life insurance from Canada Life. We use lawyers to draw up our wills, and E*TRADE to trade our shares. In our leisure time, we stop by a Cineplex Odeon theatre to catch a flick. We might even visit one of the casinos run by the Great Canadian Gaming Corporation.

We might use an online travel service, such as Travelocity, to book our well-deserved vacation and stay and ski at Whistler Resort. While we are there, we might use a TD debit card to pay for everything. Of course, we always need to stay in touch, and so the wireless telecommunications services provided by Rogers come in handy. While the Whistler Resort does allow dogs, we have to decide whether to take her or to use a boarding kennel or a personal pet-watching service to care for our border collie. When we get home, we realize the car needs an oil change, and so we drive to Mr. Lube to get it done. The washing machine also sounds a little funny, and so we call the Maytag repairman. After a long day, we just might watch some digital cable provided by Cogeco and order in from Boston Pizza. Because the television looks a little blurry, we decide that it is time to get rid of our eyeglasses and contact TLC Laser Eye Centres to see if they might help. Then, we might sign into Facebook to update our status or send a tweet to our friends on Twitter. And because we believe in future planning, we have already decided on a nursing home for our parents and even pre-purchased their funerals and burial plots. Services—from the cradle to the grave, we rely on them.

Services have become one of the most important components of the Canadian and global economies. The services sector is now responsible for over 70 percent of Canada's total economic output, as well as over 75 percent of its workforce. According to a recent Canadian study by Industry Canada, the top high-growth industries in Canada—overall, not just within the services sector—are professional, scientific, and technical services. And, as one looks across Canada, the services landscape is indeed growing. For example, in Vancouver, the hot services businesses are life coaching, personal training, health care for the elderly, massage therapy, interior design, immigration consulting, pet services, and beauty salons. In Calgary, in addition to the oil and gas sector, hot services businesses include medical research, financial services, and hospitality services. In Toronto, hot services businesses include medical and legal firms and financial services. And in Ottawa, hot services businesses are government services companies and tourism firms.[4] Also, according to the Canadian Franchise Association, the top franchise businesses in Canada are almost exclusively service-based businesses, including business consulting, beauty/health care, and senior care. Finally, research shows that three of Canada's fastest-growing exports are services: financial and insurance services, management services, and IT services.[5]

LO1　The Uniqueness of Services

As we noted in Chapter 10, when consumers buy products, they are purchasing a bundle of tangible and intangible attributes that deliver value and satisfaction. In general, it is very difficult to define a pure good or a pure service. A *pure good* implies that the consumer obtains benefits from the good alone without any added value from service; conversely, a *pure service* assumes there is no "goods" element to the service that the customer receives. In reality, most services contain some goods element. For example, at McDonald's, you receive a hamburger; at TD Bank, you are provided with a bank statement. And most goods offer some service—even if it is only delivery. In fact, many goods-producing firms are adding service offerings as a way to differentiate their products from those of their competitors.

But there are certain commonalities between services as products that set them apart from tangible goods. The four unique elements to services are *intangibility, inconsistency, inseparability,* and *inventory.* These elements are sometimes referred to as the **four Is of services**.

Why do many services emphasize their tangible benefits? The answer appears in the text.

Fairmont Hotels & Resorts
www.fairmont.com

Courtesy of Fairmont Hotels & Resorts

Intangibility

Services are intangible; that is, they cannot be held, touched, or seen before the purchase decision. In contrast, before purchasing a traditional product, a consumer can touch a box of laundry detergent, kick the tire of an automobile, or sample a new breakfast cereal. A major marketing need for services is to make them tangible or to show the benefits of using a service. American Express emphasizes the gifts available to cardholders through its Membership Rewards program; a leading insurance company says, "You're in Good Hands with Allstate"; Fairmont Hotels tells business travellers that they will have the convenience of their offices away from their offices, including computer hookups and personal services.

Inconsistency

Developing, pricing, promoting, and delivering services is challenging because the quality of a service is often inconsistent. Because services depend on the people who provide them, their quality varies with each person's capabilities and day-to-day job performance. Inconsistency is much more of a problem with services than it is with tangible goods. Tangible products can be good or bad in terms of quality, but with modern production lines, the quality will at least be consistent. On the other hand, the Toronto Maple Leafs hockey team may look like potential Stanley Cup winners on a particular day but lose by ten goals the next day. Or a cello player with the Vancouver Symphony may not be feeling well and give a less-than-average performance. Whether the service involves tax assistance at Ernst & Young or guest relations at the Sheraton, organizations attempt to reduce inconsistency through standardization and training. Standardization through automation is becoming increasingly popular in many service industries, including banking.

Inseparability

A third difference between services and goods is inseparability. There are two dimensions to inseparability. The first is inseparability of production and consumption. Whereas goods are first produced, then sold, and then consumed, services are sold first and then produced and consumed simultaneously. For example, you can buy a ticket at **AirCanada.com**, then fly and consume in-flight service as it is being produced. The second dimension of inseparability is that, in most cases, the consumer cannot (and does not) separate the deliverer of the service from the service itself. For example, to receive an education, a person may attend a college or university. The quality of the education may be high, but if the student has difficulty interacting with instructors, finds counselling services poor, or does not receive adequate library or computer assistance, he or she may not be satisfied with the educational experience. In short, a student's evaluations of education will be influenced primarily by how the instructors, counsellors, librarians, and other people at the college or university responsible for delivering the education are perceived.

The amount of interaction between the consumer and the service deliverer or provider depends on the extent to which the consumer must be physically present to receive the service. Some services, such as golf lessons and medical diagnoses, require the customer to participate in the delivery process. Other services that process tangible objects, such as car repair or dry cleaning, require less involvement from the customer. Finally, many services, such as banking and insurance, can now be delivered electronically, often requiring no face-to-face customer interaction, as with, for example, Bank of Montreal's online banking service.[6]

Inventory

Inventory of services is different from that of goods. Inventory problems exist with goods because many items are perishable and because there are costs associated with handling inventory. With services, inventory-carrying costs are more subjective and are related to **idle production capacity**, which occurs when the service provider is available but there is no demand. The inventory cost of a service is the cost of paying the person used to provide the service, along with any needed equipment. If a physician is paid to see patients but no one schedules an appointment, the fixed cost of the idle physician's salary is a high inventory-carrying cost. In some service businesses, however, the provider of the service is on commission (the Merrill Lynch stockbroker) or is a part-time employee (a counterperson at McDonald's). In these businesses, inventory-carrying costs can be significantly lower or nonexistent because the idle production capacity can be cut back by reducing hours or not having to pay salary because of the commission compensation system.

Figure 12–1 shows a scale of inventory-carrying costs, represented on the high end by airlines and hospitals and on the low end by real estate agencies. The inventory-carrying costs of airlines are high because of high-salaried pilots and very expensive equipment. In contrast, real estate agencies have employees who work on commission and need little expensive equipment to conduct business. One reason why service providers must maintain production capacity is because of the importance of time to today's customers. People do not want to wait long for service.

People play an important role in the delivery of many services. Many services ads emphasize the personal element of the offering.

Merrill Lynch

www.wealthmanagement.ml.com

Bank of America Corporation

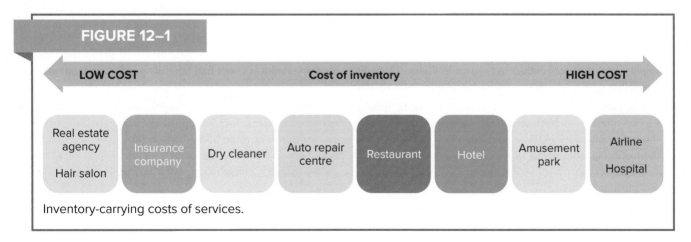

FIGURE 12–1

LOW COST — Cost of inventory — HIGH COST

| Real estate agency Hair salon | Insurance company | Dry cleaner | Auto repair centre | Restaurant | Hotel | Amusement park | Airline Hospital |

Inventory-carrying costs of services.

(LO2) The Service Continuum

The four Is of services differentiate services from goods in most cases, but as we mentioned earlier, most products sold cannot be defined as pure goods or pure services. For example, does IBM Canada sell goods or services? While the company sells computers and software, a major component of its business is information technology services, including consulting and training. Does Rogers Communications provide only goods when it publishes *Marketing Magazine,* or does it consider itself a service because it presents up-to-date Canadian business information? As companies look at what they bring to the market, there is a range from the tangible to the intangible or good-dominant to service-dominant offerings referred to as the **service continuum** (Figure 12–2).

FIGURE 12–2

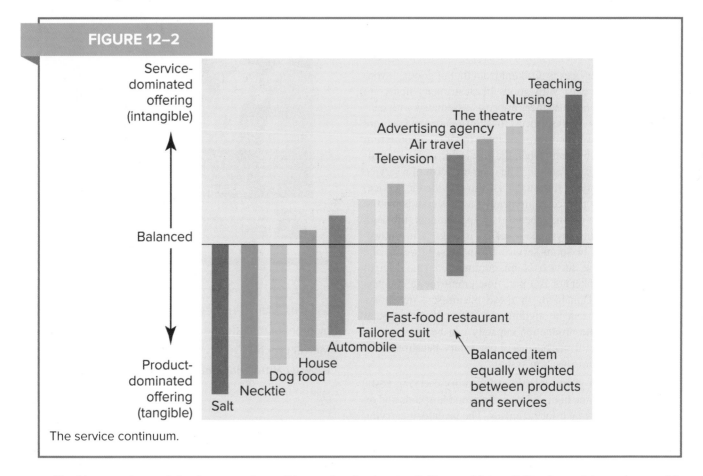

The service continuum.

Teaching, nursing, and the theatre are intangible, service-dominant activities, and intangibility, inconsistency, inseparability, and inventory are major concerns in their marketing. Salt, neckties, and dog food are tangible goods, and the problems represented by the four Is of services are not relevant in their marketing. However, some businesses are a mix of intangible-service and tangible-good factors. A clothing tailor provides a service but also a good, the finished suit. How pleasant, courteous, and attentive the tailor is to the customer is an important component of the service, and how well the clothes fit is an important part of the product. As shown in Figure 12–2, a fast-food restaurant is about half tangible goods (the food) and half intangible services (courtesy, cleanliness, speed, convenience).

For many businesses today, it is useful to distinguish between their core service and their supplementary services. A core service offering—a bank account, for example—also has supplementary services, such as deposit assistance, parking or drive-through availability, ABMs, and monthly statements. Supplementary services often allow service providers to differentiate their offering from competitors, and they may add value for consumers. While there are many potential supplementary services, key categories of supplementary services include information delivery, consultation, order taking, billing procedures, and payment options.[7]

LO3   HOW CONSUMERS PURCHASE SERVICES

Universities, hospitals, hotels, and lawyers are facing an increasingly competitive environment. Successful service organizations, like successful goods-producing firms, must understand how the consumer makes a purchase decision and a post-purchase evaluation. Service companies will be better able to position themselves effectively if they understand why a consumer chooses to use a particular service. Moreover, by understanding the consumer's post-purchase evaluation process, service companies can identify sources of customer satisfaction or dissatisfaction.

Purchasing a Service

Because of their intangible nature, it is generally more difficult for consumers to evaluate services before purchase than it is to evaluate goods (Figure 12–3). Tangible goods, such as clothes, jewellery, and furniture, have *search* qualities, such as colour, size, and style, which can be determined before purchase. But rarely can a consumer inspect, try out, or test a service in advance. This is because some services, such as restaurants and child care, have *experience* qualities, which can be discerned only after purchase or consumption. Other services provided by specialized professionals, such as medical diagnosis and legal services, have *credence* qualities, or characteristics that the consumer may find impossible to evaluate even after purchase and consumption.[8]

FIGURE 12–3

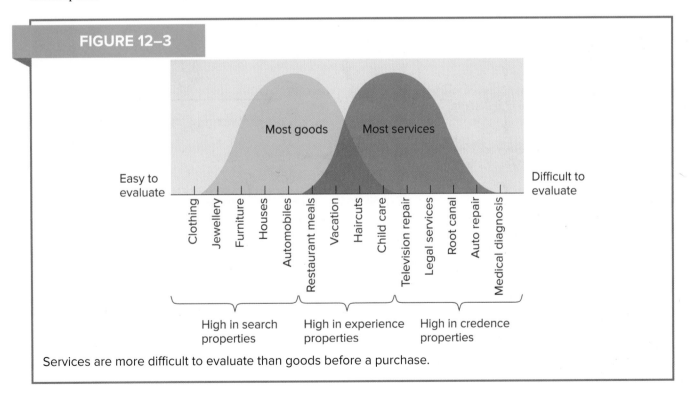

Services are more difficult to evaluate than goods before a purchase.

The experience and credence qualities of services force consumers to make a pre-purchase examination of the service by assessing the tangible characteristics that are part of, or surround, the service.[9] In other words, consumers will evaluate what they cannot see by what they can see. For example, you might consider the actual appearance of the dentist's office, or its physical location, when making a judgment about the possible quality of dental services that might be provided there. Many service organizations go to great lengths to ensure that the tangible aspects of the services convey the appropriate image and serve as surrogate indicators of the intangible service to be provided.

Services marketers recognize that because of the uncertainty created by experience and credence qualities, consumers turn to personal sources of information, such as early adopters, opinion leaders, and reference group members, during the purchase decision process. Accordingly, services marketers work to ensure customer satisfaction in order to achieve positive word-of-mouth referral.

LO4 Customer Contact Audit

To better understand the service purchasing process, service firms can develop a **customer contact audit**—a flow chart of the points of interaction between consumer and service provider.[10] These points of interaction are often referred to as *contact points, touchpoints,* or *service encounter elements.* Constructing a customer contact audit is particularly important in high-contact services, such as educational institutions, health care, and even automobile rental agencies. Figure 12–4 illustrates a customer contact audit for renting a car from Hertz. The interactions identified in a customer contact audit often serve as the basis for developing better services and delivering them more efficiently and effectively. In other words, it can help to ensure the customer has a positive experience with the service.

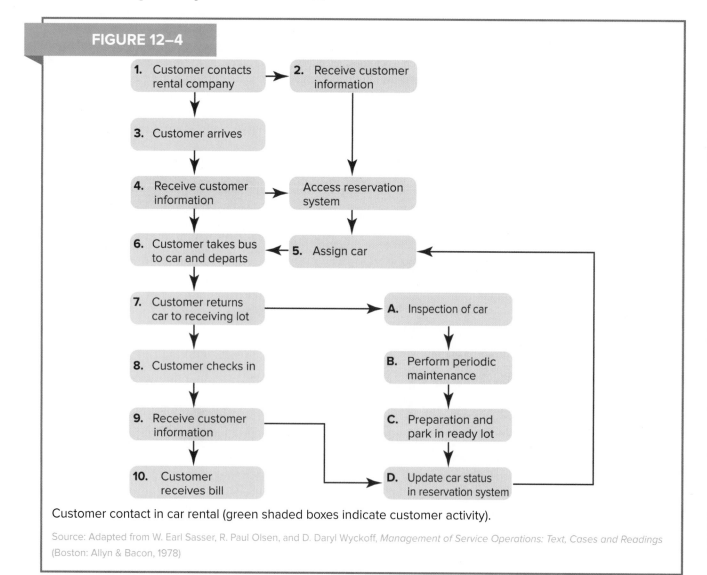

FIGURE 12–4

1. Customer contacts rental company
2. Receive customer information
3. Customer arrives
4. Receive customer information
   Access reservation system
6. Customer takes bus to car and departs
5. Assign car
7. Customer returns car to receiving lot
   A. Inspection of car
8. Customer checks in
   B. Perform periodic maintenance
9. Receive customer information
   C. Preparation and park in ready lot
10. Customer receives bill
   D. Update car status in reservation system

Customer contact in car rental (green shaded boxes indicate customer activity).

Source: Adapted from W. Earl Sasser, R. Paul Olsen, and D. Daryl Wyckoff, *Management of Service Operations: Text, Cases and Readings* (Boston: Allyn & Bacon, 1978)

When a customer decides to rent a car, the following occurs:

1. He or she contacts the rental company by phone or goes online (see Figure 12–4).
2. A customer service representative receives the information and checks the availability of the car at the desired location.
3. The customer arrives at the rental site.
4. The reservation system is again accessed, and the customer provides information regarding payment, address, and driver's licence.
5. A car is assigned to the customer.
6. The customer proceeds by bus to the car pickup.
7. The customer returns to the rental location.
8. The car is parked and the customer checks in.
9. The customer provides information on distance driven, gas consumption, and damages.
10. A bill is subsequently prepared.

Each of the steps numbered 1 to 10 is a customer contact point where the tangible aspects of Hertz service are seen by the customer. Figure 12–4, however, also shows a series of steps lettered A to D that involves two levels of inspections on the automobile. These steps are essential in providing a car that runs, but they are not points of customer interaction. To be successful, Hertz must create a competitive advantage in the sequence of interactions with the customer. In essence, Hertz must attempt to deliver the car in a seamless and timely manner, limiting the amount of time and effort required on the part of the customer. The customer contact audit is one tool that may help create that competitive advantage for Hertz or any other service firm.

LO5 Post-purchase Evaluation

Once a consumer tries a service, how is it evaluated? The primary method is by comparing expectations about the service offering with the actual experience a consumer has with the service.[11] Differences between a consumer's expectations and experience are often identified through **gap analysis**. This type of analysis asks consumers to assess their expectations and experiences on various dimensions of service quality. Expectations are influenced by word-of-mouth communications, personal needs, past experience, and marketing communications activities, while actual experiences are determined by the way an organization delivers the service.

One popular instrument developed by researchers to measure service quality and to conduct gap analysis is called SERVQUAL.[12] Researchers measure consumers' expectations and their actual service experience using a multi-item instrument. Consumers are asked to rate the importance of various dimensions of service quality and to score the service in terms of their expectations and actual experience. SERVQUAL provides the services marketer with a consumer rating of service quality and an indication of where improvements can be made.

Using SERVQUAL, these researchers have found that consumers judge service quality along five key dimensions: tangibles, reliability, responsiveness, assurance, and empathy (Figure 12–5). However, the relative importance of these various dimensions of service quality has been found to vary by type of service. For example, a recent Canadian study found that responsiveness and empathy were the most important dimensions of overall service quality in the Canadian banking context. But, for physician services, empathy and reliability were considered most important.[13]

Services marketers must understand what dimensions consumers use in judging service quality, recognize the relative importance of each dimension, find out how they rate in terms of service quality, and take actions to deliver service quality that is consistent with consumer expectations. As a consumer, you play an important role in ensuring that service firms deliver high service quality. Many service firms actively encourage customer feedback, but research shows that only 5 to 10 percent of unhappy service customers offer direct feedback to service firms.[14] Without such feedback, it is difficult for service firms to gauge how well they are doing in terms of creating and delivering quality service. What is even more vexing for service firms is the fact that your behaviour, as a customer, can affect the service experience of others. The Making Responsible Decisions box, "Customer Behaviour Can Affect the Perception of Service Quality," points out just how some customers' behaviour can negatively impact on other customers' perception of service quality.[15]

FIGURE 12–5

DIMENSION	DEFINITION	EXAMPLES OF QUESTIONS AIRLINE CUSTOMERS MIGHT ASK
Tangibles	Appearance of physical facilities, equipment, personnel, and communications materials.	Are the plane, gate, and baggage area clean?
Reliability	Ability to perform the promised service dependably and accurately.	Is my flight on time?
Responsiveness	Willingness to help customers and provide prompt service.	Are the flight attendants willing to answer my questions?
Assurance	Respectful, considerate personnel who listen to customers and answer their questions.	Are the employees knowledgeable?
Empathy	Knowing the customer and understanding their needs. Approachable and available.	Do the employees know that I have special seating and meal requirements?

Dimensions of service quality.

Source: Adapted with the permission of The Free Press, a Division of Simon & Schuster Adult Publishing Group, from *ON GREAT SERVICE: A Framework for Action* by Leonard L. Berry. Copyright © 1995 by Leonard L. Berry. All rights reserved.

MAKING RESPONSIBLE DECISIONS

Customer Behaviour Can Affect the Perception of Service Quality

Picture this. You are flying first class from Halifax to Vancouver for a well-deserved vacation. You are impressed with the amenities offered by the airline, including the courtesy and friendliness of the personnel on board. Just when you are starting to settle in and take a quick nap, right behind you in economy class is a man with very poor hygiene, who obviously has had too much to drink and who now begins to play a harmonica as loud and as poorly as possible. His behaviour is clearly disruptive and he is obviously disturbing the peace and quiet of other passengers in economy class, as well as those adjacent to him in first class, including yourself. But to your amazement, the flight attendants do not request that the drunken passenger cease his harmonica playing. He persists in his behaviour and you suffer the consequences. Your service experience with the airline has been compromised and you now rethink your perception of the airline, including its perceived quality. This is a true story.

Other customers and how they behave can contribute negatively to the functioning of service quality delivery processes and service quality outcomes. Customers who misbehave, who are uncooperative or abusive, or who simply break established social etiquette can pose serious problems for service organizations that wish to maintain service quality. You know from your own experience that the behaviour of other customers can affect your enjoyment of a service.

Customers who misbehave in a service environment are sometimes called "jaycustomers"—individuals who act thoughtlessly or abusively, causing problems for the firm, employees, and other customers. You know who they are: people who make or receive wireless phone calls during musical or theatre performances; people who cut in line in front of you as you are queuing to enter a sporting event; careless skiers who pose a risk to your health and safety; belligerent drunks on airplanes. These people break rules designed to protect the comfort and enjoyment of all customers, including unwritten social norms like not jumping the queue.

What should a service firm do about such customer misbehaviour? What should you do about it?

There are benefits to the customer and the service provider when service quality is improved. Recent research indicates that for the customer, improved service quality is connected to customer satisfaction and increases the likelihood that the customer will return to the same provider, which, in effect, offers the benefits of continuity of a single provider, customized service potential, reduced stress due to repetitive purchase process, and an absence of switching costs.[16] For the service provider, retaining existing customers is much less costly than attracting new customers, and repeat customers are clearly more profitable over time.

Most importantly, service firms see service quality as the cornerstone for customer experience management (CEM) programs. In short, poor service quality is likely to result in the customer's perception of a poor service experience and feeling dissatisfied, which, in turn, can result in the service organization losing a customer. But excellent service quality can result in the customer perceiving a good service experience and feeling satisfied, and therefore more likely to return to the service organization in the future.[17] However, what happens if there is a service failure that results in dissatisfaction and the customer complains? Research suggests that customers who experience a service failure will increase their satisfaction if the service provider makes a sincere service recovery effort. In addition, service providers can increase customer satisfaction by letting customers choose between several recovery options.[18]

Learning Review

4. What are the differences between search, experience, and credence qualities?

5. What is gap analysis?

6. An instrument or approach used to measure service quality is _____.

LO6 MANAGING THE MARKETING OF SERVICES: THE SEVEN Ps

Just as the unique aspects of services necessitate changes in the consumer's purchase process, the marketing management process requires special adaptation. As we have seen in earlier chapters, the traditional marketing mix is composed of the four Ps: product, price, place, and promotion. Careful management of the four Ps is important when marketing services. However, the distinctive nature of services requires that other additional variables be effectively managed by services marketers. The concept of an expanded marketing mix for services has been adopted by many services-marketing organizations. In addition to the traditional four Ps, the services-marketing mix includes people, physical evidence, and process, creating the **seven Ps of services marketing**. Importantly, it has been found that the proper blending of these seven Ps is important in attracting customers and ensuring customer satisfaction.[19] Let us now discuss the special nature of the marketing mix for services.

Product (Service)

To a large extent, the concepts of the product component of the marketing mix discussed in Chapters 10 and 11 apply equally to Cheerios (a good) and Visa (a service). Managers of goods and services must design the product concept, whether a good or a service, with the features and benefits desired by customers. An important aspect of the product concept is branding. Because services are intangible—and therefore more difficult to describe—the brand name or identifying logo of the service organization is particularly important when a consumer makes a purchase decision. Therefore, service organizations, such as banks, hotels, rental car companies, and restaurants, rely on branding strategies in order to distinguish themselves in the minds of the consumers. Strong brand names and symbols are important for services marketers, not only for differentiation purposes but also for conveying an image of quality. A service firm with a well-established brand reputation will also find it easier to market new services than firms without such brand reputation.[20]

Take a look at the images below to determine how successful some companies have been in branding their services by name, logo, or symbol. You will also find that these service brands and many others are leveraging social media to promote their brands. In fact, recent research has found that almost all of the top service brands (as rated by Interbrand, a branding consultancy firm) are using social media as part of their branding strategies. This includes Facebook and Twitter. In fact, 100 percent of the service brands on the Interbrand list have a Facebook page and 95 percent use Twitter.[21]

Logos create service identities.

(left): © Agencja Fotograficzna Caro; (right): Courtesy of Canadian Blood Services.

Price

In service industries, price is often referred to in many ways. Hospitals refer to *charges;* consultants, lawyers, physicians, and accountants to *fees;* airlines to *fares;* hotels to *rates;* and colleges and universities to *tuition.* Because of the intangible nature of services, price is often perceived by consumers as a possible indicator of the quality of the service. For example, would you be willing to risk a $10 dental surgery? Or a $50 divorce lawyer? In many cases, there may be few other available cues for the customer to judge a service, and so price becomes very important as a quality indicator.[22] However, in some cases, especially with experience-based services, the customer may not perceive the value of the service until after consumption. Therefore, some service companies offer their basic service for free hoping the customer will realize its value after use and then be willing to pay for it (see Chapter 13 for a discussion of freemium pricing).

Price influences perceptions of services.

Courtesy of The Redirections Group

Pricing of services also goes beyond the traditional tasks of setting the selling price. When customers buy services, they consider non-monetary costs, such as the time as well as the mental and physical efforts required to consume the service. Therefore, services marketers must also try to minimize the non-monetary costs customers may bear in purchasing and using a service. Finally, as we will see later in this chapter, pricing also plays a role in balancing consumer demand for services.

Place (Distribution)

Place (or distribution) is a major factor in developing a services-marketing strategy because of the inseparability of services from the producer. Rarely are intermediaries involved in the distribution of a service; the distribution site and the service deliverer are the tangible components of the service. And until recently, customers generally had to go to the service provider's physical location to purchase the service. Increased competition has forced many service firms to consider the value of convenient distribution and to find new ways of distributing services to demanding customers. Hair-styling chains such as First Choice Haircutters, legal firms, and accounting firms all use multiple locations for the distribution of services. Technology is also being used to deliver services beyond the provider's physical locations. For example, in the banking industry, customers of participating banks using the Interac system can access any one of thousands of ABMs across Canada and need not visit their own specific bank branch. The availability of electronic distribution of services over the Internet also allows for global reach and coverage for a variety of services, including travel services, banking, education, entertainment, and many other information-based services. With speed and convenience becoming increasingly important to customers when they select service providers, service firms can leverage the use of the Internet to deliver services on a 24/7 basis, in real time, on a global scale. In short, forward-looking firms no longer see face-to-face delivery of services as the only distribution option.[23]

Promotion

The value of promotion, especially advertising, for many services is to show consumers the benefits of purchasing the service. For example, advertising can be an effective way to demonstrate such attributes as availability, location, consistent quality, efficient and courteous service, and assurance of satisfaction.[24] While many service firms are using the Internet as an alternative distribution channel, they are also using it as an advertising or promotional medium. Many colleges and universities, for example, have their own well-designed websites to convey their messages to prospective students. Many of these websites are highly interactive, offering prospective students virtual tours and simulating the type of educational experience they should expect when they arrive on campus. Tourism marketers are also finding the Internet to be a valuable tool in reaching their prospective target markets; check out how Canada's northern territories are doing exactly that in the accompanying Going Online box, "Canada's North Tourism Initiative."

GOING ONLINE

Canada's North Tourism Initiative

Canada's three northern territories (Northwest Territories, Nunavut, and Yukon) have created a joint promotion program to attract tourism to the northern region of our country. Go to their website, **canadasnorth.com,** and click on the links for each territory, which will direct you to their respective tourism bureaus. What do you think of their approach to attracting tourists? Are they providing enough information to encourage potential tourists to consider the northern territories as a tourist destination spot? What type of "experience" are they actually trying to convey to the potential tourist?

(left): Nunavut logo, Used with permission of the Government of Nunavut; (right): Northwest Territories logo, Used with permission of the Government of the Northwest Territories.

Public relations is an important promotional tool for service firms. It is particularly useful in conveying a proper image and in helping to support a firm's positioning strategy. Public relations tools, such as event sponsorship or public-service activities, are very popular among service companies. This is particularly true for professional services firms, which are often restricted in the use of advertising by their professional governing bodies.

Personal selling also plays an important role in services marketing. It has been said that when a consumer buys a service, he or she is buying the person selling the service. Personal selling is valuable not only in attracting customers but also in retaining them. Service firms are also using social media to promote their businesses. For example, American Express is considered a leader in using social media. It has a major presence on Facebook (its page has millions of likes) and Twitter (thousands of followers) to promote its business. Increasingly, many services marketers are following the path set by packaged-goods firms; that is, they are developing integrated marketing communications plans, which include social media.[25]

People

Many services heavily depend on people for the creation and delivery of the customer service experience.[26] The nature of the interaction between employees and customers strongly influences the customer's perceptions of a service experience. In short, customers will often judge the quality of the service experience based on the performances of the people providing the service. This aspect of services marketing has led to a concept called internal marketing.[27]

Internal marketing is based on the notion that in order for a service organization to serve its customers well, it must care for and treat its employees like valued customers. In essence, it must focus on its employees (or its internal market) before successful marketing efforts can be directed at customers.[28] Internal marketing involves creating an organizational climate in general, and jobs in particular, that will lead to the right service personnel performing the service in the right way. The organization must properly select, train, and motivate all of its employees to work together to provide service quality, excellent customer experiences, and customer satisfaction. Research has shown that service organizations that want to be truly customer oriented must be employee oriented.[29] More and more, service firms are turning to social media and digital platforms to help their people better serve their customers. This means using Facebook and Twitter for customer service purposes. Telus, for example, is using social media for customer service purposes. According to the company, it sees social media as a way to improve its customer service, which has been rated negatively by customers in the past. The company actually brought in its executives to observe the conversations that customers were having with customer services representatives on social media channels in order "walk in their shoes" and to show support for these efforts.[30]

Finally, customer behaviour influences not only their own service outcomes but also the outcomes of other customers. Whether at a hockey game or in a classroom, customers can influence the perceived quality of service by their actions. Therefore, the *people* element in services includes not only the employees and the customer but also other customers.

Physical Evidence

The appearance of the environment in which the service is delivered and where the firm and customer interact can influence the customer's perception of the service. The physical evidence of the service includes all the tangibles surrounding the service: buildings, landscaping, vehicles, furnishings, signage, brochures, social media, and equipment. Service firms need to manage physical evidence carefully and systematically in order to convey the proper impression of the service to the customer. This is sometimes referred to as *impression management,* or evidence management.[31] With highly tangible services, physical evidence provides an opportunity for the firm to send consistent and strong messages about the nature of the service to be delivered.

Process

In services marketing, *process* refers to the actual procedures, mechanisms, and flow of activities by which the service is created and delivered. The actual creation and delivery steps that the customer experiences provide customers with evidence on which to judge the service. In services marketing, process involves not only "what" gets created but also "how" it gets created. The customer contact audit discussed earlier in the chapter is relevant to understanding the service process discussed here. The customer contact audit—the flow chart of the points of interaction between customer and service provider—can serve as a basis for ensuring better service creation and delivery processes. Badly designed processes are likely to create unhappy customers, and poorly conceived operational processes can make it difficult for front-line employees to do their jobs well. Mr. Lube believes that it has the right process in the vehicle oil change and fluid exchange service business. Customers do not need appointments, most stores are open seven days a week, and customers are in and out in 15 to 20 minutes. While the service is being performed, customers can drink a coffee and read the newspaper.

Most services have a limited capacity due to the inseparability of the service from the service provider and the perishable nature of the service. For example, a patient must be in the hospital at the same time as the surgeon to receive an appendectomy, and only one patient can be helped at that time. Similarly, no additional surgery can be conducted tomorrow because of an unused operating room or an available surgeon today—the service capacity is lost if it is not used. So if services marketers have a relatively fixed capacity to produce a service, they must make that capacity as productive as possible without compromising service quality.[32] This is referred to as **capacity management**. The accompanying Using Marketing Dashboards box, "Are Airline Flights Profitably Loaded?" demonstrates how an airline can use a capacity management measure called *load factor* to assess its productivity and profitability.

USING MARKETING DASHBOARDS

Are Airline Flights Profitably Loaded?

Capacity management is critical in the marketing of many services. For example, having the right number of airline seats or hotel rooms available at the right time, price, and place can spell the difference between a profitable or unprofitable service operation.

Airlines often focus on *load factor* as a capacity management measure on their marketing dashboards, along with two other measures: the operating cost per available seat flown one mile, and the revenue generated by each seat flown one mile, called *yield*. Load factor is the percentage of available seats flown one mile occupied by a paying customer.

These three measures combine to show airline operating income or loss per available seat flown one mile.

Operating income (loss) per available seat flown one mile = (Yield × Load Factor) − Operating expenses

Your Challenge As a marketing analyst for a regional Canadian airline, you have been asked to determine the operating income or loss per available seat flown one mile in the first six months of 2016. In addition, you have been asked to determine what load factor the airline must reach to break even, assuming its current yield and operating expense will not change in the immediate future.

Your Findings The airline's yield, load factor, and operating expense marketing dashboard displays are shown below. You can conclude from these measures that the airline posted about a 0.21 cent loss per available seat flown one mile in the first six months in 2016.

Operating loss per available seat flown one mile = (9.83 cents × 82.1%) − 8.28 cents = −0.2096 cents

Assuming the airline's yield and operating expenses will not change and using a little math, the airline's load factor will have to increase from 82.1% to 84.23% to break even.

Operating income (loss) per available seat flown one mile = (9.83 cents × Load factor) = 8.28 cents = 0 cents

(Load factor = 84.23%)

Your Action Assuming yield and operating expenses will not change, you should recommend that the airline consider revising its flight schedules to better accommodate traveller needs and advertise these changes. Consideration might also be given to how the airline utilizes its existing airline fleet to serve its customers and produce a profit.

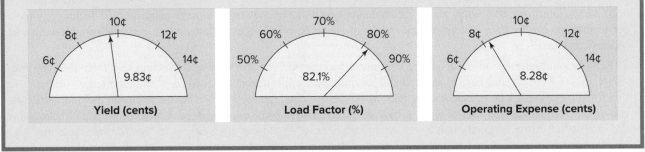

Service organizations must manage the availability of the offering so that (1) demand matches capacity over the duration of the demand cycle (e.g., one day, week, month, year), and (2) the organization's assets are used in ways that will maximize the return on investment.[33] Figure 12–6 shows how a hotel tries to manage its capacity during the high and low seasons. Differing price structures are assigned to each segment of consumers to help moderate or adjust demand for the service. Airline contracts fill a fixed number of rooms throughout the year. In the slow season, when more rooms are available, tour packages at appealing prices are used to attract groups or conventions, such as an offer for seven nights at a reduced price. Weekend packages are also offered to buyers. In high-demand season, groups are less desirable because more individual guests will be available and willing to pay higher prices. The use of **off-peak pricing**, which consists of charging different prices during different times of the day or days of the week to reflect variations in demand for the service, plays an important role in capacity management. For example, airlines offer discounts for weekend travel, movie theatres offer matinee pricing, and restaurants offer early-bird pricing in order to maintain the productivity of their service capacity.

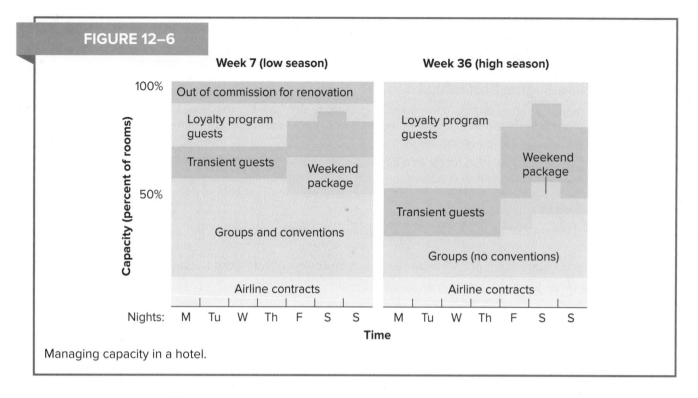

FIGURE 12–6

Managing capacity in a hotel.

SERVICES IN THE FUTURE

What can we expect from the services industry in the future? New and better services, of course, and an unprecedented variety of choices. Many of the changes will be the result of four factors: technological development, improved understanding of service delivery and consumption, the social imperative for sustainability, and the consumers' desire for unique, personable, and memorable experiences.

Technological advances are rapidly changing the services industry. The key elements of future services include mobility and personalization. AT&T, for example, recently introduced its mobile subscription service, Mobile TV, which allows consumers to view ESPN, Disney, Fox News, and other programs on their smartphones. Similarly, Google has introduced Nexus Player with Android TV, a smart TV platform that provides programming, app, and gaming options through voice recognition and app interfaces; the system makes recommendations based on viewing and usage behaviours.[34] Technology-mediated personalization can increase customers' perceptions of value; however, excessive attempts at personalization can also trigger privacy concerns.[35]

New data and information about service consumers and providers is also leading to changes in service delivery and consumption. For example, one health care study discovered that cardiac patients learned more and reported 98 percent satisfaction when they shared a 90-minute appointment with other patients, rather than meeting the doctor in the traditional, shorter, one-on-one format. Other studies of services have discovered that in some businesses, such as retailing, restaurants, and repair and installation, customer satisfaction levels are inflated because employees often engage in "service sweethearting"—giving unauthorized free products or services to customers. Many of these businesses are now changing employee recruiting and training activities to limit this type of behaviour. Both examples emphasize how understanding the details of service transactions will lead to new forms of service in the future.[36]

The growing interest in sustainability and "green" businesses is also changing the services industry. This trend began when consumers became aware of the environmental impact of many products such as automobiles, appliances, and cleaning solutions. Today, this trend has expanded to include consumers' assessment of services. Recent surveys indicate that green practices influence many consumer purchase decisions for services, including those provided by dry cleaners, contractors, and hotels. In response, many service providers are developing new approaches to their offerings. Hilton, for example, has set conservation goals to help its hotels achieve environmental management certification from the International Organization for Standardization (ISO). These and other approaches are likely to expand globally as services strive to create a competitive advantage.

Finally, both today and the future belong to service firms that can successfully create and deliver unique, personable, and memorable customer experiences. As a result of increased competition, many services have become commoditized or are seen by most consumers to be virtually identical. In that case, price often becomes the driver when making a service selection. But many consumers want something more than just a commoditized service and are prepared to pay for it. For example, consider the In-Tenta Drop Eco-Hotel. It consists of a series of portable pod hotel rooms that can be moved to different locations to take advantage of breathtaking views. Or what about the Hôtel de Glace in Quebec. At this "ice hotel," you can have a unique sub-zero experience in the individually themed rooms.

Read the accompanying Marketing Matters box, "Seven Steps to Creating Great Service Experiences!" to see just how services marketers can create real and distinctive customer experiences that differentiate themselves from commoditized services providers. Successful service firms like the Ritz-Carlton embrace comprehensive point-to-point customer experience management approaches. To do so, they place special emphasis on high-quality employee interaction with customers. Therefore, hiring, training, and motivating service-minded employees must be part of the service firm's overall customer experience management program. More importantly, research shows that the most profitable services firms focus their efforts on "money making delighters" that often do not add significant cost to the firm,[37]

MARKETING MATTERS

Seven Steps to Creating Great Service Experiences!

According to Ian Stuart, designing services that deliver memorable personal experiences is a science and an art. Using a theatre analogy, Stuart provides seven critical steps required for services marketers to make the leap from merely satisfying the customer to delivering great service experiences.

1. Stay narrowly focused and within your defined resource capabilities. This focus will ensure consistency of performance.

2. Communicate and share the service vision extensively, particularly with those with management responsibilities. This is vital for buy-in at all levels of the organization.

3. Be ever vigilant to ensure consistency and authenticity in all aspects of the service product, from the largest to smallest detail.

4. Integrate across all elements (including technical, performance, and business), using structured and unstructured communication mechanisms. Importantly, there should be an emphasis on supporting front-line service providers.

5. Create a spirit of experimentation and innovation for all service employees by encouraging everyone's involvement in the creative process. Constantly innovating to find better ways to excite the customer is key.

6. Strive for total role and performance immersion from all front-line service providers through extensive training and rehearsals.

7. Facilitate, do not direct. Integrate and lead, do not command and control.

Stuart suggests that if services marketers follow these seven steps, customers will be delighted with the service experience and remain loyal to the service organization.

Learning Review

7. Matching demand with capacity is the focus of _____ management.

8. What factors will influence the services industries in the future?

Learning Objectives Review

 Describe four unique elements of services.

The four unique elements of services—the four Is of services—are intangibility, inconsistency, inseparability, and inventory. Intangibility refers to the tendency of services to be a performance that cannot be held or touched. Inconsistency is a characteristic of services because services depend on people to deliver them, and people vary in their capabilities and in their day-to-day performance. Inseparability refers to the difficulty of separating the deliverer of the service (hair stylist) from the service itself (haircut). And services are produced and consumed simultaneously, requiring the consumer to be present for both the production and consumption processes. Inventory refers to the need to have service production capability when there is service demand.

 Explain the service continuum.

Many organizations do not market pure services or pure goods. In general, companies market products that have tangible and intangible characteristics. As companies look at what they bring to market, there is a range from the tangible to the intangible or good-dominant to service-dominant offerings, referred to as a service continuum.

 Understand how consumers purchase services.

Because services are intangible, pre-purchase evaluation is difficult for consumers. To choose a service, consumers use search, experience, and credence qualities to evaluate the good and service elements of a service offering. Because of the uncertainty created by experience and credence qualities, consumers often turn to personal sources of information, such as early adopters, opinion leaders, and reference group members, during the purchase decision process.

 Develop a customer contact audit to understand the service purchasing process.

A customer contact audit is a flow chart of the points of interaction between a consumer and a service provider. The interactions identified in the contact audit can help better understand the purchasing purchase and help create and deliver better services that ensure a satisfying experience for the customer.

 Understand how customers evaluate the services they have purchased.

Once the consumer tries a service, it is evaluated by comparing expectations with the actual service experience on five dimensions of service quality: tangibles, reliability, responsiveness, assurance, and empathy. Differences between expectations and experience are identified through gap analysis.

LO6 Explain the special nature of the marketing mix for services: the seven Ps of services marketing.

In addition to the traditional marketing mix (the four Ps) mentioned frequently throughout this text, the distinctive nature of services require that other variables be effectively managed by services marketers. These include people, physical evidence, and process. Collectively, the marketing mix for services is referred to as the seven Ps of services marketing. Many services depend on people to create and deliver services, and thus people must be hired, trained, and motivated correctly. The physical environment (physical evidence) where the services are created must be managed to convey the proper impression to the customer. The process by which services are created and delivered must also be managed effectively in order for customers to receive the service in a timely and appropriate manner. And the process must effectively manage the capacity of the service system (capacity management).

Applying Marketing Knowledge

1. Explain how the four Is of services would apply to a branch office of TD Canada Trust.

2. Idle production capacity may be related to inventory or capacity management. How would the pricing component of the marketing mix reduce idle production capacity for (a) a car wash, (b) a stage theatre group, and (c) a university?

3. Look back at the service continuum in Figure 12–2. Explain how the following points on the continuum differ in terms of consistency: (a) salt, (b) automobile, (c) advertising agency, and (d) teaching.

4. What are the search, experience, and credence properties of an airline for the business traveller and pleasure traveller? What properties are most important to each group?

5. Outline the customer contact audit for a typical check-in experience at a local hotel.

6. The text suggests that internal marketing is necessary before a successful marketing program can be directed at consumers. Why is this particularly true for service organizations?

7. Outline the capacity management strategies that an airline must consider.

8. How does off-peak pricing influence demand for services?

9. Physical evidence is one of the seven Ps of services marketing. How would a physician go about managing the physical evidence of her practice to convey the proper image to her patients?

10. This chapter suggests that consumers judge service quality along five key dimensions: tangibles, reliability, responsiveness, assurance, and empathy. Which dimension is most important to you when you judge the following services: (a) a physician, (b) a bank, (c) car rental, and (d) dry cleaning?

Building Your Marketing Plan

In this section of your marketing plan, you should distinguish between your core product—a good or a service—and your supplementary services.

1. Develop an internal marketing program that will ensure that employees are prepared to deliver the core and supplementary services.

2. Conduct a customer contact audit and create a flow chart to identify specific points of interaction with customers.

3. Describe marketing activities that will (a) address each of the seven Ps as they relate to your service, and (b) encourage the development of relationships with your customers.

Add this as an appendix to your marketing plan and use the results in developing your marketing mix strategy.

LA Galaxy: Where Sports Marketing Is a Kick!

"We have a unique product for people," exclaims Chris Klein, president of the LA Galaxy soccer club. Soccer combines many elements of athleticism, teamwork, and competition to make it fast, exciting, engaging, fun, and increasingly popular. Klein goes on to explain, "This is a cool sport, and it's something that's growing." His enthusiasm is supported by a sophisticated strategy that Klein and his marketing team have designed to help people "experience the excitement" of their product!

The LA Galaxy

The LA Galaxy is a professional soccer club competing in the Major League Soccer (MLS) league. The club was one of ten charter clubs when the league began, and is now part of the league's Western Conference. "The LA Galaxy was founded in 1996," says Klein, and "through the course of the league's history, the Galaxy has been the most successful franchise in Major League Soccer." The team has been conference champions nine times, regular season champions four times, and MLS champions five times.

The first Galaxy games were played at the Rose Bowl in Pasadena, California, until the team moved to its current location in the soccer-specific stadium StubHub Center in Carson, California. Players are primarily from the United States but also represent countries such as Brazil, Ireland, Italy, and Panama. "We have signed some of the biggest players, not only in our country, like Cobi Jones and Landon Donovan, but we've also signed some of the biggest players in the world," explains Klein. English soccer superstar David Beckham joined the LA Galaxy in 2007 and played through 2012, helping the team win two championships during that period.

Today, the LA Galaxy attracts an average of 23,000 fans to each of its games. While the hardcore fans tend to be 18- to 34-year-old men, the team also appeals to many other segments. For example, because soccer is the largest participant sport in the United States, many kids and youth soccer teams come to the games. In addition, many college students and families attend. According to Klein, it's a welcoming environment where "you can paint your face and yell" or you can bring your kids and just "have fun at the game." The team's mascot, Cozmo, is a frog-like extraterrestrial who entertains fans at the games and throughout Southern California.

Major League Soccer

As part of its negotiation to hold the 1994 FIFA (Federation Internationale de Football Association) World Cup in the United States, the U.S. Soccer Federation promised to establish a professional soccer league. The result was Major League Soccer. Since its beginning with 10 teams in 1996, Major League Soccer has expanded to 20 teams, including 3 teams in Canada. Each team plays 34 games during the regular season from March to October, and the top 12 teams participate in the playoffs, which end with the MLS Cup in December.

Even though soccer is popular around the world, introducing professional soccer in the United States presented some difficulties. Klein describes the problem:

> Soccer is the biggest sport in the world, but here in the U.S. we have a lot of competition. Major League Soccer is the equivalent to Major League Baseball, the NFL, the NBA, and the NHL. These are established leagues and MLS is the fifth major sport. In 1996, we started thinking that we had to get every baseball fan, basketball fan, and football fan to enjoy our sport.

To attempt to attract fans from other sports, MLS experimented with changes to traditional soccer rules. For example, MLS added shootouts to resolve tie games, used a countdown (to zero) clock rather than a progressive clock, allowed extra substitutions, and even considered making the goals bigger to increase the scoring. Eventually, the league concluded that the changes had alienated some traditional soccer fans without attracting new fans from other sports, so it went back to the traditional rules for MLS games.

As the league shifted from an "attract all sports fans" philosophy to a focus on people with some existing interest in soccer, it made several other changes. First, it began moving MLS games from large, rented, football facilities to new, smaller, more intimate soccer-specific stadiums. In addition, the league made efforts to internationalize the teams by allowing up to eight players per team from outside of the United States. Finally, MLS encouraged all teams to create youth development programs to help find talented local players. To complement these efforts, each team manages its own marketing program.

The LA Galaxy Marketing Program

"The primary marketing objective for the Galaxy is ticket sales," says Casey Leppanen, senior director of marketing and broadcasting. "Our product is soccer," he goes on to explain, "but we are more than that. We are an experience." So to sell single-game tickets and season tickets, the Galaxy developed a comprehensive marketing program. According to Leppanen, "Our marketing mix is pretty similar to any other sports team or company you're going to find." The key difference in marketing a sport, or any service, is that every game offers a different experience to fans. The players, the opponents, the weather, and the outcomes of the games change constantly.

How does the Galaxy sell a product that is constantly changing? The first step is to understand that different segments may attend a soccer game for different types of experiences. For example:

© Shaun Clark/Getty Images

- *Supporter clubs.* Attend to watch the strategy of a game and see the Galaxy score.

- *Families.* Want to have fun, see the mascot, and get a souvenir.

- *Latino community.* Enjoy watching soccer and forming connections with players from Central and South America.

- *Trendsetting youth.* Attend to meet friends, enjoy an event, and see star players.

- *Groups (teams, corporations, religious groups, etc.).* Want an opportunity for networking and team building.

The different interests combined with the changing "product" create a special marketing challenge. The experience the Galaxy provides to fans is much more than watching a soccer game. It includes quality of play, individual members of the team, merchandise, food, facilities, activities, and interactions with staff, other fans, and players. Some of the specific elements of the Galaxy game experience include:

- *Star players.* Robbie Keane, Steven Gerrard, Sebastian Lletget, and Giovani dos Santos are all soccer stars who attract fans.

- *Team LA Store.* Offers LA Galaxy merchandise at StubHub Center and other locations.

- *Supporter clubs.* Three clubs—the Angel City Brigade, the Riot Squad, and the Galaxians—offer the opportunity to participate in an intense and festive fan experience, complete with songs and chants.

- *Promotional nights.* Special events include Family Nights, Bobblehead Nights, Jersey-Off-The-Back Auctions, and Student Nights.

- *Name in Lights.* A donation gets your message on the home game scoreboard.

- *Cozmo.* The team mascot who entertains all fans at every game.

- *StubHub Center.* The soccer-specific stadium offers a great atmosphere, amazing sight lines, event suites, terrace cabanas, restaurants, assigned seating, general admission seating, and an inclined lawn (also called the berm) for picnic-style seating.

Of course, there are many other elements that are all part of the experience the Galaxy marketing team manages and delivers at every game.

Next, the Galaxy must deliver relevant messages to each segment. Leppanen explains that the Galaxy "want to make sure that we're delivering an authentic message, but speak[ing] to them with what they want to be spoken about." One way they accomplish this is through direct marketing, which consists of e-mail messages and direct-mail literature. These messages are complemented with traditional media advertising, outdoor advertising, and digital advertising. The traditional media include radio, TV, and print. The outdoor advertising includes billboards and bus wraps. The digital platforms, which have a total of 1.3 million Galaxy fan users, include Facebook, Twitter, YouTube, Google+, Instagram, Pinterest, Flickr, and Foursquare. Digital is a very important part of the mix because "we can get really granular and sophisticated in who we're targeting and how we speak to them," explains Leppanen.

The Galaxy also use personal selling as part of their marketing program. A team of 25 people makes personal phone calls to help sell single-game tickets, family packs, group tickets, and season tickets. There are also two teams of brand ambassadors called the Star Squad and the Galaxy Street Team who are involved in about 500 events in the community each year. Lori Nevares, a marketing coordinator at Galaxy and former Street Team member, explains, "We got to go out and do all kinds of promotional events for different communities and see the fans and how much they were devoted to the Galaxy." A skills team called the Galaxy Futboleros provides high-energy performances throughout the community as well. Finally, Cozmo makes many appearances to deliver the Galaxy soccer message to current and potential fans.

© Carrie Jesenovec/Icon SMI/ Corbis

One of the final steps in the ticket sales process is setting the price. According to Heather Pease, director of ticketing, "Every year we conduct a very in-depth analysis of our ticket sales. We go seat-by-seat, row-by-row, and category-by-category to see how many people have purchased seats and at what price." The analysis also includes a comparison of ticket prices at other sports teams in the area. Pease then uses the information to create a price and a package for every possible type of fan, ranging from Champions Lounge members, to season ticket holders, to groups or families, to single-game fans. She also offers discounted tickets for students and children.

There are a lot of marketing activities taking place at the Galaxy. In fact, Casey Leppanen says, "My role here at the Galaxy is to integrate all the pieces of our marketing department." The integration is paying off, as attendance at LA Galaxy games is well above the league average. In addition, the team currently has 8,500 season ticket holders and plans to reach 12,500 in three years.

The Business of Soccer

While ticket sales represent a substantial source of revenue for the Galaxy, there are several other important elements of the soccer "business"—broadcast rights, sponsorships, and merchandise—that the team must manage. Early in the league's history, MLS had to pay television and cable networks to broadcast its games. As the number of viewers increased, however, the league was able to attract coverage from ESPN, ABC, NBC, and Fox. The Galaxy recently began a 10-year, $55 million deal with the Time Warner Cable Sports network. Currently, all games have television and radio coverage in English and Spanish, and there is play-by-play coverage and webchat on **LAGalaxy.com**.

Sponsorships are also essential to the financial success of MLS and the Galaxy. Pepsi is the official soft drink and Aquafina is the official water of MLS. Similarly, Herbalife is the official nutrition company of the LA Galaxy. In addition, Herbalife recently announced a 10-year agreement to be the official jersey sponsor of the Galaxy. Herbalife pays $4 million annually to sponsor the team and place its logo on the front of the team jerseys. Other team sponsors include Chevrolet, Nestlé, Alaska Airlines, Shasta, and Buffalo Wild Wings. The sponsors participate in many of the team's contests, promotions, and events to support the team and to gain exposure to customers with similar values and interests.

The marketing team at the LA Galaxy is always busy. "There is a business to run," says Pease. "It is about driving revenue at the end of the day," she continues, "but the best part about it is you get to walk out on a game day and see a sold-out stadium." Seeing the sold-out stadium is a thrill not only because it's a business, however, but also because the marketing team loves soccer. Galaxy president Chris Klein, who studied business and marketing in college, is a good example of the attitude at Galaxy. "I went to college on a soccer scholarship," says Klein, "then I played professionally in our league, and I'm now president of a major club." He is thrilled by "the challenge of marketing a sport that I love, a sport that I've played, and a sport that has so much potential."

QUESTIONS

1. What is the LA Galaxy "product"?

2. Which of the seven elements of the service marketing mix are most important in the LA Galaxy marketing program?

3. How is promotion (advertising, personal selling, public relations, sales promotion, direct marketing) used by the LA Galaxy? Do these activities depend on the specific target markets?

4. How are social media integrated into the LA Galaxy's marketing strategy?

5. How does the LA Galaxy assess the impact of its marketing activities? Has its program been successful?

Case: This case was written by Steven Hartley. Sources: "Landon Donovan Retires a Champion as Galaxy Win MLS Cup," *Time*, December 8, 2014; "Galaxy's Home Has New Name," *Daily News of Los Angeles*, March 5, 2013, p. A1; Kevin Baxter, "Beckham Will Hang Up His Boots: A Star In Europe, His Late Career Move to the Galaxy Brought U.S. Fans to Soccer and Put MLS on Map," *Los Angeles Times*, May 17, 2013, p. C2; "Galaxy, Tim Warner Strike 10-Year, $55 Million Deal," *Daily News of Los Angeles*, November 16, 2011, p. C6; denz@rslsoapbox.com, "For Major League Soccer It Is All About the Numbers, TV, Attendance, and Season Tickets," rslsoapbox.com, May 18, 2012; Karl Greenberg, "Chevrolet Cleats Up for L.A. Galaxy Sponsorship," *Marketing Daily*, May 28, 2013; LA Galaxy website, www.lagalaxy.com, accessed July 26, 2013; and personal interviews with LA Galaxy personnel.

13

Pricing Products and Services

Vizio, Inc.—Delivering Beautifully Smart Products at a Great Value

Can you name North America's #1 smart TV company? Stumped? It's VIZIO, Inc., an entrepreneurial firm with a bold agenda. "Our goal is to be the next Sony in 20 to 30 years," says William Wang, VIZIO's co-founder and chief executive officer, who was born in Taiwan and immigrated to the United States at age 13.

In 2002, Mr. Wang was struck by an ad for a $10,000 flat-panel HDTV set and immediately saw an opportunity. Instead of marketing these sets as luxury items, Mr. Wang thought he could make and market an HDTV that would be affordable for the average customer.

Like many entrepreneurs, he borrowed money from friends and family and mortgaged his home. Within a year, he formed a company that is now known as VIZIO, Inc., and delivered the company's first VIZIO HDTV to Costco for distribution through that company's stores. VIZIO HDTVs are now sold through Costco, Walmart, BJ's Wholesale, Best Buy, Sam's Club, and Target stores in the U.S., along with authorized online partners such as Amazon. The company has sold more than 38 million HDTV units shipped since 2002.

VIZIO Internet Apps Plus™   VIZIO Internet Apps Plus™

YouTube: Second-Screen Experience   Full-Screen Apps Window

VIZIO's ability to deliver affordable HDTVs to the average customer is based on a novel strategy. VIZIO didn't invest in expensive manufacturing facilities but instead relied on contract manufacturers to build its products. Product development and marketing specialists in the United States handle product design and marketing. "The whole goal is to ensure that we have the right product at the right time and the right price and really drive a seamless end-to-end value chain," says a company spokesperson.

"VIZIO HDTVs are more popular and in greater demand than ever," adds Laynie Newsome, VIZIO's co-founder and chief sales officer. "Consumers want to save money without sacrificing quality or technology." Matt McRae, VIZIO's chief technology officer, adds that VIZIO's strategy is to make affordable products with innovative features, saying, "We're far from the cheapest brand on the market at present. Everybody deserves the latest technology, too."[1]

VIZIO's visionary commitment to delivering high-quality technology at a great value to consumers is evident by its pioneering role in launching smart TVs in 2010. Smart TV enables viewers to watch content from the Internet directly on their TV, for a more interactive TV-watching experience. VIZIO has sold more than 3.2 million smart TVs since 2010, making it North America's #1 smart TV company.

VIZIO's powerful and profitable price-value position clearly resonates with consumers. VIZIO is frequently ranked "Highest in Customer Satisfaction" with HDTVs by J.D. Power and Associates and listed among the largest privately held companies in the United States. Not bad for a company with about 400 employees and just 14 years old![2]

Welcome to the fascinating—and intense—world of pricing. This chapter describes the important factors organizations consider when they go about setting prices for their products and services.

NATURE AND IMPORTANCE OF PRICE

The price paid for goods and services goes by many names. You pay *tuition* for your education, *rent* for an apartment, *interest* on a bank credit card, and a *premium* for car insurance. Your dentist or physician charges you a *fee,* a professional or social organization charges *dues,* and operators of the Confederation Bridge charge you a *fare* or a *toll* to use their bridge. In business, a consultant may require a *retainer* for services rendered, an executive is given a *salary,* a salesperson receives a *commission,* and a worker is paid a *wage.* Of course, what you pay for clothes or a haircut is termed a *price.*

Among all marketing and operations factors in a business firm, price has a unique role. It is the place where all other business decisions come together. The price must be "right," in the sense that customers must be able and willing to pay it; it must generate enough sales dollars to pay for the cost of developing, producing, and marketing the product; and it must earn a profit for the company. Even small changes in price can have big effects on both the number of units sold and company profit.

What Is a Price?

The examples above highlight the many varied ways that price plays a part in our daily lives. From a marketing viewpoint, **price** is the money or other considerations (including other goods and services) exchanged for the ownership or use of a good or service. For example, Shell Oil recently exchanged one million pest-control devices for sugar from a Caribbean country, and Wilkinson Sword exchanged some of its knives for advertising used to promote its razor blades. This practice of exchanging goods and services for other goods and services rather than for money is called *barter*. These transactions account for billions of dollars annually in domestic and international trade.

For most products and services, money is exchanged, although the amount is not always the same as the list or quoted price because of the discounts, allowances, and extra fees. The factors that increase or decrease the final price of an offering help consumers construct a "price equation," which is shown in Figure 13–1.

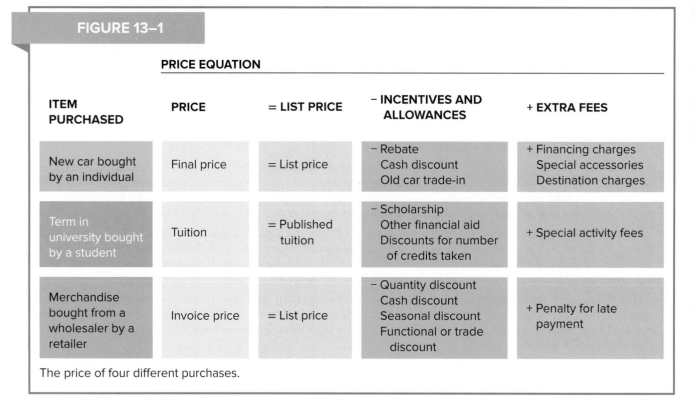

FIGURE 13–1

PRICE EQUATION

ITEM PURCHASED	PRICE	= LIST PRICE	– INCENTIVES AND ALLOWANCES	+ EXTRA FEES
New car bought by an individual	Final price	= List price	– Rebate Cash discount Old car trade-in	+ Financing charges Special accessories Destination charges
Term in university bought by a student	Tuition	= Published tuition	– Scholarship Other financial aid Discounts for number of credits taken	+ Special activity fees
Merchandise bought from a wholesaler by a retailer	Invoice price	= List price	– Quantity discount Cash discount Seasonal discount Functional or trade discount	+ Penalty for late payment

The price of four different purchases.

Price as an Indicator of Value

From a consumer's perspective, price is often used to indicate value when it is compared with the benefits of the product. Specifically, *value* is defined as the ratio of perceived benefits to price.[3] At a given price, as perceived benefits increase, perceived value increases. For example, if you are used to paying $12.99 for a medium pizza from Pizza Pizza, wouldn't a large pizza at the same price be more valuable? Many marketers often engage in the practice of *value pricing*—increasing product or service benefits while maintaining or decreasing price.

But marketers must be careful when using price as an indicator of value. For example, for many consumers, a low price might imply possible poor quality, and ultimately, poor perceived value.[4] This is particularly true for services.[5] For example, what would be your perception of a dentist who charges only $25 for a checkup and cleaning when the average dentist charges between $100 and $150? This example also illustrates that consumers will often make comparative value assessments. That is, the consumer will judge one product or service against other alternatives or substitutes. In doing so, a "reference value" emerges, which involves comparing the prices and benefits of substitute items.

However, intense competition in many industries has led to lower prices for consumers. Accordingly, some research indicates that consumers may have changed their attitudes toward lower prices in this new low-cost world. In short, consumers may not always perceive lower prices as connoting poor value or poor quality.[6] Moreover, recent Canadian research shows consumers are willing to trade off best quality for lower prices. For example, two-thirds of Canadian consumers surveyed reported "paying the lowest price was very important" in terms of their purchasing priorities, and lower prices trumped best product quality in terms of overall product attributes.[7]

Price in the Marketing Mix

Pricing is also a critical decision made by a marketing executive because price has a direct effect on a firm's profits. This is apparent from a firm's **profit equation**:

$$\text{Profit} = \text{Total revenue} - \text{Total cost}$$

or

$$\text{Profit} = (\text{Unit price} \times \text{Quantity sold}) - \text{Total cost}$$

What makes this relationship even more important is that price affects the quantity sold, as illustrated with demand curves later in this chapter. Furthermore, because the quantity sold sometimes affects a firm's costs because of efficiency of production, price also indirectly affects costs. Thus, pricing decisions influence both total revenue and total cost, which makes pricing one of the most important decisions marketing executives face.

The importance of price in the marketing mix necessitates an understanding of six major steps involved in the process organizations go through in setting prices (Figure 13–2):

1. Identifying pricing constraints and objectives
2. Estimating demand and revenue
3. Estimating cost, volume, and profit relationships
4. Selecting an approximate price level
5. Setting the list or quoted price
6. Making special adjustments to the list or quoted price

FIGURE 13–2

Step 1	Step 2	Step 3	Step 4	Step 5	Step 6
Identify pricing constraints and objectives • Constraints like demand for product class and brand, newness, costs, and competition • Objectives like profit, market share, and survival	**Estimate demand and revenue** • Demand estimation • Price elasticity estimation • Revenue estimation	**Estimate cost, volume, and profit relationships** • Cost estimation • Break-even analysis, relation to profit	**Select an approximate price level** • Demand-oriented approaches • Cost-oriented approaches • Profit-oriented approaches • Competition-oriented approaches	**Set list or quoted price** • One price or flexible prices • Company, customer, and competitive effects	**Make special adjustments to list or quoted price** • Discounts • Allowances • Geographical adjustments

Steps in setting price.

 ## STEP 1: IDENTIFYING PRICING CONSTRAINTS AND OBJECTIVES

With such a variety of alternative pricing strategies available, a marketing manager must consider the pricing constraints and pricing objectives that will narrow the range of choices. Pricing constraints relate to conditions existing in the marketplace, while pricing objectives frequently reflect corporate goals. Let us first review the pricing constraints so that we can better understand the nature of pricing alternatives. Then, we will examine pricing objectives.

Identifying Pricing Constraints

Factors that limit the latitude of prices a firm may set are **pricing constraints**. Consumer demand for the product clearly affects the price that can be charged. Other constraints on price vary from factors within the organization to competitive factors outside the organization. Moreover, legal and regulatory factors, discussed at the end of this chapter, also restrict the prices an organization can set.

Demand for the Product Class, Product, and Brand

The number of potential buyers for the product class (such as cars), product (sports cars), and brand (Dodge Viper) clearly affects the price a seller can charge. So does the question of whether the item is a luxury (a Viper) or a necessity (bread and a roof over your head). In fact, when a consumer is in urgent need of a particular necessity, a marketer may command a premium price. In this case, there may be ethical issues involved (see the accompanying Making Responsible Decisions box, "Getting an Unfair Premium Price?").[8]

MAKING RESPONSIBLE DECISIONS

Getting an Unfair Premium Price?

Consumer advocates argue that pharmaceutical companies have a general tendency to command premium prices for necessary drug products knowing that consumers usually have little choice but to pay them. For example, Pompe disease is a neuromuscular disease that is almost always fatal for infants. Genzyme has developed a drug to treat the disease but it costs an American patient over $300,000 per year and it must be used for life. In Canada, the drug costs over $80,000, but Health Canada allows for public funding for "some" sufferers of the disease. But critics of companies who charge premium pricing say the practice is not isolated to pharmaceutical companies. Oil companies, for example, are often criticized for raising prices on home heating oil during the cold Canadian winters. But the oil companies argue it is simply a supply-and-demand issue. Price-gouging claims are also levied against major airlines during peak travel periods, and individual companies are sometimes accused of price gouging during shortages. For example, during water shortages, bottled water suppliers have sometimes increased the price of their product by two to three times its original price. University students also often report paying high and unfair prices for off-campus housing when demand is high and supply is low.

The practice of commanding premium prices for luxuries and necessities appears to be gaining acceptability with marketers. Moreover, recent Canadian research suggests that some corporate executives and entrepreneurs have no ethical issues with knowingly overcharging customers for products and services.

Is the use of premium pricing for necessities fair? Is it ethical? What should be done about this practice?

Newness of the Product: Stage in the Product Life Cycle

The newer a product and the earlier it is in its life cycle, the higher the price that can usually be charged. Consider the Apple iPhone. Initially, with this new technology, Apple had no other direct competition, so it was possible to ask consumers to pay a high initial high price for this innovative product. And many consumers were interested in paying $500 for the iPhone.

Single Product versus a Product Line

When Apple introduced its iPad, not only was it unique and in the introductory stage of its product life cycle but also it was the first commercially successful tablet device sold. As a result, Apple had great latitude in setting a price. Now, with a wide range of competition in tablets from Samsung, Motorola, and others, Apple is developing a product line of iPad models with different price points.

Cost of Producing and Marketing the Product

In the long run, a firm's price must cover all the costs of producing and marketing a product. If the price does not cover the cost, the firm will fail, and so in the long term, a firm's costs set a floor under its price. Marketers must also ensure that firms in their channels of distribution make an adequate profit. Without profits for channel members, a marketer is cut off from its customers. For example, of the $200 a customer spends for a pair of designer denim jeans, 50 percent of each dollar spent goes to a specialty retailer to cover its costs and profit. The other 50 percent goes to the marketer (34 percent) and manufacturers and suppliers (16 percent). So the next time you buy a $200 pair of designer denim jeans, remember that $100 goes to the specialty retailer that stocked, displayed, and sold the jeans to you.

Cost of Changing Prices and the Time Period They Apply

If Air Canada asks General Electric (GE) to provide spare jet engines to power its Boeing 737s, GE can easily set a new price for the engines to reflect its latest information, as only one buyer has to be informed. But if Sears Canada decides that sweater prices are too low in its winter catalogues after thousands of catalogues have been mailed to customers, it has a big problem, and so it must consider the cost of changing prices and the time period for which the changes apply in developing the price list for its catalogue items. In actual practice, research indicates that most firms change the price for their major products once a year. But in the online environment, prices can change from minute to minute. So Sears, with its online virtual catalogues, can easily make price changes where it cannot with its printed versions.

Type of Competitive Markets

The seller's price is constrained by the type of market in which it competes. Economists generally delineate four types of competitive markets: pure monopoly, oligopoly, monopolistic competition, and pure competition. Figure 13–3 shows that the type of competition dramatically influences the latitude of price competition and, in turn, the nature of product differentiation and extent of advertising. A firm must recognize the general type of competitive market it is in to understand the latitude of both its price and non-price strategies. For example, prices can be significantly affected by four competitive situations:

- *Pure monopoly.* In 1994, Johnson & Johnson (J&J) revolutionized the treatment of coronary heart diseases by introducing the *stent*—a tiny mesh tube "spring" that props clogged arteries open. Initially a monopolist, J&J stuck with its early $2,235 price and achieved $1.4 billion in sales and 91 percent market share in the category. But its reluctance to give price reductions for large-volume purchases antagonized hospitals. When competitors introduced an improved stent at lower prices, J&J's market share plummeted to 8 percent just two years later.[9]

- *Oligopoly.* The few sellers of aluminum (Alcan, Alcoa) try to avoid price competition because it can lead to disastrous price wars in which all lose money. Yet firms in such industries stay aware of a competitor's price cuts or increases and may follow suit. The products can be undifferentiated (aluminum) or differentiated (jetliners), and informative advertising that avoids head-to-head price competition is used.

- *Monopolistic competition.* Dozens of regional, private brands of peanut butter compete with national brands, such as Skippy and Kraft. Both price competition (regional, private brands being lower than national brands) and non-price competition (product features and advertising) exist.

- *Pure competition.* Hundreds of local grain elevators sell corn for which price per bushel is set by the marketplace. Within strains, the corn is identical, and so advertising only informs buyers that the seller's corn is available.

Competitors' Prices and Consumers' Awareness of Them

A company must know what specific prices its present and potential competitors are charging now as well as what they are likely to charge in the near future. The company then develops a marketing mix strategy—including setting prices—to respond to its competitors' prices. Today, the Internet has increased the number of "present and potential competitors" exponentially for many products.

Competitors' prices are important only if a prospective buyer both (1) knows about those prices and (2) can act to purchase them easily. Competitor changes and price transparency through the Internet and efficient distribution make possible (1) consumer-driven pricing actions and (2) seller/retailer-driven pricing actions.

- *Consumer-driven pricing actions.* With consumers able to compare prices on the Internet, they can make more efficient buying decisions. This occurs, say, when a consumer visits the HDTV section of a store to actually examine a TV—and then goes home and orders it online at a lower price. RedLaser, an eBay-owned smartphone app, enables consumers to scan a product's barcode on a store's shelf and then compare that price to those both online and in nearby stores.

- *Seller/retailer-driven pricing actions.* Aggressive price changes through the Internet started when airlines constantly changed ticket prices to fill the seats on their planes using their yield management systems. Today, many sellers are changing online prices even faster.

Identifying Pricing Objectives

Expectations that specify the role of price in an organization's marketing and strategic plans are **pricing objectives**. To the extent possible, these organizational pricing objectives are also carried to lower levels in the organization, such as in setting objectives for marketing managers responsible for an individual brand. These objectives may change depending on the financial position of the company as a whole, the success of its products, the target segments served by the company, or the competitive environment. For example, H.J. Heinz has specific pricing objectives for its ketchup, which vary by country.

FIGURE 13–3

TYPE OF COMPETITIVE MARKET

STRATEGIES AVAILABLE	PURE COMPETITION (Many sellers who follow the market price for identical, commodity products)	MONOPOLISTIC COMPETITION (Many sellers who compete on non-price factors)	OLIGOPOLY (Few sellers who are sensitive to each other's prices)	PURE MONOPOLY (One seller who sets the price for a unique product)
Extent of price competition	Almost none: market sets price	Some: compete over range of prices	Some: price leader or follower of competitors	None: sole seller sets price
Extent of product differentiation	None: products are identical	Some: differentiate products from competitors	Various: depends on industry	None: no other producers
Extent of advertising	Little: purpose is to inform prospects that seller's products are available	Much: purpose is to differentiate firm's products from competitors	Some: purpose is to inform but avoid price competition	Little: purpose is to increase demand for product class

Pricing, product, and advertising strategies available to firms in four types of competitive markets.

Profit

Three different objectives relate to a firm's profit, usually measured in terms of return on investment (ROI) or return on assets (ROA). One objective is *managing for long-run profits,* which is followed by many Japanese firms that are willing to forgo immediate profit in cars, TV sets, or computers to develop quality products that can penetrate competitive markets in the future. A *maximizing current profit* objective, such as during this quarter or year, is common in many firms because the targets can be set and performance measured quickly. Canadian firms are sometimes criticized for this short-run orientation. A *target return* objective involves a firm, such as Irving Oil or Mohawk, setting a goal (such as 20 percent) for pretax ROI. These three profit objectives have different implications for a firm's pricing objectives.

Another profit consideration for such firms as movie studios and manufacturers is to ensure that those firms in their channels of distribution make adequate profits. Without profits for these channel members, the movie studio or manufacturer is cut off from its customers. For example, Figure 13–4 shows where each dollar of your movie ticket goes. The 51 cents the movie studio gets must cover both its production expenses and its profit. While the studio would like more than 51 cents of your dollar, it settles for this amount to make sure theatres and distributors are satisfied and willing to handle their movies. Still, with revenues close to $1 billion, the Canadian movie theatre industry has actually been raising ticket prices to increase its profitability.

Sales

Given that a firm's profit is high enough for it to remain in business, its objectives may be to increase sales revenue. The hope is that the increase in sales revenue will, in turn, lead to increases in market share and profit. Cutting price on one product in a firm's line may increase its sales revenue but reduce those of related products. Objectives related to sales revenue or unit sales have the advantage of being translated easily into meaningful targets for marketing managers responsible for a product line or brand—far more easily than with an ROI target, for example.

Market Share

Market share is the ratio of the firm's sales revenues or unit sales to those of the industry (competitors plus the firm itself). Companies often pursue a market-share objective when industry sales are relatively flat or declining. The Molson and Labatt breweries have adopted this objective in the beer market, while Pepsi-Cola Canada and Coca-Cola Canada battle for market share in the soft drink category.[10] But although increased market share is the primary goal of some firms, others see it as a means to an end: increasing sales and profits.

FIGURE 13–4

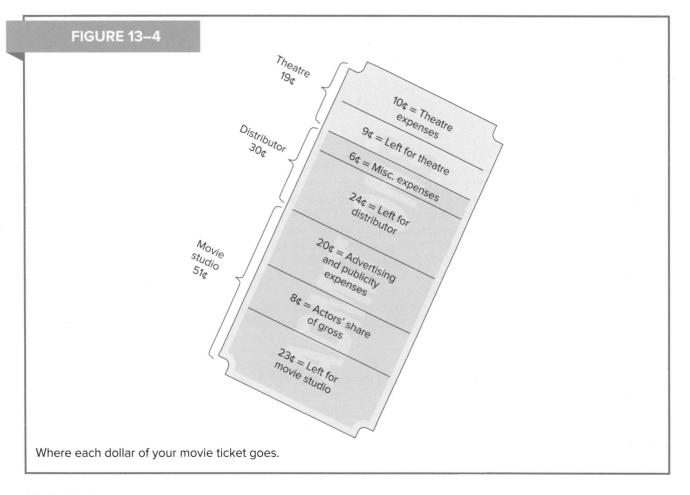

Theatre
19¢

Distributor
30¢

Movie
studio
51¢

10¢ = Theatre expenses

9¢ = Left for theatre

6¢ = Misc. expenses

24¢ = Left for distributor

20¢ = Advertising and publicity expenses

8¢ = Actors' share of gross

23¢ = Left for movie studio

Where each dollar of your movie ticket goes.

Unit Volume

Many firms use unit volume, the quantity produced or sold, as a pricing objective. These firms often sell multiple products at very different prices and need to match the unit volume demanded by customers with price and production capacity. Using unit volume as an objective can be counterproductive if a volume objective is achieved, say, by drastic price cutting that drives down company profitability.[11]

Survival

In some instances, profits, sales, and market share are less important objectives of the firm than mere survival. For example, RadioShack, an electronics retail chain, faced survival problems because it couldn't compete with the prices offered by other retailers. The company enacted price matching programs and promoted large discounts on its merchandise to raise cash and hopefully stave off bankruptcy. These efforts failed and RadioShack declared bankruptcy in 2015.

Social Responsibility

A firm may forgo higher profit on sales and follow a pricing objective that recognizes its obligations to customers and society in general. Medtronics followed this pricing policy when it introduced the world's first heart pacemaker. Gerber supplies a specially formulated product free of charge to children who cannot tolerate foods based on cow's milk. Government agencies, which set many prices for services they offer, use social responsibility as a primary pricing objective.

LO3 STEP 2: ESTIMATING DEMAND AND REVENUE

Basic to setting a product's price is the extent of customer demand for it. Marketing executives must also translate this estimate of customer demand into estimates of revenues the firm expects to receive.

Fundamentals of Estimating Demand

How much will you pay for a frozen cheese pizza you can pop in the oven for a quick dinner while you are studying for a marketing exam? $6? $8? $10? And what are some of the factors affecting this decision? Your preference for pizza compared to other quick-service food? The ease with which you can call Domino's or your local Chinese restaurant for an already-prepared meal delivered to your residence? How much money you have available in your credit card account while you're thinking about the tuition payment that's due next month? All these factors affect demand. To illustrate the fundamentals of estimating demand, let's assume you are a consultant to the marketing manager at Red Baron® pizza and your job is to start analyzing the demand for its Red Baron frozen cheese pizzas. In the process, you'll have to consider what the demand curve for frozen cheese pizza might look like, how it affects Red Baron's sales revenues, and the price elasticity of demand.

What key factors affect the demand for Red Baron frozen cheese pizzas? Read the text to find out.

© Mike Hruby

The Demand Curve

A demand curve is a graph that relates the quantity sold and price, showing the maximum number of units that will be sold at a given price. Based on secondary research you conducted regarding the annual demand for Red Baron frozen cheese pizza under circumstances that existed in 2016, you are able to construct the demand curve D1 in Figure 13–5A, which you now need to update because market conditions have changed by 2017. Note the following relationship: As price falls, more people decide to buy Red Baron frozen cheese pizza, which increases its unit sales. But price is not the complete story when estimating demand. Economists emphasize three other key factors that influence demand for a product:

1. *Consumer tastes.* As we saw in Chapter 3, these depend on many forces, such as demographics, culture, and technology. Because consumer tastes can change quickly, up-to-date marketing research is essential to estimate demand. For example, if research by nutritionists concludes that some pizzas are healthier (because they are gluten-free or vegetarian), demand for them will probably increase.

2. *Price and availability of similar products.* If the price of a competitor's pizza that is a substitute for yours—like Tombstone® pizza—falls, more people will buy it; its demand will rise and the demand for yours will fall. Other low-priced dinners are also substitutes for pizza. For example, if you want something fast so you can study, you could call Domino's or a local Chinese restaurant and order a meal for home delivery. So as the price of a substitute falls or its availability increases, the demand for your Red Baron frozen cheese pizza will fall.

3. *Consumer income.* In general, as real consumers' incomes increase (allowing for inflation), demand for a product will also increase. So if you get a scholarship and have extra cash for discretionary spending, you might eat more Red Baron frozen cheese pizzas and fewer peanut butter and jelly sandwiches to satisfy your appetite.

The first two factors influence what consumers want to buy, and the third factor affects what they can buy. Along with price, these are often called *demand factors*, or factors that determine consumers' willingness and ability to pay for products and services. As discussed in Chapters 8 and 10, it can be challenging to estimate demand for new products, especially because consumer likes and dislikes are often so difficult to read clearly.

Movement along versus Shift of a Demand Curve

The 2016 demand curve D1 for Red Baron frozen cheese pizzas in Figure 13–5A shows that as its price is lowered from $8 (point 1) to $6 (point 2), the quantity sold (demanded) increases from 2 million (Q1) to 3 million (Q2) units per year. This is an example of a *movement along a demand curve* and it assumes that other factors (consumer tastes, price and availability of substitutes, and consumers' incomes) remain unchanged.

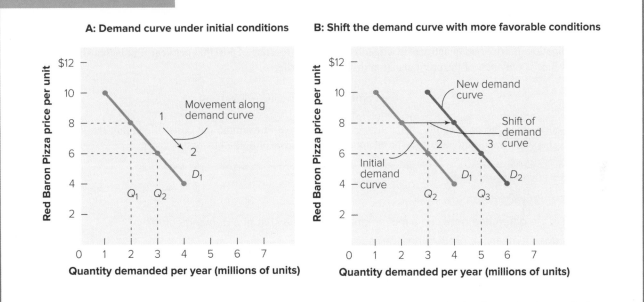

FIGURE 13–5

Demand curves for Red Baron frozen cheese pizza showing the effect on annual sales (quantity demanded per year) by change in price caused by (A) a movement along the demand curve and (B) a shift of the demand curve.

What if some of these factors do change? For example, if advertising causes more people to want Red Baron frozen cheese pizzas, demand will increase. Now the initial demand curve, D1 (the blue line in Figure 13–5B), no longer represents the demand. Instead, the new demand curve, D2 (the red line in Figure 13–5B) represents the new demand for Red Baron frozen cheese pizzas. Economists call this a *shift in the demand curve*—in this case, a shift to the right from D1 to D2. This increased demand means that more Red Baron frozen cheese pizzas are wanted for a given price. At a price of $6 (point 3), the demand is 5 million units per year (Q3) on D2 rather than 3 million units per year (Q2) on D1.

Price Elasticity of Demand

Marketing managers are especially interested in **price elasticity of demand**, or the percentage change in quantity demanded relative to a percentage change in price. Price elasticity is central to understanding a product's demand curve. It provides an indication of how sensitive consumer demand and the firm's revenues are to changes in the product's price.

For example, a product with elastic demand is one in which a slight decrease in price results in a relatively large increase in demand, or units sold. The reverse is also true. With elastic demand, a slight increase in price results in a relatively large decrease in demand. Typically, the more substitutes a product or service has, the more likely it is to be price elastic. For example, marketing experiments on soft drinks, coffee, and snack foods have been shown to have elastic demand. So marketing managers may cut price to increase the demand of their products depending on what competitors' prices are.

In contrast, a product with inelastic demand means that slight increases or decreases in price will not significantly affect the demand, or units sold, for the product. Typically, products and services considered as necessities usually have inelastic demand, as do products or services with no competitive alternatives. For example, if you have to drive to class in your car and gasoline prices increase one cent per litre, you are probably not going to start using the bus instead. Therefore, gasoline has inelastic demand, which means the increase in price will have a relatively minor impact on the number of litres of gasoline sold and may actually increase the total revenue of your local Petro-Canada or Irving gasoline station.

Fundamentals of Estimating Revenue

While economists may talk about "demand curves," marketing executives are more likely to speak in terms of "revenues generated." Demand curves lead directly to an essential revenue concept critical to pricing decisions: **total revenue**—the total money received from the sale of a product. Total revenue (TR) equals the unit price (P) times the quantity sold (Q). Or TR = P × Q. For example, assume a picture frame shop sets a price of $100 per picture and sells 400 pictures per year. In this case,

$$TR = P \times Q$$
$$= \$100 \times 400$$
$$= \$40,000$$

This combination of price and quantity sold annually shows total revenue of $40,000 per year. But is that shop making a profit? Alas, total revenue is only part of the profit equation that we saw earlier:

$$\text{Total profit} = \text{Total revenue} - \text{Total cost}$$

In order to determine the profitability of the frame shop, we have to examine the costs of running the shop. The following section covers this other important part of the profit equation—the costs of doing business.

Learning Review

3. What is the difference between a movement along and a shift of a demand curve?

4. What does it mean if a product has inelastic demand?

STEP 3: ESTIMATING COST, VOLUME, AND PROFIT RELATIONSHIPS

While revenues are the monies received by a firm from selling its products or services to customers, costs or expenses are the monies the firm pays out to its employees and suppliers. Marketing managers often use break-even analysis to relate revenues and costs, a topic covered in this section.

The Importance of Controlling Costs

Understanding the role and behaviour of costs is critical to all marketing decisions, particularly pricing decisions. Many firms go bankrupt because their costs get out of control, causing their total costs to exceed their total revenues over an extended period of time. This is why smart marketing managers make pricing decisions that balance both their revenues and costs. Three cost concepts are important in pricing decisions: total cost, fixed cost, and variable cost. **Total cost** is the total expenses incurred by a firm in producing and marketing a product. It is the sum of fixed costs and variable costs. **Fixed cost** is the firm's expenses that are stable and do not change with the quantity of product that is produced and cost. These usually include salaries of executives and lease charges on a building. **Variable cost** is the sum of the expenses of a firm that vary directly with the quantity of products that is produced and sold. Variable costs can be direct labour and materials used in producing the product or sales commissions that are tied directly to the quantity sold.

LO4 Break-Even Analysis

Marketing managers often employ an approach that considers cost, volume, and profit relationships, based on the profit equations. **Break-even analysis** is a technique that analyzes the relationship between total revenue and total cost to determine profitability at various levels of output. The *break-even point (BEP)* is the quantity at which total revenue and total costs are equal. Profit comes from any units sold beyond the BEP.

Calculating a Break-Even Point

The break-even point (BEP) is calculated as follows:

$$BEP_{Quantity} = \frac{Fixed\ cost}{Unit\ price - Unit\ variable\ cost}$$

So consider our frame shop example. Suppose the frame shop owner wanted to identify how many pictures must be sold to cover fixed costs at a given price. Also, assume that the average price a customer will pay for each picture is $100. Suppose the fixed cost (FC) for the business is $28,000 (for real estate rental, interest on a bank loan, and other fixed expenses) and unit variable cost (UVC) for a picture is $30 (for labour, glass, frame, matting). The break-even quantity (BEP$_{Quantity}$) is 400 pictures, as follows:

$$BEP_{Quantity} = \frac{Fixed\ cost}{Unit\ price - Unit\ variable\ cost}$$

$$= \frac{\$28,000}{\$100 - 30}$$

$$= 400\ pictures$$

The highlighted row in Figure 13–6 shows the break-even quantity for the frame shop at a price of $100 per picture is 400 pictures. At less than 400 pictures, the frame shop incurs a loss, and at more than 400 pictures it makes a profit.

FIGURE 13–6

QUANTITY OF PICTURES SOLD (Q)	PRICE PER PICTURE (P)	TOTAL REVENUE (TR) = (P × Q)	UNIT VARIABLE COST (UVC)	TOTAL VARIABLE COST (TVC) = (UVC × Q)	FIXED COST (FC)	TOTAL COST (TC) = (FC + TVC)	PROFIT = (TR − TC)
0	$100	$ 0	$30	$ 0	$28,000	$28,000	($28,000)
200	100	20,000	30	6,000	28,000	34,000	(14,000)
400	100	40,000	30	12,000	28,000	40,000	0
600	100	60,000	30	18,000	28,000	46,000	14,000
800	100	80,000	30	24,000	28,000	52,000	28,000
1,000	100	100,000	30	30,000	28,000	58,000	42,000
1,200	100	120,000	30	36,000	28,000	64,000	56,000

Calculating a break-even point.

Figure 13–7 shows a graphic presentation of the break-even analysis, called a *break-even chart*. It shows that total revenue and total cost intersect and are equal at a quantity of 400 pictures sold, which is the break-even point at which profit is exactly $0. The frame shop owner would obviously want to do better. So, for example, if the frame shop owner could double the quantity sold annually to 1,000 pictures, the graph in Figure 13–7 shows that an annual profit of $48,000 could be generated.

FIGURE 13–7

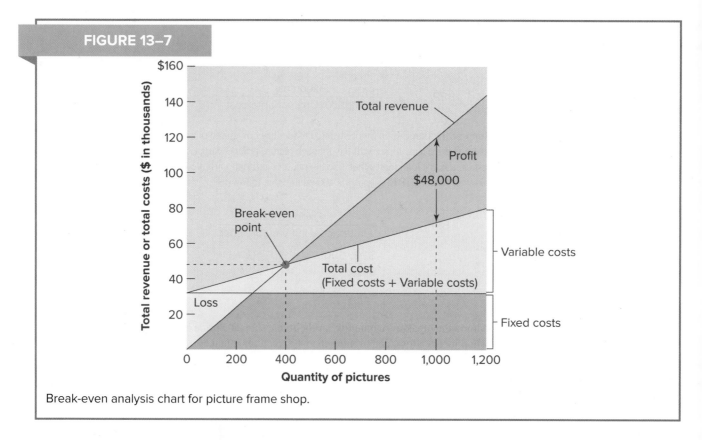

Break-even analysis chart for picture frame shop.

Application of Break-Even Analysis

Because of its simplicity, break-even analysis is used extensively in marketing, most frequently to study the impact of profit on changes in price, fixed cost, and variable cost. The mechanics of break-even analysis are the basis of the widely used electronic spreadsheets offered by such computer programs as Microsoft Excel that permit managers to answer hypothetical "what if" questions about the effect of changes in price and cost on their profit.

Learning Review

5. What is the difference between fixed cost and variable cost?

6. What is a break-even point?

STEP 4: SELECTING AN APPROXIMATE PRICE LEVEL

A key to a marketing manager's setting a final price for a product is to find an *approximate price level* to use as a reasonable starting point. Four common approaches to finding this approximate price level are (1) demand-oriented, (2) cost-oriented, (3) profit-oriented, and (4) competition-oriented approaches (Figure 13–8). Although these approaches are discussed separately below, some of them overlap, and an effective marketing manager will consider several in searching for an approximate price level.

LO5 Demand-Oriented Approaches

Demand-oriented approaches weigh factors underlying expected customer tastes and preferences more heavily than such factors as cost, profit, and competition when selecting a price level.

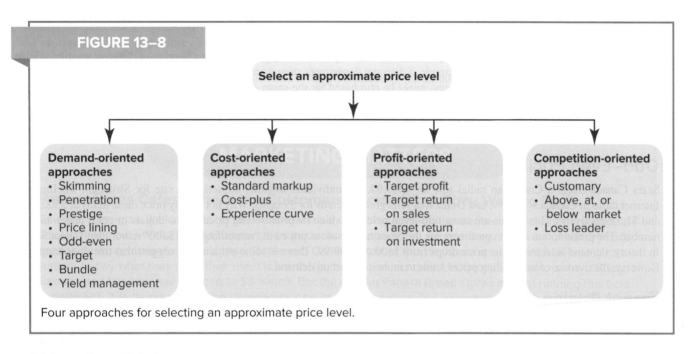

FIGURE 13–8

Select an approximate price level

Demand-oriented approaches
- Skimming
- Penetration
- Prestige
- Price lining
- Odd-even
- Target
- Bundle
- Yield management

Cost-oriented approaches
- Standard markup
- Cost-plus
- Experience curve

Profit-oriented approaches
- Target profit
- Target return on sales
- Target return on investment

Competition-oriented approaches
- Customary
- Above, at, or below market
- Loss leader

Four approaches for selecting an approximate price level.

Skimming Pricing

A firm introducing a new or innovative product can use **skimming pricing**, setting the highest initial price that customers who really desire a product are willing to pay. These customers are not very price sensitive because they weigh the new product's price, quality, and ability to satisfy their needs against the same characteristics of substitutes. As these customers' demands are satisfied, the firm lowers the price to attract another, more price-sensitive segment. Thus, skimming pricing gets its name from skimming successive layers of "cream," or customer segments, as prices are lowered in a series of steps.

Skimming pricing is an effective strategy when (1) enough prospective customers are willing to buy the product immediately at the high initial price to make these sales profitable, (2) the high initial price will not attract competitors, (3) lowering the price has only a minor effect on increasing the sales volume and reducing the unit costs, and (4) customers interpret the high price as signifying high quality. These four conditions are most likely to exist when the new product is protected by patents or copyright, its uniqueness is understood and valued by customers, or the customer perceives the new product as simply better compared to existing offerings. In fact, recent Canadian research found that 67 percent of consumers are willing to pay more for a new product that they consider superior to what is currently available on the market.[12]

Penetration Pricing

Setting a low initial price on a new product to appeal immediately to the mass market is **penetration pricing**, the exact opposite of skimming pricing. Amazon consciously chose a penetration pricing strategy when it introduced its Amazon Fire tablet computer at $199 when competitive models were being priced at $499.

The conditions favouring penetration pricing are the reverse of those supporting skimming pricing: (1) many segments of the market are price sensitive; (2) a low initial price discourages competitors from entering the market; and (3) unit production and marketing costs fall dramatically as production volumes increase. A firm using penetration pricing may (1) maintain the initial price for a time to gain profit lost from its low introductory level, or (2) lower the price further, counting on the new volume to generate the necessary profit.

In some situations, penetration pricing may follow skimming pricing. A company might initially price a product high to attract price-insensitive consumers and recoup initial research and development costs and introductory promotional expenditures. Once this is done, penetration pricing is used to appeal to a broader segment of the population and increase market share.[13]

Prestige Pricing

Prestige pricing involves setting a high price so that quality- or status-conscious consumers will be attracted to the product and buy it. Rolls-Royce cars, Chanel perfume, Cartier jewellery, and Rolex watches have an element of prestige pricing in them and may sell worse at lower prices than at higher ones. When Swiss watchmaker TAG Heuer raised the average price of its watches from $250 to $1,000, its sales volume increased sevenfold![14]

While most companies use the one-price policy, flexible pricing has grown in popularity because of increasingly sophisticated information technology. Today, many marketers have the ability to customize a price for an individual on the basis of his or her purchasing patterns, product preferences, and price sensitivity, all of which are stored in company data warehouses. Price customization is particularly prevalent for products and services bought online. Online marketers routinely adjust prices in response to purchase situations and past purchase behaviours of online buyers. Some online marketers monitor an online shopper's "clickstream"—the way that a person navigates through its website. If the visitor behaves like a price-sensitive shopper—perhaps by comparing many different products—that person may be offered a lower price. However, as noted at the end of this chapter, flexible pricing carried to the extreme could be considered price discrimination and is a practice prohibited under the *Competition Act*. Today, a popular pricing strategy for online or digital service providers is the *freemium* model, where a basic version of the service is offered for free to customers. The theory is the customer will perceive the value and then be willing to pay for the service. Or, another strategy is to offer the basic service and then provide enhanced versions or value-added versions of the service to be sold at a premium (hence the word—free-mium). Typical services using this model include software, games, and web services such as Dropbox. Finally, another dynamic pricing strategy is called *surge pricing*, which occurs when a company raises the price of its product or service if there is a spike in demand. Surge pricing, for example, is being used by car-sharing companies such as Uber and Lyft and these companies have been criticized for its use from an ethical perspective.

Company, Customer, and Competitive Effects

As the final list or quoted price is set, the effects on the company, customers, and competitors must be assessed.

Company Effects

For a firm with more than one product, a decision on the price of a single product must consider the price of other items in its product line or related product lines in its product mix. Within a product line or mix, there are usually some products that are substitutes for one another and some that complement each other. Frito-Lay recognizes that its tortilla chip product line consisting of Baked Tostitos, Tostitos, and Doritos brands are partial substitutes for one another and its bean-and-cheese dip line and salsas complement the tortilla chip line.

A manager's challenge when marketing multiple products is *product-line pricing,* the setting of prices for all items in a product line. When setting prices, the manager seeks to cover the total cost and produce a profit for the complete line, not necessarily for each item.

Product-line pricing involves determining (1) the lowest-priced product and price, (2) the highest-priced product and price, and (3) price differentials for all other products in the line.[25] The lowest- and highest-priced items in the product line play important roles. The highest-priced item is typically positioned as the premium item in quality and features. The lowest-priced item is the traffic builder designed to capture the attention of the hesitant or first-time buyer. Price differentials between items in the line should make sense to customers and reflect the differences in their perceived values of the products offered. Behavioural research also suggests that the price differentials should get larger as one moves up the product line.

Frito-Lay recognizes that its tortilla chip products are partial substitutes for one another and its bean-and-cheese dips and salsas complement tortilla chips. This knowledge is used in Frito-Lay product-line pricing.

Frito-Lay, Inc.

www.frito-lay.com

Frito-Lay North America, Inc.

Customer Effects

In setting prices, retailers weigh factors heavily that satisfy the perceptions or expectations of ultimate consumers, such as the customary prices for a variety of consumer products. Retailers have found that they should not price their store brands 20 to 25 percent below manufacturers' brands. When they do, consumers might view the lower price as signalling lower quality and they do not buy. This is also particularly true in marketing "intangible services," where low price may connote poor quality.[26]

Competitive Effects

A manager's pricing decision is immediately apparent to most competitors, who may retaliate with price changes of their own. Therefore, a manager who sets a final list or quoted price must anticipate potential price responses from competitors. Regardless of whether a firm is a price leader or follower, it wants to avoid cutthroat price wars in which no firm in the industry makes a satisfactory profit. A *price war* involves successive pricing by competitors to increase or maintain their unit sales or market share. For example, price wars in the airline industry usually result in losses for all players. Similarly, in the residential long-distance telephone industry, even price reductions as little as 1 percent can have a significant effect on company profitability.[27]

Marketers are advised to consider price cutting only when one or more conditions exist: (1) the company has a cost or technological advantage over its competitors; (2) primary demand for a product class will grow if prices are lowered; and (3) the price cut is confined to specific products or customers (as with airline tickets) and not across the board.

Social Media Impact on Pricing

Experts suggest that marketers must consider the impact social media can have on price setting. In fact, social media can have important effects on pricing. For example, think about a company planning a price increase. That company could leverage social media to listen to customers and collaborate with them when it comes to that price increase. For example, it is possible to engage the most influential customers and uncover possible acceptance or rejection of that possible price increase. If a company can convince its most influential customers to accept a price increase, it will be a lot easier to convince the overall marketplace as well. On the other hand, if influential customers are not willing to accept price increases, they will use social media to protest such increases. This was the case when Netflix attempted to raise its rental prices. Thousands of customers took to social media to protest, and Netflix had to revise its price strategy.

In order to generate greater word of mouth on social media, a company could offer customers "social media discounts" to those who spread the word. American Express, for instance, launched its Sync initiative and offered customers coupons and discounts to people who tweeted certain hashtags promoting the initiative. But companies need to size the discounts according to the social reach of the plaform (e.g., LinkedIn connections or Twitter followers).

Consumers also have better tools to compare prices of different products and can do so almost instantly. Thus, products with prices that are not in line with market standards can be quickly identified and rejected. So companies need to carefully monitor their prices and use the same price comparison tools that customers are using. Price transparency is enhanced on social media, and companies have to plan accordingly when it comes to price setting.

Finally, social media can drive up profit because companies can extend their visibility and their reach. It can also drive down costs in several areas, including advertising and PR expenditures, customer service and support, and even product design. For example, social media has been shown to reduce customer service and support costs; consider the cost of a customer service call compared to the cost of helping the same customer directly via Twitter. Social media can even reduce the costs of product design. Feedback from potential customers can be used on the front end, saving the company time, money, and guesswork. All of these savings must be considered when final prices are being set by the marketing manager. If you can increase revenue and reduce costs, then increased profit is gained, which, in turn, allows you to adapt prices, if necessary.[28]

STEP 6: MAKING SPECIAL ADJUSTMENTS TO THE LIST OR QUOTED PRICE

When you pay 75 cents for a bag of M&Ms in a vending machine or receive a quoted price of $10,000 from a contractor to renovate your kitchen, the pricing sequence ends with the last step just described: setting the list or quoted price. But when you are a manufacturer of M&M candies or gas grills and sell your product to dozens or hundreds of wholesalers and retailers in your channel of distribution, you may need to make a variety of special adjustments to the list or quoted price. Wholesalers also must adjust list or quoted prices they set for retailers. Three special adjustments to the list or quoted price are (1) discounts, (2) allowances, and (3) geographical adjustments.

Discounts

Discounts are reductions from list price that a seller gives a buyer as a reward for some activity of the buyer that is favourable to the seller. Four kinds of discounts are especially important in marketing strategy: (1) quantity, (2) seasonal, (3) trade (functional), and (4) cash discounts.[29]

Quantity Discounts

To encourage customers to buy larger quantities of a product, firms at all levels in the channel of distribution offer *quantity discounts,* which are reductions in unit costs for a larger order. For example, an instant photocopying service might set a price of 10 cents a copy for 1 to 25 copies, 9 cents a copy for 26 to 100, and 8 cents a copy for 101 or more. Because the photocopying service gets more of the buyer's business and has longer production runs that reduce its order-handling costs, it is willing to pass on some of the cost savings in the form of quantity discounts to the buyer.

Newfoundland to British Columbia have been found guilty and fined for deceptive pricing practices. However, as you examine Figure 13–9, you should remember that it is often difficult for the government to police and enforce all of these laws. It is essential to rely on the ethical standards of those making and publicizing pricing decisions. To determine how the Competition Bureau deals with deceptive pricing practices, check the accompanying Going Online box, "Checking Out Price Violations."

FIGURE 13–9

DECEPTIVE PRICING PRACTICE	DESCRIPTION
Bait and switch	This deceptive practice exists when a firm offers a very low price on a product (the bait) to attract customers to a store. Once in the store, the customer is persuaded to purchase a higher priced item (the switch) using a variety of tricks, including (1) downgrading the promoted item, (2) not having the item in stock, or (3) refusing to take orders for the item
Bargains conditional on other purchases	This practice may exist when a buyer is offered "1-Cent Sales," "Buy 1, Get 1 Free," and "Get 2 for the Price of 1." Such pricing is legal only if the first items are sold at the regular price, not a price inflated for the offer. Substituting lower quality items on either the first or second purchase is also considered deceptive.
Comparable value comparisons	Advertising such as "Retail Value $100.00, Our Price $85.00" is deceptive if a verified and substantial number of stores in the market area do not price the item at $100.
Comparisons with suggested prices	A claim that a price is below a manufacturer's suggested or list price may be deceptive if few or no sales occur at that price in a retailer's market area.
Former price comparisons	When a seller represents a price as reduced, the item must have been offered in good faith at a higher price for a substantial previous period. Setting a high price for the purpose of establishing a reference for a price reduction is deceptive.

Five most common deceptive pricing practices.

GOING ONLINE

Checking Out Price Violations

As you have read in this chapter, the Competition Bureau is responsible for administering the *Competition Act* in Canada. Competition can be lessened and/or consumers can be harmed by unfair pricing practices. Visit the Competition Bureau's home page at **www.competitionbureau.gc.ca**. Under "Resources," click on "Media Centre" and then click on "Announcements." Search through the announcements to find the following:

1. What are the types of pricing violations involving Canadian and international companies reported on the site?

2. What types of penalties were imposed?

3. What is your opinion regarding these pricing violations?

Predatory Pricing

Two types of predatory pricing are defined within the *Competition Act*. The first is called *geographic predatory pricing*. Sellers are prohibited from engaging in a policy of selling products or services in one region in Canada at a price lower than in another region with the intent or effect of lessening competition or of eliminating a competitior.

The second type of predatory pricing offence is committed when a business engages in a policy of selling products or services at "unreasonably low" prices in an attempt to substantially lessen competition. In many cases, the very low prices are designed to drive competitors out of business. Once competitors have been driven out, the firm raises its prices.

Delivered Pricing

Delivered pricing is the practice of refusing a customer delivery of an article on the same trade terms as other customers in the same location. It is a non-criminal offence, but the Competition Tribunal can prohibit suppliers from engaging in such a practice.

Learning Review

11. Why would a seller choose a flexible-price policy over a one-price policy?

12. Which pricing practices are covered by the *Competition Act?*

Learning Objectives Review

LO1   **Understand the nature and importance of pricing products and services.**

Price is the money or other considerations exchanged for the ownership or use of a product service. Although price typically involves money, the amount exchanged is often different from the list or quoted price because of allowances and extra fees.

LO2   **Recognize the constraints on a firm's pricing latitude and the objectives a firm has in setting prices.**

Pricing constraints, such as demand, product newness, costs, competitors, other products sold by the firm, and the type of competitive market, restrict a firm's pricing latitude. Pricing objectives may include profit, sales revenue, market share, unit volume, survival, or some socially responsible price level.

LO3   **Explain what a demand curve is and what price elasticity of demand means.**

A demand curve is a graph relating the quantity sold and price and shows the maximum number of product or service units that will be sold at given price. Three demand factors affect price: (a) consumer tastes, (b) price and availability of other products, and (c) consumer income. These demand factors determine consumers' willingness and ability to pay for products and services. Assuming these demand factors remain unchanged, when the price of a product is lowered or raised, the quantity demanded for it will increase or decrease, respectively. Price elasticity of demand measures the responsiveness of units of a product sold to a change in price, which is expressed as the percentage change in the quantity of a product demanded divided by the percentage change in price. It provides an indication of how sensitive consumer demand and the firm's revenue are to changes in the product's price.

LO4   **Perform a break-even analysis.**

Break-even analysis shows the relationship between total revenue and total cost at various quantities of output for given conditions of price, fixed cost, and variable cost. At the break-even point, total revenue and total cost are equal.

LO5   **Understand approaches to pricing as well as factors considered to establish prices for products and services.**

Four general approaches of finding an approximate price level for a product or service are demand-oriented, cost-oriented, profit-oriented, and competition-oriented pricing. Demand-oriented pricing stresses consumer demand; cost-oriented pricing emphasizes the costs aspects; profit-oriented pricing focuses on a balance between revenues and costs; and competition-oriented pricing stresses what competitors or the marketplace are doing. Demand, cost, profit, and competition influence the initial consideration of the price level for a product or service. To set the list or quoted price, a marketer must also consider additional factors. First, the marketer must decide whether to follow a one-price policy or a flexible-price policy. And second, the marketer must consider the effects the proposed price will have on the company, customer, and competitors. Marketers must also consider social media effects on pricing because social media, when used effectively, can reduce costs and increase profitability thus allowing greater latitude in terms of price setting, Finally, list or quoted prices are often modified through discounts, allowances, and geographical adjustments.

LO6   **Describe basic laws and regulations affecting pricing practices.**

Legal and regulatory issues in pricing focus on price fixing, price discrimination, deceptive pricing, predatory pricing, and delivered pricing. The *Competition Act* in Canada prohibits such practices.

Applying Marketing Knowledge

1. How would the price equation apply to the purchase price of (*a*) gasoline, (*b*) an airline ticket, and (*c*) a chequing account?

2. What would be your response to the following statement: "Profit maximization is the only legitimate pricing objective for the firm"?

3. Touche Toiletries, Inc. has developed an addition to its Lizardman Cologne line, tentatively branded Ode d'Toade Cologne. Unit variable costs are 45 cents for a 60-mL bottle, and heavy advertising expenditures in the first year would result in total fixed costs of $900,000. Ode d'Toade Cologne is priced at $7.50 for a 60-mL bottle. How many bottles of Ode d'Toade must be sold to break even?

4. Suppose that marketing executives for Touche Toiletries reduced the price to $6.50 for a 60-mL bottle of Ode d'Toade and the fixed costs were $1,000,000. Suppose further that the unit variable cost remained at 45 cents for a 60-mL bottle. (*a*) How many bottles must be sold to break even? (*b*) What dollar profit level would Ode d'Toade achieve if 200,000 bottles were sold?

5. Under what conditions would a digital camera manufacturer adopt a skimming price approach for a new product? A penetration approach?

6. What are some similarities and differences between skimming pricing, prestige pricing, and above-market pricing?

7. Suppose executives estimate that the unit variable costs for their DVD is $100, the fixed cost related to the product is $10 million, and the target volume for next year is 100,000 units. What sales price will be necessary to achieve a target profit of $1 million?

8. Suppose a manufacturer of exercise equipment sets a suggested price to the consumer of $395 for a particular piece of equipment to be competitive with similar equipment. The manufacturer sells its equipment to a sporting goods wholesaler who receives 25 percent of the selling price and a retailer who receives 50 percent of the selling price. What demand-oriented pricing approach is being used? And at what price will the manufacturer sell the equipment to the wholesaler?

9. To examine the psychology of pricing, we want you to do the following. Take two identical plain plastic containers and label one Brand A and one Brand B. Fill them both with the same "low-priced" hand lotion. Now, go out and find some other students or shoppers. Tell them you are testing Brand A, a $2.99 hand lotion, and Brand B, a $12.99 hand lotion. Ask them to compare Brand A and Brand B in terms of perceived quality and value and which one, if any, they prefer. Write up a short report indicating your findings. Did price influence the consumers' perception of the products?

10. The Confederation Bridge cost $1.3 billion to build. Assume a daily traffic rate of 4,000 vehicles per day with an average toll charge of $45 and the fact that the bridge opened for business in 1997. How many years would it take for the bridge to break even in the initial capital costs of $1.3 billion?

Building Your Marketing Plan

In starting to set a final price:

1. List three pricing constraints and two pricing objectives.

2. Think about your customers and competitors and set three possible prices.

3. Assume a fixed cost and unit variable cost and (*a*) calculate the break-even points using the three possible prices, and (*b*) plot a break-even chart for the three prices (see Figure 13–7).

To arrive at the final price(s) for your offering(s):

1. Modify the three prices in light of (*a*) pricing considerations for demand-, cost-, profit-, and competition-oriented approaches; and (*b*) possibilities for discounts, allowances, and geographic adjustments.

2. Prepare another break-even chart given these modified prices.

3. Choose the final price(s).

Video Case 13

Carmex: Setting the Price of the Number-One Lip Balm

"Carmex is dedicated to providing consumers with superior lip balm formulas—that heal, sooth, and protect—while ensuring lips remain healthy and hydrated," exclaims Paul Woelbing, president of Carma Laboratories, Inc.

It's an ambitious mission, but the company has been extraordinarily successful with its 75-year-old product. Woelbing and his management team at Carma Laboratories can attribute their success to a strong brand, a loyal customer base, a growing product line, financial strength, and an exceptional talent for setting prices that achieve company objectives and still provide value to customers. Even during the recession and periods of slow growth, the company has been successful. "In a rough economy, shopping habits change," Woelbing says. "People buy smaller quantities more frequently, but they still need personal care products."

© McGraw-Hill Education/ Editorial Image, LLC, photographer

The Company

Carmex was created by Paul's grandfather, Alfred Woelbing, in his kitchen in Wauwatosa, Wisconsin, in 1937. Alfred had an entrepreneurial spirit and experimented with ingredients such as camphor, menthol, phenol, lanolin, salicylic acid, and cocoa seed butter to make the new product. The name didn't have any meaning other than Alfred liked the sound of "Carma," and "ex" was a popular suffix for many brands at the time. He packaged the balm in small glass jars and sold the product for 25 cents from the trunk of his car by making personal sales calls to pharmacies in Wisconsin, Illinois, and Indiana. From the beginning, price and value were important to the product's success. If pharmacies weren't initially interested in Carmex, Alfred would leave a dozen jars for free. The samples would sell quickly and soon the pharmacies would place orders for more!

As the company grew, Alfred's son, Don, joined the business and helped add new products to the company's offerings. For example, in the 1980s, Carmex made its first significant packaging change by also offering the balm in squeezable tubes. In the 1990s, Carmex became available in stick form, which had been used by two of Carma's major competitors—ChapStick and Blistex. In the 2000s, Carmex became available in mint, cherry, and strawberry flavours. The company also expanded into larger manufacturing facilities, added a new distribution centre, and hired its first marketing experts.

Today, the company is led by Alfred's grandsons, Paul and Eric Woelbing, who continue to manage the company to new levels of success. They appeared on *The Oprah Winfrey Show* to announce the sale of the billionth jar of Carmex. The governor of Wisconsin declared a Carmex commemoration day to celebrate its 75th anniversary. NBA all-star LeBron James became a promotional partner. In addition, *Pharmacy Times* magazine recently named Carmex the number-one pharmacist-recommended brand of lip balm for the 15th consecutive year. "We are honoured to receive this unprecedented acknowledgement," said Woelbing.

© McGraw-Hill Education/Mark Dierker, photographer

Industry observers estimate that Carma Labs holds approximately 10 percent of the lip balm market. The company distributes its products through major drug, food, and mass merchant retailers, convenience stores, and online in more than 25 countries around the world. The company's most recent products—Carmex Healing Cream and Carmex Hydrating Lotion—represent a significant step from lip care to skin care. The expanded product line, multichannel distribution, growing volume, international trade, and direct competition make pricing decisions even more important today than when Alfred started the business many years ago.

Setting Prices of Carmex Products

"There are many factors that go into what results in the retail price in the store," explains Kirk Hodgdon of Bolin Marketing. As one of the marketing experts who helps Carma Labs with advertising, marketing research, and pricing decisions, Hodgdon uses information about consumer demand, production and material costs, profit goals, and competition to help Woelbing and Carmex retailers arrive at specific prices. The many factors often overlap and lead to different prices for different products, channels, and target markets. "It's a challenge!" says Hodgdon.

Consumers' tastes and preferences, for example, influence the price of Carmex products. Alisa Allen, Bolin director of marketing, explains: "Consumers will tell you that they love Carmex because it's a great value. That doesn't necessarily mean that it's the absolute lowest price. It means that it does so much; they pay a dollar and they get all kinds of benefits from the product above and beyond what they would expect." A single jar of original formula Carmex may sell for $0.99 at mass retailers such as Walmart and Target, and between $1.59 and $1.79 in drug and food retailers such as Walgreens and Kroger. These prices are a good indication of how important it is to understand consumers when setting prices. "There are magic price points for consumers," says Allen. "Any time you can drop a penny off, the consumer responds to that price."

Carmex has also introduced a premium lip balm product, Carmex Moisture Plus, at a retail price between $2.49 and $2.99. Moisture Plus is a lip balm that is packaged in a sleek silver tube, offers a slant tip–like lipstick, and is targeted toward women. The formula offers women a satin gloss shine and includes vitamin E and aloe for richer moisturization. The upscale package and additional product benefits help Carmex Moisture Plus command a higher price than the traditional Carmex jar and tube.

The cost of the ingredients that make up the Carmex lip balm formulas, the packaging, the manufacturing equipment, and the staffing are also factored into the price of the products. Volumes are a key driver of the cost of packaging and ingredients. For example, Carmex purchases up to 12 million yellow tubes each year for the traditional product, and 2 million sticks each year for the newer Moisture Plus product. The difference in quantities leads to a lower price for the traditional yellow tubes. Similarly, ingredient suppliers, label suppliers, and box suppliers all provide discounts for larger quantities. It is also more efficient for Carmex's manufacturing facility to make a large batch of traditional formula than it is to make a small batch of Moisture Plus. Carmex has also reduced its costs with efforts such as its new environmentally friendly Carmex jar, which holds the same amount of lip balm but uses 20 percent less plastic, eliminating 35 tonnes of raw material costs and the related shipping costs!

Carmex also considers retailer margins when it sets its prices. According to Allen, "We typically sell our product to two types of retailers." There are everyday low pricing (EDLP) retailers such as Walmart, and high-low retailers such as Walgreens. EDLP retailers offer consumers the lowest price every day without discounting through promotions. High-low retailers charge consumers a higher price, but they occasionally discount the product through special promotions, which Carmex often supports with "marketing discretionary funds." Carmex typically offers its products at different prices to EDLP and high-low retailers to allow each retailer to achieve its profit margin goals and to account for Carmex's promotion expenditures. When the additional expenditures are considered, however, the cost to both types of retailer is similar.

Finally, Carmex considers competitors' prices when setting its prices. Burt's Bees, ChapStick, Blistex, and many other brands offer lip balm products, and consumers often compare their prices to the price of Carmex. "We have found through research that it is extremely important that the price gap is not too great," explains Allen. "If that gap becomes too wide consumers will leave the Carmex brand and purchase a competitor's product." When Carmex was preparing to launch its premium Moisture Plus product, it conducted a thorough analysis of similar products to ensure that Moisture Plus was in an acceptable price range.

Carma Labs Inc.

Carmex in the Future

The original, and now legendary, Carmex formula and packaging will continue into the future with occasional changes to its pricing practices. New products, however, are on the horizon and likely to challenge the perceptions of the traditional products and prices in the Carmex line. Carmex Moisture Plus products, for example, will be offered in limited edition designs that ask consumers "Which personality are you?" Paul Woelbing explains the new approach:

> Lip care is an important component of a daily beauty regimen and consumers need a product they can rely on that protects and serves as an important foundation. The goal of the new Carmex Moisture Plus line is to offer our consumers a hard-working lip balm line that represent and reflects their unique style.

Some of the new styles include Chic in houndstooth, Fab in a groovy retro look, Adventurous in a leopard print, and Whimsical in an art deco design.

"We are so excited about the future of Carmex," says Hodgdon. "We are planning new products, we have new plans for retailers, and the future is nothing but bright!"

QUESTIONS

1. Which of the four approaches to setting a price does Carmex use for its products? Should one approach be used exclusively?

2. Why do many Carmex product prices end in 9? What type of pricing is this called? What should happen to demand when this approach is used?

3. Should cost be a factor in Carmex's prices? What do you think is a reasonable markup for Carmex and for its retailers?

4. What is the difference between an EDLP retailer and a high-low retailer? Why does Carmex charge them different prices?

5. Conduct an online search of lip balm products and compare the price of a Carmex product with three similar products from competitors. How do you think the competitors are setting their prices?

Case: This case was written by Steven Hartley and Alisa Allen. Sources: Kristen Scheuing, "The Man Behind Carmex," *Wisconsin Trails*, March/April 2011; "Carmex and Carma Laboratories: Pharmacy Times Names Carmex Number One Recommended Lip Balm," *IndiaPharma News*, June 21, 2013; "New Lip Balm Offers Sun Protection While Drenching Lips in Moisture," *Postmedia Breaking News*, May 21, 2013; Carma Laboratories website, www.mycarmex.com, accessed September 2, 2013; and interviews with Bolin Media personnel.

B Appendix
Financial Aspects of Marketing

Basic concepts from accounting and finance provide valuable tools for marketing executives. This appendix describes an actual company's use of accounting and financial concepts and illustrates how they assist the owner in making marketing decisions.

THE CAPLOW COMPANY

An accomplished artist and calligrapher, Jane Westerlund, decided to apply some of her experience to the picture framing business. She bought an existing retail frame store, The Caplow Company, from a friend who owned the business and wanted to retire. She avoided the do-it-yourself end of the framing business and chose three kinds of business activities: (1) cutting the frame, mats, and glass for customers who brought in their own pictures or prints to be framed; (2) selling prints and posters that she had purchased from wholesalers; and (3) restoring high-quality frames and paintings.

To understand how accounting, finance, and marketing relate to each other, let us analyze (1) the operating statement for her frame shop, (2) some general ratios of interest that are derived from the operating statement, and (3) some ratios that pertain specifically to her pricing decisions.

The Operating Statement

The *operating statement* (also called an *income statement* or *profit-and-loss statement*) summarizes the profitability of a business firm for a specific time period, usually a month, quarter, or year. The title of the operating statement for The Caplow Company shows it is for a one-year period (Figure B–1). The purpose of an operating statement is to show the profit of the firm and the revenues and expenses that led to that profit. This information tells the owner or manager what has happened in the past and suggests actions to improve future profitability.

The left side of Figure B–1 shows that there are three key elements to all operating statements: (1) sales of the firm's goods and services, (2) costs incurred in making and selling the goods and services, and (3) profit or loss, which is the difference between sales and costs.

Sales Elements

The sales element of Figure B–1 has four terms that need explanation:

- *Gross sales* are the total amount billed to customers. Dissatisfied customers or errors may reduce the gross sales through returns or allowances.
- *Returns* occur when a customer gives the item purchased back to the seller, who either refunds the purchase price or allows the customer a credit on subsequent purchases. In any event, the seller now owns the item again.
- *Allowances* are given when a customer is dissatisfied with the item purchased and the seller reduces the original purchase price. Unlike returns, in the case of allowances the buyer owns the item.
- *Net sales* are simply gross sales minus returns and allowances.

FIGURE B-1

THE CAPLOW COMPANY Operating Statement For The Year Ending December 31, 2017				
Sales	Gross sales			$80,500
	Less: Returns and allowances			500
	Net sales			$80,000
Costs	Cost of goods sold:			
	Beginning inventory at cost		$ 6,000	
	Purchases at billed cost	$21,000		
	Less: Purchase discounts	300		
	Purchases at net cost	20,700		
	Plus freight-in	100		
	Net cost of delivered purchases		20,800	
	Direct labour (framing)		14,200	
	Cost of goods available for sale		41,000	
	Less: Ending inventory at cost		5,000	
	Cost of goods sold			36,000
	Gross margin (gross profit)			$44,000
	Expenses:			
	Selling expenses:			
	Sales salaries	2,000		
	Advertising expense	3,000		
	Total selling expense		5,000	
	Administrative expenses:			
	Owner's salary	18,000		
	Bookkeeper's salary	1,200		
	Office supplies	300		
	Total administrative expense		19,500	
	General expenses:			
	Depreciation expense	1,000		
	Interest expense	500		
	Rent expense	2,100		
	Utility expenses (heat, electricity)	3,000		
	Repairs and maintenance	2,300		
	Insurance	2,000		
	Canada Pension Plan	2,200		
	Total general expenses		13,100	
	Total expenses			37,600
Profit or loss	Profit before taxes			$ 6,400

Example of an operating statement.

The operating statement for The Caplow Company shows the following:

Gross sales	$80,500
Less: Returns and allowances	$ 500
Net sales	$80,000

The low level of returns and allowances shows the shop generally has done a good job in satisfying customers, which is essential in building the repeat business necessary for success.

Cost Elements

The *cost of goods sold* is the total cost of the products sold during the period. This item varies according to the kind of business. A retail store purchases finished goods and resells them to customers without reworking them in any way. In contrast, a manufacturing firm combines raw and semi-finished materials and parts, uses labour and overhead to rework these into finished goods, and then sells them to customers. All these activities are reflected in the cost of goods sold item on a manufacturer's operating statement. Note that the frame shop has some features of a pure retailer (prints and posters it buys that are resold without alteration) and some of a pure manufacturer (assembling the raw materials of moulding, matting, and glass to form a completed frame).

Some terms that relate to cost of goods sold need clarification:

- *Inventory* is the physical material that is purchased from suppliers, may or may not be reworked, and is available for sale to customers. In the frame shop, inventory includes moulding, matting, glass, prints, and posters.

- *Purchase discounts* are reductions in the original billed price for such reasons as prompt payment of the bill or the quantity bought.

- *Direct labour* is the cost of the labour used in producing the finished product. For the frame shop, this is the cost of producing the completed frames from the moulding, matting, and glass.

- *Gross margin (gross profit)* is the money remaining to manage the business, sell the products or services, and give some profit. Gross margin is net sales minus cost of goods sold.

The two right-hand columns in Figure B–1 between "Net sales" and "Gross margin" calculate the cost of goods sold:

Net sales		$80,000
Cost of goods sold		
Beginning inventory at cost	$ 6,000	
Net cost of delivered purchases	20,800	
Direct labour (framing)	14,200	
Cost of goods available for sale	41,000	
Less: ending inventory at cost	5,000	
Cost of goods sold		36,000
Gross margin (gross profit)		$44,000

This section considers the beginning and ending inventories, the net cost of purchases delivered during the year, and the cost of the direct labour going into making the frames. Subtracting the $36,000 cost of goods sold from the $80,000 net sales gives the $44,000 gross margin.

Three major categories of expenses are shown in Figure B–1 below the gross margin:

- *Selling expenses* are the costs of selling the product or service produced by the firm. For The Caplow Company, there are two such selling expenses: sales salaries of part-time employees waiting on customers, and the advertising expense of simple newspaper ads and direct-mail ads sent to customers.

- *Administrative expenses* are the costs of managing the business and, for The Caplow Company, include three expenses: the owner's salary, a part-time bookkeeper's salary, and office supplies expense.

- *General expenses* are miscellaneous costs not covered elsewhere; for the frame shop, these include seven items: depreciation expense (on her equipment), interest expense, rent expense, utility expense, repair and maintenance expense, insurance expense, and employment insurance and Canada Pension Plan.

As shown in Figure B–1, selling, administrative, and general expenses total $37,600 for The Caplow Company.

Profit Element

What the company has earned, the *profit before taxes,* is found by subtracting cost of goods sold and expenses from net sales. For The Caplow Company, Figure B–1 shows that profit before taxes is $6,400.

General Operating Ratios to Analyze Operations

Looking only at the elements of The Caplow Company's operating statement that extend to the right column highlights the firm's performance on some important dimensions. Using operating ratios, such as *expense-to-sales ratios,* for expressing basic expense or profit elements as a percentage of net sales gives further insights:

ELEMENT IN OPERATING STATEMENT	DOLLAR VALUE	PERCENTAGE OF NET SALES
Gross sales	$80,500	
Less: Returns and allowances	500	100%
Net sales	80,000	
Less: Cost of goods sold	36,000	45
Gross margin	44,000	55
Less: Total expenses	37,600	47
Profit (or loss) before taxes	$ 6,000	8%

Westerlund can use this information to compare her firm's performance in one time period with that in the next. To do so, it is especially important that she keep the same definitions for each element of her operating statement, also a significant factor in using the electronic spreadsheets discussed in Chapter 13. Performance comparisons between periods are more difficult if she changes definitions for the accounting elements in the operating statement.

She can use either the dollar values or the operating ratios (the value of the element of the operating statement divided by net sales) to analyze the firm's performance. However, the operating ratios are more valuable than the dollar values for two reasons: (1) the simplicity of working with percentages rather than dollars, and (2) the availability of operating ratios of typical firms in the same industry, which are published by Dun & Bradstreet and trade associations. Thus, Westerlund can compare her firm's performance not only with that of *other* frame shops but also with that of *small* frame shops that have annual net sales, for example, of under $100,000. In this way, she can identify where her operations are better or worse than other similar firms. For example, if trade association data showed a typical frame shop of her size had a ratio of cost of goods sold to net sales of 37 percent, compared with her 45 percent, she might consider steps to reduce this cost through purchase discounts, reducing inbound freight charges, finding lower-cost suppliers, and so on.

Ratios to Use in Setting and Evaluating Price

Using The Caplow Company as an example, we can study four ratios that relate closely to setting a price: (1) markup, (2) markdown, (3) stockturns, and (4) return on investment. These terms are defined in Figure B–2 and explained below.

Markup

Both markup and gross margin refer to the amount added to the cost of goods sold to arrive at the selling price, and they may be expressed either in dollar or percentage terms. However, the term *markup* is more commonly used in setting retail prices. Suppose the average price Westerlund charges for a framed picture is $80. Then, in terms of the first two definitions in Figure B–2 and the earlier information from the operating statement,

ELEMENT OF PRICE	DOLLAR VALUE
Cost of goods sold	$36
Markup (or gross margin)	44
Selling price	$80

FIGURE B–2

NAME OF FINANCIAL ELEMENT OR RATIO	WHAT IT MEASURES	EQUATION
Selling price ($)	Price customer sees	Cost of goods sold (COGS) + Markup
Markup ($)	Dollars added to COGS to arrive at selling price	Selling price − COGS
Markup on selling price (%)	Relates markup to selling price	$\dfrac{\text{Markup}}{\text{Selling price}} \times 100 = \dfrac{\text{Selling price} - \text{COGS}}{\text{Selling price}} \times 100$
Markup on cost (%)	Relates markup to cost	$\dfrac{\text{Markup}}{\text{COGS}} \times 100 = \dfrac{\text{Selling price} - \text{COGS}}{\text{COGS}} \times 100$
Markdown (%)	Ability of firm to sell its products at initial selling price	$\dfrac{\text{Markdowns}}{\text{Net sales}} \times 100$
Stockturn rate	Ability of firm to move its inventory quickly	$\dfrac{\text{COGS}}{\text{Average inventory at cost}}$ or $\dfrac{\text{Net sales}}{\text{Average inventory at selling price}}$
Return on investment (%)	Profit performance of firm compared with money invested in it	$\dfrac{\text{Net profit after taxes}}{\text{Investment}} \times 100$

How to calculate selling price, markup, markdown, stockturn, and return on investment.

The third definition in Figure B–2 gives the percentage markup on selling price:

$$\text{Markup on selling price (\%)} = \frac{\text{Markup}}{\text{Selling price}} \times 100$$

$$= \frac{44}{80} \times 100 = 55\%$$

And the percentage markup on cost is obtained as follows:

$$\text{Markup on cost (\%)} = \frac{\text{Markup}}{\text{Cost of goods sold}} \times 100$$

$$= \frac{44}{36} \times 100 = 122.2\%$$

Inexperienced retail clerks sometimes fail to distinguish between the two definitions of markup, which (as the preceding calculations show) can represent a tremendous difference, and so it is essential to know whether the base is cost or selling price. Marketers generally use selling price as the base for talking about "markups" unless they specifically state that they are using cost as a base.

Retailers and wholesalers that rely heavily on markup pricing (discussed in Chapter 15) often use standardized tables that convert markup on selling price to markup on cost, and vice versa. The two equations below show how to convert one to the other:

$$\text{Markup on selling price (\%)} = \frac{\text{Markup on cost (\%)}}{100\% + \text{Markup on cost (\%)}}$$

$$\text{Markup on cost (\%)} = \frac{\text{Markup on selling price (\%)}}{100\% - \text{Markup on selling price (\%)}}$$

Using the data from The Caplow Company gives the following:

$$\text{Markup on selling price (\%)} = \frac{\text{Markup on cost (\%)}}{100\% + \text{Markup on cost (\%)}} \times 100$$

$$= \frac{122.2}{100 + 122.2} \times 100 = 55\%$$

$$\text{Markup on cost (\%)} = \frac{\text{Markup on selling price (\%)}}{100\% - \text{Markup on selling price (\%)}} \times 100$$

$$= \frac{55}{100} - 55 \times 100 = 122.2\%$$

The use of an incorrect markup base is shown in Westerlund's business. A markup of 122.2 percent on her cost of goods sold for a typical frame she sells gives 122.2% × $36 = $44 of markup. Added to the $36 cost of goods sold, this gives her a selling price of $80 for the framed picture. However, a new clerk working for her who erroneously priced the framed picture at 55 percent of cost of goods sold set the final price at $55.80 ($36 of cost of goods sold plus 55% × $36 × $19.80). The error, if repeated, can be disastrous: Frames would be mistakenly sold at $55.80, or $24.20 below the intended selling price of $80.

Markdown

A markdown is a reduction in a retail price that is necessary if the item will not sell at the full selling price to which it has been marked up. The item might not sell for a variety of reasons: The selling price was set too high or the item is out of style or has become soiled or damaged. The seller "takes a markdown" by lowering the price to sell it, thereby converting it to cash to buy future inventory that will sell faster.

The markdown percentage cannot be calculated directly from the operating statement. As shown in the fifth item of Figure B–2, the numerator of the markdown percentage is the total dollar markdowns. Markdowns are reductions in the prices of goods that are purchased by customers. The denominator is net sales.

Suppose that The Caplow Company had a total of $700 in markdowns on the prints and posters that are stocked and available for sale. Because the frames are custom made for individual customers, there is little reason for a markdown there. Caplow's markdown percentage then is as follows:

$$\text{Markdown (\%)} = \frac{\text{Markdown}}{\text{Net sales}} \times 100$$

$$= \frac{\$700}{\$80,000} \times 100$$

$$= 0.875\%$$

Other kinds of retailers often have markdown ratios several times this amount. For example, women's dress stores have markdowns of about 25 percent, and menswear stores have markdowns of about 2 percent.

Stockturn Rate

A business firm is anxious to have its inventory move quickly, or "turn over." Stockturn rate, or simply stockturns, measures this inventory movement. For a retailer, a slow stockturn rate may show it is buying merchandise customers do not want, and so this is a critical measure of performance. When a firm sells only a single product, one convenient way to measure stockturn rate is simply to divide its cost of goods sold by average inventory at cost. The sixth item in Figure B–2 shows how to calculate stockturn rate using information in the following operating statement:

$$\text{Stockturn rate} = \frac{\text{Cost of goods sold}}{\text{Average inventory at cost}}$$

The dollar amount of average inventory at cost is calculated by adding the beginning and ending inventories for the year and dividing by 2 to get the average. From Caplow's operating statement, we have the following:

$$\begin{aligned}
\text{Stockturn rate} &= \frac{\text{Cost of goods sold}}{\text{Average inventory at cost}} \\[2mm]
&= \frac{\text{Cost of goods sold}}{\dfrac{\text{Beginning inventory} + \text{Ending inventory}}{2}} \\[2mm]
&= \frac{\$36{,}000}{\dfrac{\$6{,}000 \ + \ \$5{,}000}{2}} \\[2mm]
&= \frac{\$36{,}000}{\$5{,}500} \\[2mm]
&= 6.5 \text{ stockturns per year}
\end{aligned}$$

What is considered a "good stockturn" varies by the kind of industry. For example, supermarkets have limited shelf space for thousands of new products from manufacturers each year, and so they watch stockturn carefully by product line. The stockturn rate in supermarkets for breakfast foods is about 17 times per year, for pet food about 22 times, and for paper products about 25 times per year.

Return on Investment

A better measure of the performance of a firm than the amount of profit it makes in a year is its ROI, which is the ratio of net income to the investment used to earn that net income. To calculate ROI, it is necessary to subtract income taxes from profit before taxes to obtain net income, and then divide this figure by the investment that can be found on a firm's balance sheet (another accounting statement that shows the firm's assets, liabilities, and net worth). While financial and accounting experts have many definitions for "investment," an often-used definition is "total assets."

For our purposes, let us assume that Westerlund has total assets (investment) of $20,000 in The Caplow Company, which covers inventory, store fixtures, and framing equipment. If she pays $1,000 in income taxes, her store's net income is $5,400, and so her ROI is given by the seventh item in Figure B–2:

$$\begin{aligned}
\text{Return on investment} &= \text{Net incomes} \,/\, \text{investment} \times 100 \\[2mm]
&= \$5{,}400/\$20{,}000 \times 100 \\[2mm]
&= 27\%
\end{aligned}$$

If Westerlund wants to improve her ROI next year, the strategies she might take are found in this alternative equation for ROI:

$$\text{ROI} = \text{Net sales/investment} \times \text{Net income/net sales}$$

$$= \text{Investment turnover} \times \text{Profit margin}$$

This equation suggests that The Caplow Company's ROI can be improved by raising turnover or increasing profit margin. Increasing stockturns will accomplish the former, whereas lowering cost of goods sold to net sales will cause the latter.

14 Managing Marketing Channels and Supply Chains

Learning Objectives

After reading this chapter, you should be able to:

LO1 Explain what is meant by a marketing channel of distribution and why intermediaries are often needed.

LO2 Distinguish among traditional marketing channels, electronic marketing channels, multichannel distribution, and different types of vertical marketing systems.

LO3 Describe factors considered by marketing executives when selecting and managing a marketing channel.

LO4 Recognize how conflict, cooperation, and legal considerations affect marketing channels' relationships.

LO5 Recognize the relationship among marketing channels, logistics, and supply chain management, and how a company's supply chain aligns with its marketing strategy.

LO6 Identify the major logistics costs and customer service factors that managers consider when making supply chain decisions.

LO7 Describe the key logistics functions in a supply chain.

Callaway Golf: Designing and Delivering the Goods for Great Golf

What do Morgan Pressel and Phil Mickelson, two world-class golf professionals, have in common? Both use Callaway Golf equipment, accessories, and apparel when playing their favourite sport.

With annual sales approaching $900 million, Callaway Golf is one of the most recognized and highly regarded companies in the golf industry. With its commitment to continuous product innovation and broad distribution in North America and more than 100 countries worldwide, Callaway Golf has built a strong reputation for designing and delivering the goods for golfers of all skill levels, both amateur and professional. Callaway Golf primarily markets its products through more than 15,000 on- and off-course authorized golf retailers and sporting goods retailers, such as Golf Town; Golf Galaxy, Inc.; Dick's Sporting Goods, Inc.; and PGA Tour Superstores, which sell quality golf products and provide a level of customer service appropriate for the sale of such products. Callaway Golf considers its retailers a valuable marketing asset.

The company also has its own online store (**CallawayGolf.com**), which makes it a full-fledged multichannel marketer, and a successful one as well. Soon after Callaway's online store was launched, the chief executive of PGA of America called the store "innovative in that it combines that old legacy relationship with the retail channel with the new innovation of the Web." According to a Marketing Group spokesperson, "Callaway produces in-house a wide-ranging, high volume of original content from instructional videos to interviews with R&D leads and tour pros, blog posts, and even live streams of Callaway events. This commitment to creating original content helps to give consumers a better feel for the company and its products when they go to purchase equipment online and at retail."

Today, **CallawayGolf.com** is a dynamic, engaging, and interactive website that constantly delivers new in-depth product information and media, original social content, user-generated content, and e-commerce capabilities. All of this helps consumers become better informed during the purchasing process. Not surprisingly, **CallawayGolf.com** is listed among the top Internet retailers in North America. Golfers in Canada can go to **CaCallawayGolf.com** for a similar online experience.[1]

Providing Callaway's authorized golf retailers and sporting goods retailers with the right products, at the right place, at the right time, and in the right quantity and condition is the responsibility of the company's supply chain. Callaway sources raw materials for its golf equipment, accessories, and all apparel from around the world. At the same time, Callaway delivers its finished products to company retailers through external shipping companies, such as United Parcel Service (UPS).[2]

This chapter first focuses on marketing channels of distribution and why they are an important component in the marketing mix. It then shows how such channels benefit consumers and the sequence of firms that make up a marketing channel. Finally, it describes factors that influence the choice and management of marketing channels, including channel conflict and cooperation. The discussion then turns to the significance of supply chains and logistics management. In particular, attention is placed on the necessary alignment between supply chain management and marketing strategy and the trade-offs managers make between total distribution costs and customer service.

NATURE AND IMPORTANCE OF MARKETING CHANNELS

Reaching prospective buyers, either directly or indirectly, is a prerequisite for successful marketing. At the same time, buyers benefit from distribution systems used by firms.

LO1 Defining Marketing Channels of Distribution

You see the results of distribution every day. You may have purchased Lay's potato chips at Mac's Milk, a book through **Chapters.Indigo.ca**, and Levi's jeans at Sears. Each of these items was brought to you by a marketing channel of distribution, or simply a **marketing channel**, which consists of individuals and firms involved in the process of making a product or service available for use or consumption by consumers or industrial users.

Marketing channels can be compared with a pipeline through which water flows from a source to a terminus. Marketing channels make possible the flow of goods from a producer, through intermediaries, to a buyer. Intermediaries go by various names (Figure 14–1) and perform various functions. Some intermediaries actually purchase items from the seller, store them, and resell them to buyers. For example, Sunshine Biscuits produces cookies and sells them to food wholesalers. The wholesalers then sell the cookies to supermarkets and grocery stores, which, in turn, sell them to consumers. Other intermediaries, such as brokers and agents, represent sellers but do not actually take title to products—their role is to bring a seller and buyer together. Century 21 real estate agents are examples of this type of intermediary. The importance of intermediaries is made even clearer when we consider the functions they perform and the value they create for buyers.

FIGURE 14–1

TERM	DESCRIPTION
Middleman	Any intermediary between the manufacturer and end-user markets
Agent or broker	Any intermediary with legal authority to act on behalf of the manufacturer
Wholesaler	An intermediary who sells to other intermediaries, usually to retailers; term usually applies to consumer markets
Retailer	An intermediary who sells to consumers
Distributor	An imprecise term, usually used to describe intermediaries who perform a variety of distribution functions, including selling, maintaining inventories, extending credit, and so on; a more common term in business markets but may also be used to refer to wholesalers
Dealer	A more imprecise term than *distributor* that can mean the same as distributor, retailer, wholesaler, and so forth

Terms used for marketing intermediaries.

Source: American Marketing Association. Used by permission.

Value Created by Intermediaries

Few consumers appreciate the value created by intermediaries. However, producers recognize that intermediaries make selling goods and services more efficient because they minimize the number of sales contacts necessary to reach a target market. Figure 14–2 shows a simple example of how this comes about in the digital camera industry. Without a retail intermediary (such as Best Buy), Kodak, Sony, Panasonic, and Hewlett-Packard would each have to make four contacts to reach the four buyers shown, who are in the target market. However, each producer has to make only one contact when Best Buy acts as an intermediary. Equally important from a macromarketing perspective, the total number of industry transactions is reduced from 16 to 8, which reduces producer cost and hence benefits the consumer.

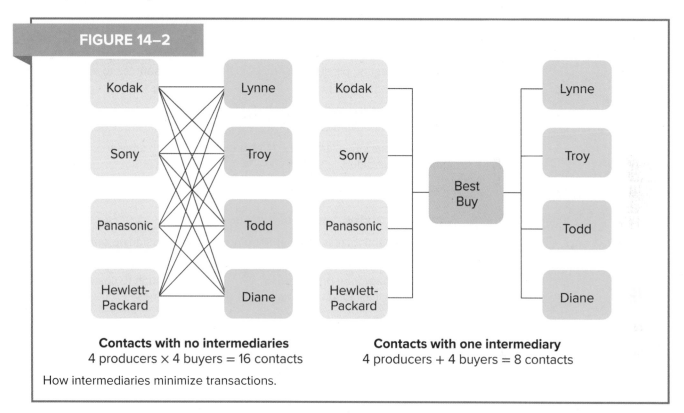

FIGURE 14–2

Contacts with no intermediaries
4 producers × 4 buyers = 16 contacts

Contacts with one intermediary
4 producers + 4 buyers = 8 contacts

How intermediaries minimize transactions.

Functions Performed by Intermediaries

Intermediaries make possible the flow of products from producers to buyers by performing three basic functions (Figure 14–3). Most prominently, intermediaries perform a transactional function that involves buying, selling, and risk taking because they stock merchandise in anticipation of sales. Intermediaries perform a logistical function evident in the gathering, storing, and dispersing of products. Finally, intermediaries perform facilitating functions, which assist producers in making goods and services more attractive to buyers.

All three functions must be performed in a marketing channel, even though each channel member may not participate in all three. Channel members often negotiate about which specific functions they will perform. Sometimes disagreements result, and a breakdown in relationships among channel members occurs. This happened when PepsiCo's bottler in Venezuela switched to Coca-Cola. Because all marketing channel functions had to be performed, PepsiCo either had to set up its own bottling operation to perform the marketing channel functions or find another bottler, which it did.

Consumer Benefits from Intermediaries

Consumers also benefit from intermediaries. Having the goods and services you want, when you want them, where you want them, and in the form you want them is the ideal result of marketing channels. For example, FedEx provides next-morning delivery, Esso offers gas stations along Canadian highways, and airlines allow tickets to be generated by online travel agencies.

TYPE OF FUNCTION	ACTIVITIES RELATED TO FUNCTION
Transactional function	• *Buying*: Purchasing products for resale or as an agent for supply of a product • *Selling*: Contacting potential customers, promoting products, and seeking orders • *Risk taking*: Assuming business risks in the ownership of inventory that can become obsolete or deteriorate
Logistical function	• *Assorting*: Creating product assortments from several sources to serve customers • *Storing*: Assembling and protecting products at a convenient location to offer better customer service • *Sorting*: Purchasing in large quantities and breaking into smaller amounts desired by customers • *Transporting*: Physically moving a product to customers
Facilitating function	• *Financing*: Extending credit to customers • *Grading*: Inspecting, testing, or judging products and assigning them quality grades • *Marketing information and research*: Providing information to customers and suppliers, including competitive conditions and trends

Marketing channel functions performed by intermediaries.

Learning Review

1. What is meant by a marketing channel?
2. What are the three basic functions performed by intermediaries?

CHANNEL STRUCTURE AND ORGANIZATION

A product can take many routes on its journey from a producer to buyers, and marketers search for the most efficient route from the many alternatives available.

Marketing Channels for Consumer Goods and Services

Figure 14–4 shows the four most common marketing channels for consumer goods and services. It also shows the number of levels in each marketing channel, as evidenced by the number of intermediaries between a producer and ultimate buyers. As the number of intermediaries between a producer and buyer increases, the channel is viewed as increasing in length. Thus, the producer → wholesaler → retailer → consumer channel is longer than the producer → consumer channel.

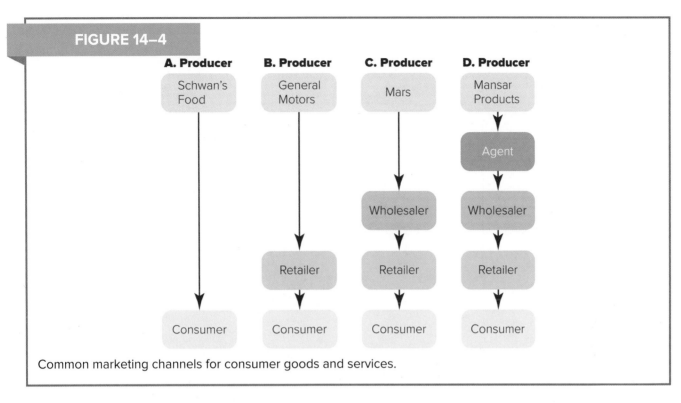

FIGURE 14–4

A. Producer	B. Producer	C. Producer	D. Producer
Schwan's Food	General Motors	Mars	Mansar Products
			Agent
		Wholesaler	Wholesaler
	Retailer	Retailer	Retailer
Consumer	Consumer	Consumer	Consumer

Common marketing channels for consumer goods and services.

Channel A represents a **direct channel** because a producer and ultimate consumers deal directly with each other. Many products and services are distributed this way. A number of insurance companies sell their financial services using a direct channel and branch sales offices. The Schwan Food Company markets a full line of frozen foods using door-to-door salespeople who sell to customers from refrigerated trucks. Because there are no intermediaries with a direct channel, the producer must perform all channel functions.

The remaining three channel forms are considered **indirect channels** because intermediaries are inserted between the producer and consumers and perform numerous channel functions. Channel B, with a retailer added, is most common when a retailer is large and can buy in large quantities from a producer, or when the cost of inventory makes it too expensive to use a wholesaler. Such manufacturers as General Motors and Ford use this channel, and a local car dealer acts as a retailer. Why is there no wholesaler? So many variations exist in the product that it would be impossible for a wholesaler to stock all the models required to satisfy buyers; in addition, the cost of maintaining an inventory would be too high. However, large retailers, such as Sears Canada, Hudson's Bay, and Target, buy in sufficient quantities to make it cost effective for a producer to deal with only a retail intermediary.

Adding a wholesaler in Channel C is most common for low-cost, low-unit-value items that are frequently purchased by consumers, such as candy, confectionary items, and magazines. For example, Mars sells its line of candies to wholesalers in case quantities; wholesalers can then break down (sort) the cases so that individual retailers can order in boxes or much smaller quantities.

Channel D, the most indirect channel, is employed when there are many small manufacturers and many small retailers and an agent is used to help coordinate a large supply of the product. Mansar Products, Ltd. is a Belgian producer of specialty jewellery that uses agents to sell to wholesalers, which then sell to many small retailers.

Marketing Channels for Business Goods and Services

The four most common channels for business goods and services are shown in Figure 14–5. In contrast to channels for consumer products, business channels typically are shorter and rely on one intermediary or none at all because business users are fewer in number, tend to be more concentrated geographically, and buy in larger quantities (see Chapter 6).

Channel A, represented by IBM's large, mainframe computer business, is a direct channel. Firms using this channel maintain their own salesforce and perform all channel functions. This channel is employed when buyers are large and well defined, the sales effort requires extensive negotiations, and the products are of high unit value and require hands-on expertise in terms of installation or use.

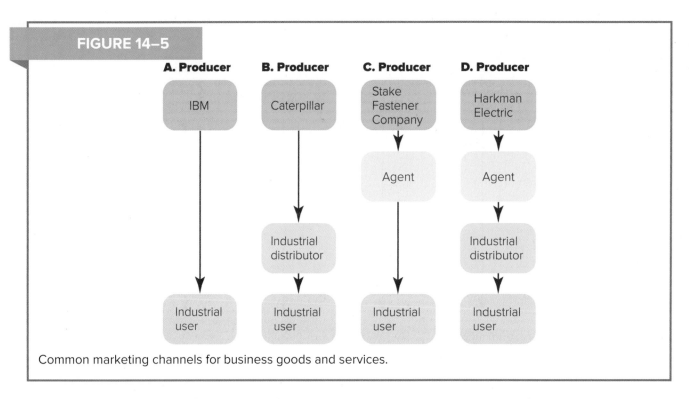

FIGURE 14–5

Common marketing channels for business goods and services.

Channels B, C, and D are indirect channels with one or more intermediaries to reach business customers. In Channel B, a **business distributor** performs a variety of marketing channel functions, including selling, stocking, and delivering a full product assortment and financing. In many ways, business distributors are like wholesalers in consumer channels. Caterpillar relies on business distributors to sell its construction and mining equipment in over 200 countries. In addition to selling, Caterpillar distributors stock 40,000 to 50,000 parts, and service equipment using highly trained technicians.[3]

Channel C introduces a second intermediary, an *agent,* who serves primarily as the independent selling arm of producers and represents a producer to industrial users. For example, Stake Fastener Company, a producer of industrial fasteners, has an agent call on business customers rather than employing its own salesforce.

Channel D is the longest channel and includes both agents and distributors. For instance, Harkman Electric, a producer of electric products, uses agents to call on electrical distributors, who sell to business customers.

Internet Marketing Channels

These common marketing channels for consumer and business goods and services are not the only routes to the marketplace. Advances in electronic commerce have opened new avenues for reaching buyers and creating customer value. **Internet marketing channels** employ the Internet to make products and services available for consumption or use by consumers or business buyers. A unique feature of these channels is that they combine electronic and traditional intermediaries to create value for buyers.[4]

Figure 14–6 shows the electronic marketing channels for books (**Amazon.ca**), automobiles (**autoTRADER.ca**), reservation services (**Travelocity.ca**), and personal computers (**Dell.ca**). Are you surprised that they look a lot like the common marketing channels? An important reason for the similarity resides in channel functions detailed in Figure 14–3. Electronic intermediaries can and do perform transactional and facilitating functions effectively and at a relatively lower cost than traditional intermediaries because of efficiencies made possible by information technology. However, electronic intermediaries are incapable of performing elements of the logistical function, particularly for such products as books and automobiles. This function remains with traditional intermediaries or with the producer, as evident with Dell, Inc. and its direct channel.

Many services can be distributed through electronic marketing channels, such as travel reservations marketed by **Travelocity.ca**, financial securities by Scotia iTRADE, and insurance by **MetLife.ca**. Software, too, can be marketed this way. However, many other services, such as health care and auto repair, still involve traditional intermediaries. With the growth of social media platforms such as Facebook, many companies are also turning to social media as a distribution channel.

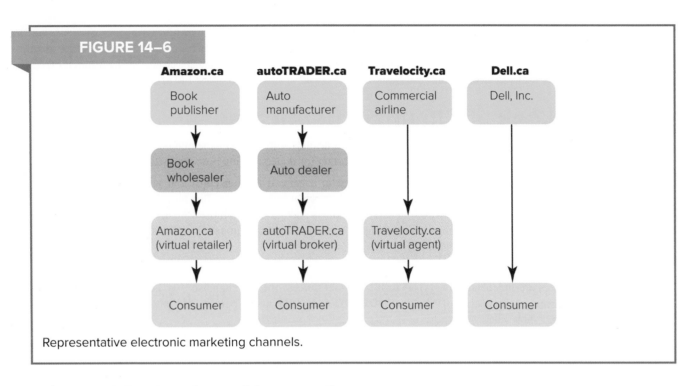

FIGURE 14–6

Representative electronic marketing channels.

Direct Marketing Channels

Many firms also use direct marketing channels to reach buyers. **Direct marketing channels** (sometimes referred to as *direct-to-customer,* or *DTC* or *D2C*) allow consumers to buy products by interacting with various media without a face-to-face meeting with a salesperson. Direct marketing includes mail-order selling, direct-mail sales, catalogue sales, telemarketing, interactive media, social media, and televised home shopping.[5]

Some firms sell products almost entirely through direct marketing channels. These firms include L.L. Bean (apparel) and **Dell.ca** (personal computers). Such manufacturers as Nestlé and Sunkist, in addition to using traditional channels composed of wholesalers and retailers, employ direct marketing through websites, catalogues, and telemarketing to reach more buyers. At the same time, retailers such as Sears Canada use direct marketing techniques to augment conventional store merchandising activities.

Multiple Channels and Strategic Alliances

Historically, most organizations used a single channel of distribution to reach their customers. Today, however, many firms engage in multichannel distribution. **Multichannel marketing**, sometimes called *omnichannel marketing*, is the blending of different communication and delivery channels that are mutually reinforcing in attracting, retaining, and building relationships with consumers who shop and buy from traditional intermediaries and online. Multichannel marketing seeks to integrate a firm's electronic marketing and delivery channels. At Eddie Bauer, for example, every effort is made to make the apparel shopping and purchase experience for its customers the same across its retail store, catalogue, and website channels.

Multichannel marketing also can leverage the value-adding capabilities of different channels. For example, retail stores leverage their physical presence by allowing customers to pick up their online orders at a nearby store or return or exchange non-store purchases if they wish. Catalogues can serve as shopping tools for online purchasing, as they do for store purchasing. Websites can help consumers do their homework before visiting a store. For example, Staples has leveraged its store, catalogue, and website channels with impressive results.

In some situations, producers use *dual distribution*, an arrangement whereby a firm reaches different buyers by employing two or more different types of channels for the same basic product. For example, GE sells its large appliances directly to home and apartment builders but uses retail stores, including Lowe's home centres, to sell to consumers. In some instances, firms pair multiple channels with a multibrand strategy. This is done to minimize cannibalization of the firm's family brand and differentiate the channels. For example, Hallmark sells its Hallmark greeting cards through Hallmark stores and select department stores and its Ambassador brand of cards through discount and drugstore chains.

Another innovation in marketing channels is the use of **strategic channel alliances**, whereby one firm's marketing channel is used to sell another firm's products. An alliance between Kraft Foods and Starbucks is an example. Kraft distributes Starbucks coffee in supermarkets. Strategic alliances are also popular in global marketing, where the creation of marketing and channel relationships is expensive and time consuming. For example, General Mills and Nestlé have an extensive alliance that spans 140 markets worldwide.[6]

A Closer Look at Channel Intermediaries

Channel structures for consumer and business products assume various forms based on the number and type of intermediaries. Knowledge of the roles played by these intermediaries is important for understanding how channels operate in practice.

The terms *wholesaler, agent,* and *retailer* have been used in a general fashion consistent with the meanings given in Figure 14–1. However, on closer inspection, a variety of specific types of intermediaries emerges. These intermediaries engage in wholesale activities—those activities involved in selling products and services to those who are buying for the purposes of resale or business use. Intermediaries engaged in retailing activities are discussed in detail in Chapter 15.

Merchant Wholesalers

Merchant wholesalers are independently owned firms that take title to the merchandise they handle. They go by various names, including business or industrial distributor (described earlier). About 83 percent of the firms engaged in wholesale activities are merchant wholesalers.

Merchant wholesalers are classified as either full-service or limited-service wholesalers, depending on the number of functions performed. Two major types of full-service wholesalers exist. *General merchandise (or full-line) wholesalers* carry a broad assortment of merchandise and perform all channel functions. This type of wholesaler is most prevalent in the hardware, drug, and clothing industries. However, these wholesalers do not maintain much depth of assortment within specific product lines. *Specialty merchandise (or limited-line) wholesalers* offer a relatively narrow range of products but have an extensive assortment within the product lines carried. They perform all channel functions and are found in the health foods, automotive parts, and seafood industries. Four major types of specialty merchandise or limited-service wholesalers exist: (1) rack jobbers, (2) cash-and-carry wholesalers, (3) drop shippers, and (4) truck jobbers.

Agents and Brokers

Unlike merchant wholesalers, agents and brokers do not take title to merchandise and typically provide fewer channel functions. They make their profit from commissions or fees paid for their services, whereas merchant wholesalers make their profit from the sale of the merchandise they own.

Manufacturer's agents and selling agents are the two major types of agents used by producers. **Manufacturer's agents**, or *manufacturer's representatives,* work for several producers and carry non-competitive, complementary merchandise in an exclusive territory. Manufacturer's agents act as a producer's sales arm in a territory and are principally responsible for the transactional channel functions, primarily selling. They are used extensively in the automotive supply, footwear, and fabricated steel industries. By comparison, **selling agents** represent a single producer and are responsible for the entire marketing function of that producer. They design promotional plans, set prices, determine distribution policies, and make recommendations on product strategy. Selling agents are used by small producers in the textile, apparel, food, and home furnishing industries.

Brokers are independent firms or individuals whose principal function is to bring buyers and sellers together to make sales. Brokers, unlike agents, usually have no continuous relationship with the buyer or seller but negotiate a contract between two parties and then move on to another task. Brokers are used extensively by producers of seasonal products (such as fruits and vegetables) and in the real estate industry.

A unique broker that acts in many ways like a manufacturer's agent is a food broker, representing buyers and sellers in the grocery industry. Food brokers differ from conventional brokers because they act on behalf of producers on a permanent basis and receive a commission for their services. For example, Nabisco uses food brokers to sell its candies, margarine, and Planters peanuts, but it sells its line of cookies and crackers directly to retail stores.

Manufacturer's Branches and Offices

Unlike merchant wholesalers, agents, and brokers, manufacturer's branches and sales offices are wholly owned extensions of the producer that perform wholesale activities. Producers assume wholesale functions when there are no intermediaries to perform these activities, customers are few in number and geographically concentrated, or orders are large or require significant attention. A *manufacturer's branch office* carries a producer's inventory and performs the functions of a full-service whole-saler. A *manufacturer's sales office* does not carry inventory, typically performs only a sales function, and serves as an alternative to agents and brokers.

Vertical Marketing Systems and Channel Partnerships

The traditional marketing channels described so far represent a loosely knit network of independent producers and intermediaries brought together to distribute goods and services. However, new channel arrangements have emerged for the purpose of improving efficiency in performing channel functions and achieving greater marketing effectiveness. These new arrangements are called vertical marketing systems and channel partnerships. **Vertical marketing systems (VMS)** are professionally managed and centrally coordinated marketing channels designed to achieve channel economies and maximum marketing impact.[7] Figure 14–7 depicts the major types of vertical marketing systems: corporate, contractual, and administered.

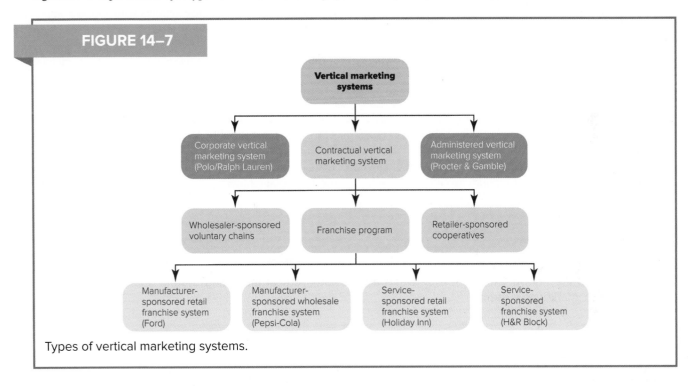

FIGURE 14–7

Types of vertical marketing systems.

Corporate Systems

The combination of successive stages of production and distribution under a single ownership is a *corporate vertical marketing system.* For example, a producer might own the intermediary at the next level down in the channel. This practice, called *forward integration,* is exemplified by Irving Oil, which refines gasoline and also operates retail gasoline stations. Other examples of forward integration include Goodyear, Singer, Sherwin Williams, and the building materials division of Boise Cascade. Alternatively, a retailer might own a manufacturing operation, a practice called *backward integration.* For example, Safeway supermarkets operate their own bakeries, and Tim Hortons operates its own coffee-roasting facilities.

Companies seeking to reduce distribution costs and gain greater control over supply sources or resale of their products pursue forward and backward integration. However, both types of integration increase a company's capital investment and fixed costs. For this reason, many companies favour contractual vertical marketing systems to achieve channel efficiencies and marketing effectiveness.

Sherwin-Williams represents a type of vertical marketing system.
Sherwin-Williams
www.sherwin-williams.com

Contractual Systems

Under a *contractual vertical marketing system,* independent production and distribution firms integrate their efforts on a contractual basis to obtain greater functional economies and marketing impact than they could achieve alone. Contractual systems are the most popular among the three types of vertical marketing systems.

Three variations of contractual systems exist: (1) *wholesaler-sponsored voluntary chains* where a wholesaler develops a contractual relationship with small, independent retailers to standardize and coordinate buying practices, merchandising programs, and inventory management efforts; (2) *retailer-sponsored cooperatives* where small, independent retailers form an organization that operates a wholesale facility cooperatively; and (3) *franchising.* **Franchising** is a contractual arrangement between a parent company (a franchisor) and an individual or firm (a franchisee) that allows the franchise to operate a certain type of business under an established name and according to specific rules. Four types of franchise arrangements are most popular: (1) manufacturer-sponsored retail franchise systems (prominent in the automobile industry), (2) manufacturer-sponsored wholesale systems (evident in the soft-drink industry), (3) service-sponsored retail franchise systems with a unique approach for performing a service (such as McDonald's), and (4) service-sponsored franchise systems where franchisors license individuals or firms to dispense a service under a trade name and specific guidelines (e.g., H&R Block tax services). Service-sponsored franchise arrangements are the fastest-growing type of franchise. Franchising is discussed further in Chapter 15.

Administered Systems

In comparison, *administered vertical marketing systems* achieve coordination at successive stages of production and distribution by the size and influence of one channel member rather than through ownership. Procter & Gamble, given its broad product assortment ranging from disposable diapers to detergents, is able to obtain cooperation from supermarkets in displaying, promoting, and pricing its products. Walmart can obtain cooperation from manufacturers in terms of product specifications, price levels, and promotional support, given its position as the world's largest retailer.

Learning Review

3. What is the difference between a direct channel and an indirect channel?

4. What is the principal distinction between a corporate vertical marketing system and an administered vertical marketing system?

LO3   CHANNEL CHOICE AND MANAGEMENT

Marketing channels not only link a producer to its buyers but also provide the means through which a firm implements various elements of its marketing strategy. Therefore, choosing a marketing channel is a critical decision.

Factors Affecting Channel Choice and Management

The final choice of a marketing channel by a producer depends on a number of factors that often interact with each other.

Environmental Factors

The changing environment described in Chapter 3 has an important effect on the choice and management of a marketing channel. For example, the Fuller Brush Company, a name synonymous with door-to-door selling, now uses catalogues and telemarketing to reach customers. Rising employment among women, resulting in fewer being at home during working hours, prompted this action. Advances in the technology of growing, transporting, and storing perishable cut flowers has allowed many retailers, such as Calgary's Kensington Florist, to eliminate flower wholesalers and buy direct from flower growers. Additionally, the Internet has created new marketing channel opportunities for online marketing of flowers as well as consumer electronics, books, and music and video products.

Consumer Factors

Consumer characteristics have a direct bearing on the choice and management of a marketing channel. Determining which channel is most appropriate is based on answers to some fundamental questions, such as: Who are potential customers? Where do they buy? When do they buy? How do they buy? What do they buy? And what experience are they seeking? The answers to these questions also indicate the type of intermediary best suited to reaching target buyers.

Product Factors

In general, highly sophisticated products, such as large, scientific computers; unstandardized products, such as custom-built machinery; and products of high unit value are distributed directly to buyers. Unsophisticated, standardized products with low unit value, such as table salt, are typically distributed through indirect channels. A product's stage in the life cycle also affects marketing channels.

Company Factors

A firm's financial, human, or technological capabilities affect channel choice. For example, firms that are unable to employ a salesforce might use manufacturer's agents or selling agents to reach wholesalers or buyers. If a firm has multiple products for a particular target market, it might use a direct channel, whereas firms with a limited product line might use intermediaries of various types to reach buyers.

Channel Design Considerations

Recognizing that numerous routes to buyers exist and also recognizing the factors just described, marketing executives typically consider three questions when choosing a marketing channel and intermediaries:

1. Which channel and intermediaries will provide the best coverage of the target market?
2. Which channel and intermediaries will best satisfy the buying requirements of the target market?
3. Which channel and intermediaries will be the most profitable?

Target Market Coverage

Achieving the best coverage of the target market requires attention to the density and type of intermediaries to be used at the retail level of distribution. Three degrees of distribution density exist: intensive, exclusive, and selective. *Intensive distribution* means that a firm tries to place its products and services in as many outlets as possible. Intensive distribution is usually chosen for convenience products or services—for instance, candy, fast food, newspapers, and soft drinks. Increasingly, medical services are distributed in this fashion. Cash—yes, cash—is also distributed intensively by Visa. Visit Visa's website, described in the Going Online box, "Need Cash Fast? Check the Visa ATM Locator," to locate the nearest Visa automated teller machine.

GOING ONLINE

Need Cash Fast? Check the Visa ATM Locator

Short of cash? Visa offers a valuable web resource in its ATM Locator, which can be accessed at **www.visa.com/atmlocator**. Visa has some 1.4 million automatic teller machines in more than 200 countries. One is probably in your neighbourhood, wherever that is in the world! To find the nearest Visa ATM, follow the easy ATM Locator directions and request a site map. You will be in the money in no time.

Dario Pignatelli/Bloomberg via Getty Images

Exclusive distribution is the extreme opposite of intensive distribution because only one retail outlet in a specified geographical area carries the firm's product. Exclusive distribution is typically chosen for specialty products or services—for example, automobiles, some women's fragrances, men's suits, and yachts. Sometimes, retailers sign exclusive distribution agreements with manufacturers. Gucci, one of the world's leading luxury goods companies, uses exclusive distribution, while luxury retailer Saks Inc. seeks exclusive product lines for its stores.[8]

Selective distribution lies between these two extremes and means that a firm selects a few retail outlets in a specific geographical area to carry its products. Selective distribution weds some of the market coverage benefits of intensive distribution to the control over resale evident with exclusive distribution. For this reason, selective distribution is the most common form of distribution intensity and is usually associated with shopping goods or services, such as Rolex watches and Ping golf clubs.

Satisfying Buyer Requirements

A second consideration in channel design is gaining access to channels and intermediaries that satisfy at least some of the interests buyers might want fulfilled when they purchase a firm's products or services. These interests fall into four categories: (1) information, (2) convenience, (3) variety, and (4) pre- or post-sale services.

Information is an important requirement when buyers have limited knowledge or desire specific data about a product or service. Properly chosen intermediaries communicate with buyers through in-store displays, demonstrations, and personal selling. Personal computer manufacturers, such as Apple Inc., have opened their own retail outlets staffed with highly trained personnel to inform buyers how their products can better meet each customer's needs.

Convenience has multiple meanings for buyers, such as proximity or driving time to a retail outlet. For example, Mac's Milk stores, with outlets nationwide, satisfy this interest for buyers, and candy and snack food firms benefit by gaining display space in these stores. For other consumers, convenience means a minimum of time and hassle. Jiffy Lube and Mr. Lube, which promise to change engine oil and filters quickly, appeal to this aspect of convenience. For those who shop on the Internet, convenience means that websites must be easy to locate and navigate, and image downloads must be fast.

Variety reflects buyers' interest in having numerous competing and complementary items from which to choose. Variety is evident in both the breadth and depth of products and brands carried by intermediaries, which enhances their attraction to buyers. Thus, manufacturers of pet food and supplies seek distribution through pet superstores, such as Petco and PetsMart, which offer a wide array of pet products.

Pre- or post-sale services provided by intermediaries are an important buying requirement for such products as large household appliances that require delivery, installation, and credit. Therefore, Whirlpool seeks dealers that provide such services.

Profitability

The third consideration in designing a channel is profitability, which is determined by the margins earned (revenues minus cost) for each channel member and for the channel as a whole. Channel cost is the critical dimension of profitability. These costs include distribution, advertising, and selling expenses associated with different types of marketing channels. The extent to which channel members share these costs determines the margins received by each member and by the channel as a whole.

Companies routinely monitor the performance of their marketing channels. Read the Using Marketing Dashboards box to see how ABC Furniture views the sales and profit performance of its marketing channels.

USING MARKETING DASHBOARDS

Channel Sales and Profit at ABC Furniture

ABC is a mid-size furniture manufacturer. It sells its furniture through furniture store chains, independent furniture stores, and department store chains. The company has traditionally allocated its marketing funds for cooperative advertising, in-store displays, and retail sales support on the basis of dollar sales by channel.

Your Challenge   As the vice president of sales and marketing at ABC Furniture, you have been asked to review the company's sales and profit in its three channels and recommend a course of action. The question: Should ABC Furniture continue to allocate its marketing funds on the basis of channel dollar sales or profit?

Your Findings   ABC Furniture tracks the sales and profit from each channel (and individual customer) and sales trends on its marketing dashboard. This information is displayed in the marketing dashboard below.

Several findings stand out. Furniture store chains and independent furniture stores account for 85.2 percent of ABC Furniture sales and 93 percent of company profit. These two channels also evidence growth as measured by annual percentage change in sales. By comparison, department store chains annual percentage sales growth has declined and recorded negative growth in 2017. This channel accounts for 14.8 percent of company sales and 7 percent of company profit.

Your Action   ABC Furniture should consider abandoning the practice of allocating marketing funds solely on the basis of channel sales volume. The importance of independent furniture stores to ABC's profitability warrants further spending, particularly given this channel's favourable sales trend. Doubling the percentage allocation for marketing funds for this channel may be too extreme, however. Rather, an objective and task promotional budgeting method should be adopted (see Chapter 16). ABC Furniture might also consider the longer-term role of department store chains as a marketing channel.

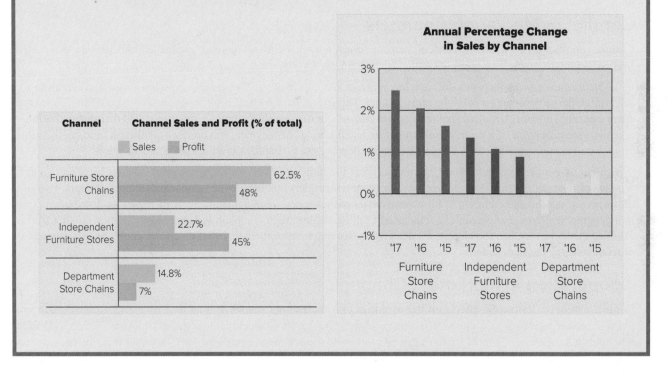

Global Dimensions of Marketing Channels

Marketing channels around the world reflect traditions, customs, geography, and the economic history of individual countries and societies. Even so, the basic marketing channel functions must be performed. But differences do exist and are illustrated by highlighting marketing channels in Japan.

Intermediaries outside Western Europe and North America tend to be small, numerous, and often owner-operated. Japanese marketing channels tend to include many intermediaries based on tradition and lack of storage space. As many as five intermediaries are involved in the distribution of soap in Japan compared with one or two in North America.

Understanding marketing channels in global markets is often a prerequisite to successful marketing. For example, Gillette attempted to sell its razors and blades through company salespeople in Japan as it does in North America, thus eliminating wholesalers traditionally involved in marketing toiletries. Warner-Lambert Company sold its Schick razors and blades through the traditional Japanese channel involving wholesalers. The result? Schick achieved a commanding lead over Gillette in the Japanese razor and blade market.[9]

Channel relationships also must be considered. In Japan, the distribution *keiretsu* (translated as "alignments") bonds producers and intermediaries together. The bond, through vertical integration and social and economic ties, ensures that each channel member benefits from the distribution alignment. The dominant member of the distribution *keiretsu,* which is typically a producer, has considerable influence over channel member behaviour, including which competing products are sold by other channel members. Well-known Japanese companies, such as Matsushita (electronics), Nissan and Toyota (automotive products), Nippon Gakki (musical instruments), and Kirin (and other brewers and distillers), employ the distribution *keiretsu* extensively. Shiseido and Kanebo, for instance, influence the distribution of cosmetics through Japanese department stores.

(LO4) Channel Relationships: Conflict, Cooperation, and Law

Unfortunately, because channels consist of independent individuals and firms, there is always potential for disagreements concerning who performs which channel functions, how profits are allocated, which products and services will be provided by whom, and who makes critical channel-related decisions. These channel conflicts necessitate measures for dealing with them. Sometimes, they result in legal action.

Conflict in Marketing Channels

Channel conflict arises when one channel member believes another channel member is engaged in behaviour that prevents it from achieving its goals. Two types of conflict occur in marketing channels: vertical conflict and horizontal conflict.[10]

Vertical conflict occurs between different levels in a marketing channel—for example, between a manufacturer and a wholesaler or retailer or between a wholesaler and a retailer. Three sources of vertical conflict are most common. First, conflict arises when a channel member bypasses another member and sells or buys products direct, a practice called **disintermediation**. Second, disagreements over how profit margins are distributed among channel members produce conflict. A third conflict situation arises when manufacturers believe wholesalers or retailers are not giving their products adequate attention.

Horizontal conflict occurs between intermediaries at the same level in a marketing channel, such as between two or more retailers (Target and Walmart), or between two or more wholesalers that handle the same manufacturer's brands. Two sources of horizontal conflict are common.[11] First, horizontal conflict arises when a manufacturer increases its distribution coverage in a geographical area. For example, a franchised Cadillac dealer might complain to General Motors that another franchised Cadillac dealer has located too close to its dealership. Second, multichannel distribution causes conflict when different types of retailers carry the same brands.

Cooperation in Marketing Channels

Conflict can have destructive effects on the workings of a marketing channel, and so it is necessary to secure cooperation among channel members. One means is through a *channel captain,* a channel member that coordinates, directs, and supports other channel members. Channel captains can be producers, wholesalers, or retailers. P&G assumes this role because it has a strong consumer following in such brands as Crest, Tide, and Pampers. Therefore, it can set policies or terms that supermarkets will follow. Walmart and Home Depot are retail channel captains because of their strong consumer image, number of outlets, and purchasing volume.

A firm becomes a channel captain because it is typically the channel member with the ability to influence the behaviour of other members.[12] Influence can take four forms. First, economic influence arises from the ability of a firm to reward other members given its strong financial position or customer franchise. Microsoft Corporation has such influence. Expertise is a second source of influence over other channel members. Third, identification with a particular channel member may also create influence for that channel member. For instance, retailers may compete to carry the Ralph Lauren line, or clothing manufacturers may compete to be carried by well-known retailers. In both instances, the desire to be associated with a channel member gives that firm influence over others. Finally, influence can arise from the legitimate right of one channel member to direct the behaviour of other members. This situation would occur under contractual vertical marketing systems where a franchisor could legitimately direct how a franchisee behaves. Other means for securing cooperation in marketing channels rest in the different variations of vertical marketing systems.

Channel influence can be used to gain concessions from other channel members. For instance, some large supermarket chains expect manufacturers to pay allowances, in the form of cash or free goods, to stock and display their products. Some manufacturers call these allowances "extortion," as described in the Making Responsible Decisions box, "The Ethics of Slotting Allowances."[13]

MAKING RESPONSIBLE DECISIONS

The Ethics of Slotting Allowances

Have you ever wondered why your favourite cookies are no longer to be found at your local supermarket? Or why that delicious tortilla chip you like to serve at parties is missing from the shelves and replaced by another brand?

Blame it on slotting allowances. Some large supermarket chains demand slotting allowances from food manufacturers, paid in the form of money or free goods, to stock and display products. These allowances can run up to $25,000 per item for a supermarket chain. Not surprisingly, slotting allowances have been labelled "ransom," "extortional allowances," and "commercial bribery" by manufacturers because they already pay supermarkets "trade dollars" to promote and discount their products. Small food manufacturers, in particular, view slotting allowances as an economic barrier to the distribution of their products. Supermarket operators see these allowances as a reasonable cost of handling business for manufacturers.

Is the practice of charging slotting allowances unethical behaviour?

Legal Considerations

Conflict in marketing channels is typically resolved through negotiation or the exercise of influence by channel members. Sometimes, conflict produces legal action. Therefore, knowledge of legal restrictions affecting channel strategies and practices is important. Some restrictions were described in Chapter 13, namely, vertical price fixing and price discrimination. However, other legal considerations unique to marketing channels warrant attention.

In general, suppliers have the right to choose the intermediaries that carry or represent their products. However, suppliers can run into legal difficulty over *refusing to deal* with customers who can meet the usual trade terms offered by the supplier. The *Competition Act* looks seriously at cases where a supplier withholds or withdraws products from a customer if such behaviour will adversely affect the customer.

Dual distribution is a situation where a manufacturer distributes through its own vertically integrated channel in direct competition with wholesalers and retailers that also sell its products. If the manufacturer's behaviour is viewed as an attempt to unduly lessen competition by eliminating wholesalers or retailers, then such action may violate the *Competition Act* and would be examined by the Competition Bureau.

Vertical integration is viewed in a similar light. Like dual distribution, it is not illegal, but the practice could be subject to legal action if such integration were designed to eliminate or lessen competition unduly.

Exclusive dealing and tied selling are prohibited under the *Competition Act* if they are found to unduly lessen competition or create monopolies. *Exclusive dealing* exists when a supplier requires channel members to sell only its products or restricts distributors from selling directly competitive products. *Tied selling* occurs when a supplier requires a distributor purchasing some products to buy others from the supplier. These arrangements often arise in franchising. Tied selling would be investigated by the Competition Bureau if the tied products could be purchased at fair market value from other suppliers at desired standards of the franchisor and if the arrangements were seen as restricting competition. Full-line forcing is a special kind of tied selling. This is a supplier's requiring that a channel member carry its full line of products to sell a specific item in the supplier's line.

Resale or market restrictions refer to a supplier's attempt to stipulate to whom distributors may resell the supplier's products and in what specific geographical areas or territories they may be sold. These practices could be subject to review under the *Competition Act* if such restrictions were deemed to be restraining or lessening competition.

5. What are the three degrees of distribution density?

6. What are the three questions marketing executives consider when choosing a marketing channel and intermediaries?

7. What is meant by "exclusive dealing"?

LO5 LOGISTICS AND SUPPLY CHAIN MANAGEMENT

A marketing channel relies on logistics to actually make products available to consumers and business users—a point emphasized earlier in this chapter. Logistics involves those activities that focus on getting the right amount of the right products to the right place at the right time at the lowest possible cost. The performance of these activities is **logistics management**, the practice of organizing the *cost-effective flow* of raw materials, in-process inventory, finished goods, and related information from point of origin to point of consumption to satisfy *customer requirements*. This perspective is represented in the concept of a supply chain and the practice of supply chain management.

A **supply chain** is a sequence of firms that perform activities required to create and deliver a good or service to consumers or industrial users. It differs from a marketing channel in terms of membership. A supply chain includes suppliers who provide raw material inputs to a manufacturer as well as the wholesalers and retailers who deliver finished goods to you. The management process is also different. **Supply chain management** is the integration and organization of information and logistics activities *across firms* in a supply chain for the purpose of creating and delivering goods and services that provide value to consumers. The relationship among marketing channels, logistics management, and supply chain management is shown in Figure 14–8. An important feature of supply chain management is its application of sophisticated information technology, which allows companies to share and operate systems for order processing, transportation scheduling, and inventory and facility management.

FIGURE 14–8

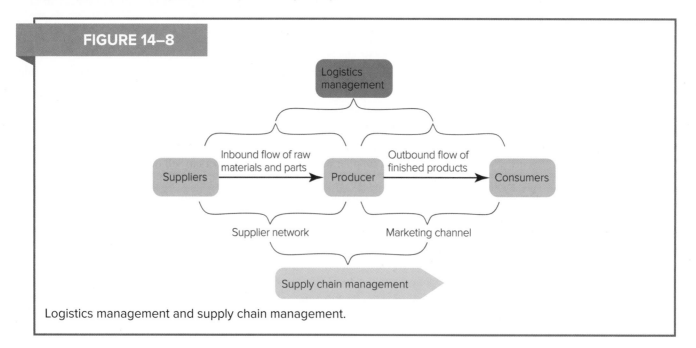

Logistics management and supply chain management.

Sourcing, Assembling, and Delivering a New Car: The Automotive Supply Chain

All companies are members of one or more supply chains. A supply chain is essentially a sequence of linked suppliers and customers in which every customer is, in turn, a supplier to another customer until a finished product reaches the final consumer. Even the simplified supply chain diagram for car makers shown in Figure 14–9 illustrates how complex a supply chain can be.[14] A car maker's supplier network includes thousands of firms that provide the 5,000 or so parts in a typical automobile. They provide items ranging from raw materials, such as steel and rubber, to components, including transmissions, tires, brakes, and seats, to complex subassemblies and assemblies evident in chassis and suspension systems that make for a smooth, stable ride. Coordinating and scheduling material and component flows for their assembly into actual automobiles by car makers is heavily dependent on logistical activities, including transportation, order processing, inventory control, materials handling, and information technology. A central link is the car maker supply chain manager, who is responsible for translating customer requirements into actual orders and arranging for delivery dates and financial arrangements for automobile dealers. This is not an easy task, given the different consumer preferences and the amounts consumers are willing to pay.

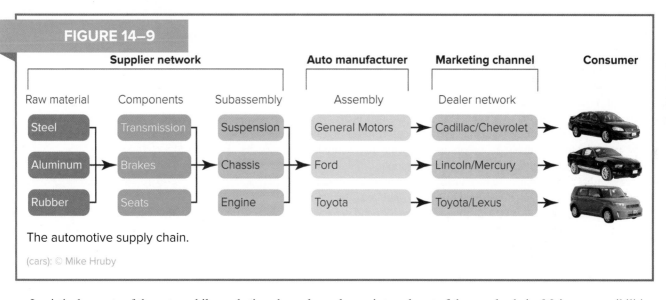

FIGURE 14–9

The automotive supply chain.

(cars): © Mike Hruby

Logistical aspects of the automobile marketing channel are also an integral part of the supply chain. Major responsibilities include transportation, which involves the selection and oversight of external carriers (trucking, airline, railroad, and shipping companies) for cars and parts to dealers; the operation of distribution centres; the management of finished goods inventories; and order processing for sales. Supply chain managers also play an important role in the marketing channel. They work with extensive car dealer networks to ensure that the right mix of automobiles is delivered to different locations. In addition, they make sure that spare and service parts are available so that dealers can meet the car maintenance and repair needs of consumers. All of this is done with the help of information technology that links the entire automotive supply chain. What does all of this cost? It is estimated that logistics costs represent 25 to 30 percent of the retail price of a typical new car.

Supply Chain Management and Marketing Strategy

The automotive supply chain illustration shows how information and logistics activities are integrated and organized across firms to create and deliver a car for you. What is missing from this illustration is the link between a specific company's supply chain and its marketing strategy. Just as companies have different marketing strategies, they also manage supply chains differently. More specifically, the goals to be achieved by a firm's marketing strategy determine whether its supply chain needs to be more responsive or efficient in meeting customer requirements.

Aligning a Supply Chain with Marketing Strategy

There are a variety of supply chain configurations, each of which is designated to perform a different task well. Marketers today recognize that the choice of a supply chain follows from a clearly defined marketing strategy and involves three steps:[15]

1. *Understand the customer.* To understand the customer, a company must identify the needs of the customer segment being served. These needs, such as a desire for a low price or convenience of purchase, help a company define the relative importance of efficiency and responsiveness in meeting customer requirements.

2. *Understand the supply chain.* Second, a company must understand what a supply chain is designed to do well. Supply chains range from those that emphasize being responsive to customer requirements and demand to those that emphasize efficiency with a goal of supplying products at the lowest possible delivered cost.

3. *Harmonize the supply chain with the marketing strategy.* Finally, a company needs to ensure that what the supply chain is capable of doing well is consistent with the targeted customer's needs and its marketing strategy. If a mismatch exists between what the supply chain does particularly well and a company's marketing strategy, the company will either need to redesign the supply chain to support the marketing strategy or change the marketing strategy. The bottom line is that a poorly designed supply chain can do serious damage to an otherwise brilliant marketing strategy.

How are these steps applied and how are efficiency and responsive considerations built into a supply chain? Let us briefly look at how two market leaders—Dell Computer Corporation and Walmart, Inc.—have harmonized their supply chain and marketing strategies.[16]

Dell Computer Corporation: A Responsive Supply Chain

The Dell marketing strategy targets customers who wish to have the most up-to-date personal computer equipment customized to their needs. These customers are also willing to (1) wait to have their customized personal computer delivered in a few days rather than picking out a model at a retail store, and (2) pay a reasonable, though not the lowest, price in the marketplace. Given Dell's customer segment, the company has the option of adopting an efficient or responsive supply chain. An efficient supply chain may use inexpensive but slower modes of transportation, emphasize economies of scale in its production process by reducing the variety of PC configurations offered, and limit its assembly and inventory storage facilities to a single location. If Dell opted only for efficiency in its supply chain, it would be difficult, if not

World-class marketers Dell Computer and Walmart emphasize responsiveness and efficiency in their supply chains.

(left): Courtesy of Dell, Inc.; (right): Courtesy of WalMart Stores, Inc.

impossible, to satisfy its target customer's desire for rapid delivery and a wide variety of customizable products. Dell, instead, has opted for a responsive supply chain. It relies on more expensive express transportation for receipt of components from suppliers and delivery of finished products to customers. The company achieves product variety and manufacturing efficiency by designing common platforms across several products and using common components. Dell operates manufacturing facilities in various countries to ensure rapid delivery. Moreover, Dell has invested heavily in information technology to link itself with suppliers and customers.

Walmart, Inc.: An Efficient Supply Chain

Now, let us consider Walmart. Walmart's marketing strategy is to be a reliable, lower-price retailer for a wide variety of mass-consumption consumer goods. This strategy favours an efficient supply chain designed to deliver products to consumers at the lowest possible cost. Efficiency is achieved in a variety of ways. For instance, Walmart keeps relatively low inventory levels, and most inventory is stocked in stores available for sale, not in warehouses gathering dust. The low inventory arises from Walmart's innovative use of *cross-docking*—a practice that involves unloading products from suppliers, sorting products for individual stores, and quickly reloading products onto trucks for a particular store. No warehousing or storing of products occurs, except for a few hours or at most a day. Cross-docking allows Walmart to operate only a small number of distribution centres to service its vast network of Walmart stores, Supercentres, and Sam's Clubs, which contributes to efficiency. On the other hand, the company runs its own fleet of trucks to service its stores. This does increase cost and investment, but the benefits in terms of responsiveness justify the cost, in Walmart's case. Walmart has invested significantly more than its competitors have in information technology to operate its supply chain. The company feeds information about customer requirements and demand from its stores back to its suppliers, which manufacture only what is being demanded. This large investment has improved the efficiency of Walmart's supply chain and made it responsive to customer needs.

Three lessons can be learned from these two examples. First, there is no one best supply chain for every company. Second, the best supply chain is the one that is consistent with the needs of the customer segment being served and complements a company's marketing strategy. And finally, supply chain managers are often called upon to make trade-offs between efficiency and responsiveness on various elements of a company's supply chain.

INFORMATION AND LOGISTICS MANAGEMENT OBJECTIVE IN A SUPPLY CHAIN

The objective of information and logistics management in a supply chain is to minimize logistics costs while delivering maximum customer service. The Dell Computer and Walmart examples highlight how two market leaders have realized this objective by different means. An important similarity between these two companies is that both use information to leverage logistics activities, reduce logistics costs, and improve customer service.

Information's Role in Supply Chain Responsiveness and Efficiency

Information consists of data and analysis regarding inventory, transportation, distribution facilities, and customers throughout the supply chain.[17] Continuing advances in information technology make it possible to track logistics activities and customer service variables and manage them for efficiency and responsiveness. For example, information on customer-demand patterns allows pharmaceutical companies, such as Eli Lilly and GlaxoSmithKline, to produce and stock medicines in anticipation of customer needs. This improves supply chain responsiveness because customers will find the medicines when and where they want them. Demand information improves supply chain efficiency because pharmaceutical firms are better able to forecast customer needs and produce, transport, and store the required amount of inventory.

A variety of technologies are used to transmit and manage information in a supply chain. An *electronic data interchange* (EDI) combines proprietary computer and telecommunication technologies to exchange electronic invoices, payments, and information between suppliers, manufacturers, and retailers. When linked with store scanning equipment and systems, EDI provides a seamless electronic link from a retail checkout counter to suppliers and manufacturers. Walmart and Procter & Gamble actually pioneered the use of EDI, and it is commonly used in the retail, apparel, transportation, pharmaceutical, grocery, health care, and insurance industries, as well as by local, provincial, and federal government agencies. About 95 percent of the companies listed in the *Fortune 1000* use EDI, as do most of the Canadian companies listed in the *Financial Post 500*. At Hewlett-Packard, for example, one million EDI transactions are made every month.

Another technology, the *extranet,* permits secure business-to-business communication between a manufacturer and its suppliers, distributors, and sometimes other partners (such as advertising agencies). Extranets are less expensive and more flexible to operate than EDI because of their connection to the public Internet. This technology is prominent in private electronic exchanges described in Chapter 6.

Whereas EDI and extranets transmit information, other technologies help manage information in a supply chain. Enterprise resource planning (ERP) technology and supply chain management software track logistics cost and customer service variables, both of which are described next.

Total Logistics Cost Concept

For our purposes, **total logistics cost** includes expenses associated with transportation, materials handling and warehousing, inventory, stockouts (being out of inventory), order processing, and return goods handling. Note that many of these costs are interrelated, and so changes in one will impact the others. For example, as the firm attempts to minimize its transportation costs by shipping in larger quantities, it will also experience an increase in inventory levels. Larger inventory levels will not only increase inventory costs but should also reduce stockouts. It is important, therefore, to study the impact on all of the logistics decision areas when considering a change.

Customer Service Concept

Because a supply chain is a *flow,* the end of it—or *output*—is the service delivered to customers. Within the context of a supply chain, **customer service** is the ability of logistics management to satisfy users in terms of time, dependability, communication, and convenience. As suggested by Figure 14–10, a supply chain manager's key task is to balance these four customer service factors against total logistics cost factors.

FIGURE 14–10

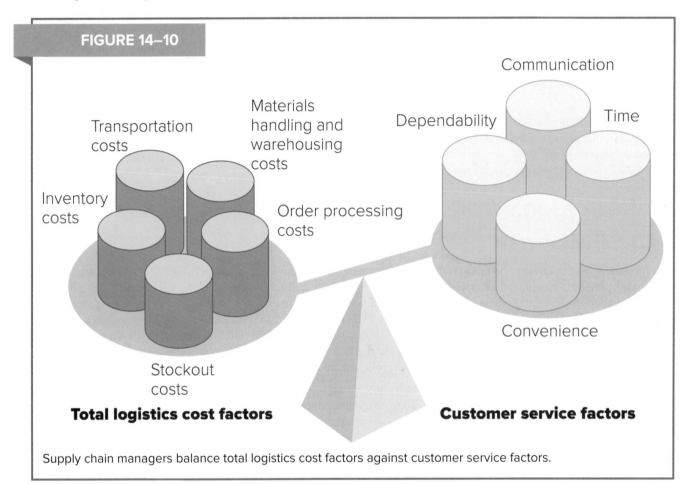

Total logistics cost factors   **Customer service factors**

Supply chain managers balance total logistics cost factors against customer service factors.

Time

In a supply chain setting, time refers to *lead time* for an item, which means the lag from ordering an item until it is received and ready for use or sale. This is also referred to as *order cycle time* or *replenishment time* and may be more important to retailers or wholesalers than consumers. The various elements that make up the typical order cycle include recognition of the need to order, order transmittal, order processing, documentation, and transportation. A current emphasis in supply chain management is to reduce lead time so that the inventory levels of customers may be minimized. Another emphasis is to make the process of reordering and receiving products as simple as possible, often through electronic data and inventory systems called *quick response* and *efficient consumer response* delivery systems. These inventory management systems are designed to reduce the retailer's lead time for receiving merchandise, thereby lowering a retailer's inventory investment, improving customer service levels, and reducing logistics expense.

Dependability

Dependability is the consistency of replenishment. This is important to all firms in a supply chain and to consumers. It can be broken into three elements: consistent lead time, safe delivery, and complete delivery. Consistent service allows planning (such as appropriate inventory levels), whereas inconsistencies create surprises. Intermediaries may be willing to accept longer lead times if they know about them in advance and can thus make plans.

Communication

Communication is a two-way link between buyer and seller that helps in monitoring service and anticipating future needs. Status reports on orders are a typical example of improved communication between buyer and seller.

Convenience

The concept of convenience for a supply chain manager means that there should be a minimum of effort on the part of the buyer in doing business with the seller. Is it easy for the customer to order? Are the products available from many outlets? Does the buyer have to buy huge quantities of the product? Will the seller arrange all necessary details, such as transportation? The seller must concentrate on removing unnecessary barriers to customer convenience.

Learning Review

10. The objective of information and logistics management in a supply chain is to _____.

11. How does consumer demand information increase supply chain responsiveness and efficiency?

LO7   KEY LOGISTICS FUNCTIONS IN A SUPPLY CHAIN

The four key logistic functions in a supply chain include (1) transportation, (2) warehousing and materials handling, (3) order processing, and (4) inventory management. These functions have become so complex and interrelated that many companies have outsourced them to third-party logistics providers. *Third-party logistics providers* are firms that perform most or all of the logistics functions that manufacturers, suppliers, and distributors would normally perform themselves.[18] Today, many of Canada's top manufacturers outsource one or more logistics functions, at least on a limited basis. UPS Supply Chain Solutions, FedEx Supply Chain Services, DHL, and Penske Logistics are just a few of the companies that specialize in handling logistics functions for their clients.

The four major logistics functions and the involvement of third-party logistics providers are described in detail next.

Transportation

Transportation provides the movement of goods necessary in a supply chain. There are five basic modes of transportation—railroads, motor carriers, air carriers, pipelines, and water carriers—and modal combinations involving two or more modes, such as highway trailers on a rail flatcar.

All transportation modes can be evaluated on six basic service criteria:

- *Cost.* Charges for transportation.
- *Time.* Speed of transit.
- *Capability.* What can be realistically carried with this mode.
- *Dependability.* Reliability of service regarding time, loss, and damage.
- *Accessibility.* Convenience of the mode's routes (such as pipeline availability).
- *Frequency.* Scheduling.

Figure 14–11 summarizes service advantages and disadvantages of the five basic modes of transportation available.[19] To read about a unique transportation concept that provides vital supplies to Canada's diamond mines in the north, check out the Marketing Matters box, "Canada's Ice Road," which describes Canada's ice road and the truckers who risk their lives travelling it.[20]

FedEx and UPS are two third-party logistics providers that perform most or all of the logistics functions that manufacturers, suppliers, and distributors would normally perform.

FedEx

www.fedex.com

UPS

www.ups.com

(left): Courtesy of FedEx Corporation; (right): © Douglas C. Pizac/AP Photo/The Canadian Press

FIGURE 14–11

MODE	RELATIVE ADVANTAGES	RELATIVE DISADVANTAGES
Rail	• Full capability • Extensive routes • Low cost	• Some reliability, damage problems • Not always complete pickup and delivery • Sometimes slow
Truck	• Complete pickup and delivery • Extensive routes • Fairly fast	• Size and weight restrictions • Higher cost • More weather sensitive
Air	• Fast • Low damage • Frequent departures	• High cost • Limited capabilities
Pipeline	• Low cost • Very reliable • Frequent departures	• Limited routes (accessibility) • Slow
Water	• Low cost • Huge capacities	• Slow • Limited routes and schedules • More weather sensitive

Advantages and disadvantages of five modes of transportation.

MARKETING MATTERS

Canada's Ice Road

When it comes to epic engineering, nothing tops the Tibbitt to Contwoy to Winter Road, a superhighway of ice that extends hundreds of kilometres from Yellowknife, Northwest Territories, into the neighbouring territory of Nunavut over frozen lakes and spongy tundra. To build it, workers from Nuna Logistics put in 20-hour days and fight cold wind chills that dip to 70 below zero. By the end of January, the workers complete the longest heavy-haul ice road in the world. It is as wide as an eight-lane highway, and 75 percent of it is built over frozen lakes. When the ice thickens by late February, it is capable of supporting 70-tonne super trucks. This ice road and the trucks that travel it supply the diamond mines of northern Canada. Without the ice road and the vital supplies that travel across it, the diamond mines could not operate effectively. In about a decade, Canada has gone from producing and marketing no diamonds to being the third-largest producer by value in the world, producing more than 12 million carats worth over $1.5 billion. In many ways, the ice road and the truckers who use it have made this industry possible.

To stay in operation, the mines require 300,000 tonnes of fuel, explosives, steel, and concrete, all hauled over the ice each year. If the ice roads do not hold up and truckers cannot make their runs, stranded freight has to be flown in, at six to eight times the cost. This results in added costs to the diamond mines of tens of millions of dollars each year. And, because of weather conditions, many flights are cancelled or delayed, resulting in curtailed operations of the mines. Thus, the ice road plays a vital logistics function in the supply chain of Canada's growing diamond industry. The truckers take great risks driving the ice roads, and people have lost their lives when the ice surface gives way. But the truckers take the risk because they can make almost a year's salary in only nine to ten

James Reeve/Getty Images

weeks of work. The ice road only lasts a few months, and close to 10,000 loads must make it through from February to April. Then, the next January, they will rebuild the road all over again, and the supply chain to the diamond mines will be re-established.

Warehousing and Materials Handling

Warehouses may be classified in one of two ways: (1) storage warehouses, and (2) distribution centres. In *storage warehouses,* the goods are intended to come to rest for some period of time, as in the aging of products or in storing household goods. *Distribution centres,* on the other hand, are designed to facilitate the timely movement of goods and represent a very important part of a supply chain. They represent the second-most significant cost in a supply chain after transportation.

Distribution centres not only allow firms to hold their stock in decentralized locations but also are used to facilitate sorting and consolidating products from different plants or different suppliers. Some physical transformation can also take place in distribution centres, for example, mixing or blending different ingredients, labelling, and repackaging. Paint companies, such as Sherwin-Williams and Benjamin Moore, use distribution centres for this purpose. In addition, distribution centres may serve as manufacturer sales offices and order processing centres.

Materials handling, which involves moving goods over short distances into, within, and out of warehouses and manufacturing plants, is a key part of warehouse operations. The two major problems with this activity are high labour costs and high rates of loss and damage. Every time an item is handled, there is a chance for loss or damage. Common materials handling equipment includes forklifts, cranes, and conveyors. Today, materials handling in warehouses is automated by using computers and robots to reduce the cost of holding, moving, and recording inventories.

Order Processing

There are several stages in the processing of an order, and a failure at any one of them can cause a problem with the customer. The process starts with transmitting the order by a variety of means, such as the Internet, an extranet, or electronic data interchange (EDI). This is followed by entering the order in the appropriate databases and sending the information to those who need it. For example, a regional warehouse is notified to prepare an order. After checking inventory, a new quantity may need to be reordered from the production line, or purchasing may be requested to reorder from a vendor. If the item is currently out of stock, a *backorder* is created, and the whole process of keeping track of a small part of the original order must be managed. In addition, credit may have to be checked for some customers, all documentation for the order must be prepared, transportation must be arranged, and an order confirmation must be sent. Order processing systems are evaluated in terms of speed and accuracy.

Electronic order processing has replaced manual processing for most large Canadian companies. For example, 96 percent of IBM's purchase transactions with suppliers are conducted on the Internet. Kiwi Brands, the marketer of Kiwi shoe polish, Endust, and Behold, receives 75 percent of its retailers' purchase orders via EDI. The company has also implemented financial EDI, sending invoices to retailers and receiving payment order/remittance advice documents and electronic funds transfer (EFT) payments. Shippers as well are linked to the system, allowing Kiwi to receive shipment status messages electronically.

Inventory Management

Inventory management is one of the primary responsibilities of the supply chain manager. The major problem is maintaining the delicate balance between too little and too much. Too little inventory may result in poor service, stockouts, brand switching, and loss of market share; too much leads to higher costs because of the money tied up in inventory and the risk that it may become obsolete.

Materials handling through automation is now common in distribution centres.

© Chuck Savage/Getty Images

Reasons for Inventory

Traditionally, carrying inventory has been justified on several grounds: (1) to offer a buffer against variations in supply and demand, often caused by uncertainty in forecasting demand; (2) to provide better service for those customers who wish to be served on demand; (3) to promote production efficiencies; (4) to provide a hedge against price increases by suppliers; (5) to promote purchasing and transportation discounts; and (6) to protect the firm from such contingencies as strikes and shortages. However, companies today view inventory as something to be moved, not stored, and more of a liability than an asset. The traditional justification for inventory has resulted in excessive inventories that have proven costly to maintain. Consider the North American automobile industry. Despite efforts to streamline its supply chain, industry analysts estimate that more than $230 billion worth of excess inventory piles up annually in the form of unused raw materials, parts waiting to be delivered, and vehicles sitting on dealers' lots.[21]

Inventory Costs

Specific inventory costs are often hard to detect because they are difficult to measure and occur in many different parts of the firm. A classification of inventory costs includes the following:

- *Capital costs.* The opportunity costs resulting from tying up funds in inventory instead of using them in other, more profitable investments; these are related to interest rates.
- *Inventory service costs.* Such items as insurance and taxes that are present in many provinces.
- *Storage costs.* Warehousing space and materials handling.
- *Risk costs.* Possible loss, damage, pilferage, perishability, and obsolescence.

Storage costs, risk costs, and some service costs vary according to the characteristics of the items inventoried. For example, perishable products or highly seasonal items have higher risk costs than a commodity-type product, such as lumber. Capital costs are always present and are proportional to the *values* of the item and prevailing interest rates. The costs of carrying inventory vary with the particular circumstances but quite easily could range from 10 to 35 percent for different firms.

Supply Chain Inventory Strategies

Conventional wisdom a decade ago was that a firm should protect itself against uncertainty by maintaining a reserve inventory at each of its production and stocking points. This has been described as a "just-in-case" philosophy of inventory management and led to unnecessarily high levels of inventory. In contrast is the **just-in-time (JIT) concept**, which is an inventory supply system that operates with very low inventories and requires fast, on-time delivery. When parts are needed for production, they arrive from suppliers "just in time," which means neither before nor after they are needed. Note that JIT is used in situations where demand forecasting is reliable, such as when supplying an automobile production line, and is not suitable for inventories that are to be stored over significant periods of time.

Electronic data interchange and electronic messaging technology coupled with the constant pressure for faster response time in replenishing inventory have also changed the way suppliers and customers do business in a supply chain. The approach, called **vendor-managed inventory (VMI)**, is an inventory-management system whereby the *supplier* determines the product amount and assortment a customer (such as a retailer) needs and automatically delivers the appropriate items.

Campbell's Soup's system illustrates how VMI works.[22] Campbell's first establishes EDI links with retailers. Every morning, retailers electronically inform the company of their demand for all Campbell's products and the inventory levels in their distribution centres. Campbell's uses that information to forecast future demand and determine which products need replenishment based on upper and lower inventory limits established with each retailer. Trucks leave the Campbell's shipping plant that afternoon and arrive at the retailer's distribution centres with the required replenishments the same day.

Closing the Loop: Reverse Logistics

The flow of goods in a supply chain does not end with the consumer or industrial user. Companies today recognize that a supply chain can work in reverse. **Reverse logistics** is a process of reclaiming recyclable and reusable materials, returns, and reworks from the point of consumption or use for repair, remanufacturing, redistribution, or disposal. The effect of reverse logistics can be seen in the reduced waste in landfills and lowered operating costs for companies.

Such companies as Nokia (return and reuse of mobile phones), and HP, Caterpillar, Xerox, and IBM (remanufacturing and recycling) have acclaimed reverse logistics programs.[23] Other firms have enlisted third-party logistics providers to handle this process along with other supply chain functions.

Learning Review

12. What are the basic trade-offs among the modes of transportation?

13. What types of inventory should use storage warehouses, and which types should use distribution centres?

14. What are the strengths and weaknesses of a just-in-time system?

Learning Objectives Review

LO1 **Explain what is meant by a marketing channel of distribution and why intermediaries are often needed.**

A marketing channel of distribution, or simply a marketing channel, consists of individuals and firms involved in the process of making a product or service available for use or consumption by consumers and business users. Intermediaries make possible the flow of products from producers to buyers by performing three basic functions. The transactional function involves buying, selling, and risk taking because intermediaries stock merchandise in anticipation of sales. The logistics function involves the gathering, storing, and dispensing of products. The facilitating function assists producers in making products and services more attractive to buyers.

LO2 **Distinguish among traditional marketing channels, electronic marketing channels, multichannel distribution, and different types of vertical marketing systems.**

Traditional marketing channels describe the route taken by products and services from producers to buyers. This route can range from a direct channel with no intermediaries, because a producer and ultimate consumers deal directly with each other, to indirect channels where intermediaries (agents, wholesalers, distributors, or retailers) are inserted between a producer and consumer and perform numerous channel functions. Internet marketing channels employ the Internet to make products and services available for consumption and use by consumer or business buyers. Today, many firms engage in multichannel distribution including multichannel marketing, sometimes called *omnichannel marketing*, which is the blending of different communication and delivery channels that are mutually reinforcing in attracting, retaining, and building relationships with consumers who shop and buy in traditional intermediaries and online. Dual distribution and strategic alliances are used. Vertical marketing systems (VMS) are professionally managed and centrally coordinated marketing channels designed to achieve channel economics and maximum marketing impact. There are three types of VMS: corporate, contractual, and administered.

LO3 **Describe factors considered by marketing executives when selecting and managing a marketing channel.**

Four factors affect a company's choice and management of a marketing channel: environmental factors, consumer factors, product factors, and company factors. Recognizing that numerous routes to buyers exist and also recognizing the factors just described, marketers consider three questions when choosing and managing a marketing channel. Which channel and intermediaries will provide the best coverage of the target market? Marketers typically choose one of three levels of coverage: intensive, selective, and exclusive distribution. Which channel and intermediaries will best satisfy the buying requirements of the target market? These buying requirements include information, convenience, variety, and pre- and post-sale services. Which channel and intermediaries will be the most profitable?

LO4 **Recognize how conflict, cooperation, and legal considerations affect marketing channels' relationships.**

Because marketing channels consist of independent individuals and firms, there is the potential for conflict. Two types of conflict can occur: vertical and horizontal. Vertical conflict occurs between different levels of a marketing channel while horizontal conflict occurs between intermediaries at the same level in a marketing channel. One way to reduce the prospect of conflict is to have a channel captain—a channel member that coordinates, directs, and supports other channel members. However, sometimes channel conflict can result in legal action. Such legal action arises from channel practices that are perceived to restrain competition or to create monopolies.

 Recognize the relationship among marketing channels, logistics, and supply chain management, and how a company's supply chain aligns with its marketing strategy.

A marketing channel relies on logistics to make products available to consumers and business users. Logistics involves those activities that focus on getting the right amount of the right products to the right place at the right time at the lowest possible cost. The performance of these activities is logistics management—the practice of organizing the cost-effective flow of raw materials, in-process inventory, finished goods, and related information from point of origin to point of consumption to satisfy customer requirements.

A supply chain is a sequence of firms that perform activities required to create and deliver a product or service to consumers or business users. It differs from a marketing channel in terms of membership. A supply chain includes suppliers that provide raw material inputs to a manufacturer as well as the wholesalers and retailers that deliver products and services. The management process is also different. Supply chain management is the integration and organization of information and logistics activities across firms in a supply chain for the purpose of creating and delivering products and services that provide value to consumers.

A company's supply chain follows from its defined marketing strategy. The alignment of a company's supply chain with its marketing strategy involves three steps: (*1*) a supply chain must reflect the needs of the customer being served, (*2*) a company must understand what a supply chain is designed to do well, and (*3*) a supply chain must be consistent with the customer's needs and the company's marketing strategy.

 Identify the major logistics costs and customer service factors that managers consider when making supply chain decisions.

Companies strive to provide superior customer service while controlling logistics costs. The major customer service factors include the time between orders and deliveries, dependability in replenishing inventory, communication between buyers and sellers, and convenience in buying from the seller. Logistics cost factors include transportation, materials handling and warehousing, order processing, inventory, and stockouts.

LO7   **Describe the key logistics functions in a supply chain.**

The four logistics functions in a supply chain include transportation, warehousing and materials handling, order processing, and inventory management. Transportation provides the movement of goods necessary in a supply chain. Five major transport modes are railroads, motor carriers, air carriers, pipelines, and water carriers. Warehousing and materials handling include the storing, sorting, and handling of products at storage warehouse or distribution centres. Order processing includes order receipt, delivery, invoicing, and collection from customers. Inventory management involves minimizing inventory-carrying costs while maintaining sufficient stocks of products to satisfy customer needs. Two popular inventory management practices are just-in-time (JIT) and vendor-managed inventory (VMI) systems.

Applying Marketing Knowledge

1. Suppose that the president of a carpet manufacturing firm has asked you to look into the possibility of bypassing the firm's wholesalers (who sell to carpet, department, and furniture stores) and sell direct to these stores. What caution would you voice on this matter, and what type of information would you gather before making this decision?

2. How does the channel captain idea differ among corporate, administered, and contractual vertical marketing systems with particular reference to the use of different forms of influence available to firms?

3. How do specialty, shopping, and convenience goods generally relate to intensive, selective, and exclusive distribution? Give a brand name that is an example of each goods–distribution matchup.

4. List several companies to which logistical activities might be unimportant. Also, list some whose focus is only on the inbound or outbound side.

5. List the logistics customer service factors that would be important to buyers in the following types of companies: (*a*) manufacturing, (*b*) retailers, (*c*) hospitals, and (*d*) construction.

6. The auto industry is a heavy user of just-in-time concept. Why? What other industries would be good candidates for its application? What do they have in common?

7. What are some types of business in which order processing may be among the most important success factors in terms of logistics management?

Building Your Marketing Plan

Does your marketing plan involve selecting channels and intermediaries? If so:

1. Identify which channel and intermediaries will provide the best coverage of the target market for your product and service.
2. Specify which channel and intermediaries will best satisfy the important buying requirements of the target market.
3. Determine which channel and intermediaries will be the most profitable.

Select your channel(s) and intermediary(ies). Now, does your marketing plan involve a product? If so:

1. If inventory is involved, (*a*) identify the three or four kinds of inventory needed for your organization (retail stock, finished goods, raw materials, supplies, and so on), and (*b*) suggest ways to reduce their costs.
2. (*a*) Rank the four customer service factors (time, dependability, communication, and convenience) from most important to least important from your customers' point of view, and (*b*) identify actions for the one or two most important factors to serve customers better.

Video Case 14

Amazon: Delivering the Earth's Biggest Selection!

"The secret is we are on our seventh generation of fulfillment centres and we have gotten better every time," explains Jeff Bezos, CEO of **Amazon.com**, Inc. The global online retailer is a pioneer of fast, convenient, low-cost shopping that has attracted millions of consumers. Of course, while Amazon has changed the way many people shop, the company still faces the traditional and daunting task of creating a seamless flow of deliveries.

The Company

Bezos started **Amazon.com** with a simple idea: Use the Internet to transform book buying into the fastest, easiest, and most enjoyable shopping experience possible. The company was incorporated in 1994 and launched its website in July 1995. At the forefront of a huge growth of dot-com businesses, Amazon pursued a get-big-fast business strategy. Sales grew rapidly and Amazon began adding products and services other than books. In fact, Amazon soon set its goal on being "Earth's most customer-centric company, where customers can find and discover virtually anything they might want to buy online."

Today, **Amazon.com** continues to grow by providing low prices, vast selection, and convenience. Its selection of products covers a broad range of categories including books; movies, music, and games; electronics and computers; home, garden, and tools; beauty, health, and grocery; toys; clothing, shoes, and jewellery; sports and outdoors; and automotive and industrial. In addition, Amazon offers digital music, an app store for Android, Amazon Cloud Drive, Kindle e-readers, Kindle Fire tablets, Amazon Fire TV, and the Amazon Fire phone. Other services allow customers to:

* Search for a product or brand using all or part of its name.

* Place orders with one click using the "Buy Now with 1-Click" button on the website, and the "Mobile 1-Click" button for phones.

* Receive personalized recommendations based on past purchases through opt-in e-mails.

These products and services have attracted millions of people around the globe. Further, the company's growth has made **Amazon.com**, along with its international sites in Australia, Brazil, Canada, China, France, Germany, India, Italy, Japan, Mexico, Spain, and the United Kingdom, the world's largest online retailer.

Amazon's e-commerce platform is also used by more than 2 million small businesses, retail brands, and individual sellers. For example, programs such as Selling on Amazon, Fulfillment by Amazon, Amazon Webstore, and Checkout by Amazon allow small businesses to use Amazon's e-commerce platform to facilitate sales. Online retailers store their products at Amazon's fulfillment centres and when they sell a product, Amazon ships it! Amazon also operates retail websites for brands such as bebe, Marks & Spencer, Lacoste, and AOL's Shop@AOL. Individual sellers use the Amazon network to reach millions of potential customers. These business partnerships all contribute to Amazon's sales, which now exceed $75 billion.

Bezos defines Amazon by its "big ideas, which are customer centricity, putting the customer at the centre of everything we do, and invention—we like to pioneer, we like to explore." Amazon's success is also the result of an intense focus on cost and efficiency that leads to lower prices. More specifically, Amazon is exceptional at managing the elements of its supply chain, which make up one of the most complex and expensive aspects of the company's business.

Supply Chain and Logistics Management at **Amazon.com**

What happens after an order is submitted on Amazon's website but before it arrives at the customer's door? A lot. Amazon maintains huge distribution, or "fulfillment," centres where it keeps inventory of millions of products. This is one of the key differences between Amazon and some of its competitors—it actually stocks products. Bezos describes how they have improved: "Years ago, I drove the Amazon packages to the post office every evening in the back of my Chevy Blazer. My vision extended so far that I dreamed we might one day get a forklift. Fast-forward to today and we have 96 fulfillment centres." So Amazon must manage the flow of products from its 15 million-plus suppliers to its U.S. and international fulfillment centres with the flow of customer orders from the fulfillment centres to individuals' homes or offices.

The process begins with the suppliers. Amazon collaborates with its suppliers to increase efficiencies and improve inventory turnover. For example, Amazon uses software to forecast purchasing patterns by region, which allows it to give its suppliers better information about delivery dates and volumes. After the products arrive at the fulfillment centre, they are scanned and placed on shelves in what often appear to be haphazard locations. That is, books may be on the same shelf next to toys and kitchen utensils. Dave Clark, vice president of worldwide operations and customer service at Amazon, explains: "If you look at how these items fit in the bin, they are optimized to utilize the available space, we have computers and algorithms that tell people the areas of the building that have the most space to put the product that's coming in at that time." Clark observes that one of its 1-million-square-foot fulfillment centres (the size of more than 20 football fields) represents a "physical manifestation of earth's biggest selection."

At the same time, Amazon has been improving the part of the process that sorts the products into the individual orders. Once an order is placed in the computer system, sophisticated software generates a map of the location of each product and a "pick ambassador" walks the aisles to select the products. Each item is scanned as it is selected so that inventory levels and locations are always up to date. Packers ensure that all items are included in the box before it is taped and labelled. The boxes then travel along a conveyor belt and are diverted into groups based on the delivery location. A network of trucks and regional postal hubs then conclude the process with delivery of the order. Amazon actually uses more trucks than planes!

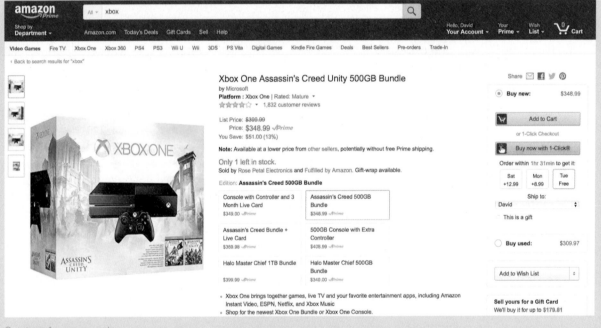

Courtesy Amazon.com Inc.

The success of Amazon's logistics and supply chain management activities may be most evident during the year-end holiday shopping season. Amazon received orders for 36.8 million items on Cyber Monday (the Monday following American Thanksgiving), including orders for Xbox and PlayStation gaming consoles that reached more than 1,000 units per minute. During the entire holiday season, Amazon shipped orders to 185 countries. Well over 99 percent of the orders were shipped and delivered on time.

Continuous Improvement at Amazon

In a recent letter to Amazon shareholders, Bezos reported that Amazon employees are "always asking how do we make this better?" He also described the Amazon Kaizen program (named for the Japanese term meaning "change for the better") and how it is used to streamline processes and reduce defects and waste.

As a result, there are many new changes and improvements under way at Amazon, many of which are related to its supply chain and logistics management approach.

One example of a new service at Amazon is Amazon Fresh, its online, same-day-delivery service for groceries. The service has been in trial stage in Seattle for several years and recently expanded to Los Angeles and San Francisco. The success of the service in these cities is likely to influence how quickly Amazon expands into other cities. Another new service at Amazon is based on its agreement with the United States Postal Service to offer Sunday delivery to select cities. The demand for this service in the trial cities will also influence how quickly it is rolled out to other cities. Finally, Amazon received a lot of attention when it revealed that it is developing unmanned aerial drones that could fly small shipments to customers within 30 minutes. "We can carry objects up to 5 pounds, which covers 86 percent of the items that we deliver," explains Bezos. The Federal Aviation Administration granted Amazon permission to fly drones experimentally in early 2015.

Amazon.com has come a long way since 1995. Its logistics and supply chain management activities have provided Amazon with a cost-effective and efficient distribution system that combines automation and communication technology with superior customer service. To continue its drive to increase future sales, profits, and customer service, Amazon continues to use its inventive spirit to encourage innovation. According to Bezos, "what we are doing is challenging and fun—we get to work in the future."

QUESTIONS

1. How do Amazon's logistics and supply chain management activities help the company create value for its customers?

2. What systems did Amazon develop to improve the flow of products from suppliers to Amazon fulfillment centres? What systems improved the flow of orders from the fulfillment centres to customers?

3. Why will logistics and supply chain management play an important role in the future success of **Amazon.com**?

Case: Amazon.com: This case was written by Steven Hartley. Sources: Tim Worstall, "Both Amazon and WalMart Are Really Logistics Companies, Not Retailers," *Forbes.com*, April 11, 2014; Dan Mitchell, "Next Up for Disruption: The Grocery Business," *Fortune.com*, April 4, 2014; Mae Anderson, "Amazon's Bezos Outlines Grocery, Drone Plans," *Businessweek.com*, April 10, 2014; Jeff Bercovici, "The Same-Day War: Amazon, Google and Walmart Race to Bring Your Groceries," *Forbes*, May 5, 2014; Brad Stone, "Why Amazon's Going Up In the Air," *Bloomberg Businessweek*, December 9–15, 2013, pp. 12–13; "Record-Setting Holiday Season for Amazon Prime," Amazon press release, December 26, 2013; "Company Info: Overview," http://phx.corporate-ir.net/phoenix.zhtml?c=176060&p=irol-mediaKit; Jeff Bezos, "2013 Letter to Shareholders," http://phx.corporate-ir.net/phoenix.zhtml?c=97664&p=irol-reportsannual; "Amazon's Jeff Bezos Looks to the Future," *60 Minutes* episode, December 1, 2013; and Mark Veverka, "The World's Best Retailer," *Barron's*, March 30, 2009.

15 Retailing

What Is Trending in Canadian Retailing?

Plenty of interesting things are happening in Canadian retailing. Here are just a few examples. Indochino, which began as an online retailer selling made-to-measure suits, plans to expand into the bricks-and-mortar world in a big way. The company was founded by two university students with no fashion expertise, but they managed to design the perfect way for men to buy a custom suit online at an affordable price. After years of optimizing that process, Indochino is making an aggressive push into the real world, with plans to open 150 bricks-and-mortar locations by 2020, in addition to greatly expanding its product line. Currently, it has several permanent physical locations in cities such as Vancouver and Boston. To guide this growth, Indochino landed one of the biggest rounds of financing in Canadian e-commerce history and recruited a management team of fashion and retail veterans.

High-end Canadian-based clothing retailer Kit and Ace is looking to build its brand among global jetsetters by hosting a series of pop-up shops in luxury hotels in major cities around the world. The pop-up series, known as "The Carry-on," is taking place in cities such as San Francisco, Los Angeles, and New York, as well as London in the United Kingdom and Sydney and Melbourne in Australia. The campaign will also take place online through social media sites such as Facebook, Instagram, and Snapchat, where brand followers can see what's happening at each pop-up event and also get some tips on the best places to eat, shop, and visit in each city, based on input from local influencers. Vancouver-based Kit and Ace uses pop-up stores as a way to establish a presence in neighbourhoods where it plans to open permanent locations, but this is the first time the company has tried a travelling pop-up campaign. The goal with its hotel campaign is to promote its clothing as being ideal for travellers. Kit and Ace sells shirts, pants, and jackets that it says are "perfect for long flights," with technical features that ensure the material doesn't wrinkle and holds its shape. Canadian hotels aren't on the list because the company has several stores in Canada. But the company is considering doing similar hotel pop-ups in Canada in the future.

Andrew Francis Wallace/ZUMA Press/Newscom

Starbucks Canada is now pouring beer and wine along with coffee and cappuccinos. Several Starbucks cafés in Canada have launched the Starbucks Evenings menu, which is available after 2 p.m. and includes Canadian craft beer, cider, and a selection of Canadian and international wines. New food offerings include small plates designed for sharing, such as artichoke and goat cheese flatbread, and Parmesan-crusted chicken skewers. "The opportunity was to offer new occasions for our customers to come in a little bit later in the day and to connect as they normally would over a cup of coffee, but also expand the [food and beverage] offerings," said Jessica Mills, director of brand communications at Starbucks Canada. Mills said the new menu is aimed at existing Starbucks customers (over the legal drinking age of 19, of course).

McDonald's is on a mission to reinvent its customer experience. It has introduced kiosks at restaurants in the U.S. and Canada where customers can order customized meals, delivering on its goal of personalizing the customer experience.

Finally, Hudson's Bay Co. (HBC), the owner of Saks Fifth Avenue, Lord & Taylor, and Hudson's Bay department stores, is now going deeper into global retailing with its plans to open 40 Saks Off 5th discount stores in Germany, beginning in 2017. The Saks Off 5th stores will open in locations already owned by the company in Germany, while it keeps an eye out for more expansion opportunities in other parts of Europe. The store openings are part of a nearly $1.5 billion investment that HBC plans on pumping into its European properties over the next seven years, including renovations to its Kaufhof department stores in Germany.[1]

This chapter examines the concept of **retailing**, which includes all activities involved in selling, renting, and providing goods and services to ultimate consumers for personal, family, or household use. We will look at the critical role of retailing in the marketplace and the challenging decisions retailers face as they strive to create value and customer satisfaction. In the channel of distribution, retailing is where the customer meets the product. According to the Retail Council of Canada, a non-profit association representing more than 40,000 stores of all formats across Canada, "Retail is the face of Canadian business."[2]

THE VALUE AND SCOPE OF RETAILING

Retailing is an important marketing activity. Not only do producers and consumers meet through retailing actions, but retailing also creates customer value and has a significant impact on the economy. In fact, retailing is critically important to the Canadian and global economies. Retail sales in Canada exceed $480 billion.[3] And the retail sector also employs over two million people in Canada, or one in eight Canadian jobs, making it the second-largest labour force in the country.[4] Major retail categories in Canada include automotive, food, furniture, and clothing.

The magnitude of retail sales is hard to imagine. Some of Canada's top retailers have annual sales revenues that surpass the gross domestic product (GDP) of several nation-states. For example, Canada's top three grocery store rivals (Loblaws, Empire, and Metro) have combined sales greater than the GDP of Luxembourg. On a global basis, just the top 250 retailers in the world (based on sales) had combined sales of over $4.4 trillion. Walmart is the world's number one retailer with over $476 billion in sales. Some of the other top retailers in the world include Carrefour (France), Tesco (U.K.), and Schwartz (Germany). Some Canadian retailers also made the top 250 list, including Loblaws, Empire Company, Canadian Tire, and Shoppers Drug Mart.[5]

The scope of retailing has reached all corners of the globe. But the retail marketplace is evolving. China, for example, is now the world's third-largest retail market. India, too, is attracting the attention of global retailers, and many South American countries are experiencing strong retail growth, including Argentina and Chile. But despite this changing and competitive global marketplace, leading Canadian retailers are thriving in this new environment.[6] As we will see later in the chapter, in order to sustain their growth, Canadian retailers will have to overcome several challenges in this new global retail arena.

LO1 Classifying Retail Outlets

For manufacturers, consumers, and the economy, retailing is an important component of marketing that has several variations. Because of the large number of alternative forms of retailing, it is easier to understand the differences among retail institutions by recognizing that outlets can be classified in several ways. First, **form of ownership** distinguishes retail outlets based on whether individuals, corporate chains, or contractual systems own the outlet. Second, **level of service** is used to describe the degree of service provided to the customer ranging from self-, limited-, and full-service retailers. Finally, the type of **merchandise line** describes how many different types of products a store carries and in what assortment. A more in-depth discussion of the alternative types of outlets follows.

Form of Ownership

Independent Retailer

One of the most common forms of retail ownership is the independent business, owned by an individual. The independent retailer accounts for over 60 percent of total retail trade in Canada. Small retailers tend to dominate in bakeries, sporting goods stores, jewellery shops, and gift stores. They are also popular retailers of auto supplies, books, paint, flowers, and women's accessories. The advantage of this form of ownership for the owner is that he or she can be his or her own boss. For customers, the independent store can offer convenience, quality, personal service, and lifestyle compatibility.

Corporate Chain

A second form of ownership, the corporate chain, involves multiple outlets under common ownership. If you have ever shopped at Hudson's Bay, Target, or Loblaws, or had your hair cut at First Choice Haircutters, you have shopped at a chain outlet.

In a chain operation, centralization in decision making and purchasing is common. Chain stores have advantages in dealing with manufacturers, particularly as the size of the chain grows. A large chain can bargain with a manufacturer to obtain good service or volume discounts on orders. The buying power of chains allows them to offer consumers competitive prices on merchandise. Walmart's large volume makes it a strong negotiator with manufacturers of most products. Consumers also benefit in dealing with chains because there are multiple outlets with similar merchandise and consistent management policies. The Retail Council of Canada reports tremendous growth in corporate chain stores across the nation.

Contractual System

Contractual systems involve independently owned stores that band together to act like a chain. The three kinds described in Chapter 14 are retailer-sponsored cooperatives, wholesaler-sponsored voluntary chains, and franchises. One retailer-sponsored cooperative is Guardian Drugs, which consists of neighbourhood pharmacies that all agree to buy their products from the same wholesaler. In this way, members can take advantage of volume discounts commonly available to chains and also give the impression of being a large chain, which may be viewed more favourably by some consumers. Wholesaler-sponsored voluntary chains, such as Ace Hardware, try to achieve similar benefits.

As noted in Chapter 14, in a franchise system an individual or firm (the franchisee) contracts with a parent company (the franchisor) to set up a business or retail outlet. The franchisor usually assists in selecting the location, setting up the store or facility, advertising, and training personnel. The franchisee usually pays a one-time franchise fee and an annual royalty, usually tied to the franchise's sales. There are two general types of retail franchises: *business-format franchises,* such as McDonald's, and *product-distribution franchises,* such as a Ford dealership or a Coca-Cola distributor. In business-format franchising, the franchisor provides step-by-step procedures for most aspects of the business and guidelines for the most likely decisions a franchisee will face.

Franchising is attractive because it offers an opportunity for people to enter a well-known, established business for which managerial advice is provided. Also, the franchise fee may be less than the cost of setting up an independent business.

Franchise fees paid to the franchisor can range from $15,000 for a Subway franchise to $50,000 for a McDonald's restaurant franchise. When the fees are combined with other costs, such as real estate and equipment, however, the total investment can be much higher. Figure 15–1 shows the top five franchises in North America in 2016, as rated by *Entrepreneur* magazine, based on such factors as size, financial strength, stability, growth rate, years in business, and costs.[7] By selling franchises, an organization reduces the cost of expansion but loses some control. A good franchisor, however, will maintain strong control of the outlets in terms of delivery and presentation of merchandise and try to enhance recognition of the franchise name. Canadian entrepreneurs have plenty of franchise opportunities, from automotive care to wine making. You can check it out at the Canadian Franchise Association website (**www.cfa.ca**).

McDonalds is an example of a successful retail franchise.

Martin Good/Shutterstock.com

FIGURE 15–1

Franchise	Type of Business	Start-Up Costs	Number of Franchises (global)
Jimmy John's Sandwhiches	Sandwich restaurant	$326,000–$555,000	2,434
Hampton by Hilton	Hotel	$4,200,000–$7,800,000	2,122
Supercuts	Hair salon	$144,000–$294,000	1,548
Servpro	Cleaning and restoration	$156,000–$210,000	1,715
Subway	Sandwich restaurant	$116,000–$263,000	44,702

The top five franchises in North America (2016).

Level of Service

Even though most customers perceive little variation in retail outlets by form of ownership, differences among retailers are more obvious in terms of level of service. In some department stores, very few services are provided. Some warehouse grocery stores have customers bag the food themselves. Other retail outlets, such as Holt Renfrew, provide a wide range of customer services from gift wrapping to wardrobe consultation.

Self-Service

Self-service is at the extreme end of the level of service continuum because the customer performs many functions and little is provided by the outlet. Home building-supply outlets and gas stations are often self-service. Warehouse stores, usually in buildings several times larger than a conventional store, are self-service with all non-essential customer services eliminated. Similarly, many gas stations are self-service. New forms of self-service are being developed in grocery stores, airlines, and hotels. For example, when you fly, you can often choose to use self-service kiosks to check in, find a seat, and print a boarding pass without the help of an attendant. In short, with self-service you are actually a co-creator of the value you receive.

Limited Service

Limited-service outlets provide some services, such as return of credit and merchandise, but not others, such as return of custom-made clothes. General merchandise stores, such as Walmart and Target, are usually considered limited-service outlets. Customers are responsible for most shopping activities, although salespeople are available in such departments as consumer electronics, jewellery, and lawn and garden.

Full Service

Full-service retailers, which include most specialty stores and some department stores, provide many services to their customers. Services can include more knowledgeable and friendly salespeople on the floor assisting the customer with purchases or offering special delivery of purchases to customers' homes. Often, this full-service strategy can serve as a competitive advantage for such stores, especially in this new customer experience management era.

Merchandise Line

Retail outlets also vary by their merchandise lines, the key distinction being the breadth and depth of the items offered to customers (Figure 15–2). **Depth of product line** means that the store carries a large assortment of each item, such as a shoe store that offers running shoes, dress shoes, and children's shoes. **Breadth of product line** refers to the variety of different items a store carries.

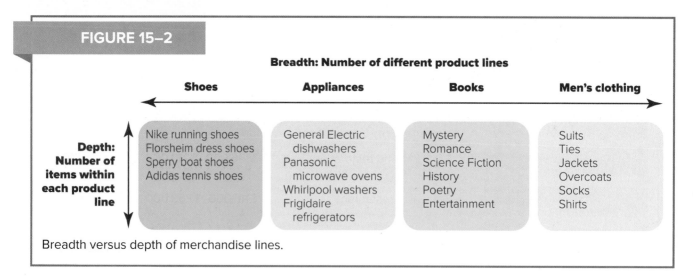

FIGURE 15–2

Breadth versus depth of merchandise lines.

Depth of Line

Stores that carry a considerable assortment (depth) of a related line of items are limited-line stores. Black's photography stores carry considerable depth in photography equipment. Stores that carry tremendous depth in one primary line of merchandise are single-line stores. La Senza carries great depth in women's lingerie, while Lids is a retail outlet that specializes in selling hats to teens. Both limited- and single-line stores are often referred to as *specialty outlets.*

Specialty discount outlets focus on one type of product, such as electronics, business supplies, or books, at very competitive prices. These outlets are referred to in the trade as *category killers* because they often dominate the market.

Breadth of Line

Stores that carry a broad product line, with limited depth, are referred to as *general merchandise stores.* For example, large department stores carry a wide range of different types of products but not unusual sizes. The breadth and depth of merchandise lines are important decisions for a retailer. For example, Bulk Barn is Canada's largest bulk food retailer. Its tagline emphasizes the breadth of its product line: "At Bulk Barn we carry over 4,000 products—everything from soup to nuts." Traditionally, outlets carried related lines of goods. Today, however, **scrambled merchandising**, offering several unrelated product lines in a single store, is common. The modern drugstore carries food, camera equipment, magazines, paper products, toys, small hardware items, and pharmaceuticals. Supermarkets rent DVDs, process photos, and sell flowers.

A form of scrambled merchandising, the **hypermarket**, has been successful in Europe. These hypermarkets are large stores (more than 200,000 square feet) based on a simple concept: Offer consumers everything in a single outlet, eliminating the need to stop at more than one location. The stores provide variety, quality, and low price for food and groceries and general merchandise. In France, the concept is so successful that hypermarkets maintain a 51 percent share of the grocery market. Carrefour, one of the largest retailers in this category, has 1,459 hypermarkets, including 237 in France, 489 in the rest of Europe, 291 in Latin America, and 375 in Asia. The growth of hypermarkets may be slowing in Europe, however, as consumers' interest in smaller stores and convenient locations has increased. In response, retailers have been cutting prices on food to attract customers and lure them away from competitors. Despite its declining popularity in some parts of the world, the original hypermarket concept is still growing in popularity in many countries; in China, for example, Carrefour, Tesco, and Walmart are expanding the number of stores they operate.[8]

In North America, retailers discovered that many shoppers were uncomfortable with the huge size of hypermarkets. So they developed a variation of the hypermarket called the *supercentre,* which combines a typical merchandise store with a full-size grocery. These supercentres tend to range in size between 100,000 and 200,000 square feet. Loblaws, one of Canada's top retail grocery chains, uses the supercentre concept very successfully. Its McCowan Market in Markham, Ontario, is 115,000 square feet and offers its traditional grocery line along with other merchandise selection, including housewares, office supplies, cosmetics, and electronics. Walmart Canada is also a major player in the supercentre category.

Scrambled merchandising is convenient for consumers because it eliminates the number of stops required in a shopping trip. However, for the retailer, this merchandising policy means that there is competition between very dissimilar types of retail outlets, or **intertype competition**. A local bakery may compete with a department store, discount outlet, or even a local gas station. Scrambled merchandising and intertype competition make it more difficult to be a retailer.

Learning Review

1. Centralized decision making and purchasing are an advantage of _____ ownership.

2. What are some examples of new forms of self-service retailers?

3. Would a shop for big men's clothes carrying pants in sizes 40 to 60 have a broad or deep product line?

 ## NON-STORE RETAILING

Most of the retailing examples discussed earlier in the chapter, such as corporate chains, department stores, and limited- and single-line specialty stores, involve store retailing. Many retailing activities today, however, are not limited to sales in a store. Non-store retailing occurs outside a retail outlet through activities that involve varying levels of customer and retailer involvement. Figure 15–3 shows six forms of non-store retailing: automatic vending, direct mail and catalogues, television home shopping, online retailing, telemarketing, and direct selling.

Automatic Vending

Non-store retailing includes vending machines, or *v-commerce,* which make it possible to serve customers when and where stores cannot. Maintenance and operating costs are high, and so product prices in vending machines tend to be higher than those in stores. Typically, small convenience products are available in vending machines. In fact, most of the machines in use in Canada are soft-drink or beverage machines. But more complex products are being sold in vending machines, too. For example, Best Buy uses vending machines to sell smartphones, digital cameras, flash drives, and other consumer electronics in airports, hospitals, and businesses. Improved technology is making vending machines easier to use by reducing the need for cash. Many machines already accept credit cards, and some even accept cashless purchases using smartphones. Coca-Cola Canada was the first company in Canada to offer Interac Flash payment capabilities in vending machines, starting the rollout at the Calgary Stampede.[9]

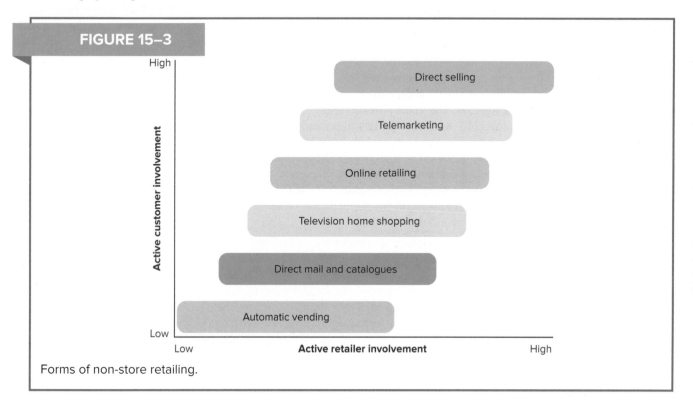

FIGURE 15–3

Forms of non-store retailing.

Another improvement in vending machines is the use of wireless technology to notify vendors when their machines are empty. Nestlé, for example, is installing hundreds of ice cream vending machines in France and England that send wireless messages to supply-truck drivers. Finally, there are "smart-interactive" vending machines such as Coca-Cola's new 100-flavour interactive soda fountain (called Freestyle) that allows you to mix your own flavoured soda. Plus, this machine sends sales data back to headquarters, and Coke corporate can also talk to the machine telling it whether certain flavours need to be discontinued.[10] Another trend in vending machines is "green machines," which consume less energy by using more efficient compressors, more efficient lighting, and better insulation. Finally, new portable vending machines now offer Wi-Fi and social media connectivity for busy consumers.

Direct Mail and Catalogues

Direct mail and catalogue retailing has been called "the store that comes to the door." It is attractive because it eliminates the cost of a store and clerks. In addition, it improves marketing efficiency through segmentation and targeting and creates customer value by providing a fast and convenient means of making a purchase. And many catalogues now serve as a tool to encourage consumers to visit a website, a social media page, or even a store. Canadians have been increasing the amount they spend on direct mail catalogue merchandise. Internationally, catalogue shopping is also popular. For example, Swedish furniture retailer IKEA delivers close to 200 million copies of

For the latest trends in retail vending, read the text.

HealthyYOU® Vending

its catalogue to over 30 countries in over 25 languages, including several million to Canada.[11] Perhaps the hottest trend today is subscription services, where products are delivered automatically to your door after you sign up with a provider. These subscription services will supply everything from fresh fruit to underwear.

As consumers' direct mail and catalogue purchases have increased, the numbers of direct mailings, catalogues, and products sold have also increased. A typical household now receives dozens of catalogues per year. The competition, combined with higher paper and postal costs, however, has caused direct retailers to focus on proven customers rather than "prospects." A successful approach now used by many catalogue retailers is to send specialty catalogues to market niches identified in their databases. L.L. Bean, a long-standing catalogue retailer, has developed an individual catalogue for fly-fishing enthusiasts.

New, creative forms of direct-mail and catalogue retailing are also being developed. Sears, for example, has invested in social media technologies to make its Wish Book available through smartphones and iPads. In addition, Sears and other retailers are adding QR codes to their catalogues so that consumers can scan them using a smartphone app to view more product information and videos. Other innovations include digital catalogues that are searchable in PDF format and embedded with links to complementary products. You will also see merchants using direct mail and catalogues to direct customers to personalized URLs, which are web pages preloaded with information and offerings specific to an individual.

IKEA is a major global player that uses catalogue retailing.

Inter IKEA Systems B.V.

Television Home Shopping

Television home shopping is possible when consumers watch a shopping channel on which products are displayed; orders are then placed over the telephone or on the Internet. Two popular networks, the Home Shopping Network and QVC, reach millions of Canadian households. A limitation of TV shopping has been the lack of buyer–seller interaction and the inability of consumers to control the items they see. But new technologies now allow consumers to simultaneously shop, chat, and interact with their favourite show host while watching TV.

Online Retailing

Online retailing allows consumers to search for, evaluate, and order products through the Internet. For many consumers, the advantages of this form of retailing, sometimes called *e-tailing,* are 24-hour access, the ability to comparison shop, in-home privacy, and variety. Online retail sales are expected to hit $35 billion by 2018.[12]

Today, traditional and online retailers—"bricks and clicks"—are melding, using experiences from both approaches to create better value and experiences for customers. For example, Walmart has a "Pick Up Today" service that allows customers to order online and receive same-day pickup at a local store. In addition, Walmart offers site-to-store service for online items not available in stores, as well as free shipping for pickup at a FedEx Office location. The Walmart mobile app allows shoppers to browse and order products using their smartphones.

Online retail purchases can occur in several ways. Consumers can pay a fee to become a member of an online discount service; they can use an online shopping agent or "bot," such as MySimon (**www.mysimon.com**); or they can go directly to online malls or online shopping directories (portals), such as the Canadian Online Shopping Mall (**http://homer.ca/shopping/index.htm**). Online retailing can also be done via auction on such sites as **www.ebay.ca**. Or, you could simply go to a specific online retailer's site. Currently, over 22 million Canadians visit online retailers' sites.[13] A final approach to online retailing is "flash sales" at sites such as **www.gilt.com** and **www.hautelook.com**, which will send you text messages announcing limited-time offers at big discounts.

One interesting shopping portal is **Cangive.ca**. It allows shoppers to donate up to 15 percent of their online purchases to a cause or charity designated by the shopper. Popular causes or charities include Mothers Against Drunk Driving (MADD) and the Canadian Diabetes Association. Many major Canadian retail companies are part of this portal including **Amazon.ca**, Canadian Tire, and Chapters-Indigo.[14]

Online retailing has also had an impact in terms of physical cross-border shopping. For example, many Americans now use the Internet to order prescription drugs from online Canadian pharmacies, avoiding the hassle of travelling across the border to do their shopping in person. At the same time, online retailing is enabling Canadians to buy from American merchants. For example, for every $100 spent online, only $51 is going to Canadian retailers with $34 going south of the border and the rest to Asia-Pacific and European retailers.[15]

One of the biggest problems online retailers face is that nearly two-thirds of online shoppers make it to "checkout" and then leave the website to compare shipping costs and prices on other sites. Of the shoppers who leave, 70 percent do not return. Experts suggest that online retailers should think of their websites as dynamic billboards if they are to attract and retain customers, and they should be easy to use, customizable, and facilitate interaction to enhance the online customer experience. For example, BMW, Mercedes, and Jaguar encourage website visitors to "build" a vehicle by selecting interior and exterior colours, packages, and options; view the customized virtual car; and then use Facebook, Twitter, or e-mail to share the configuration.[16]

Cangive is an example of a novel retail portal.

Online retailing is also evolving to include social shopping options, including *intermediaries*, such as Groupon and Living-Social, that match consumers with merchants; *marketplaces*, such as Google Offers and Storenvy, that provide a self-service advertising site; and *aggregators*, such as Yipit, that crawl the Web to find deals to list on their own site. Many consumers also use online resources as price comparison sites that influence their offline shopping at local stores.[17]

Telemarketing

Another form of non-store retailing, called **telemarketing**, involves using the telephone to interact with and sell directly to consumers. Compared with direct mailing, telemarketing is often viewed as a more efficient means of targeting consumers. Insurance companies, brokerage firms, and newspapers have often used this form of retailing as a way to cut costs but still maintain access to their customers. According to the Canadian Marketing Association, annual telemarketing sales exceed $16 billion.[18]

The telemarketing industry has gone through some changes as a result of past and proposed legislation related to telephone solicitations. Such issues as consumer privacy, industry standards, and ethical guidelines have encouraged discussion among consumer groups, government, and businesses. New legislation and regulation has evolved to provide a balance between consumer privacy and the right to engage in ethical business practices.

Direct Selling

Direct selling, sometimes called door-to-door retailing, involves direct sales of goods and services to consumers through personal interactions and demonstrations in their homes or offices. A variety of companies, including such familiar names as Fuller Brush, Avon, World Book, and Mary Kay Cosmetics, have created a multibillion-dollar industry by providing consumers with personalized service and convenience. In Canada, however, sales have been declining as retail chains such as Walmart begin to carry similar products at discount prices and as the increasing number of dual-career households reduces the number of potential buyers at home.

In response to the changes, many direct-selling retailers are expanding into other markets. Avon, for example, has millions of sales representatives in more than 100 countries, including Mexico, Poland, Argentina, and China. Direct selling is likely to continue to grow in markets where the lack of effective distribution channels increases the importance of door-to-door convenience and where the lack of consumer knowledge about products and brands will increase the need for a person-to-person approach.

Learning Review

4. Successful catalogue retailers often send _____ catalogues to _____ markets identified in their databases.

5. How are retailers increasing consumer interest and involvement in online retailing?

6. Where are direct-selling retail sales growing? Why?

RETAILING STRATEGY

This section identifies how a retailer develops and implements a retailing strategy by positioning the store and taking specific retailing mix actions. Figure 15–4 identifies the relationship between positioning and the retailing mix.

FIGURE 15–4

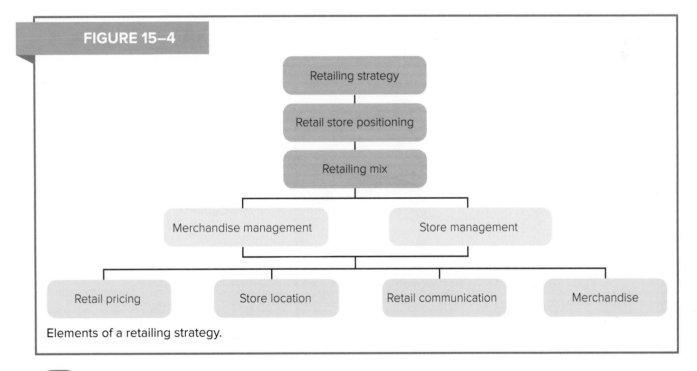

Elements of a retailing strategy.

LO3 Positioning a Retail Store

The classification alternatives presented in the previous sections help determine one store's position relative to its competitors.

Retail Positioning Matrix

The **retail positioning matrix** was developed by the MAC Group, Inc., a management consulting firm.[19] This matrix positions retail outlets on two dimensions: breadth of product line and value added. As defined previously, breadth of product line is the range of products sold through each outlet. The second dimension, *value added,* includes such elements as location (as with 7-Eleven stores), product reliability (as with Holiday Inn or McDonald's), or prestige (as with Birks).

The retail positioning matrix in Figure 15–5 shows four possible positions. An organization can be successful in any position, but unique strategies are required within each quadrant. Consider the four stores shown in the matrix:

1. *Hudson's Bay has high value added and a broad product line.* Retailers in this quadrant pay great attention to store design and product lines. Merchandise often has a high margin of profit and is of high quality. The stores in this position typically provide high levels of service.

2. *Walmart has low value added and a broad product line.* Walmart and similar firms typically trade a lower price for increased volume in sales. Retailers in this position focus on price with low service levels and an image of being a place for good buys.

3. *Birks has high value added and a narrow product line.* Retailers of this type typically sell a very restricted range of products that are of high-status quality. Customers are also provided with high levels of service.

4. *Payless ShoeSource has low value added and a narrow product line.* Such retailers are specialty mass merchandisers. Payless, for example, carries attractively priced shoes for the entire family. These outlets appeal to value-conscious consumers. Economies of scale are achieved through centralized advertising, merchandising, buying, and distribution. Stores are usually the same in design, layout, and merchandise; hence, they are often referred to as "cookie-cutter" stores.

Walmart offers a broad product line but also low value added.

© Helen Sessions/Alamy Stock Photo

FIGURE 15–5

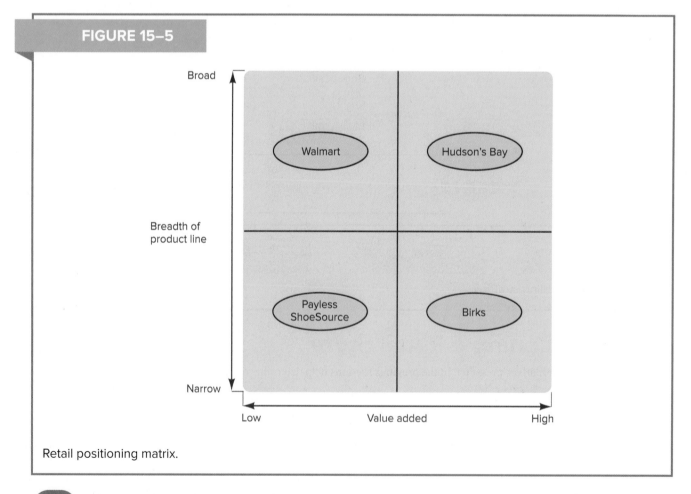

Retail positioning matrix.

LO4 Retailing Mix

In developing retailing strategy, managers work with the **retailing mix**, which includes activities related to managing the store and the merchandise in the store. The retailing mix is similar to the marketing mix and includes retail pricing, store location, retail communication, and merchandise.

Retail Pricing

In setting prices for merchandise, retailers must decide on the markup, markdown, and timing for markdowns. As mentioned in Appendix B, *markup* refers to how much should be added to the cost the retailer pays for a product to reach the final selling price. Retailers decide on the *original markup,* but by the time the product is sold, they end up with a *maintained markup.* The original markup is the difference between retailer cost and initial selling price. When products do not sell as quickly as anticipated, their price is reduced. The difference between the final selling price and retailer cost is the maintained markup, which is also called the *gross margin.*

Discounting a product, or taking a *markdown,* occurs when the product does not sell at the original price and an adjustment is necessary. Often, new models or styles force the price of existing models to be marked down. Discounts may also be used to increase demand for complementary products. For example, retailers might take a markdown on the price of cake mix to generate frosting purchases. The *timing* of a markdown can be important. Many retailers take a markdown as soon as sales fall off to free up valuable shelf space and cash. However, other stores delay markdowns to discourage bargain hunters and maintain an image of quality. There is no clear answer, but retailers must consider how the timing might affect future sales.

Although most retailers plan markdowns, many retailers use price discounts as part of their regular merchandising policy. Walmart and Home Depot, for example, emphasize consistently low prices and eliminate most markdowns with a strategy often called *everyday low pricing.* Because consumers often use price as an indicator of product quality, however, the brand name of the product and the image of the store become important decision factors in these situations. Another strategy, *everyday fair pricing,* is advocated by retailers that may not offer the lowest price but try to create value for customers through service and the total buying experience. A special issue for retailers trying to keep prices low is **shrinkage**, or theft of merchandise by customers and employees. Retail theft costs Canadian retailers over $3 billion a year, and the cost of this theft gets passed along to the consumer in the form of higher retail prices. The Retail Council of Canada is working with its members on numerous loss-prevention programs.[20]

Off-price retailing is a retail pricing practice that has become quite common. **Off-price retailing** involves selling brand-name merchandise at lower than regular prices. The difference between the off-price retailer and a discount store is that off-price merchandise is bought by the retailer from manufacturers with excess inventory at prices below wholesale prices, while the discounter buys at full wholesale price (but takes less of a markup than do traditional department stores). Because of this difference in the way merchandise is purchased by the retailer, selection at an off-price retailer is unpredictable, and searching for bargains has become a popular activity for many consumers where savings can often make up for the search effort.

There are several variations of off-price retailing. One is the warehouse club. These large stores (more than 100,000 square feet) are rather stark outlets with no elaborate displays, customer service, or home delivery. They require an annual membership fee for the privilege of shopping there. While a typical Walmart store stocks 30,000 to 60,000 items, warehouse clubs carry about 4,000 to 8,000 items and usually stock just one brand name of appliance or food product. Service is minimal, and customers usually must pay by cash or cheque. However, the extremely competitive pricing of merchandise makes warehouse clubs attractive. Some major warehouse clubs you may be familiar with include Costco, Walmart's Sam's Club, and BJ's Wholesale Club. Sales at these off-price retailers have grown dramatically over the past decade.

A second variation is the outlet store. Factory outlets, such as Van Heusen Factory Store, Bass Shoe Outlet, Gap Factory Store, and Oneida Factory Store, offer products for 25 to 75 percent off the suggested retail price. Manufacturers use the stores to clear excess merchandise and to reach consumers who focus on value shopping. Some retail outlets, such as Brooks Brothers Outlet Store, allow retailers to sell excess merchandise and still maintain an image of offering merchandise at full price in their primary store.

A third variation of off-price retailing is offered by single-price, or extreme value, retailers, such as Family Dollar, Dollar General, and Dollar Tree. These stores average about 6,000 square feet in size and attract customers who want value and a "corner store" environment rather than a large supercentre experience.

Store Location

A second aspect of the retailing mix involves deciding where to locate the store and how many stores to have. Most stores today locate near each other in one of several settings: central business district, regional shopping centre, community shopping centre, strip location, power centre, off-mall, or lifestyle centre.

The **central business district** is the oldest retail setting, the community's downtown area. Until the regional outflow to suburbs, it was the major shopping area, but the suburban population has grown at the expense of the downtown area. However, recently, there has been some downtown revitalization, with even some "big box" retailers, such as Home Depot and

Costco, locating in the downtown core. But some consumers are put off by big-box stores and large department stores. So some downtowns are revitalizing themselves by offering smaller boutiques and specialty stores where product quality and customer service are the focus.

A **regional shopping centre** consists of 50 to 150 stores that typically attract customers who live or work within an 8- to 16-km range. These large shopping areas often contain two or three anchor stores, which are well-known national or regional stores, such as Sears and Hudson's Bay. The largest variation of a regional shopping centre is the West Edmonton Mall in Alberta. This shopping centre is a conglomerate of 800 stores, an indoor amusement park, 110 restaurants, and a world-class hotel.

Another new concept in regional shopping centres is Vaughan Mills, a 1.2 million-square-foot complex with more than 200 retailers and a unique merchandising concept. It is the first new enclosed regional shopping centre built in Canada in more than a decade. It is distinctive in that it is organized into six "themed neighbourhoods," each emphasizing an aspect of Ontario culture. One focuses on urban cities and contains urban youth-oriented retailers, such as Bluenotes and West 49. Another focuses on fashion and houses stores, such as Aritzia and BCBG Max Azria Outlet. The complex also houses Bass Pro Shops Outdoor World—which features an indoor trout pond—a NASCAR SpeedPark go-cart track, and the largest Tommy Hilfiger outlet in the world.

A more limited approach to retail location is the **community shopping centre**, which typically has one primary store (usually a department store branch) and often about 20 to 40 smaller outlets. Generally, these centres serve a population of consumers who are within a 10- to 20-minute drive.

Not every suburban store is located in a shopping mall. Many neighbourhoods have clusters of stores, referred to as a **strip location** (or strip mall), to serve people who are within a 5- to 10-minute drive. Gas station, hardware, laundry, grocery, and pharmacy outlets are commonly found in a strip location. Unlike the larger shopping centres, the composition of these stores is usually unplanned. A variation of the strip shopping location is called the **power centre**, which is a huge shopping strip with multiple anchor (or national) stores. Power centres are seen as having the convenient location found in many strip centres and the additional power of national stores. These large strips often have two to five anchor stores and usually contain a supermarket, which brings the shopper to the power centre on a weekly basis. For example, Deerfoot Meadows in Calgary is anchored by IKEA, Walmart, and Loblaws and has 50 other retailers in its complex.[21]

Another trend in Canada in terms of locating stores is **off-mall retailing**. In this case, retailers that traditionally locate in malls are building on stand-alone sites. For example, Sears Canada, a common anchor at malls, has opened new-format stores across Canada away from the malls, while the Hudson's Bay Company has launched Designer Depot outlets as free-standing stores.

Another retail location that is growing in popularity in Canada is the **lifestyle centre**—an open-air cluster of specialty retailers, along with theatres, restaurants, fountains, play areas, and green spaces. These lifestyle centres offer the consumer a back-to-community feel and a shopping and entertainment "experience." The Village at Park Royal in West Vancouver was Canada's first lifestyle centre. It has a

Lifestyle centres are emerging as a popular retail concept in Canada.

Photo courtesy of Musson Cattell Mackey Partnership and F&A Architecture (Joint Venture Architect)
Photographer: Michael Boland Photography

lighthouse, old-fashioned gas lamps, and West Coast–style architecture where each store differs in appearance, height, design, and colour. Customers do not go there to comparison shop; instead they go to visit the specialty shops, get a bite to eat, or meet friends for a drink.[22]

Finally, other types of retail locations include carts, kiosks (including electronic kiosks), and wall units. These forms of retailing have been popular in airports and mall common areas because they provide consumers with easy access and also provide rental income for the property owner. Retailers benefit from the relatively low cost compared with a regular store. Another hot trend in is the concept of *pop-up stores,* or flash retailing. A pop-up's location is temporary and could be used for one day or for a particular buying season. You probably see pop-ups around Halloween or Christmas. An interesting twist on pop-ups occurred recently when Walmart Canada partnered with Procter & Gamble and turned 50 Toronto bus shelters into mobile-enabled pop-up stores. Shoppers were able to use smart mobile devices to scan QR codes on posters featuring popular P&G products, with the items shipped to customers' homes for free.[23]

In Canada, there has been a shift in the retail landscape in terms of store location and consumer patronage. For example, power centres and lifestyle centres are attracting customers away from traditional shopping centres, especially the large regional shopping centres. In response, these regional shopping centres are reinventing themselves as "mix use" communities where consumers can shop, be entertained, dine, and participate in sports and leisure, as well as other activities.[24]

Retail Communication

A retailer's communication activities can play an important role in positioning a store and creating its image. While the traditional elements of communication and promotion are discussed in Chapter 17 (advertising) and Chapter 18 (personal selling), the message communicated by the many other elements of the retailing mix is also important.

Deciding on the image of a retail outlet is an important retailing mix factor that has been widely recognized and studied since the late 1950s. Pierre Martineau described image as "the way in which the store is defined in the shopper's mind," partly by its functional qualities and partly by an aura of psychological attributes.[25] In this definition, *functional* refers to such elements as price ranges, store layouts, and breadth and depth of merchandise lines. The psychological attributes are the intangibles, such as a sense of belonging, excitement, style, or warmth. Image has been found to include impressions of the corporation that operates the store, the category or type of store, the product categories in the store, the brands in each category, merchandise and service quality, and the marketing activities of the store.[26] Closely related to the concept of image is the store's atmosphere or ambience. Many retailers believe that sales are affected by layout, colour, lighting, and music in the store, and other elements of the retail environments. This concept leads many retailers to use *shopper marketing*—the use of displays, coupons, product samples, and other brand communications to influence shopping behaviour in a store. Shopper marketing can also influence behaviour in an online shopping environment and when shoppers use smartphone apps to identify shopping needs or make purchase decisions.[27] In creating the right image and atmosphere, a retail store tries to attract its target audience and fortify beliefs about the store, its products, and the shopping experience in the store.[28] While store image perceptions can exist independently of shopping experiences, consumers' shopping experiences also influence their perceptions of a store. In addition, the physical surroundings also influence a store's employees.[29]

Merchandise

A final element of the retailing mix is the merchandise offering. Managing the breadth and depth of the product line requires retail buyers who are familiar with the needs of the target market and the alternative products available from the many manufacturers that might be interested in having a product available in the store. A popular approach to managing the assortment of merchandise today is called **category management**. This approach assigns a manager with the responsibility for selecting all products that consumers in a market segment might view as substitutes for each other, with the objective of maximizing sales and profits in the category. For example, a category manager might be responsible for shoes in a department store or paper products in a grocery store.

Retailers have a variety of marketing metrics that can be used to assess the effectiveness of a store or retail format. First, there are measures related to customers such as the number of transactions per customer, the average transaction size per customer, the number of customers per day or per hour, and the average length of store visit. Second, there are measures related to products such as number of returns, inventory turnover, inventory carrying cost, and average number of items per transaction. Finally, there are financial measures, such as gross margin, sales per employee, return on sales, and markdown percentage.[30] The two most popular measures for retailers are sales per square foot and same-store sales growth. The Using Marketing Dashboards box describes the calculation for these measures for Apple Stores.[31]

USING MARKETING DASHBOARDS

Why Apple Stores May Be the Best Retailer

How effective is my retail format compared to other stores? How are my stores performing this year compared to last year? Information related to this question is often displayed in a marketing dashboard using two measures: (1) sales per square foot, and (2) same-store sales growth.

Your Challenge   You have been assigned to evaluate the Apple Store retail format. The store's simple, inviting, and open atmosphere has been the topic of discussion among many retailers. Apple, however, is relatively new to the retailing business and many experts have been skeptical of the format. To allow an assessment of Apple Stores, use *sales per square foot* as an indicator of how effectively retail space is used to generate revenue and *same-store sales growth* to compare the increase in sales of stores that have been open for the same period of time. The calculations for these two indicators are:

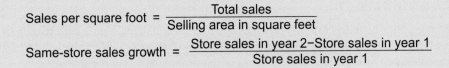

$$\text{Sales per square foot} = \frac{\text{Total sales}}{\text{Selling area in square feet}}$$

$$\text{Same-store sales growth} = \frac{\text{Store sales in year 2} - \text{Store sales in year 1}}{\text{Store sales in year 1}}$$

Your Findings   You decide to collect sales information for Target, Neiman Marcus, Best Buy, Tiffany, and Apple Stores to allow comparisons with other successful retailers. The information you collect allows the calculation of sales per square foot and same store growth for each store. The results are then easy to compare in the graphs below.

Your Action   The results of your investigation indicate that sales per square foot at Apple Stores are higher than any of the comparison stores at approximately $4,800. In addition, Apple's same-store growth rate of 22 percent is higher than all of the other retailers. You conclude that the elements of Apple's format are very effective and even indicate that Apple may currently be the best retailer.

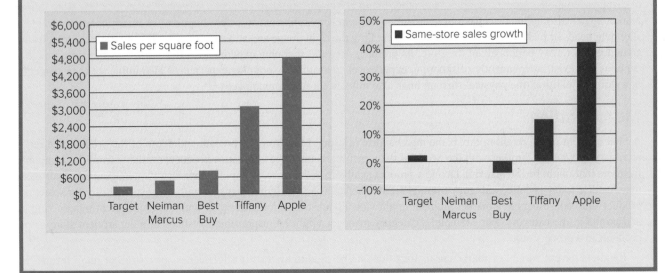

Learning Review

7. What are the two dimensions of the retail positioning matrix?

8. How does original markup differ from maintained markup?

9. A huge shopping strip with multiple anchor stores is a _____ centre.

THE CHANGING NATURE OF RETAILING

Retailing is the most dynamic aspect of a channel of distribution. Such stores as factory outlets show that new retailers are always entering the market, searching for a new position that will attract customers. The reason for this continual change is explained by two concepts: the wheel of retailing and the retail life cycle.

The Wheel of Retailing

The **wheel of retailing** describes how new forms of retail outlets enter the market.[32] Usually, they enter as low-status, low-margin stores, such as a drive-through hamburger stand with no indoor seating and a limited menu (Figure 15–6, box 1). Gradually, these outlets add fixtures and more embellishments to their stores (in-store seating, plants, and chicken sandwiches as well as hamburgers) to increase the attractiveness for customers. With these additions, prices and status rise (see box 2). As time passes, these outlets add still more services, and their prices and status increase even further (see box 3). These retail outlets now face some new form of retail outlet that again appears as a low-status, low-margin operator (see box 4), and the wheel of retailing turns as the cycle starts to repeat itself.

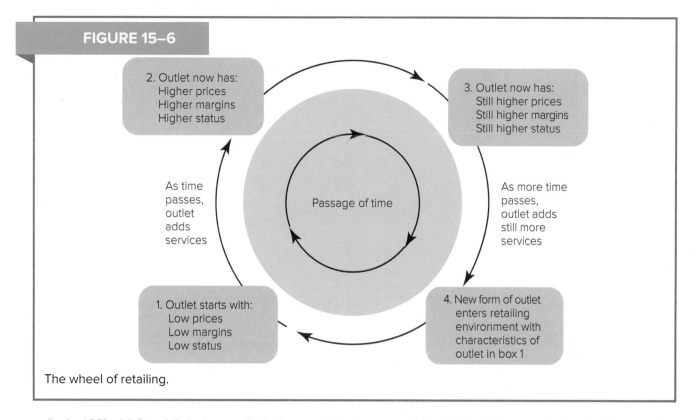

FIGURE 15–6

2. Outlet now has:
   Higher prices
   Higher margins
   Higher status

3. Outlet now has:
   Still higher prices
   Still higher margins
   Still higher status

As time passes, outlet adds services

Passage of time

As more time passes, outlet adds still more services

1. Outlet starts with:
   Low prices
   Low margins
   Low status

4. New form of outlet enters retailing environment with characteristics of outlet in box 1

The wheel of retailing.

In the 1950s, McDonald's had a very limited menu of hamburgers and french fries. Most stores had no inside seating for customers. Over time, the wheel of retailing for fast-food restaurants has turned. These chains have changed by altering their stores and expanding their menus. Today, McDonald's has new format stores and many new products, including specialty coffees and more healthful offerings such as salads. In fact, it recently opened a new coffee chain in Japan, called McCafé, which it believes will compete effectively with Starbucks. And it now even offers table service at some of its restaurants. These changes are leaving room for new forms of outlets that offer only the basics—burgers, fries, and cola; a drive-through window; and no inside seating. For still others, the wheel has come full circle. Taco Bell is now opening small, limited-offering outlets in gas stations or "wherever a burrito and a mouth might possibly intersect."

Discount stores were a major new retailing form in the 1960s and priced their products below those of department stores. As prices in discount stores rose, in the 1980s, they found themselves overpriced compared with a new form of retail outlet—the warehouse retailer. Today, off-price retailers and factory outlets are offering prices even lower than warehouses!

The Retail Life Cycle

The process of growth and decline that retail outlets, like products, experience is described by the **retail life cycle**.[33] Figure 15–7 shows the retail life cycle and the position of various current forms of retail outlets on it. *Early growth* is the stage of emergence of a retail outlet, with a sharp departure from existing competition. Market share rises gradually, although profits may be low because of start-up costs. In the next stage, *accelerated development,* both market share and profit achieve their greatest growth rates. Usually, multiple outlets are established as companies focus on the distribution element of the retailing mix. In this stage, some later competitors may enter. Wendy's, for example, appeared on the hamburger chain scene almost 20 years after McDonald's had begun operation. The key goal for the retailer in this stage is to establish a dominant position in the fight for market share.

FIGURE 15–7

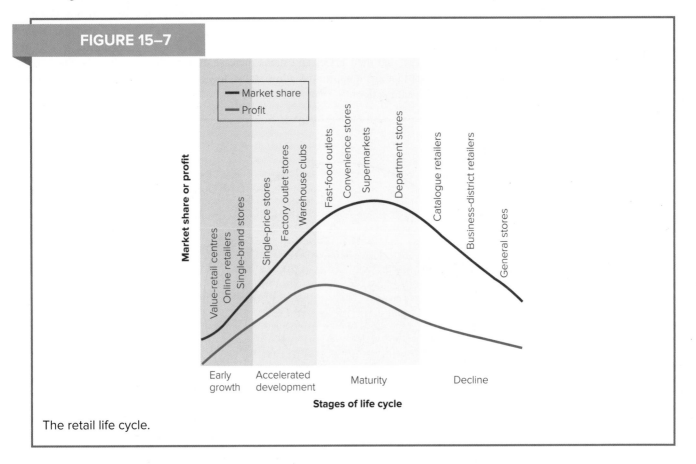

The retail life cycle.

The battle for market share is usually fought before the *maturity* phase, and some competitors drop out of the market. New retail forms enter in the maturity phase, stores try to maintain their market share, and price discounting occurs. For example, when McDonald's introduced its Extra Value Meal, a discounted package of burger, fries, and drink, Wendy's followed with its 99¢ Value Menu.

The challenge facing retailers is to delay entering the *decline* stage, in which market share and profit fall rapidly. Specialty apparel retailers, such as The Gap, Benetton, and Ann Taylor, have noticed a decline in market share after a decade of growth. To prevent further decline, these retailers will need to find ways of discouraging their customers from moving to low-margin, mass-volume outlets or high-price, high-service boutiques.

FIVE IMPORTANT TRENDS THAT ARE SHAPING THE RETAIL LANDSCAPE

There are five important trends that are shaping the retail landscape on a global basis: (1) travel retailing, (2) mobile retailing, (3) faster retailing, (4) experience retailing, and (5) innovative retailing.[34] You can also check out other relevant trends facing Canadian retailers by completing the Going Online exercise and checking out the Retail Council of Canada.

Travel Retailing

Over a billion people travel internationally each year— approximately 15 percent of the global population—and they spend the equivalent of more than a trillion U.S. dollars in the process. As a result, companies such as Pernod Ricard and L'Oréal refer to travel retail as their "sixth continent," and Luxottica describes airport sales as "the Formula One of retail." International tourism continues to rise above expectations despite continuing global geopolitical and economic challenges, and sales have grown by more than 12 percent a year since 2009. Half of that growth has come from an increase in travellers, especially from emerging countries like China. Much of the rest is due to the willingness of travellers to shop en route and abroad (and retailers' improved capability to serve them).

GOING ONLINE

Welcome to the Retail Council of Canada

Founded in 1963, Retail Council of Canada (RCC) is the "Voice of Retail." RCC is a not-for-profit association representing all retail formats, including national and regional department stores, mass merchants, specialty chains, independent stores, and online merchants. It speaks for an industry that touches the daily lives of Canadians in every corner of the country—by providing jobs, consumer value, world-class product selection, and the colour, sizzle, and entertainment of the marketplace. RCC promotes retail as a career, as an economic driver, and as a barometer of consumer tastes and confidence. Go to the RCC's Media Centre on its website (**www.retailcouncil.org/media**) and then select "News Releases." Read about the latest trends and developments in retailing in Canada.

The expanding middle classes of emerging markets are travelling to the world's capitals and boosting sales, especially of luxury products, and this is benefiting the developed economies of the United States, Canada, and Europe. For example, over half of France's 16-billion-euro luxury industry depends on tourists. Therefore, now and in the future, retailers will continue catering to high-spending travellers, especially emerging market tourists, to drive growth. Travel retail provides new opportunities to engage with consumers. Travellers often have time for leisurely shopping due to lengthy wait times at airports, and international travel often promotes a sense of personal achievement, both conditions providing a good atmosphere for experimentation and indulgence. In response to these opportunities, many companies are investing in building brand awareness in emerging countries, even when the targeted consumers may not purchase those brands at home. This is because these consumers are keen to acquire foreign and luxury brands while travelling, especially in developed markets which offer superior product selection and availability as well as advantageous price comparisons due to high import taxes in home countries.

As a result, airports have become retail destinations and airport retail design has evolved, now dominated by luxury fashion trends rather than the duty-free shops of the past. Airports have also become laboratories and an important source of data, allowing companies to experiment.

Mobile Retailing

A projected 65 percent of the global population will be using a mobile phone by 2017, and an estimated 83 percent of Internet usage will be through handheld devices. It is no surprise then that mobile retailing is expected to continue to grow aggressively. In the next three years, global e-commerce sales made via mobile devices are expected to top US$638 billion, which is about the size of the world's entire e-commerce market just a short time ago.

The introduction of wearables, such as Google Glass and Apple Watch, opens new opportunities for reaching consumers, and retailers will keep an eye on developments in this arena. The smart watch sector is currently estimated at US$1.4 billion to US$1.8 billion but is expected to surge to US$10 billion by 2018. The full range of the wearable technology market is projected to hit US$30 billion in sales during the same period.

Retailers will need to respond by offering free in-store Wi-Fi and mobile-friendly retail websites optimized for different kinds of personal devices. Mobile payments will play a large role—Forrester expects mobile payments to amount to US$90 billion by 2017—as will location-based marketing. Walmart, eBay, and Amazon have already created convenient mobile customer experiences and others will follow. However, while shoppers want real-time, relevant, and personalized information and offers, retailers will need to surround this service with very strong privacy and security. Trust, transparency, and protecting customer information will be critical in retaining loyalty as mobile retailing becomes the norm.

Faster Retailing

Speed has been an important trend in retail for over a decade. This includes "fast fashion," that is, getting runway styles to the stores as soon as possible; limited-time-only products and flash sales to drive urgency and immediate purchase; pop-up establishments to quickly get products and services to market and build buzz; and self-service check-out and kiosks to reduce or eliminate waiting. Millennials will be driving much of this as they are the largest generation, with a lot of spending power, and they carry a lot of influence. They prefer fast response and immediate gratification, and retailers will cater to that. With Amazon and Google offering same-day delivery in certain areas, expect other companies to follow; the delivery window will become more narrow and specific.

This won't happen overnight, of course, but the first movers in this area are aggressively testing possibilities. Amazon expanded its same-day delivery service in parts of the U.S. to certain cities in the U.K., Germany, and Canada. It recently tested delivery by taxi, and is waiting for U.S. Federal Aviation Administration permission to begin its Prime Air service in which drones will deliver packages within 30 minutes. The ability to meet the consumer's need for speed makes an efficient end-to-end supply chain more important than ever.

While same-day product delivery will not likely be the norm for everyone, instant availability of information will be. More and more consumers are expecting it, and retailers will need to deliver. Retailers will need to optimize their information to provide as much content as shoppers need without the load time, especially over Wi-Fi and cellular networks on mobile devices, so shoppers can easily and quickly find the information or product they need.

Experience Retailing

Retailing is no longer just about the product, but the experience. Consumers want shopping to include entertainment, education, emotion, engagement, and enlightenment. Retailers are exploring innovative ways to enhance the buying experience for their customers: fashion shows, music festivals, tablet and interactive displays, social media campaigns, and product and marketing co-creation. The Legaspi Company has even rebuilt failing shopping malls into Hispanic cultural centres serving all the needs of a family: grocery stores, dental and medical care, clothes, entertainment, banking, a department of motor vehicles, and spaces for religious activities; these locations have seen income and foot traffic increase, typically by 30 percent.

It should be noted that with all these new forms of engagement, regardless of in-store, online, at home, or on the street, consumers still want a seamless and consistent experience. They expect to be able to view online information, access coupons, learn about promotions, and review inventory at any time on any device. They expect messaging and product and pricing information to be consistent across all channels: advertising and social media; in-store and online; pushed or pulled; the sales people on the floor as well as the customer service representative on the phone. They want to order, pick up, ship, receive, and return anywhere. To become nimble enough to respond to these consumer expectations, some retailers may have to change their internal operations, removing silos and improving cross-functional collaboration.

Personalized websites and e-mails have become the norm, and consumers are looking for this personalization to extend into their in-store experiences. Retailers can now send customized text messages to shoppers in-store, and adapt interactions to each individual. Retailers will therefore be investing in analysis of big data to enable personalization. However, trust will be critical since violation of privacy will be a concern for consumers. Retailers will need to be transparent in their collection and use of data, and educate shoppers about the value they are delivering with personalized shopping experience.

Innovative Retailing

The retail industry continues to be disrupted by new technologies and innovative competition. There will be no single formula for success, which will come in all shapes and sizes, formats and channels. There will be a further blurring of sectors as well as single-product retailing, such as Warby Parker. There will continue to be non-traditional retailers innovating in the retail space, such as Verizon with its Mall of America destination store. Mobile POS systems will continue to enable inventive pop-up stores, trucks, and kiosks. Retailers will be vertically integrated and vertically transparent, such as Zady. In some cases, the middleman will be cut out completely, with no physical stores, no inventory, no warehouses, but rather made-to-order direct from manufacturer, such as Awl & Sundry and **Made.com**.

The line between retailer and producer will begin to blur in new ways, such as Amazon's Creative Expressions, part of its 3-D Printing Store. Expect more retailers to be innovators. Numerous retailers have invested heavily in their own innovation labs, including Nordstrom, Walmart, Staples, Amazon, and The Home Depot. Retailers are embracing technology and using it in creative ways. For example, Lowe's has introduced a multilingual robot that can scan a part a shopper brings in, identify it, instantly access information about it, and help the customer find it in the store. With the Internet of Things, we can soon expect retail innovations like automatic purchasing and delivery with connected homes and refrigerators. For a good example of innovative retailing, read the Marketing Matters box, "The Shopping Bag of the Future Is Here!" which discusses the shopping bag of the future![35] Finally, retailers are also getting innovative when it comes to sustainable practices as the Making Responsible Decision box, "Innovative Retailing Includes Sustainability Practices," points out![36]

MARKETING MATTERS

The Shopping Bag of the Future Is Here!

Adobe is bringing the intelligence of e-commerce to the bricks-and-mortar world with a new smart shopping bag that functions like a virtual shopping cart. The Adobe Smart Bag is a collaboration with Capgemini and tech startup Twyst. Once customers place items in the bag, it starts a running total of those products. The checkout process is determined by the retailer, but the bag's technology allows for an automatic checkout via a store app. It is designed with a hard exterior (Adobe's prototype is made of leather) and a reusable interior bag that the customer can remove at the end of their shopping trip, triggering the purchase of all of the items inside.

The Smart Bag makes use of Bluetooth low energy (BLE) and radio-frequency identification (RFID) technology to allow communication between the bag and product tags. It has a lightweight BLE device built into the bag's base that can recognize when an item with a RFID tag is placed inside. (RFID tags are stickers that emit a signal that can be placed on a product tag and cost just a fraction of a cent.) The bag is also lined with mylar that blocks out other signals so when a customer passes items in the store, they're not added to the customer's shopping cart.

Once the interior bag is removed, it sends a signal to the app triggering a mobile purchase, using payment information stored in the retailer's app. The store can then follow-up with a digital receipt via e-mail. Ben Gilchriest, digital innovation lead at Capgemini, said this technology was customizable based on the needs of the retailer. The design and production of the bag itself, for example, is at the discretion of the retailer, meaning the store can choose to make it out of either luxe or inexpensive materials and customize it with their own branding. Stores can also use the technology without pairing it with a mobile app. In that case, the BLE device could be built into a kiosk or a traditional checkout, allowing the customer to pay using a terminal instead of a phone.

Gilchriest said this had the potential to massively cut down checkout times, a key pain point for retailers. Marc Eaman, Adobe's director of marketing cloud technical marketing, demonstrated the bag on stage using the outdoor apparel brand REI Co-Op as an example. Eaman entered into a mock store and picked up the bag, then purchased a bicycle helmet, using it with the back-end of REI's app showing how the purchase worked on-screen. REI Co-Op is not currently using the Smart Bag, but Gilchriest said several retailers are currently testing it in "clean lab" simulated retail spaces for potential use.

The near future of the retail industry is about adaptation and embracing change. The speed of innovation and the disruption it causes won't cease, and the demands of customers will continue to escalate. To thrive in this environment, retailers will respond quickly to threats and opportunities with innovations of their own. This requires connecting strategy, capabilities, and specific initiatives, guided by the insights provided by market data. The right talent with the right skill set is key to successful execution, of course. Retailers will need to focus on finding, recruiting, and retaining the best people. But the reality is that no retailer will have all the appropriate talent in-house, making it essential that they develop an arrangement of partnerships and specialized resources. So when needed, they can quickly call upon the right expertise to drive the kind of innovation in product offerings, business models, and customer engagement that will enable them to stay ahead of the competition. With market disruption comes opportunities, and obviously, the retailers who can be nimble, adapt, and innovate in the face of these changes will be in a better position for success than those who cannot.

MAKING RESPONSIBLE DECISIONS

Innovative Retailing Includes Sustainability Practices

Sustainability has been a topic of interest for some retailers for many years. Recently, however, it has become a movement for the entire industry and is being driven by innovative retailers who embrace the concept of sustainability. These retailers are discovering that not only does sustainability save money, it also means winning the hearts and minds of customers! These innovative retailers are building sustainability practices into their overall business strategies. For example, Canadian Tire has implemented hundreds of sustainability initiatives in recent years, from lighting retrofits to efficiency improvements in product transport, saving the retailer approximately $6 million. Home Depot has created a program that gives Canadian manufacturers the opportunity to pitch innovative, environmentally sustainable products. By supporting great ideas, the retailer hopes to help transform the market by ensuring that sustainable products are always on their store shelves. It also saved $16 million a year when it switched its in-store fixtures to compact fluorescent light bulbs.

Sears Canada replaced more than 116,000 incandescent lights in all of its Sears Home and full-line stores across Canada, making it the first Canadian retailer to install an LED retrofit. This resulted in a 75 percent annual reduction in energy consumption and two-year payback on investment. Walmart commissioned an assessment of its heating, ventilation, and air conditioning (HVAC) and energy systems at over 200 stores, resulting in adjustment changes that created a 20 percent increase in energy efficiency and will provide a payback on investment of less than three years. Mountain Equipment Co-op is also being innovative by collecting rainwater to water grass at the store and to use in its toilets. Finally, IKEA Canada no longer offers customers plastic bags in any of its stores and reserves prime parking spaces for customers driving hybrid vehicles. Other companies are using motion detectors to turn lights on and off, improving the fuel economy of delivery vehicles, and designing "zero waste" stores.

Are your favourite retailers being innovative when it comes to sustainability? And do sustainability efforts influence your retail purchase decisions?

Learning Review

10. According to the wheel of retailing, when a new retail form appears, how would you characterize its image?

11. Market share is usually fought out before the _____ stage of the retail life cycle.

Learning Objectives Review

Explain the alternative ways to classify retail outlets.

Retail outlets can be classified by form of ownership, level of service, and type of merchandise line. The forms of ownership include independent retailers, corporate chains, and contractual systems that include retailer-sponsored cooperatives, wholesaler-sponsored voluntary chains, and franchises. The levels of service include self-service, limited-service, and full-service outlets. Stores classified by their merchandise line include stores with depth, such as sporting good specialty stores, and stores with breadth, such as large department stores.

Describe the many methods of non-store retailing.

Non-store retailing includes automatic vending, direct mail and catalogues, television home shopping, online retailing, telemarketing, and direct selling. The methods of non-store retailing vary by the level of involvement of the retailer and the level of involvement of the customer. Vending, for example, has low involvement, whereas both the consumer and the retailer have high involvement in direct selling.

Classify retailers in terms of the retail positioning matrix.

The retail positioning matrix positions retail outlets on two dimensions: breadth of product line and value added. There are four possible positions in the matrix. Such stores as Hudson's Bay have a broad product line and high value added. Such stores as Walmart also have a broad product line but have low value added because they offer fewer services. Birks represents a narrow product line and high value added. Finally, such stores as Payless ShoeSource offer a narrow product line and low value added.

Develop retailing mix strategies over the life cycle of a retail store.

The retail life cycle describes the process of growth and decline for retail outlets through four stages: early growth, accelerated development, maturity, and decline. The retail mix—pricing, store location, communication, and merchandise—can be managed to match the retail strategy with the stage of the life cycle. The challenge facing retailers is to delay entering the decline stage, where market share and profit fall rapidly.

LO5
Identify the challenges Canadian retailers face as they pursue sustainable growth, including the five important trends that are shaping the retail landscape.

There are five important trends that are shaping the retail landscape on a global basis, including Canadian retailing: (1) travel retailing, (2) mobile retailing, (3) faster retailing, (4) experience retailing, and (5) innovative retailing.

Applying Marketing Knowledge

1. Discuss the impact of the growing number of dual-income households on (*a*) non-store retailing, and (*b*) the retail mix.

2. How does value added affect a store's competitive position?

3. In retail pricing, retailers often have a maintained markup. Explain how this maintained markup differs from original markup and why it is so important.

4. What are the similarities and differences between product and retail life cycles?

5. How would you classify Walmart in terms of its position on the wheel of retailing versus that of an off-price retailer?

6. Develop a chart to highlight the role of each of the three main elements of the retailing mix across the four stages of the retail life cycle.

7. In Figure 15–5, Payless ShoeSource was placed on the retail positioning matrix. What strategies should Payless follow to move itself into the same position as Birks?

8. Breadth and depth are two important components in distinguishing among types of retailers. Discuss the breadth and depth implications of the following retailers: (*a*) La Senza, (*b*) Walmart, (*c*) L.L. Bean, and (*d*) Best Buy.

9. According to the wheel of retailing and the retail life cycle, what will happen to factory outlet stores?

10. The text discusses the development of online retailing. How does the development of this retailing form agree with the implications of the retail life cycle?

Building Your Marketing Plan

Does your marketing plan involve using retail? If the answer is no, read no further and do not include a retailing element in your plan. If the answer is yes:

1. Use Figure 15–4 to develop your retailing strategy by (*a*) selecting a position in the retail positioning matrix, and (*b*) specifying the details of the retailing mix.

2. Develop a positioning statement describing the breadth of the product line (broad versus narrow) and value added (low versus high). See Figure 15–5.

3. Describe an appropriate combination of retail pricing, store location, retail communications, and merchandise assortment.

Video Case 15

The Mall of America: America's Biggest Mall Knows the Secret to Successful Retailing!

The secret to success at the Mall of America is continually creating "new experiences for our guests" explains Jill Renslow, senior vice president of business development and marketing. "We want to make not only our locals but also our tourists have a unique experience every time they come and visit," she adds.

That's an ambitious undertaking for any retailer, but it is particularly challenging for the Mall of America because it attracts more than 40 million guests each year. To create new experiences, the mall uses a combination of constantly changing retail offerings, entertainment options, and special attractions. From new stores to musical acts to celebrity book signings to fashion shows and even to appearances by Taylor Swift, the Mall of America has become the "Hollywood of the Midwest."

"The key truly is being fresh and exciting" says Renslow.

The Big Idea for a Big Mall

The concept of a huge mall was the result of several trends. First, covered shopping centres began to replace downtown main-street shopping areas in the United States. Second, retail developers observed that casinos were adding non-gambling activities to attract entire families. Taking their cue from Las Vegas, a Canadian family, the Ghermezians, built the West Edmonton Mall as a destination venue with shopping, restaurants, hotels, and a theme park. The success of the West Edmonton Mall led to the search for another location for the destination mall concept, and soon the Mall of America was under construction in Minneapolis, Minnesota! The West Edmonton Mall was the largest mall in North America until 2004, only to be eclipsed by the Mall of America.

According to Dan Jasper, vice president of communications at the Mall of America, the Ghermezians are a "wonder family that are visionaries. . . . They dream really big dreams, and they bring them to reality; they did that in Edmonton with the West Edmonton Mall, and they did that here in Minnesota with the Mall of America," he explains. Today, the Mall of America is the largest mall in North America with 4.8 million square feet of shopping and entertainment space. And it's getting bigger! "We're opening our new grand front entrance and that will bring us to 5.5 million square feet, making us by far not only the busiest, not only the most successful, but the largest, most massive mall in the nation," says Jasper.

Executives at the Mall of America face several important challenges. First, they must keep a huge and diverse portfolio of retailers and attractions in the mall. Second, they must attract millions of visitors each year. Finally, they must increase its marketing and social media presence in the marketplace. The combination of these three activities is essential to the mall's continued success. This is particularly true at a time when e-commerce and online shopping are growing in popularity.

Managing the Mall

The size of the Mall of America is difficult to comprehend. There are more than four miles (6.5 km) of storefront in an area the size of 88 football fields. Three anchor stores—Macy's, Nordstrom, and Sears—are complemented by more than 500 specialty stores. The diversity of the retail offerings is also amazing. The types of stores range from familiar names such as Banana Republic, Apple, and True Religion to unique stores such as Brickmania, which offers custom LEGO® building kits, and Games by James, which offers thousands of board games and puzzles. According to Renslow, "That's what's special about the Mall of America, that's what attracts people from around the world."

To encourage entrepreneurs to come to the mall, there is a specialty leasing program that offers new retailers an affordable entry-level lease in exchange for flexibility related to their location. Mike Pohl, owner of the ACES Flight Simulation store, is one example of the unique businesses the program attracts. "I decided to locate at the Mall of America because it's the single biggest retail location in the country," Mike explains. "There are 40 million people that come here every year, and it's primarily an entertainment mall compared to a traditional mall, so it was a wonderful match for ACES," he adds.

The Mall of America also includes more than 20 restaurants, the House of Comedy for touring comedians, and an American Girl store with a doll hair salon and party facilities. The 14 theatres at the Mall of America include a 200-seat 3D theatre, equipped with D-Box motion seating, and a 148-seat theatre for guests 21 and older. In addition, some additional unique features of the Mall of America include:

- Nickelodeon Universe®, a 7-acre theme park with more than 20 attractions and rides including a roller coaster, a Ferris wheel, and a water chute in a sky-lighted area with more than 400 trees.

- Sea Life® Minnesota Aquarium, where visitors can see jellyfish, rays, and sea turtles; snorkel with tropical fish; or even dive with sharks!

- The Amazing Mirror Maze, Moose Mountain Adventure Golf, and the Universe of Light show.

- Two connected-access hotels, including a 342-room JW Marriott and a 500-room Radisson Blu.

- The Chapel of Love, which offers custom weddings and wedding packages and has performed more than 5,000 weddings in the mall!

Regular events and activities include the Art + Style Series, Toddler Tuesdays, the Mall Stars program for people who want to walk and exercise in the mall, and the Mall of America Music Series. The Mall of America also hosts corporate events for organizations with large groups. There are more than 12,000 free parking spaces available to accommodate any size group.

Attracting Visitors

From its opening day, visitors have been going to the Mall of America at the extraordinary rate of 10,000 visitors per day (or almost 40 million visitors annually), the most of any mall in the world. This is possible because the mall attracts shoppers from more than 18 states, including Minnesota, Wisconsin, Kentucky, Michigan, Ohio, and Pennsylvania, and from more than 11 countries, including Canada, Great Britain, France, Mexico, Germany, Scandinavia, Italy, Netherlands, Japan, China, and Spain. However, 80 percent of visitors are from Minnesota, Wisconsin, Iowa, the Dakotas, Illinois, Ohio, and Canada. The mall has worked closely with airlines and other partners to offer "Shop Till You Drop" packages that bring shoppers from throughout the world.

As Resnlow explains, "Mall of America shoppers are literally from age 3 to 83, which is a great opportunity for us but also a challenge. We need to be able to make sure that we communicate with each one of our guests. So we focus on the local market, which are 60 percent of our shoppers, and we also focus on our tourists, which are 40 percent of our shoppers, and we have different messages to those different audiences." Another key target audience for the mall includes young women. Unmarried women have disposable income and like to travel, and married women are the primary purchase decision makers in their households and often bring their spouses, children, and girlfriends to the mall.

Marketing, Social Media, and the Mall of America

Another key to the Mall of America's success has been its ability to manage its presence in the marketplace. According to Sarah Schmidt, public relations manager for the Mall of America, "A typical campaign for the Mall of America includes TV, radio, and print, and we also include social media campaigns as well." A recent campaign, "The Scream Collector," started with TV ads and then followed up with progress reports on billboards. Another campaign created a blizzard in the mall. The "blizzard was a tweet-powered blizzard where guests had to tweet #twizzard in, and once it hit a certain number of tweets, it started snowing in the mall," Schmidt says.

Social media are an important element of the Mall of America campaigns. Dan Jasper explains, "The Mall of America is at the forefront of social media and digital technology within the retail industry. For shopping malls, nobody has us beat." The mall has created a communication hub that integrates social media, texting, phone, and security all in a single system. "What that allows us to do is to speak with one voice, and to give real-time answers, suggestions, and advice to consumers," he says.

What is in the future for the Mall of America? According to Jasper, the answer is an even bigger mall. "In the coming years we're going to double the size of the Mall of America" he says. So, prepare yourself for an even more extraordinary retailing experience!

QUESTIONS

1. What is the key to success at the Mall of America?
2. What trends contributed to the idea for the Mall of America? How did it get started?
3. What challenges does the Mall of America face as it strives to continue its success?
4. What specific actions has the Mall of America taken to address each challenge?

Case: Mall of America: This case was written by Steven Hartley. Sources: Jennifer Latson, "Why America's Biggest Mall is Getting Bigger," *Time*, August 12, 2015; Samuel Greengard, "Mall of America Increases Its Social Presence," *CIO Insight*, July 28, 2015, p. 2; "This Is How You Resurrect America's Dying Malls," *Time*, April 15, 2014, p. 1; "JW Mall of America Hotel Set To Open In November," *Travel Weekly*, April 9, 2015, p. 17; Erika Fry, "Why Mall of America Is Expanding As Many Retailers Implode," *Fortune*, March 10, 2014; "Mall of America Marks 20 Years," *Women's Wear Daily*, November 5, 2012, p. 8; Jerry Gerlach and James Janke, "The Mall of America as a Tourist Attraction," *Focus*, Summer 2001, p. 32; and the Mall of America website www.mallofamerica.com.

16

Integrated Marketing Communications and Direct Marketing

Learning Objectives

After reading this chapter, you should be able to:

LO1 Discuss integrated marketing communications and the communication process.

LO2 Describe the promotional mix and the uniqueness of each component.

LO3 Select the promotional approach appropriate to a product's life cycle and characteristics as well as stages of the buying decision.

LO4 Discuss the characteristics of push and pull strategies.

LO5 Describe the elements of the promotion decision process.

LO6 Explain the value of direct marketing for consumers and sellers.

Taco Bell Loves Twitter!

More than 1.5 million people follow Taco Bell on Twitter. Many more are reached by other elements of its engaging integrated marketing campaign. If you've ever had a late-night snack at Taco Bell, you may be one of them!

Taco Bell has been wildly successful with its Cool Ranch Doritos Locos Tacos campaign. It began three weeks before the new taco was launched with password-only social media events. Taco Bell listened to real-time conversations on Twitter (@TacoBell) and rewarded fans with "epic deliveries." A woman who asked Taco Bell to be her Valentine, a student who promised to gather enough friends to eat 1,000 tacos, and a fan who posted a message about tacos on YouTube all received early tastes of the new product.

The campaign then used television, radio, outdoor, and cinema ads, as well as public relations support. The television ads included two 15-second spots titled "Wow" and "Duh" that were supported by a contest (printed on taco wrappers) inviting customers to post photos to Instagram or Twitter using the #wow and #duh hashtags for a chance to have their entry appear on a billboard. The most unique element of the campaign was a 3D ad showing a Dorito chip exploding and then morphing into a Cool Ranch Doritos Locos Taco chip. The ad appeared in more than 8,000 movie theatres, and the new product quickly became the company's most liked, shared, retweeted, and talked-about product on Facebook, Twitter, and Vine.

© Mike Hruby

© Mike Hruby

One reason for Taco Bell's success is that all of the elements of its Doritos Locos Tacos campaign are integrated to have the same message and tone, and they focus on engaging consumers. Some marketers have observed that our marketplace is in the midst of a shift from traditional branding to an "age of engagement" and that social media promotions are the best way to accommodate this shift. In addition, they suggest that several aspects of social media promotions are essential to engage today's customers. They are as follows:

1. Post relevant content about the benefits and uses of the product.
2. Supplement text with photos and videos.
3. Create sweepstakes, contests, and deals that reward current and new customers.
4. Encourage and respond to comments and feedback, both positive and negative.
5. Be current and timely with all interactions.

In addition to a presence on Twitter, many brands are using other new forms of engagement, such as Facebook Pages, RSS (rich site summary) feeds, mobile apps, blogs, websites, and QR (quick response) codes. Even traditional media are engaging customers—for example, TV reality shows like *Dancing with the Stars* and *America's Got Talent* encourage online and telephone voting. In the future, successful integrated marketing communications campaigns will certainly be engaging you!

Taco Bell's successful Doritos Locos Tacos campaign demonstrates the opportunity for engaging potential customers and the importance of integrating the various elements of a marketing communication program.[1] Promotion represents the fourth element in the marketing mix. The promotional element consists of five communication tools, including advertising, personal selling, sales promotion, public relations, and direct marketing. The combination of one or more of these communication tools is called the **promotional mix**. All of these tools can be used to (1) inform prospective buyers about the benefits of the product, (2) persuade them to try it, and (3) remind them later about the benefits they enjoyed by using the product.

In the past, marketers often viewed these communication tools as separate and independent. The advertising department, for example, often designed and managed its activities without consulting departments or agencies that had responsibility for sales promotion or public relations. The result was often an overall communication effort that was uncoordinated and, in some cases, inconsistent. Today, the concept of designing marketing communications programs that coordinate all promotional activities—advertising, personal selling, sales promotion, public relations, and direct marketing—to provide a consistent message across all audiences is referred to as **integrated marketing communications (IMC)**. In addition, by taking consumer expectations into consideration, IMC is a key element in a company's customer experience management strategy.[2]

This chapter provides an overview of the communication process, a description of the promotional mix elements, several tools for integrating the promotional mix, and a process for developing a comprehensive promotion program. One of the promotional mix elements, direct marketing, is also discussed in this chapter. Chapter 17 covers advertising, sales promotion, and public relations, and Chapter 18 discusses personal selling.

LO1 THE COMMUNICATION PROCESS

Communication is the process of conveying a message to others and requires six elements: a source, a message, a channel of communication, a receiver, and the processes of encoding and decoding (Figure 16–1).[3] The **source** may be a company or person who has information to convey. The information sent by a source, such as a description of a new wireless telephone, forms the **message**. The message is conveyed by means of a **channel of communication**, such as a salesperson, advertising media, or public relations tools. Consumers who read, hear, or see the message are the **receivers**.

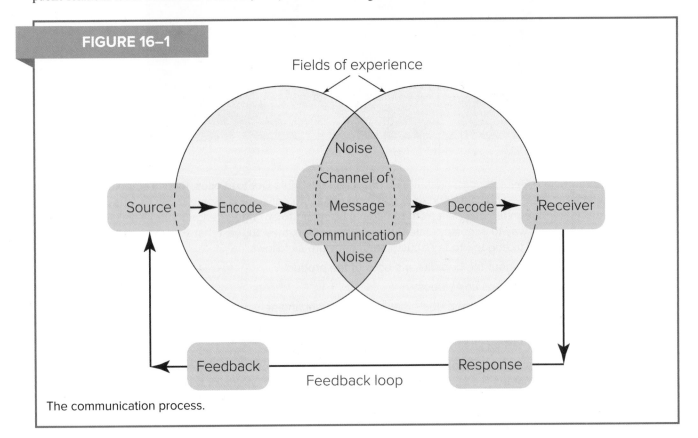

FIGURE 16–1

The communication process.

Encoding and Decoding

Encoding and decoding are essential to communication. **Encoding** is the process of having the sender transform an abstract idea into a set of symbols. **Decoding** is the reverse, or the process of having the receiver take a set of symbols, the message, and transform them back to an abstract idea. Look at the accompanying The North Face advertisement: Who is the source, and what is the message? Decoding is performed by the receivers according to their own frame of reference: their attitudes, values, and beliefs.[4] In the ad, The North Face is the source, and the message is the advertisement, which appeared in *Wired* magazine (the channel). The picture and text in the advertisement show that the source's intention is to generate interest in its products with the headline "Never stop exploring"—a statement the source believes will appeal to the readers of the magazine.

The process of communication is not always a successful one. Errors in communication can happen in several ways. The source may not adequately transform the abstract idea into an effective set of symbols, a properly encoded message may be sent through the wrong channel and never make it to the receiver, the receiver may not properly transform the set of symbols into the correct abstract idea, or finally, feedback may be so delayed or distorted that it is of no use to the sender. Although communication appears easy to perform, truly effective communication can be very difficult.

For the message to be communicated effectively, the sender and receiver must have a mutually shared **field of experience**—similar understanding and knowledge. Figure 16–1 shows two circles representing the fields of experience of the sender and receiver, which overlap in the message. For example, some communication problems have occurred when companies have taken their messages to cultures with different fields of experience, resulting in translation problems or misinterpretations. For example, KFC made a mistake when its "finger-lickin' good" slogan was translated into Mandarin Chinese as "eat your fingers off."[5]

How would you decode this ad? What message is The North Face trying to send?

Courtesy of The North Face

Feedback

Figure 16–1 shows a line labelled *feedback loop,* which consists of a response and feedback. A **response** is the impact the message had on the receiver's knowledge, attitudes, or behaviours. **Feedback** is the sender's interpretation of the response and indicates whether the message was decoded and understood as intended. Chapter 17 reviews approaches called *pre-testing* that ensure that messages are decoded properly.

Noise

Noise includes extraneous factors that can work against effective communication by distorting a message or the feedback received (see Figure 16–1). Noise can be a simple error, such as a printing mistake that affects the meaning of a newspaper advertisement, or using words or pictures that fail to communicate the message clearly. Noise can also occur when a salesperson's message is misunderstood by a prospective buyer, such as when a salesperson's accent, use of slang terms, or communication style makes hearing and understanding the message difficult.

Learning Review

1. What are the six elements required for communication to occur?
2. A difficulty for companies advertising in foreign markets is that the audience does not share the same _____.
3. A misprint in a newspaper ad is an example of _____.

LO2 THE PROMOTIONAL ELEMENTS

To communicate with consumers, a company can use one or more of five promotional alternatives: advertising, personal selling, public relations, sales promotion, and direct marketing. Figure 16–2 summarizes the distinctions among these five elements. Three of these elements—advertising, sales promotion, and public relations—are often said to use *mass selling* because they are used with groups of prospective buyers. In contrast, personal selling uses *customized interaction* between a seller and a prospective buyer. Personal-selling activities include face-to-face, telephone, and interactive electronic communication. Direct marketing also uses messages customized for specific customers.

FIGURE 16–2

PROMOTIONAL ELEMENT	MASS OR CUSTOMIZED	PAYMENT	STRENGTHS	WEAKNESSES
Advertising	Mass	Fees paid for space or time	• Efficient means for reaching large numbers of people	• High absolute costs • Difficult to receive good feedback
Personal selling	Customized	Fees paid to salespeople as either salaries or commissions	• Immediate feedback • Very persuasive • Can select audience • Can give complex information	• Extremely expensive per exposure • Messages may differ between salespeople
Public relations	Mass	No direct payment to media	• Often most credible source in the consumer's mind	• Difficult to get media cooperation
Sales promotion	Mass	Wide range of fees paid, depending on promotion selected	• Effective at changing behaviour in short run • Very flexible	• Easily abused • Can lead to promotion wars • Easily duplicated
Direct marketing	Customized	Cost of communication through mail, telephone, or computer	• Messages can be prepared quickly • Facilitates relationship with customer	• Declining customer response • Database management is expensive

The promotional mix.

Advertising

Advertising is any paid form of non-personal communication about an organization, good, service, or idea by an identified sponsor. The *paid* aspect of this definition is important because the space for the advertising message normally must be bought. An occasional exception is the public service announcement, where the advertising time or space is donated. A full-page, four-colour ad in *Canadian Living* magazine, for example, costs over $40,000, and over $36,000 in *Maclean's*. The *non-personal* component of advertising is also important. Advertising involves mass media (such as TV, radio, and magazines), which are non-personal and do not have an immediate feedback loop as does personal selling. So before the message is sent, marketing research plays a valuable role; for example, it determines that the target market will actually see the medium chosen and that the message will be understood.

There are several advantages to a firm using advertising in its promotional mix. It can be attention-getting—as with the Klondike ad shown here—and also can communicate specific product benefits to prospective buyers. By paying for the advertising space, a company can control *what* it wants to say and, to some extent, to *whom* the message is sent. Advertising also allows the company to decide *when* to send its message (which includes how often). The non-personal aspect of advertising also has its advantages. Once the message is created, the same message is sent to all receivers in a market segment. If the message is properly pre-tested, an advertiser can ensure the ad's ability to capture consumers' attention and trust that the same message will be decoded by all receivers in the market segment.[6]

Advertising has some disadvantages. As noted in Figure 16–2 and discussed in depth in Chapter 17, the costs to produce and place a message are significant, and the lack of direct feedback makes it difficult to know how well the message was received. However, direct-response advertising, including television and Internet or online advertising, now offers greater possibility of interactivity between advertiser and customer, including more feedback potential. Direct-response advertising and Internet or online advertising are discussed further in Chapter 17.

An attention-getting advertisement.

Courtesy of Unilever

Personal Selling

The second major promotional alternative is **personal selling**, defined as the two-way flow of communication between a buyer and seller, designed to influence a person's or group's purchase decision. Unlike advertising, personal selling is usually face-to-face communication between the sender and receiver (although telephone and electronic sales are growing). Why do companies use personal selling?

There are important advantages to personal selling, as summarized in Figure 16–2. A salesperson can control to *whom* the presentation is made, reducing the amount of *coverage,* or communication with consumers who are not in the target audience. The personal component of selling has another advantage over advertising in that the seller can see or hear the potential buyer's reaction to the message. If the feedback is unfavourable, the salesperson can modify the message.

The flexibility of personal selling can also be a disadvantage. Different salespeople can change the message so that no consistent communication is given to all customers. The high cost of personal selling is probably its major disadvantage. On a cost-per-contact basis, it is generally the most expensive of the five promotional elements.

Public Relations

Public relations is a form of communication management that seeks to influence the feelings, opinions, or beliefs held by customers, prospective customers, shareholders, suppliers, employees, and other publics about a company and its products or services. Many tools, such as special events sponsorship, lobbying efforts, annual reports, press conferences, social media, and image management, may be used by a public relations department, although publicity often plays the most important role. **Publicity** is a non-personal, indirectly paid presentation of an organization, good, or service. It can take the form of a news story, editorial, or product announcement. A difference between publicity and both advertising and personal selling is the *indirectly paid* dimension. With publicity, a company does not pay for space in a mass medium (such as television or radio) but attempts to get the medium to run a favourable story on the company. In this sense, there is an indirect payment for publicity in that a company must support a public relations staff.

An advantage of publicity is credibility. When you read a favourable story about a company's product (such as a glowing restaurant review), there is a tendency to believe it. Travellers throughout the world have relied on Fodor's travel guides. These books outline out-of-the-way, inexpensive restaurants, hotels, inns, and bed-and-breakfast rooms, giving invaluable publicity to these establishments. Such businesses do not (nor can they) buy a mention in the guides, which have sold millions of copies.

The disadvantages of publicity relate to the lack of the user's control over it. A company can invite a news team to preview its innovative exercise equipment and hope for a favourable mention on the 6 P.M. newscasts. But without buying advertising time, there is no guarantee of any mention of the new equipment or that it will be aired when the target audience is watching. Social media, such as blogs, have grown dramatically and allow uncontrollable public discussions of almost any company activity. Many public relations departments now focus on facilitating and responding to online discussions. Generally, publicity is an important element of many promotional campaigns, although the lack of control means that it is rarely the primary element.

Sales Promotion

A fourth promotional element is **sales promotion**, a short-term inducement of value offered to arouse interest in buying a good or service. Used in conjunction with advertising or personal selling, sales promotions are offered to intermediaries as well as to ultimate consumers. Coupons, rebates, samples, and sweepstakes are just a few examples of sales promotions discussed in Chapter 17.

The advantage of sales promotion is that the short-term nature of these programs (such as a coupon or sweepstakes with an expiration date) often stimulates sales for their duration. Offering value to the consumer in terms of a cents-off coupon or rebate may increase store traffic from consumers who are not store-loyal.[7]

Sales promotions cannot be the sole basis for a campaign because gains are often temporary and sales drop off when the deal ends.[8] Advertising support is needed to convert the customer who tried the product because of a sales promotion into a long-term buyer.[9] If sales promotions are conducted continuously, they lose their effectiveness. Customers begin to delay purchase until a coupon is offered, or they question the product's value. Some aspects of sales promotions also are regulated by the federal government. These issues are reviewed in detail later in Chapter 17.

Fodor's travel guides offer free publicity for companies.

© McGraw-Hill Education/ Editorial Image

Direct Marketing

Another promotional alternative, **direct marketing**, uses direct communication with consumers to generate a response in the form of an order, a request for further information, or a visit to a retail outlet.[10] The communication can take many forms, including face-to-face selling, direct mail, catalogues, telephone solicitations, and direct response advertising on television, radio, print, e-mail, social media, or mobile communication devices. Like personal selling, direct marketing often consists of interactive communication. It also has the advantage of being customized to match the needs of specific target markets. Messages can be developed and adapted quickly to facilitate one-to-one relationships with customers.

While direct marketing has been one of the fastest-growing forms of promotion, it has several disadvantages. First, most forms of direct marketing require a comprehensive and up-to-date database with information about the target market. Developing and maintaining the database can be expensive and time-consuming. In addition, growing concern about privacy has led to a decline in response rates among some customer groups. Companies with successful direct marketing programs are sensitive to these issues and often use a combination of direct marketing alternatives together, or direct marketing combined with other promotional tools, to increase value for customers.

Learning Review

4. Explain the difference between advertising and publicity when both appear on television.

5. Which promotional element should be offered only on a short-term basis?

6. Cost per contact is high with the _____ element of the promotional mix.

INTEGRATED MARKETING COMMUNICATIONS— DEVELOPING THE PROMOTIONAL MIX

A firm's promotional mix is the combination of one or more of the promotional elements it chooses to use. In putting together the promotional mix, a marketer must consider several issues. First, the balance of the elements must be determined. Should advertising be emphasized more than personal selling? Should a promotional rebate be offered? Would public relations activities be effective? Would a combination of online and traditional media work best? Several factors affect such decisions: the target audience for the promotion,[11] the stage of the product's life cycle, the characteristics of the product, the decision stage of the buyer, and even the channel of distribution. Second, because the various promotional elements are often the responsibility of different departments, coordinating a consistent promotional effort is necessary. A promotional planning process designed to ensure integrated marketing communications can facilitate this goal. To see an example of an integrated marketing communications campaign, read the accompanying Marketing Matters box, "Sears Canada Goes Integrated!"[12]

MARKETING MATTERS

Sears Canada Goes Integrated!

Sears Canada, a struggling retailer, is attempting to right the ship by employing an integrated approach to its communication. It recently launched a new springtime campaign called "Everything's springing up Sears." The campaign includes TV, radio, and PR. It also features reality-TV star Debbie Travis (and her new patio and home decor collection for Sears). The campaign starts with a 30-second, brightly coloured TV spot featuring people lounging in their yards.

The word "everything" has become important for Sears, says Vincent Power, vice-president, corporate affairs and communications at Sears Canada. The "everything under one roof" concept was launched during the 2015 holiday season with the "For everything under the tree, there's Sears" campaign. For this campaign, Sears will use an integrated, multifaceted digital, public, social, and influencer relations strategy to promote the company and its offerings. "The traditional flyer by itself isn't enough anymore," Power says. Today's customer responds to everything from Instagram and email to Twitter, he says. "We need to interact with that person over separate platforms."

IVY Photos/Shutterstock.com

The goal is to execute "everything under one roof" in store and online to recapture consumers aged 35 to 50 with school-age kids "that have drifted away from Sears over the past decade," Power says. He also believes there was previously too much separation among Sears' channels, including catalogues and stores. For important events in families' lives, such as Mother's Day or Back to School, Power says, "We need to be a much more integrated company." The company tested its new approach with the #HappyRenewYear program, showcasing Sears' health and wellness products. It was supported by PR, blogger partnerships, a feature on **Sears.ca**, and direct mail.

The new Travis line of Tuscan-inspired home products is being promoted with large-scale booths at the National Home Show in Toronto and at the Cottage Life Show in Mississauga, Ontario. Travis is doing media interviews and autograph signings at both shows. She will also be doing a national media tour to support her new partnership with Sears and will participate in a Twitter party. Additional elements include a contest to win a trip to Travis's new villa in Tuscany, Italy.

Travis will be on the front cover of a retail flyer and on the cover of a new 40-page Outdoor Style magalogue that will be mailed to Sears Loyalty Club members. Travis previously launched her own paint and home products line in 2005 at Canadian Tire, which has since been discontinued. "We have her across all platforms," Power says. "She's a perfect fit with Sears. She's got good quality, great design, but at affordable prices." The Travis line will expand to include indoor furniture, tabletop, home decor, and bed and bath items.

The Target Audience

Promotional programs are directed to the ultimate consumer, to an intermediary (retailer, wholesaler, or industrial distributor), or to both. Promotional programs directed to buyers of consumer products often use mass media because the number of potential buyers is large. Personal selling is used at the place of purchase, generally the retail store. Direct marketing may be used to encourage first-time or repeat purchases. Combinations of many media alternatives are a necessity for many target audiences today, as you read in the preceding Marketing Matters box.

Advertising directed to business buyers is used selectively in trade publications, such as *Fence Industry* magazine for buyers of fencing material. Because business buyers often have specialized needs or technical questions, personal selling is particularly important. The salesperson can provide information and the necessary support after sales.

Intermediaries are often the focus of promotional efforts. As with business buyers, personal selling is the major promotional ingredient. The salespeople assist intermediaries in making a profit by coordinating promotional campaigns sponsored by the manufacturer and by providing marketing advice and expertise. Intermediaries' questions often pertain to the allowed markup, merchandising support, and return policies.

(LO3) The Product Life Cycle

All products have a product life cycle (see Chapter 11), and the composition of the promotional mix changes over the four life-cycle stages, as shown for Purina Dog Chow in Figure 16–3.

Introduction Stage

Informing consumers in an effort to increase their level of awareness is the primary promotional objective in the introduction stage of the product life cycle. In general, all the promotional mix elements are used at this time, although the use of specific mix elements during any stage depends on the product and situation. News releases about Purina's new nutritional product are sent to veterinary magazines, trial samples are sent to registered dog owners, advertisements are placed in *Dog World* magazine, and the salesforce begins to approach supermarkets to get orders. Advertising is particularly important as a means of reaching as many people as possible to build up awareness and interest. Purina Dog Chow, for example, uses social media, specifically its Facebook page, to reach dog owners. Publicity may even begin slightly before the product is commercially available.

Growth Stage

The primary promotional objective of the growth stage is to persuade the consumer to buy the product—Purina Dog Chow—rather than substitutes, and so the marketing manager seeks to gain brand preference and solidify distribution. Sales promotion assumes less importance in this stage, and publicity is not a factor because it depends on novelty of the product. The primary promotional element is advertising, which stresses brand differences. Personal selling is used to solidify the channel of distribution. For consumer products, such as dog food, the salesforce calls on wholesalers and retailers in hopes of increasing inventory levels and gaining shelf space. For business products, the salesforce often tries to get contractual arrangements to be the sole source of supply for the buyer.

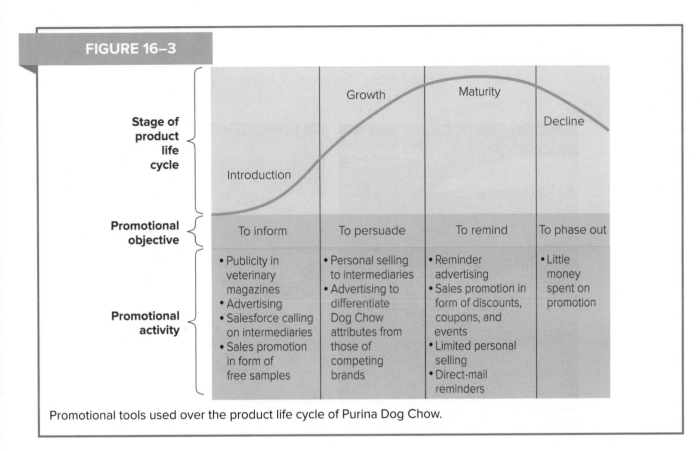

FIGURE 16–3

Stage of product life cycle	Introduction	Growth	Maturity	Decline
Promotional objective	To inform	To persuade	To remind	To phase out
Promotional activity	• Publicity in veterinary magazines • Advertising • Salesforce calling on intermediaries • Sales promotion in form of free samples	• Personal selling to intermediaries • Advertising to differentiate Dog Chow attributes from those of competing brands	• Reminder advertising • Sales promotion in form of discounts, coupons, and events • Limited personal selling • Direct-mail reminders	• Little money spent on promotion

Promotional tools used over the product life cycle of Purina Dog Chow.

Maturity Stage

In the maturity stage, the need is to maintain existing buyers, and advertising's role is to remind buyers of the product's existence. Sales promotion, in the form of discounts and coupons offered to both ultimate consumers and intermediaries, is important in maintaining loyal buyers. In a test of one mature consumer product, it was found that 80 percent of the product's sales at this stage resulted from sales promotions.[13] Since 1998, Purina has sponsored the Incredible Dog Challenge, which is now covered by ESPN.[14] Purina also ran a sweepstakes program on Facebook called "Strong Dogs." Direct marketing actions, such as direct mail, are used to maintain involvement with existing customers and to encourage repeat purchases. Price cuts and discounts can also significantly increase a mature brand's sales. The salesforce at this stage seeks to satisfy intermediaries. An unsatisfied customer who switches brands is hard to replace.

Decline Stage

The decline stage of the product life cycle is usually a period of phase-out for the product, and little money is spent in the promotional mix. The rate of decline can be rapid, when a product is replaced by an improved or lower cost product, for example, or slow, if there is a loyal group of customers.

Purina Dog Chow: a product in the maturity stage of its life cycle

Product Characteristics

The proper blend of elements in the promotional mix also depends on the type of product. Three specific characteristics should be considered: complexity, risk, and ancillary services. *Complexity* refers to the technical sophistication of the product and hence the amount of understanding required to use it. It is hard to provide much information in a one-page magazine ad or 30-second television ad; the more complex the product, the greater is the emphasis on personal selling. Gulfstream asks potential customers to call its senior vice president in its ads. No information is provided for simple products, such as Heinz ketchup, a familiar household staple.

A second element is the degree of *risk* represented by the product's purchase. Risk for the buyer can be assessed in terms of financial risk, social risk, and physical risk. A private jet, for example, might represent all three risks—it is expensive, employees and customers may see and evaluate the purchase, and safety and reliability are important. Although advertising helps, the greater the risk, the greater is the need for personal selling. Consumers are unlikely to associate any of these risks with, say, cereal.

How do Gulfstream aircraft and Heinz ketchup, a familiar food product, differ on complexity, risk, and ancillary services?

Gulfstream www.gulfstream.com

Heinz www.heinz.com

(left): General Dynamics; (right): Courtesy of Kraft Heinz Company. Used with permission

The level of ancillary services required by a product also affects the promotional strategy. *Ancillary services* pertain to the degree of service or support required after the sale. This characteristic is common to many business products and consumer purchases. Who will provide maintenance for the plane? Advertising's role is to establish the seller's reputation. Direct marketing can be used to describe how a product or service can be customized to individual needs. However, personal selling is essential to build buyer confidence and provide evidence of customer service.

Stages of the Buying Decision

Knowing the customer's stage of decision making can also affect the promotional mix. Figure 16–4 shows how the importance of the promotional elements varies with the three stages in a consumer's purchase decision.

Pre-purchase Stage

In the pre-purchase stage, advertising is more helpful than personal selling because advertising informs the potential customer of the existence of the product and the seller. Sales promotion in the form of free samples also can play an important role to gain low-risk trial. When the salesperson calls on the customer after heavy advertising, there is some recognition of what the salesperson represents. This is particularly important in business settings in which sampling of the product is usually not possible.

Purchase Stage

At the purchase stage, the importance of personal selling is highest, whereas the impact of advertising is lowest. Sales promotion in the form of coupons, deals, point-of-purchase displays, and rebates can be very helpful in encouraging demand. In this stage, although advertising is not an active influence on the purchase, it is the means of delivering the coupons, deals, and rebates that are often important. In this stage, social media can also play an important role in the final decision by delivering promotions and giving consumers control of the process.

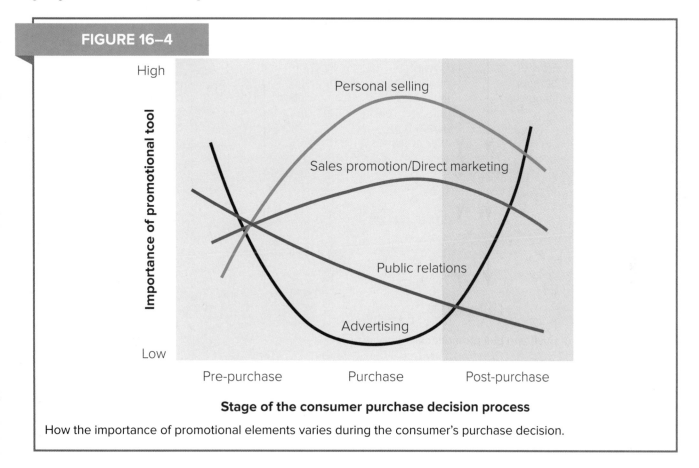

FIGURE 16–4

How the importance of promotional elements varies during the consumer's purchase decision.

Post-purchase Stage

In the post-purchase stage, the salesperson is still important. In fact, the more personal contact after the sale, the more the buyer is satisfied. Advertising is also important to assure the buyer that the right purchase was made. Advertising and personal selling help reduce the buyer's post-purchase anxiety.[15] Sales promotion in the form of coupons and direct marketing reminders can help encourage repeat purchases from satisfied first-time users. Public relations plays a small role in the post-purchase stage.

Channel Strategies

Chapter 14 discussed the channel flow from producer to intermediaries to consumer. Achieving control of the channel is often difficult for the manufacturer, and promotional strategies can assist in moving a product through the channel of distribution. This is where a manufacturer has to make an important decision about whether to use a push strategy, a pull strategy, or both in its channel of distribution.[16]

 Push Strategy

Figure 16–5A shows how a manufacturer uses a **push strategy**, directing the promotional mix to channel members to gain their cooperation in ordering and stocking the product. In this approach, personal selling and sales promotions play major roles. Salespeople call on wholesalers to encourage orders and provide sales assistance. Sales promotions, such as case discount allowances (20 percent off the regular case price), are offered to stimulate demand. By pushing the product through the channel, the goal is to get channel members to push it to their customers.

FIGURE 16–5

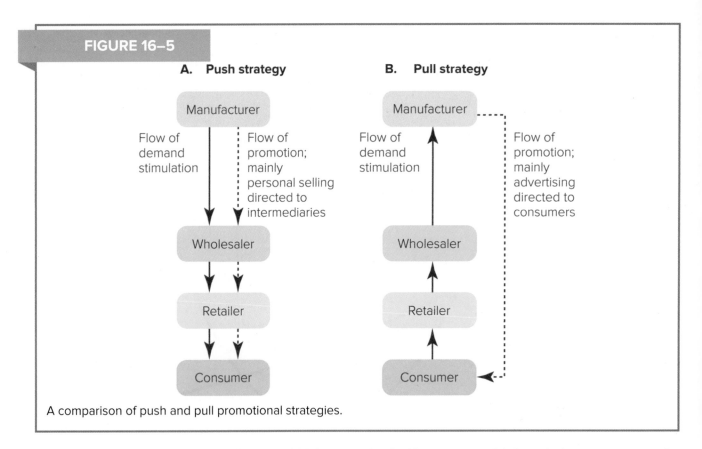

A comparison of push and pull promotional strategies.

Canadian firms, such as Pepsi-Cola Canada and Molson, spend a significant amount of their marketing resources on maintaining their relationships with their distributors and, through them, with retailers. In general, Canadian consumer goods firms are allocating greater percentages of their promotional budgets toward intermediaries. In some cases, as much as 60 percent of the promotional budget is being allocated to personal selling and sales promotions designed to reach intermediaries, while 40 percent is spent on promotional activities directed toward ultimate consumers.[17]

Pull Strategy

In some instances, manufacturers face resistance from channel members who do not want to order a new product or increase inventory levels of an existing brand. As shown in Figure 16–5B, a manufacturer may then elect to implement a **pull strategy** by directing its promotional mix at ultimate consumers to encourage them to ask the retailer for the product. Seeing demand from ultimate consumers, retailers order the product from wholesalers and thus the item is pulled through the intermediaries. Such firms as Procter & Gamble and Heinz Canada use pull strategies, including e-mail marketing campaigns, online websites with electronic couponing, and Facebook pages directed at ultimate consumers to create consumer pull. Pampers Village at **www.pampers.ca** is an example of how P&G engages in pull strategy activities.[18]

A novel pull strategy is one being used by B.C. hemlock producers and their Coastal Forest and Lumber Association as they seek greater market share in Japan. B.C. hemlock, now rebranded as Canada Tsuga, uses a Japanese sumo wrestler in advertising that is directed toward home builders, who are now, in turn, demanding the product from lumber suppliers. The product is now the preferred product in post-and-beam construction, and the Japanese consumer now views the Canadian Tsuga very positively.[19]

Learning Review

7. Describe the promotional objective for each stage of the product life cycle.

8. At what stage of the consumer purchase decision is the importance of personal selling highest? Why?

9. Explain the differences between a push strategy and a pull strategy.

DEVELOPING THE IMC PROGRAM

Because media costs are high, promotion decisions must be made carefully, using a systematic approach. Paralleling the planning, implementation, and evaluation steps described in the strategic marketing process (Chapter 2), the promotion decision process is divided into (1) developing, (2) executing, and (3) evaluating the promotion program (Figure 16–6). Development of the promotion program focuses on the four Ws:

- *Who* is the target audience?
- *What* are (1) the promotion objectives, (2) the amounts of money that can be budgeted for the promotion program, and (3) the kinds of promotion to use?
- *Where* should the promotion be run?
- *When* should the promotion be run?

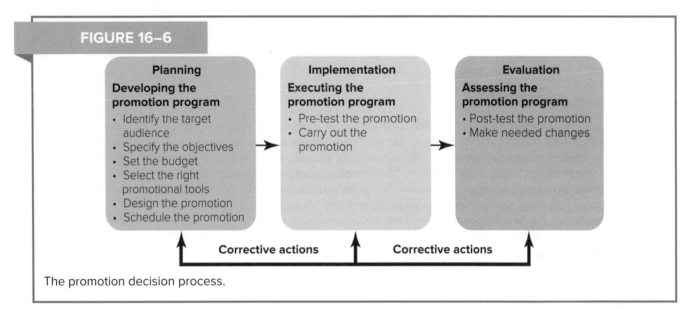

FIGURE 16–6

The promotion decision process.

Identifying the Target Audience

The first decision in developing the promotion program is identifying the *target audience,* the group of prospective buyers toward which a promotion program is directed. To the extent that time and money permit, the target audience for the promotion program is the target market for the firm's product, which is identified from marketing research and market segmentation studies. The more a firm knows about its target audience's profile—including their needs, demographics, lifestyle, attitudes, values, media use, and purchase behaviours—the easier it is to develop a promotion program. If a firm wanted to reach you with television and magazine ads, for example, it would need to know what TV shows you watch and what magazines you read. A firm might also use *behavioural targeting*—collecting information about your web-browsing behaviour—to determine the online ads that you will see as you surf the web. This has led to a new form of online behavioural advertising (see Chapter 17).

Specifying Promotion Objectives

After the target audience is identified, a decision must be reached on what the promotion should accomplish. Consumers can be said to respond in terms of a **hierarchy of effects**, which is the sequence of stages a prospective buyer goes through, from initial awareness of a product to eventual action (either trial or adoption of the product).[20]

- *Awareness.* The consumer's ability to recognize and remember the product or brand name.
- *Interest.* An increase in the consumer's desire to learn about some of the features of the product or brand.
- *Evaluation.* The consumer's appraisal of the product or brand on important attributes.

- *Trial.* The consumer's actual first purchase and use of the product or brand.

- *Adoption.* Through a favourable experience on the first trial, the consumer's repeated purchase and use of the product or brand.

For a totally new product, the sequence applies to the entire product category, but for a new brand competing in an established product category, it applies to the brand itself. These steps can serve as guidelines for developing promotion objectives.

Although sometimes an objective for a promotion program involves several steps in the hierarchy of effects, it often focuses on a single stage. Regardless of what the specific objective might be, from building awareness to increasing repeat purchases,[2][1] promotion objectives should possess three important qualities. They should (1) be designed for a well-defined target audience, (2) be measurable, and (3) cover a specified time period.

Setting the Promotion Budget

After setting the promotion objectives, a company must decide on how much to spend. The promotion expenditures needed to reach millions of Canadian households are enormous. Canadian companies are expected to spend over $15 billion on advertising and billions more on sales promotion and direct marketing to reach these households.[22] Some companies, such as McDonald's Canada, Procter & Gamble, and General Motors of Canada, spend hundreds of millions of dollars each year.

Determining the ideal amount for the budget is difficult because there is no precise way to measure the exact results of spending promotion dollars. However, several methods are used to set the promotion budget.[23]

Percentage of Sales

In the **percentage of sales budgeting** approach, funds are allocated to promotion as a percentage of past or anticipated sales, in terms of either dollars or units sold. A common budgeting method,[24] this approach is often stated in such terms as, "Our promotion budget for this year is 3 percent of last year's gross sales." The advantage of this approach is obvious: It is simple and provides a financial safeguard by tying the promotion budget to sales. However, there is a major fallacy in this approach, which implies that sales cause promotion. Using this method, a company may reduce its promotion budget because of a downturn in past sales or an anticipated downturn in future sales—situations where it may need promotion the most. See the Using Marketing Dashboards box, "How Much Should You Spend on IMC?" for an application of the promotion-to-sales ratio for the automotive industry.

Competitive Parity

A second common approach, **competitive parity budgeting**, is matching the competitor's absolute level of spending or the proportion per point of market share. This approach has also been referred to as *matching competitors* or *share of market*. It is important to consider the competition in budgeting.[25] Consumer responses to promotion are affected by competing promotional activities; thus, if a competitor runs 30 radio ads each week, it may be difficult for another firm to get its message across with only five messages.[26] The competitor's budget level, however, should not be the only determinant in setting a company's budget. The competition might have very different promotional objectives, which require a different level of promotion expenditures.

All You Can Afford

Common to many small businesses is **all-you-can-afford budgeting**, in which money is allocated to promotion only after all other budget items are covered. As one company executive said in reference to this budgeting process, "Why, it's simple. First, I go upstairs to the controller and ask how much they can afford to give us this year. She says a million and a half. Later, the boss comes to me and asks how much we should spend, and I say 'Oh, about a million and a half.' Then we have our promotion appropriation."[27]

Fiscally conservative, this approach has little else to offer. Using this budgeting philosophy, a company acts as though it does not know anything about a promotion-to-sales relationship or what its promotion objectives are.

USING MARKETING DASHBOARDS

How Much Should You Spend on IMC?

Integrated marketing communications programs coordinate a variety of promotion alternatives to provide a consistent message across audiences. The amount spent on the various promotional elements, or on the total campaign, may vary depending on the target audience, the type of product, where the product is in the product life cycle, and the channel strategy selected. Managers often use the promotion-to-sales ratio on their marketing dashboard to assess how effective the IMC program expenditures are at generating sales.

Your Challenge As a manager at General Motors, you've been asked to assess the effectiveness of all promotion expenditures during the past year. The promotion-to-sales ratio can be used by managers to make year-to-year comparisons of their programs, to compare the effectiveness of their program with competitor's programs, or to make comparisons with industry averages. You decide to calculate the promotion-to-sales ratio for General Motors. In addition, to allow a comparison, you decide to make the same calculation for one of your competitors, Ford, and for the entire automobile industry. The ratio is calculated as follows:

$$\text{Promotion-to-sales ratio} = \text{Total promotion expenditures}/\text{Total sales}$$

Your Findings The information needed for these calculations is readily available from trade publications and annual reports. The following graph shows the promotion- to-sales ratio for General Motors and Ford and the automotive industry. General Motors spent $2.21 billion on its IMC program to generate $49 billion in sales for a ratio of 4.5 (percent). Ford's ratio was 2.8, and the industry average was 3.2.

Your Action General Motors' promotion-to-sales ratio is higher than Ford's and higher than the industry average. This suggests that the current mix of promotional activities and the level of expenditures may not be creating an effective IMC program. In the future, you will want to monitor the factors that may influence the ratio.

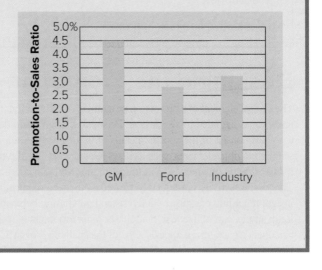

Objective and Task

The best approach to budgeting is **objective and task budgeting**, whereby the company (1) determines its promotion objectives, (2) outlines the tasks to accomplish these objectives, and (3) determines the promotion cost of performing these tasks.[28]

This method takes into account what the company wants to accomplish, and requires that the objectives be specified.[29] Strengths of the other budgeting methods are integrated into this approach because each previous method's strength is tied to the objectives. For example, if the costs are beyond what the company can afford, objectives are reworked and the tasks revised. The difficulty with this method is the judgment required to determine the tasks needed to accomplish objectives. Would two or four insertions in *Time* magazine be needed to achieve a specific awareness level? Figure 16–7 shows a sample media plan with objectives, tasks, and budget outlined. The total amount to be budgeted is $430,000. If the company can afford only $300,000, the objectives must be reworked, tasks redefined, and the total budget recalculated.

Selecting the Right Promotional Tools

Once a budget has been determined, the combination of the five basic integrated marketing communications (IMC) tools—advertising, personal selling, sales promotion, public relations, and direct marketing—can be specified. While many factors provide direction for selection of the appropriate mix, the large number of possible combinations of the promotional tools means that many combinations can achieve the same objective. Therefore, an analytical approach and experience are particularly important in this step of the promotion decision process. The specific mix can vary from a simple program using a single tool to a comprehensive program using all forms of promotion. The Olympic Games have become a very visible example of a comprehensive IMC program. Because the Games are repeated every two years, the promotion is almost continuous. Included in the program are advertising campaigns; personal selling efforts by the Olympic committee and organizers; sales promotion activities, such as product tie-ins and sponsorships; public relations programs managed by the host cities; and direct marketing efforts targeted at a variety of audiences, including governments, organizations, firms, athletes, and individuals.[30] At this stage, it is also important to assess the relative importance of the various tools. While it may be desirable to utilize and integrate several forms of promotion, one may deserve emphasis. The Olympic Games, for example, place exceptional importance on public relations and publicity.

FIGURE 16–7

OBJECTIVE	
To increase awareness among university students for a new video game. Awareness at the end of one semester should be 20 percent of all students from the existing 0 percent today.	
TASKS	
Advertisements once a week for a semester in 500 university papers	$280,000
Direct-mail samples to student leaders on 500 university campuses	50,000
Sponsor a national contest for video-game players	100,000
Total budget	$430,000

The objective and task approach.

Designing the Promotion

The central element of a promotion program is the promotion itself. Advertising consists of advertising copy and the artwork that the target audience is intended to see or hear. Personal selling efforts depend on the characteristics and skills of the salesperson. Sales promotion activities consist of the specific details of inducements, such as coupons, samples, and sweepstakes. Public relations efforts are readily seen in tangible elements, such as news releases and social media; and direct marketing actions depend on written, verbal, and electronic forms of delivery. The design of the promotion will play a primary role in determining the message that is communicated to the audience. This design activity is frequently viewed as the step requiring the most creativity. In addition, successful designs are often the result of insight regarding consumers' interests and purchasing behaviour. All of the promotion tools have many design alternatives. Advertising, for example, can utilize fear, humour, or other emotions in its appeal.[31] Similarly, direct marketing can be designed for varying levels of personal or customized appeals. One of the challenges of IMC is to design each promotional activity to communicate the same message. Coca-Cola Canada, for example, was able to ensure that its "Taste the Feeling" message was fully integrated into each of the elements of its recent IMC campaign that included traditional media as we as social and digital media.

Scheduling the Promotion

Once the designs of all of the promotional program elements are complete, it is important to determine the most effective timing of their use. The promotion schedule describes the order in which each promotional tool is introduced and the frequency of its use during the campaign.

Several other factors, such as seasonality and competitive promotion activity, can also influence the promotion schedule. Such businesses as ski resorts, airlines, and professional sports teams are likely to reduce their promotional activity during the off-season. Similarly, restaurants, retail stores, and health clubs are likely to increase their promotional activities when new competitors enter the market.

EXECUTING AND EVALUATING THE IMC PROGRAM

Carrying out the promotion program can be expensive and time-consuming. One researcher estimates that "an organization with sales less than $10 million can successfully implement an IMC program in one year, one with sales between $200 million and $500 million will need about three years, and one with sales between $2 billion and $5 billion will need five years." To facilitate the transition, there are hundreds of IMC agencies, large and small, all across Canada that are available to assist companies that are making the shift to IMC. Moreover, some of the largest global agencies have also adopted approaches that embrace "total communications solutions." While many agencies still have departments dedicated to advertising, direct marketing, and other specialties, the trend is clearly toward a long-term perspective in which all forms of promotion are integrated.[32] Check out the Going Online box, "Canadian Agencies Adopt IMC Approaches," to learn more about how one agency approaches integrated marketing communications.

An important factor in developing successful IMC programs is to create a process that facilitates their design and use. A tool used to evaluate a company's current process is the *IMC audit*. The audit analyzes the internal communication network of the company; identifies key audiences; evaluates customer databases; assesses messages in recent ads, public relations releases, packaging, video news releases, signage, sales promotion programs, direct mail, and online, including presence on social media; and determines the IMC expertise of the company and agency personnel. This process is becoming increasingly important as consumer-generated media such as blogs, RSS, podcasts, and social networks become more popular and as the use of search engines increases. Now, in addition to ensuring that traditional forms of communication are integrated, companies must be able to monitor consumer content, respond to inconsistent messages, and even answer questions from individual customers. Still, although many organizations are interested in improving their IMC processes, they have not been successful at implementing them because of lack of expertise, lack of budget, and lack of management approval.

GOING ONLINE

Canadian Agencies Adopt IMC Approaches

Many traditional ad agencies in Canada have shifted their approach away from offering clients only strict advertising solutions to comprehensive marketing communications solutions, including an IMC and interactive advertising approach. Cossette is one such Canadian firm. It offers its Canadian clients a host of marketing communications solutions, many of which combine the promotional elements discussed in this chapter. Go to Cossette's website at **www.cossette.com**, click on "Portfolio Reel," and then review some of case studies provided to find out which promotional elements Cossette used and when.

1. Which campaigns seem to embrace an IMC or interactive approach?

2. How effective do you think these campaigns are? How should they be evaluated in terms of success?

As shown earlier in Figure 16–6, the ideal execution of a promotion program involves pre-testing each design before its actual use to allow for changes and modifications that improve its effectiveness. Similarly, post-tests are recommended to evaluate the impact of each communication and the contribution it makes in achieving program objectives. The most sophisticated pre-test and post-test procedures have been developed for advertising and are discussed in Chapter 17. Testing procedures for sales promotion and direct marketing efforts currently focus on comparisons of different designs and/or responses to programs by the target audience and even different segments within the target audience. To fully benefit from IMC programs, companies must create and maintain a test-result database that allows comparisons of the relative impact of the promotional tools and their execution options in varying situations. Information from the database allows informed design and execution decisions and provides support for IMC activities during internal reviews by financial or administrative personnel.

Currently, about one-fourth of all businesses assess promotion program effectiveness by measuring "most of their communication tactics."[33] For most organizations, the assessment focuses on trying to determine which element of promotion works better or which ones work best in combination. In an integrated program, for example, media advertising might be used to build awareness, sales promotion to generate trial, direct marketing to generate additional information on individual prospects, and personal sales to complete a transaction. These tools are obviously used for different reasons to achieve specific objectives, but their combined use creates a synergy that should be the focus of the assessment. Another level of assessment is necessary when firms have global IMC programs.

Learning Review

10. What are the characteristics of good promotion objectives?

11. What is the weakness of the percentage of sales budgeting approach?

12. How have advertising agencies changed to facilitate the use of IMC programs?

LO6 DIRECT MARKETING

Direct marketing has many forms and utilizes a variety of media. Several forms of direct marketing—direct mail and catalogues, television home shopping, telemarketing, and direct selling—were discussed as methods of non-store retailing in Chapter 15. In addition, although advertising is discussed in Chapter 17, a form of advertising—direct response advertising—is an important form of direct marketing, as is direct mail advertising, also discussed in Chapter 17. Finally, online advertising, especially interactive online advertising, is also discussed in Chapter 17 and is now an important part of many Canadian companies' direct marketing activities. The Canadian Direct Marketing Association recently defined direct marketing in this way: It is a marketing technique that affords institutions to communicate in a targeted or personalized fashion with a customer. It is channel-agnostic, meaning it can include any technique or medium, including digital (e-mail, social media, mobile, web) and promotional (sampling, displays, couponing, direct-response TV, big data, call centres, database marketing, analytics). Unique to direct marketing is its call to action and its measureable results. In this section, the growth of direct marketing, its value to consumers and sellers, and key global, technological, and ethical issues are discussed.

The Growth of Direct Marketing

The increasing interest in customer relationship management (CRM) is reflected in the dramatic growth of direct marketing in Canada. The ability to customize communication efforts and create one-to-one interactions is appealing to most marketers, particularly those with IMC programs. While direct marketing methods are not new (e.g., direct mail), the ability to design and use them has increased with the availability of customer information databases and new printing technologies. In recent years, direct marketing growth—in terms of spending, revenue generation, and employment—has outpaced total economic growth. The Canadian Marketing Association (CMA) reports that its members employ over 480,000 people and generate more than $51 billion in annual sales through direct marketing activities in Canada.[34] Telemarketing, including call-centre-based direct marketing, is responsible for close to one-half of that employment.

According to the CMA, one of the fastest-growing direct marketing mediums in Canada is *e-mail marketing*.[35] E-mail marketing is considered a fast and easy way to stay in touch with customers. Marketers use e-mail to promote special offers and announce new products and upgrades. E-mail is also often used as a component of well-designed IMC programs. For example, the Hudson's Bay Company utilizes e-mail marketing as part of its IMC program. Many Canadian companies are also using e-mail newsletters, or *ezines,* as a way to increase their contact points with customers. There has also been explosive growth in mobile direct marketing and social network direct marketing. In fact, many marketers who wish to reach Generation Y are using mobile and social network direct marketing. Generation Y are considered "digital natives"—they have grown up with technology and use their smartphones and tablets to access Facebook, Netflix, and Twitter. In fact, on average, this group checks their mobile phones over 100 times a day! They also use SMS and MMS messaging. Therefore, mobile and social network direct marketing are being added to IMC campaigns designed to reach Gen Y members.

Just about any offer communicated through traditional direct marketing methods can be promoted through an electronic or digital channel. However, many Canadians have complained about unsolicited and often unwanted communications from marketers, often referred to as spam. So recently, the Government of Canada put in place legislation and regulation to combat this practice (Bill C-28). Basically, *spam* is defined as any electronic commercial message sent without the express consent of the recipient(s).[36]

The Value of Direct Marketing

One of the most visible indicators of the value of direct marketing for consumers is the level of use of the various forms of direct marketing. For example, over one-half of the Canadian population has ordered merchandise or services by phone or mail; millions purchase items from television offers; about 20 percent of Canadian adults purchase from a catalogue each year; and over 56 percent of Canadian households order goods and services online. Additionally, more than 42 percent of Canadians have purchased goods and services from direct-sales consultants.[37] Consumers report many benefits purchasing via direct marketing, including the following: They do not have to go to a store; they can usually shop 24/7; buying direct saves time; they avoid hassles with salespeople; they can save money; it is fun and entertaining; and direct marketing offers more privacy than does in-store shopping. Many consumers also believe that direct marketing companies provide excellent customer service. Toll-free telephone numbers, customer service representatives with access to information regarding purchase preferences, overnight delivery services, and unconditional guarantees all help create value for direct marketing customers.

Direct mobile marketing, especially via smartphone, is growing in popularity in Canada.

© Alex Segre/Alamy Stock Photo

The value of direct marketing for marketers can be described in terms of the responses it generates.[38] **Direct orders** are the result of offers that contain all the information necessary for a prospective buyer to make a decision to purchase and complete the transaction. Club Med, for example, uses e-mail marketing to sell "last-minute specials" to people in its database. The messages, which are sent midweek, describe rooms and air transportation available at 30 to 40 percent discount if the customer can make the decision to travel on such short notice. **Lead generation** is the result of an offer designed to generate interest in a product or service and a request for additional information. Four Seasons Hotels now sells private residences in several of its properties and sends direct mail to prospective residents asking them to request additional information on the telephone or through a website. Finally, **traffic generation** is the outcome of an offer designed to motivate people to visit a business. Home Depot, for example, uses an opt-in e-mail alert to announce special sales that attract consumers to the store. Similarly, Target uses direct mail to generate traffic to its new stores.[39]

Technological, Global, and Ethical Issues in Direct Marketing

The information technology and databases described in Chapter 8 are key elements of any direct marketing program. Databases are the result of organizations' efforts to create profiles of customers so that direct marketing tools, such as e-mail, catalogues, direct mail, and telemarketing, can be directed at specific customers.

While most companies try to keep records of their customers' past purchases, many other types of data are needed to use direct marketing to develop one-to-one relationships with customers. Some data, such as lifestyles, media use, and demographics, are best collected from the consumer. Other types of data, such as price, quantity, and brand, are best collected from the businesses where purchases are made. New integrated marketing databases match consumers' postal addresses, telephone numbers, and e-mail addresses. In addition, many businesses are beginning to match their customer records with Facebook profiles, Twitter following behavior, and Google search activity. In fact, many marketers capture online customer data, including clickstream behaviour (how someone navigates a website), and some direct marketers rely on cookies to focus their direct marketing efforts. *Cookies* are computer files that a marketer can upload onto the computer of an online shopper who visits the marketer's website. Cookies allow the marketer to record a user's visit, track visits to other websites, and store and retrieve this information in the future. Cookies can also contain information provided by the visitors, such as expressed product preferences, personal data, passwords, and financial information. Clearly, cookies make it possible for customized direct marketing, including targeted online advertising. And there is some controversy over the use of this practice, especially when it comes to consumer privacy.

Direct marketers also face several challenges and opportunities in global markets today. Several countries, such as Italy and Denmark, for example, have requirements for mandatory "opt-in"—that is, potential customers must give permission to include their name on a list for direct marketing solicitations. In addition, the mail, telephone, and Internet systems in many countries are not as well developed as they are in Canada. The need for improved reliability and security in these countries has slowed the growth of direct mail, while the dramatic growth of mobile phone penetration has created an opportunity for direct mobile marketing campaigns. Another issue for global direct marketers is payment. The availability of credit and credit cards varies throughout the world, creating the need for alternatives such as C.O.D. (cash on delivery), bank deposits, and online payment accounts.

Global and domestic direct marketers also face ethical challenges. For example, considerable attention has been given to some annoying direct marketing activities, such as telephone solicitations during dinner and evening hours. And concerns about consumer privacy have also been raised. In fact, the Canadian government established the Office of Privacy Commissioner of Canada (**www.priv.gc.ca**) and enacted legislation, including the *Personal Information Protection and Electronic Documents Act (PIPEDA),* as a way of protecting the privacy of Canadians. Industry associations, such as the CMA, have also developed guidelines for their members to follow when it comes to consumer privacy, including online privacy. See the accompanying Making Responsible Decisions box, "Consumer Privacy and Direct Marketing in the Future," which discusses consumer privacy, especially what the future may have in store when it comes to your privacy.[40]

MAKING RESPONSIBLE DECISIONS

Consumer Privacy and Direct Marketing in the Future

What does the future hold with regard to our personal privacy when it comes to direct marketing activities? Recently, a privacy expert at Competia, Estelle Metayer, provided some insight at a conference hosted by the Canadian Marketing Association. The highlights of her talk are as follows:

- Approximately 62 percent of consumers are vulnerable to security attacks simply because they do not change their passwords regularly.

- Ever heard of "voyeur-gasm"? It relates to people's extremely curious nature about what others are doing and saying. For example, the information made available about others on social media has become a great source of entertainment for many people.

- Do you like to invest in stocks? You can now join **Empire.Kred**, a platform where individuals can virtually invest in other people based on the extent and quality of their social media activity. Think about it as a stock exchange for individual reputations.

- What might Canada look like in 2030 from a privacy perspective? Here are Estelle's four potential scenarios:

  - *Data lockdown.* Consumers have massive privacy concerns, demand more law and government control, and organize massive demonstrations following concerns over data breaches; a Ministry of Data/Privacy exists; hefty fines are issued to corporations and this leads to a surge in data encryption technologies.

  - *Centurions.* Consumers turn to government for guidelines to safeguard their privacy; there is a heavy load on companies to comply and explain how data is used; e-residency and e-identity cards are in place nationwide; education curriculum includes privacy courses.

  - *Icarus or data chaos.* Consumers are concerned about privacy and citizen-led guerillas emerge; government sites are hacked on a regular basis; new business models emerge and consumers are charged for privacy; private firms emerge to police data and privacy.

  - *Wild West.* Consumers happily trade info for personalization and market their personal data for sale; algorithms predict future behaviour and are hidden from public view; business models all rely on data monetization. In this scenario, four companies dominate the market: Amazon, Google, Facebook, and Über.

What do you think of her predictions? Who should be responsible for consumer privacy? Is a principles-based approach to privacy a better option or would a more heavily regulatory approach work better?

Learning Review

13. The ability to design and use direct marketing programs has increased with the availability of _____ and _____.

14. The fastest-growing direct market medium in Canada is _____.

15. What are the three types of responses generated by direct marketing activities?

Learning Objectives Review

 Discuss integrated marketing communications and the communication process.

Integrated marketing communication is the concept of designing marketing communications programs that coordinate all promotional activities—advertising, personal selling, sales promotion, public relations, and direct marketing—to provide a consistent message across all audiences and to maximize the promotional budget and impact of communication. The communication process conveys messages with six elements: a source, a message, a channel of communication, a receiver, and encoding and decoding. The communication process also includes a feedback loop and can be distorted by noise.

 Describe the promotional mix and the uniqueness of each component.

There are five promotional alternatives. Advertising, sales promotion, and public relations are mass-selling approaches, whereas personal selling and direct marketing use customized messages. Advertising can have high absolute costs but reaches large numbers of people. Personal selling has a high cost per contact but provides immediate feedback. Public relations is often difficult to obtain but is very credible. Sales promotion influences short-term consumer behaviour. Direct marketing can help develop customer relationships, although maintaining a database can be very expensive.

 Select the promotional approach appropriate to a product's life cycle and characteristics as well as stages of the buying decision.

The promotional mix changes over the four product life-cycle stages. During the introduction stage, all the promotional mix elements are used. In the growth stage, the primary promotional element is advertising. The maturity stage utilizes sales promotion and direct marketing. During the decline stage, little money is spent on the promotional mix. Product characteristics also help determine the promotion mix. The level of complexity, risk, and ancillary services required will determine which element is needed. Knowing the customer's stage in the buying process can help select appropriate promotions. Advertising and public relations can create awareness in the pre-purchase stage, personal selling and sales promotion can facilitate the purchase, and advertising can help reduce anxiety in the post-purchase stage.

 Discuss the characteristics of push and pull strategies.

A push strategy directs the promotional mix to channel members to gain their cooperation in ordering and stocking the product. Personal selling and sales promotion are commonly used in push strategies. A pull strategy directs the promotional mix at ultimate customers to encourage them to ask the retailer for the product. Direct-to-consumer advertising is typically used in pull strategies.

LO5 Describe the elements of the promotion decision process.

The promotion decision process consists of three steps: planning, implementation, and control. The planning step consists of six elements: identifying the target audience, specifying the objectives, setting the budget, selecting the right promotional elements, designing the promotion, and scheduling the promotion. The implementation step includes pre-testing. The control step includes post-testing.

LO6 **Explain the value of direct marketing for consumers and sellers.**

The value of direct marketing for consumers is indicated by its level of use. The value of direct marketing for sellers can be measured in terms of three types of responses: direct orders, lead generation, and traffic generation. Growth in electronic forms of direct marketing, including e-mail marketing, and direct mobile marketing is evident in Canada.

Applying Marketing Knowledge

1. After listening to a recent sales presentation, Mary Smith signed up for membership at the local health club. On arriving at the facility, she learned there was an additional fee for racquetball court rentals. "I don't remember that in the sales talk; I thought they said all facilities were included with the membership fee," complained Mary. Describe the problem in terms of the communication process.

2. Develop a matrix to compare the five elements of the promotional mix on three criteria—to whom you deliver the message, what you say, and when you say it.

3. Explain how the promotional tools used by an airline would differ if the target audience were (a) consumers who travel for pleasure, and (b) corporate travel departments that select the airlines to be used by company employees.

4. Suppose you introduced a new consumer food product and invested heavily both in national advertising (pull strategy) and in training and motivating your field salesforce to sell the product to food stores (push strategy). What kinds of feedback would you receive from both the advertising and your salesforce? How could you increase both the quality and quantity of each?

5. Fisher-Price Company, long known as a manufacturer of children's toys, has introduced a line of clothing for children. Outline a promotional plan to get this product introduced in the marketplace.

6. Many insurance companies sell health insurance plans to companies. In these companies, the employees pick the plan, but the set of offered plans is determined by the company. Recently, Blue Cross–Blue Shield, a health insurance company, ran a television ad stating, "If your employer doesn't offer you Blue Cross–Blue Shield coverage, ask why." Explain the promotional strategy behind the advertisement.

7. Identify the sales promotion tools that might be useful for (a) Tastee Yogurt, a new brand introduction; (b) 3M self-sticking Post-it Notes; and (c) Wrigley's Spearmint Gum.

8. Design an integrated marketing communications program—using each of the five promotional elements—for Spotify, an online music service.

9. BMW introduced the activity vehicle, the X5, to compete with other popular 4 × 4 vehicles, such as the Mercedes-Benz M-class and Jeep Grand Cherokee. Design a direct marketing program to generate (a) leads, (b) traffic in dealerships, and (c) direct orders.

10. Develop a privacy policy for database managers that provides a balance of consumer and seller perspectives. How would you encourage voluntary compliance with your policy? What methods of enforcement would you recommend?

Building Your Marketing Plan

To develop the promotion strategy for your marketing plan, follow the steps suggested in the planning phase of the promotion decision process described in Figure 16–6.

1. You should (*a*) identify the target audience, (*b*) specify the promotion objectives, (*c*) set the promotion budget, (*d*) select the right promotion tools, (*e*) design the promotion, and (*f*) schedule the promotion.

2. Also specify the pre-testing and post-testing procedures needed in the implementation and control phases.

3. Finally, describe how each of your promotion tools is integrated to provide a consistent message.

Video Case 16

Taco Bell: Using IMC to Help Customers Live Más!

"Every touch point is considered," explains Stephanie Perdue, Taco Bell's senior director of marketing, "from the posters in the restaurants down to the packaging, and all of the different media channels." Stephanie is describing the integrated marketing communications (IMC) approach used by Taco Bell, North America's leading Mexican-style quick service restaurant. IMC is one of the key factors that has contributed to the extraordinary success of the food chain, which serves more than 36 million customers each week!

The Company

The story behind Taco Bell and its success is fascinating. After World War II, a young marine named Glen Bell returned to his home state of California with an entrepreneurial spirit and an observation that people were hungry for fast, good food. He opened his first restaurant, Bell's Burgers, based on the simple concept that customers might want to walk up and get their food from a service window. Not far away, two brothers named McDonald were operating their new restaurant using a "drive-in" concept. For several years, Bell and the McDonald brothers enjoyed friendly competition as pioneers of the growing fast-food industry. However, when the burger restaurant market became crowded with competitors, Bell decided to try something new—tacos!

Tacos were new to most Americans, so Bell experimented with many concepts. First he developed a crunchy taco shell and opened a restaurant called Taco Tia. His marketing activities consisted of handing out sombreros and having Mariachis play outside the restaurant. Next, Bell started another restaurant, El Taco, with a group of celebrity partners. Finally, after a friend suggested that Glen should use his name in his business, the first Taco Bell was opened in Downey, California.

Taco Bell grew quickly and as Bell began opening additional locations, he decided that the restaurants should resemble the appearance of California's historic missions. With the help of an architect, he created

© David Paul Morris/Bloomberg via Getty Images

an inviting design based on an adobe-like exterior with a red clay-tile roof. The name and logo utilized a mission-style bell, a version of which is still in use today. Through franchises and additional corporate locations, Taco Bell soon reached from coast to coast.

Today Taco Bell is a subsidiary of Yum! Brands, which also owns and operates KFC, Pizza Hut, and WingStreet. Taco Bell now has more than 6,500 locations and $7 billion in sales. Many locations are co-branded with KFC, Pizza Hut, and Long John Silver stores. Taco Bell also operates Taco Bell Express locations in convenience stores, truck stops, shopping malls, and airports.

Integrated Marketing Communications at Taco Bell

From its beginning, Taco Bell has used very creative promotional activities. For example, when the Mir space station was about to reenter the Earth's atmosphere, Taco Bell placed a target in the Pacific Ocean and announced that every person in the United States would receive a free taco if any piece of the falling space station hit the target. Similarly, in its "Steal a Base, Steal a Taco" promotion, Taco Bell promises to give everyone a free taco if any player steals a base in the World Series. While the space station did not hit the target, several players have stolen bases in the World Series, leading to free tacos for everyone! Taco Bell has also offered special promotions with Mountain Dew, partnered with the NBA as its official fast food, and created videos for movie-thearer advertising.

You might remember some of Taco Bell's advertising campaigns such as "Yo quiero Taco Bell," "Grand Taste. Loco Value," or "Get it at The Bell." The more recent "Think Outside the Bun" campaign was designed for Millennials. Then as that group changed, Taco Bell executives recognized that they had an opportunity to reposition the chain. Tracee Larocca, brand creative director at Taco Bell, explains, "We realized there was a big opportunity as the culture shifted from 'food as fuel' to 'food as experience.'" Taco Bell considered many new taglines, such as "Keep Life Spicy" and "Hunger for Más," and eventually developed the "Live Más" campaign. As campaigns and positioning changes, integrated marketing becomes increasingly important. According to Larocca, "as the brand's creative director, my job is to make sure that all of our communications have the same look, tone, and feel across all platforms, making sure we maintain consistency in our brand voice no matter what we're doing internally or externally."

Advertising Age magazine recently named Taco Bell the winner of its Marketer of the Year award for its extraordinary use of integrated marketing in the launch of its Doritos Locos Tacos. The new product went through three years of development and 45 prototypes before its launch, which led to sales of 100 million units in its first 10 weeks. Taco Bell allocates approximately 70 percent of its budget to traditional media, 20 percent to digital media, and 10 percent to new media where it can "explore." The traditional media budget included a Super Bowl ad utilizing the "Live Más" theme. "It was all about a mindset and not necessarily an age range or a demographic," explains Larocca. The ad, called "Forever Young," showed "a group of old people breaking out of a retirement home and having a great night on the town," she adds.

The social media component of the campaign included Facebook, Twitter, Vine, Snapchat, and Instagram. The Twitter campaign, for example, included a Hometown Tweet-off where anyone could send a tweet saying why a Taco Bell truck should visit their hometown. Similarly, Taco Bell posted pictures to Facebook and watched the responses in the comments and the "likes." Some of the new media budget was used to try things such as Taco Bell's own video channels for web and mobile, and a live stream to a billboard in Times Square. As Rob Poetsch, director of public affairs and engagement, observed about the Doritos Locos Tacos launch, "for the first time, we had a fully integrated plan that engaged all of our constituents."

The Future at Taco Bell

Taco Bell continues to develop new products, brand concepts, and promotions. For example, waffle tacos, Cinnabon Delights, and the A.M. Crunchwrap are new additions to the menu. In addition, a new brand concept called Taco Bell Cantina, which is testing its first locations in Chicago and San Francisco, will offer "tapas-style" appetizers for customers to share, and beer and wine, in an urban setting. Finally, a new breakfast menu campaign used 25 men named Ronald McDonald to help suggest that a new generation of fast-food breakfast items is now available at Taco Bell. All of these activities are contributing to the company's continued growth. Yum! Brands expects Taco Bell's domestic sales to double by 2021!

QUESTIONS

1. What factors contributed to Taco Bell's early success?

2. Which of the promotional elements described in Figure 16–2 were used by Taco Bell in its Doritos Locos Tacos campaign?

3. How does Taco Bell ensure the continued success of the food chain?

Case: This case was written by Steven Hartley. Sources: Maureen Morrison, "In Breakfast Wars, Taco Bell's Bold Marketing Pays Off with Big Sales," *Advertising Age,* July 28, 2014, p. 6; "Taco Bell Serving Alcohol in Wicker Park Officially Opens Tuesday," *WLS-TV,* September 22, 2015; Maureen Morrison, "Taco Bell's New Concept: Designer Tacos in California," *Advertising Age,* April 28, 2014, p. 4; Vanessa Wong, "Taco Bell's Secret Recipe for New Products," *Bloomberg Businessweek,* June 2–8, 2014, pp. 18–20; Maureen Morrison, "Marketer of the Year 2013," *Advertising Age,* September 2, 2013, p. 15; Mark Brandau, "Yum Plans to Double U.S. Taco Bell Sales," *Restaurant News,* May 22, 2013; "The Glen Bell Legacy," www.tacobell.com/static_files/TacoBell/StaticAssets/documents/GlenBellLegacy.pdf; "Taco Bell," http://www.yum.com/brands/tb.asp; and interviews with Taco Bell executives.

17 Advertising, Sales Promotion, and Public Relations

Learning Objectives

After reading this chapter, you should be able to:

LO1 Explain the differences between product advertising and institutional advertising and the variations within each type.

LO2 Describe the steps used to develop, execute, and evaluate an advertising program.

LO3 Explain the advantages and disadvantages of alternative advertising media.

LO4 Discuss the strengths and weaknesses of consumer-oriented and trade-oriented sales promotions.

LO5 Recognize public relations as an important form of communication.

Virtual Reality Is the New Reality for Advertising

You may remember when Facebook announced that it had paid $2 billion for a small company called Oculus Rift, and you wondered what could that company be doing that was so important. The answer is: virtual reality.

Oculus Rift manufactures wearable virtual reality (VR) headsets that look a little like ski goggles but when worn create a 360-degree immersive experience through high-quality video and audio. Many marketers believe VR will soon become an important way for advertisers to reach consumers. As Terry Block, a former Skype executive, explains, "When Facebook is involved, you know advertising is going to be a big piece of the picture."

So how will virtual reality work for businesses? According to Alex Lirtsman, co-founder of digital marketing agency Ready Set Rocket, "It's the ultimate way a car company can showcase their latest car, a retailer can provide a view of their Fashion Week event, a travel destination can showcase activities, or any advertiser can truly take a 30-second spot to the next level." Virtual reality could also allow consumers to shop and browse at stores such as Nordstrom, IKEA, or Safeway at any time and without crowds.

Oculus Rift won't be the only company with a VR product on the market. Microsoft describes its HoloLens as a VR product that can be used for gaming, video conferencing, and 3D modelling. Sony's Project Morpheus headset will potentially augment the gaming experience of the 10 million households that already own Sony Playstation game systems. And Samsung's Gear VR is compatible with its Galaxy line of phones. Other entrants include HTC, Valve, and MergeVR. While current sales of VR products are approximately $60 million, experts suggest that sales will reach $150 billion in just five years.

© Rex Features via AP Images

Several companies have already implemented virtual reality campaigns. Mountain Dew, for example, created the VR Skate experience, which simulates a ride through the streets of Las Vegas with Dew Tour pro-skaters. Mountain Dew then followed up with another campaign for snowboarders. The TV series *Game of Thrones* created a VR experience where users ascend a 700-foot ice wall, and Marriott hotels created an experience that "teleported" people to London or Maui. In the future, VR products will also link to your phone, watch, and other devices to add other sensory elements to the experience.

While some of this sounds like enthusiasm for a new gadget, advertisers are preparing for a substantial new medium. According to film director Chris Milk, "From an advertising perspective, it's a very powerful tool. Advertisers are looking for two main things: penetrating people's consciousness and getting their undivided attention. With virtual reality, you have their undivided attention because they can't see or hear anything else." VR headsets also have the potential to be addressable like a computer or a phone so that advertisers can target specific market segments.

Watch for exciting new VR experiences in the near future. Fox Sports, for example, is testing VR offerings of NASCAR races in 180-degree and 360-degree viewing options. To participate in these and other virtual reality immersion experiences consumers are predicted to purchase 12 million VR headsets in 2016![1] The growth of virtual reality is just one of the many exciting changes occurring in the field of advertising today. They illustrate the importance of advertising as one of the five promotional mix elements in marketing communications programs.

This chapter describes three of the promotional mix elements—advertising, sales promotion, and public relations. Direct marketing was covered in Chapter 16, and personal selling is covered in Chapter 18

TYPES OF ADVERTISEMENTS

Chapter 16 described *advertising* as any paid form of non-personal communication about an organization, good, service, or idea by an identified sponsor. This chapter will detail the alternative types of advertisement and the advertising decision process, as well as introduce you to the concepts of sales promotion and public relations.

As you look through any magazine, watch television, listen to the radio, or browse the Internet, many advertisements you see or hear may give you the impression that they have few similarities. Advertisements are prepared for different purposes, but they basically consist of two types: product and institutional. These two types of ads can also be classified on the basis of whether they are intended to get the consumer to take immediate action (*direct-response advertising*) or to influence future purchase or actions (*delayed-response advertising*).

LO1 Product Advertisements

Focused on selling a good or service, **product advertisements** take three forms: (1) pioneering (or informational), (2) competitive (or persuasive), and (3) reminder. Look at the ads in this section and determine the type and objective of each ad.

Used in the introductory stage of the product life cycle, *pioneering* advertisements tell people what a product is, what it can do, and where it can be found. The key objective of a pioneering advertisement is to inform the target market. Informative ads have been found to be interesting, convincing, and effective.[2]

Advertising that promotes a specific brand's features and benefits is *competitive*. The objective of these messages is to persuade the target market to select the firm's brand rather than that of a competitor. An increasingly common form of competitive advertising is *comparative* advertising, which shows one brand's strengths relative to those of competitors.[3] Studies indicate that comparative ads attract more attention and increase the perceived quality of the advertiser's brand.[4] Firms that use comparative advertising need market research to provide legal support for their claims.[5]

Product advertisements serve varying purposes. Would these ads be considered (1) pioneering, (2) competitive, or (3) reminder?

(left): Levi Strauss & Co; (middle): Samsung; (right): Shaw's

Reminder advertising is used to reinforce previous knowledge of a product. The Shaw's ad shown here reminds consumers about the association between its product and a special event—in this case, Valentine's Day. Reminder advertising is good for products that have achieved a well-recognized position and are in the mature phase of their product life cycle. Another type of reminder ad, *reinforcement,* is used to assure current users they made the right choice. One example: "Aren't you glad you use Dial? Don't you wish everybody did?"

Institutional Advertisements

The objective of **institutional advertisements** is to build goodwill or an image for an organization, rather than promote a specific good or service. Institutional advertising has been used by such companies as Pfizer and IBM Canada to build confidence in the company name.[6] Often, this form of advertising is used to support the public relations plan or to counter adverse publicity. Four alternative forms of institutional advertisements are often used:

- *Advocacy institutional* advertisements state the position of a company or organization on an issue. For example, Health Canada ads encourage parents to vaccinate their children with its "Be a Champion. Get Vaccinated" campaign.

- *Pioneering institutional* advertisements, like the pioneering ads for products discussed earlier, are used for announcements about what a company is, what it can do, or where it is located. Recent Bayer ads stating "We cure more headaches than you think" are intended to inform consumers that the company produces many products in addition to aspirin.

- *Competitive institutional* advertisements promote the advantages of one product class over another and are used in markets where different product classes compete for the same buyers. The Dairy Farmers of Canada (DFC), made up of more than 13,000 dairy farmers in Canada, promotes the consumption of milk as it competes against other beverages.

- *Reminder institutional* advertisements, like the product form, simply bring the company's name to the attention of the target market again.

As mentioned earlier, advertising can also be classified as either direct-response advertising or delayed-response advertising. *Direct-response advertising* seeks to motivate the customer to take immediate action, such as a television ad asking you to phone a toll-free telephone number and place an order immediately. Lavalife, for example, uses direct-response television ads. The primary objective of the ads is to generate calls to the company about its online dating services.[7] *Delayed-response advertising,* on the other hand, presents images and/or information designed to influence the consumer in the near future when making purchases or taking other actions. Direct marketers often rely on direct-response advertising as part of their direct-marketing efforts. However, more and more often, traditional marketers are using this form of advertising as they attempt to obtain an immediate return on their advertising dollar and measured response in terms of advertising effectiveness.

An advocacy institutional ad promotes immunization for Canadians.

Courtesy of Immunize Canada. © 2016 Canadian Public Health Association.

Learning Review

1. What is the difference between pioneering and competitive ads?

2. What is the purpose of an institutional advertisement?

3. What is direct-response advertising?

LO2   DEVELOPING THE ADVERTISING PROGRAM

The promotion decision process described in Chapter 16 can be applied to each of the promotional elements. Advertising, for example, can be managed by following the three steps of the process: developing, executing, and evaluating.

Identifying the Target Audience

To develop an effective advertising program, advertisers must identify the target audience. All aspects of an advertising program are likely to be influenced by the characteristics of the prospective consumer. Understanding the needs, lifestyles, attitudes, and demographics of the target market is essential. Diet Mountain Dew, for example, is targeted at Generation X males, while Kraft's Crystal Light Liquid is targeted at calorie-conscious women. Both campaigns emphasize advertising techniques that match their target audiences. To appeal to Generation X males, Diet Mountain Dew became the sponsor of a NASCAR team. Meanwhile, to attract calorie-conscious women, Crystal Light began providing nutritional information on a dedicated Facebook page and on Twitter. Similarly, the placement of the advertising depends on the audience. When Under Armour introduced its "I Will What I Want" campaign featuring women's apparel, it created a website (**https://www.underarmour.com/en-ca/iwillwhatiwant**), made deals with flash-sale website Gilt, posted a video on its YouTube channel that has been viewed 8 million times, and used traditional print, digital, and outdoor advertising to reach competitive women. Similarly, the placement of the advertising depends on the audience.[8] Even scheduling can depend on the audience. Nike schedules advertising, sponsorships, deals, and endorsements to correspond with the Olympic Games to appeal to amateur, college and university, and professional athletes.[9] To eliminate possible bias that might result from subjective judgments about some population segments, advertising program decisions should be based on market research about the target audience. For example, Home Depot tweaked its target audience and its message in Quebec after research revealed its ad campaigns were not connecting with French consumers.[10]

Specifying Advertising Objectives

The guidelines for setting promotion objectives described in Chapter 16 also apply to setting advertising objectives. This step helps advertisers with other choices in the promotion decision process, such as selecting media and evaluating a campaign. Advertising with an objective of creating awareness, for example, would be better matched with a magazine than a directory, such as the Yellow Pages.[11] Similarly, an advertiser looking to induce consumers to trial or to take other direct action, such as visit a store location, would use a direct-response form of advertising, such as direct mail. The Institute of Communication Agencies, which represents Canada's communications and advertising agencies, believes that establishing advertising objectives is so important that it created the CASSIE Awards, whereby advertisers are recognized for achieving ad campaign objectives. For example, Mitsubishi Canada sur-

A successful ad campaign achieves its objectives.

Used with permission from autoTrader

passed its sales objectives with an integrated as campaign consisting of TV, radio, print, digital and social including Facebook and Twitter. A&W also surpassed its unaided ad awareness objectives with a campaign consisting of TV, website, online display, social media, and in-store POS.[12]

Setting the Advertising Budget

The methods used to set the overall promotion budget as outlined in Chapter 16 can be used to establish a specific advertising budget. As with the promotional or integrated marketing communications (IMC) budget, the best approach to setting the ad budget is the objective and task approach. There are numerous advertising options available to the advertiser, and most of the alternatives require substantial financial commitments. A formal budgeting process that involves matching the target audience to the available advertising options, evaluating the ability of those options to achieve specified objectives, and weighing the relative costs of the advertising options is definitely a requirement for effective advertising.

Designing the Advertisement

An advertising message usually focuses on the key benefits of the product that are important to a prospective buyer in making trial and adoption decisions. The message depends on the general form or appeal used in the ad and the actual words included in the ad.

Message Content

Most advertising messages are made up of both informational and persuasive elements. These two elements, in fact, are so intertwined that it is sometimes difficult to tell them apart. For example, basic information contained in many ads, such as the product name, benefits, features, and price, is presented in a way that tries to attract attention and encourage purchase. On the other hand, even the most persuasive advertisements must contain at least some basic information to be successful.

Information and persuasive content can be combined in the form of an appeal to provide a basic reason for the consumer to act. Although the marketer can use many different types of appeals, common advertising appeals include fear appeals,[13] sex appeals, and humorous appeals.

Fear appeals suggest to the consumer that he or she can avoid some negative experience through the purchase and use of a product or service, a change in behaviour, or a reduction in the use of a product. Examples with which you may be familiar include fire or smoke detector ads that depict a home burning, or social cause ads warning of the serious consequences of drug and alcohol use or high-risk sexual behaviour. Pacific Blue Cross of Burnaby, B.C., for example, runs ads asking people to think about the adequacy of their health insurance coverage and the "unthinkable" consequences if they do not have enough coverage.[14] However, when using fear appeals, the advertiser must be sure that the appeal is strong enough to get the audience's attention and concern but not so strong that it will cause them to tune out the message.

In contrast, *sex appeals* suggest to the audience that the product will increase the attractiveness of the user. Sex appeals can be found in almost any product category, from automobiles to toothpaste. Unfortunately, many commercials that use sex appeals are successful only at gaining the attention of the audience; they have little impact on how consumers think, feel, or act. Some advertising experts even argue that such appeals get in the way of successful communication by distracting the audience from the purpose of the ad.

Humorous appeals imply either directly or more subtly that the product is more fun or exciting than competitors' offerings. As with fear and sex appeals, the use of humour is widespread in Canadian advertising and can be found in many product categories. In fact, no product sector appears immune. For example, unlike Pacific Blue Cross health insurance, mentioned above, BCAA Life Insurance uses a humorous ad campaign to promote life insurance.[15] However, humour has to be used with care. Jokes tend to wear out quickly, eventually boring the consumer. Moreover, sometimes, the humour may offend the target audience, and some humorous appeals may not travel well across cultures. Still, recent Canadian research reveals that consumers prefer humorous appeals over sex appeals. A full 67 percent of Canadians say humour is the secret ingredient that makes an advertisement most persuasive, compared to only 7 percent who feel that, ultimately, sex sells.[16]

Creating the Actual Message

The "creative people" in an advertising agency—copywriters and art directors—have the responsibility to turn appeals and such features as quality, style, dependability, economy, and service into attention- getting, believable advertisements. Translating creative ideas into actual advertisements is a complex process. Designing quality artwork, layout, and production for the advertisements is also often costly and time-consuming. It typically costs more than $200,000 to produce a 30-second high-quality TV commercial. High-visibility integrated ad campaigns can be even more expensive. Other costs can include paying celebrity spokespersons to appear in the ads. In fact, Canadians are seeing many celebrities featured in advertising today, including sports heroes and entertainers. For example, Sidney Crosby represents Gatorade and Reebok, while Michael J. Fox is a spokesperson for Toyota. Non-profits also use spokespeople in their ads, but these spokespeople are not compensated. For example, March of Dimes Canada uses Willian Shatner as its spokesperson, while Don Cherry is a spokesperson for organ donation awareness for the Kidney Foundation of Canada.[17]

How would they get by without you?

BCAA Life Insurance is one of the most important purchases you can make when it comes to securing your family's financial future. Whether you're a new parent or a first time homeowner, BCAA has a plan that's right for you and your family. Call toll-free 1-800-663-1956 or 604-268-5555 to speak with a Life Insurance advisor.

This ad campaign for BCAA Life Insurance uses humour to underscore the importance of life insurance for family security.

Photo: Philip Jarmain, 2009. Used with permission of British Columbia Automotive Associates (BCAA), www.bcaa.com.

SELECTING THE RIGHT MEDIA

Every advertiser must decide where to place its advertisements. The alternatives are the advertising media, the means by which the message is communicated to the target audience. Newspapers, magazines, radio, and TV are examples of *advertising media*. This "media selection" decision is related to the target audience, type of product, nature of the message, campaign objectives, available budget, and the costs of the alternative media. Figure 17–1 shows the distribution of the over $14 billion spent on advertising in Canada among the many media alternatives.[18] One trend that experts are seeing is advertising dollars being shifted from several traditional media to online advertising. In less than ten years, spending on online advertising has gone from virtually zero dollars to over $5 billion in Canada.[19] Some of Canada's leading advertisers include General Motors of Canada, Sears Canada, BCE (Bell Canada Enterprises), the Government of Canada, Procter & Gamble, Rogers Communications, the Hudson's Bay Company, and Ford Motor Company of Canada. And many of them are major Internet advertisers, including those investing heavily in social media platforms.

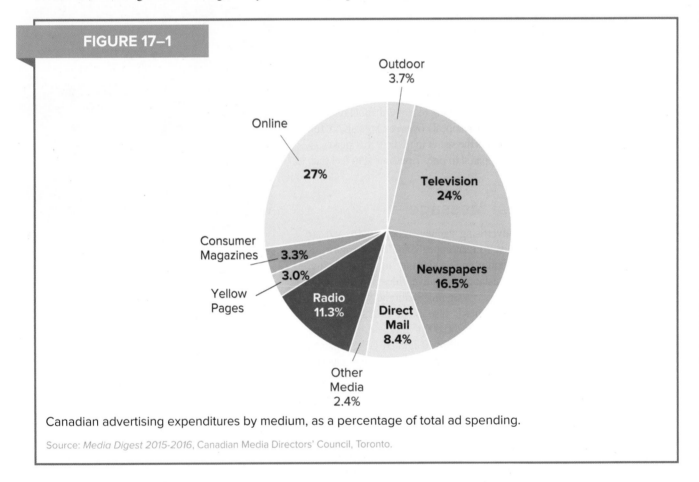

FIGURE 17–1

Canadian advertising expenditures by medium, as a percentage of total ad spending.

Source: *Media Digest 2015-2016*, Canadian Media Directors' Council, Toronto.

Choosing a Medium and a Vehicle within That Medium

In deciding where to place advertisements, a company has several media to choose from and a number of alternatives, or vehicles, within each medium. Often, advertisers use a mix of media forms and vehicles to maximize the exposure of the message to the target audience while minimizing costs. These two conflicting goals of (1) maximizing exposure and (2) minimizing costs are of central importance to media planning.

Basic Terms

Media buyers speak a language of their own, and so every advertiser involved in selecting the right media for their campaigns must be familiar with some common terms used in the advertising industry. Figure 17–2 shows the most common terms used in media decisions.

Because advertisers try to maximize the number of individuals in the target market exposed to the message, they must be concerned with reach. **Reach** is the number of different people or households exposed to an advertisement. The exact definition of reach sometimes varies among alternative media. Newspapers often use reach to describe their total circulation or the number of different households that buy the paper. Television and radio stations, in contrast, describe their reach using the term **rating**—the percentage of households in a market that are tuned to a particular TV show or radio station. In general, advertisers try to maximize reach in their target market at the lowest cost.

Like greater reach, greater frequency has been historically viewed by advertisers as desirable. This was because it was believed that consumers often do not pay close attention to the advertising message. Therefore, many advertisers wanted to expose the same audience more than once to their message. This involves **frequency**, or the average number of times a person in the target audience is exposed to a message or advertisement. In fact, the traditional 3+ *effective-frequency model* (exposing the target audience 3+ times to an ad) has dominated the advertising industry for years. Now, however, there is evidence that this model may be flawed. So, many Canadian advertisers have turned to a new approach called *recency*—delivering media messages in a way that increases the likelihood of reaching more people with a message close to the time of their purchase. This is sometimes called *just-in-time communications.*[20]

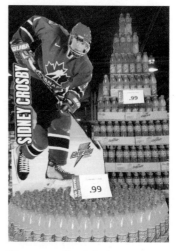

The use of celebrity spokespersons is popular in Canadian advertising.

© Halifax Daily News/Jeff Harper/ The Canadian Press

When reach (expressed as a percentage of the total market) is multiplied by frequency, an advertiser will obtain a commonly used reference number called **gross rating points (GRPs)**. To obtain the appropriate number of GRPs to achieve an advertising campaign's objectives, the media planner must balance reach and frequency. The balance will also be influenced by cost. **Cost per thousand (CPM)** refers to the cost of reaching 1,000 individuals or households with the advertising message in a given medium (*M* is the Roman numeral for 1,000). See the accompanying Using Marketing Dashboards box for an example of the use of CPM in media selection.

FIGURE 17–2

TERM	WHAT IT MEANS
Reach	The number of different people or households exposed to an advertisement.
Rating	The percentage of households in a market that are tuned to a particular TV show or radio station.
Frequency	The average number of times an individual is exposed to an advertisement.
Gross rating points (GRPs)	Reach (expressed as a percentage of the total market) multiplied by frequency.
Cost per thousand (CPM)	The cost of advertising divided by the number of thousands of individuals or households who are exposed.
Programmatic ad purchasing	An automated-based (the use of software), data-driven way of buying advertising.

The language of the media buyer.

USING MARKETING DASHBOARDS

What Is the Best Way to Reach 1,000 Customers?

Marketing managers must choose from many advertising options as they design a campaign to reach potential customers. Because there are so many media alternatives (television, radio, magazines, etc.) and multiple options within each of the media, it is important to monitor the efficiency of advertising expenditures on your marketing dashboard.

Your Challenge As the marketing manager for a company about to introduce a new soft drink into the market, you are preparing a presentation in which you must make recommendations for the advertising campaign. You have observed that competitors use magazine ads, newspaper ads, and even Super Bowl ads! To compare the cost of some of the alternatives, you decide to use one of the most common measures in advertising: cost per thousand impressions (CPM). The CPM is calculated as follows:

Cost per thousand impressions = Advertising cost ($) / Impressions generated (in 1000s)

Your challenge is to determine the most efficient use of your advertising budget.

Your Findings Your research department helps you collect cost and audience size information for three options: full-page colour ads in the *Globe and Mail* (newspaper) and *Maclean's* magazine, and a 30-second television ad during the Super Bowl (Canada only). With this information, you are able to calculate the cost per thousand impressions for each alternative.

Your Action Based on the calculations for these options, you see that there is a variation in the cost of reaching 1,000 potential customers (CPM) and also in the absolute cost of the advertising. Although advertising on the Super Bowl has the lowest CPM, $29 for each 1,000 impressions, it also has the largest absolute cost! Your next step will be to consider other factors such as your total available budget, the profiles of the audiences each alternative reaches, and whether the type of message you want to deliver is better communicated in print or on television.

Media Alternative	Cost of Ad	Audience Size	Cost per Thousand Impressions
Globe and Mail (newspaper)	$13,000	400,000	$32
Maclean's (magazine)	$36,000	385,000	$93
Super Bowl (TV)	$100,000	9,000,000	$11

The media buyer has now added a new term to his/her language. **Programmatic ad purchasing** is an automated-based (the use of software), data-driven way of buying advertising. It originated from the online or digital advertising space but now has expanded into other traditional forms of media, including broadcast television and out-of-home ads. Basically, instead of the labour-intensive human-based approach to ad buying, programmatic involves the use of technology to make the ad purchases. The media buyer is often faced with an incredible variety of advertising options, including how and where ads appear. Developing the best ad solutions for brands requires intelligence gathering and tough decision making. Programmatic ad purchasing now assists the media buyer by automating many of the ad evaluation and buying processes involved.

LO3 Different Media Alternatives

Figure 17–3[21] summarizes the advantages and disadvantages of the important advertising media, which are described in more detail below.

Television

Television is a valuable medium because it communicates with sight, sound, and motion. Print advertisements alone could never give you the sense of a new sports car accelerating from a stop or cornering at high speed. In addition, network television is the only medium that can reach 98 percent of the homes in Canada over an average week. And 90 percent of Canadian households are cable- or satellite-equipped. *Out-of-home* TV viewing also reaches millions of Canadians in bars, hotels, and university campuses each week. The average Canadian watches almost 30 hours of TV per week. Importantly, many Canadians are now watching TV online using providers such as Netflix, Shomi, and Crave TV. The major national (English) networks include CBC Television, CTV—the largest private broadcaster—CITY-TV, and Global TV.[22]

FIGURE 17–3

MEDIUM	ADVANTAGES	DISADVANTAGES
Television	Reaches extremely large audience; uses picture, print, sound, and motion for effect; can target specific audiences	High cost to prepare and run ads; short exposure time and perishable message; difficult to convey complex information
Radio	Low cost; can target specific local audiences; ads can be placed quickly; can use sound, humour, and intimacy effectively	No visual element; short exposure time and perishable message; difficult to convey complex information
Magazines	Can target specific audiences; high-quality colour; long life of ad; ads can be clipped and saved; can convey complex information	Long time needed to place ad; relatively high cost; competes for attention with other magazine features
Newspapers	Excellent coverage of local markets; ads can be placed and changed quickly; ads can be saved; quick consumer response; low cost	Ads compete for attention with other newspaper features; short lifespan; poor colour
Yellow Pages	Excellent coverage of geographic segments; long use period; available 24 hours/365 days	Proliferation of competitive directories in many markets; difficult to keep up-to-date
Online	Video and audio capabilities; animation can capture attention; ads can be interactive and link to advertiser	Animation and interactivity require large files and more time to load; effectiveness is still uncertain
Outdoor	Low cost; local market focus; high visibility; opportunity for repeat exposures	Message must be short and simple; low selectivity of audience; criticized as a traffic hazard
Direct mail	High selectivity of audience; can contain complex information and personalized messages; high-quality graphics	High cost per contact; poor image (junk mail)

Advantages and disadvantages of major advertising media.

Source: William F. Arens, *Contemporary Advertising*, 9th ed. Copyright © 2004 by The McGraw-Hill Companies; Figure 17–3 from William G. Nickels, James M. McHugh, and Susan M. McHugh, *Understanding Business*, 7th ed. © 2005 by The McGraw-Hill Companies.

Television's major disadvantage is cost. For example, the cost of a 30-second spot on CTV during the Super Bowl can be over $100,000.[23] Because of these high charges, many advertisers have reduced the length of their commercials from 30 seconds to 15 seconds. This practice, referred to as *splitting 30s,* reduces costs but severely restricts the amount of information and emotion that can be conveyed. Research indicates, however, that two different versions of a 15-second commercial, run back-to-back, will increase recall over long intervals. Additionally, some advertisers are shifting their ad spends to live events rather than programs that might be watched on PVRs days later.[24]

Another problem with television is the likelihood of *wasted coverage*—having people outside the market for the product see the advertisement. In recent years, the cost and wasted-coverage problems of TV have been reduced through the introduction of specialized digital or cable and direct broadcast (satellite) channels. Advertising time is often less expensive on cable and direct broadcast channels than on the major networks. There are currently many channel options—such as CMT, MuchMusic, HGTV, YTV, and Food Network Canada—that reach very narrowly defined audiences. Other forms of television are changing television advertising also. On-demand and pay-per-view movie services such as Disney and HBO, as well as PVRs, for example, offer the potential of commercial-free viewing. Almost 60 percent of Canadian households have PVRs. Finally, as mentioned, online television (OTV) is growing in popularity and viewing time using tablets, smartphones, or other devices. This has led to the emergence of *addressable television advertising*—precision targeting of a message to specific individuals through their digital device.

Another popular form of television advertising is the infomercial. **Infomercials** are program-length (30-minute) advertisements that take an educational approach to communication with potential customers. Volvo, Club Med, General Motors, Mattel, Revlon, and many other companies are using infomercials as a means of providing information that is relevant, useful, and entertaining to prospective customers. In many cases, marketers are using infomercials for direct-response purposes, asking customers to order products and/or to request further information during the airing. Over $25 million is spent on infomercials in Canada.[25]

Radio

There are over 600 commercial radio stations in Canada. Radio reaches 90 percent of the population aged 12 and over in an average week. And the average radio listener spends close to 11 hours per week listening to radio. However, Canadians are also listening to radio online for an additionally six hours per week. The major advantage of radio is that it is a segmented medium offering distinctive formats. There are jazz stations, classical music stations, all-talk shows, and hard rock stations, all catering to different market segments. The top formats in Canada are news/talk, adult contemporary, country, hot AC (hot adult contemporary), current hits, and rock.

The disadvantage of radio is that it has limited use for products that must be seen. Another problem is the ease with which consumers can tune out a commercial by switching stations. Radio is also a medium that competes for people's attention as they do other activities, such as driving, working, or relaxing. Peak radio listening time, for example, is during peak rush-hour commuting (6 to 10 A.M. and 4 to 7 P.M.). Radio listeners also have another radio listening option—satellite radio services (SiriusXM) that offer digital-quality radio channels for a monthly subscription, with some channels being commercial-free. Additionally, SiriusXM has also rolled out online streaming products in addition to iPhone, iPad, Android, and BlackBerry listening applications.[26]

Magazines

Magazines have become a very specialized medium. There are almost 1,300 consumer magazines produced in Canada and over 700 business publications and trade journals. According to the Print Measurement Bureau (PMB), almost 80 percent of Canadians aged 12 or over read a magazine in the past month.[27] The marketing advantage of this medium is the great number of special-interest publications that appeal to narrowly defined segments. Runners read *Runner's World,* golfers buy *Golf Canada,* gardeners subscribe to *Gardening Life,* and children peruse *Famous Kids* or *Owl.* Each magazine's readership often represents a unique profile. Take the *Rolling Stone* reader, who tends to travel, backpack, and ski more than do most people—and so a manufacturer of ski equipment that places an ad in *Rolling Stone* knows that it is reaching the desired target audience. In addition to the distinct audience profiles of magazines, good colour production is an advantage that allows magazines to create strong images.

The cost of advertising in national magazines is a disadvantage, but many national publications, such as *Canadian Living* and *Maclean's,* publish regional and even metro editions, which reduce the absolute cost and wasted coverage. In addition to cost, a limitation to magazines is their infrequency. At best, magazines are printed on a weekly basis, with many specialized publications appearing only monthly or less often. However, one major trend is transforming the magazine business and that is the emergence of digital editions that are available on websites, smartphones, tablets, and eReaders. While printed magazines remain the number-one choice of magazine readers, digital editions offer many advantages to readers, especially for mobile consumers.

Newspapers

Newspapers are an important local medium with excellent reach potential. There are over 100 daily newspapers in Canada, including more than a dozen French-language papers. There are also over 1000 community newspapers. Because of the daily publication of most papers, they allow advertisements to focus on specific current events, such as a "24-hour sale." Local retailers often use newspapers as their sole advertising medium.

Newspapers, however, are rarely saved by the purchaser, and so companies are generally limited to ads that call for an immediate customer response (although customers can clip and save the ads they are interested in). Companies also cannot depend on newspapers for the same colour reproduction quality as that in most magazines.

National advertising campaigns rarely include this medium except in conjunction with local distributors of their products. In these instances, both parties often share the advertising costs using a cooperative advertising program, which is described later in this chapter. Another exception is the use of newspapers, such as the *Globe and Mail,* that have national distribution.

According to Canadian research, newspapers are thriving in a digital world. For example, print readership is up and website readership of digital or online newspapers is also growing rapidly. More than half of newspaper readers read a newspaper website. Print versions tend to be read early in the day and after dinner while digital versions are read early, between breakfast and lunch, and after dinner. Smartphones are used for updates all day, and tablets are used mainly in the evening. Other research shows that Canadians trust newspaper advertising and that newspaper ads influence purchase decisions.[28]

Yellow Pages

Close to $400 million is spent on Yellow Pages advertising in Canada. This is almost as much as what is spent on magazine advertising in Canada.[29] Yellow Pages directories reach almost every household in Canada and are a *directional* medium because they help consumers know where purchases can be made after other media have created awareness and demand.

Yellow Pages have several other advantages. First, they are available 24 hours each day and 365 days each year. In addition, Yellow Pages have a long lifespan—directories are typically published once each year and provide advertisers with many advertising size options. A disadvantage of Yellow Pages advertising is the proliferation of similar directories. Many markets now have competing directories for specific neighbourhoods and even ethnic groups. Another disadvantage is the lack of

Magazines such as *Runner's World* appeal to narrowly defined segments such as athletes who are interested in running.

timeliness because Yellow Pages can be updated with new information only once each year. Yellow Pages are typically used for local advertising—more than 80 percent of all Yellow Pages expenditures are local—because of the difficulty of coordinating a nationwide campaign in Yellow Pages directories. However, many of these problems have been overcome with the advent of Internet or online Yellow Pages and phone directories, including **www.canada411.ca**.

Direct Mail

Direct mail advertising is often considered the cornerstone of the efforts of many direct marketers (see Chapters 15 and 16) to reach consumers. But any advertiser looking for good audience selectivity can find direct mail advertising effective. Also, direct mail advertising allows marketers to provide more information to the customer than is possible in a television or radio spot. In many cases, direct mail advertising is being used in conjunction with other media, particularly broadcast, as part of an integrated marketing communications (IMC) solution. Mass media are used to create awareness, while direct mail advertising is used to build a relationship and facilitate a purchase.

One disadvantage of direct mail advertising is its rising costs due to postal rate increases. Another limitation is that people often view direct mail advertising as junk mail and are reluctant to open such mail. A novel approach to overcome that problem is the use of *self-mailers*—simple white envelopes without any promotional messaging—that consumers are more likely to open. Also, the availability of robust databases now allows the advertiser to send mail only to well-defined targets with very specific and appealing offers, which is helping to improve consumer response rates.

Online

Online advertising is the fastest-growing advertising medium in Canada. *Online advertising,* sometimes referred to as Internet or *web advertising,* now exceeds over $5 billion in total ad spending already surpassing spending on television advertising. This form of advertising includes online classified and directory advertising, online e-mail, search engine, social media advertising, and traditional display ads. Quebecor Media, for example, has a classified advertising site called **classifiedextra.ca**, which integrates ads from more than 200 daily and community newspapers and the **Canoe.ca** portal. And then there is Kijiji, one of Canada's most popular free local classified sites.

One of the major reasons for this explosive growth is the trend toward integrated marketing communications with traditional advertisers now using Internet advertising more and more often as part of their integrated campaigns.[30]

Online advertising is similar to print advertising in that it offers a visual message, but it has additional advantages because it can also use the audio and video capabilities of the Internet. Sound and movement may attract more attention or make the message more entertaining. Online advertising also has the unique feature of being interactive. Interactive online advertising, sometimes called *rich media,* has drop-down menus, built-in games, videos, short films, or search engines to engage viewers.

There are a variety of venues to advertise online, including (1) portal sites, such as **Sympatico.ca** or **Canoe.ca**; (2) network buys through multi-site vendors, such as 24/7 Canada; (3) individual site advertising; (4) and search engines, such as Google. Advertisers also have a choice of the type of online ads that they wish to present to the customer. The most common is the display or banner ad. Other forms of online advertising include skyscrapers, pop-ups, interstitials, and microsites, which use streaming video and audio and are very similar to traditional television advertising. And, of course, growing in popularity is advertising on social media sites. Additionally, paid search is also a fast-growing form of online advertising as the bulk of Internet traffic begins at a search engine such as Google or Bing. Moreover, online mobile advertising is the fastest growing form of online advertising in Canada

One concern many advertisers have had with online advertising is measuring the effectiveness of the medium. But several companies are now involved in attempting to measure Internet advertising effectiveness. For example, Nielsen Media Research measures click-by-click behaviour through meters installed on the computers of hundreds of thousands of individuals in more than two dozen countries both at home and at work (see **www.nielsennetratings.com** for recent ratings). Another method being tested to provide some indication of the effectiveness of online advertising is *permission-based advertising,* where viewers agree to watch a commercial online in exchange for points, samples, or access to premium content, and advertisers only pay for completed views. The Interactive Advertising Bureau of Canada is also working to advance the use and effectiveness of Internet advertising in Canada. For example, it has a research program called the Canadian Media Optimization (CMOST) designed to measure the impact of online advertising. It has already conducted research for Molson, RBC Insurance, General Motors, Canadian Tire, and AIM Trimark. Recently, its research showed that Tetley Red Tea, using print and online advertising achieved higher levels of awareness for the brand as well as higher brand favourability measures and higher levels of purchase intent.[31]

Online advertisers are now also using a new tool to improve online advertising effectiveness, *online behavioural advertising* or *interest-based advertising.* In this case, advertisers track the online activities of online individuals and deliver ads targeted to the customer's interests. For example, if you click on a site to buy airline tickets from Toronto to Vancouver, you are then likely to see an ad for hotels in Vancouver!

Another new concept in online advertising is the concept of *real-time bidding (RTB).* RTB is a method of selling and buying online display advertising in real time, one ad impression at a time. There are three entities involved in RTB: buyers and systems that use demand-side platforms (DSP), sellers who use supply-side platforms (SSP), and online real-time ad exchanges. This is all made possible because of big data and data analytics. A simple example of how it works is as follows: An individual enters a website page and it starts loading. A bid request is sent out by the website publisher to potential advertisers saying, "There is a 30-year-old French-Canadian male living in Montreal looking for airline tickets to Paris. How much are you willing to bid for being the only advertiser on this page?" Within milliseconds, the website publisher receives bids from different advertisers. The website publisher then analyzes who the highest bidder is and the winner is alerted and allowed to place the ad. This occurs in real time and causes no delay for the individual doing the search. RTB is not the same of programmatic ad purchasing but is one way programmatic ad buying can occur, especially with online advertising.

Outdoor

A very effective medium for reminding consumers about your product is outdoor advertising. Outdoor and transit advertising expenditures in Canada are estimated at almost $500 million.[32] The most common form of outdoor advertising, called *billboards,* often results in good reach and frequency. The visibility of this medium is good supplemental reinforcement for well-known products, and it is a relatively low-cost and flexible alternative. A company can buy space just in the desired geographical market. A disadvantage of bill-boards, however, is that no opportunity exists for long advertising copy. Also, the effectiveness of a billboard site depends on traffic patterns and sight lines. In many areas, environmental laws have limited the use of this medium.

If you have ever lived in a metropolitan area, chances are you might have seen another frequently used form of outdoor advertising: *transit advertising.* This medium includes messages on the interior and exterior of buses, subway cars, taxis, and transit shelters. In fact, the advertiser can actually purchase an entire bus, called a *superbus,* for about $100,000 and place its message over the entire vehicle. If selectivity is important, space can be bought in specific neighbourhoods or even transit routes. One disadvantage to this medium is that anxious travel times, when audiences are largest, are not conducive to reading advertising copy. People are standing shoulder to shoulder, hoping not to miss their stop, and little attention is paid to the advertising.

But billboards can play an important part of an integrated marketing communications cam-paign. For example, Nova Scotia Tourism used an IMC campaign involving television, digital, online, and outdoor media to promote its "Take Yourself There" campaign. In addition to tradi-tional outdoor billboards, the agency actually installed a 28-foot replica of the Peggy's Cove Lighthouse at a busy intersection in Toronto's business district. Additionally, a traditional bill-board was put up showing people skipping stones into the ocean. Anyone within 600 metres of the billboard could tune into a radio frequency and hear the sounds of the ocean.[33]

An effective outdoor media display.

User-Generated Content

A growing trend in the advertising business is **user-generated content (UGC)**, also referred to as user-generated media. This is media generated by users (customers) and disseminated via various channels, in particular, the Internet. There are numerous ways marketers can interface with such media. They can (1) simply advertise on user-generated content sites, such as YouTube; (2) allow the user to create the content themselves, and then sponsor that content and allow it to be shared with others online; (3) sponsor an actual contest encouraging the user to create media; or (4) partner with the consumer to co-create the media and the message and then disseminate it. The "Become the Doritos Guru" campaign is an example of a very successful UGC campaign. Basically, consumers were asked to "name the new Doritos flavour and create an ad to support it." In return, the company would pay one winner $25,000, plus 1 percent of the flavour's sales, forever. The company used an online platform strategy to engage their target (teens) and encourage them to participate. They created a brand website, DoritosGuru.ca, and integrated it with Facebook and YouTube. Over 75,000 people registered as users at DoritosGuru.ca; over 30,000 fans registered on Facebook; and over 1.7 million people viewed the user-generated ads. In the end, there were over 2,000 approved submissions, and after 500,000 votes, Ryan Coopersmith's "Scream Cheese" entry was declared the winner. Sales results were impressive, up 25 percent over the previous year.[34]

Other Media

As traditional media have become more expensive and cluttered, advertisers have been attracted to a variety of non-traditional advertising options, called *place-based media.* Messages are placed in locations that attract a specific target audience, such as airports, doctors' offices, health clubs, theatres (where ads are played on the screen before the movies are shown), even washrooms of bars, colleges and universities, restaurants, and nightclubs! You have probably also seen advertising on video screens on gas pumps, ATMs, in elevators, and even within video games (in-game advertising, or "advergam-ing"). St. Joseph's Healthcare in Hamilton, Ontario, for example, uses place-based media by advertising in theatres or cinemas to recruit health-care workers. Finally, another new form of advertising is growing very quickly in Canada—mobile advertising—where companies are reaching consumers on their mobile smartphones and tablets.[35] Check out the Going Online exercise to read about the trends in mobile advertising.

Advertisers can buy space inside a washroom—captive audiences.

Learning Review

9. Explain the difference between pre-testing and post-testing advertising copy.
10. What is the difference between aided and unaided recall post-tests?

 SALES PROMOTION

The Importance of Sales Promotion

At one time, sales promotion was considered by many to be a supplemental ingredient of the promotional mix. But more recently, the use of sales promotion has increased, and so has its perceived importance to marketers. In fact, in Canada, more money is now spent on sales promotion than on advertising.[40]

There are several reasons for the growth in importance of sales promotion. For one, many marketers are looking for measurable results from their promotional efforts. Sales promotion is viewed as an effective tool in this regard. Second, consumers and the trade (e.g., retailers) have become more value-conscious and thus more responsive to sales promotion activities. Third, some suggest that the use of sales promotion has grown because it has become contagious. In short, many marketers are simply responding to the increased use of sales promotion by competitors. Finally, the availability of information technology, allowing electronic delivery and processing of sales promotion offers, has also served as a stimulus for the growth of sales promotion.

While sales promotion techniques have grown in use and in stature, they are rarely used in isolation or as a stand-alone promotional tool. With the trend toward IMC, sales promotion techniques are used more commonly in conjunction with other promotional activities. However, the selection and integration of the many sales promotion techniques requires a good understanding of the relative advantages and disadvantages of each kind of sales promotion.

Consumer-Oriented Sales Promotions

Directed to ultimate consumers, **consumer-oriented sales promotions**, or simply *consumer promotions,* are sales tools used to support a company's advertising and personal selling efforts. Consumer-oriented sales promotion tools include coupons, deals, premiums, contests, sweepstakes, samples, loyalty programs, point-of-purchase displays, rebates, and product placement (Figure 17–5).

Coupons

Coupons are typically printed certificates that give the bearer a savings or a stated price reduction when purchasing a specific product. Coupons can be used to stimulate demand for mature products or to promote the early trial of a new brand. Billions of direct-to-consumer coupons are distributed annually in Canada. Canadians redeem millions of these coupons resulting in savings of over $100 million on products. The most popular coupons redeemed in Canada are for personal care and food products.[41]

The number of coupons generated online and on mobile platforms is also growing, and the redemption rate for these types of coupons is higher than other forms of coupons. Couponing is growing in popularity, with many daily coupon services companies such as Groupon springing up, as well as social media companies such as Facebook getting into the game. But do coupons help boost revenue or market share for companies? Studies show that when coupons are used, a company's market share does increase during the period immediately after they are distributed.[42] There are indications, however, that couponing can reduce gross revenues by lowering the price paid by already-loyal consumers.[43] Therefore, manufacturers and retailers are particularly interested in coupon programs directed at potential first-time buyers. One means of focusing on these potential buyers is through electronic in-store coupon machines that match coupons to your most recent purchases.

Deals

Deals are short-term price reductions, commonly used to increase trial among potential customers or to retaliate against a competitor's actions. There are two basic types of deals: cents-off deals and price-pack deals. Cents-off deals offer a brand at less than a regular price, and the reduced prices are generally marked directly on the label or package. Cents-off deals can be very effective, even more so than coupons in stimulating short-term sales.

FIGURE 17–5

KIND OF SALES PROMOTION	OBJECTIVES	ADVANTAGES	DISADVANTAGES
Coupons	Stimulate demand	Encourage retailer support	Consumers delay purchases
Deals	Increase trial; retaliate against competitor's actions	Reduce consumer risk	Consumers delay purchases; reduce perceived product value
Premiums	Build goodwill	Consumers like free or reduced-price merchandise	Consumers buy for premium, not product
Contests	Increase consumer purchases; build business inventory	Encourage consumer involvement with product	Require creative or analytical thinking
Sweepstakes	Encourage present customers to buy more; minimize brand switching	Get customer to use product and store more often	Sales drop after sweepstakes
Samples	Encourage new product trial	Low risk for consumer	High cost for company
Loyalty programs	Encourage repeat purchases	Help create loyalty	High cost for company
Point-of-purchase displays	Increase product trial; provide in-store support for other promotions	Provide good product visibility	Hard to get retailer to allocate high-traffic space
Rebates	Encourage customers to purchase; stop sales decline	Effective at stimulating demand	Easily copied; steal sales from future; reduce perceived product value
Product placements	Introduce new products; demonstrate product use	Positive message in a noncommercial setting	Little control over presentation of product

Sales promotion alternatives.

Price-pack deals offer consumers something extra, such as "20 percent more for the same price," or "Two packages for the price of one." Price-pack deals can be very effective in retaliating against or pre-empting a competitor's actions. For example, if a rival manufacturer introduces a new cake mix, the company could respond with the price-pack deal (e.g., 2 for 1), building up the stock on the kitchen shelves of cake mix buyers and making the competitor's introduction more difficult. Marketers must be careful, however, of overusing deals. If consumers expect a deal, they may delay a purchase until the deal occurs. Moreover, frequent deals may erode the perceived value of the brand to the consumer.

Premiums

Premiums are items offered free or at significant savings as incentives to buy a product. A premium offered at below its normal price is known as *self-liquidating* because the cost charged to the consumers covers the cost of the item. Offering premiums at no cost or at low cost encourages customers to return frequently or to use more of the product. However, the company must be careful that the consumer does not just buy the premium.

Contests

In the fourth sales promotion shown in Figure 17–5—the contest—consumers apply their analytical or creative thinking to try to win a prize. Most often, a consumer submits an entry to be judged by a panel. Many companies use contests not only to increase consumer purchases but also to obtain the names and addresses of consumers for direct marketing purposes. Many contests have gone online and are often highly interactive. For example, M&M Meat Shops ran an "M&M Meat Shops Saves a Day" contest, based on a series of television ads. For the contest, consumers were invited to visit a microsite and view all the commercials. They then had to answer multiple-choice questions based on the spots and also indicate which one was their favourite. Those who answered the five questions correctly were entered into a draw to win $1,000 of M&M gift cards. In another example, Teletoon created a site for Maynards candy that included an online game and details for a contest where winners received a variety of prizes, including MP3 players.[44]

Sweepstakes

Sweepstakes require participants to submit some kind of entry forms but are purely games of chance requiring no analytical or creative effort from the consumer. Tim Hortons's Roll Up the Rim to Win and Publisher's Clearing House are examples of well-known sweepstakes. Canada has federal and provincial regulations covering sweepstakes, contests, and games regarding fairness, to ensure that the chance of winning is represented honestly and to guarantee that the prizes are awarded.

Samples

Another common consumer sales promotion is sampling, or offering the product free or at a greatly reduced price. Often used for new products, sampling puts the product in the consumer's hands; a trial size is generally offered that is smaller than the regular package size. If consumers like the sample, it is hoped they will remember and buy the product. Many Canadian firms have successfully used sampling as part of their marketing strategy. For example, recently, Martin's Family Fruit Farm of Waterloo, Ontario, got into the snack chip business by launching its Martin's Crispy Apple Chips snack. Targeting health-conscious consumers, it used a major sampling campaign to reach its target—45,000 GoodLife Fitness customers. It also provided samples in 35,000 knapsacks given to kids in 500 Ontario daycare centres.[45]

Loyalty Programs

Loyalty programs are a sales promotion tool used to encourage and reward repeat purchases by acknowledging each purchase made by a consumer and offering a premium as purchases accumulate. The most popular loyalty programs today are credit card reward programs and frequent-flyer and frequent traveller programs used by airlines, hotels, and car rental companies to reward loyal customers. Some programs are free, such as Air Canada's Aeroplan, while others require the customer to pay an annual membership fee. For example, Chapters-Indigo offers its iRewards loyalty program that provides online and in-store discounts on purchases for a $35 annual membership fee. But perhaps the most famous and most successful loyalty program in Canada is the Canadian Tire 'Money'™ program. Now, in addition to receiving your Canadian Tire 'Money'™ at the checkout when you make your purchases, you can also collect "virtual" money through the use of a Canadian Tire credit card, and even through the use of the company's website. Recently, more and more loyalty programs are going mobile. That is, companies are leveraging mobile smartphones to deliver and maintain loyalty programs.

Canadian Tire 'Money'™ is an example of a successful loyalty program.

Courtesy of Canadian Tire Corporation

Point-of-Purchase Displays

In a store aisle, you often encounter a sales promotion called a point-of-purchase display. These product displays take the form of advertising signs, which sometimes actually hold or display the product, and are often located in high-traffic areas near the cash register or the end of an aisle. The accompanying picture shows a point-of-purchase display for Nabisco's annual Back-to-School program. The display is designed to maximize the consumer's attention to lunch-box and after-school snacks and to provide storage for the products.

Some studies estimate that one-third of a consumer's buying decisions are made in the store. This means that grocery product manufacturers want to get their message to you at the instant you are next to their brand in your supermarket aisle—perhaps through a point-of-purchase display. Digital signage and video displays are now growing in popularity at point-of-purchase, including those equipped with near-field communication technology that is activated when a shopper walks by a product and a video message begins.

Rebates

Another consumer sales promotion in Figure 17–5—the cash rebate—offers the return of money based on proof of purchase. This tool has been used heavily by car manufacturers facing increased competition. When the rebate is offered on lower-priced items, the time and trouble of mailing in a proof-of-purchase to get the rebate cheque means that many buyers—attracted by the rebate offer—never take advantage of it. However, this "slippage" is less likely to occur with frequent users of rebate promotions. Additionally, online consumers are more likely to take advantage of rebates.[46]

Product Placement

A final consumer promotion, **product placement**, involves the use of a brand-name product in a movie, television show, video, or commercial for another product. Companies are usually eager to gain exposure for their products, and the studios believe that product placements add authenticity to the film or program. You have probably noticed numerous examples of product placement, such as Dr. Pepper and Facebook in the movie *Thor,* and Apple, Google, and Prius in *Little Fockers.* Product placement has also grown in television programs. For example, Canadian TV shows such as *Little Mosque in the Prairie* and *Heartland* feature product placements on a regular basis, including even building in mini-subplots around such brands as TD Bank and Apple iPad. Product placement can be economical, too. The cost of product placement is about 10 percent of the cost of a 30-second ad spot on Canadian TV.[47] The U.S. is the world's largest paid product placement market, but product placement is also growing in popularity around the world, including, as mentioned, in Canada.

Point-of-purchase displays help increase consumers' attention in a store.

© McGraw-Hill Education/Mark Dierker, photographer

Trade-Oriented Sales Promotions

Trade-oriented sales promotions, or simply *trade promotions,* are sales tools used to support a company's advertising and personal selling directed to wholesalers, retailers, or distributors. Some of the sales promotions just reviewed are used for this purpose, but there are three other common approaches targeted uniquely to these intermediaries: (1) allowances and discounts, (2) cooperative advertising, and (3) training of distributors' salesforces.

Allowances and Discounts

Trade promotions often focus on maintaining or increasing inventory levels in the channel of distribution. An effective method for encouraging such increased purchases by intermediaries is the use of allowances and discounts. However, overuse of these "price reductions" can lead to retailers changing their ordering patterns in the expectation of such offerings. Although there are many variations that manufacturers can use with discounts and allowances, three common approaches include the merchandise allowance, the case allowance, and the finance allowance.[48]

Reimbursing a retailer for extra in-store support or special featuring of the brand is a *merchandise allowance.* Performance contracts between the manufacturer and trade member usually specify the activity to be performed, such as a picture of the product in a newspaper with a coupon good at only one store. The merchandise allowance then consists of a percentage deduction from the list case price ordered during the promotional period. Allowances are not paid by the manufacturer until it sees proof of performance (such as a copy of the ad placed by the retailer in the local newspaper).

A second common trade promotion, a *case allowance,* is a discount on each case ordered during a specific time period. These allowances are usually deducted from the invoice. A variation of the case allowance is the "free goods" approach whereby retailers receive some amount of the product free based on the amount ordered, such as one case free for every ten cases ordered.

A final trade promotion, the *finance allowance,* involves paying retailers for financing costs or financial losses associated with consumer sales promotions. This trade promotion is regularly used and has several variations. One type is the floor stock protection program—manufacturers give retailers a case allowance price for products in their warehouses, which prevents shelf stock from running down during promotional periods. Also common are freight allowances, which compensate retailers that transport orders from the manufacturer's warehouse.

Cooperative Advertising

Resellers often perform the important function of promoting the manufacturer's products at the local level. One common sales promotional activity is to encourage both better quality and greater quantity in the local advertising efforts of resellers through **cooperative advertising**. These are programs by which a manufacturer pays a percentage of the retailer's local advertising expense for advertising the manufacturer's products.

Usually, the manufacturer pays a percentage, often 50 percent, of the cost of advertising up to a certain dollar limit, which is based on the amount of the purchases the retailer makes of the manufacturer's products. In addition to paying for the advertising, the manufacturer often furnishes the retailer with a selection of different ad executions, sometimes suited for several different media. A manufacturer may provide, for example, several different print layouts as well as a few broadcast ads for the retailer to adapt and use.

Training of Distributors' Salesforces

One of the many functions the intermediaries perform is customer contact and selling for the producers they represent. Both retailers and wholesalers employ and manage their own sales personnel. A manufacturer's success often rests on the ability of the reseller's salesforce to represent its products.

Thus, it is in the best interests of the manufacturer to help train the reseller's salesforce. Because the reseller's salesforce is often less sophisticated and less knowledgeable about the products than the manufacturer might like, training can increase their sales performance. Training activities include producing manuals and brochures to educate the reseller's salesforce. The salesforce then uses these aids in selling situations. Other activities include national sales meetings sponsored by the manufacturer and field visits to the reseller's location to inform and motivate the salesperson to sell the products. Manufacturers also develop incentive and recognition programs to motivate reseller's salespeople to sell their products.

Learning Review

11. Which sales promotional tool is most common for new products?

12. What's the difference between a coupon and a deal?

13. Which trade promotion is used on an ongoing basis?

(LO5) PUBLIC RELATIONS

As noted in Chapter 16, *public relations* is a form of communication management that seeks to influence the feelings, opinions, or beliefs held by various publics about a company and its products or services. PR efforts may utilize a variety of tools and may be directed at many distinct audiences. While public relations personnel usually focus on communicating the positive aspects of the business, they may also be called on to minimize the negative impact of a problem or crisis, sometimes called crisis management.

Public Relations Tools

In developing a public relations campaign, several tools and tactics are available to the marketer. The most frequently used public relations tool is *publicity*, which we defined in Chapter 16 as a non-personal, indirectly paid presentation of an organization, good, or service. Publicity usually takes the form of a *news release,* consisting of an announcement regarding changes in the company, or the product line.

The objective of a news release is to inform a newspaper, radio station, or other medium of an idea for a story. A study found that more than 40 percent of all free mentions of a brand name occur during news programs.[49] A second common publicity tool is the *news conference*. Representatives of the media are invited to an informational meeting, and advance materials regarding the content are sent. This tool is often used when negative publicity requires a company response.

Non-profit organizations rely heavily on publicity to spread their messages. *Public service announcements (PSAs),* for which free space or time is donated by the media, are a common mode of publicity for these organizations. For example, ABC Canada Literacy Foundation uses televised PSAs to promote adult literacy, while the Canadian Cancer Society and the Heart and Stroke Foundation of Canada use both television and radio PSAs to encourage Canadians to eat more fruits and veggies. The Canadian Women's Foundation is also using PSAs to raise awareness of the sexist messages on female clothing and in the media and the negative effects it has on girls.

A growing area of public relations is event or cause sponsorship, sometimes referred to as *sponsorship marketing.* The goal of sponsorship marketing is to create a forum to disseminate company information and/or to create brand identification for the company or its product with members of the target audience. You are obviously aware of the biggest and most visible sponsorship opportunity in the world: the Olympic Games. But there are numerous other sponsorships that are available to companies. For example, annual Canadian Interuniversity Sports (CIS) championships are sponsored by some of Canada's leading companies. Petro-Canada is an official sponsor of the Trans Canada Trail project, and CIBC is the official sponsor the Canadian Breast Cancer Foundation's "Run for Life" campaign.

Sponsorship marketing has become so popular that there is now a national organization that has been created to help enhance the development of this concept. Check out the Sponsorship Marketing Council of Canada at **www.sponsorshipmarketing.ca**. The council sponsors an annual sponsorship marketing awards show to showcase the effectiveness of sponsorship marketing programs. For example, recent winners include Ford Celebrity Face-off for Charity (a celebrity hockey game with funds going to the Montreal Canadiens Children's Foundation); Captain Morgan Tall Ships sponsorship; BMO's sponsorship of the Calgary Stampede; and the Canadian Tire NHL Junior Skills Competition.[50]

The development of collateral materials, such as annual reports, brochures, newsletters, corporate websites, or videos about the company and its product, are also basic public relations tools. These materials provide information to target publics and often generate good publicity.

Good public relations activities, however, should always be carefully planned and made part of an organization's IMC effort. This also includes recognizing that social media is allowing public discussions online about every possible company, product, or brand. While these discussions are seemingly uncontrollable, many public relations departments are now facilitating and responding to what happens on social media sites. McDonald's, for example, responds to comments about its products and corporate behaviour using a blog called "Open for Discussion." Canadian research has also revealed that use of social media as active PR campaigns has grown rapidly. For example, Twitter usage by PR professionals has jumped to almost 80 percent. PR professionals are also using Facebook, YouTube, LinkedIn, Wikipedia, and Skype. And the reason why PR professionals are leveraging social media is because consumers are reporting that social media does influence their purchasing behaviour.[51] Therefore, the use and leveraging of social media for PR purposes is now imperative.

Finally, however, public relations activities, both traditional and digital, must be used wisely and in an ethical and socially responsible manner (see the Making Responsible Decisions box, "Ethics and PR Activities.").[52]

MAKING RESPONSIBLE DECISIONS

Ethics and PR Activities

Kim Harrison, a recognized authority in the PR field suggests, "Public relations is one of the most maligned professions. Our critics flay us with criticism: 'PR stunt,' 'PR ploy,' 'Spin doctors,' or 'Public relations is organized lying.'"

He suggests that this denigration arose because public relations is an umbrella term that covers a multitude of activities and practitioners who are located at all points of the ethical spectrum.

Public relations practitioners don't have to be registered, don't need to be qualified, and don't need to belong to a professional association requiring high standards of professional and ethical practice. Anyone can call himself or herself a public relations practitioner, even the untrained, the incompetent, and the unscrupulous.

Harrison argues that most high-profile problems relating to the profession originate from non-members of public relations professional bodies. These people can legitimately engage in public relations as they see fit and are subject to only laws, not ethical standards of behaviour. Furthermore, he suggests that the profession is vulnerable because many practitioners are merely technicians or implementers—messengers for the management of the organization or client. The PR persons in these situations have no authority over what they do; they are merely mouthpieces for other people who may or may not be ethical. However, the PR practitioners are held responsible by recipients of the messages they disseminate.

Also, there are many cases of practitioners who allow themselves to fall short of good practice.

PR practitioners, Harrison states, should ask themselves how equipped they are to deal with ethical decision-making that will stand up to scrutiny? For example, how would you handle some of these real-life scenarios?

- Do you wait to return the telephone call from a journalist who wants some sensitive information until just after their deadline so they can't use the information?

- What angle do you take in writing an article on a staff member you don't respect?

- Do you avoid saying "no" to a senior manager or client whose expectations of communication are unrealistic, because you don't want to jeopardize the relationship?

- Your marketing department has made dubious claims about a new product. How do you handle this?

- Your organization is in the middle of a difficult issue, and your CEO decides to make public statements only after the lawyers have watered down your draft statement. What can you do?

Harrison suggests there are practical ways to build ethics into PR:

1. Define in writing the specific issue or conflict. (The act of writing or typing it out as hard copy helps to clarify it in your mind.)

2. Identify the relevant internal or external factors (e.g., political, social, financial) that may influence the decision.

3. Identify and rank the key values and principles involved. What reasons can you provide for prioritizing one competing value or principle over another?

4. Identify the parties who will be affected by the decision and define your obligation to each. Do you need to confer with those parties about the potential risks and consequences of alternative courses of action?

5. Select ethical principles to guide your decision-making process.

6. Make a decision.

7. Develop and implement an action plan that is consistent with the ethical priorities you have determined as central to the dilemma.

8. Reflect on the outcome of this ethical decision-making process. How would you evaluate the consequences of this process for those involved?

This process, according to Harrison should help PR professionals deal with ethical dilemmas. What do you think?

Learning Review

14. What is a news release?

15. A growing area of public relations is _____

Learning Objectives Review

LO1 **Explain the differences between product advertising and institutional advertising and the variations within each type.**

Product advertisements focus on selling a good or service and take three forms: Pioneering advertisements tell people what a product is, what it can do, and where it can be found; competitive advertisements persuade the target market to select the firm's brand rather than a competitor's; and reminder advertisements reinforce previous knowledge of a product. Institutional advertisements are used to build goodwill or an image for an organization. They include advocacy advertisements, which state the position of a company on an issue, and pioneering, competitive, and reminder advertisements, which are similar to the product ads but focus on the institution.

LO2 **Describe the steps used to develop, execute, and evaluate an advertising program.**

The promotion decision process can be applied to each advertising element. The steps to develop an advertising program include identify the target audience, specify the advertising objectives, set the advertising budget, design the advertisement, create the message, select the media, and schedule the advertising. Executing the program requires pre-testing, and evaluating the program requires post-testing.

LO3 **Explain the advantages and disadvantages of alternative advertising media.**

Television advertising reaches large audiences and uses picture, print, sound, and motion; its disadvantages, however, are that it is expensive and ephemeral. Radio advertising is inexpensive and can be placed quickly, but it has no visual element and is also ephemeral. Magazine advertising can target specific audiences and can convey complex information, but it takes a long time to place the ad and is relatively expensive. Newspapers provide excellent coverage of local markets and can be changed quickly, but they have a short lifespan and poor colour. Yellow Pages advertising has a long use period and is available 24 hours per day; its disadvantages, however, are that there is a proliferation of directories and they cannot be updated frequently. Online advertising can be interactive, and used with traditional media for integrated communications purposes. However, work is still being done to measure its effectiveness. Outdoor advertising provides repeat exposures, but its message must be very short and simple. Direct mail can be targeted at very selective audiences, but its cost per contact is high. Finally, user-generated content (UGC), media generated by consumers and disseminated via various channels, in particular, the Internet, is growing in popularity as companies attempt to engage and interact with their customers. The consumer absorbs the costs of the activity, but companies do not always have control over what is communicated and how it is communicated.

LO4 **Discuss the strengths and weaknesses of consumer-oriented and trade-oriented sales promotions.**

Coupons encourage retailer support but may delay consumer purchases. Deals reduce consumer risk but also reduce perceived value. Premiums offer consumers additional merchandise they want, but they may be purchasing only for the premium. Contests create involvement but require creative thinking. Sweepstakes encourage repeat purchases, but sales drop after the sweepstakes. Samples encourage product trial but are expensive. Loyalty programs help create loyalty but are expensive to run. Displays provide visibility but are difficult to place in retail space. Rebates stimulate demand but are easily copied. Product placement provides a positive message in a non-commercial setting but is difficult to control. Trade-oriented sales promotions include (*a*) allowances and discounts, which increase purchases but may change retailer ordering patterns; (*b*) cooperative advertising, which encourages local advertising; and (*c*) salesforce training, which helps increase sales by providing the salespeople with product information and selling skills.

LO5 **Recognize public relations as an important form of communication.**

Public relations activities usually focus on communicating positive aspects of the business. A frequently used public relations tool is publicity, which includes new releases and news conferences or public service announcements. A growing area of public relations is sponsorship marketing as is the use of social media.

Applying Marketing Knowledge

1. How does competitive product advertising differ from competitive institutional advertising?

2. Suppose you are the advertising manager for a new line of children's bath products. Which form of media would you use for this new product?

3. You have recently been promoted to be director of advertising for the Timkin Tool Company. In your first meeting with Mr. Timkin, he says, "Advertising is a waste! We've been advertising for six months now and sales haven't increased. Tell me why we should continue." Give your answer to Mr. Timkin.

4. A large life insurance company has decided to switch from using a strong fear appeal to a humorous approach. What are the strengths and weaknesses of such a change in message strategy?

5. Which medium has the lowest cost per thousand?

MEDIUM	COST	AUDIENCE
TV show	$5,000	25,000
Magazine	2,200	6,000
Newspaper	4,800	7,200
FM radio	420	1,600

6. Some national advertisers have found that they can have more impact with their advertising by running a large number of ads for a period and then running no ads at all for a period. Why might such a flighting schedule be more effective than a continuous or steady schedule?

7. Each year, managers at Bausch & Lomb evaluate the many advertising media alternatives available to them as they develop their advertising program for contact lenses. What advantages and disadvantages of each alternative should they consider? Which media would you recommend to them?

8. What are two advantages and two disadvantages of the advertising post-tests described in the chapter?

9. The RBC is interested in consumer-oriented sales promotions that would encourage senior citizens to direct-deposit their Canada Pension cheques with the bank. Evaluate the sales promotion options, and recommend two of them to the bank.

Building Your Marketing Plan

To augment your promotion strategy from Chapter 16:

1. Use Figure 17–3 to select the advertising media you will include in your plan by analyzing how combinations of media (e.g., television and Internet advertising, radio, Yellow Pages, etc.) can complement each other.

2. Use Figure 17–5 to select your consumer-oriented sales promotion activities.

3. Specify which trade-oriented sales promotions and public relations activities you will use.

Video Case 17

Google, Inc.: The Right Ads at the Right Time

"So what we did, in essence, is we said advertising should be useful to a consumer just as much as the organic search results, and we don't want people just to buy advertising and be able to show an ad if it's irrelevant to the consumer's need," says Richard Holden, director of product management at Google. To accomplish this, Google developed a "Quality Score" model to predict how effective an ad will be. The model uses many factors such as click-through rates, advertiser history, and keyword

© Justin Sullivan/Getty Images

performance, to develop a score for each advertisement. "Essentially, what we're trying to do is predict ahead, before we actually show an ad, how a consumer will react to that ad, and our interest is in showing fewer ads, not more ads; just the right ads at the right time," Holden continues. The Google advertising model has revolutionized the advertising industry, and it continues to improve every day!

The Company

Google began in 1996 as a research project for Stanford computer science students Larry Page and Sergey Brin. They started with a simple idea—that a search engine based on the relationships between websites would provide a better ranking than a search engine based only on the number of times a key term appeared on a website. The success of their model led to rapid growth and the founders moved the company from their dorm room, to a friend's garage, to offices in Palo Alto, California, and eventually to its current location, known as the Googleplex, in Mountain View, California. In 2000, Google began selling advertising as a means of generating revenue. Its advertising model allowed advertisers to bid on search words and pay for each "click" by a search-engine user. The ads were required to be simple and text-based so that the search result pages remained uncluttered and the search time was as fast as possible.

Page and Brin's first search engine was called "BackRub" because their technique was based on relationships, or backlinks, between websites. The name quickly changed, however. The name "Google" is a misspelling of the word "googol," which is a mathematical term for a 1 followed by 100 zeros. Page and Brin used the name in the original domain, **www.google.stanford.edu**, to reflect their interest in organizing the immense amount of information available on the web. The domain name, of course, became **www.google.com**, and eventually Webster's dictionary added the verb "google" with the definition "to use the Google search engine to obtain information on the Internet." The name has become so familiar that *Advertising Age* recently reported that Google is "the world's most powerful brand"!

Today, Google receives several hundred million inquiries each day as it pursues its mission: to organize the world's information and make it universally accessible and useful. The company generates more than $21 billion in annual revenue and has more than 20,000 employees. As Google has grown, it has developed ten guidelines that represent the corporate philosophy:

1. Focus on the user and all else will follow.
2. It's best to do one thing really, really well.
3. Fast is better than slow.
4. Democracy on the web works.
5. You don't need to be at your desk to need an answer.
6. You can make money without doing evil.
7. There's always more information out there.
8. The need for information crosses all borders.
9. You can be serious without a suit.
10. Great just isn't good enough.

Using these guidelines, Google strives to continually improve its search engine. "The perfect search engine," explains Google co-founder Larry Page, "would understand exactly what you mean and give back exactly what you want."

Online Advertising

Google generates revenue by offering online advertising opportunities—next to search results or on specific web pages. The company always distinguishes ads from the search results or the content of a web page and it never sells placement in the search results. This approach ensures that Google website visitors always know when someone has paid to put a message in front of them. The advantage of online advertising is that it is measurable and allows immediate assessment of its effectiveness. As Gopi Kallayil, product marketing manager, explains, "There is a very high degree of measurability and trackability that you get through online advertising." In addition, he says, "With online advertising, you can actually track the value of every single dollar that you spend, understand which particular customers the ad reached, and what they did after they received the advertising message."

The online advertising market has grown from its initial focus on simple text ads to a much larger set of options. There are five key categories of online advertising:

- Search: 47%
- Display: 35%
- Classified: 10%
- Referral: 7%
- E-mail: 1%

Google is the dominant provider of online search requests and receives more than 60 percent of the search advertising revenue. The fastest-growing advertising category, however, is display advertising where Yahoo! and Microsoft are established providers. Google believes that there is an opportunity to grow its display advertising sales by making the ads useful information instead of visual clutter. According to Google co-founder Sergey Brin, "It's like search—matching people with information they want. It just happens to be promotional."

Several improvements in technology and business practice tools contributed to Google's success. First, Google developed its patented PageRank™ algorithm, which evaluates the entire link structure of the web and uses the link structure to determine which pages are most important. Then the process uses hypertext-matching analysis to determine which pages are relevant to a specific search. A combination of the importance and the relevance of web pages provides the search results—in just a fraction of a second. Second, Google developed two business practice tools—AdWords and AdSense—to help (1) advertisers create ads, and (2) content providers generate advertising revenue. Both tools have become essential elements of Google's advertising model.

AdWords

To help advertisers place ads on their search-engine results, Google developed an online tool called AdWords. Advertisers can use AdWords to create ad text, select target keywords, and manage their account. The process allows advertisers to reach targeted audiences. Frederick Vallaeys, AdWords evangelist, explains, "One of my favourite things about AdWords is the fact that it really helps you find the right customer at the right time and show them the right message. With AdWords, you can very specifically target your market because you're targeting them at a time when they do a search on Google. At that time, they've told you a keyword, you know exactly what they're looking for, and here is your opportunity as a marketer to give them the exact answer to what they've just told you they wanted to find." Google has found that text ads that are relevant to the person reading them have much higher response ("click-through") rates than ads that are not targeted.

AdWords is also easy for any advertiser to use. Large or small businesses can simply open an account with a credit card and have ads appear within minutes. "When AdWords rolled out their self-service product, it really was one of the first times when it was very easy for a small business to put their ad up on the Internet on a search engine and compete on a level playing field alongside Fortune 1000 companies," says Vallaeys. Google has an experienced sales service team available to help any advertiser select appropriate keywords, generate ad copy, and monitor campaign performance. The team is dedicated to helping its advertisers improve click-through rates because high click-through rates are an indication that ads are relevant to a user's interests. Methods of improving advertising performance include changing the keywords and rewriting copy. Because there is no limit to the number of keywords that an advertiser can select and each keyword can be matched with different ad copy, the potential for many very customer-specific options is high.

Another advantage of Google's AdWords program is that it allows advertisers to easily control costs. The ads appear as a "Sponsored Link" next to search results each time the Google search engine matches the search request with the ad's keywords and Quality Score, although the advertiser is not charged unless someone "clicks" on the link. In a traditional advertising model, advertisers were charged using a CPM (cost-per-thousand) approach, which charged for the impressions made by an ad. According to Holden, the Google model "transformed that to what we call a CPC, or a cost-per-click model, and this is a model that an advertiser, instead of paying for an impression, only pays when somebody actually clicks on that ad and is delivered to their website. So, in effect, they may be getting the benefit from impressions being shown, but we're not actually charging them anything unless there's a definite lead being delivered to their website." Google also offers advertisers real-time analytical services to allow assessment of and changes to any component of an advertising campaign.

AdSense

The AdSense program was designed for website owners as a tool for placing ads next to their web page content rather than next to search results. Currently, thousands of website managers use AdSense to place ads on their sites and generate revenue. Google applies the same general philosophy to matching ads with websites as it does to matching ads to search requests. By delivering ads that precisely target the content on the site's pages, Google believes the advertising enhances the experience for visitors to the website. In this way, advertisers, website publishers, and information seekers all benefit.

AdSense is one of the tools Google is using to pursue its goal of increasing its display advertising business. Yahoo! and Microsoft's Bing are leaders in display advertising because they can put ads on their own websites such as Yahoo! Finance and MSN Money. To provide additional outlets for display ads, Google recently purchased YouTube. In addition, Google purchased DoubleClick, an advertising exchange where websites put space up for auction and ad agencies bid to place ads for their clients. Google is also trying to make it easy for anyone to create a display ad by introducing a new tool called Display Ad Builder. Some experts observe that because Google is so dominant at search advertising, its future growth will depend on success in display advertising.

Google's Future Strategy

How will Google continue its success? One possibility is that it will begin to try to win advertising away from the U.S. TV industry. While this is a new type of advertising requiring creative capabilities and relationships with large advertising agencies, Google has dedicated many of its resources to becoming competitive for television advertising expenditures. For example, Google recently helped Volvo develop a campaign that included a YouTube ad and Twitter updates. Google is also likely to develop new websites, establish blogs, and build relationships with existing sites.

Another opportunity for Google will be mobile telephone advertising. There are currently more than 5.4 billion mobile phones in use, and 1 billion of those are Internet-capable. Just as Google's search engine provides a means to match relevant information with consumers, phones offer a chance to provide real-time and location-specific information. Some of the challenges in mobile advertising will be that the networks are not fast and that the ad formats are not standardized. Google believes its new phone and its Android operating system will also help.

Finally, as Google pursues its mission it will continue to expand throughout the world. Search results are already available in 35 languages and volunteers are helping with many others. It is obvious that Google is determined to "organize the world's information" and make it "accessible and useful."

QUESTIONS

1. Describe several unique characteristics about Google and its business practices.

2. What is Google's philosophy about advertising? How can less advertising be preferred to more advertising?

3. Describe the types of online advertising available today. Which type of advertising does Google currently dominate? Why?

4. How can Google be successful in the display advertising business? What other areas of growth are likely to be pursued by Google in the future?

Case: This case was written by Steven Hartley. Sources: "2 Billion Consumers Worldwide to Get Smart(phones) by 2016," *emarketer*, December 11, 2014; Jessica E. Vascellaro, "Google Decides to Find Its Creative Side," *The Wall Street Journal*, October 7, 2009; Robert D. Hof, "Google's New Ad Weapon," *BusinessWeek*, June 22, 2009, p. 52; Maria Bartiromo, "Eric Schmidt on Where Google Is Headed," *BusinessWeek*, August 17, 2009, p. 11; "Why Microsoft–Yahoo Deal Could Be Good for Google," *Advertising Age*, August 10, 2009, p. 10; Peter Burrow, "Apple and Google: Another Step Apart," *BusinessWeek*, August 17, 2009, p. 24; Jeff Jarvis, "How the Google Model Could Help," *BusinessWeek*, February 9, 2009, p. 32; Abbey Klaasen, "Google Says Print Ads Isn't the Answer for Newspapers," *Advertising Age*, January 26, 2009, p. 17; Matthew Creamer, "Recession Doesn't Dent Total Value of Top 100 Brands," *Advertising Age*, April 27, 2009; "The 500 Largest U.S. Corporations," *Fortune*, May 4, 2009, p. F-1; "ComScore Releases August 2009 U.S. Search Engine Rankings," www.comscore.com, October 10, 2009; interviews with Google personnel; and information contained on the Google website (www.google.com).

Personal Selling and Sales Management

Learning Objectives

After reading this chapter, you should be able to:

LO1 Discuss the nature and scope of personal selling and sales management in marketing.

LO2 Identify the different types of personal selling.

LO3 Explain the stages in the personal selling process.

LO4 Describe the major functions of sales management.

Meet Today's Sales Professional

Have you been considering sales as a career opportunity? If so, then consider Lindsey Smith as a role model. Lindsey Smith began her career representing molecular imaging products within the medical diagnostics division of GE Healthcare. She joined the company 11 years ago right out of college with a bachelor of business administration (BBA) degree. The epitome of today's sales professional, she lists integrity, motivation, trust and relationship building, and a team orientation as just a few of the ingredients necessary for a successful sales career today.

As a sales professional, she recognizes the importance of constantly updating and refining her product knowledge, analytical and communication skills, and strategic thinking about opportunities to more fully satisfy each customer's clinical, economic, and technical requirements. And for good reason. Her customer contacts include physicians (radiologists, neurologists, and cardiologists), medical technologists, nurses, and health care provider CEOs, CFOs, and other administrators.

Lindsey Smith's selling orientation and customer relationship philosophy rest on four pillars:

1. *A commitment to creating value for clients.* Lindsey believes "every sales call and client interaction should create value for both the customer and the company."

2. *Seek to serve clients as a trusted consultant.* Lindsey emphasizes "being a resource for my customers by providing novel solutions for them."

3. *Reinforce the company's competitive advantage.* Lindsey continually reinforces GE Healthcare's competitive advantage: "I emphasize my company's value proposition and showcase the company's product innovation, solutions, and service."

© Hillsman Stuart Jackson

4. *Regard challenges as opportunities.* Lindsey says, "I consider challenges as opportunities to provide innovative solutions and resources to customers and to build client trust and long-term relationships." Lindsey Smith's approach to selling and customer relationships has served her customers and her well. She is among the company's top revenue producers and has a long list of loyal customers. Not surprisingly, Ms. Smith has been a recipient of the company's Commercial Excellence Award in six of the last eight years.

In 2014, Lindsey Smith was promoted to her current position as senior client director at GE Healthcare. Then, in 2016, she was named executive client director. In this capacity, she represents and manages the entire GE Healthcare company portfolio, including medical technology, health care consulting, information technology, service operations, and finance solutions for one of GE's largest strategic health care systems. She manages 75 commercial and operations personnel.[1]

This chapter describes the scope and significance of personal selling and sales management in marketing and creating value for customers. It first highlights the many forms of personal selling. Next, the major steps in the selling process are outlined with an emphasis on building buyer–seller relationships.

The chapter then focuses on salesforce management and its critical role in achieving a company's broader marketing objectives. Three major salesforce management functions are then detailed. They are sales plan formulation, sales plan implementation, and salesforce evaluation. Finally, technology's persuasive influence on how selling is done and how salespeople are managed is described.

SCOPE AND SIGNIFICANCE OF PERSONAL SELLING AND SALES MANAGEMENT

Chapter 16 described personal selling and management of the sales effort as being part of the firm's promotional mix. Although it is important to recognize that personal selling is a useful vehicle for communicating with present and potential buyers, it is much more. Take a moment to answer the questions in the personal selling and sales management quiz in Figure 18–1. As you read on, compare your answers with those in the text.

FIGURE 18–1

1. What percentage of the average field sales representative's time each workweek is spent actually selling to customers? (check one)

   40% _____   50% _____   60% _____

2. "A salesperson's job is finished when a sale is made." True or false? (circle one)

   True   False

3. About what percentage of companies include customer satisfaction as a measure of salesperson performance? (check one)

   10% _____   30% _____   50% _____
   20% _____   40% _____   60% _____

Personal selling and sales management quiz.

(LO1) Nature of Personal Selling and Sales Management

As discussed in Chapter 16, *personal selling* involves the two-way flow of communication between a buyer and seller, often in a face-to-face encounter, designed to influence a person's or group's purchase decision. However, with advances in telecommunications, personal selling also takes place over the telephone, through video teleconferencing, and via the Internet.

However, personal selling remains a highly human-intensive activity despite the use of technology. Accordingly, the people involved must be managed. **Sales management** involves planning the selling program and implementing and controlling the personal selling effort of the firm. The tasks involved in managing personal selling include setting objectives; organizing the salesforce; recruiting, selecting, training, and compensating salespeople; and evaluating the performance of individual salespeople.

Pervasiveness of Selling

"Everyone lives by selling something," wrote author Robert Louis Stevenson a century ago. His observation still holds true today. In Canada, more than one million people are employed in sales positions.[2] Included in this number are manufacturing sales personnel, real estate brokers, stockbrokers, and salesclerks who work in retail stores. In reality, however, virtually every occupation that involves customer contact has an element of personal selling. For example, lawyers, accountants, bankers, and company personnel recruiters perform sales-related activities, whether or not they acknowledge it.

Many executives in major companies have held sales positions at some time in their careers. Selling often serves as a stepping-stone to top management, as well as being a career path in itself.

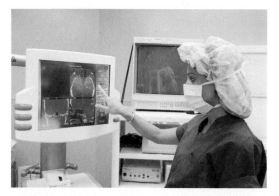

Could this be a salesperson in the operating room? Read the text to find why Medtronic salespeople visit hospital operating rooms.

Medtronic

www.medtronic.com

© Radius Images/Getty Images

Personal Selling in Marketing and Entrepreneurship

Personal selling serves three major roles in a firm's overall marketing effort. First, salespeople are the critical link between the firm and its customers. This role requires that salespeople match company interests with customer needs to satisfy both parties in the exchange process. Second, salespeople *are* the company in a consumer's eyes. They represent what a company is or attempts to be and are often the only personal contact that a customer has with the company. For example, the "look" projected by Gucci salespeople is an important factor in communicating the style of the company's apparel line. Moreover, as acknowledged by IBM's former chief executive officer, his company's 40,000-strong salesforce is "our face to the client. Third, personal selling may play a dominant role in a firm's marketing program. This situation typically arises when a firm uses a push marketing strategy, described in Chapter 16. Avon, for example, pays almost 40 percent of its total sales dollars for selling expenses. Pharmaceutical firms and office and educational equipment manufacturers also rely heavily on personal selling in the marketing of their products.

Personal selling has been also shown to be critical to successful entrepreneurial efforts for three reasons.[3] First, selling a business concept to potential investors is an entrepreneur's first sales effort. Second, selling the business concept to prospective employees necessary for the success of the venture is essential. Finally, the more traditional sales art of convincing customers to buy one's product or service, getting referrals, and building professional networks is necessary. In short, highly successful entrepreneurs have a great sales talent.

Creating Customer Value through Salespeople: Relationship and Partnership Selling

As the critical link between the firm and its customers, salespeople can create customer value in many ways. For instance, by being close to the customer, salespeople can identify creative solutions to customer problems. Salespeople at Medtronic, Inc., the world leader in the heart pacemaker market, are in the operating room for more than 90 percent of the procedures performed with their product, and are on call, through pagers, 24 hours a day. "It reflects the willingness to be there in every situation, just in case a problem arises—even though nine times out of ten, the procedure goes just fine," notes a satisfied customer.[4]

Salespeople can create value by easing the customer buying process. This happened at TE Connectivity, a producer of electrical products. Salespeople and customers had a difficult time getting product specifications and performance data on the company's 70,000 products quickly and accurately. The company now has all its information on its website, which can be downloaded instantly by salespeople and customers. Customer value is also created by salespeople who follow through after the sale. At Jefferson Smurfit Corporation, a multibillion-dollar supplier of packaging products, one of its salespeople juggled production from three of the company's plants to satisfy an unexpected demand for boxes from General Electric. This person's action led to the company being given GE's "Distinguished Supplier Award."

Customer value creation is made possible by **relationship selling**, the practice of building ties to customers based on a salesperson's attention and commitment to customer needs over time. Relationship selling involves mutual respect and trust among buyers and sellers. It focuses on creating long-term customers, not a one-time sale. In fact, a recent survey of 300 senior sales executives revealed that 96 percent consider "building long-term relationships with customers" to be the most important activity affecting sales performance.[5] Such companies as Merck Frosst Canada, IBM Canada, Bell Canada, and Kraft Canada have made relationship building a core focus of their sales effort.

Some companies have taken relationship selling a step further and forged partnerships between buyer and seller organizations. With **partnership selling**, sometimes called *enterprise selling,* buyers and sellers combine their expertise and resources to create customized solutions; to commit to joint planning; and to share customer, competitive, and company information for their mutual benefit, and ultimately the customer's benefit. As an approach to sales, partnership selling relies on cross-functional business specialists who apply their knowledge and expertise to achieve higher productivity, lower cost, and greater customer value. Partnership selling complements supplier and channel partnering, described in Chapters 6 and 14. This practice is embraced by such companies as IBM Canada, 3M Canada, DuPont, and Honeywell, which have established partnerships with their customers, such as Air Canada, Ford, and McDonald's.

Relationship and partnership selling represent another dimension of customer relationship management (CRM). Both emphasize the importance of learning about customer needs and wants and tailoring solutions to customer problems as a means to create customer value. Finally, in the customer experience management (CEM) era, sales personnel can play a critical role in ensuring customers perceive a positive experience with the company and its brands.

Learning Review

1. What is personal selling?
2. What is involved in sales management?

LO2 THE MANY FORMS OF PERSONAL SELLING

Personal selling assumes many forms based on the amount of selling done and the amount of creativity required to perform the sales task. Broadly speaking, three types of personal selling exist: order taking, order getting, and sales support activities. While some firms use only one of these types of personal selling, others use a combination of all three.

Order Taking

Typically, an **order taker** processes routine orders or reorders for products that have already been sold by the company. The primary responsibility of order takers is to preserve an ongoing relationship with existing customers and maintain sales. Two types of order takers exist. *Outside order takers* visit customers and replenish inventory stocks of resellers, such as retailers or wholesalers. For example, Frito-Lay salespeople call on supermarkets, neighbourhood grocery stores, and other establishments to ensure that the company's line of snack products is in adequate supply. In addition, outside order takers often provide assistance in arranging displays. *Inside order takers,* also called *order clerks* or *salesclerks,* typically answer simple questions, take orders, and complete transactions with customers. Many retail clerks are inside order takers. Inside order takers are often employed by companies that use *inbound telemarketing,* the use of toll-free telephone numbers that customers can call to obtain information about products or services and make purchases. In business-to-business settings, order taking arises in straight rebuy situations. Order takers generally do little selling in a conventional sense and engage in only modest problem solving with customers. They often represent products that have few options, such as confectionary items, magazine subscriptions, and highly standardized industrial products.

Portable communications technology enables Frito-Lay salespeople with the order-taking process.

Frito-Lay, Inc.

www.fritolay.com

© Fuse/Corbis/Getty Images

Inbound telemarketing is also an essential selling activity for more "customer service" driven firms, such as Dell Computer. Order takers in such firms undergo extensive training so that they can better assist callers with their purchase decisions.

Order Getting

An **order getter** sells in a conventional sense and identifies prospective customers, provides customers with information, persuades customers to buy, closes sales, and follows up on customers' use of a product or service. Like order takers, order getters can be inside (an automobile salesperson) or outside (a Xerox salesperson). Order getting involves a high degree of creativity and customer empathy and is typically required for selling complex or technical products with many options, and so considerable product knowledge and sales training are necessary. In modified-rebuy or new-buy purchase situations in organizational selling, an order getter acts as a problem solver who identifies how a particular product may satisfy a customer's need. Similarly, in the purchase of a service, such as insurance, a Metropolitan Life insurance agent can provide a mix of plans to satisfy a buyer's needs depending on income, stage of the family's life cycle, and investment objectives.

Order getting is not a 40-hour-per-week job. Industry research indicates that outside order getters, or field service representatives, often work over 50 hours per week. As shown in Figure 18–2, 41 percent of their time is spent selling by phone or face-to-face. What percent did you check for question 1 in Figure 18–1? Another 24 percent is devoted to generating leads and researching customer accounts. The remainder of a sales representative's workweek is occupied by administrative tasks, meetings, service calls, travel, customer follow-up and training.[6]

Order getting by outside salespeople is also expensive. It is estimated that the average cost of a single field sales call on a business customer is about $500, factoring in salespeople compensation, benefits, and travel and entertainment expenses. This cost illustrates why outbound telemarketing is so popular today. *Outbound telemarketing* is the practice of using the telephone rather than personal visits to contact customers. A significantly lower cost per sales call (in the range of $20 to $25) and little or no field expense accounts for its widespread appeal. Accordingly, outbound telemarketing has grown significantly.

FIGURE 18–2

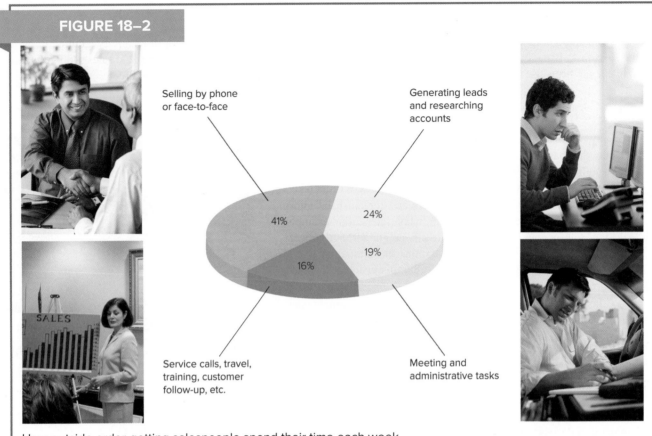

How outside order-getting salespeople spend their time each week.

Source: Gerhard Gschwandtner, "How Much Time Do Your Salespeople Spend Selling?" *Selling Power,* March/April 2011, p. 8. Photos: (top left): Asia Images/Getty Images; (top right) © Susan Van Etten/PhotoEdit, Inc.; (bottom right) © Royalty-Free/Corbis; (bottom left) Tetra Images/Getty Images

Customer Sales Support Personnel

Customer sales support personnel augment the selling effort of order getters by performing a variety of services. For example, **missionary salespeople** do not directly solicit orders but rather concentrate on performing promotional activities and introducing new products. They are used extensively in the pharmaceutical industry, where they persuade physicians to prescribe a firm's product. Actual sales are made through wholesalers or directly to pharmacists who fill prescriptions. A **sales engineer** is a salesperson who specializes in identifying, analyzing, and solving customer problems and who brings know-how and technical expertise to the selling situation but often does not actually sell products and services. Sales engineers are popular in selling industrial products, such as chemicals and heavy equipment. In many situations, firms engage in cross-functional **team selling**, the practice of using an entire team of professionals in selling to and servicing major customers.[7]

   Team selling is used when specialized knowledge is needed to satisfy the different interests of individuals in a customer's buying centre. For example, a selling team might consist of a salesperson, a sales engineer, a service representative, and a financial executive, each of whom would deal with a counterpart in the customer's firm. Selling teams have grown in popularity due to partnering, and they take different forms. In *conference selling,* a salesperson and other company resource people meet with buyers to discuss problems and opportunities. In *seminar selling,* a company team conducts an educational program for a customer's technical staff, describing state-of-the-art developments. IBM and Xerox pioneered cross-functional team selling in working with prospective buyers. Other firms have embraced this practice and have created and sustained value for their customers.[8]

3. What is the principal difference between an order taker and an order getter?

4. What is team selling?

LO3 THE PERSONAL SELLING PROCESS: BUILDING RELATIONSHIPS

Selling, and particularly order getting, is a complicated activity that involves building buyer–seller relationships. Although the salesperson–customer interaction is essential to personal selling, much of a salesperson's work occurs before this meeting and continues after the sale itself. The **personal selling process** consists of six stages: (1) prospecting, (2) preapproach, (3) approach, (4) presentation, (5) close, and (6) follow-up (Figure 18–3).

Prospecting

Personal selling begins with *prospecting*—the search for and qualification of potential customers. For some products that are one-time purchases, continual prospecting is necessary to maintain sales. There are three types of prospects. A *lead* is the name of a person who may be a possible customer. A *prospect* is a customer who wants or needs the product. If an individual wants the product, can afford to buy it, and is the decision maker, this individual is a *qualified prospect.*

Leads and prospects are generated using several sources. For example, advertising may contain a coupon or a toll-free number to generate leads. Some companies use exhibits at trade shows, professional meetings, and conferences to generate leads or prospects. Staffed by salespeople, these exhibits are used to attract the attention of prospective buyers and disseminate information. Others use lists and directories or the Internet for generating leads and prospects. Websites, e-mail, and social media networks such as LinkedIn are used by salespeople to connect with individuals and companies

Trade shows are a popular source for leads and prospects.

© Urbanmyth/Alamy Stock Photo

that may be prospects. Another approach for generating leads is through *cold canvassing* in person or by telephone. This approach simply means that a salesperson may open a directory, pick a name, and visit or call that individual or business. Although the refusal rate is high with cold canvassing, this approach can be successful.[9] However, cold canvassing is frowned upon in most Asian and Latin American societies. Personal visits, based on referrals, are expected.

Cold canvassing is also often criticized by Canadian consumers. Many consumers see cold canvassing as an intrusion into their privacy, and many find it simply distasteful.[10] Many trade associations, including the Canadian Marketing Association, have codes of ethics for dealing with this issue, such as adhering to consumers' "do not call," "do not mail," or "do not visit" requests. The Canadian government has also attempted to more closely regulate cold canvassing with the Canadian Radio-television and Telecommunications Commission (CRTC) requiring telemarketers to inform consumers that they have the right to say no to such solicitations.

Preapproach

Once a salesperson has identified a qualified prospect, preparation for the sale begins with the preapproach. The *preapproach* stage involves obtaining further information on the prospect and deciding on the best method of approach. Knowing how the prospect prefers to be approached, and what the prospect is looking for in a product or service, is essential regardless of cultural setting. For example, a Merrill Lynch stockbroker will need information on a prospect's discretionary income, investment objectives, and preference for discussing brokerage services over the telephone or in person. For business product companies, such as Texas Instruments, the preapproach involves identifying the buying role of a prospect (for example, influencer or decision maker), important buying criteria, and the prospect's receptivity to a formal or informal presentation. Identifying the best time to contact a prospect is also important. For example, insurance companies have discovered the best times to call on people in different occupations: dentists before 9:30 a.m., lawyers between 11 a.m. and 2 p.m., and university professors between 7 and 8 p.m.

FIGURE 18–3

STAGE	OBJECTIVE	COMMENTS
1. Prospecting	Search for and qualify prospects	Start of the selling process; prospects produced through advertising, referrals, and cold canvassing
2. Preapproach	Gather information and decide how to approach the prospect	Information sources include personal observation, other customers, and own salespeople
3. Approach	Gain a prospect's attention, stimulate interest, and make transition to the presentation	First impression is critical; gain attention and interest through reference to common acquaintances, a referral, or product demonstration
4. Presentation	Begin converting a prospect into a customer by creating a desire for the product or service	Different presentation formats are possible; however, involving the customer in the product or service through attention to particular needs is critical; important to deal professionally and ethically with prospect skepticism, indifference, or objections
5. Close	Obtain a purchase commitment from the prospect and create a customer	Salesperson asks for the purchase; different approaches include the trial close and assumptive close
6. Follow-up	Ensure that the customer is satisfied with the product or service	Resolve any problems faced by the customer to ensure customer satisfaction and future sales possibilities

Stages and objectives of the personal selling process.

This stage is very important in global selling where customs dictate appropriate protocol. In many South American countries, for example, buyers expect salespeople to be punctual for appointments. However, prospective buyers are routinely 30 minutes late. South Americans take negotiating seriously and prefer straightforward presentations, but a hard-sell approach will not work.[11]

Successful salespeople recognize that the preapproach stage should never be short-changed. Their experience coupled with research on customer complaints indicates that failure to learn as much as possible about the prospect is unprofessional and the ruin of a sales call.

Approach

The *approach* stage involves the initial meeting between the salesperson and prospect, where the objectives are to gain the prospect's attention, stimulate interest, and build the foundation for the sales presentation itself and the basis for a working relationship. The first impression is critical at this stage, and it is common for salespeople to begin the conversation with a reference to common acquaintances, a referral, or even the product or service itself. Which tactic is used will depend on the information obtained in the prospecting and preapproach stages.

The approach stage is very important in international settings. In many societies outside Canada, considerable time is devoted to non-business talk designed to establish a rapport between buyers and sellers. For instance, it is common for two or three meetings to occur before business matters are discussed in the Middle East and Asia. Gestures are also very important. The initial meeting between a salesperson and a prospect in Canada customarily begins with a firm handshake. Handshakes also apply in France, but they are gentle, not firm. Forget the handshake in Japan. A bow is appropriate. What about business cards? Business cards should be printed in English on one side and the language of the prospective customer on the other. Knowledgeable Canadian salespeople know that their business cards should be handed to Asian customers using both hands, with the name facing the receiver. In Asia, anything involving names demands respect.[12]

How business cards are exchanged with Asian customers is very important. Read the text to learn the appropriate protocol in the approach stage of the personal selling process.

© Phillip Jarrell/Taxi/Getty Images

Presentation

The *presentation* is at the core of the order-getting selling process, and its objective is to convert a prospect into a customer by creating a desire for the product or service. Three major presentation formats exist: (1) stimulus response, (2) formula selling, and (3) need satisfaction.

Stimulus-Response Presentation

The **stimulus-response presentation** format assumes that given the appropriate stimulus by a salesperson, the prospect will buy. With this format, the salesperson tries one appeal after another, hoping to "hit the right button." A counter clerk at McDonald's is using this approach when he or she asks whether you would like an order of french fries or a dessert with your meal. The counter clerk is engaging in what is called *suggestive selling.* Although useful in this setting, the stimulus-response format is not always appropriate, and for many products, a more formalized format is necessary.

Formula-Selling Presentation

The **formula-selling presentation** format, a more formalized presentation, is based on the view that a presentation consists of information that must be provided in an accurate, thorough, and step-by-step manner to inform the prospect. A popular version of this format is the *canned sales presentation,* which is a memorized, standardized message conveyed to every prospect. Used frequently by firms in telephone and door-to-door selling of consumer products (for example, Kirby vacuum cleaners), this approach treats every prospect the same, regardless of differences in needs or preference for certain kinds of information. Canned sales presentations can be advantageous when the differences between prospects are unknown or with novice salespeople who are less knowledgeable about the product and the selling process than are experienced salespeople. Although it guarantees a thorough presentation, it often lacks flexibility and spontaneity and, more importantly, does not provide for feedback from the prospective buyer—a critical component in the communication process and the start of a relationship.

Need-Satisfaction Presentation

The stimulus-response and formula selling formats share a common characteristic: the salesperson dominates the conversation. By comparison, the **need-satisfaction presentation** format emphasizes probing and listening by the salesperson to identify the needs and interests of prospective buyers. Once these are identified, the salesperson tailors the presentation to the prospect and highlights product benefits that may be valued by the prospect. The need-satisfaction format, which emphasizes problem solving and customer solutions, is the most consistent with the marketing concept and relationship building.

Two selling styles are associated with this format.[13] **Adaptive selling** involves adjusting the presentation to fit the selling situation, such as knowing when to offer solutions and when to ask for more information. Sales research and practice show that knowledge of the customer and sales situation are key ingredients for adaptive selling. Many consumer service firms, such as brokerage and insurance firms and consumer product firms effectively apply this selling style. **Consultative selling** focuses on problem identification, where the salesperson serves as an expert on problem recognition and resolution. With consultative selling, problem solution options are not simply a matter of choosing from an array of existing products or services. Rather, novel solutions often arise thereby creating unique value for the customer. Consultative selling is prominent in business-to-business marketing. IBM Canada is often recognized for its consultative selling style, as is Xerox. In fact, according to a senior Xerox sales executive, "Our business is no longer about selling boxes. It's about selling digital, networked-based information management solutions, and this requires a highly customized and consultative process." But what does a customer solution really mean? From a buyer's perspective, a solution is one that (1) meets their requirements, (2) is designed to uniquely solve their problem, (3) can be implemented, and (4) ensures follow-up. In order to accomplish this a salesperson has to do three things. First, the salesperson must spend considerable time and effort to fully understand a specific customer's requirements. Second, the salesperson must understand that effective customer solutions are based on relationships between sellers and buyers. And finally, the salesperson must engage in consultative selling in order to provide novel solutions and value for the customer.[14]

Handling Objections

A critical concern in the presentation stage is handling objections. *Objections* are excuses for not making a purchase commitment or decision. Some objections are valid and are based on the characteristics of the product or service or price. However, many objections reflect prospect skepticism or indifference. Whether valid or not, experienced salespeople know that objections do not put an end to the presentation. Rather, techniques can be used to deal with objections in a courteous, ethical, and professional manner. The following six techniques are the most common:[15]

- *Acknowledge and convert the objection.* This technique involves using the objection as a reason for buying. For example, a prospect might say, "The price is too high." The reply: "Yes, the price is high because we use the finest materials. Let me show you . . ."

- *Postpone.* The postpone technique is used when the objection will be dealt with later in the presentation: "I'm going to address that point shortly. I think my answer would make better sense then."

- *Agree and neutralize.* Here, a salesperson agrees with the objection, then shows that it is unimportant. A salesperson would say, "That's true, and others have said the same. However, they concluded that this issue was outweighed by the other benefits."

- *Accept the objection.* Sometimes, the objection is valid. Let the prospect express such views, probe for the reason behind it, and attempt to stimulate further discussion on the objection.

- *Denial.* When a prospect's objection is based on misinformation and clearly untrue, it is wise to meet the objection head on with a firm denial.

- *Ignore the objection.* This technique is used when it appears that the objection is a stalling mechanism or is clearly not important to the prospect.

Each of these techniques requires a calm, professional interaction with the prospect and is most effective when objections are anticipated in the preapproach stage. Handling objections is a skill requiring a sense of timing, appreciation for the prospect's state of mind, and adeptness in communication. Objections also should be handled ethically. Lying or misrepresenting product or service features are grossly unethical practices.

Close

The *closing* stage in the selling process involves obtaining a purchase commitment from the prospect. This stage is the most important and the most difficult because the salesperson must determine when the prospect is ready to buy. Telltale signals indicating a readiness to buy include body language (prospect re-examines the product or contract closely), statements ("This equipment should reduce our maintenance costs"), and questions ("When could we expect delivery?").

The close itself can take several forms. Three closing techniques are used when a salesperson believes a buyer is about ready to make a purchase: (1) trial close, (2) assumptive close, and (3) urgency close. A *trial close* involves asking the prospect to make a decision on some aspect of the purchase: "Would you prefer the blue or grey model?" An *assumptive close* entails asking the prospect to consider choices concerning delivery, warranty, or financing terms under the assumption that a sale has been finalized. An *urgency close* is used to commit the prospect quickly by making reference to the timeliness of the purchase: "The low-interest financing ends next week" or "That is the last model we have in stock." Of course, these statements should be used only if they accurately reflect the situation; otherwise, such claims would be unethical. When a prospect is clearly ready to buy, the final close is used, and a salesperson asks for the order.

Follow-Up

The selling process does not end with the closing of a sale; rather, professional selling requires customer follow-up. One marketing authority equated selling and follow-up with courtship and marriage, by observing ". . . the sale merely consummates the courtship. Then the marriage begins. How good the marriage is depends on how well the relationship is managed."[16] The *follow-up stage* includes making certain that the customer's purchase has been properly delivered and installed and that any difficulties experienced with the use of the item are addressed. Attention to this stage of the selling process solidifies the buyer–seller relationship. Moreover, research shows that the cost and effort to obtain repeat sales from a satisfied customer is roughly half of that necessary to gain a sale from a new customer.[17] In short, today's satisfied customers become tomorrow's qualified prospects or referrals. (What was your answer to question 2 in the quiz in Figure 18–1?)

Learning Review

5. What are the six stages in the personal selling process?

6. What is the distinction between a lead and a qualified prospect?

7. Which presentation format is most consistent with the marketing concept? Why?

LO4   # THE SALES MANAGEMENT PROCESS

Selling must be managed if it is going to contribute to a firm's overall objectives. Although firms differ in the specifics of how salespeople and the selling effort are managed, the sales management process is similar across firms. Sales management consists of three interrelated functions: (1) sales plan formulation, (2) sales plan implementation, and (3) evaluation and control of the salesforce (Figure 18–4).

Sales Plan Formulation: Setting Direction

Formulating the sales plan is the most basic of the three sales management functions. According to the vice president of the Harris Corporation, a global communications company, "If a company hopes to implement its marketing strategy, it really needs a detailed sales planning process."[18] The **sales plan** is a statement describing what is to be achieved and where and how the selling effort of salespeople is to be deployed. Formulating the sales plan involves three tasks: (1) setting objectives, (2) organizing the salesforce, and (3) developing account management policies.

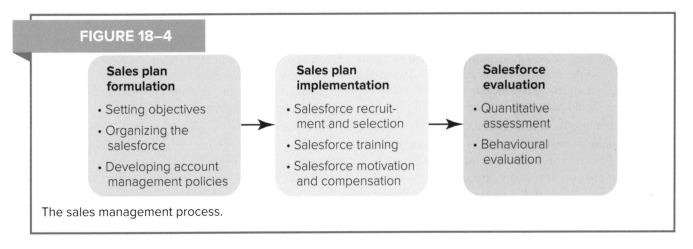

The sales management process.

Setting Objectives

Setting objectives is central to sales management because this task specifies what is to be achieved. In practice, objectives are set for the total salesforce and for each salesperson. Selling objectives can be output related and focus on dollar or unit sales volume, number of new customers added, and profit. Alternatively, they can be input related and emphasize the number of sales calls and selling expenses. Output- and input-related objectives are used for the salesforce as a whole and for each salesperson. A third type of objective that is behaviourally related is typically specific for each salesperson and includes his or her product knowledge, customer service, and selling and communication skills. Increasingly, firms are also emphasizing knowledge of competition as an objective, as salespeople are calling on customers and should see what competitors are doing.[19] But should salespeople explicitly ask their customers for information about competitors? Read the accompanying Making Responsible Decisions box, "The Ethics of Asking Customers about Competitors," to find out how salespeople view this practice.[20]

MAKING RESPONSIBLE DECISIONS

The Ethics of Asking Customers about Competitors

Salespeople are a valuable source of information about what is happening in the marketplace. By working closely with customers and asking good questions, salespeople often have first-hand knowledge of customer problems and wants. They also are able to spot the activities of competitors. However, should salespeople explicitly ask customers about competitor strategies, such as pricing practices, product development efforts, and trade and promotion programs? Gaining knowledge about competitors by asking customers for information is a ticklish ethical issue. Research indicates that 25 percent of North American salespeople engaged in business-to-business selling consider this practice unethical, and their companies have explicit guidelines for this practice. It is also noteworthy that Japanese salespeople consider this practice to be more unethical than do salespeople in North America.

Do you believe that asking customers about competitor practices is unethical? Why or why not?

Whatever objectives are set, they should be precise and measurable and specify the time period over which they are to be achieved. Once established, these objectives serve as performance standards for the evaluation of the salesforce—the third function of sales management.

Organizing the Salesforce

Organizing a selling organization is the second task in formulating the sales plan. Three questions are related to organization. First, should the company use its own salesforce, or should it use independent agents, such as manufacturer's representatives? Second, if the decision is made to employ company salespeople, then should they be organized according to geography, customer type, or product or service? Third, how many company salespeople should be employed?

The decision to use company salespeople or independent agents is made infrequently. However, recently, Coca-Cola's Food Division replaced its salesforce with independent agents (food brokers). The Optoelectronics Division of Honeywell, Inc. has switched back and forth between agents and its own salesforce over the last 25 years and now uses both. The decision is based on an analysis of economic and behavioural factors. An economic analysis examines the costs of using both types of salespeople and is a form of break-even analysis.

Consider a situation in which independent agents would receive a 5 percent commission on sales, and company salespeople would receive a 3 percent commission, salaries, and benefits. In addition, with company salespeople, sales administration costs would be incurred for a total fixed cost of $500,000 per year. At what sales level would independent or company salespeople be less costly? This question can be answered by setting the costs of the two options equal to each other and solving for the sales level amount, as shown in the following equation:

$$\frac{\text{Total cost of company salespeople}}{0.03(X) + \$500,000} = \frac{\text{Total cost independent agents}}{0.05(X)}$$

where X = sales volume. Solving for X, sales volume equals $25 million, indicating that below $25 million in sales, independent agents would be cheaper, but above $25 million, a company salesforce would be cheaper. This relationship is shown in Figure 18–5.

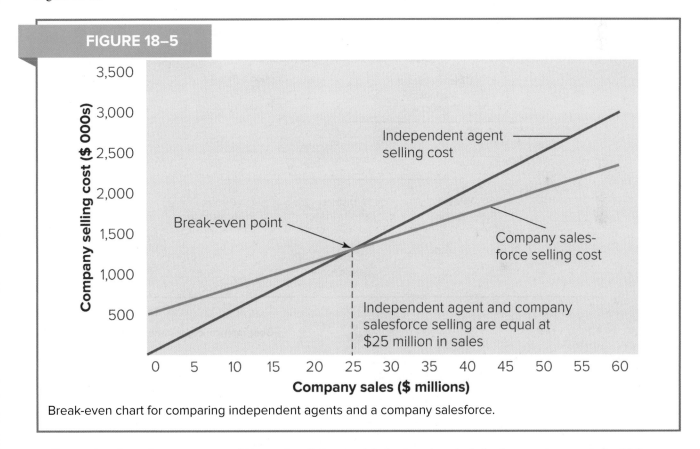

FIGURE 18–5

Break-even chart for comparing independent agents and a company salesforce.

Economics alone does not answer this question, however. A behavioural analysis is also necessary and should focus on issues related to the control, flexibility, effort, and availability of independent and company salespeople.[21] An individual firm must weigh the pros and cons of the economic and behavioural considerations before making this decision.

If a company elects to employ its own salespeople, then it must choose an organizational structure based on (1) geography, (2) customer, or (3) product (Figure 18–6). A geographical structure is the simplest organization, where Canada or, indeed, the globe is first divided into regions and each region is divided into districts or territories. Salespeople are assigned to each district with defined geographical boundaries and call on all customers and represent all products sold by the company. The principal advantage of this structure is that it can minimize travel time, expenses, and duplication of selling effort. However, if a firm's products or customers require specialized knowledge, then a geographical structure is not suitable.

FIGURE 18–6

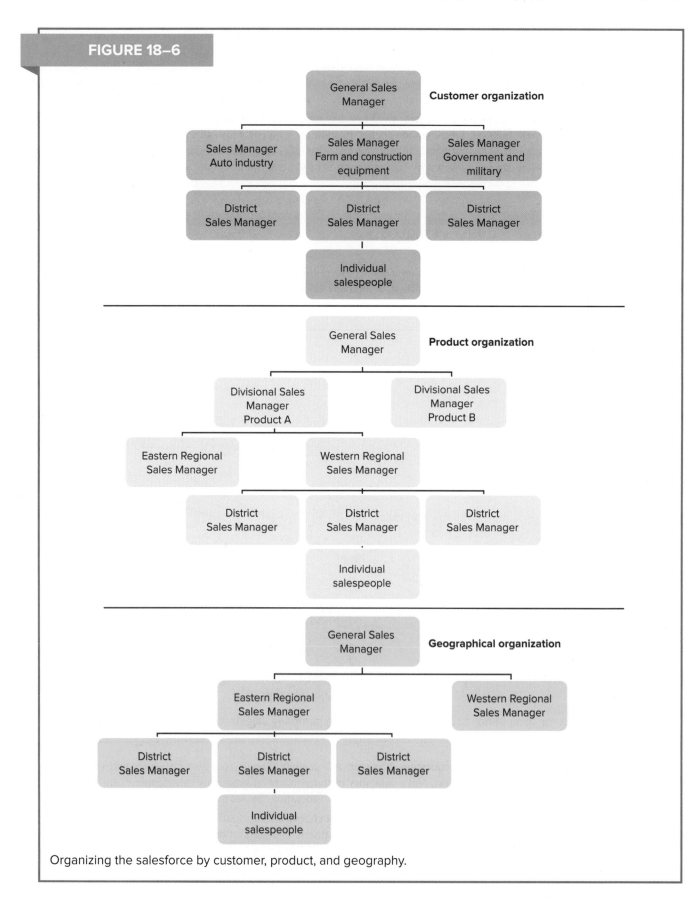

Organizing the salesforce by customer, product, and geography.

When different types of buyers have different needs, a customer sales organizational structure is used. In practice, this means that a different salesforce calls on each separate type of buyer or marketing channel. For example, Kodak switched from a geographical to a marketing channel structure, with different sales teams serving specific retail channels: mass merchandisers, photo specialty outlets, and food and drug stores. The rationale for this approach is that more effective, specialized customer support and knowledge are provided to buyers. However, this structure often leads to higher administrative costs and some duplication of selling effort because two separate salesforces are used to represent the same products.

An important variation of the customer organizational structure is **key account management**—the practice of using team selling to focus on important customers so as to build mutually beneficial, long-term, cooperative relationships.[22] Key account management involves teams of sales, service, and often technical personnel who work with purchasing, manufacturing, engineering, logistics, and financial executives in customer organizations. This approach, which often assigns company personnel to a customer account, results in "customer specialists" who can provide exceptional service. Procter & Gamble uses this approach with Walmart, as does Black & Decker with Home Depot.

When specific knowledge is required to sell certain types of products, then a product sales organization is used. For example, a steel manufacturer has a salesforce that sells drilling pipe to oil companies and another that sells specialty steel products to manufacturers. The primary advantage of this structure is that salespeople can develop expertise with technical characteristics, applications, and selling methods associated with a particular product or family of products. However, this structure also produces high administrative costs and duplication of selling effort because two company salespeople may call on the same customer.

In short, there is no one best sales organization for all companies in all situations. Rather, the organization of the salesforce should reflect the marketing strategy of the firm. Each year, about 10 percent of firms change their sales organizations to implement new marketing strategies.

The third question related to salesforce organization involves determining the size of the salesforce. For example, why does Frito-Lay have about 17,500 salespeople who call on supermarkets, grocery stores, and other establishments to sell snack foods? The answer lies in the number of accounts (customers) served, the frequency of calls on accounts, the length of an average call, and the amount of time a salesperson can devote to selling.

A common approach for determining the size of a salesforce is the **workload method**. This formula-based method integrates the number of customers served, call frequency, call length, and available selling time to arrive at a figure for the salesforce size. For example, Frito-Lay needs about 17,500 salespeople according to the following workload method formula:

$$NS = \frac{NC \times CF \times CL}{AST}$$

where:

NS = Number of salespeople

NC = Number of customers

CF = Call frequency necessary to service a customer each year

CL = Length of an average call

AST = Average amount of selling time available per year

Frito-Lay sells its products to 350,000 supermarkets, grocery stores, and other establishments. Salespeople should call on these accounts at least once a week, or 52 times a year. The average sales call lasts an average of 81 minutes (1.35 hours). An average salesperson works 2,000 hours a year (50 weeks × 40 hours a week), but 12 hours a week are devoted to non-selling activities, such as travel and administration, leaving 1,400 hours a year. Using these guidelines, Frito-Lay would need:

$$NS = \frac{350,000 \times 52 \times 1.35}{1,400} = 17,550 \text{ salespeople}$$

The value of this formula is apparent in its flexibility; a change in any one of the variables will affect the number of salespeople needed. Changes are determined, in part, by the firm's account management policies.

Developing Account Management Policies

The third task in formulating a sales plan involves developing **account management policies** that specify whom the salespeople should contact, what kinds of selling and customer service activities should be engaged in, and how these activities should be carried out. These policies might state which individuals in a buying organization should be contacted, the amount of sales and service effort that different customers should receive, and the kinds of information that the salespeople should collect before or during a sales call.

An example of an account management policy in Figure 18–7 shows how different accounts or customers can be grouped according to level of opportunity and the firm's competitive sales position.[23] When specific account names are placed in each cell, salespeople clearly see which accounts should be contacted, with what level of selling and service activity, and how to deal with them. Accounts in cells 1 and 2 might have high frequencies of personal sales calls and increased time spent on a call. Cell 3 accounts will have lower call frequencies, and cell 4 accounts might be contacted through telemarketing or direct mail rather than in person.[24]

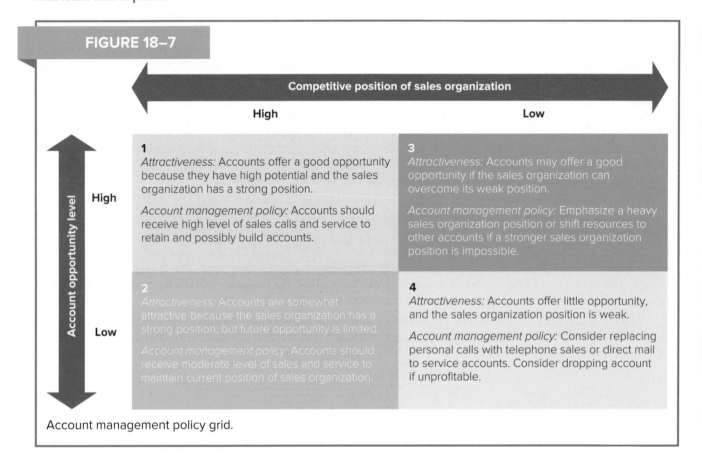

FIGURE 18–7

Competitive position of sales organization

Account opportunity level

1
Attractiveness: Accounts offer a good opportunity because they have high potential and the sales organization has a strong position.

Account management policy: Accounts should receive high level of sales calls and service to retain and possibly build accounts.

3
Attractiveness: Accounts may offer a good opportunity if the sales organization can overcome its weak position.

Account management policy: Emphasize a heavy sales organization position or shift resources to other accounts if a stronger sales organization position is impossible.

2
Attractiveness: Accounts are somewhat attractive because the sales organization has a strong position, but future opportunity is limited.

Account management policy: Accounts should receive moderate level of sales and service to maintain current position of sales organization.

4
Attractiveness: Accounts offer little opportunity, and the sales organization position is weak.

Account management policy: Consider replacing personal calls with telephone sales or direct mail to service accounts. Consider dropping account if unprofitable.

Account management policy grid.

Sales Plan Implementation: Putting the Plan into Action

The sales plan is put into practice through the tasks associated with sales plan implementation. Whereas sales plan formulation focuses on "doing the right things," implementation emphasizes "doing things right." The three major tasks involved in implementing a sales plan are (1) salesforce recruitment and selection, (2) salesforce training, and (3) salesforce motivation and compensation.

Salesforce Recruitment and Selection

Effective recruitment and selection of salespeople is one of the most crucial tasks of sales management. It entails finding people who match the type of sales position required by a firm. Recruitment and selection practices would differ greatly between order-taking and order-getting sales positions, given the differences in the demands of these two jobs. Therefore, recruitment and selection begin with a carefully crafted job analysis and job description followed by a statement of job qualifications.[25]

A *job analysis* is a study of a particular sales position, including how the job is to be performed and the tasks that make up the job. Information from a job analysis is used to write a *job description,* a written document that describes job relationships and requirements that characterize each sales position. It explains (1) to whom a salesperson reports, (2) how a salesperson interacts with other company personnel, (3) the customers to be called on, (4) the specific activities to be carried out, (5) the physical and mental demands of the job, and (6) the types of products and services to be sold. The job description is then translated into a statement of job qualifications, including the aptitudes, knowledge, skills, and a variety of behavioural characteristics considered necessary to perform the job successfully. Qualifications for order-getting sales positions often mirror the expectations of buyers: (1) imagination and problem-solving ability, (2) honesty, (3) intimate product knowledge, and (4) attentiveness reflected in responsiveness to buyer needs and customer loyalty and follow-up.[26] Firms use a variety of methods for evaluating prospective salespeople. Personal interviews, reference checks, and background information provided on application forms are the most frequently used methods.

Successful selling also requires a high degree of emotional intelligence. **Emotional intelligence** is the ability to understand one's own emotions and the emotions of people with whom one interacts on a daily basis. These qualities are important for adaptive selling and may spell the difference between effective and ineffective order-getting salespeople.[27] Are you interested in what your emotional intelligence might be? Read the accompanying Going Online box, "What Is Your Emotional Intelligence?" and test yourself.

GOING ONLINE

What Is Your Emotional Intelligence?

A person's success at work depends on many talents, including intelligence and technical skills. Recent research indicates that an individual's emotional intelligence is also important, if not more important! Emotional intelligence (E-IQ) has five dimensions: (1) self-motivation skills; (2) self-awareness, or knowing one's own emotions; (3) the ability to manage one's emotions and impulses; (4) empathy, or the ability to sense how others are feeling; and (5) social skills, or the ability to handle the emotions of other people.

What is your E-IQ? Visit the website **www.ihhp.com/free-eq-quiz**. Answer 17 questions to learn what your emotional intelligence is and obtain additional insights.

The search for qualified salespeople has produced an increasingly diverse salesforce in Canada. Women now represent half of all professional salespeople, and minority representation is growing.

Salesforce Training

Whereas recruitment and selection of salespeople is a one-time event, salesforce training is an ongoing process that affects both new and seasoned salespeople. Sales training covers much more than selling practices. For example, IBM Global Services salespeople, who sell consulting and various information technology services, take at least two weeks of in-class and web-based training on both consultative selling and the technical aspects of business.

On-the-job training is the most popular type of training, followed by individual instruction provided by experienced salespeople. Formal classes and seminars conducted by sales trainers and computer-based training are also popular.

Two areas with regard to salesforce training in Canada are training salespeople to respect and connect with female buyers, and training salespeople for their new roles in enterprise-wide customer relationship management (CRM). Evidence suggests that many Canadian companies are failing to do both.[28] For example, a study asked Canadian women to name a company that actually markets or sells well to women. Twenty-five percent of respondents could not come up with an answer. Moreover, respondents then went on to fail all 22 industries examined in the study based on their inability to satisfy women's needs. Women gave poor marks, for example, to the banking, investment, and insurance industries, citing the poor treatment they received because of their gender. Additionally, they ranked car dealers at 21 out of 22 industry categories in terms of meeting their needs as buyers.

Many experts are suggesting that Canadian companies should start focusing their efforts on training their salespeople to become more gender intelligent. Fortunately, some companies are heeding the call and are investing in gender intelligent salesforces. Toyota Canada created a sales process called Access, designed specifically to meet the needs of women consumers. All salespeople are trained to be gender sensitive and to understand and approach women in such a way as to ensure a satisfying car-shopping experience. According to Toyota Canada, Access has been a major success, and its women-friendly program has driven market share and customer satisfaction numbers. Finally, Rona has also seen close to a 40 percent annual compounded growth rate in revenue since it implemented gender-intelligent sales strategies.[29]

Salesforce Motivation and Compensation

A sales plan cannot be successfully implemented without motivated salespeople. Research on salesperson motivation suggests that (1) a clear job description, (2) effective sales management practices, (3) a personal need for achievement, and (4) proper compensation, incentives, or rewards will produce a motivated salesperson.[30]

The importance of compensation as a motivating factor means that close attention must be given to how salespeople are financially rewarded for their efforts. Salespeople are paid using one of three plans: (1) straight salary, (2) straight commission, or (3) a combination of salary and commission. Under a *straight salary compensation plan,* a salesperson is paid a fixed fee per week, month, or year. With a *straight commission compensation plan,* a salesperson's earnings are directly tied to the sales or profit generated. For example, an insurance agent might receive a 2 percent commission of $2,000 for selling a $100,000 life insurance policy. A *combination compensation plan* contains a specified salary plus a commission on sales or profit generated.

Each compensation plan has its advantages and disadvantages.[31] A straight salary plan is easy to administer and gives management a large measure of control over how salespeople allocate their efforts. However, it provides little incentive to expand sales volume. This plan is used when salespeople engage in many non-selling activities, such as account servicing. A straight commission plan provides the maximum amount of selling incentive but can detract salespeople from providing customer service. This plan is common when non-selling activities are minimal. Combination plans are most preferred by salespeople and attempt to build on the advantages of salary and commission plans while reducing the potential shortcomings of each. Today, a majority of companies use combination plans.

Non-monetary rewards are also given to salespeople for meeting or exceeding objectives. These rewards include trips, honours societies, distinguished salesperson awards, and letters of commendation. Some unconventional rewards include the new pink Cadillacs and jewellery given by Mary Kay Cosmetics to outstanding salespeople. Mary Kay, with 12,000 cars, has the largest fleet of General Motors cars in the world![32]

Mary Kay Cosmetics recognizes a top salesperson at its annual sales meeting.

Mary Kay Cosmetics, Inc. www.marykay.com

Courtesy Mary Kay, Inc.

Effective recruitment, selection, training, motivation, and compensation programs combine to create a productive salesforce. Ineffective practices often lead to costly salesforce turnover. The expense of replacing and training a new salesperson, including the cost of lost sales, can be high. Also, new recruits are often less productive than seasoned salespeople.[33]

Salesforce Evaluation: Measuring Results

The final function in the sales management process involves evaluating the salesforce. It is at this point that salespeople are assessed as to whether sales objectives were met and account management policies were followed. Both quantitative and behavioural measures are used to tap different selling dimensions.[34]

Quantitative Assessments

Quantitative assessments, called quotas, are based on input- and output-related objectives set forth in the sales plan. Input-related measures focus on the actual activities performed by salespeople, such as those involving sales calls, selling expenses, and account management policies. The number of sales calls made, selling expense related to sales made, and the number of reports submitted to superiors are frequently used input measures.

Output measures often appear in a sales quota. A **sales quota** contains specific goals assigned to a salesperson, sales team, branch sales office, or sales district for a stated time period. Dollar or unit sales volume, last year/current year sales ratio, sales of specific products, new accounts generated, and profit achieved are typical goals. The time period can range from one month to one year.

Behavioural Evaluation

Behavioural measures are also used to evaluate salespeople. These include assessments of a salesperson's attitude, attention to customers, product knowledge, selling and communication skills, appearance, and professional demeanour. Even though these assessments are sometimes subjective, they are frequently considered and, in fact, inevitable in salesperson evaluation. Moreover, these factors are often important determinants of quantitative outcomes.

Almost 60 percent of companies now include customer satisfaction as a behavioural measure of salesperson performance.[35] (What percentage did you check for question 3 in Figure 18–1?) IBM Canada has been the most aggressive in using this behavioural measure. Forty percent of an IBM salesperson's evaluation is linked to customer satisfaction; the remaining 60 percent is linked to profits achieved. Eastman Chemical Company surveys its customers with eight versions of its customer satisfaction questionnaire printed in nine languages. Some 25 performance items are studied, including on-time and correct delivery, product quality, pricing practice, and sharing of market information. The survey is managed by the salesforce, and salespeople review the results with customers. Eastman salespeople know that "the second most important thing they have to do is get their customer satisfaction surveys out to and back from customers," says Eastman's sales training director. "Number one, of course, is getting orders."

Increasingly, companies are using marketing dashboards to track salesperson performance for evaluation purposes. An illustration appears in the accompanying Using Marketing Dashboards box.

USING MARKETING DASHBOARDS

Tracking Salesperson Performance at Moore Chemical & Sanitation Supply, Inc.

Moore Chemical & Sanitation Supply, Inc. (MooreChem) is a large supplier of cleaning chemicals and sanitary products. MooreChem sells to janitorial companies that clean corporate and professional office buildings.

MooreChem recently installed a sales and account management planning software package that included a dashboard for each of its sales representatives. Salespeople had access to their dashboards as well. These dashboards included seven measures—sales revenue, gross margin, selling expense, profit, average order size, new customers, and customer satisfaction. Each measure was gauged to show actual salesperson performance relative to target goals.

Your Challenge As a newly promoted district sales manager at MooreChem, your responsibilities include tracking each salesperson's performance in your district. You are also responsible for directing the sales activities and practices of district salespeople.

In anticipation of a performance review with one of your salespeople, Brady Boyle, you review his dashboard for the previous quarter. Provide a constructive review of his performance.

Your Findings Brady Boyle's quarterly performance is displayed below. Boyle has exceeded targeted goals for sales revenue, selling expenses, and customer satisfaction. All of these measures show an upward trend. He has met his target for gaining new customers and average order size. But Boyle's gross margin and profit are below targeted goals. These measures evidence a downward trend as well. Brady Boyle's mixed performance requires a constructive and positive correction.

Your Action Brady Boyle should already know how his performance compares with targeted goals. Remember, Boyle has access to his dashboard. Recall that he has exceeded his sales target, but is considerably under his profit target. Boyle's sales trend is up, but his profit trend is down.

You will need to focus attention on Boyle's gross margin and selling expense results and trend. Boyle, it seems, is spending time and money selling lower margin products that produce a targeted average order size. It may very well be that Boyle is actually expending effort selling more products to his customers. Unfortunately, the product mix yields lower gross margins, resulting in a lower profit.

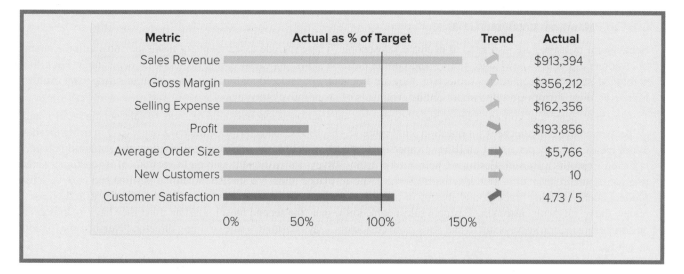

Salesforce Automation and Customer Relationship Management

Personal selling and sales management are undergoing a technological revolution with the integration of salesforce automation and customer relationship management processes. In fact, the emergence of information and communication technologies (ICTs) has transformed the sales function in many companies and made the promise of customer relationship management a reality. **Salesforce automation (SFA)** is the use of technology to make the sales function more effective and efficient. SFA applies to a wide range of activities, including each stage in the personal selling process and management of the salesforce itself.

Salesforce automation exists in many forms. Examples of SFA applications include computer hardware and software for account analysis, lead management, contact management, time management, territory management, order processing and follow-up, sales presentations, proposal generation, and product and sales training. Each application is designed to ease administrative tasks and free up time for salespeople to be with customers building relationships and providing service.

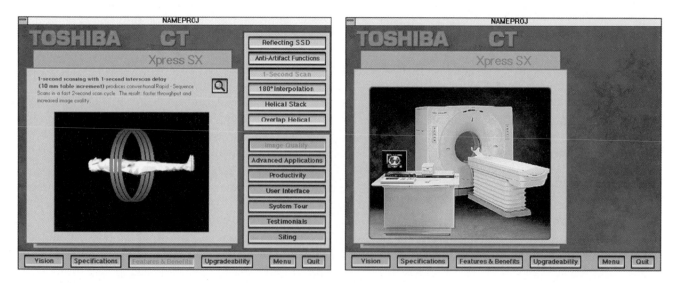

Toshiba America Medical Systems salespeople have found computer technology to be an effective sales presentation tool and training device.

Toshiba America Medical Systems www.toshiba.com

Courtesy of Toshiba Medical Systems & Interactive Media.

Salesforce Technology

Technology has become an integral part of field selling. Today, most companies supply their field salespeople with laptop or notebook computers as well as smartphones and tablets. For example, salespeople for Godiva Chocolates use their laptop computers to process orders, plan time allocations, forecast sales, and communicate with other Godiva personnel and with customers. While in a department store candy buyer's office, a salesperson can calculate the order cost, transmit the order, and obtain a delivery date within a few minutes from Godiva's order processing department.[36]

Toshiba America Medical System salespeople use laptop computers with built-in DVD capabilities to provide interactive presentations for their computerized tomography (CT) and magnetic resonance imaging (MRI) scanners. In it, the customer sees elaborate three-dimensional animations, high-resolution scans, and video clips of the company's products in operation as well as narrated testimonials from satisfied customers. Toshiba has found this application to be effective both for sales presentations and for training its salespeople.[37]

Salesforce Communication

Technology has changed the way salespeople communicate with customers, other salespeople and sales support personnel, and management. Electronic mail, text messaging, and voice mail are common communication technologies used by salespeople today. In particular, tablet device technology and robust smartphones now allow salespeople to exchange data, text, and voice transmissions in an instant. Whether travelling or in a customer's office, this type of technology provides information at the salesperson's fingertips to answer customer questions and solve problems.

Advances in communication and computer technologies have made possible the mobile and home sales office. Some salespeople now equip minivans with a fully functional desk, swivel chair, light, computer, printer, fax machine, smartphone, and satellite dish. Other sales representatives, like those at Symetra Financial, for example, use their BlackBerry smartphones to look up customers' addresses and to retrieve notes on past visits. They can even get maps and directions from MapQuest so that they don't get lost! After they visit with the customer, they enter information on the visit into the customer files stored on the device as well as into the company's database.[38] At EDS, a professional services firm, salespeople access its intranet to download client material, marketing content, account information, technical papers, and competitive profiles. In addition, EDS offers 7,000 training classes that salespeople can take anytime and anywhere.

Home offices are now common. Hewlett-Packard is a case in point. The company shifted its salesforce into home offices, closed several regional sales offices, and saved millions of dollars in staff salaries and office rent. A fully equipped home office for each salesperson includes a notebook computer, fax/copier, smartphone, VOIP (voice over Internet protocol) phones, and office furniture.

Salesforce automation is clearly changing how selling is done and how salespeople are managed. Its numerous applications promise to boost selling productivity, improve customer relationships, and decrease selling cost. But importantly, along with this technology is the realization that all organizations must empower their salesforces to use the technology wisely and ethically in order to build long-term profitable relationships with the customers. It is also apparent that in this new era of customer experience management, organizations must recognize that the experience the customer has with a salesperson might be the greatest opportunity to win or lose customers, and therefore, organizational support for the salespeople must be a major priority.[39] Finally, the emergence of social media is having and will continue to have an impact on the selling function. In fact, successful salespeople are now utilizing a variety of social media platforms including LinkedIn, Facebook, and Twitter not only to prospect but also to build and sustain relationships with customers. For a look at how social media can be used as a sales tool, read the accompanying Marketing Matters box, "How to Use Twitter as a Sales Tool."[40]

MARKETING MATTERS

How to Use Twitter as a Sales Tool

Most people think of Twitter as a tool to socialize and connect with others all over the world. However, a growing number of businesses realize the great potential Twitter has as a sales tool. Some experts provide the following guidance as to how to best utilize Twitter to boost sales:

1. *Complete a profile and Twitter page.* The first thing sales companies or reps should do on Twitter is complete their profile and customize their account. Creating a custom background that contains the company phone number, website, and other contact information is a great way to display the information that isn't in the profile.

2. *Find prospects and leads with search filters.* People are very quick to express their gripes, needs, and concerns on Twitter. If someone has a problem, they tweet about it. There are tools available to help search for tweets containing certain keywords in real time. One of the most popular tools for this is HootSuite. When used in conjunction with a CRM management tool, social media management becomes much easier.

3. *Follow industry leaders.* Staying up to date on industry news and events is extremely important in sales. Sales reps that are "in the know" have a leg up on the competition because they are aware of the current trends of the industry. By following reporters, news sites, and other related users in your field, you are able to get the news first.

4. *Tweet helpful information regularly.* One of the biggest mistakes sales reps make on Twitter is using it as an advertising platform. People on Twitter do not want to be sold to. Twitter is used to get news, to be entertained, and to connect with others. In order to gain recognition from future clients, reps should tweet links to free resources, helpful tips, and company news. If a tweet contains an informative link, is entertaining, or creates conversation, there is a much higher chance of the tweet being retweeted and replied to.

5. *Utilize hashtags.* Hashtags can be great for finding like-minded people who have similar interests. Hashtags are meant to be shared. By finding industry-related hashtags, reps are able to access large groups of people with the same needs. Hashtags can also be used by sales reps in order to entice others to retweet or to gain followers. If the hashtag starts trending, it can be a huge PR boost for the company.

6. *Be personal.* Even the most affluent and professional companies on Twitter realize the importance of being personable. It is possible to be less formal and still maintain a certain level of professionalism. Tweeting technical jargon and speaking generically gives the impression that a robot is handling the Twitter account. Twitter has a fun atmosphere and people like the ability to interact casually. With sales, people buy into the salesperson before they buy the product or service. Twitter allows people to see a bit of the salesperson's personality.

7. *Capitalize on the public nature of Twitter.* When a tweet is sent to a user using the "@" symbol, all of the user's followers will be able to see that tweet. This is an excellent way to share white papers and other free resources with the public. If the user's followers see the tweet sent to them, they will naturally be interested in the free resource as well, and this can create a chain reaction.

Learning Review

8. What are the three types of selling objectives?
9. What three factors are used to structure sales organizations?
10. How does emotional intelligence tie to adaptive selling?

Learning Objectives Review

LO1   **Discuss the nature and scope of personal selling and sales management in marketing.**

Personal selling involves the two-way flow of communication between a buyer and seller, often in a face-to-face encounter, designed to influence a person's or group's purchase decision. Sales management involves planning the selling program and implementing and controlling the personal selling effort of the firm. The scope of selling and sales management is apparent in three ways. First, virtually every occupation that involves customer contact has an element of personal selling. Second, selling plays a significant role in a company's overall marketing effort. Salespeople occupy a boundary position between buyers and sellers; they *are* the company to many buyers and account for a major cost of marketing in a variety of industries; and they can create value for customers. Finally, through relationship and partnership selling, salespeople play a central role in tailoring solutions to customer problems as a means to customer value creation.

LO2   **Identify the different types of personal selling.**

Three types of personal selling exist: (*a*) order taking, (*b*) order getting, and (*c*) customer sales support activities. Each type differs from the others in terms of actual selling done and the amount of creativity required to perform the sales task. Order takers process routine orders or reorders for products that were already sold by the company. They generally do little selling in a conventional sense and engage in only modest problem solving with customers. Order getters sell in a conventional sense and identify prospective customers, provide customers with information, persuade customers to buy, close sales, and follow up on customers' use of a product or service. Order getting involves a high degree of creativity and customer empathy and is typically required for selling complex or technical products with many options. Customer sales support personnel augment the sales effort of order getters by performing a variety of services. Sales support personnel are prominent in cross-functional team selling, the practice of using an entire team of professionals in selling to and servicing major customers.

LO3   **Explain the stages in the personal selling process.**

The personal selling process consists of six stages: (*a*) prospecting, (*b*) preapproach, (*c*) approach, (*d*) presentation, (*e*) close, and (*f*) follow-up. Prospecting involves the search for and qualification of potential customers. The preapproach stage involves obtaining further information on the prospect and deciding on the best method of approach. The approach stage involves the initial meeting between the salesperson and prospect. The presentation stage involves converting a prospect into a customer by creating a desire for the product or service. The close involves obtaining a purchase commitment from the prospect. The follow-up stage involves making certain that the customer's purchase has been properly delivered and installed and difficulties experienced with the use of the item are addressed.

LO4   **Describe the major functions of sales management.**

Sales management consists of three interrelated functions: (*a*) sales plan formulation, (*b*) sales plan implementation, and (*c*) evaluation and control of the salesforce. Sales plan formulation involves setting objectives, organizing the salesforce, and developing account management policies. Sales plan implementation involves salesforce recruitment, selection, training, motivation, and compensation. Finally, evaluation and control of the salesforce focuses on quantitative assessments of sales performance and behavioural measures, such as customer satisfaction, that are linked to selling objectives and account management policies.

Applying Marketing Knowledge

1. Jane Dawson is a new sales representative for the Charles Schwab brokerage firm. In searching for clients, Jane purchased a mailing list of subscribers to the *Financial Post* and called them all regarding their interest in discount brokerage services. She asked if they had any stocks and if they had a regular broker. Those people without a regular broker were asked about their investment needs. Two days later, Jane called back with investment advice and asked if they would like to open an account. Identify each of Jane Dawson's actions in terms of the personal selling process.

2. For the first 50 years of business, the Johnson Carpet Company produced carpets for residential use. The salesforce was structured geographically. In the past five years, a large percentage of carpet sales has been to industrial users, hospitals, schools, and architects. The company also has broadened its product line to include area rugs, Oriental carpets, and wall-to-wall carpeting. Is the present salesforce structure appropriate, or would you recommend an alternative?

3. Where would you place each of the following sales jobs on the order taker/order getter continuum shown below: (*a*) Tim Hortons counter clerk, (*b*) automobile insurance salesperson, (*c*) IBM salesperson, (*d*) life insurance salesperson, and (*e*) shoe salesperson?

4. Listed here are two different firms. Which compensation plan would you recommend for each firm, and what reasons would you give for your recommendations: (*a*) A newly formed company that sells lawn care equipment on a door-to-door basis directly to consumers; and (*b*) the Nabisco Company, which sells heavily advertised products in supermarkets by having the salesforce call on these stores and arrange shelves, set up displays, and make presentations to store buying committees?

5. The TDK company services 1,000 electronic stores throughout the country. Each store is called on 12 times a year, and the average sales call lasts 30 minutes. Assuming a salesperson works 40 hours a week, 50 weeks a year, and devotes 75 percent of the time to actual selling, how many salespeople does TDK need?

6. A furniture manufacturer is currently using manufacturer's representatives to sell its line of living room furniture. These representatives receive a 4 percent commission. The company is considering hiring its own salespeople and has estimated that the fixed cost of managing and paying their salaries would be $1 million annually. The salespeople would also receive a 4 percent commission on sales. The company has saless of $25 million dollars, and sales are expected to grow by 15 percent next year. Would you recommend that the company switch to its own salesforce? Why or why not?

7. Suppose someone said to you, "The only real measure of a salesperson is the amount of sales produced." How might you respond?

Building Your Marketing Plan

Does your marketing plan involve a personal selling activity? If the answer is no, read no further and do not include a personal selling element in your plan. If the answer is yes:

1. Identify likely prospects for your product or service.

2. Determine what information you should obtain about the prospect.

3. Describe how you would approach the prospect.

4. Outline the presentation you would make to the prospect for your product or service.

5. Develop a sales plan, focusing on the organizational structure you would use for your salesforce (geography, product, or customer).

Xerox: Building Customer Relationships Through Personal Selling

"I'm like the quarterback of the team. I manage 250 accounts, and anything from billing issues, to service issues, to selling the products. I'm really the face to the customer," says Alison Capossela, a Washington, D.C.–based Xerox sales representative.

As the primary company contact for Xerox customers, Alison is responsible for developing and maintaining customer relationships. To accomplish this, she uses a sophisticated selling process that requires many activities, from making presentations, to attending training sessions, to managing a team of Xerox personnel, to monitoring competitors' activities. The face-to-face interactions with customers, however, are the most rewarding for Capossela. "It's an amazing feeling; the more they challenge me, the more I fight back. It's fun!" she explains.

The Company

Xerox Corporation's mission is to "help people find better ways to do great work by constantly leading in document technologies, products, and services that improve customers' work processes and business results." To accomplish this mission Xerox employs 130,000 people in 160 countries. Xerox is the world's leading document management enterprise and a Fortune 500 company.

Xerox offers a wide range of products and services. These include printers, copiers and fax machines, multifunction and network devices, high-speed color presses, digital imaging and archiving products and services, and supplies such as toner, paper, and ink. The entire company is guided by customer-focused and employee-centred core values (e.g., "We succeed through satisfied customers") and a passion for innovation, speed, and adaptability.

The Selling Process at Xerox

In 2001, Xerox began a shift to a consultative selling model that focused on helping customers solve their business problems rather than just placing more equipment in their office. The shift meant that sales reps needed to be less product-oriented and more relationship-and value-oriented. Xerox wanted to be a provider of total solutions. Today, Xerox has more than 8,000 sales professionals throughout the world who spend a large amount of their day developing customer relationships Capossela explains: "Fifty percent of my day is spent with my customers, 25 percent is following up with phone calls or e-mails, and another 25 percent involves preparing proposals." The approach has helped Xerox attract new customers and keep existing customers.

The sales process at Xerox typically follows the six stages of the personal selling process identified in Figure 18–3: (1) Xerox identifies potential clients through responses to advertising, referrals, and telephone calls; (2) the salesforce prepares for a presentation by familiarizing themselves with the potential client and its document needs; (3) a Xerox sales representative approaches the prospect and suggests a meeting and presentation; (4) as the presentation begins, the salesperson summarizes relevant information about potential solutions Xerox can offer, states what he or she hopes to get out of the meeting, explains how the products and services work, and reinforces the benefits of working with Xerox; (5) the salesperson engages in an action close (gets a signed document or a firm confirmation of the sale); and then (6) continues to meet and communicate with the client to provide assistance and monitor the effectiveness of the installed solution.

19

Pulling It All Together: The Strategic Marketing Process

Strategic Marketing Helps General Mills Adapt to New Tastes!

Consumer tastes are changing and so are consumer expectations for new products. This is particularly true in the supermarket where consumers are increasingly demanding convenient, healthy, and good-tasting food. At consumer foods manufacturer General Mills, that means Vivian Milroy Callaway faces exciting challenges as she helps the company adapt to the changes.

As vice president of the Center for Learning and Experimentation at General Mills, Callaway is responsible for helping uncover and introduce new-product ideas for the company. The strategic marketing process—planning, implementation, and evaluation—is essential to her job and recently played an important role in the development of a new dessert concept called Warm Delights.

To start the process, Callaway did not look at the new dessert concept alone—but in relation to all the other sweet treats people were eating. "One of my challenges," she says, "is that consumers often say one thing in marketing research studies and then do something else when facing a supermarket shelf." To overcome this problem, Callaway and her team ran marketing experiments that involved putting a prototype dessert in a store, measuring the results, improving the prototype, and then repeating the process.

The research helped better understand many aspects of the product that were important to consumers. For example, the research revealed that extending the black microwaveable bowl outside the edges of the Warm Delights package would better communicate its cooking convenience to prospective buyers. So the unique packaging with the bowl edges exposed was adopted. After many additional experiments, the result was a successful nationwide launch of Warm Delights microwaveable desserts, followed quickly by a product line extension, Warm Delights Minis. Growth of both products suggests that the process provided a good match with consumer tastes.

General Mills

Planning for Even More Changes

General Mills' retail sales in the U.S. and Canada now exceed $10 billion from several divisions, including baking products, snacks, frozen foods, yogurt, and cereal. While consumer tastes in each category are changing, a quick environmental scan of the largest division—cereal—shows how important a good strategic marketing process is for the company. Consider the following:

- *Expense.* The launch of a new cereal typically costs up to $30 million and usually involves replacing one of more than 300 competing breakfast cereals already sitting on retailers' shelves.

- *Success rate.* Only one out of four brands "succeeds," which is defined as maintaining distribution for three to four years in the $10 billion-a-year U.S. and Canadian ready-to-eat (RTE) cereal market. Adding to the challenge: Retail food industry sales did not grow while costs increased.

- *Market trends.* The lack of growth in the RTE cereal market is being caused by several factors, including (1) consumers are moving away from products with too much sugar, genetically modified ingredients, or artificial food dyes, and toward products perceived as healthy or labelled organic; and (2) consumers are avoiding higher shelf prices, which are the result of rising costs.

Creative Initiatives at General Mills

General Mills introduces more than 300 new food products each year in response to consumers' changing tastes. In fact, the company website emphasizes the perspective that drives the company to continually offer what consumers are asking for: "We serve the world by making food people love." In light of these consumer trends and the intense competition it faces in the consumer foods industry, General Mills is offering a variety of new products, among them:

- Fibre 1 snack bars
- Chex gluten-free mix
- Nature Valley Protein granola
- Trix with four colours (instead of six, to eliminate artificial colours and flavours)

The success or failure of these and other products is related to the planning, implementation, and evaluation phases of the strategic marketing process General Mills uses.[1]

This chapter elaborates on some of the issues and techniques presented in Chapter 2 and introduces additional tools and strategies to help marketing, product, and brand managers succeed in the ever-changing, competitive marketplace. Marketing strategies now emerging at General Mills and other firms provide examples.

MARKETING BASICS: DOING WHAT WORKS AND ALLOCATING RESOURCES

As noted in Chapter 2, corporate and marketing executives search continuously to find a competitive advantage—a unique strength relative to what competitors are doing now and are likely to do in the future.[2] Having identified this competitive advantage, they must figure out how to exploit it.[3] This involves (1) finding and using what works for their organization and industry given both the organizational situation and industry situation, and (2) allocating resources effectively to exploit those situations. However, research suggests most organizations are not doing a good job when it comes to strategy formulation and implementation.[4] So, next we will discuss finding and using what really works as opposed to what does not work.

Finding and Using What Really Works

In a five-year study, researchers conducted in-depth analysis of 160 companies and more than 200 management tools and techniques, such as supply chain management, customer relationship management (CRM), and the use of information and communications technologies. The result? Individual management tools and techniques had no direct relationship to superior business performance.[5]

What did matter? The researchers concluded that what matters are four basic business and management practices—"what really works," to use a phrase. These are (1) strategy, (2) execution, (3) culture, and (4) structure. Firms with excellence in all four of these areas are likely to achieve superior business performance. And in terms of individual tools and techniques, the researchers concluded that the firm's choice of a tool or technique is less important than the flawless execution of it.

Industry leaders such as Home Depot do all four of the basic practices extremely well, not just two or three,

Costco achieves excellence in what really matters.

and are vigilant about continuing to do them well when conditions change. In contrast, Lululemon, BlackBerry, and Groupon are struggling today to get these basics right and regain their past success. Let's look at companies that stand out today in each of the four key business practices:

- *Strategy: Devise and maintain a clearly stated, focused strategy.* Walmart may be the unstoppable force in mass-merchandise retailing, but among warehouse clubs, its Sam's Club is not. The winner, to date, is Costco, with 60 percent as many stores as Sam's Club but almost twice the sales revenue. A key reason is Costco's focused strategy based on the knowledge that, of all retail channels, warehouse clubs attract the largest proportion of affluent shoppers. Costco's strategy: sell a limited selection of branded high-end merchandise at low prices.[6]

- *Execution: Develop and maintain flawless operational execution.* Toyota is generally acknowledged as the best in the world in revolutionizing auto manufacturing. It created the doctrine of *kaizen*, or continuous improvement, which is now used throughout the auto industry. Toyota has also launched a new program called "bundled development," which allows suppliers to develop parts three or four years in advance, independent of a vehicle's design, to create "better performance, easier manufacturing, and higher quality."[7]

- *Culture: Develop and maintain a performance-oriented culture.* Several high-performing companies point to their culture as central to their success. Janssen-Ortho, for example, promotes leadership development and innovation teams as part of its organizational culture. Flight Centre keeps its organization performing well by promoting from within, thus motivating its employees and perpetuating its winning culture. Spin Master Toys promotes a fun and positive environment that keeps its company humming along, while Dofasco leverages employee profit-sharing to promote a performance-oriented culture. Finally, for the sixth time in seven years, Google was recently ranked number 1 on Fortune's list of the 100 Best Companies to Work For. Its culture is based on several key principles including: "Focus on the user and all else will follow," "You can make money without doing evil," and "Great just isn't good enough." The performance result? High employee job satisfaction, 17 percent growth in sales, and 11 percent growth in profits.[8]

- *Structure: Build and maintain a fast, flexible, flat organization.* Successful small organizations often grow into bureaucratic large ones with layers of managers and red tape that slow down the decision-making process. High-performing firms, on the other hand, empower their employees to make decisions and provide an environment where internal communications are encouraged, as is active problem-solving, all within simple and flat organizational structures. The unquestioned all-time leader in delivering world-class aircraft with only a small team of engineers, designers, and machinists: Lockheed Martin's Skunk Works. Discussed later in the chapter, its first director set key organizational guidelines, like "use a small number of good people who can talk to anyone in the organization to solve a problem."[9]

Of course, in practice, a firm cannot allocate unlimited resources to achieving each of these business basics. It must make choices on where its resources can give the greatest return, the topic of the next section.

LO1 Allocating Marketing Resources Using Sales Response Functions

A **sales response function** relates the expense of the marketing effort to the marketing results obtained.[10] For simplicity, in the examples that follow, only the effects of the annual marketing effort on annual sales revenue will be analyzed, but the concept applies to other measures of marketing success—such as profit, units sold, or level of awareness—as well.

Maximizing Incremental Revenue Minus Incremental Cost

Economists give managers a specific guideline for optimal resource allocation: allocate the firm's marketing, production, and financial resources to the markets and products where the excess of incremental revenues over incremental costs is greatest.

Figure 19–1 illustrates the resource allocation principle that is inherent in the sales response function. The firm's annual marketing effort, such as sales and advertising expenses, is plotted on the horizontal axis. As the annual marketing effort increases, so does the resulting annual sales revenue, which is plotted on the vertical axis. The relationship is assumed to be S-shaped, showing that an additional $1 million of marketing effort, from $3 million to $4 million, results in far greater increases of sales revenue in the midrange ($20 million) of the curve than at either end (an increase from $2 million to $3 million in spending yields an increase of $10 million in sales; an increase from $6 million to $7 million in spending leads to an increase of $5 million in sales).

A Numerical Example of Resource Allocation

Suppose that Figure 19–1 shows the situation for a new General Mills product called Cheerios + Ancient Grains, the first mainstream cereal featuring Kamut, spelt, and quinoa grains. It is targeted at health-conscious consumers who want a great-tasting cereal. Cheerios + Ancient Grains is an extension of Cheerios, a top-selling cereal brand.[11]

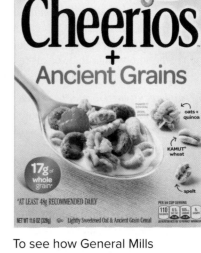

Also assume that the sales response function does not change through time as a result of changing consumer tastes and incomes. Point A shows the position of the firm in year 1, whereas Point B shows it three years later in year 4. Suppose General Mills decides to launch new advertising and sales promotions that, say, increase its marketing effort for the brand from $3 million to $6 million a year. If the relationship in Figure 19–1 holds true and is a good picture of consumer purchasing behaviour, the sales revenues of Cheerios + Ancient Grains should increase from $30 million to $70 million a year.

Let us look at the major resource allocation question: What are the probable increases in sales revenue for Cheerios + Ancient Grains in year 1 and year 4 if General Mills were to spend an additional $1 million in marketing effort? As Figure 19–1 reveals:

Year 1

Increase in marketing effort from $3 million to $4 million = $1 million

Increase in sales revenue from $30 million to $50 million = $20 million

Ratio of incremental sales revenue to effort = $20,000,000:$1,000,000 = 20:1

Year 4

Increase in marketing effort from $6 million to $7 million = $1 million

Increase in sales revenue from $70 million to $73 million = $3 million

Ratio of incremental sales revenue to effort = $3,000,000:$1,000,000 = 3:1

To see how General Mills allocated resources to its Cheerios + Ancient Grains cereal, read the text.

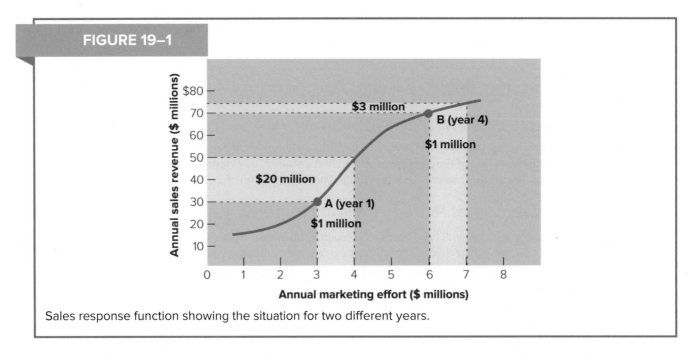

FIGURE 19–1

Sales response function showing the situation for two different years.

Thus, in year 1, a dollar of extra marketing effort returned $20 in sales revenue, whereas in year 4, it returned only $3. If no other expenses are incurred, it might make sense to spend $1 million in year 4 to gain $3 million in incremental sales revenue. However, it may be far wiser for General Mills to invest the money in products in one of its other business units, such as its Warm Delights microwaveable desserts. The essence of resource allocation is simple: put incremental resources where the incremental returns are greatest over the foreseeable future. For General Mills, this means that it must allocate its available resources (talent and dollars) more efficiently when developing its broad portfolio of products and brands and creating the marketing actions required to reach their respective target market segments. Professors Clayton Christensen and Derek van Bever have observed, however, that since the recession of 2008, some companies have preferred to retain capital rather than invest in new products—a circumstance they call the *capitalist's dilemma*.[12]

Allocating Marketing Resources in Practice

General Mills, like many firms in these businesses, does extensive analysis using **share points**, or percentage points of market share, as the common basis of comparison to allocate marketing resources effectively for different product lines within the same firm. This allows it to seek answers to the question, "How much is it worth to us to try to increase our market share by another 1 (or 2, or 5, or 10) percentage point?"

This analysis enables higher-level managers to make resource allocation trade-offs among different kinds of business units owned by the company. To make these resource allocation decisions, marketing managers must estimate (1) the market share for the product, (2) the revenues associated with each point of market share (a share point in breakfast cereals may be five times what it is in cake mixes), (3) the contribution to overhead and profit (or gross margin) of each share point, and (4) possible cannibalization effects on other products in the line (for example, new Cheerios + Ancient Grains might reduce the sales of regular Cheerios). Fortunately, in the case of Cheerios + Ancient Grains, the brand was a success for General Mills.[13]

Resource Allocation and the Strategic Marketing Process

Company resources are allocated effectively in the strategic marketing process by converting marketing information into marketing actions. Figure 19–2 summarizes the strategic marketing process introduced in Chapter 2, along with some details of the marketing actions and information that comprise it. Figure 19–2 is really a simplification of the actual strategic marketing process: While the three phases of the strategic marketing process have distinct separations in the figure and the marketing actions are separated from the marketing information, in practice, these blend together and interact.

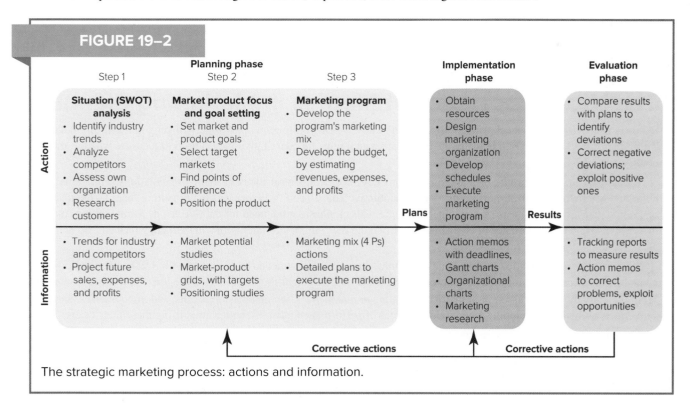

FIGURE 19–2

The strategic marketing process: actions and information.

PHASE	OUTPUT REPORT
Planning	Marketing plans (or programs) that define goals and the marketing mix strategies to achieve them
Implementation	Results (memos or computer outputs) that describe the outcomes of implementing the plans
Evaluation	Corrective action memos, triggered by comparing results with goals, often using the firm's marketing metrics and dashboards

The upper half of each box in Figure 19–2 highlights the actions involved in that part of the strategic marketing process and the lower half summarizes the information and reports used. Note that each phase has an output report.

The corrective action memos become feedback loops in Figure 19–2 that help improve decisions and actions in the earlier phases of the strategic marketing process.

Learning Review

1. What is the significance of the S-shape of the sales response function in Figure 19–1?

2. What are the main output reports from each phase of the strategic marketing process?

THE PLANNING PHASE OF THE STRATEGIC MARKETING PROCESS

Four aspects of the strategic marketing process deserve special mention: (1) the vital importance of metrics in marketing planning, (2) the varieties of marketing plans, (3) marketing planning frameworks that have proven useful, and (4) some marketing planning and strategy lessons.

The Vital Importance of Metrics in Marketing Planning

Planners have a tongue-in-cheek truism: "If you don't know where you're going, any road will get you there." In making marketing plans, the "road" chosen is really the quantitative goal plus the quantitative metric used to measure whether the goal is being achieved.

Today, measuring the results of marketing actions has become a central focus in many organizations. This boils down to defining "where the organization is going"—the quantitative goals—and "whether it is really getting there"—the quantitative marketing metrics used to measure actual performance. This emphasizes the need for data-driven decision making (mentioned in Chapter 2) and the importance of choosing and displaying the right marketing metrics in marketing dashboards so that managers can quickly view the results.

Most firms stress innovation to help achieve growth. Marketing departments work closely with R&D and operations departments to complete successful innovation projects. So what metrics might they use to measure their innovation performance? Well, typically most firms use several metrics, including *output metrics*, which measure results, and *input metrics*, which measure efforts going into developing new products. Areas of performance most often measured using these metrics are:

- Revenue growth due to new products or services and customer satisfaction with new products or services (output metrics).
- Number of ideas or concepts in the new-product pipeline and R&D spending as a percentage of sales (input metrics).

A careful look at these innovation metrics reveals that it is generally far easier to measure marketing inputs than marketing outputs. For example, measuring "the number of ideas or concepts in the new-product pipeline" (an input) is far easier than measuring "customer satisfaction with new products or services" (an output). But the evaluation phase of the strategic marketing process seeks to compare actual results—an output metric—with the goals set. So where possible, marketing managers prefer to use effective output metrics if they are available.

The Variety of Marketing Plans

The planning phase of the strategic marketing process usually results in a marketing plan that sets the direction for the marketing activities of an organization. As noted earlier in Appendix A (following Chapter 2), a marketing plan is the heart of a business plan. Like business plans, marketing plans are not all from the same mould; they vary with the length of the planning period, the purpose, and the audience. Let us look briefly at two kinds: long-range plans and annual marketing plans.

Long-Range Marketing Plans

Typically, long-range marketing plans cover marketing activities from two to five years into the future. Except for firms in such industries as autos, steel, or forest products, marketing plans rarely go beyond five years into the future because the tremendous number of uncertainties present make the benefits of planning less than the effort expended. Such plans are often directed at top-level executives and the board of directors.

Annual Marketing Plans

Usually developed by a marketing or product manager (discussed later in the chapter) in a consumer products firm, such as General Mills, annual marketing plans deal with marketing goals and strategies for a product, product line, or entire firm for a single year. Typical steps that such firms as Kellogg's, Coca-Cola, and Johnson & Johnson take in developing their annual marketing plans for their existing

FIGURE 19–3

	Weeks before approval of plan
Steps in annual marketing planning process	50 40 30 20 10 0
1. Obtain up-to-date marketing information from marketing research study of product users.	
2. Brainstorm alternatives to consider in next year's plan with marketing research and ad agency.	
3. Meet with internal media specialists to set long-run guidelines in purchase of media.	
4. Obtain sales and profit results from last fiscal year, which ended 16 weeks earlier.	
5. Identify key issues to address by talks with marketing researchers, ad agency, and so on.	
6. Hold key issues meeting with marketing director; form task force of line managers, if needed.	
7. Write and circulate key issues memo; initiate necessary marketing research to reduce uncertainty.	
8. Review marketing mix elements and competitors' behaviour with key managers, marketing director.	
9. Draft marketing plan, review with marketing director, and revise, as necessary.	
10. Present plan to marketing director, task force, key line departments; make necessary changes.	
11. Present marketing plan to division general manager for approval, 10 weeks before start of fiscal year.	

KEY: ◣ Planned period of work   ▲ Planned completion date

Steps that a large consumer packaged-goods firm takes in developing its annual marketing plan.

Source: Stasch, S. F., & Lanktree, P. (1980). Can Your Marketing Planning Procedures be Improved? *Journal of Marketing*, 44(3), p. 82. pp. 79–90. Reprinted with permission from Journal of Marketing, published by the American Marketing Association.

products are shown in Figure 19–3.[14] This annual planning cycle typically starts with a detailed marketing research study of current users and ends after 48 weeks, with the approval of the plan by the division general manager—10 weeks before the fiscal year starts. Between these points, there are continuing efforts to uncover new ideas through brainstorming and key-issues sessions with specialists both inside and outside the firm. The plan is fine-tuned through a series of often-excruciating reviews by several levels of management, which leaves few surprises and very little to chance.

Marketing Planning Frameworks: The Search for Growth

Marketing planning for a firm with many products competing in many markets—a multiproduct, multimarket firm—is a complex process. Three techniques that are useful in helping corporate and marketing executives in such a firm make important resource allocation decisions are (1) Porter's generic business strategies, (2) profit enhancement options, and (3) market–product synergies. All of these techniques are based on elements introduced in earlier chapters.

Porter's Generic Business Strategies

As shown in Figure 19–4, Michael E. Porter has developed a framework in which he identifies four basic, or "generic," strategies.[15] A **generic business strategy** is one that can be adopted by any firm, regardless of the product or industry involved, to achieve a competitive advantage.

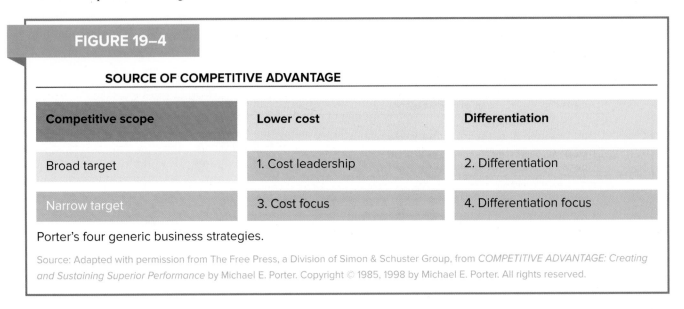

FIGURE 19–4

Porter's four generic business strategies.

Although all of the techniques discussed here involve generic strategies, the phrase is most often associated with Porter's framework. In this framework, the columns identify the two fundamental alternatives firms can use in seeking competitive advantage: (1) becoming the low-cost producer within the markets in which it competes, or (2) differentiating itself from competitors through developing points of difference in its product offerings or marketing programs. In contrast, the rows identify the competitive scope: (1) a broad target by competing in many market segments, or (2) a narrow target by competing in only a few segments or even a single segment. The columns and rows result in four generic business strategies, any one of which can provide a competitive advantage among similar business units in the same industry:

1. A **cost leadership strategy** (cell 1) focuses on reducing expenses and lowering product prices while targeting a broad array of market segments. One way is by securing raw materials from a lower-cost supplier. Also, significant investments in capital equipment may be necessary to improve the production or distribution process and achieve these lower unit costs. The cost leader still must have adequate quality levels. Ikea's sophisticated systems of regional warehouses and electronic data interchange with its suppliers have led to huge cost savings, and its cost leadership strategy results in lower prices for customers.

2. A **differentiation strategy** (cell 2) requires products to have significant points of difference in product offerings, brand image, higher quality, advanced technology, or superior service to charge a higher price while targeting a broad array of market segments. This allows the firm to charge a price premium. For example, Canada Goose has become the world's best brand when it comes to outerwear—it really works in extreme weather and customers love the brand. The Marketing Matters box, "Canada Goose's Differentiation Strategy Is Working," discusses how the company achieved its success leveraging a differentiation strategy.[16]

3. A **cost focus strategy** (cell 3) involves controlling expenses and, in turn, lowering product prices, targeting a narrow range of market segments. Retail chains targeting only a few market segments in a restricted group of products often use a cost focus strategy successfully. IKEA has become the world's largest furniture retailer by selling flat-pack, self-assembly furniture, accessories, and bathroom and kitchen items to cost-conscious consumers.

Which of Porter's generic strategies is Ikea using? For the answer and a discussion of the strategies, see the text.

IKEA.

4. A **differentiation focus strategy** (cell 4) requires products to have significant points of difference to target one or only a few market segments. Volkswagen has achieved spectacular success by targeting the "nostalgia segment," 35- to 55-year-old baby boomers, with its technology-laden Beetle, while Stratus Vineyards focuses on a niche market of consumers looking for a high-priced, ultra-premium wine.

MARKETING MATTERS

Canada Goose's Differentiation Strategy Is Working

Dani Reiss has been CEO of Canada Goose since 2001. Over this period, he has grown the company's revenue by close to 4,000 percent, and Canada Goose has become the country's premier brand of outerwear. Mr. Reiss, whose grandfather, Sam Tick, founded the company in 1957, talks about the (differentiation) strategy that has worked so well for the company.

When Reiss started with the company, the company's focus was exclusively on the outerwear part of the business and growing it around the globe. Originally, Canada Goose was worn by people who lived and worked in the coldest places on earth. While this is still the case, the brand has gained broader appeal with other market segments. In short, the product has moved beyond a pure utilitarian product to being a luxury, premium-priced, self-expressive brand. And one of the pillars of this differentiation strategy used by Canada Goose is the fact that the product is "Made in Canada." Being made in Canada, according to Reiss, has helped propel the brand forward because history and heritage matters to the customers who buy Canada Goose. Reiss suggests that many brands have "lost an element of their soul by outsourcing to Asia." He argues, "If you look at some of the world's greatest brands, like Louis Vuitton—it is all made at 27 factories in France. It was a calculated risk for us, but the truth is, had we decided to go offshore and manufacture like everyone else was doing, I am certain that we would not be where we are today." At the end of the day, he insists that being made in Canada is a clear point of differentiation—it is what makes Canada Goose special. Granted, one of the powers of the brand that truly differentiates Canada Goose is the fact that it is the warmest jacket on the planet, so that is also very important. But being a traditional, authentic Canadian luxury brand is also imperative and it helps set it apart from competitors.

When asked about the importance of social media with regard to its marketing strategy, Reiss had this to say: "Social media [tools are] very important because of the way people communicate about our product. People have this experience of extreme warmth and then they go talk to somebody else about it. Our Facebook page is very active and engaged and the growth was organic. It is not commercial; it is social. We tell our stories a lot more than we push our products. We are not going to take out some ad just to get millions of [Facebook] fans." In the end, Canada Goose is a great example of how a firm can leverage a differentiation strategy to achieve tremendous success in the marketplace. And people talk about this differentiation, thus supporting the growth of the brand.

These strategies also form the foundation for Michael Porter's theory about what makes a nation's industries successful, as was discussed in Chapter 7.

Profit Enhancement Options

If a business wants to increase, or "enhance," its profits, it can (1) increase revenues, (2) decrease expenses, or (3) do both. Among these "profit enhancement options," let us look first at the strategy options of increasing revenues and then at those for decreasing expenses.

The strategy option of increasing revenues can be achieved only by using one or a combination of four ways to address present or new markets and products (Figure 19–5): (1) market penetration, (2) product development, (3) market development, and (4) diversification (all of which were described in Chapter 2).

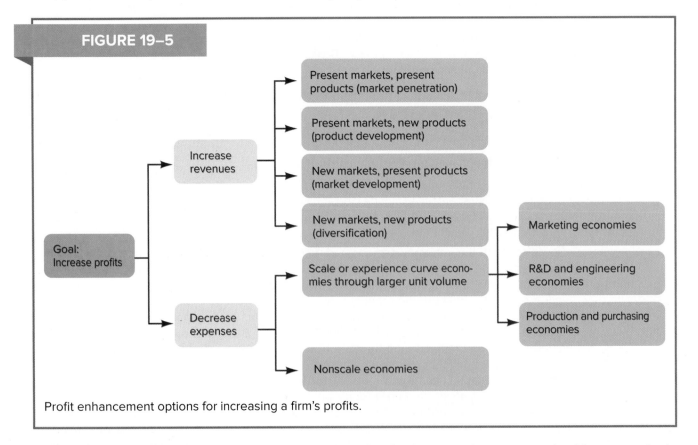

FIGURE 19–5

Profit enhancement options for increasing a firm's profits.

Procter & Gamble has followed a successful strategy of market penetration (present markets, present products) by concentrating its effort on becoming the market leader in each of its more than 30 product categories. It is currently first in market share in more than half these product categories. Efforts to increase customer satisfaction have also helped increase market penetration. It has also increased its market share in 19 of its 20 largest core brands by introducing product improvements and trimming retail prices.[17]

In contrast, Johnson & Johnson has succeeded with a product development strategy—finding new products for its present markets—to complement popular brands, such as Tylenol pain reliever and Acuvue contact lenses. To compete with Bristol-Myers and other companies, Johnson & Johnson developed Tylenol PM, a combination pain killer and sleeping pill, and Acuvue Oasis, a comfortable and disposable contact lens.

Walt Disney Co. pursued a market development strategy (new market, present product) following the success of the original Disneyland in Anaheim, California. The first market expansion was to Orlando, Florida, and then Tokyo and Paris. Disney has also pursued a diversification strategy by entering into the motion picture business with the development of Touchstone Pictures, a film studio, and Disney Cruise Line, a family-oriented cruise ship line.

Canadian Tire has pursued a multipronged strategy, including increased market penetration in existing markets; market development (geographic expansion); introducing new products to expand its current product line; and diversification through the acquisition of FGL Sports Ltd., the establishment of retail gasoline stations and retail car washes, and participation in the financial services business, including banking, insurance, and credit card services.

Strategy options for decreasing expenses fall into two broad categories (see Figure 19–5). One is relying on scale economies or experience-curve benefits from an increased volume of production to drive unit costs down and gross margins up, the best-known examples being consumer electronic devices such as smartphones and tablets where prices have dropped significantly over just a few years. Scale economies may occur in marketing, as well as in R&D, engineering, production, and purchasing.

The other strategy option to decrease expenses is simply finding other ways to reduce costs, such as cutting the number of managers, increasing the effectiveness of the salesforce through more training, or reducing product rejects by improving quality. Procter & Gamble concluded that the world did not really need 31 varieties of Head & Shoulders shampoo, and so it cut the number of packages, sizes, and formulas and thereby reduced expenses and increased profits.

Market–Product Synergies

Using the market–product grid framework introduced in Chapter 9, we can see two kinds of synergy that are critical in developing corporate and marketing strategies: (1) marketing synergy and (2) R&D–manufacturing synergy. While the following example involves external synergies through mergers and acquisitions, the concepts apply equally well to internal synergies sought in adding new products or seeking new markets.

A critical step in the external analysis is to assess how these merger and acquisition strategies provide the organization with synergy—the increased customer value achieved through performing organizational functions more efficiently. The "increased customer value" can take many forms: more products, improved quality on existing products, lower prices, improved distribution, and so on. But the ultimate criterion is that customers should be better off as a result of the increased synergy. The firm, in turn, should be better off by gaining more satisfied customers.

A market–product grid helps identify important trade-offs in the strategic marketing process. As noted in the nearby Marketing Matters box, "A Key Strategy Issue: Finding Synergies,"[18] assume you are vice president of marketing for Great Lawns Corporation's line of non-powered lawn mowers and powered walking mowers sold to the consumer market. You are looking for new product and new market opportunities to increase your revenues and profits.

MARKETING MATTERS

A Key Strategy Issue: Finding Synergies

A good example of synergy is the transformational partnership between Loblaw and Shoppers Drug Mart. Loblaw's purchase of Shoppers Drug Mart provides both companies additional scale, added internal capabilities, market coverage, and significant operating cost savings ($300 million over three years), allowing the company to better compete against U.S. chains such as Walmart by offering a combination of merchandise, pharmacy products, and groceries.

Another major merger that created plenty of synergy was the Procter & Gamble and Gillette merger. It resulted in one of the largest packaged-goods companies in the world. Finally, Toronto-Dominion (TD) Bank acquired BankNorth of New England and then Commerce Bank of New Jersey to achieve synergy and obtain a presence in the lucrative U.S. retail banking market. This merged firm resulted in cost savings, technology sharing, and increased revenues. TD also acquired Ameritrade to gain a presence in the wealth management and brokerage segment of the financial services market.

To try your hand in this synergy game, assume that you are a vice president of marketing for Great Lawns Corporation, which markets a line of non-powered and powered walking and riding lawn mowers. A market–product grid for your business is shown below. You distribute your non-powered mowers in all three market segments shown and powered walking mowers only in suburban markets. However, you do not offer powered riding mowers for any of the three markets.

Here are your strategy dilemmas:

1. Where are the marketing synergies (efficiencies)?
2. Where are the R&D and manufacturing synergies (efficiencies)?
3. What would a market–product grid look like for an ideal company that Great Lawns could merge with for it to achieve both marketing and R&D/manufacturing synergies (efficiencies)?

For answers to these questions, read the text and study Figures 19–6 and 19–7.

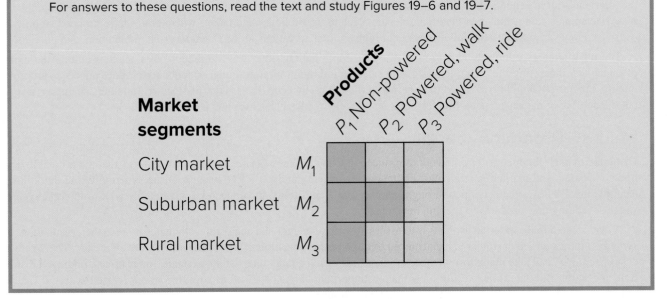

You conduct a market segmentation study and develop a market–product grid to analyze future opportunities. You identify three major segments in the consumer market based on geography: (1) city, (2) suburban, and (3) rural households. These market segments relate to the size of lawn a consumer must mow. The product clusters are (1) non-powered, (2) powered walking, and (3) powered riding mowers. Five alternative marketing strategies are shown in the market–product grids in Figure 19–6. The important marketing efficiencies—or synergies—run horizontally across the rows in Figure 19–6. Conversely, the important R&D and production efficiencies—or synergies—run vertically down the columns. Let us look at the synergy effects for the five combinations in Figure 19–6:[19]

1. *Market–product concentration.* The firm benefits from "focus" on a single product line and market segment, but it loses opportunities for significant synergies in both marketing and R&D–manufacturing.

2. *Market specialization.* The firm gains marketing synergy through providing a complete product line, but R&D–manufacturing have the difficulty of developing and producing three different products.

3. *Product specialization.* The firm gains R&D–manufacturing synergy through production economies of scale, but gaining market distribution in the three different geographic areas will be costly.

4. *Selective specialization.* The firm does not get either marketing or R&D–manufacturing synergies because of the uniqueness of the market–product combinations.

5. *Full coverage.* The firm has the maximum potential synergies in both marketing and R&D–manufacturing. The question is whether it is spread too thin due to the resource requirements needed to reach all market–product combinations.

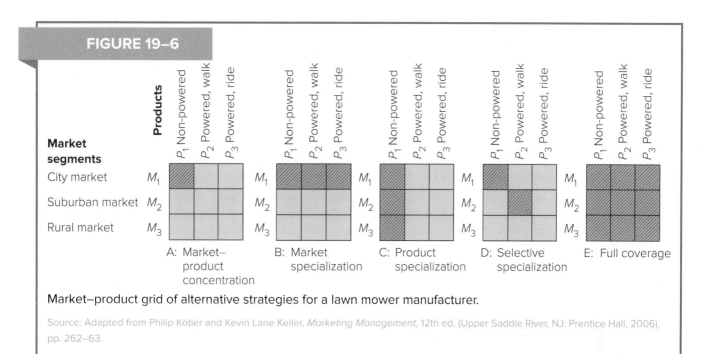

Market–product grid of alternative strategies for a lawn mower manufacturer.

Source: Adapted from Philip Kotler and Kevin Lane Keller, *Marketing Management,* 12th ed. (Upper Saddle River, NJ: Prentice Hall, 2006), pp. 262–63.

The Marketing Matters box, "A Key Strategy Issue: Finding Synergies," posed the question of what the ideal partner for Great Lawns would be if it merged with another firm, given the market–product combinations shown in the box. If, as vice president of marketing, you want to follow a full-coverage strategy, then the ideal merger partner is shown in Figure 19–7. This would give the maximum potential synergies—if you are not spreading your merged companies too thin. Marketing gains by having a complete product line in all regions, and R&D–manufacturing gains by having access to new markets that can provide production economies of scale through producing larger volumes of its existing products.

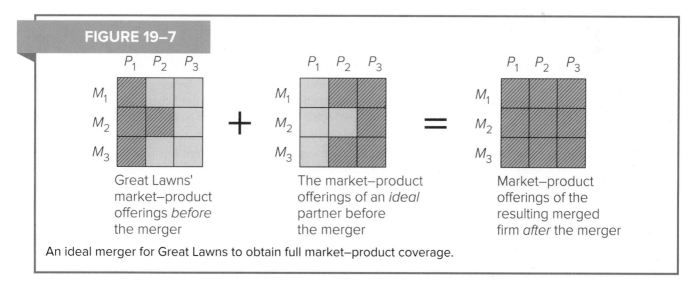

An ideal merger for Great Lawns to obtain full market–product coverage.

LO3 Some Planning and Strategy Lessons

Applying these frameworks is not automatic but requires a great deal of managerial judgment. Common-sense requirements of an effective marketing plan are discussed next, followed by problems that can arise.

Guidelines for an Effective Marketing Plan

Dwight D. Eisenhower, when he commanded the Allied armies in World War II, made his classic observation, "Plans are nothing; planning is everything." It is the process of careful planning that focuses an organization's efforts and leads to success. The plans themselves, which change with events, are often secondary. Effective planning and plans are inevitably characterized by identifiable objectives, specific strategies or courses of action, and the means to execute them. Here are some guidelines in developing effective marketing plans:

- *Set measurable, achievable goals.* Ideally, goals should be quantified and measurable in terms of what is to be accomplished and by when. "Increase market share from 18 to 22 percent by December 31, 2017" is preferable to "Maximize market share given our available resources." Also, to motivate people, the goals must be achievable.

- *Use a base of facts and valid assumptions.* The more a marketing plan is based on facts and valid assumptions, rather than guesses, the less are the uncertainty and risk associated with executing it. Good marketing research helps. For example, General Mills' research indicates a basic fact that busy consumers on the go want very convenient food products—ones they can eat with one hand. So, when Steve Sanger, CEO of General Mills, receives plans for a new food product from his employees, he asks one question: Does it have the "one-handedness" feature that consumers want? Without that feature, the marketing plan for that product is not likely to be successful.

- *Utilize simple but clear and specific plans.* Effective execution of plans requires that people at all levels in the firm understand what, when, and how they are to accomplish their tasks.

- *Have complete and feasible plans.* Marketing plans must incorporate all the key marketing mix factors and be supported by adequate resources.

- *Make plans controllable and flexible.* Marketing plans must enable results to be compared with planned targets, often using precise marketing metrics and dashboards. This allows replanning—the flexibility to alter the original plans based on recent results.

- *Find the right person to implement the plans.* But make sure that person is heavily involved in making the plans.

- *Work toward consensus-building.* "Ownership" of the plan by team members and stakeholders increases the chances for its success.

Problems in Marketing Planning and Strategy

From post-mortems on company plans that did work and on those that did not work, a picture emerges of where problems occur in the planning phase of a firm's strategic marketing process. The following list explores these problems:

1. Plans may be based on very poor assumptions about environmental factors, especially changing economic conditions and competitors' actions. Canadians used to equate the name Listerine with mouthwash. But Scope started an anti-Listerine campaign and successfully convinced Canadians that mouthwash did not have to taste bad to work. The result? Listerine lost its position as market leader.

2. Planners and their plans may have lost sight of their customers' needs. But not the Papa John's pizza chain. The "better ingredients, better pizza" slogan makes the hair stand up on the back of the necks of Pizza Hut executives. The reason is that this slogan of Papa John's reflects the firm's obsessive attention to detail, which is stealing market share from the much bigger Pizza Hut. Sample detail: If the cheese on the pizza shows a single air bubble or the crust is not golden brown, the offending pizza is not served to the customer.

3. Too much time and effort may be spent on data collection and writing the plans. Westinghouse has cut its planning instructions for operating units "that looked like an auto repair manual" to five or six pages.

4. Line operating managers often feel no sense of ownership in implementing the plans. Andy Grove, when he was CEO of Intel, observed, "We had the very ridiculous system . . . of delegating strategic planning to strategic planners. The strategies these [planners] prepared had no bearing on anything we actually did."[20] The solution is to assign more planning activities to line operating managers—the people who actually carry them out.

Balancing Value and Values in Strategic Marketing Plans

Two important trends are likely to influence the strategic marketing process in the future. The first, *value-based planning,* combines marketing planning ideas and financial planning techniques to assess how much a division or strategic business unit (SBU) contributes to the price of a company's shares (or shareholder wealth). Value is created when the financial return of a strategic activity exceeds the cost of the resources allocated to the activity.

The second trend is the increasing interest in *value-driven strategies,* which incorporate concerns for ethics, integrity, employee health and safety, and environmental safeguards with more common corporate values, such as growth, profitability, customer service, and quality. As the nearby Making Responsible Decisions box, "Strategy Includes Good Citizenship and Sustainable Development," points out, many Canadian companies are engaging in socially responsible and sustainable development practices and have integrated such activities as central components of their strategic plans.[21]

MAKING RESPONSIBLE DECISIONS

Strategy Includes Good Citizenship and Sustainable Development

Many companies have integrated corporate social responsibility and sustainable development business practices into both their short-term and long-term strategic plans. For example, Transcontinental Inc. of Montreal is Canada's largest printing company. It has embedded the concepts of corporate citizenship and environmental responsibility into the company's strategic planning and implementation processes. Every year, it develops a list of worthy causes and makes cash donations or provides free printing services to those causes. The company focuses on health, education, culture, and community development. It supports many hospitals and research centres, provides funds to major universities, and supports Centraide/United Way and the Heritage Canada fund. It also has a comprehensive environmental policy aimed to protect the natural environment. In fact, it establishes corporate objectives to improve its environmental performance in the same way it establishes its more traditional corporate objectives such as revenue and profitability.

Potash Corp. of Saskatchewan also engages in sustainable business practices. It was recently ranked among the top 50 global companies by SustainAbility, Inc, a global think tank that works in partnerships with the United Nations Environment Program. One area of focus for the company is demanding adherence to human rights standards from its suppliers, and this practice is an inherent part of the company's strategic sourcing process. Canadian Tire is another company that integrates good citizenship and the protection of the environment into its traditional strategic planning and implementation processes. For example, the company has a comprehensive environment, health, and safety program, and managers of this program report to the company's board of directors outlining their activities and the goal-achievement with regard to this program.

Finally, Vancity is Canada's largest credit union. It is guided by its commitment to corporate social responsibility and to improve the quality of life in the communities in which it operates. It has a clear "statement of values" that includes the concepts of integrity, innovation, and responsibility. To ensure that it achieves its objectives with regard to these values, the company conducts a social audit process. It then publishes the results in an "accountability report" to provide a picture of its social and environmental performance. According to the company, "It's the business decisions you make as an organization, the people you hire to make them and the impact you leave on the community in which you do business that matter. And, at the end of day, how you do all these things is based on your organizational values. While [our accountability] report covers everything from our employee engagement scores to how much paper we recycle, it's really about what counts most: our values of integrity, innovation, and responsibility."

What are your thoughts on these companies who make value-driven strategies an important part of the strategic focus? Importantly, what about the companies who do not make such a commitment?

Finally, remember that it is easier to talk about planning than to do it well. Try your hand as a consultant to help Trevor's Toys make some strategic decisions, as described in the nearby Going Online box, "Want to Be a BCG Consultant? Solve the Trevor's Toys Online Case."

GOING ONLINE

Want to Be a BCG Consultant? Solve the Trevor's Toys Online Case

The Boston Consulting Group, or BCG, is probably best known for its "growth–share" portfolio matrix. As a very active and respected management consulting organization, BCG maintains a website to describe its services. Included on its website is an interactive strategy case that asks potential employees to analyze typical strategic challenges faced by BCG clients.

   Go to the BCG website and assess the e-commerce strategy for Trevor's Toys. You can access the case by going to **http://www.bcg.it/Shared/InteractiveCase.swf**. Read the case carefully, solve it within the time limits, and consider becoming a BCG consultant after graduation!

Disruptive Innovations and Long-Range Marketing Plans

Disruptive innovations create a new market by initially reaching new customers through displacing an existing market's low-end product. The innovation eventually displaces the original product or technology, creating havoc for organizations that operate in the old, displaced market and disrupting their long-range marketing plans.

However, these disruptive innovations don't replace an existing product or technology overnight. Instead, established firms in the industry initially conclude the disruptive innovation isn't worth pursuing because the new market is too small and takes scarce resources away from improving their existing products. Eventually, the disruptive innovation becomes pervasive enough to invade the large, traditional markets, often driving the original firms out of business. Examples include Wikipedia, which caused Encyclopedia Britannica to stop print production after 244 years, and digital media, which replaced CDs and DVDs.

How can marketing managers recognize and incorporate disruptive innovations in their long-range plans? While no perfect answer exists, the first giant step toward an answer: Ask tough, focused, disruptive questions. Research shows that (1) disruptive innovators ask more questions than they get answers to and (2) good questions provide greater value than good answers![22]

Learning Review

3. What are two kinds of marketing plans?

4. Describe Porter's four generic business strategies.

5. What are four alternative ways to increase a firm's profit when considering profit enhancement options and strategies?

6. Where do (a) marketing synergies and (b) R&D–manufacturing synergies appear in a market–product grid framework?

7. Why is it important to include line operating managers in the planning process?

THE IMPLEMENTATION PHASE OF THE STRATEGIC MARKETING PROCESS

The postgame summary of a losing sports team coach often runs something like, "We had an excellent game plan; we just didn't execute it."

Is Planning or Implementation the Problem?

The planning-versus-execution issue applies to the strategic marketing process as well: A difficulty when a marketing plan fails is determining whether the failure is due to a poor plan or poor implementation.[23]

Effective managers tracking progress on a struggling plan first try to identify whether the problems involve (1) the plan and strategy, (2) its implementation, or (3) both, and then they try to correct the problems. But as discussed earlier in the chapter, research on what really works shows that successful firms have excellence on both the planning and strategy side and the implementation and execution side. For example, General Electric's continuing leadership in lighting combines strong innovative products (planning and strategy) with excellent advertising and distribution (implementation and execution). Figure 19–8 shows the outcomes of (1) good and bad marketing planning, and (2) good and bad marketing implementation.

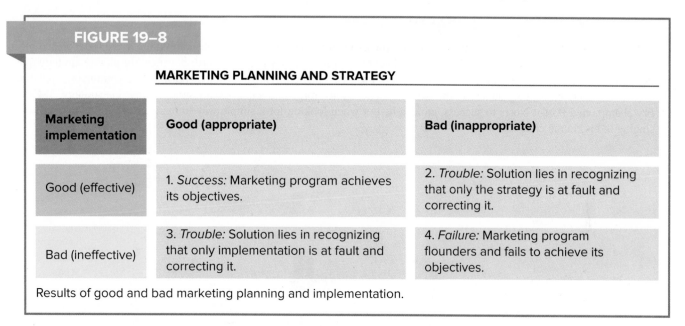

FIGURE 19–8

MARKETING PLANNING AND STRATEGY

Marketing implementation	Good (appropriate)	Bad (inappropriate)
Good (effective)	1. *Success:* Marketing program achieves its objectives.	2. *Trouble:* Solution lies in recognizing that only the strategy is at fault and correcting it.
Bad (ineffective)	3. *Trouble:* Solution lies in recognizing that only implementation is at fault and correcting it.	4. *Failure:* Marketing program flounders and fails to achieve its objectives.

Results of good and bad marketing planning and implementation.

Increasing Emphasis on Marketing Implementation

The implementation phase of the strategic marketing process has emerged as a key factor to success by moving many planning activities away from the duties of planners to those of line managers.

General Electric's Jack Welch has become a legend in making GE far more efficient and far better at implementation. When Welch became CEO of GE, he faced an organization mired in red tape, turf battles, and slow decision making. Further, Welch saw GE bogged down with 25,000 managers and close to a dozen layers between him and the factory floor. In his "delayering," he sought to cut GE's levels in half and to speed up decision making and implementation by building an atmosphere of trust and autonomy among his managers and employees.

In terms of implementation and meeting key goals, Welch also insisted that GE's departments be "winners"—or #1 or #2 in their industry in terms of revenues and profits. Welch had another mantra for these departments: "Fix, close, or sell!" Under his leadership, more than 100 GE businesses were closed or sold. An example is GE's small appliance division that was sold to Black & Decker. The remaining GE businesses were either running well or were "fixed"—in Welch's terms. Although there are debates on some Welch strategies, businesses around the world are using GE's focus on implementation as a benchmark.

An example of where GE combines both planning and implementation is its much-publicized "ecomagination" initiative. This campaign includes goals of doubling its investment in research and development, reducing greenhouse gas emissions, and increasing revenues from its ecomagination-products that aid the environment—such as more efficient lighting, lower-emission aircraft engines, and solar-energy hybrid locomotives. This ecomagination program led GE to re-lamp 62 of its facilities using the products from its lighting division, both to reduce greenhouse emissions and to lower its energy costs.[24]

Improving Implementation of Marketing Programs

No magic formula exists to guarantee effective implementation of marketing plans. In fact, the answer seems to be equal parts of good management skills and practices, from which have come some guidelines for improving program implementation.

Communicate Goals and the Means to Achieve Them

Those called on to implement plans need to understand both the goals sought and how they are to be accomplished. Everyone in Papa John's—from founder John Schnatter to telephone order takers and make-line people—is clear on what the firm's goal is: to deliver better pizzas using better ingredients. The firm's orientation packet for employees lists its six "core values," which executives are expected to memorize. Sample: Core value no. 4 is "PAPA," or "People Are Priority No. 1, Always."[25]

Have a Responsible Program Champion Willing to Act

Successful programs almost always have a **product (or program) champion** who is able and willing to cut red tape and move the program forward. Such people often have the uncanny ability to move back and forth between big-picture strategy questions and specific details when the situation calls for it. Program champions are notoriously brash in overcoming organizational hurdles. In many cases, they adhere to the axiom, "Better to ask forgiveness than permission." Using this strategy, 3M's Art Fry championed Post-it Notes to success, an idea he got when looking for a simple way to mark places in his hymnal while singing in his church choir.

What are some of the benefits General Electric achieved in its "ecomagination" initiative? For the answer, which shows GE's world-class program planning and implementation, see the text.

General Electric Company

www.ge.com

© Inganielsen/Dreamstime.com

Reward Successful Program Implementation but Don't Punish Failure

When an individual or a team is rewarded for achieving the organization's goal, they have maximum incentive to see a program implemented successfully because they have personal ownership and a stake in its success. At the same time, progressive organizations encourage their employees to take risks and are not punished if those risks do not pay off. In many cases, the lessons learned from failure can be as instructive as the lessons learned from success.

Take Action and Avoid "Paralysis by Analysis"

Management experts warn against paralysis by analysis, the tendency to excessively analyze a problem instead of taking action. To overcome this pitfall, they call for a "bias for action" and recommend a "do it, fix it, try it" approach.[26] Conclusion: Perfectionists finish last, so getting 90 percent perfection and letting the marketplace help in the fine-tuning makes good sense in implementation.

Lockheed Martin's Skunk Works got its name from the comic strip *L'il Abner* and its legendary reputation from achieving superhuman technical feats with a low budget and ridiculously short deadlines by stressing teamwork. Under the leadership of Kelly Johnson, Skunk Works turned out a series of world-class aircraft, from the world's fastest (the SR-71 Blackbird) to the most untraceable aircraft (the F-117 Stealth fighter). Two of Kelly Johnson's basic tenets: (1) make decisions promptly, and (2) avoid paralysis by analysis. In fact, one study showed that Johnson's Skunk Works could carry out a program on schedule with 126 people, whereas a competitor in a comparable program was behind schedule with 3,750 people.[27]

Foster Open Communication to Surface the Problems

Success often lies in fostering a work environment that is open enough so that employees are willing to speak out without fear of recrimination when they see problems. The focus is placed on trying to solve the problem as a group rather than finding someone to blame. Solutions are solicited from anyone who has a creative idea to suggest— from the caretaker to the president—without regard to status or rank in the organization.

Two more Kelly Johnson axioms from Lockheed Martin's Skunk Works apply here: (1) When trouble develops, surface the problem immediately, and (2) get help; do not keep the problem to yourself. This may mean getting ideas from competitors. Moreover, it may also mean combing your own entire firm as well as key suppliers and distributors to find talented people with solutions.

Open communication at Lockheed Martin's Skunk Works has led to state-of-the-art aircraft like this F-35 Lightning II Joint Strike Fighter.

U.S. Navy photo courtesy Lockheed Martin/Released

Schedule Precise Tasks, Responsibilities, and Deadlines

Successful implementation requires that people know the tasks for which they are responsible and the deadline for completing them. To implement the tasks required to carry out its marketing plans, many organizations, including the Royal Canadian Mint, prepare an **action item list** that has four columns: (1) the task, (2) the name of the person responsible for accomplishing that task, (3) the date by which the task is to be finished; (4) and what is to be delivered. Action item lists are forward-looking, clarify the targets, and put strong pressure on people to achieve their designated tasks by the deadline.

Related to the action item lists are formal *program schedules,* which show the relationships through time of the various program tasks. Scheduling an action program involves (1) identifying the main tasks, (2) determining the time required to complete each, (3) arranging the activities to meet the deadline, and (4) assigning responsibilities to complete each task.

Scheduling program activities can be done efficiently with *Gantt charts* developed by Henry L. Gantt. This method is the basis for the scheduling techniques used today, including elaborate computerized methods. The key to all scheduling techniques is to distinguish tasks that must be done sequentially from those that *can* be done concurrently. Scheduling tasks concurrently often reduces the total time required for a program. Software programs, such as Microsoft Project, simplify the task of developing a schedule or a Gantt chart.

Finally, in an attempt to be more efficient and productive when conducting marketing implementation meetings, many organizations are now using something called a *time-based agenda* when conducting such meetings. With a time-based agenda approach, a meeting agenda shows the running time allocated to each agenda item. In short, time is shown as running time (2:00, 2:03, etc.) and not target time (3 minutes, 10 minutes, etc.), which lets participants know better how the meeting is progressing.

(LO4) Organizing for Marketing

A marketing organization is needed to implement the firm's marketing plans. Basic issues in today's marketing organizations include understanding (1) how line versus staff positions and divisional groupings interrelate to form a cohesive marketing organization, and (2) the role of the marketing or product manager.

The Evolving Role of the Chief Marketing Officer

The senior executive responsible for a firm's marketing activities shown in Figure 19–9 is increasingly given the title of chief marketing officer (CMO) rather than vice president of marketing. This reflects the broadening of the CMO's role as the inside-the-company "voice of the consumer." So today, it is critical that CMOs understand (1) the changing characteristics of domestic and global consumers, (2) the role of digital media and mobile marketing in integrated marketing efforts, and (3) the benefits of the many new multichannel data streams in decision making and marketing effectiveness assessment. These broadened responsibilities have led to increasing influence also. For example, a recent survey of CMOs in Canadian firms found over 75 percent of CMOs believed their influence in organization success has grown. Additionally, the survey found most CMOs believe that harnessing data analytics is one of the most important challenges that they face.[28]

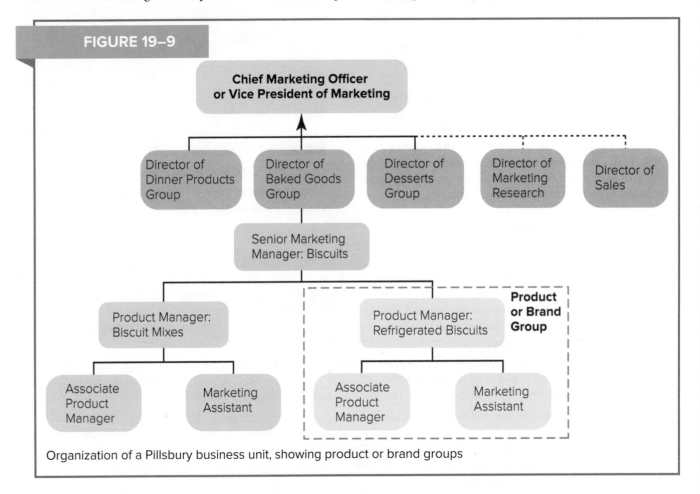

FIGURE 19–9

Organization of a Pillsbury business unit, showing product or brand groups

Line versus Staff and Divisional Groupings

Although simplified, Figure 19–9 shows the organization of a typical business unit in a consumer packaged goods firm, such as Kraft Canada. This business unit shown in Figure 19–9 consists of Dinner Products, Baked Goods, and Desserts. It highlights the distinction between line positions and staff positions in marketing. People in **line positions**, such as senior marketing manager for Biscuits, have the authority and responsibility to issue orders to the people who report to them, such as the two product managers shown in Figure 19–9.

In this organizational chart, line positions are connected with solid lines. Those in **staff positions** (shown by dotted lines) have the authority and responsibility to advise people in line positions but cannot issue direct orders to them.

Most marketing organizations use divisional groupings—such as product line, functional, geographical, and market-based—to implement plans and achieve their organizational objectives. Some of these appear in some form in the organizational chart in Figure 19–9. The top of the chart shows organization by **product line groupings**, in which a unit is responsible for specific product offerings, such as Dinner Products or Baked Goods.

At levels higher than those shown in Figure 19–9, firms may be organized by **functional groupings**, such as manufacturing, marketing, and finance, which are the different business activities within a firm.

Many packaged goods firms use **geographical groupings**, in which sales territories are subdivided according to geographic location. Each director of sales has several regional sales managers reporting to him or her, such as western, eastern, and so on. These, in turn, have district managers reporting to them, with the field sales representatives at the lowest levels.

Many packaged-goods firms use **market-based groupings**, which utilize specific customer segments, such as the banking, health care, or manufacturing segments. When this method of organizing is combined with product groupings, the result is a *matrix organization*.

A relatively recent position in consumer products firms is the *category manager* (senior marketing manager in Figure 19–9). Category managers have profit-and-loss responsibility for an entire product line—all biscuit brands, for example. They attempt to reduce the possibility of one brand's actions hurting another brand in the same category. Procter & Gamble uses category managers to organize by "global business units," such as baby care and beauty care. Cutting across country boundaries, these global business units implement standardized worldwide pricing, marketing, and distribution.[29]

Role of the Product Manager

The key person in the product or brand group shown in Figure 19–10 is the manager who heads it. This person is often called the *product manager* or *brand manager*. This person and the assistants in the product group are the basic building blocks in the marketing department of most consumer and industrial product firms. The function of a product manager is to plan, implement, and evaluate the annual and long-range plans for the products for which he or she is responsible.

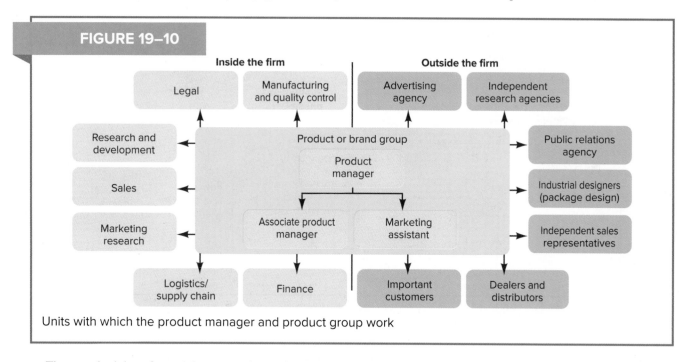

FIGURE 19–10

Units with which the product manager and product group work

There are both benefits and dangers to the product manager system. On the positive side, product managers become strong advocates for the assigned products, cut red tape to work with people in various functions both inside and outside the organization (see Figure 19–10), and assume profit-and-loss responsibility for the performance of the product line. On the negative side, even though product managers have major responsibilities, they have relatively little direct authority, and so most groups and functions shown in Figure 19–10 must be coordinated to meet the product's goals.[30] To coordinate the many units, product managers must use persuasion rather than orders.

But as more Canadian firms embrace customer-intimacy, customer relationship management (CRM), and customer experience management (CEM) strategies, product managers are no longer the only ones responsible for managing the product or customer base. Some Canadian firms have created new positions, such as "manager of student segment," "VP of financial services clients," or "director of customer management," which shadow the traditional product manager roles. These firms have divided their organizations into "customer-facing roles" (such as segment managers). More and more often, it is the segment managers, not the product managers, who make the final decisions on product, price, promotion, and place (distribution).

LO5 THE EVALUATION PHASE OF THE STRATEGIC MARKETING PROCESS

The essence of evaluation, the final phase of the strategic marketing process, is to compare results with planned goals for the marketing program in order to take necessary corrective actions.

The Marketing Evaluation Process

Ideally, quantified goals from the marketing plans developed in the planning phase have been accomplished by the marketing actions taken in the implementation phase (Figure 19–11) and measured as results in the evaluation phase. A marketing manager then uses *management by exception*, which means identifying results that deviate from plans to diagnose their causes and take new actions.

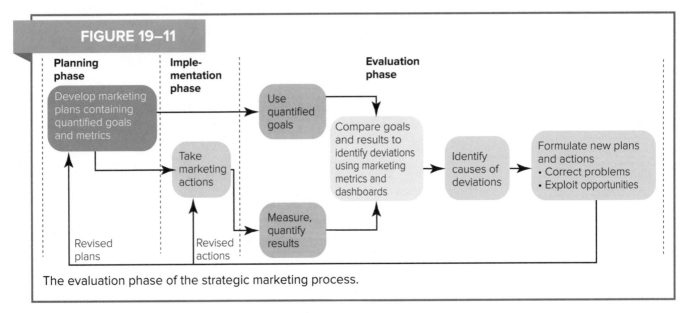

FIGURE 19–11

The evaluation phase of the strategic marketing process.

Often, results fall short of plans, and a corrective action is needed. For example, after 50 years of profits, Caterpillar accumulated losses of $1 billion. To correct the problem, Caterpillar focused its marketing efforts on core products and reduced its manufacturing costs. When results are better than plans, the marketing manager tries to identify the reason and move quickly to exploit the unexpected opportunity.

"Hiring a Milkshake" and Digging Beneath the Numbers

The "goals" used in marketing metrics are almost always quantitative goals. But sometimes the numbers can hide what is really happening and digging beneath the surface is needed to reveal the insights that lead to better marketing actions. Here's an example: A fast-food chain asked a team of consultants to beef up sales of its milkshakes. The chain had huge files about the likes of loyal milkshake customers. But changing the milkshakes based on those likes had no impact on sales. So consultants tried a different approach and asked: "What job is a customer trying to do when he hires a milkshake?" After looking at the results, the consultants found that: (1) half the milkshakes were bought by men in the early morning; (2) it was the only thing they bought; and (3) they then drove off in their car with it. Research on why these customers "hired the milkshake" revealed they (1) all had a similar job (2) with a long, boring drive to work and (3) needed something to do while driving. By understanding what job the customers were trying to get done, how to improve the milkshake product became clear: You make the milkshake more viscous and put chunks of fruit into it to make sucking through a straw on the commute more unpredictable, interesting, and rewarding!

Evaluation Involves Marketing ROI, Metrics, and Dashboards

In the past decade, measuring the performance of marketing activities has become a central focus in many organizations. This boils down to some form of the question, "What measure can I use to determine if my company's marketing is effective?"

No single measure exists to determine if a company's marketing is effective. In finance, the return on investment (ROI) measure relates the total investment made to the total return generated from the investment. The concept has been extended to trying to measure the effectiveness of marketing expenditures with **marketing ROI**, the application of modern measurement technologies to understand, quantify, and optimize marketing spending.[31]

The evaluation phase of the strategic marketing process tries to improve marketing ROI through the effective use of marketing metrics and dashboards:

- *Marketing metrics.* Depending on the specific goal or objective sought, one or a few key marketing metrics are chosen, such as market share, cost per lead, retention rate, cost per click, sales per square foot, and so on.[32] This is the "quantified goals" step in Figure 19–11.

- *Marketing dashboards.* Ideally, the marketing metrics are displayed—often daily or weekly—on the marketing dashboard on the manager's computer. With today's syndicated scanner data, Internet clicks, and TV viewership tracking, the typical manager faces information overload. So an effective marketing dashboard displays highlights—often in colour—where actual results vary significantly from plans. This alerts the manager to potential problems.[33]

These highlighted exceptions, or deviations from plans in Figure 19–11, are the immediate focus of the marketing manager. Marketing managers then try to improve their marketing ROI by correcting shortfalls and exploiting results that exceed plans.

Evaluation Using Marketing Metrics and Marketing Dashboards at General Mills

Let's assume it is mid-January and you are part of Vivian Callaway's Warm Delights team at General Mills. Your team is using the marketing data and metrics shown in the marketing dashboard in Figure 19–12. We can summarize the evaluation step of the strategic marketing process using this dashboard and the three-step challenge-findings-actions format used in the Using Marketing Dashboards boxes in this book.

The Distribution Challenge for Warm Delights Minis

You've been asked to analyze the channel of distribution strategy of the Warm Delights Minis product. This hypothetical example is based on the type of scanner data General Mills uses, but details have been modified to simplify the data and analysis.

The marketing dashboard in Figure 19–12 focuses on the distribution of the six existing Warm Delights Minis flavours and the impact of adding two new flavours introduced in the fall—Lemon Swirl Cake and Cinnamon Swirl Cake.[34] As with all new grocery products, the challenge is to gain distribution on retailers' shelves. So the marketing metrics in Figure 19–12 focus on the distribution of Warm Delights Minis in the five main channels of distribution used by General Mills. These five channels and their shortened names in Figure 19–12 are:

- Grocery stores/supermarkets: Grocery
- Mass merchandisers: Mass
- Warehouse/club stores: Warehouse
- Convenience stores: Convenience
- Drug stores/pharmacies: Drug

FIGURE 19–12

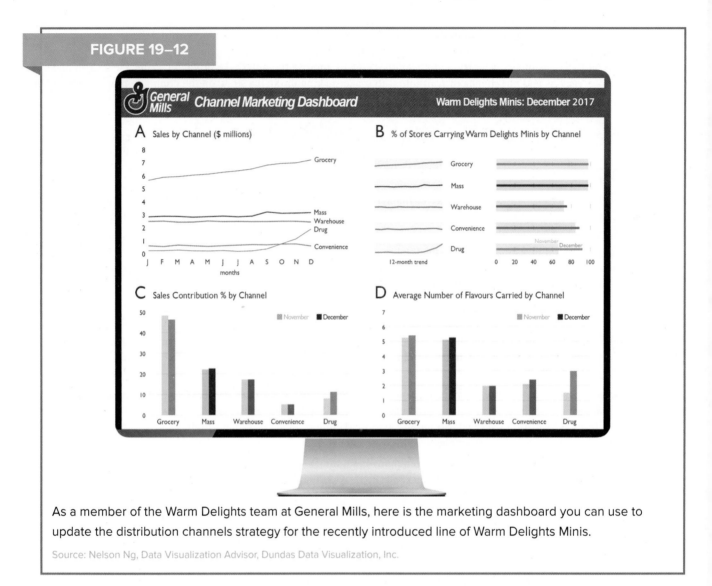

As a member of the Warm Delights team at General Mills, here is the marketing dashboard you can use to update the distribution channels strategy for the recently introduced line of Warm Delights Minis.

Source: Nelson Ng, Data Visualization Advisor, Dundas Data Visualization, Inc.

The Findings for Warm Delights Minis

The marketing dashboard in Figure 19–12 describing the 2017 performance of Warm Delights Minis is divided into four charts, each with different marketing metrics:

- *Chart A: Monthly Unit Sales by Channel (Millions).* This shows sales revenues for warehouse and convenience stores are flat or trending down while those for mass merchandisers and grocery are up slightly. The grocery channel is clearly the most important. But the really encouraging news is the jump in sales in the drugstore channel from September to December.

- *Chart B: % of Stores Carrying Warm Delights Minis by Channel.* The horizontal bar chart—a narrow December bar within the wider November bar—explains much of the major increase in September to December drugstore unit sales seen in Chart A. Chart B shows that from November to December the percentage of drugstores carrying the Warm Delights Minis jumped from about 64 percent to 91 percent.

- *Chart C: % of Total Sales Revenues by Channel.* The monthly bars total 100 percent. While the chart shows the importance of the grocery channel, it also shows the increased monthly sales revenue in the drug channel.

- *Chart D: Average Number of Flavours Carried by Channel.* This paints the picture more clearly. An important reason for the increased unit and dollar sales from the drug channel is due to increasing the average number of flavours carried in a drugstore from 1.4 to 3.0 from November to December.

The Actions for Warm Delights Minis

Further analysis of the dashboard showing the sales by channel of individual flavours of Warm Delights Minis reveals the jump in sales in the drugstore channel is because (1) a major chain (like Walmart) added the line, and (2) drugstores are embracing the new flavours, which have made many customers more aware that drugstores are now actively selling many food lines.

Your investigation reveals a different situation for the four channels other than drugstores. The minor changes in sales there are due to the two new flavours simply replacing older, slower-moving ones.

Hot desserts normally experience an increased seasonal demand in winter. So because sales and distribution are growing, you decide to invest in the brand and schedule additional national TV advertising in late January and throughout February to exploit both the seasonal demand and recent sales trends. Seeing the jump in sales from adding a major drugstore chain, you research ways to attract other potential chains in all five main channels that Warm Delights Minis uses.

Learning Review

11. What are four groupings used within a typical marketing organization?

12. What two components of the strategic marketing process are compared to evaluate a marketing program?

Learning Objectives Review

 Explain how marketing managers allocate their limited resources.

Marketing managers use the strategic marketing process and marketing information, such as marketing plans, sales reports, and action memos, to effectively allocate their scarce resources to exploit the competitive advantages of their products. Marketers may use either sales response functions or market share (share point) analysis to help them assess what the market's response will be to additional marketing efforts.

LO2 **Describe three marketing planning frameworks: Porter's generic strategies, profit enhancement options, and market–product synergies.**

Three useful frameworks to improve marketing planning are (*a*) Porter's generic business strategies, (*b*) profit enhancement options, and (*c*) market–product synergies. Porter identifies four generic business strategies that firms can adopt: (*1*) a cost leadership strategy, which focuses on reducing expenses to lower product prices while targeting a broad array of market segments; (*2*) a differentiation strategy, which requires products to have significant points of difference to charge a premium price while targeting a broad array of market segments; (*3*) a cost focus strategy, which involves controlling costs to lower prices of products targeted at a narrow range of market segments; and (*4*) a differentiation focus strategy, which requires products to have significant points of difference to reach one or only a few market segments.

A second marketing planning framework is to use profit enhancement options to increase sales revenues, decrease costs, or both. To increase revenues, marketers can use one or a combination of four strategies to focus on present or new products or markets: market penetration (selling more of a product to existing markets); (*1*) market penetration (selling more of a product to existing markets); (*2*) market development (selling an existing product to new markets); (*3*) product development (selling a new product to existing markets); and (*4*) diversification (selling a new product to new markets). To reduce expenses, marketers can (*a*) generate additional economies of scale in marketing and production costs, and (*b*) reduce personnel and other non-marketing costs, product rejects through improved quality, and so forth.

The third framework is to use a market–product grid that results in two kinds of synergies: marketing synergies (efficiencies), which run horizontally across the row of the various products offered by the firm to a single market segment; and R&D–manufacturing synergies (efficiencies), which run vertically down a column of the various market segments targeted for a given product or product class. The interactions or synergy effects of these marketing and production efficiencies results in five alternative combinations: market–product concentration, market specialization, product specialization, selective specialization, and full coverage.

LO3 **Explain what makes an effective marketing plan and some problems that often exist with it.**

An effective marketing plan has measurable, achievable goals; uses facts and valid assumptions; is simple, clear, and specific; is complete and feasible; and is controllable and flexible. Some problems that arise with marketing plans are that marketers (*a*) base them on poor assumptions about the marketing environment; (*b*) lose sight of their customers' needs; (*c*) spend too much time and effort on data collection for and writing the actual plan; and (*d*) do not seek ownership of the plan by operating managers and others charged with its implementation. Improving implementation of marketing plans can be achieved by clearly communicating goals and means to achieve them; having a program champion willing to act, rewarding successful implementation and not punishing failure; taking action and avoiding paralysis by analysis; fostering open communication; and scheduling precise tasks, responsibilities, deadlines and deliverables.

 Describe the alternatives for organizing a marketing department and the role of a product manager.

A marketing department must be organized to effectively implement a marketing plan. First, marketing organizations must distinguish between line positions, those individuals in the marketing organization who have the authority and responsibility to issue orders to people that report to them to carry out a particular aspect of the marketing plan, and staff positions, those individuals who have the authority and responsibility to advise but not directly order people in line positions to do something.

The role of the product manager is to interact with numerous people and groups both inside and outside the firm to coordinate the planning, implementation, and evaluation of the marketing plan and its budget on an annual and long-term basis for the products responsible.

 Explain how marketing ROI, metrics, and dashboards relate to evaluating programs.

The evaluation phase of the strategic marketing process involves measuring the results of the actions from the implementation phase and comparing them with goals set in the planning phase. Marketing metrics, used to help quantify the goals in the planning stage, are of two kinds: input and output metrics. The marketing manager then takes action to correct negative deviations from the plan and to exploit positive ones. Today, managers want an answer to the question, "Are my marketing activities effective?" One answer is in using marketing ROI, which is the application of modern measurement technologies to understand, quantify, and optimize marketing spending. Quantifying a marketing goal with a carefully defined marketing metric and tracking this metric on a marketing dashboard can improve marketing ROI.

Applying Marketing Knowledge

1. Assume a firm faces an S-shaped sales response function. What happens to the ratio of incremental sales revenue to incremental marketing effort at the (*a*) bottom, (*b*) middle, and (*c*) top of this curve?

2. What happens to the ratio of incremental sales revenue to incremental marketing effort when the sales response function is an upward-sloping straight line?

3. Assume General Mills has to decide how to spend millions of dollars to try and expand its cereal and yogurt businesses. To allocate this money between these two businesses, what information would General Mills like to have?

4. Suppose your Great Lawns lawn mower company has the market–product concentration situation shown in Figure 19–6A. What are both the synergies and potential pitfalls of following expansion strategies of (*a*) market specialization and (*b*) product specialization?

5. Are value-driven strategies inconsistent with value-based planning? Give an example that supports your position.

6. The first Domino's Pizza restaurant was near a college campus. What implementation problems are (*a*) similar and (*b*) different for restaurants near a college campus versus a military base?

7. A common theme among managers who succeed repeatedly in program implementation is fostering open communication. Why is this so important?

8. Why are quantified goals in the planning phase of the strategic marketing process important for the evaluation phase?

Building Your Marketing Plan

Do the following activities to complete your marketing plan:

1.   Draw a simple organization chart for your organization.

2.   In terms of evaluation, list (*a*) the four or five critical factors (such as revenues, number of customers, variable costs) and (*b*) how frequently (monthly, quarterly) you will monitor them to determine if special actions are needs to exploit opportunities or correct deviations.

3.   Read Appendix A, "Creating an Effective Marketing Plan." Then, write a 600-word executive summary for your marketing plan using the numbered headings shown in Appendix A.

Video Case 19

General Mills Warm Delights™: Indulgent, Delicious, and Gooey!

Vivian Milroy Callaway, vice president for the Center for Learning and Experimentation at General Mills, retells the story for the "indulgent, delicious, and gooey" Warm Delights™. She summarizes, "When you want something that is truly innovative, you have to look at the rules you have been assuming in your category and break them all!"

When a new business achieves a breakthrough, it looks easy to outsiders. The creators of Betty Crocker Warm Delights stress that if the marketing decisions had been based on the traditions and history of the cake category, a smaller, struggling business would have resulted. The team chose to challenge the assumptions and expectations of accumulated cake category business experience. The team took personal and business risks, and Warm Delights is a roaring success.

Planning Phase: Innovation, but a Shrinking Market

"In the typical grocery store, the baking mix aisle is a quiet place," says Callaway. Shelves sigh with flavours, types, and brands. Prices are low, but there is little consumer traffic. Cake continues to be a tradition for birthdays and social occasions. But consumer demand declines. The percentage of U.S. households that bought at least one baking mix in 2000 was 80 percent. Four years later, the percentage of households was 77 percent, a very significant decline.

Today, a promoted price of 89 cents to make a 9 x 12-inch cake is common. Many choices, but little differentiation, gradually falling sales, and low uniform prices are the hallmarks of a mature category. But it's not that consumers don't buy cake-like treats. In fact, indulgent treats are growing. The premium prices for ice cream ($3.00 a pint) and chocolate ($3.00 a bar) are not slowing consumer purchases.

The Betty Crocker marketing team challenged the food scientists at General Mills to create a great-tasting, easy-to-prepare, single-serve cake treat. The goal: Make it indulgent, delicious, and gooey. The team focused the scientists on a product that would have the following:

- Consistently great taste
- Quick preparation
- A single portion
- No cleanup

The food scientists delivered the prototype! Now, the marketing team began hammering out the four Ps. They started with a descriptive name "Betty Crocker Dessert Bowls" and a plan to shelve it in the "quiet" cake aisle. This practical approach would meet the consumer need for a "small, fast, microwave cake" for dessert. Several marketing challenges emerged:

- *The comparison problem.* The easy shelf price comparison to 9 x 12-inch cakes selling for 89 cents would make it harder to price Dessert Bowls at $2.00.
- *The communication problem.* The product message, "a small, faster-to-make cake," wasn't compelling. For example, after-school snacks should be fast and small, but "dessert" sounds too indulgent.
- *The quiet aisle problem.* The cake-aisle shopper is probably not browsing for a cake innovation.
- *The dessert problem.* Consumer's on-the-go, calorie-conscious meal plans don't generally include a planned dessert.
- *The microwave problem.* Consumers might not believe it tastes good.

In sum, the small, fast-cake product didn't resonate with a compelling consumer need. But it would be a safe bet because the Dessert Bowls positioning fit nicely with the family-friendly Betty Crocker brand.

Implementation Phase: Leaving the Security of Family Behind

The consumer insights team really enjoyed the hot, gooey cake product. They feared that it would languish in the cake aisle under the Dessert Bowls name because it didn't fully describe the essence of what the food delivered. They explored who really are the indulgent treat customers. The data revealed that the heaviest buyers of premium treats are women without children. This focused the team on a target consumer: "What does she want?" They enlisted an ad agency and consultants to come up with a name that would appeal to "her." Several independently suggested the "Warm Delights" name, which became the brand name.

An interesting postscript to the team's brand name research: A competitor apparently liked not only the idea of a quick, gooey, microwaveable dessert but also the "Dessert Bowls" name! You may now see its competitive product on your supermarket's shelves.

Targeting the on-the-go women who want a small, personal treat had marketing advantages:

- The $2.00 Warm Delights price compared favourably to the price of many single-serve indulgent treats.
- The product food message "warm, convenient, delightful" is compelling.
- On-the-go women's meal plans do include the occasional delicious treat.

© Daniel Hundley/Token Media

One significant problem remained: The cake-aisle shopper is probably not browsing for an indulgent, single-serve treat. The marketing team solved this shelving issue by using advertising and product displays outside the cake aisle. This would raise women's awareness of Warm Delights. Television advertising and in-store display programs are costly, so Warm Delights sales would have to be strong to pay back the investment.

Vivian Callaway and the team turned to market research to fine-tune the plan. The research put Warm Delights (and Dessert Bowls) on the shelf in real (different) stores. A few key findings emerged. First, the name "Warm Delights" beat "Dessert Bowls." Second, the Warm Delights with nuts simply wasn't easy to prepare, so nuts were removed. Third, the packaging with a disposable bowl beat the typical cake-mix packaging involving using your own bowl. Finally, by putting the actual product on supermarket shelves and in displays in the stores, sales volumes could be analyzed.

Evaluation Phase: Turning the Plan into Action!

The marketing plan isn't action. Sales for "Warm Delights" required the marketing team to (1) get the retailers to stock the product, preferably somewhere other than the cake aisle, and (2) appeal to consumers enough to have them purchase, like, and repurchase the product.

The initial acceptance of a product by retailers is important. But each store manager must experience good sales of Warm Delights to be motivated to keep its shelves restocked with the product. Also, the Warm Delights team must monitor the display activity in the store. Are the displays occurring as expected? Do the sales increase when a display is present? Watching distribution and display execution on a new product is very important so that sales shortfalls can be addressed proactively.

Did the customer buy one or two Warm Delights? Did the customer return for a second purchase a few weeks later? The syndicated services that sell household panel purchase data provide the answer. The Warm Delights team evaluates these reports to see if the number of people who tried the product matches with expectations and how the repeat purchases occur. Often, the "80/20 rule" applies. So, in the early months, is there a group of consumers that buys repeatedly and will fill this role?

For ongoing feedback, calls by Warm Delights consumers to the free consumer information line are monitored. This is a great source of real-time feedback. If a pattern emerges and these calls are mostly about the same problem, that is bad. However, when consumers call to say "thank you" or "it's great," that is good. This is an informal quick way to identify if the product is on track or further investigation is warranted.

Good Marketing Makes a Difference

The team took personal and business risks by choosing a Warm Delights plan over the more conservative Dessert Bowls plan. Today, General Mills has loyal Warm Delights consumers who are open to trying new flavours, new sizes, and new forms. If you were a consultant to the Warm Delights team, what would you do to grow this brand?

QUESTIONS

1. What is the competitive set of desserts in which Warm Delights is located?

2. (*a*) Who is the target market? (*b*) What is the point of difference on the positioning for Warm Delights? (*c*) What are the potential opportunities and hindrances of the target market and positioning?

3. (*a*) What marketing research did Vivian Callaway execute? (*b*) What were the critical questions that she sought research and expert advice to get answers to? (*c*) How did this affect the product's marketing mix price, promotion, packaging, and distribution decisions?

4. (*a*) What initial promotional plan directed to consumers in the target market did Callaway use? (*b*) Why did this make sense to Callaway and her team when Warm Delights was launched?

5. If you were a consultant to Vivian Callaway, what product changes would you recommend to increase sales of Warm Delights?

Case: This case was prepared by Roger Kerin, Steven Hartley, and William Rudelius.

Using Social Media and Mobile Marketing to Connect with Consumers

Learning Objectives

After reading this chapter, you should be able to:

LO1 Define social media and describe how they differ from traditional advertising media.

LO2 Identify the four major social networks and how brand managers integrate them into their organizations' marketing actions.

LO3 Describe the differing roles of those receiving messages through traditional media versus social media, as well as the factors brand managers use to select a social network.

LO4 Compare the performance measures of social media linked to costs (inputs) versus revenues (outputs)

LO5 Identify the cause of the convergence of the real and digital worlds and how this will affect the future of social media.

The Ultimate Marketing Machine . . . Is in Your Pocket!

Few aspects of business have changed as quickly as the marketing discipline during the past five years. And more change is inevitable. To see the future, however, you need look no further than your pocket. Social media and mobile marketing will soon make your phone the ultimate marketing machine!

Consumers regularly engage the marketplace with many forms of media. Each month, millions of people watch television, millions listen to radio, and millions access the Internet on a computer. While these are astounding numbers, it is the growth in the use of smartphones that is getting marketers' attention. Currently, millions of people use their phone to access an app, while millions more use social media on their phones. Smartphones and tablets are quickly replacing computers as the way most people access the Internet, apps, and social media. The always-on and always-connected aspects of these devices are adding mobility as an important dimension of marketing and creating mobile marketing as an essential tool for the future.

As the use of smartphones has grown, businesses have created a wide variety of mobile experiences for consumers. In a recent survey, the most popular smartphone apps were Facebook, Google Search, YouTube, Google Play, Google Maps, Gmail, Facebook Messenger, Google+, and Instagram. These and other mobile experiences have attracted more than $1 billion in annual advertising revenue, and experts predict that they will soon account for a major percentage of all online display ad budgets.

Mobile marketing is continuing to evolve though. The current apps and social media experiences are designed for the small screen of a mobile phone, but they do not necessarily take advantage of the user's location or mobility. The future of mobile marketing will focus on the ability to interact with a world of connected devices. As author Tina Desai explains, "In this connected world, it is the mobile device that becomes the digital remote control for the real world."

Courtesy of Estimote

Shopping is one example of this interaction. When a customer walks into a store, a Bluetooth low energy (BLE) beacon will sense that the customer has arrived, then it will access customer loyalty data, create a personalized promotion, and send it to the shopper's smartphone. The shopper can select products from the ad and then follow in-store navigation to the selected products. Other areas where mobile marketing will have immediate applications is in health monitoring and fitness, home security and comfort, and automobile safety.

What are some other new elements of this dynamic environment? Watch for sponsored videos on Instagram, a buy button on Twitter, mobile payments with Apple Pay, self-destructing ads on Snapchat, and even virtual reality experiences![1]

This chapter defines social media, describes four widely used social media, explains how organizations use them in developing marketing strategies, and considers where social media are headed in the future.

LO1 UNDERSTANDING SOCIAL MEDIA

Defining *social media* is challenging, but it's necessary to help a brand or marketing manager select the right one. This section defines social media, positions a number of social networks, and compares social and traditional media. As you read this, consider how you might choose from the social media alternatives if you—like college and university students around the globe—were using one to launch a start-up business or expand a small business.

What Are Social Media?

This section describes how social media came about, defines social media, and provides a means of classifying the countless social media available to assist marketing managers in choosing among them.

Defining Social Media

Social media represent a unique blending of technology and social interaction to create personal value for users. **Social media** are online media where users submit comments, photos, and videos—often accompanied by a feedback process to identify "popular" topics.[2] Most social media involve a genuine online conversation among people about a subject of mutual interest, one built on their personal thoughts and experiences. However, other social media sites involve games and virtual worlds in which the online interaction includes playing a game, completing a quest, controlling an avatar, and so on. Business firms also refer to social media as "consumer-generated media." A single social media site with millions of users interacting with each other, such as Facebook, Twitter, and LinkedIn, is referred to as a *social network.*

How Social Media Came About

The term "social media" is sometimes used interchangeably with the terms "Web 2.0" and "user-generated content"—two concepts that are the foundations of today's social media. Web 2.0 does not refer to any technical update of the World Wide Web, but identifies functionalities that make possible today's high degree of interactivity among users. So with Web 2.0, content is no longer seen as being created and published in final form exclusively by one author. Instead, the content can be modified continuously by all users in a participatory fashion, such as with blogs and wikis. The next generation web, Web 3.0, will include new functionalities that are customized to each individual and their location, activity, interests, and needs.[3]

A *blog*—a contraction of "web log"—is a web page that serves as a publicly accessible personal journal and online forum for an individual or organization. Companies like Hewlett-Packard and Frito-Lay routinely monitor blogs to gain insight into customer complaints and suggestions. A *wiki* is a website whose content is created and edited by the ongoing collaboration of end users, for example, to generate and improve new product ideas. They differ in that a blog is a diary that shows a sequential journey while a wiki shows the end result as a single entry.

As we saw in Chapter 17, *user-generated content (UGC)* is media generated by users (consumers) and disseminated via various channels, in particular, the Internet. The term "user-generated content" was in common use by 2005 and covers all the ways people can use social media. UGC satisfies three basic criteria:

1. It is published either on a publicly accessible website or on a social networking site, so it is not simply an e-mail.

2. It shows a significant degree of creative effort, so it is more than simply posting a newspaper article on a personal blog without editing or comments.

3. It is consumer generated by an individual outside of a professional organization, without a commercial market in mind.

Classifying Social Media

Most of us would probably say that Facebook, Twitter, LinkedIn, and YouTube are well-known social networks. But brand or marketing managers trying to reach potential customers need a system to classify the more than 400 specialized and diverse social networks to select the best among them. Kaplan and Haenlein have proposed a classification system for marketers based on two factors:[4]

1. *Media richness.* This involves the degree of acoustic, visual, and personal contact between two communication partners—face-to-face communications, say, being higher in media richness than telephone or e-mail communications. The higher the media richness and quality of presentation, the greater the social influence that communication partners have on each other's behaviour.

2. *Self-disclosure.* In any type of social interaction, individuals want to make a positive impression to achieve a favourable image with others. This favourable image is affected by the degree of self-disclosure about a person's thoughts, feelings, likes, and dislikes—where greater self-disclosure is likely to increase one's influence on those reached.

The text describes how Web 2.0 and user-generated content are the foundations of today's social media.

© Equinox Imagery/Alamy Stock Photo

Figure 20–1 uses these two factors of media richness and self-disclosure to position a number of social media sites in two-dimensional space. For example, Wikipedia is a collaborative project that is low on both self-disclosure and media richness.[5] LinkedIn, on the other hand, contains detailed career and résumé information for business networking and is high in self-disclosure but only moderate in media richness. Marketing managers look carefully at the positioning of the social media shown in Figure 20–1 when selecting those to use in their plans. For example, LinkedIn, positioned in the Social Networking Sites segment in Figure 20–1, is a professional networking service with 360 million members in 200 countries. LinkedIn recently generated $454 million in annual advertising revenue from companies such as Citigroup, Microsoft, Chevron, HP, and Volkswagen, which promote their companies' career opportunities to people with specific job titles.[6]

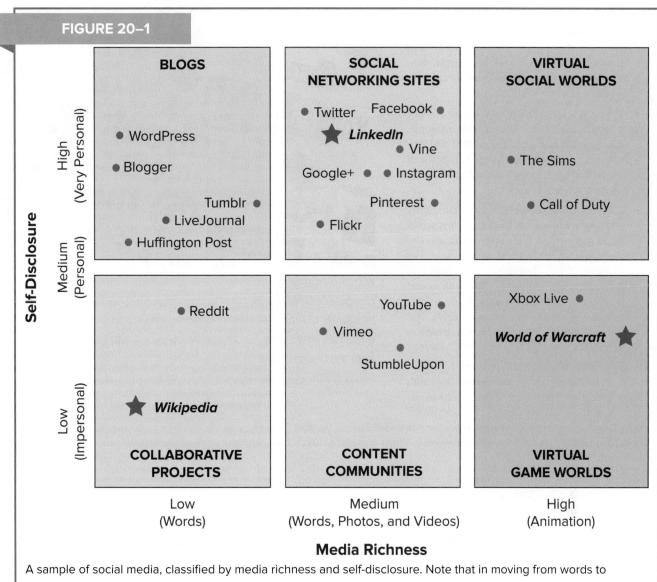

FIGURE 20–1

A sample of social media, classified by media richness and self-disclosure. Note that in moving from words to photos, videos, and animation, media richness increases. Also, in moving from very impersonal messages to highly personal ones, self-disclosure increases.

Comparing Social and Traditional Media

Consumers receive information, news, and education from print (newspapers, magazines) and electronic media (radio, television). But brand and marketing managers know that social media are very different from traditional media like newspapers or even radio or television. Social media and traditional media have both similarities and differences that impact marketing strategies, as described below:[7]

- *Ability to reach both large and niche audiences.* Both kinds of media can be designed to reach either a mass market or specialized segments; however, good execution is critical, and audience size is not guaranteed.

- *Expense and access.* Messages and ads in traditional media like newspapers or television generally are expensive to produce and have restricted access by individuals. Also, traditional media are typically owned privately or by the government. In contrast, messages on social media networks are generally accessible everywhere to those with smartphones, computers, and tablet devices and can be produced cheaply.

- *Training and number of people involved.* Producing traditional media typically requires specialized skills and training and often involves teams of people. In contrast, sending messages on social media requires only limited skills, so practically anyone can post a message that includes words and images.

- *Time to delivery.* Traditional media can involve days or even months of continuing effort to deliver the communication, and time lags can be extensive. In contrast, individuals using social media can post virtually instantaneous content.

- *Permanence.* Traditional media, once created, cannot be altered. For example, once a magazine article is printed and distributed, it cannot be changed. But social media can be altered almost instantaneously by comments or editing.

- *Credibility and social authority.* Individuals and organizations can establish themselves as an "expert" in their given field, thereby becoming an "influencer" in that field. For example, CBC Television has credibility among television media. But with social media, a sender often simply begins to participate in the "conversation," hoping that the quality of the message will establish credibility with the receivers, thereby enhancing the sender's influence.

In terms of privacy and anonymity, with minor exceptions, recipients of traditional media like TV or radio ads are completely anonymous.

With the countless social networks available on smartphones and computer screens, how do brand or marketing managers choose the best ones to reach their target markets? As a first step, the text describes how social media can be classified and how they differ from traditional media.

© Anatolii Babii/Alamy Stock Photo

Subscribers to newspapers or magazines are somewhat less so because publishers can sell subscription lists to advertisers. Social media have much less privacy and anonymity. When a social network breaches expectations for privacy, unethical outsiders can access users' names.[8]

Learning Review

1. What do we mean by social media?
2. In classifying social media, what do we mean by (*a*) media richness and (*b*) self-disclosure?
3. Compare traditional media and social media in terms of time to delivery of the communication.

LO2　A LOOK AT FOUR IMPORTANT SOCIAL NETWORKS

Facebook, Twitter, LinkedIn, and YouTube are four widely used networks in the world of social media. So, brand or marketing managers need a special understanding of these four website platforms as they integrate social media into their marketing strategies to supplement the traditional media they already use. This section briefly defines and describes each of these four major social media and outlines some guidelines for a brand manager using each of them. Because of its importance, Facebook merits more detailed coverage.

Comparing Four Social Media

Figure 20–2 compares four major social media networks (Facebook, Twitter, LinkedIn, and YouTube) from the point of view of a brand manager.[9] Facebook can increase brand exposure by enabling convenient user posting of links, photos, and videos. Twitter makes it easy to place brand messages and gain online customer support. While primarily a powerful network in helping users find jobs, LinkedIn has also found a niche in helping small businesses network to reach potential customers, as well as filling its traditional role of connecting job seekers and jobs. YouTube's videos make it especially useful in explaining a complex product.

FIGURE 20–2

BASIS OF COMPARISON	SOCIAL MEDIA			
	facebook.	**twitter**	**Linked in**	**You Tube**
Male–Female Breakdown	42% male, 58% female	50% male, 50% female	56% male, 44% female	58% male, 42% female
Brand Exposure	Powerful for gaining brand exposure through convenient user posting of links, photos, and videos.	Consistent placement of brand messages is easy with applications like HootSuite and TweetCastor. Sponsored tweets promote brands.	Free opportunities exist, like Business Pages and LinkedIn Influencer posts. Paid Sponsored Updates provide added reach.	Powerful in gaining attention, explaining a complex product, and branding. Channels unite users on content and heighten viewership.
Customer Communication	Great for people who like your brand and want to share their opinions. Leads all social networks for this.	Twitter is powerful for gaining online customer support. Engaging one-on-one is simple and easy to track.	Half of those using social media for customer service use a LinkedIn Company Page while 40% do so with LinkedIn Groups.	YouTube gains user's ready attention in attracting customer support. Easy to allow responses to user comments and ratings.
Traffic to Website	Is the traffic leader through rewording engaging content with better news feed placement. But its share of referred visits is falling.	Referral traffic from Twitter is growing faster than any other social network. Photos and videos make tweets even more clickable.	LinkedIn generates referrals—though less than many other social networks—but can be valuable for B2B and business development.	YouTube is an important source of traffic. Get traffic back to user's site by adding a hyperlink in the video description.

How brand managers can use four social media networks in developing their marketing strategies.

Sources: The 2014 Male–Female Breakdowns are provided by Compete, Inc.; and DMR Directory of Social Network, App and Digital Stats; the other information is adapted from "The CMO's Guide to the 2014 Social Landscape."
(Facebook): © Craig Ruttle/AP Photo; (Twitter): © Ingvar Björk/Alamy Stock Photo; (LinkedIn): Kristoffer Tripplaar/Alamy Stock Photo; (YouTube): © TP/Alamy Stock Photo

Facebook

Facebook is the first choice among people seeking to create and maintain online connections with others by using photos, videos, and short text entries. Facebook enhanced its photo-sharing capability with its recent acquisition of Instagram. With over 1.4 billion active users—one in every five people on the planet—Facebook is truly the 900-pound gorilla among all social media and is accessible in more than 70 languages. Canada is the most active Facebook country on the planet. More than 19 million Canadians log on to Facebook once a month (half of the entire Canadian population!), and 14 million check their newsfeeds daily. Importantly, many are doing so via a mobile device (smartphone or tablet).[10]

Facebook: An Overview

Facebook is a website where users may create a personal profile, add other users as friends, and exchange comments, photos, videos, and "likes" with them. Facebook users today can keep friends and family updated on what they are thinking, doing, and feeling. In addition, users may chat with friends and create and join common interest groups, and businesses can create Facebook Pages as a means of advertising and building relationships with customers. Facebook is open to anyone age 13 and older.

CEO Mark Zuckerberg and COO Sheryl Sandberg have managed Facebook through incredible growth. To understand the magnitude of the company, consider the following facts about Facebook:

- Facebook has over 1.4 billion active users.
- Facebook processes 350 million photos, 4.5 billion likes, and 10 billion messages each day.
- Eighty-two percent of Facebook users living outside of the United States.
- Facebook generates revenue from more than 2 million advertisers. Half of all Facebook users have more than 200 friends in their network, and 18- to 29-year-olds have 300![11]

Facebook in a Brand Manager's Strategy

Facebook Pages were created as a method for brand managers to generate awareness for their product, service, or brand within Facebook. They allow brand managers to promote their business on Facebook, separate from their private and personal profiles. Done well, these pages are magnets for feedback. Additionally, Facebook Page information is generally public and is catalogued by search engines so that brand managers can identify influencers within their customer base.

To generate new customers and increase traffic to their Facebook Pages, brand managers can use paid ads and sponsored stories within the Facebook advertising platform. An advantage of these Facebook ads is that the content can migrate into Facebook conversations among friends—to the delight of advertisers.

The marketing challenge for an organization's Facebook Page is to post content that will generate the best response. Brand managers using Facebook seek to maintain a conversation with their fans. Research suggests the following guidelines to engage fans on Facebook:[12]

- Be creative in using links, photos, and videos.
- Make it familiar, but with a twist. Focus content strategy on imagery and messaging that is familiar to fans—punctuated with something unique. Aflac uses its Aflac Duck—the well-known "spokes-duck"—to treat fans to Aflac Duck commercials, virtual Duck gifts, and supplemental insurance offers.
- Keep it fresh. Redbox uses frequent posts to keep fans informed about its latest film releases.
- Learn users' passions and let them guide content. Taco Bell polls users to see which menu item they'd like featured in the following week's menu profile photo.

Gaining meaningful user loyalty enables a company to target promotional offers to its best customers. A recent study found that "Likes" or "Followers" on a brand's Facebook Page are worth an astounding $174 in terms of product spending, brand loyalty, and "propensity to recommend" the site to others.[13]

Launching a New Social Network Using Facebook

Want to launch your own social network? For example, StuffDOT is a place for people to post the things they like and earn rewards for their recommendations and online purchases. It differs from other social-sharing websites because users "dot" their favourite things to StuffDOT and receive financial rewards or commissions when someone purchases that item. Commissions can be redeemed for gift cards with many major retailers, such as Amazon and Target.[14]

Figure 20–3 shows the Facebook Page for StuffDOT, a start-up that targets college- and university-aged women. The notes in the margins in Figure 20–3 show how elements on the StuffDOT Facebook Page seek to connect with fans, generate conversations, and help measure the success of the Facebook Page:

- *Profile and Cover Image.* Show StuffDOT's attention-getting logo.
- *People Like This Page.* Tells the number of people clicking the "Like" button.
- *Facebook Page Posts.* Pictures items like clothes and travel information shared with users.

Facebook offers its business customers a variety of ad templates that help measure the results of an ad, such as "Page Likes" (chosen by StuffDOT) or "Clicks to Website." StuffDOT also uses Facebook's "App Install" template to inform and encourage people to download the StuffDOT app.

FIGURE 20–3

Profile and Cover Image
Brand identifying image; usually includes a logo or promotional image

People Reached
The number of people who saw a specific post

People Like This Page
The number of people who have clicked the Like button

Facebook Page Posts
Messages that appear in the News Feed of people who Like the Page

People Like This Post
Indicates when people like a post

StuffDOT's Facebook Page shows elements of interest to both its marketing team and potential users.

StuffDOT's challenge is to break through the social media clutter and attract loyal users. So the StuffDOT marketing team works continuously to present an attention-getting, user-friendly Facebook Page.

As a start-up, StuffDOT finds new users and website testers by recruiting Campus Ambassadors from colleges and universities. StuffDOT Campus Ambassadors actively promote the site through workshops, social media marketing, word-of-mouth, and promotional partnerships with events and businesses on college and university campuses. To learn more about what StuffDOT is up to now, go to **www.stuffdot.com**.

Mobile Marketing at Facebook

Keeping 1.4 billion users happy is a tall order—even for Facebook. As the most common method of accessing Facebook shifts from computers to mobile smartphones, the company is continually making changes to its mobile capabilities. As CEO Mark Zuckerberg explains: "Moving from just being a single service to a family of world-class apps to help people share in different ways is the biggest shift in our strategy to connect people in many years."[15] Some recent examples include the following:

- *Faster news publishing.* An initiative called Instant Articles provides content, rather than links, from media organizations such as the *New York Times*, *National Geographic*, and Buzzfeed directly to a user's News Feed. This makes access 10 times faster, prevents the Facebook experience from being interrupted, and acknowledges that two-thirds of all American adults now own a smartphone.[16]

- *Photo-sharing and facial recognition.* Facebook recently introduced an app called Moments, which uses facial recognition to identify which "friends" are in the photos and then asks if the user would like to share the photo. It is Facebook's response to the mobile situation where a user takes a photo and someone asks, "Will you send that to me?"[17]

- *E-mail marketing for Facebook app.* In a program called Custom Audiences, Facebook helps advertisers target customers as they scroll through Facebook's mobile app by matching e-mail addresses provided by the advertisers with the e-mail addresses it has for many of its users. Facebook also identifies "lookalikes," people who are similar to an advertiser's customers, for targeted ads. Currently, more than half of Facebook's sales revenues come from mobile devices![18]

- Integration of mobile app enhancements. Facebook is building a suite of mobile apps, which includes Messenger, Instagram, WhatsApp, and about 40 others that connect through the Messenger platform. The goal is to better enable e-commerce through smartphones.[19]

What other changes will Facebook make as part of its mobile marketing strategy? Perhaps only Mark Zuckerberg knows!

Twitter

Now that "tweets" have become part of our everyday language, it's apparent that Twitter has entered the mainstream of Canadian life. Globally, Twitter has over 500 million registered users. It has over 10 million users in Canada, and this number is growing rapidly. This growth has not gone unrecognized, with Canadian broadcasters Shaw and Bell signing agreements with Twitter Canada to be part of the Twitter Amplify program, which allows advertisers to embed video clips and other content on its sites. Overall, globally, "active" Tweeter users, estimated at over 300 million, send over 500 million tweets per day.[20]

Twitter: An Overview

Twitter is a website that enables users to send and receive *tweets,* messages up to 140 characters long. Introduced in 2006, Twitter is based on the principle of "followers." So when you choose to follow another Twitter user, that user's tweets appear in reverse chronological order on your Twitter page.

Because of its short message length, the ease of posting and receiving tweets, and its convenience on a smartphone, Twitter can be a good source of information about a brand or product. Carma Laboratories, the maker of Carmex lip balm and skin care products, uses Twitter as an important tool in its social media program to communicate brand messages to its followers. As part of Carmex's social media outreach, the brand is active on Twitter with daily messages, retweets, and replies.

The immediacy of Twitter messaging allows brands like Carmex to operate promotions in real time. For example, Carmex partnered with **LeBronJames.com** to conduct a scavenger hunt on Twitter where members of TeamLeBron tweeted clues to their location. The first person to arrive at the destination won a jar of Carmex with a 14-karat-gold cap.

Beyond sending out messages, Carmex relies on Twitter as a listening device. Carmex's social media team monitors mentions of Carmex on Twitter to see what people are saying. If there are product concerns, Carmex can reach out to consumers to make sure their concerns are quickly addressed. For more about Carmex and how it uses social media to conduct marketing research, see Chapter 8.

Twitter in a Brand Manager's Strategy

With the 140-character limit on tweets, brand managers cannot expect extensive comments on their brands. But they can use social media management tools like TweetDeck or HootSuite to see what Twitter users are saying—good and bad—about both their own brands and competitive ones. They can then respond to the negative comments and retweet the positive ones.

Brand managers have various other strategies for listening to and interacting with current and potential consumers using Twitter. For example, they can:[21]

- Generate brand buzz by developing an official Twitter profile, recruiting followers, and showing photos of their products.

- Follow the Twitter profiles that mention their product and monitor what is being said, responding to user criticisms to develop happier customers.

- Tweet on topics that provide information of value to their consumers.

As with Facebook, Twitter can actively engage customers if done creatively. For example, Wine Country Ontario used a clever Twitter contest, encouraging wine enthusiasts who visited Ontario's wine region to respond to the challenge, "Untweetable but You Can Try." Winners received a Wine Country Ontario experience.[22] To further enhance this engagement, Twitter recently introduced new features to make the site more appealing and acquired Grip to analyze tweets for businesses hungry for user insights.[23]

LinkedIn

Unlike Facebook and Twitter, the LinkedIn site's main purpose is professional networking and job searching.

LinkedIn: An Overview

An example of a clever Twitter campaign.

Courtesy Wine Country Ontario

LinkedIn is a business-oriented website that lets users post their professional profiles to connect to a network of businesspeople. The people in this network are called *connections*. With more than 350 million users in over 200 countries, including over 7 million Canadian users, this social network helps users gain an introduction to someone they wish to know through a mutual, trusted contact. Because of its popularity, over 3 million companies have LinkedIn Company Pages to post news and job openings.[24]

Here are some other ways that LinkedIn members can use its network:

- To find jobs, people, and business opportunities recommended by someone in the network and bookmark jobs to apply for.
- To review and profile a manager offering a job and find a contact to introduce them.
- To enable advertisers to reach targeted people based upon job titles, seniority, age, and location.

LinkedIn in a Brand Manager's Strategy

Marketing managers can use LinkedIn to promote their brand in subtle ways. This is done mainly for business-to-business (B2B) image building and networking with industry-related groups. Using LinkedIn, brand managers can demonstrate the organization's expertise and create and moderate discussion groups.

According to a recent survey of small business owners, 41 percent see LinkedIn as potentially beneficial to their company—more than twice that for Facebook, Twitter, or YouTube.[25] LinkedIn recently streamlined its research process for finding qualified employees so that an employer can type its needs into the LinkedIn "search box," which results in a summary that includes people, jobs, groups, and companies. Brand managers also use LinkedIn for business development to identify sales leads and locate vendors.[26] Sales representatives often use LinkedIn to see the profiles of purchasing personnel or managers with whom they are meeting.

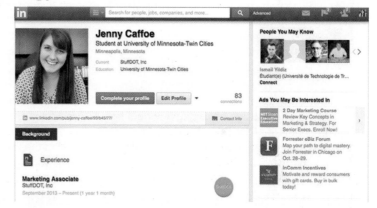

LinkedIn members like Jenny Caffoe, above, connect to a network of businesspeople. Brand managers can use it to build their company's image and find sales leads and vendors.

Courtesy of StuffDOT, Inc.

YouTube

The ability of YouTube to reach its audience stretches the imagination. Think about this: YouTube's one billion users (1) make four billion views per day, (2) upload 300 hours of video each minute, and (3) generate 40 percent of YouTube's traffic from mobile devices.[27]

YouTube: An Overview

YouTube is a video-sharing website in which users can upload, view, and comment on videos. YouTube uses streaming video technology to display user-generated video content that includes movie and TV clips, music videos, and original videos developed by amateurs. While most of the content is uploaded by amateurs, many companies offer material on the site through a YouTube channel.

YouTube redesigns its home page periodically to provide a more organized structure to steer users to "channels," rather than simply encourage them to browse like in the past. Recently, YouTube also redesigned the format for its YouTube channels. These channels serve as home pages for organizations and individuals and allow them to upload their own videos, as well as post and share videos created by others.

What are the most watched videos on YouTube? They are Psy's "Gangnam Style," Justin Bieber's "Baby," and Taylor Swift's "Blank Space" with 2.3 billion, 1.1 billion, and 1.0 billion views, respectively. Each of these artists has YouTube channels that aggregate their music and other videos they have uploaded for fans and other users to view.[28]

YouTube in a Brand Manager's Strategy

YouTube offers great opportunity for a brand manager to produce and show a video that explains the benefits of a complex product. Since YouTube is owned by Google, it incorporates a search engine, so users interested in a specific topic can find it easily. In terms of cost advantages, while a brand manager must pay the cost of creating a video, launching a new channel on YouTube is free. YouTube also offers a program to help small businesses create video ads and buy and manage key words for their video ads on the website. For insight regarding new ways online video is becoming part of mobile marketing strategies, see the Marketing Matters box, "Mobile Marketing Discovers Video Bloggers."[29]

MARKETING MATTERS

Mobile Marketing Discovers Video Bloggers

Fifty percent of all YouTube views now take place on a smartphone or a tablet. This incredible shift from just a few years ago signals a new era of consumer behaviour and the essential role online video must have in mobile marketing strategies.

Research suggests that when Millennials watch a video on their phones, they are twice as engaged as they are when watching on a television. They are also more likely to (1) change their opinion about the brands represented in the ads or the content, (2) discuss the brands with someone else, (3) visit a store carrying the brand, and (4) make a purchase. So getting video messages online is of growing importance to marketers.

Of course, placing ads or posting branded content on YouTube is the first level of a mobile marketing strategy. Some marketers, however, have observed that video bloggers, or vloggers, are becoming the online versions of traditional celebrities. Snickers, for example, created an online version of its popular "You're Not You When You're Hungry" campaign by having vloggers from F2Freestyles and Ultimate Handyman create videos for their YouTube channels. As Dan Burdett, Snickers global brand director, explains, "Between them, the international vloggers in this campaign have over 7.5 million subscribers, giving the brand campaign huge global reach."

How will mobile marketing utilize online video in the future? Experts think 360-degree videos, 4K videos, virtual reality videos, and augmented reality videos are not far into the future!

Three guidelines on marketing and promoting a brand using YouTube videos include the following:[30]

- Exploit visual aspects of your message, perhaps sacrificing product messages to tell a more entertaining story.

- Create a branded channel rich in keywords to improve the odds of the video showing up in user searches.

- Target viewers by using YouTube's insights and analytics research to reveal the number of views, the number of visits to your website, and what keywords are driving user visits.

Of special interest to brand managers: YouTube recently started guaranteeing its audience size to advertisers—airing additional ads across its channels until they reach a specified percentage of the target audience.

Learning Review

4. How is user-generated content presented by someone using Facebook?

5. What are some ways brand managers use Facebook to converse with a brand's fans? How does Facebook facilitate mobile marketing activities?

6. How can brand managers use YouTube to converse with customers? What is a new form of mobile marketing using online video?

INTEGRATING SOCIAL MEDIA INTO TODAY'S MARKETING STRATEGIES

Thousands of marketing managers around the globe understand how to use traditional media to generate sales for their brand. Some are successful, and others are not. But many of these same managers will admit that social networks are so new and complex, they are not sure how best to use them.

This section looks at (1) how social media tie to the strategic marketing process, (2) how to select social media, (3) how social media can be used to generate sales, and (4) how to measure the results of social media programs.

Social Media and the Strategic Marketing Process

The strategic marketing process described in Chapter 2 and the communications process running from sender to receiver discussed in Chapter 16 apply to both traditional and social media. But note these important differences in the communication process:

- Traditional media such as magazine or TV ads generally use one-way communication from sender to receiver, who the marketer hopes will buy the product advertised. A little word-of-mouth chatting may occur among the consumer "passive receivers," but communication generally ends with the receiver.

- Social media deliberately seek to ensure that the message *does not end* with an individual receiver. Instead, the goal is to reach "active receivers," those who will become "influentials" and be "delighted" with the brand advertised. These will then become "evangelists," who will send messages—user-generated content—to their online friends and then back to the advertiser about the joys of using the brand.

So, success in social media marketing relies heavily on the ability of a marketing program to convert passive "receivers" of the message to active "evangelists" who will spread favourable messages about the brand.

Selecting the Social Media

In using social media, a brand manager tries to select and use one or more of the options from the hundreds that exist. This often entails assessing (1) the characteristics of the website's visitors and (2) the number of users or unique visitors to the website.

Audience Data Available for Social Media

Both marketing research organizations and the social media themselves provide user-profile data for the social media to help brand managers choose among them. As presented earlier, the top row of Figure 20–2 shows a recent profile of the male–female audience breakdown for four major social media. As shown in the figure, Facebook users are 58 percent female and 42 percent male, while YouTube users are the reverse, important differences to brand managers allocating promotion budgets.

Recent Activity on the Four Social Media

Brand managers must also evaluate the number of users and the monthly market share of visits for the various social media platforms. Number of users is a measure of the size of the audience. Market share is an indication of the use of the website relative to the other sites. In terms of the number of users, Facebook and YouTube have 1 billion or more users, although Facebook's market share is three times larger. Similarly, Twitter and LinkedIn have between 300 and 350 million users, but Twitter has a higher market share indicating more frequent use.[31]

How Social Media Produce Sales

An example shows how a PepsiCo brand manager can use social media to produce sales and profits for her product or brand. Consider the roles of both the PepsiCo brand manager and social media in the following example.[32]

Role of the PepsiCo Brand Manager

The PepsiCo brand manager composes title, copy, and images or photos for the social media ad. She often specifies the web address to which its ad should link based on the brand's social media marketing goals.

To increase awareness and build up a fan base, she might link the ad to the PepsiCo website or its Facebook, Twitter, or Pinterest sites. Ideally, to encourage and produce new sales that can be tracked, she must link the ad to a coupon code, a specific product on the PepsiCo website, or another promotional offer.

The brand manager then defines the characteristics of the one or more market segments she wants to reach on the social media she has selected. This starts with demographic characteristics like geographic region, sex, age range, and education. She then adds factors like relationship status and user interests.

Role of Social Media

Ads and videos on social media such as YouTube and Facebook are less likely than traditional print ads to have a marketing objective of immediate sales. This is because social media images are often on the screen for only seconds. A more likely goal is to have viewers go to the advertiser's website and post it on their Facebook Pages or forward it to friends. The key for a brand manager using social media is to gain viewers' attention for a few extra seconds.

PepsiCo's "Test Drive" YouTube video is an example of this strategy. Building on its highly successful "Uncle Drew" videos and TV ads, PepsiCo used its entertaining "Test Drive" video to promote its Pepsi MAX beverages—a zero-calorie cola. In the video, NASCAR driver Jeff Gordon is disguised as "Mike," an average guy taking a test drive at a local dealership. The unsuspecting car salesman riding along will never forget it!

"Test Drive" was a huge hit for Pepsi MAX, with over 35 million views in its first two months. Even better, the video reinforces the product's tag line of "a great-tasting, zero-calorie cola in disguise." As a product in the mature stage of its product life cycle, Pepsi MAX uses an entertaining message to make its diet beverages relevant to a younger target audience. The video captures the viewer's attention by replacing some product messaging with entertainment.[33]

Measuring the Results of Social Media Programs

Performance measures for social media divide into (1) those linked to inputs or costs (Figure 20–4) and (2) those tied to the outputs or revenues resulting from social media. Clearly, the ideal performance measure for both conventional and social media is one that ties actual sales revenues to the cost of the ad or other promotion. With the explosion in the growth of social media, marketing and brand managers are being challenged to connect the cost of these new social network promotions to the sales they generate. The result has been an emergence of many new performance measures, often requiring a whole new language.

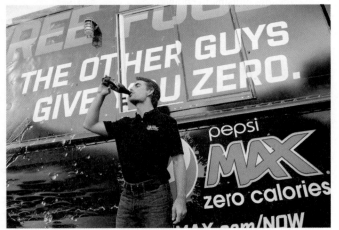

In choosing to run a social media ad campaign like this Pepsi MAX video on YouTube, brand managers must assess the potential sales likely to result compared to a campaign using traditional media.

© Brian Blanco/Invision for Pepsi/ AP Images

Performance Measures Linked to Inputs or Costs

Figure 20–4 shows three performance measures for social media linked mainly to inputs or costs. Moving down the list of measures shown in Figure 20–4, one starts with a measure tied only to costs (cost per thousand, or CPM), then moves to a measure of interest in a product (cost per click, or CPC), and finally moves to a measure linked more closely to the sales revenues generated from the social media ad or action (cost per action, or CPA).

The cost per thousand (CPM) measure ties to the number of times the ad loads and a user might see it—but not whether the user has actually reacted to it. This measure is roughly equivalent to the CPM for traditional media discussed in Chapter 17. The cost per click (CPC) measure gives the rate the advertiser pays, say to Facebook, every time a visitor clicks on the ad and jumps from that page to the advertiser's website. Finally, the cost per action (CPA) measure ties loosely to actual sales—for example, paying $5 for every purchase that originates from an ad, say, on the Facebook site. By summing up the revenues from all these purchases, a difficult task, this CPA measure most closely ties the cost of the social media ad to the sales revenues the ad generates.

FIGURE 20–4

Performance Measure	Costs to Advertisers	Who Provides It	Who Uses It	An Assessment	
				Advantages	Disadvantages
Cost per thousand (CPM)	"I will pay $0.50 for every 1,000 times this ad loads, up to $100 per month."	Small websites that sell ads directly (may be using a third-party service)	Advertisers who simply want to build "awareness"	Simple to use	Impressions don't always lead to sales
Cost per click (CPC)	"I will pay $1.00 for every visitor who clicks on this ad and goes from your website to mine."	Most websites use this method—executed by a third party such as Google AdWords	Advertisers who want to pay for success, but may not be able to track sales from advertisement to purchase	Only pay for a visitor who has expressed an interest in my ad	Ads may not display if they are a poor fit for the viewing audience
Cost per action (CPA)	"I will pay $5 for every purchase that originated from an ad on your site."	Usually executed through third parties; Google AdSense recently added this feature	Sophisticated advertisers who want to pay for success	Only pay for what works	Similar to CPC but harder to track and more expensive per action

Performance measures for social media linked mainly to inputs or costs, as seen by a brand manager.

Performance Measures Linked to Outputs or Revenues

Many of the measures for evaluating how a brand manager's social network promotion is doing reflect the two-way communications present in social media. These measures often tie to output results in terms of "friends," "followers," or "visitors" to a social network site, which can be a first step to estimating the sales revenue generated. From a brand manager's viewpoint, here are some of the frequently used Facebook measures, moving from the more general to the more specific:

- *Users/members.* Individuals who have registered on a social networking site by completing the process involved, such as providing their name, user ID (usually an e-mail address), and password, as well as answering a few questions (date of birth, gender, etc.).

- *Fans.* The number of people who have opted in to a brand's messages through a social media platform at a given time.

- *Share of voice.* The brand's share or percentage of all the online social media chatter related to, say, its product category or a topic.

- *Page views.* The number of times a Facebook Page is loaded in a given time period.

- *Visitors.* The total number of visitors to a Facebook Page in a given time period; if someone visits three times in one day, she is counted three times.

- *Unique visitors.* The total number of unique visitors to a Facebook Page in a given time period; if someone visits three times in one day, he is counted only once.

- *Average page views per visitor.* Page views divided by visitors in a given time period.

- *Interaction rate.* The number of people who interact with a post ("like," make a comment, and so on) divided by the total number of people seeing the post.

- *Click-through rate (CTR).* Percentage of recipients who have clicked on a link on the page to visit a specific site.

- *Fan source.* Where a social network following comes from—with fans coming from a friend being more valuable than those coming from an ad.

Note that while sales revenues resulting from social media do not appear in these measures, as we move down the list above, the measures are often more specific than comparable ones used in traditional media. This is because it is far simpler to electronically track the social network users who click on a website or ad than it is to track consumers who receive traditional media.

Specialized Focus for Other Social Media

One of the advantages of social media is that communities can form around ideas and commonalities, regardless of the physical location of their members. While major social media such as Facebook or YouTube may garner the majority of the traffic, smaller media such as Pinterest may be more successful for some products and services.

Pinterest, a virtual pinboard and content-sharing social network, allows people to "pin" or share images of their favourite things such as clothing, craft ideas, home decor, and recipes. Pinterest members create customized, themed "pinboards" to categorize their images such as "Odds & Ends," "Food," and "Knitting" shown on the Pinterest screen. These images are shared with other members of the Pinterest community. Members can also share their pinned images on Facebook and Twitter.

Pinterest has over 72 million users, 85 percent of whom are women—with 75 percent of daily traffic coming through mobile applications.[34] So it has become a major sales driver for retailers and manufacturers that target women. In using Pinterest, brand managers can post images of their company's products on their Pinterest board and link them back to their websites.

Pinterest allows users to "pin" or share images of favourite interests on its site, which is useful for brand managers promoting their company's products.

© Lenscap/Alamy Stock Photo

Learning Review

7. What is the difference between (and marketing significance of) a "passive receiver" for conventional media and an "active receiver" for social media?

8. Stated simply, how can an advertiser on Facebook expect to generate sales?

LO5 SOCIAL MEDIA + SMARTPHONES + EXOTIC APPS

Trends in marketing's use of social media reflect what scientists call "mirror worlds" or "smart systems" that are really the convergence of the real and digital worlds. A *smart system* is a computer-based network that triggers actions by sensing changes in the real or digital world. This section discusses (1) the convergence of real and digital worlds, (2) how this convergence links social media to marketing actions, and (3) where all this *may* be headed in *your* future. The section closes by describing social media and global marketing.

The Convergence of Real and Digital Worlds

Saying that our physical and virtual worlds are converging sounds like science fiction. This convergence of real and digital worlds is the result of a proliferation of interlinked smartphones, tablet devices, sensors, special identification tags, databases, algorithms, apps, and other elements. A look at several of these elements helps explain this real world–digital world convergence and what it means for marketing.

Smartphones

Seeing today's smartphones, users often forget how far they've come in 15 years and how they've changed marketing. In 1998, the RIM 950 revolutionized mobile e-mail. The device had a screen and a keyboard—but no phone. The revolution was completed in 2007 with Apple's legendary iPhone. It had all three basics—screen, multitouch keyboard, and phone. Today's GPS-enabled smartphones give mobile consumers access to online ads, local restaurant promotions, and time-sensitive discounts at retailers. And, Canadians love smartphones. Almost seven in ten Canadians have a smartphone, and they are using them in a big way. In fact, over half of Canadians' time spent online is through their smartphones. And over 30 percent of Canadians are using their smartphones to watch TV. This is opening up opportunities for marketers to reach consumers in dynamic and engaging ways.[35]

Databases and Algorithms

As discussed in Chapters 8 and 9, finding prospective customers often involves market segmentation that requires databases searched with exotic algorithms—models used to query, organize, manipulate, and present data. The owners of these databases, among them Google and Facebook, must make them as useful as possible to potential advertisers in order to succeed.

Among databases, Google is the hands-down winner—indexing 30 trillion unique web pages across 230 million sites. Its search engine now gives results in answers to research queries in photos, facts, and "direct answers," and not just the "blue links" of website addresses. Google now offers its own social networking service, Google+, to obtain data about individuals by name, personal interests, and identities of friends.[36]

Facebook recently entered Google's territory by announcing Graph Search, its own search engine algorithm. Facebook users can conduct their own queries about people, places, photos, and interests. An example is "restaurants recommended by friends." This lets Facebook give advertisers real value in the "likes" found on its site. For example, a small chocolate retail shop can target young parents who buy lots of organic food products.[37] So it's not difficult to see how a casual "like" for a brand by a user in a database's "digital world" can converge into an actual "real-world" purchase by the user through a very targeted promotion planned by a brand manager.

Apps

The apps for smartphones are accelerating the convergence of the real and digital worlds. Apps (or mobile apps or applications) are small, downloadable software programs that run on smartphones and tablet devices. When Apple launched its iPhone, it didn't expect smartphone apps to be very important. Wrong! Apple's App Store currently offers 1.5 million apps either free or for sale, and Google Play offers 1.6 million apps for users of Android devices. With the wide array of apps to choose from, today's consumers typically spend two hours a day using about eight apps.[38]

Many apps are video games. Angry Birds, for example, has been downloaded more than 2 billion times since its 2009 release, which is one reason Angry Birds–themed products now range from mascara to toys and entertainment parks. The popularity of the game is declining though as it enters the decline stage of its product life cycle (PLC).[39]

The video games Farmville, Temple Run, QuizUp, 4Pics1Word, and Fruit Ninja also show the short PLC for these apps in today's tough competitive environment.

Enter Clash of Clans and Candy Crush Saga video games that exploit the real world–digital world convergence. Today's successful new video games (1) build on a huge personal-rewards psychology for players; (2) can be played on the small smartphone screens; (3) top the most-downloaded charts of Apple iOS, Google, Android, and Facebook; and (4) often use a "freemium strategy"—where the download is free but users pay for extra features, such as for ways to speed up the game.

The Candy Crush app has now been installed over 500 million times across Facebook, iOS, and Android devices. Even Angry Birds has changed its strategy from charging a download cost to a freemium strategy with its recently launched Angry Birds Go. Sound easy to build an app? Maybe. But hundreds of creative apps die a quiet death each year!

Mobile Marketing: Tightening Links to Marketing Actions

This convergence of the real and digital worlds has also contributed to the growth of mobile marketing, or the broad set of interactive messaging options that are used to communicate through personal mobile devices.[40] This continuous connection present in mobile marketing has led to important smartphone apps, such as:

- *Price-comparison searches.* Scan product bar codes or QR codes and research 500,000 stores, synchronizing searches between your computer and your smartphone.
- *Location-based promotions.* Use your GPS-enabled smartphone for location check-ins to receive discounts at stores such as JCPenney.
- *Loyalty programs.* Win loyalty points for walking into stores like Canadian Tire and receive discounts from them.

The number of smartphone shopping searches and purchases has exploded in recent years, causing huge challenges (such as showrooming) for conventional bricks-and-mortar retailers.

The clear point of difference in mobile marketing is its unique ability to empower users by connecting with them individually and continuously—learning about their likes and personal characteristics and sharing this information with online friends and (often) marketers selling products. This socially networked world will lead to connected users having more direct interactions with sellers.

The convergence of social media, smartphones, tablet devices, and new apps will lead to companies having a more dynamic interaction with their customers. But is this an unqualified success for buyers? Consider the following perspectives.

A Consumer Purchase Where Sensors Have Some Control

A vending machine scans your face to identify your age and sex and changes its display and—in the future—may give you a quantity discount for buying two of your favourite candy bars (it knows about your Facebook "likes") while showing an electronic dinner coupon for a nearby restaurant if you appear between 7 and 9 p.m. this evening. The results of the candy and dinner offer are directly measurable for marketers. While it offers unusual convenience, does this buying situation start to interfere with your personal privacy?

A Consumer Purchase Where the Buyer Controls All

Some cities in South Korea and China are on the leading edge of virtual supermarket shopping. Tesco Home Plus, a supermarket chain, provides a quick spur-of-the-moment opportunity for grocery shopping. Shoppers use their smartphones to scan images

Too busy to visit your supermarket this week? If you are in China or Korea, do it on the wall of your subway station with your smartphone—and have your purchases delivered to your door.

© Imaginechina/Corbis

on the wall of a subway station to buy Tesco's grocery products while waiting for their train. They use the smartphone app to pay for the groceries, which are delivered to their door right after they get home. In this example, buyers achieve great convenience—probably an unqualified success.

On Privacy: How Much "Convergence" Is Too Much?

Smart systems are fine up to a point. For example, most of us are comfortable letting convergence find us a timely deal at a local restaurant using a location-based app on our smartphone. It may even be all right if Google's latest database breakthrough automatically proposes an "ideal vacation plan" for us based on our normal preferences, weather conditions, and available hotel and airline prices.

But we may be concerned if retailers now place sensors in several hundred locations to track us, following the signals emitted from our Wi-Fi-enabled smartphone. Here are some other numbers that may frighten you:

- *2,000-plus.* Estimated number of times the online activity of an average Internet user is tracked every day.
- *3,000-plus.* Number of "shopping tendencies" Acxiom says it can measure for nearly every household.
- *700 million.* Approximate number of adult consumers in the global database of Acxiom Corp., a leading data broker.

About 68 percent of Internet users today feel that privacy laws don't protect them adequately. So 86 percent of them have used privacy technologies to take online steps to remove or mask their digital data.[41] The future? Concerned about Internet privacy, the Canadian government has enacted legislation to define the rights of consumers in the use of data involving their personal characteristics and activities.

Social Media and Global Marketing

Computers, television, the Internet, smartphones, tablet devices, and social media have changed forever the way individuals around the world communicate. This dramatically affects global marketing. However, as you read in Chapter 7, a "one-size-fits-all" approach is not recommended when it comes to social media and global marketing. For example, there are language barriers when marketers reach across borders. But simply translating content will not be enough to achieve a successful global marketing campaign. In other words, there are other factors at work that inhibit the use of a "one-size-fits-all" approach. These factors include cultural, economic, and political-regulatory variables.

Experts provide some basic advice regarding the use of social media and global marketing.[42] *First,* pick the right social media platforms. This means researching and finding out where the customers are in terms of social media usage. Facebook and Twitter have established international audiences, but local competitors such as Orkut (huge in Brazil and India) or VK (Russia) can also be important, depending on the customer being sought. It's also worth bearing in mind that, with Facebook and Twitter still offically banned in China, local alternatives such as Weibo and Renren are essential for maintaining a presence there. *Second,* once the social media platforms are selected, organize them in a hub-and-spoke fashion. Align the main hub (one owned and managed by the company, not a third-party platform like Facebook) with the largest and most active market. Use the other social media platforms as spokes to promote the hub and drive traffic to the hub. Starbucks, for example, uses its global brand page as its hub and associated country pages as the spokes.

Third, develop the right content that meets your customers' needs. This means to first carefully listen to your customers to find out what content they want. For example, audiences in the United Kingdom react well to humorous content. The basic rules to create relevant and appropriate content are (1) speak to the customer in their language and always use a back-translation process and use a local experts to check it (Dell's Direct2Dell blog, for example, has Twitter feeds in English, Spanish, Japanese, and Chinese), (2) use images wherever possible (pictures are much easier to convey a message), and (3) identify the right influencers in each market and invest to engage them so that they can help spread the word.

Fourth, establish ground rules for using social media. Outline who can and cannot create a social media channel or profile for the company, as well as what is permissible content and what is not. *Fifth,* measure the performance of the social media campaign using key metrics (e.g., growth in unique visitors or number of conversations).

Successful global marketers realize that a good social media strategy is not just a website or Facebook Page. It involves understanding where your customers are in terms of social media usage and engaging them with relevant and appealing content. They also understand it is also about incorporating social media into an IMC program, channel strategy, and overall marketing strategy.

Learning Review

9. What is an example of how the real (physical) and digital (virtual) worlds are converging?

10. What are apps and why are they important?

11. What is an example of the reach of social media in (*a*) global marketing and (*b*) international affairs?

Learning Objectives Review

 Define social media and describe how they differ from traditional advertising media.

Social media are online media where active users submit news, photos, videos, and opinions, often accompanied by a feedback process to identify "popular" topics. Social media can be classified based on two factors: (*1*) media richness, which involves the degree of acoustic, visual, and physical contact between the social network and the user, and (*2*) self-disclosure, which is the degree to which individuals can control the impressions they want to make to others. Social media differ from traditional advertising media (newspapers, magazines, radio, and television) in that user-generated content (*1*) is relatively inexpensive to create, publish, and access; (*2*) requires little training to develop; (*3*) can deliver virtually instantaneous responses; (*4*) can quickly alter and repost; and (*5*) may not be as private or anonymous as users expect.

 Identify the four major social networks and how brand managers integrate them in their organizations' marketing actions.

The four major social networks are Facebook, Twitter, LinkedIn, and YouTube. Facebook is a social network where users create a personal profile, add other users as "friends," and exchange messages, photos, videos, and opinions with them. When incorporating Facebook into their promotional strategies, brand managers should know that Facebook content generally cannot be catalogued or reported by an outside search engine such as Google. One way to respond to this is to create a Facebook Page for the brand. Twitter enables users to send and receive "tweets," messages up to 140 characters long. For Twitter, brand managers can use monitoring programs such as CoTweet to track what people are saying about their organization's brand. LinkedIn lets users post their personal profiles to a network of businesspeople. LinkedIn can be used to create a company profile to share brand information and career opportunities with LinkedIn users and to demonstrate the company's expertise and professionalism. YouTube is a video-sharing social network where users can upload, distribute, view, and comment on videos. YouTube also allows marketers to create a brand channel to promote a product, show ads for it, and have viewers comment on it. YouTube also allows a company to inform consumers about itself and direct traffic by featuring a link back to its website.

 Describe the differing roles of those receiving messages through traditional media versus social media and the factors brand managers use to select a social network.

With promotional messages received through traditional media, recipients are generally "passive receivers" and the communication ends with them. In contrast, recipients of social media messages are "active receivers," and the company sending them messages hopes they will become "evangelists" and send positive messages back to the company and to online friends. The factors a marketer uses to select a specific social network involve assessing (*1*) the number of daily visitors to the company's website, (*2*) the characteristics (or profile) of those visitors, and (*3*) the focus of the social network. Of the four major social networks, Facebook has the largest number of daily visitors, followed by YouTube, Twitter, and LinkedIn. Each of these has a unique user profile that allows marketers to develop marketing programs to reach specific target segments. Also, because each social network has a unique focus (videos, short messaging, and so on), marketers can modify their marketing programs to take advantage of these differences.

LO4 **Compare the performance measures of social media linked to costs (inputs) versus revenues (outputs)**

Performance measures linked to costs (inputs) include (*1*) cost per thousand (similar to the CPM for a print ad), which is the number of times an ad is displayed to a user; (*2*) cost per click (CPC), which gives the rate the advertiser pays each time a visitor clicks on the ad and then jumps to the advertiser's web page; and (*3*) cost per action (CPA), which is the amount paid for every purchase that originates from an ad on a social media site. Examples of performance measures linked to revenues (outputs) include (*1*) users/members that have registered on social media websites; (*2*) the number of unique monthly users viewing the website at a given time; (*3*) page views, or the number of times a specific web page is loaded; and (*4*) visitors, or the total number of users viewing a particular web page during a specified time period.

 Identify the cause of the convergence of the real and digital worlds and how this will affect the future of social media.

The convergence of the real and digital worlds in social media is the result of the proliferation of interlinked smart-phones, tablet devices, sensors, special identification tags, databases, algorithms, apps, and other elements. This convergence will allow consumers and marketers to increase the exchange of personal and product-related information with each other. For consumers, however, this could lead to a loss of privacy and possible exploitation by unscrupulous marketers. Finally, social media are global and marketers must be able to effectively harness their use in global marketing campaigns.

Applying Marketing Knowledge

1. How could your college or university more effectively use Facebook and Twitter to promote its brand to potential students?

2. You and three university friends have decided to launch an online business selling clothes that students wear—T-shirts, shorts, sweats, and so on. You plan to use Facebook ads. What "likes" or interests do (*a*) college and university men and (*b*) women have that might help you in planning your Facebook strategy?

3. You graduated from college four years ago and now have an information technology (IT) job. Your company just announced it will move all its IT work overseas in three months. Go to the LinkedIn site and determine what information you would put on your LinkedIn site to help you find a new job.

4. What is the significance of user-generated content when contrasted with social media and traditional media?

5. You are a brand manager for a sneaker manufacturer like Nike or Under Armour and are trying to use Facebook to reach (*a*) college- and university-aged women and (*b*) men over 55 years of age. What three or four "likes" or interests would you expect each segment to have when you try to reach it with Facebook?

6. In measuring the results of a social network, what are the (*a*) advantages and (*b*) disadvantages of performance measures linked directly to revenues versus costs?

7. You have a location-based app such as Foursquare on your GPS-enabled smartphone that tells you about a discount at your favourite local restaurant. How does this reflect the convergence of real and digital worlds?

Building Your Marketing Plan

Remembering the target market segments you identified in Chapter 9 for your marketing plan:

1. (*a*) Identify which one of the four social networks described in this chapter would be most useful and (*b*) give your reasons.

2. Briefly describe (*a*) how you would use this social network to try to increase sales of your products and (*b*) why you expect target market customers to respond to it.

StuffDOT™, Inc.: Rewarding Users for Actively Shopping and Sharing!

"Coming from a rewards and loyalty background, I often wondered how to combine the best of rewards and commissions with the expanding universe of social media," says Jennifer Katz, founder and chief executive officer of StuffDOT, Inc.

"Further, it seemed really unfair that only a few people were benefiting from all the content millions of people were providing for free online. I believe the individuals creating all this online content deserve to benefit from their efforts," says Katz.

"Thinking about this, one day our marketing director came into a meeting and explained how a really cute anchor bracelet that she posted on a social-sharing site went viral. But now she faced a six-week backlog to purchase it. So we all said, if she made a commission on every anchor bracelet that was sold because of that one post, she could have bought five. Right then and there, StuffDOT was born," explains Katz.

While the young social network is constantly changing, its beginnings offer a valuable case study.

StuffDOT's Vision, Brand Name, and Logo

StuffDot is designed to be the all-in-one site for online shopping and sharing. StuffDOT's vision is to reward users for what they are already doing online. Most other sites tend to keep all the affiliate fees and commissions for themselves. StuffDOT, however, enables users to benefit from all this online shopping and sharing. This is the first time, to StuffDOT's knowledge, that a firm has developed a platform where the people posting to social media are the same people who are rewarded for it. In addition, the StuffDOT team has added coupons, cash-back shopping from thousands of retailers, and a feature that allows users to create their own stores, called DOT shops.

"We chose the brand name StuffDOT because it was catchy and [we] felt we could really build on it," says Katz. "With the name StuffDOT, we could use Stuff, DOT, and StuffDOT, which also gives flexibility. The name also is great for campaigns like 'CareDot,' 'Spot the Dot,' or 'Stuff I Like.' The team tried other names, but they just didn't have that fun stickiness that the name StuffDOT does," says Jennifer Katz.

The StuffDOT team also tried and tested several different logos before coming up with the memorable, attention-getting logo shown below. People see the orange dot as friendly, familiar, and eye-catching, and it has proven to be an easy logo to build on.

Courtesy of StuffDOT, Inc.

How StuffDOT Works

Kelsey Fisher, StuffDOT's creative director, explains what a "dot" is and the steps in "dotting"—keys to understanding how StuffDOT users earn and redeem their resulting commissions.

What Is a "Dot"?

"Dots are posts ranging from products, to do-it-yourself projects, to recipes, to funny videos and random photos," Fisher explains. "A dot is something posted to view, to share, or to track for a future purchase. A dot is simply a post of anything you want to display on the StuffDOT site," she says.

How to "Dot"

Kelsey Fisher explains the three steps to dot:

1. "Use the simple drag-and-drop process to add the 'Dot It' button to your toolbar in your web browser.

2. "Dot or post items you 'like' online by clicking on that button on your toolbar. For example, if you are browsing Macy's online store and see something you like, you can click on the 'Dot It' button in your toolbar and it will show up on your StuffDOT page.

3. "Watch your commissions grow as people share, buy, or click on the stuff you've 'dotted.' You can also earn commissions on your own purchases!"

Earning and Redeeming StuffDOT Commissions

So how does an online user actually earn commissions? When users find things they want to share or purchase online, they dot or post the item to StuffDOT. If the item appears with a sticker showing a commission percentage, this means it is from one of StuffDOT's retail partners and is commission-eligible.

When a dot leads to a purchase or a click-through view, or a share by the "dotter" or someone else, the dotter will receive a commission. Users can also earn commissions by posting and purchasing their own items. Once a user's balance reaches $15, they can start redeeming gift cards from a variety of popular retailers.

Enhancing StuffDOT's User-Friendliness

A challenge for the StuffDOT team is keeping it simple, yet having features that make StuffDOT fun and rewarding.

"I work closely with the StuffDOT team to turn the concepts they create into user-friendly features on StuffDOT," says Sudipta Tripathy, StuffDOT's chief technology officer. "For example, we want to ensure that all new features have the same look and feel across all parts of the StuffDOT platform—website, Android app, or iOS app," he says.

Courtesy of StuffDOT, Inc.

Recent updates and features now enable StuffDOT users more ways to earn commissions. By moving many features to its mobile apps (photo), StuffDOT has added the flexibility to share, shop, and earn anywhere at any time. Some other examples of user-friendly features include:

- *Retailer list.* Adding a list of retailers and their commission percentages lets StuffDOT shoppers know the exact rewards from each store. Also, users can discover reward-eligible shops they did not even know about.

- *Search shops and deals.* Users can search for products and deals from StuffDOT's retailers without leaving the site. StuffDOT members can then find, dot, and buy commission-eligible items in one easy-to-use platform.

- *Commission status.* The redesigned commissions section shows users the values of their lifetime, current, and pending commissions. So they can track their purchase commissions and confirm their purchases are commission-eligible.

Marketing StuffDOT

StuffDOT has focused its initial marketing efforts on three areas: (1) partnerships, (2) the StuffDOT Internship and Campus Ambassador Program, and (3) social sharing.

StuffDOT's partnerships include online affiliate aggregators that give users access to over 20,000 online retailers that share affiliate fees and commissions. In addition, StuffDOT has been working with select retailers to create unique promotional programs that benefit users and make the partner brand more prominent. For example, a recent promotion featured a free pair of running shoes for signing up, referring friends, and dotting. This not only built awareness for the brand of running shoes but also created a new user base for StuffDOT.

The StuffDOT Internship and Campus Ambassador Program (see photo) not only gives students a rich experience working in new social media but also has greatly enhanced the benefits of the StuffDOT platform. Student interns work both at the home office and on campus to create StuffDOT promotions. Depending on their interests, students may focus on organizing new-user workshops and street-team promotions or finding new partners and users through social networks. StuffDOT is looking continuously for new Campus Ambassadors.

Social-sharing features throughout the StuffDOT site make it very convenient for users to share items with friends or family. For example, a student who wants a new laptop for her birthday can share that item with friends on Facebook, and she can also e-mail that item with an embedded link to her parents as a reminder. That student can also earn a StuffDOT reward on the purchase—a "double" birthday present.

Courtesy of StuffDOT, Inc.

QUESTIONS

1. What recent StuffDOT actions have added to its user-friendliness?

2. (a) Who are StuffDOT's major competitors and (b) what point(s) of difference should StuffDOT use to distinguish itself from them?

3. How should StuffDOT be marketed so that it becomes an integral part of everyday life?

4. How can the team create "buzz" for StuffDOT and grow its user base most effectively (a) using social media platforms (like Facebook and Twitter) and (b) using its own website?

Case: This case was written by Jennifer Katz, Amanda Axvig, and William Rudelius.

GLOSSARY

80/20 rule A concept that suggests 80 percent of a firm's sales are obtained from 20 percent of its customers.

above-, at-, or below-market pricing Setting prices based on pricing of similar products in the market.

account management policies Policies that specify whom the salespeople should contact, what kinds of selling and customer service activities should be engaged in, and how these activities should be carried out.

action item list An aid to implementing a market plan, consisting of four columns: (1) the task, (2) the name of the person responsible for accomplishing that task, (3) the date by which the task is to be finished; and (4) what is to be delivered.

adaptive selling A need-satisfaction sales presentation that involves adjusting the presentation to fit the selling situation.

advertising Any paid form of non-personal communication about an organization, good, service, or idea by an identified sponsor.

all-you-can-afford budgeting Allocating funds to promotion only after all other budget items are covered.

attitude A learned predisposition to respond to an object or class of objects in a consistently favourable or unfavourable way.

baby boomers The generation of those born between 1946 and 1964.

back translation Retranslating a word or phrase into the original language by a different interpreter to catch errors.

balance of trade The difference between the monetary value of a nation's exports and imports.

barriers to entry Business practices or conditions that make it difficult for new firms to enter a market.

beliefs A consumer's subjective perception of how well a product or brand performs on different attributes.

benchmarking Discovering how others do something better than your own firm so that you can imitate or leapfrog competition.

bidders' list A list of firms believed to be qualified to supply a given item.

blended family Family formed by the merging into a single family of two previously separated units.

bottom of the pyramid The largest, but poorest socio-economic group of people in the world, consisting of 4 billion people who reside in developing countries and live on less than $2 per day.

brand community A specialized group of consumers with a structured set of relationships involving a particular brand, fellow customers of that brand, and the product in use.

brand equity The added value that a given brand name gives to a product beyond the functional benefits provided.

brand licensing A contractual agreement whereby a company allows another firm to use its brand name, patent, trade secret, or other property for a royalty or fee.

brand loyalty A favourable attitude toward and consistent purchase of a single brand over time.

brand name Any word, device (design, shape, sound, or colour), or combination of these used to distinguish a seller's goods or services.

brand personality A set of human characteristics associated with a brand name.

branding Activity in which an organization uses a name, phrase, design, symbols, or combination of these to identify its products and distinguish them from those of competitors.

breadth of product line The variety of different items a store carries.

break-even analysis A technique that analyzes the relationship between total revenue and total cost to determine profitability at various levels of output.

brokers Independent firms or individuals whose principal function is to bring buyers and sellers together to make sales.

bundle pricing The marketing of two or more products in a single "package" price.

business The clear, broad, underlying industry or market sector of an organization's offering.

business analysis The stage of the new-product process that involves specifying the product features and marketing strategy and making financial projections needed to commercialize a product.

business distributor Performs a variety of marketing channel functions, including selling, stocking, delivering a full product assortment, and financing for business goods and services.

business goods Products that assist directly or indirectly in providing products for resale (also known as B2B goods, industrial goods, or organizational goods).

business marketing The marketing of goods and services to companies, governments, and not-for-profit organizations for use in the creation of goods and services that they can produce and market to others.

business model The strategies an organization develops to provide value to the customers it serves.

buy classes Three types of organizational buying situations: new buy, straight rebuy, and modified rebuy.

buying centre The group of people in an organization who participate in the buying process and share common goals, risks, and knowledge important to a purchase decision.

buzz marketing Popularity created by consumer word of mouth.

capacity management Making service capacity as productive as possible without compromising service quality.

category management An approach that assigns a manager with the responsibility for selecting all products that consumers in a market segment might view as substitutes for each other, with the objective of maximizing sales and profits in the category.

cause marketing Occurs when the charitable contributions of a firm are tied directly to the customer revenues produced through the promotion of one of its products.

caveat emptor The legal concept of "let the buyer beware" that was pervasive in Canadian business culture before the 1960s.

census metropolitan areas (CMAs) Geographic labour markets having a population of 100,000 persons or more.

central business district The oldest retail setting, the community's downtown area.

channel conflict Arises when one channel member believes another channel member is engaged in behaviour that prevents it from achieving its goals.

channel of communication The means of conveying a message to a receiver.

co-branding The pairing of two or more recognized brands on a single product or service.

code of ethics A formal statement of ethical principles and rules of conduct.

cognitive dissonance Feeling of post-purchase psychological tension or anxiety.

cohort brand management The bundling of one company's multiple brands into a single marketing effort aimed at a common consumer group.

commercialization The stage of the new-product process that involves positioning and launching a new product in full-scale production and sales.

communication The process of conveying a message to others, which requires six elements: a source, a message, a channel of communication, a receiver, and the processes of encoding and decoding.

community shopping centre A retail location that typically has one primary store (usually a department store branch) and 20 to 40 smaller outlets, serving a population of consumers who are within a 10- to 20-minute drive.

competencies An organization's special capabilities, including skills, technologies, and resources, that distinguish it from other organizations and provide value to its customers.

competition Alternative firms that could provide a product to satisfy a specific market's needs.

Competition Act The key legislation designed to protect competition and consumers in Canada.

competitive advantage A unique strength relative to competitors, often based on quality, time, cost, innovation, customer intimacy, or customer experience management.

competitive parity budgeting Matching the competitors' absolute level of spending or the proportion per point of market share.

consideration set The group of brands that a consumer would consider acceptable from among all the brands of which he or she is aware.

consultative selling Focuses on problem definition, where the salesperson serves as an expert on problem recognition and resolution.

consumer behaviour The actions that a person takes in purchasing and using products and services, including the mental and social processes that precede and follow these actions.

consumer ethnocentrism The tendency to believe that it is inappropriate, indeed immoral, to purchase foreign-made products.

consumer goods Products purchased by the ultimate consumer.

consumer socialization The process by which people acquire the skills, knowledge, and attitudes necessary to function as consumers.

consumerism A grassroots movement started in the 1960s to increase the influence, power, and rights of consumers in dealing with institutions.

consumer-oriented sales promotions Sales tools used to support a company's advertising and personal selling efforts directed to ultimate consumers; examples include coupons, sweepstakes, and samples.

convenience goods Items that the consumer purchases frequently and with a minimum of shopping effort.

cooperative advertising Advertising programs by which a manufacturer pays a percentage of the retailer's local advertising expense for advertising the manufacturer's products.

core values An organization's core values are the fundamental, passionate, and enduring principles that guide its conduct over time.

corporate level Level at which top management directs overall strategy for the entire organization.

cost focus strategy Involves controlling expenses and, in turn, lowering product prices targeting a narrow range of market segments.

cost leadership strategy Focuses on reducing expenses and lowering produce prices while targeting a broad array of market segments.

cost per thousand (CPM) The cost of reaching 1,000 individuals or households with an advertising message in a given medium.

cost-plus pricing Summing the total unit cost of providing a product or service and adding a specific amount to the cost to arrive at a price.

countertrade The practice of using barter rather than money for making global sales.

cross-cultural analysis Involves the study of similarities and differences among consumers in two or more nations or societies.

cross-functional teams A small number of people from different departments in an organization who are mutually accountable to accomplish a task or common set of performance goals.

cultural symbols Things that represent ideas and concepts.

culture The set of values, ideas, and attitudes that are learned and shared among the members of a group.

currency exchange rate The price of one country's currency expressed in terms of another country's currency.

customary pricing Setting prices dictated by tradition, standardized channels of distribution, or other competitive factors.

customer contact audit A flow chart of the points of interaction between consumer and service provider.

customer experience management (CEM) Managing the customers' interactions with the organization at all levels and at all touchpoints (direct and indirect contacts of the customer with an organization) so that the customer has a positive impression of the organization, is satisfied with the experience, and will remain loyal to the organization.

customer lifetime value (CLV) The profit generated by the customer's purchase of an organization's product or service over the customer's lifetime.

customer relationship management (CRM) The process of building and developing long-term relationships with customers by delivering customer value and satisfaction.

customer satisfaction The match between customer expectations of the product and the product's actual performance.

customer service The ability of logistics management to satisfy users in terms of time, dependability, communication, and convenience.

customer value The unique combination of benefits received by the customer that include quality, price, convenience, on-time delivery, and both before-sale and after-sale service.

customer value proposition A cluster of benefits that an organization promises customers to satisfy their needs.

customs Norms and expectations about the way people do things in a specific country.

data mining The extraction of hidden predictive information from large databases.

decoding The process of having the receiver take a set of symbols, the message, and transform them back to an abstract idea.

demographics The study of the characteristics of a human population. These characteristics include population size, growth rate, gender, marital status, ethnicity, income, and so forth.

depth interviews Detailed, individual interviews with people relevant to a research project.

depth of product line The store carries a large assortment of each item.

derived demand Demand for business products and services is driven by, or derived from, demand for consumer products and services.

development The stage of the new-product process that involves turning the idea on paper into a prototype.

differentiation focus strategy Requires products to have significant points of difference to target one or only a few market segments.

differentiation strategy Requires products to have significant points of difference in product offerings, brand image, higher quality, advanced technology, or superior service to charge a higher price while targeting a broad array of market segments.

direct channel A marketing channel where a producer and ultimate consumers deal directly with each other.

direct forecast Estimating the value to be forecast without any intervening steps.

direct investment A domestic firm actually investing in and owning a foreign subsidiary or division.

direct marketing Promotional element that uses direct communication with consumers to generate a response in the form of an order, a request for further information, or a visit to a retail outlet.

direct marketing channels Allow consumers to buy products by interacting with various advertising media without a face-to-face meeting with a salesperson.

direct orders The result of offers that contain all the information necessary for a prospective buyer to make a decision to purchase and complete the transaction.

discretionary income The money that remains after paying for taxes and necessities.

disintermediation Channel conflict that arises when a channel member bypasses another member and sells or buys products direct.

disposable income The money a consumer has left after paying taxes to use for such necessities as food, shelter, clothing, and transportation.

downsizing Reducing the content of packages without changing package size and maintaining or increasing the package price.

dumping Occurs when a firm sells a product in a foreign country below its domestic price or below its actual cost.

economic espionage The clandestine collection of trade secrets or proprietary information about a company's competitors.

economy Pertains to the income, expenditures, and resources that affect the cost of running a business and household.

eCRM A web-centric, personalized approach to managing long-term customer relationships electronically.

electronic commerce The activities that use electronic communication in the inventory, promotion, distribution, purchase, and exchange of products and services.

e-marketplaces Online trading communities that bring together buyers and supplier organizations.

emotional intelligence The ability to understand one's own emotions and the emotions of people with whom one interacts on a daily basis.

encoding The process of having the sender transform an abstract idea into a set of symbols.

environmental forces The uncontrollable factors involving social, economic, technological, competitive, and regulatory forces.

environmental scanning The process of continually acquiring information on events occurring outside the organization to identify and interpret potential trends.

ethics The moral principles and values that govern the actions and decisions of an individual or group.

ethnic marketing Combinations of the marketing mix that reflect the unique attitudes, race or ancestry, communication preferences, and lifestyles of ethnic Canadians; sometimes called multicultural marketing.

ethnographic research Observational approach to discover subtle emotional reactions as consumers encounter products in their "natural use environment."

evaluative criteria Factors that represent both the objective attributes of a brand (such as display screen) and the subjective ones (such as brand prestige) you use to compare different products and brands.

experience curve pricing Pricing method based on production experience; that is, the unit cost of many products and services declines by 10 to 30 percent each time a firm's experience at producing and selling them doubles.

experiment Obtaining data by manipulating factors under tightly controlled conditions to test cause and effect.

exporting Producing goods in one country and selling them in another country.

failure fee A penalty payment a manufacturer makes to compensate a retailer for failed sales from its valuable shelf space.

family life cycle The distinct phases that a family progresses through, from formation to retirement, each phase bringing with it identifiable purchasing behaviours.

feedback The communication flow from receiver back to the sender that helps the sender know whether the message was decoded and understood as intended.

field of experience Similar understanding and knowledge; to communicate effectively, a sender and a receiver must have a mutually shared field of experience.

fixed cost The firm's expenses that are stable and do not change with the quantity of product that is produced and cost.

focus groups An informal session of six to ten customers—past, present, or prospective—in which a discussion leader, or moderator, asks their opinions about the firm's and its competitors' products.

form of ownership Distinguishes retail outlets based on whether individuals, corporate chains, or contractual systems own the outlet.

formula-selling presentation Providing information in an accurate, thorough, and step-by-step manner to inform the prospect.

four Is of services Four unique elements to services: intangibility, inconsistency, inseparability, and inventory.

franchising Contractual arrangement between a parent company (a franchisor) and an individual or firm (a franchisee) that allows the franchise to operate a certain type of business under an established name and according to specific rules.

frequency The average number of times a person in the target audience is exposed to a message or advertisement.

full-service agency An advertising agency providing the most complete range of services, including market research, media selection, copy development, artwork, and production.

functional groupings Organizational groupings, such as manufacturing, marketing, and finance, which are the different business activities within a firm.

functional level The level in an organization where groups of specialists actually create value for the organization.

gap analysis An evaluation tool that compares expectations about a service offering to the actual experience a consumer has with the service.

Generation X The population of those born between 1965 and 1976.

Generation Y (Millennials) Those born between 1977 and 1994.

generic business strategy Strategy that can be adopted by any firm, regardless of the product or industry involved, to achieve a competitive advantage.

geographical groupings Organizational groupings in which a unit is subdivided according to geographical location.

global brand A brand marketed under the same name in multiple countries with similar and centrally coordinated marketing programs.

global competition Exists when firms originate, produce, and market their products and services worldwide.

global consumers Consumer groups living in many countries or regions of the world that have similar needs or seek similar features and benefits from products or services.

global marketing strategy The practice of standardizing marketing activities when there are cultural similarities and adapting them when cultures differ.

goals or objectives Statements of an accomplishment of a task to be achieved, often by a specific time.

government units The federal, provincial, and local agencies that buy goods and services for the constituents they serve.

green marketing Marketing efforts to produce, promote, and reclaim environmentally sensitive products.

greenwashing Disinformation disseminated by an organization so as to present an environmentally responsible public image.

grey market A situation where products are sold through unauthorized channels of distribution.

gross domestic product (GDP) The monetary value of all goods and services produced in a country during one year.

gross income The total amount of money made in one year by a person, household, or family unit.

gross rating points (GRPs) A reference number for advertisers, created by multiplying reach (expressed as a percentage of the total market) by frequency.

hierarchy of effects The sequence of stages a prospective buyer goes through, from initial awareness of a product to eventual action.

hypermarket A large store (more than 200,000 square feet) offering consumers everything in a single outlet.

idea generation Developing a pool of concepts as candidates for new products.

idle production capacity When the service provider is available but there is no demand.

indirect channels Marketing channels where intermediaries are inserted between the producer and consumers and perform numerous channel functions.

industrial firms Organizational buyers that, in some way, reprocess a good or service they buy before selling it again to the next buyer.

infomercials Program-length (30-minute) advertisements that take an educational approach to communication with potential customers.

in-house agency A company's own advertising staff, which may provide full services or a limited range of services.

institutional advertisements Advertisements designed to build goodwill or an image for an organization, rather than promote a specific good or service.

integrated marketing communications (IMC) The concept of designing marketing communications programs that coordinate all promotional activities—advertising, personal selling, sales promotion, public relations, and direct marketing—to provide a consistent message across all audiences and to maximize the promotional budget and impact of the communications.

interactive marketing Involves two-way buyer–seller electronic communication in which the buyer can control the kind and amount of information received from the seller.

internal marketing The notion that in order for a service organization to serve its customers well, it must care for and treat its employees like valued customers.

Internet marketing channels Employ the Internet to make goods and services available for consumption or use by consumers or business buyers.

Internet of Things (IoT) The network of products embedded with connectivity-enabled electronics.

intertype competition Competition between very dissimilar types of retail outlets.

involvement The personal, social, and economic significance of the purchase to the consumer.

ISO 14000 Worldwide standards for environmental quality and green marketing practices.

ISO 9000 standards Registration and certification of a manufacturer's quality management and quality assurance system.

joint venture An arrangement in which a foreign company and a local firm invest together to create a local business, sharing ownership, control, and profits of the new company.

just-in-time (JIT) concept An inventory supply system that operates with very low inventories and requires fast, on-time delivery.

key account management The practice of using team selling to focus on important customers so as to build mutually beneficial, long-term, cooperative relationships.

label An integral part of the package that typically identifies the product or brand, who made it, where and when it was made, how it is to be used, and package contents and ingredients.

laws Society's values and standards that are enforceable in the courts.

lead generation The result of an offer designed to generate interest in a product or service and a request for additional information.

learning Those behaviours that result from (1) repeated experience, and (2) thinking.

level of service The degree of service provided to the customer by self-, limited-, and full-service retailers.

licensing Offering the right to a trademark, patent, trade secret, or other similarly valued items of intellectual property in return for a royalty or a fee.

lifestyle A mode of living that is identified by how people spend their time and resources, what they consider important in their environment, and what they think of themselves and the world around them.

lifestyle centre An open-air cluster of specialty retailers, along with theatres, restaurants, fountains, play areas, and green spaces.

limited-service agencies Specialize in one aspect of the advertising process, such as providing creative services to develop the advertising copy or buying previously unpurchased media space.

line positions People, such as senior marketing managers, who have the authority and responsibility to issue orders to the people who report to them, such as product managers.

linear trend extrapolation The pattern is described with a straight line.

logistics management The practice of organizing the cost-effective flow of raw materials, in-process inventory, finished goods, and related information from point of origin to point of consumption to satisfy customer requirements.

loss-leader pricing Selling products below their customary prices to attract attention to them in the hope that customers will buy other products as well.

lost-horse forecast Making a forecast using the last known value and modifying it according to positive or negative factors expected in the future.

macromarketing The aggregate flow of a nation's goods and services to benefit society.

make-buy decision An evaluation of whether components and assemblies will be purchased from outside suppliers or built by the company itself.

manufacturer's agents Work for several producers and carry non-competitive, complementary merchandise in an exclusive territory; also called manufacturer's representatives.

market People with the desire and ability to buy a specific product.

market (industry) potential The maximum total sales of a product by all firms to a segment during a specified time period under specified environmental conditions and marketing efforts of the firms.

market modification Strategy in which a company tries to find new customers, increase a product's use among existing customers, or create new-use situations.

market orientation Focusing efforts on (1) continuously collecting information about customers' needs and competitors' capabilities, (2) sharing this information throughout the organization, and (3) using the information to create value, ensure customer satisfaction, and develop customer relationships.

market segmentation Aggregating prospective buyers into groups, or segments, that (1) have common needs and (2) will respond similarly to a marketing action.

market segments The relatively homogeneous groups of prospective buyers that result from the market segmentation process.

market share The ratio of sales revenue of the firm to the total sales revenue of all firms in the industry, including the firm itself.

market testing Exposing actual products to prospective consumers under realistic purchase conditions to see if they will buy.

market-based groupings Organizational groupings that utilize specific customer segments.

marketing The activity, set of institutions, and processes for creating, communicating, delivering, and exchanging offerings that have value for customers, clients, partners, and society at large.

marketing accountability The responsibility for the systematic management of marketing resources and processes to achieve measurable gains in return on marketing investment and increased marketing efficiency, while maintaining quality and increasing the value of the corporation.

marketing channel Individuals and firms involved in the process of making a product or service available for use or consumption by consumers or industrial users.

marketing concept The idea that an organization should strive to satisfy the needs of consumers, while also trying to achieve the organization's goals.

marketing dashboard The visual computer display of the essential information related to achieving a marketing objective.

marketing metric A measure of the quantitative value or trend of a marketing activity or result.

marketing mix The marketing manager's controllable factors; the marketing actions of product, price, promotion, and place that he or she can take to create, communicate, and deliver value.

marketing plan A road map for the marketing activities of an organization for a specified future period of time, such as one year or five years.

marketing program A plan that integrates the marketing mix to provide a good, service, or idea to prospective buyers.

marketing research The process of defining a marketing problem and opportunity, systematically collecting and analyzing information, and recommending actions to improve an organization's marketing activities.

marketing ROI The application of modern measurement technologies to understand, quantify, and optimize marketing spending.

marketing strategy The means by which a marketing goal is to be achieved, usually characterized by a specified target market and a marketing program to reach it.

marketing tactics Detailed day-to-day operational decisions essential to the overall success of marketing strategies.

market–product grid A framework to relate the market segments of potential buyers to products offered or potential marketing actions by the firm.

marketspace An information- and communication-based electronic exchange environment occupied by sophisticated computer and telecommunication technologies and digital offerings.

materials handling Moving goods over short distances into, within, and out of warehouses and manufacturing plants.

merchandise line How many different types of products a store carries and in what assortment.

merchant wholesalers Independently owned firms that take title to the merchandise they handle.

message The information sent by a source to a receiver in the communication process.

microfinance The practice of offering small, collateral-free loans to individuals who otherwise would not have access to the capital necessary to begin small businesses or other income-generating activities.

micromarketing How an individual organization directs its marketing activities and allocates its resources to benefit its customers.

mission A statement of the organization's function in society, often identifying its customers, markets, products, and technologies.

missionary salespeople Sales support personnel who do not directly solicit orders but rather concentrate on performing promotional activities and introducing new products.

mixed branding A firm markets products under its own name and that of a reseller because the segment attracted by the reseller is different from its own market.

moral idealism A personal moral philosophy that considers certain individual rights or duties as universal, regardless of the outcome.

motivation The energizing force that causes behaviour that satisfies a need.

multibranding A manufacturer's branding strategy giving each product a distinct name.

multichannel marketing Sometimes called omnichannel marketing, the blending of different communication and delivery channels that are mutually reinforcing in attracting, retaining, and building relationships with consumers who shop and buy from traditional intermediaries and online.

multidomestic marketing strategy Strategy that uses as many different product variations, brand names, and advertising programs as countries in which they do business.

multiproduct branding Use by a company of one name for all its products in a product class.

national character A distinct set of personality characteristics common among people of a country or society.

need-satisfaction presentation A selling format that emphasizes probing and listening by the salesperson to identify the needs and interests of prospective buyers.

new-product process The stages a firm uses to identify business opportunities and convert them to a saleable good or service.

new-product strategy development The first stage of the new-product process, providing the necessary focus, structure, approach, and guidelines for pursuing innovation.

noise Extraneous factors that can work against effective communication by distorting a message or the feedback received.

nonprobability sampling Using arbitrary judgments to select the sample so that the chance of selecting a particular element may be unknown or zero.

objective and task budgeting A budgeting approach whereby the company (1) determines its promotion objectives, (2) outlines the tasks to accomplish these objectives, and (3) determines the promotion cost of performing these tasks.

observation Watching, either mechanically or in person, how people behave.

odd–even pricing Setting prices a few dollars or cents under an even number.

off-mall retailing Occurs when retailers that traditionally locate in malls build on stand-alone sites.

off-peak pricing Charging different prices during different times of the day or days of the week to reflect variations in demand for the service.

off-price retailing Selling brand-name merchandise at lower than regular prices.

opinion leaders Those knowledgeable about users of particular products and services, and so their opinions influence others' choices.

order getter A salesperson who sells in a conventional sense and identifies prospective customers, provides customers with information, persuades customers to buy, closes sales, and follows up on customers' use of a product or service.

order taker Processes routine orders or reorders for products that have already been sold by the company.

organizational buyers Those manufacturers, wholesalers, retailers, and government agencies that buy goods and services for their own use or for resale.

organizational buying behaviour The decision-making process that organizations use to establish the need for products and services, and to identify, evaluate, and choose among alternative brands and suppliers.

organizational buying criteria The objective attributes of the supplier's products and services and the capabilities of the supplier itself.

organizational culture A set of values, ideas, attitudes, and norms of behaviour that is learned and shared among the members of an organization.

packaging Any container in which a product is offered for sale and on which label information is communicated.

partnership selling The practice, sometimes called enterprise selling, whereby buyers and sellers combine their expertise and resources to create customized solutions; to commit to joint planning; and to share customer, competitive, and company information for their mutual benefit, and ultimately the customer's benefit.

penetration pricing Setting a low initial price on a new product to appeal immediately to the mass market.

perceived risk The anxiety felt because the consumer cannot anticipate the outcomes of a purchase but believes that there may be negative consequences.

percentage of sales budgeting Allocating funds to advertising as a percentage of past or anticipated sales, in terms of either dollars or units sold.

perception The process by which an individual selects, organizes, and interprets information to create a meaningful picture of the world.

perceptual map A means of displaying or graphing in two dimensions the location of products or brands in the minds of consumers to enable a manager to see how consumers perceive competing products or brands relative to its own and then take marketing actions.

personal selling The two-way flow of communication between a buyer and seller, often in a face-to-face encounter, designed to influence a person's or group's purchase decision.

personal selling process Sales activities occurring before and after the sale itself, consisting of six stages: (1) prospecting, (2) preapproach, (3) approach, (4) presentation, (5) close, and (6) follow-up.

personality A person's consistent behaviours or responses to recurring situations.

points of difference Characteristics of a product that make it superior to competitive substitutes.

post-tests Tests conducted after an advertisement has been shown to the target audience to determine whether it has accomplished its intended purpose.

power centre A huge shopping strip with multiple anchor (or national) stores, a convenient location, and a supermarket.

prestige pricing Setting a high price on a product to attract quality- or status-conscious consumers.

pre-tests Tests conducted before an advertisement is placed to determine whether it communicates the intended message or to select among alternative versions of an advertisement.

price The money or other considerations (including other goods and services) exchanged for the ownership or use of a good or service.

price elasticity of demand The percentage change in quantity demanded relative to a percentage change in price.

price lining Pricing a line of products at a number of different specific pricing points.

pricing constraints Factors that limit the latitude of price a firm may set.

pricing objectives Expectations that specify the role of price in an organization's marketing and strategic plans.

primary data Facts and figures that are newly collected for the project.

private branding When a company manufactures products but sells them under the brand name of a wholesaler or retailer (often called private labelling or reseller branding).

probability sampling Using precise rules to select the sample such that each element of the population has a specific known chance of being selected.

product A good, service, or idea consisting of a bundle of tangible and intangible attributes that satisfies consumers and is received in exchange for money or some other unit of value.

product (or program) champion A person who is able and willing to cut red tape and move the program forward.

product advertisements Advertisements that focus on selling a good or service and take three forms: (1) pioneering (or informational), (2) competitive (or persuasive), and (3) reminder.

product class The entire product category or industry.

product differentiation Strategy that involves a firm using different marketing mix activities, such as product features and advertising, to help consumers perceive the product as being different from and better than competing products.

product form Variations of a product within the product class.

product life cycle The stages a new product goes through in the marketplace: introduction, growth, maturity, and decline.

product line A group of products that are closely related because they satisfy a class of needs, are used together, are sold to the same customer group, are distributed through the same outlets, or fall within a given price range.

product line groupings Organizational groupings in which a unit is responsible for specific product offerings.

product mix The number of product lines offered by a company.

product modification Altering a product's characteristics, such as its quality, performance, appearance, features, or package to try to increase and extend the product's sales.

product placement Using a brand-name product in a movie, television show, video, or a commercial for another product.

product positioning The place an offering occupies in consumers' minds on important attributes relative to competitive products.

product repositioning Changing the place an offering occupies in a consumer's mind relative to competitive products.

production goods Items used in the manufacturing process that become part of the final product.

profit The money left after a business firm's total expenses are subtracted from its total revenue; the reward for the risk it undertakes in marketing its offerings.

profit equation Profit = Total revenue − Total cost, or Profit = (Unit price × Quantity sold) − Total cost.

profit responsibility Idea that companies have a simple duty—to maximize profits for their owners or shareholders.

programmatic ad purchasing An automated-based (the use of software), data-driven way of buying advertising.

promotional mix The combination of one or more of these communications tools: advertising, personal selling, sales promotion, public relations, and direct marketing.

protectionism The practice of shielding one or more industries within a country's economy from foreign competition through the use of tariffs or quotas.

protocol A statement that, before product development begins, identifies (1) a well-defined target market; (2) specific customers' needs, wants, and preferences; and (3) what the product will be and do.

public relations A form of communication management that seeks to influence the feelings, opinions, or beliefs held by customers, prospective customers, shareholders, suppliers, employees, and other publics about a company and its products or services.

publicity A non-personal, indirectly paid presentation of an organization, good, or service.

pull strategy Directing the promotional mix at ultimate consumers to encourage them to ask the retailer for the product.

purchase decision process The stages a buyer passes through in making choices about which products and services to buy.

push strategy Directing the promotional mix to channel members to gain their cooperation in ordering and stocking a product.

quality Those features and characteristics of a product that influence its ability to satisfy customer needs.

quota A restriction placed on the amount of a product allowed to enter or leave a country.

rating The percentage of households in a market that are tuned to a particular TV show or radio station.

reach The number of different people or households exposed to an advertisement.

receivers Consumers who read, hear, or see the message sent by a source in the communication process.

reciprocity An industrial buying practice in which two organizations agree to purchase each other's products and services.

reference groups People to whom an individual looks as a basis for self-appraisal or as a source of personal standards.

regional shopping centre Consists of 50 to 150 stores that typically attract customers who live within an 8- to 16-km range, often containing two or three anchor stores.

regulation Restrictions that provincial and federal laws place on business with regard to the conduct of its activities.

relationship selling The practice of building ties to customers based on a salesperson's attention and commitment to customer needs over time.

resellers Wholesalers or retailers that buy physical products and sell them again without any processing.

response The impact the message had on the receiver's knowledge, attitudes, or behaviours.

retail life cycle The process of growth and decline that retail outlets, like products, experience.

retail positioning matrix Positions retail outlets on two dimensions: breadth of product line and value added.

retailing All activities involved in selling, renting, and providing goods and services to ultimate consumers for personal, family, or household use.

retailing mix Activities related to managing the store and the merchandise in the store—including retail pricing, store location, retail communication, and merchandise.

reverse auction A buyer communicates a need for a product or service, and would-be suppliers are invited to bid in competition with each other.

reverse logistics A process of reclaiming recyclable and reusable materials, returns, and reworks from the point of consumption or use for repair, remanufacturing, redistribution, or disposal.

sales (company) forecast The total sales of a product that a firm expects to sell during a specified time period under specified environmental conditions and its own marketing efforts.

sales engineer A salesperson who specializes in identifying, analyzing, and solving customer problems and who brings know-how and technical expertise to the selling situations but does not actually sell goods and services.

sales management Planning the selling program and implementing and controlling the personal selling effort of the firm.

sales plan A statement describing what is to be achieved and where and how the selling effort of salespeople is to be deployed.

sales promotion A short-term inducement of value offered to arouse interest in buying a good or service.

sales quota Contains specific goals assigned to a salesperson, sales team, branch sales office, or sales district for a stated time period.

sales response function Relates the expense of the marketing effort to the marketing results obtained.

salesforce automation (SFA) The use of technology to make the sales function more effective and efficient.

salesforce survey forecast Asking the firm's salespeople to estimate sales during a coming period.

sampling The process of gathering data from subsets of a total population.

scrambled merchandising Offering several unrelated product lines in a single retail store.

screening and evaluation The stage of the new-product process that involves internal and external evaluations of the new-product ideas to eliminate those that warrant no further action.

secondary data Facts and figures that have been recorded before the project at hand.

self-concept The way people see themselves and the way they believe others see them.

self-regulation An alternative to government control where an industry attempts to police itself.

selling agents Represent a single producer and are responsible for the entire marketing function of that producer.

semiotics The field of study that examines the correspondence between symbols and their role in the assignment of meaning for people.

service continuum A range from the tangible to the intangible or goods-dominant to service-dominant offerings available in the marketplace.

services Intangible activities, benefits, or satisfactions that an organization provides to consumers in exchange for money or something else of value.

seven Ps of services marketing Product, price, place, and promotion, as well as people, physical evidence, and process that constitute the services-marketing mix.

share points Percentage points of market share; often used as the common basis of comparison to allocate marketing resources effectively.

shopping goods Items for which the consumer compares several alternatives on such criteria as price, quality, or style.

shrinkage Breakage and theft of merchandise by customers and employees.

situation analysis Taking stock of where the firm or product has been recently, where it is now, and where it is headed in terms of the organization's plans and the external factors and trends affecting it.

situational influences Conditions that have an impact on your purchase decision process: (1) the purchase task, (2) social surroundings, (3) physical surroundings, (4) temporal effects, and (5) antecedent states.

Six Sigma A means to "delight the customer" by achieving quality through a highly disciplined process that focuses on developing and delivering near-perfect products and services.

skimming pricing The highest initial price that customers really desiring a product are willing to pay.

slotting fee A payment a manufacturer makes to place a new item on a retailer's shelf.

social audit A systematic assessment of a firm's objectives, strategies, and performance in the domain of social responsibility.

social class The relatively permanent, homogeneous divisions in a society into which people sharing similar values, lifestyles, interests, and behaviour can be grouped.

social CRM The use of social media to enable organizations to engage customers in collaborative conversations for mutually beneficial value.

social enterprise An organization that applies business strategies to maximize improvements in human and environmental well-being as well as social impact, rather than profits for external shareholders.

social forces Forces of the environment that include the demographic characteristics of the population and its values.

social marketing Marketing designed to influence the behaviour of individuals in which the benefits of the behaviour accrue to those individuals or to the society in general and not to the marketer.

social media Where online users submit comments, photos, and videos—often accompanied by a feedback process to identify "popular" topics.

social media marketing Consumer-generated online-marketing efforts to promote brands and companies for which they are fans (or conversely, negatively promoting brands and companies for which they are non-fans), and the use by marketers of online tools and platforms to promote their brands or organizations.

social responsibility Individuals and organizations are part of a larger society and are accountable to that society for their actions.

societal marketing concept The view that an organization should discover and satisfy the needs of its consumers in a way that also provides for society's well-being.

societal responsibility Refers to obligations that organizations have to (1) the preservation of the ecological environment, and (2) the general public.

source A company or person who has information to convey.

specialty goods Items that a consumer makes a special effort to search out and buy.

staff positions People who have the authority and responsibility to advise people in the line positions but cannot issue direct orders to them.

stakeholder responsibility Focuses on the obligations an organization has to those who can effect achievement of its objectives, including customers, employees, suppliers, and distributors.

standard markup pricing Adding a fixed percentage to the cost of all items in a specific product class.

stimulus-response presentation A selling format that assumes the prospect will buy if given the appropriate stimulus by a salesperson.

strategic alliances Agreements among two or more independent firms to cooperate for the purpose of achieving common goals, such as a competitive advantage or customer value creation.

strategic business unit (SBU) A subsidiary, division, or unit of an organization that markets a set of related offerings to a clearly defined group of customers.

strategic business unit level A business unit level where managers set a more specific strategic direction for their businesses to exploit value-creating opportunities.

strategic channel alliances A practice whereby one firm's marketing channel is used to sell another firm's products.

strategic marketing process Process whereby an organization allocates its marketing mix resources to reach its target markets.

strategy An organization's long-term course of action designed to deliver a unique customer experience while achieving its goals.

strip location A cluster of stores serving people who live within a 5- to 10-minute drive.

subcultures Subgroups within the larger, or national, culture with unique values, ideas, and attitudes.

subliminal perception Means that you see or hear messages without being aware of them.

supplier development The deliberate effort by organizational buyers to build relationships that shape suppliers' products, services, and capabilities to fit a buyer's needs and those of its customers.

supply chain A sequence of firms that perform activities required to create and deliver a good or service to consumers or industrial users.

supply chain management The integration and organization of information and logistics activities across firms in a supply chain for the purpose of creating and delivering goods and services that provide value to customers.

supply partnership A relationship that exists when a buyer and its supplier adopt mutually beneficial objectives, policies, and procedures for the purpose of lowering the cost and/or increasing the value of products and services delivered to the ultimate consumers.

support goods Items used to assist in producing other goods and services.

survey A research technique used to generate data by asking people questions and recording their responses on a questionnaire.

survey of buyers' intentions forecast Asking prospective customers if they are likely to buy a product during some future time period.

sustainable development Conducting business in a way that protects the natural environment while making economic progress.

sustainable marketing Refers to seeking to meet today's (global) economic, environmental, and social needs without compromising the opportunity for future generations to meet theirs.

SWOT analysis An acronym describing an organization's appraisal of its internal Strengths and Weaknesses and its external Opportunities and Threats.

target market One or more specific groups of potential consumers toward which an organization directs its marketing program.

target pricing The practice of deliberately adjusting the composition and features of a product to achieve the target price to consumers.

target profit pricing Pricing method based on an annual target of a specific dollar volume of profit.

target return-on-investment pricing Setting prices to achieve return-on-investment (ROI) targets.

target return-on-sales pricing Setting typical prices that will give a firm a profit that is a specific percentage.

tariffs Government taxes on goods or services entering a country, which primarily serve to raise prices on imports.

team selling Using an entire team of professionals in selling to and servicing major customers.

technology Inventions or innovations from applied science or engineering research.

telemarketing Using the telephone to interact with and sell directly to consumers.

total cost The total expenses incurred by a firm in producing and marketing a product.

total logistics cost Expenses associated with transportation, materials handling and warehousing, inventory, stockouts, order processing, and return goods handling.

total revenue The total money received from the sale of a product.

trade feedback effect A country's imports affect its exports and exports affect its imports.

trade name A commercial, legal name under which a company does business.

trademark Identifies that a firm has legally registered its brand name or trade name so that the firm has its exclusive use.

trade-oriented sales promotions Sales tools used to support a company's advertising and personal selling efforts directed to wholesalers, distributors, or retailers. Three common approaches are allowances and discounts, cooperative advertising, and salesforce training.

trading down Reducing the number of features, quality, or price.

trading up Adding value to a product (or line) through additional features or higher-quality materials.

traditional auction A seller puts an item up for sale, and would-be buyers are invited to bid in competition with each other.

traffic generation The outcome of an offer designed to motivate people to visit a business.

trend extrapolation Extending a pattern observed in past data into the future.

triple-bottom-line Recognition of the need for organizations to improve the state of people, the planet, and profit simultaneously, if they are to achieve sustainable, long-term growth.

ultimate consumers People—whether 80 years or 8 months old—who use the goods and services purchased for a household.

unsought goods Items that the consumer either does not know about or knows about but does not initially want.

usage rate Quantity consumed or patronage—store visits—during a specific period; varies significantly among different customer groups.

user-generated content (UGC) Media generated by users (customers) and disseminated via various channels, in particular, the Internet.

utilitarianism A personal moral philosophy that focuses on the "greatest good for the greatest number" by assessing the costs and benefits of the consequences of ethical behaviour.

value analysis A systematic appraisal of the design, quality, and performance of a product to reduce purchasing costs.

value consciousness The concern for obtaining the best quality, features, and performance of a product or service for a given price.

values Personally or socially preferable modes of conduct or states of existence that are enduring.

variable cost The sum of the expenses of a firm that vary directly with the quantity of products that is produced and sold.

vendor-managed inventory (VMI) An inventory management system whereby the supplier determines the product amount and assortment a customer (such as a retailer) needs and automatically delivers the appropriate items.

vertical marketing systems (VMS) Professionally managed and centrally coordinated marketing channels designed to achieve channel economies and maximum marketing impact.

viral marketing The online version of word of mouth, involving the use of messages "infectious" enough that consumers wish to pass them along to others through online communication.

warranty A statement indicating the liability of the manufacturer for product deficiencies.

wheel of retailing A concept that describes how new retail outlets enter the market as low-status, low-margin stores and gradually add embellishments that raise their prices and status. They now face a new low-status, low-margin operator, and the cycle starts to repeat itself.

whistle-blowers Employees who report unethical or illegal actions of their employers.

word of mouth The influencing of people during conversations.

workload method A formula-based method for determining the size of a salesforce that integrates the number of customers served, call frequency, call length, and available selling time to arrive at a salesforce size.

yield management pricing The charging of different prices to maximize revenue for a set amount of capacity at any given time.

CHAPTER NOTES

Chapter 1

1. Danny Kucharsky, "Hamilton Aims to Shatter Stereotypes Built on Steel," *Marketing,* October 22, 2015, **http://www.marketingmag.ca/brands/ hamilton-aims-to-shatter-stereotypes-built-on-steel-159701**; and **www.hamilton.ca** (downloaded November 3, 2015).

2. Regis McKenna, "Marketing Is Everything," *Harvard Business Review* (Jan/Feb 1991), pp. 65–79.

3. Lisa M. Keefe, "Marketing Defined," *Marketing News* (January 15, 2008), pp. 28–29.

4. Philip Kotler and Sidney J. Levy, "Broadening the Concept of Marketing," *Journal of Marketing* (January 1969), pp. 10–15.

5. George G. Brenkert, "Ethical Challenges in Social Marketing," *Journal of Public Policy & Marketing* (Spring 2002), pp. 14–25; and Alan R. Andreasen, "Marketing Social Marketing in the Social Change Marketplace," *Journal of Public Policy & Marketing* (Spring 2002), pp. 3–13.

6. Mintel Global New Products Database, **http://www.mintel.com/global-new-products-database**, accessed March 20, 2015; George Castellion and Stephen K. Markham, "Perspective: New Product Failure Rates: Influence of Argumentum ad Populum and Self-Interest," *Journal of Product Innovation Management* 30, no. 5 (2013), pp. 976–979; Robert M. McMath and Thom Forbes, *What Were They Thinking?* (New York: Times Business, 1998), pp. 3–22.

7. From the Hot Pockets website, **www.facebook.com/hotpockets**.

8. "Body Image," **http://mediasmarts.ca/body-image/body-image-girls**, downloaded October 10, 2015.

9. E. Jerome McCarthy, *Basic Marketing: A Managerial Approach* (Homewood, IL: Richard D. Irwin, 1960); and Walter van Waterschoot and Christophe Van den Bulte, "The 4P Classification of the Marketing Mix Revisited," *Journal of Marketing* (October 1992), pp. 83–93.

10. Frederick G. Crane, *Marketing for Entrepreneurs* (Thousand Oaks, CA: Sage, 2013); Frederick G. Crane and Marc H. Meyer, "Key Caveats and Emerging Creative Solutions to Achieve Successful Corporate Innovation," *Current Opinion in Creativity, Innovation and Entrepreneurship* (2012), Vol. 1 (2), pp. 1–6; and Frederick G. Crane and Marc H. Meyer, "The Challenges of Innovation in American Companies: An Executive Ethnographic Investigation." *Journal of Technology Management and Innovation* (2011), Vol. 6 (4), pp. 193–204.

11. Danny Kucharsky, "Hamilton Aims to Shatter Stereotypes Built on Steel," *Marketing*; and **www.hamilton.ca** (downloaded November 3, 2015).

12. Robert F. Keith, "The Marketing Revolution," *Journal of Marketing* (January 1960), pp. 35–38.

13. *Annual Report* (New York: General Electric Company, 1952), p. 21.

14. Michael Treacy and Fred D. Wiersema, *The Discipline of Market Leaders* (Reading, MA: Addison-Wesley, 1995); Michael Treacy and Fred Wiersema, "How Market Leaders Keep Their Edge," *Fortune* (February 6, 1995), pp. 88–89; and Michael Treacy, "You Need a Value Discipline—But Which One?" *Fortune* (April 17, 1995), p. 195.

15. Frederick G. Crane and Jeffrey E. Sohl, "Imperatives for Venture Success: Entrepreneurs Speak," *International Journal of Entrepreneurship and Innovation* (May 2004), pp. 99–106.

16. "What's a Loyal Customer Worth?" *Fortune* (December 11, 1995), p. 182; and Lauren Keller Johnson, "The Real Value of Customer Loyalty," *MIT Sloan Management Review* (Winter 2002), pp. 14–17.

17. G.R. Iyer and David Bejou, *Customer Relationship Management in Electronic Markets* (New York: The Haworth Press Inc., 2004).

18. "Worldwide CRM Spending Growing Dramatically, but for Best Results Managers Need to Know How to Use it," *True Clarity*, July 16, 2013; **http://www.trueclarityintl.com/news/140-worldwide-crm-spending-growing-dramatically**.

19. Mark Whitmore and Jonathan Copulsky, "CRM R.I.P.?" *Marketing* (April 7, 2003), **www.marketingmag.ca** (downloaded June 10, 2005).

20. Bruce Temkin, "Companies Deliver Subpar Customer Experiences," Forrester Research (January 7, 2005).

21. Bob Thompson, *Customer Experience Management: A Winning Business Strategy in a Flat World* (CustomerThinkCorp, 2006).

22. "10 Companies with the Best Customer Experience," *The Huffington Post*, September 20, 2011, **http://www.huffingtonpost.com/2011/09/20/the-top-10-companies-with-most-admired-customer-experience_n_972027.html**, downloaded January 10, 2013.

23. Rob Gerlsbeck, "Sweeeet," *Marketing Magazine* (December 11/18, 2006), p. 8; and Peter Kim, "Reinventing the Marketing Organization," Forrester Research (July 13, 2006).

24. "Lessons from the Leading Edge of Customer Experience Management," *A Report by Harvard Business Review Analytic Services* (Brighton, MA: Harvard Business School Publishing, 2014).

25. Mark Schaefer, *Social Media Explained* (Mark Schaefer, 2014); and Guy Kawasaki and Peg Fitzpatrick, *The Art of Social Media* (Portfolio, 2014).

26. Ilya Pozin, "20 Companies You Should Be Following on Social Media," *Forbes*, March 6, 2014, **http://www.forbes.com/sites/ilyapozin/2014/03/06/20-companies-you-should-be-following-on-social-media/**.

27. Paul Greenberg, *CRM at the Speed of Light* (McGraw-Hill, 2010); "Social CRM spend set to surpass $1 billion in 2012," **http://www.socialmedia-forum.com/blog/2012/02/london/social-crm-spend-set-to-surpass-1billion-in-2012/**.

28. Andrew Crane and John Desmond, "Societal Marketing and Morality," *European Journal of Marketing* (Spring 2002), pp. 548–70.

29. Shelby D. Hunt and John Burnett, "The Macromarketing/Micromarketing Dichotomy: A Taxonomical Model," *Journal of Marketing* (Summer 1982), pp. 9–26.

Chapter 2

1. "Our Values," from Ben & Jerry's website, **http://www. benjerry.com/values**, April 3, 2015; and "Ice Cream History Revealed! What Was Ben & Jerry's First Ice Cream Flavor?" *BusinessWire*, November 15, 2011, **http://www.businesswire.com/news/home/20111115007275/en/Ice-Cream-History-Revealed!-Ben-Jerry%E2%80%99s-Ice#.VR8B7J50yM8**.

2. Nick Craig and Scott Snook, "From Purpose to Impact," *Harvard Business Review*, May 2014, pp. 105–11; Joe Van Brussel, "Ben & Jerry's Become B-Corp Certified, Adds Credibility to Impact Investing Movement," *Huffington Post: Business*, October 23, 2012, **http://www.huffingtonpost.com/ 2012/10/23/ben-and-jerrys-b-corp-impactinvesting_n_2005315.html**; and "What Are B-Corps?" B-Corporation website, see **http://www.bcorporation.net/what-are- b-corps**.

3. "Global Ice Cream," press release posted at **www.marketresearch.com**, October 10, 2014.

4. Roger Kerin and Robert Peterson, *Strategic Marketing Problems: Cases and Comments*, 13th ed. (Upper Saddle River, NJ: Prentice Hall, 2013), p. 140.

5. W. Chan Kim and Reneé Mauborgne, "Blue Ocean Strategy: From Theory to Practice," *California Management Review* 47, no. 3 (Spring 2005), p. 10.

6. Michael E. Porter, "What Is Strategy?" *Harvard Business Review*, November–December 1996, p. 2.

7. Frank Holland, "Tomorrow's CMO Will Be Plugged into the Entire Marketing Cycle," *Adweek*, January 9, 2015, p. 1; George S. Day and Robert Malcolm, "The CMO and the Future of Marketing," *Marketing Management*, Spring 2012, pp. 34–43.

8. AMA (2011), **http://marketingpower.com**, retrieved January 5, 2013. Also see, Adam Gaskill and Hume Winzar, "The Capabilities of Accountable Marketing Practitioners: A Finance Perspective," *Journal of the Academy of Business Education*, Spring 2013.

9. Taken in part from Jim Collins and Morten T. Hansen, *Great By Choice* (New York: HarperCollins Publishers, 2011); and Jim Collins and Jerry I. Porras, *Built to Last: Successful Habits of Visionary Companies* (New York: HarperCollins Publishers, 2002), p. 54.

10. Ibid, p. 54; and Jim Collins, *Good to Great: Why Some Companies Make the Leap . . . and Others Don't* (New York: HarperCollins Publishers, 2001), p. 195.

11. Collins and Porras, *Built to Last*, p. 73; Patrick M. Lencioni, "Make Your Values Mean Something," *Harvard Business Review*, July 2002, p. 6.

12. Catherine M. Dalton, "When Organizational Values Are Mere Rhetoric," *Business Horizons* 49 (September–October 2006), p. 345.

13. Collins and Porras, *Built to Last*, pp. 94–95; and Tom Krattenmaker, "Write a Mission Statement That Your Company Is Willing to Live," *Harvard Management Communication Letter*, March 2002, pp. 3–4.

14. Collins and Porras, *Built to Last*, pp. 94–95; and Tom Krattenmaker, "Write a Mission Statement That Your Company Is Willing to Live," *Harvard Management Communication Letter*, March 2002, pp. 3–4.

15. Nikos Mourkogiannis, "The Realist's Guide to Moral Purpose," *Strategy + Business*, no. 41 (Winter 2005), pp. 42, 45, 47.

16. Sheila M. J. Bonini, Lenny T. Mendonca, and Jeremy M. Oppenheim, "When Social Issues Become Strategic," *The McKinsey Quarterly*, 2006, no. 2, pp. 23, 25, 30–31.

17. Theodore Levitt, "Marketing Myopia," *Harvard Business Review* (July–August 1960), pp. 45–56.

18. "Top 50 Socially Responsible Corporations in Canada," *Maclean ' s*, June 9, 2011, **http://www2.macleans.ca/2011/06/09/better-business/**; and Katherine Ellison, "The Bottom Line Redefined," *Nature Conservancy* (Winter 2002), pp. 45–50.

19. See **http://www.ic.gc.ca/eic/site/icgc.nsf/eng/home**.

20. Marc H. Meyer and Frederick G. Crane, *Venturing: Innovation and Business Planning for Entrepreneurs* (Boston, MA: The Institute for Enterprise Growth, 2015).

21. George Stalk, Philip Evans, and Lawrence E. Shulman, "Competing on Capabilities: The New Rules of Corporate Strategy," *Harvard Business Review*, March–April 1992, pp. 57–69; and Darrell K. Rigby, *Management Tools 2007: An Executive's Guide* (Boston: Bain & Company, 2007), p. 22.

22. Roger A. Kerin and Robert A. Peterson, *Strategic Marketing Problems: Cases and Comments*, 10th edition (Englewood Cliffs, NJ: Prentice Hall, 2004), pp. 2–3; and Derek F. Abell, *Defining the Business* (Englewood Cliffs, NJ: Prentice Hall, 1980), pp. 57–69.

23. **http://shop.lululemon.com/home.jsp**; and **http://www.abebooks. com/books/CompanyInformation/**.

24. "The 20 Most Innovative Companies in BC, 2012," *BC Business*, **http://www.bcbusinessonline.ca/2012/innovators**.

25. Adapted from The Experience Curve Reviewed, IV: The Growth Share Matrix of the Product Portfolio (Boston: The Boston Consulting Group, 1973). See also **https://www.bcgperspectives. com/content/classics/strategy_the_ product_portfolio** (registration and login required for access).

26. Roger A. Kerin, Vijay Mahajan, and P. Rajan Varadarajan, *Contemporary Perspectives on Strategic Marketing Planning* (Boston: Allyn & Bacon, 1990), p. 52.

27. "The Top 100 Brands: Best Global Brands 2014," Interbrand, **http://bestglobalbrands.com/2014/ranking/** pp. 2–3.

28. Julie Moreland, "Steve Jobs, Apple, And The Importance Of Company Culture," *Fast Company*, November 2, 2011, **https://www.fastcompany.com/ 1792485/steve-jobs-apple-and-importance-company-culture**.

29. See the Apple press release library at **http://www.apple. com/pr/library/**.

30. Joseph Palenchar, "Apple Watch the One to Watch," The Week in Consumer Electronics, March 16, 2015, **www.twice.com**.

31. Parmy Oson, "Apple's U.S. iPhone Sales Surpass Android for First Time in Years," **Forbes.com**, February 4, 2014, p. 22; and "Worldwide Smartphone Growth Forecast to Slow from a Boil to a Simmer as Prices Drop and Markets Mature, According to IDC," press release, December 1, 2014, International Data Corporation (IDC), **http://www.idc.com/getdoc. jsp?containerId= prUS25282214**.

32. Jack Linshi, "5 Charts That Show Why the iPad's Fifth Birthday Is Bittersweet," **www.time.com**, April 6, 2015; "The State of the Tablet Market," *TabTimes Weekly*, April 10, 2015, **http://tabtimes.com/resources/the-state-of-the-tablet-market/**; and Larry Magid, "Apple's Tablets Selling Well but Market Share Slips While Samsung Grows, *Forbes*, May 1, 2013, **http://www.forbes.com/ sites/larrymagid/2013/05/01/apples-tablet-market-share-slips-and-samsunggrows**.

33. Don Reisinger, "iPod History: 10 Milestones in the Wearable Music Player's Evolution," eWeek, October 31, 2014, p. 1-1; James Hall, "MP3 Players Are Dead," Business Insider, December 26, 2012, **http://www.businessinsider.com/ mp3-players-are-dead-2012-12**; Zak Islam, "Smartphones Heavily Decrease Sales of iPod, MP3 Players," Tom's Hardware, December 31, 2012,

http://www.tomshardware.com/news/SmartphonesiPod-
MP3-Players-Sales,20062.html.

34. "Company Profile: Apple Inc." MarketLine, November 6, 2014,
www.marketline.com.

35. Strengths and weaknesses of the BCG technique are based on Derek F. Abell and
John S. Hammond, *Strategic Market Planning: Problem and Analytic Approaches*
(Englewood Cliffs, NJ: Prentice Hall, 1979); Yoram Wind, Vijay Mahajan, and
Donald Swire, "An Empirical Comparison of Standardized Portfolio Models,"
Journal of Marketing, Spring 1983, pp. 89–99; and J. Scott Armstrong and
Roderick J. Brodie, "Effects of Portfolio Planning Methods on Decision Making:
Experimental Results," *International Journal of Research in Marketing*, Winter
1994, pp. 73–84.

36. H. Igor Ansoff, "Strategies for Diversification," *Harvard Business Review*
(September–October 1957), pp. 113–24.

37. "Dairy Producers Pour More Milk," *Marketing* (September 26, 2006), p. 4.

38. www.secondcup.ca.

39. "Second Cup Adds Music to its Menu," *Marketing* (September 26, 2006), p. 4;
www.mccain.com; and www.heinz.com.

40. The definition is adapted from Stephen Few, *Information Dashboard Design: The
Effective Visual Communication of Data* (Sebastopol, CA: O'Reilly Media, Inc.
2006), pp. 2–46.

41. Ibid.; Bruce H. Clark, Andrew V. Abela, and Tim Ambler, "Behind the Wheel,"
Marketing Management, May–June 2006, pp. 19–23; Spencer E. Ante, "Giving the

Boss the Big Picture," *Business Week*, February 13, 2006, pp. 48–49; and
Dashboard Tutorial (Cupertino, CA: Apple, Inc, 2006).

42. Few, *Information Dashboard Design*.

43. Stephen Few, *Now You See It* (Oakland, CA: Analytics Press, 2009); Michael
Krauss, "Balance Attention to Metrics with Intuition," *Marketing News*, June 1,
2007, pp. 6–8; John Davis, *Measuring Marketing: 103 Key Metrics Every Marketer
Needs* (Singapore: John Wiley & Sons, 2007); Paul W. Farris, Neil T. Bendle,
Phillip E. Pfeifer, and David J. Reibstein, *Marketing Metrics* (Upper Saddle River,
NJ: Wharton School Publishing, 2006); and Marcel Corstjens and Jeffrey Merrihue,
"Optimal Marketing," *Harvard Business Review*, October 2003, pp. 114–21.

44. The now-classic reference on effective graphic presentation is Edward R. Tufte, *The
Visual Display of Quantitative Information*, 2nd Edition (Cheshire, CT: Graphic
Press, 2001); also see Stephen Few, *Information Dashboard Design*.

45. "Car2go North America Names Daniel Florence COO and Amber Quist CMO,"
PR Newswire, October 19, 2015, http://www.prnewswire.com/news-releases/
car2go-north-america-names-daniel-florence-as-chief-operating-officer-
amber-quist-as-chief-marketing-officer-300161308.html.

46. Jordan Elkind, "5 Steps to Becoming a Customer-Centric Organization," May 13,
2014, http://marketingland.com/5-steps-becoming-customer-centric-
marketing-organization-83202.

47. Information provided by Masterfoods (February 2013).

Appendix A

1. Personal interview with Arthur R. Kydd, St. Croix Management Group.

2. Examples of guides to writing marketing plans include William A. Cohen, *The
Marketing Plan* (New York: Wiley, 1995); Mark Nolan, *The Instant Marketing
Plan* (Santa Maria, CA: Puma Publishing Company, 1995); and Roman G.
Hiebing, Jr., and Scott W. Cooper, *The Successful Marketing Plan*, 2nd ed.
(Lincolnwood, IL: NTC Business Books, 1997).

3. Examples of guides to writing business plans include Rhonda M. Abrams, *The
Successful Business Plan: Secrets & Strategies*, 3rd ed. (Grants Pass, OR: Oasis
Press/PSI Research, 2000); Joseph A. Covello and Brian J. Hazelgren, *The

Complete Book of Business Plans (Naperville, IL: Sourcebooks, 1995); Joseph A.
Covello and Brian J. Hazelgren, *Your First Business Plan*, 3rd ed. (Naperville, IL:
Sourcebooks, 1998); and Angela Shupe, ed., *Business Plans Handbook*, vols. 1–4
(Detroit: Gale Research, 1997).

4. Abrams, *The Successful Business Plan*, p. 30.

5. Some of these points are adapted from Abrams, pp. 30–38; others are adapted from
William Rudelius, *Guidelines for Technical Report Writing* (Minneapolis:
University of Minnesota, undated). See also William Strunk, Jr., and E. B. White,
The Elements of Style (New York, Macmillan, 1979).

Chapter 3

1. "Company Profile: Facebook, Inc.," MarketLine, February 6, 2015, www.
marketline.com; Ben Geier, "Zuckerberg Says Facebook's Giant Internet Drones
Are Already Flying," *Fortune.com*, April 1, 2015; Aaron Tilley, "Looking
Beyond Mobile, Facebook Is Getting into The Internet of Things," *Forbes.com*,
March 25, 2015; Jack Linshi, "Facebook Will Now Help Your Photos Look Way
Better," *Time.com*, December 18, 2014; Michael L. Best, "Global Computing:
The Internet That Facebook Built," Communications of the ACM, December 2014;
Trefis Team, "Facebook Through the Lens of Porter's Five Forces," *Forbes.com*,
November 28, 2014; Austin Carr, "Facebook Everywhere," *Fast Company*, July/
August 2014, pp. 56–92; Brad Stone and Sarah Frier, "Facebook's Next Decade,"
Bloomberg Businessweek, February 3, 2014, pp. 44–49.

2. Mark Cardwell, "Coffee-Loving Canadians Brewing up New Store Sales,"
Canadian Grocer, March 6, 2015, www.canadiangrocer.com, accessed October
10, 2015.

3. "Tea Fact Sheet and Trends," Tea Association of Canada, www.tea.ca, accessed
October 10, 2015.

4. Peter Coy, Shobhana Chandra, and Rich Miller, "Go," *Bloomberg Businessweek*,
April 13, 2015, pp. 11–12; Sarah Vizard, "The Marketing Year: Key Trends 2014,"
Marketing Week, December 4, 2014, p. 1; Matthew Idema, "Digital Market Trends
in the New Year," businesstoday.co.om, May 4, 2015; "2015 Emerging Top 10
Trends," management.co.nz, April 2015; Linda A. Goldstein, "Current FTC Hot
Buttons and Trends," *Response*, April 2015, p. 60; Jonathan Bacon, "The
Marketing Year: Technology Trends 2014," *Marketing Week*, December 5, 2014,
p. 1; Karen Nayler, "Trends and Issues," *Marketing Magazine*, September 29, 2014,
pp. 10–12; Mindi Chahal, "Five Trends Marketers Need to Know for 2015,"
Marketing Week, December 3, 2014, p. 1; and Juan M. Sanchez, "Growth Around
the World Is Still Below the Trend," *The Regional Economist*, January 2015,
pp. 4–7.

5. *World Population Prospects, 2015,* United Nations, New York.

6. Ibid.

7. Ibid.

8. Ibid.; Canadian Media Directors' Council, *Media Digest, 2015–2016,* Toronto.

9. *Population Projections for Canada, Provinces and Territories, 2009-2036,* Statistics Canada Catalogue no. 91-520.

10. Chris Matthews, "America's Most Indebted Generation, Gen X," **Fortune.com**, August 29, 2014; Leonard Klie, "Gen X: Stuck in the Middle," **destinationCRM. com**, February 1, 2012; Michele Hammond, "Gen X Pips Boomers to Lead Online Retail Spending," **www.startupsmart.com.au**, January 10, 2013; Chris Johns, "Hotels for Hipsters," *Globe and Mail*, November 13, 2012, p. E1; and Piet Levy, "Segmentation by Generation," *Marketing News*, May 15, 2011, p. 20.

11. "Understanding Canada's Millenial Audience," eMarketer.com, October 17, 2013, **http://www.emarketer.com/Article/Understanding-Canadarsquos-Millennial-Audience/1010304**.

12. Tracy Bains, "Engaging Canada's Ethnic Communities Online," *DX3 Digest,* November 22, 2011, **http://digest.dx3canada.com/2011/11/22/engaging-canadas-ethnic-communities-online/**.

13. Chris Daniels, "Multicultural Marketing: The Visible Majority, *Marketing,* March 12, 2012, **http://www.marketingmag.ca/news/marketer-news/multicultural-marketing-the-visible-majority-48428**.

14. Rebecca Harris, "Skin Deep," *Marketing* (January 29, 2007), pp. 18–19; and Kristin Laird, "Walmart Marks EID with Facebook Recipe Ad," *Marketin,* July 23, 2014; **http://www.marketingmag.ca/brands/walmart-marks-eid-with-facebook-recipe-ad-120452**.

15. Sarah Cunningham-Scharf, "What You Missed at the Ethnic Consumer Marketing Conference," *Canadian Grocer,* May 07, 2015, **http://www.canadiangrocer. com/top-stories/what-you-missed-at-the-ethnic-consumer-marketing-conference-53024**; and Sarah Barmak, "New BrandSpark Study Shows How Canadian Ethnic Buyers Shop," *Canadian Grocer,* July 22, 2014, **http://www. canadiangrocer.com/top-stories/new-brandspark-study-shows-how-canadian-ethnic-buyers-shop-43031**.

16. "Food Statistics," Statistics Canada, Ottawa (2010), catalogue no. 21-020-X.

17. Michelle Halpern, "Flavour Nation," *Marketing* (January 23, 2006), p. 10.

18. "Survey of Household Spending 2012," Statistics Canada, *The Daily,* April 25, 2012.

19. Marco Vriens and Patricia Kidd, "The Big Data Shift," *Marketing Insights,* November/December 2014, pp. 22–29; and Cliff Saran, "Big Data Technology Has Its Work Cut Out to Harness Web Analytics," *Computer Weekly,* May 13–19, 2014, p. 12.

20. Michael Porter, *Competitive Advantage* (New York: Free Press, 1985); and Michael Porter, *Competitive Strategy* (New York: Free Press, 1980).

21. Bruce H. Clark, Andrew V. Abela, and Time Ambler, "Behind the Wheel," *Marketing Management,* June 2006, p. 19–23; and Paul W. Farris, Neil T. Bendle, Phillip E. Pfeifer, and David J. Reibstein, *Marketing Metrics: 501 Metrics Every Executive Should Master* (Philadelphia: Wharton School Publishing, 2007).

22. Canadian Federation of Independent Business, **www.cfib.ca** (downloaded October 20, 2015); "Small Business Statistics, August 2013," Industry Canada, **www.ic.gc. ca/sbstatistics** (downloaded October 20, 2015); Vincent Ferrao, "Women in Canada," Statistics Canada, 89-503-X, 2011; and Frederick G. Crane, *Marketing for Entrepreneurs, Second Edition* (Thousand Oaks, CA: Sage Publications, 2013).

23. **www.ic.gc.ca**.

24. Jeff Fraser, "Cross-Device Tracking Raises Consumer Privacy Concerns," *Marketing,* March 17, 2015, **http://www.marketingmag.ca/advantage/cross-device-tracking-is-the-next-big-threat-to-consumer-privacy-140588**.

25. Ibid.

Chapter 4

1. Susan Adams, "The World's Most Ethical Companies, 2014," *Forbes*, March 20, 2014, **http://www.forbes.com/sites/susanadams/2014/03/20/the-worlds-most-ethical-companies/**; Julie Smyth, "Canada's Top 50 Socially Responsible Corporations, 2015," *Maclean's*, June 8, 2015, **http://www.macleans.ca/economy/business/canadas-top-50-most-socially-responsible-companies/**.

2. Patrick Murphy and Gene Laczniak, *Marketing Ethics: Cases and Readings* (Upper Saddle River, NJ, Prentice Hall, 2006); and D. Robin and S. J. Vitell, *Theoretical Foundations in Marketing Ethics* (London: Elsevier, 2006).

3. Verne E. Henderson, "The Ethical Side of Enterprise," *Sloan Management Review* (Spring 1982), pp. 37–47. See also Joseph L. Badaracco, Jr., *Defining Moments: When Managers Must Choose Between Right and Right* (Boston: Harvard Business School Press, 1997).

4. M. Bommer, C. Gratto, J. Grauander, and M. Tuttle, "A Behavioral Model of Ethical and Unethical Decision Making," *Journal of Business Ethics,* vol. 6 (1987), pp. 265–80.

5. Frederick G. Crane, "Ethics, Entrepreneurs and Corporate Managers," *Journal of Small Business & Entrepreneurship* (2009), vol. 22 (3), pp. 267–74.

6. "Nurses Top Honesty and Ethics List for 11th Year," **www.gallup.com**, December 3, 2010.

7. F. G. Crane, "Teaching Business Ethics in B-Schools: A Cross-Cultural Examination," *Journal of the Academy of Business Education* (2005), 6(2), pp. 63–67.

8. Frederick G. Crane, "The Ethics of Canadian and American Entrepreneurs: A Cross-Cultural Study," *Business Journal for Entrepreneurs,* 2012, Issue 3, pp. 125–39.

9. See, for example, Linda Trevino and Katherine A. Nelson, *Managing Business Ethics: Straight Talk and How to Get It Right,* 5th Edition (New York: John Wiley & Sons, 2011).

10. See Murphy and Laczniak, *Marketing Ethics;* and Robin and Vitell, *Theoretical Foundations in Marketing Ethics.*

11. Dan T. Swartwood and Richard J. Hefferman, *Trends in Intellectual Property Loss, Survey Report* (Alexandria, VA: American Society for Industrial Security, 1998).

12. Vern Terpstra and Kenneth David, *The Cultural Environment of International Business,* 3rd ed. (Cincinnati: South-Western Publishing, 1991), p. 12.

13. For an extended treatment of ethics in the exchange process, see Gregory T. Gundlach and Patrick E. Murphy, "Ethical and Legal Foundations in Relational Marketing Exchanges," *Journal of Marketing* (October 1993), pp. 35–46.

14. For an extensive examination on slotting fees, see Paul N. Bloom, Gregory T. Gundlach, and Joseph P. Cannon, "Slotting Allowances and Fees: Schools of Thought and Views of Practicing Managers," *Journal of Marketing* (April 2000), pp. 92–109.

15. Hedieh Nasheri , *Economic Espionage and Industrial Spying* (Cambridge: Cambridge University Press, 2005).

16. John Dalla Costa, "Ethics & Marketing," *Marketing* (May 22/29, 2006), p. 13.

17. Laura Pratt, "Everyday Ethics," *Marketing* (September 11, 2006), pp. 16–17.

18. R. Eric Reidenbach and Donald P. Robin, *Ethics and Profits* (Englewood Cliffs, NJ: Prentice Hall, 1989).

19. "Scotchgard Working Out Recent Stain on Its Business," **www.mercurynews.com** (downloaded June 2003).

20. James Q. Wilson, "Adam Smith on Business Ethics," *California Management Review* (Fall 1989), pp. 59–72; and George M. Zinkham, Michael Bisesi, and Mary Jane Saxon, "MBAs: Changing Attitudes Toward Marketing Dilemmas," *Journal of Business Ethics,* vol. 8 (1989), pp. 963–74.

21. **www.nestlecanada.ca** (downloaded April 25, 2001).

22. Robert B. Reich, "The New Meaning of Corporate Social Responsibility," *California Management Review* (Winter 1998), pp. 8–17.

23. Harvey S. James and Farhad Rassekh, "Smith, Friedman, and Self-Interest in Ethical Society," *Business Ethics Quarterly* (July 2000), pp. 659–74.

24. Toni Clarke, "FDA Approves Sanofi's Gaucher Disease Drug Cerdelga," Reuters, August 19, 2014, **www.reuters.com**.

25. For an extended description of the Perrier decision, see "Perrier— Overresponding to a Crisis," in Robert F. Hartley, *Marketing Mistakes and Successes,* 8th ed. (New York: Wiley, 2001), pp. 127–37.

26. Julie Smyth, "Canada's Top 50 Socially Responsible Corporations, 2015," *Maclean's,* June 8, 2015, **http://www.macleans.ca/economy/business/ canadas-top-50-most-socially-responsible-companies/**; and "Top 50 Socially Responsible Corporations," *Maclean's,* June 9, 2011, **http://www2. macleans. ca/2011/06/09/better-business/**.

27. *The ISO Survey of Management System Standard Classifications—2011* (Geneva, Switzerland: International Organization for Standardization, 2015).

28. P. Rajan Varadarajan and Anil Menon, "Cause-Related Marketing: A Coalignment of Marketing Strategy and Corporate Philanthropy," *Journal of Marketing,* July 1988, pp. 58–74.

29. The examples given are found in "The Socially Correct Corporation," *Fortune* (July 24, 2000), special section; "The Wider Benefits of Backing a Good Cause," *Marketing* (September 2, 1999), pp. 18–22; and "Top 50 Socially Responsible Corporations," *Maclean's,* June 9, 2011, **http://www2.macleans.ca/2011/06/09/better-business/**.

30. These steps are adapted from J. J. Carson and G. A. Steiner, *Measuring Business Social Performance: The Corporate Social Audit* (New York: Committee for Economic Development, 1974); see also Sandra Waddock and Neil Smith, "Corporate Responsibility Audits: Doing Well by Doing Good," *Sloan Management Review* (Winter 2000), pp. 75–84.

31. Unmesh Kher, "Getting Smart at Being Good. . . . Are Companies Better Off for It?" *Time,* January, 2006, pp. A1–A37; and Pete Engardio, "Beyond the Green Corporation," *Bloomberg Businessweek,* January 29, 2007, pp. 50–64.

32. "Economics-Creating Environmental Capital," *The Wall Street Journal,* March 24, 2008, Section R; and Remi Trudel and June Cotte, "Does Being Ethical Pay?" *The Wall Street Journal,* May 12, 2008, p. R4.

33. Angela Kryhul, "The Consumer Connection," *Marketing* (June 5, 2006), pp. 12–13.

34. "The 2015 Best 50 Corporate Citizens in Canada," *Corporate Knights,* **http://www.corporateknights.com/reports/2015-best-50/2015-best-50-results-14333042/**; also see Tara Perkins, "The Company Spotlight, Desjardin Group," *Corporate Knights,* The Best 50 Corporate Citizens 2012, **http://www. corporateknights.com/report/2012-best-corporate-citizens-canada**.

35. "Green buying: how to make true eco-friendly purchases," Environment Canada, February 27, 2012, **www.ec.gc.ca**, downloaded February 12, 2013.

36. See Wayne D. Hoyer and Deborah J. MacInnis, *Consumer Behavior,* 5th ed. (New York: Houghton Mifflin Company, 2008), pp. 535–37.

37. Hollie Shaw, "Canadians Won't Pay More for Eco-Friendly Products," **www. financialpost.com**, October 6, 2011 (downloaded January 14, 2013).

38. "National Geographic Explores the World of Green Consumers," GlobeScan, September 25, 2012, **http://www.globescan.com/84-press-releases-2012/ 241-canadian-consumers-among-the-least-green-and-least-guilty-about-their-environmental-impact.html**.

39. "Corporate Knights Special Reports," **www.corporateknights.ca** (downloaded August 28, 2013).

Chapter 5

1. Andrew Clarke, "What Women Want. . . . .in a Car," *The Globe and Mail,* September 6, 2012, **www.theglobeandmail.com** (downloaded February 4, 2013); and "What Matters the Most When People Buy Cars," *BrandWeek,* October 11, 2010, p. 23; "Americans Rethinking How They Buy Cars," **money.msn.com**, April 4, 2014; "Car-Buying Tips Men Can Learn from Women," **www. leasetrader.com**, January 30, 2012; "New Efforts to Shorten the Car-Buying Process," *Wall Street Journal*, February 27, 2013, p. D3; Jerry Hirsh, "Car Buying: How Men and Women Compare," **www.latimes.com**, April 7, 2011; "What Matters the Most When People Buy Cars," *BrandWeek,* October 11, 2010, p. 23; "Gender Wars and Car Shopping: Men Want Power, Women Want Cloth Seats," **www.autos.aol.com**, July 16, 2010; and Michael J. Silverstein and Kate Sayre, "The Female Economy," *Harvard Business Review,* September 2009, pp. 46–53.

2. Roger D. Blackwell, Paul W. Miniard, and James F. Engel, *Consumer Behavior,* 10th ed. (Mason, OH: South-Western Publishing, 2005).

3. For thorough descriptions of consumer expertise, see Joseph W. Alba and J. Wesley Hutchinson, "Knowledge Calibration: What Consumers Know and What They Think They Know," *Journal of Consumer Research* (September 2000), pp. 123–57.

4. For in-depth studies on external information search patterns, see Sridhar Moorthy, Brian T. Ratchford, and Debabrata Tulukdar, "Consumer Information Search Revisited: Theory and Empirical Analysis," *Journal of Consumer Research* (March 1997), pp. 263–77; Joel E. Urbany, Peter R. Dickson, and William L. Wilkie, "Buyer Uncertainty and Information Search," *Journal of Consumer Research* (March 1992), pp. 452–63.

5. Michelle Sexsmith, "Today's Trends in Online Shopping," *Environics,* August 16, 2012, **http://en.environicsanalytics.ca/media_room.aspx?tab= news&item=CR_Summer2012**.

6. For an extended discussion on evaluative criteria, see Del J. Hawkins, David L. Mothersbaugh, and Roger J. Best, *Consumer Behavior,* 10th ed. (Burr Ridge, IL: McGraw-Hill/Irwin, 2007), pp. 572–77.

7. Hawkins, Mothersbaugh, and Best, *Consumer Behavior,* pp. 534–35. For an extended discussion on consumer choice sets, see Allan D. Shocker, Moshe Ben-Akiva, Bruno Boccara, and Prakesh Nedungadi, "Consideration Set Influences on Consumer Decision Making and Choice: Issues, Models, and Suggestions." *Marketing Letters* (August 1991), pp. 181–98.

8. William J. McDonald, "Time Use in Shopping: The Role of Personal Characteristics," *Journal of Retailing* (Winter 1994), pp. 345–66; Robert J. Donovan, John R. Rossiter, Gillian Marcoolyn, and Andrew Nesdale, "Store Atmosphere and Purchasing Behavior," *Journal of Retailing* (Fall 1994), pp. 283–94; and Eric A. Greenleaf and Donald R. Lehman, "Reasons for Substantial

Delay in Consumer Decision Making," *Journal of Consumer Research* (September 1995), pp. 186–99.

9. Sunil Gupta and Valarie Zeithaml, "Customer Metrics and Their Impact on Financial Performance," *Marketing Science,* November–December 2006, pp. 718–739.

10. Jagdish N. Sheth and Banwari Mitral, *Consumer Behavior,* 2nd ed. (Mason, OH: South-Western Publishing, 2003), p. 32.

11. Sunil Gupta and Donald R. Lehmann, *Managing Customers as Investments* (Upper Saddle River, NJ: Pearson Education, Inc., 2005).

12. For an overview of research on involvement, see John C. Mowen and Michael Minor, *Consumer Behavior,* 5th ed. (Upper Saddle River, NJ: Prentice Hall, 2001); and Wayne D. Hoyer and Deborah J. MacInnis, *Consumer Behavior,* 5th ed. (Florence, KY: South-Western Education Publishing, 2009).

13. For an overview on the three problem-solving variations, see Hawkins, Mothersbaugh, and Best, *Consumer Behavior,* pp. 510–14.

14. Russell Belk, "Situational Variables and Consumer Behavior," *Journal of Consumer Research* (December 1975), pp. 157–63.

15. A.H. Maslow, *Motivation and Personality* (New York: Harper & Row, 1970). Also see Richard Yalch and Frederic Brunel, "Need Hierarchies in Consumer Judgments of Product Design: Is It Time to Reconsider Maslow's Hierarchy?" in Kim Corfman and John Lynch, eds., *Advances in Consumer Research* (Provo, UT: Association for Consumer Research, 1996), pp. 405–10.

16. Bernardo J. Carducci, *The Psychology of Personality,* 2nd ed. (Oxford, UK: John Wiley & Sons, 2009).

17. Terry Clark, "International Marketing and National Character: A Review and Proposal for an Integrative Theory," *Journal of Marketing* (October 1990), pp. 66–79; and John-Benedict E. M. Steenkamp, "The Role of National Culture in International Marketing Research," *International Marketing Review* 18, no. 1 (2001), pp. 30–44.

18. Jane Spencer, "Lenovo Puts Style in New Laptop," *Wall Street Journal,* January, 2008, p. B5.

19. This example provided in Michael R. Solomon, *Consumer Behavior,* 4th ed. (Upper Saddle River, NJ: Prentice Hall, 1999), p. 59.

20. For further reading on subliminal perception, see B. Bahrami, N. Lavie and G. Rees, "Attentional Load Modulates Responses of Human Primary Visual Cortex to Invisible Stimuli," *Current Biology,* March 2007, pp. 39–47.

21. August Bullock, *The Secret Sales Pitch* (San Jose, CA: Norwich Publishers, 2004); "GOP Commercial Resurrects Debate on Subliminal Ads," *Wall Street Journal* (September 13, 2000), p. B10; "I Will Love This Story," *U.S. News & World Report* (May 12, 1997), p. 12; and "Firm Gets Message Out Subliminally," *Dallas Morning News* (February 2, 1997), pp. 1H, 6H.

22. Sholnn Freeman, "Brand Breakdown," *The Washington Post,* March 26, 2006, p. F1ff.

23. Martin Fishbein and I. Aizen, *Belief, Attitude, Intention and Behavior: An Introduction to Theory and Research* (Reading, MA: Addison-Wesley 1975), p. 6.

24. Richard J. Lutz, "Changing Brand Attitudes through Modification of Cognitive Structure," *Journal of Consumer Research* (March 1975), pp. 49–59. See also Mowen and Minor, *Consumer Behavior,* pp. 287–88.

25. "Lunch at Tim's Lifestyle Segment Profile," Environics Analytics, 2015.

26. This discussion is based on Ed Keller and Jon Berry, *The Influentials* (New York: Simon and Schuster, 2003).

27. Michele Sexsmith, "Today's Trends in Online Shopping," *Environics Analytics,* August 16, 2012, **http://en.environicsanalytics.ca/media_room.aspx?tab= news&item=CR_Summer2012**.

28. F.G. Crane and T.K. Clarke, "The Identification of Evaluative Criteria and Cues Used in Selecting Services," *Journal of Services Marketing* (Spring 1988), pp. 53–59.

29. **www.the-cma.org.** Also see, Emanuel Rosen, *Anatomy of Buzz Marketing Revisited* (New York: Broadway Business, 2009).

30. For an extensive review on consumer socialization of children, see Deborah Roedder John, "Consumer Socialization of Children: A Retrospective Look at Twenty-Five Years of Research," *Journal of Consumer Research* (December 1999), pp. 183–213.

31. "Special Issues for Young Children," and "How Marketers Target Kids," **www.media-awareness.ca** (downloaded January 10, 2007).

32. J. Paul Peter and Jerry C. Olson, *Consumer Behavior and Marketing Strategy,* 9th ed. (Burr Ridge, IL: McGraw Hill/Irwin, 2010).

33. This discussion is based on Hawkins, Mothersbaugh, and Best, *Consumer Behavior: Building Marketing Strategy;* **www.teenresearch.com**, downloaded April 1, 2007; "Teens Rule," **MediaBuyer.com**, downloaded April 7, 2007; Jennifer Saranow, "This Is the Car We Want, Mommy," *Wall Street Journal,* November 9, 2006, pp. D1, D4; and "Trillion-Dollar Kids," *The Economist,* December 2, 2006, p. 66.

34. Harold R. Kerbo, *Social Stratification and Inequality* (Burr Ridge, IL: McGraw-Hill, 2000). For an extensive discussion on social class, see Eric Arnould, Linda Price, and George Zinkhan, *Consumers,* 2nd ed. (Burr Ridge, IL: McGraw Hill/Irwin, 2004), chap. 6.

35. Astrid Van Den Broek, "Fighting Cultural Fade," *Strategy Magazine* (February 11, 2004), p. 21.

36. "Ethnic Marketing in Canada," Environics, August 23, 2013, **http://www.slidesh are.net/Environics/ethnic-marketing-in-canada**; Stan Sutter, "The Quebec Connection," **http://www.headspacemarketing.com/** (accessed December 10, 2015); Susan Krashinsky, "Target Take Note: Quebec Market Tricky for Outsiders," *Globe and Mail,* March 4, 2013, **http://www.theglobeandmail.com/report- on-business/industry-news/marketing/target-take-note-quebec-market- tricky-for-outsiders/article9259193/**.

37. Sutter, "The Quebec Connection."

38. Ibid.

39. Ibid.

40. "Ethnic Marketing in Canada."

41. Ibid.

Chapter 6

1. Information provided by Campus Living Centres (2016).

2. "Interview: industry vets on the future of Canadian manufacturing," *Canadian Business,* April 30, 2015, **http://www.canadianbusiness.com/innovation/the- future-of-manufacturing/** (downloaded February 7, 2016); "Manufacturing in Canada," Canadian Manufacturing Coalition, n.d., **http://www. manufacturingourfuture.ca/english/manufacturing-in-canada/ manufacturing-in-canada.html** (downloaded February 7, 2016).

3. Statistics Canada, **www.statcan.ca**, CANSIM, 380-0002 and 13-001 XIB (2016).

4. Statistics Canada, **www.statcan.gc.ca/eng/subjects/standard/naics/2012/index** (downloaded January 17, 2016).

5. An argument that consumer buying and organizational buying do not have important differences is found in Edward F. Fern and James R. Brown, "The Industrial/Consumer Marketing Dichotomy: A Case of Insufficient Justification," *Journal of Marketing* (Spring 1984), pp. 68–77. However, most writers on the subject do draw distinctions between the two types of buying. See, for example, Michael D. Hutt and Thomas W. Speh, *Business Marketing Management,* 7th ed. (Fort Worth, TX: Dryden Press, 2001); and H. Michael Hayes, Per V. Jenster, and Nils-Erik Aaby, *Business Marketing: A Global Perspective* (Chicago: Richard D. Irwin, 1996).

6. This list of characteristics and portions of the discussion in this section are based on F. Robert Dwyer and John F. Tanner, Jr., *Business Marketing*, 4th ed. (Burr Ridge, IL: McGraw-Hill/ Irwin, 2009); and Michael D. Hutt and Thomas W. Speh, *Business Marketing Management: B2B*, 11th ed. (Mason, OH: South-Western, 2012).

7. Dwyer and Tanner, *Business Marketing*, 2009.

8. Rich Smith, "Boeing Lands a Blockbuster Sale—That No One Has Heard About," The Motley Fool, March 30, 2015, **www.fool.com/investing/general/2015/03/30/boeing-lands-a-blockbuster-sale-that-no-one-has-he.aspx**.

9. "Boise Cascade Turns Green," *Wall Street Journal* (September 3, 2003), p. B6.

10. Hutt and Speh, *Business Marketing Management: B2B*.

11. For an overview on ISO 9000 certification, see Thomas H. Stevenson and Frank C. Barnes, "What Industrial Marketers Need to Know about ISO 9000 Certification: A Review, Update, and Integration with Marketing," *Industrial Marketing Management* (November 2002), pp. 695–703.

12. P.K. Humphreys, W.L. Li, and L.Y. Chan, "The Impact of Supplier Development on Buyer-Supplier Performance," *Omega,* 32(2), 2004, pp. 131–143.

13. This example is found in Sandy D. Jap and Jakki J. Mohr, "Leverage Internet Technologies in B2B Relationships," *California Management Review* (Summer 2002), pp. 24–38.

14. "Harley-Davidson Company," *Purchasing Magazine Online* (September 4, 2003).

15. Emi Kolawole, "IBM's 'Sequoia' Unseats Fujitsu; Tops the List as Fastest Supercomputer," *Washington Post*, June 18, 2012, **www.washingtonpost.com/blogs/innovations/post/ibms-sequoia-unseats-fujitsu-tops-the-list-as-fastest-supercomputer/2012/06/18/gJQAG0nUIV_blog.html**.

16. Pratibha A. Dabholkar, Wesley J. Johnston, and Amy S. Cathey, "The Dynamics of Long-Term Business-to-Business Exchange Relationships," *Journal of Academy of Marketing Science,* vol. 22(2) (1994), pp. 130–45.

17. "EDS Signs $1.7 Billion IT Services Agreement with Kraft Foods," EDS news release, April 28, 2006; and "HP Finalizes $3 Billion Outsourcing Agreement to Manage Procter & Gamble's IT Infrastructure," Hewlett-Packard news release, May 6, 2003.

18. James C. Anderson and James A. Narus, *Business Market Management* (Upper Saddle River, NJ: Prentice Hall, 1999); and Neil Rackham, Lawrence Friedman, and Richard Ruff, *Getting Partnering Right* (New York: McGraw-Hill, 1996); and Joseph P. Cannon and Christian Homburg, "Buyer-Supplier Relationships and Customer Firm Costs," *Journal of Marketing* (January 2001), pp. 29–43.

19. Starbucks Global Responsibility Report: Goals and Progress 2013, downloaded January 5, 2015; Helen Walker and Wendy Phillips, "Sustainable Procurement: Emerging Issues," *International Journal of Procurement Management* 2, no. 1 (2009), pp. 41–61.

20. Thomas V. Bonoma, "Major Sales: Who Really Does the Buying?" *Harvard Business Review*, May–June 1982, pp. 11–19. Also see, Philip L. Dawes, Don Y. Lee, and Grahame R. Dowling, "Information Control and Influence in Emerging Buying Centers," *Journal of Marketing*, July 1998, pp. 55–68; and Thomas Tellefsen, "Antecedents and Consequences of Buying Center Leadership: An Emergent Perspective," *Journal of Business-to-Business Marketing* 13, no. 1 (2006), pp. 53–59.

21. Paul A. Herbig, *Handbook of Cross-Cultural Marketing* (New York: The Halworth Press, 1998).

22. Julia M. Bristor, "Influence Strategies in Organizational Buying: The Importance of Connections to the Right People in the Right Places," *Journal of Business-to-Business Marketing,* vol. 1 (1993), pp. 63–98.

23. These definitions are adapted from Frederick E. Webster, Jr., and Yoram Wind, *Organizational Buying Behavior* (Englewood Cliffs, NJ: Prentice Hall, 1972), p. 6.

24. "Can Corning Find Its Optic Nerve?" *Fortune* (March 19, 2001), pp. 148–50.

25. Jeffrey E. Lewin and Naveen Donthu, "The Influence of Purchase Situation on Buying Center Structure and Involvement: A Select Meta-Analysis of Organizational Buying Behavior Research," *Journal of Business Research*, October 2005, 1381–90.

26. See, for example, R. Vekatesh, Ajay Kohli, and Gerald Zaltman, "Influence Strategies in Buying Centers," *Journal of Marketing* (October 1995), pp. 61–72; Gary L. Lilien and Anthony Wong, "An Exploratory Investigation of the Structure of the Buying Center in the Metal Working Industry," *Journal of Marketing Research* (February 1984), pp. 1–11. See also, Christopher P. Puto, Wesley E. Patton III, and Ronald H. King, "Risk Handling Strategies in Industrial Vendor Selection Decisions," *Journal of Marketing* (Winter 1985), pp. 89–98.

27. "B2B E-Commerce Headed for Trillions," **www.clickz.com** (downloaded September 1, 2009); and "Electronic Commerce and Technology," *The Daily,* Statistics Canada (April 20, 2009).

28. This discussion is based on Jennifer Reinhold, "What We Learned in the New Economy," *Fast Company* (March 4, 2004), pp. 56ff; Mark Roberti, "General Electric's Spin Machine," *Industry Standard* (January 22–29, 2001), pp. 74–83; and **www.boeing.com/procurement** (downloaded February 6, 2004).

29. "B2B, Take 2," *BusinessWeek* (November 25, 2003).

30. Mark Krauss, "eBay 'Bids' on Small-Biz Firms to Sustain Growth," *Marketing News* (December 8, 2003), pp. 6, 7; "eBay Realizes Success in Small-Biz Arena," *Marketing News* (May 1, 2004), p. 11; and **www.ebay.com/chp/business-industrial**.

31. This discussion is based on Robert J. Dolan and Youngme Moon, "Pricing and Market Making on the Internet," *Journal of Interactive Marketing* (Spring 2000), pp. 56–73; and Ajit Kambil and Eric van Heck, *Marking Markets: How Firms Can Benefit from Online Auctions and Exchanges* (Boston: Harvard Business School Press, 2002).

32. Susan Avery, "Supply Management Is Core of Success at UTC," *Purchasing,* September 7, 2006, pp. 36–39.

33. Shawn P. Daley and Prithwiraz Nath, "Reverse Auctions for Relationship Marketers," *Industrial Marketing Management*, February 2005, pp. 157–66; and Sandy Jap, "The Impact of Online Reverse Auction Design on Buyer-Supplier Relationships," *Journal of Marketing,* January 2007, pp. 146–59.

Chapter 7

1. "Dell India regains Top Spot in Domestic PC Market," **ibnlive.in.com**, May 24, 2014; "Dell India Plans to Open More Exclusive Brand Outlets in India," **www. business-standard.com**, December 13, 2013; "Dell's Next Big Agenda," **www.crn.in**, February 21, 2012; "Dell India Opens Its Exclusive Store in Hyderabad," **www.greatandhra.com**, September 12, 2012; and "How Dell Conquered India," **www.CNNMoney.com**, February 10, 2011.

2. These estimates are based on data from *International Trade Statistics 2016* (Geneva: World Trade Organization). Global trade statistics reported in this chapter also came from this source, unless otherwise indicated.

3. Ibid.

4. S. Kim and S. Kim, *Global Corporate Finance,* 6th ed. (Oxford, UK: Blackwell Publishing, 2006).

5. "Canada's State of Trade: Trade and Investment Update 2016," Foreign Affairs, Trade and Development Canada, **http://www.international.gc.ca/economist-economiste/assets/pdfs/SoT_2016_eng.pdf**.

6. Ibid.

7. Ibid.

8. Danielle Goldfarb, "Five trade trends for 2015 and how Canada can take advantage of them," *Ottawa Citizen,* January 1, 2015, **http://ottawacitizen.com/news/national/danielle-goldfarb-five-trade-trends-for-2015-and-how-canada-can-take-advantage-of-them**.

9. Michael E. Porter, *The Competitive Advantage of Nations* (New York: Free Press, 1990), pp. 577–615. For another view that emphasizes cultural differences, see David S. Landes, *The Wealth and Poverty of Nations* (New York: Norton, 1998).

10. Roger L. Martin and Michael E. Porter, "Canadian Competitiveness: Nine Years After the Crossroads," **www.mgmt.utoronto.ca/research/competitive.htm** (downloaded May 5, 2002).

11. Dennis R. Appleyard and Alfred J. Field, Jr., *International Economics,* 4th ed. (Burr Ridge, IL: McGraw-Hill/Irwin, 2001), chap. 15; "A Fruit Peace," *The Economist* (April 21, 2001), pp. 75–76; and Gary C. Hufbauer and Kimberly A. Elliott, *Measuring the Cost of Protection in the United States* (Washington, DC: Institute for International Economics, 1994).

12. This discussion is based on information provided by the World Trade Organization, **www.wto.org** (downloaded March 17, 2007).

13. **www.juniper.net/company** (downloaded March 15, 2004); and "Alliances in Consumer and Packaged Goods," **www.corporatefinance.mckinsey.com** (downloaded Autumn 2003).

14. For an excellent overview of different types of global companies and marketing strategies, see Warren J. Keegan, *Global Marketing Management,* 7th ed. (Upper Saddle River, NJ: Prentice Hall, 2002), chap. 2.

15. Johnny K. Johansson and Ilkka A. Ronkainen, "The Brand Challenge," *Marketing Management* (March–April 2004), pp. 54–55.

16. Kevin Lane Keller, *Strategic Brand Management,* 2nd ed. (Upper Saddle River, NJ: Prentice Hall, 2003), p. 693.

17. For an extensive discussion on identifying global consumers, see Jean-Pierre Jeannet and H. David Hennessey, *Global Marketing Strategies,* 4th ed. (Boston: Houghton Mifflin, 1998).

18. "Number of internet users worldwide from 2005 to 2016 (in millions)," Statista: The Statistics Portal website (2016), **www.statista.com/statistics/186370/number-of-internet-users-worldwide-time-series/** (accessed September 4, 2016).

19. For comprehensive references on cross-cultural aspects of marketing, see Paul A. Herbig, *Handbook of Cross-Cultural Marketing* (New York: Halworth Press, 1998); Jean-Claude Usunier, *Marketing across Cultures,* 2nd ed. (London: Prentice Hall Europe, 1996); and Philip R. Cateora and John L. Graham, *International Marketing,* 12th ed. (Burr Ridge, IL: McGraw-Hill/Irwin, 2005). Unless otherwise indicated, examples found in this section appear in these excellent sources.

20. "Clash of Cultures," *BrandWeek* (May 4, 1998), p. 28. Also see R. L. Tung, *Business Negotiations with the Japanese* (Lexington, MA: Lexington Books, 1993).

21. For examples on cross-cultural marketing, see Hawkins, Mothersbaugh, and Best, *Consumer Behavior,* 10th ed. (Burr Ridge, IL: McGraw-Hill, 2007).

22. "Greeks Protest Coke's Use of Parthenon," *Dallas Morning News* (August 17, 1992), p. D4.

23. "Japanese Products are Popular in the U.S.," *Research Alert* (November 17, 2000), p. 8; and "Buying American," *American Demographics* (March 1998), pp. 32–38; and Sharon Younger, "Marketing Overseas? Keep it Canadian," *Strategy Magazine* (February 11, 2002), p. 23.

24. "Marketing by Language: Oracle Trims Teams, Sees Big Savings," *Advertising Age International* (July 2000), pp. 4, 38.

25. Terrence A. Shimp and Subhash Sharma, "Consumer Ethnocentrism, Construction and Validation of the CETSCALE," *Journal of Marketing Research* (August 1987), pp. 280–89.

26. Subhash Sharma, Terrence Shimp, and Jeongshin Shin, "Consumer Ethnocentrism: A Test of Antecedents and Moderators," *Journal of the Academy of Marketing Science* (Winter 1995), pp. 26–37; Joel Herche, "A Note on the Predictive Validity of the CETSCALE," *Journal of the Academy of Marketing Science* (Summer 1992), pp. 261–64.

27. Vijay Mahajan and Kamini Banga, *The 86 Percent Solution: How to Succeed in the Biggest Market Opportunity of the Next 50 Years* (Upper Saddle River, NJ: Pearson Education, 2006); and C.K. Pralahad, *The Fortune at the Bottom of the Pyramid: Eradicating Poverty Through Profits* (Upper Saddle River, NJ: Pearson Education, 2005).

28. "Betting on a New Label: Made in Russia," *BusinessWeek* (April 12, 1999), p. 122; "Russia and Central-Eastern Europe: Worlds Apart," *BrandWeek* (May 4, 1998), pp. 30–31; and "We Will Bury You . . . with a Snickers Bar," *U.S. News & World Report* (January 26, 1998), pp. 50–51.

29. **www.wto.com** (downloaded February 15, 2004).

30. Pralahad, *The Fortune at the Bottom of the Pyramid;* and Jay Greene, "Taking Tiny Loans to the Next Level," *BusinessWeek,* November 27, 2006, pp. 76–79.

31. Cateora and Graham, *International Marketing.*

32. For an extensive and recent examination of these market entry options, see, for example, Johnny K. Johansson, *Global Marketing: Foreign Entry, Local Marketing, and Global Management,* 3rd ed. (Burr Ridge, IL: McGraw Hill/Irwin, 2003); Keegan, *Global Marketing Management;* Kotabe and Helson, *Global Marketing Management;* and Cateora and Graham, *International Marketing.*

33. McDonald's 2009 Annual Report.

34. "A Survey of Business in China," *The Economist* (March 20, 2004), special section.

35. This discussion is based on Keller, *Strategic Brand Management,* pp. 709–10; "Machines for the Masses," *Wall Street Journal* (December 9, 2003), pp. A19, A20; "The Color of Beauty," *Forbes* (November 22, 2000), pp. 170–76; "It's Goo, Goo, Goo, Goo Vibrations at the Gerber Lab," *Wall Street Journal* (December 4, 1996), pp. A1, A6; Donald R. Graber, "How to Manage a Global Product Development

Process," *Industrial Marketing Management* (November 1996), pp. 483–98; and Herbig, *Handbook of Cross-Cultural Marketing.*

36. Jagdish N. Sheth and Atul Parvatiyar, "The Antecedents and Consequences of Integrated Global Marketing," *International Marketing Review* 18, no. 1 (2001), pp. 16–29. Also see D. Szymanski, S. Bharadwaj, and R. Varadarajan, "Standardization versus Adaptation of International Marketing Strategy: An Empirical Investigation," *Journal of Marketing* (October 1993), pp. 1–17.

37. "Global Marketing Confronts the Digital Age," *Ideas@Beedie,* December 19, 2012, **http://beedie.sfu.ca/ideas/?p=5.**

38. This discussion is based on John Fahy and Fuyuki Taguchi, "Reassessing the Japanese Distribution System," *Sloan Management Review* (Winter 1995), pp. 49–61; and Edward Tse, "The Right Way to Achieve Profitable Growth in the Chinese Consumer Market," *Strategy & Business* (Second Quarter 1998), pp. 10–21.

39. "With Profits Elusive, Wal-Mart to Exit Germany," *Wall Street Journal,* July 29, 2006, pp. A1, A6.

Chapter 8

1. Pedro Garcia, "Using Social Media for Marketing Research," LinkedIn, September 18, 2014, **https://www.linkedin.com/pulse/20140918095916-59226101-using-social-media-for-marketing-research**; Ray Nelson, "How to Use Social Media for Market Research," *Social Media Today*, March 19, 2013, **http://www.socialmediatoday.com/content/how-use-social-media-market-research**.

2. For a lengthier, expanded discussion, consult the American Marketing Association's website at **www.marketingpower.com**; for a researcher's comments on this and other definitions of marketing research, see Lawrence D. Gibson, "Quo Vadis, Marketing Research?" *Marketing Research* (Spring 2000), pp. 36–41.

3. Joseph Pereira, "Unknown Fruit Takes on Unfamiliar Markets," *Wall Street Journal* (September 9, 1995), pp. B1, B5.

4. Lisa D'Innocenzo, "Focus Groups for a New Age," *Strategy Magazine* (August 23, 2004), p. 10.

5. Rob Gerlsbeck, "Canadian Forces," *Marketing* (November 26, 2007), p. 22.

6. "Focus on Consumers," *General Mills Midyear Report* (Minneapolis, MN: General Mills, January 8, 1998), pp. 2–3.

7. Michael J. McCarthy, "Stalking the Elusive Teenage Trendsetter," *Wall Street Journal* (November 19, 1998), pp. B1, B10.

8. See **www.trendhunter.com/about-trend-hunter**.

9. "Measurement for the Future," BBM Canada, **http://www.bbm.ca/en/products-services/the-portable-people-meter/measurement-for-the-future** (downloaded February 4, 2013).

10. Scott Moore, "The New Currency," *Marketing* (September 14, 2009), p. 41.

11. Mark Maremont, "New Toothbrush Is Big-Ticket Item," *Wall Street Journal* (October 27, 1998), pp. B1, B6; Emily Nelson, "P&G Checks Out Real Life," *Wall Street Journal* (May 17, 2001), pp. B1, B4.

12. Kenneth Chang, "Enlisting Science's Lessons to Entice More Shoppers to Spend More," *New York Times,* September 19, 2006, p. D3; and Janet Adamy, "Cooking Up Changes at Kraft Foods," *Wall Street Journal,* February 20, 2007, pp. B1, B4.

13. Dina Elboghdady, "Naked Truth," *Portland Press* (March 5, 2002), pp. C1, C5. For more information on Ethnography, see Hy Mariampolski, *Ethnography for Marketers: A Guide to Consumer Immersion* (Thousand Oaks, CA: Sage Publications, 2006).

14. Laurie Burkitt, "Battle for the Brain," *Forbes* (November 16, 2009), pp. 76–78.

15. Marketing Research and Intelligence Association, **www.mria-arim.ca** (downloaded November 11, 2009).

16. Patrick E. Murphy and Gene R. Lacznick, *Marketing Ethics: Cases and Readings* (Upper Saddle River, NJ: Pearson Education, 2006).

17. "Charter of Respondent Rights," Marketing Research and Intelligence Association, **www.mria-arim.ca** (downloaded March 27, 2007).

18. Janakiraman Moorthy, Rangin Lahiri, Neelanjan Biswas, Dipyaman Sanyal, Jayanthi Ranjan, Krishnadas Nanath, and Pulak Ghosh, "Big Data: Prospects and Challenges," *Vikalpa*, January–March 2015, pp. 74–96; Karthik Kambatla, Giorgos Kollias, Vipin Kumar, and Ananth Grama, "Trends in Big Data Analytics," *Journal of Parallel and Distributed Computing*, January 2014, pp. 2561–73.

19. Joel Stein, "Your Data, Yourself," *Time*, March 21, 2011, pp. 39–46; and Ryan Flinn, "The Big Business of Sifting through Social Media Data," *Bloomberg Businessweek,* October 25–October 31, 2010, pp. 20–22.

Chapter 9

1. Liz Torlee, "Not My News," *Marketing* (November 28, 2005), pp. 29, 32.

2. Ken Wong, "Why Johnny Can't Segment," *Marketing,* January 9, 2006, p. 11; Marc H. Meyer, *FASTPATH to Growth* (Oxford: Oxford University Press, 2007); Malcolm McDonald, "The Marketing Leaders," **www.themarketingleaders.com/articles/oct06/malcolm_mcdonald.htm** (downloaded April 24, 2007); and Roger J. Best, *Market-Based Management* (Saddle River, NJ: Prentice-Hall, 2000).

3. Patti Summerfield, "The Death of Demographics," *Strategy Magazine* (October 20, 2003).

4. These examples were gleaned from the PRIZM5 Clusters developed by Environics.

5. Chris H.S. Choi, Iain Murray, and Karen Kwan, "Activity-Based Segmentation of Canadian Domestic Pleasure Travelers to New Brunswick," *International Journal of Hospitality & Tourism Administration,* (July–September 2011), vol. 12 (3), pp. 202–24.

6. The discussion of fast-food trends and market share is based on: *National Consumer Survey © Choices 3 Crosstabulation Report: Fast-Food Restaurants* (New York: Simmons Market Research Bureau, Inc., Spring 2001).

7. "Zinc Research Releases Canadian Social Media Segmentation Research Findings," Zinc Research, April 29, 2010, **http://www.zincresearch.com/modules/news/newsitem.php?ItemId=16**; "New Database Reveals Social Media Habits Tied to Canadian Lifestyles," *Environics,* March 21, 2011, **http://www.environicsanalytics.ca/media_room.aspx?tab=news&item=2011Mar21_Database**.

8. Del J. Hawkins, David L. Mothersbaugh, and Roger J. Best, *Consumer Behavior,* 10th ed. (Burr Ridge, IL: McGraw-Hill/Irwin, 2007).

9. **www.ginchgonch.com** (2013).

10. **www.leadingbrandsinc.com** (2013).

11. "Niche Markets: Natural Health Products Show Canadian Success," *The Canadian,* February 26, 2012, **http://www.agoracosmopolitan.com/news/business/2012/02/26/3106.html**.

12. This discussion is based on Roger A. Kerin and Robert A. Peterson, *Strategic Marketing Problems: Cases and Comments,* 11th ed. (Upper Saddle River, NJ: Prentice Hall, 2007), pp. 147–49; John M. Mullins, Orville C. Walker Jr., Harper W. Boyd Jr., and Jean-Claude Larreche, *Marketing Management: A Strategic Decision-Marketing Approach,* 5th ed. (Burr Ridge, IL: McGraw-Hill/Irwin, 2005),

Chapter 10

1. Information supplied by Thoth Technology, 2016.

2. Debora Viana Thompson, Rebecca W. Hamilton, and Roland Rust, "Feature Fatigue: When Product Capabilities Become Too Much of a Good Thing," *Journal of Marketing Research,* November 2005, pp. 431–42; and Roland T. Rust, Debora Viana Thompson, and Rebecca W. Hamilton, "Defeating Feature Fatigue," *Harvard Business Review,* February 2006, pp. 98–107.

3. This discussion is based on Christopher Lovelock and Jochen Wirtz, *Services Marketing,* 5th edition (Upper Saddle River, NJ: Prentice-Hall, 2004).

4. Leonard Berry, Venkatesh Shankar, Janet Turner Parish, Susan Cadwallader, and Thomas Dotzel, "Creating New Markets Through Service Innovation," *MIT Sloan Management Review* (Winter 2006), 56–71.

5. Greg A. Stevens and James Burley, "3,000 Raw Ideas = 1 Commercial Success!" *Research-Technology Management* (May–June 1997), pp. 16–27.

6. R. G. Cooper and E. J. Kleinschmidt, "New Products—What Separates Winners from Losers?" *Journal of Product Innovation Management* (September 1987), pp. 169–84; Robert G. Cooper, *Winning at New Products,* 2nd ed. (Reading, MA: Addison-Wesley, 1993), pp. 49–66; Thomas D. Kuczmarski, "Measuring Your Return on Innovation," *Marketing Management* (Spring 2000), pp. 25–32; and Merle Crawford and Anthony D. Benedetto, *New Products Management,* 9th ed (New York: McGraw-Hill/Irwin, 2008).

7. Julie Fortser, "The Lucky Charm of Steve Sanger," *BusinessWeek* (March 26, 2001), pp. 75–76.

8. Robert Cooper, *The Accelerate to Market—Small-Medium Enterprise: A Stage-Gate Roadmap from Idea to Launch* (Ontario, Canada: Product Development Institute, 2002); and Pierre Loewe and Jennifer Dominiquini, "Overcoming the Barriers to Effective Innovation," *Strategy & Leadership* 34, no. 1 (2006), pp. 24–31.

9. Dan P. Lovallo and Olivier Sibony, "Distortions and Deceptions in Strategic Decisions," *The McKinsey Quarterly,* no. 1 (2006), pp. 19–29; and Byron G. Augusto, Eric P. Harmon, and Vivek Pandit, "The Right Service Strategies for Product Companies," *The McKinsey Quarterly,* no. 1 (2006), pp. 41–51.

10. Isabelle Royer, "Why Bad Projects Are So Hard to Kill," *Harvard Business Review,* February 2003, pp. 48–56; John T. Morn, Dan P. Lovallo, and S. Patrick Viguerie, "Beating the Odds in Market Entry," *The McKinsey Quarterly,* no. 4 (2005), pp. 35–45; Leslie Perlow and Stephanie Williams, "Is Silence Killing Your Company?" *Harvard Business Review,* May 2003, pp. 52–58; Beverly K. Brockman and Robert M. Morgan, "The Moderating Effect of Organizational Cohesiveness in Knowledge Use and New Product Development," *Journal of Marketing Science,* no. 3 (Summer 2006), pp. 295–306; Eyal Biyalogorsky, William Boulding, and Richard Staelin, "Stuck in the Past: Why Managers Persist with New Product Failures," *Journal of Marketing,* April 2006, pp. 108–21; and Irwin L. Janis, *Groupthink* (New York: Free Press, 1988).

p. 216; and Carol Traeger, "What Are Automakers Doing for Women? Part III: Volvo," **www.edmund.com**, July 26, 2005.

13. Nicholas Zamiska, "How Milk Got a Major Boost by Food Panel," *Wall Street Journal,* August 30, 2004, pp. B1, B5.

14. Rebecca Winter, "Chocolate Milk," *Time,* April 30, 2001, p. 20.

15. Mark A. Moon, John T. Mentzer, Carlo D. Smith, and Michael S. Garver, "Seven Keys to Better Forecasting," *Business Horizons* (September–October 1998), pp. 44–52.

11. Jena McGregor, "How Failure Breeds Success," *BusinessWeek,* July 10, 2006, pp. 42–52.

12. Ibid.

13. "Manning Awards Reveal Canadian Innovators Winning $161 000 in Prizes," Ernest C. Manning Awards Foundation, news release, October 9, 2012, retrieved from **www.manningawards.ca**; "The 20 Most Innovative Companies in B.C. 2012," *BCBusiness,* **http://www.bcbusiness.ca/the-20-most-innovative-companies-in-bc-2012**.

14. Amy Merrick, "As 3M Chief, McNerney Wastes No Time Starting Systems Favored by Ex-Boss Welch," *Wall Street Journal* (June 5, 2001), pp. B1, B4; see General Electric's website (**www.ge.com**) for an in-depth explanation of Six Sigma that 3M and other Fortune 500 companies use to improve quality: "The Road to Customer Impact: What Is Six Sigma?"

15. Jonas Matthing, Per Kristensson, and Andres Gustafsson, "Developing Successful Technology-based Services: The Issue of Identifying and Involving Innovative Users," *Journal of Services Marketing,* 20 (2006), 288–97.

16. Janice Griffiths-Hemans and Rajiv Grover, "Setting the Stage for Creative New Products: Investigating the Idea Fruition Process," *Journal of the Academy of Marketing Science,* Winter 2006, pp. 27–39.

17. C. K. Prahalad and Venkat Ramswamy, *The Future of Competition* (Boston: Harvard Business School Press, 2004); Steve Hamm, "Adding Customers to the Design Team," *BusinessWeek* (March 1, 2004), pp. 22–23; and Anthony W. Ulwick, "Turn Customer Input into Innovation," *Harvard Business Review* (January 2002), pp. 91–97.

18. Elisabeth A. Sullivan, "A Group Effort," *Marketing News,* February 28, 2010, pp. 22–29.

19. Jeffrey Pfeffer, "Why Employees Should Lead Themselves," **CCNMoney.com** (February 6, 2006), **http://money.cnn.com/magazines/business2**; "Ideas That Bloom," *BusinessWeek* (Spring 2006), **www.businessweek.com/magazine/content**; and William Taylor, "Here's an Idea: Let Everyone Have Ideas," *New York Times* (March 26, 2006).

20. "Ideas That Bloom," *BusinessWeek.*

21. "Consumer Trends Revealed as More Than 100,000 Canadians Share Their Shopping Habits in One of Canada's Largest Consumer Studies," Canada Newswire, January 7, 2013, **http://www.newswire.ca/en/story/1095725/consumer-trends-revealed-as-more-than-100-000-canadians-share-their-shopping-habits-in-one-of-canada-s-largest-consumer-studies**.

22. Bruce Nussbaum, "The Power of Design," *BusinessWeek* (May 17, 2004), pp. 86–94; the article gives many techniques for idea and concept generation, as do Appendixes A, B, and C in Merle Crawford and Anthony Di Benedetto, *New Products Management,* 10th ed. (Burr Ridge, IL: McGraw-Hill/Irwin, 2011).

23. **www.myhappycheeks.com**.

24. Kristin Tillotson, "Crowdfunding Gears Up for a Fresh Kick Start," *Star Tribune*, November 6, 2012, pp. A1, A10; and Brett Molina, "Pebble Time Most Funded Kickstarter Ever," *USA Today*, March 3, 2015.

25. See Ipsos Canada's website at **www.ipsos.ca**.

26. Marc H. Meyer and Frederick G. Crane, *Innovation: The Workbook*, Boston, MA (Institute for Enterprise Growth, 2016).

27. Jessica Bennett, "Marissa Mayer on the Day She Broke the Internet," *Newsweek*, July 25, 2011, p. 74.

28. Gilbert A. Churchill, Jr., Tom J. Brown, and Tracy A. Suter, *Basic Marketing Research*, 7th ed (Mason, OH: South-Western, Cengage Learning, 2010), pp. 122–130.

29. Yuhong Wu, Sridhar Balasubramanian, and Vijay Mahajan, "When Is a Preannounced New Product Likely to Be Delayed?" *Journal of Marketing* (April 2004), pp. 101–13.

30. Kerry A. Dolan, "Speed: The New X Factor," *Forbes,* December 26, 2005, pp. 74–77.

31. Gail Edmonson, "BMW's Dream Factory," *BusinessWeek,* October 16, 2006, pp. 70–80; Steve Hamm, "Speed Demons," *BusinessWeek,* March 27, 2006, pp. 68–76; and Amy Barrett, "J & J: Reinventing How It Invents," *BusinessWeek,* April 17, 2006, pp. 60–61.

32. For more information on how to reduce the risks of new product development, see Susuma Ogawa, "Reducing the Risks of New Product Development," *MIT Sloan Management Review* (Winter 2006), pp. 65–71.

Chapter 11

1. "Most Trusted by Shoppers," Brandspark 2016, **http://brandsparkmosttrusted.com/2016winners_cdn.html**; and Serus Lu, "Tim Hortons, President's Choice Top List of Canadians' Most-Trusted Brands," *Globe and Mail*, June 23, 2015, **http://www.theglobeandmail.com/report-on-business/industry-news/marketing/tim-hortons-presidentschoice-top-list-of-canadians-most-trusted-brands/article25067708/**.

2. For an extended discussion of the generalized product life cycle, see Donald R. Lehmann and Russell S. Winer, *Product Management,* 5th ed (Burr Ridge, IL: McGraw-Hill, 2008).

3. Gillette Fusion Case Study (New York: Datamonitor, June 6, 2008). All subsequent references to Gillette Fusion are based on this case study.

4. Orville C. Walker, Jr., and John W. Mullins, *Marketing Management: A Strategic Decision-Making Approach*, 8th ed. (Burr Ridge, IL: McGraw-Hill/Irwin, 2014), p. 209.

5. Kate MacArthur, "Coke Energizes Tab, Neville Isdell's Fave," *Advertising Age,* August 29, 2005, pp. 3, 21.

6. Julia Boorstin, "Can Fusion Become a Billion-Dollar Razor?" **MoneyCentral.msn.com**, downloaded January 10, 2007.

7. Everett M. Rogers, *Diffusion of Innovations,* 5th ed. (New York: Free Press, 2003).

8. Jagdish N. Sheth and Banwasi Mitral, *Consumer Behavior: A Managerial Perspective,* 2nd ed. (Mason, OH: South-Western College Publishing, 2003).

9. "When Free Samples Become Saviors," *The Wall Street Journal* (August 14, 2001), pp. B1, B4; and **www.marketingmag.ca** (March 9, 1998).

10. For a historical perspective on the product/brand manager system, see George S. Low and Ronald A. Fullerton, "Brands, Brand Management, and the Brand Manager System: A Critical-Historical Evaluation," *Journal of Marketing Research* (May 1994), pp. 173–90.

11. **www.newbalance.com** (downloaded May 6, 2007).

12. Sheth and Mitral, *Consumer Behavior;* and Marsha Cohen, *Marketing to the 501 Population* (New York: EPM Communications, Inc., 2007).

13. "Food Marketers Latch on to Health," *Advertising Age* (February 23, 2004), pp. 4, 41; and Daniel Kadlec, "The Low Carb Frenzy," *Time* (May 3, 2004), pp. 47–54.

14. "Shrinkflation: Consumer Goods that Got Downsized," **money.msn.com**, April 25, 2014; "Pop(sicle) Quiz," *Consumer Reports*, August 2012, p. 63; "Downsized: More and More Products Lose Weight," *Consumer Reports*, February 2011, p. 32ff; "P&G Lightens the Load on Diapers," *Wall Street Journal*, September 9, 2013, p. B2; and Bruce Horovitz, "Shoppers Beware: Products Shrink but Prices Stay the Same," *USA Today*, June 11, 2008.

15. "Building Brands in a Complex Environment," Canadian Marketing Association, Ottawa (May 2007).

16. This discussion is based on Kevin Lane Keller, *Strategic Brand Management*, 4th ed. (Upper Saddle River, NJ: Prentice Hall, 2013).

17. Keller, *Strategic Brand Management.*

18. Sharon Morrison and Frederick G. Crane, "Building the Service Brand by Creating and Managing an Emotional Brand Experience," *Journal of Brand Management,* (May 2007), pp. 410–21.

19. Frederick G. Crane, *Marketing for Entrepreneurs,* Second Edition (Thousand Oaks, CA: Sage Publications, 2013); Frederick G. Crane and Jeffrey E. Sohl, "Imperatives for Venture Success: Entrepreneurs Speak," *The International Journal of Entrepreneurship and Innovation* (May 2004), pp. 99–106.

20. Jeff Fraser, "Small Business Like Branding, Not Brand Experts," *Marketing Daily,* July 13, 2013, **http://www.marketingmag.ca/news/marketer-news/infographic-small-businesses-like-big-branding-not-brand-experts-83672?p83672?utm_sourceEmailMarketing&utm_mediumemail&utm_campaignmarketing_daily_AM**.

21. "Best Canadian Brands," Interbrand, 2012, **http://www.interbrand.com/en/Interbrand-offices/Interbrand-Toronto/Best-Canadian-Brands-2012.aspx**.

22. "Best Global Brands 2015," Interbrand, **http://interbrand.com/best-brands/best-global-brands/2015/ranking/**; and "Best Canadian Brands 2014," Interbrand, **http://interbrand.com/wp-content/uploads/2015/08/Interbrand-Best-Canadian-Brands-2014.pdf**.

23. "Hummer Markets Shoes for Offroad Set," *Advertising Age* (January 12, 2004), pp. 3, 40; Bruce Orwell, "Disney's Magic Transformation?" *The Wall Street Journal* (October 4, 2000), pp. A1, A15; and Keller, *Strategic Brand Management.*

24. Marc Fetscherin, et al., "In China? Pick Your Brand Name Carefully," *Harvard Business Review*, September 2012, p. 26; Beth Snyder Bulik, "What's in a (Good) Product Name? Sales," *Advertising Age*, February 2, 2009, p. 10; and Keller, *Strategic Brand Management.*

25. "When Brand Extension Becomes Brand Abuse," *BrandWeek* (October 26, 1998), pp. 20, 22.

26. Piyush Kumar, "The Impact of Cobranding on Customer Evaluations of Brand Counterextensions," *Journal of Marketing* (July 2005).

27. This discussion is based on David Aaker, *Brand Portfolio Strategy* (New York: Free Press, 2004); and "To LureOlder Girls, Mattel Brings in Hip Hop Crowd, " *The Wall Street Journal* (July 18, 2003).

28. "P&G Brand Divestitures Will Be Bigger than Original Targets," *Advertising Age*, February 19, 2015, **http://adage.com/article/cmo-strategy/p-g-brand-divestitures-bigger-original-targets/297240/**.

29. "2013 BrandSpark Canadian Shopper Study," PR in Canada, January 8, 2013, **www.princanada.com/2013-brandspark-canadian-shopper-study**.

30. **www.pez.com**, downloaded February 1, 2015; "So Sweet: William and Kate PEZ Dispensers," **www.today.msnbc.com**, March 30, 2012; David Welch, *Collecting Pez* (Murphysboro, IL: Bubba Scrubba Publications, 1995); and "Elements Design Adds Dimension to Perennial Favorite Pez Brand," *Package Design Magazine*, May 2006, pp. 37–38.

31. "Market Statistics," **www.Packaging-Gateway.com**, downloaded March 25, 2012.

32. "Green Bean Casserole Turns 50," *Dallas Morning News*, November 19, 2005, p. 10D.

33. "Packaging Is the Capper," *Advertising Age* (May 5, 2003), p. 22.

34. Theresa Howard, "Frito-Lay's New Stax to Take a Stand," *USA Today* (August 14, 2003), p. 12B.

35. Jeff Fraser, "Molson Coors Debuts Vented Can for Smoother Pour," *Marketing* magazine, July 12, 2013, **www.marketingmag.ca/news/marketer-news/molson-coors-debuts-vented-can-for-smoother-pour-**

83392?p83392?utm_sourceEmailMarketing&utm_medium email&utm_campaign marketing_daily_AM.

36. Representative recent scholarly research on packaging and labelling perceptions includes Priya Rgahubir and Eric A. Greenleaf, "Ratios in Proportion: What Should the Shape of the Package Be?" *Journal of Marketing*, April 2006, pp. 95–107; Peter H. Bloch, Frederic F. Brunel, and Todd Arnold, "Individual Differences in the Centrality of Visual Product Aesthetics: Concept and Measurement," *Journal of Consumer Research*, March 2003, pp. 551–65: and Pamela Anderson, Joan Giese, and Joseph A. Cote, "Impression Management Using Typeface Design," *Journal of Marketing*, October 2004, pp. 60–72.

37. "Asian Brands Are Sprouting English Logos in Pursuit of Status, International Image," *The Wall Street Journal* (August 7, 2001), p. B7C.

38. Susanna Hamner, "Packaging that Pays," *Business 2.0*, July 26, 2006, pp. 68–69.

39. "Wal-Mart: Use Less Packaging," *Dallas Morning News*, September 23, 2006, p. 2D. For an overview of Procter & Gamble's environmental efforts, see *Sustainability Report 2005* (Cincinnati, OH: Procter & Gamble Company, 2006).

40. "Packaging," **www.hp.com**, downloaded January 17, 2007.

41. Christian Twigg-Flesner, *Consumer Product Guarantees* (Aldershot, England: Ashgate Publishing, 2003).

Chapter 12

1. Tx Zhuo, "Airbnb and Uber Are Just the Beginning," **Entrepreneur.com**, March 25, 2015; Tomio Geron, "The Share Economy," *Forbes*, February 11, 2013, pp. 58–66; "How Couchsurfing Epitomizes the 'Sharing Economy,'?" *Huffington Post*, January 25, 2013; "adverCar Invites Drivers to Rent Car 'Real Estate' to Showcase Favorite Brands," GlobeNewswire, January 14, 2013; "Will You Leave Your Job to Join the Sharing Economy?" *VentureBeat*, January 22, 2013; "Airbnb's Brian Chesky: It's Only Day Two in the Sharing Economy," *PandoDaily*, January 11, 2013; and "A Step Forward for Ride-Sharing: California Suspends Fines against Lyft," *VentureBeat*, January 30, 2013.

2. Ibid.

3. John E. G. Bateson and Douglas Hoffman, *Services Marketing*, 4th ed. (KY: Cengage, 2010).

4. Karen Milde, "Small Business Special: The Hottest Industries in Canada Today," *Canadian Immigrant*, October 12, 2012, **http://canadianimmigrant.ca/work-and-education/small-business-special-the-hottest-industries-in-canada-today**.

5. Canadian Franchise Association, **www.cfa.ca** (downloaded March 25, 2016); and John Greenwood, "The services industry: Canada's secret economic playground?" *Maclean's*, April 1, 2015. **http://www.macleans.ca/economy/economicanalysis/the-services-industry-canadas-secret-economic-playground/** (downloaded April 20, 2016).

6. Christopher Lovelock and Evert Gummesson, "Whither Services Marketing?" *Journal of Services Research* 7 (August 2004), pp. 20–41.

7. Christopher Lovelock and Jochen Wirtz, *Services Marketing: People, Technology, Strategy*, 7th ed. (Englewood Cliffs, NJ: Prentice Hall, 2011).

8. Valarie A. Zeithhaml, "How Consumer Evaluation Processes Differ Between Goods and Services," in James H. Donnelly and William R. Georges, eds., *Marketing of Services* (Chicago, IL; American Marketing Association, 1981).

9. Keith B. Murray, "A Test of Services Marketing Theory: Consumer Information Acquisition Activities," *Journal of Marketing* (January 1991), pp. 10–25; and

F. G. Crane, *Professional Services Marketing: Strategy and Tactics* (New York: The Haworth Press, Inc., 1993).

10. Marc H. Meyer, Eliot Jekowsky, and Frederick G. Crane (2007). "Applying Platform Design to Improve Patient Services Across the Continuum of Care," *Managing Service Quality*, vol. 17 (1), (2007), pp. 23–40; and Mark R. Testa and Lori J. Sipe, "A Systems Approach to Service Quality," *Cornell Hotel and Restaurant Administration Quarterly*, vol. 47 (1) (February 2006), pp. 36–48; and W. Earl Susser, R. Paul Olsen, and D. Daryl Wyckoff, Management of Service Operations (Boston: Allyn & Bacon, 1978).

11. John Ozment and Edward Morash, "The Augmented Service Offering for Perceived and Actual Service Quality," *Journal of the Academy of Marketing Science* (Fall 1994), pp. 352–63.

12. A. Parasuraman, Valarie A. Zeithaml, and Leonard L. Berry, "Reassessment of Expectations as a Comparison Standard in Measuring Service Quality: Implications for Further Research," *Journal of Marketing* (January 1994), pp. 111–24; and Leonard L. Berry, *On Great Service* (New York: Free Press, 1995).

13. Riadh Ladhari, "Assessment of the Psychometric Properties of SERVQUAL in the Canadian banking industry," *Journal of Financial Services Marketing* (June 2009), vol. 14, no. 1, pp. 70–82; and Jacquelyn Crane, Brenna Crane, and Frederick Crane, "Patient Satisfaction with Family Physicians in Canada," *Journal of Medical Marketing*, vol. 6, no. 1 (2006), pp. 63–66.

14. Stephen S. Tax and Stephen W. Brown, "Recovering and Learning from Service Failure," *Sloan Management Review* (Fall 1998), pp. 75–88.

15. Lovelock and Wirtz, *Services Marketing: People, Technology, Strategy*, 7th ed.

16. Francois Carillat, Fernando Jaramillo, and Jay Mulki, "Examining the Impact of Service Quality: A Meta-Analysis of Empirical Evidence," *Journal of Marketing Theory & Practice* (Spring 2009), vol. 17, no. 2, pp. 95–110; Richard Spreng, Linda Hui Shi, and Thomas Page, "Service Quality and Satisfaction in Business-to-Business Services," *Journal of Business & Industrial Marketing*, 2009, vol. 24, no. 7/8, pp. 537–48; and Crane, Crane, and Crane, "Patient Satisfaction with Family Physicians in Canada," *Journal of Medical Marketing*. Also see Gordon

Fullerton and Shirley Taylor, "Mediating, Interactive, and Non-linear Effects in Service Quality and Satisfaction with Services Research," *Canadian Journal of Administrative Sciences* (June 2002).

17. Katherine N. Lemon, Tiffany Barnett White, and Russell S. Winer, "Dynamic Customer Relationship Management: Incorporating Future Considerations into the Service Retention Decision," *Journal of Marketing* (January 2002), pp. 1–14.

18. Anna S. Mattila, "Do Women Like Options More than Men? An Examination in the Context of Service Recovery," *Journal of Services Marketing,* 2010 (7), pp. 499–508.

19. Lovelock and Wirtz, *Services Marketing: People, Technology, Strategy,* 7th ed.; and Valarie A. Zeithaml, Mary Jo Bitner, and Dwayne D. Gremler, *Services Marketing,* 5th ed. (New York: McGraw-Hill, 2009).

20. Sundar G. Bharedwaj, P. Rajan Varadarajan, and John Fahy, "Sustainable Competitive Advantage in Services Industries: A Conceptual Model and Research Propositions," *Journal of Marketing* (October 1993), pp. 83–99.

21. Lenna Garibian, "Top Brands Using Twitter for Customer Support," *MarketingProfs* (December 10, 2012), **http://www.marketingprofs.com/charts/2012/9654/top-brands-using-twitter-for-customer-support#ixzz2LML8XMGw.**

22. F. G. Crane, "The Relative Effect of Price and Personal Referral Cues on Consumers' Perceptions of Dental Services," *Health Marketing Quarterly,* vol. 13, no. 4 (1996), pp. 91–105.

23. Lovelock and Wirtz, *Services Marketing: People, Technology, Strategy,* 7th ed.

24. Robert E. Hite, Cynthia Fraser, and Joseph A. Bellizzi, "Professional Service Advertising: The Effects of Price Inclusion, Justification, and Level of Risk," *Journal of Advertising Research* 30 (August/September 1990), pp. 23–31; and F. G. Crane, *Professional Services Marketing: Strategy and Tactics.*

25. F. G. Crane, *Professional Services Marketing: Strategy and Tactics;* and Kathleen Mortimer "Services Advertising: The Agency Viewpoint," *Journal of Services Marketing,* No. 2 (2001), pp. 131–46.

26. Patriya Tansuhaj, Donna Randall, and Jim McCullough, "A Services Marketing Management Model: Integrating Internal and External Marketing Functions," *Journal of Services Marketing* (Winter 1988), pp. 31–38.

27. Christian Gronroos, "Internal Marketing Theory and Practice," in Tim Bloch, G. D. Upah, and V. A. Zeithaml, eds., *Services Marketing in a Changing Environment* (Chicago, IL: American Marketing Association, 1984); and Dennis J. Cahill, *Internal Marketing* (New York: The Haworth Press Inc., 1996).

28. Ibid.

29. Rita Di Mascio, "The Service Models of Frontline Employees," *Journal of Marketing,* July 2010, pp. 63–80; Stephen W. Brown, "The Employee Experience," *Marketing Management* 12 (March–April 2003), pp. 12–13; and Lawrence A. Crosby and Sheree L. Johnson, "Watch What I Do," *Marketing Management* 12 (November–December 2003), pp. 10–11.

30. Rohit Bhargava, "9 Ways Top Brands Use Social Media for Better Customer Service," Mashable.com (October 28, 2011), **http://mashable.com/2011/10/28/social-customer-service-brands/.**

31. F.G. Crane, *Professional Services Marketing: Strategy and Tactics;* and Leonard L. Berry and Neeli Bendapudi, "Clueing in Customers," *Harvard Business Review* (February 2003), pp. 100–6.

32. Frederick H. deB. Harris and Peter Peacock, "Hold My Place, Please," *Marketing Management* (Fall 1995), pp. 34–46, and Lovelock and Wirtz, *Services Marketing: People, Technology, Strategy,* 7th ed.

33. Lovelock and Wirtz, *Services Marketing: People, Technology, Strategy,* 7th ed.

34. Dan Kedmey, "Google Unveils 'First-of-its-Kind,' Android TV Streaming Device," *Time,* October 17, 2014; and Angel Moscaritolo, "AT&T Rebrands U-verse as Mobile TV," *PC Magazine,* February 4, 2013.

35. Anyuan Shen and A. Dwayne Ball, "Is Personalization of Services Always a Good Thing? Exploring the Role of Technology- Mediated Personalization (TMP) in Service Relationships," Journal of Services Marketing 23 (2009), pp. 80–92.

36. Kamalini Ramdas, Elizabeth Teisberg, and Amy L. Tucker, "4 Ways to Reinvent Service Delivery," *Harvard Business Review,* December 2012, pp. 99–106; Michael K. Brady, Clay M. Voorhees, and Michael J. Brusco, "Service Sweethearting: Its Antecedents and Customer Consequences," *Journal of Marketing,* March 2012, pp. 81–98.

37. Timothy Keiningham, Sunil Gupta, Lerzan Aksoy and Alexander Buoye, "The High Cost of Customer Satisfaction," MIT Sloan Review, Spring 2014: **http://sloanreview.mit.edu/article/the-high-price-of-customer-satisfaction/.**

Chapter 13

1. "The Vizio Story," **vizio.com**, downloaded May 15, 2015; "America's Largest Private Companies," **forbes.com**, November 5, 2014; "How Vizio Conquered TV," **fortune.com**, July 25, 2012; and "Vizio Extends Battle Plan," *Wall Street Journal,* January 3, 2011, p. B3.

2. Ibid.

3. Adapted from Kent B. Monroe, *Pricing: Making Profitable Decisions,* 3rd ed. (Burr Ridge, IL: McGraw-Hill/Irwin, 2003). See also David J. Curry, "Measuring Price and Quality Competition," *Journal of Marketing* (Spring 1985), pp. 106–17.

4. Del J. Hawkins, David L. Mothersbaugh, and Roger J. Best, *Consumer Behavior,* 10th ed. (Burr Ridge, IL: McGraw-Hill/Irwin, 2007).

5. Carmer Salvador, Enrique Rebolloso, Baltasar Fernandez-Ramirez, and Maria del Pilar Canton, "Service Price Components and their Relationship with Customer Satisfaction," *Journal of Revenue and Pricing Management* (2007), 6, pp. 40–50. Also see F.G. Crane, *Professional Services Marketing: Strategy and Tactics* (New York: The Howard Press, Inc, 1993); and F. G. Crane, "The Relative Effect of Price and Personal Referral Cues on Consumers' Perceptions of Dental Services," *Health Marketing Quarterly,* vol. 13, no. 4 (1996), pp. 91–105.

6. Ian Yeoman and Una McMahon-Beattie, "The UK Low-Cost Economy," *Journal of Revenue and Pricing Management* (2007), 6, pp. 40–50.

7. "Canadians Value Price Before Safety, Style When Car Shopping," *Driving,* February 17, 2015; **http://driving.ca/auto-news/news/canadians-consider-price-before-safety-and-style-when-car-shopping-survey**; and Jeff Fraser, "Consumerology Shows Canadians Getting Thriftier," *Marketing Daily,* June 25, 2013, **http://www.marketingmag.ca/news/marketer-news/infographic-consumerology-shows-canadians-getting-thriftier-82317?p=82317?utm_source?EmailMarketing&utm_medium?email&utm_campaign?marketing_daily_AM.**

8. **www.cadth.ca/media** (downloaded January 15, 2009); and Frederick G. Crane, "Ethics, Entrepreneurs and Corporate Managers: A Canadian Study," *Journal of Small Business & Entrepreneurship,* vol. 22, no. 3 (2009), pp. 267–74. Also see N. Craig Smith and John A. Quelch, *Ethics in Marketing* (Homewood, IL: Richard D. Irwin, 1993).

9. Ron Winslow, "How a Breakthrough Quickly Broke Down for Johnson & Johnson," *Wall Street Journal* (September 18, 1998), pp. A1, A5.

10. Jeff Lobb, "The Right (Pepsi) Stuff," *Marketing* (July 8, 1996), p. 15.

11. "Price War Is Raging in Europe," *Business Week* (July 6, 1992), pp. 44–45.

12. "Consumer Trends Revealed as More Than 100,000 Canadians Share Their Shopping Habits in One of Canada's Largest Consumer Studies," January, 7, 2013, **http://finance.yahoo.com/news/consumer-trends-revealed-more-100-151400145.html**.

13. Wilson, Dominic, "Penetration Pricing," *Blackwell Encyclopedic Dictionary of Marketing,* 2005, p. 259.

14. "Time Is Money," *Forbes* (September 18, 2000), pp. 178–85.

15. "Why That Deal Is Only $9.99," *BusinessWeek* (January 10, 2000), p. 36. For further reading on odd–even pricing, see Jianping Liang and Vinay Kanetkar, "Price Endings: Magic and Math," *Journal of Product & Brand Management,* vol.15, no. 6 (2006), pp. 377–85.

16. Adam Nguyen, Roger Heeler and Cheryl Buff, "Consumer Perceptions of Bundles," *Journal of Product & Brand Management,* vol. 18, no. 3 (2009), pp. 218–25.

17. Thomas T. Nagle and Reed K. Holden, *The Strategy and Tactics of Pricing,* 4th ed. (Englewood Cliffs, NJ: Prentice Hall, 2006), pp. 243–49.

18. Monroe, *Pricing: Making Profitable Decisions.*

19. Scott McCartney, "You Paid What for That Flight?" *The Wall Street Journal,* August 26, 2010, pp. D1, D2.

20. "Panera Cares" What We Do," **http://paneracares.org/what-we-do/** (downloaded February 20, 2013); Aaron Kagan, "Cash Register-less Panera Cares Opens January 23," January 10, 2013, **http://boston.eater.com/archives/2013/01/10/cash-registerless-panera-cares-opens-january-23.php**.

21. Peter M. Noble and Thomas S. Gruca, "Industrial Pricing: Theory and Managerial Practice," *Marketing Science,* vol. 18, no. 3 (1999), pp. 435–54.

22. George E. Belch and Michael A. Belch, *Introduction to Advertising and Promotion,* 9th ed. (New York: Irwin/McGraw-Hill, 2012),

23. Nicolas Van Praet, "From one buck to $3: How high will Dollarama go on its price points," *Financial Post,* September 11, 2014, **http://business.financialpost.com/news/retail-marketing/from-one-buck-to-3-how-high-will-dollarama-go-on-its-price-points** (accessed May 2, 2016).

24. "Variable Pricing on the Way for Yellow Pages," *Marketing Daily* (June 14, 2007), **www.marketing.ca**.

25. Monroe, *Pricing: Making Profitable Decisions.*

26. F.G. Crane, "The Relative Effect of Price and Personal Referral Cues on Consumers' Perceptions of Dental Services." Also see, Akshay R. Rao, "The Quality of Price as a Quality Cue," *Journal of Marketing Research,* November 2005, pp. 401–5.

27. Charles Fishman, "Which Price Is Right," *FastCompany* (March 2003), p. 92, **www.fastcompany.com/magazine/68/pricing.html**.

28. "Four Effects of Social Media and Digital Marketing on Pricing," Deloitte Consulting, July 2012; "Social Media Marketing: Increase Your Reach, Reduce Your Marketing Costs," LaunchHouse, June 15, 2012, **http://www.launchhouse.com/news/social-media-marketing-increase-your-reach-reduce-your-marketing-costs/**.

29. For an extensive discussion on discounts, see Monroe, *Pricing: Making Profitable Decisions.*

Chapter 14

1. Interview with Jeff Newton, Callaway Golf, July 3, 2014; "Callaway Golf.com: The Social Sport," Internetretailer.com, December 5, 2013; **www. callawaygolf.com**, downloaded April 15, 2015; and Stephanie Kang, "Callaway Will Use Retailers to Sell Goods Directly to Consumers Online," *Wall Street Journal,* November 6, 2006, p. B5.

2. Ibid.

3. Donald V. Fites, "Make Your Dealers Your Partners," *Harvard Business Review* (March–April 1996), pp. 84–95.

4. Bert Rosenbloom, *Marketing Channels: A Management View,* 7th ed. (Cincinnati, OH: South-Western College Publishing, 2004).

5. **www.the-cma.org**.

6. Mike Hughlett, "General Mills, with Nestle, is trying to make cereal more popular overseas," *Star Tribune,* May 24, 2015, **http://www.startribune.com/general-mills-with-nestl-xe9-is-trying-to-make-cereal-more-popular-overseas/304770161/**.

7. For an overview of vertical marketing systems, see Lou Pelton, David Stutton, and James R. Lumpkin, *Marketing Channels,* 2nd ed. (Chicago: Irwin, 2002), chapter 14.

8. "Saks to Add Exclusive Lines," *Wall Street Journal,* February 25, 2010, p. B2.

9. "Gillette Tries to Nick Schick in Japan," *Wall Street Journal* (February 4, 1991), pp. B3, B4.

10. Christine B. Bucklin, Pamela A. Thomas-Graham, and Elizabeth Webster, "Channel Conflict: When Is It Dangerous?" *The McKinsey Quarterly,* No. 3, (1997), pp. 36–43.

11. "Dealer Surplus," *Forbes,* October 16, 2006, pp. 50–52; and Kevin Kelleher, "Giving Dealers a Raw Deal," *Business 2.0,* December 2004, pp. 82–83.

12. F. Robert Dwyer and Julie Gassenheimer, "Relational Roles and Triangle Dramas: Effects on Power Play and Sentiments in Industrial Channels," *Marketing Letters,* vol. 3 (1992), pp. 187–200.

13. Paul N. Bloom, Gregory T. Gundlach, and Joseph P. Cannon, "Slotting Allowances and Fees: Schools of Thought and Views of Practicing Managers," *Journal of Marketing,* April 2000, pp. 92–109; and William L. Wilkie, Debra M. Desrochers, and Gregory T. Gundlach, "Marketing Research and Public Policy: The Case of Slotting Fees," *Journal of Public Policy & Marketing,* Fall 2002, pp. 275–89.

14. *The Smarter Supply Chain of the Future: Industry Edition* (Somer, NY: IBM Corporation, 2009); and John Paul MacDuffie and Takahiro Fujimoto, "Why Dinosaurs Will Keep Ruling the Automobile Industry," *Harvard Business Review,* June 2010, pp. 23–25.

15. Major portions of this discussion are based on Sunil Chopra and Peter Meindl, *Supply Chain Management: Strategy, Planning, and Operations,* 6th ed. (Upper Saddle River, NJ: Prentice Hall, 2016), Chapters 1–3; and Hau L. Lee, "The Triple-A Supply Chain," *Harvard Business Review* (October 2004), pp. 102–12.

16. This discussion is based on Dave Blanchard, "Top 25 Supply Chains of 2015," **www.industryweek.com**, June 1, 2015; "The 2014 Supply Chain Top 25: Leading the Decade," *Supply Chain Management Review,* September-October, 2014, pp. 8–17. "Harvard Business Review, on Managing Supply Chains," *Harvard Business Review,* June, 2011; "The Lessons from Dell's Supply Chain Transformation," **www.supplychaindigest.com**, March 18, 2011; Brett Booen, "Walmart's Supply Chain Acts as If Every Day Is Black Friday," *Supply Chain Digital,* November 19, 2010; and Chopra and Meindl, *Supply Chain Management.*

17. David Simchi-Levi, Philip Kaminsky, and Edith Simchi-Levi, *Designing and Managing the Supply Chain*, 3rd ed. (Burr Ridge, IL: McGraw-Hill/Irwin, 2007). Also, Fan Wu, Sengun Yeniyurt, Daekwan Kim, and S. Tamer Cavusgil, "The Impact of Information Technology on Supply Chain Capabilities and Firm Performance: A Resource-Based View," *Industrial Marketing Management*, October 2006, pp. 593–4.

18. Erik Schonfeld, "The Total Package," *eCompany* (June 2001), pp. 91–97; and Kurt Hoffman, "Snapple Found Handling Logistics In-House Left a Sour Taste," **www.supplychainbrain.com** (April 2002).

19. Douglas M. Lambert, *Supply Chain Management: Processes. Partnerships, and Performance*, 2nd ed. (Sarasota, FL: Supply Chain Management Institute, 2006).

20. Jeff Wise, "Building Canada's Epic Ice Road," *Popular Mechanics* (February 2007). **www.popularmechanics.com**

21. Jeffrey Davis and Martha Baer, "Some Assembly Required," *Business 2.0* (February 12, 2001), pp. 78–87.

22. Jean Murphy, "Better Forecasting, S&OP Support Transformation at Campbell's Soup Co.," *Global Logistics & Supply Chain Strategies*, June 2004, pp. 28–30.

23. "Product Return and Recycling," **hp.com**, May 10, 2015; Second Annual Report of the eCycling Leadership Initiative (Consumer Electronics Association, April 2013);

Chapter 15

1. Murhad Hemmadi, "Indochino Suits Up for an Aggrressive Retail Expansion," *Marketing*, March 31, 2016, **http://www.marketingmag.ca/brands/indochino-suits-up-for-an-aggressive-retail-expansion-171220**; Brenda Bouw, "Kit and Ace Looks to Take Off with Global Jetsetters," *Marketing*, March 31, 2016, **http://www.marketingmag.ca/brands/kit-and-ace-looks-to-take-off-with-global-jetsetters-171240**; Rebecca Harris, "Starbucks Canada Launches Beer, Wine Menu," *Marketing*, April 1, 2016, **http://www.marketingmag.ca/brands/starbucks-canada-launches-beer-wine-menu-171405**; Ross Martin, "How McDonald's Reinventing Its Customer Experience," *Marketing*, March 28, 2016, **http://www.marketingmag.ca/brands/how-mcdonalds-is-reinventing-its-customer-experience-170827**; Canadian Press, "HBC to Open 40 Saks Off 5th Stores in Germany," *Marketing*, April 5, 2016, **http://www.marketingmag.ca/brands/hbc-to-open-40-saks-off-5th-stores-in-germany-171609**.

2. Retail Council of Canada, Annual Report, **www.retailcouncil.org** (downloaded February 2016).

3. *Media Digest 2015-2016*, Canadian Media Directors' Council, Toronto.

4. Retail Fast Facts, Retail Council of Canada (March 2016), **www.retailcouncil.org** (downloaded May 10, 2016).

5. *Global Powers of Retailing 2016*, Deloitte (2016).

6. Ibid.

7. "2016 Top Franchises from *Entrepreneur*'s Franchise 500 List," *Entrepreneur*, **https://www.entrepreneur.com/franchise500**.

8. "Store Network Under Banners," Carrefour website, **http://www.carrefour.com/sites/default/files/PARCEN311214.pdf**; Nadya Masidlover, "Corporate News: Carrefour Stems a Slide in Its Domestic Market," *Wall Street Journal*, January 18, 2013, p. B7; "Mass Grocery Retail-Q3 2012," *BMI Food & Drink Report*, July 2012; and Tom Orlik and Bob David, "Relief on China Growth Comes with Caveats," *Wall Street Journal*, January 19, 2013, p. A10.

9. Michelle DiPardo, "Coke to Unveil First Interac Flash Vending Machines at Stampede," *Marketing Daily*, July 4, 2013, **http://www.marketingmag.ca/news/marketer-news/coke-to-unveil-first-interac-flash-vending-machines-at-stampede-82966?p?82966?utm_source?EmailMarketing&utm_medium?email&utm_campaign?marketing_daily_AM**.

10. Zachary Wilson, "Coca-Cola's 100-Flavour Interactive Freestyle Soda Fountain," *FastCompany*, **www.fastcompany.com**, downloaded January 20, 2010.

11. **www.ikea.com**, accessed January 25, 2016.

12. **www.retailcouncil.org** (May 2016).

13. "Retail Ecommerce Sales in Canada to Near C$30 Billion," *eMarketer*, January 15, 2015, **http://www.emarketer.com/Article/Retail-Ecommerce-Sales-Canada-Near-C30-Billion/1011853**.

14. **www.cangive.ca**.

15. "Retail Ecommerce Sales in Canada to Near C$30 Billion," *eMarketer*, January 15, 2015, **http://www.emarketer.com/Article/Retail-Ecommerce-Sales-Canada-Near-C30-Billion/1011853**.

16. Susan Rose, Moira Clark, Phillip Samouel, and Neil Hair, "Online Customer Experience in e-Retailing: An Empirical Model of Antecedents and Outcomes," *Journal of Retailing* 2 (2012), pp. 308–22; and Feng Zhu and Xiaoquan (Michael) Zhang, "Impact of Online Consumer Reviews on Sales: The Moderating Role of Product and Consumer Characteristics," *Journal of Marketing* 74 (March 2010), pp. 133–48.

17. Onur H. Bodur, Noreen M. Klein, and Neeraj Arora, "Online Price Search: Impact of Price Comparison Sites on Offline Price Evaluations," *Journal of Retailing*, March 2015, pp. 125–139; and Lee and Kyoochun Lee, "Social Shopping Promotions from a Social Merchant's Perspective," *Business Horizons*, October 2012, pp. 441–51.

18. **www.the-cma.org**.

19. The following discussion is adapted from William T. Gregor and Eileen M. Friars, *Money Merchandizing: Retail Revolution in Consumer Financial Services* (Cambridge, MA: Management Analysis Center, Inc., 1982).

20. "A Changing Attitude: Loss Prevention," from the Annual Report of the Retail Council of Canada, **www.retailcouncil.org** (downloaded June 10, 2007).

21. **http://www.deerfootmeadows.com/about-us/**

22. Eve Lazarus, "Main Street Malls," *Marketing* (April 3, 2006), pp. 11–12.

23. "Walmart Creates 50 Mobile-Enabled Pop-Up Shops with P&G," *Retail Info Systems News*, June 17, 2013, **http://risnews.edgl.com/retail-news/Walmart-Creates-50-Mobile-Enabled-Pop-Up-Shops-with-P-G86959**.

24. *Retail Market Trends, North America*, Grubbs & Ellis (Summer 2007).

25. Pierre Martineau, "The Personality of the Retail Store," *Harvard Business Review* (January–February 1958), p. 47.

26. Julie Baker, Dhruv Grewal, and A. Parasuraman, "The Influence of Store Environment on Quality Inferences and Store Image," *Journal of the Academy of Marketing Science* (Fall 1994), pp. 328–39; and Dhruv Grewal, R. Krishnan, Julie Baker, and Norm Burin, "The Effect of Store Name, Brand Name and Price Discounts on Consumers' Evaluations and Purchase Intentions," *Journal of Retailing* (Fall 1998), pp. 331–52.

27. Jack Neff, "Shopper Marketing's New Frontier: e-Commerce," *Advertising Age*, March 14, 2011, p. 14.

28. Jans-Benedict Steenkamp and Michel Wedel, "Segmenting Retail Markets on Store Image Using a Consumer-Based Methodology," *Journal of Retailing* (Fall 1991), p. 300.

29. Mary Jo Bitner, "Servicescapes: The Impact of Physical Surroundings on Customers and Employees," *Journal of Marketing* (April 1992), pp. 57–71.

30. John Davis, *Measuring Marketing* (Singapore: Wiley and Sons, 2007).

31. *2011 Chain Store Productivity Report,* September 23, 2011, **http://retailsails. files.wordpress.com/2011/09/rsspsf.pdf**.

32. The wheel of retailing theory was originally proposed by Malcolm P. McNair, "Significant Trends and Development in the Postwar Period," in A. B. Smith, ed., *Competitive Distribution in a Free, High-Level Economy and Its Implications for the University* (Pittsburgh: University of Pittsburgh Press, 1958), pp. 1–25; see also Stephen Brown, "The Wheel of Retailing—Past and Future," *Journal of Retailing* (Summer 1990), pp. 143–49; and Malcolm P. McNair and Eleanor May, "The Next

Revolution of the Retailing Wheel," *Harvard Business Review* (September–October 1978), pp. 81–91.

33. William R. Davidson, Albert D. Bates, and Stephen J. Bass, "Retail Life Cycle," *Harvard Business Review* (November–December 1976), pp. 89–96.

34. This discussion is based on *Global Powers of Retailing 2016,* Deloitte (2016),

35. Russ Martin, "Adobe Introduces Shopping Bag of the Future," *Marketing*, March 23, 2016, **http://www.marketingmag.ca/tech/adobe-introduces-shopping-bag-of-the-future-170750**.

36. "Whole Foods Opens Green Store in California," Green Retail Decisions, May 5, 2016 **http://www.greenretaildecisions.com/news/2016/05/05/whole-foods-opens-green-store-in-california**; "Best Environmental Practices of Leading Retailers Around the World," **http://www.greeningretail.ca** (accessed August 25, 2010). Also see, "Top Green Retailers Find Sustainability Makes Good Business Sense," February 18, 2010, **http://www.ryerson.ca/news/news/Research_News/20100218_green.html** (accessed August 25, 2010).

Chapter 16

1. Sara Boboltz, "Whoever Runs Taco Bell's Twitter Account Deserves a Raise," *Huffington Post*, February 28, 2014; Jenni Romaniuk, "Are You Ready for the Next Big Thing?" *Journal of Advertising Research*, December 2012, pp. 397–99; "Taco Bell Implements Its Largest Marketing Campaign Ever," QSRweb, March 7, 2013; "Highly Anticipated, Most Socially Requested Taco Bell Product Launch to Be Largest Marketing Campaign in Brand's History," Business Wire, March 7, 2013; "Yo Quiero Engagement? Taco Bell Charms the Twittersphere," **www. Business2Community.com**, February 4, 2013; Lynne D. Johnson, "Customer Engagement Is the New Marketing," *Journal of Advertising Research*, June 2010, pp. 118–19; Natalie Zmuda, "QR Codes Gaining Prominence Thanks to a Few Big Players," *Advertising Age*, March 21, 2011, p. 8; Alyssa S. Groom, "Integrated Marketing Communication Anticipating the 'Age of Engage,'" *Communication Research Trends*, December 1, 2008, p. 3; "How to Get More Followers on Twitter: Engage with Social Promotions," **www.Business2Community.com**, March 16, 2013; and "How to Engage Your Audience on Social Media," **www. Business2Community.com**, March 28, 2013.

2. Sita Mishra and Sushma Muralie, "Managing Dynamism of IMC – Anarchy to Order." *Journal of Marketing and Communication,* September 2010, pp. 29–37.

3. Wilbur Schramm, "How Communication Works," in Wilbur Schramm, ed., *The Process and Effects of Mass Communication* (Urbana, IL: University of Illinois Press, 1955), pp. 3–26.

4. F. G. Crane and T. K. Clarke, *Consumer Behaviour in Canada: Theory and Practice,* 2nd ed. (Toronto: Dryden, 1994), pp. 287–98.

5. "Mistakes in Advertising," on the Learn English website, **http://www. learningenglish.de/mistake/HorrorMistakes.htm**, accessed May 5, 2011; Bianca Bartz, "Advertising Bloopers," TrendHunter Marketing website, **http://www.trendhunter.com/trends/advertising-bloopers-international-ads-lost-in-translation**, accessed May 5, 2011.

6. Rik Pieters and Michel Wedel, "Attention Capture and Transfer in Advertising: Brand Pictorial, and Text-Size Effects," *Journal of Marketing* (April 2004), pp. 36–50.

7. Kusum L Ailawadi, Scott A. Neslin, and Karen Gedenk, "Pursuing the Value-Conscious Consumer: Store Brands versus National Brand Promotions," *Journal of Marketing* (January 2001), pp. 71–89.

8. B. C. Cotton and Emerson M. Babb, "Consumer Response to Promotional Deals," *Journal of Marketing,* vol. 42 (July 1978), pp. 109–13.

9. Robert George Brown, "Sales Response to Promotions and Advertising," *Journal of Advertising Research,* vol. 14 (August 1974), pp. 33–40.

10. Adapted from *Economic Impact: U.S. Direct Marketing Today* (New York: Direct Marketing Association, 1998), p. 25.

11. Siva K. Balasubramanian and V. Kumar, "Analyzing Variations in Advertising and Promotional Expenditures: Key Correlates in Consumer, Industrial, and Service Markets," *Journal of Marketing* (April 1990), pp. 57–68.

12. Danny Kucharsky, "Sears Canada's new campaign is everything," *Marketing*, March 17, 2016, **http://www.marketingmag.ca/advertising/sears-canadas-new-campaign-is-everything-170368**.

13. Dunn Sunnoo and Lynn Y. S. Lin, "Sales Effects of Promotion and Advertising," *Journal of Advertising Research,* vol. 18 (October 1978), pp. 37–42.

14. John Palmer, "Animal Instincts," *PROMO* (May 2001), pp. 25–33.

15. F. G. Crane and T. K. Clarke, *Consumer Behaviour in Canada: Theory and Practice*, pp. 237–38, 346.

16. "Push vs. Pull Strategies," *Daily News*, May 3, 2011; James M. Oliver and Paul W. Farris, "Push and Pull: A One-Two Punch for Packages Products," *Sloan Management Review* (Fall 1989), pp. 53–61.

17. Ken Riddell, "Advertising Sees Share of Pie Dwindling," *Marketing* (January 7, 1994), p. 2.

18. **www.pampers.ca** (downloaded May 5, 2013).

19. Eve Lazarus, "Branching Out," *Marketing* (October 20, 2003), **www.marketingmag.ca** (downloaded June 22, 2005).

20. Robert J. Lavidge and Gary A. Steiner, "A Model for Predictive Measurement of Advertising Effectiveness," *Journal of Marketing* (October 1961), p. 61.

21. Brian Wansink and Michael Ray, "Advertising Strategies to Increase Usage Frequency," *Journal of Marketing* (January 1996), pp. 31–46.

22. *Media Digest 2015-2016,* Canadian Media Directors' Council, Toronto.

23. Don E. Schultz and Anders Gronstedt, "Making Marcom an Investment," *Marketing Management* (Fall 1997), pp. 41–49; and J. Enrique Bigne, "Advertising Budget Practices: A Review," *Journal of Current Issues and Research in Advertising* (Fall 1995), pp. 17–31.

24. John Philip Jones, "Ad Spending: Maintaining Market Share," *Harvard Business Review* (January–February 1990), pp. 38–42; and Charles H. Patti and Vincent

Blanko, "Budgeting Practices of Big Advertisers," *Journal of Advertising Research,* vol. 21 (December 1981), pp. 23–30.

25. James A. Schroer, "Ad Spending: Growing Market Share," *Harvard Business Review* (January–February 1990), pp. 44–48.

26. Jeffrey A. Lowenhar and John L. Stanton, "Forecasting Competitive Advertising Expenditures," *Journal of Advertising Research,* vol. 16, no. 2 (April 1976), pp. 37–44.

27. Daniel Seligman, "How Much for Advertising?" *Fortune* (December 1956), p. 123.

28. James E. Lynch and Graham J. Hooley, "Increasing Sophistication in Advertising Budget Setting," *Journal of Advertising Research,* vol. 30 (February–March 1990), pp. 67–75.

29. Jimmy D. Barnes, Brenda J. Muscove, and Javad Rassouli, "An Objective and Task Media Selection Decision Model and Advertising Cost Formula to Determine International Advertising Budgets," *Journal of Advertising,* vol. 11, no. 4 (1982), pp. 68–75.

30. "The Olympic Brand Maintains Its Global Strength and Recognition," States News Service, February 12, 2013; Graham Ruddock, "London Olympics Sponsors Are Already into Their Stride," *Daily Telegraph,* May 6, 2011, p. 8; "The Olympics Come But Once Every Two Years," *Marketing News,* November 1, 2008, p. 12; "Olympics Will Bring Online Opportunities for Many Brands," *Revolution,* July 14, 2008, p. 13; and Don E. Schultz, "Olympics Get the Gold Medal in Integrating Marketing Event," *Marketing News,* April 27, 1998, pp. 5, 10.

31. Cornelia Pechman, Guangzhi Zhao, Marvin E. Goldberg, and Ellen Thomas Reibling, "What to Convey in Antismoking Advertisements for Adolescents: The

Use of Protection Motivation Theory to Identify Effective Message Themes," *Journal of Marketing* (April 2003), pp. 1–18.

32. Kate Fitzgerald, "Beyond Advertising, " *Advertising Age* (August 3, 1998), pp. 1, 14; Curtis P. Johnson, "Follow the Money: Sell CFO on Integrated Marketing's Merits, " *Marketing News* (May 11, 1998).

33. "Measure for Measure," *Marketing Management* (January–February 2004), p. 7.

34. **www.the-cma.org** (downloaded on May 10, 2016).

35. Ibid.

36. "Government of Canada Protects Canadians with Electronic Commerce Protection Act," **www.ic.gc.ca**, downloaded January 30, 2010.

37. Mai Nguyen, "The Marketing Blend behind Steeped Tea's Brand Success," *Marketing,* May 19, 2016, **http://www.marketingmag.ca/brands/the-marketing-blend-behind-steeped-teas-brand-success-174827** (downloaded May 20, 2016); "Internet Use and E-Commerce," Statistics Canada, November 19, 2014; **http://www.statcan.gc.ca/pub/11-627-m/11-627-m2014003-eng.htm**.

38. Carrie A. Johnson, "Getting Multichannel Retailing Right," **www.forrester.com** (downloaded January 7, 2005).

39. Theresa Howard, "Email Grows as Direct-Marketing Tool: They're Quicker to Make, Cheap to Send," *USA Today,* November 28, 2008, p. 5B.

40. Cristina Onosé, "The Latest on Privacy Compliance, Consumer Trends and Our Privacy World in 2030," Canadian Marketing Association, May 4, 2016, **https://www.the-cma.org/about/blog/privacy-summit-the-latest-on-privacy-compliance-consumer-trends-and-our-privacy-world-in-2030**.

Chapter 17

1. Dan Kedmey, "Virtually Real," *Time,* February 9, 2015, p. 12; Maria Minsker, "Facebook Gets Real about Virtual Reality," *Customer Relationship Management,* March 2015, p. 16; Michelle Castillo, "How Virtual Reality Could Revolutionize Ads in the Sports Industry," *Adweek,* May 22, 2015, p. 1; Rae Ann Fera, "Get the Most Out of VR," *Marketing,* January 5 2015, p. 18; Ann-Christine Diaz, "Grab Your Headset: Producer Plunge into Virtual Reality," *Advertising Age,* February 9, 2015, p. 26; Madeline Berg, "From HDR to Virtual Reality: Inside the Future of Entertainment," **Forbes.com**, June 10, 2015; and John Gaudiosi, "How Augmented Reality and Virtual Reality will Generate $150 Billion in Revenue by 2020," **Fortune.com**, April 29, 2015.

2. Karen V. Fernandex and Dennis L. Rosen, "The Effectiveness of Information and Color in Yellow Pages Advertising," *Journal of Advertising,* Summer, 2000, p. 61; David A. Aaker and Donald Norris, "Characteristics of TV Commercials Perceived as Informative," *Journal of Advertising Research,* vol. 22, no. 2 (April–May 1982), pp. 61–70.

3. Larry D. Compeau and Dhruv Grewal, "Comparative Price Advertising: An Integrative Review," *Journal of Public Policy & Marketing* (Fall 1998), pp. 257–73.

4. Chingching Chang, "The Relative Effectiveness of Comparative and Noncomparative Advertising: Evidence for Gender Differences in Information-Processing Strategies," *Journal of Advertising,* Spring 2007, p. 21; Jerry Gotlieb and Dan Sorel, "The Influence of Type of Advertisement, Price, and Source Credibility on Perceived Quality," *Journal of the Academy of Marketing Science* (Summer 1992), pp. 253–60; and Cornelia Pechman and David Stewart, "The Effects of Comparative Advertising on Attention, Memory, and Purchase Intentions," *Journal of Consumer Research* (September 1990), pp. 180–92.

5. Kathy L. O'Malley, Jeffrey J. Bailey, Chong Leng Tan, and Carl A. Bozman, "Effects of Varying Web-Based Advertising-Substantiation Information on Attribute Beliefs and Perceived Product Quality," *Academy of Marketing Sciences*

Journal, 2007, p. 19; Bruce Buchanan and Doron Goldman, "Us vs. Them: The Minefield of Comparative Ads," *Harvard Business Review* (May–June 1989), pp. 38–50.

6. Lewis C. Winters, "Does It Pay to Advertise to Hostile Audiences with Corporate Advertising?" *Journal of Advertising Research* (June/July 1988), pp. 11–18; and Robert Selwitz, "The Selling of an Image," *Madison Avenue* (February 1985), pp. 61–69.

7. Matt Semansky, "Lavalife Spot Looks on Bright Side of Dating," *Marketing Daily* (July 10, 2007), **www.marketingmag.ca** (downloaded July 18, 2007).

8. "New Crystal Light Liquid Drink Mix Frees You from the Choice between Taste or Calories," PR Newswire, February 11, 2013; Natalie Zmuda, "Diet Mtn Dew Steps Out from Shadow of Flagship Brand," *Advertising Age,* March 5, 2012, p. 4; Ashley Ross, "Why Models Are Addicted to This Fitness Trend," **Time.com**, May 7, 2015; and Andrew Adam Newman, "Under Armour Heads Off the Sidelines for a Campaign Aimed at Women," *New York Times,* July 31, 2014, p. 3.

9. Shareen Pthak, "How Nike Ambushed the Olympics with This Neon Shoe," *Advertising Age,* August 20, 2012, p. 1.

10. "Cassies Silver: Home Depot is 'beau' in Quebec," *Strategy,* February 19, 2014, **http://strategyonline.ca/2014/02/19/cassies-silver-home-depot-is-beau-in-quebec/**.

11. Bob Donath, "Match Your Media Choice and Ad Copy Objective," *Marketing News* (June 8, 1998), p. 6.

12. **http://cassies.ca/home/winners2016cassies.ca/** (downloaded May 20, 2016).

13. Michael S. LaTour and Herbert J. Rotfeld, "There Are Threats and (Maybe) Fear-Caused Arousal: Theory and Confusions of Appeals to Fear and Fear Arousal Itself," *Journal of Advertising* (Fall 1997), pp. 45–59.

14. Eve Lazarus, "Think About the Unthinkable in New Blue Cross Ads," *Marketing Daily* (June 6, 2007), **www.marketingmag.ca** (downloaded July 4, 2007).

15. This example has been supplied by Rethink Canada, agency of record for BCAA Life Insurance.

16. "If Sex Sells, Humour Sells Way More," Institute of Communication Agencies, **www.icacanada.ca** (downloaded February 3, 2010).

17. **www.kidney.ca** and **www.marchofdimes.ca**.

18. *Media Digest 2015-2016,* Canadian Media Directors' Council, Toronto.

19. Ibid.

20. Lowell L. Lunden, "Secrets for Powerful Advertising: Strategic Implications of Recency," *Canadian Advertising Research Foundation Newsletter* (December 2003), pp. 9–13.

21. William F. Arens, *Contemporary Advertising,* 9th ed. (New York: McGraw-Hill/Irwin, 2004); and William G. Nickels, James M. McHugh, and Susan M. McHugh, *Understanding Business,* 7th ed. (Burr Ridge, IL: McGraw-Hill, 2005, p. 493).

22. *Media Digest 2015-2016,* Canadian Media Directors' Council, Toronto.

23. **www.ctv.ca**.

24. Kate Newsstead and Jenni Romaniuk, "Cost per Second: The Relative Effectiveness of 15- and 30-Second Television Advertisements," *Journal of Advertising Research,* 2009, pp. 68–76.

25. "Net Advertising Revenue by Medium in Canada," Television Bureau of Canada (2010).

26. *Media Digest 2015-2016,* Canadian Media Directors' Council, Toronto.

27. Ibid.

28. Ibid.

29. Ibid.

30. **www.iabcanada.com** (downloaded May 12, 2016).

31. **http://iabcanada.com/research/cmost/** (downloaded May 27, 2016)

32. *Media Digest 2015-2016,* Canadian Media Directors' Council, Toronto.

33. Michelle DiPardo, "Extreme Brings a Bit of Peggy's Cove to Toronto," *Marketing Daily,* May 21, 2013, **www,marketingmag.ca**.

34. "Become the Doritos Guru," **www.cassies.ca/caselibrary** (downloaded March 10, 2010).

35. **www.iabcanada.com** (downloaded May 12, 2013).

36. Danny Kucharsky, "Agency Opens Inside Clothing Shop," *Marketing Daily* (May 28, 2007), **www.marketingmag.ca** (downloaded July 20, 2007).

37. The discussion of post-testing is based on William F. Arens, *Contemporary Advertising,* 9th ed. (Burr Ridge, IL: Richard D. Irwin, 2004).

38. **www.adstandards.com** (downloaded May 27, 2016).

39. *ASC Research: Consumer Perspectives on Advertising 2016,* Advertising Standards Council, 2016, **http://www.adstandards.com/en/ASCLibrary/consumerResearch.aspx**.

40. Lisa D'Innocenzo, "Selling to the Store," *Strategy Magazine* (February 9, 2004), p. 1.

41. "Coupon Redemption in Canada," Canadian Deals Association, May 16, 2013, **http://www.canadiandealsassociation.com/coupon-redemption-in-canada-some-interesting-data/**.

42. Kapil Bawa and Robert W. Shoemaker, "Analyzing Incremental Sales from a Direct-Mail Coupon Promotion," *Journal of Marketing* (July 1998), pp. 66–78.

43. Roger A. Strang, "Sales Promotion—Fast Growth, Faulty Management," *Harvard Business Review,* vol. 54 (July–August 1976), pp. 115–24; and Ronald W. Ward and James E. Davis, "Coupon Redemption," *Journal of Advertising Research,* vol. 18 (August 1978), pp. 51–58. Similar results on favourable mail-distributed coupons were reported by Alvin Schwartz, "The Influence of Media Characteristics on Coupon Redemption," *Journal of Marketing,* vol. 30 (January 1966), pp. 41–46.

44. Matt Semansky, "M&M Ads Spawn New Contest," *Marketing Daily* (June 8, 2007), **www.marketingmag.ca** (downloaded July 20, 2007); and Matt Semansky, "Teltoon Contesting with General Mills, Maynards," *Marketing Daily* (June 6, 2007), **www.marketingmag.ca** (downloaded July 20, 2007).

45. Eve Lazarus, "Martin's Puts New Apple Snack on Ontario Shelves," *Marketing Daily,* July 2, 2013, **http://www.marketingmag.ca/news/marketer-news/martins-puts-new-apple-snack-on-ontario-shelves-82737?p?82737?utm_source?EmailMarketing&utm_medium?email&utm_campaign?marketing_daily_AM**.

46. "The Case for Rebates," *Chief Marketer,* July 1, 2011.

47. Stefania Moretti, "Canadian TV Takes Product Placement Further Than Hollywood," *Toronto Sun,* April 7, 2010, **http://www.torontosun.com/money/2010/04/07/13492491.html**.

48. This discussion is drawn particularly from John A. Quelch, *Trade Promotions by Grocery Manufacturers: A Management Perspective* (Cambridge, MA: Marketing Science Institute, August 1982).

49. Scott Hue, "Free 'Plugs' Supply Ad Power," *Advertising Age* (January 29, 1990), p. 6.

50. **www.sponsorshipmarketing.ca**.

51. Laurie Smith, "Study: Use of Social Media in PR Campaigns Growing," Canadian Newswire, June 7, 2011, **http://www.newswire.ca/en/story/744063/study-use-of-social-media-in-public-relations-campaigns-growing**; and Melinda Emerson, "How to Use Social Media to Drum Up PR for your Small Business," March 28, 2013, **http://succeedasyourownboss.com/03/2013/how-to-use-social-media-to-drum-up-pr-for-your-small-business/**.

52. Kim Harrison, "Ensure You Bring Ethics into Your PR Activities, " **http:// www.cuttingedgepr.com/articles/bring-ethics-into-pr-activities.asp** (downloaded May 27, 2016).

Chapter 18

1. Interview with Lindsey Smith, GE Healthcare, June 6, 2015.

2. Statistics Canada, *Canada Year Book,* (Ottawa, 2016).

3. Jim Clifton and Sangeeta Bharadwaj Badal, *Entrepreneurial StrengthsFinder* (New York: Gallup Press, 2014); and Meghan Casserly, "The Five Sales Tactics Every Entrepreneur Must Master," **forbes.com**, January 30, 2013.

4. "Surgical Visits," Business 2.0, April 2006, p. 94.

5. Mark W. Johnston and Greg W. Marshall, *Contemporary Selling: Building Relationships, Creating Value,* 4th ed. (Burr Ridge, IL: McGraw-Hill/Irwin, 2014).

6. Gerhard Gschwandtner, "How Much Time Do Your Salespeople Spend Selling?" *Selling Power,* March/April 2011, p. 8.

7. For an overview of team selling, see Eli Jones, Andrea Dickson, Lawrence B. Chonko, and Joseph P. Cannon, "Key Accounts and Team Selling: A Review,

Framework, and Research Agenda," *Journal of Personal Selling & Sales Management,* Spring 2005, pp. 181–98.

8. "Team Selling Works!" **www.sellingpower.com**, March 24, 2013.

9. Scott Sterns, "Cold Calls Have Yet to Breathe Their Last Gasp," *Wall Street Journal*, December 14, 2006, p. D2.

10. Jim Edwards, "Dinner, Interrupted," *BrandWeek* (May 26, 2003), pp. 28–32.

11. Paul A. Herbing, *Handbook of Cross-Cultural Marketing* (New York: The Haworth Press, 1998).

12. Philip R. Cateora, Mary C. Gilly, and John L. Graham, *International Marketing*, 16th ed. (Burr Ridge, IL: McGraw-Hill/Irwin, 2013).

13. Mark W. Johnston and Greg W. Marshall, *Contemporary Selling: Building Relationships, Creating Value*, 4th ed. (Burr Ridge, IL: McGraw-Hill/Irwin, 2014).

14. Kapil R. Tuli, Ajay K. Kohli, and Sundar G. Bharadwaj, "Rethinking Customer Solutions: From Product Bundles to Relational Processes," *Journal of Marketing,* July 2007, pp. 1–17.

15. For an extensive discussion of objections, see Charles M. Futrell, *Fundamentals of Selling*, 13th ed. (Burr Ridge, IL: McGraw-Hill/ Irwin, 2014), chapter 12.

16. Theodore Levitt, *The Marketing Imagination* (New York: Free Press, 1983), p. 111.

17. Stephen B. Castleberry, and John F. Tanner, Jr., *Selling: Building Partnerships*, 9th ed. (Burr Ridge, IL: McGraw-Hill, 2014).

18. *Management Briefing: Sales and Marketing* (New York: Conference Board, October 1996), pp. 3–4.

19. Ellen Neuborne, "Know Thy Enemy," *Sales & Marketing Management* (January 2003), pp. 29–33.

20. Douglas E. Hughes, Joel LeBon, and Adam Rapp, "Gaining and Leveraging Customer-based Competitive Intelligence: The Pivotal Role of Social Capital and Salesperson Adaptive Selling Skills," *Journal of the Academy of Marketing Science,* January 2013, pp. 91–110; Stephen Schultz, "Capturing CI through Your Sales Force," *Competitive Intelligence Magazine*, January– February 2002, pp. 15–17.

21. See Mark W. Johnston and Greg W. Marshall, *Sales Force Management*, 11th ed. (Burr Ridge, IL: McGraw-Hill/ Irwin, 2014), pp. 100–4; and William T. Ross, Jr., Frederic Dalsace, and Erin Anderson, "Should You Set Up Your Own Sales Force or Should You Outsource It? Pitfalls in the Standard Analysis," *Business Horizons*, January–February 2005, pp. 23–36.

22. Eli Jones, et al., "Key Accounts and Team Selling." Also see, Arun Sharma, "Success Factors in Key Accounts," *Journal of Business & Industrial Marketing* 21, no. 3 (2006), pp. 141–50.

23. This discussion is based on William L. Cron and Thomas E. DeCarlo, *Dalrymple's Sales Management,* 9th ed. (Hoboken, NJ: John Wiley & Sons, Inc., 2006).Also see Rene Darmon, "Joint Assessment of Optimal Sales Force Sizes and Sales Call Guidelines: A Management-Oriented Tool," *Canadian Journal of Administrative Sciences* (September 2007), pp. 200–19.

24. René Y. Darmon, "Joint Assessment of Optimal Sales Force Sizes and Sales Call Guidelines: A Management-Oriented Tool"; and "Look Who's Calling," *Sales & Marketing Management* (May 1998), pp. 43–46.

25. This discussion is based on Dalrymple, Cron, and DeCarlo, *Sales Management.*

26. Julia Chang, "Born to Sell?" *Sales & Marketing Management* (July 2003), pp. 34–38.

27. "Look for Employees with High EQ Over IQ," **forbes.com**, March 18, 2013; and Blair Kidwell, David M. Hardesty, Brian R. Murtha, and Shibin Sheng, "Emotional Intelligence in Marketing Exchanges," *Journal of Marketing,* January 2011, pp. 78–93.

28. Joanne Thomas Yaccato, "Through the Gender Lens," *Marketing Magazine* (June 30, 2003); and Lesley Young, "Strange Hybrids," *Marketing* (February 11, 2002), **www.marketingmag.ca** (downloaded June 22, 2005).

29. Ibid.

30. Thomas Steenburgh and Michael Ahearne, "Motivating Salespeople: What Really Works," *Harvard Business Review*, July-August 2012, pp. 71–75; and Rosann L. Spiro, Gregory A. Rich, and William J. Stanton, *Management of the Sales Force,* 12th ed. (Burr Ridge, IL: McGraw-Hill/Irwin, 2008), chapter 7.

31. This discussion is based on Johnston and Marshall, *Sales Force Management*, chapter 11.

32. **www.marykay.com/recognition** (downloaded June 21, 2016).

33. Jeffrey E. Lewin and Jeffrey K. Sager, "The Influence of Personal Characteristics and Coping Strategies on Salespersons' Turnover Intentions," *Journal of Personal Selling & Sales Management*, Fall 2010, pp. 355–70; and René Y. Darmon, "The Concept of Salesperson Replacement Value: A Sales Force Turnover Management Tool," *Journal of Personal Selling & Sales Management*, Summer 2008, pp. 211–32.

34. For further reading, see Goutam N. Challagolla and Tasadduq A. Shervani, "A Measurement Model of the Dimensions and Types of Output and Behavior Control: An Empirical Test in the Salesforce Context," *Journal of Business Research* (July 1997), pp. 159–72; and Gregory A. Rich, William H. Bommer, Scott B. McKenzie, Philip M. Podsakoff, and Jonathan L. Johnson, "Apples and Apples or Apples and Oranges? A Meta-Analysis of Objective and Subjective Measures of Salesperson Performance," *Journal of Personal Selling & Sales Management* (Fall 1999), pp. 41–52.

35. "Measuring Sales Effectiveness," *Sales & Marketing Management* (October 2000), p. 136; "Quota Busters," *Sales & Marketing Management* (January 2001), pp. 59–63.

36. "Corporate America's New Sales Force," *Fortune,* August 11, 2003, special advertising section.

37. **www.toshiba.com/technology** (downloaded May 15, 2004).

38. Sue Hildreth, "Mobile CRM Makes Its Move," **SearchCRM.com** (June 13, 2006), **www.searchcrm.com** (downloaded July 29, 2007).

39. Christopher Plouffe and Donald Barcley, "Salesperson Navigation: The Intraorganizational Dimension of the Sales Role," *Industrial Marketing Management* (May 2007), pp. 528–39.

40. Angela Hausman, "How to Use Twitter as a Marketing Tool," February 11, 2016, **https://www.hausmanmarketingletter.com/how-to-use-twitter-as-a-marketing-tool/** (downloaded June 2, 2016); and Kfir Bar-Levav, "8 Keys to Turning Twitter into a Great Sales Tool," NISM, **http://nismonline.org/8-keys-to-turning-twitter-into-a-great-sales-tool/** (downloaded June 2, 2016).

Chapter 19

1. Scott Stoddard, "Top Dividend Stock General Mills Adapts to New Tastes," *Investors Business Daily*, May 28, 2015, p. B9; Lucy Maher and Susie Stulz, "Millennials Take Over the Store Aisle," *Adweek*, June 22, 2015, pp. S1–15; and Personal interviews with Vivian Milroy Callaway; Sarah Nassauer, "What If We All Bought Organic?" *Wall Street Journal*, March 18, 2015, p. D1; Annie Gasparro, "General Mills to Cut Costs—Company Announces New Initiatives Amid Slow U.S. Sales," *Wall Street Journal*, June 26, 2014, p. B4; "General Mills Overview," and "General Mills 2014 Annual Report," see General Mills website,

http://www.generalmills.com/en/Company/Overview; Lisa Belfuss, "Why Trix Cereal Will Soon Have Four Colors Instead of Six," *Wall Street Journal*, June 23, 2015, p. B2; and "Betty's Must-Have New Products," see **http://www. bettycrocker.com/products/new-products**.

2. Hugh Courtney, John T. Horn, and Jayanti Kar, "Getting into Your Competitor's Head," *The McKinsey Quarterly*, February 2009.

3. Richard Rumelt, *Good Strategy/Bad Strategy* (New York: Crown Business, 2011).

4. Ibid.

5. Nitin Nohria, William Joyce, and Bruce Roberson, "What Really Works," *Harvard Business Review* (July, 2003), pp. 42–52; and "Who Gets Eaten and Who Gets to Eat," *The Economist* (July 12, 2003), pp. 61–63.

6. "Costco Brand of Retailing Continues to Resonate," *MMR*, May 25, 2015, p. 56; and Armin Harris et al., "The Directors: Costco Wholesale," *Fortune*, May 4, 2009, pp. 100–1.

7. David Sedgwick, "Toyota's New Plan: Design Parts, Then Cars," *Automotive News*, June 15, 2015, p. 33; Geoff Colvin, "How It Works," *Fortune*, February 27, 2012, pp. 71–79; and Kathleen Kerwin and Paul Magnusson, "Can Anything Stop Toyota?" *BusinessWeek*, November 17, 2003, pp. 114–22.

8. Milton Moskowitz and Robert Levering, "The 100 Best Companies to Work For," *Fortune*, March 15, 2015, pp. 143–144; and "The 500 Largest U.S. Corporations," *Fortune*, June 15, 2015, p. F4.

9. Ben R. Rich and Leo Janos, *Skunk Works* (Boston: Little, Brown and Company, 1994).

10. Murali K. Mantrala, Prabhakant Sirha, and Andris A. Zoltners, "Impact of Resource Allocation Rules on Marketing Investment-Level Decisions and Profitability," *Journal of Marketing Research* (May 1992), pp. 162–75.

11. Mike Hughlett, "General Mills Adds New Cereals to Take On Trends," **www.startribune.com**, December 14, 2014; and Bridget Christenson, "New Products Deliver on Taste," Taste of General Mills, **www.blog.generalmills.com**, December 16, 2014.

12. Clayton M. Christensen and Derek van Bever, "The Capitalist's Dilemma," *Harvard Business Review*, June 2014, pp. 60–68.

13. *2016 Annual Report* (Minneapolis: General Mills, Inc., 2016).

14. This discussion and Figure 19–3 are adapted from Stanley F. Stasch and Patricis Longtree, "Can Your Marketing Planning Procedures Be Improved?" *Journal of Marketing* (Summer 1980), p. 82, by permission of the American Marketing Association.

15. Adapted with permission of The Free Press, a Division of Macmillan, Inc., from *Competitive Advantage: Creating and Sustaining Superior Performance* by Michael E. Porter. Copyright 1985 by Michael E. Porter.

16. Hollie Shaw, "Canada Goose's Made-in-Canada Marketing Strategy Translates into Success," *Financial Post*, May 18, 2012, **http://business.financialpost.com/ 2012/05/18/canada-gooses-made-in-canada-marketing-strategy- translates-into-success/**.

17. Patricia Sellers, "P&G: Teaching an Old Dog New Tricks," *Fortune* (May 31, 2004), pp. 167–80.

18. "Grocery giant Loblaw to buy Shoppers Drug Mart for $12.4 billion," *Marketing Daily*, July 15, 2013, **http://www.marketingmag.ca/news/marketer-news/**

grocery-giant-loblaw-to-buy-shoppers-drug-for-12-4-billion- 83556?p?83556?utm_source?EmailMarketing&utm_ medium?email&utm_campaign?marketing_daily_PM**.

19. Adapted from Philip Kotler and Kevin Lane Keller, *Marketing Management*, 12th ed. (Upper Saddle River, NJ: Prentice Hall, 2006), pp. 262–63.

20. Stratford Sherman, "How Intel Makes Spending Pay Off," *Fortune* (February 22, 1993), pp. 57–61.

21. **www.transcontinental.com; www.potashcorp.com; www.canadiantire. com; and www.vancity.com**.

22. Anirban Sen, "Disruptive Innovation Is a Strategy, Not Just the Technology," *Business Today*, January 4, 2015, pp. 150–158; Hal B. Gregerson, Jeff Dyer, and Clayton M. Christensen, "Why Ask Why?" *Chief Executive.Net*, January/February 2012, pp. 40–43.

23. Charles H. Noble and Michael P. Mokwa, "Implementing Marketing Strategies: Developing and Testing a Managerial Theory," *Journal of Marketing* (October 1999), pp. 57–74.

24. "Ecomagination," see **www.ge.com/company/citizenship/-ecomagination/ index.html**, July 24, 2007.

25. Daniel Roth, "This Ain't No Pizza Party," *Fortune* (November 9, 1998), pp. 158–64.

26. Thomas J. Peters and Robert H. Waterman, Jr., *In Search of Excellence: Lessons from America's Best-Run Companies* (New York: Harper & Row, 1982).

27. Tom Peters, "Winners Do Hundreds of Percent over Norm," *Minneapolis Star Tribune* (January 8, 1985), p. 5B; and Ben Rich and Leo Janos, *Skunk Works* (Boston: Little Brown, 1994), pp. 51–53.

28. "CMO-mentum: Critical new challenges face CMOs," Deloitte, n.d., **http:// www2.deloitte.com/ca/en/pages/chief-marketing-officer/articles/cmo- mentum.html** (downloaded June 7, 2016).

29. Peter Galuska, Ellen Neuborne, and Wendy Zeliner, "P&G's Hottest New Product: P&G," *BusinessWeek* (October 5, 1998), pp. 92–96.

30. Robert W. Ruekert and Orville C. Walker, Jr., "Marketing's Interaction with Other Functional Units: A Conceptual Framework and Empirical Evidence," *Journal of Consumer Marketing* (Spring 1987), pp. 1–19; Shikhar Sarin and Vijay Mahajan, "The Effect of Reward Structures on the Performance of Cross-Functional Product Development Teams," *Journal of Marketing* (April 2001), pp. 35–53; and Amy Edmondson, Richard Bohmer, and Gary Pisano, "Speeding Up Team Learning," *Harvard Business Review* (October 2001), pp. 125–32.

31. James D. Lenskold, *Marketing ROI* (New York: McGraw-Hill, 2003).

32. Michael Krauss, "Balance Attention to Metrics with Intuition," *Marketing News*, June 1, 2007, pp. 6–8; John Davis, *Measuring Marketing: 103 Key Metrics Every Marketer Needs* (Singapore: John Wiley & Sons, 2007); and Paul W. Farris, Neil T. Bendle, Phillip E. Pfeifer, and David J. Reibstein, *Marketing Metrics* (Upper Saddle River, NJ: Wharton School Publishing, 2006).

33. Malcolm Craig, *Thinking Visually: Business Applications of 14 Core Diagrams* (New York and London: Continuum, 2000).

34. The illustrative example of using a marketing dashboard at General Mills was developed by David Ford and Vivian Milroy Callaway.

Chapter 20

1. "Connecting with the Cosmos: The Total Audience Media Universe, Newswire, Nielsen, March 19, 2015; Marc de Swaan Arons, Frank van den Driest, and Keith

Weed, "The Ultimate Marketing Machine," *Harvard Business Review*, July–August 2014, pp. 55–63; Gian Fulgoni and Andrew Lipsman, "Digital Game Changers:

How Social Media Will Help Usher In the Era of Mobile and Multi-Platform Campaign-Effectiveness Measurement," *Journal of Advertising Research*, March 2014, pp. 11–16; Tina Desai, "The Future of Mobile Marketing: Connecting the Physical with Digital," *Marketing Week*, November 26, 2014, p. 1; Peter Roesler, "Why Mobile Marketing Is Still the Next Big Thing," www.inc.com, August 18, 2014; Steven Tweedie, "The 10 Most Popular Apps of 2014," *Business Insider*, December 29, 2014; and Lauren Johnson, "This Year's 10 Biggest Shifts, Shake-Ups and Surprises in Mobile Marketing," *Adweek*, December 21, 2014, p. 1.

2. Dave Evans, *Social Media Marketing: An Hour a Day* (Indianapolis, IN: Wiley Publishing, Inc., 2009), pp. 57–59.

3. Andreas M. Kaplan and Michael Haenlein, "Users of the World, Unite! The Challenges and Opportunities of Social Media," *Business Horizons* 53, no. 1 (2010), pp. 59–68.

4. Kaplan and Haenlein, "Users of the World, Unite!" pp. 62–64.

5. Drake Bennett, "Ten Years of Inaccuracy and Remarkable Detail," *Bloomberg Businessweek*, January 10–January 16, 2011, pp. 57–61.

6. Michael Sebastian, "LinkedIn Sells Nearly Half a Billion Dollars in Ads Last Year," **adage.com**, February 5, 2015; and Jim Edwards, "This LinkedIn Deck Shows the ROI for 8 Of Its Biggest Ad Clients," *Business Insider*, August 3, 2012.

7. Chiranjeev Kohli, Rajneesh Suri, and Anuj Kapoor, "Will Social Media Kill Branding?" *Business Horizons*, 58 (2015), pp. 35–44; Starr Hall and Chadd Rosenberg, *Get Connected: The Social Networking Toolkit for Business* (Madison, WI: Entrepreneur Press, 2009), pp. 17–20.

8. Emily Steel and Geoffrey Fowler, "Facebook in Privacy Breach," *Wall Street Journal*, October 18, 2010, pp. A1, A2; and Geoffrey Fowler and Emily Steel, "Facebook Says User Data Sold to Broker," *Wall Street Journal*, November 1, 2010, p. B3.

9. Figure 20–2 is adapted from "The CMO's Guide to the 2014 Social Landscape." See **http://visual.ly/cmos-guide-2014-social-landscape**.

10. "Facebook Statistics," accessed June 26, 2016, www.facebook.com; and *2015-2016 Media Digest*, Canadian Media Directors' Council, Toronto.

11. Aaron Smith, "6 New Facts about Facebook," www.pewresearch.org, Pew Research Center, February 3, 2014; "Announcing 2 Million Advertisers on Facebook," press release, Facebook website, **http://newsroom.fb.com**, February 24, 2015; Ashlee Vance, "Your Facebook Data Are Here," *Bloomberg Businessweek*, October 7–October 13, 2013, pp. 42–44; and Cooper Smith, "7 Statistics about Facebook Users That Reveal Why It's Such a Powerful Marketing Platform," *Business Insider*, November 16, 2013.

12. "Top 10 Ways to Engage Fans on Facebook," Buddy Media, Inc., 2010.

13. Ned Smith, "How Much Is a Facebook Friend Worth? $174.17," *BusinessNewsDaily*, April 26, 2013. See **http://www.businessnewsdaily.com/4402-value-facebook-friend-marketing.html**.

14. The discussion of StuffDOT was provided by Kelsey Fisher, Jenny Caffoe, Lexi Diderich, and Malyn Mueller of StuffDOT, Inc.

15. Deepa Seetharaman, "Facebook to Enhance Messenger App," *Wall Street Journal*, March 26, 2015, p. B8.

16. Deepa Seetharaman, "Facebook Pushes Speedier News Publishing," *Wall Street Journal*, May 14, 2015, p. B4

17. Deepa Seetharaman, "Facebook's Facial Recognition Is Latest AI Step," *Wall Street Journal*, June 24, 2015, p. B5; and Molly McHugh, "Facebook Moments Is a Smarter Photo App—Much Smarter," www.wired.com, June 15, 2015.

18. Rolfe Winkler and Jack Marshall, "Google Imitates Facebook with E-mail Marketing," *Wall Street Journal*, April 15, 2015, p. B4; Vindu Goel, "Rise in

Mobile Ads Pushes Up Facebook Results," *Star Tribune*, January 30, 2014, p. D3; and Evelyn M. Rusli, "For Mark Zuckerberg, Tumult and Turnaround," *Wall Street Journal*, January 6, 2014, pp. A1,10.

19. Seetharaman, "Facebook to Enhance Messenger App."

20. Twitter website, **https://about.twitter.com/company**; Knowlton Thomas, "Twitter Passes 500 Million Users," TechVibes, July 30, 2012, **http://www.techvibes.com/blog/twitter-passes-500-million-users-study-reveals-canada-accounts-for-2-of-all-users-2012-07-30**; Sunny Freeman, "Twitter Canada Promises Not to Bombard Users with Its New Ads," *Huffington Post Business Canada*, August 7, 2013, **http://www.huffingtonpost.ca/2013/06/13/twitter-canada-launch_n_3430365.html**; Hayley Tsukayama, "Twitter Turns 7: Users Send over 400 Million Tweets per Day," *The Washington Post*, March 21, 2013, **http://articles.washingtonpost.com/2013-03-21/business/37889387_1_tweets-jack-dorsey-twitter**.

21. Thomas Lee, "Social-Media Bees Create Target Buzz," *Star Tribune*, April 13, 2013, pp. A1, A6; and Jeff Herring and Maritza Parra, "Make the Most of Tweeting," *Star Tribune*, January 6, 2011, p. E4.

22. Michelle DiPardo, "Wine Country Ontario Promotes Its Untweetable Experience," *Marketing Daily*, June 25, 2013, **http://www.marketingmag.ca/news/marketer-news/wine-country-ontario-promotes-its-%e2%80%9cuntweetable%e2%80%9d-experience-82368?p?82368?utm_source?EmailMarketing&utm_medium?email&utm_campaign?marketing_daily_AM**.

23. Elizabeth Dwoskin and Yoree Koh, "Twitter Pushes Deeper into Data," *Wall Street Journal*, April 16, 2014, p. B2.

24. LinkedIn website, **https://press.linkedin.com/about-linkedin**; and Craig Smith, "By the Numbers: 80 Amazing LinkedIn Statistics," DMR Digital Marketing Ramblings, February 9, 2014; and Jessi Hempel, "LinkedIn: How It Is Changing Business," *Fortune*, July 1, 2013, pp. 69–74.

25. "LinkedIn Is Trying to Quicken Its Pulse," *Bloomberg Businessweek*, April 22–April 28, 2013, pp. 32–33; Emily Moltby and Shira Ovide, "Which Social Media Work?" *Wall Street Journal*, January 31, 2013, p. B8; and Brandon Bailey, "Who Needs Friends? LinkedIn Has Success with Members," *Star Tribune*, April 25, 2013, pp. D1, D3.

26. Johnathon Podensky, "LinkedIn Search Just Got Smarter," LinkedIn Official Blog, March 25, 2013, **http://blog.linkedin.com/2013/03/25/linkedIn-search-just-got-smarter/**.

27. YouTube website, **https://www.youtube.com/yt/press/statistics.html**; Craig Smith, "By the Numbers: 90+ Amazing YouTube Statistics," DMR Digital Marketing Ramblings, June 8, 2015; and Amanda Axvig, Vice President of Marketing, AOI Marketing, Inc.

28. Daisy Wyatt, "Most Viewed YouTube Videos of All Time: From 'Gangnam Style' to Katy Perry's 'Dark Horse,'" *The Independent*, June 26, 2015, **http://www.independent.co.uk/artsentertainment/music/features/most-viewedyoutube-videos-from-gangnam-style-to-wreckingball-9607483.html**; and YouTube website, **https://www.youtube.com/results?search_query=most+viewed+video+on+youtube+of+all+time**.

29. "Neal Mohan, "How to Win the Moments That Matter with Mobile Video," Adweek, April 3, 2015, p. 1; "Why Online Video Is a Must-Have for Your Mobile Marketing Strategy," www.thinkwithgoogle.com, April 2015; Alison Millington, "Snickers Seeking Global Reach with New Vlogger-led Digital Campaign," Marketing Week, April 8, 2015; and Sarah Vizard, "YouTube at 10: How It Plans to Stay Ahead," Marketing Week, May 15, 2015.

30. Lauren Drell, "Hashtags, and Infographics, and Videos! Oh My!" *Marketing Insights*, March/April 2014, pp. 40–47; Christa Toole, "Ten Tips for Those Who

Still Aren't Using YouTube," *Advertising Age*, www.adage.com, October 19, 2010; and Felix Gillette, "On YouTube, Seven-Figure Views, Six-Figure Paychecks," *Bloomberg Businessweek*, September 27–October 3, 2010, pp. 35–36.

31. "Most Popular Social Media Website in the United States in March 2015, Based on Share of Visits," The Statistics Portal, www.statista.com, 2015; and DMR Digital Marketing Ramblings.

32. This example and the section on measuring results were provided by Brian Stuckey and Amanda Axvig of StuffDOT, Inc.

33. The Jeff Gordon—Pepsi Max example was provided by Nancy Harrower, Concordia University—St. Paul; and Sheila Shayon, "Pepsi Continues to Bask in Branded Content Glory with Top YouTube Views," Brand Channel, April 8, 2013. See **http://www.brandchannel.com/home/post/2013/04/08/Pepsi-Tops-YouTube-Leaderboard-040813.aspx**.

34. Craig Smith, "By the Numbers: 90+ Amazing Pinterest Statistics," DMR Digital Marketing Ramblings, May 23, 2015.

35. *Media Digest 2015-2016*, Canadian Media Directors' Council, Toronto.

36. Evelyn M. Rusli and Amir Efrati, "Facebook on Collision Course with Google on Web Searches," *Wall Street Journal*, January 16, 2013, pp. A1, A10.

37. Evelyn M. Rusli, "Buy Signal: Facebook Widens Data Targeting," *Wall Street Journal*, April 10, 2013, p. B4; and Hayley Tsukayama, "Facebook's Big Reveal: Social Search," *Star Tribune*, January 16, 2013, p. D6.

38. Jessi Hempel, "Smartphones: The War to Be No. 3," *Fortune*, February 4, 2013, pp. 35–36.

39. Juhana Rossi, "Angry Birds' Maker Perches for Global Growth Takeoff," *Wall Street Journal*, April 4, 2013, p. B4; Spencer E. Ante, "Rovio Mines Video with 'Angry Birds Toons,'" *Wall Street Journal*, March 12, 2013, p. B6; and John Gaudiosi, "Rovio Execs Explain What Angry Birds Toons Channel Opens Up to Its 1.7 Billion Gamers," *Forbes*, March 13, 2013. See **http://www. forbes.com/sites/ johngaudiosi/2013/03/11/rovio-execs-explain-what-angry-birdstoons-channelopens-up-to-its-1-7-billion-gamers**.

40. Andreas M. Kaplan, "If You Love Something, Let It Go Mobile: Mobile Marketing and Mobile Social Media 4x4," *Business Horizons* 55, no. 2 (2012), pp. 129–39.

41. Elizabeth Dwoskin, "Give Me Back My Privacy," *Wall Street Journal*, March 24, 2014, pp. R1–2; Georgia Wells, "Real-Time Marketing in a Real-Time World," *Wall Street Journal*, March 24, 2014, p. R3; and Elizabeth Dwoskin, "What Your Phone Is Sharing about Your Secrets," *Wall Street Journal*, January 14, 2014, pp. B1, 4.

42. Christian Arno, "Using Social Media for International Marketing Campaigns," SwissMadeMarketing, Jan 31, 2013, **http://swissmademarketing.com/social-media-international-marketing-campaigns/**; and Andres Wittermann, "The global social media challenge: a social marketer's guide to managing brands across borders," **http://www.ipra.org/itl/04/2013/the-global-social-media-challenge-a-social-marketer-s-guide-to-managing-brands-across-borders**.

NAME INDEX

A

Abrams, Rhonda M., 55
Adashynski, Aina, 56
Adkins-Green, Sheryl, 189, 191, 192
Allen, Alisa, 347, 348
Allen, Chelsea, 25
Armstrong, Lance, 158
Ash, Mary Kay, 189
Auchinleck, Geoffrey, 252

B

Beckham, David, 314
Bell, Glen, 439
Bennett, Craig, 208
Bennett, Laura, 263
Berthon, Pierre, 184
Beyers, Nico, 24
Bezos, Jeff, 386–388
Bieber, Justin, 542
Bigsby, Terry, 252
Block, Terry, 442
Bodden, Jim, 34
Boyle, Brady, 491
Briggs, Nicki, 23
Brin, Sergey, 469, 470
Bullock, August, 125
Burdett, Dan, 542
Burke, Richard, 158

C

Callaway, Vivian Milroy, 500, 523, 528–530
Capossela, Alison, 497–498
Cherry, Don, 447
Chesky, Brian, 295
Christensen, Clayton, 505
Clark, Dave, 388
Cohen, Ben, 26
Cook, Tim, 35, 37
Coopersmith, Ryan, 455
Coughlin, Natalie, 263
Crosby, Sidney, 129, 447, 449f

D

Dell, Michael, 162
Deming, W. Edwards, 39
Desai, Tina, 532
Dirksing, Peter, 264, 265
Dogan, Mustafa, 21
Donovan, Landon, 314
dos Santos, Giovani, 316

E

Eaman, Marc, 409
Eisenhower, Dwight D., 514

F

Felice, Steve, 162
Fisher, Kelsey, 552–553
Fleming, Anne, 117
Fontaine, Réjean, 252
Ford, Henry, 10, 221
Fox, Michael J., 447
Friedman, Milton, 105
From, Kathryn, 255
Fry, Art, 518

G

Gadhafi, Moammar, 102
Gantt, Henry L., 519
Gates, Bill, 10
Gebbia, Joe, 295
Gerard, Steven, 316

Gerst, Jeff, 216, 217
Gilchriest, Ben, 409
Glassel, Linda, 239, 240, 242
Glover, Richard, 95
Goertz, Andrea, 96
Gordon, Jeff, 544
Green, Kerry, 252
Greenfield, Jerry, 26
Greiner, Helen, 251
Grove, Andy, 514
Gyles, Geoff, 252

H

Haas, Edward, III, 285
Haenlein, Michael, 534
Hamilton, Laird, 263
Harrison, Kim, 465–466
Hartline, Jana, 111
Hartzell, Dane, 216
Heath, John, 23
Herle, David, 459
Herring, Tyler, 240
Hochman, Kevin, 291–294
Hodgdon, Kirk, 347, 348
Hogg, Bevill, 158
Holden, Richard, 469, 471
Hurd, Bo, 139

J

James, Lebron, 347
Jasper, Dan, 413, 414
Jeffries, Courtney, 256
Jobs, Steve, 10
Johnson, Kelly, 518–519
Jones, Cobi, 314
Joslyn, Mark, 159, 160

K

Kallayil, Gopi, 470
Kaplan, Andreas M., 534
Kaplan, Belinda, 56, 62
Katz, Jennifer, 552
Keane, Robbie, 316
Keith, Robert, 12, 13
Kennedy, John, 51
Kennedy, John F., 88
Kilbourne, Jean, 9
Klein, Chris, 314, 315, 317
Kydd, Arthur R., 54

L

Larocca, Tracee, 440
Lecomte, Roger, 252
Lee, Ian, 24, 25
Leighton, Michael, 159, 160
Leppanen, Casey, 315, 316
Leroux, Monique, 108
Levitt, Theodore, 31
Lirtsman, Alex, 442
Lletget, Sebastian, 316

M

Macko, Dean, 207
Marini, Michael, 1–3
Martineau, Pierre, 403
Mason, Andrew, 137, 138, 140
Matson, Holly, 217
McCarthy, E. Jerome, 9
McKenzie, Barney, 60
McMath, Robert M., 8
McRae, Matt, 319
Metayer, Estelle, 436
Mickelson, Phil, 358
Milk, Chris, 443

Mills, Jessica, 391
Monfils, Gael, 242
Mossler, Julie, 138, 140
Mukherjee, Ann, 208

N

Nagarajan, Gina, 191
Nagel, Linda J., 459
Nevares, Lori, 316
Nickerson, Mary, 113
Niczowski, Susan, 252

O

O'Brien, Kyle, 22

P

Page, Larry, 469, 470
Palmisano, Sam, 51, 52
Pease, Heather, 316
Perdue, Stephanie, 439
Perlman, David, 139
Phelps, Michael, 263
Pitt, Leyland, 184
Plangger, Kirk, 184
Poetsch, Rob, 440
Pohl, Mike, 413
Porter, Michael, 166–167, 167f,
    508–509, 508f
Power, Vincent, 423, 424
Pressel, Morgan, 358
Psy, 542

Q

Quine, Brendan, 243
Quist, Amber, 45

R

Reiss, Dani, 509–510
Renslow, Jill, 412–414
Roberts, Caroline, 244
Rogers, Richard, 189
Rometty, Virginia, 51
Rubin, Ann, 50, 52

S

Sandberg, Sheryl, 538
Sanger, Steve, 514
Schmidt, Sarah, 414
Schnatter, John, 518
Shapiro, Daniel, 184
Sharapova, Maria, 242
Shasteen, Rhonda, 190
Shatner, William, 447
Shepherd, Connie, 56
Shepherd, John, 56
Skally, Nick, 240, 242
Smith, Lindsey, 473–474
Solheim, Jostein, 27
Sparrow, Ben, 252
Stephens, Robert, 91–93
Stevenson, Robert Louis, 475
Stuart, Ian, 311
Swanson, Dana, 265, 266
Swift, Taylor, 542

T

Thomas, Carl, 263, 264
Thomas, Dave, 202
Tick, Sam, 509
Toyoda, Kiichiro, 111
Travis, Debbie, 423–424
Tripathy, Sudipta, 553

Trudeau, Justin, 5
Turner, Neil, 297
Twain, Mark, 209

U
Ulukaya, Hamdi, 21–23

V
Vallaeys, Frederick, 471
Van Bever, Derek, 505

W
Wang, William, 318
Warren, Kevin, 498
Welch, Jack, 517
Westerlund, Jane, 350, 353, 355, 356, 357
Wilkinson, Catherine, 56, 62
Woelbing, Alfred, 346, 347
Woelbing, Don, 346
Woelbing, Eric, 347
Woelbing, Paul, 346, 347, 348
Wolfman, Ian, 292

Z
Zoshi, Joshua, 252
Zuckerberg, Mark, 72, 73, 538, 539, 540

COMPANY/PRODUCT INDEX

A

Abbott Laboratories, 154
ABC, 317
ABC Canada Literacy Foundation, 465
ABC Life Literacy Canada, 5, 5f
AbeBooks, 34
ABI Inform/Proquest, 199f
AC Nielsen Canada, 199f
ACES Flight Simulation, 413
Accutron, 281
Ace Hardware, 392
Acuvue, 511
Acuvue Oasis, 511
adidas Group, 105, 281, 394f
Adobe Smart Bag, 409
adverCar, 297
Advertising Age, 199f, 469
Advertising Standards Canada
    (ASC), 459
Advertising Standards Council, 88
Aeroplan, 462
Aflac, 538
Agentrics, 154
AIM Trimark, 454
Air Canada, 5, 78f, 144, 227, 297, 297,
    323, 332, 462, 476
Air Team Maria 19, 241f
Airbnb, 295–297
Airbus Industrie, 143, 171
AirO Lightning MP, 241f
AirO Maria Lite OS, 241f
AirO Team Maria 23, 241f
Alaska Airlines, 317
Alcan Aluminum, 182, 323
Alcoa, 323
Alfred Sung, 336
Allied Lyons, 178
Allstate, 298
Amazing Mirror Maze, 414
Amazon Creative Expressions, 408
Amazon Fire, 331, 387
Amazon Fresh, 389
Amazon Kindle, 31, 37, 248, 249, 387
Amazon LivingSocial, 138, 398
Amazon Prime Air, 408
Amazon.ca, 364, 365f, 398
Amazon.com, 14, 83, 266, 281, 318, 331,
    386–389, 407, 408, 436
American Demographics, 199f
American Express, 283, 298, 307, 339
American Express Gold Card, 123
American Girl, 413
American Marketing Association (AMA), 3, 4,
    29, 102, 102f
America's Got Talent, 417
Ameritrade, 512
Anacin, 281
Andrés Wines, 181
Android, 256, 452, 547
Android TV, 310

Angry Birds, 547
Ann Taylor, 224, 406
Anne Klein Couture, 166
AOL Shop@AOL, 387
App Store, 547
Apple Computer, 250
Apple II, 247, 248
Apple, Inc., 6, 9, 14, 31, 35, 36, 36f, 37, 118, 119, 132,
    183, 223, 229, 245, 247, 248, 250, 255, 278, 279,
    280, 281, 294, 322, 370, 413, 463, 547
Apple Industrial Design Group, 255
Apple iOS, 547
Apple Pay, 83, 533
Apple Stores, 403–404
Apple Watch, 36, 37, 255, 407
Arctic Power, 225
Ariba, 153
Ariel, 251
Aritzia, 402
Arm & Hammer, 282, 283
Art Institute, 92
Asana, 24
Aspenware, 252
AT&T, 175, 310
Audobon, 113
Automatic Merchandiser, 63
autoTRADER.ca, 364, 365f, 446f
Avis, 233
Avis Budget Group, 297
Avon Products, Inc., 106, 172, 398, 476
A&W, 283, 446
Awl & Sundry, 408

B

Baked Lay's, 271
Baked Tostitos, 338
Banana Republic, 224, 413
Bank of Montreal (BMO), 14, 102,
    299, 465
BankNorth, 511
Barbie, 283
Baskin-Robbins, 178
Bass Pro Shops Outdoor World, 401, 402
Bass Shoe Outlet, 401
Bath & Body Works, 283
Bauer, 278
The Bay. *See* Hudson's Bay Company
Bayer Corporation, 127, 445
BBM Canada, 205
BCAA Life Insurance, 447
BCBG Max Azri Outlet, 402
Bean Around the World, 60, 61
The Beanery Coffee House, 67
bebe, 387
Bebo, 239
Behold, 382
Bell Canada Enterprises (BCE), 14, 102, 281,
    283, 297, 448, 476, 540
Bell Mobility, 226
Bell's Burgers, 439

Ben & Jerry's, 26–27, 43, 44, 44f
Ben & Jerry's Canada, 27
Ben & Jerry's Scoop Shops, 43
Benetton, 173, 406
Benjamin Moore, 381
Best Buy, 92–94, 148, 154, 318, 361,
    396, 404
Better Business Bureau (BBB), 88
Better Cotton Initiative, 105
Betty Crocker, 236, 529
Betty Crocker Dessert Bowl, 529–530
Betty Crocker Warm Delights, 528–530
B.F. Goodrich, 146
Bic, 280, 281
Bing, 454, 471
Birks, 124, 399, 400, 400f
BJ's Wholesale Club, 318, 401
Black & Decker, 170, 184, 283, 284, 487, 503, 517
Blackberry, 452, 493
Black's Photography, 394
Blenz Coffee, 61
Bleu Blanc Rouge, 458
Blistex, 347, 348
Blogger, 535f
BloodTrak® Blood Transfusion Management
    System, 252
Bloomspot, 138
Blue Book of Canadian Business, 199f
Bluenotes, 402
Bluetooth, 533
BMW, 112, 134, 259, 398
Boeing, 145, 153, 171, 236, 323
Boeing 737, 146, 323
Boeing 777, 146
Boeing 787, 146
Boise Cascade, 367
Bold, 281
Bolin Digital, 216
Bolin Marketing, 216, 217, 347
Bombardier, 106, 144, 146, 165, 174
Bombardier Aerospace, 143
Bombardier ECO4, 106
Bontrager, 159
Borden, Inc., 336–337
Bose, 278
Boston Consulting Group (BCG), 34,
    36f, 516
Boston Pizza International, 297
BrandSpark International, 79
Bratz, 283
Bravado! Designs, 255
Brawny, 277
Breyers, 205
The Brick, 79, 268
Brickmania, 413
Bristol-Myers, 511
British Airways, 119
Brooks Brothers Outlet Store, 401
Bruno Magli, 166
Buckley Mixture, 181

Budweiser Light, 126
Buffalo Wild Wings, 317
Buick, 120
Bulk Barn, 395
Burger King, 123, 232
Burt's Bees, 348
Business Week, 199f
BuyWithMe, 138
Buzzfeed, 540
BW, 458
By Terry, 224

C

Cabbage Patch Snacktime Kids, 100
Cadbury Schweppes, 176
Cadillac, 124, 288, 372
Cadillac/Chevrolet, 375f
Café Card, 38
Caffe Artigiano, 61
Calgary Stampede, 465
Call of Duty, 535f
Callaway Golf, 358–359
Camay, 283
Campbell Soup Company, 106, 121, 154, 275,
    278, 282, 286, 383
Campus Living Centres, 141–142
Canada Goose Inc., 278, 509–510
Canada Life, 297
Canada Post, 297
Canada Tsuga, 428
canada411.ca, 453
Canadian Advertising Foundation, 88
Canadian Blood Services
    (Sociète Canadienne du Sang), 306f
Canadian Breast Cancer Foundation, 465
Canadian Broadcasting Association, 88
Canadian Broadcasting Corporation (CBC), 5, 124, 143
Canadian Business, 199f
Canadian Cancer Society, 6, 465
Canadian Code of Advertising
    Standards, 459
Canadian Coffee Drinking Study, 62
Canadian Diabetes Association, 398
Canadian Direct Marketing
    Association, 434
Canadian Forces, 200
Canadian Franchise Association, 297, 393
Canadian Geographic, 129
Canadian Health and Lifestyle, 129
Canadian Intellectual Property Office, 282
Canadian Interuniversity Sports
    (CIS), 465
*Canadian Journal of Marketing
    Research*, 199f
Canadian Living, 420, 452
Canadian Manufacturers & Exporters (CME-MEC), 143
Canadian Manufacturing Coalition, 143
Canadian Marketing Association (CMA), 88, 102, 102f,
    130, 277–278, 398, 434, 436, 479
Canadian Media Optimization
    (CMOST), 454
Canadian Museum of Civilization, 5
Canadian National Railway, 106
Canadian Online Shopping Mall, 397

Canadian Outlook Long-Term Economic Forecast, 81
Canadian Pacific, 143
Canadian Radio-television and Telecommunication
    Commission (CRTC), 88, 479
Canadian Red Cross, 5, 30, 33
Canadian Standards Association
    (CSA), 125
Canadian Tire Corporation, Limited, 5, 13, 13f, 30, 32,
    34, 143, 268, 340, 392, 398, 410, 424, 454, 462,
    465, 511, 515, 547
Canadian Tire Money, 462
Canadian Tourism Commission
    (CTC), 220
Canadian Trade Index, 199f
Canadian Turkey Marketing Agency,
    274, 275
Canadian Women's Foundation, 465
Candy Crush Saga, 547
Cangive.ca, 398
Canoe.ca, 454
Canon, 332
CanWest Global TV System, 278
Capgemini, 409
The Caplow Company, 350–357
Captain Morgan Tall Ships, 465
Cargill, 143
Carleton University, 24
Carma Laboratories, Inc., 346–349, 540
CarMax, 337
Carmex, 216–219, 346–349, 540
Carrefour, 392, 395
Carter's, 268
Cartier, 331
car2go, 46
CASSIE Awards, 446
Catalyst Accord, 96
Caterpillar, Inc., 147, 172, 181, 364,
    383, 522
CBC Television, 124, 451, 536
Celestial Seasonings, 286, 287
Center for Learning and Experimentation
    (General Mills), 500
Centraide/United Way, 515
Centrum, 80, 268
Centrum Select, 225
Century 21, 360
Cerdelga, 105
Cereal Partners Worldwide, 171
Chanel, 173, 186, 331
Chapel of Love, 414
Chaps, 280
ChapStick, 347, 348
Chapters, 62
Chapters-Indigo, 360, 398, 462
Cheerios, 250, 305, 504, 505
Cheerios + Ancient Grains, 504, 505
Cheerios Snack Mix, 125
Cheese Nips, 286
Cheetos, 208
Chevrolet (Chevy), 17, 317, 340
Chevron, 534
Chex, 502
Chips Ahoy!, 287
Chobani Bite, 23
Chobani Champions, 23

Chobani Culture, 23
Chobani Flip, 23
Chobani Greek Yogurt, 21, 22, 23
Chobani, Inc., 21–25
Chobani SoHo, 24
Chocolate Fudge Brownie, 44
Christian Dior, 166, 166f, 336
Christie's, 173
Christmas Wish Book, 14
Chrysler LLC, 81
Church & Dwight, 282
CIBC, 465
Cineplex Odeon, 297
Citigroup, 534
City of Calgary, 96
City of Hamilton, 1–3, 11, 11f
City of Surrey, 61, 62, 64
City of Vancouver, 57, 61
CityDeal, 139
CITY-TV, 451
Clairol Haircolouring, 125
Clash of Clans, 547
classifiedextra.ca, 454
Cling-Free, 281
Clinique, 225
Cloverleaf, 286
Club Med, 435, 452
CMT, 452
CNN, 249
Coastal Forest and Lumber
    Association, 428
Coca-Cola Canada, 325, 396, 432
Coca-Cola Company, 106, 119, 171, 172, 173, 175, 177,
    178, 183, 205, 250, 271, 278, 281, 286, 287, 361,
    392, 396, 485, 507
Coccolino, 172
Coffee Break Coffee House, 56–71
Cogeco, 297
Coke, 177, 185, 271, 396
Colgate, 127, 171
Colgate-Palmolive Company, 126f, 127, 171, 225
Colgate Total, 126f, 127
Commerce Bank, 511
Compass Group, 61
Competia, 436
Competition Bureau, 86, 341, 342, 373
Competition Tribunal, 86, 343
ComputerWorld, 4, 5
ConAgra, 140
Confederation Bridge, 319
Conference Board of Canada, 2, 33,
    81, 199f
Consumer Electronics Association, 92
Consumer Reports, 118, 151f
Consumers Association of Canada (CAC), 88
Cool Ranch Doritos Locos Tacos, 416–417
Coors Light, 287
Coppertone, 268
Corning, Inc., 149
Corona Extra, 130
Corporate Knights, 107, 109
Cosmair, 280
Cossette Communications, 297, 433, 458, 502f, 503
CoTweet, 550

Couchsurfing.com, 296
Courtyard, 283
Cover Girl, 273
Cracker Jack, 336–337
Craftsman, 288, 332
Craisins, 274
Crave, 451
Cray, Inc., 245
Crest, 6, 127, 372
Crest Neat Squeeze, 255
Croma, 162
Crowdsaver, 140
Crunch 'n Munch, 336–337
CTV, 124, 451
Customer Service Institute of Canada, 15
Cyanamid Canada Inc., 225

D

Daimler AG, 164
Dairy Farmers of Canada (DFC),
    195, 445
Dairy Foods, 63
Dancing with the Stars, 417
Dannon, 23
Danone, 24, 268
Darberry, 139
Dave Matthews Band, 44
DDB, 457
DeBeers, 173
Deere & Company, 147
Deerfoot Meadows, 402
Del Monte, 284
Deli Creations, 207
Dell.ca, 364, 365, 365f
Dell Computer, 83, 93, 154, 162, 181, 255, 364, 365f,
    376, 377, 477, 549
Dempster's Bread, 129
Department of Consumer and Corporate Affairs, 88
Designer Depot, 402
Desjardins Group, 107–108
DeWalt, 283, 284
DHL, 379
Dial, 284, 444
Dialog, 199f
Diamant, 158
Dick's Sporting Goods, 358
DieHard, 281
Diet Mountain Dew, 445
Diet Pepsi, 458, 458f
Digital Advertising Alliance of Canada (DAAC), 459
Dior. *See* Christian Dior
Disney, 14, 31, 278, 280, 283, 310,
    452, 511
Disney Cruise Line, 511
Disneyland, 511
Diver Entertainment, 263
Dodge Viper, 322
Dofasco, 503
Dog World, 424
DogVacay, 296
Dollar, 233
Dollar General, 401
Dollar Tree, 401
Dollarama, 332, 337

Domino's, 280, 326
Donna Karan, 124
Doritos, 277, 283, 338, 455
DoritosGuru.ca, 455
DoubleClick, 471
Dove, 14, 268
Dove Cream Oil, 14
Dow Jones Sustainability North America Index, 96
Downy, 244
Dr. Pepper, 278, 463
Dream Bikes, 160
Dropbox, 338
Dun & Bradstreet, 199f, 353
Duncan Hines, 236
Dunkin' Donuts, 61
DuPont, 476
DuPont Canada, 143
Duracell, 278, 281

E

Earthcycle Packaging, 81
Eastern Mountain Sports, 266
Eastman Chemical Company, 491
Eastman Kodak. *See* Kodak
Easy Off, 281
EasyTech, 93
eBay, Inc., 83, 153, 154, 249, 279, 323, 397, 407
eBayBusiness, 153, 154
ECOLOGO, 108, 108f
Economic Developers Association of Canada, 2
Eddie Bauer, 365
Edelman Public Relations, 297
Edmonton Symphony Orchestra, 33
Edo Japan, 81
EDS, 493
Ektelon, 240
Electric Drive Transportation
    Association, 113
Electronic Data Systems, 147
Eli Lilly, 377
Elizabeth Arden, 284
Empire Company, 391, 392
Empire.Kred, 436
Encana Corporation, 95
Encyclopedia Brittanica, 516
Endust, 382
ENMAX Corporation, 96
Entrepreneur, 393
Environics Analytics Group Ltd.,
    127, 133
Environmental Media Association, 113
Epoch Times, 134
Ericsson, 171
Ericsson Canada, 5
Ernst & Young, 21, 182, 298
ESPN, 310, 317, 425
Esquires Coffee, 61
Essex, 139
Esso, 80, 361
E*TRADE, 297
Euphrates, 21
Eveready, 281
Excedrin, 281

EXO³, 240
EXO³ Ignite 95, 241f
EXO³ Red 95, 241f
Extra Strength Bayer Plus Aspirin, 127
Exxon, 281
EZ Squirt Ketchup, 248, 249
eZone, 162,

F

F-117 Stealth Fighter, 519
F-35 Lightning II Joint Strike
    Fighter, 519f
Facebook, 16, 23, 27, 39, 72–73, 75f, 89, 100, 138, 140,
    184, 212, 216–219, 227, 228, 239, 242, 281, 293,
    296, 297, 306–308, 316, 390, 398, 416, 417, 424,
    425, 428, 434, 435, 436, 440, 442, 445, 446, 455,
    460, 463, 465, 493, 510, 532, 534, 535f, 536–541,
    537f, 539f, 543–547,
    549, 554
Facebook Deals, 138
Facebook Pages, 538, 544, 545, 549
Facebook Messenger, 532, 540
Fairfield Inns, 256, 283
Fairmont Hotels & Resort, 298
Family Dollar, 401
Famous Kids, 452
FarmTrade.com, 153
FarmVille, 547
Febreze, 284
Federal Aviation Administration, 389, 408
Federal Express (FedEx), 15, 145, 249, 297,
    361, 379, 380
Federated Co-Operatives, 143
Fédération des producteurs de lait du Québec, 38, 38f
Federation Internationale de Football Association
    (FIFA), 314
FedEx Office, 249, 397
FedEx Supply Chain Services, 379
Fence Industry, 424
FGL Sports Ltd., 511
Fibre 1, 502
Fiddle Faddle, 336
Financial Post 500, 377
Financial Post's Canadian
    Demographics, 199f
Fingos, 250
First Choice Haircutters, 297, 307, 392
Fitbit, 36
Fitness, 266
Flava, 283
Flickr, 316, 535f
Flight Centre, 503
Florsheim, 394f
Fodor's, 421, 422
Folgers, 286
Food Banks Canada, 106
Food Network Canada, 452
Forbes, 50, 137, 199f, 295
Ford Celebrity Face-off for Charity, 465
Ford Motor Company, 93, 114, 152, 171, 182, 221, 223,
    246, 363, 375f, 392, 431, 476
Ford Motor Company of Canada, 448
Ford Mustang, 281
Ford Thunderbird, 223, 281
Forrester, 407

Fortune, 199f, 503
Fortune Brands, 245
Fortune 1000, 377
4-H Clubs of Canada, 5
4Pics1Word, 547
Four Seasons, 82, 297, 435
Foursquare, 23, 316
Fox, 317
Fox News, 266, 310
Fraser Institute, 33
Fraser's Canadian Trade Directory, 199f
Freestyle, 396
Fresh Express, 256
Fresh Step Crystals, 125
Frigidaire, 394f
Frito-Lay, 77, 208, 257, 271, 277, 283, 286,
  336, 338, 477, 487, 534
Frosty, 229
Fruit Ninja, 547
Fruitopia, 205
Fuji Photo, 169
Fuller Brush Company, 368, 398

G

Game of Thrones, 443
Games by James, 413
Gandalf Group, 459
Ganong Brothers, 182
The Gap, 137, 224, 406
Gap Factory Store, 401
Gardening Life, 452
Gary Fisher, 159
Gatorade, 129, 269, 278, 279, 280, 447
GE Healthcare, 473–474
GE Medical Systems, 154
Geek Squad, 91–93
Genentech, 113
General Electric (GE), 12, 13, 29, 106, 119, 153, 225,
  254, 281, 282, 323, 365, 394f, 476, 517, 518f
General Mills, 12, 171, 200, 250, 273, 366, 500–502,
  504–505, 507, 514, 523, 524f, 528–530
General Mills Cheerios Snack Mix, 125
General Motors (GM), 221, 280, 297, 335, 363, 372,
  375f, 431, 452, 454, 490
General Motors of Canada, 5, 430, 448
Genzyme, 105, 322
GeorgiaPacific, 277
Gerber, 183, 282, 325
Getaround, 296
GHX Canada, 154
Gigante, 171
Gillette, 172, 178, 183, 184, 206, 268, 274, 275, 371, 511
Gillette Body, 275
Gillette Fusion, 268, 270, 272
Gilt, 139
Gilt.com, 397, 445
Ginch Gonch, 234
Girl Guides of Canada, 5
Glass Plus, 281
GlaxoSmithKline, 377
Global Healthcare Exchange, 154
Global News, 134
Global TV, 278, 451
The Globe and Mail, 450, 453

*The Globe and Mail Report of
  Business*, 199f
Gmail, 532
Godiva Chocolates, 493
Golden Beauty, 184
Golf Canada, 452
Golf Galaxy, Inc., 358
Golf Town, 358
Good Housekeeping, 125, 286
GoodLife Fitness, 462
Goodyear, 367
Google, 73, 83, 184, 198, 212, 250, 258, 280, 281, 408,
  435, 436, 454, 463, 469–472, 503, 542, 547, 548
Google+, 16, 316, 532, 535f, 547
Google AdSense, 471–472
Google AdWords, 471
Google Display Ad Builder, 472
Google Glass, 407
Google Lab, 23
Google Maps, 532
Google Nexus, 310
Google Offers, 138, 398
Google Play, 532
Google PageRank, 470
Google Search, 532
Government of Canada, 434, 448
Graph Search, 547
GrassRoots Café, 62, 67
Great Canadian Gaming Corporation, 297
Great Lawns Corporation, 512–513, 513f
Great Little Box Company, 32
Great Pizza, 62
Greater Toronto Area, 3
GREE, 184
Grey Cup, 130
Grey Jungle Media, 458
Grey Poupon, 207
Greyston Bakery, 44
Groupon, 80, 137–140, 398, 460, 503
Groupon Now, 138, 14
Groupon Stores, 138
Grumman Aircraft, 152
Guardian Drugs, 392
Gucci, 124, 173, 370, 475
Gulberg Restaurant, 62
Gulfstream, 425, 426

H

HaagenDazs, 277
Haggar Clothing Co., 132
Hallmark Cards, 78, 365
Hamburger Helper, 200
Hampton Hotels, 393f
Happy Cheeks, 256
Harkman Electric, 364
Harley-Davidson, 130, 147, 182, 183, 274, 278, 279
Harley Owners Group (HOG), 130
Harris Corporation, 483
Harry Rosen, 123
Harvard Business Review, 199f
Hautelook.com, 397
Hawaiian Punch, 273, 275, 276
HBC.com, 80

HBO, 452
Head & Shoulders, 511
Health Canada, 6, 322, 444
Healthy Choice, 140
Heart and Stroke Foundation of
  Canada, 465
Heart and Stroke Foundation of Nova Scotia, 6
Heartland, 463
Heinz, 248, 249, 268, 286, 332, 425, 426
Heinz Canada, 39, 274, 428
Helena Rubinstein, 184
Henredon, 280
Herbalife, 317
Heritage Canada, 515
Hershey, 335
Hertz, 233, 302–303, 302f
Hewlett-Packard (HP), 147, 178, 259, 273,
  361, 377, 493, 534
HGTV, 452
Hi5, 239
Hilton, 310
Hindustan Lever, 178
Hitachi, 166, 172
H.J. Heinz, 106, 323
H&M, 106
Holiday Inn, 80, 283, 399
Holiday Inn Express, 80
Holiday Inn Worldwide, 80
Holt Renfrew, 336, 393
Home Depot, 147, 297, 372, 401, 408,
  410, 435, 446, 487, 502
Home Shopping Network, 397
HomeMadeSimple.com, 284
Homestyle Pop Secret, 200
Honda, 114, 178, 259, 283
Honda Accord, 223
Honeywell Inc., 143, 476, 485
Hoover's, 199f
Hot Pockets, 8
Hot Pockets Pizza Snacks, 8
Hot Pockets Snackers, 8
Hotel Association of Canada, 80
Hôtel de Glace, 311
House of Comedy, 413
HP, 245, 383
H&R Block, 368
HTC, 118, 442
H_2O Audio, 263–265
Hudson's Bay Company (HBC), 80, 268, 277, 336, 363,
  391, 392, 399, 400f, 402, 434, 448
Huffington Post, 3, 535f
Huggies, 171
Hulu, 296
Hyundai Motors, 182, 207, 288

I

IAd Network, 294
IBM, 50–52, 101, 147, 176, 181, 281,
  363, 382, 383, 476, 478
IBM Canada, 6, 32, 300, 444, 476,
  482, 491
IBM Global Services, 489
Ideale, 184

IDEO, 255, 256
IGA, 308
IKEA, 79, 173, 396–397, 402, 442, 508, 509
IKEA Canada, 410
Imc2, 291
Immunize Canada, 445f
In-Tenta Drop Eco-Hotel, 311
Inc., 263
Inco, 143
Incredible Dog Challenge, 425
Indochino, 390
Industry Canada, 33, 86, 147, 247, 278, 281, 282, 297
Inniskillin Wines of Ontario, 165
Innovation, Science and Economic Development Canada, 33, 199f
Instagram, 23, 316, 390, 440, 532, 535f, 540
Institute of Communication Agencies (ICA), 446
Intel, 148, 172, 273, 281, 514
Interac Flash, 396
Interactive Advertising Bureau (lAB) of Canada, 199f, 454, 456
Interbrand, 36, 280–281, 306
Intercon Security, 297
International Olympic Committee, 292
International Standards Organization (ISO), 106, 147, 310
iPad, 9, 31, 37, 248, 255, 270, 322, 397, 452, 463
iPhone, 37, 118, 119, 248, 250, 255, 256, 264, 294, 322, 452, 547
iPod, 37, 250, 263, 264, 281, 294
Ipsos Canada, 205, 257
IPTV, 75f
iRewards, 462
iRobot, 251
Irving Oil, 324, 328, 367

J
J. Walter Thompson, 457
Jaguar, 223, 398
Janssen-Ortho, 503
Java Hut, 61
Jawbone, 36
JC Penney, 547
J.D. Power and Associates, 319
Jefferson Smurfit Corporation, 476
Jeopardy!, 51
Jiffy Lube, 370
Jimmy John's Sandwiches, 393f
Joffrey Ballet, 137
John Deere, 147
Johnson & Johnson (J&J), 29, 119, 132, 154, 276, 283, 323, 507, 511
Jolly Joes, 287
Journal of Advertising, 199f
Journal of Consumer Research, 199f
Journal of Marketing, 199f
Journal of Marketing Research, 199f
Journal of Retailing, 199f
Joy, 281
Juniper Networks, Inc., 171
Just Born Inc., 287

JVC, 166

K
Kanebo, 372
Kelloggs, 132, 507
Kelloggs Canada, 146
Kensington Florist, 368
Keurig, 74
KFC, 62, 419, 440
Kia Motors, 125
Kickstarter.com, 256
Kidney Foundation of Canada, 447
Kijiji, 454
Kimberly-Clark, 14, 171
Kirby, 481
Kirin, 372
Kirovsky Zvod, 181
Kit and Ace, 390
Kit Kat, 176
Kiwi Brands, 382
Klein, 159
Kleenex, 14, 279, 280, 287
Klondike, 421
Kmart, 130
Kodak, 169, 251, 361, 487
Komatsu, 172
Kraft Canada, 147, 323, 476, 520
Kraft Crystal Light Liquid, 445
Kraft Foods, 21, 206, 268, 287, 366
Kraft Miracle Whip, 286
Kroger, 347
Kuschelweich, 172
Kwantlen Chronicle, 68
Kwantlen Polytechnic University, 56–58, 60–65, 67–68
Kwantlen Student Association (KSA), 62

L
LA Galaxy, 314–317
La Senza, 394
Labatt, 325
LabPET, 252
Lacoste, 387
Land Rover, 223
Lavalife, 445
Lawrence Livermore National Laboratory, 147
Lay's Potato Chips, 77, 277, 360
Lay's Stax, 286
Leading Brands, 234
Leaky Bucket Report, 61
LeBronJames.com, 540
The Legaspi Company, 408
LEGO, 172, 413
Lenovo, 124
Leo Burnett Co., 291
Les Chics, 127
Let Her Jump, 292–293
LevelUp, 138
Lever, 178
Lever Europe, 172
Levi Strauss, 107, 173, 183, 360, 444f
LexisNexis, 199f

Lexus, 14, 82
Lexus RX 450, 258
LG, 118
Lids, 394
Life, 80, 283
LifeScan Canada, 80
Lincoln/Mercury, 375f
Lindemans, 165
LinkedIn, 16, 184, 194, 227, 339, 465, 479, 493, 534, 535f, 536, 537f, 541, 543
Liquid Paper, 270
Listerine, 514
Little Fockers, 463
Little Mosque on the Prairie, 463
LiveJournal, 535f
Liz Claiborne, 107
L.L. Bean, 365, 397
Lloyds of London, 60
Loblaw Companies Ltd., 5, 24, 32, 106, 283, 333, 391, 392, 395, 402, 511
Lockheed Martin, 503, 518–519
LOFT, 224
London Stock Exchange, 60
Long John Silver, 440
L'Oréal, 172, 184, 406
Lord & Taylor, 391
Louis Vuitton, 278, 509
Lowe's, 148, 365, 408
Lululemon Athletica Inc., 34, 281, 503
Lunch at Tim's, 127, 128–129, 128f
Lung Association, 113
Luvs, 277
Luxottica Group, 280, 406
Lyft, 296, 338

M
MAB, 166
MAC Group, 399
Maclean's, 129, 132, 223, 420, 450, 452
MacMillan Bloedel, 145
Mac's Milk, 146, 360, 370
Macy's, 413
Made.com, 408
Major League Soccer, 314–317
Mall of America, 408, 412–414
Manchu Wok, 81
Mansar Products Ltd., 363
Manulife, 103
Maple Leaf Foods, 143
MapQuest, 493
March of Dimes Canada, 447
Marina Maher Communications, 291
Maritime Life Assurance Company, 32
Marketing Group, 359
Marketing Magazine, 199f, 300
Marketing News, 199f
Marketing Research and Intelligence Association (MRIA), 210–211, 212, 213
Marriott Corporation, 256
Marriott International, 283
Marriott Marquis, 283
Mars, 178, 363
Mars, Inc., 46, 223, 275

Mars Canada, 102
Martin's Crispy Apple Snacks, 462
Martin's Family Fruit Farm, 462
Mary Kay Cosmetics, 189, 398, 490
Mary Kay Inc., 189–192
Mary Kay India, 190–191
Mary Kay MelaCEP Whitening System, 191
Mary Kay Velocity, 125
Master Lock, 245
MasterCard International, 106, 174
Mastro Limpio, 172
Matsushita, 166, 372
Mattel, 100, 107, 172, 283, 452
Maybelline, 183
Maynards, 462
Maytag, 297
McCafé, 405
McCain Foods, 5, 38, 182, 183
McCowan Market, 395
McDonald's, 6, 62, 67, 106, 107f, 130, 172–173, 174, 181, 232, 281, 297, 298, 299, 306f, 368, 391, 392, 393, 399, 405, 406, 465, 476, 481
McDonald's Canada, 38, 430
McDonald's Extra Value Meal, 406
McKesson Corporation, 154
McMaharajah, 174
Mean Stinks, 292, 293–294
Medis Health, 143
Medtronic, Inc., 54, 325, 475f, 476
MEplusYOU, 291, 292
Mercedes-Benz, 112, 186, 398
Merck Frosst Canada, 476
MergeVR, 442
Merrill Lynch, 299, 480
MetLife.ca, 364
Metro Inc., 391
Metropolitan Life, 477
MGA Entertainment, 283
Michelin, 10, 123, 171, 277, 279
Microsoft Canada, 6, 102
Microsoft Corporation, 247, 250, 277, 278, 281, 372, 470, 471, 534
Microsoft Excel, 273, 330
Microsoft HoloLens, 442
Microsoft Office, 273
Microsoft PowerPoint, 273
Microsoft Project, 519
Microsoft Windows Vista, 250
Microsoft Windows XP, 250
Microsoft Word, 273
Microsoft Xbox, 247, 272
Mike and Ike Treats, 287
Mimosin, 172
MindMeld, 83
MINI USA, 176
Minister of International Affairs, 24
Mintel, 8
Minute Maid Squeeze-Fresh, 250
Miramax, 283
Mitsubishi Canada, 446
M&M Meat Shops, 462
M&Ms, 9, 223, 275, 339

Mobile TV, 310
Model T, 221
Moen Inc., 207, 245
Mohawk, 324
Molly Maid, 297
Molson, 268, 325, 428, 454
Molson Canadian, 287
Montgomery Ward, 138
Montreal Canadiens Children's Foundation, 465
Montreal Museum for Fine Arts, 33
Moore Chemical & Sanitation Supply, Inc. (Moore-Chem), 491–492
Moose Mountain Adventure Golf, 414
Moosehead, 165
Motel Bar, 137
Mothers Against Drunk Driving (MADD), 398
Motorola, 36
Motorola Networks, 172, 177, 322
Mountain Dew, 440, 443
Mountain Equipment Co-op, 107, 410
Mr. Clean, 172, 284
Mr. Greek, 81
Mr. Lube, 297, 308, 370
Mr. Proper, 172
MSN Money, 471
MSN News, 266
MuchMusic, 452
MySimon, 397
MySpace, 239

N
Nabisco, 132, 286, 366, 462
NASCAR, 443, 445
NASCAR SpeedPark, 402
National Basketball Association (NBA), 440
National Defence, 143
National Geographic, 540
Nature Valley Protein, 502
NBC, 317
NDP Group, 202
Neiman Marcus, 404
Nescafé, 184
Nestlé Canada, 103
Nestlé S.A., 54, 171, 173, 176, 184, 317, 365, 366, 396
Netflix, 83, 339, 434, 451
NEVAMASH, 181
New Balance, Inc., 275
New York Times, 540
Newton Computer, 250
Newton Town Centre, 62
Nexen, Inc., 101–102
NHL Junior Skills Competition, 465
Nickelodeon Universe, 413
Nielsen Media Research, 74, 205, 206, 454
Nielsen PRIZM, 127
Nike, 107, 173, 244, 275, 279, 280, 394f, 445
Nikon, 6, 246
Nintendo Wii U, 247, 272
Nippon Gakki, 372

Nissan Motor Company, 146–147, 178, 372
Nokia, 383
Nordstrom, 408, 413, 442
Nortel, 171
North Face, The, 419
Nova Scotia Tourism, 455
Novartis Consumer Health Canada, 181
Nuna Logistics, 381
Nuprin, 281

O
Obsession, 281
Ocean Park Pizza, 62
Ocean Spray, 197, 198, 274
Ocean Spray Cranberries, 286
Oculus Rift, 442
Oculus VR, 73
Off the Hook, 458
Office Depot, 93
Office Max, 206
Office of the Privacy Commissioner, 435
Olay, 77
Old Navy, 224
Old Spice, 294
Oliberté, 108
Olympics, 431, 445,465
Olympus, 186
One Sweet Whirled, 44
Oneida Factory Outlet, 401
Ontario Dairy Council, 24
Ontario Ministry of Agriculture, Food and Rural Affairs, 24
Ontario Power Generation, 297
OpenTable, 138, 139
Operation Bear Hug, 22
The Oprah Winfrey Show, 347
Oracle Corporation, 176
Oral-B, 83
Oral-B CrossAction, 206
Oreos, 286
Orkut, 239, 549
Oscar Mayer, 132, 207
Owl, 452

P
PACER's National Bullying Prevention Center, 294
Pacific Blue Cross, 447
PackBot, 251
Pampers, 171, 277, 372, 428
Panasonic, 361, 394f
Pandora, 296
Panera Bread, 333
Panera Cares Cafe, 333
Pantene, 274
Papa John's, 514, 518
Parking Panda, 296
Payless ShoeSource, 128, 400, 400f
PCjr, 281
Pebble, 36
Pebble Time, 256
Penske Logistics, 379

Pentium, 281
People, 132
Pepsi, 278, 317
Pepsi Ginger Cola, 248
Pepsi MAX, 544
PepsiCo Beverages Canada, 95
PepsiCo Canada, 248, 325, 428
PepsiCo, Inc., 23, 95, 127, 164, 171, 172, 178, 185, 208, 273, 277, 361, 543–544
Performance Tennis Racquets, 240
Pernod Ricard, 406
Perrier, 105, 105f
Pert, 176
Petco, 370
Petro-Canada, 283, 327, 465
PetsMart, 370
Pez Candy Inc., 285
Pfizer, 444
PGA Tour Superstores, 358
Pharmacy Times, 347
Piece Brewery & Pizzeria, 138
Pillsbury, 12–13, 236, 520f
Ping, 370
Pinterest, 23, 316, 535f, 543, 546
Pioneer, 166
Pizza Hut, 164, 440, 514
Pizza Hut Express, 283
Pizza Pizza, 145, 320
PlantBottle Packaging, 106
Planters, 366
PlasticsNet, 153
Playboy, 280
PlayStation 3, 247
PlayStation 4, 247
Polo, 280
Porsche, 283
Post Cereal, 121, 121f
Post-It Notes, 518
Potash Corp., 515
PowerBook, 281
Pratt & Whitney, 143
President's Choice, 283
Pret, 176
Prince Sports, Inc., 239–242
Princess Margaret Secondary School, 65
Pringles, 286
Print Measurement Bureau (PMB), 452
PRIZM, 127
PRIZM C2, 226f
PRIZM QC, 127, 133
PRIZM5, 127, 128–129, 128f, 133, 226
PRIZM5 QC, 133
Procter & Gamble (P&G), 101, 106, 132, 147–149, 171, 368, 372, 377, 402, 428, 430, 448, 487, 510, 511, 521
Profit Magazine, 199f
Progressive Grocer, 199f
Provigo, 153
PRS Group, 179
Prudential, 77
Publisher's Clearing House, 462
Purina Dog Chow, 424, 425, 425f

Q

Quaker Oats Company, 276
QualiData Research Inc., 207
Quality Institute, 147
Quattro, 227
Quebecor Media, 454
QuizUp, 547
QVC, 397
Qpod, 139

R

Radio Shack, 283, 325
Radisson Blu, 414
Ralph Lauren, 280, 372
Ralston Purina, 277
Raymond Weil, 247
RBC Financial Group, 281
RBC Insurance, 454
R.C. Purdy's Chocolates, 34
Reader's Digest, 223
Ready Set Rocket, 442
Red Baron, 326–327, 327f
Red Bull, 61, 281
Red Lobster, 38
Redbook, 132
Redbox, 538
Reddit, 535f
RedLaser, 323
Reebok, 107, 129, 275, 447
REI, 266
REI Co-op, 409
Reif Estate Winery, 181
RelayRides, 296
Renaissance Hotels, 283
Renren, 549
Rentoid, 296
Restaurants and Institutions, 61
Retail Council of Canada (RCC), 391, 392, 401, 406, 407
Rethink, 457
Revlon, 336, 452
Revolution, 207
RIM 950, 547
Ritz-Carlton, 311
Robin Hood, 268
Rockport, 280
Rogers Communications, 134, 281, 297, 300, 448
Rogers Wireless, 226
Rolex, 82, 331, 336, 370
Rolling Stone, 452
Rolls Royce, 173, 331
Rona Inc., 106, 489
Ronald McDonald House, 106
Roots Canada, 80
Rossimoda, 166
Royal Canadian Mint, 143, 519
Royal Doulton, 82
The Runner, 68
Runner's World, 452, 453f

S

Safeguard, 283
Safeway, 333, 367, 442
Saint Joseph's Hospital, 33
Saks Fifth Avenue, 391
Saks Inc., 370
Sales and Marketing Management, 199f
Saltworks Technologies, 34, 252
Salvation Army, 6
Sam's Club, 318, 376, 377, 401, 503
Samsung, 36, 37, 118, 119, 165, 281, 282, 322, 444f
Samsung Galaxy, 37, 442
Samsung Gear VR, 442
Sanford, 270
Santitas, 283
Sanyo, 166
SaveOurEnvironment.org, 44
Schick, 226, 371
Schwan's Food Company, 363
Schwartz, 392
Schweppes Tonic Water, 176
Schweppes Tonica, 176
Scion, 112
Scooba, 251
Scope, 514
Scotch-Brite, 175
Scotchgard, 103
Scotia iTRADE, 5, 364
Scotiabank, 78, 281, 297
Scott's Directories, 199f
Scoutmob, 138
Scripto, 288
Sea Life Minnesota Aquarium, 414
Sears, 14, 283, 288, 360, 397, 402, 413
Sears Canada, 14, 79, 323, 332, 336, 363, 365, 402, 410, 423–424, 448
Sears *Christmas Wish Book*, 14
Sears Home, 410
Second Cup, 38
Secret, 291–294
Secrete Clinical Strength, 291
Seiko, 172, 186
The Secret Sales Pitch, 125
Service Canada, 143
ServiceMaster, 297
Servpro, 393f
7-Eleven, 399
7UP, 281
Sharp, 166, 281
Shasta, 317
Shaw Communications, 32, 278, 540
Shaws, 444f
Shell Oil, 320
Shepherd Gift Foundation, 23
Sheraton, 298
Sherwin Williams, 280, 367, 381
Shian Naturals Health & Beauty Products, 234
Shishedo, 172, 372
Shomi, 451
Shoppers Drug Mart, 5, 14, 80, 268, 281, 283, 392, 511
Siemens, 152, 171
Simon Fraser University, 184
The Sims, 535
Singer, 267
SiriusXM, 332, 452

Skippy, 211, 323
Skippy Squeez'It, 286
Skunk Works. *See* Lockheed Martin
Skype, 442, 465
Small Business Canada Magazine, 199f
Smart Choice, 283
Smarter Planet, 50–52
SmartThings, 256
SMG, 291
Snake Light Flexible Flashlight, 184
Snapchat, 73, 390, 440
SNC-Lavalin, 102
Snickers, 130, 542
Snow Master, 124
Snow Pup, 124
Snuggle, 172
Sobeys Inc., 79, 80, 283, 333
Sodexo Canada, 61
Sony, 132, 166, 173, 178, 183, 247, 254,
    259, 272, 282, 361
Sony PlayStation, 442
Sony PlayStation 3, 247
Sony PlayStation 4, 247
Sony PlayStation Portable (PSP), 272
Sony Project Morpheus, 442
Sotheby's, 173
Source Perrier S.A., 105, 105f
SPCA, 68
Special Olympics, 106
Speedpass, 80
Sperry, 394f
Spic and Span, 287
Spin Master Toys, 503
Spinlister, 296
Sponsorship Marketing Council of Canada, 465
Sporting Goods Manufacturing Association, 240
Sports Chalet, 266
SR-71 Blackbird, 518
SRI Consulting Business Intelligence (SRIC-BI), 127
St. Croix Venture Partners, 55
St. Joseph Aspirin, 276
St. Joseph's Healthcare, 455
Stake Fastener Company, 364
Standards Council of Canada (SCC), 147
Staples, 14, 93, 153, 365, 408
Starbucks Canada, 391
Starbucks Coffee, 13, 13f, 14, 61–63, 67, 74,
    148, 366, 391, 405, 549
Starkist, 277
Statistics Canada, 76, 78, 80, 82,
    198, 199f
Storenvy, 398
Strategy Magazine, 199f
Stratus Vineyards, 17, 38, 81, 509
Strawberry Hill Shopping Mall, 62
StuffDOT, 538–539, 539f, 552–554
StumbleUpon, 535f
Subway, 393, 393f
The Successful Business Plan, 55
Summer Fresh Salads, 252
Sun Chips, 257
Sunkist, 278, 365
Sunshine Biscuits, 360
Super Bowl, 46, 130, 450, 451

Supercuts, 393f
Sure, 281
Survey Monkey, 201
SustainAbility, Inc., 515
Swatch, 172, 335
Swiffer, 284
Sylvania, 147
Symetra Financial, 493
Sympatico, 297, 454
SymphonyIRI Group, 258

T

Tab, 271
Taco Bell, 405, 416–417, 439–440, 538
Taco Tia, 439
TAG Heuer, 331
Target, 154, 171, 242, 277, 318, 336, 347, 363,
    372, 392, 394, 404, 435
TaskRabbit, 296
Tassimo, 74
Taxi, 458
TD Canada Trust, 78, 107, 281, 297, 298, 463, 511–512
TD Waterhouse, 6
TE Connectivity, 476
Tech Depot, 93
Teenage Research Unlimited, 200
Teletoon, 462
Telus Group, 6, 14, 32, 96, 281, 308
Telus Mobility, 226
Temple Run, 547
Tesco, 392, 395
Tesco Home Plus, 548
Tesla, 83
Tetley Red Tea, 454
Texas Instruments (TI), 172, 480
Texture, 83
The Shopping Channel, 102
ThePoint.org, 137
Thomson Reuters, 281
Thor, 463
ThothX Technology Inc., 243–244
ThothX Tower, 243–244
3Com, 171
3M Canada, 32, 476
3M Company, 32, 34, 103, 103f, 175, 254,
    256, 259, 269, 518
3M Post-It Notes, 518
3M Scotchgard, 103, 103f
3 MUSKETEERS, 46
Tide, 268, 372
Tidy Bowl, 281
Tiffany & Company, 175, 224, 404
Tim Hortons, 6, 30, 38, 61, 62, 67, 69, 107,
    128, 268, 281, 367, 462
Time, 431
Time Warner Cable Sports, 317
Timex, 172
Tippr, 138
TLC Laser Eye Centres, 297
Tommy Hilfiger, 402
TOMS, 285
Toro Company, 124, 340
Toronto Dominion Bank. *See* TD
    Canada Trust

Toronto Hospital for Sick Children, 244
Toronto Maple Leafs, 298
Toronto Zoo, 5
Toshiba America Medical System,
    492f, 493
Tostitos, 283, 338
Touchstone Pictures, 283, 511
TownePlace Suites, 283
Toyota, 100, 111–115, 182, 202, 281, 340, 372,
    375f, 447, 503
Toyota Canada, 489
Toyota Corolla, 111
Toyota Prius, 112–113, 258, 463
Toyota Tundra, 111
Toyota USA Foundation, 112
Toyota/Lexus, 111–112, 375f
Trans Canada Trail, 6, 465
Transcontinental Inc., 515
Transparency International, 101
Travel Weekly, 266
Travelocity.ca, 297, 364, 365f
Trek, 159
Trek Bicycle Corporation, 158–160
Trek Wear, 158
Trend Hunter, 200
Trevor's Toys, 515–516
Trimark Investments, 225
Trix, 502
Trojan, 268
Tropicana, 277
True Religion, 413
TrueBlue, 234
Tumblr, 535f
Turo, 296, 297
TweetCastor, 537f
24/7 Canada, 454
Twitter, 16, 16f, 23, 27, 73, 75f, 138, 184, 193, 194, 212,
    227, 239, 242, 297, 306–308, 316, 339, 398,
    416–417, 434, 435, 440, 445, 446, 465, 472,
    493–494, 533, 534, 535f, 536, 537f, 540, 541,
    543, 549
Twitter Canada, 540
Twyst, 409
Tylenol, 283, 511
Tylenol Cold & Flu, 126, 283
Tylenol 8-Hour, 126
Tylenol PM, 126, 283, 511

U

UBC, 67
Uber, 296, 297, 338, 436
Ultralife, 251
Uncle Ben's Calcium Plus, 276
Under Armour, 445
Underwriters Laboratories (UL), 108
Unilever, 27, 43, 172, 276, 277
United Nations, 32, 76
United Nations Environment
    Program, 515
United Nations World Food
    Programme, 106
United Technologies Corp., 154
Universe of Light, 414
University of Chicago, 137
UPS, 359, 379, 380

UPS Supply Chain Solutions, 379
Urban Masala, 62
U.S. Department of Energy, 52
U.S. National Coffee Association, 63
U.S. National Parks, 113
U.S. Postal Service, 389
U.S. Secret Service, 158
U.S. Small Business Administration, 21

V

V8, 121
Vacation Club, 283
VALS, 127
Valve, 442
Van Heusen Factory Store, 401
Vancity, 95, 515
Vancouver Canucks, 5
Vancouver International Airport, 69
Vancouver Sun, 134
Vancouver Symphony, 298
Vanity Fair, 132
Vaughan Mills, 402
Venus, 183f
Verizon, 408
VIA Rail, 5, 143, 297
Vicks, 176
Viking, 240
Village at Park Royal, 402
Villiger, 158
Vimeo, 535f
Vine, 416, 440, 535f
Visa, 174, 305, 369
VIZIO, Inc., 318–319
VK, 78, 549
Volkswagen, 111, 178, 182, 509, 534
Volkswagen Beetle, 92, 509
Volvo, 223, 452, 472
Volvo of North America, 234

W

Walgreens, 347, 348
Wall Street Journal, 266

Walmart, Inc., 10, 13, 13f, 79, 93, 128, 140, 143, 148,
    171, 185, 203, 205, 224, 242, 284, 287, 318, 335,
    336, 347, 368, 372, 376, 377, 391, 394, 395, 397,
    400, 400f, 401, 402, 407, 408, 487, 503, 511, 525
Walmart Canada, 395, 402
Walmart Supercentres, 376
Walt Disney Company. *See* Disney
Warby Parker, 408
Warm Delights, 500–501, 505, 523, 528–530
Warm Delights Minis, 523–525, 524f
Warner-Lambert Company, 371
Waterford, 165
Watson, 51
Weibo, 549
Weight Watchers, 38
Welch's, 211
Wendy's Restaurants, 202, 203f, 204f, 225, 227,
    228, 229, 230, 231, 232, 233f, 406
West Edmonton Mall, 402, 413
West 49, 402
Western Union, 134
Westinghouse, 514
WestJet, 6, 33, 283
WhatsApp, 540
Whirlpool Corporation, 145, 171, 173, 184,
    284, 370, 394f
Whistler Resort, 297
Wicks, 176
Wikipedia, 465, 516, 534, 535f
WildPlay Element Parks, 33
Wilkinson Sword, 320
Wilson, 236
Wilson Cirrus One BLX, 337
Wine Country Ontario, 540
WingStreet, 440
Winnie the Pooh, 280
Winnipeg Ballet, 5
Wired, 419
Wolf Trax DDP Micronutrient Technology, 252
Women-Drivers.com, 117
Women's Running, 266
Woot, 139
WordPress, 535f
Workopolis, 297
WorkSafeBC, 5

World Book, 398
World of Warcraft, 535f
World Trade Organization (WTO), 169
World Wildlife Fund, 113
Wow-1Day! Painting Inc., 34
Wrigley's, 183, 245

X

X-1, 263–266
Xbox Live, 535f
Xerox Corporation, 153, 228, 383, 477,
    478, 482, 497–499

Y

Yahoo!, 208, 470, 471
Yahoo! Deals, 138
Yahoo! Finance, 471
Yellow Chilli Restaurant, 62
Yellow Pages Group, 61, 138, 337, 446, 451f, 453
Yelp, 138
Yipit, 398
Yoplait, 23, 24
YouTube, 16, 16f, 316, 455, 465, 471, 472, 532, 534,
    535f, 536, 537f, 541–542, 543–544, 546
YTV, 452
Yum! Brands, 440
Yves St. Laurent, 124

Z

Zady, 408
Zappos, 14
Zara, 105
Zinc Research, 227
Zipcar, 297
Zippo, 288
Zoomerang, 201
Zune, 250

SUBJECT INDEX

A

above-market pricing, 335–336
abuse of dominant position, 86
Acadian subculture, 133–134
accelerated development stage, retail life cycle, 405–406
accessory equipment, 247
account management policies, 487–488, 488f
action item list, 519
actual self, 124
adaptive selling, 482
addressable television advertising, 452
administered systems, 368
administered vertical marketing systems, 368
administrative expenses, 352
adopters, 272–273, 272f
adoption, 430
advergaming, 455
advertising
    advantages and disadvantages, 421
    advertising program. *See* advertising program
    advocacy advertisements, 444
    Canadians' opinions, 459
    comparative advertising, 444
    competitive advertising, 444
    competitive institutional advertisements, 445
    complaints about ads, 459
    cooperative advertising, 464
    defined, 420, 443
    delayed-response advertising, 443, 445
    described, 420–421
    direct-response advertising, 443, 445
    institutional advertisements, 444–445
    Internet, 435, 451f, 454
    vs. marketing, 3
    media. *See* advertising media
    mobile advertising, 455, 456
    online, 435, 451f, 454
    permission-based advertising, 454
    pioneering advertisements, 444
    pioneering institutional advertisements, 445
    product advertisements, 444
    in promotional mix, 420–421
    reinforcement advertising, 444
    reminder advertising, 444
    reminder institutional advertisements, 445
    services, 307
    targeted online advertising, 435
    teaser advertising campaigns, 130
    types of advertisements, 443–445
    web advertising, 435, 454
advertising agencies, 334, 432, 433, 446, 447, 457–458, 457f
advertising media
    advantages and disadvantages, 451f
    basic terms, 448–449, 449f
    Canadian advertising expenditures by medium, 448f
    choosing medium and vehicle, 448
    cost per thousand (CPM), 449, 449f
    different media alternatives, 450–456
    direct mail, 453
    frequency, 449, 449f
    gross rating points (GRPs), 449, 449f
    Internet, 454
    magazines, 452
    mobile advertising, 456
    newspapers, 452–453
    outdoor advertising, 454–455
    place-based media, 455
    radio, 452
    rating, 449, 449f
    reach, 449, 449f
    selection criteria, 456
    selection of, 448–450
    television, 450–452
    user-generated content, 455
    Yellow Pages, 453
advertising program
    advertising budget, 446
    advertising objectives, 446
    aided recall, 458
    attitude tests, 458
    carrying out, 457–458, 457f
    changes, 459
    creation of actual message, 447
    designing the advertisement, 446–447
    evaluation of, 458–459
    execution of, 457
    inquiry tests, 458
    jury tests, 457
    media alternatives, 450–456
    media selection, 448–450
    message content, 446–447
    portfolio tests, 457
    post-tests, 458
    pre-tests, 457
    sales tests, 458
    scheduling the advertising, 456
    target audience, 445–446
    theatre tests, 457
    unaided recall, 458
advocacy institutional advertisements, 444
Afghanistan, 177
Africa, 76, 78, 172, 178, 179
agents, 360f, 364, 364, 364f, 366
aggregators, 398
aggression, 124
aided recall (recognition-readership), 458
algorithms, 547
all-you-can-afford budgeting, 430
allowances, 340–341, 350, 463–464
alternative branding strategies, 282f
alternative evaluation, 118, 151f, 152
AMA statement of ethics, 102f
ambience, 403
ambiguous question, 202, 203f
ancillary services, 426
Andean trade group, 171
annual marketing plans, 507–508, 507f
anti-spam legislation, 88
Anytime Anywhere Media Measurement (A2/M2), 206
approach, 480f, 481
approximate price level, 330–337, 331f
apps, 547
Argentina, 171
ASEAN Free Trade Area (AFTA), 171
Asia, 76, 78, 107, 163, 164, 171, 172, 173, 178, 189, 479, 481
Asia-Pacific Economic Cooperation (APEC), 171
aspiration group, 130
assertiveness, 124
assumptive close, 483
at-market pricing, 335–336
atmosphere, 403
attitude tests, 458
attitudes
    attitude change, 127
    changing attitudes, 79–81
    and consumer behaviour, 127
    defined, 127
auctions, 154–155
Australia, 165, 171
authentic experiencers, 221
authenticity, 280
automatic vending, 395–396
automotive industry, 116–117
automotive supply chain, 375, 375f
average page views per visitor, 545
awareness, 429
awareness set, 118

B

B2B goods. *See* business goods
baby boomers, 77
back translation, 176
backorder, 382
backward integration, 367
bad timing, 250
bait-and-switch selling, 86, 342f
balance of trade, 165
Bangladesh, 76f
bargains conditional on other purchases, 342f
barriers to entry, 85
barter, 164, 320
basic service improvements, 249
BCG analysis, 34–35, 36f
behavioural evaluation, 491
behavioural learning, 126
behavioural segmentation, 226–227, 226f, 228, 229f
behavioural targeting, 429
beliefs, 127
below-market pricing, 335–336
benchmarking, 34
benefit corporation (B Corp), 108
benefits sought, 226
bid rigging, 86, 97
bidders' list, 152
big data, 211
billboards, 454–455
blended family, 78
blog, 534
board of directors, 28f, 29
Bolivia, 171
bottom of the pyramid, 177
brain-wave marketing, 207–208
brand
    see also brand management
    consumer evaluation of, 118
    demand, 322
    drivers, 211, 212f
    fighting brands, 283
    global brand, 172–173
    top global and Canadian brands, 280–281
brand ambassadors, 280
brand community, 130
brand development index (BDI), 273, 275–276
brand equity
    brand licensing, 280
    creating brand equity, 279–280
    customer-based brand equity pyramid, 279f
    defined, 278
    valuing brand equity, 280
brand extension, 283
brand licensing, 280
brand loyalty, 126
brand management
    brand equity, 279–280
    brand licensing, 280
    brand name selection, 278, 281, 282
    brand personality, 278
    branding strategies, 282–285
    cohort brand management, 284
    described, 277–278
brand manager, 273, 521
brand name, 278, 281, 282
brand personality, 278
brand trust, 267
branding, 278
    see also brand management
branding strategies
    alternative branding strategies, 282f
    brand extension, 283
    co-branding, 283

cohort brand management, 284
corporate branding, 282
family branding, 282
green bands, 285
line extensions, 283
mixed branding, 284
multibranding, 283
multiproduct branding, 282–283
private branding, 283–284
private labelling, 283
product line extension, 282
reseller branding, 283
social benefit brands, 285
sub-branding, 283
Brazil, 76f, 166, 171, 174, 177, 184
breadth of marketing, 5–6
breadth of product line, 394, 394f, 395, 399
break-even analysis, 328–330, 330f
break-even chart, 329, 485, 485f
break-even point, 329, 329f
bribery, 98, 101
brokers, 360f, 366
Brunei, 171
budget
    advertising budget, 446
    all-you-can-afford budgeting, 430
    competitive parity budgeting, 430
    marketing budget in marketing plan, 70
    objective and task budgeting, 431, 432f
    percentage of sales budgeting, 430
    promotion budget, 430–431
build-to-order (BTO), 223
bullet graphs, 39
bundle pricing, 332
business, 31
business analysis, 257
business buying. *See* organizational buyers;
    organizational buying behaviour
business cards, 481
business culture, 100–101
business distributor, 364
business firm, 28
business-format franchises, 392
business goods
    classification of, 246–247
    defined, 245
    marketing channels, 363–364, 364f
    production goods, 246
    support goods, 247
business marketing, 142
business markets. *See* organizational markets
business model, 31
business plans, 55, 55f
    see also marketing plan
business portfolio analysis, 34–37, 36f
business practices, 86, 503
business services, 363–364, 364f
business-to-business (B2B) marketing, 142
buy classes, 149
buyer requirements, 370
buyer-seller relationships, 147–148
buyer turnover, 456
buyers
    organizational buyers. *See* organizational buyers
    power of, 85
    role in buying centre, 149
buying centre, 148–150, 150f
buying situations and, 149–150
defined, 148
people in, 149
roles in, 149
buying committee, 148
buying decision. *See* purchase decision process
buzz marketing, 130

C

Cambodia, 171
Canada
    Acadian subculture, 133–134
    advertising agencies adopt IMC approaches, 433
    advertising, opinions about, 459

advertising expenditures by medium, 448f
and APEC, 171
anti-spam legislation, 88
balance of trade, 165
challenges faced by retailers, 406–409
Chinese-Canadian subculture, 134
cultural symbols, 175
cultural mosaic, 133
developed country, 177
diamond mines, 379, 381
disposable income, 82
e-commerce, 173
engaging ethnic groups using social media, 79
environmental scan of, 74, 75f
ethical perceptions of entrepreneurs, 98–99
ethnic diversity, 78–79
ethnic subculture, 133, 134
export future, 165–166
export markets, 164–165, 169
the family, 78
family income, 82
federal legislation, 87f
food manufacturers, 143
free trade agreements, 171
French-Canadian subculture, 133
generational cohorts, 77–78
global imports, 164f
and global marketplace, 165
gross domestic product (GDP), 165
gross income, 82
health, 80
ice highway, 381
innovation success stories, 251–252
and the Internet, 79
ISO certification, 147
language, 176
lifestyles and social media, 127–129
manufacturing sector, 143, 144
measurement of economic activities in
    organizational markets, 145
military recruitment, 200
mobile advertising, 456
national character, 124
North tourism initiative, 307
per capita income, 77
population, 77
population shifts, 78
protectionism, 168
quotas, 169
retail sales, 391
safety standards, 100
salad bowl phenomenon, 133
services and the economy, 297
shifting age structure, 77
small- and medium-sized enterprises (SMEs), 85
social class, 132
social enterprise, 108
social responsibility, 109
South-Asian Canadian subculture, 134
surplus, 165
thumbs-up, 175
top Canadian brands, 280–281
top retailers, 391
trade regulations, 179
trade partners, 165–166
underperforming provinces, 40–41
word of mouth, 129–130
and world trade, 163–165
Canada-EFTA agreement, 171
Canada-Israel Free Trade Agreement, 171
Canadian Code of Advertising Standards, 459
Canadian Outlook Long-Term Economic Forecast, 81
canned sales presentation, 481–482
cannibalization, 224
capacity management, 308–309, 310f
capital costs, 382
capitalist's dilemma, 505
car dashboards, 39
Caribbean, 171
carts, 402
case allowance, 464
cash cows, 36

cash discounts, 340
catalogues, 396–397
category development index (CDI), 273, 275–276
category killers, 394
category management, 403
category manager, 521
causal research, 195
cause marketing, 106
caveat emptor, 100
census metropolitan areas (CMAs), 78
central business district, 401
cents-off deals, 460
Chad, 177
"challenge-findings-action" format, 39
channel captain, 372
channel conflict, 372
channel influence, 372
channel of communication, 418
charges, 306
charitable contributions, 106
Charter of Respondent Rights, 210–211
chief executive officer (CEO), 29
chief experience officer, 15
chief marketing officer (CMO), 29, 39, 45, 520, 520f
child labour, 107
children
    consumer socialization, 131
    family life cycle, 131–132
    influence on family purchases, 132
    obesity, 80
Chile, 171
China, 76, 76f, 77, 78, 99, 101, 134, 158, 162–164, 164f,
    171, 173, 174, 177, 178, 182, 184, 185, 189–191
Chinese-Canadian subculture, 134
Chinese communities, 78, 79
click-through rate (CTR), 546
clickstream, 338
closed-end question, 202
closing stage, 480f, 483
CMA Code of Ethics, 102, 102f
co-branding, 283
co-workers
    and ethics, 102–103
    suggestions, and new products, 255
code of ethics, 101–102, 102f
cognitive dissonance, 119
cognitive learning, 126
cohort brand management, 284
cola war, 171
cold canvassing, 479
collateral materials, 465
Colombia, 171
combination compensation plan, 490
commercialization, 259
commissions, 319
communication
    see also communication process
    defined, 418
    open, 519
    retail communication, 403
    salesforce communication, 493
    and supply chain, 379
communication infrastructures, 177
communication process
    channel of communication, 418
    decoding, 419
    described, 418f
    encoding, 419
    errors in communication, 419
    feedback, 419
    field of experience, 419
    message, 418
    noise, 419
    receivers, 418
    response, 419
    source, 418
community shopping centre, 402
company. *See* organizations
company description, 57–58
company effects, 338
company factors, channel choice and management, 369
company forecast. *See* sales forecast
company rivalry, 166

company strategy, 166
company structure, 166
comparable value comparisons, 342f
comparative advertising, 444
comparisons with suggested prices, 342f
compensation of salesforce, 490
competencies, 34, 58
competition
    see also competitors
    alternative forms of, 83
    assessment of, 84–85
    barriers to entry, 85
    competitive market, and price, 323, 324f
    components of, 84–85
    defined, 83
    economic espionage, 100–101
    ethics of competition, 100–101
    existing competitors and substitutes, 85
    global competition, 171
    intertype competition, 395
    legislation, 86
    for market share, 32
    monopolistic competition, 83, 323, 324f
    monopoly, 83, 323, 324f
    oligopoly, 83, 323, 324f
    power of buyers and suppliers, 85
    pure competition, 83, 323, 324f
    pure monopoly, 323, 324f
    and world trade, 166–167
Competition Act, 86, 97, 338, 341, 343, 373
competition-oriented approaches (pricing),
    331f, 335–337
Competition Tribunal Act, 86
competitive advantage, 34, 58, 286
    national, 166–167, 167f
competitive advertising, 444
competitive analysis, 61–62
competitive effects, 338–339
competitive forces, 73, 83–85
competitive institutional
    advertisements, 445
competitive parity budgeting, 430
competitive position, 275
competitive products, 256
competitors
    see also competition
    asking customers about competitors, 484
    existing competitors, 85
    prices, 323
    pure-play online competitors, 85
    reaction to competitor's position, 275
    small businesses as, 85
    and strategic direction, 34
complexity, 54, 425
compliance, 124
concept tests, 257
conference selling, 478
conflicts of interest, 101
connections, 541
consideration set, 118
consignment selling, 86
consistency, 378
conspiracy, 86
consultative selling, 482
consumer behaviour
    attitudes, 127
    beliefs, 127
    culture and subculture, 132–134
    defined, 117
    ethical behaviour, 109
    family influence, 130–132
    influences on, 122f
    learning, 125–126
    lifestyle, 127–129
    motivation, 123
    perception, 124–125
    personal influence, 129–130
    personality, 124
    psychological influences, 122–128
    purchase decision process, 117–122
    reference groups, 130
    service quality, perception of, 304–305
    situational influences, 121

social class, 132
social responsibility, 109
socio-cultural influences, 129–134
values, 126
consumer buying process. See purchase decision process
consumer confidence index, 81
consumer demand, 145
consumer-driven pricing actions, 323
consumer ethics, 109
consumer ethnocentrism, 177
consumer expectations, 81
consumer factors, channel choice and management, 369
consumer-generated media, 534
consumer goods
    classification of, 245–246, 246f
    convenience goods, 245
    defined, 245
    marketing channels, 362–363, 363f
    shopping goods, 245
    specialty goods, 245
    unsought goods, 245
consumer income, 81–82, 178, 326
    see also income
consumer markets
    consumer behaviour. See consumer behaviour
    market segmentation, 221–224
    segmentation variables and breakdowns, 222f
consumer needs. See needs
consumer-oriented sales promotions
    contests, 462
    coupons, 460
    deals, 460
    defined, 460
    loyalty programs, 462
    point-of-purchase displays, 462–463
    premiums, 461
    product placement, 463
    rebates, 463
    samples, 462
    sweepstakes, 462
consumer promotions. See consumer-oriented sales
    promotions
consumer protection
    legislation, 86, 87f
    packaging and labelling, 286
consumer rights, 88, 100
consumer sentiment index, 81
consumer services, 362–363, 363f
consumer socialization, 131
consumer trends, 276
consumer wants, 8f
consumerism, 88
consumers
    adopters, 272–273, 272f
    caveat emptor, 100
    characteristics, and marketing channels, 369
    competitors' prices, 323
    connecting with, 287
    expectations, 81, 303
    experiences. See experiences
    gap analysis, 303
    global consumers, 173
    income, 81–82, 326
    intermediaries, benefits from, 361
    legislation, 86
    newness, meaning of, 248
    paying what they want, 333
    and product life cycle, 276
    purchasing services, 301–305
    and strategic direction, 34
    suggestions, and new products, 255
    tastes, and demand, 326
    technology, impact of, 82–83
    ultimate consumers, 6
    understanding the customer, 34
    value perception, 119
    voice, ignoring, 251
consumption experience, 119
contact points, 302
contests, 462
continuous innovation, 248, 248f, 250
continuous (steady) schedule, 456

contract assembly, 181
contract manufacturing, 181
contractual systems, 368, 392–393
contractual vertical marketing system, 368
controllable factors, 10
controlled test markets, 258
convenience, 370, 379
convenience goods, 245
convenience products, 80
cookies, 435
cooperation in marketing channels, 372
cooperative advertising, 464
copyright, 99
core competencies, 34
core service, 300
core values, 30, 58
corporate branding, 282
corporate chain, 392
corporate culture, 101–103
corporate level, 29
corporate social responsibility (CSR), 104, 107, 515
    see also social responsibility
corporate systems, 367
corporate vertical marketing system, 367
corporation. See organizations
correcting a negative deviation, 47
Corruption Perceptions Index (CPI), 101
cost-effective flow, 374
cost focus strategy, 509
cost leadership strategy, 508
cost of goods sold, 352
cost-oriented approaches (pricing), 331f, 333–334
cost per action (CPA), 544, 545f
cost per click (CPC), 545, 545f
cost per thousand (CPM), 449, 449f, 450, 544, 545f
cost-plus pricing, 334
Costa Rica, 171
costs
    capital costs, 382
    controlling costs, importance of, 328
    cost reduction, and packaging, 288
    estimating cost relationships, 328–33-
    fixed cost, 328
    incremental cost, 503
    integrated marketing communications (IMC), 431
    inventory costs, 382–383
    inventory service costs, 382
    marketing costs, and pricing, 322
    in operating statement, 352
    performance measures linked to, 544, 545f
    production costs, 322
    risk costs, 382
    storage costs, 382
    total cost, 328
    total logistics cost, 377
    variable cost, 328
countertrade, 164
coupons, 460
credence qualities, 301
credibility, 421
criminal offences, 86
critical factors, 43, 250
cross-border shopping, 398
cross-cultural analysis, 174
cross-device tracking, 88–89
cross-functional teams, 29, 254
crowdfunding, 256
crowdsourcing, 7, 255
cue, 126
cultural diversity, 174–177
cultural ethnocentricity, 177
cultural explorers, 221
cultural mosaic, 133
cultural symbols, 175
culture
    changing attitudes and values, 79–81
    and consumer behaviour, 132–134
    defined, 79
    and ethics, 99–100
    marketing, 503
    national character, 124
    organizational, 31
    as social force, 79–81

societal, 99–100
and subculture, 132–134
currency exchange rate, 178
customary pricing, 335
customer analysis, 63–65
customer-based brand equity pyramid, 279f
customer-centric marketing organization (CCMO), 15, 46
customer contact audit, 302–303, 302f
customer effects, 338
customer experience management (CEM)
described, 14
practices, 15–16
retailing, 394
and salesforce, 493
service quality, 305
and services, 305
customer experience management era, 14–15
customer lifetime value (CLV), 14
customer relationship management (CRM)
data mining, 211–212
defined, 13
direct marketing, growth of, 434
eCRM, 14
interactive marketing, 14
partnership selling, 476
relationship selling, 476
salesforce automation, 492–493
training for roles in, 489
customer requirements, 374
customer sales support personnel, 478
customer satisfaction
as behavioural measure of salesperson performance, 491
defined, 13
as goal, 32
customer service, 378–379
customer solution, 482
customer value
creating through salespeople, 476
defined, 13
and labelling, 286–287
and packaging, 285, 286–287
relationship selling, 476
customer value proposition, 10
customers. See consumers
customized interaction, 420
customs, 175

D

dashboard. See marketing dashboard
dashboard dining, 80
data analysis, 83, 209
data analytics, 211
data collection, 209
data mining, 211–212
data scientists, 211
data visualization, 39
data warehouse, 211
databases, 211, 547
de-selection of customer segments, 231–232
dealers, 360f
deals, 460
deceptive advertising, 97
deceptive marketing practices, 86
deceptive pricing, 341–342, 342f
deceptive sales practices, 100
deceptive trade practices, 88
deciders, 149
decline stage
product life cycle, 269f, 270–271, 425
retail life cycle, 406
decoding, 419
deficit, 165
delayed-response advertising, 443, 445
deletion, 270
delivered pricing, 86, 343
demand
consumer demand, 145
demand characteristics, 145
demand conditions, 166
demand curve, 326–327, 327f

derived demand, 145
estimating, 326–327
organizational markets, 145
price elasticity of demand, 327
and pricing, 322
primary demand, 268
selective demand, 268
demand characteristics, 145
demand conditions, 166, 167f
demand curve, 326–327, 327f
demand factors, 325
demand-oriented approaches (pricing), 330–333, 331f
Democratic Republic of Congo, 76f
demographic segmentation, 225, 226f, 228, 229f
demographics
Canadian population, 77
defined, 76
ethnic diversity, 78–79
family, 78
generational cohorts, 77–78
population shifts, 78
world population, 76–77
department, 29
dependability, 378
depth interviews, 200
depth of marketing, 5–6
depth of product line, 394, 394f
derived demand, 145, 246
descriptive research, 195
deterministic tracking, 89
developed countries, 177
developing countries, 177
development, 258
device, 278
diamond mines, 378, 381
"diamond" of national competitive advantage, 166–167, 167f
dichotomous question, 202
differentiation focus strategy, 509
differentiation positioning, 233–234
differentiation strategy, 509–510
diffusion of innovation, 272
digital natives, 434
direct channel, 363
direct exporting, 181
direct forecast, 236
direct investment, 182
direct labour, 352
direct mail, 396–397, 451f, 453
direct marketing
advantages and disadvantages, 422
consumer privacy, 436
defined, 422
direct orders, 435
e-mail marketing, 434
and ethics, 435
forms of, 433
global issues, 435
growth of, 434
and the Internet, 435
lead generation, 435
mobile direct marketing, 434
in promotional mix, 422
technological issues, 435
traffic generation, 435
value of, 434–435
direct marketing channels, 365
direct mobile marketing, 434
direct orders, 435
direct-response advertising, 443, 445
direct selling, 398
direct-to-customer (DTC), 365
direction of organization, 31–33
discontinuous innovation, 248, 248f
discount stores, 405
discounts, 339–340, 463–464
discretionary income, 82
discriminatory pricing, 86
disintermediation, 372
disposable income, 82
disruptive innovations, 516
dissociative group, 130
distribution. See place (distribution)

distribution centres, 381
distribution strategy
and global channels of distribution, 185, 371–372
global marketing, 185
distribution systems, 177
distributors, 202, 360f, 364, 464
diversification, 37f, 38, 511
divisional groupings, 520–521
divisions, 172
divorce, 78
dogs, 36
dominance, 124
door-to-door retailing, 398
double ticketing, 86
downsizing, 277
drive, 126
drivers, 203, 211, 212f
dual adaptation strategy, 184
dual distribution, 365, 373
dues, 319
dumping, 185
durable good, 245
dynamic pricing, 337
dynamically continuous innovation, 248, 248f

E

e-commerce, 83, 173
see also e-marketing; Internet
e-mail marketing, 434
e-marketplaces, 153–154
e-services, 307
e-tailing, 397
early adopters, 272f
early growth stage, retail life cycle, 405
early majority, 272f
Eastern Europe, 32, 164, 177, 178, 182
eco-consciousness, 80–81
economic considerations, 177–178
economic data, 82
economic development stages, 177
economic espionage, 100–101, 174
economic forces, 72, 81–82, 177–178
economic infrastructure, 177–178
economic integration, 169–171
economy, 81
ecopreneurs, 81
eCRM, 14
Ecuador, 164, 168, 171
effective-frequency model, 449
efficient consumer response, 378
efficient supply chain, 376
80/20 rule, 227
elderly populations, 77
electronic data interchanges (EDI), 377, 382, 383
electronic kiosks, 202, 402, 408
electronic marketing channels, 364, 365f
electronic order processing, 382
emotional intelligence, 489
emotional trust, 267
employee welfare, 32
employees
and retailing, 403
salespeople. See salesforce
suggestions, and new products, 255
welfare of, 32
whistle-blowers, 103
encoding, 419
endorsements, 125
entrepreneurs, ethical perceptions of, 98–99
entrepreneurship, personal selling, 476
enterprise resource planning (ERP), 377
enterprise selling, 476
entry into markets, 85
environmental concerns
see also social responsibility
consumer social responsibility, 109
eco-consciousness, 80–81
going green, 80
green marketing, 105, 106

greenwashing, 108
packaging, 287–288
sustainable procurement, 148
environmental factors, channel choice and management, 368
environmental forces, 10, 72–73, 74f
environmental scanning
Canada, environmental scan of, 74, 75f
competitive forces, 83–85
defined, 73
economic data, collection of, 82
economic forces, 10, 81–82
environmental trends, 73–74, 74f
global environmental scan. *See* global
environmental scan
importance of, 73–75
regulatory forces, 86–89
social forces, 75–81
technological forces, 82–83
environmental trends, 73–74, 74f
environmentally friendly retailing, 410
espionage, 100–101, 174
ethical marketing behaviour, 99–103, 99f
ethics
see also social responsibility
asking customers about competitors, 484
bribery, 98, 101
business culture, 100–101
caveat emptor, 100
Charter of Respondent Rights, 210–211
co-workers, 102–103
code of ethics, 101–102, 102f
cold canvassing, 479
of competition, 100–101
consumer behaviour and, 109
corporate culture, 101–103
current perceptions of ethical behaviour, 98
defined, 17, 96
and direct marketing, 435, 436
of downsizing, 277
economic espionage, 100–101
entrepreneurs' perceptions, 98–99
ethical/legal framework in marketing, 97–98, 97f
ethical marketing behaviour, 99–103, 99f
of exchange, 100
global marketing, 98
industry practices, 100–101
kickbacks, 101
management, behaviour of, 102–103
and marketing, 17
in marketing research, 210
and marketing strategy, 515
moral idealism, 103
personal moral philosophy, 103
pharmaceutical companies, and premium prices, 322
privacy issues, 88–89, 435, 436
and protectionism, 168
and public relations, 465–466
slotting allowances, 372
societal culture and norms, 99–100
students' concerns about ethical climate, 98
subliminal messages, 125
utilitarianism, 103
value-driven strategies, 515
whistle-blowers, 103
ethnic diversity, 78–79
ethnic marketing, 78, 79
ethnic subculture, 133, 134
ethnographic research, 206–207
euro, 169
European Free Trade Association (EFTA), 171
European Union (EU), 165, 168, 169–170, 170f, 176, 179, 181, 288
evaluation, 429, 432–433, 490–491
evaluation phase
digging beneath the numbers, 522–523
strategic marketing process, 47, 522–525, 522f
marketing dashboards, 523–525
marketing evaluation process, 522–523
marketing metrics, 523–525
marketing plan, 70
marketing ROI, 523
evaluative criteria, 118
everyday fair pricing, 401

everyday low pricing (EDLP), 341, 401
evidence management, 308
evoked set, 118
evolution of North American businesses, 12–17, 12f
exchange, 4–5, 100
exchange-rate fluctuations, 178
exclusive dealing, 86, 373
exclusive distribution, 370
execution, 432–433, 503
see also implementation phase
executive summary, 57
existing products, 247
expectations, 81, 303
expense-to-sales ratios, 353
experience curve pricing, 334
experience qualities, 301
experience retailing, 408
experiences, 6, 81, 119, 121, 397, 403, 407, 408
see also services
experiments, 203, 205
exploiting a positive deviation, 47
exploratory research
basic exploratory research, 197
depth interviews, 200
described, 195
focus groups, 198, 200
fuzzy front-end methods, 200
secondary data, 197–198, 199f
social listening, 200
trend hunting, 200
explorer quotient (EQ), 220
exporting, 180–181
exports, 164–165, 171
express warranties, 288
extended problem solving, 120
external approach (screening and evaluation), 257
external search, 118
extranet, 83, 377
extreme value retailers, 401
extroversion, 124
ezines, 434

F

face-to-face surveys, 201, 201f
facilitating function, 361, 362f
factor conditions, 166
factory outlets, 401, 404, 405
fad product, 271f, 272
failure fee, 259
failures (new product), 8, 250–252
family, 78
family branding, 282
family decision making, 132
family income, 82
family influence, 130–132
family life cycle, 131–132, 131f
family roles in purchase process, 132
fan source, 546
fans, 545
fares, 306, 319
fashion product, 271f, 272
fast fashion, 408
fast prototyping, 259
faster retailing, 408
fear appeals, 446–447
feature bloat, 247
feedback, 419
feedback loop, 418f, 419
fees, 306, 319
female body dissatisfaction, and marketing, 9
field experiments, 203
field of experience, 419
field service representatives, 477
fieldwork, 209
fighting brands, 283
finance allowance, 464
financial aspects of marketing
administrative expenses, 352
allowances, 350
cost of goods sold, 352
direct labour, 352

general expenses, 352
gross margin (gross profit), 352, 401
gross sales, 350
income statement, 350–352, 351f
inventory, 352
markdown, 354f, 355, 401
markup, 353–355, 354f, 401
net sales, 350
operating ratios, 353
operating statement, 350–352, 351f
profit-and-loss statement, 350–352, 351f
profit before taxes, 352
purchase discounts, 352
ratios used in setting and evaluating price, 353–357
return on assets (ROA), 324
return on investment (ROI), 354f, 356–357
returns, 350
selling expenses, 352
selling price, 354f
stockturn rate, 354f, 356
financial objectives, 58
financial systems, 177
firm. *See* organizations
firmographics, 228–229
fitness, 80
fixed alternative question, 202
fixed cost, 328
fixed pricing, 337
flash retailing, 397
flash sales, 408
flexible-price policy, 337–338
flighting (intermittent) schedule, 456
flow, 378
FOB origin pricing, 341
focus groups, 198, 200
follow-up stage, 483
food broker, 366
food manufacturers, 143
forecasting. *See* sales forecast
forgetting rate, 456
form of ownership, 392–394
formal research design. *See* research design
former price comparisons, 342f
former Soviet Union, 32
formula selling presentation, 481–482
forward integration, 367
foundation of an organization, 30–31
four Is of services, 298–299
four Ps, 9–10
France, 164, 164f, 172, 175, 176
franchise fees, 393
franchisees, 392
franchises, 393f
franchising, 181, 368, 393, 393f
"free goods" approach, 464
free spirits, 220
free trade agreements, 169–171
free trials, 125
freemium model, 338
French-Canadian subculture, 133
frequency, 449, 449f
frequent usage, 275
full coverage, 512
full-line wholesalers, 366
full-service agency, 457–458, 457f
full-service retailers, 394
full warranty, 288
functional discounts, 340
functional groupings, 521
functional level, 29
functional trust, 267
fuzzy front-end methods, 200

G

Gantt charts, 519
gap analysis, 303
gatekeepers, 149
gender sensitivity, 489
General Agreement on Tariffs and Trade (GATT), 169
general expenses, 352
general merchandise stores, 395

general merchandise wholesalers, 366
generalized life cycle, 271
Generation X, 77
Generation Y, 77–78, 434
generational cohorts, 77–78
generational marketing, 78
generic business strategy, 508–510, 508f
geographic adjustments (pricing), 341
geographic labour markets, 78
geographic predatory pricing, 343
geographic segmentation, 225, 226f, 228, 229f
geographical groupings, 521
Germany, 164, 164f, 165, 171, 172, 173, 174, 175, 176, 182, 185, 288
gestures, 481
global brand, 172–173
global companies, 172–173
global competition, 171
global consumers, 173
global economics, 168
global environmental scan
    consumer income and purchasing power, 178
    cross-cultural analysis, 174
    cultural diversity, 174–177
    cultural ethnocentricity, 177
    cultural symbols, 175
    currency exchange rate, 178
    customs, 175
    economic considerations, 177–178
    economic infrastructure, 177–178
    language, 176
    political-regulatory climate, 179
    political risk rating, 179
    political stability, 179
    stages of economic development, 177
    trade regulations, 179
    values, 174
global ethics, 168
global market entry strategies, 180–182, 180f
global marketing
    see also world trade
    approach stage, 481
    in borderless economic world, 168–174
    Canadian companies and, 165
    cultural diversity, 174–177
    direct investment, 182
    and direct marketing, 435
    distribution strategy, 185
    economic considerations, 177–178
    economic espionage, 174
    entry strategies, 180–182, 180f
    ethics and, 98
    exporting, 180–181
    global environmental scan. See global environmental scan
    global marketing channels, 185f, 371–372
    income levels, 77
    and ISO certification, 147
    joint venture, 181–182
    and language, 176
    licensing, 181
    lifestyle segments, 127–129
    living standards, 77
    marketing program, 182–186
    political-regulatory climate, 179
    preapproach, 479–481
    pricing strategy, 185–186
    product strategies, 182–184, 183f
    promotion strategies, 182–184, 183f
    and services, 310
    shifting age structure, 77
    and social media, 184, 548–549
    sustainable development, 32
    top global brands, 280–281
    top retailers, 392
    trademark protection, 278
    world population, 76–77
global marketing program, 182–186
global marketing strategy, 172
global organizational markets, 144–145

global strategic alliances, 171
goals
    see also objectives
    communicating, 518
    defined, 31
    goal setting, 43, 65–66
    SMART goals, 31
    types of goals, 32
going green, 80
good citizenship, 515
goods
    business goods, 245, 246–247, 362–364, 364f
    consumer goods, 245, 245–246, 246f, 362–363, 363f
    convenience goods, 245
    defined, 6
    durable good, 245
    marketing of, 6
    nondurable good, 245
    production goods, 246
    pure good, 298
    search qualities, 301
    shopping goods, 245
    specialty goods, 245
    support goods, 247
    unsought goods, 245
government agencies, 33
government markets, 144–145
government units, 144
Greece, 179
green business, 310
green brands, 285
green machines, 396
green marketing, 105–106, 107
green technology, 82
greenwashing, 108
grey market, 186
gross domestic product (GDP), 165
gross income, 82
gross margin, 352, 401
gross profit, 352
gross rating points (GRPs), 449, 449f
gross sales, 350
groupthink, 251
growth, 269, 508–513
growth-share matrix, 35, 36f
growth stage (product life cycle), 269f, 270, 424
growth strategies
    business portfolio analysis, 34–37, 36f
    market-product strategies, 37–38, 37f
guarantees, 125
Guatemala, 168

H

handling objections, 482
harvesting, 27, 271
head-to-head positioning, 233
health, 79–80
health issues, 288
hierarchy of effects, 429
hierarchy of needs, 123, 123f
high-learning product, 271, 271f
high-technology products, 10
history of marketing, 12–17
Holland, 166
Honduras, 168
Hong Kong, 134, 139, 164f, 173
horizontal channel conflict, 372
horizontal price fixing, 341
human capital. See employees
humorous appeals, 447
Hungary, 177
hypermarket, 395

I

ice highway, 381
Iceland, 171
idea generation, 255–256
ideal self, 124
ideas, 6

idle production capacity, 299
illegal downloading, 109
IMC audit, 432–433
immigration, 77
implementation phase
    chief marketing officer, 520, 520f
    communicating goals, 518
    fostering communication, 519
    improving implementation, 517–519
    line vs. staff and divisional groupings, 520–521, 520f
    marketing implementation, emphasis on, 517
    marketing organization, 519–521
    vs. planning, 516–517, 517f
    product manager, 521, 521f
    program champion, 518
    rewarding success, 518
    scheduling tasks, responsibilities, and deadlines, 519
    strategic marketing process, 42f, 45–47, 516–521, 517f
    taking action, 518
implementation plan, 70
implied warranties, 288
import quotas, 169
imports, 164–165
impression management, 308
in-game ads, 455
in-house agencies, 457f, 458
inbound telemarketing, 477
income
    bottom of the pyramid, 177
    consumer income, 82, 178, 326
    discretionary income, 82
    disposable income, 82
    global income, 77, 178
    gross income, 82
    per capita income, 77, 178
income statement, 69f, 350–352, 351f
inconsistency, 298, 378
incremental cost, 503
incremental revenue, 503
independent retailer, 392
independent trading communities, 153
India, 76, 76f, 77, 78, 101, 162–163, 164, 171, 173, 174, 176, 177–178, 184, 189–191
indirect channels, 363
indirect exporting, 180
Indonesia, 76f, 171
industrial firm, 143
industrial goods. See business goods
industrial markets, 143, 144–145
industry, 28, 54
industry analysis, 60–61
industry classification system, 144–145, 144f
industry potential, 236
industry practices, 100–101
influencers, 149
infomercials, 452
information, and supply chain responsiveness and efficiency, 377–379
information and communication technologies (ICTs), 83, 153, 492
information search, 118, 151f, 152
information technology, 211
innovation, 34, 370
innovative retailing, 408–409, 410
innovators, 272f
input metrics, 506
inquiry tests, 458
inseparability, 298–299
inside order takers, 477
insider trading, 100
installations, 247
institutional advertisements, 444–445
intangibility, 298
integrated marketing communications (IMC)
    see also promotion
    billboards, 454–455
    combining online and traditional media, 423
    costs of, 431
    defined, 418
    designing the promotion, 432
    development of IMC program, 429–432
    evaluation, 432–433
    execution of, 432–433

IMC audit, 432–433
promotion budget, 430–431
promotion decision process, 429f
promotion objectives, 429–430
promotional mix, development of, 423–428
scheduling the promotion, 432
selection of promotional tools, 431
social media, 422
target audience, 424, 429
intellectual property, 181
intelligent enterprise, 211
intelligent failures, 251
intelligent marketing enterprise platform, 211–212, 212f
intensive distribution, 369
interaction rate, 46
interactive marketing, 14
interactive websites, 77
interest, 319, 429
interest-based advertising, 454
intermediaries, 360, 360f, 361, 361f, 362f, 366–367, 398, 424, 463–464
internal approach (screening and evaluation), 256
internal marketing, 308
internal search, 118
international firm, 172
Internet
    see also e-marketing
    advertising, 435, 451f, 454
    auctions, 154–155
    blog, 534
    bots, 398
    Canadians and, 79
    combining online and traditional media, 423
    concept tests, 257
    cookies, 435
    copyright, 99
    cross-border shopping, 398
    and direct marketing, 435
    e-commerce, 83, 173
    e-mail marketing, 434
    e-marketplaces, 153–154
    e-tailing, 397
    eCRM, 14
    extranet, 83, 377
    flash sales, 398
    focus groups, 198, 200
    illegal downloading, 109
    independent trading communities, 153
    interactive websites, 77
    Internet of Things (IoT), 83
    intranet, 83
    market testing, 205
    marketing channels, 364, 365f
    marketspace, 83
    and mass customization, 223–224
    networked global marketspace, 173
    organizational buying, 153–155
    panel results, 205–206
    permission-based advertising, 454
    price customization, 338
    privacy issues, 435
    private exchanges, 153
    pure-play online competitors, 85
    retailing, 397–398
    rich media, 454
    services, promotion of, 307
    shopping portals, 397–398
    social media, 16–17, 79, 422, 532–549
    spam, 434
    surveys, 201, 202
    targeted online advertising, 435
    tourism marketers, 307
    user behaviour, 206
    user-generated content, 455
    video blogging, 542
    viral marketing, 130
    virtual reality market testing, 259
    virtual reality testing, 205
    virtual shopping cart, 409
    Yellow Pages or phone directories, 453
Internet marketing channels, 364, 365f
Internet of Things (IoT), 83, 409
intertype competition, 395

intranet, 83
introduction stage (product life cycle), 268–269, 269f, 424
inventors, 256
inventory, 299, 352, 382
inventory-carrying costs, 299, 299f
inventory costs, 382–383
inventory management, 382–383
inventory of services, 299
inventory service costs, 382
inventory strategies, 383
involvement, 120–121
Ireland, 165, 169
ISO 9000 standards, 147, 179
ISO 14000, 106
Israel, 171, 177
Italy, 164, 164f, 172, 176, 182

J

Japan, 126, 139, 162, 164, 164f, 166, 168, 169, 171, 173, 175–179, 182, 183–184, 185, 198, 371–372, 387, 405, 414, 481
jaycustomers, 304
job analysis, 488
job description, 488–489
joint decision making, 132
joint venture, 181–182
judgments of the decision maker, 236
jury tests, 457
just-in-time communications, 449
just-in-time (JIT) concept, 147, 383

K

kaizen, 503
keiretsu, 371–372
key account management, 487
kickbacks, 101
kiosks, 408
Korea, 99, 164, 164f, 165, 189

L

label, 285
    see also labelling
labelling
    communication benefits, 286
    connecting with customers, 287
    consumer protection, 286
    contemporary challenges, 287
    and customer value, 286–287
    functional benefits, 286–287
    open dating, 286
    perceptual benefits, 287
laboratory test markets, 259
laggards, 272f
language, 176
Laos, 171
late majority, 272f
Latin America, 76, 107, 132, 139, 162, 171, 172, 175, 176, 178, 182, 184
laws, 97
lead generation, 435
lead time, 378
lead users, 254
leading question, 202, 203f
leads, 479
learning, 125–126
legal forces, 73
legal systems, 178
legislation. *See* regulation
length of product life cycle, 271
level of service, 392, 393–394
licensing, 181
Liechtenstein, 171
life cycle, product. *See* product life cycle
lifestyle, 127
lifestyle centre, 402, 403
Likert scale, 202
limited-coverage warranty, 288

limited-line wholesalers, 366
limited problem solving, 120
limited-service agencies, 457f, 458
limited-service outlets, 394
limited-time-only products, 408
line extensions, 283, 501
line positions, 520
linked prosperity, 26
linear trend extrapolation, 237, 237f
list price, 337–339
load factor, 308, 309
location-based marketing, 407
location-based promotions, 547
logistical function, 361, 362f
logistics management
    automotive supply chain, 375, 375f
    customer service, 378–379
    defined, 374
    described, 374f
    inventory management, 382–383
    key logistics functions, 379–383
    materials handling, 381
    order processing, 382
    reverse logistics, 383
    total logistics cost, 377, 378f
    transportation, 379, 380f
    warehousing, 381
logotype (logo), 278
long-range marketing plans, 507, 516
long-run profits, 324
loss-leader pricing, 337
lost-horse forecast, 236
low-learning product, 271f, 272
lower classes, 132
loyalty programs, 462, 547

M

machine vision systems, 151–153
macroeconomic conditions, 81
macromarketing, 7
magazine advertising, 451f, 452
mail surveys, 201, 201f
maintained markup, 401
major process innovations, 249
major service innovations, 249
make-buy decision, 152
Malaysia, 166, 171, 179, 189
mall intercept interviews, 201
management
    brand management. *See* brand management
    brand manager, 273, 521
    category manager, 521
    chief executive officer (CEO), 29
    chief marketing officer (CMO), 29, 39, 45, 520, 520f
    ethical behaviour, 102–103
    organizing for marketing. *See* marketing organization
    of product life cycle, 273–277
    product manager, 273, 521, 521f
    top management, 29
management by exception, 522
manufacturer-sponsored retail franchise systems, 368
manufacturer-sponsored wholesale systems, 368
manufacturer's agents, 366
manufacturer's branch office, 367
manufacturer's representatives, 366
manufacturer's sales office, 367
manufacturing operations, 172
manufacturing sector, 143, 144
markdown, 354f, 355, 401
market
    consumer markets. *See* consumer markets
    defined, 5
    expected growth, 231
    global organizational markets, 144–145
    government markets, 144–145
    industrial markets, 143, 144–145
    new market, 276
    organizational markets. *See* organizational markets
    reseller markets, 143, 144–145
    size, 231
    target market. *See* target market

market analysis, 59–65
market attractiveness, 251
market-based groupings, 521
market definition, 251
market development, 37f, 38, 511
market growth rate, 35
market modification, 274–275
market orientation, 13
market orientation era, 13–14
market penetration, 37f, 38, 510
market potential, 64–65, 236
market-product analysis, 37–38, 65–66
market-product concentration, 512
market-product focus, 43, 65–66
market-product grid, 37, 37f, 222, 222f, 230, 230f,
    511–513, 513f
market-product strategies, 37–38, 37f
market-product synergies, 224, 511–513
market restriction, 86
market restrictions, 373
market segmentation
    behavioural segmentation, 226–227, 226f, 228, 229f
    challenges of, 224
    choosing segments, 231
    criteria for forming segments, 225
    de-selection of segments, 231–232
    defined, 43, 221–222
    demographic segmentation, 225, 226f, 228, 229f
    effective use of, 223–224
    80/20 rule, 227
    estimate size of markets, 230
    fast-food market, 227–228, 232
    firmographics, 228–229
    geographic segmentation, 225, 226f, 228, 229f
    group products into categories, 229
    grouping potential buyers into segments, 225–229
    linking needs to action, 222, 222f
    market-product grid, 222, 222f, 230, 230f
    marketing actions to reach target markets, 232
    meaning of, 221–222
    multiple products and multiple market segments, 223
    need for, 221
    one product and multiple market segments, 223
    organizational (business) markets, 228–229, 229f
    psychographic segmentation, 225–226, 226f
    reasons for, 221–224
    segmentation variables and breakdowns, 226f
    segments of one, 223–224
    select target markets, 230–231, 230f
    social media users, 227–228
    steps in, 224–233, 224f
    synergies versus cannibalization, 224
    usage rate, 227
    ways to segment consumer markets, 225–226, 226f
    when to segment markets, 223–224
market segments, 222
market share, 32, 35, 325, 405–406, 430
market specialization, 512
market testing, 205, 258–259
marketer-dominated source of information, 118
marketing
    vs. advertising, 3
    basics, 502–506
    benefits, 6
    breadth and depth of marketing, 5–6
    business marketing, 142
    buyers and users of, 6
    buzz marketing, 130
    careers in marketing, 519–521
    cause marketing, 106
    vs. common sense, 3
    and consumer needs, 7–10, 8f
    costs, and pricing, 322
    defined, 3–4
    direct marketing. See direct marketing
    direct mobile marketing, 434
    e-mail marketing, 434
    e-marketing. See e-marketing
    and ethics, 97–98
    ethnic marketing, 78, 79
    and female body dissatisfaction, 9
    financial aspects of marketing. See financial aspects of
        marketing

finding and using what really works, 502–503
green marketing, 105, 106
history of marketing, 12–17
influencing factors, 6–7
interactive marketing, 14
internal marketing, 308
macromarketing, 17
micromarketing, 17
multicultural marketing, 78
new-product failures, 250–251
non-profit organizations, causes, and places, 5, 5f
organizations and, 5, 519–521, 520f
personal selling in, 475–476
requirements for marketing to occur, 4–5
resource allocation, 503–506
vs. selling, 3
skills, 29
social marketing, 6
social media marketing, 16, 543
and social responsibility, 104–109
sponsorship marketing, 465
technology, impact of, 82–83
terms and concepts, 4
understanding marketing, 3–4
viral marketing, 130
what is marketed, 6
marketing accountability, 27, 29
marketing activities plan, 70, 71f
marketing budget, 70, 70f
marketing channels
    agents, 360f, 364, 364f, 366
    brokers, 360f, 366
    business goods and services, 363–364, 364f
    business distributor, 364
    buyer requirements, 370
    channel captain, 372
    channel choice and management, 368–373
    channel conflict, 372
    channel partnerships, 367–368
    channel relationships, 372–373
    channel strategies, and promotional mix,
        427–428
    company factors, 369
    consumer benefits from intermediaries, 361
    consumer factors, 369
    consumer goods and services, 363–364, 364f
    cooperation, 372
    defined, 360
    design considerations, 369–370
    direct channel, 363
    direct marketing channels, 365
    disintermediation, 372
    dual distribution, 365, 373
    electronic marketing channels, 364, 365f
    environmental factors, 368
    global channels of distribution, 185f, 371–372
    importance of, 360–362
    indirect channels, 363
    influence, 372
    intermediaries, 360, 360f, 361, 361f, 362f,
        366–367, 398
    Internet marketing channels, 364, 365f
    legal considerations, 373
    manufacturer's agents, 366
    manufacturer's branches and offices, 366–367
    merchant wholesalers, 366
    multichannel marketing, 365
    multichannel distribution, 365
    multiple channels, 365–366
    nature of, 360–362
    organization, 362–368
    product factors, 369
    profitability, 370–371
    pull strategy, 428, 428f
    push strategy, 427–428, 428f
    selling agents, 366
    strategic channel alliances, 366
    structure, 362–368
    target market coverage, 369–370
    vertical marketing systems (VMS),
        367–368, 367f
marketing concept, 13
marketing concept era, 13

marketing dashboard
    brand development index (BDI), 275–276
    capacity management, 309
    car dashboards and, 39
    category development index (CDI), 275–276
    channel sales and profit, 370–371
    competition, assessment of, 84–85
    defined, 39
    example of, 40f, 523–524, 524f
    integrated marketing communications (IMC),
        costs of, 430–431
    load factor, 309
    marketing ROI using, 523
    monitoring your new-product launch, 252–253
    new-product failures, reducing, 252
    online panel results, 205–206
    price premium measure, 336–337
    reach, 450
    retail format, 403–404
    tracking salesperson performance, 491–492
    tracking strategic performance, 39–40
    underperforming provinces, 40–41
    use of, 523
marketing department, 6, 7f, 11f
marketing drivers, 203
marketing environment. See environmental scanning
marketing information system
    big data, 211
    data analytics, 211
    data mining, 211–212
    described, 198, 211, 212f
    key elements of, 211
    primary data, 197
    sales "drivers," 211, 212f
marketing metric, 39, 506
marketing mix
    defined, 10
    development of, 44–45
    elements of, 10, 45f
    four Ps, 9–10
    place (distribution). See place (distribution)
    poor execution, and new product failures, 250
    price. See price
    product. See product
    and product life cycle, 269
    promotion. See promotion
"Marketing Myopia" (Levitt), 31
marketing organization, 46, 46f, 70, 519–521, 520f
marketing orientations
    customer experience management era, 14–15
    described, 12f
    market orientation era, 13–14
    marketing concept era, 13
    production era, 12
    sales era, 12–13
    social media marketing era, 16–17
marketing plan
    annual marketing plans, 507–508, 507f
    audience, 54–55
    balancing value and values in, 515
    company description, 57–58
    competencies, 58
    competitive advantage, 58
    competitive analysis, 61–62
    core values, 58
    customer analysis, 63–64
    defined, 33, 54
    described, 54–55
    disruptive innovations, 516
    elements in typical marketing plan, 55f
    evaluation phase, 70, 522–525
    executive summary, 57
    financial objectives, 58
    frameworks, 508–513
    guidelines, 54–55, 514
    implementation phase, 70, 516–521
    industry, 54
    industry analysis, 60–61
    interpreting the marketing plan, 56
    kind and complexity of organization, 55
    long-range marketing plans, 507, 516
    market analysis, 59–65
    market potential, 64–65

market-product focus, 65–66
marketing activities plan, 70, 71f
marketing and product objectives, 65
marketing budget, 70, 70f
marketing organization, 70
marketing program, 66–69, 517–519
meaning, 54–55
metrics, 506, 523
mission, 58
most-asked questions by outside audiences, 55
non-financial objectives, 58
place (distribution) strategy, 68–69
points of difference, 66
positioning, 66
price strategy, 67
problems, 514
product strategy, 67
promotion strategy, 68
purposes, 54
sales forecast, 69–70
sample five-year marketing plan, 56–71
strategic focus and plan, 58
substantive notes, 56
SWOT analysis, 59, 59f–60f
table of contents, 57
target audience and purpose, 54
variety of marketing plans, 507–508
writing and style suggestions, 56
writing style, format and layout notes, 56
marketing planning. *See* marketing plan; planning phase
marketing planning frameworks
described, 508
generic business strategy, 508–510, 508f
market-product synergies, 511–513
profit enhancement options, 510–511, 510f
marketing program, 10, 11, 44–45, 45f, 46–47, 66–69,
517–519
see also marketing strategy
marketing program, global, 182–186
marketing research
big data, 211
causal research, 195
Charter of Respondent Rights, 210–211
conclusions, 209–210
data analytics, 211
data collection and analysis, 209
data mining, 211–212
defined, 194
depth interviews, 200
descriptive research, 195
ethical issues, 210
ethnographic research, 206–207
experiments, 203–205
exploratory research, 195, 197–200
focus groups, 198, 200
fuzzy front-end methods, 200
intelligent marketing enterprise platform, 211–212,
212f
marketing information system. *See* marketing
information system
neuromarketing, 207–208
news, 213
observation, 205–207
optimal research design, 208
primary data, 197
problem definition, 197–200
process, 196–197, 196f
report, 209–210
research design, 201–209
sampling, 208–209
secondary data, 197–198, 199f
single source data, 198
social listening, 200
social media and, 193–194
statistical procedures, 208
survey, 201–202
trend hunting, 200
types of, 195
marketing resources, 503–506
marketing ROI, 523
marketing strategy
see also strategy
aligning with supply chain, 375–376

branding strategies, 282–285
cost focus strategy, 509
cost leadership strategy, 508
defined, 46
differentiation focus strategy, 509
differentiation strategy, 509–510
diversification, 37f, 38, 511
and ethics, 515
generic business strategy, 508–510, 508f
global marketing strategy, 172
and involvement, 121
market development, 37f, 38, 511
market penetration, 37f, 38, 510
multidomestic marketing strategy, 172
new-product strategy development, 254
and organizational buying situations, 150
place (distribution) strategy, 68–69
pricing strategies. *See* pricing strategy
problems, 514
product development, 37f, 38, 511
product differentiation, 222
product strategies. *See* product strategies
promotion strategies. *See* promotion strategies
pull strategy, 428, 428f
push strategy, 427–428, 428f
retailing strategy, 399–403
and shape of product life cycle, 271
Six Sigma, 254
social media, 543
and supply chain management, 375–376
value-driven strategies, 515
marketing tactics, 47
marketplaces, 398
marketspace, 83
markup, 353–355, 354f, 401
mass customization, 223–224
mass selling, 420
matching competitors, 430
matching market share, 430
materials handling, 381
matrix organization, 521
maturity stage
product life cycle, 269f, 270, 425
retail life cycle, 406
maximization of current profit, 324
media. *See* advertising media
media richness, 534
members, 545
membership group, 130
merchandise allowance, 463
merchandise line, 392, 394–395
merchandise offering, 403
merchant wholesalers, 366
MERCOSUR, 171
mergers, 86, 511–512, 513f
message, 418
message content, 446–447
message creation, 447
metrics, 39, 506, 523
Mexico, 99, 101, 126, 144, 165, 168, 171, 189
micro-enterprise, 85
microfinance, 178
micromarketing, 17
middle-aged married couples, 132
middle classes, 132
Middle East, 172, 175, 179, 481
middleman, 360f
Millennials, 77–78
minimally viable product (MVP), 258
misleading advertising, 86, 88
mission, 30, 58
mission statement, 30
missionary salespeople, 478
mixed branding, 284
mobile advertising, 456
mobile marketing, 542, 547–548
mobile retailing, 407
mobile technology, 407
modification of market, 274–275
modification of product, 273–274
modified rebuy, 149
monopolistic competition, 83, 323, 324f
monopoly, 83

moral idealism, 103
moral philosophy, 103
motivation, 123, 490
multibranding, 283
multichannel distribution, 365
multichannel marketing, 365
multicultural marketing, 78
multidomestic marketing strategy, 172
multinational firm, 172
multiple channels, 365–366
multiple market-product strategies, 38–39
multiproduct branding, 282–283
Myanmar, 171
mystery shoppers, 207

N

national character, 124
national competitive advantage, 166–167, 167f
need-satisfaction presentation, 482
needs
described, 8
desire to satisfy needs, 4
discovering consumer needs, 7–9, 8f
hierarchy of needs, 123, 123f
motivation, 123
personal needs, 123
physiological needs, 123
safety needs, 123
satisfying consumer needs, 9–10, 11f
self-actualization needs, 123
segmentation, and linking needs to action, 222
social needs, 123
unsatisfied needs, 4
vs. wants, 8
net sales, 350
Netherlands, 164, 164f
network buy, 454
networked global marketspace, 173
neuromarketing, 207–208
new buy, 149
new market, 276
new-product process
business analysis, 257
commercialization, 259
concept tests, 257
controlled test markets, 258
defined, 254
development, 258
external approach, 257
idea generation, 255–256
internal approach, 256
market testing, 258–259
marketing information and methods, 260f
new-product strategy development, 254
screening and evaluation, 256–257
simulated test markets (STMs), 259
Six Sigma, 254
skipping steps in, 251
stages in, 254
standard test markets, 258
test marketing, 258
virtual reality market testing, 259
new-product strategy development, 254
new products
company's perspective, 248
consumer's perspective, 248
consumption effects, and newness, 246–247, 247f
continuous innovation, 248, 248f
described, 247–249
discontinuous innovation, 248, 248f
dynamically continuous innovation, 248, 248f
vs. existing products, 247
failure fee, 259
failures, 8, 250–252
legality, 247
and marketing dashboards, 252
monitoring your new-product launch, 252–253
new-product process. *See* new-product process
vs. new services, 249
newness, meaning of, 247–248
organizational problems, 251

slotting fee, 259
success or failure, 250–252
new services
see also new-product process
categories of, 249–250
vs. product innovations, 249
new-to-world products, 10
new-use situations, 275
new users, 274
newness, 247–248
news conference, 465
news release, 465–465
newspaper advertising, 451f, 452–453
Nigeria, 76f
noise, 419
non-criminal reviewable matters, 86
nondurable good, 245
non-financial objectives, 58
non-monetary rewards, 490
non-profit organization, 28, 33
non-store retailing
automatic vending, 395–396
catalogues, 396–397
described, 395, 396f
direct mail, 396–397
direct selling, 398
door-to-door retailing, 398
online retailing, 397–398
telemarketing, 398
television home shopping, 397
non-exhaustive question, 203f
nonprobability sampling, 209
norms, 99–100
North America, 162, 168, 171, 172, 173, 175, 176, 178, 184
North American Free Trade Agreement (NAFTA), 144, 169, 171
North American Industry Classification System (NAICS), 144–145, 144f, 228
Norway, 165, 171
notice in time, 89

O

obesity, 80
objections, 482
objective and task budgeting, 431, 432f
objectives
see also goals
advertising objectives, 446
defined, 31
financial objectives, 58
marketing and product objectives, 65
non-financial objectives, 58
organizational buying objectives, 146–147
personal selling process, 480f
pricing objectives, 323–325
profit objectives, 324
promotion objectives, 429–430
sales management, 484
observation, 205–207
odd-even pricing, 332
off-mall retailing, 402
off-peak pricing, 309
off-price retailing, 401, 405
offerings, 27, 34
older married couples, 131, 132
older unmarried singles, 131, 132
oligopoly, 83, 323, 324f
Olympic Games, 465
omnichannel marketing, 365
on-the-job training, 489
one-price policy, 337–338
online advertising, 435, 454
online auctions, 154–155, 155f
online behavioural advertising, 454
online buying, 153–155
online market testing, 205
online marketing. *See* e-marketing
online panels, 205–206
online retailing, 397–398
online shopping agents, 397
online surveys, 201, 201f

open dating, 286
open-end question, 202
open innovation, 255
operating ratios, 353
operating statement, 350–352, 351f
opinion leaders, 129
optimal research design, 208
order clerks, 477
order cycle time, 378
order getter, 477, 478f
order processing, 382
order size, 145–146
order taker, 477
organization chart, 46f
organizational buyers
see also organizational buying behaviour
defined, 6, 142
global organizational markets, 144–145
government markets, 144–145
industrial markets, 143, 144–145
reseller markets, 143, 144–145
organizational buying behaviour
buyer-seller relationships, 147–148
buying centre, 148–150, 150f
buying committee, 148
characteristics of, 145–150, 146f
defined, 145
demand characteristics, 145
number of potential buyers, 146
objectives, 146–147
organizational buying criteria, 147
reciprocity, 147
size of order or purchase, 145–146
supply partnerships, 147–148
organizational buying criteria, 147
organizational buying process, 150–153, 151f
organizational culture, 31, 503
organizational direction, 31–33
organizational foundation, 30–31
organizational goods. *See* business goods
organizational markets
see also organizational buying behaviour
e-marketplaces, 153–154
economic activities, measurement of, 144–145
global organizational markets, 144
government markets, 144
independent trading communities, 153
industrial markets, 143
market segmentation, 228–229, 229f
measurement of, 144–145
nature of, 142–144
online auctions, 154–155
online buying, 153–155
organizational buying process, 150–153, 151f
private exchanges, 153
reseller markets, 143
size of, 142–144
virtual, 153–154
organizational strategies, 33
organizational structure. *See* structure of organizations
organizational synergy, 224
organizations
business firm, 28
core values, 30
corporate level, 29
customer-centric marketing organization (CCMO), 15, 46
culture, 31
defined, 27
direction, 31–33
distinct life stages, 12–17
evolution of North American businesses, 12–17, 12f
foundation, 30–31
functional level, 29
global companies, 172–173
industrial firms, 143
kinds of organizations, 27–28
and marketing channels, 362–368
marketing department, 7f, 9
marketing organization, 46, 46f, 519–521, 520f
mission, 30
new-product failures, 251
newness, meaning of, 248

non-profit organization. *See* non-profit organization
strategic business unit level, 29
strategy. *See* strategy
structure of, 28–29, 28f
visionary organizations, 30–33, 30f
organizing for marketing. *See* marketing organization
original markup, 401
outbound telemarketing, 477
outdoor advertising, 451f, 454–455
outlet stores, 401
output, 378
output metrics, 506
outside order getters, 477, 478f
outside order takers, 477

P

Pacific Rim, 171, 173
packaging
communication benefits, 286
connecting with customers, 287
consumer protection, 286
contemporary challenges, 287–288
cost reduction, 288
and customer value, 285, 286–287
defined, 285
environmental concerns, 287–288
functional benefits, 286–287
health, safety, and security issues, 288
perceptual benefits, 287
shelf life, 288
page views, 545
Pakistan, 76f
Paraguay, 171
parallel development, 259
parallel importing, 186
paralysis by analysis, 518–519
partnership selling, 476
patents, 99
pay what you want, 333
penetration pricing, 269, 331
people, and services, 308
people meter, 205
per capita income, 77, 178
perceived risk, 125
percentage of sales budgeting, 430
perception, 124–125
perceptual maps, 234, 235f
performance contracts, 463
performance measures
linked to inputs or costs, 545
linked to outputs or revenues, 545–546
social networks, 544–546, 545f
performance-oriented culture, 503
permission-based advertising, 454
personal influence, 129–130
Personal Information Protection and Electronic Documents Act (PIPEDA), 88, 100, 435
personal interview surveys, 201, 201f
personal moral philosophy, 103
personal needs, 123
personal selling
see also sales management
adaptive selling, 482
advantages and disadvantages, 421
consultative selling, 482
customer sales support personnel, 478
customer solution, 482
customer value and salespeople, 476
defined, 421, 475
enterprise selling, 476
in entrepreneurship, 476
forms of, 477–478
in marketing, 475–476
nature of, 475
order getter, 477, 478
order taker, 477
partnership selling, 476
pervasiveness of selling, 475
process. *See* personal selling process
in promotional mix, 421

quiz, 475f
relationship selling, 476
scope and significance, 474–476
services, 307
personal selling process
approach, 481
close, 483
defined, 479
follow-up, 483
handling objections, 482
preapproach, 479–481
presentation, 481–482
prospecting, 479
stages and objectives, 480f
personal sources of information, 118
personality, 124
personality traits, 124
Peru, 171
pharmaceutical industry, 322
Philippines, 76f, 171, 173, 175, 185
phone directories, 453
physical evidence, 308
physiological needs, 123
pioneering advertisements, 444
pioneering institutional advertisements, 445
place (distribution)
defined, 10
dual distribution, 365, 373
exclusive distribution, 370
intensive distribution, 369
marketing channels. See marketing channels
in marketing plan, 68–69
multichannel distribution, 365
selective distribution, 370
services, 306–307
strategy, 68–69
place-based media, 455
planning phase
goal setting, 43
growth, search for, 508–513
vs. implementation, 516–517, 517f
market-product focus, 43
marketing plan. See marketing plan
marketing planning frameworks, 508–513
marketing program, 44–45, 45f
metrics, 506
planning and strategy lessons, 513–516
problems, 514
situation analysis, 43
steps in, 42–43
strategic marketing process, 42–44, 506–516
SWOT analysis, 43, 44f
value-values balance, 515
point-of-purchase displays, 462–463
points of difference, 43, 66, 250
Poland, 175, 177, 183
political-regulatory climate, 179
political risk rating, 179
political stability, 179
pop-up stores, 402, 408
population
Canadian population, 77
elderly populations, 77
ethnic population, 78–79
population shifts, 78
shifting age structure, 77
ten most populous countries by 2050, 76f
world population, 76–77
population explosion, 76
population shifts, 78
portable people meter (PPM), 205
portable vending machines, 396
portals, 397–398, 454
Porter's generic business strategies, 508–510, 508f
portfolio tests, 457
positioning
differentiation positioning, 233–234
head-to-head positioning, 233
in marketing plan, 66
product positioning, 233–234
repositioning the product, 275–277
retail store, 399f, 399–400

positioning statement, 234
postpone technique, 482
post-purchase behaviour, 119–120, 151f, 152–153
post-purchase evaluation (services), 303–305
post-purchase stage, 427
post-tests, 458
power centre, 402
pre- or post-sale service, 370
pre-purchase stage, 426
pre-tests, 419, 457
preapproach, 479–481, 480f
predatory pricing, 343
premium prices, 322
premiums, 319, 461
presentation, 480f, 481–482
president, 29
prestige pricing, 331
price
see also pricing
availability of other products, and, 326
competitors' prices, 323
cost of changing prices and time period, 323
customization, online, 338
defined, 9, 318
examples, 320f
importance of, 319–321
as indicator of value, 320
list price, 337–339
in marketing mix, 321
nature of, 319–321
of other products, 326
perception, 320, 338
premium prices, 322
and profit equation, 321
quoted price, 337–339
regulation and legislation, 86
services, 306
setting prices. See pricing
suggested retail price, 341
and tariffs, 168
price-comparison searches, 547
price discrimination, 41
price elasticity of demand, 327
price equation, 320f
price fixing, 341
price lining, 332
price maintenance, 86
price-pack deals, 460–461
price premium measure, 336–337
price setting. See pricing
price violations, 342
price war, 339
prices, 319
pricing
see also pricing strategy
allowances, 340–341
approximate price level, selection of, 330–337, 331f
break-even analysis, 328–330, 330f
break-even point, 329, 329f
company effects, 338
competitive effects, 338–339
competitive markets, type of, 323, 324f
consumer-driving pricing actions, 323
controlling costs, importance of, 328
cost of changing prices and time period, 323
customer effects, 338
and demand, 322
discounts, 339–340
dynamic pricing, 337
estimating cost, volume, and profit relationships, 328–330
estimating demand, 326–327
estimating revenue, 328
fixed pricing, 337
flexible-price policy, 337–338
FOB origin pricing, 341
geographical adjustments, 341
legal and regulatory aspects, 86, 341–343
list or quoted price, setting, 337–339
market share, 325
marketing costs, 322
newness of product, 322
one-price policy, 337–338

pay what you want, 333
pricing constraints, identification of, 321, 322–323
pricing objectives, identification of, 321, 323–325
and product life cycle stage, 322
product-line pricing, 338
production costs, 322
and profit, 324
ratios for, 353–357, 354f
and sales, 324
seller/retailer-driven pricing actions, 323
single product vs. product line, 322
social media impact on, 339
social responsibility, 325
special adjustments, 339–343
steps, 321, 321f
surge pricing, 338
and survival, 325
uniform delivered pricing, 341
and unit volume, 325
pricing constraints, 321, 322–323
pricing objectives, 321, 323–325
pricing strategy
above-market pricing, 335–336
at-market pricing, 335–336
below-market pricing, 335–336
bundle pricing, 332
competition-oriented approaches, 313f, 335–337
cost-oriented approaches, 331f, 333–334
cost-plus pricing, 334
customary pricing, 335
demand-oriented approaches, 330–333, 331f
dumping, 185
everyday fair pricing, 401
everyday low pricing (EDLP), 341, 401
experience curve pricing, 334
global marketing, 182–186
grey market, 186
loss-leader pricing, 337
in marketing plan, 67
odd-even pricing, 332
off-peak pricing, 309
off-price retailing, 401
penetration pricing, 269, 331
prestige pricing, 331
price lining, 332
profit-oriented approaches, 331f, 334–335
retail pricing, 401
skimming pricing, 269, 331
standard markup pricing, 333–334
target pricing, 332
target profit pricing, 334
target return-on-investment pricing, 335
target return-on-sales pricing, 334
value pricing, 320
yield management pricing, 332–333
primary data, 197
primary demand, 268
Privacy Act (PA), 88
privacy issues, 88–89, 435, 436, 548
private branding, 283–284
private exchanges, 153
private labelling, 283
PRIZM5, 127, 128–129, 133
PRIZM5 QC, 133
probability sampling, 208–209
problem definition, 197–200
problem recognition, 117–118, 151f, 152
problem-solving variations, 120–121, 121f
process, 308–309
process innovations, 249
process-line extensions, 249
product
adopters, 272, 272f
ancillary services, 426
business goods, 246–247
characteristics, and promotional mix, 425–426
classification of products, 245
competitive products, 256
complexity, 425
consumer goods, 245–246, 246f
defined, 9, 244
degree of tangibility, 245
deletion, 270

demand, 322
drivers, 211, 212f
existing products, 247
fad product, 271f, 272
fashion product, 271f, 272
grouping into categories, 229
harvesting, 271
high-learning product, 271, 271f
high-technology products, 10
level, 272
low-learning product, 271f, 272
and marketing channels, 368
new products. *See* new products
new-to-world products, 10
points of difference, 43
poorly conceived, 251
price, and availability of, 326
product definition, 250
product line, 244
product mix, 245
quality, 250
risk, 426
service as product, 305–306
substitute products, 320, 326
types of user, 245
variations of products, 244–245
product adaptation strategy, 183
product advertisements, 444
product bundling, 273
product champion, 518
product class, 245, 272, 322
product counterfeiting, 278
product definition, 250
product development, 37f, 38, 511
product differentiation, 222
product-distribution franchises, 392
product extension strategy, 183
product factors, and channel choice, 369
product form, 272
product invention strategy, 184
product item, 244
product life cycle
    and consumers, 272–273
    decline stage, 269f, 270–271, 425
    defined, 268
    fad product, 271f, 272
    fashion product, 271f, 272
    four dimensions of, 271–273
    generalized life cycle, 271
    growth stage, 269f, 270, 424
    high-learning product, 271, 271f
    introduction stage, 268–268, 269f, 424
    length of, 271
    low-learning product, 271f, 272
    management of, 273–277
    market modification, 274–275
    and marketing mix, 269
    maturity stage, 269f, 270, 425
    pioneering advertisements, 444
    and price, 322
    product adopters, 272, 272f
    product class, 272
    product form, 272
    product level, 272
    product manager, role of, 273
    product modification, 273–274
    product repositioning, 275–277
    and promotional mix, 424–425
    reminder advertisements, 444
    shape of, 271
    stages of, 269f, 322, 424–425, 425f
product line, 244, 322, 394
product line extensions, 282
product line groupings, 520
product-line pricing, 338
product manager, 273, 521, 521f
product mix, 245
product modification, 273–274
product newness, 322
product placement, 463
product positioning
    approaches to, 233–234
    defined, 233

differentiation positioning, 233–234
head-to-head positioning, 233
perceptual maps, 234, 235f
positioning statement, 234
product repositioning, 234, 235f
product repositioning, 234, 235f, 275–277
product specialization, 512
product strategies
    deletion, 270
    global marketing, 182–184, 183f
    harvesting, 271
    in marketing plan, 67
    product adaptation, 183
    product extension, 183
    product invention, 184
product warranty, 288
production costs, 322
production era, 12
production goods, 246
profit
    current profits, 24
    defined, 28
    estimating profit relationship, 328–330
    as goal, 32
    gross profit, 352
    long-run profits, 324
    in operating statement, 352
    and price, 324
    profit before taxes, 352
profit-and-loss statement, 350–352, 351f
profit enhancement options, 510–511, 510f
profit equation, 321
profit objectives, 324
profit-oriented approaches (pricing), 331f,
    334–335
profit responsibility, 105
profitability, 370
program champion, 518
program schedules, 519
programmatic ad purchasing, 450
promotion
    see also integrated marketing communications (IMC)
    decision process, 429, 429f
    defined, 10
    design of promotion, 432
    multibranding, 283
    objectives, 429–430
    promotion budget, 430–431
    promotion program, development of, 429–432
    promotion program, evaluation of, 432–433
    promotion program, execution of, 432–433
    promotion schedule, 432
    promotional mix. *See* promotional mix
    sales promotion. *See* sales promotion
    services, 307
    tools, selection of, 431
promotion budget, 430–431
promotion strategies, 68, 182–184, 183f
promotional allowances, 340–341
promotional mix
    advertising, 420–421
    channel strategies, 427–428
    defined, 418
    described, 420f
    development of, 423–428
    direct marketing, 422
    personal selling, 421
    product characteristics, 425–426
    and product life cycle, 424–425, 425f
    public relations, 421–422
    pull strategy, 428, 428f
    push strategy, 427–428, 428f
    sales promotion, 422
    stages of buying decision, 426–427, 427f
    target audience, 424
proprietary information, 100
prospecting, 479, 480f
prospects, 479
protectionism, 168–169, 169f
protocol, 250
prototype, 257
psychographic segmentation, 225–226, 226f
psychographics, 127–129

psychological influences
    attitudes, 27
    beliefs, 127
    learning, 125–126
    lifestyle, 127–129
    motivation, 123
    perception, 124–125
    personality, 124
    psychographics, 127–129
    values, 126
public relations
    advantages and disadvantages, 421–422
    collateral materials, 465
    defined, 421
    ethical issues, 465–466
    news conference, 465
    news release, 464–465
    in promotional mix, 421–422
    public service announcement (PSA), 420, 465
    publicity, 421–422, 464
    services, 307
    social media, 465
    sponsorship marketing, 465
    tools of, 482–483
public service announcement (PSAs), 420, 465
public sources of information, 118
publicity, 421–422, 465
pull strategy, 428, 428f
pulse (burst) schedule, 456
purchase decision, 119, 151f, 152
purchase decision process
    see also consumer behaviour
    alternative evaluation, 118
    cognitive dissonance, 119
    defined, 117
    illustration of, 118f
    influences on, 122f
    information search, 118
    involvement, level of, 120–121
    post-purchase behaviour, 119–120
    post-purchase stage, 427
    pre-purchase stage, 426
    problem recognition, 117–118
    problem-solving variations, 120–121, 120f
    and promotional mix, 426–447, 447f
    purchase decision, 119
    purchase stage, 426–427
    services, 301–305
    situational influences, 121
purchase discounts, 352
purchase frequency, 456
purchase patterns, 211
purchase size, 145–146
purchase stage, 426–427
purchasing power, 178
pure competition, 83, 323, 324f
pure good, 298
pure monopoly, 323, 324f
pure-play online competitors, 85
pure service, 298
push strategy, 427–428, 428f

Q

qualified prospects, 479
quality
    defined, 34
    as goal, 32
    poor quality product, and failures, 250
    service quality, 303–305, 304f
quality-of-life issues, 107
quantitative assessments, 490
quantity discounts, 339
Quebec, 86, 133–134
question marks, 35
questionnaires, 201–202, 201f, 202f
questions (surveys), 202, 203f
quick response, 378
quotas, 169
quoted price, 337–339

R

radio advertising, 451, 452
radio-frequency identification devices (RFID), 212
rates, 306
rating, 449, 449f
ratios
    markdown, 354, 355
    markup, 353–355, 354f
    operating ratios, 353
    return on assets (ROA), 324
    return on investment (ROI), 324, 354
    stockturn rate, 354f, 356
    used in setting and evaluating price, 353–357
reach, 449, 449f
real-time bidding (RTB), 454
rebates, 463
receivers, 418
recency, 449
recession, 81
reciprocity, 147
reference groups, 130
reference value, 320
refusal to deal, 86, 373
regional shopping centre, 402
regulation
    anti-spam, 88
    competition legislation, 86
        see also *Competition Act*
    consumer protection legislation, 86
    consumerism, 88
    defined, 86
    e-mail, 435
    ethical/legal framework in marketing, 97–99, 97f
    federal competition and consumer legislation, 87f
    global political-regulatory climate, 179
    laws, 97
    and marketing channels, 373
    newness, in legal terms, 247
    package tampering, 286
    pricing, legal and regulatory aspects of, 86, 341–343
    privacy issues, 88–89, 435, 436
    in Quebec, 86
    self-regulation, 88
    trade regulations, 179
    warranties, 288
regulatory forces, 73, 86–89, 179
reinforcement, 126
reinforcement advertising, 444
related diversification, 38
related industries, 166
relationship selling, 476
relative market share, 35
reliability, 196
remarriage, 78
reminder advertising, 444
reminder institutional advertisements, 445
rent, 319
repeat purchasers, 270
replenishment time, 378
report (research), 209–210
repositioning the product, 275–277
resale price maintenance, 341
resale restrictions, 373
research. *See* marketing research
research and development (R&D), 251
research and development (R&D) innovations, 255–256
research conclusions, 209–210
research design
    ethnographic research, 206–207
    experiments, 203, 205
    neuromarketing, 207–208
    observation, 205–207
    optimal research design, 208
    sampling, 208–209
    survey, 201–202, 201f, 203f, 204f
research methods. *See* research design
reseller branding, 283
reseller markets, 143, 144–145
resellers, 143
resource allocation, 45, 503–506, 504f
response, 126, 419

responsive supply chain, 376
retail communication, 403
retail life cycle, 405–406, 406f
retail outlets, classification of, 392
retail positioning matrix, 399–400, 400f
retail pricing, 401
retailer-sponsored cooperatives, 368, 392
retailers
    see also retailing
    independent retailer, 392
    as intermediaries, 360, 360f, 366–367
    pricing actions, 323
    resellers, 143
    top Canadian and global retailers, 391–392
retailing
    automatic vending, 395–396
    changing nature of, 404–406
    classification of retail outlets, 392
    defined, 391
    direct mail and catalogues, 396–397
    direct selling, 398
    environmentally friendly retailing, 410
    experience retailing, 408
    faster retailing, 408
    form of ownership, 392–394
    green machines, 396
    innovative retailing, 408–409, 410
    level of service, 392, 393–394
    merchandise line, 392, 394–395
    mobile retailing, 407
    non-store retailing, 395–398, 396f
    online retailing, 397–398
    retail life cycle, 405–406, 406f
    scope of, 391–395
    sustainability, 410
    telemarketing, 398
    television home shopping, 397
    travel retailing, 406–407
    trends, 406–409
    value of, 391–395
    wheel of retailing, 405, 405f
retailing mix
    communication, 403
    defined, 400
    merchandise offering, 403
    retail pricing, 401
    store location, 401–403
retailing strategy
    category management, 403
    communication, 403
    elements of, 399f
    merchandise offering, 403
    off-price retailing, 401
    positioning a retail store, 399–400, 399f
    pricing, 401
    retailing mix, 399f, 400–403
    store location, 401–403
retainers, 319
return on assets (ROA), 324
return on investment (ROI), 324, 354f, 356–357, 523
returns, 350
revenue
    estimating, 328
    incremental revenue, 503
    performance measures linked to, 545–546
    total revenue, 328
reverse auction, 154–155
reverse logistics, 383
rich media, 454
right to be heard, 100
right to be informed, 100
right to choose, 100
right to safety, 100
rising trends, 276
risk
    perceived risk, 125
    product's purchase, 426
risk costs, 382
routine problem solving, 121
rural areas, 78
Russia, 101, 164, 171. 174, 175, 178, 182, 189

S

safety issues, 288
safety needs, 123
salad bowl phenomenon, 133
salaries, 319
sales
    as goal, 32
    gross sales, 350
    net sales, 350
    in operating statement, 350–351
    and pricing, 324
    social media and, 543–544
sales "drivers," 211, 212f
sales engineer, 478
sales era, 12–13
sales forecast
    defined, 236
    direct forecast, 236
    judgments of the decision maker, 236
    linear trend extrapolation, 237, 237f
    lost-horse forecast, 236
    main techniques, 236–237
    in marketing plan, 69–70
    salesforce survey forecast, 236
    statistical methods, 237
    survey of buyers' intentions forecast, 236
    surveys of knowledgeable groups, 236
    trend extrapolation, 237
sales management
    account management policies, 487–488, 488f
    customer sales organizational structure, 486f, 487
    defined, 475
    geographical structure, 485, 486f
    key account management, 487
    nature of, 475–476
    objectives, 484
    process, 483–493, 484f
    product sales organization, 486f, 487
    quiz, 475f
    sales plan formulation, 483–488
    sales plan implementation, 488–490
    salesforce, organization of, 484–487, 486f
    salesforce automation (SFA), 492–493
    salesforce evaluation, 490–491
    scope and significance, 474–476
    workload method, 487
sales plan
    defined, 483
    formulation of, 483–488
    implementation, 488–490
sales promotion
    advantages and disadvantages, 422
    allowances, 463–464
    alternatives, 461f
    consumer-oriented sales promotions, 460–463
    contests, 462
    cooperative advertising, 464
    coupons, 460
    deals, 460
    defined, 422
    discounts, 463–464
    importance of, 460
    loyalty programs, 462
    point-of-purchase displays, 462–463
    premiums, 461
    product placement, 463
    in promotional mix, 422
    rebates, 463
    samples, 462
    sweepstakes, 462
    trade-oriented sales promotions, 463–464
    training of distributors' salesforces, 464
sales quota, 490
sales response function, 503–506, 504f
sales revenue, 32
sales teams, 478
sales tests, 458
salesclerks, 477
salesforce
    see also sales management
    automation, 492–493

communication, 493
compensation, 490
customer value, creation of, 476
emotional intelligence, 489
evaluation, 490–491
motivation, 490
organization of, 484–487, 486f
recruitment and selection, 488–489
sales quota, 490
size of, 487
technology, 493
tracking salesperson performance, 491–492
training, 464, 489
workload method, 487
salesforce automation (SFA), 492–493
salesforce survey forecast, 236
salespeople. *See* personal selling; sales management;
   salesforce
samples, 208, 462
sampling, 208–209
sandwich generation, 77
schedules for implementation, 46, 519
scientific method, 196
scrambled merchandising, 395
screening and evaluation, 256–257
search engine advertising, 454
search qualities, 301
seasonal discounts, 340
secondary data, 197–198, 199f
The Secret Sales Pitch: An Overview of Subliminal
   Advertising (Bullock), 125
security issues, 288
segmentation. *See* market segmentation
selective attention, 124
selective comprehension, 124
selective demand, 268
selective distribution, 370
selective exposure, 124
selective perception, 124
selective retention, 124
selective specialization, 512
self-actualization needs, 123
self-concept, 124
self-disclosure, 534
self-liquidating premiums, 461
self-mailers, 453
self-regulation, 88
self-service, 394
self-service check-outs, 408
seller/retailer-driven pricing actions, 323
selling
   adaptive selling, 482
   conference selling, 478
   consultative selling, 482
   vs. marketing, 3
   partnership selling, 476
   personal selling. *See* personal selling
   relationship selling, 476
   seminar selling, 478
   suggestive selling, 481
   team selling, 478
selling agents, 366
selling expenses, 352
selling price, 354f
semantic differential scale, 202
seminar selling, 478
semiotics, 175
sensitivity analysis, 211
service continuum, 300, 300f
the service economy, 297–300
   see also services
service encounter elements, 302
service encounters, 258
service industries, 143
service innovations, 249
service level. *See* level of service
service-line extensions, 249
service quality, 303, 304–305, 304f
service-sponsored franchise systems, 368
service-sponsored retail franchise
   systems, 368
service sweethearting, 310

services
   ancillary services, 426
   authenticity, dimensions of, 280
   business services, 363–364, 364f
   Canadian economy, 297
   capacity management, 308–309, 310f
   changes in consumer interests, 311
   consumer services, 301–305, 362–363, 363f
   core services, 300
   credence qualities, 301
   customer contact audit, 302–303, 302f
   defined, 6, 245, 247, 297
   evaluation of, 301f
   experience qualities, 301
   exportation of, 165
   four Is of services, 298–299
   in the future, 310–311
   gap analysis, 303
   global economy, 297
   idle production capacity, 299
   inconsistency, 298
   inseparability, 298–299
   intangibility, 298
   internal marketing, 308
   Internet promotion, 307
   inventory-carrying costs, 299, 299f
   inventory of services, 299
   marketing of, 6, 305–309
   new services, 249–250
   off-peak pricing, 309
   people, 308
   physical evidence, 308
   place (distribution), 306–307
   post-purchase evaluation, 303–305
   price, 306
   process, 308–309
   product (service), 305–306
   promotion, 307
   public relations, 307
   purchase of services, 301–302
   pure service, 298
   service continuum, 300, 300f
   the service economy, 297–300
   service job growth, 297
   service quality, 303–305, 304f
   seven Ps of services marketing, 305–309
   steps to great service experiences, 311
   success or failure, 250–252
   supplementary services, 300
   and technological improvements, 310
   uniqueness of services, 298–299
SERVQUAL, 303
seven Ps of services marketing
   defined, 305
   people, 308
   physical evidence, 308
   place (distribution), 306–307
   price, 306
   process, 308–309
   product (service), 305–306
   promotion, 307
sex appeals, 447
shape of product life cycle, 271
share of market, 430
share of voice, 545
share points, 505
shelf life, 288
shopper marketing, 403
shopping goods, 245
shrinkage, 401
simulated test markets (STMs), 259
Singapore, 171, 179, 189
single-parent family, 132
single-price retailers, 401
single source data, 198
situation analysis, 43
situational influences, 121
Six Sigma, 254
skimming pricing, 269, 331
sleeping positions, 222, 222f
slotting allowances, 100, 259, 373
slugging, 97
small- and medium-sized enterprises (SMEs), 85

small businesses, as competitors, 85
small technology firms, 256
SMART goals, 31
smart-interactive vending machines, 396
smart system, 546
smartphones, 547
social audit, 106–108
social benefit brand, 285
social class, 132
social CRM, 16–17
social enterprise, 108
social forces
   culture, 79–81
   defined, 75
   demographics, 76–79
   influence of, 72
social listening, 200
social marketing, 6
social media
   classification of, 534, 535f
   convergence of real and digital worlds, 546–547
   defined, 533
   described, 533–534
   discounts, 339
   engaging Canada's ethnic groups, 79
   future of, 548
   global marketing and, 184, 548–549
   history of, 534
   integrating into marketing strategies, 543–546
   lessons for brand managers, 543–544
   linking to marketing actions, 547–548
   and marketing research, 193–194
   mobile marketing, 547–548
   performance measures, 544–546, 545f
   pricing, 339
   public relations, 421–422, 454
   sales and, 543–544
   salesforce automation, 492–493
   segmentation, 227–228
   selection of, 543
   smartphones and exotic apps, 546–549
   social media marketing, 16, 79
   social media marketing era, 16–17
   social networks, 536–542, 543
   strategic marketing process, 543
   vs. traditional marketing research, 193–194
   vs. traditional media, 535–536
   understanding, 533–536
   usage, 227–228
social media marketing, 16, 79
social media marketing era, 16–17
social media users, 227–228
social needs, 123
social networks
   audience data, 543
   comparison of, 536, 537f
   described, 534
   Facebook, 537–540
   LinkedIn, 541
   recent growth of, 543
   selecting, 543
   specialized focus of, 546
   Twitter, 540
   YouTube, 541–542
social responsibility
   see also environmental concerns; ethics
   cause marketing, 106
   concepts of, 104–106, 104f
   consumer behaviour and, 109
   consumer ethics and, 109
   defined, 17, 104
   favourable word-of-mouth, 107
   as goal, 32
   green marketing, 105–106, 107
   greenwashing, 108
   ISO 14000, 106
   macromarketing, 17
   and marketing, 104–109
   micromarketing, 17
   and pricing, 325
   profit responsibility, 105
   rewards for, 107
   social audit, 106–108

social enterprise, 108
societal marketing concept, 17, 104
societal responsibility, 105
stakeholder responsibility, 105
sustainable development, 107
sustainable marketing, 104–109
triple-bottom line, 105
societal culture. *See* culture
societal marketing concept, 17
societal responsibility, 105
socio-cultural influences
consumer socialization, 131
culture and subculture, 132–134
described, 129
family decision making, 132
family influence, 130–132
family life cycle, 131–132, 131f
opinion leaders, 129
personal influence, 129–130
reference groups, 130
social class, 132
word of mouth, 129–130
source, 418
sources of information, 118
South Africa, 177, 184
South America, 171, 172, 173
South Asia, 178, 182
South-Asian Canadian subcultures, 134
South Asian communities, 78, 79
Spain, 176
spam, 434
spark lines, 39
specialization, 512
specialty goods, 245
specialty merchandise wholesalers, 366
specialty outlets, 394
splitting 30s, 451
sponsorship marketing, 465
spouse-dominant decision making, 132
Sri Lanka, 177
staff positions, 520
stages of economic development, 177
stakeholder responsibility, 105
standard markup pricing, 333–334
standard test markets, 258
Starch test, 458
stars, 36
statistical methods, 237
stimulus discrimination, 126
stimulus generalization, 126
stimulus-response presentation, 481
stock-keeping unit (SKU), 244
stockturn rate, 354f, 356
storage costs, 382
storage warehouses, 381
store location, 401–403
straight commission compensation
plan, 490
straight rebuy, 149, 150
straight salary compensation plan, 490
strategic alliances, 171, 365–366
strategic business unit (SBU), 29, 35–36
strategic business unit level, 29
strategic channel alliances, 366
strategic directions, 33–38
strategic marketing process
actions and information, 505f
defined, 41
designing the marketing organization, 46
developing schedules, 46
evaluation phase, 47, 522–525, 522f
executing the marketing program, 47–48
goal setting, 43
illustration of, 42f
implementation phase, 45–47, 516–521, 517f
market-product focus, 43
marketing organization. *See* marketing organization
marketing program, 44–45, 45f
planning phase, 42–45, 506–516
and resource allocation, 503–506, 505f
resources, 45
situation analysis, 43
social media and, 543

SWOT analysis, 43, 44f
value-values balance, 515
strategy
see also marketing strategy
business portfolio analysis, 34–37, 36f
business unit level strategy, 28f, 29
citizenship, 515
competencies, 34
competitors, 34
corporate-level strategy, 28f, 29
cost focus strategy, 509
cost leadership strategy, 508
customers, 34
defined, 28
differentiation focus strategy, 509
differentiation strategy, 509–510
finding and using what really works, 503
functional level, 28f, 29f
generic business strategy, 508–510, 508f
growth strategies, 34–38
market-product strategies, 37–38, 37f
marketing dashboard, 39–40, 523, 524f
marketing metric, 39, 523
organizational foundation, 30–31
organizational strategies, 33
planning and strategy lessons, 513–516
problems, 514
strategic directions, 33–38
sustainable development, 515
tracking strategic performance, 39–40
variation by level, 33
variation by offering, 33
in visionary organizations, 30–33, 30f
strip location, 402
structure of organizations
corporate level, 29
finding and using what really works, 502–503
functional level, 29
illustration of, 28f
strategic business unit level, 29
style changes, 250
sub-branding, 283
subcultures, 132–134
subliminal messages, 125
subliminal perception, 124
subsidiaries, 172
substitute products, 320, 326
substitutes, 85
The Successful Business Plan (Abrams), 55
suggested retail price, 341
suggestive selling, 481
superbus, 455
supercentre, 395
supplementary-service innovations, 249
supplementary services, 300
supplier development, 147
suppliers
power of, 85
suggestions, and new products, 255
supplies, 247
supply chain
see also logistics management; supply chain management
aligning with marketing strategy, 375–376
automotive supply chain, 375, 375f
customer service, 378–379, 378f
defined, 374
efficient supply chain, 376
as flow, 378f
information and logistic management objective, 377–379
information, role of, 377
inventory costs, 382–383
inventory management, 382–383
inventory purpose, 382
inventory strategies, 383
key logistics functions, 379–383
materials handling, 381
order processing, 382
responsive supply chain, 376
reverse logistics, 383
total logistics cost, 377

transportation, 379, 380f
warehousing, 381
supply chain management
see also supply chain
defined, 374
described, 375
and marketing strategy, 375–376
total logistics cost, 377, 378f
supply partnerships, 147–148
support goods, 247
supporting industries, 166
surge pricing, 338
surplus, 165
survey, 201–202, 201f, 203f, 204f
survey of buyers' intentions forecast, 236
survey panel, 202
surveys of knowledgeable groups, 236
survival, 325
sustainability, 310, 410
sustainable development, 32, 107, 515
sustainable marketing
defined, 105
understanding social responsibility for, 104–109
sustainable procurement, 148
Sweden, 165, 171, 173, 179
sweepstakes, 462
Switzerland, 171, 176
SWOT analysis, 43, 44f, 59, 59f–60f
synergies, 224, 511–513

T

Taiwan, 173, 181, 189, 198
tangibility, 245
Tanzania, 177
target audience, 54, 424, 429, 445–446
target market
see also target marketing
coverage, and channel design, 369–370
defined, 9
market size, 230, 231
marketing actions to reach, 232, 233f
selection of, 230–231, 230f
target marketing
see also target market
estimate size of markets, 230
selection of target markets, 230–231
steps in, 224–232, 224f
target pricing, 332
target profit pricing, 334
target return objective, 324
target return-on-investment pricing, 335
target return-on-sales pricing, 334
targeted online advertising, 435
tariff, 168
team selling, 478
teaser advertising campaigns, 130
technological forces, 73, 82–83
technology
customers, impact on, 82–83
data analytics, 83
defined, 82
and direct marketing, 435
green, 82
innovation, and business model change, 82
marketers, impact on, 83
marketing information system. *See* marketing information system
mobile, 407
radio-frequency identification devices (RFID), 212
and retailing, 407
salesforce technology, 493
and services, 310–311
and surveys, 202
3D, 82
video blogging, 542
virtual reality market testing, 259
telemarketing, 398, 434, 477, 479
telephone surveys, 201, 201f
television advertising, 450–452, 451f
television home shopping, 397
television ratings, 205

temporal effects, 121
test marketing, 203, 258
Thailand, 171, 173, 182, 184
theatre tests, 457
third-party logistics providers, 379
3D technology, 82
"thumbs-up," 175
Tibbitt to Contwoy to Winter Road, 381
tied selling, 373
time poverty, 79
time to market (TtM), 259
time-based agenda, 519
tolls, 319
top management, 29
total cost, 328
total logistics cost, 377, 378f
total revenue, 328
touchpoints, 302
tracking strategic performance, 39–40
trade agreements, 169–171
trade feedback effect, 164
trade (functional) discounts, 340
trade-in allowances, 340
Trade-marks Act, 278
trade name, 278, 282
trade-oriented sales promotions, 463–464
trade promotions, 463–464
trade regulations, 179
trade secrets, 100–101
trademarks, 99, 278
trading down, 277
trading up, 277
traditional auction, 154
traditional media, 535–536
traffic generation, 435
training
    of distributors' salesforces, 464
    salesforce, 464, 489
transactional function, 361, 362f
transit advertising, 455
transnational firm, 172
Trans-Pacific Partnership (TPP), 171
transportation, 379, 380f
transportation systems, 179
travel retailing, 406–407
trend extrapolation, 237
trend hunting, 200
trends
    changing, 276
    hunting, 200
    tracking, 73–74
    trade, 165–166
trial, 268, 430
trial close, 483
triple-bottom line, 105
tuition, 306, 319
Turkey, 177, 178
tweets, 540

U

ultimate consumers, 6
ultra-customization, 223
unaided recall, 458
unanswerable question, 203f
underperforming provinces, 40–41
uniform delivered pricing, 341
unique visitors, 545
uniqueness of services, 298–299
unit sales, 35
unit volume, 325
United Kingdom, 132, 164, 164f, 169, 173, 175
United States
    and APEC, 171
    deficit, 165
    developed country, 177
    e-commerce, 173
    ethical perceptions of entrepreneurs, 98–99
    exports to Canada, 165

global exports and imports, 164f
importer of Canadian goods, 164, 165–166
measurement of economic activities in
    organizational markets, 145
population, 76f
psychographics survey, 127
social class, 132
universities, 256
unreasonably low prices, 343
unrelated diversification, 38
unsatisfied needs, 4
unsought goods, 245
upper classes, 132
urban centres, 78
urgency close, 483
Uruguay, 171
usage instructions, 125
usage rate, 227
use experience, 119
user-generated content (UGC), 455, 534
users
    in buying centre, 149
    social media, 545
    types of, 245
utilitarianism, 103

V

validity, 196
VALS system, 127
value added, 399
value analysis, 152
value-based planning, 515
value change, 277
value consciousness, 80
value-driven strategies, 515
value perception, 118
value pricing, 320
value-values balance, 515
values
    changing values, 79–81, 277
    and consumer behaviour, 126
    core values, 30, 58
    defined, 126, 174
    and global marketing, 174
variable cost, 328
variety, 370
v-commerce, 395–396
vending machines, 395–396
vendor-managed inventory (VMI), 383
Venezuela, 171, 177
vertical channel conflict, 372
vertical integration, 373
vertical marketing systems (VMS), 367–368, 367f
vertical price fixing, 341
video blogging, 542
video cases
    Amazon.com, 386–389
    Carmex, 216–219, 346–348
    Chobani, Inc., 21–25
    Geek Squad, 91–93
    General Mills, 528–530
    Google, Inc., 469–472
    Groupon, 137–140
    IBM, 49–52
    LA Galaxy, 314–317
    Mall of America, 412–414
    Mary Kay, 189–192
    Prince Sports, Inc., 239–242, 241f
    Procter & Gamble, 291–294
    StuffDOT, Inc., 552–554
    Taco Bell, 439–440
    Toyota, 111–115
    Trek, 158–160
    X-1, 263–266
    Xerox, 497–499
Vietnam, 171, 178
viral marketing, 130
virtual organizational markets, 153–154
virtual reality, 442–443

virtual reality market testing, 259
virtual shopping cart, 409
visible minorities, 78
vision, 30
visionary organizations, 30–33, 30f
visitors, 545
volume relationships, 328–330

W

wages, 319
wall units, 402
wants, 8
warehouse clubs, 401
warehousing, 381
warranties, 125
warranty, 288
wasted coverage, 452
web advertising, 435, 454
web log. See blog
Web 2.0, 534
Western Europe, 132, 162, 163, 171, 173, 177, 178, 184
"what really works," 502–503
wheel of retailing, 405, 405f
whistle-blowers, 103
wholesaler-sponsored voluntary chains, 368, 392
wholesalers, 143, 360, 360f, 366
wiki, 534
women
    and automotive industry, 116–117
    marketing to women, 489
    time poverty, 79
    in the workforce, 79
word of mouth, 129–130
workload method, 487
world population, 76–77
world trade
    see also global marketing
    balance of trade, 165
    barter, 164
    Canadian perspective, 165–166
    company strategy, structure, and rivalry, 166
    competitive advantage, 166–167, 167f
    countertrade, 164
    demand conditions, 166
    dollar value of, 163
    dynamics of, 163–167
    economic espionage, 174
    economic integration, rise of, 169–171
    economic protectionism, decline of, 168–169, 169f
    exports and imports, 164–165, 164f
    factor conditions, 166
    global brand, 172–173
    global companies, 172–173
    global competition, 171
    global consumers, 173
    global environmental scan. See global
        environmental scan
    global marketing program, 182–186
    global perspective, 164, 164f
    grey market, 185–186
    networked global marketspace, 173
    political risk rating, 179
    related and supporting industries, 166
    strategic alliances, 171
    and tariffs, 168
    top ten global exporters and importers, 164f
    trade feedback effect, 164
World Trade Organization (WTO), 169

Y

Yellow Pages, 451f, 453
yield management pricing, 332–333
young married couples, 131
young singles, 131